# Warship Identification

# Warship Identification

Lieut-Commander E. C. Talbot-Booth RD, RNR
and David G. Greenman, Group Officer SC, SRC

IAN ALLAN LONDON

First published 1971

SBN 7110 0166 9





Published by Ian Allan Ltd, Shepperton, Surrey,
and printed in the United Kingdom by
Ian Allan (Printing) Ltd.

# Contents

# Introduction

The importance of warship identification should need no stressing.

Notwithstanding sophisticated electronics, radar and other instrumentations, visual recognition is essential.

There is no need for every individual to accumulate a mass of intelligence nor to try and memorize ship outlines. In any case ships frequently undergo considerable structural changes.

Knowledge of types is helpful but may be misleading as a vessel designated a Destroyer in one navy may be known as a Frigate or an Escort in another.

It is dangerous to try and identify by a single feature instead of by a number collectively and naturally much depends upon weather conditions, distances, bearings and accuracy of observation.

A coded description modelled on method is less likely to be misinterpreted than the result of free impressions by an untrained observer.

A submariner sees things differently from a surface observer or from an airman.

The *Reporting Code* outlined in this book enables the main silhouette characteristics to be reduced to a simple form readily learnt by those hitherto unfamiliar with ships.

Three separate stages have been elaborated: the *First Sighting or Distant View;* the *Medium View* and the *Close View* although for operational value the vessel sighted may then be too close to do much about it.

In this manner identification proceeds steadily and from the information obtained by the combined views, an outline may be reproduced for transmission to base.

Other matters relevant or helpful in identification are examined and illustrated together with a glossary of terms most frequently employed but bearing in mind that visual recognition is always based upon what an object looks like and not what might be technically correct.

Having thoroughly analysed the subject the volume complements this by nearly 1,400 solid silhouettes of ships arranged according to the coding system which has undergone operational and practical testing and as a result of which has received commendation.

These silhouettes are then repeated as outline drawings to a larger scale grouped more or less in types or classes, cross referenced to the silhouettes and with relevant details.

A fairly comprehensive list of *Pendant Numbers* or other identification markings actually appearing on ships may help recognition in peace time although it must be remembered that these are subject to alteration from time to time.

Any constructive criticism, information, photographs or drawings will always be welcome.

# Glossary

**Abaft**  Behind an object.

**Abeam**  An object bearing at right angles to the centre line.

**Aft**  Towards the stern. The *after* part.

**After-Castle**  Raised portion of hull or an *island* at the after end of a ship. Also termed *poop*. Common in merchant ships and in some naval auxiliaries.

**Ahead**  Directly in advance of a vessel.

**Amidships**  Midway between bow and stern.

**Armament**  Weapons carried: guns, launchers, torpedo tubes etc.

**Astern**  Directly to the rear of, or behind, a vessel.

**Athwartships**  Across a vessel. At right angles to the centre line.

**Barbette**  As seen for recognition, is the lower circular section on deck upon which a turret revolves. It is the top of a cylinder which goes far down into the ship and protects the mechanism for working and loading the guns.

**Beam**  The greatest width of a ship. *On the beam* indicates a bearing at right angles to the centre line.

**Bearing**  The relative direction of one object from another.

**Blast Screen**  Raised projection on superstructure in front of a gun to protect the deck and gun crew from the blast.

**Boom**  Heavy derrick or spar attached to the base of a mast or kingpost for working boats or other gear.

**Bow Wave**  Wave formed under or near the bows when a ship is under way. Not necessarily any indication of speed.

**Bows**  Adjacent to the stem. Either side near the front.

**Break**  The point where an upper deck forms a step with the deck below.

**Breakwater**  Low wall on the forecastle to prevent water sweeping aft: usually apexed.

**Bridge**  Superstructure foreward often with *wings* athwartships for navigation or signalling purposes.

**Bridge Deck**  Centre island or mid-castle. Found in merchant ships and some naval auxiliaries.

**Broadside**  Complete view of a ship from stem to stern: not fore-shortened.

## PRINCIPAL PARTS OF A WARSHIP

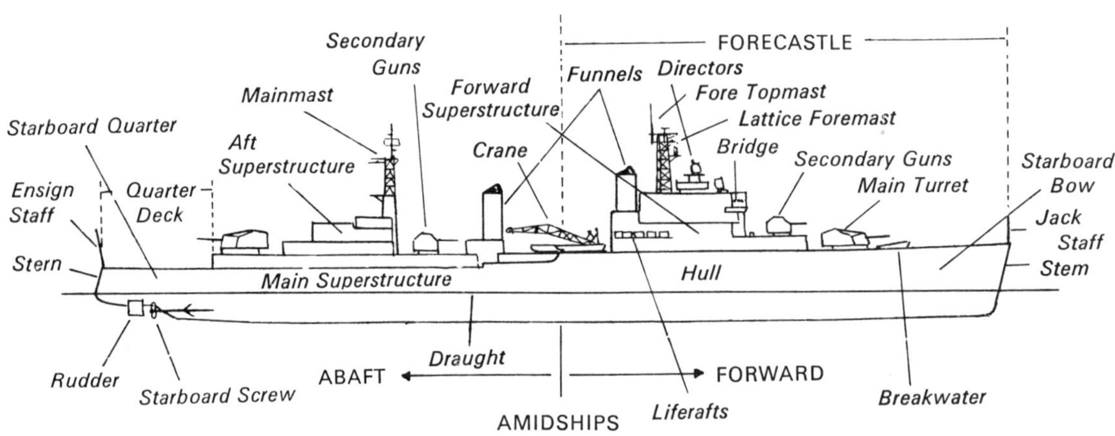

**Bulkhead**  A wall which divides a ship either transversely or longitudinally.

**Bulwark**  Plating on deck side to give protection from the weather, in place of railings.

**Castle**  Raised portion of hull above the upper deck. Same as *island*.

**Catwalk**  A light fore and aft bridge raised above the deck and joining two islands or parts of superstructure. Particularly prominent in oil tankers. Also known as flying bridges.

**Centre Line**  Imaginary line drawn on deck from stem to stern.

**Chine**  Where the bottom of a ship meets the sides at an angle instead of the usual curve. Very noticeable in small coastal craft such as motor torpedo boats which are said to have a *hard chine.*.

**Cinder or Clinker Screen**  Small screen round the front of a funnel top.

**Control Tower**  Protected revolving tower for housing gunnery and other instruments.

**Conning Tower**  Armoured compartment from which a ship is navigated and controlled in action. Superstructure in a submarine but now more-often termed a *sail* or *fin*.

**Cowl**  Smoke deflecting baffle on a funnel top. Larger than a clinker screen and covering whole top.

**Counter**  Stern of a ship.

**Crow's Nest**  Look-out platform on foremast. Prominent in some small craft.

**Cutwater**  Extreme front of a ship. The stem.

**Davits**  Curved fittings for supporting and handling the small boats of a ship.

**Depth Charge Rack**  At the stern of many ships to carry depth charges.

**Depth Charge Throwers**  Of various kinds for throwing depth charges either astern or ahead of a ship.

**Derrick**  Same as a boom. Spar attached to foot of a mast for handling boats, gear or stores.

**Director**  Instrument for directing gunfire or missile launching.

**Displacement**  Weight of water displaced or pushed aside by a vessel, equal to her own weight. See separate notes on *Tonnage*.

**Draught**  Depth from waterline to keel.

**Ensign**  Flag denoting nationality; not always the same as that worn ashore as the national flag.

**Ensign Staff**  Flagstaff at stern from which Ensign is worn if not from the Peak. Nearly always worn at this position when not under way.

**Fin**  A modern term for the *sail* or *conning tower* of a submarine.

**Flare**  Slope outwards of a ship's hull from waterline to upper deck—particularly at bows and stern.

**Flagship**  Ship in a squadron which wears the flag of an Admiral commanding the squadron. Ship which accommodates the staff.

**Flush Deck**  Uninterrupted upper deck line without castles or islands.

**Flying Bridge**  Light platforms projecting athwartships from main bridge structure on either side for signalling or other purposes. In RFA tankers the islands or castles are joined on the centre line by light, narrow platforms. These are also

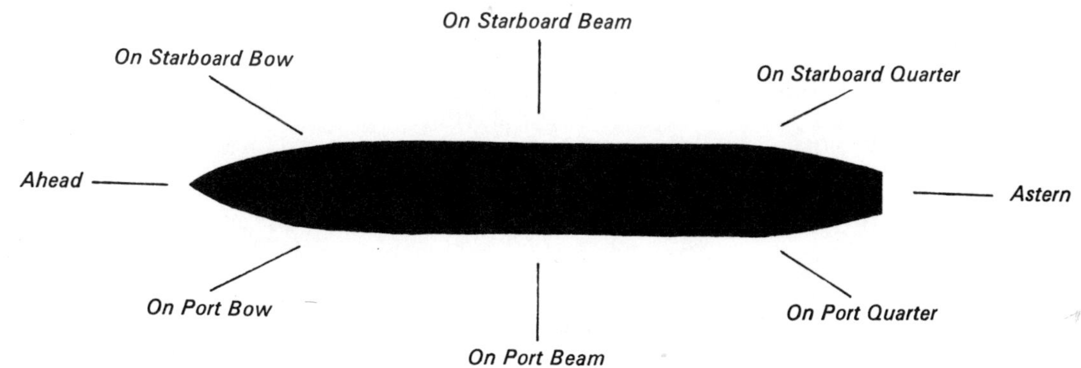


## RELATIVE BEARINGS

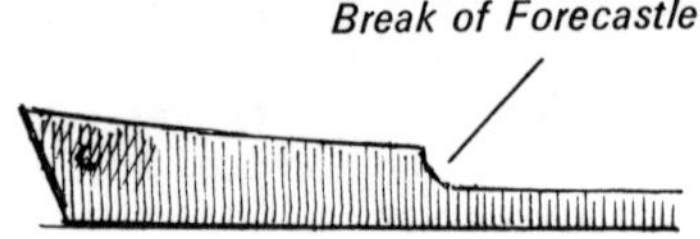


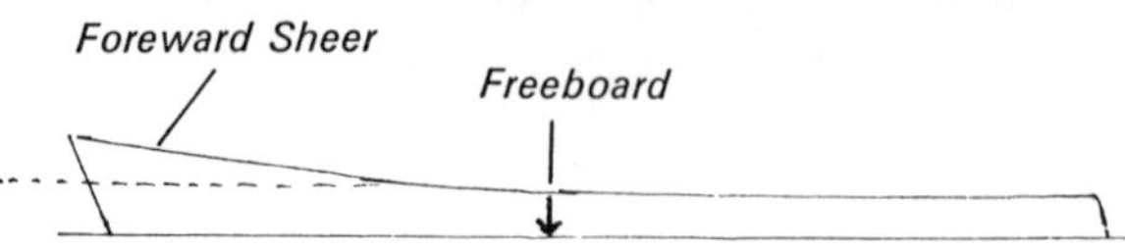


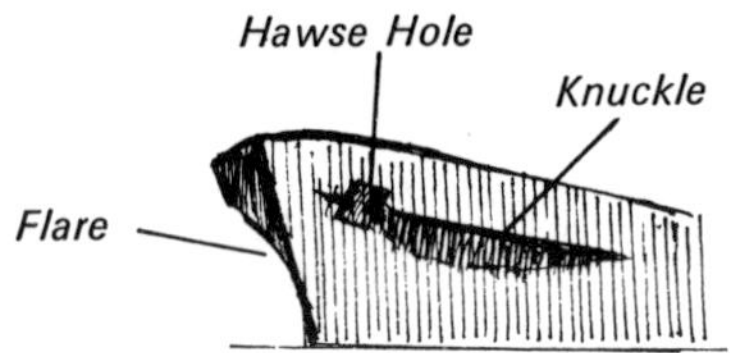

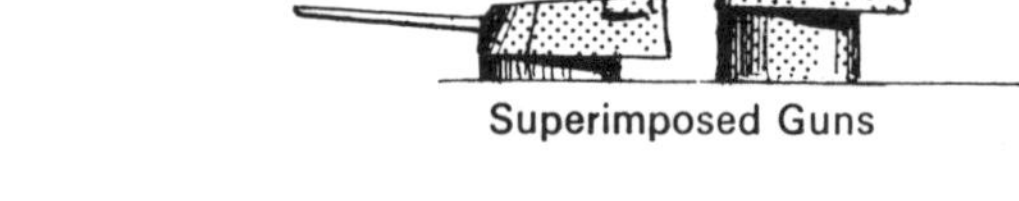


called flying bridges, but more often, cat walks.

**Fore and Aft**  Along the length of a vessel.

**Foreward**  Towards the fore or front part of a ship.

**Forecastle**  Raised portion of hull at foreward end.

**Freeboard**  For recognition purposes, indicates the depth from waterline to upper deck.

**Gaff**  Light fore and aft spar projecting at an angle from a mast and from which Ensign is usually worn at sea.

**Gallows**  Inverted U-shaped fittings at sides or stern of a trawler or minesweeper for handling nets or sweeping gear.

**Gun House**  Lightly armoured mount for completely protecting guns but lighter than a turret.

**Gun Shield**  Protection for gun's crew but not completely enclosing the gun mounting.

**Hance**  Curved or sloping portion of side plating or bulwark at breaks of islands or castles. Sometimes termed 'Fashion Plate'

**Hull**  The main body of a ship. Without superstructure etc.

**Island**  The same as castle. A raised portion of the hull above the upper deck.

**Jack**  A small flag worn at the Jack staff foreward when a vessel is not under way. Exception in HM ships is that a Union Jack is worn under way by Royal Yacht or escorting ships.

**Jack Staff**  Small staff on stem at which a Jack or small flag is worn as above.

**Kingpost**  Short vertical or raking pole to which a derrick, boom or spar is attached. Lighter and shorter than a mast. RFA Replenishment ships have particularly tall and heavy kingposts.

**Knot**  A measure of speed in nautical miles (6,080.20 feet) per hour.

**Knuckle**  Where the flare becomes angular near the upper deck Foreward or sometimes in Russian ships, at the stern also

**Launcher**  For recognition purposes this comprises any kind of rocket or missile projector.

**List**  Angle of a ship from the vertical when rolling or a permanent angle assumed as the result of damage or shifting cargo.

**Mack**  A combined mast and funnel (stack). Sometimes incorrectly used to indicate an enclosed or covered mast only.

**Main Armament**  The heaviest armament.

**Main Deck**  Topmost continuous deck.

**Mast**  Vertical or raked poles to support radar installations, controls etc. or for signalling purposes. Of many types and they now tend to become heavier to support complexity of gear.

**Midcastle**  Raised portion — an island or castle amidships. Same as bridge deck or centre castle.

**Peak**  Extreme outward end of a gaff from which Ensigns are worn.

**Pendant Numbers**  Two or more numeral

flags, frequently preceded by a superior or alphabetical flag allocated to most warships as a means of communication and identification. Usually painted on sides in peace time and/or on counter.

**Quarter**  Adjacent to the stern on either side.

**Quarter Deck**  Deck near the stern over the quarters. Position of authority and reserved normally for officers.

**Poop**  Raised island or castle at the stern. Same as after-castle.

**Port Side**  That side of a vessel which is on the left when facing foreward. Indicated by red light at night—usually close to or on the bridge.

**Radio Direction Finder**  Instrument for determining the source of radio impulses.

**Rake**  Slope or inclination of mast, funnel, stem or stern. Anything out of the perpendicular.

**Rangefinder**  Instrument for determining distances from an object. Fitted on turrets or towers or incorporated into the superstructure.

**Rubbing Strake**  Heavy wooden strakes or battens along the hull sides to protect the latter from contact with dock walls and quays. A very characteristic feature of small craft such as minesweepers and coastal craft which have frequent occasion to go alongside.

**Run-Away**  When the upper deck runs in an uninterrupted diagonal line from stem to stern. A distinctive feature in Russian, Swedish or United States' destroyers.

**Sail**  The modern term for conning tower or fin of a submarine.

**Searchlight Platform**  For recognition purposes indicates a light platform, usually circular, raised above the deck.

**Secondary Armament**  Subsidiary armament next in calibre to the main battery.

**Silhouette**  Strictly and for recognition purposes indicates a representation of a ship or object in *solid* black or dark colour on a lighter background to show outline more clearly. A term often incorrectly applied to an outline drawing.

**Sheer**  Slope upwards of a hull at foreward and after ends.

**Sponson**  Projection from the side, particularly in aircraft carriers. Usually to support guns light on the flight deck level.

**Starboard**  That side of a vessel which is on the right when facing foreward. Indicated by a green light at night.

**Stem**  Extreme foreward part of a ship's hull. That portion which cuts the water. Sometimes called a *Cut-water.*

**Stern**  Extreme after portion of a ship's hull.

**Superstructure**  Upperworks or deck-houses above the upper deck, usually not extending the whole width.

**Superimposed**  Turret or gun placed on a higher level than another.

**Sweep**  Gear on the after deck of a minesweeper and towed astern for cutting mines loose from their mooring wires. Sometimes seen in conjunction with a power winch.

**Tonnage**  The size of a ship. In warships it is based on actual weight. In merchant ships it is volume. See separate chapter on Tonnage.

**Transom**  In recognition, implies a completely flat stern above the waterline.

**Turrets**  Heavily armoured revolving structures for protecting the main armament. May contain one, two or even three, guns.

**Torpedo Tubes**  Tubes for launching torpedoes. Rotating and mounted singly or in sets up to five. Normally positioned on the centre line and in small ships, on the upper deck or superstructure. Homing torpedo tubes are usually fixed athwartships or diagonally.

**Trim**  Condition of a ship at any time. *Light trim* or *Load trim* etc. Whether a vessel is down to her correct *mark* and riding correctly.

**Truck**  The extreme top of a mast. Usually a flat plate.

**Upper Deck**  Topmost or weather deck. It may vary however with different types of vessel.

**Wake**  Disturbed water left astern

**Waterline**  Line formed by surface of water on the hull.

**Wells**  The spaces between the islands or castles of a ship.

**Yard**  Light spar rigged athwartships on a mast for signalling purposes. In sail ships it is a heavier spar to which the head of a sail is attached.

# Some Abbreviations and Technical Terms

ABM   Anti Ballistic Missile.
ADA   Action Data Automation System.
ASDIC   Anti Submarine Detection Indication (Committee).
ASROC   Anti Submarine Rocket Launcher.
ASTOR   Anti Submarine Torpedo.
ASW   Anti Submarine Warfare (or Weapon).
BEEHIVE   Colloquial term for TACAN qv
BPDMS   Basic Point Defence Missile System (Modified 8 tube Asroc Missile Launcher).
BQR-4   Passive Submarine Detection Sonar.
CF 299   Small Ships Guided Weapons.
CENTO   Central Treaty Organization.
DC   Depth Charge.
DCM   Depth Charge Mortar.
DCT   Depth Charge Thrower.
DRT   Dead Reckoning Tracer.
DSRV   Deep Submergence Rescue Vehicle.
DASH   Drone Anti Submarine Helicopter.
ECM   Electronic Countermeasures.
ELINT   Electronic Intelligence (Russian) Trawler.
EWA   Early Warning.
FAST   Fast Automatic Shuttle Transfer.
FBM   Fleet Ballistic Missile.
FRAM   Fleet Rehabilitation and Modernisation.
GUPPY   Greater Underwater Propulsion Programe. (Method to improve performance of existing submarines.)
HAYRAKE   Very large two-tiered Radar Scanner. Similar to "Bedstead" and "Matress".
HEDGEHOG   Anti-submarine Weapon.
ICBM   Inter–Continental Ballistic Missile.
IRBM   Intermediate Range Ballistic Missile.
LASER   Light Amplification by Stimulated Emission of radiation.
LIMBO   Anti Submarine Mortar.
LORAN   Long Range Navigation. Electronic system used to position the ship by radio waves.

MCLWG   Major Calibre Light Weight Gun.
MRS 3   Medium Range System for Gun Mounting.
MSBS   Submarine borne Intermediate Range Ballistic Missile.
NATO   North Atlantic Treaty Organisation.
ORI   Operational Readiness Inspection.
PARAVANE   Apparatus for cutting wires of floating mines.
PDMS   Point Defence Missile System.
PUFFS   Passive Underwater Control Feasibility Study. (Small fin-like structure; hydrophone).
RADAR   Radio Detection and Ranging.
RDF   Radio Direction Finder.
RPD   Radar Picket Destroyer.
SABMIS   Sea Based Anti Ballistic Missile Interception System.
SAM   Surface (or ship) to Air Missile.
SEATO   South East Asia Treaty Organisation.
SINS   Ships Inertial Navigation System (enables ships to establish position without reference to external aids).
SIRS   Ship Installed Radio System.
SLBM   Submarine Launched Ballistic Missile.
SNORKEL   Breathing tube to enable conventional submarines to remain submerged.
SNORT   Another term for Snorkel.
SONAR   Sound Navigation and Ranging.
SONODOME   Plastic dome, usually in bow structure which acts as window for sonar beams (sound waves).
STANAVFORLANT   Standing Naval Force Atlantic. (NATO)
STOL   Short Take Off and Landing (Aircraft).
SQUID   Anti Submarine Mortar.
TACAN   Tactical Air Navigation System; coloquially termed BEEHIVE.
ULMS   Underwater Launched Missile System.
VDS   Variable Depth Sonar.
VTOL   Vertical Take Off and Landing (Aircraft).

# SECTION ONE

# Aids to Identification

# First Sighting or Distant View

First sighting will probably be masts and possibly funnels and *not* smoke as warships endeavour to reduce this to a minimum.

The ship will be *hull down* but as the distance between observer and ship decreases, other features appear. Much also depends upon the height of the observer above the waterline and sighting may vary from about 2 miles to 15 or so.

Masts, funnels and superstructure are followed by turrets but these will probably look mere humps at first. Very often *spaces between* features are more significant than actual shapes.

It is very unlikely even when the hull emerges, that anything definite about it can be noted and certainly not the shapes of stem and stern. In fact, even when closer, the forms of these features may never be completely ascertained, especially at speed and possibly little reliance can be attached to their shape in practice.

If possible it is always better to take time before reporting until a vessel is seen more or less broadside, as foreshortening tends to distort or obscure important features.

Eventually objects will appear until a complete Distant View is possible.

The vessel must then be studied according to a definite plan and the most obvious method is to start foreward and work aft noting the prominent features in sequence as described below.

Naturally all vessels do not have every object that is coded in the accompanying example which is given to incorporate all the objects that are covered by the Distant View.

**B**     BUBBLE (or Golf Ball). A Plastic covering for delicate instrumentation; cannot be mistaken.

**Con**     CONTROL TOWER Very heavy towers incorporating directors, range finders etc. Almost exclusively a Russian feature.

**C**     CRANE Mostly in auxiliaries or minesweepers but may still be seen in cruisers. Not always easy to distinguish from a kingpost, especially if jib is stowed horizontally.

**D**     DIRECTORS All types of Directors and Detectors are coded if sufficiently large or prominent.

**Dr**     DIRECTORS (Raised) This implies that the Director is mounted on its own tall base and *not* that it is placed high up on superstructure.

**F**     FUNNELS Coded in this view simply as **F** regardless of shape but adding **r** if prominently raked.

**G**     GUNS Vary in size and shape. Guns in turrets or large gun houses may be reported as GT if desired.
If a ship has large *and* small guns the latter are coded as Gs.
Large mortars if *looking* like guns are coded G.

**K**     KINGPOST Short vertical pole mostly in auxiliaries or minesweepers to which a boom is attached for handling boats or other gear.

**L**     LAUNCHER All coded as **L** regardless of type or function.

**M**     MASTS Coded in this view simply as **M** but adding **r** if heavily raked, or **s** if very small.
Examples are shown to indicate the various structures that are classed as masts.

# FIRST SIGHTING OR DISTANT VIEW

1. HULL DOWN.
   Cruiser.
2. Complete distant view of same ship.
3. Same ship in different weather conditions.
4. Complete distant view of Destroyer or Frigate. Very clear weather.
5. Distant view of Destroyer; medium visibility.
6. Heavy ship; poor weather.
7. Destroyer at night as under searchlight and very calm weather conditions.

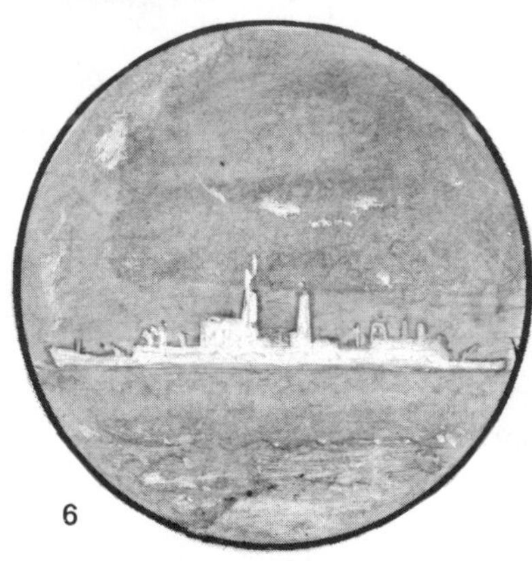

# CODING DISTANT VIEW

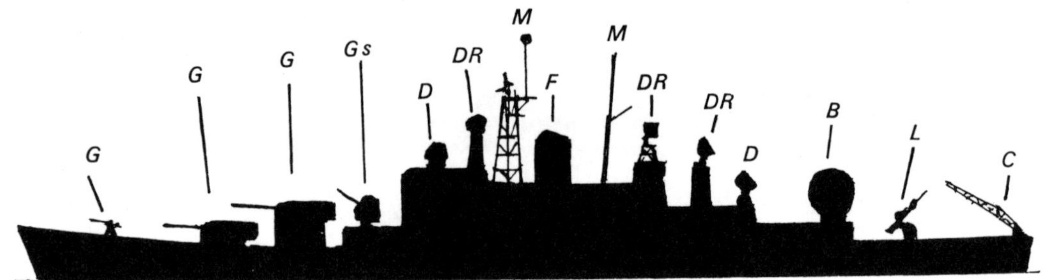


EXAMPLE OF FEATURES CODED IN THE DISTANT VIEW.

G. GUN. Actually in coding a ship of this size, this gun would not be reported at all as it would appear very insignificant but when appearing as the *Main Armament* and looking comparatively large as in examples Number 3 and 6 of the tests on next page, it would be.

G. GUN.

G. GUN.

Gs. GUN (small)—that is to say, in this ship it appears smaller than the main turrets.

D. DIRECTOR.

DR. DIRECTOR (Raised).

M. MAST.

F. FUNNEL.

M. MAST—actually "R" should be added to indicate raking.

DR. DIRECTOR (Raised).

DR. DIRECTOR (Raised).

D. DIRECTOR.

B. BUBBLE.

L. LAUNCHER.

C. CRANE.

## FUNNELS (F)

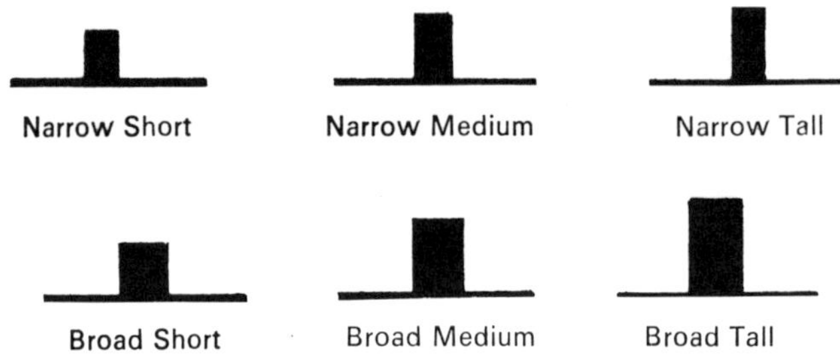


## BUBBLE (B)

# CRANES (C)

Cruiser Type

Depot Ships etc.

Minesweeper Type
(situated aft)

# DIRECTORS (D)

USSR

USSR

USSR

UK

## RAISED DIRECTOR (DR)

USA

USA

USA

# GUNS (G)

**TURRET GUN (GT)**

USSR

USA

ITALY

Gun (G)
(open)

Depth Charge Mortars
Coded as GT

# SOME LAUNCHERS (L)

USA

USSR

USSR

USSR

NATO

UK

FRANCE

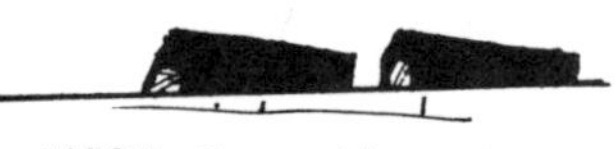

USSR  Covered Launchers

# MASTS (M)

1

2

3

4

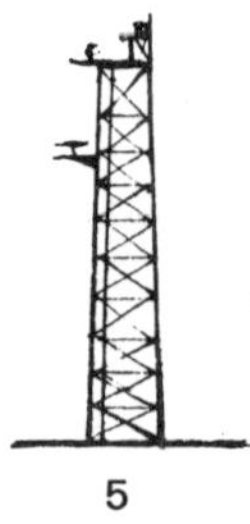

5

6

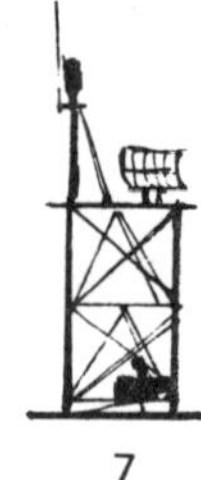

7

8

(Coded simply as "M" in the Distant View, adding "r" if raked and "s" if very small.)

1. POLE.
2. TRIPOD.⎤ Vary in height and angle of
3. TRIPOD.⎬ legs; some rake forward and
4. TRIPOD.⎦ others aft. U.S. Type—very heavy and usually very tall.
5. LATTICE or CAGE. (Uprights may rake).
6. LATTICE or CAGE—small. Frequently U.S. or Russian.
7. LATTICE or CAGE—heavy. Comparatively short or quadpod. Frequently U.S. or Russian.
8. ENCLOSED. May be combined with a funnel or a heavy mast alone. Technically when combined with funnel it is a "MACK" (Mast & Stack). If no other funnel was visible it could be reported as "F", even if tall.
9. MAST AND FUNNEL COMBINED. Coded as MF *not* FM.
10. MAST AND FUNNEL COMBINED. Coded as MF *not* FM.
11.⎤ Various types of Complex masts. CON-
12.⎢ TROL TOWER AND MAST. Coded as
13.⎢ Con M. A distinctive Russian feature.
14.⎦

9

10

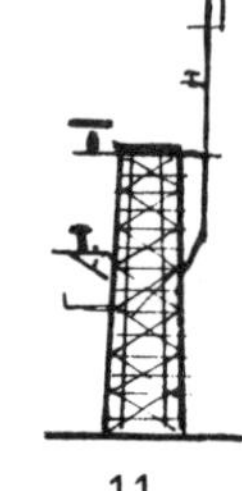

11

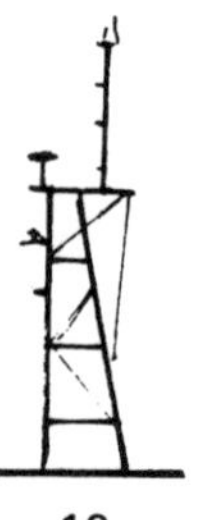

12

13

14

# The Basic Hull Forms

As mentioned previously, it is extremely un-likely that the hull form will be sufficiently distinct at a distance to enable an accurate report to be made. Nevertheless, in certain conditions it may be and for this reason the accompanying diagrams are given in silhouette form.

They are amplified on a larger scale later in the book.

In any case the hull form is the most difficult

## HULL FORMS

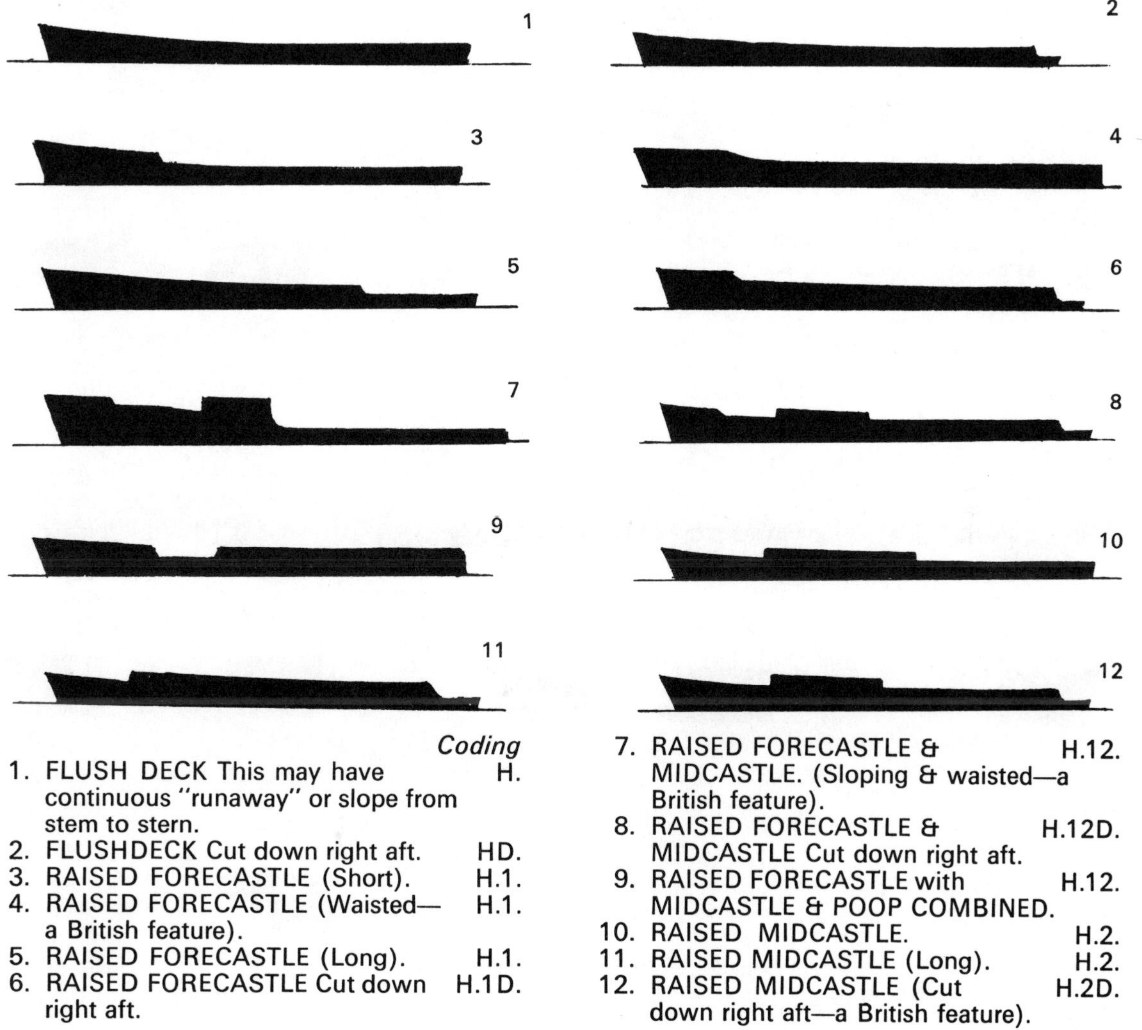

| | *Coding* |
|---|---|
| 1. FLUSH DECK This may have continuous "runaway" or slope from stem to stern. | H. |
| 2. FLUSHDECK Cut down right aft. | HD. |
| 3. RAISED FORECASTLE (Short). | H.1. |
| 4. RAISED FORECASTLE (Waisted—a British feature). | H.1. |
| 5. RAISED FORECASTLE (Long). | H.1 |
| 6. RAISED FORECASTLE Cut down right aft. | H.1D. |
| 7. RAISED FORECASTLE & MIDCASTLE. (Sloping & waisted—a British feature). | H.12. |
| 8. RAISED FORECASTLE & MIDCASTLE Cut down right aft. | H.12D. |
| 9. RAISED FORECASTLE with MIDCASTLE & POOP COMBINED. | H.12. |
| 10. RAISED MIDCASTLE. | H.2. |
| 11. RAISED MIDCASTLE (Long). | H.2. |
| 12. RAISED MIDCASTLE (Cut down right aft—a British feature). | H.2D. |

feature in ship recognition as several factors tend to confuse.

Some ships are *flush decked* that is to say the topmost deck runs clean from stem to stern.

Others have *castles* or *islands* showing above the upper deck level and these are classed as *one, two-* or *three-island* vessels according to the positions.

An *island* is an integral part of the hull structure as distinct from superstructure and deck houses which are built onto the deck, usually being of lighter construction or not extending to the full width of a vessel.

The lengths of islands varies or there may be a combination of two.

Many British frigates have a distinctive hull form although somewhat difficult to code.

The diagram below indicates the 12 basic types and the addition of D, *drop,* indicates that the hull is cut down right aft as in Royal Navy Frigates or *County* Class Destroyers.

## TYPES OF STEMS (B)

(Reported as "B"—Bows—to avoid confusion with "S" for Sterns.)
1. Straight or Vertical.
2. Raking. (Angle of rake varies.)
3. Curved and Raking.
4. Inward Curve. Noticeable in some Italian Corvettes or Frigates, on Ice-breakers and in fast Motor Patrol Craft.

## TYPES OF STERNS (S)

1. Straight or Vertical. (Probably minelaying or transom.)
2. Cruiser—sloping *outwards.* (Angle varies.)
3. *Inwards* Sloping.
4. Minelaying. (Particularly a Russian feature.)
5  Number of drawing in grey or second section

# CODING OF SILHOUETTES

HULL FORMS, STEMS AND STERNS are not always very definite at this distance but should be attempted and reported if possible.

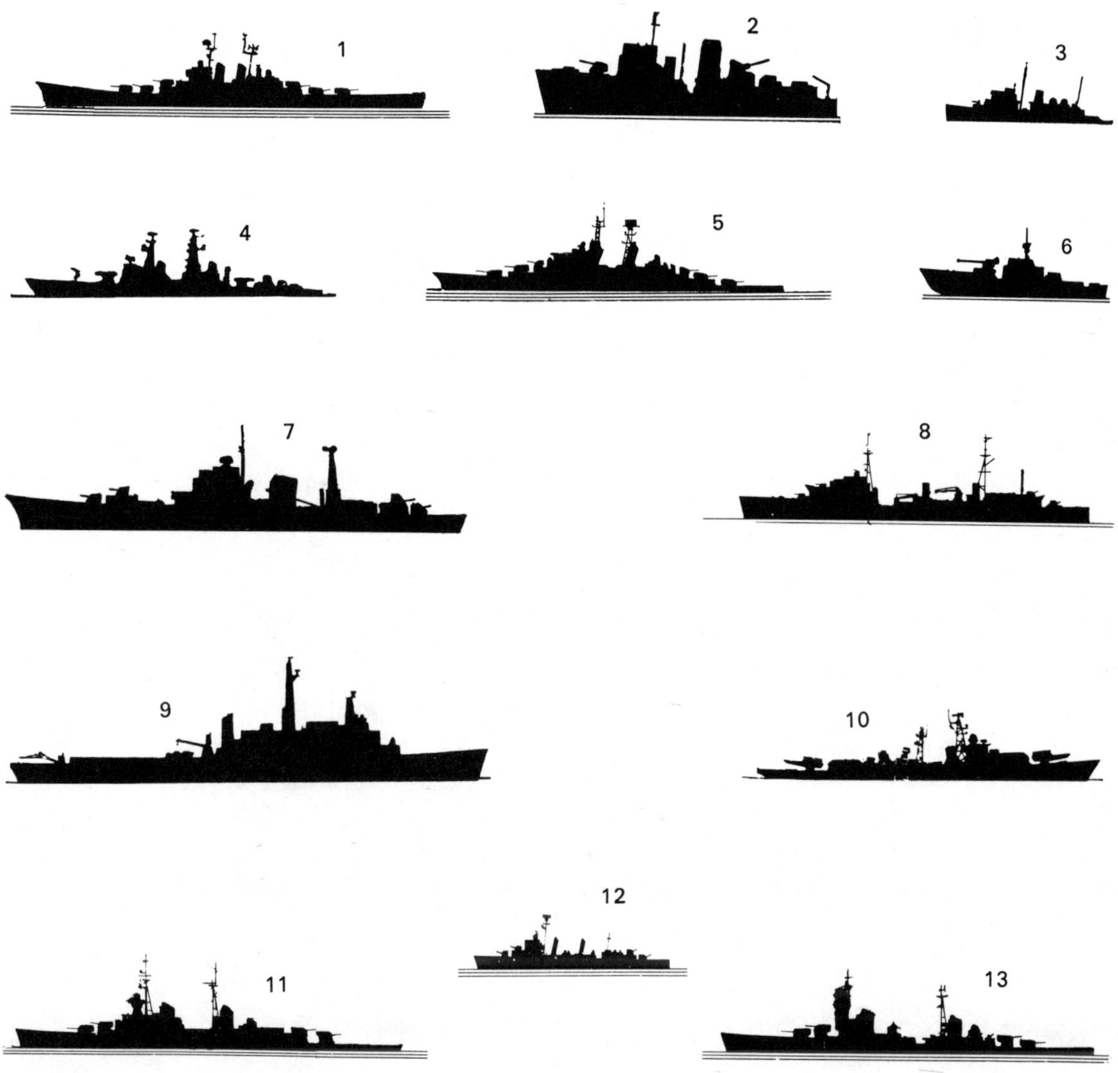

1. G G G D M F(r) F(r) M(r) D G G G H B3 S3
2. G M(r) K F(r) G C H1 B2 S1
3. G M(r) F(r) M(r) H1 D B1 S3
4. L L D M F(r) M F(r) DR L H B2 S3
5. G G Gs D M F(r) M F(r) D Gs G G H1 B3 S1
6. G M H B4 S3
7. G G D M F(r) K M G G H B3 S3
8. G G D M C F C F M K G G H1 B2 S1
9. D R M F C C H (or H1) B2 S3
10. L D M(r) F(r) M D R F(r) L H (or H1) B2 S4
11. G G Con. M F M F D G G H1 B2 S3
12. G G D M(r) F(r) F(r) M(r) G G H B2 S1
13. G G Con. M F D M F D G G H1 B2 S1

# The Medium View

This is probably the most important of all as it indicates that a vessel is well above the horizon and ceasing to be a solid mass or silhouette. Distinctive features begin to appear and others may be more readily picked out, or a re-assessment of the first sighting made.

Types of funnels, masts and armament become clearer, allowing for a more detailed description. Hull forms may be seen for the first time and possibly stems and sterns and these features may be added to the observer's report which will now cover Sequence, Hull Form, Bows and Stern.

The accompanying solid silhouettes (A) of two similar classes of Russian cruisers show similarities in the number of turrets, control towers and so on. The two Medium Views below them (B), show the same ships, when it can clearly be seen that *Sverdlov*, at the top, has a forecastle extending to beneath the third turret while *Chapaev*, at the bottom, has one which extends only to below the bridge. Secondary turrets along the forecastle deck can also be seen in *Sverdlov* and other distinctions become clear. The wider spacing of funnels and masts in *Chapaev* would not be noticeable if the ship was foreshortened.

The solid silhouette of a destroyer (C) also makes clear the difficulties of hull form when compared with No 3 in the grey hull forms that follow.

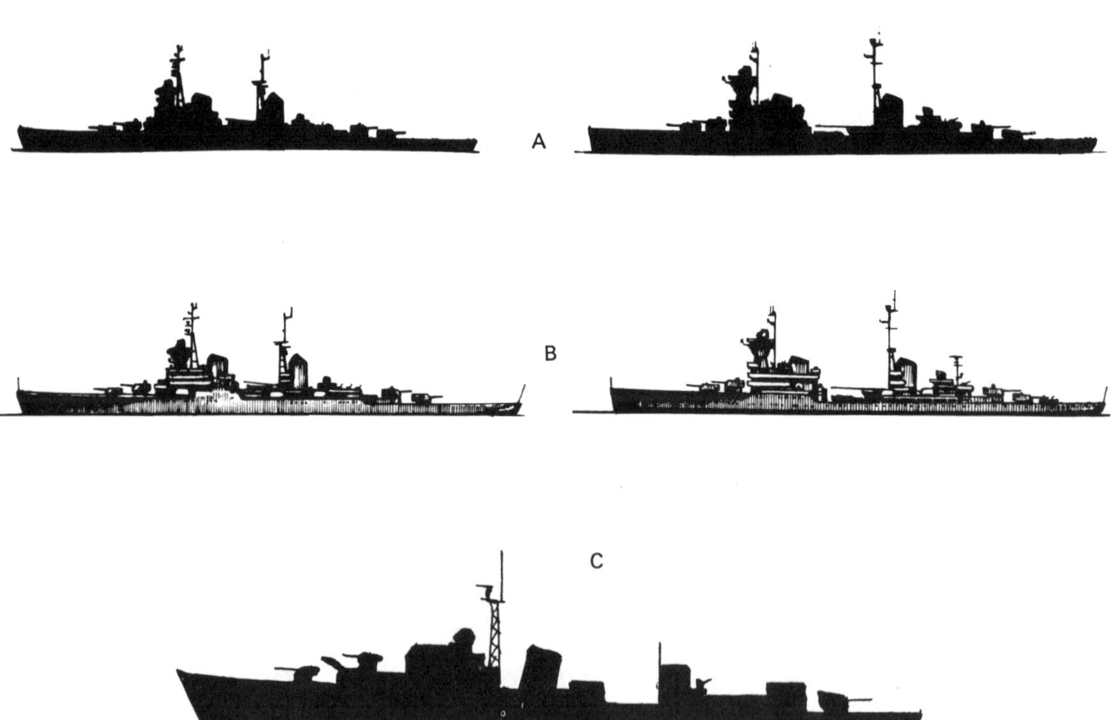

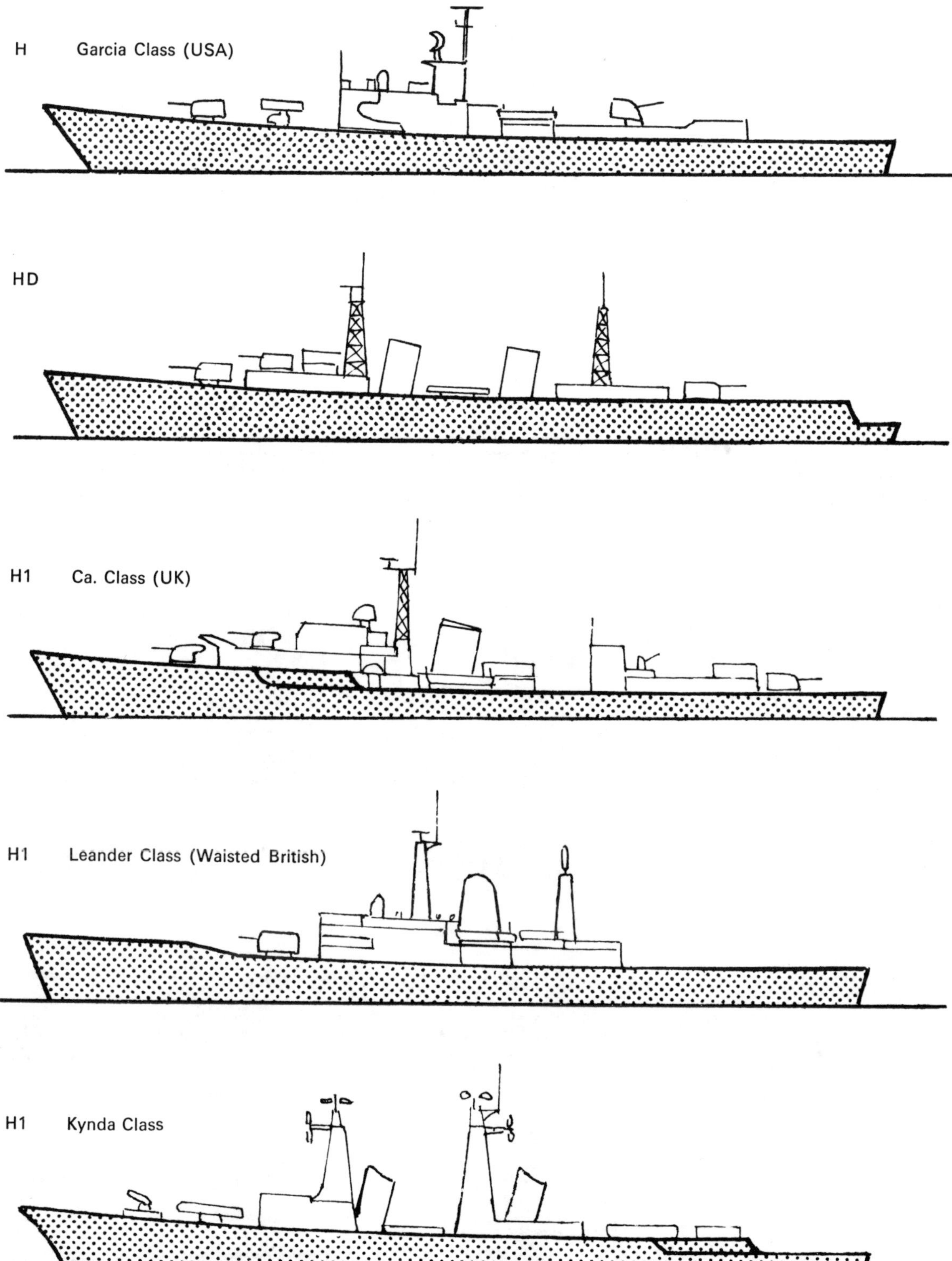

H       Garcia Class (USA)
HD
H1      Ca. Class (UK)
H1      Leander Class (Waisted British)
H1      Kynda Class

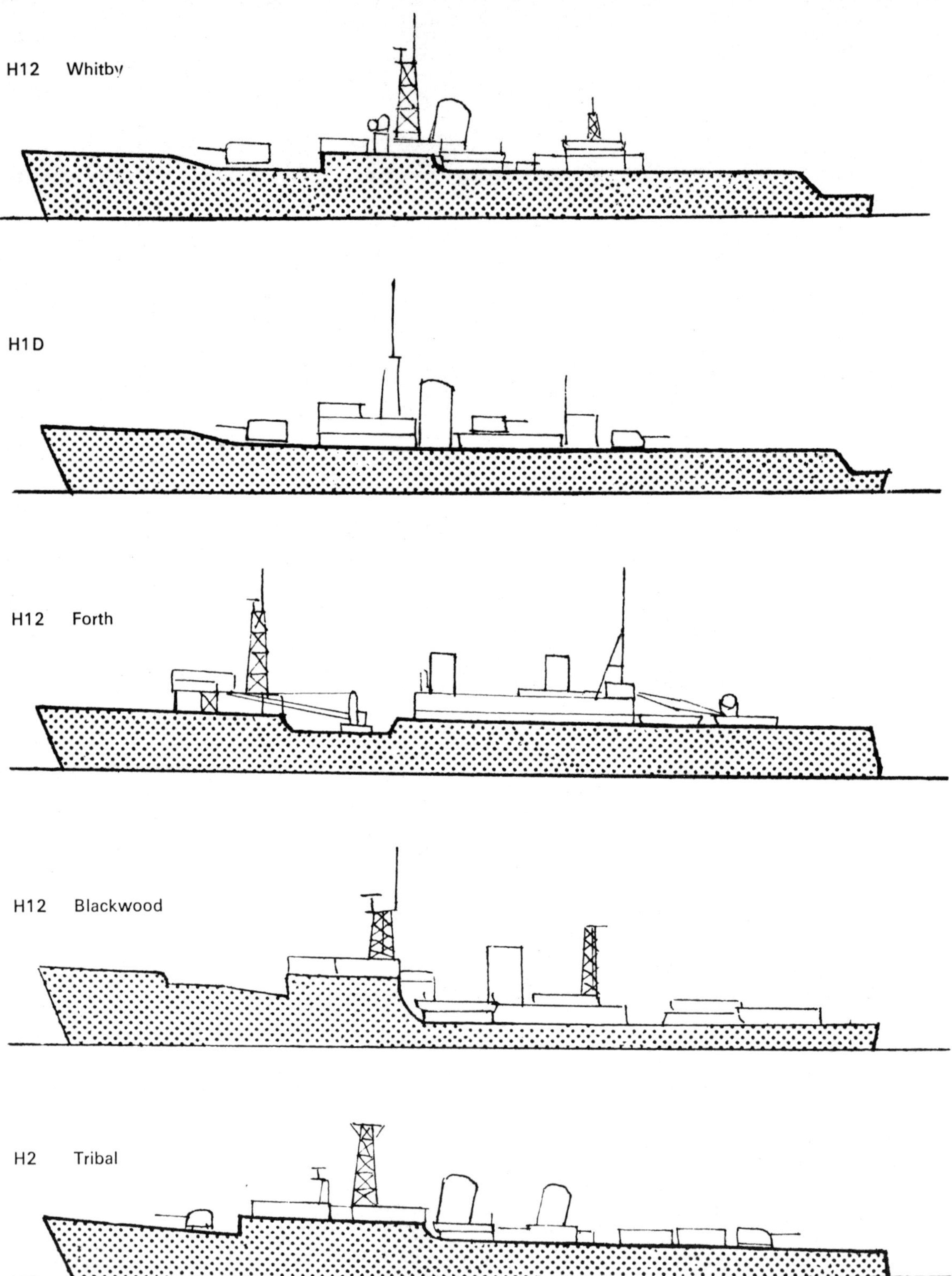

H12    Whitby
H1D
H12    Forth
H12    Blackwood
H2    Tribal

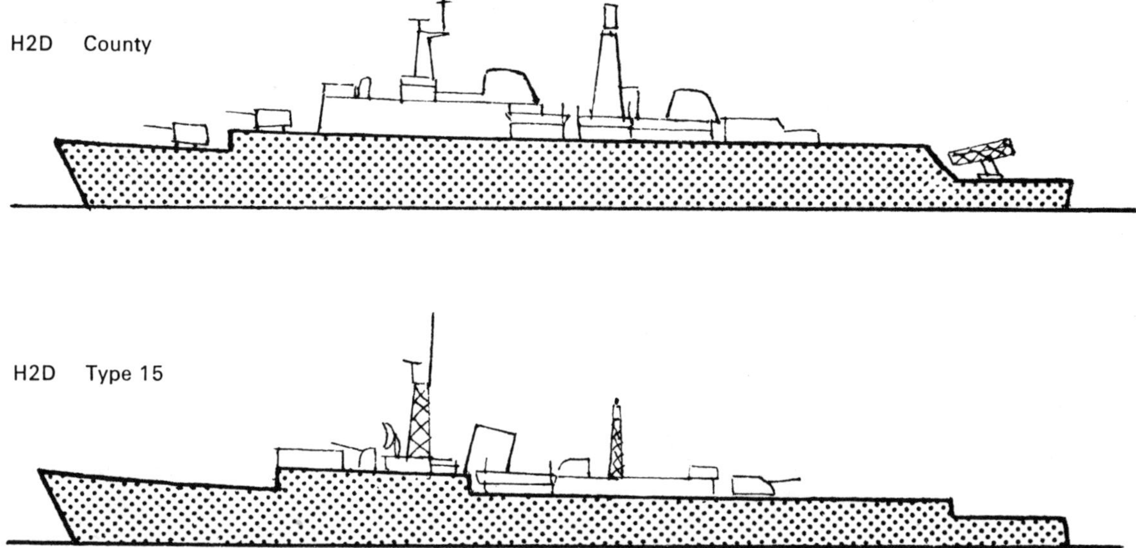


# TYPES OF STEMS (B)

**Bows (B)** These are enlargements of those on page 20 and with some aircraft carrier types added—the first being a British and the latter, an American type.

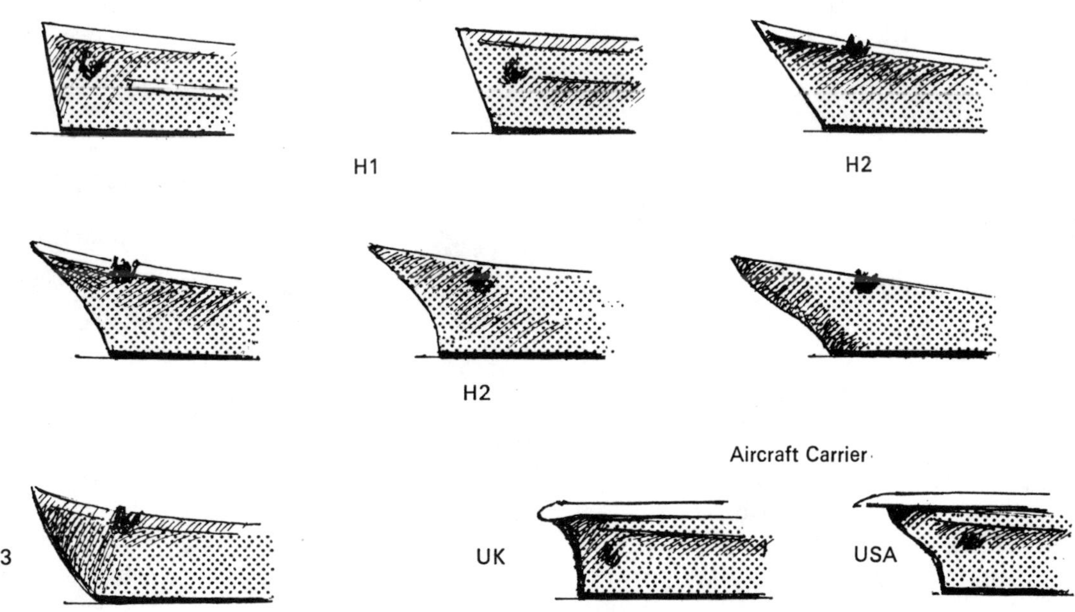

# TYPES OF STERNS (S)

**Sterns (S)** Enlargements of those on page 20, No 5 being of British and American aircraft carriers.

Added to No 2 is a typical Canadian destroyer stern.

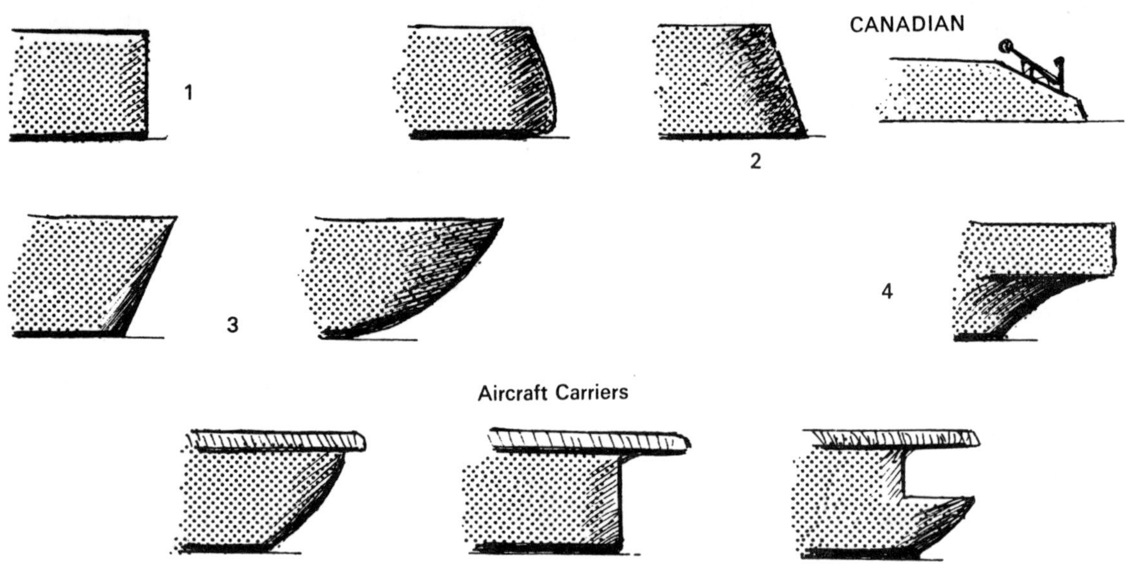



# FUNNELS (F)

**Funnels (F)** The presence of funnels noted on the Distant View now needs amplification by an estimation of size. Two groups, each of three variants, are used. The size is relative to the height above the structure or deck upon which it stands. Varying shapes may also be noted or left to the Close View. If a funnel is raked, always add r to the report.

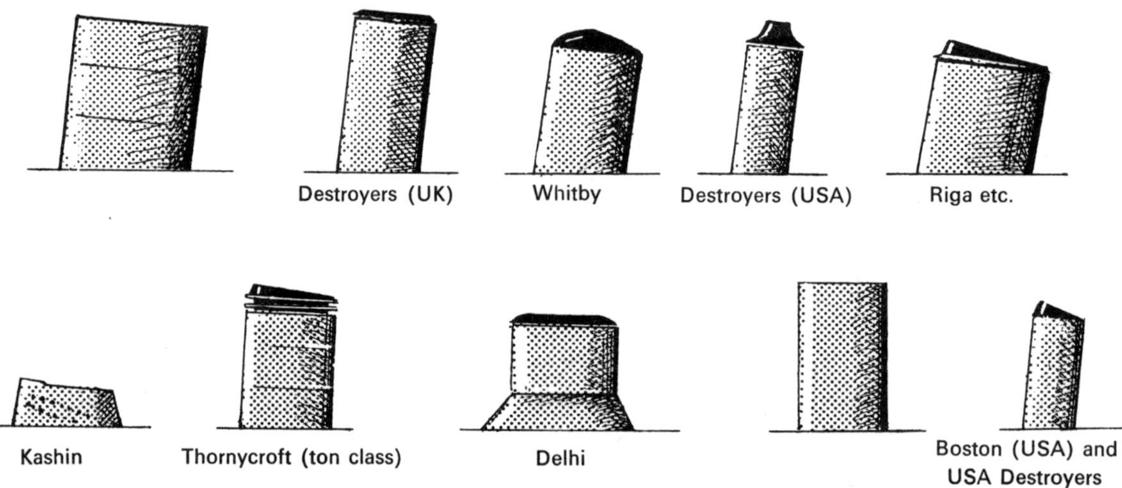

DU

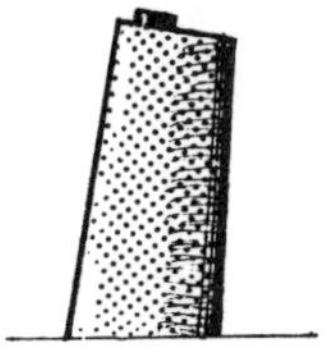

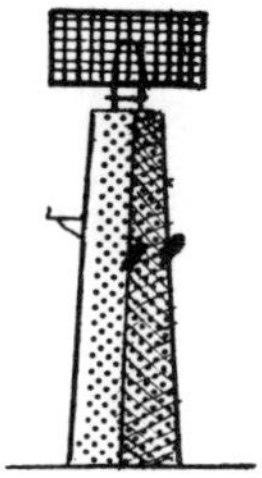

Modern Conical

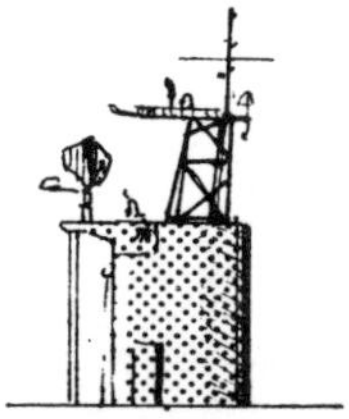

Bergamini (ITALY)
Modern Complex type

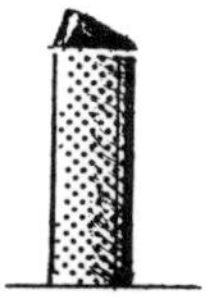

Modern Matchstick.
Fearless Tiger

Daring

Tiny modern type.
De Cristofaro class (ITALY)

**Turrets, Guns, Torpedo Tubes, Laun-
chers, Mortars, Directors** etc. may be
noted or amplified by studying the accompanying drawings or variations.

# GUNS (G)

Small Gun

Shield

AA gun

Turret

Mortar

USSR

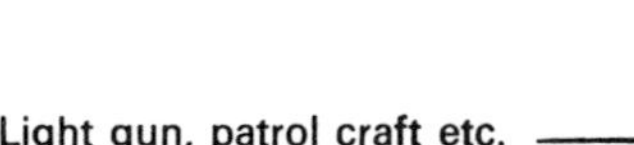

Light gun, patrol craft etc.

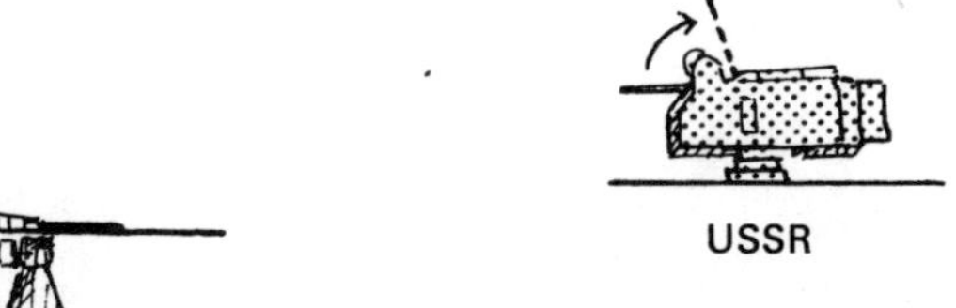

USSR

# LAUNCHERS (L)

Twin Terrier
(USA, DU, ITALY)

Single Tartar

Seacat (UK)

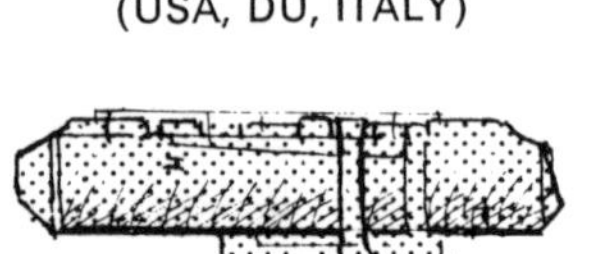

Shaddock (USSR)

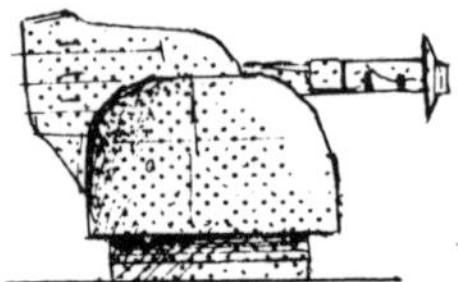

Anti Submarine weapon.
Able/Alpha     (USA)

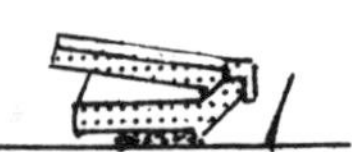

Seaslug (UK)

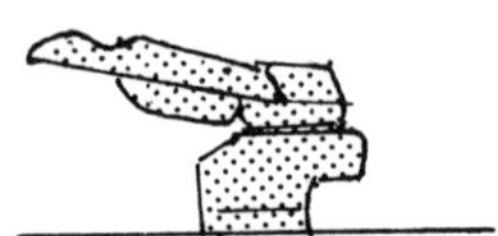

Twin Goa (USSR)

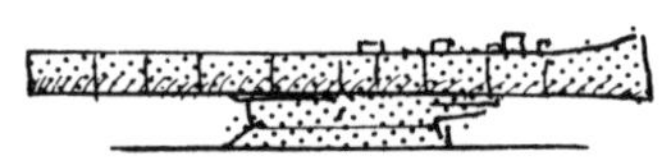

Torpedo Tubes (USSR)

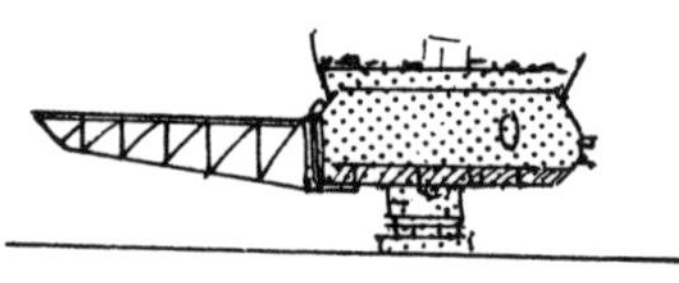

Strela (USSR)

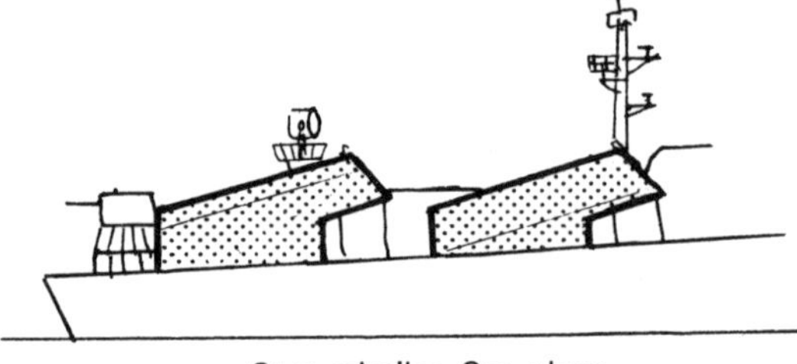

Styx missiles Osa class

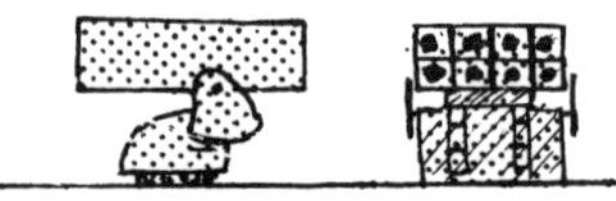

Asroc (USA)

6 barrelled rocket launcher
(also **12** barrelled) (USSR)

Rocket   Launchers   (Coded 'L' when
clearly visible)

DU

Squid

Limbo

# DIRECTORS AND RADAR

USA

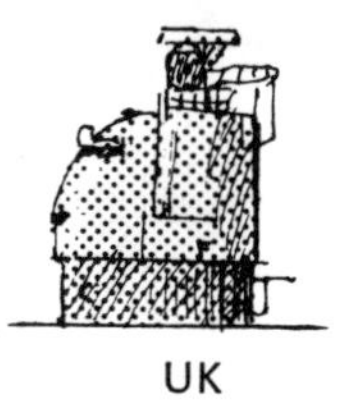

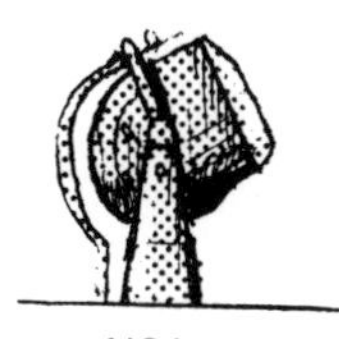
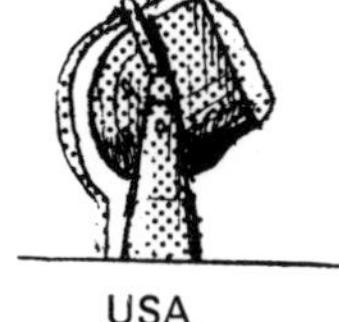

UK

USA

USSR

USSR (Kashin)

USSR

Radar (UK)
Warning and Control System
Aircraft Carriers

UK

984 Radar Aerial (UK)

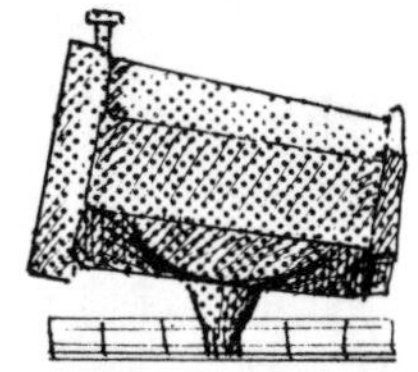
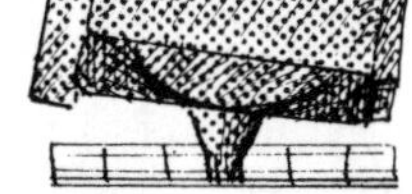

Tacan—Not coded. Usually
on top of mast

965 Radar Aerial (UK). Some single

Aircraft Direction   Aerial (UK).
Salisbury Class

# CRANES (C)

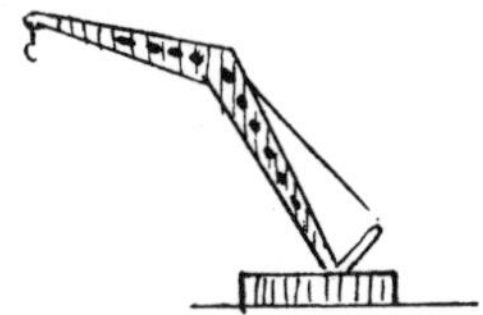

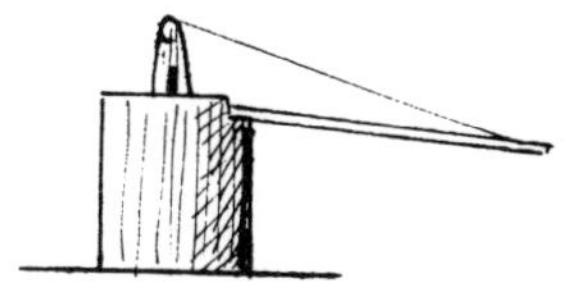

# The Close View

As mentioned earlier, the Close View may be largely of academic interest, as when a warship comes really close, if she is a friend she is ready at hand to protect you and if an enemy, nothing much matters.

On the other hand for general interest and even for the acquisition of knowledge that may be very valuable on future occasions, it must not be neglected.

It may well be that opportunities to see various fittings in their setting have never occurred before and even some of the features that should have been visible in the Medium View may have been overlooked or they may have been obscured for some reason or other.

The presence of mine rails or of an helicopter deck may become apparent.

The accompanying drawing shows a Russian destroyer of the *Kynda* Class.

Details such as boat stowage, booms, smaller guns, launchers, breakwaters and other features show up for the first time.

Every opportunity should be taken of looking at ships close up, even in dock, to familiarize oneself with small points that may all add a link to the chain of correct observation.

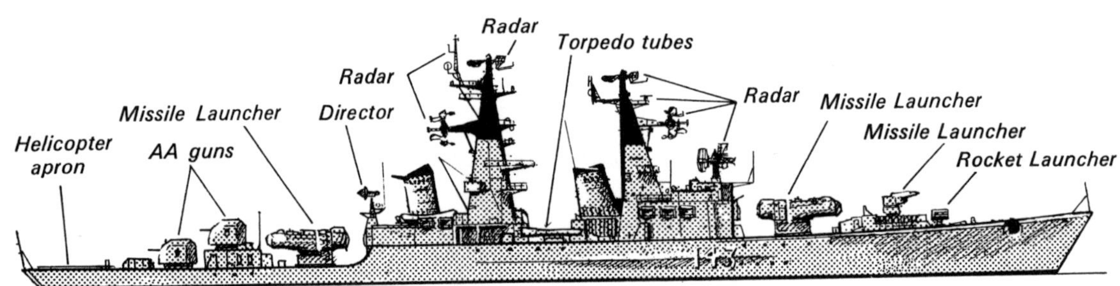

# Naval Ensigns

Naval Ensigns may differ considerably from the Merchant Ensigns and from the National Flag as worn ashore, or they may be the same for all three as in the case of France and the United States.

Others, are differenced by being swallow tailed or with three tails as in Finland, Norway and Sweden.

A number of British Commonwealth countries retain the white field and Cross of St. George but with their own National Flag replacing the British Union Flag in the Canton, while Australia and New Zealand retain the Union Flag but replace the Cross of St. George with the Stars of the Southern Cross.

In navies of most countries the Ensign is worn from the Ensign staff while in harbour or at anchor and from the peak when at sea. In action Masthead Ensigns are nearly always worn in addition.

In some cases the flags are incorrect heraldically as there is no fimbriation of metal dividing colour from colour. Notable exceptions to this occur in the ensigns of South Africa and Yugoslavia.

It has been impossible to show in much detail the sometimes very complicated badge or central design on such a small scale.

Flags are arranged first in four principal categories:

1 Flags with prominent crosses—Numbers 1-14.
2 Flags divided vertically—Numbers 15-20.
3 Flags divided horizontally—Numbers 21-41.
4 Flags with field predominately of one colour.

Within each of these sections they are next arranged in *strict alphabetical order* of colours; for example—Numbers 1-3 have blue fields but Number 1 has *red* and *white* markings while Number 3 has *yellow*.

Again, Numbers 4 and 5 both have red fields but Number 4 has *blue* and *white* markings while Number 5 has *white* alone (B & W before W).

In the Vertical flags Number 15 has *blue, white* and red stripes, Number 16 has *blue, yellow* and red and Numbers 17 and 18 have *green,* white and red.

Finally in the Number 4 section there are *blue* flags, *green* flags, *red* flags, *white* flags and *yellow* flags.

## ALPHABETICAL LIST OF COUNTRIES REPRESENTED

Libya 23

Malaysia 10
Mexico 18

Netherlands 26
New Zealand 56
Nigeria 12
North Vietnam 53
Norway 4

Pakistan 46
Persia (Iran) 35
Peru 20
Philippines 25
Poland 40

Portugal 47

Royal Fleet Auxiliary (UK) 43
Russia (USSR) 58
Rumania 16

Siam (Thailand) 27
South Africa 7
South Korea 42
South Vietnam 60
Spain 41
Sweden 3
Syria 21

Taiwan 51
Thailand 27

Turkey 52

United Arab Republic (Egypt)
 22
United Kingdom 9
United States 37
Uruguay 33
USSR (Russia) 48

Venezuela 28
Vietnam (North) 53
Vietnam (South) 60

Yugoslavia 50

West Germany 24

1. ICELAND.

2. DOMINICAN REPUBLIC.

3. SWEDEN.

4. NORWAY.

5. DENMARK.

6. FINLAND.

7. SOUTH AFRICA.

8. BURMA.

9. UNITED KINGDOM.

10. MALAYSIA.

11. INDIA.

12. NIGERIA.

13. CEYLON.

14. BELGIUM.

15. FRANCE.

★16. RUMANIA.

17. ITALY.

18. MEXICO.

19. CANADA.

20. PERU.

★21. SYRIA.

★22. UNITED ARAB REPUBLIC
(EGYPT).

23. LIBYA.

24. WEST GERMANY.

25. PHILIPPINES.

26. NETHERLANDS (HOLLAND)

27. THAILAND (SIAM).

28. VENEZUELA.

29. ECUADOR.

30. COLOMBIA.

Black STARS indicate countries in the Communist Bloc or countries whose navies consist largely of Russian supplied vessels.

★31. CUBA.

32. GREECE.

33. URUGUAY.

34. ARGENTINA.

35. IRAN (PERSIA).

36. GHANA.

37. UNITED STATES.

38. CHILE.

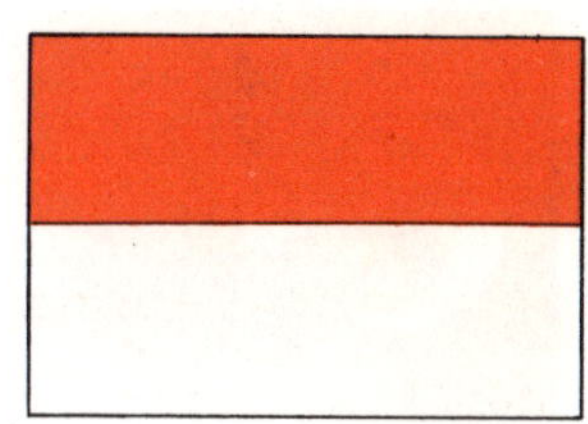

39. INDONESIA.

★40. POLAND.

41. SPAIN.

42. SOUTH KOREA.

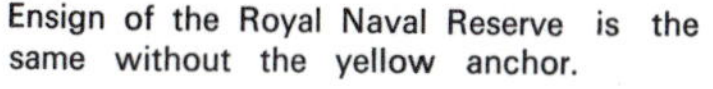

43. UNITED KINGDOM. (ROYAL FLEET AUXILIARY).

Ensign of the Royal Naval Reserve is the same without the yellow anchor.

44. ISRAEL.

45. BRAZIL.

46. PAKISTAN.

47. PORTUGAL.

48. ALBANIA.

★49. EAST GERMANY.

Naval Auxiliaries have the same device and horizontal stripes but on a Blue Field with various badges such as a yellow lighthouse for Hydrographic Service.

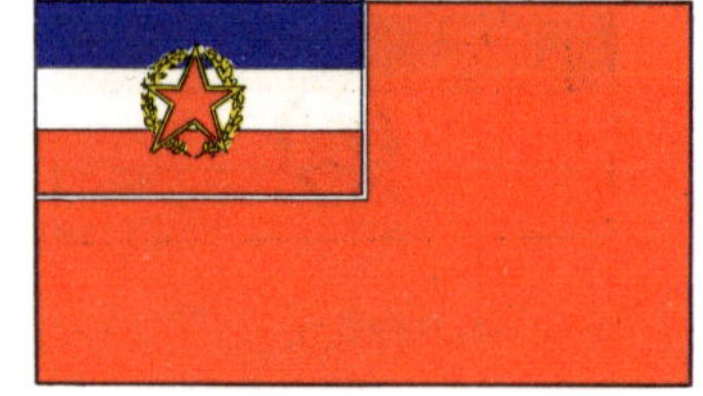

★50. YUGOSLAVIA.

51. NATIONALIST CHINA (TAIWAN).

52. TURKEY.

★53. NORTH VIETNAM.

★54. COMMUNIST CHINA.

55. AUSTRALIA.

56. NEW ZEALAND.

57. JAPAN.

★58. U.S.S.R. (RUSSIA)

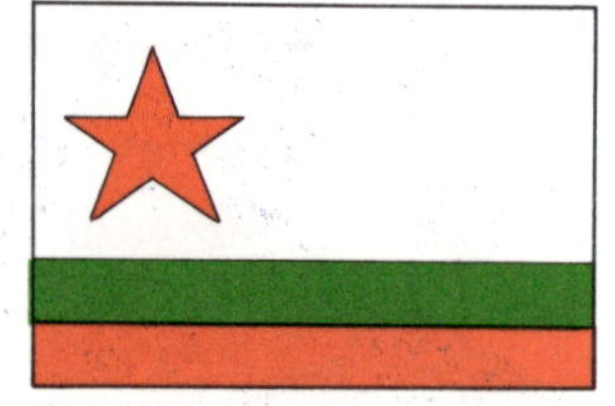

★59. BULGARIA.

60. SOUTH VIETNAM.

# Positioning

It has already been stated that spaces between features may be of more value in identification of a particular ship, than the features themselves.

Positioning is the most important step in coding for there may be many ships with the same or similar sequences and hull form but the positions, lengths and spacing vary greatly.

The length of a vessel is divided *visually* (or *actually* on a drawing or photograph), into twelve equal parts, 0 at the stem and 12 at the stern. Every feature is estimated against this grid and any feature between two divisions is coded as Q.

The ship shown above is therefore now coded as follows:

> G G Con. M F M F D G G. H/I. B2. S2. F6.
> FL (Forecastle Length) 0–9.
> Con. (Control Tower) at 3Q.  M (Masts) at 4, 6Q.
> F (Funnel) at 4Q, 6Q.
> G (Turrets) at 2, 2Q, 9, 9Q.

Positions of smaller turrets along the forecastle deck, plating below first funnel, torpedo tubes, bridge and all other objects may all be similarly positioned, coded and reported.

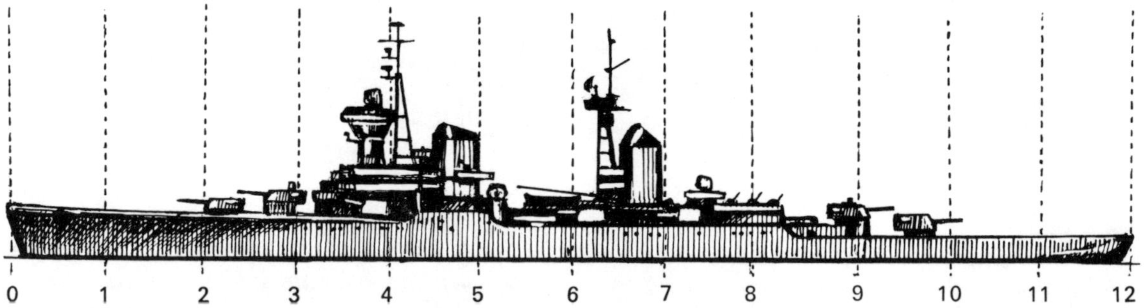

# Armament

In a conventional ship the heaviest weapons constitute the *main armament* and the next heaviest, the *secondary armament.*

The largest guns are usually in turrets or large gun houses which totally enclose the weapons and they are almost invariably placed in positions along the centre line of the vessel.

In vessels such as cruisers, there may also be a row of smaller turrets, usually along the sides of the upper deck. The *Sverdlov* Class of the USSR are excellent examples.

The secondary armament in smaller ships probably consists of anti-aircraft or dual purpose guns. These are grouped at various positions and may be individual, massed around the bridges or at other strategic and advantageous positions both for attack and defence. Most of these small weapons are not enclosed but probably have a light protecting shield in front.

Missile launchers of various sizes, types and functions, are rapidly taking the place of the large guns and some ships have their main armament entirely consisting of surface to air, surface to surface or anti-submarine launchers.

The accompanying diagram shows the plan of a ship with the general positioning of weapons although all those indicated are unlikely to be found in any one ship.

The main turrets when on the centre line, are lettered as shown. Thus A is always the first and perhaps the only turret forward, followed by B if a second and by C if a third.

C turret may sometimes be on the same level as A as in some of the older United States' cruisers, or superimposed over B as it was originally in the British *Dido* Class.

Should there be a midship turret it is designated Q, and X and Y are aft.

Smaller guns are coded and positioned in the same manner.

Conventional torpedo tubes (which are not sequenced in the distant view), are usually on the upper deck of surface ships or in the waist. Homing torpedo tubes are generally fixed pointing outboard on either beam, diagonally or at right angles to the centre line.

*Limbos* or *Squids* are positioned aft, frequently in a recessed portion of the upper deck.

Some anti-submarine mortars are placed forward in the neighbourhood of the bridge.

There are many sizes of rocket or missile launchers and they may be found in many varying positions although the larger ones are normally on the centre line like turrets.

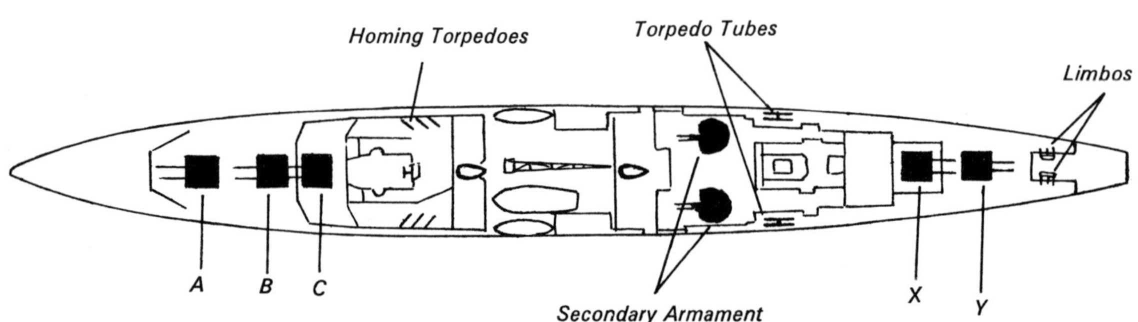


**Superimposed Turrets**

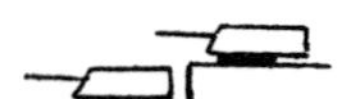

# SOME SHIP-BORNE GUIDED MISSILES

ASROC   Anti Submarine Rocket Launcher. (USA)

EXOCET   Short Range Surface to Surface Missile. (France)

GOA   Anti-Aircraft Missile. (USSR)

IKARA   Long Range Anti-Submarine Missile. (Au.)

MALAFON   Long Range anti-submarine weapon system. (France)

MASURCA   Marine Supersonic Rocket Contre Avions. (France)

POLARIS   Fleet Ballistic Missile. (USA)

POSEIDON   Improved Polaris. (USA)

SAWFLY   Intermediate Range Surface to Surface Ballistic Missile. (USSR)

SEACAT   Short Range Ship to Air Missile. (UK)

SEA DART   Medium Range Ship to Air Missile. (UK)

SEA KILLER   Short Range Surface to Surface Missile. (Italy)

SEA LANCE   Close Range Surface to Surface Missile. (USA)

SEASLUG   Medium Range Ship to Air Missile. (UK)

SHADDOCK   Medium Range Surface to Surface Missile. (USSR)

STANDARD   Medium to Long Range Supersonic Surface to Air Missile. (USA)

STYX   Close Range Surface to Surface Missile. (USSR)

TALOS   Long Range Surface to Air Missile. (USA)

TARTAR   Supersonic Surface to Air Missile. (USA)

TERNE   Short Range Surface to Surface Missile. (Norway)

TERRIER   Supersonic Surface to Surface Missile. (USA)

# Tonnage and Size Estimation

A floating object displaces or pushes aside its own weight in water.

**Warships** are always calculated on this *displacement* or actual weight in tons. It varies from light trim when a vessel has few stores and little ammunition as on trials to full or loaded trim when she has full magazines, fuel tanks and stores as in war time. The difference between the two is very considerable.

*Standard displacement* is that shown in most reference books and implies full magazines and stores but no fuel or reserve water.

**Merchant Ships** are usually spoken of in terms of *gross tons.*

This is volume and has nothing to do with weight—100 cubic feet of enclosed space being equal to one ton and this capacity tonnage had its origin in the number of tuns

## RELATIVE SIZES

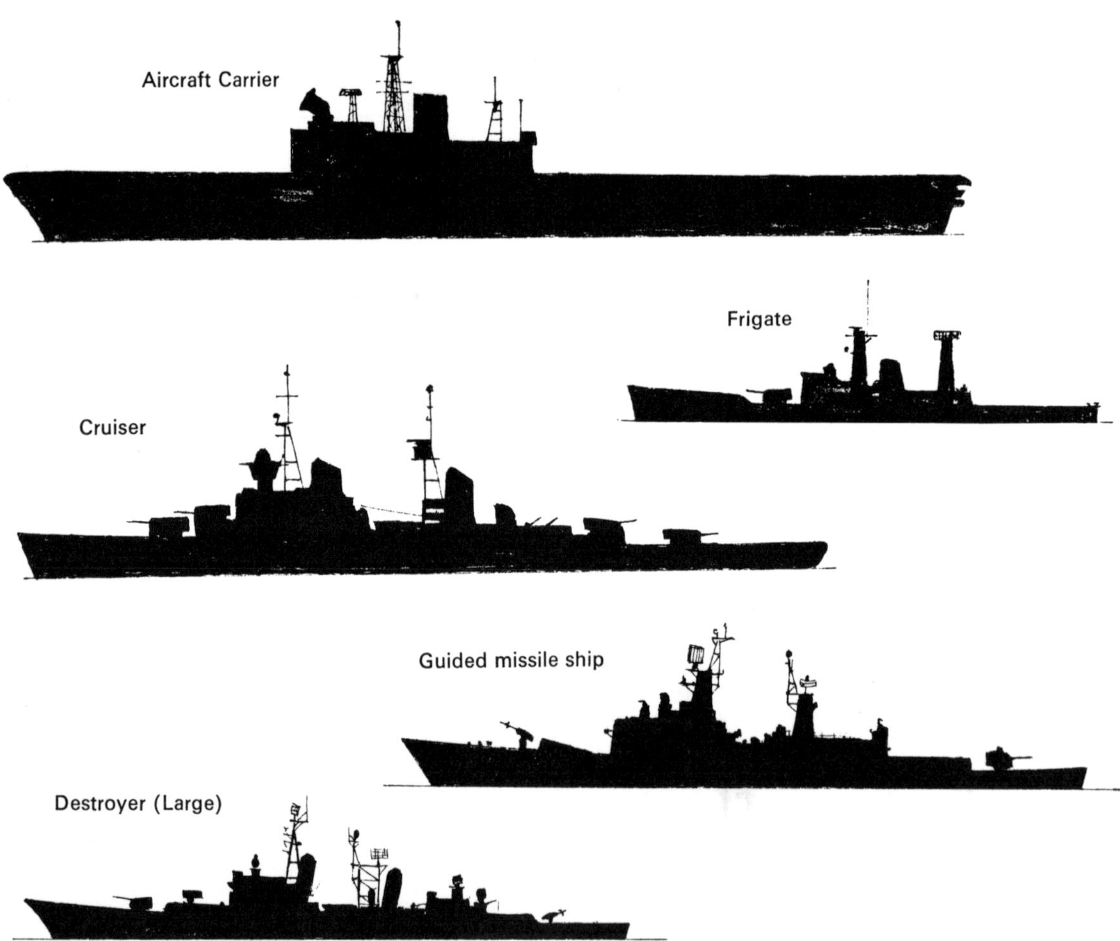

or casks of wine that a ship could carry.

*Length of* a ship varies considerably, that along the waterline frequently being considerably less than that over all, especially in a ship having a heavily raked stem.

Estimation of the size of a ship at sea is difficult as there is nothing by which to measure her. Some observers have a feeling for it and it is probably few who cannot form some estimation as to whether a ship is large or small, a Cruiser or a Minesweeper, but this is relative and whether either is a large or small example of its type is another matter. The general tendency is to *over estimate*. As a guide, the larger such fittings as boats and guns appear, the smaller the ship. Similarly a vessel with six turrets is fairly obviously larger than one with two but this may not always be the case.

**Over Estimation** of size is often noticeable when:
1 The object is silhouetted with the sun or light behind it.
2 In dull or foggy weather.
3 When ship and sky or sea are more or less of the same colour.
4 When the observer is close to sea level as in a small boat or a submarine.
5 When a ship is seen other than broadside.

**Under Estimation** occurs when:
1 The sun is directly on the ship.
2 In very clear weather. This might be occasioned by mirage.
3 In a very calm sea.
4 When viewed from the air.
5 When fore-shortened. (Not necessarily the same as No 5 above.)

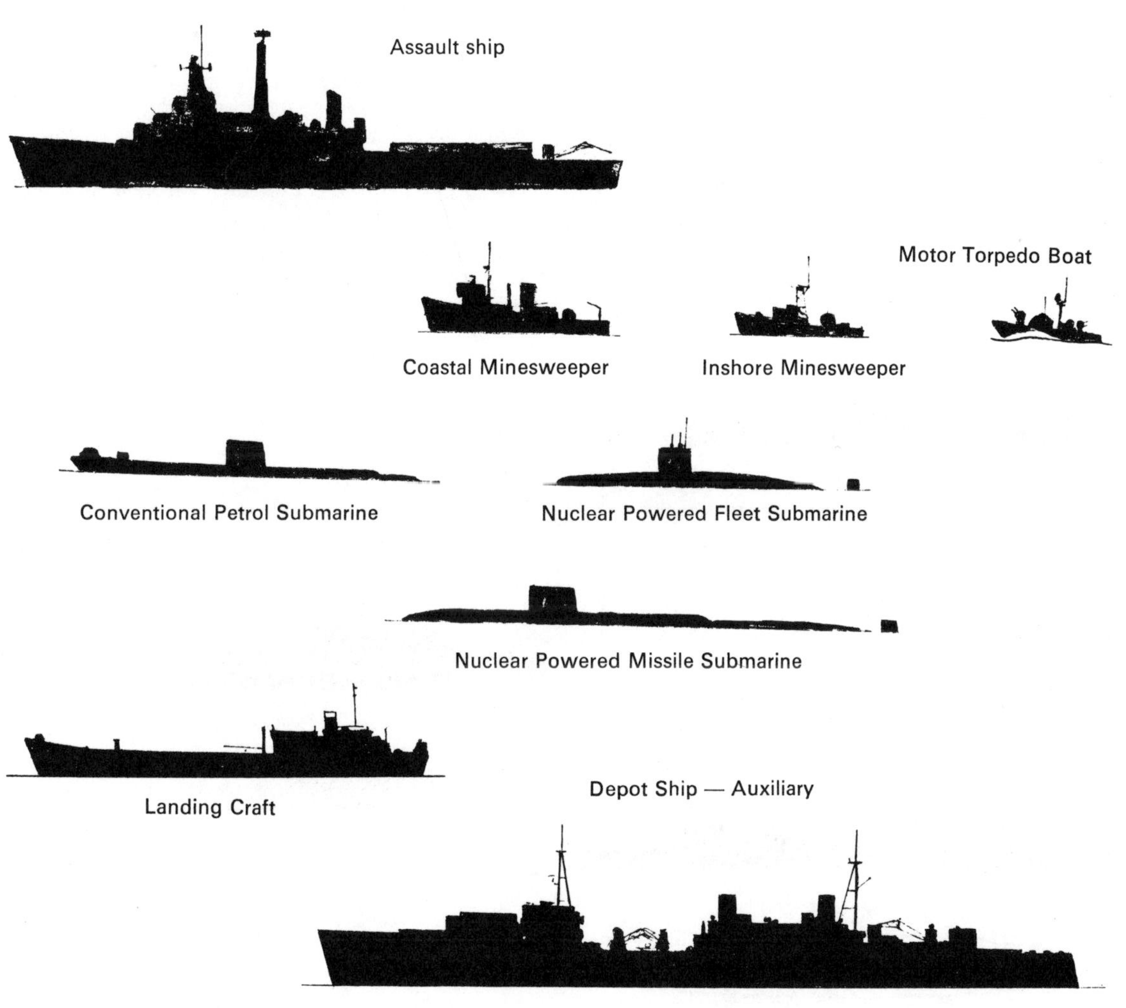

# Warship Types

All ships designed and built to perform a common duty, constitute a *Type.* Thus there is an Aircraft Carrier Type, a Destroyer Type and so on. A basic similarity obtains among ships of a Type in most navies although considerable confusion reigns, even in closely knit associations such as NATO, as to designation.

A type designated a Destroyer by one country may be known as a Frigate or an Escort in another. Again a vessel may be downgraded during her career, starting life as a Fleet Destroyer and ending as a Light Escort. In spite of this, for identification purposes and reporting, there remain certain categories which by and large hold good.

From the air, Types may be identified from their hull shapes showing ratio of length to beam which remain fairly constant. The overlapping of Types must be borne in mind although the actual function of the vessel sighted, is at this stage, not too relevant.

By adopting a standardized method of sighting and reporting, the task is easier for observers and the system is designed to aid them in this.

In the last war things were in some cases, a little easier, as for example, no Battleship had more than two funnels and therefore a ship with three, could not possibly have come into this category unless disguise was employed—a factor always to be borne in mind.

In the Type Characteristics described below, the boldest outlines enveloping the entire shape as first sighted, are termed *hallmarks* and these can be memorized—can be seen at a great distance, and provide one link with identification.

## HALLMARKS

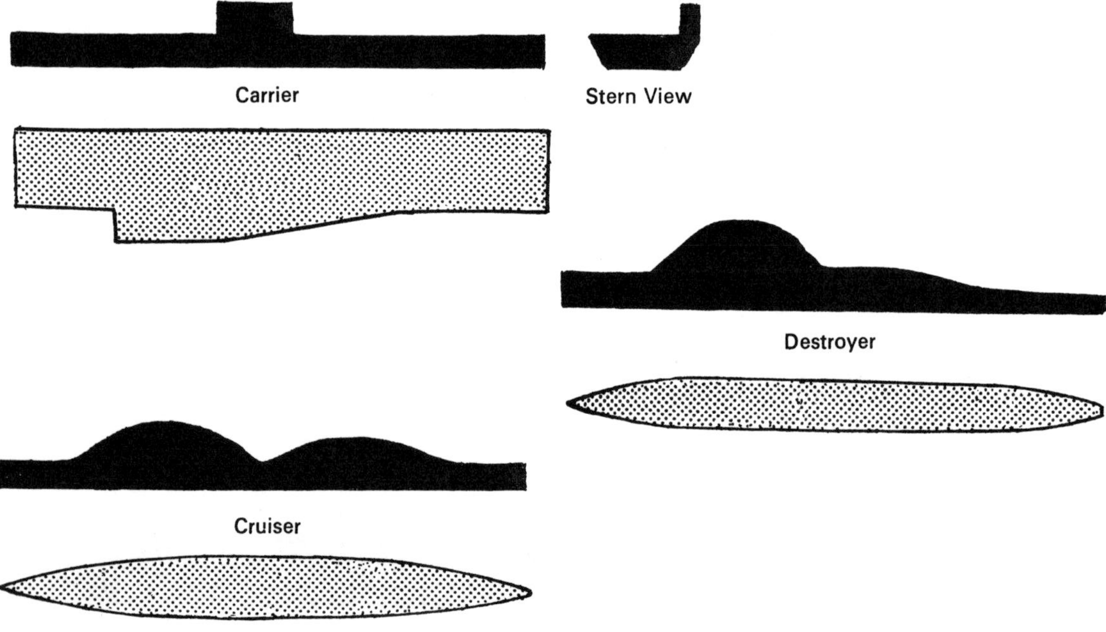

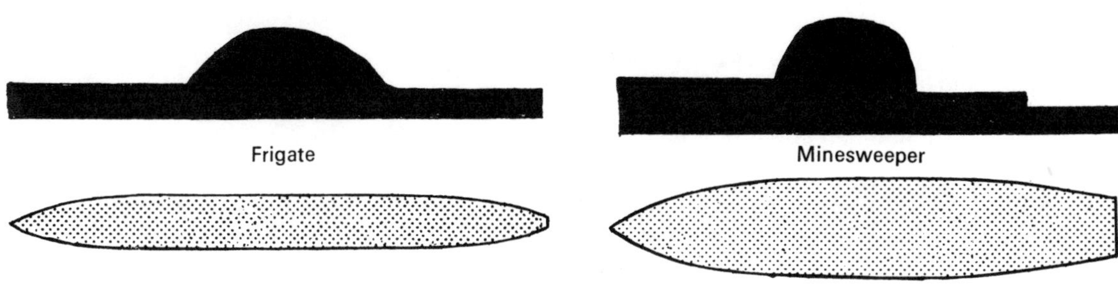


# TYPE CHARACTERISTICS

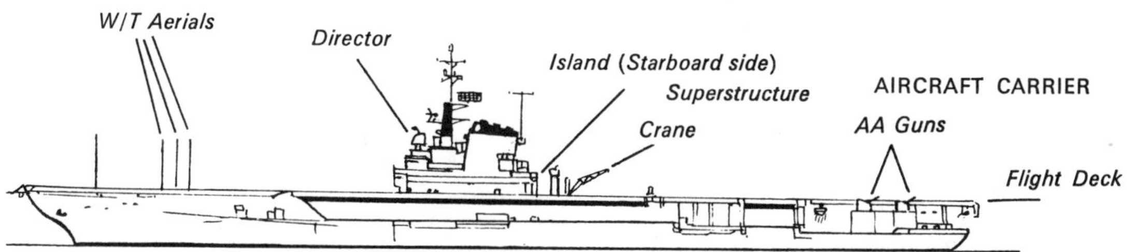


## Carrier Types

HALLMARKS (Whether attack, commando carriers or carriers that have been converted to other uses.) Briefly, a box with a clean, small superstructure amidships.

PLAN Rectangular or with sharp angled-deck on the port side. Superstructure always on starboard side.

FEATURES High freeboard. No sheer. Characteristic stems and sterns. Sponsons from sides to support overhanging flight deck or light guns. Light wireless masts at sides, swung outboard when flying is in progress.

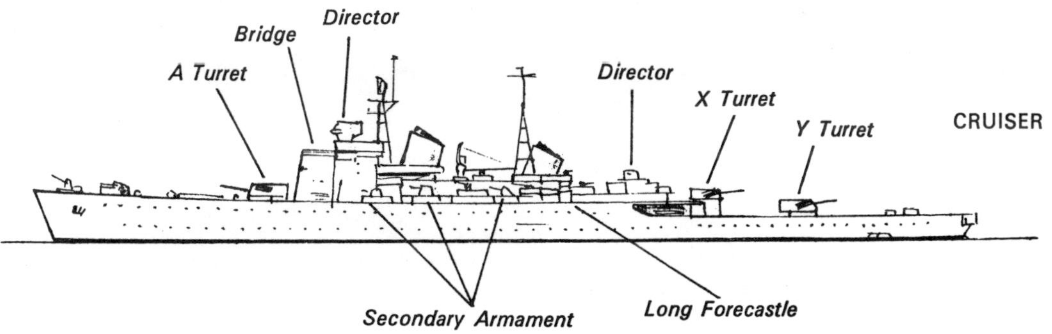


## Cruiser Types

HALLMARK Almost triangular block of superstructure or in two large curves. Plenty of weather deck fore and aft.

PLAN Cigar shape. Beam about one-ninth to one-eleventh of ship. Sometimes have a transom stern.

FEATURES Large bridges. Flush decked or with long forecastle. Conspicuous turrets. Frequently two funnels, sometimes thin and raking. Probably light masts with foremast clear of bridge. Rakish appearance except Russian, which are *stiff*.

**Destroyer Types (Conventional)**
HALLMARK  Tall hump well foreward. After part comparatively low.
PLAN  Pencil shaped with straight sides and tapering stern. Beam about one-tenth of length.
FEATURES  Bridge well foreward on tall forecastle. Probably two large funnels with considerable rake. Light, raking masts. Gun houses frequently look very large. Torpedo tubes. Anti-submarine gear aft. Space between features.

**Frigate Types**
(Those converted or partially converted from destroyers naturally more nearly resemble them.)
HALLMARK  Similar to Destroyers but hump more centralized and cone shaped. Shorter.
PLAN  Similar to Destroyers but shorter.
FEATURES  Generally *lighter* in appearance. Probably flush-decked or with very long forecastles. Fewer and smaller guns. Probably only a single funnel. More bunched up.

**Escort Types**
(Most ships classed as Escorts are either older types of small Destroyers or even former Minesweepers.)
HALLMARK  Similar to Destroyers.
PLAN  Similar to Destroyers.
FEATURES  Box bridge. Probably single raking funnel. Light masts. Guns very small and without screens. May have long forecastle and prominent sheer. Considerable anti-submarine gear aft.

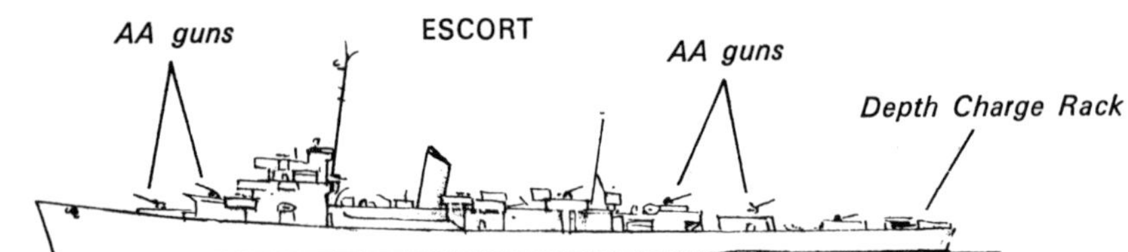


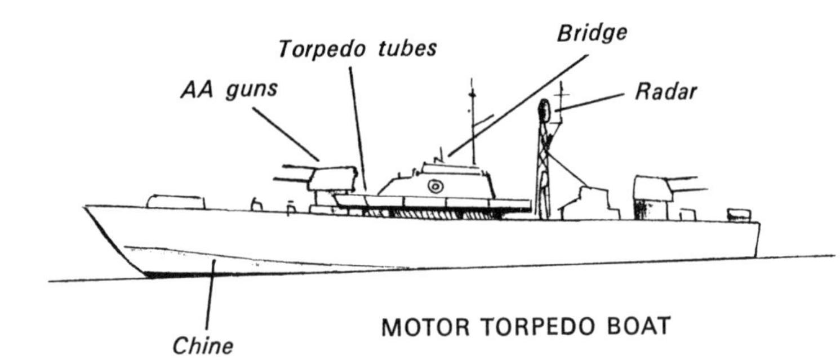


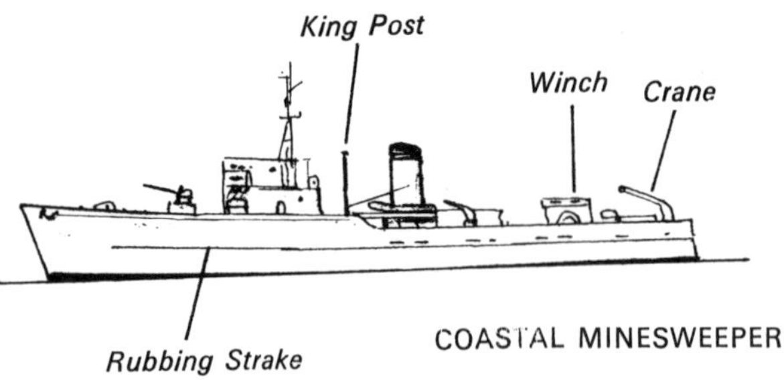

## Minesweeper Types

(This covers a very wide variety in appearance

HALLMARK  Short and squat with tall hump amidships. Hull low aft.

PLAN  Short and with wide beam.

FEATURES  Squat and with bridge well foreward. High freeboard. Short sheer foreward. Prominent rubbing strakes. Funnel large and vertical, about amidships. Tall kingpost near funnel. Small cranes like davits right aft to handle sweeping gear. Large winches which may be covered with grating or canvas and look box like.

## Motor Torpedo Craft

These are mostly self evident and need no amplification. When at speed, lift their foot right clear and are enveloped in heavy spray.

They mostly have a small bridge or superstructure somewhere about amidships, gun barrels look very long, and sometimes they have very prominent torpedo tubes or rocket launchers.

## Submarines

Self evident and dealt with in a later chapter. It is just possible and in certain lights, to mistake a submarine for a small surface ship, especially such craft as the R Class of the USSR.

## Auxiliaries

These cover such a variety of types that it is impossible to generalize. Mostly of the same build as merchant cargo vessels or tankers. Fleet Oilers equipped with fuelling at sea gear are distinctive by reason of the very tall kingposts and lengthy booms or derricks.

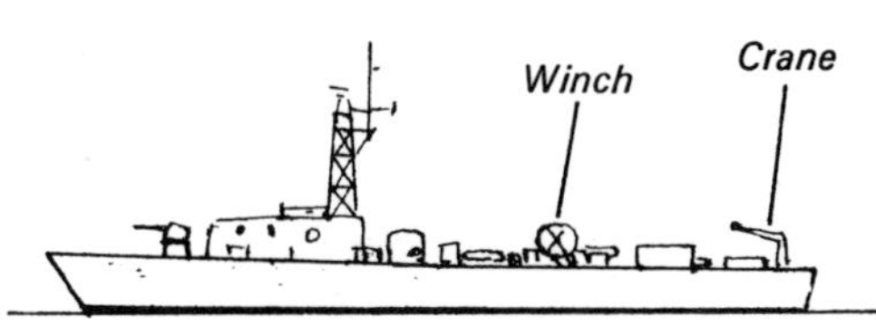


INSHORE MINESWEEPER

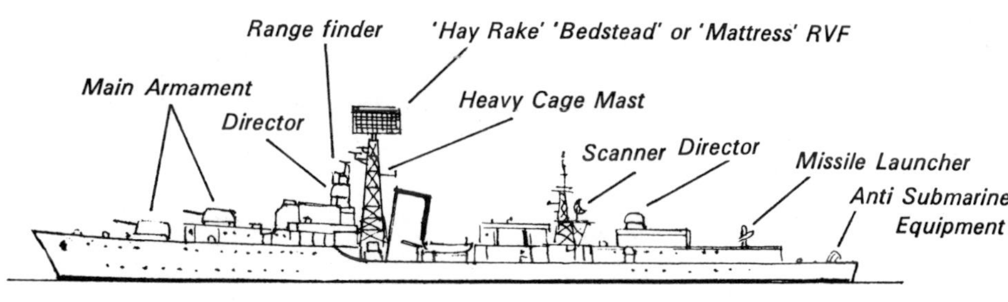


DESTROYER

# Submarines

Submarines are in a class of their own from several aspects. They come to the surface comparatively rarely and if they do they may be seen in varying stages of diving or rising to the surface. Even when travelling in surface trim, their freeboard is so slight that reporting has to be made on what is visible at the time. Further, if on the surface, a submarine may be coming to attack or intercept and it is by then probably too late to achieve much by reporting at all.

Much of the above is undoubtedly true and some may therefore conclude that attempts at identification or reporting are completely pointless and yet, paradoxically, ability to do so is most important for there are occasions when a submarine may be disabled and unable to dive or it may be necessary to track her in exercises.

If shape of hull can be seen it is useful and a few of the most common hull forms, together with bows or stems and characteristic sterns, are featured in the accompanying diagram, 3. The shape of the stern is however almost immaterial and it is usually underwater anyway.

Periscopes and snorkels can be withdrawn

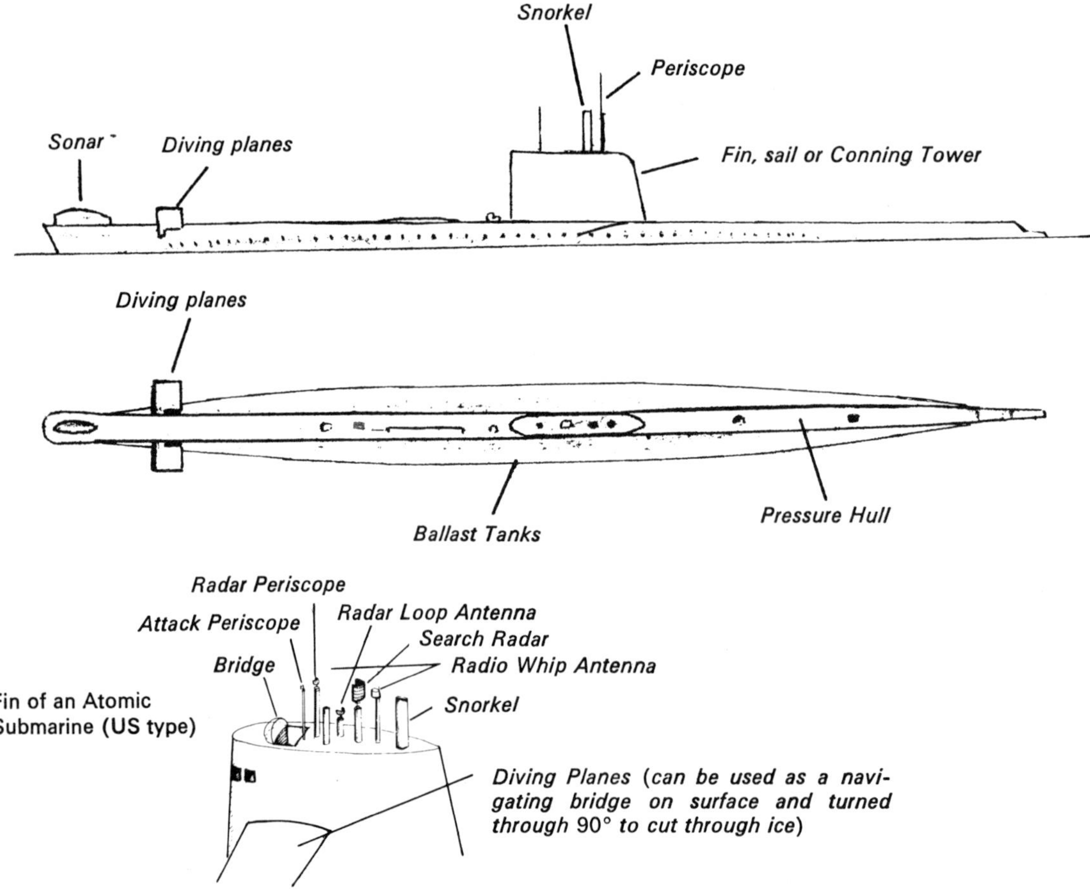

or raised at will, are not constant, and are therefore not a reliable feature. Clearly the principal and sometimes the only, feature of any value is the size, shape and positioning of the *Fin, Sail* or *Conning Tower.*

Position of diving planes should be noted as these vary, some being low down on the hull while others are on or near deck level. Many United States' nuclear powered submarines have planes in varying positions on the fin.

Diagram 4 shows a submarine positioned on the grid system as for surface vessels. This example would be coded; Hull Form 3, Fin 5 to $6\frac{1}{2}$, S (Sonar) $\frac{1}{2}$, G (Gun) $4\frac{1}{2}$, R (Rudder) $12\frac{1}{2}$

Using the system described immediately below, the Fin would be coded as: $U\frac{1}{2}$, A1, $U1\frac{1}{2}$, A2, $DA2\frac{1}{2}$. This may sound a little complicated but very short practice will prove that it is easily applied. As heights as well as lengths are used for coding fins it is necessary to use a piece of graph paper or alternatively to draw the shape on a piece of plain paper and then roughly square it up. Only an approximation is necessary.

Always code from bottom foreward to bottom aft using the following abbreviations: U = Up, D = Down, A = sloping Aft and F = sloping Foreward, adding O = Outward slope and N (instead of I which could be confused with figure 1) = Inward Slope. Thus the examples on Diagram 5 would be coded as follows: **Example A** U3, A2, DA3,I. **Example B** U1, A1,U1,A3,$D\frac{1}{2}$,A1,$D\frac{1}{2}$,A1,D1. **Example C** UA2,I, A2, D2,I,O.

The only other letters in this code to cover most of the remaining features that might be encountered are: Hu = Hump. That is, any other raised object not obviously a Sonar. R = Rudder. This is sometimes so far aft that it appears to be unconnected with the above—water hull and on the grid system must be reported as 13, 14 or 15, remembering that the 0–12 scale covers obvious visible waterline. So = Sonar.

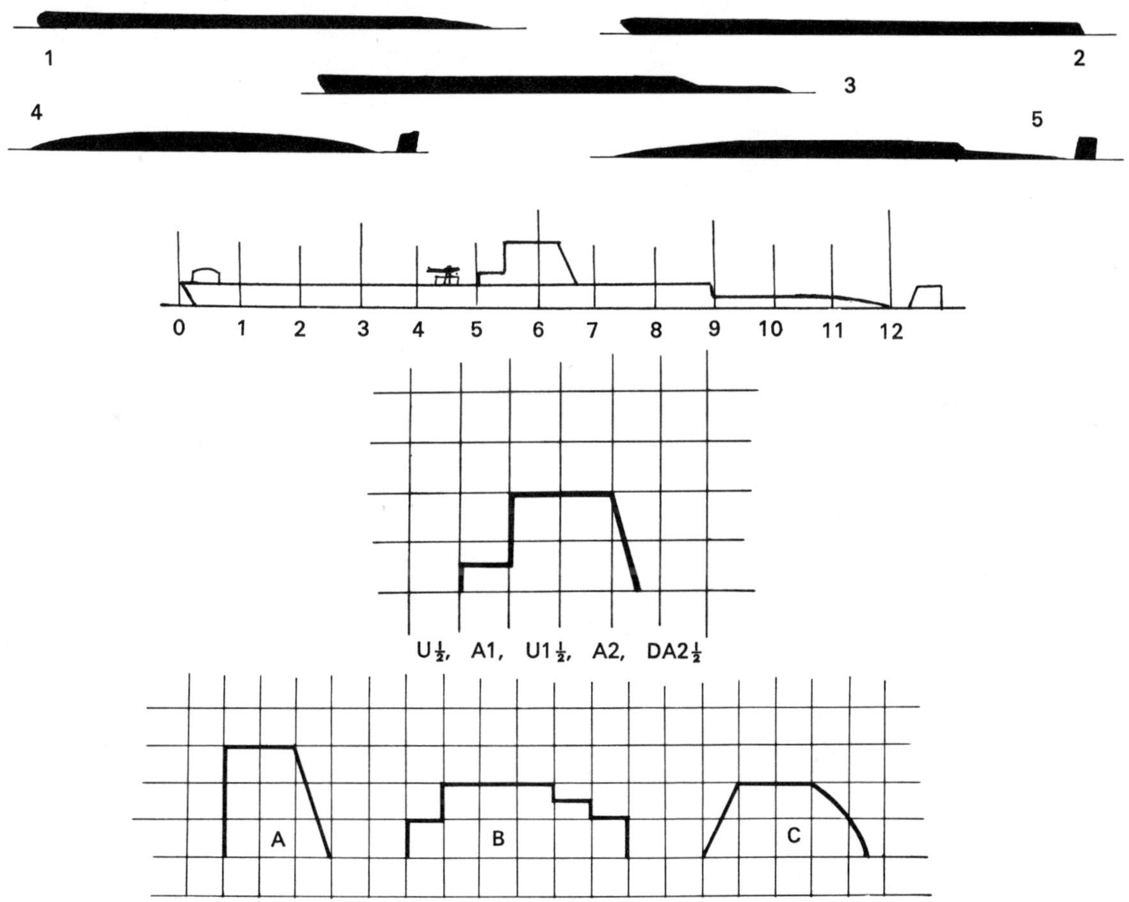

# Warship Classes

In each type of warship there are *Classes* or groups of ships built to the same design, sometimes by different builders but frequently by the same yard. These ships may therefore have almost identical features.

Usually a Class is named after the first or prototype but sometimes it is referred to by a generic term such as *County* Class, *Town* Class or *Battle* Class. The difference between Classes may often be very slight and may be confined to type of machinery rather than to any very noticeable difference in external appearance.

To attempt to define a Class is extremely risky especially as any original variation may be negatived or accentuated by reconstruction.

Occasionally a Class is very obvious however, such as a *Leander* Class Frigate although when supplied to other navies it probably bears a different designation.

Occasionally also a few details may differentiate conclusively between superficially similar Classes. For example the Russian *Sverdlov* Class Cruisers have very *long* forecastles while the earlier *Chapaevs* have *short* ones

In the United States and Russian Navies ships may be built in very large Classes indeed, numbering perhaps 50 or 60 ships.

If there is need for differentiation of Class this should be left for reference to special charts, reference books or to those qualified by specialist study and who are right up to date with their knowledge.

# Nationality or Country of Origin

Warships of some nations possess certain peculiarities in outward appearance but it would be dangerous for an untrained observer to attempt identification by this means. The most that might be attempted at first is to state the *possible* nation of origin. So many Navies of NATO, Commonwealth and other countries have craft designed by or formerly belonging to another nation. For example, Australia has Destroyers of a United States' Class and the Netherlands has Frigates of the British *Leander* Class.

The following notes may however be of some little help although too much reliance must not be placed on the features stressed. They might be borne in mind when piecing together the whole picture.

**NATO** Many ships have cage or enclosed masts of various complexities.

**USSR Cruisers** All have forecastles, frequently very long. Very heavy control towers and foremasts combined. Large funnels (mostly without rake) and sequence MF-MF not unlike certain ships of an earlier Italian design. Mine-laying sterns.

**Destroyers** Many are flush decked with very short and very steep sheer foreward. Very large gun houses and short gun barrels. Heavily raking masts and funnels, the latter often being very short. Sequence frequently MF-MF. Funnels well separated. Large bridges. Mine-laying sterns. Very raking stems. Some of the lighter guns have two barrels mounted vertically, a feature otherwise in one or two small Italian ships.

**USA Cruisers and Destroyers** Largely flush decked. Heavily raking stems, straight sterns. Frequently have prominent *run away* over entire length. Most Destroyers have a short section of low side plating abreast or just abaft the bridge. (A feature also of some Russian Destroyers.) Frequently have two tall thin funnels. Very heavy or tall tripod masts with widely stretched legs. Also heavy square cage masts. Sometimes have three turrets forward and/or aft. Large number of director towers.

**UK Destroyers and Frigates** Very often have a distinctive and somewhat complex hull form. Short cage masts or enclosed masts. Conspicuous life rafts on most types—white painted. Generally of low silhouette. Single funnels.

**JAPAN Destroyers** Flush-decked with continuous *run away* or else have extremely long forecastle. Small, heavily raking funnels. Heavy tripod masts. Heavily raking or curved and raking stems.

**NETHERLANDS Cruisers and Destroyers** Funnels bent back at an angle or trunked into masts. Mostly have raised forecastle and high freeboard.

**SWEDEN Destroyers** Mostly flush decked with very prominent *run away* over whole length. Very small funnels and small, low superstructure.

**ITALY Destroyers, Escorts etc.** Frequently have MF-MF sequence and must not be confused with Russian ships of similar characteristic.

# Colouring of Warships

Colouring as a guide to identification is of no great value as the greater proportion of the world's combatant surface ships are painted some shade of grey all over, with black boot-topping. The shade certainly varies and by and large, ships of countries in warm or sunny climates, are usually of a lighter hue than those in more northern waters.

It is true that some countries favour a rather distinctive shade, with perhaps more blue or green than normal in so called battleship grey, but these colours are not necessarily constant and are subject to alteration.

Undoubtedly all greys do have a large element of camouflage effect compared to other colours and when light and other weather conditions have to be taken into account, they do tend to blend or merge into the background.

Colouring of individual portions, such as masts may vary from Class to Class or even in vessels of the same Class in one Navy. Tops of masts may be white or black or the latter may be carried lower down as in some vessels with enclosed masts. Some may have black top to the funnel of varying depths or even bands of black, white or red.

Squadron badges are sometimes displayed on funnels and in the case of the NATO Standing Force, the ships comprising it bear the NATO insignia on the funnels.

Colouring of boats varies considerably and they may be grey, white, blue, green, black or red. Gun barrels are sometimes black.

Decks may be all-over grey or with portions in green, red, black, or brown Other decks may be plain wood.

Pendant numbers when appearing, are usually white or black and possibly outlined or shadowed by a contrasting colour. Deck landing numbers are also usually white.

It would probably confuse if an attempt was made to detail colours currently in use, nevertheless the following generalisations may be of some value.

SWEDEN  Some ships adopt a form of camouflage painting (not dazzle-painting) in dull shades.

USSR  Most combatant ships have a very thin white line between the topsides and the black boot-topping.

SUBMARINES  Various shades of grey in most Navies but some are black all over, including Royal Navy and other NATO countries.
Russian craft vary and some are dark blue or dark brownish green.

AUXILIARIES  Most auxiliaries and support ships are grey all over with black boot-topping and plain grey funnels or grey with black tops.

ROYAL FLEET AUXILIARY  Grey all over with black boot-topping, grey funnel or grey with black top.

ROYAL MARITIME AUXILIARY SERVICE  Comprises sea or ocean going craft not operated by the RFA such as cable ships, mooring craft, and large salvage tugs. Black hulls and boot-topping, grey upperworks and funnels.

PORT AUXILIARY SERVICE  Operating the smaller, harbour craft such as tugs and water carriers etc. Black hull, red boot-topping, buff upperworks and buff funnels with black top.

CANADIAN COAST GUARD  White or black hulls except icebreakers or Arctic patrol vessels, which have red. White upperworks, white funnels with black top and small red maple leaf beneath.

JAPANESE MARITIME SAFETY AGENCY  White hulls and superstructure. White or buff funnels with black top, red band and white or yellow star or chrysanthemum.

MILITARY SEA LIFT COMMAND (US)  Formerly the Military Sea Transport Service. Grey all over, black boot-topping, grey funnels with black top, below which is a blue band above a yellow one.

UNITED STATES COAST GUARD  White or black hulls, black or red boot-topping, white or buff funnels with black top.

Most ships have a wide diagonal band extending from upper deck to waterline, abaft the bows, on which is a large Coast Guard Insignia.

SURVEY & RESEARCH SHIPS Ships in most Navies are all white with buff funnels or buff with black top.

ICEBREAKERS: **Canadian** Red hulls and other colours as for Coast Guard vessels. Boats usually red.

**USA** White all over with buff or white funnel and black top.

**USSR** Black hulls. Red boot-topping with thin white dividing line. Buff or white funnel with black top and possibly a red band or red star beneath.

# Some Pitfalls and Confusing Factors

Possible distortions caused by weather conditions and variations in light have already been mentioned. In addition there are more permanent causes of confusion. Hull forms are frequently difficult to pick out, particularly in the distant view by reason of many items and pieces of equipment cluttering the upper deck. These tend to merge into one another and break up the outline.

Stems and sterns are frequently hidden by heavy weather or by bow waves and wake when a ship is at high speed. Port and Starboard views may differ by reason of small boats or deck houses on one side only. Life rafts and floats may vary in position. Canvas screens round bridges or platforms may not always be in position. Guns, launchers, winch gear, torpedo tubes and similar items are frequently covered against the weather by all-embracing canvas screens. They may also be covered with the intention of rendering them less conspicuous. Light guns may be temporarily removed from their mountings and even gun barrels turned from the fore and aft line may make observation difficult. Large ventilators may be turned or unshipped. Topmasts may be struck.

Naturally in war time, deliberate disguise or break up of outline by dazzle painting still further confuses the issue but that is another story.

No counters to any of the above can be suggested beyond a very careful comparison of a ship sighted with the solid black silhouettes. For this reason stress is again laid on the fact that *positioning* or *spacing* of the main objects such as masts and funnels is frequently of greater importance than looking for more details at an early stage. It is for this reason that in the second part of the book, the definite sequence is replaced by grouping those vessels together whose main outlines are similar. For example *Fletcher* Class ships will be found together regardless of whether they have three, four or five guns—the important thing being to recognize that she belongs to this Class. Functions and differences will then the more readily be discovered.

# Countries Having Naval Forces

## BRITISH COMMONWEALTH

**United Kingdom of Great Britain and Northern Ireland**  The Royal Navy.
**Australia**  The Royal Australian Navy.
**Canada**  The Canadian Armed Forces (Navy) 1964. Formerly the Royal Canadian Navy. (1910)
**Ceylon**  The Royal Ceylon Navy.
**Cyprus**  Coastal Patrol.
**India**  Indian Naval Service. 1947. Formerly Royal Indian Navy.

**Jamaica**  Jamaican Defence Force. Coast Guard.
**Kenya**  Kenya Navy. (1964).
**Malaysia**  The Royal Malay Navy.
**New Zealand**  The Royal New Zealand Navy.
**Nigeria**  Nigerian Navy.
**Pakistan**  Pakistan Navy. (Formerly Royal Pakistan Navy) 1947.
**Singapore**  Coast Guard.
**Trinidad & Tobago**  Coast Guard.

## COMMUNIST BLOC (WARSAW PACT) AND OTHER COMMUNIST COUNTRIES

**Albania**
**Bulgaria**
**China**  (People's Republic).
**Cuba**
**Germany**  (East).

**Korea**  (North).
**Poland**
**Rumania**
**Vietnam**  (North).
**Yugoslavia**

## VARIOUS TREATY ORGANISATIONS

**CENTO (Central Treaty Organization)**
**Iran**
**Pakistan**
**Turkey**
**United Kingdom**
**United States**

**NATO (North Atlantic Treaty Organisation)**
**Belgium**
**Canada**
**Denmark**
**Germany**  (West)
**Greece**
**Iceland**  (Coastguard)
**Italy**
**Netherlands**
**Norway**

**Portugal**
**Turkey**
**United Kingdom**
**United States**
**France** withdrew from NATO in 1966 but close co-operation is maintained in some exercises.

**SEATO (South East Asia Treaty Organisation)**
**Australia**
**France**
**New Zealand**
**Pakistan**
**Philippines**
**Thailand**
**United Kingdom**
**United States**

# Flag Abbreviations

| | | | | | | |
|---|---|---|---|---|---|
| AD | Abu Dhabi | Fr | France | Po | Portugal |
| Ag | Algeria | Ge | Germany | Pv | Peru |
| Al | Albania | Gh | Ghana | Py | Paraguay |
| Am | America (United States) | Gr | Greece | RC | Republic of China (Communist) |
| Ar | Argentina | Ia | Indonesia | RK | Republic of North Korea (Communist) |
| Au | Australia | Ic | Iceland | | |
| Be | Belgium | In | India | Rm | Rumania |
| Bm | Burma | Iq | Iraq | Ru | Russia |
| Br | Great Britain | Ir | Iran (Persia) | SA | South Africa |
| Bu | Bulgaria | Is | Israel | SAr | South Arabia |
| Bz | Brazil | It | Italy | Se | Senegal |
| Ca | Canada | Iv | Ivory Coast | Sg | Singapore |
| Cd | Cambodia | Ja | Japan | Si | Saudi Arabia |
| Ce | Ceylon | Ke | Kenya | So | Somalia |
| Ch | Chile | KO | South Korea | Sp | Spain |
| Cn | Cameroon | Ku | Kuwait | Sw | Sweden |
| Co | Colombia | Le | Lebanon | Sy | Syria |
| Cs | China (Nationalist) | Li | Liberia | Ta | Tanzania |
| Cu | Cuba | Ly | Libya | Th | Thailand (Siam) |
| Cy | Cyprus | Me | Mexico | Tn | Tunisia |
| Da | Denmark | Mo | Morocco | Tr | Trinidad |
| Do | Dominica | My | Malaysia | Tu | Turkey |
| Du | Netherlands | Ng | Nigeria | Ur | Uruguay |
| Ec | Ecuador | No | Norway | Ve | Venezuela |
| EG | East German | NV | North Vietnam | VN | Viet Nam (South) |
| Eg | Egypt | NZ | New Zealand | Ys | Yugoslavia |
| Et | Ethiopia | Ph | Poland | Za | Zambia |
| Fi | Finland | Pi | Philippines | | |
| | | Pk | Pakistan | | |

# SECTION TWO

# Solid Silhouettes

# Arrangement of Solid Silhouette Section

**Scale** 200 feet to 1 inch except for smaller craft which are drawn to a larger scale. In these cases the 200 foot scale is indicated by the horizontal line above each drawing.

Silhouettes are divided into six sections as below but *within* each section, strict *sequence* coding is adhered to, as indicated above the drawings.

*Hull Form* is not adhered to but in each case it is mentioned immediately after the consecutive number.

**1 Carrier Types** which includes all those ships converted to other functional types but which still retain the unmistakeable carrier silhouette.

**2 All other Combat Types** but excluding SUBMARINES which are dealt with only in Section 2.

**3 Merchant Ship Types** Profiles 1 & 2. Engines amidships. Including auxiliaries, some depot ships, boom defence craft, Icebreakers, tugs, etc.

**4 Merchant Ship Types** Profile 3. Engines aft but bridge amidships. Oilers, water carriers and other auxiliaries.

**5 Merchant Ship Types** Profile 4. Engines aft and all superstructure aft.

**6 Merchant Ship Types** Profile 5. Engines aft but bridge right foreward.

## EXPLANATION OF LEGENDS BENEATH SOLID SILHOUETTES

1 Consecutive Number
2 Hull Form
3 Type of Ship

4 Nationality
5 Number of drawing in grey
   or second section

# ABBREVIATIONS OF SHIP TYPES BENEATH BLACK DRAWINGS

| | |
|---|---|
| AC | Aircraft Carrier |
| Amph/AsltS | Amphibious Assault Ship |
| Amph/CmdS | Amphibious Command Ship |
| AmphTr | Amphibious Transport |
| Aslt | Assault |
| ATr | Aircraft Transport |
| Ax | Auxiliary |
| BDV | Boom Defence Vessel |
| C | Cutter |
| CblS | Cable Ship |
| CDVsl | Coast Defence Vessel |
| CG | Coast Guard |
| Cgo/AF | Cargo/Aircraft Ferry |
| CgoS | Cargo Ship |
| CmdS | Command Ship |
| CmdoC | Commando Carrier |
| Cmns/RlyS | Communications Relay Ship |
| Cr | Cruiser |
| Cvt | Corvette |
| D | Destroyer |
| DTdr | Destroyer Tender |
| DpoS | Depot Ship |
| DvgTdr | Diving Tender |
| E | Escort |
| EPB | Escort Patrol Boat |
| Exp | Experimental |
| F | Frigate |
| FPB | Fast Patrol Boat |
| FPVsl | Fast Patrol Vessel |
| FSptS | Fire Support Ship |
| FyPnL | Fishery Protection Launch |
| Gbt | Gunboat |
| GMCr | Guided Missile Cruiser |
| GMD | Guided Missile Destroyer |
| GME | Guided Missile Escort |
| GMF | Guided Missile Frigate |
| GMPB | Guided Missile Patrol Boat |
| HRprS | Heavy Repair Ship |
| HC | Helicopter Carrier |
| HC/Cr | Helicopter Cruiser |
| HplS | Hospital Ship |
| HyGB | Hydrofoil Gunboat |
| Ibr | Icebreaker |
| LCI | Landing Craft (Infantry) |
| LCT | Landing Craft (Tank) |
| LhtTdr | Lighthouse Tender |
| LS | Landing Ship |
| LSD | Landing Ship (Dock) |
| LSR | Landing Ship (Rocket) |
| MGB | Motor Gunboat |
| ML | Motor Launch |
| Mnhtr | Minehunter |
| Mnlyr | Minelayer |
| Mnswpr | Minesweeper |
| MnTdr | Mining Tender |
| MslRgeS | Missile Range Ship |
| MTB | Motor Torpedo Boat |
| MtcS | Maintenance Ship |
| Ntlyr | Netlayer |
| O | Oiler |
| ORS | Oceanographic Research Ship |
| PB | Patrol Boat |
| PlcV | Police Vessel |
| PVsl | Patrol Vessel |
| PY | Presidential Yacht |
| RchS | Research Ship |
| RdrPkt | Radar Picket |
| RO | Replenishment Oiler |
| RprS | Repair Ship |
| RscuS | Rescue Ship |
| RvrGbt | River Gunboat |
| RY | Royal Yacht |
| S | Ship |
| SC | Submarine Chaser |
| Sly | Supply |
| SptS | Support Ship |
| SubTdr | Submarine Tender |
| Svg | Salvage |
| SvyS | Survey Ship |
| TB | Torpedo Boat |
| Tg | Tug |
| Tr | Transport |
| TrgS | Training Ship |
| Vsl | Vessel |
| WrC | Water Carrier |
| WthrS | Weather Ship |

**DFM**

1. AC. Br. 3

**DMFB**

2. AC. Am. 24

**DMFDC**

3. AC. Am. 29

**DMFDC**

4. AC. Am. 28

**DMFMD**

5. AC. Br. 2

DMFMDC

6.   AC. Am. 30

GCMFFG

7.   A.Tr. Am. 17

GCMFMFG

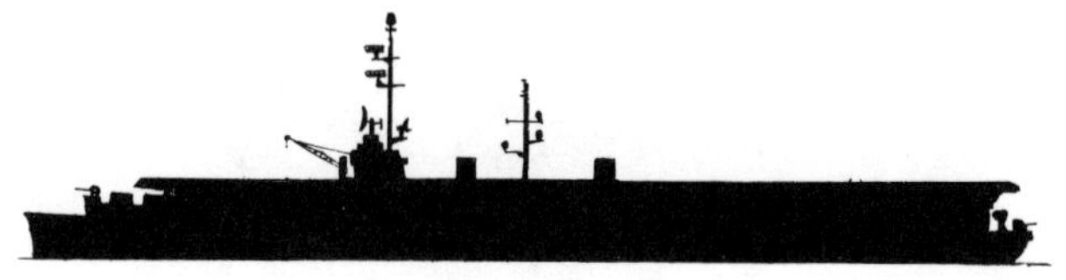

8.   HC. Sp. 18

GGMFGG

9.   AC. Ar. 11

GGMFM

10.   Amph.Aslt.S.
Am. 14

GMFG

11.   Rpr.S. Br. 13

GMFG

12.   AC. Bz. 12

GMMGMFMB

13.   Amph.Cmd.S.
Am. 31

LLLDDDMF

   14.   HC/Cr. Ru. 33

M

15.   AC. Am. 27

M

**16.   Cgo./A.F. Am. 22**

MCFC

**17.   Cgo./A.F. Am. 15**

MF

**19.   ACs. Am. 25**

MF

**20.   Cmdo. Cs. Br. 9**

MFB

**21.   AC. Fr. 23**

MFC

**22.   AC. In. 5**

MFC

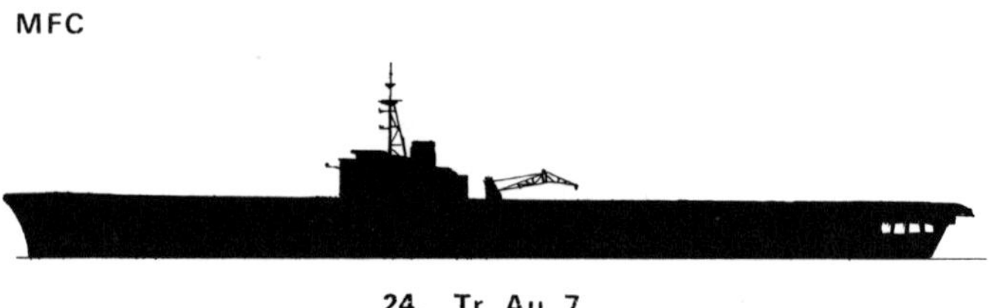

**24.   Tr. Au. 7**

MFC

**25.   AC. Au. 6**

MFM

26.   AC. Am. 26

MFMC

27.   AC. Fr. 8

MFG

28.   HC. Fr. 32

MMCFC

29.   Cgo./A.F. Am. 15

MMCFC

30.   Cgo./A.F. Am. 16

MMFMB

31.   AC. Br. 1

MMFMFFM

32.   Cmd.S. Am. 20

MMKMMFFFMM

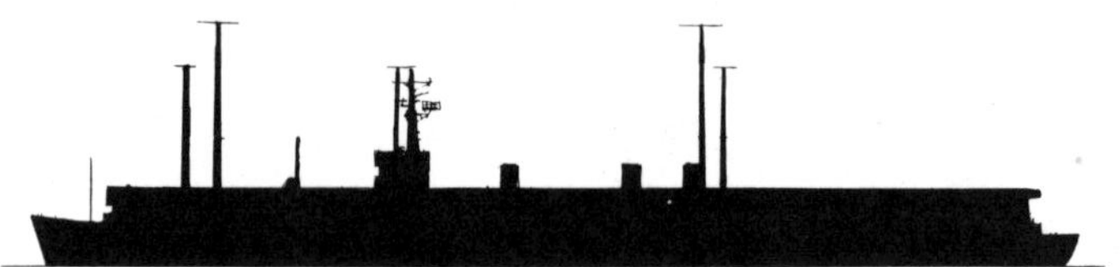

33.   Cmns.Rly.S. Am. 19

MMMMM

34.   Cmns.Rly.S. Am. 21

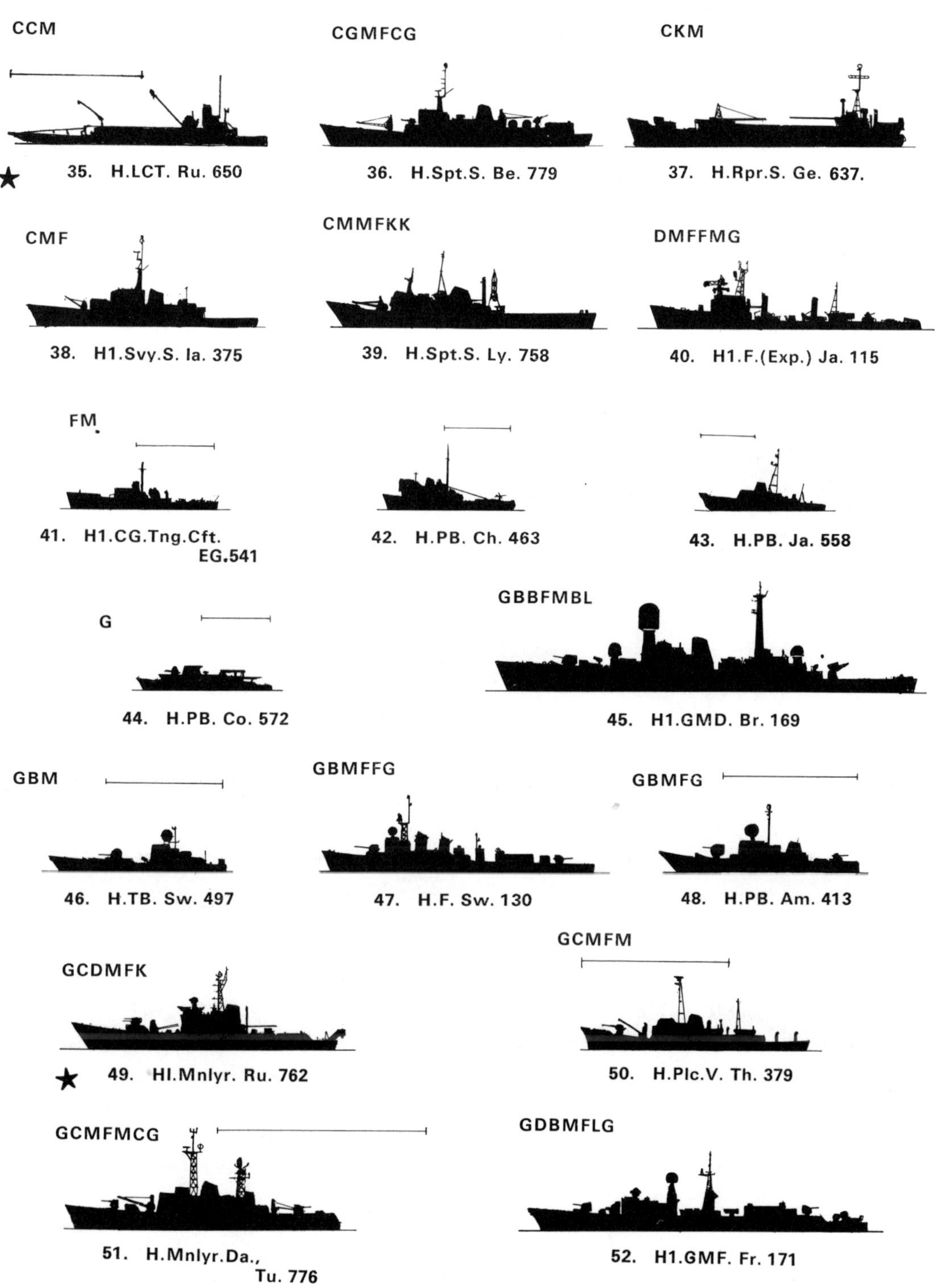

CCM
CGMFCG
CKM
35. H.LCT. Ru. 650
36. H.Spt.S. Be. 779
37. H.Rpr.S. Ge. 637.
CMF
CMMFKK
DMFFMG
38. H1.Svy.S. Ia. 375
39. H.Spt.S. Ly. 758
40. H1.F.(Exp.) Ja. 115
FM
41. H1.CG.Tng.Cft.
EG.541
42. H.PB. Ch. 463
43. H.PB. Ja. 558
G
GBBFMBL
44. H.PB. Co. 572
45. H1.GMD. Br. 169
GBM
GBMFFG
GBMFG
46. H.TB. Sw. 497
47. H.F. Sw. 130
48. H.PB. Am. 413
GCMFM
GCDMFK
49. Hl.Mnlyr. Ru. 762
50. H.Plc.V. Th. 379
GCMFMCG
GDBMFLG
51. H.Mnlyr.Da.,
Tu. 776
52. H1.GMF. Fr. 171

GDDMFLMFDDGL

53.  H.GMD. Ge. 82

GDDMFM

54.  H12.E. Au. 192

GDDMFMMFDG

★  55.  H.D. Ru. 85

GDMC

★  56.  H.Mnswpr. EG. 482

GDMDFGFCC

57.  H2.LSD. Am. 610

GDMF

58.  H.MTB. It. 404

GDMFCMFDGG

59.  H1.Cr. Sw. 55

GDMFCMGG

60.  H1.Cmd.S. Fr. 333

GDMFF

61.  H2.F. Br. 129

GDMFFDDGL

62.  H.GMD. Au. 81

GDMFFG

63.  H2.F. Br. 129

GDMFFGG

64.  H1.D. Bz. 143

GDMFFGG

65.  H1.D. Ja.142

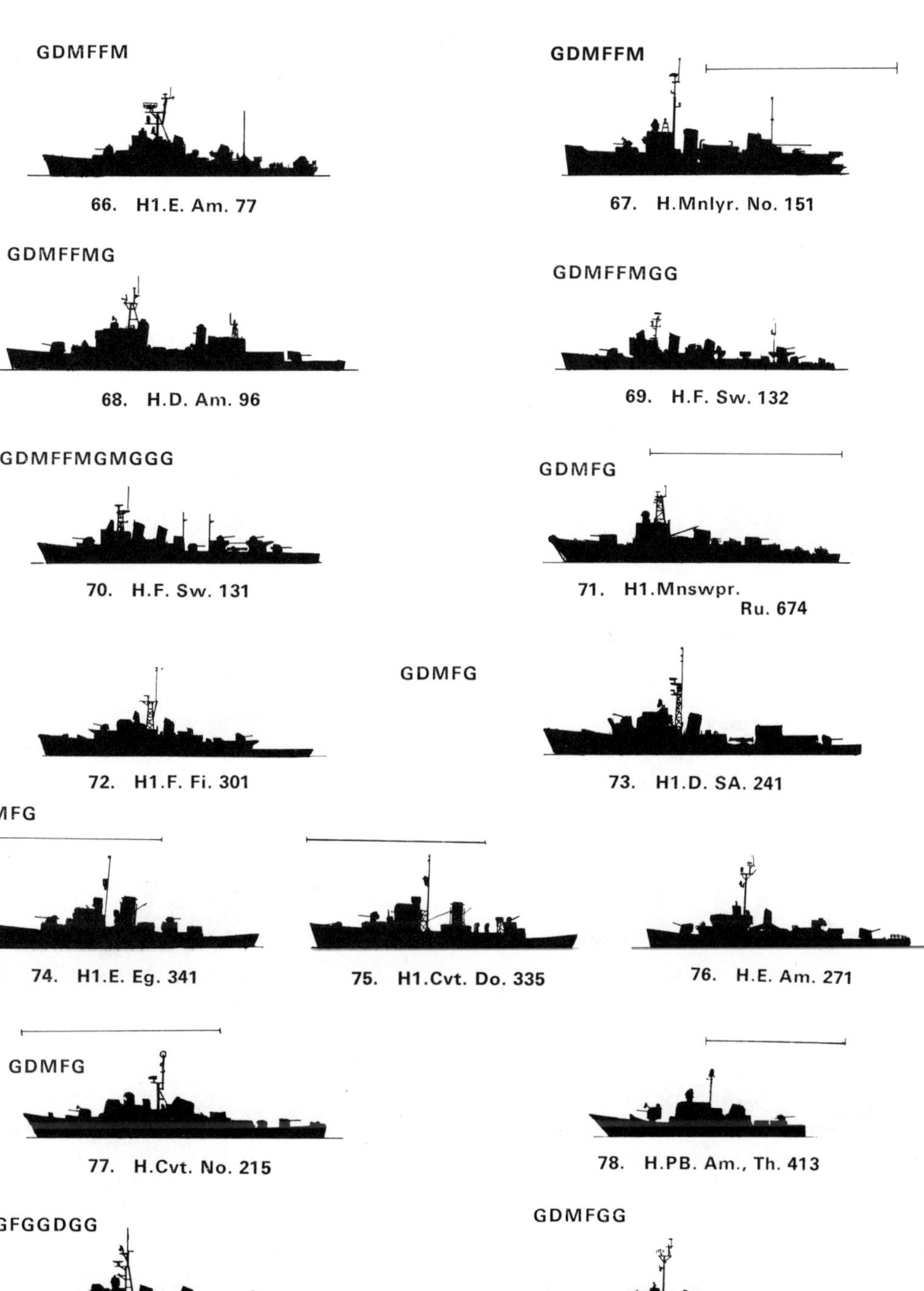


GDMFFM
GDMFFM
66.   H1.E. Am. 77
67.   H.Mnlyr. No. 151
GDMFFMG
GDMFFMGG
68.   H.D. Am. 96
69.   H.F. Sw. 132
GDMFFMGMGGG
GDMFG
70.   H.F. Sw. 131
71.   H1.Mnswpr.
Ru. 674
GDMFG
72.   H1.F. Fi. 301
73.   H1.D. SA. 241
GDMFG
74.   H1.E. Eg. 341
75.   H1.Cvt. Do. 335
76.   H.E. Am. 271
GDMFG
77.   H.Cvt. No. 215
78.   H.PB. Am., Th. 413
GDMFGFGGDGG
GDMFGG
79.   H1.D. Sp. 125
80.   H.E. Am. 271

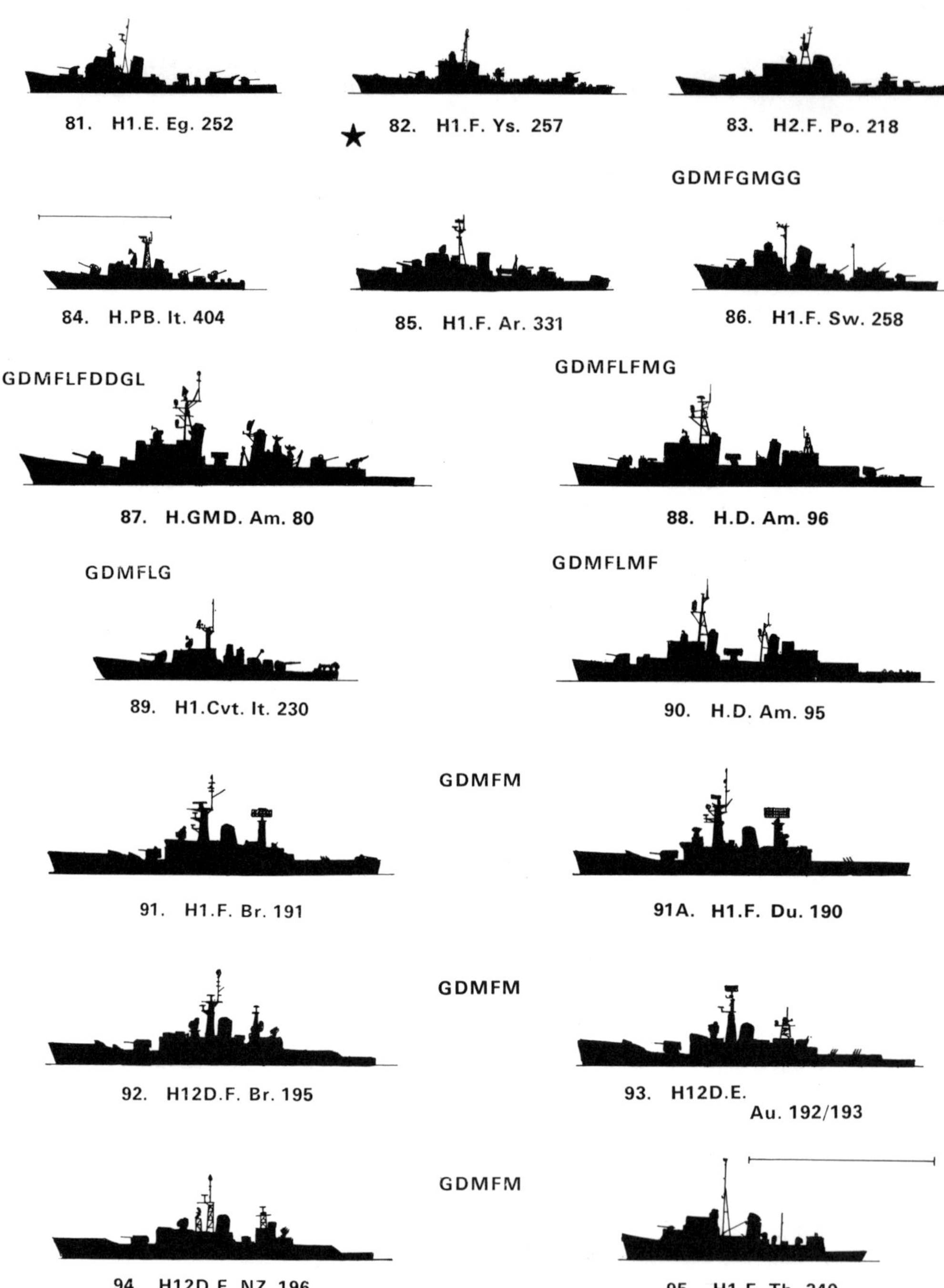



81.  H1.E. Eg. 252

★ 82.  H1.F. Ys. 257

83.  H2.F. Po. 218



84.  H.PB. It. 404

85.  H1.F. Ar. 331

86.  H1.F. Sw. 258



87.  H.GMD. Am. 80



88.  H.D. Am. 96



89.  H1.Cvt. It. 230



90.  H.D. Am. 95



91.  H1.F. Br. 191

91A.  H1.F. Du. 190



92.  H12D.F. Br. 195

93.  H12D.E.
Au. 192/193



94.  H12D.F. NZ. 196

95.  H1.F. Th. 340

**GDMFMCF**

96.   H2.Amph.Aslt.S.
Am. 609

**GDMFMD**

97.   H1.F. Br., In.,
NZ.190

**GDMFMD**

98.   HD.F. My. 197

**GDMFMFDDL**

99.   H2.GMD. It. 60

**GDMFMFDGGG**

100.   H1.D. Fr. 110

**GDMFMFDLG**

101.   H.D. Am. 99

**GDMFMFG**

102.   H.F. Am. 57

**GDMFMFGGG**

★   103.   H1.D. Ru,Eg.,Ia.,
Ph. 93

**GDMFMFGGG**

104.   H.D. It. 107

**GDMFMFLDL**

105.   H.GMD. Am. 59

**GDMFMG**

106.   H2.Rdr.Pkt.
Am. 279

107.   H.E. Am. 272

★   108.   H1.F. RC. 380

**GDMFMG**

109.   H1D.F. In. 194

110.   H12D.F. Br. 194

GDMFMG

111.  H12D.Fs.
Br.,In., SA. 194

112.  H12D.F. Br. 194

GDMFMG

113.  H12D.F. Br. 196

114.  H1.Dpo.S. Po. 326

GDMFMG

115.  H1.D. Au. 224

GDMFMGG

116.  H1.D. In. 253

GDMFMM

117.  H.Cmd.S. Am.311

GDMFMMGG

118.  H.D. Sw. 25

GDMGFCF

119.  H2.Amph.Aslt.S.
Am. 607

GDMM

120.  H12D.F. Br. 187

GDMMDDL

121.  H1.GMF. Am. 185

GDMMDG

122.  H12D.F.
Br., In. 189

GDMMFCF

123.  H2.Amph.Aslt.S.
Am. 608

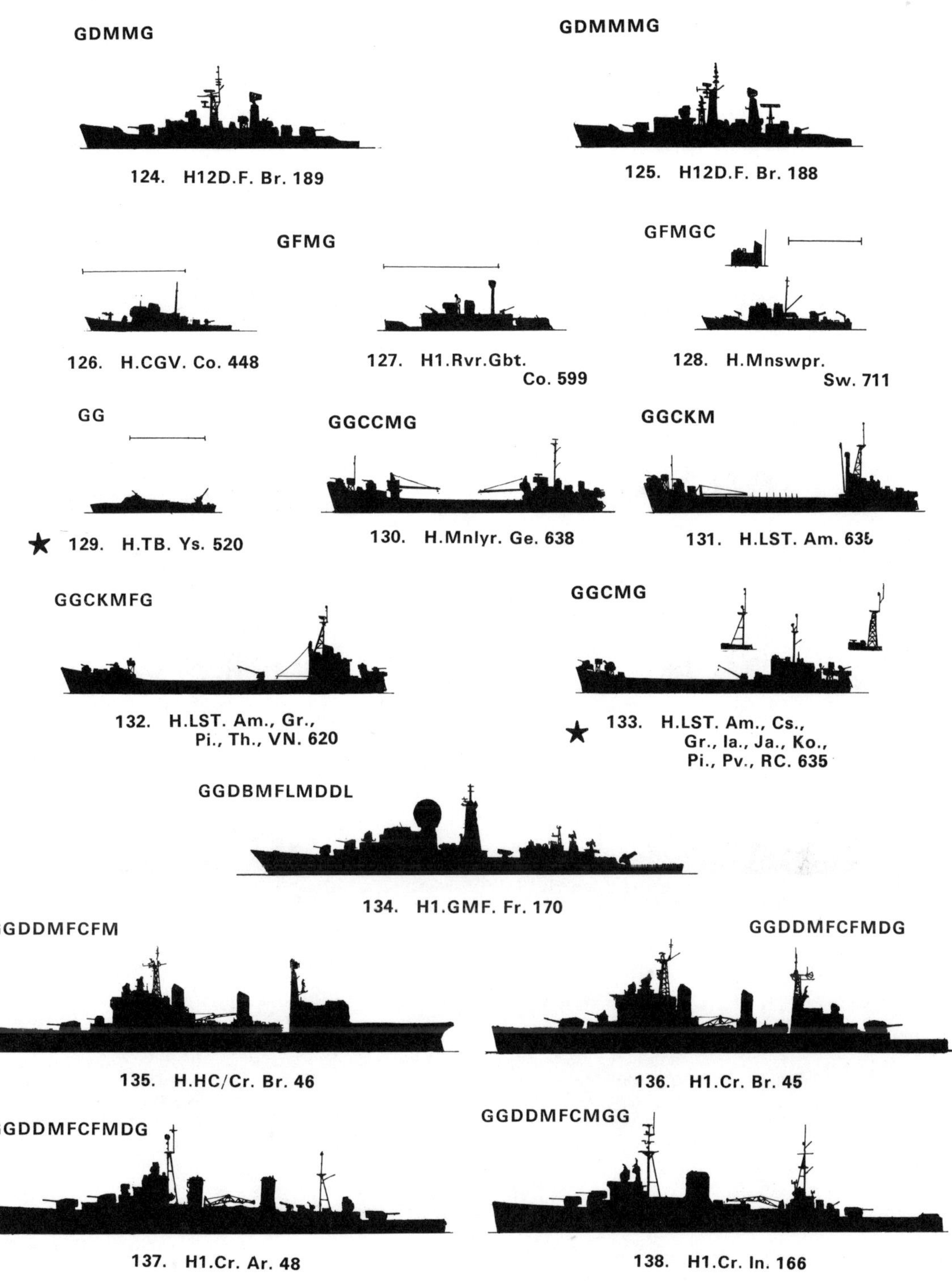

**GDMMG**

124. H12D.F. Br. 189

**GDMMMG**

125. H12D.F. Br. 188

**GFMG**

126. H.CGV. Co. 448

127. H1.Rvr.Gbt. Co. 599

**GFMGC**

128. H.Mnswpr. Sw. 711

**GG**

★ 129. H.TB. Ys. 520

**GGCCMG**

130. H.Mnlyr. Ge. 638

**GGCKM**

131. H.LST. Am. 635

**GGCKMFG**

132. H.LST. Am., Gr., Pi., Th., VN. 620

**GGCMG**

★ 133. H.LST. Am., Cs., Gr., Ia., Ja., Ko., Pi., Pv., RC. 635

**GGDBMFLMDDL**

134. H1.GMF. Fr. 170

**GGDDMFCFM**

135. H.HC/Cr. Br. 46

**GGDDMFCFMDG**

136. H1.Cr. Br. 45

**GGDDMFCFMDG**

137. H1.Cr. Ar. 48

**GGDDMFCMGG**

138. H1.Cr. In. 166

GGDDMFMDFGG

★ 139. H.D. Ru. 90

★. 140. H.D. Ru. 91

GGDDMFMFL

GGDMFCFMGG

★ 141. H.GMD. Ru. 89

142. H1.Cr. In., Pv. 47

GGDMFFDGGG

143. H.D. Am., Ar.,    Ge., Gr., It., Ja.,
Bz., Ch., Cs., Co.,    Pv., Sp., Tu. 105

144. H.D. Am. 100

GGDMFFG

145. H.D. Am. 101

146. H1.D. Sp. 124

GGDMFFGDGG

GGDMFFGG

147. H.D. It. 103

148. H1.D. Sp. 134

GGDMFFGGG

149. H.D. It., Ja. 108

150. H.D. Am., Bz., Gr.,
Ko., Sp. 106

GGDMFFL

GGDMFFMDGG

151. H1.D. Fr. 112

152. H1.D. Ch. 116

GGDMFFMG

153.   H1.D. Ja. 120

154.   H1.D. Am., Cs. 138

GGDMFFMG

155.   H.D. Am., Cs. 104

156.   H.D. Am. 97

GGDMFFMG

157.   H1.D. Tu. 137

GGDMFFMGG

158.   H1.D., It. 139

GGDMFFMGG

159.   H1.D. Am., Cs. 140

160.   H1.D. Am., Cs. 141

161.   H1.D.
          Gr., It., Tu. 137

GGDMFG

★   162.   H.E. Ru., Bu., Fi.,
              EG., Ia., RC. 259

GGDMFG

163.   H1.D. Br. 244

164.   H1.D. Pk. 245

GGDMFG

164a   H.E.
          Am., Cs., Ko. 274

165.   H1.D.
          Br., Au., Pv. 225

GGDMFGG

166.   H1.F. Sp. 328

167.   H.E. Am., Bz., Cs.,
       Gr., It., Ja., Ko.,
       Pv., Th., Ur. 266

GGDMFGG

168.   H2.F. Ia. 220

169.   H1.D. Is. 238

GGDMFGG

★   170.   H1.D. Ys. 240·

GGDMFGGGG

171.   H1.D. Ve. 231

GGDMFGGGG

★   172.   H1.D. Ph. 247

GGDMFGMGG

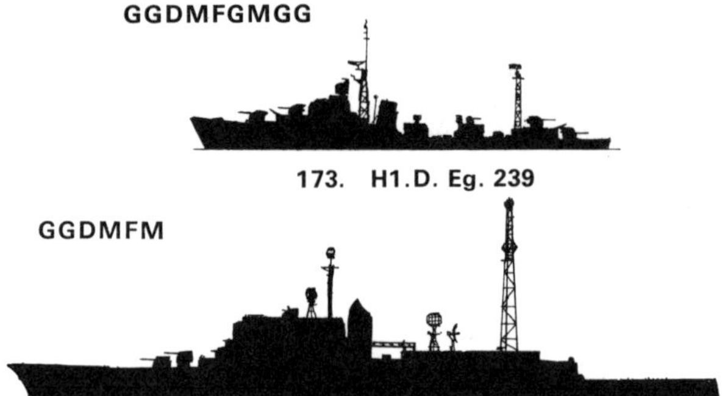

173.   H1.D. Eg. 239

GGDMFLFM

GGDMFM

174.   H.D. Am. 96

175.   H1.Cr., Fr. 168

176.   H.F. Ng. 319

GGDMFM

177   H1.D. Au. 232

GGDMFM

GGDMFMDDL

178.   H1.Rdr.Pkt. Br. 234

179.   H1.GMCr. It. 166

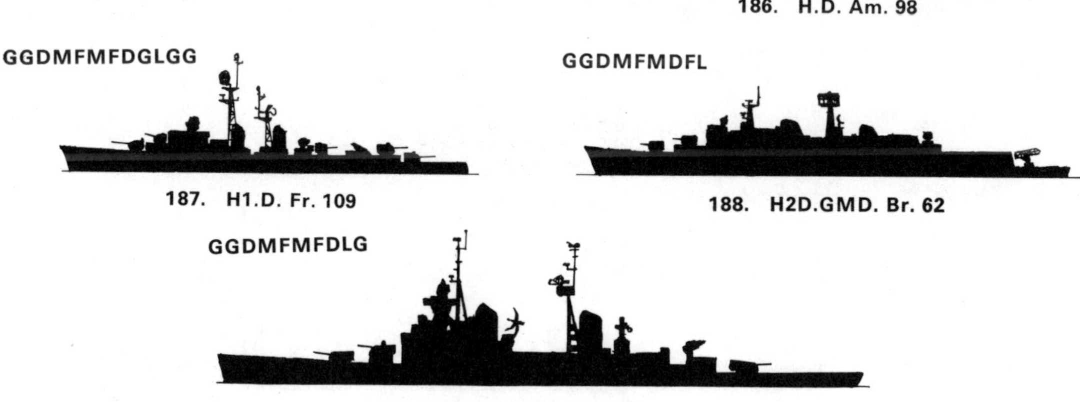


GGDMFMFDL
GGDMFMFDDLC
180.   H.D. Ru. 87
181.   H.D. Ja. 79
GGDMFMFDG
182.   H.F. Da. 63
GGDMFMFDGG
183.   H1.Cr. Ru., Ia. 52
184.   H1.Cr. Ru. 53
GGDMFMFDGGG
186.   H.D. Am. 98
GGDMFMFDGLGG
187.   H1.D. Fr. 109
GGDMFMDFL
188.   H2D.GMD. Br. 62
GGDMFMFDLG
189.   H1.GMCr. Ru. 51

GGDMFMFG

190.   H.D. Am. 97

GGDMFMFGG

★   191.   H.F. Ru. 92

GGDMFMG

192.   H1.D. Tu. 237

193.   H1.D. Br. 226

GGDMFMGG

★   194.   H1.D. Ys. 246

195.   H1.D. In. 242

GGDMFMGG

196.   H1.D. Bz. 270

197.   H1.D. RC. 248

GGDMFMGG

★   198.   H1.Spt.S. Ru. 318

GGGDDMFFMDDGGC

199.   H.Cr. Am. 36

GGGDDMFFMDDGGC

200.   H.Cr.
          Ar., Bz., Ch. 43

GGGDDMFFMDDGGC

**201. H.Cr. Bz. 41**

GGDDMFFDDGGGC

**202. H.Cr. Am. 35**

GGGDDMFFMDGGGC

**GGGDDMFFMGG**

**203. H.Cr. Am. 37**

**204. H1.Cr. Pk. 49**

GGGDDMFMDDGGC

**205. H.Cr. Am. 164**

GGGDDMFMDDGGGC

**GGGDMF**

**206. H.Cr. Am. 165**

**207. H1.D. Pk. 235**

GGGDMFCMFDLGG

**208. H.F. Am. 56**

GGGDMFMFDGGG

**GGGDMFMFGGG**

**209. H1.D. Ja. 118**

**210. H1.D. Ja. 123**

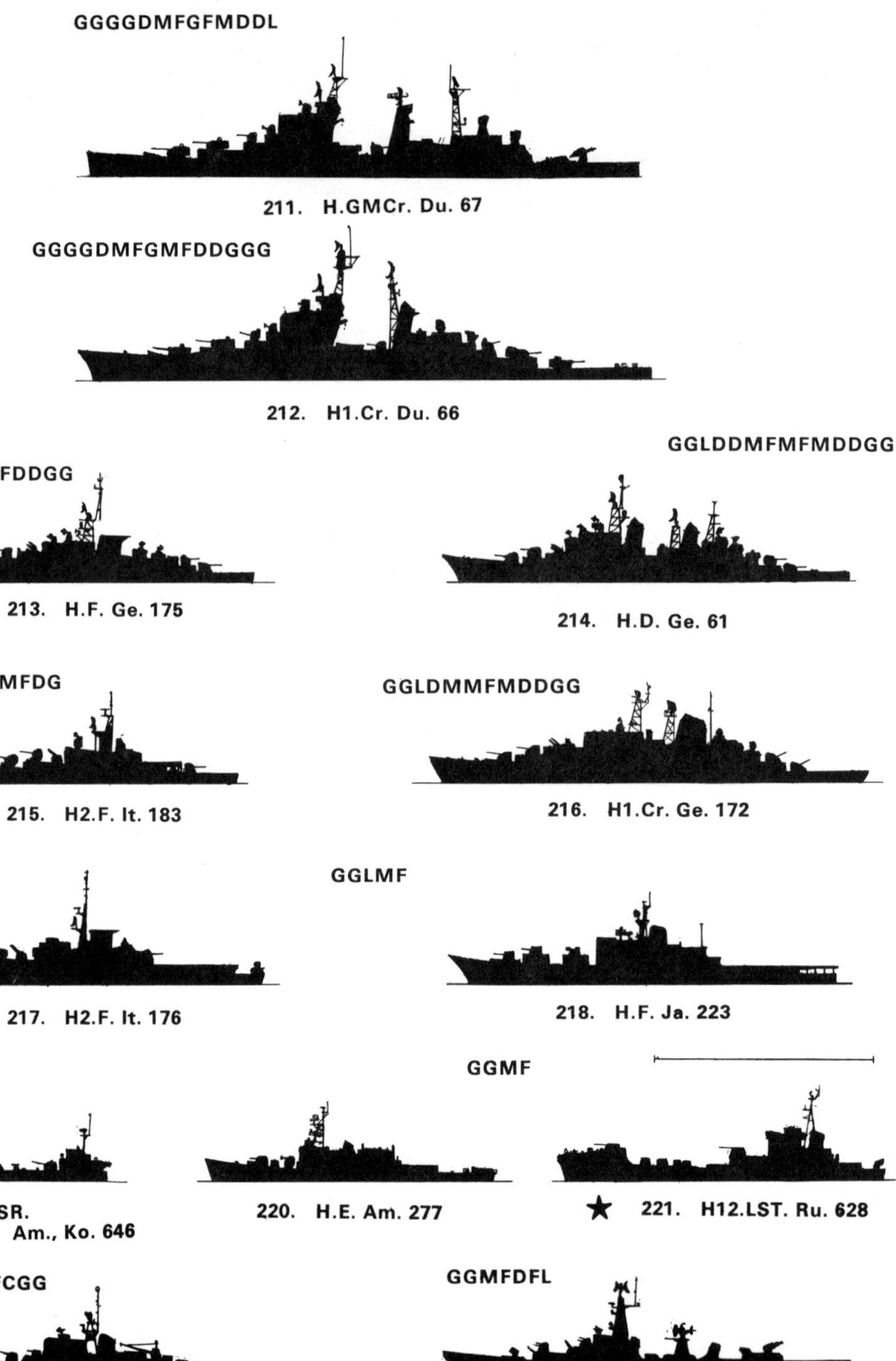

**GGGGDMFGFMDDL**

211.  H.GMCr. Du. 67

**GGGGDMFGMFDDGGG**

212.  H1.Cr. Du. 66

**GGLDDMFDDGG**

213.  H.F. Ge. 175

**GGLDDMFMFMDDGG**

214.  H.D. Ge. 61

**GGLDMFDG**

215.  H2.F. It. 183

**GGLDMMFMDDGG**

216.  H1.Cr. Ge. 172

217.  H2.F. It. 176

**GGLMF**

218.  H.F. Ja. 223

**GGM**

219.  H1.LSR.
Am., Ko. 646

220.  H.E. Am. 277

**GGMF**

★ 221.  H12.LST. Ru. 628

**GGMFCGG**

222.  H1.Spt.S. Ge. 320

**GGMFDFL**

★ 223.  H2.GMD.Ru. 86

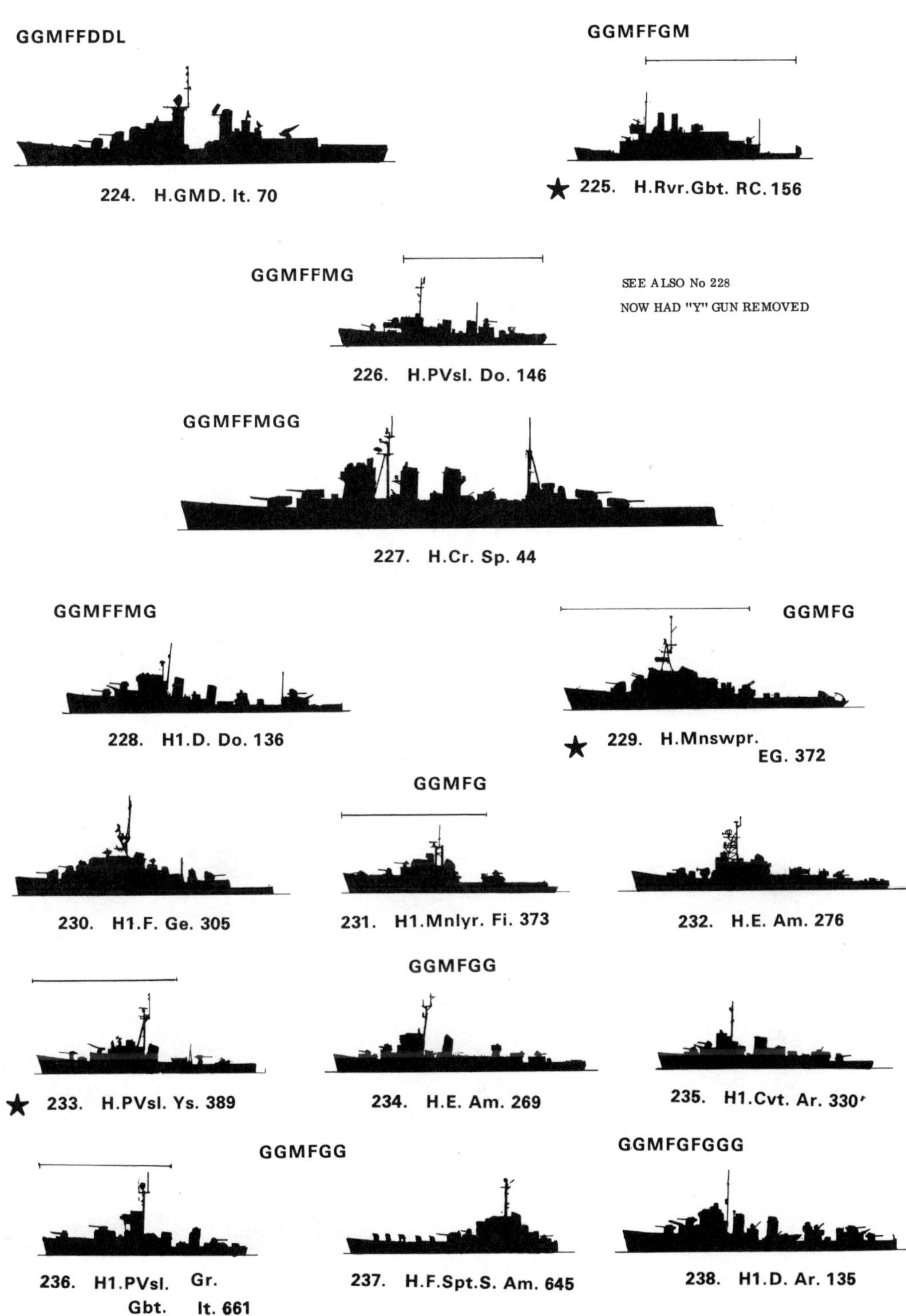

GGMFFDDL
224. H.GMD. It. 70

GGMFFGM
225. H.Rvr.Gbt. RC.156

GGMFFMG
226. H.PVsl. Do. 146

SEE ALSO No 228
NOW HAD "Y" GUN REMOVED

GGMFFMGG
227. H.Cr. Sp. 44

GGMFFMG
228. H1.D. Do. 136

GGMFG
229. H.Mnswpr. EG. 372

GGMFG
230. H1.F. Ge. 305
231. H1.Mnlyr. Fi. 373
232. H.E. Am. 276

GGMFGG
233. H.PVsl. Ys. 389
234. H.E. Am. 269
235. H1.Cvt. Ar. 330'

GGMFGG
236. H1.PVsl. Gr.
Gbt. It. 661
237. H.F.Spt.S. Am. 645

GGMFGFGGG
238. H1.D. Ar. 135

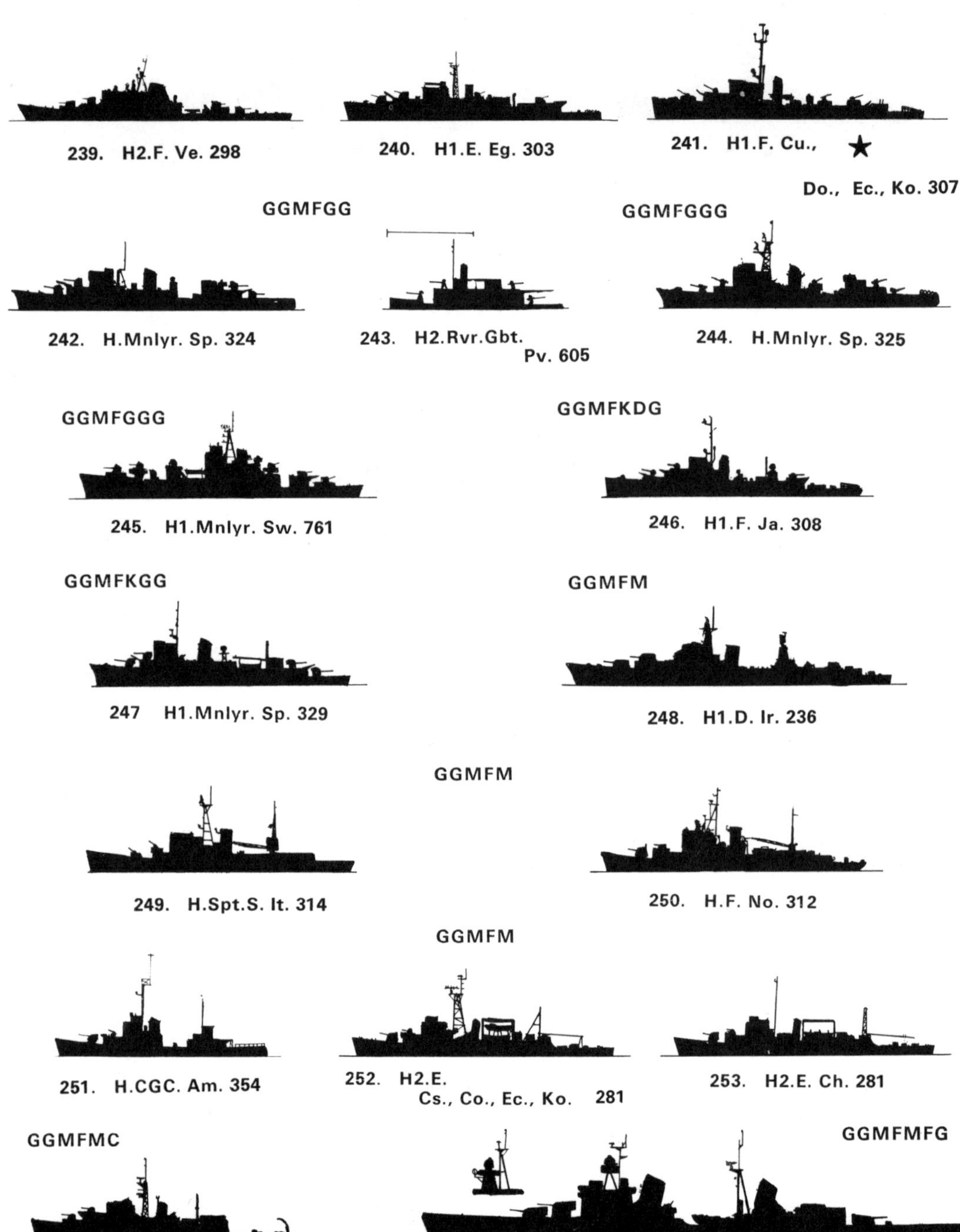


GGMFGG

239.   H2.F. Ve. 298
240.   H1.E. Eg. 303
241.   H1.F. Cu.,
Do.,   Ec., Ko. 307

GGMFGG
242.   H.Mnlyr. Sp. 324
243.   H2.Rvr.Gbt.
Pv. 605

GGMFGGG
244.   H.Mnlyr. Sp. 325

GGMFGGG
245.   H1.Mnlyr. Sw. 761

GGMFKDG
246.   H1.F. Ja. 308

GGMFKGG
247   H1.Mnlyr. Sp. 329

GGMFM
248.   H1.D. Ir. 236

GGMFM
249.   H.Spt.S. It. 314

250.   H.F. No. 312

GGMFM
251.   H.CGC. Am. 354
252.   H2.E.
Cs., Co., Ec., Ko.   281
253.   H2.E. Ch. 281

GGMFMC
254.   H1.F. In. 304

GGMFMFG
255.   H1.Cr. Ru. 54

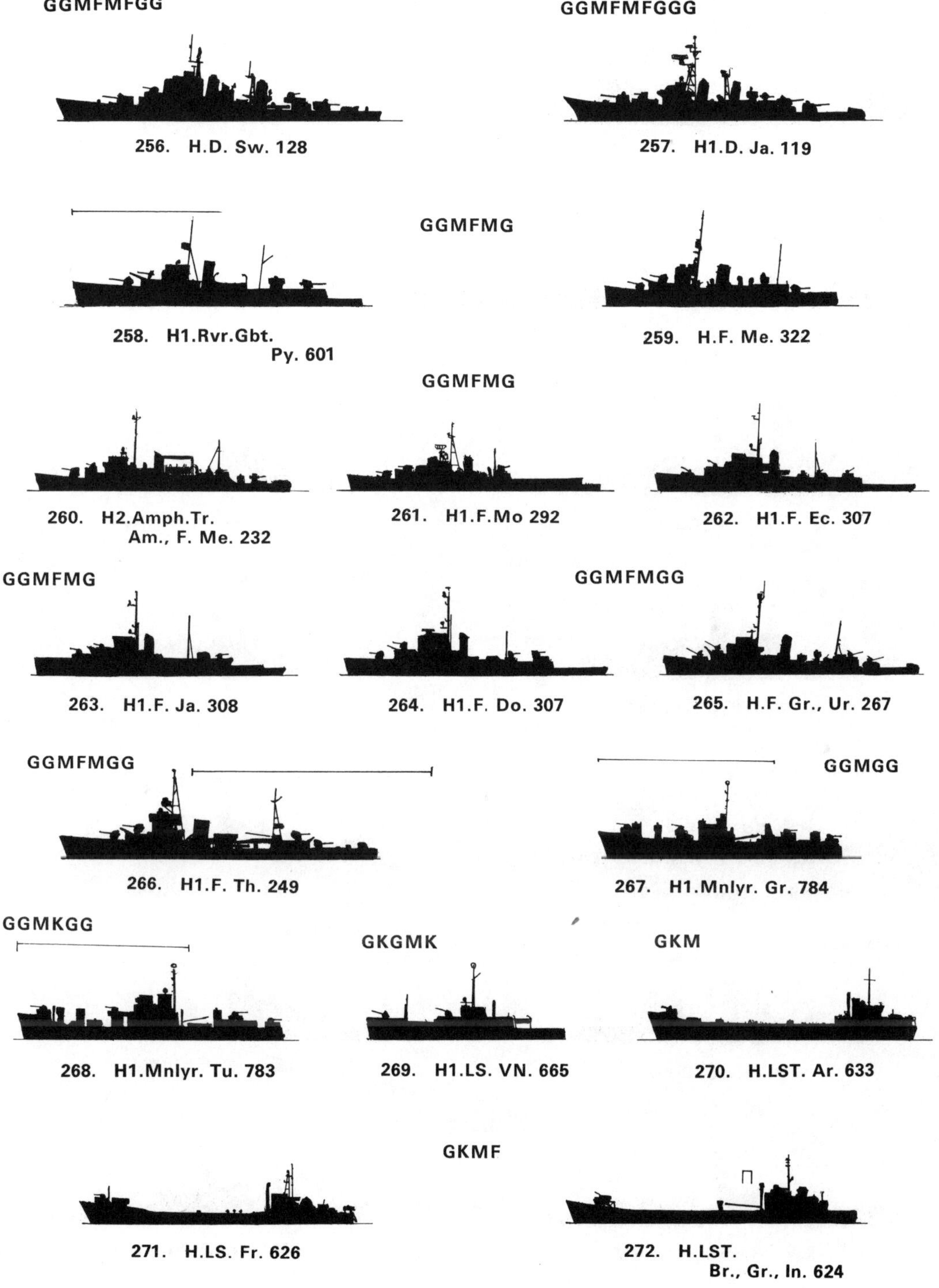

GGMFMFGG
256.   H.D. Sw. 128
GGMFMFGGG
257.   H1.D. Ja. 119
GGMFMG
258.   H1.Rvr.Gbt.
Py. 601
259.   H.F. Me. 322
GGMFMG
260.   H2.Amph.Tr.
Am., F. Me. 232
261.   H1.F.Mo 292
262.   H1.F. Ec. 307
GGMFMG
263.   H1.F. Ja. 308
GGMFMGG
264.   H1.F. Do. 307
265.   H.F. Gr., Ur. 267
GGMFMGG
266.   H1.F. Th. 249
GGMGG
267.   H1.Mnlyr. Gr. 784
GGMKGG
268.   H1.Mnlyr. Tu. 783
GKGMK
269.   H1.LS. VN. 665
GKM
270.   H.LST. Ar. 633
GKMF
271.   H.LS. Fr. 626
272.   H.LST.
Br., Gr., In. 624

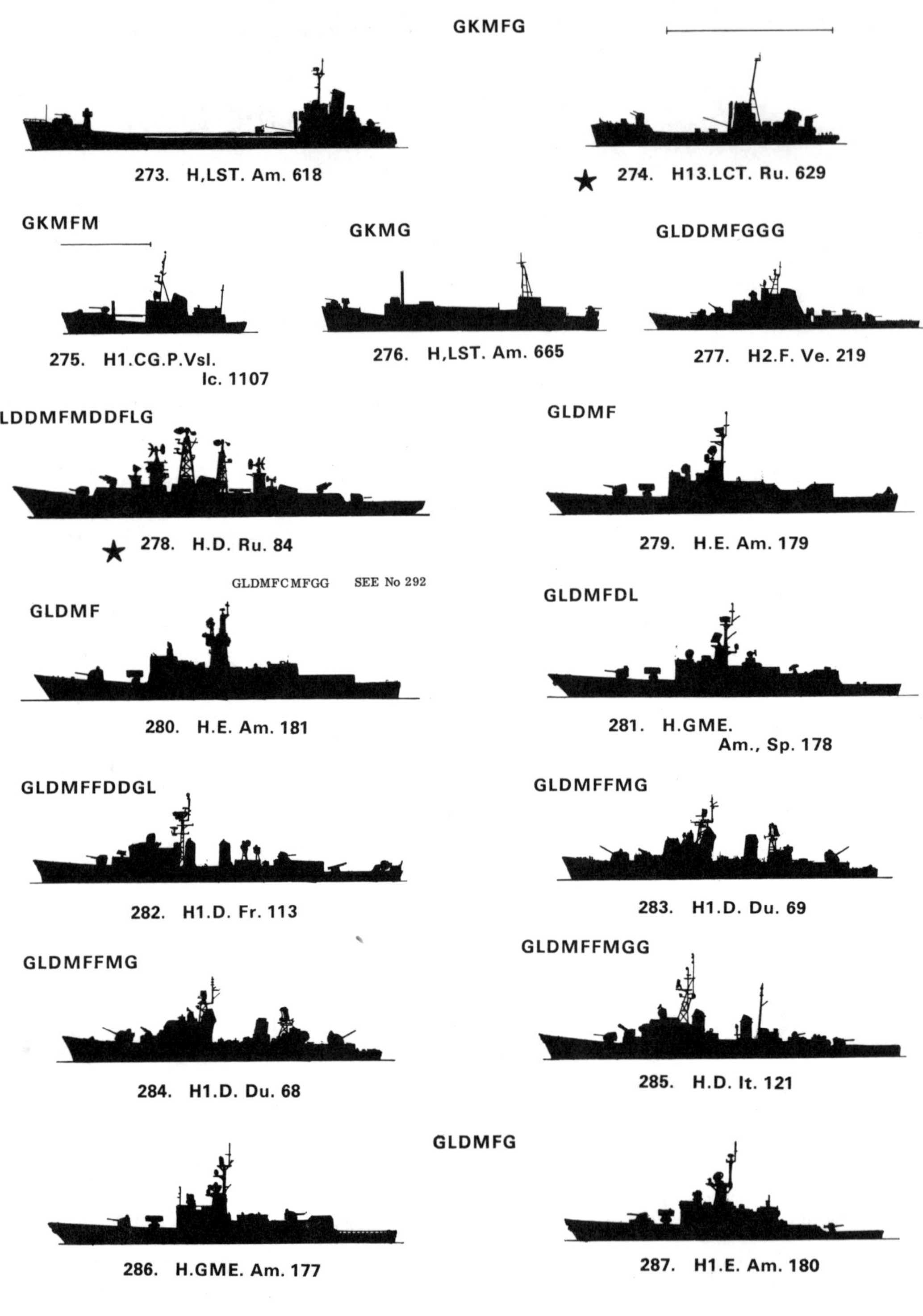

GKMFG

273. H,LST. Am. 618

★ 274. H13.LCT. Ru. 629

GKMFM

275. H1.CG.P.Vsl.
Ic. 1107

GKMG

276. H,LST. Am. 665

GLDDMFGGG

277. H2.F. Ve. 219

GLDDMFMDDFLG

★ 278. H.D. Ru. 84

GLDMF

279. H.E. Am. 179

GLDMFCMFGG    SEE No 292

GLDMF

280. H.E. Am. 181

GLDMFDL

281. H.GME.
Am., Sp. 178

GLDMFFDDGL

282. H1.D. Fr. 113

GLDMFFMG

283. H1.D. Du. 69

GLDMFFMG

284. H1.D. Du. 68

GLDMFFMGG

285. H.D. It. 121

GLDMFG

286. H.GME. Am. 177

287. H1.E. Am. 180

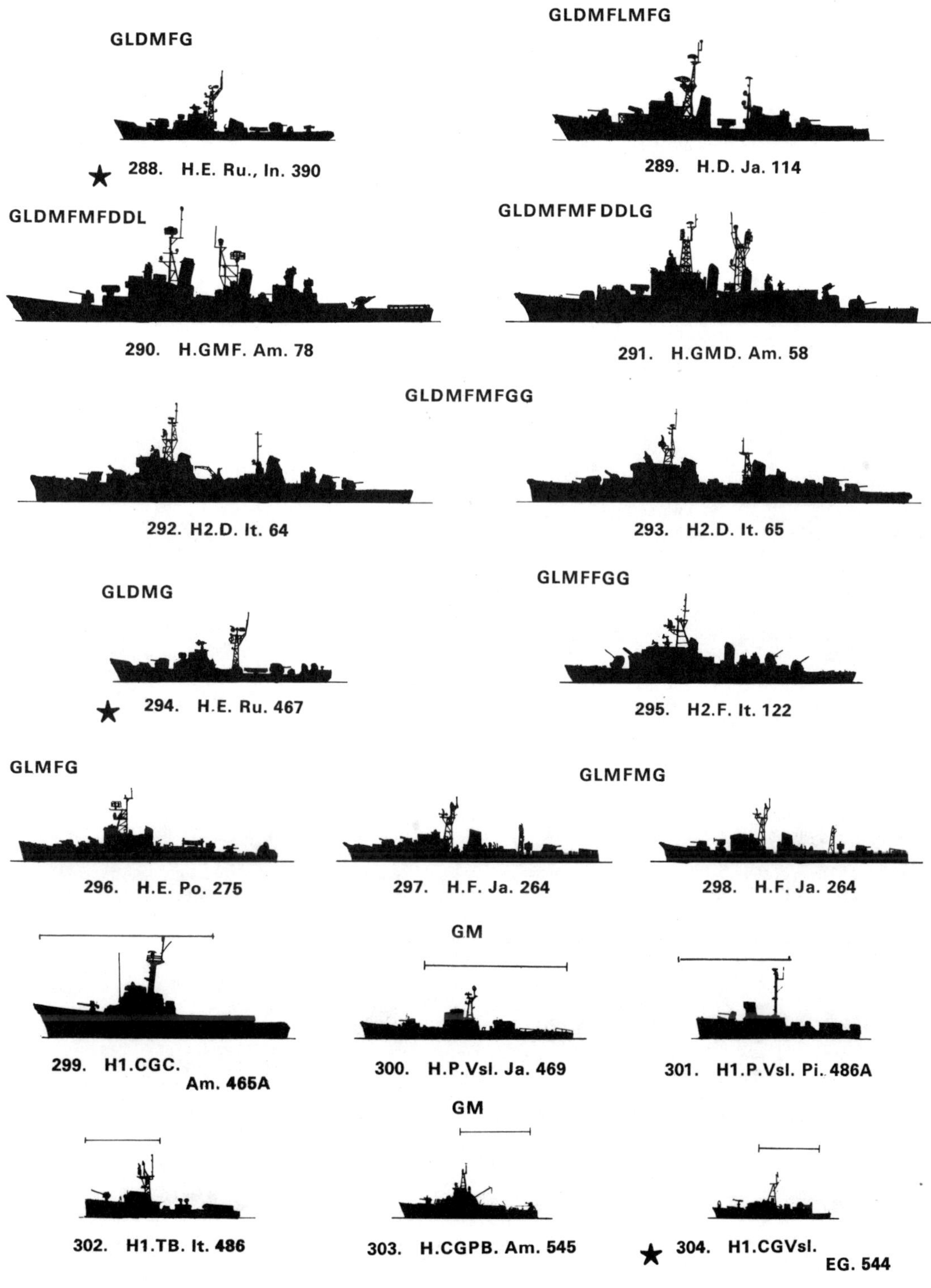


GLDMFG
288. H.E. Ru., In. 390

GLDMFLMFG
289. H.D. Ja. 114

GLDMFMFDDL
290. H.GMF. Am. 78

GLDMFMFDDLG
291. H.GMD. Am. 58

GLDMFMFGG
292. H2.D. It. 64
293. H2.D. It. 65

GLDMG
294. H.E. Ru. 467

GLMFFGG
295. H2.F. It. 122

GLMFG
296. H.E. Po. 275

GLMFMG
297. H.F. Ja. 264
298. H.F. Ja. 264

299. H1.CGC. Am. 465A

GM
300. H.P.Vsl. Ja. 469

301. H1.P.Vsl. Pi. 486A

302. H1.TB. It. 486

GM
303. H.CGPB. Am. 545

304. H1.CGVsl. EG. 544

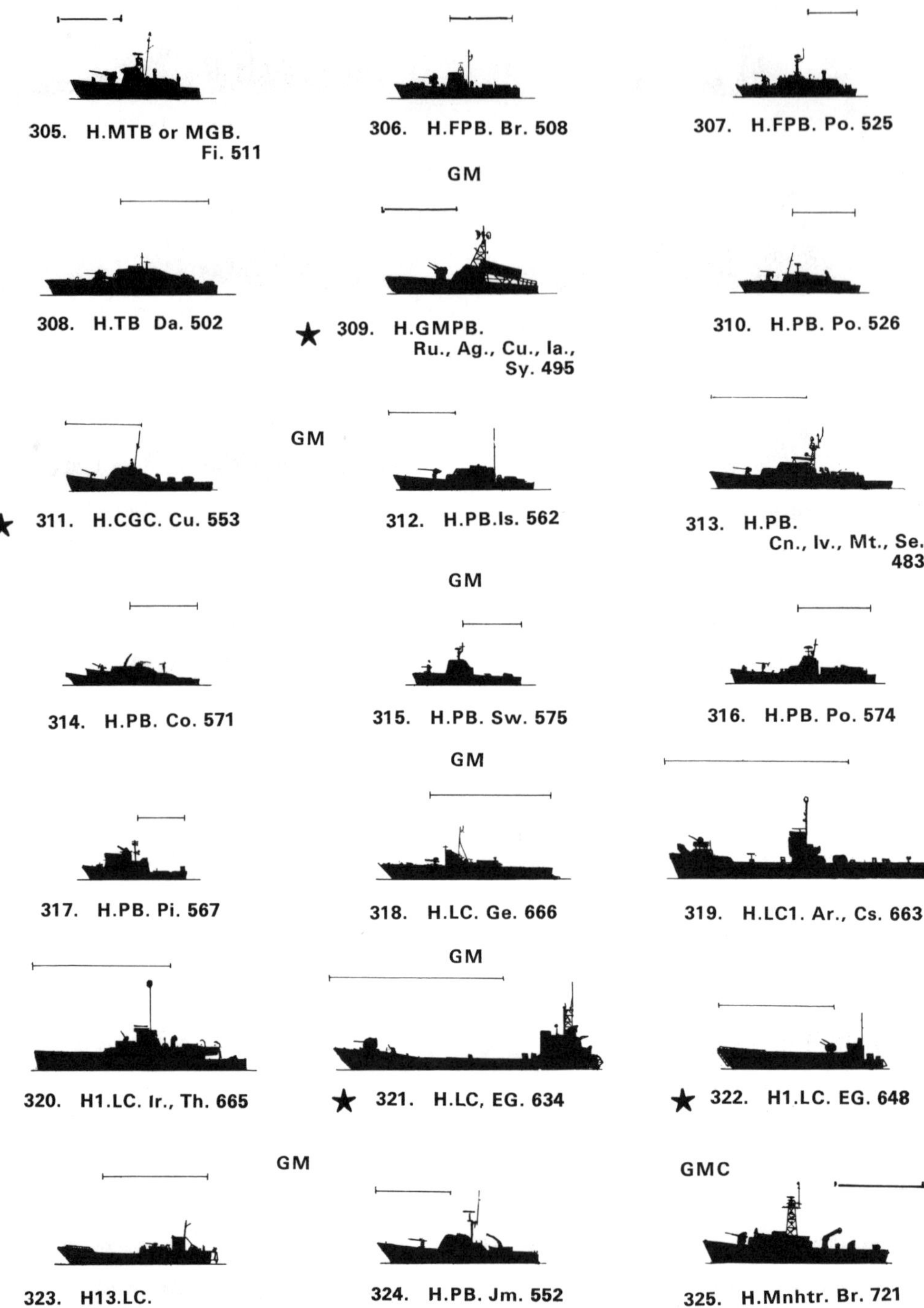

GM

305.   H.MTB or MGB.
            Fi. 511

306.   H.FPB. Br. 508

307.   H.FPB. Po. 525

GM

308.   H.TB  Da. 502

309.   H.GMPB.
            Ru., Ag., Cu., Ia.,
            Sy. 495

310.   H.PB. Po. 526

GM

311.   H.CGC. Cu. 553

312.   H.PB.Is. 562

313.   H.PB.
            Cn., Iv., Mt., Se.
            483

GM

314.   H.PB. Co. 571

315.   H.PB. Sw. 575

316.   H.PB. Po. 574

GM

317.   H.PB. Pi. 567

318.   H.LC. Ge. 666

319.   H.LC1. Ar., Cs. 663

GM

320.   H1.LC. Ir., Th. 665

321.   H.LC, EG. 634

322.   H1.LC. EG. 648

GM

323.   H13.LC.
            Am., Cd., Ch., Cs.,
            Gr., Th., Rc. 656

324.   H.PB. Jm. 552

GMC

325.   H.Mnhtr. Br. 721

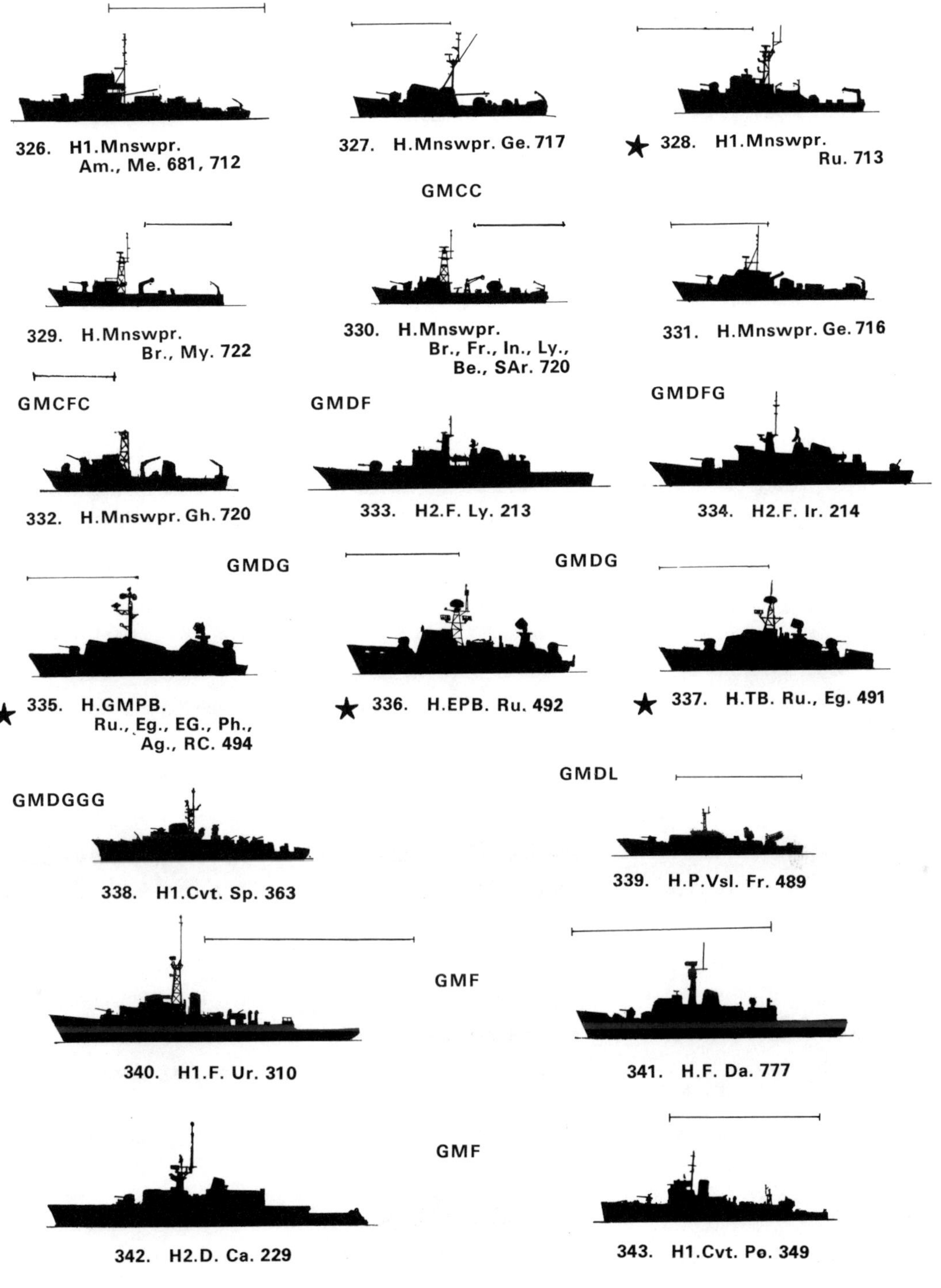


GMC

326. H1.Mnswpr.
Am., Me. 681, 712

327. H.Mnswpr. Ge. 717

★ 328. H1.Mnswpr.
Ru. 713

GMCC

329. H.Mnswpr.
Br., My. 722

330. H.Mnswpr.
Br., Fr., In., Ly.,
Be., SAr. 720

331. H.Mnswpr. Ge. 716

GMCFC

332. H.Mnswpr. Gh. 720

GMDF

333. H2.F. Ly. 213

GMDFG

334. H2.F. Ir. 214

GMDG

★ 335. H.GMPB.
Ru., Eg., EG., Ph.,
Ag., RC. 494

GMDG

★ 336. H.EPB. Ru. 492

★ 337. H.TB. Ru., Eg. 491

GMDGGG

338. H1.Cvt. Sp. 363

GMDL

339. H.P.Vsl. Fr. 489

340. H1.F. Ur. 310

GMF

341. H.F. Da. 777

GMF

342. H2.D. Ca. 229

343. H1.Cvt. Po. 349

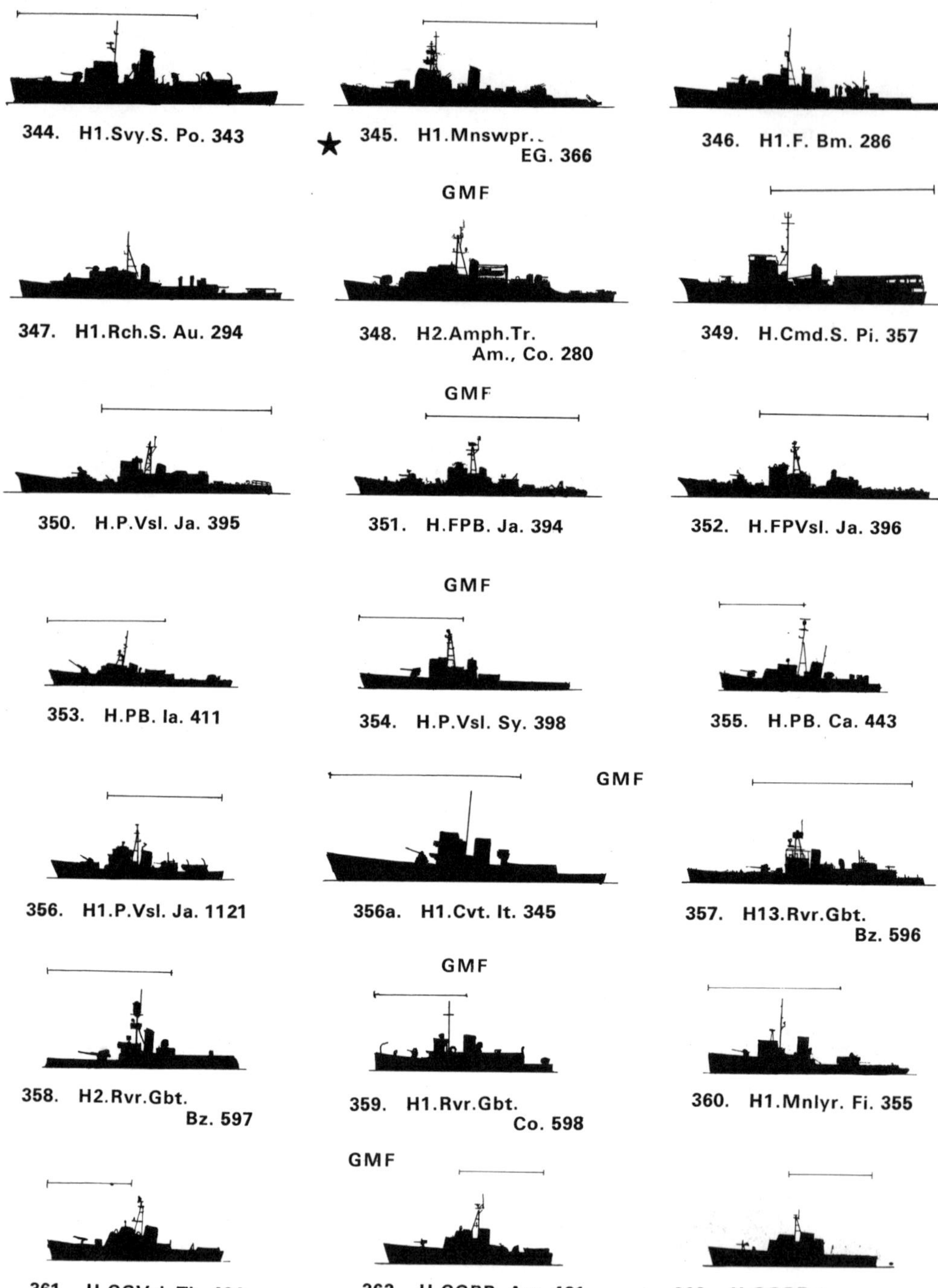


GMF

344.  H1.Svy.S. Po. 343
345.  H1.Mnswpr..
EG. 366
346.  H1.F. Bm. 286

GMF

347.  H1.Rch.S. Au. 294
348.  H2.Amph.Tr.
Am., Co. 280
349.  H.Cmd.S. Pi. 357

GMF

350.  H.P.Vsl. Ja. 395
351.  H.FPB. Ja. 394
352.  H.FPVsl. Ja. 396

GMF

353.  H.PB. Ia. 411
354.  H.P.Vsl. Sy. 398
355.  H.PB. Ca. 443

GMF

356.  H1.P.Vsl. Ja. 1121
356a.  H1.Cvt. It. 345
357.  H13.Rvr.Gbt.
Bz. 596

GMF

358.  H2.Rvr.Gbt.
Bz. 597
359.  H1.Rvr.Gbt.
Co. 598
360.  H1.Mnlyr. Fi. 355

GMF

361.  H.CGVsl. Th. 434
362.  H.CGPB. Am. 431
363.  H.CGPB.
Am., Ko. 430

GMF

364.  H1.PB. Me 447

365.  H1.PB Fi. 416

366.  H.Svy.S. Ar. 435

GMF

367.  H.MTB or MGB.
      It. 399

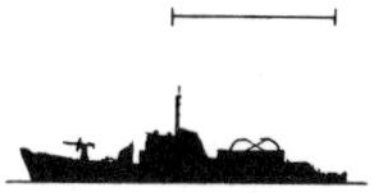

368.  H.PB. Me. 454

★ 369.  H.CGC. Cu. 458A

GMF

370.  H.Rvr.Gbt. Py. 602

371.  H.PB. Sg. 442

372.  H.Hy.Gb. Am. 585

GMF

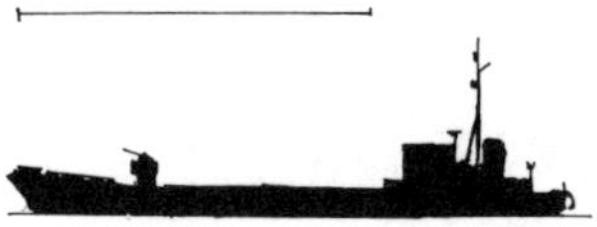

373.  H13.LC. Ng. 622

GMFC

374.  H1.CGVsl. Ly. 419

GMFC

374a.  H1.E. Th. 337

375.  H1.E. SA. 337

GMFC

376.  H1.Mnhtr.
      Br., Ar. 691

377.  H1.Mnswpr.
      Fr., Ge. 688

378.  H1.Mnswpr.
      Ge. 684

379.  H1.Mnswpr.
      Am. 677

GMFC

380.  H.Mnswpr.
      Ge. 704

★ 381.  H.Mnswpr. Ru. 709

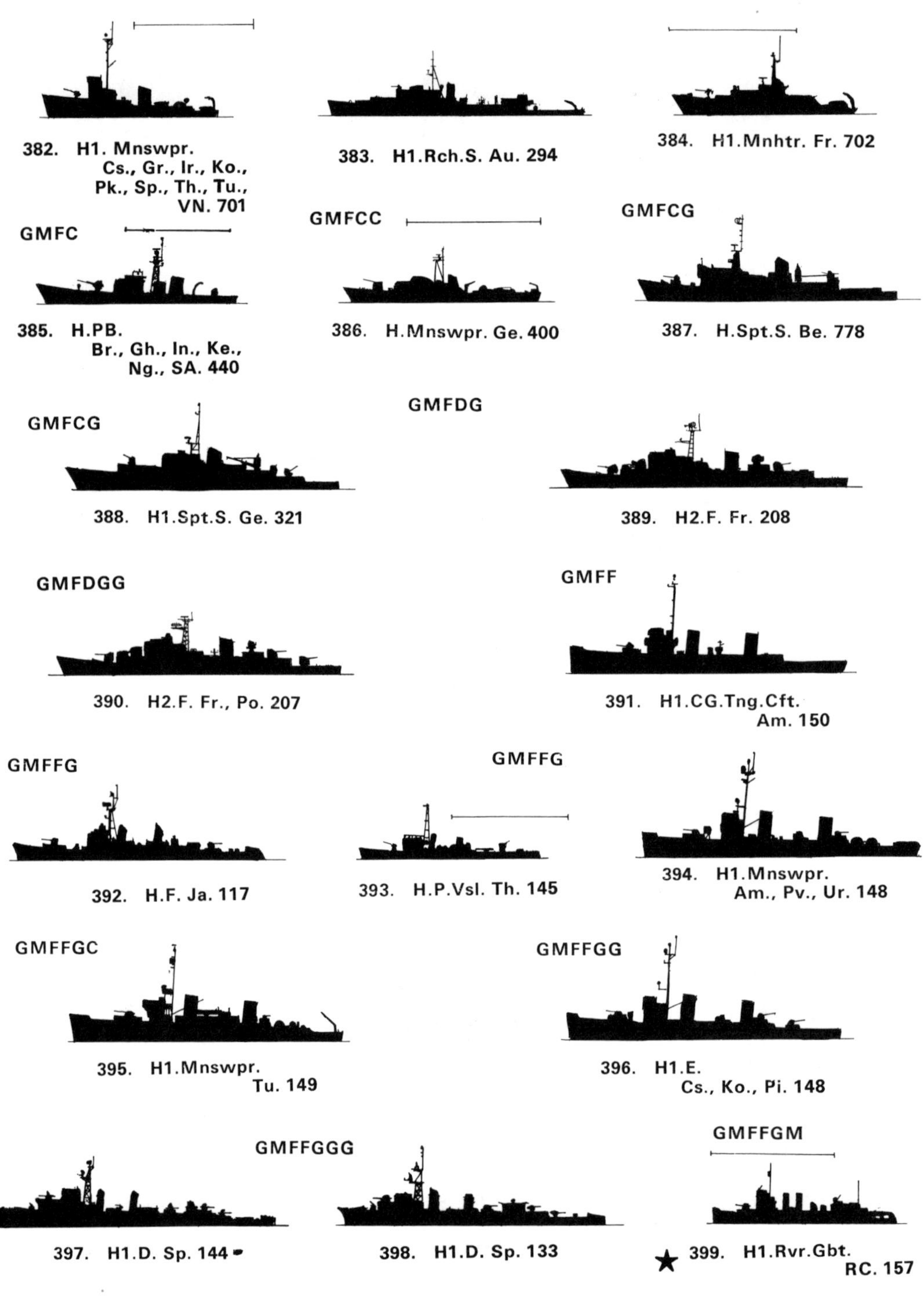



382. H1. Mnswpr.
Cs., Gr., Ir., Ko.,
Pk., Sp., Th., Tu.,
VN. 701

383. H1.Rch.S. Au. 294

384. H1.Mnhtr. Fr. 702

385. H.PB.
Br., Gh., In., Ke.,
Ng., SA. 440

386. H.Mnswpr. Ge. 400

387. H.Spt.S. Be. 778

388. H1.Spt.S. Ge. 321

389. H2.F. Fr. 208

390. H2.F. Fr., Po. 207

391. H1.CG.Tng.Cft.
Am. 150

392. H.F. Ja. 117

393. H.P.Vsl. Th. 145

394. H1.Mnswpr.
Am., Pv., Ur. 148

395. H1.Mnswpr.
Tu. 149

396. H1.E.
Cs., Ko., Pi. 148

397. H1.D. Sp. 144

398. H1.D. Sp. 133

399. H1.Rvr.Gbt.
RC. 157

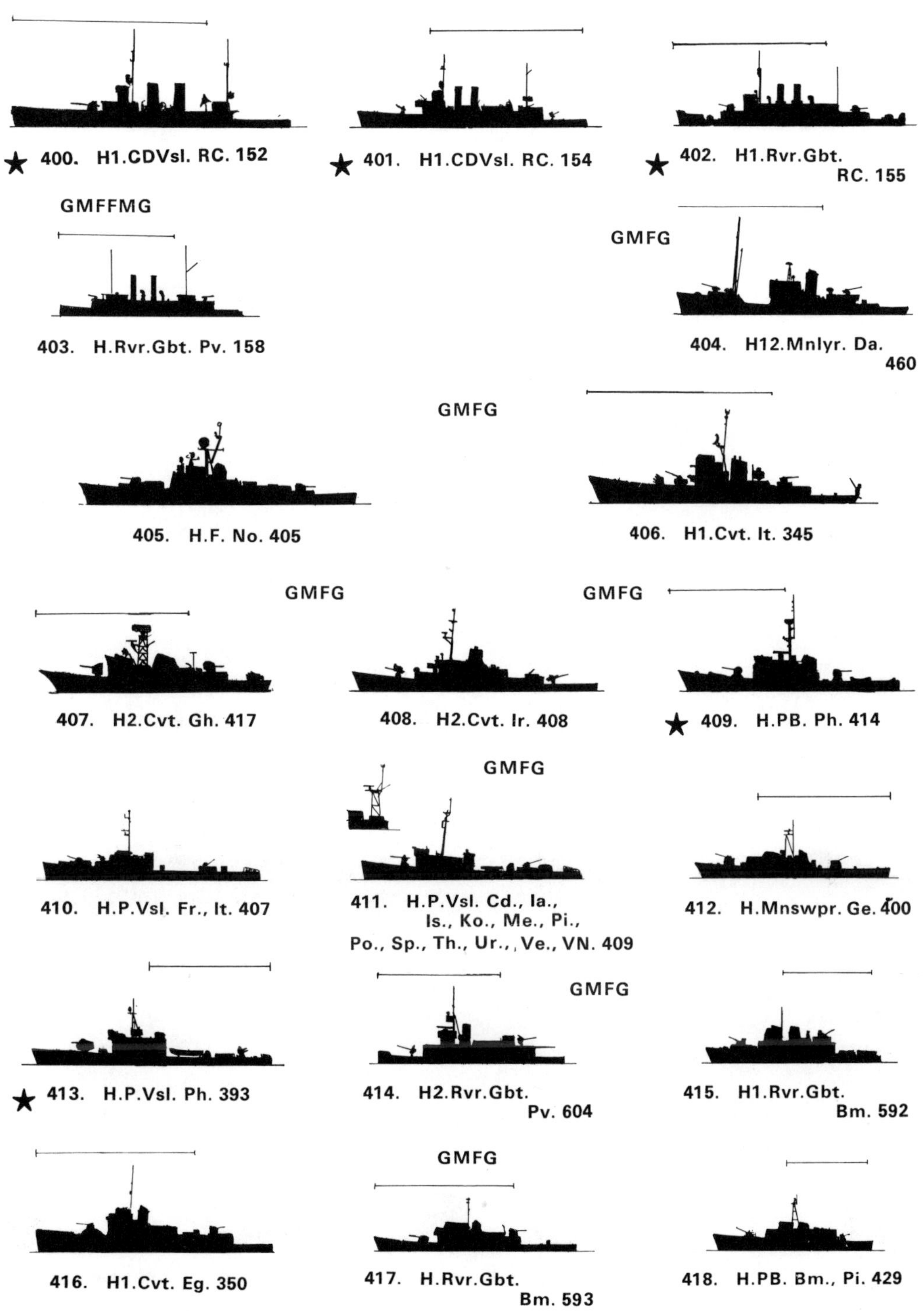

GMFFMG

★ 400.  H1.CDVsl. RC. 152

★ 401.  H1.CDVsl. RC. 154

★ 402.  H1.Rvr.Gbt. RC. 155

GMFFMG

403.  H.Rvr.Gbt. Pv. 158

GMFG

404.  H12.Mnlyr. Da. 460

GMFG

405.  H.F. No. 405

406.  H1.Cvt. It. 345

GMFG

407.  H2.Cvt. Gh. 417

GMFG

408.  H2.Cvt. Ir. 408

GMFG

★ 409.  H.PB. Ph. 414

410.  H.P.Vsl. Fr., It. 407

GMFG

411.  H.P.Vsl. Cd., Ia., Is., Ko., Me., Pi., Po., Sp., Th., Ur., Ve., VN. 409

412.  H.Mnswpr. Ge. 400

★ 413.  H.P.Vsl. Ph. 393

414.  H2.Rvr.Gbt. Pv. 604

GMFG

415.  H1.Rvr.Gbt. Bm. 592

416.  H1.Cvt. Eg. 350

GMFG

417.  H.Rvr.Gbt. Bm. 593

418.  H.PB. Bm., Pi. 429

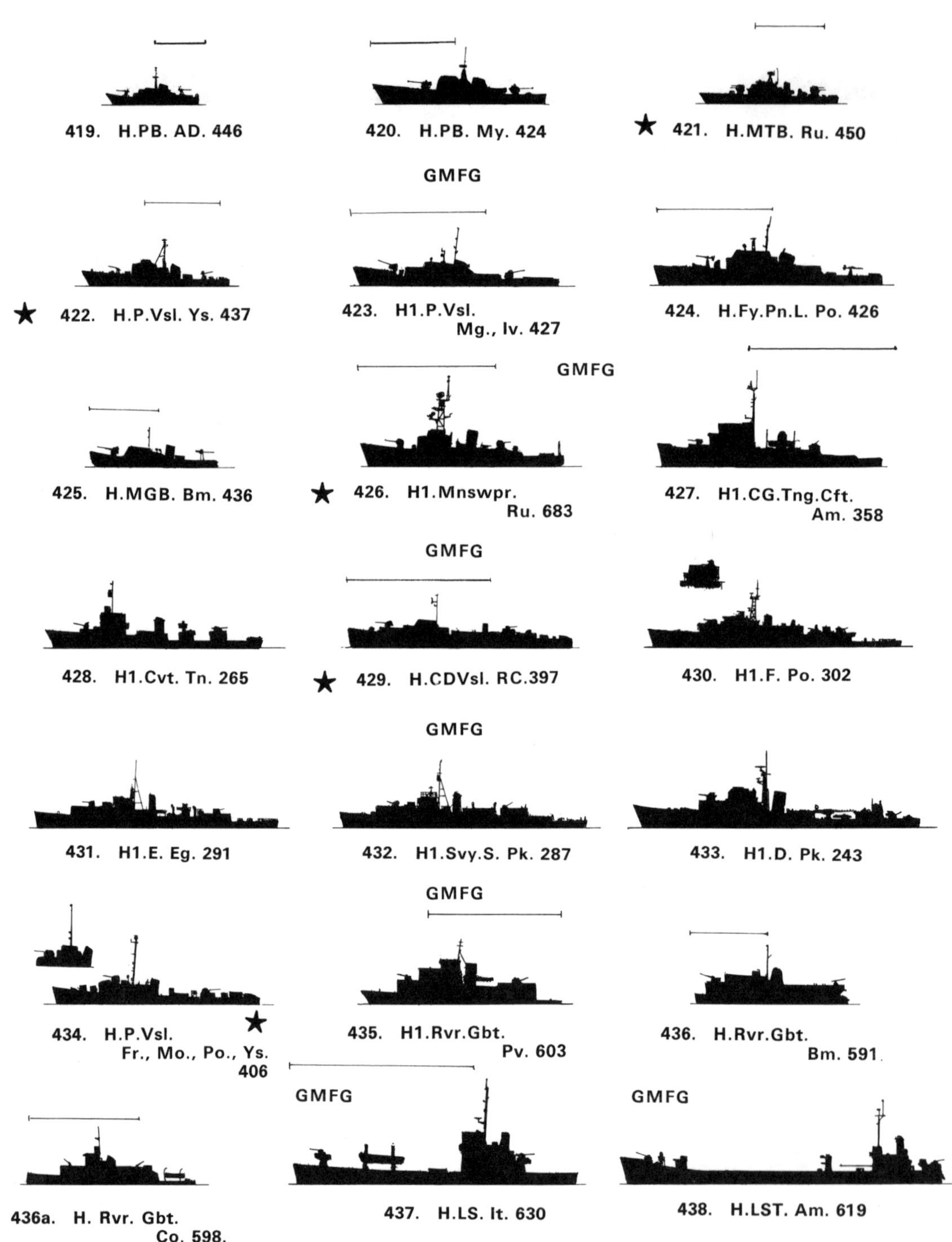

GMFG
419. H.PB. AD. 446
420. H.PB. My. 424
421. H.MTB. Ru. 450
GMFG
422. H.P.Vsl. Ys. 437
423. H1.P.Vsl.
Mg., Iv. 427
424. H.Fy.Pn.L. Po. 426
425. H.MGB. Bm. 436
GMFG
426. H1.Mnswpr.
Ru. 683
427. H1.CG.Tng.Cft.
Am. 358
428. H1.Cvt. Tn. 265
GMFG
429. H.CDVsl. RC.397
430. H1.F. Po. 302
GMFG
431. H1.E. Eg. 291
432. H1.Svy.S. Pk. 287
433. H1.D. Pk. 243
GMFG
434. H.P.Vsl.
Fr., Mo., Po., Ys.
406
435. H1.Rvr.Gbt.
Pv. 603
436. H.Rvr.Gbt.
Bm. 591
GMFG
436a. H. Rvr. Gbt.
Co. 598.
437. H.LS. It. 630
GMFG
438. H.LST. Am. 619

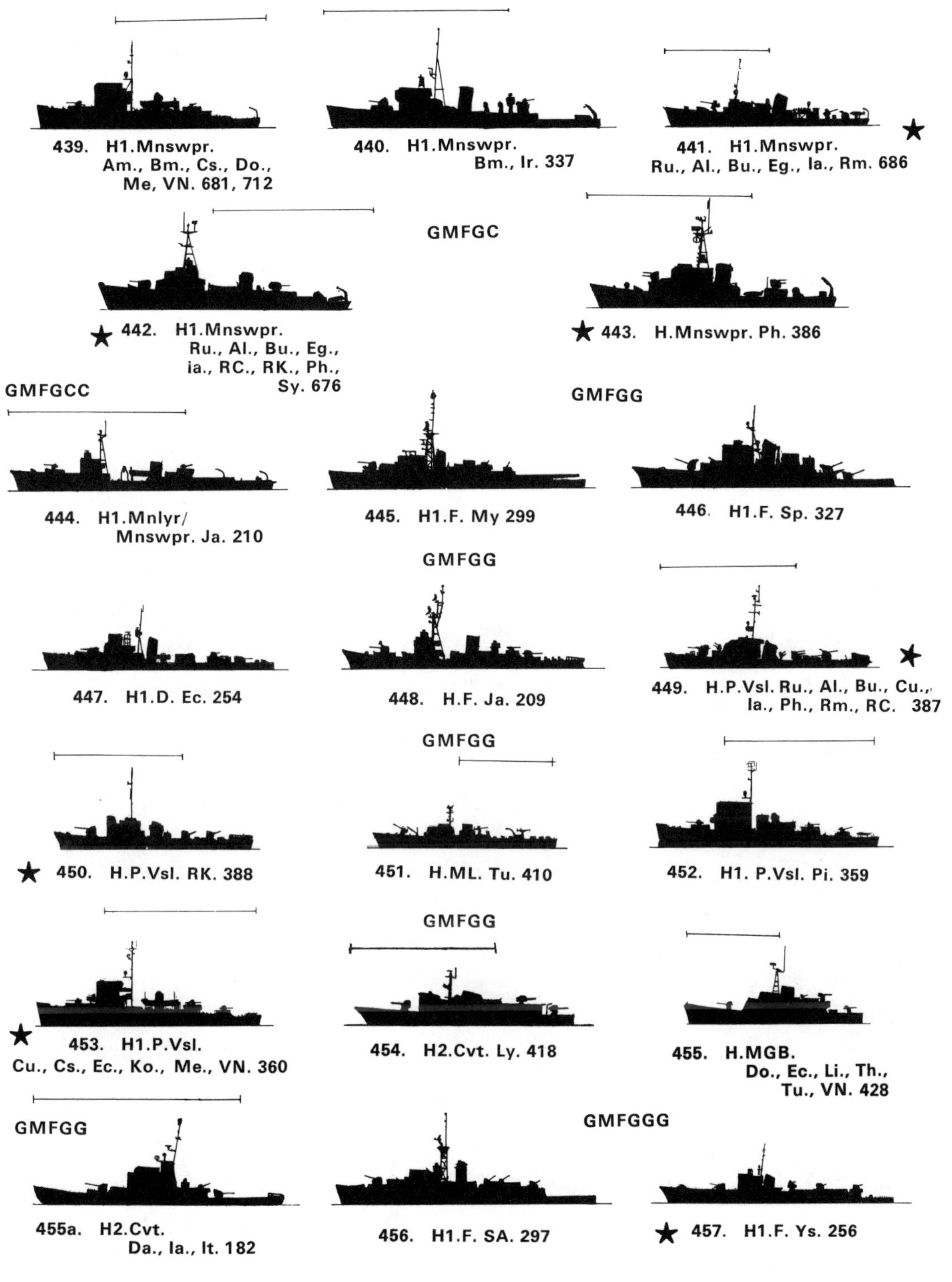


GMFGC

439. H1.Mnswpr.
Am., Bm., Cs., Do.,
Me, VN. 681, 712

440. H1.Mnswpr.
Bm., Ir. 337

441. H1.Mnswpr.
Ru., Al., Bu., Eg., Ia., Rm. 686

GMFGC

442. H1.Mnswpr.
Ru., Al., Bu., Eg.,
ia., RC., RK., Ph.,
Sy. 676

443. H.Mnswpr. Ph. 386

GMFGCC

444. H1.Mnlyr/
Mnswpr. Ja. 210

445. H1.F. My 299

GMFGG

446. H1.F. Sp. 327

GMFGG

447. H1.D. Ec. 254

448. H.F. Ja. 209

449. H.P.Vsl. Ru., Al., Bu., Cu.,
Ia., Ph., Rm., RC. 387

GMFGG

450. H.P.Vsl. RK. 388

451. H.ML. Tu. 410

452. H1. P.Vsl. Pi. 359

GMFGG

453. H1.P.Vsl.
Cu., Cs., Ec., Ko., Me., VN. 360

454. H2.Cvt. Ly. 418

455. H.MGB.
Do., Ec., Li., Th.,
Tu., VN. 428

GMFGG

455a. H2.Cvt.
Da., Ia., It. 182

GMFGGG

456. H1.F. SA. 297

457. H1.F. Ys. 256

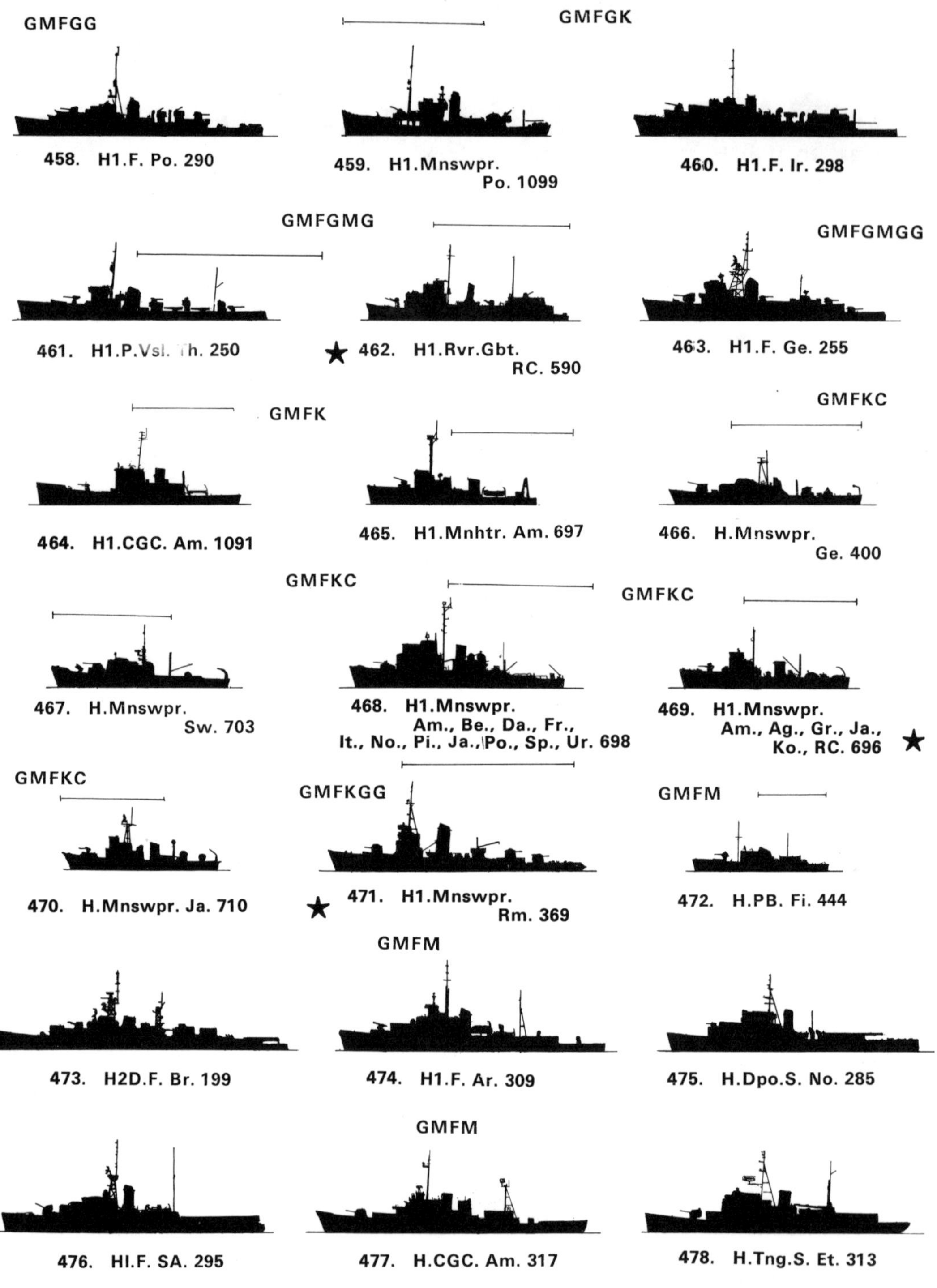


GMFGG
GMFGK
458.   H1.F. Po. 290
459.   H1.Mnswpr. Po. 1099
460.   H1.F. Ir. 298
GMFGMG
GMFGMGG
461.   H1.P.Vsl. Th. 250
462.   H1.Rvr.Gbt. RC. 590
463.   H1.F. Ge. 255
GMFK
GMFKC
464.   H1.CGC. Am. 1091
465.   H1.Mnhtr. Am. 697
466.   H.Mnswpr. Ge. 400
GMFKC
GMFKC
467.   H.Mnswpr. Sw. 703
468.   H1.Mnswpr. Am., Be., Da., Fr., It., No., Pi., Ja., Po., Sp., Ur. 698
469.   H1.Mnswpr. Am., Ag., Gr., Ja., Ko., RC. 696
GMFKC
GMFKGG
GMFM
470.   H.Mnswpr. Ja. 710
471.   H1.Mnswpr. Rm. 369
472.   H.PB. Fi. 444
GMFM
473.   H2D.F. Br. 199
474.   H1.F. Ar. 309
475.   H.Dpo.S. No. 285
GMFM
476.   HI.F. SA. 295
477.   H.CGC. Am. 317
478.   H.Tng.S. Et. 313

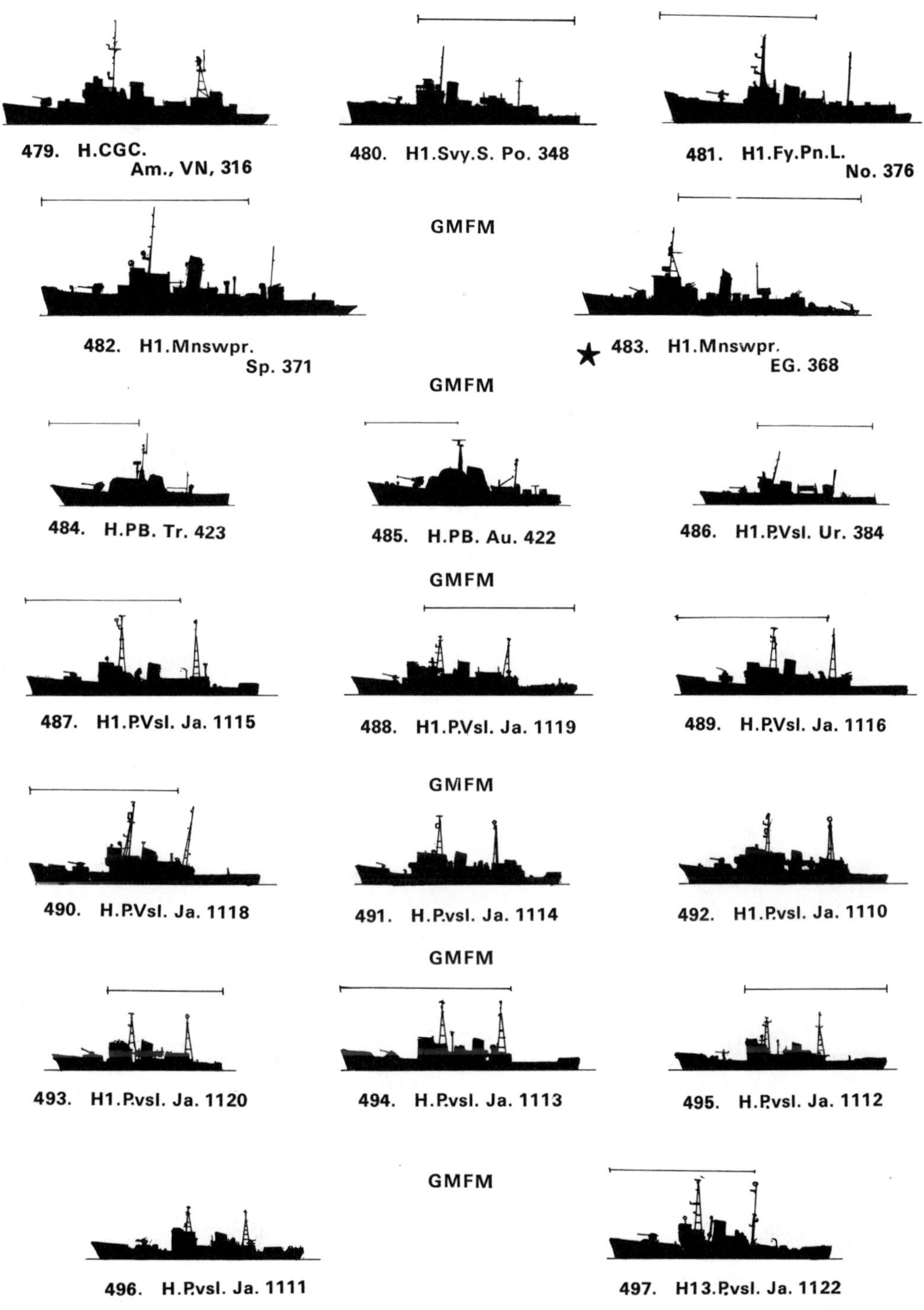

GMFM
479.  H.CGC.
Am., VN, 316
480.  H1.Svy.S. Po. 348
481.  H1.Fy.Pn.L.
No. 376
GMFM
482.  H1.Mnswpr.
Sp. 371
483.  H1.Mnswpr.
EG. 368
GMFM
484.  H.PB. Tr. 423
485.  H.PB. Au. 422
486.  H1.P.Vsl. Ur. 384
GMFM
487.  H1.P.Vsl. Ja. 1115
488.  H1.P.Vsl. Ja. 1119
489.  H.P.Vsl. Ja. 1116
GMFM
490.  H.P.Vsl. Ja. 1118
491.  H.P.vsl. Ja. 1114
492.  H1.P.vsl. Ja. 1110
GMFM
493.  H1.P.vsl. Ja. 1120
494.  H.P.vsl. Ja. 1113
495.  H.P.vsl. Ja. 1112
GMFM
496.  H.P.vsl. Ja. 1111
497.  H13.P.vsl. Ja. 1122

**GMFM**

**498.  H1.D. Au. 233**

**499.  H2.D. Ca. 227**

NOW GMFML & SHOULD COME 539a

**GMFM**

**500.  H.FPB. Ja. 395**

★ **501.  H.CGC. Cu. 457**

**GMFMC**

**502.  H1.Tng.S. In. 289**

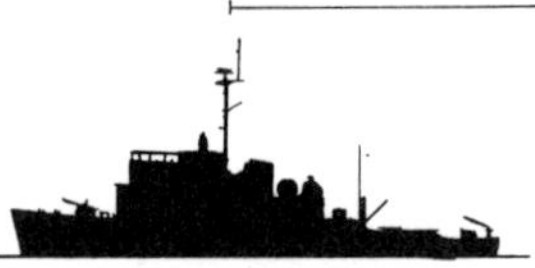

**503.  H1.Mnswpr.
Am. 678, 679**

**504.  H1.Mnswpr.
Am., Be., Fr., It. 680**

**505.  H1.PVsl. Sp. 687**

**GMFMC**

**506.  H1.Mnswpr.
Da., Fr., It. 698**

**507.  H1.Mnswpr.
Fr., Du., Po. 682**

**GMFMDG**

**508.  H2D.F. Au. 202**

**509.  H.F. Fr. 262**

**GMFMDGG**

**510.  H.F. Fr. 260**

**GMFMFCC**

**511.  H1.Mnswpr.
Pv. 147**

**GMFMFGG**

★ **512.  H1.D. Ru. 94**

**GMFMG**

**513.  H2D.F. Ca., 198**

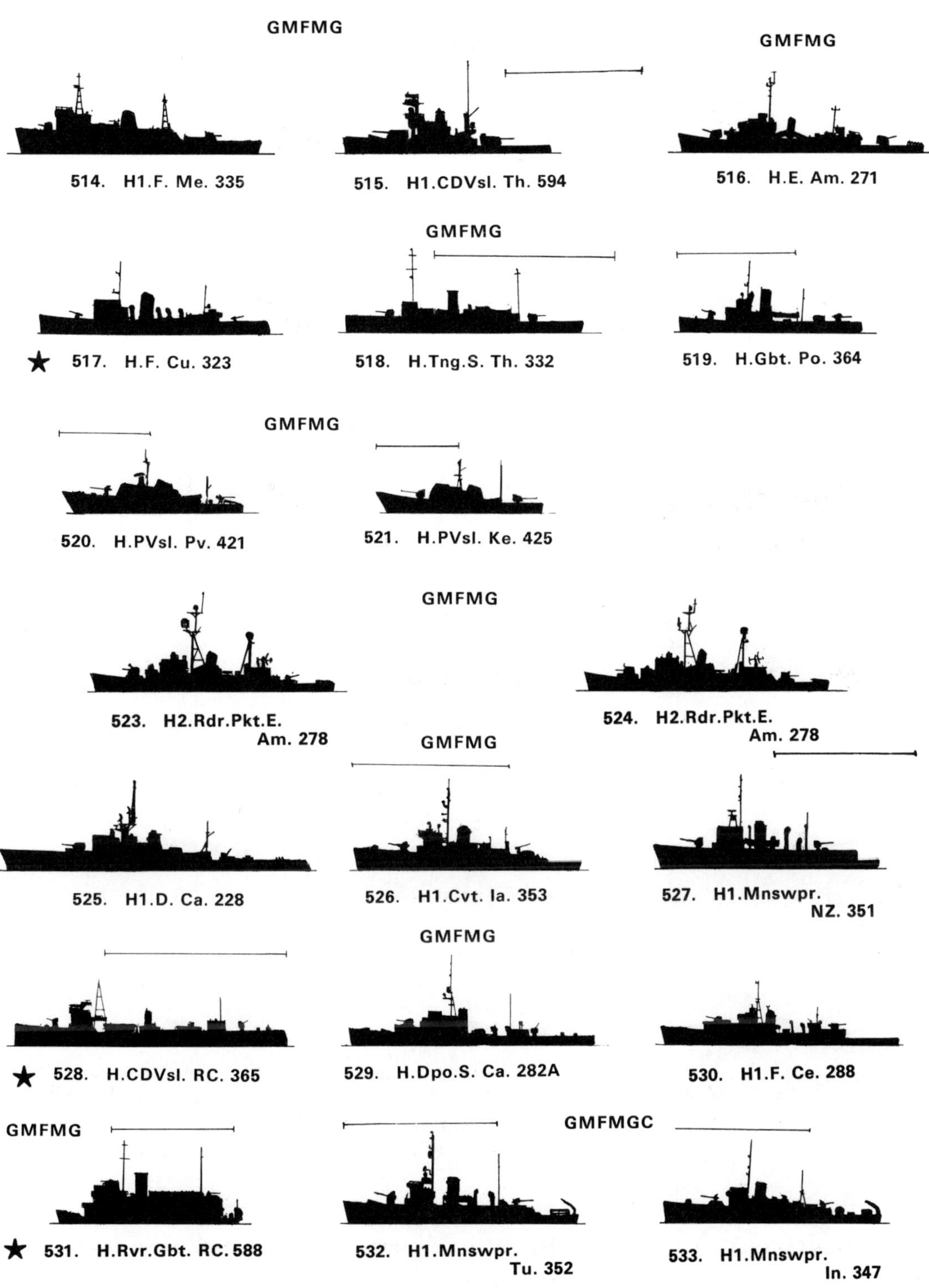


GMFMG
514.   H1.F. Me. 335
GMFMG
515.   H1.CDVsl. Th. 594
GMFMG
516.   H.E. Am. 271
517.   H.F. Cu. 323
GMFMG
518.   H.Tng.S. Th. 332
519.   H.Gbt. Po. 364
GMFMG
520.   H.PVsl. Pv. 421
521.   H.PVsl. Ke. 425
GMFMG
523.   H2.Rdr.Pkt.E.
Am. 278
524.   H2.Rdr.Pkt.E.
Am. 278
525.   H1.D. Ca. 228
GMFMG
526.   H1.Cvt. Ia. 353
527.   H1.Mnswpr.
NZ. 351
528.   H.CDVsl. RC. 365
GMFMG
529.   H.Dpo.S. Ca. 282A
530.   H1.F. Ce. 288
GMFMG
531.   H.Rvr.Gbt. RC. 588
532.   H1.Mnswpr.
Tu. 352
GMFMGC
533.   H1.Mnswpr.
In. 347

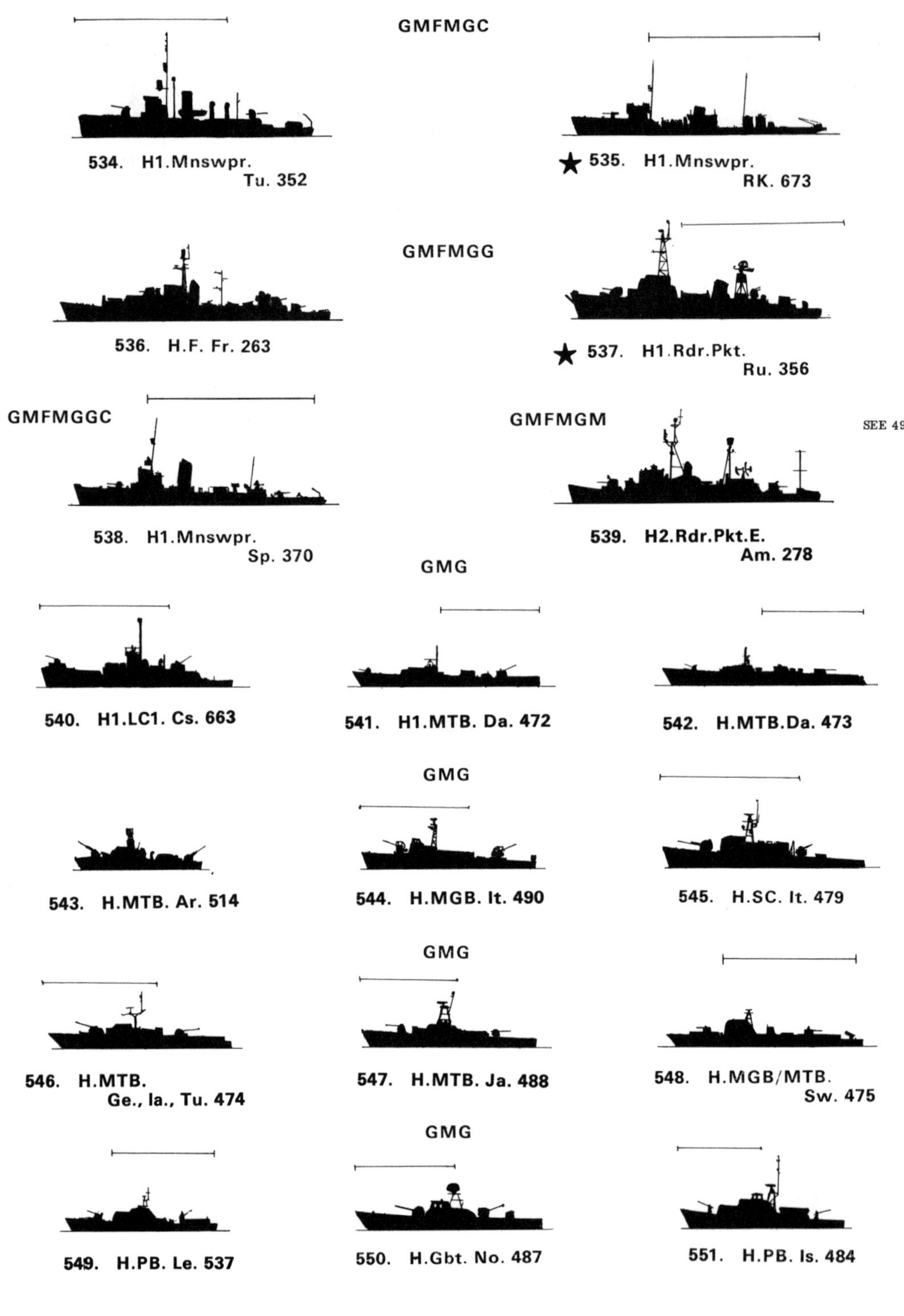

GMFMGC

534.   H1.Mnswpr.
Tu. 352

535.   H1.Mnswpr.
RK. 673

GMFMGG

536.   H.F. Fr. 263

537.   H1.Rdr.Pkt.
Ru. 356

GMFMGGC

GMFMGM

SEE 499.

538.   H1.Mnswpr.
Sp. 370

539.   H2.Rdr.Pkt.E.
Am. 278

GMG

540.   H1.LC1. Cs. 663

541.   H1.MTB. Da. 472

542.   H.MTB.Da. 473

GMG

543.   H.MTB. Ar. 514

544.   H.MGB. It. 490

545.   H.SC. It. 479

GMG

546.   H.MTB.
Ge., Ia., Tu. 474

547.   H.MTB. Ja. 488

548.   H.MGB/MTB.
Sw. 475

GMG

549.   H.PB. Le. 537

550.   H.Gbt. No. 487

551.   H.PB. Is. 484

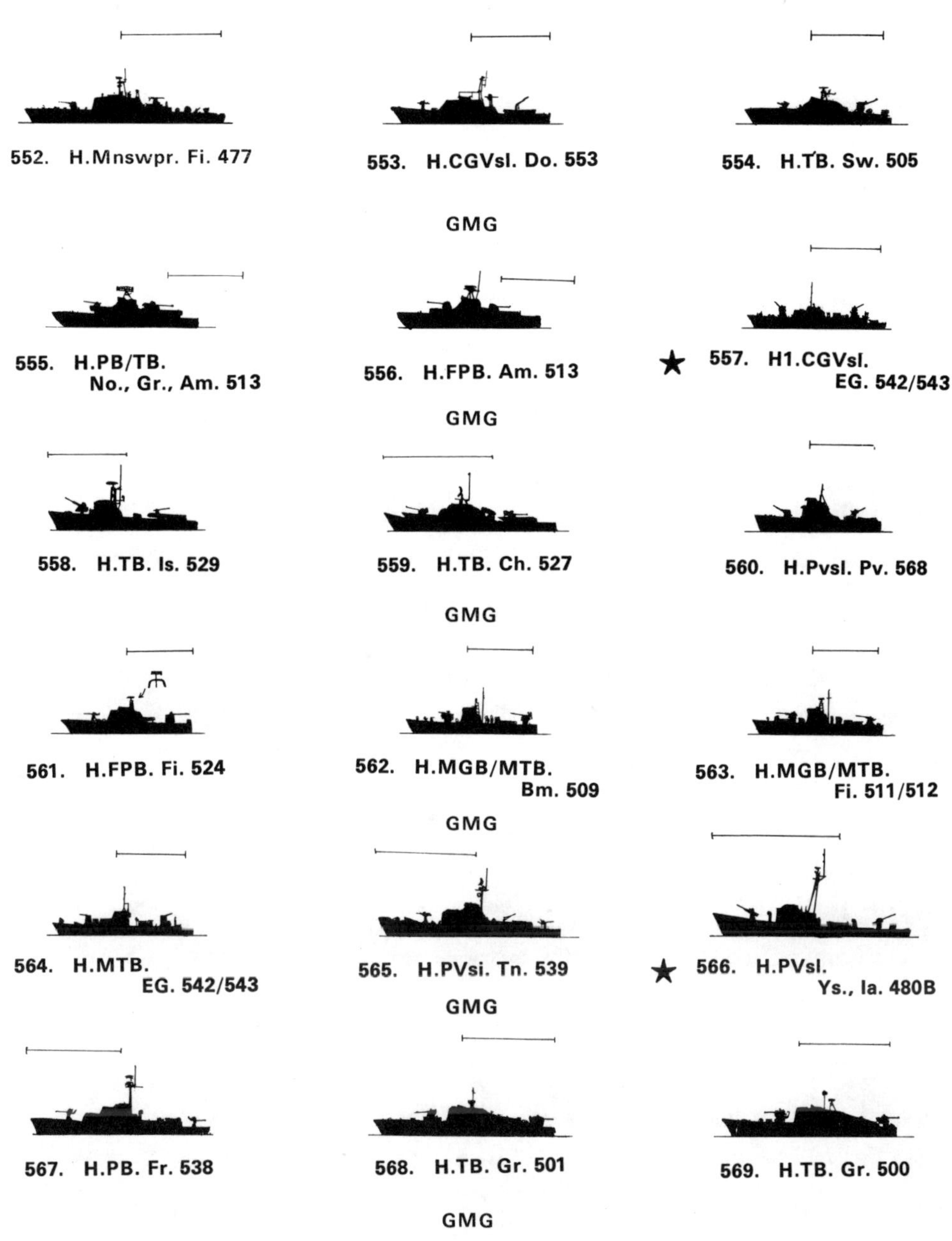



552.  H.Mnswpr. Fi. 477

553.  H.CGVsl. Do. 553

554.  H.TB. Sw. 505

555.  H.PB/TB.
No., Gr., Am. 513

556.  H.FPB. Am. 513

★ 557.  H1.CGVsl.
EG. 542/543

558.  H.TB. Is. 529

559.  H.TB. Ch. 527

560.  H.Pvsl. Pv. 568

561.  H.FPB. Fi. 524

562.  H.MGB/MTB.
Bm. 509

563.  H.MGB/MTB.
Fi. 511/512

★ 564.  H.MTB.
EG. 542/543

565.  H.PVsi. Tn. 539

★ 566.  H.PVsl.
Ys., Ia. 480B

567.  H.PB. Fr. 538

568.  H.TB. Gr. 501

569.  H.TB. Gr. 500

570.  H.TB. Da. 570

571.  H.PB. Pk. 485

572.  H.Hy.GB. Am. 583

GMG

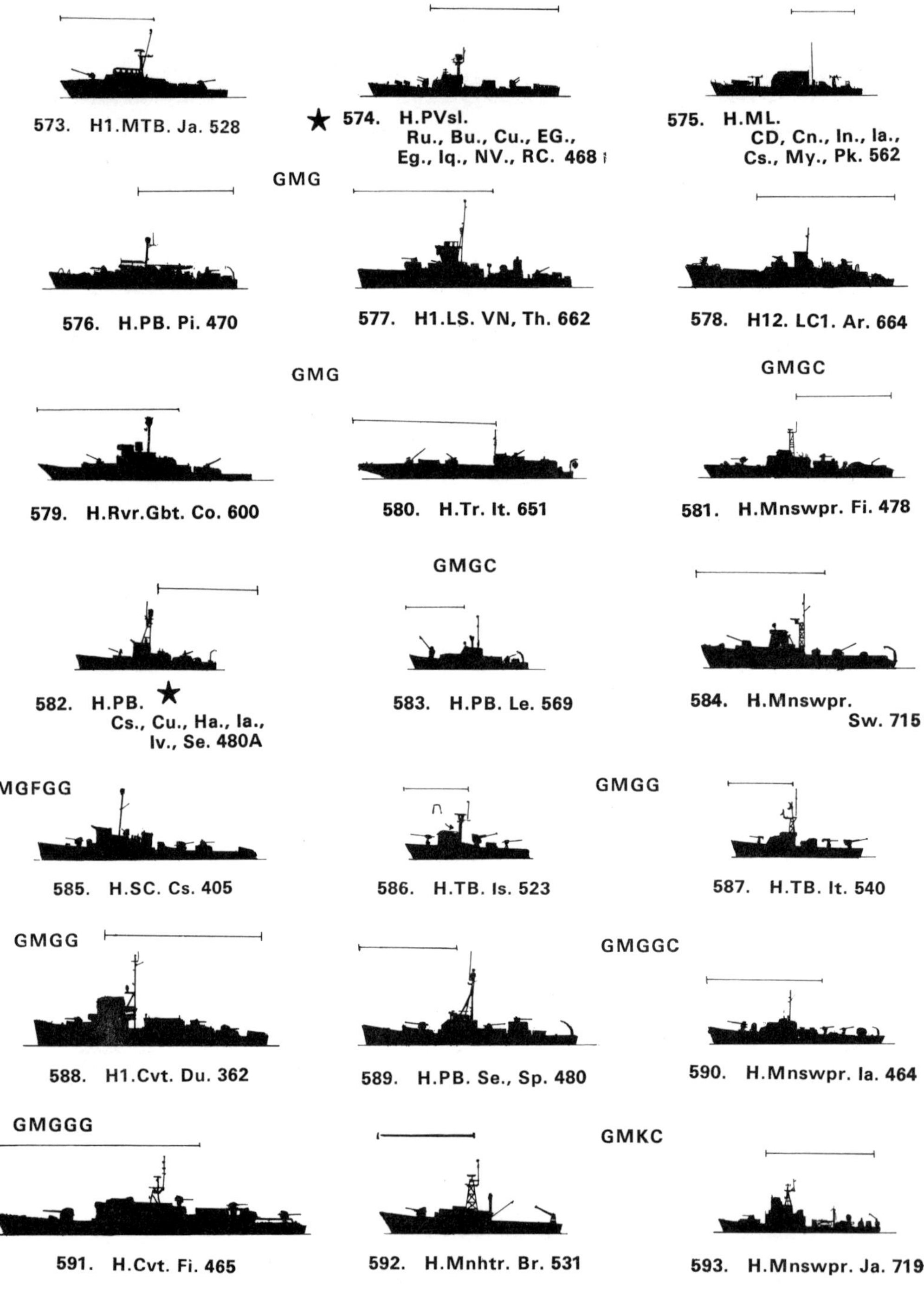

573.  H1.MTB. Ja. 528

574.  H.PVsl.
Ru., Bu., Cu., EG.,
Eg., Iq., NV., RC. 468

575.  H.ML.
CD, Cn., In., Ia.,
Cs., My., Pk. 562

GMG

576.  H.PB. Pi. 470

577.  H1.LS. VN, Th. 662

578.  H12. LC1. Ar. 664

GMG

GMGC

579.  H.Rvr.Gbt. Co. 600

580.  H.Tr. It. 651

581.  H.Mnswpr. Fi. 478

GMGC

582.  H.PB.
Cs., Cu., Ha., Ia.,
Iv., Se. 480A

583.  H.PB. Le. 569

584.  H.Mnswpr.
Sw. 715

GMGFGG

GMGG

585.  H.SC. Cs. 405

586.  H.TB. Is. 523

587.  H.TB. It. 540

GMGG

GMGGC

588.  H1.Cvt. Du. 362

589.  H.PB. Se., Sp. 480

590.  H.Mnswpr. Ia. 464

GMGGG

GMKC

591.  H.Cvt. Fi. 465

592.  H.Mnhtr. Br. 531

593.  H.Mnswpr. Ja. 719

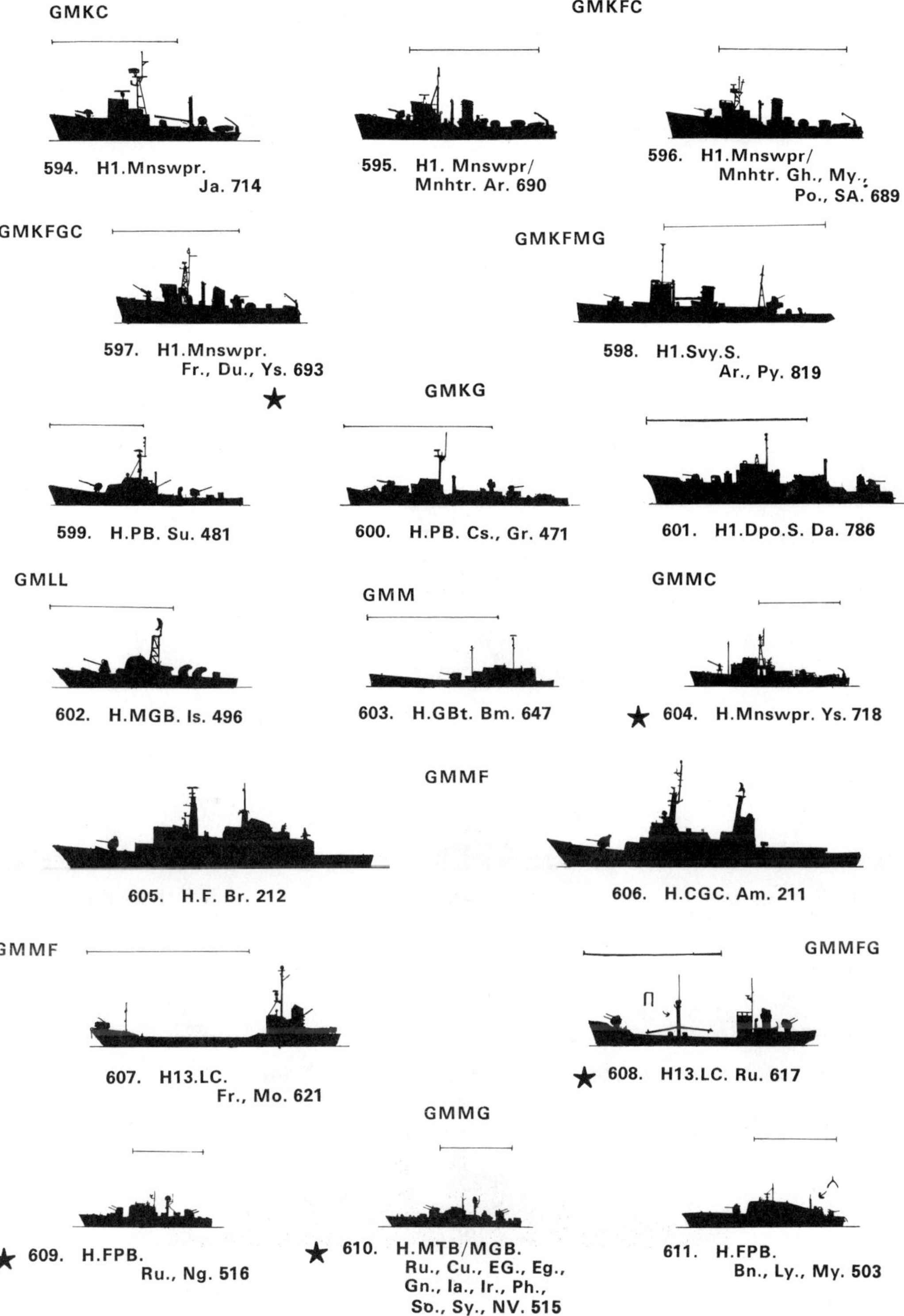

GMKC

594. H1.Mnswpr.
Ja. 714

GMKFC

595. H1. Mnswpr/
Mnhtr. Ar. 690

596. H1.Mnswpr/
Mnhtr. Gh., My.,
Po., SA. 689

GMKFGC

597. H1.Mnswpr.
Fr., Du., Ys. 693
★

GMKFMG

598. H1.Svy.S.
Ar., Py. 819

GMKG

599. H.PB. Su. 481

600. H.PB. Cs., Gr. 471

601. H1.Dpo.S. Da. 786

GMLL

602. H.MGB. Is. 496

GMM

603. H.GBt. Bm. 647

GMMC

★ 604. H.Mnswpr. Ys. 718

GMMF

605. H.F. Br. 212

606. H.CGC. Am. 211

GMMF

607. H13.LC.
Fr., Mo. 621

GMMFG

★ 608. H13.LC. Ru. 617

GMMG

★ 609. H.FPB.
Ru., Ng. 516

★ 610. H.MTB/MGB.
Ru., Cu., EG., Eg.,
Gn., Ia., Ir., Ph.,
So., Sy., NV. 515

611. H.FPB.
Bn., Ly., My. 503

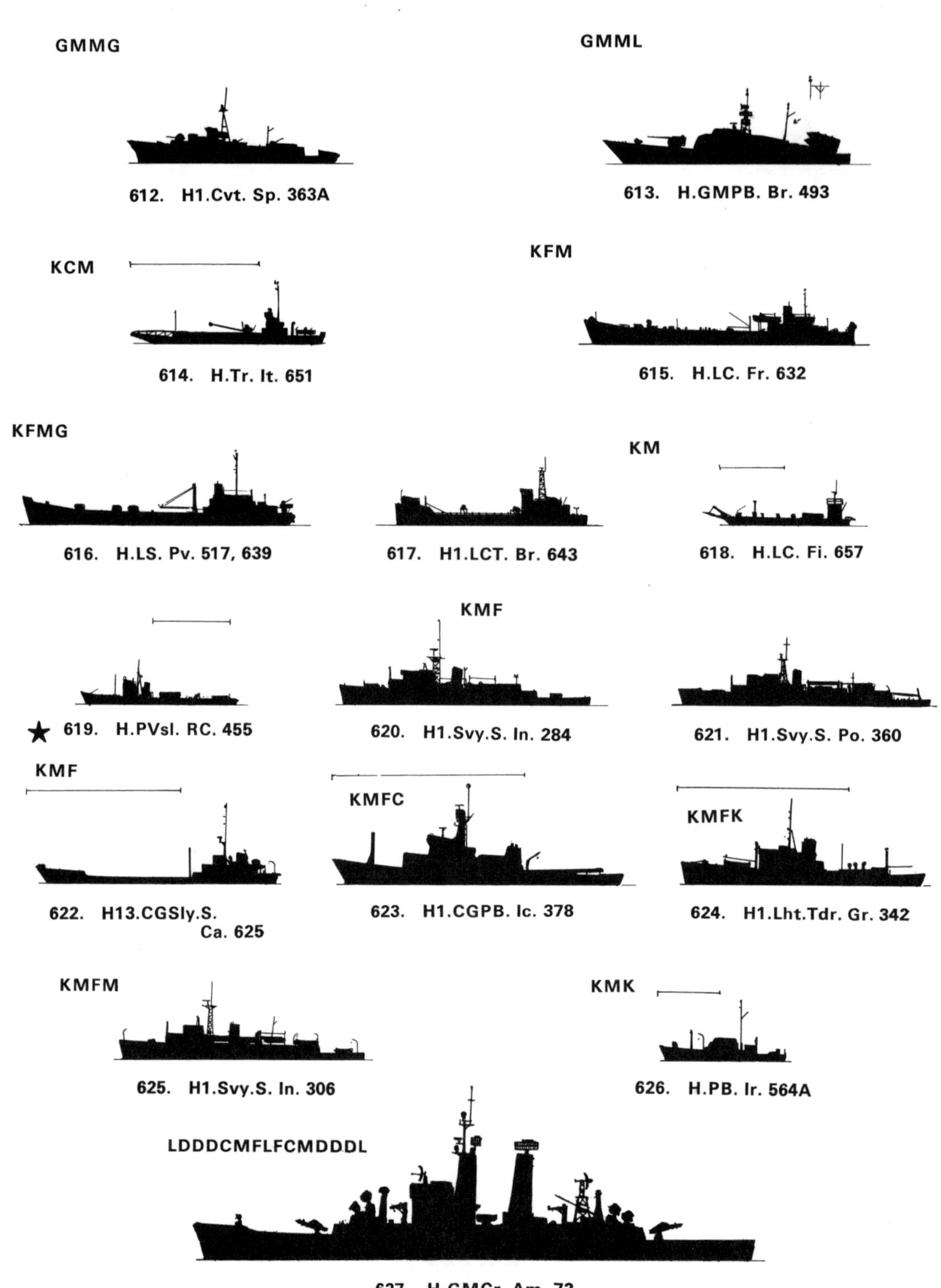

GMMG
612.   H1.Cvt. Sp. 363A
GMML
613.   H.GMPB. Br. 493
KCM
614.   H.Tr. It. 651
KFM
615.   H.LC. Fr. 632
KFMG
616.   H.LS. Pv. 517, 639
617.   H1.LCT. Br. 643
KM
618.   H.LC. Fi. 657
619.   H.PVsl. RC. 455
KMF
620.   H1.Svy.S. In. 284
621.   H1.Svy.S. Po. 360
KMF
622.   H13.CGSly.S. Ca. 625
KMFC
623.   H1.CGPB. Ic. 378
KMFK
624.   H1.Lht.Tdr. Gr. 342
KMFM
625.   H1.Svy.S. In. 306
KMK
626.   H.PB. Ir. 564A
LDDDCMFLFCMDDDL
627.   H.GMCr. Am. 72

**LDDMFCMFG**

628.   H,GMCr. It. 76

**LDDMFFDG**

629.   H1,GMF. Am. 73

**LDMFDL**

★ 630.   H1.GMD. Ru. 173/4

**LGDDMFMFG**

631.   H2.GMCr. It. 75

**LGDMF**

★ 632.   H.LS. Ru. 627

**LGDMFMDFGL**

★ 633.   H.GMD. Ru. 88

**LGDMFMDGG**

634.   H.E. Fr. 261

635.   H.E. Fr. 260

**LGDMFMFDDL**

636.   H1.D. Fr. 111

**LGGMFFFMG**

637.   H1.D. Co. 126

**LGLMFCFDG**

638.   H.D. Ja. 71

**LGLMFMFDGL**

639.   H.GMF. Am. 186

**LGMFG**

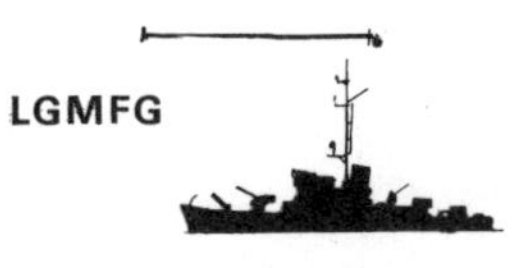

640.   H.PVsl. Du. 452

**LLDDDDMLGKMDDL**

641.  H.GMCr. Am. 160

**LLDDMFMFDDL**

642.  H1.GMF. Am. 74

**LLDDMMDDL**

643.  H1.GMF. Am. 184

**LLDMFMFDL**

644.  H1.GMF. Am. 74

**LLDMFMFDLGG**

★ 645.  H1.GMD. Ru. 83

**LLGGMFFMGG**

646.  H1.D. Sw. 127

**LLGMFBG**

★ 647.  H.PB. EG. 392

**LLGMFGG**

★ 648.  H.PB. EG. 391

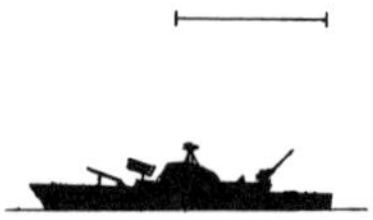

649.  H.TB. Sw. 506

**LLMG**

★ 650.  H3.E. Ru. 466

**LM**

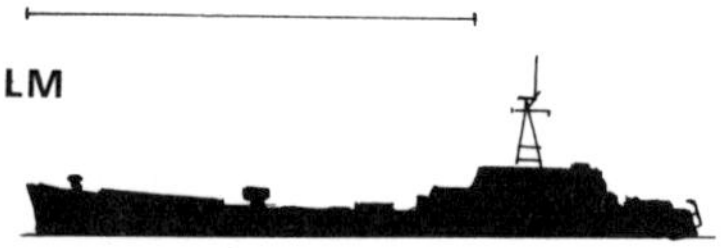

★ 651   H.LS. Ru. 627

**LMFCG**

652.  H.Cvt. Ge. 374

**LMFG**

653.  H1.Cvt. Ge. 377

654.  H.ML. Tu. 439

**LMFM**

655.  H.CGVsl. Th. 438

LMG

M

656.   H.MTB. Ja. 517

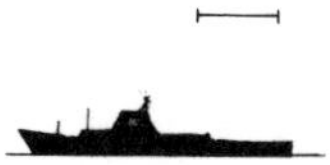

657.   H.PB. Li. 577

658.   H.LC. Sw. 534

M

★ 659.   H.TB. EG. 522

660.   H.TB. Sp. 476

★ 661.   H.ML. Cu. 545

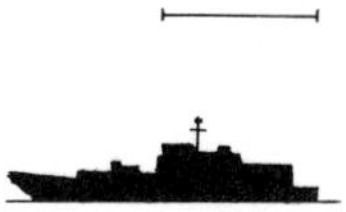

M

662.   H1.Tr. Co. 668

663.   H.CG.Rscu.S.
              Ca. 557

664.   H.PB. Ce. 556

M

665.   H.PB. Ja. 550

666.   H Tng.S.Br. 504

667.   H.CGC. Da. 578

M

668.   H.PB. Au. 564

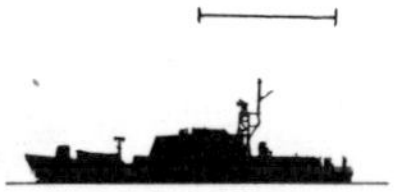

669.   H.PB. NZ. 565

670.   H.PB. Pk. 563

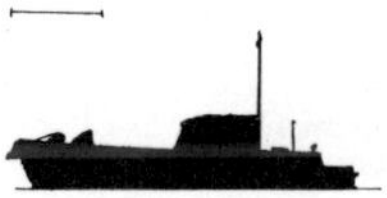

M

671.   H1.PB. Ce. 566

672.   H.PB. In. 532

673.   H.CGVsl. Do. 570

M

674.   H.LC. Am. 667

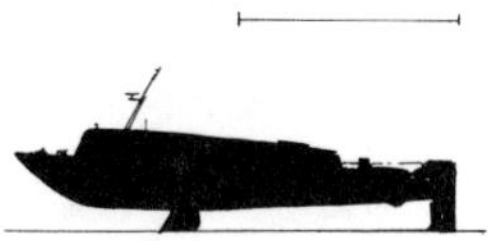

675.   H.Hy.(Exp.).
              Am. 579

676.   H.Hy.PB. Pi. 586

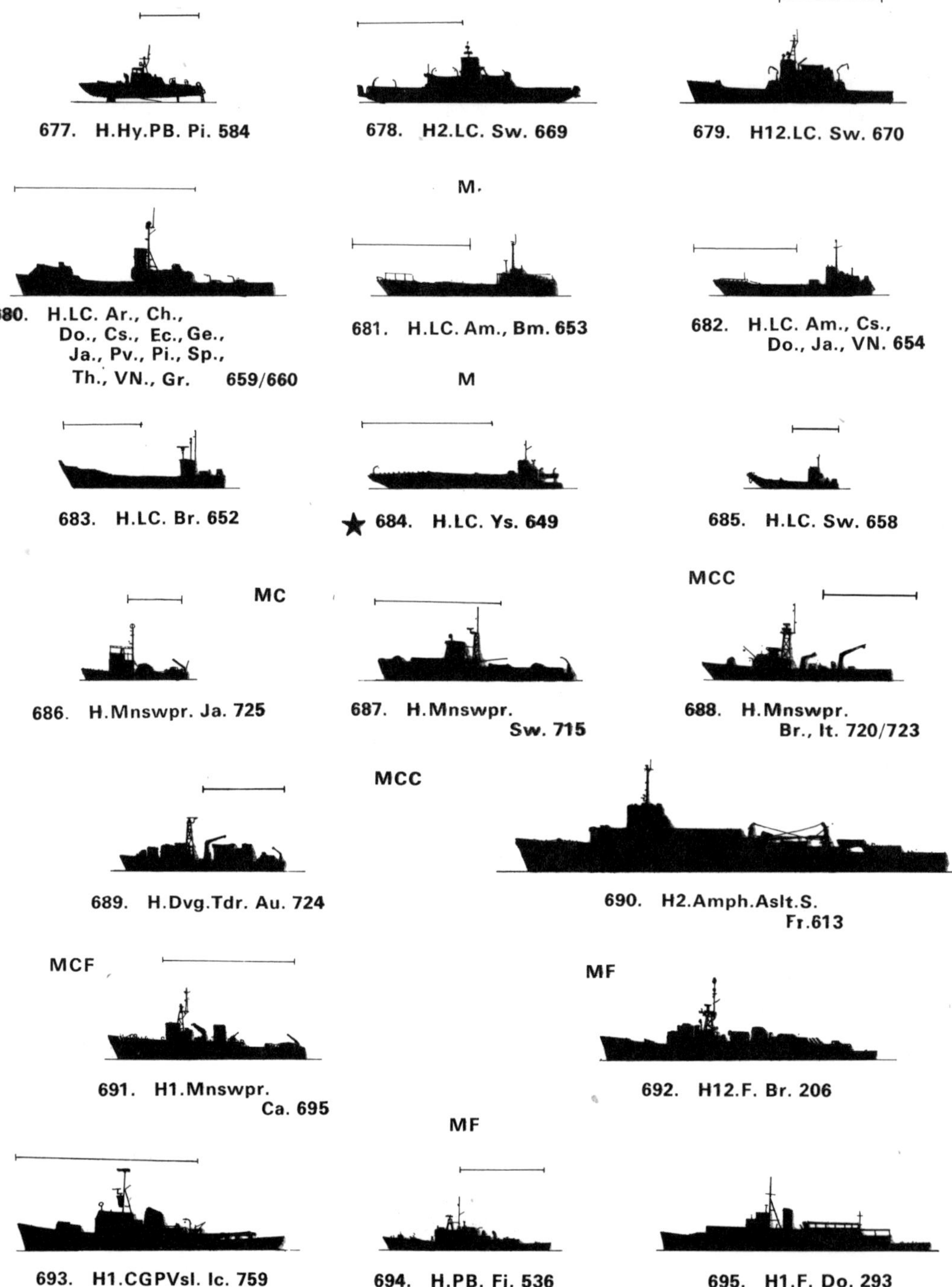


M

677.   H.Hy.PB. Pi. 584
678.   H2.LC. Sw. 669
679.   H12.LC. Sw. 670

M.

680.   H.LC. Ar., Ch.,
       Do., Cs., Ec., Ge.,
       Ja., Pv., Pi., Sp.,
       Th., VN., Gr.     659/660
681.   H.LC. Am., Bm. 653
682.   H.LC. Am., Cs.,
       Do., Ja., VN. 654

M

683.   H.LC. Br. 652
684.   H.LC. Ys. 649
685.   H.LC. Sw. 658

MC

686.   H.Mnswpr. Ja. 725
687.   H.Mnswpr.
       Sw. 715
MCC
688.   H.Mnswpr.
       Br., It. 720/723

MCC

689.   H.Dvg.Tdr. Au. 724
690.   H2.Amph.Aslt.S.
       Fr.613

MCF

691.   H1.Mnswpr.
       Ca. 695
MF
692.   H12.F. Br. 206

MF

693.   H1.CGPVsl. Ic. 759
694.   H.PB. Fi. 536
695.   H1.F. Do. 293

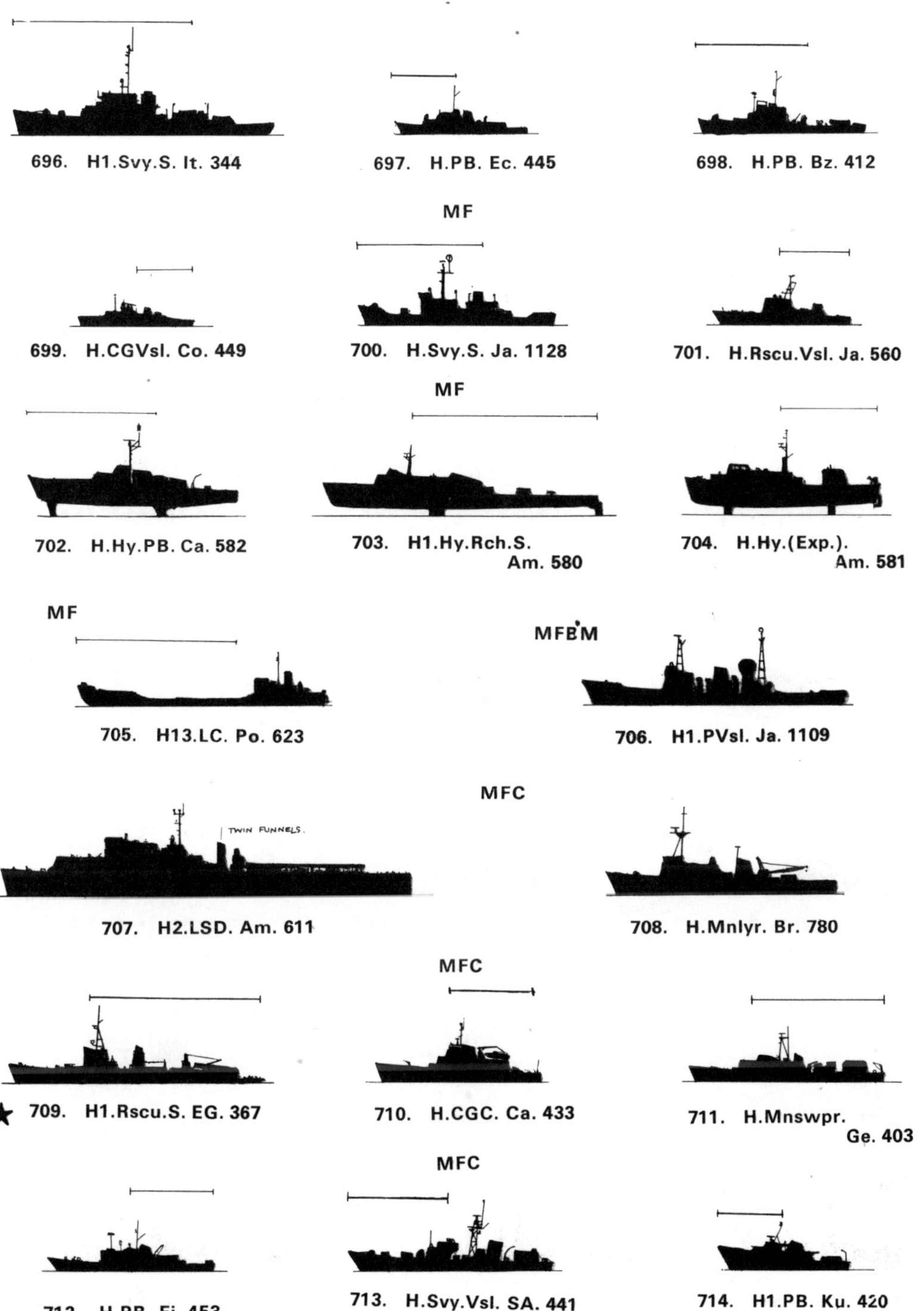



696.  H1.Svy.S. It. 344

697.  H.PB. Ec. 445

698.  H.PB. Bz. 412

699.  H.CGVsl. Co. 449

700.  H.Svy.S. Ja. 1128

701.  H.Rscu.Vsl. Ja. 560

702.  H.Hy.PB. Ca. 582

703.  H1.Hy.Rch.S. Am. 580

704.  H.Hy.(Exp.). Am. 581

705.  H13.LC. Po. 623

706.  H1.PVsl. Ja. 1109

707.  H2.LSD. Am. 611

708.  H.Mnlyr. Br. 780

709.  H1.Rscu.S. EG. 367

710.  H.CGC. Ca. 433

711.  H.Mnswpr. Ge. 403

712.  H.PB. Fi. 453

713.  H.Svy.Vsl. SA. 441

714.  H1.PB. Ku. 420

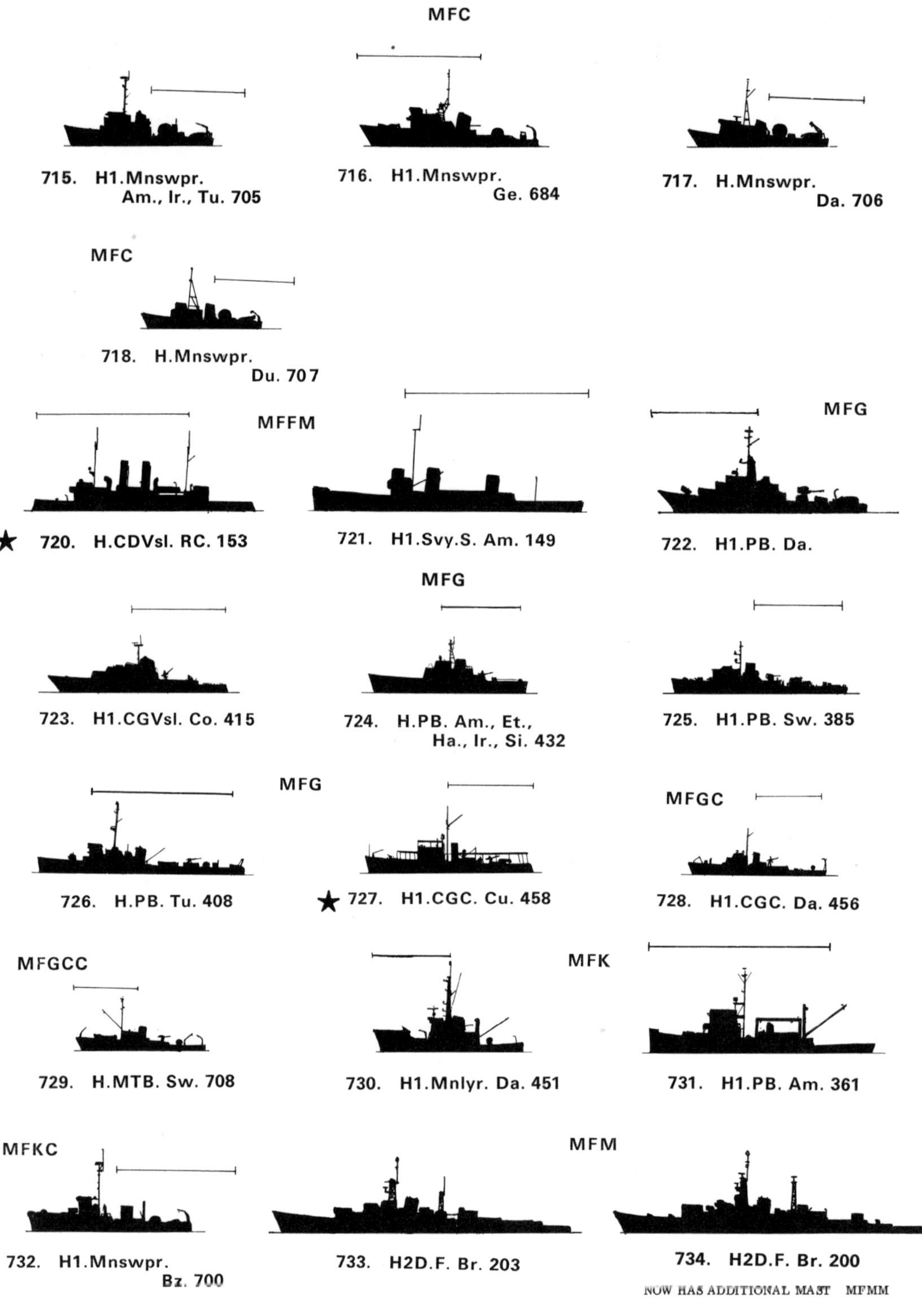


MFC
715. H1.Mnswpr.
Am., Ir., Tu. 705
716. H1.Mnswpr.
Ge. 684
717. H.Mnswpr.
Da. 706
MFC
718. H.Mnswpr.
Du. 707
MFFM
720. H.CDVsl. RC. 153
721. H1.Svy.S. Am. 149
MFG
722. H1.PB. Da.
MFG
723. H1.CGVsl. Co. 415
724. H.PB. Am., Et.,
Ha., Ir., Si. 432
725. H1.PB. Sw. 385
MFG
726. H.PB. Tu. 408
727. H1.CGC. Cu. 458
MFGC
728. H1.CGC. Da. 456
MFGCC
729. H.MTB. Sw. 708
MFK
730. H1.Mnlyr. Da. 451
731. H1.PB. Am. 361
MFKC
732. H1.Mnswpr.
Bz. 700
733. H2D.F. Br. 203
MFM
734. H2D.F. Br. 200
NOW HAS ADDITIONAL MAST   MFMM

**MFM**

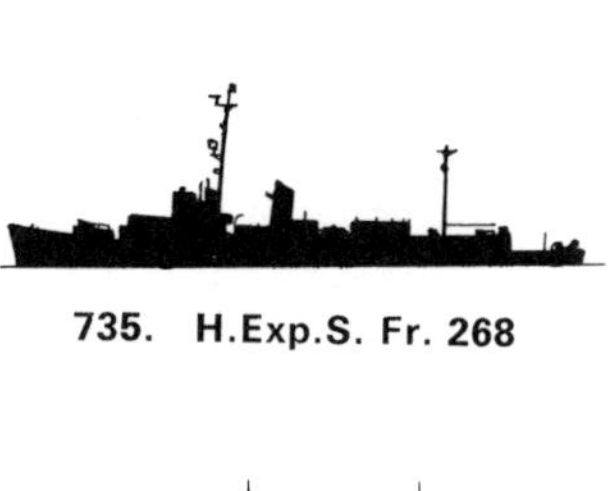

735. H.Exp.S. Fr. 268

736. H.Svy.S. Am. 315

737. H1.Svy.S. SA. 296

**MFM**

738. H1.Svy.S. NZ 283

★ 739. H1.F. RC. 382

★ 740. H1.F. RC. 381

**MFM**

741. H.PVsl. Ja. 998

742. H12.Svy.Vsl.
Ja. 1127

743. H.PVsl. Ja. 1126

**MFM**      **MFMC**

★ 744. H1.F. RC. 383

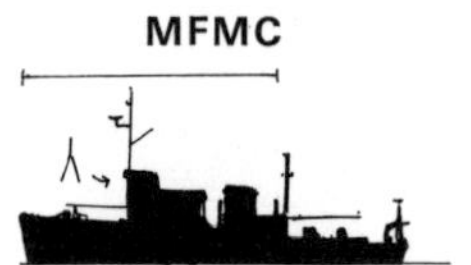

★ 745. H.Rvr.Gbt. RC. 587

746. H1.Exp.Vsl.
Ge. 836

**MFMC**

747. H1.Rch.S. Be. 699

**MFMC**

748. H1.Spt.S. Be. 336

**MFMCC**

749. H1.Mnswpr.
Gr. 337

**MFMDG**

750. H2D.F. Br. 204

751. H2D.F. SA. 201

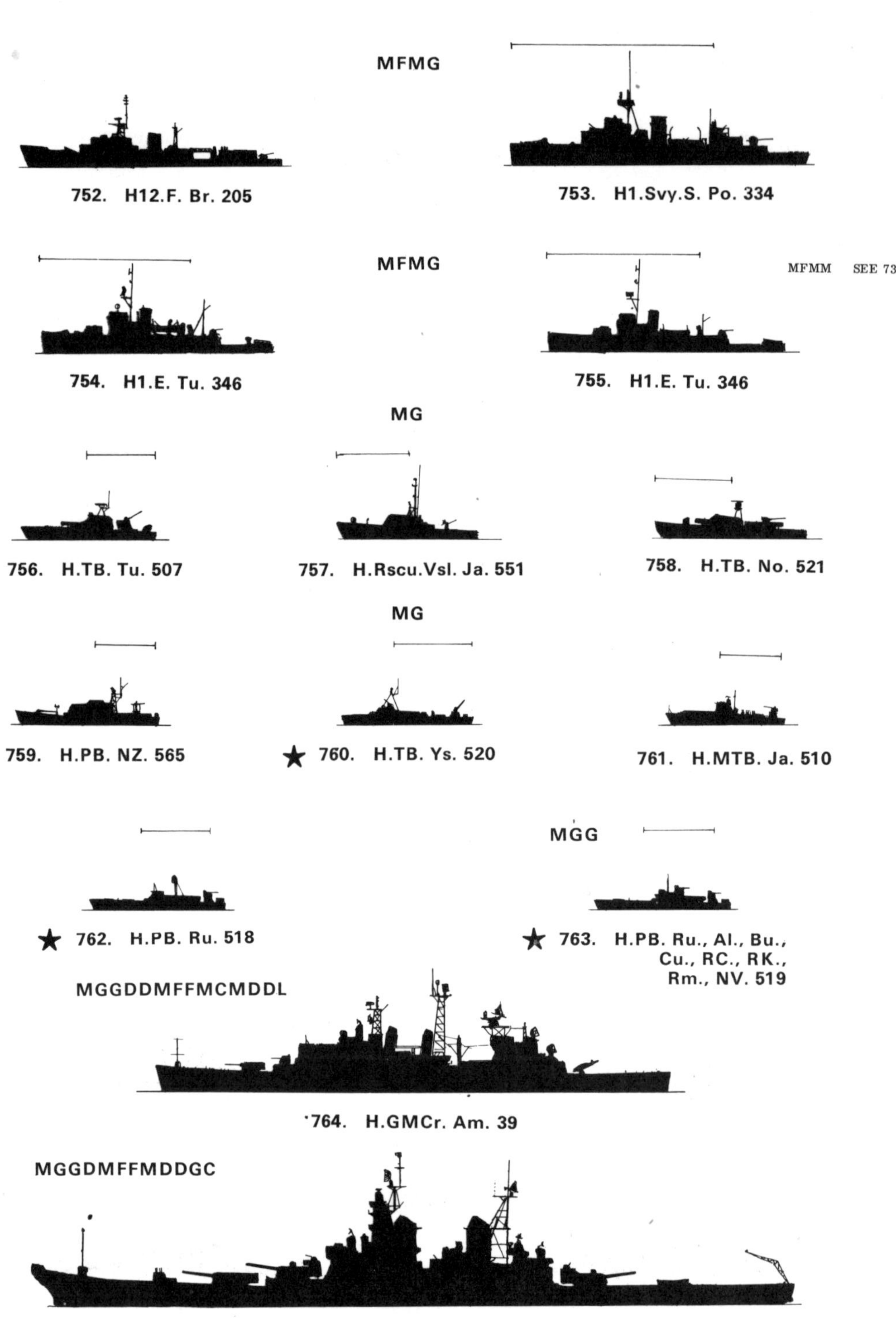


MFMG

752.   H12.F. Br. 205

753.   H1.Svy.S. Po. 334

MFMG

MFMM    SEE 734

754.   H1.E. Tu. 346

755.   H1.E. Tu. 346

MG

756.   H.TB. Tu. 507

757.   H.Rscu.Vsl. Ja. 551

758.   H.TB. No. 521

MG

759.   H.PB. NZ. 565

760.   H.TB. Ys. 520

761.   H.MTB. Ja. 510

MGG

762.   H.PB. Ru. 518

763.   H.PB. Ru., Al., Bu.,
Cu., RC., RK.,
Rm., NV. 519

MGGDDMFFMCMDDL

764.   H.GMCr. Am. 39

MGGDMFFMDDGC

765.   H.BS. Am. 34

MGGDMFFMDDGGC

**766.   H.Cr. Am. 36**

MGGDMFFMKMDDL

**767.   H.GMCr. Am. 40**

MGGGDDMFFMKMDDL

**768.   H.GMCr. Am. 41**

MGGGDDMFFMMDDL

**769.   H.GMCr. Am. 38**

MGGGDDMFMDDDLL

**770.   H.Cr. Am. 162**

MGGGDDMFMDDGGC

**771.   H.Cr. Am. 163**

MGMDMFMDG

**772.   H.Cmd.S. Am. 161**

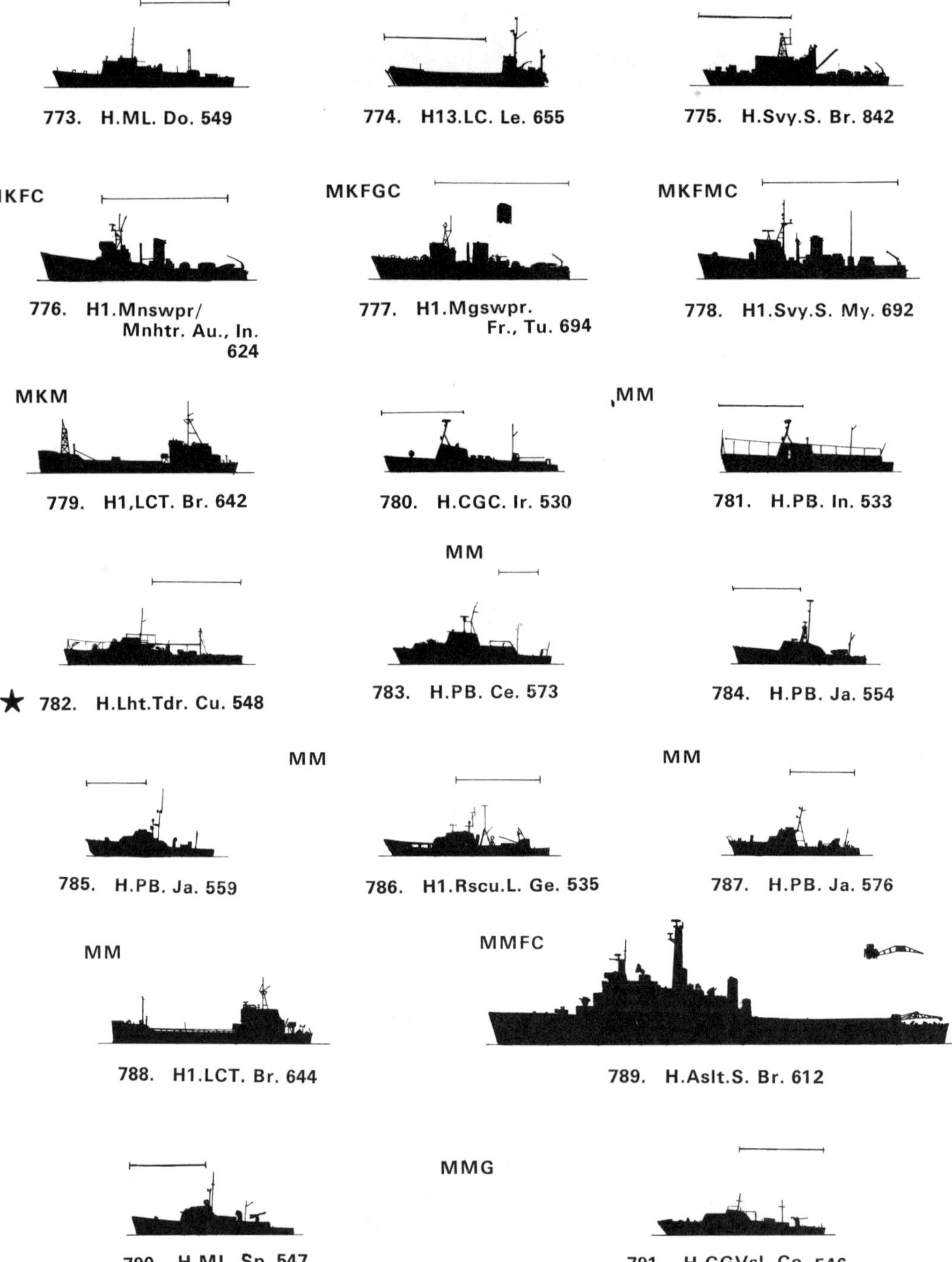

MK
773. H.ML. Do. 549
774. H13.LC. Le. 655
775. H.Svy.S. Br. 842
MKFC
776. H1.Mnswpr/
Mnhtr. Au., In.
624
MKFGC
777. H1.Mgswpr.
Fr., Tu. 694
MKFMC
778. H1.Svy.S. My. 692
MKM
779. H1,LCT. Br. 642
780. H.CGC. Ir. 530
MM
781. H.PB. In. 533
MM
782. H.Lht.Tdr. Cu. 548
783. H.PB. Ce. 573
784. H.PB. Ja. 554
MM
785. H.PB. Ja. 559
786. H1.Rscu.L. Ge. 535
MM
787. H.PB. Ja. 576
MM
788. H1.LCT. Br. 644
MMFC
789. H.Aslt.S. Br. 612
MMG
790. H.ML. Sp. 547
791. H.CGVsl. Co. 546

# NON-COMBATANT TYPES

## HULL FORM

The most difficult feature in recognition as several factors tend to confuse.

In the Distant View only parts above the upper deck are visible. Some ships have no raised "castles" and these are classed as "Flush Decked" vessels.

Other ships have *castles* showing like islands above the deck level and these are classed as one, two or three-island ships.

Islands or castles are: (1) *Forecastle:* (2) *Midcastle* and (3) *Aftercastle.*

By numbering the castles from foreward to aft as in *Fig. 1* an indication of the hull form can be given. For example, a three-island ship is described as having *hull form 1-2-3.* Islands vary in length and may be joined: thus a long forecastle *joined* to a midcastle would be *H 1* and not *H 1-2.*

## THE BASIC HULL FORMS  *Fig. 1*

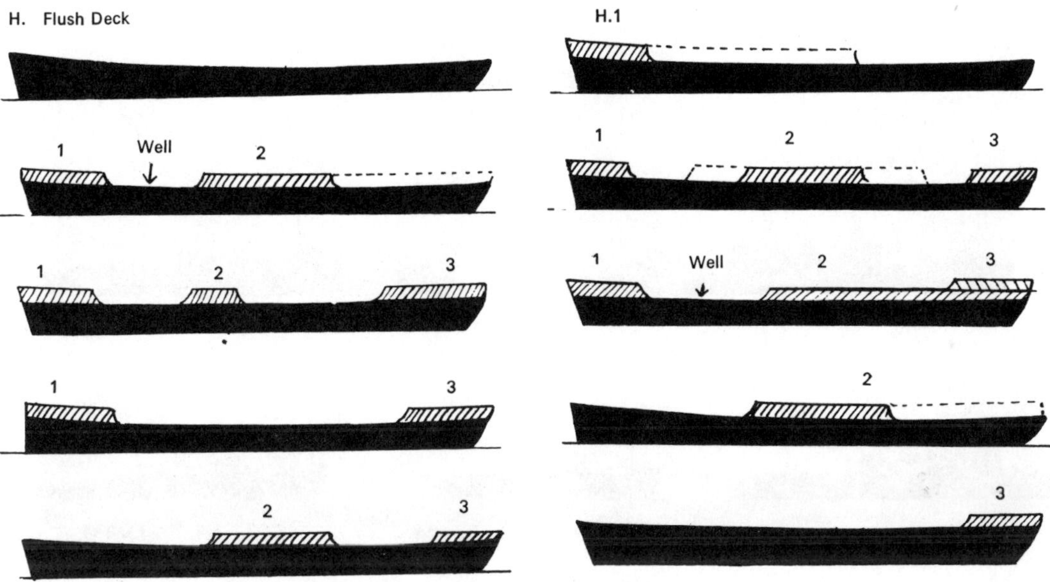



## PROFILE (P)

Profile in recognition implies the position of the navigating bridge structure relative to the main superstructure and the funnel.

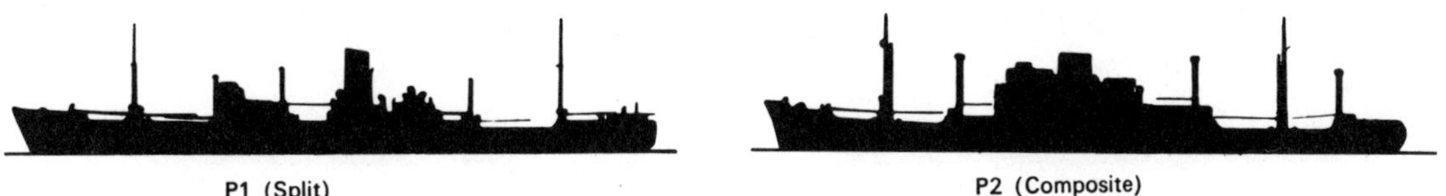

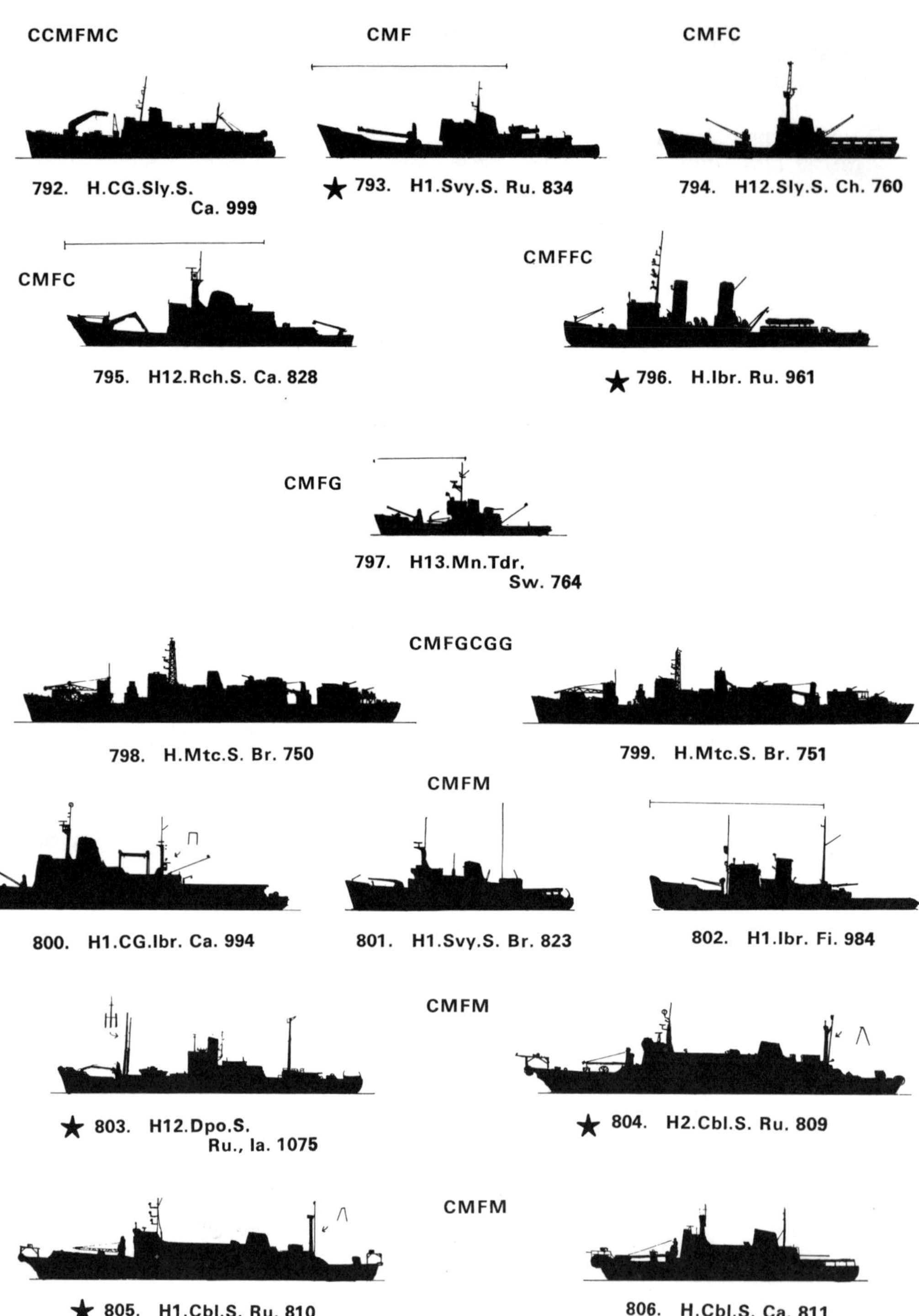

CCMFMC
792.  H.CG.Sly.S.
Ca. 999

CMF
793.  H1.Svy.S. Ru. 834

CMFC
794.  H12.Sly.S. Ch. 760

CMFC
795.  H12.Rch.S. Ca. 828

CMFFC
796.  H.Ibr. Ru. 961

CMFG
797.  H13.Mn.Tdr.
Sw. 764

CMFGCGG
798.  H.Mtc.S. Br. 750

799.  H.Mtc.S. Br. 751

CMFM
800.  H1.CG.Ibr. Ca. 994

801.  H1.Svy.S. Br. 823

802.  H1.Ibr. Fi. 984

CMFM
803.  H12.Dpo.S.
Ru., Ia. 1075

804.  H2.Cbl.S. Ru. 809

CMFM
805.  H1.Cbl.S. Ru. 810

806.  H.Cbl.S. Ca. 811

★ 807.   H1.Ibr. Ru. 974

809.   H1.Sub.Tdr.
Am. 738

811.   H1.Msl.Rge.S.
Am. 754

808.   H1.Svy.S. Br. 824

★ 810.   H12.Msl.Rge.S.
Ru. 768

812.   H13.Exp.GMS.
Fr. 767

813.  H1.   Rch.S. Am. 755


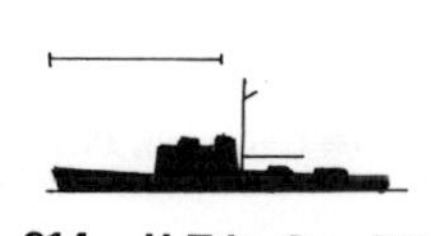
814.   H.Tdr. Sw. 711

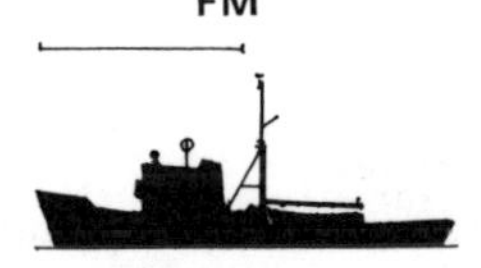
815.   H1.CG.PB. Ic. 763

816.   H.Tg. Do. 1335

817.   H12.D.Tdr. Au. 747

819.   H.D.Tdr. Am. 739

★ 818.   H13.Dpo.S.
Ru. 734

★ 820.   H13.Spt.S. Ru. 748

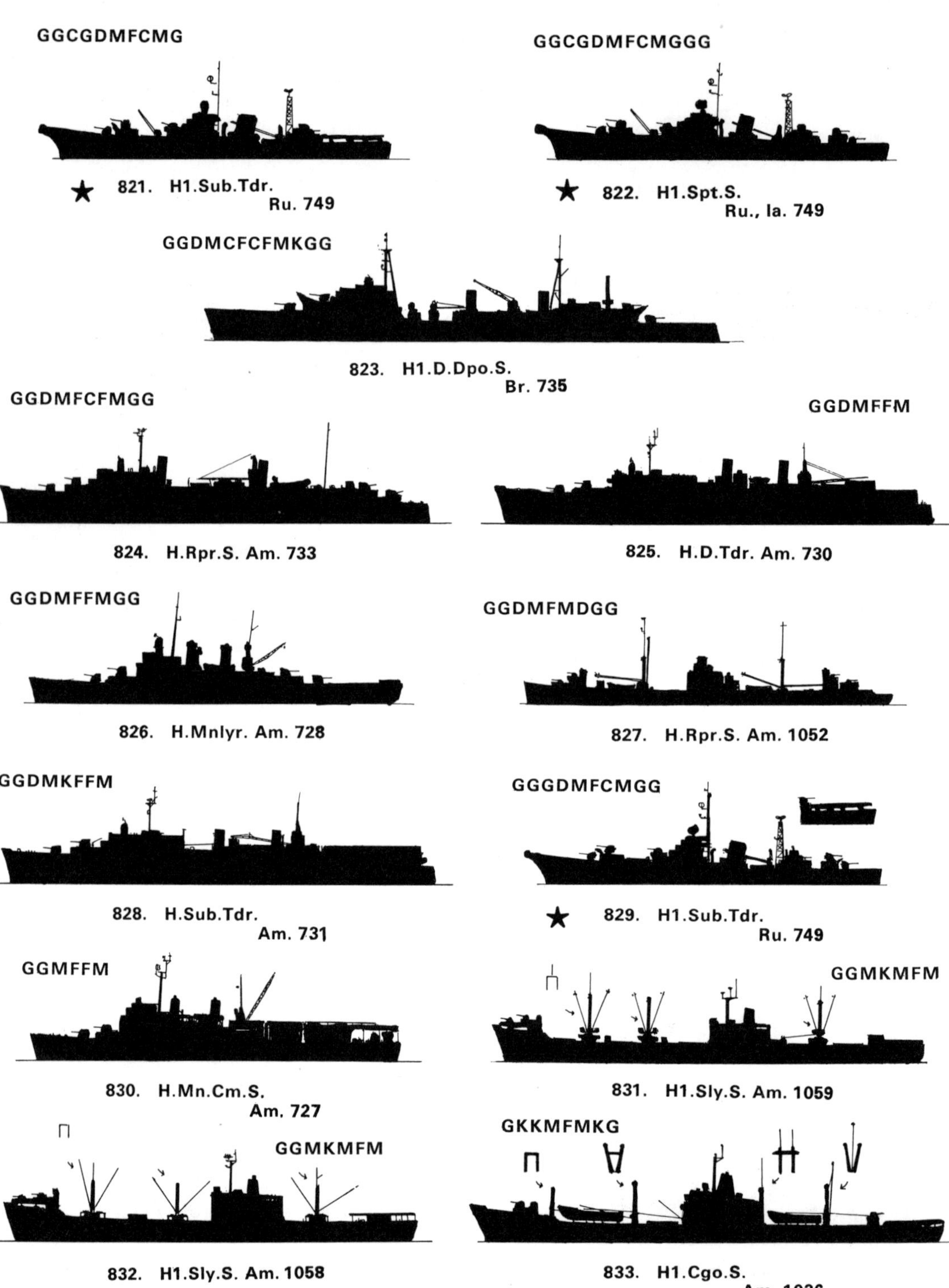

GGCGDMFCMG
821. H1.Sub.Tdr.
Ru. 749

GGCGDMFCMGGG
822. H1.Spt.S.
Ru., Ia. 749

GGDMCFCFMKGG
823. H1.D.Dpo.S.
Br. 735

GGDMFCFMGG
824. H.Rpr.S. Am. 733

GGDMFFM
825. H.D.Tdr. Am. 730

GGDMFFMGG
826. H.Mnlyr. Am. 728

GGDMFMDGG
827. H.Rpr.S. Am. 1052

GGDMKFFM
828. H.Sub.Tdr.
Am. 731

GGGDMFCMGG
829. H1.Sub.Tdr.
Ru. 749

GGMFFM
830. H.Mn.Cm.S.
Am. 727

GGMKMFM
831. H1.Sly.S. Am. 1059

GGMKMFM
832. H1.Sly.S. Am. 1058

GKKMFMKG
833. H1.Cgo.S.
Am. 1036

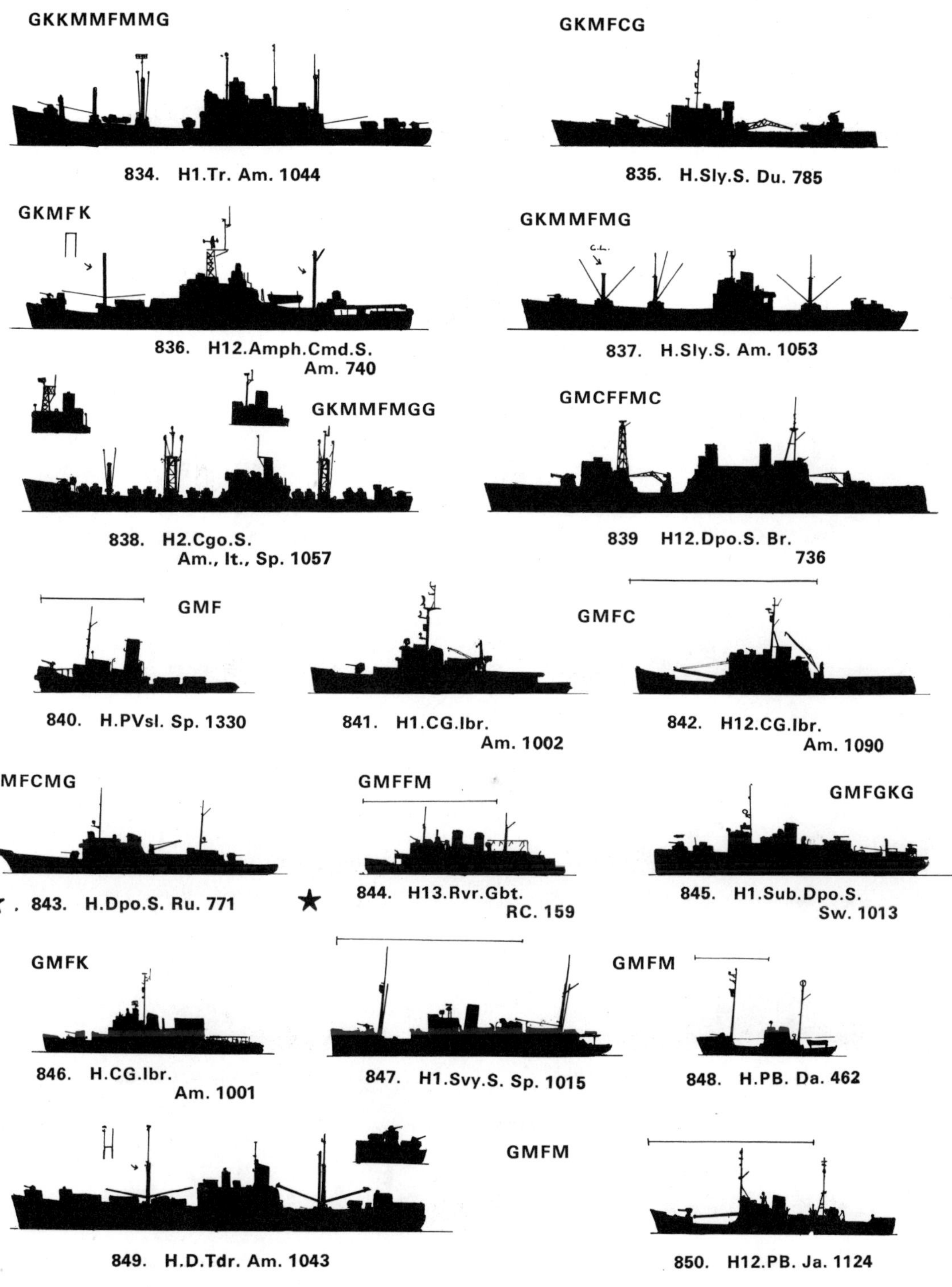


GKKMMFMMG
834. H1.Tr. Am. 1044

GKMFCG
835. H.Sly.S. Du. 785

GKMFK
836. H12.Amph.Cmd.S.
Am. 740

GKMMFMG
837. H.Sly.S. Am. 1053

GKMMFMGG
838. H2.Cgo.S.
Am., It., Sp. 1057

GMCFFMC
839 H12.Dpo.S. Br.
736

GMF
840. H.PVsl. Sp. 1330

GMFC
842. H12.CG.lbr.
Am. 1090

841. H1.CG.lbr.
Am. 1002

GMFCMG
843. H.Dpo.S. Ru. 771

GMFFM
844. H13.Rvr.Gbt.
RC. 159

GMFGKG
845. H1.Sub.Dpo.S.
Sw. 1013

GMFK
846. H.CG.lbr.
Am. 1001

847. H1.Svy.S. Sp. 1015

GMFM
848. H.PB. Da. 462

849. H.D.Tdr. Am. 1043

GMFM
850. H12.PB. Ja. 1124

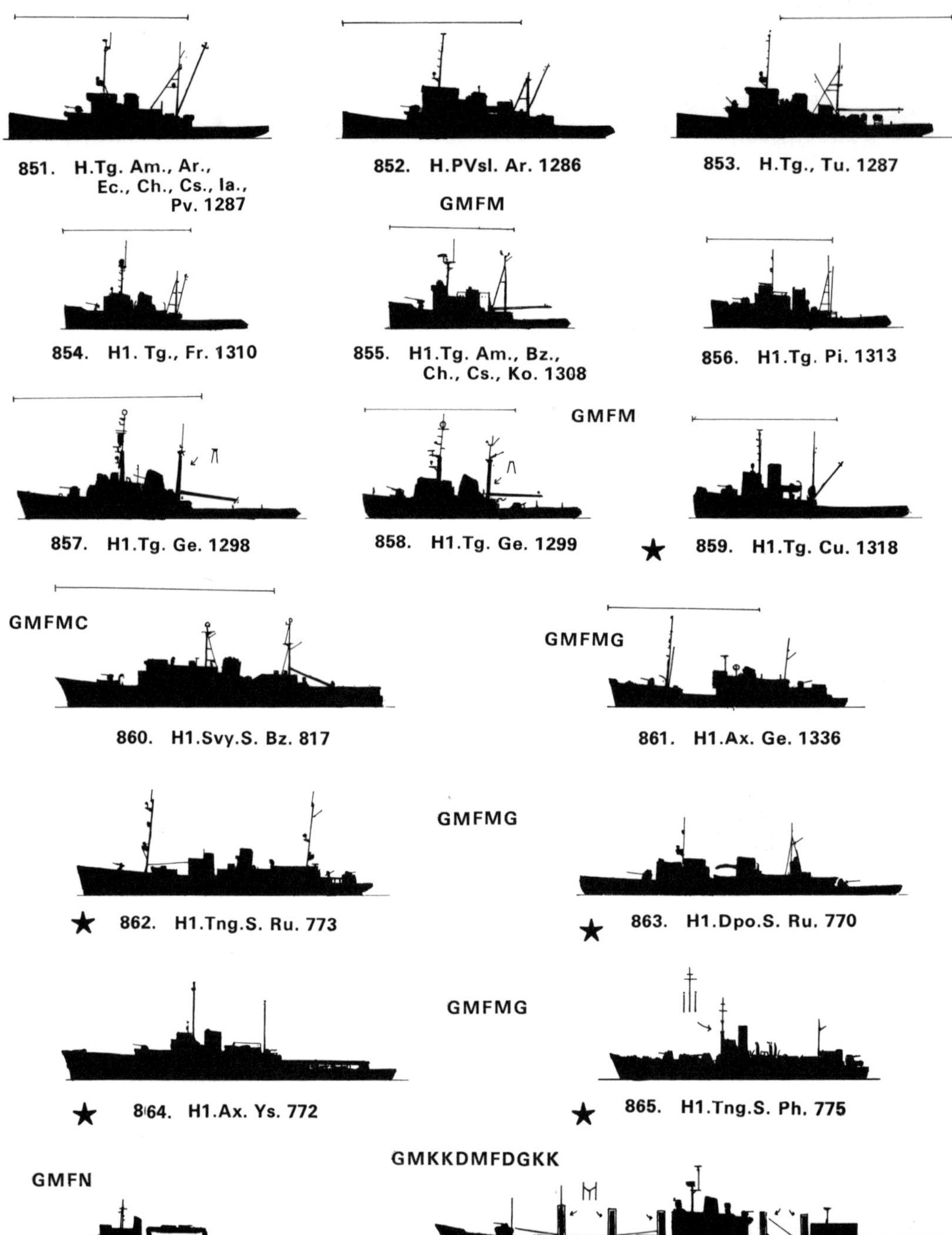


GMFM

851. H.Tg. Am., Ar., Ec., Ch., Cs., Ia., Pv. 1287
852. H.PVsl. Ar. 1286
853. H.Tg., Tu. 1287

GMFM

854. H1. Tg., Fr. 1310
855. H1.Tg. Am., Bz., Ch., Cs., Ko. 1308
856. H1.Tg. Pi. 1313

857. H1.Tg. Ge. 1298
858. H1.Tg. Ge. 1299

GMFM

859. H1.Tg. Cu. 1318

GMFMC

860. H1.Svy.S. Bz. 817

GMFMG

861. H1.Ax. Ge. 1336

GMFMG

862. H1.Tng.S. Ru. 773
863. H1.Dpo.S. Ru. 770

GMFMG

864. H1.Ax. Ys. 772
865. H1.Tng.S. Ph. 775

GMFN

866. H13.Rscu.S. Am. 787

GMKKDMFDGKK

867. H1.Sly.S. Am. 1038

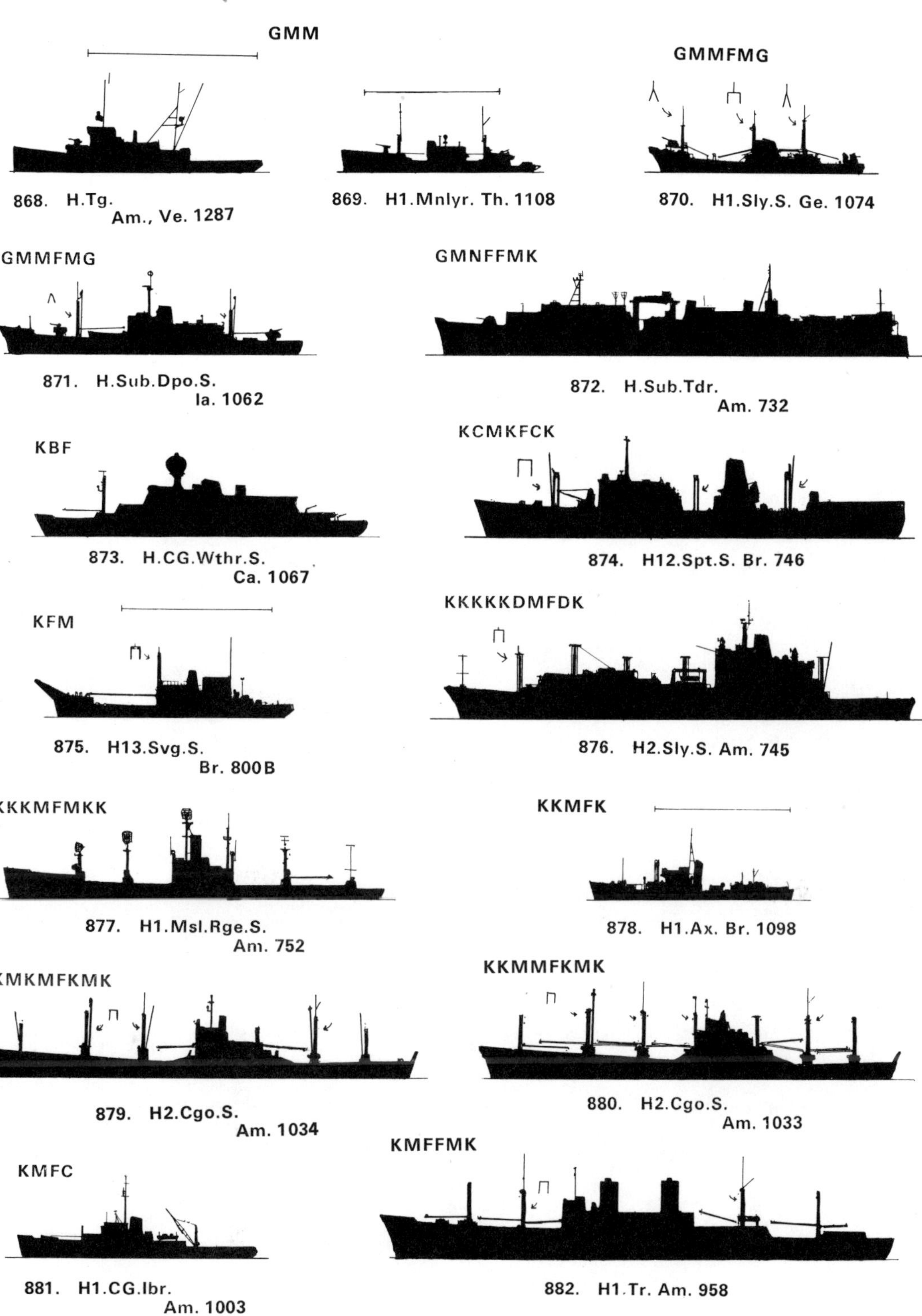

GMM
868.  H.Tg.
Am., Ve. 1287
869.  H1.Mnlyr. Th. 1108
GMMFMG
870.  H1.Sly.S. Ge. 1074
GMMFMG
871.  H.Sub.Dpo.S.
Ia. 1062
GMNFFMK
872.  H.Sub.Tdr.
Am. 732
KBF
873.  H.CG.Wthr.S.
Ca. 1067
KCMKFCK
874.  H12.Spt.S. Br. 746
KFM
875.  H13.Svg.S.
Br. 800B
KKKKKDMFDK
876.  H2.Sly.S. Am. 745
KKKMFMKK
877.  H1.Msl.Rge.S.
Am. 752
KKMFK
878.  H1.Ax. Br. 1098
KKMKMFKMK
879.  H2.Cgo.S.
Am. 1034
KKMMFKMK
880.  H2.Cgo.S.
Am. 1033
KMFC
881.  H1.CG.Ibr.
Am. 1003
KMFFMK
882.  H1.Tr. Am. 958

KMFG

KMFK

883.  H12.CG.Vsl.
         Am. 1087

884.  H12.Svy.S.
         Ja. 1125

885.  H.Cmd.S. Pi. 1027

886.  H.CG.Ibr. Ca. 1000

KMFK

887.  H.Svy.S. Du. 825

888.  H.Cbl.S. Br. 808

KMFKK

889.  H123.Tr. Sp. 1071

KMFM

890.  H12.Rpr.S. In. 1072

KMFM

891.  H1.Sub.Tdr.
         Am. 1045

892.  H.Sub.Tdr.
         Am. 1045

KMFM

893.  H1.Cgo.S.
         Am. 1037

KMFM

894.  H1.Rch.S. Ca. 1103

895.  H1.Svy.S. Ar. 1104

896.  H12.CG.Vsl.
         Am. 1092

897.  H13.Ibr. Ru. 970

KMFM

898.  H.CG.Ibr. Ca. 995

899.  H.Svy.S. Ng. 1094

KMFM

**900.   H.CG.Ibr. Ca. 996**

KMFMK

**901.   H.Tr. Am. 1006**

KMFMM

**902.   H1.Svy.S.
Am. 1047**

KMKFM

**903.   H.Spt.S. Br. 1067**

KMKMFKKD

**904.   H1.Msl.Rge.S.
Am. 753**

KMKMFKM

**905.   H2.Sly.S. Am. 1055**

KMKMFKM

**906.   H1.Sly.S. Am. 1048**

**907.   H1.Cgo.S.
Am. 1049**

KMKMFKM

**908.   H1.Cgo.S.
Am. 1049**

KMKMFMK

**909.   H1.Spt.S. Br. 1061**

KMMFKM

**910.   H1.Tr.
Am., Sp. 1046**

KMMFM

**911.   H2.Sly.S.
Am. 1054**

KMMFM

**912.   H12.Tr. Bz. 1064**

**913.   H2.Sly.S. Am. 1056**

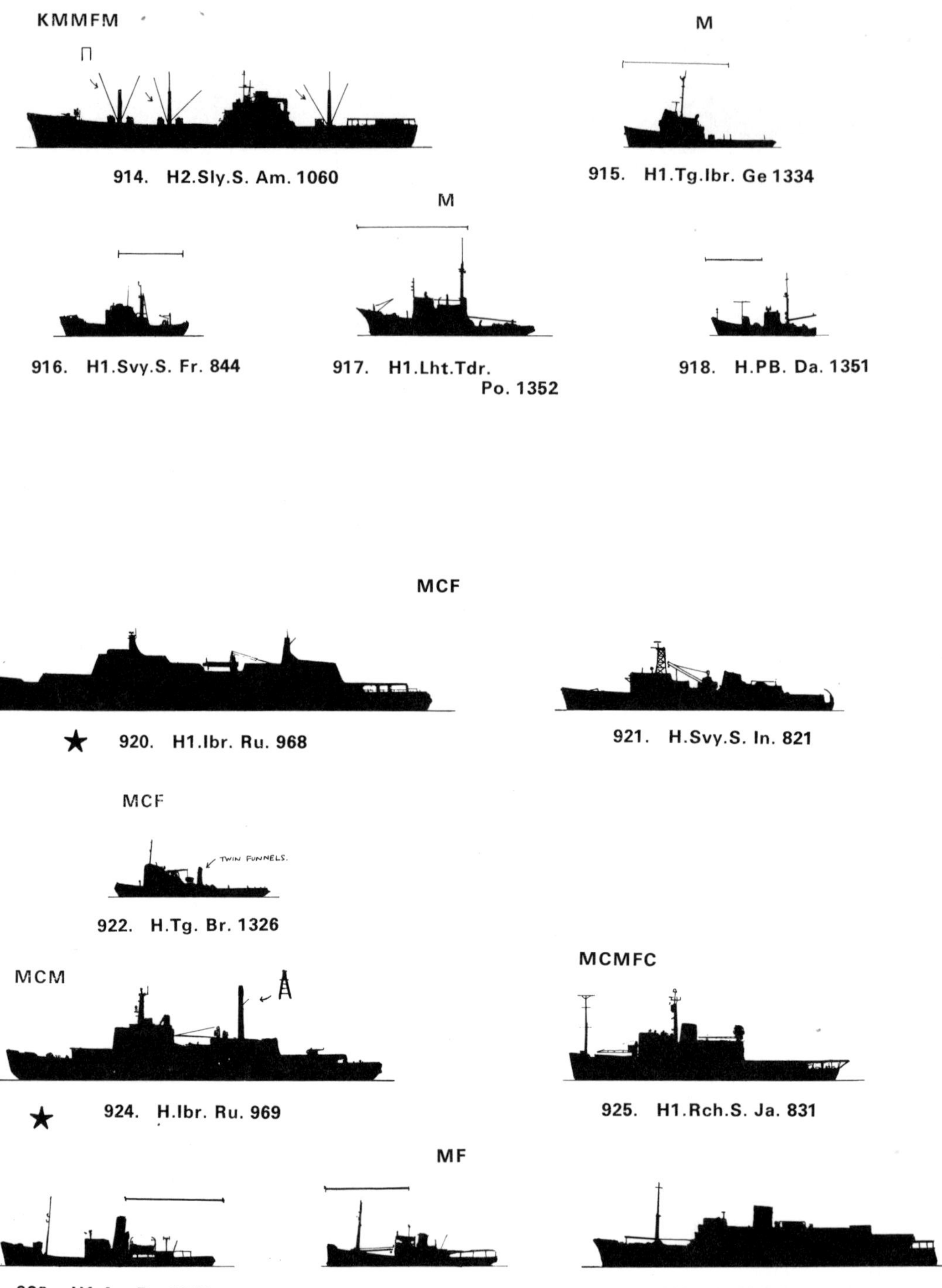


KMMFM
914.  H2.Sly.S. Am. 1060
M
915.  H1.Tg.Ibr. Ge 1334
M
916.  H1.Svy.S. Fr. 844
M
917.  H1.Lht.Tdr.
Po. 1352
918.  H.PB. Da. 1351
MCF
920.  H1.Ibr. Ru. 968
921.  H.Svy.S. In. 821
MCF
TWIN FUNNELS.
922.  H.Tg. Br. 1326
MCM
924.  H.Ibr. Ru. 969
MCMFC
925.  H1.Rch.S. Ja. 831
MF
926.  H1.Ax. Br. 1346
927.  H.Tg. Co. 1100
928.  H.Mtc.S. Fr. 1008.

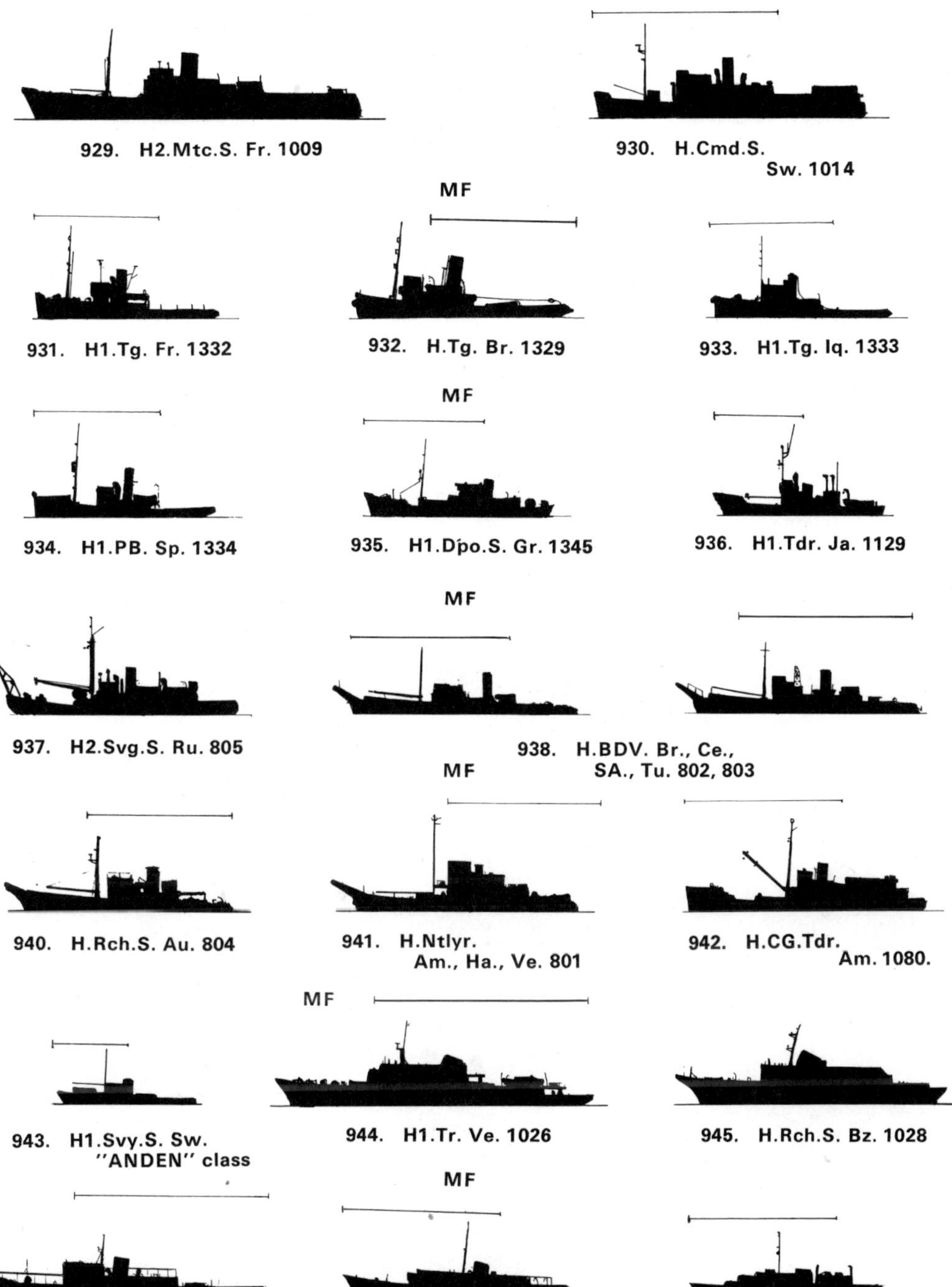

MF
929. H2.Mtc.S. Fr. 1009
930. H.Cmd.S. Sw. 1014
MF
931. H1.Tg. Fr. 1332
932. H.Tg. Br. 1329
933. H1.Tg. Iq. 1333
934. H1.PB. Sp. 1334
MF
935. H1.Dpo.S. Gr. 1345
936. H1.Tdr. Ja. 1129
937. H2.Svg.S. Ru. 805
MF
938. H.BDV. Br., Ce., SA., Tu. 802, 803
MF
940. H.Rch.S. Au. 804
941. H.Ntlyr. Am., Ha., Ve. 801
942. H.CG.Tdr. Am. 1080.
MF
943. H1.Svy.S. Sw. "ANDEN" class
944. H1.Tr. Ve. 1026
945. H.Rch.S. Bz. 1028
MF
946. H1.Ax. Ys. 1031
947. H.Tng.S. Gh. 1030
948. H.Svy.S. Me. 1032

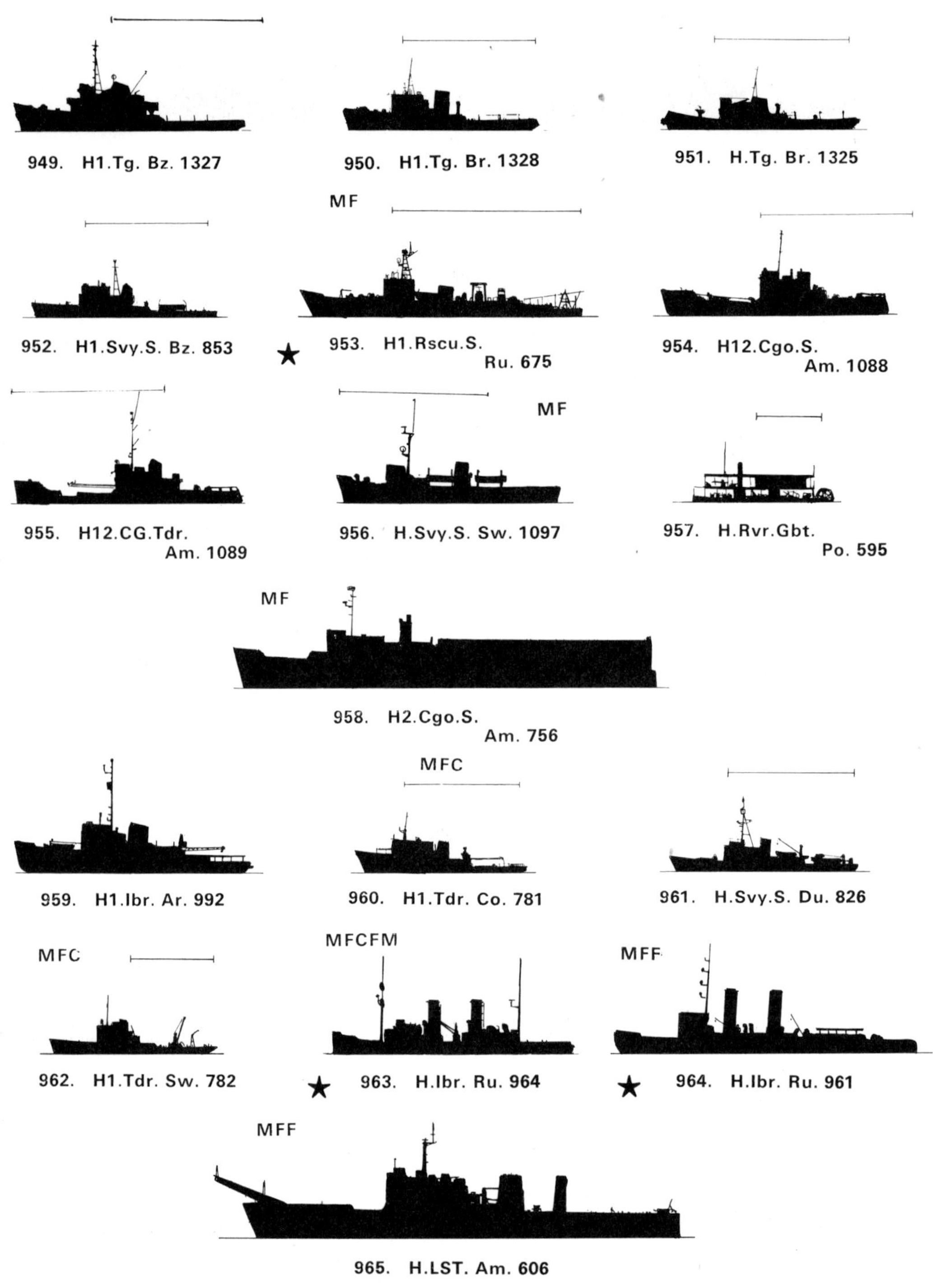

MF

949. H1.Tg. Bz. 1327

950. H1.Tg. Br. 1328

951. H.Tg. Br. 1325

MF

952. H1.Svy.S. Bz. 853

953. H1.Rscu.S. Ru. 675

954. H12.Cgo.S. Am. 1088

955. H12.CG.Tdr. Am. 1089

MF

956. H.Svy.S. Sw. 1097

957. H.Rvr.Gbt. Po. 595

MF

958. H2.Cgo.S. Am. 756

959. H1.Ibr. Ar. 992

MFC

960. H1.Tdr. Co. 781

961. H.Svy.S. Du. 826

MFC

962. H1.Tdr. Sw. 782

MFCFM

963. H.Ibr. Ru. 964

MFF

964. H.Ibr. Ru. 961

MFF

965. H.LST. Am. 606

MFFM

966.   H.Tr. Am. 959

967.   H.Tng.S. Tu. 960

MFFM

968.   H1.Cbl.S. Am. 726

★   969.   H.Ibr. Ru. 962

MFFM

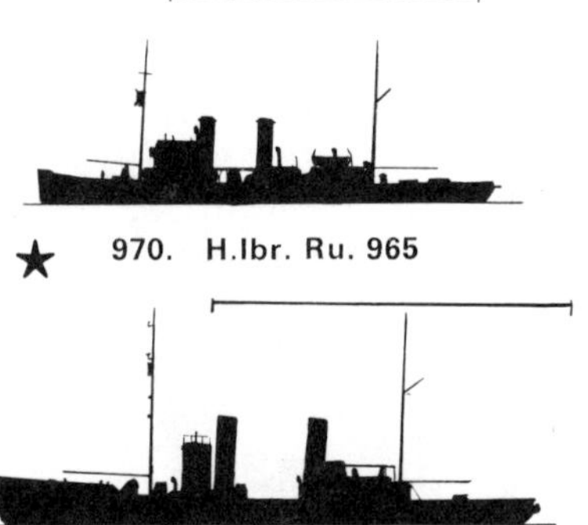

★   970.   H.Ibr. Ru. 965

971.   H.Ibr. Fi. 966

MFFM

★   972.   H1.Ibr. Ru. 963

973.   H.CG.Ibr. Ca. 967

MFFMC

974.   H.Rpr.S. Am. 729

MFK

975.   H1.Svy.S. Th. 1029

976.   H.PB. Fi. 1096

977.   H1.Svy.S. Fr. 843

MFK

978.   H1.Tg. Br. 1331

979.   H1.Tdr. Ge. 1316

MFKM

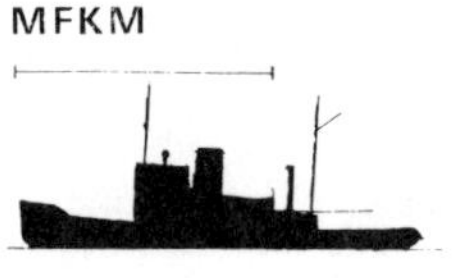

980.   H.Ibr. Fi. 986

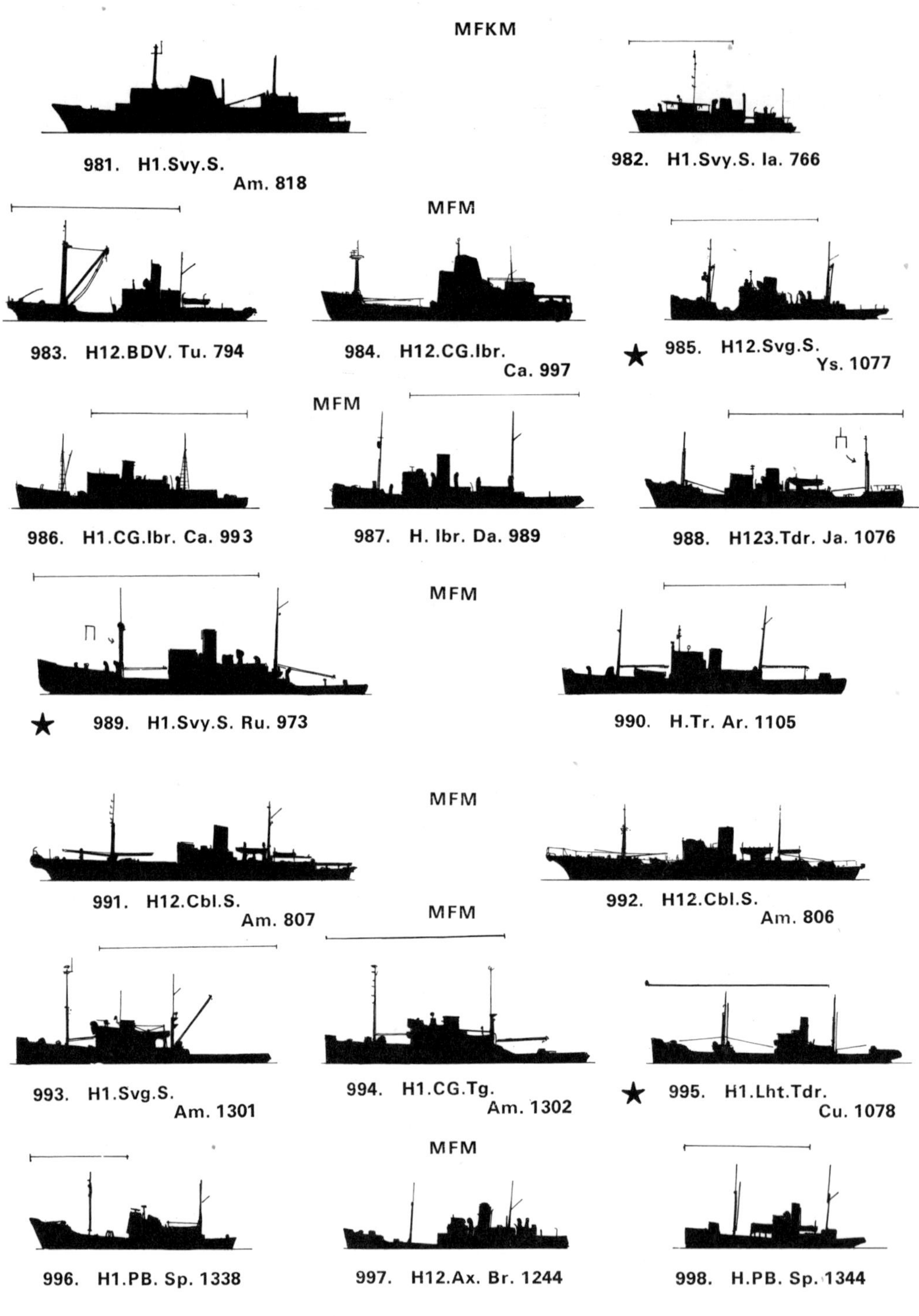


MFKM
981. H1.Svy.S. Am. 818
982. H1.Svy.S. Ia. 766
MFM
983. H12.BDV. Tu. 794
984. H12.CG.Ibr. Ca. 997
985. H12.Svg.S. Ys. 1077
986. H1.CG.Ibr. Ca. 993
987. H. Ibr. Da. 989
988. H123.Tdr. Ja. 1076
MFM
989. H1.Svy.S. Ru. 973
990. H.Tr. Ar. 1105
MFM
991. H12.Cbl.S. Am. 807
992. H12.Cbl.S. Am. 806
MFM
993. H1.Svg.S. Am. 1301
994. H1.CG.Tg. Am. 1302
995. H1.Lht.Tdr. Cu. 1078
MFM
996. H1.PB. Sp. 1338
997. H12.Ax. Br. 1244
998. H.PB. Sp. 1344

MFM

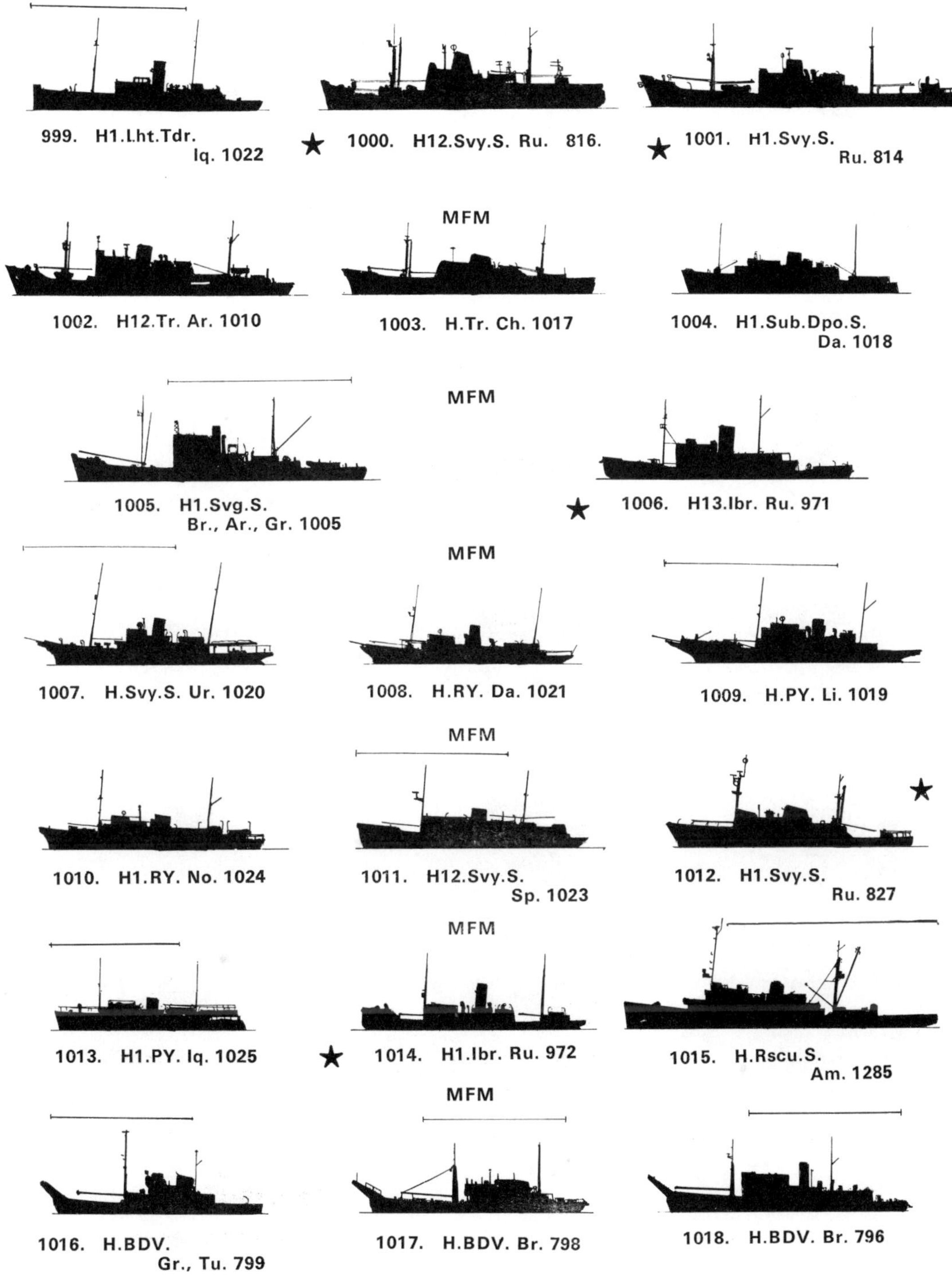

999. H1.Lht.Tdr.
Iq. 1022

1000. H12.Svy.S. Ru. 816.

1001. H1.Svy.S.
Ru. 814

1002. H12.Tr. Ar. 1010

MFM

1003. H.Tr. Ch. 1017

1004. H1.Sub.Dpo.S.
Da. 1018

MFM

1005. H1.Svg.S.
Br., Ar., Gr. 1005

1006. H13.Ibr. Ru. 971

MFM

1007. H.Svy.S. Ur. 1020

1008. H.RY. Da. 1021

1009. H.PY. Li. 1019

MFM

1010. H1.RY. No. 1024

1011. H12.Svy.S.
Sp. 1023

1012. H1.Svy.S.
Ru. 827

MFM

1013. H1.PY. Iq. 1025

1014. H1.Ibr. Ru. 972

1015. H.Rscu.S.
Am. 1285

MFM

1016. H.BDV.
Gr., Tu. 799

1017. H.BDV. Br. 798

1018. H.BDV. Br. 796

1019.   H1.CG.Tdr.
Am. 1079

1020.   H2.Tdr. Ja. 1086

1021.   H1.Tdr. Ja. 1084

1022.   H12.CG.lbr.
Ca. 1081

1023.   H.Tdr. Ja. 1085

1024.   H.Lht.Tdr.
Do. 1082

1025.   H.Tg. Th. 1293

1026.   H1.Tg. Br. 1320

1027.   H1.Tg. Br. 1321

1028.   H1.Tg. Ar. 1323

★ 1029.   H1.Tg. Ru. 1303

1030.   H1.Tg. Br. 1300

1031.   H1.Tg. Sp. 1307

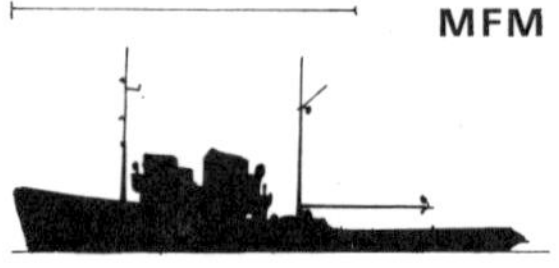



1032.   H1.PB. Sp. 1306

1033.   H.Tg. Pk. 1291

1034.   H1.Spt.S.
Th. 1319

1035.   H1.Svg.S.
Br. 1305

1036.   H1.lbr. Da. 990

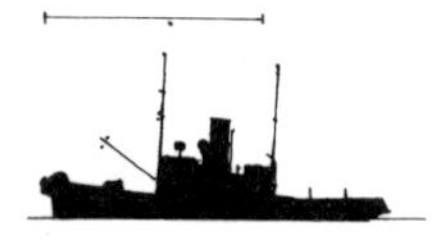

1037.   H.Tg. Ch. 1322

1038.   H1.Tdr. Fr. 991

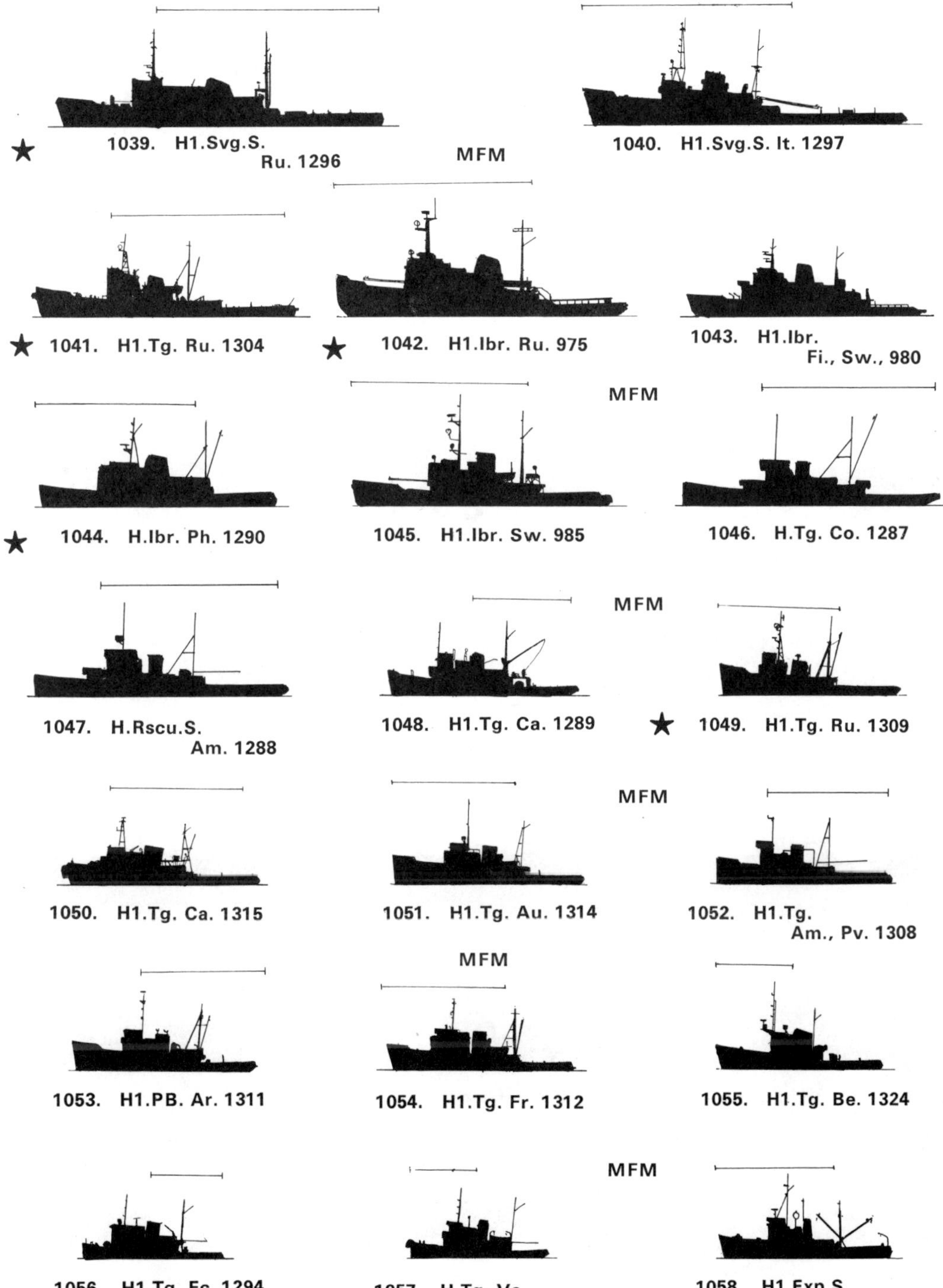


MFM
1039. H1.Svg.S.
Ru. 1296
MFM
1040. H1.Svg.S. It. 1297
MFM
1041. H1.Tg. Ru. 1304
1042. H1.Ibr. Ru. 975
1043. H1.Ibr.
Fi., Sw., 980
1044. H.Ibr. Ph. 1290
1045. H1.Ibr. Sw. 985
MFM
1046. H.Tg. Co. 1287
1047. H.Rscu.S.
Am. 1288
1048. H1.Tg. Ca. 1289
MFM
1049. H1.Tg. Ru. 1309
1050. H1.Tg. Ca. 1315
1051. H1.Tg. Au. 1314
MFM
1052. H1.Tg.
Am., Pv. 1308
1053. H1.PB. Ar. 1311
MFM
1054. H1.Tg. Fr. 1312
1055. H1.Tg. Be. 1324
1056. H1.Tg. Ec. 1294
1057. H.Tg. Ve.
"FERNANDO
GOMEZ"
MFM
1058. H1.Exp.S.
Ge. 837

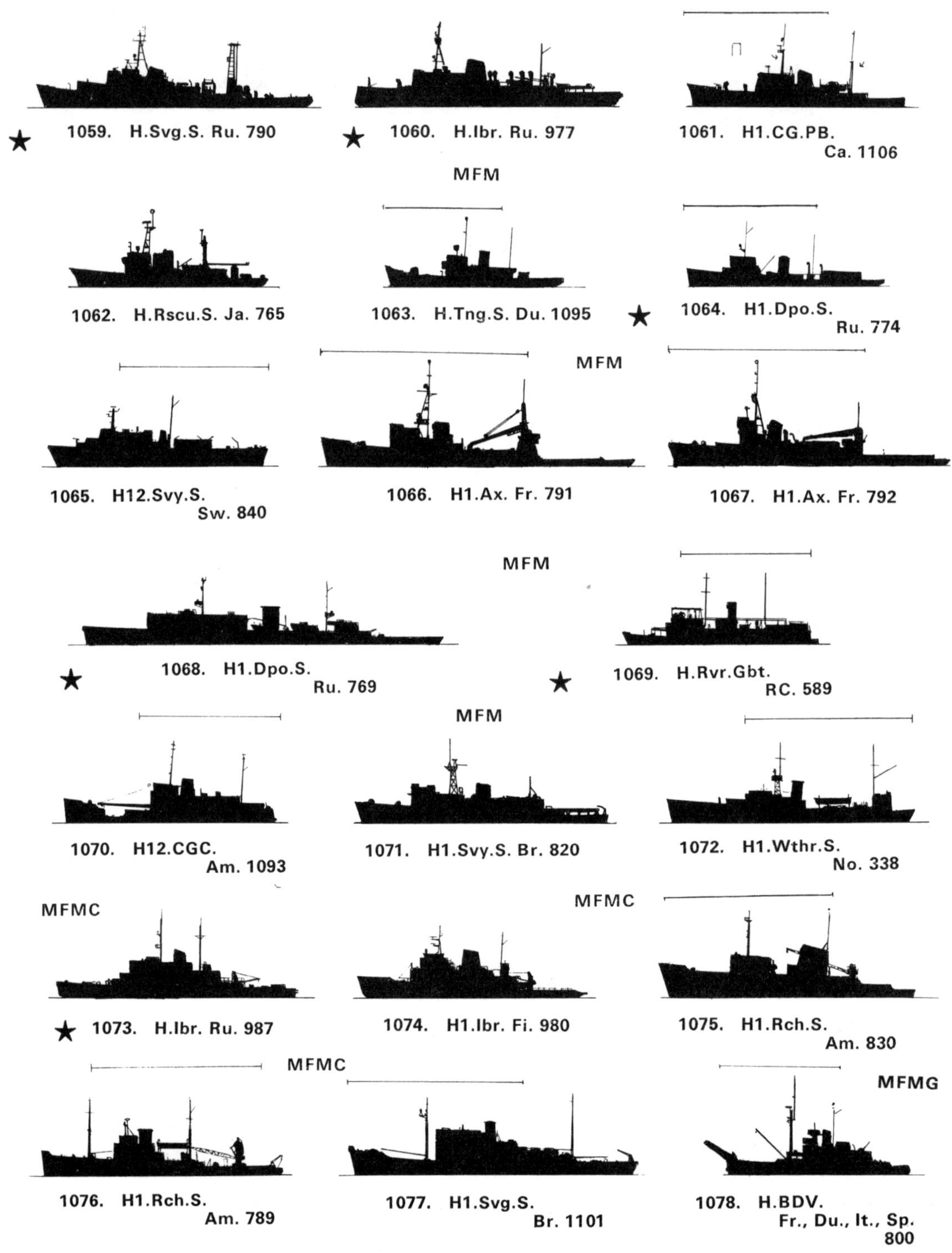


MFM

1059.   H.Svg.S. Ru. 790
1060.   H.Ibr. Ru. 977
1061.   H1.CG.PB.
Ca. 1106

MFM

1062.   H.Rscu.S. Ja. 765
1063.   H.Tng.S. Du. 1095
1064.   H1.Dpo.S.
Ru. 774

1065.   H12.Svy.S.
Sw. 840

MFM

1066.   H1.Ax. Fr. 791
1067.   H1.Ax. Fr. 792

MFM

1068.   H1.Dpo.S.
Ru. 769
1069.   H.Rvr.Gbt.
RC. 589

MFM

1070.   H12.CGC.
Am. 1093
1071.   H1.Svy.S. Br. 820
1072.   H1.Wthr.S.
No. 338

MFMC

1073.   H.Ibr. Ru. 987
1074.   H1.Ibr. Fi. 980

MFMC

1075.   H1.Rch.S.
Am. 830

MFMC

1076.   H1.Rch.S.
Am. 789
1077.   H1.Svg.S.
Br. 1101

MFMG

1078.   H.BDV.
Fr., Du., It., Sp.
800

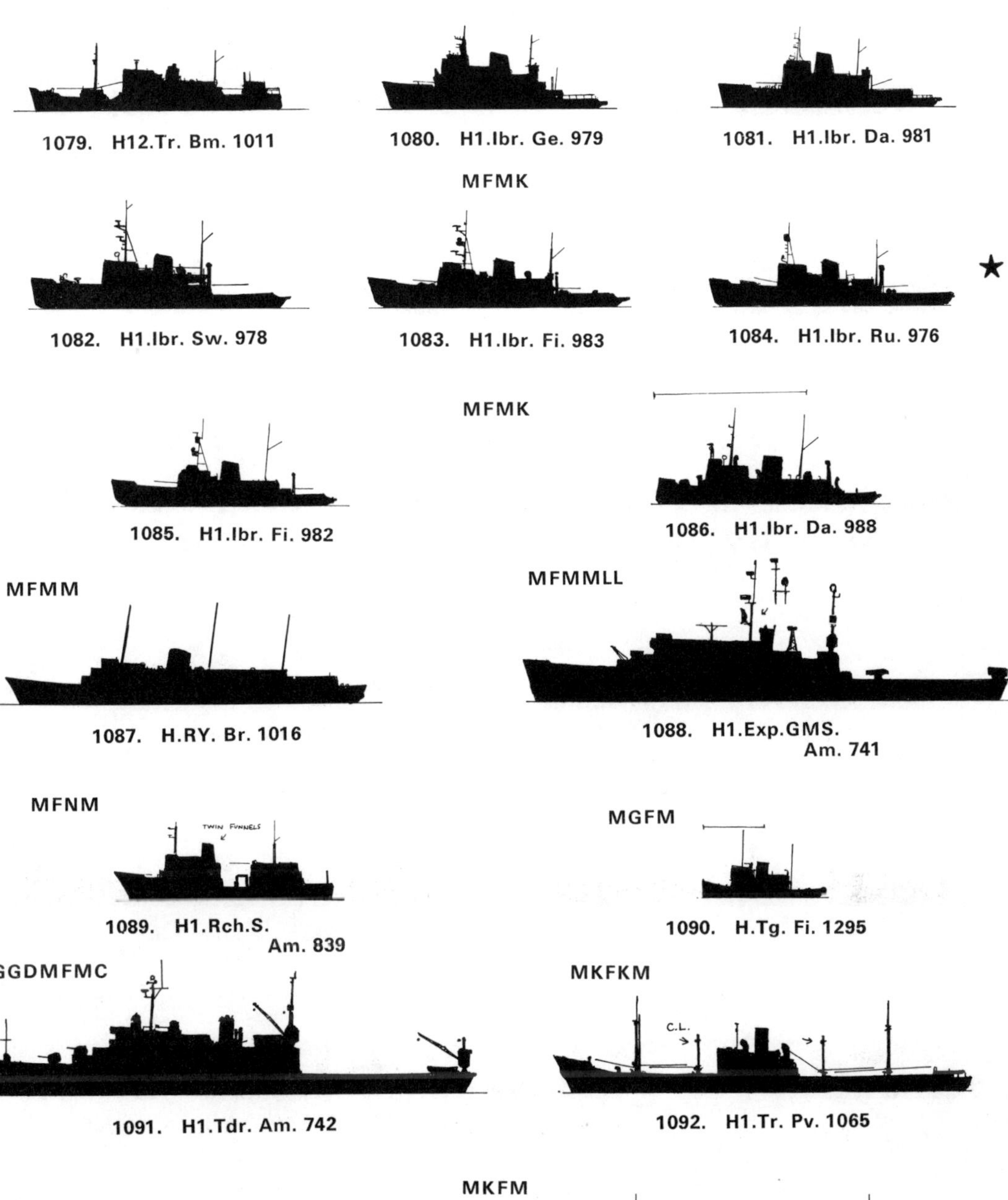


MFMK

1079.   H12.Tr. Bm. 1011
1080.   H1.Ibr. Ge. 979
1081.   H1.Ibr. Da. 981

MFMK

1082.   H1.Ibr. Sw. 978
1083.   H1.Ibr. Fi. 983
1084.   H1.Ibr. Ru. 976

MFMK

1085.   H1.Ibr. Fi. 982
1086.   H1.Ibr. Da. 988

MFMM

1087.   H.RY. Br. 1016

MFMMLL

1088.   H1.Exp.GMS.
Am. 741

MFNM

TWIN FUNNELS

1089.   H1.Rch.S.
Am. 839

MGFM

1090.   H.Tg. Fi. 1295

MGGDMFMC

1091.   H1.Tdr. Am. 742

MKFKM

C.L.

1092.   H1.Tr. Pv. 1065

MKFM

1093.   H1.Tr. Cs. 1069
1094.   H1.Tdr. Am. 1045

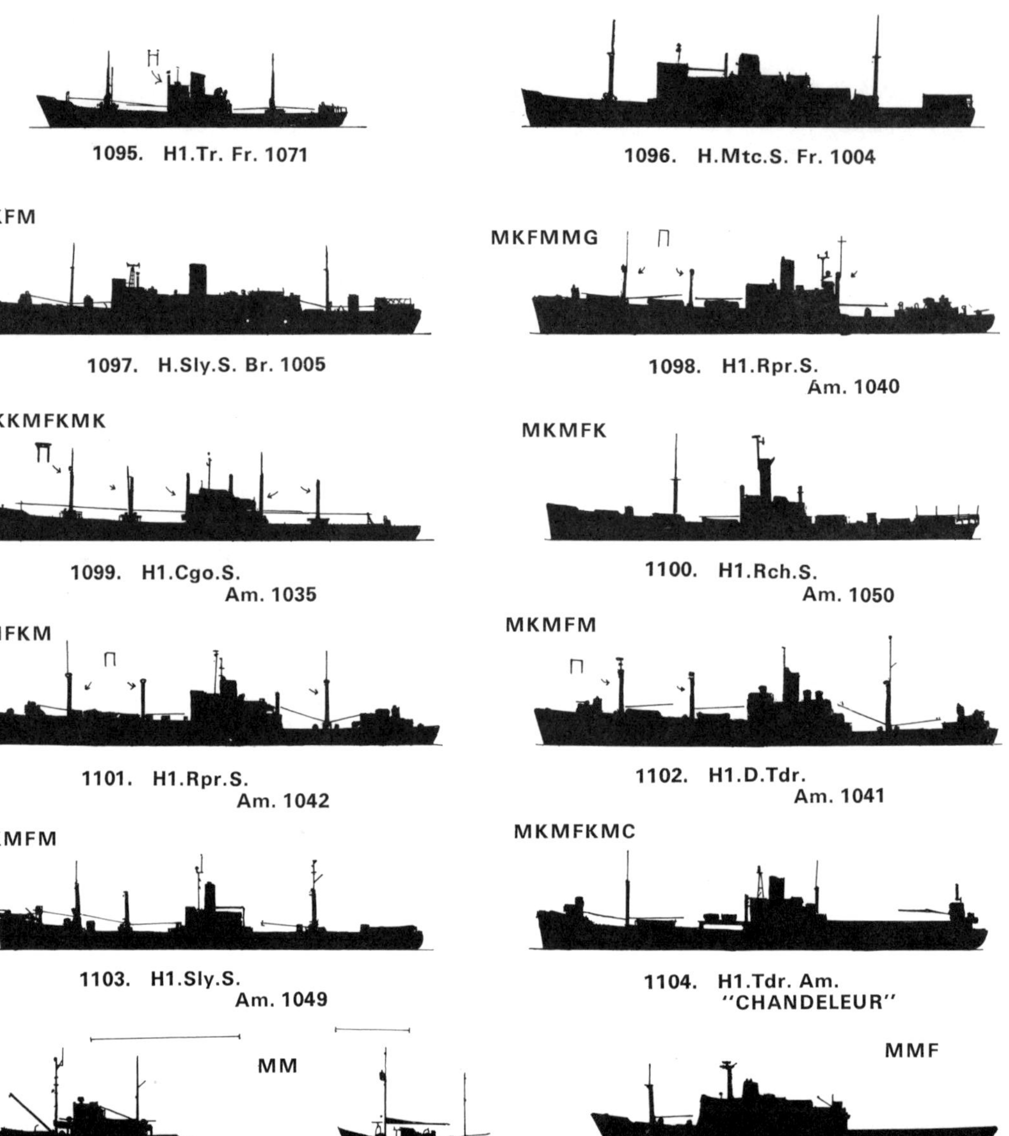

MKFM

1095.  H1.Tr. Fr. 1071

1096.  H.Mtc.S. Fr. 1004

MKFM

1097.  H.Sly.S. Br. 1005

MKFMMG

1098.  H1.Rpr.S.
Am. 1040

MKKMFKMK

1099.  H1.Cgo.S.
Am. 1035

MKMFK

1100.  H1.Rch.S.
Am. 1050

MKMFKM

1101.  H1.Rpr.S.
Am. 1042

MKMFM

1102.  H1.D.Tdr.
Am. 1041

MKMFM

1103.  H1.Sly.S.
Am. 1049

MKMFKMC

1104.  H1.Tdr. Am.
"CHANDELEUR"

MM

1105.  H.Ntlyr.
Am., Ec., Fr., Tu.    797

1106.  H.PB. Da. 1347

MMF

1107.  H.Spt.S. Br. 757

MMF

1108.  H1.PVsl.  Br. 832

1109.  H1.Exp.S.
Am. 744

MMF

1110.   H1.Exp.S.
Am. 743

★ 1111.   H1.Svy.S.
Ph. 1240

MMF

1112.   H1.Rch.S.
Am. 841

MMFC

1113.   H1.Rch.S.
Am. 829/830

MMFK

1114.   H1.Svg.S.
Am. 793

MMFKM

1115.   H.Rpr.S.
Am. 1039

MMFM

1116.   H1.Sly.S.   Ge. 1073

1117.   H1.Tr. Am. 1037

MMFM

1118.   H12.Amph.
Cmd.S. Am. 740

MMFM

1119.   H13.Tr. Bz. 1063

★ 1120.   H.Svy.S.
Ru. 815

MMFM

1121.   H2.Tr. Ar. 1012

1122.   H.PVsl. Ja. 998

MMFM

1123.   H.Mtc.S. Ca. 1066

1124.   H.Rch.S.
Am. 1051

MMFM

MN

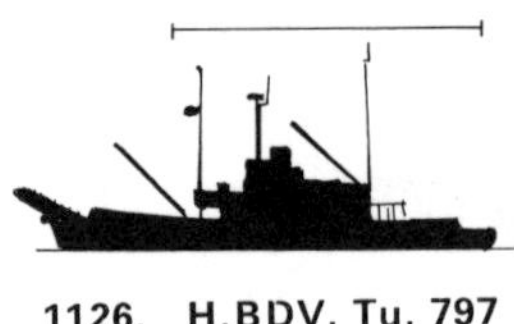

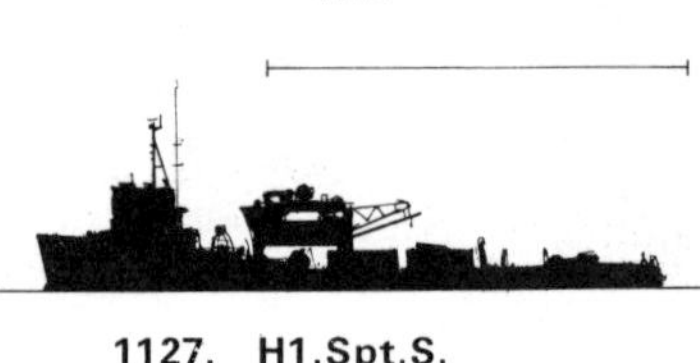

1125.  H.Wthr.S.
Du. 838

1126.  H.BDV. Tu. 797

1127.  H1.Spt.S.
Am. 788

## PROFILE 3

P3 (Engines Aft)

CKCMKKMFC

1128.  H1.RO. Du. 846

GGMDMKMKKGFGG

GKDMMKMF

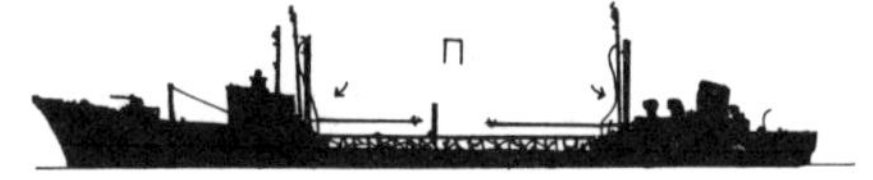

1129.  H13.O. Am. 1134

1130.  H13.O. Ja. 1281

GKMMFG

KMF

1131.  H13.Sly.S.
Ge. 847

1132.  H123.O. Ru. 1176

KMKF

1133.  H123.O. Br. 1146

1134.  H13.Tr. Fr. 1184

**KMKFK**

1135.   H123.O. Ur. 1151

**KMKFK**

1136.   H13.O. Ch. 1152

**KMKKF**

1137.   H123.O. Fr. 1148

**KMKKFK**

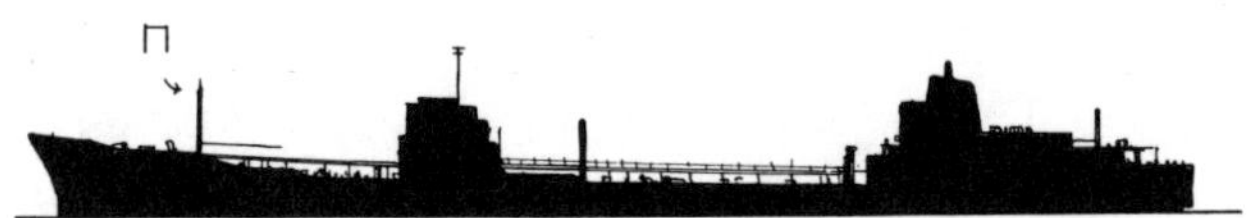

1138.   H13.O. Am. 1150

**KMKKKKF**

1139.   H123.O. Am. 1135

**KMKKMFC**

1140.   H13.Sly.S.
Ca. 845

**KMKMF**

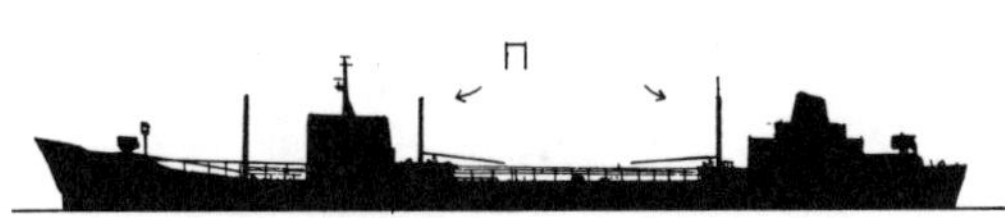

1141.   H123.O. Ch. 1153

**KMMMF**

1142.   H123.RO.
Br. 1143

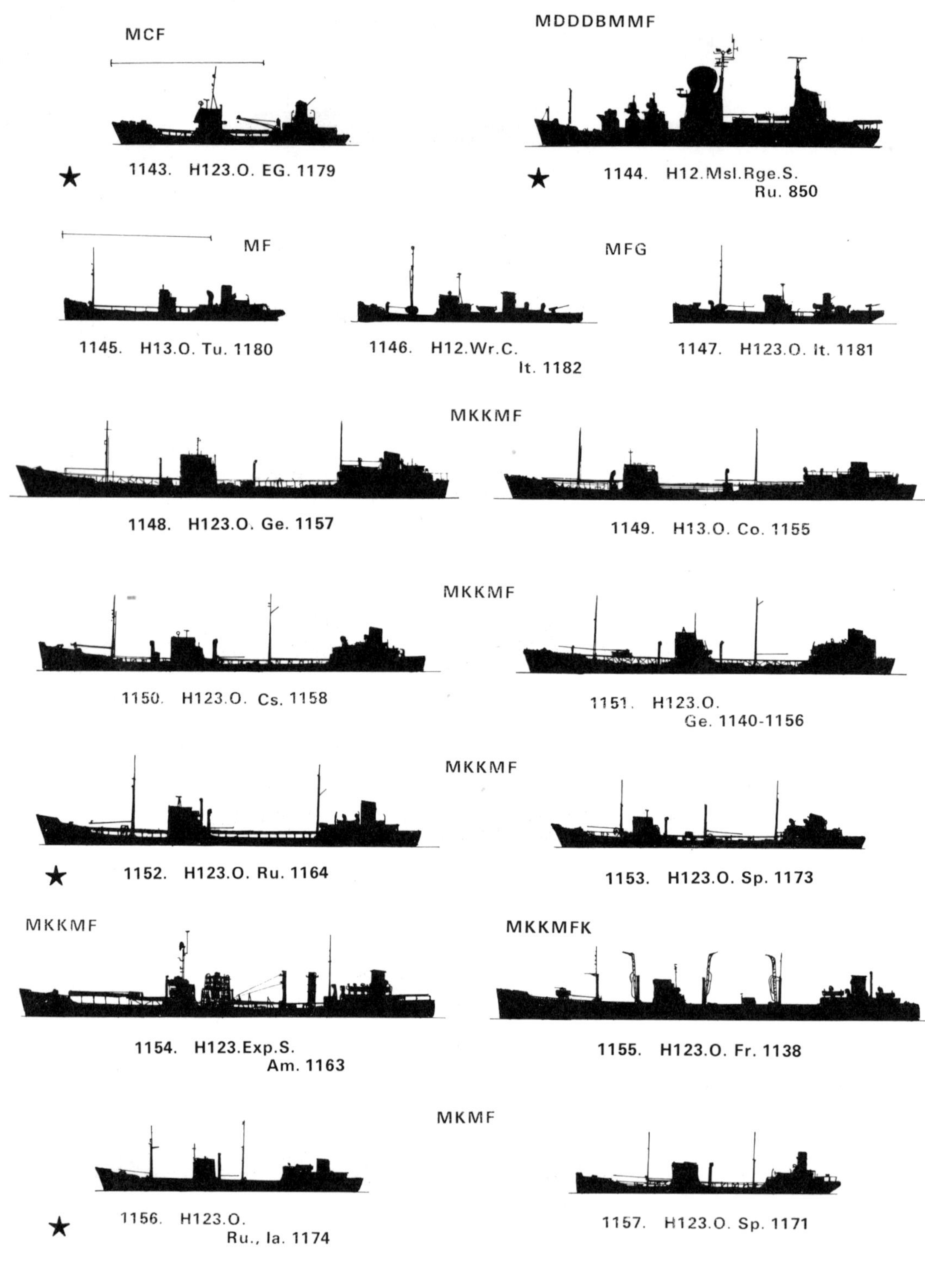


MCF
1143.   H123.O. EG. 1179
MDDDBMMF
1144.   H12.Msl.Rge.S.
Ru. 850
MF
1145.   H13.O. Tu. 1180
1146.   H12.Wr.C.
It. 1182
MFG
1147.   H123.O. It. 1181
MKKMF
1148.   H123.O. Ge. 1157
1149.   H13.O. Co. 1155
MKKMF
1150.   H123.O. Cs. 1158
1151.   H123.O.
Ge. 1140-1156
MKKMF
1152.   H123.O. Ru. 1164
1153.   H123.O. Sp. 1173
MKKMF
1154.   H123.Exp.S.
Am. 1163
MKKMFK
1155.   H123.O. Fr. 1138
MKMF
1156.   H123.O.
Ru., Ia. 1174
1157.   H123.O. Sp. 1171

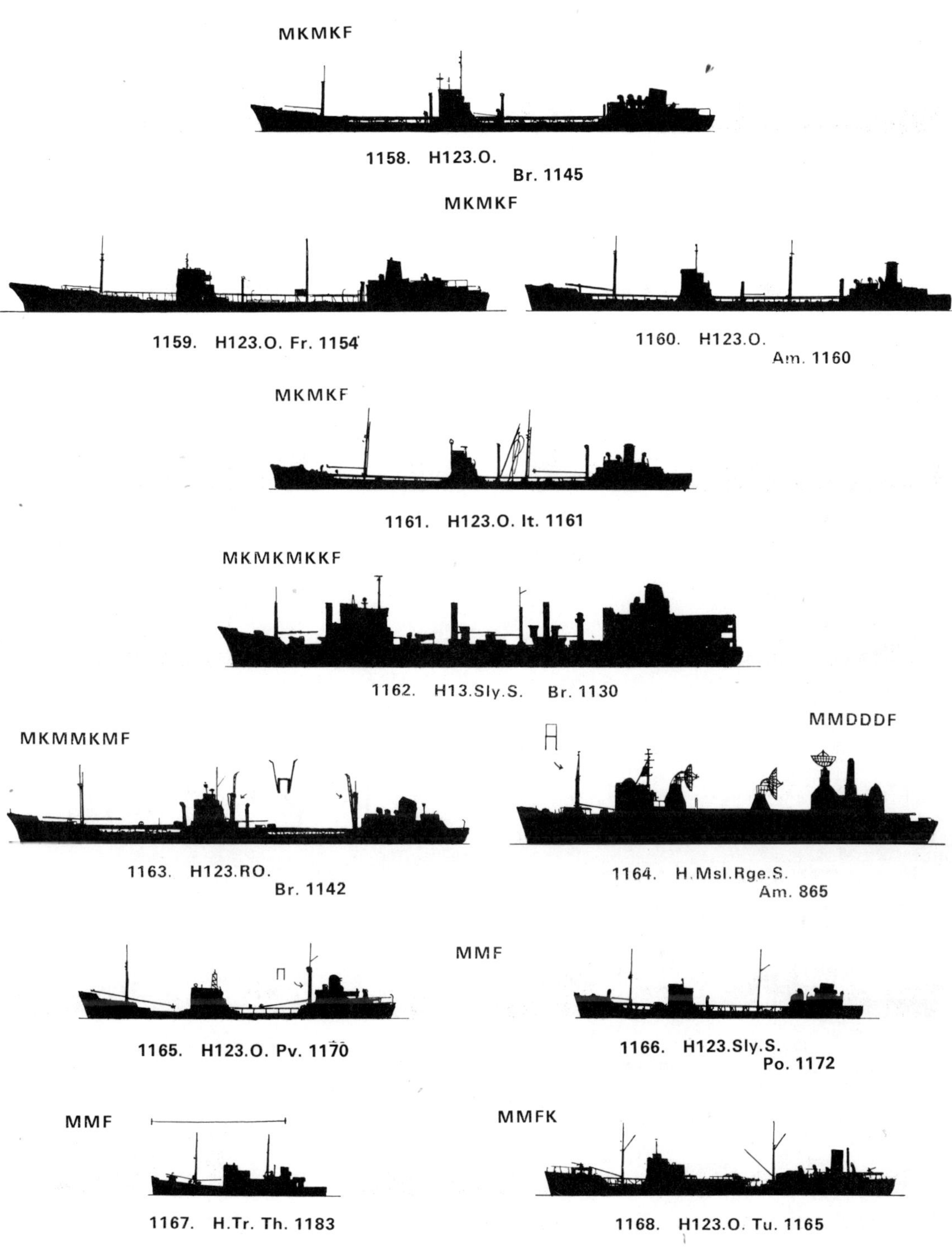


MKMKF
1158. H123.O.
Br. 1145

MKMKF
1159. H123.O. Fr. 1154
1160. H123.O.
Am. 1160

MKMKF
1161. H123.O. It. 1161

MKMKMKKF
1162. H13.Sly.S. Br. 1130

MKMMKMF
1163. H123.RO.
Br. 1142

MMDDDF
1164. H.Msl.Rge.S.
Am. 865

1165. H123.O. Pv. 1170

MMF
1166. H123.Sly.S.
Po. 1172

MMF
1167. H.Tr. Th. 1183

MMFK
1168. H123.O. Tu. 1165

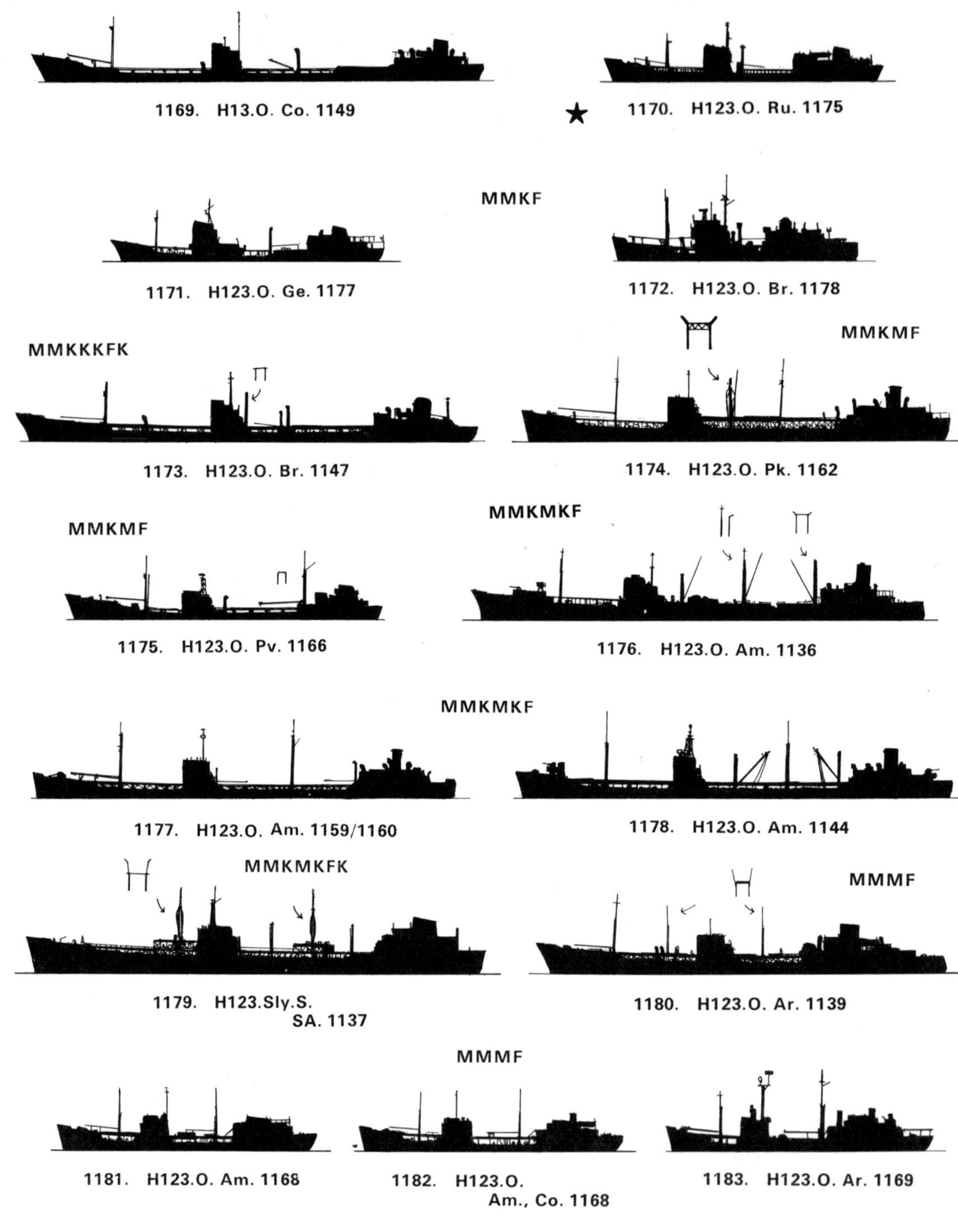


MMKF
1169.   H13.O. Co. 1149
1170.   H123.O. Ru. 1175
MMKF
1171.   H123.O. Ge. 1177
1172.   H123.O. Br. 1178
MMKKKFK
1173.   H123.O. Br. 1147
MMKMF
1174.   H123.O. Pk. 1162
MMKMF
1175.   H123.O. Pv. 1166
MMKMKF
1176.   H123.O. Am. 1136
MMKMKF
1177.   H123.O. Am. 1159/1160
1178.   H123.O. Am. 1144
MMKMKFK
1179.   H123.Sly.S.
         SA. 1137
MMMF
1180.   H123.O. Ar. 1139
MMMF
1181.   H123.O. Am. 1168
1182.   H123.O.
         Am., Co. 1168
1183.   H123.O. Ar. 1169

MMMKMF

MMMMF

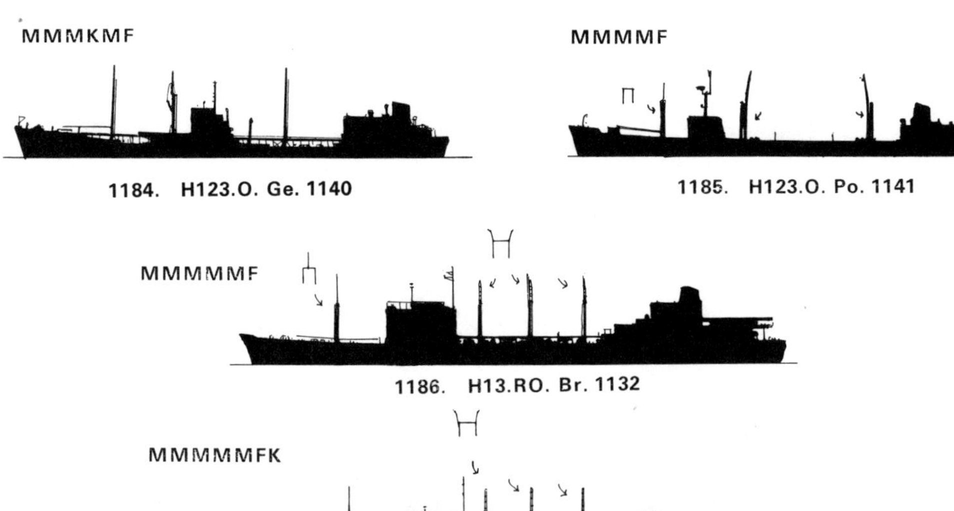

1184.   H123.O. Ge. 1140

1185.   H123.O. Po. 1141

MMMMMF

1186.   H13.RO. Br. 1132

MMMMMFK

1187.   H123.RO.   Br., Au. 1133

MMMMMMF

1188.   H13.RO. Br. 1131

# P4

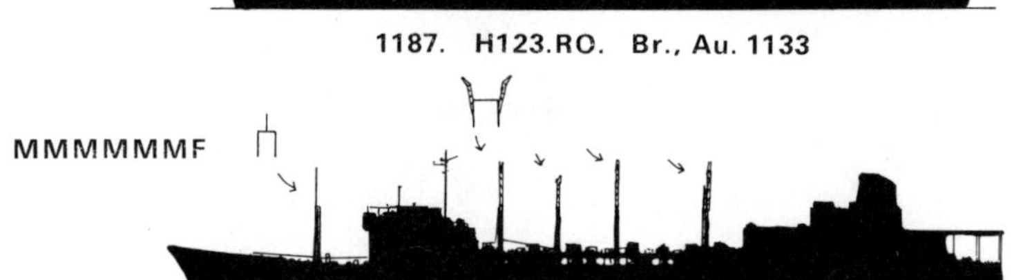

P4  (Engines and Bridge Aft)

CCMF

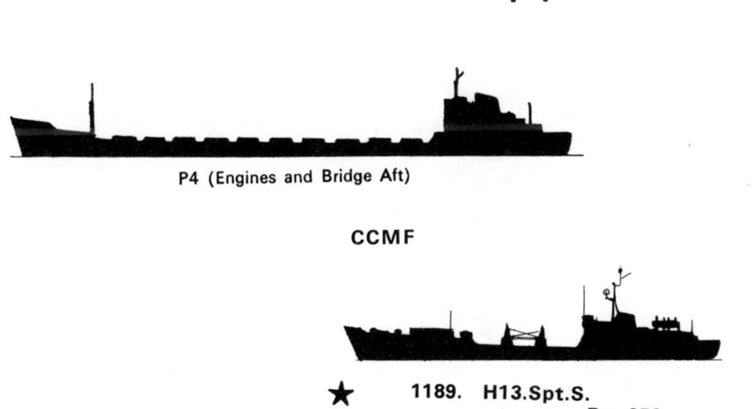

★   1189.   H13.Spt.S.
                    Ru. 852

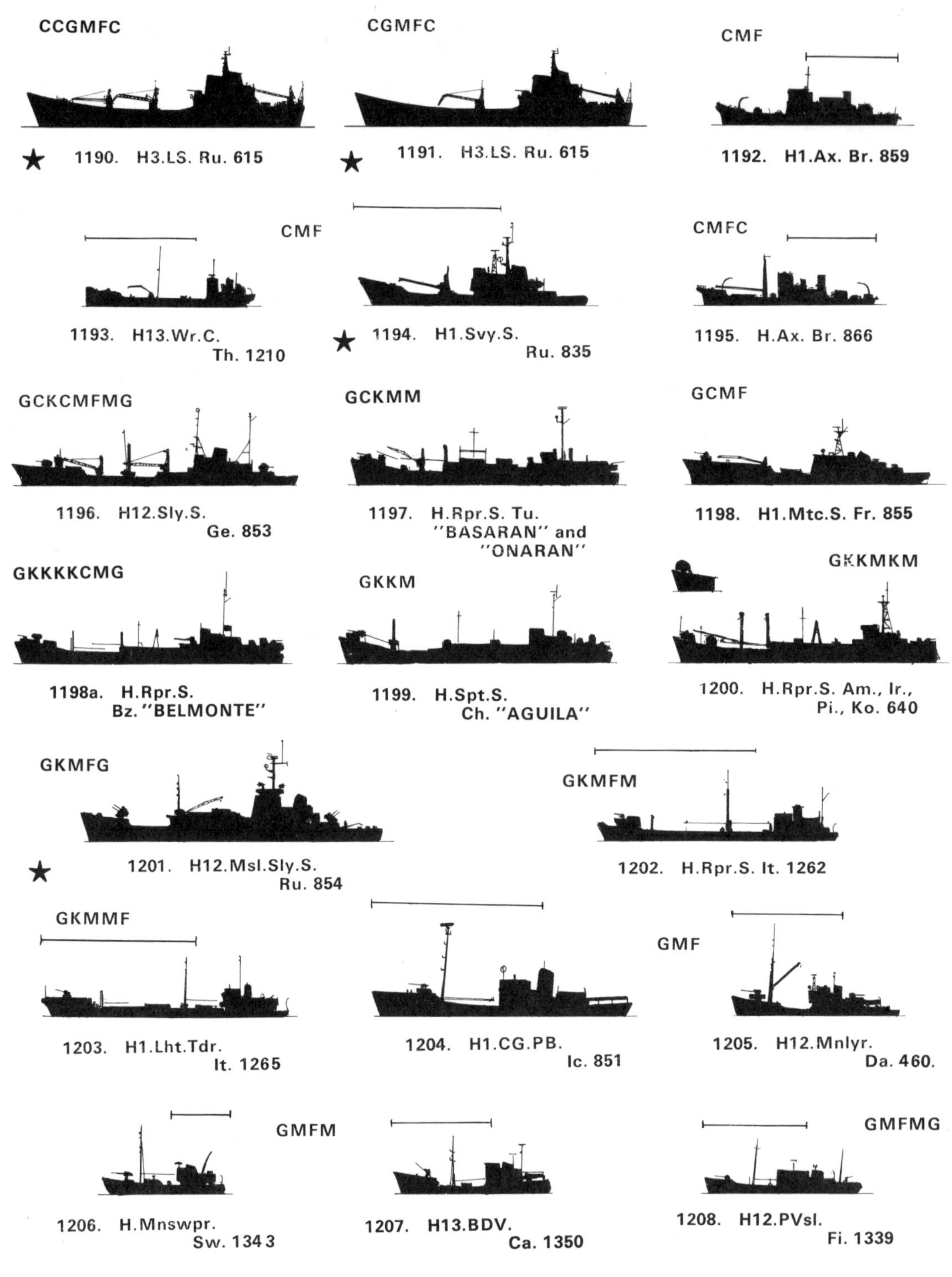


CCGMFC
1190. H3.LS. Ru. 615

CGMFC
1191. H3.LS. Ru. 615

CMF
1192. H1.Ax. Br. 859

CMF
1193. H13.Wr.C. Th. 1210

1194. H1.Svy.S. Ru. 835

CMFC
1195. H.Ax. Br. 866

GCKCMFMG
1196. H12.Sly.S. Ge. 853

GCKMM
1197. H.Rpr.S. Tu. "BASARAN" and "ONARAN"

GCMF
1198. H1.Mtc.S. Fr. 855

GKKKKCMG
1198a. H.Rpr.S. Bz. "BELMONTE"

GKKM
1199. H.Spt.S. Ch. "AGUILA"

GKKMKM
1200. H.Rpr.S. Am., Ir., Pi., Ko. 640

GKMFG
1201. H12.Msl.Sly.S. Ru. 854

GKMFM
1202. H.Rpr.S. It. 1262

GKMMF
1203. H1.Lht.Tdr. It. 1265

1204. H1.CG.PB. Ic. 851

GMF
1205. H12.Mnlyr. Da. 460.

GMFM
1206. H.Mnswpr. Sw. 1343

1207. H13.BDV. Ca. 1350

GMFMG
1208. H12.PVsl. Fi. 1339

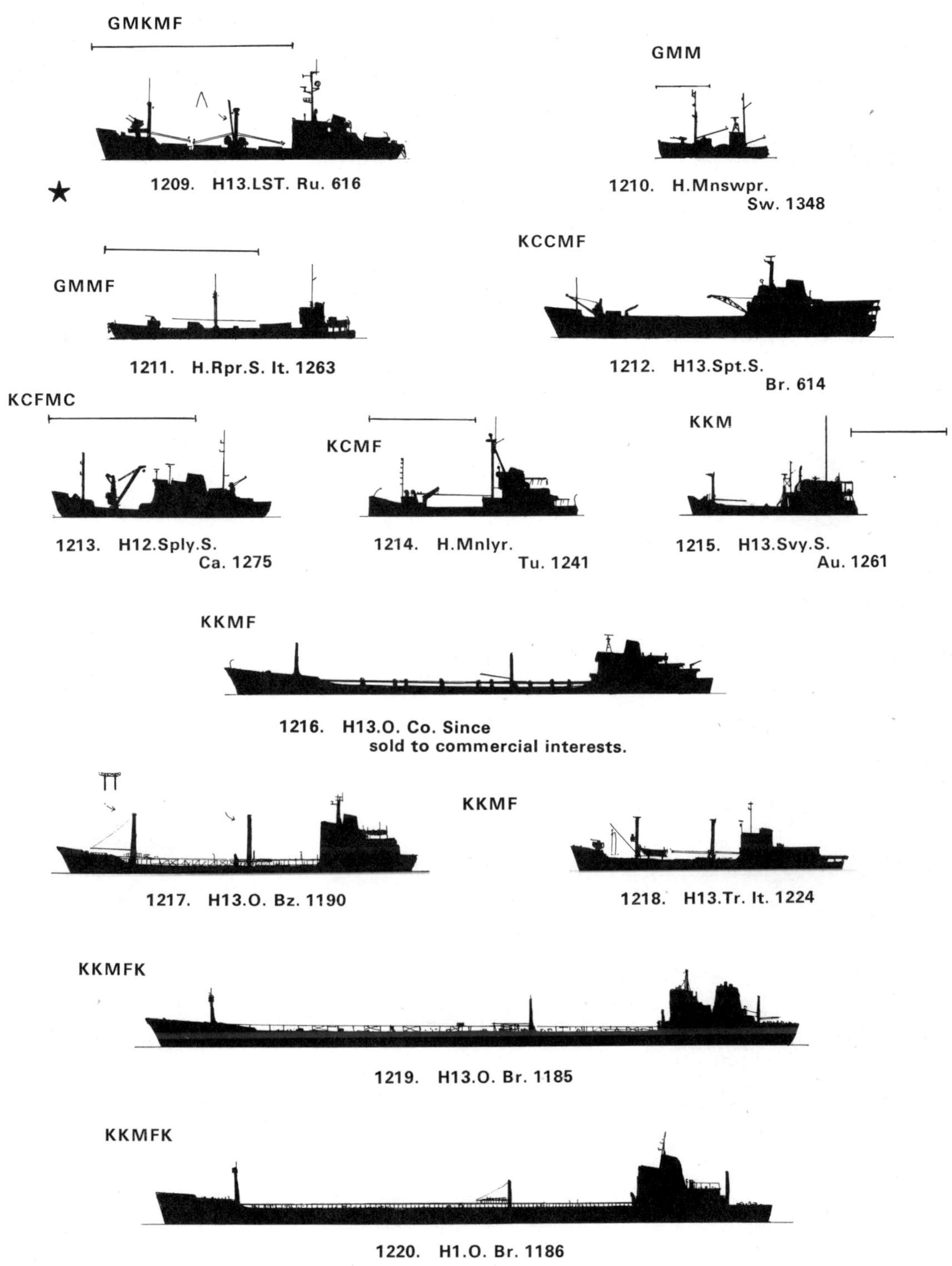


GMKMF
GMM
1209. H13.LST. Ru. 616
1210. H.Mnswpr.
Sw. 1348
GMMF
KCCMF
1211. H.Rpr.S. It. 1263
1212. H13.Spt.S.
Br. 614
KCFMC
KCMF
KKM
1213. H12.Sply.S.
Ca. 1275
1214. H.Mnlyr.
Tu. 1241
1215. H13.Svy.S.
Au. 1261
KKMF
1216. H13.O. Co. Since
sold to commercial interests.
KKMF
1217. H13.O. Bz. 1190
1218. H13.Tr. It. 1224
KKMFK
1219. H13.O. Br. 1185
KKMFK
1220. H1.O. Br. 1186

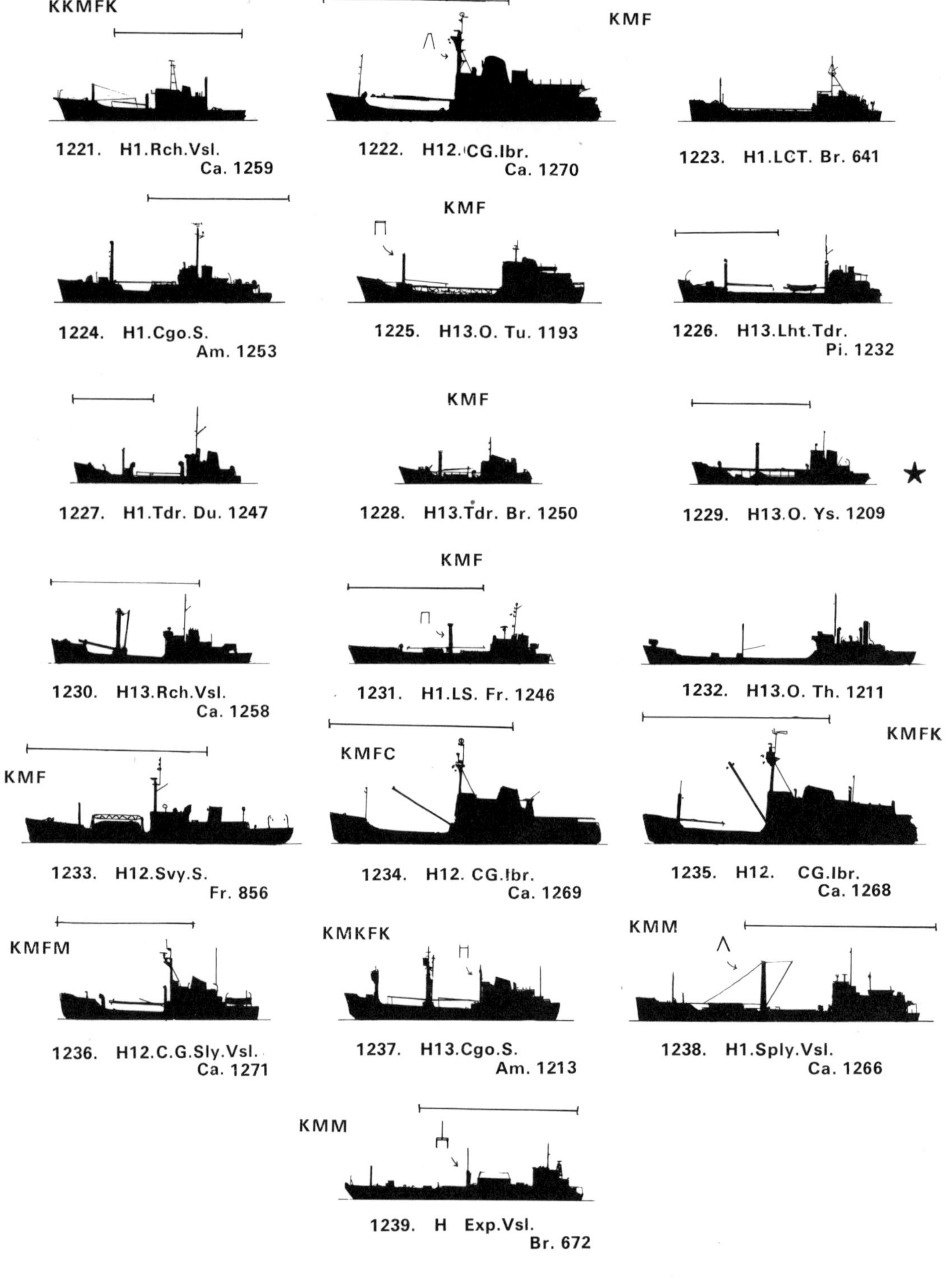

KKMFK
1221. H1.Rch.Vsl.
Ca. 1259
KMF
1222. H12.CG.Ibr.
Ca. 1270
1223. H1.LCT. Br. 641
1224. H1.Cgo.S.
Am. 1253
KMF
1225. H13.O. Tu. 1193
1226. H13.Lht.Tdr.
Pi. 1232
1227. H1.Tdr. Du. 1247
KMF
1228. H13.Tdr. Br. 1250
1229. H13.O. Ys. 1209
1230. H13.Rch.Vsl.
Ca. 1258
KMF
1231. H1.LS. Fr. 1246
1232. H13.O. Th. 1211
KMF
1233. H12.Svy.S.
Fr. 856
KMFC
1234. H12. CG.Ibr.
Ca. 1269
KMFK
1235. H12. CG.Ibr.
Ca. 1268
KMFM
1236. H12.C.G.Sly.Vsl.
Ca. 1271
KMKFK
1237. H13.Cgo.S.
Am. 1213
KMM
1238. H1.Sply.Vsl.
Ca. 1266
KMM
1239. H Exp.Vsl.
Br. 672

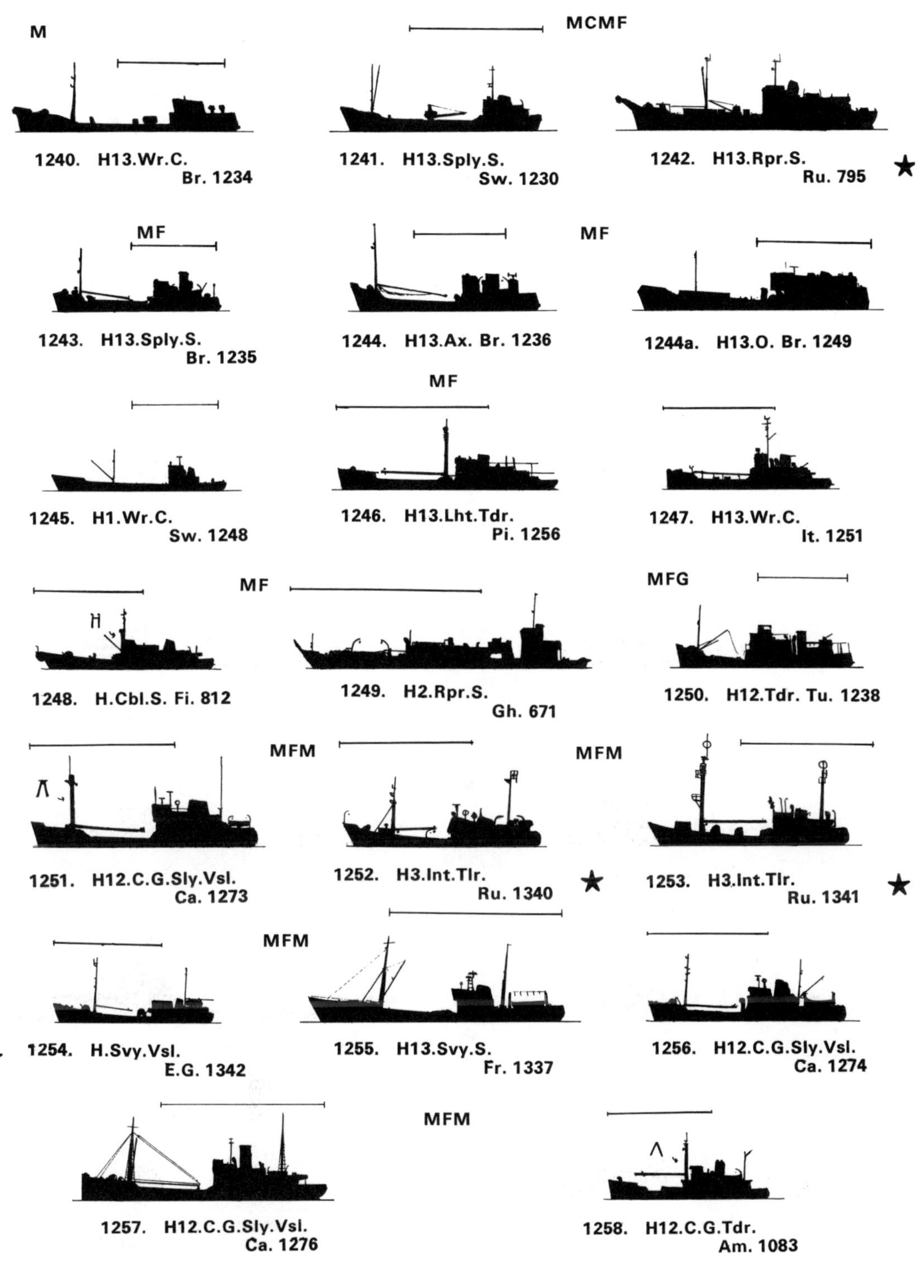



1240. H13.Wr.C. Br. 1234
1241. H13.Sply.S. Sw. 1230
1242. H13.Rpr.S. Ru. 795 ★
1243. H13.Sply.S. Br. 1235
1244. H13.Ax. Br. 1236
1244a. H13.O. Br. 1249
1245. H1.Wr.C. Sw. 1248
1246. H13.Lht.Tdr. Pi. 1256
1247. H13.Wr.C. It. 1251
1248. H.Cbl.S. Fi. 812
1249. H2.Rpr.S. Gh. 671
1250. H12.Tdr. Tu. 1238
1251. H12.C.G.Sly.Vsl. Ca. 1273
1252. H3.Int.Tlr. Ru. 1340 ★
1253. H3.Int.Tlr. Ru. 1341 ★
★ 1254. H.Svy.Vsl. E.G. 1342
1255. H13.Svy.S. Fr. 1337
1256. H12.C.G.Sly.Vsl. Ca. 1274
1257. H12.C.G.Sly.Vsl. Ca. 1276
1258. H12.C.G.Tdr. Am. 1083

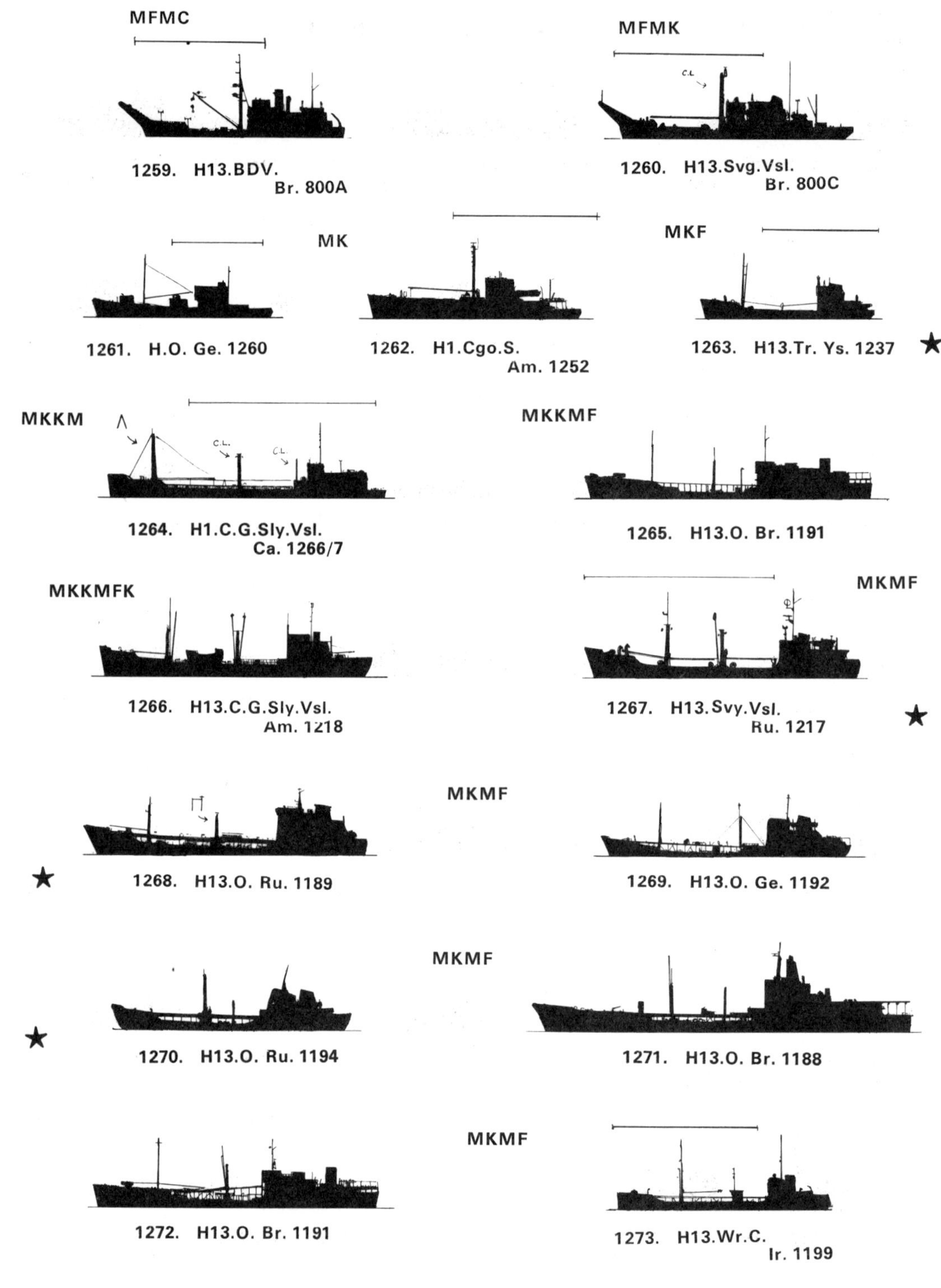


MFMC
1259. H13.BDV.
Br. 800A

MFMK
1260. H13.Svg.Vsl.
Br. 800C

MK
1261. H.O. Ge. 1260

1262. H1.Cgo.S.
Am. 1252

MKF
1263. H13.Tr. Ys. 1237

MKKM
1264. H1.C.G.Sly.Vsl.
Ca. 1266/7

MKKMF
1265. H13.O. Br. 1191

MKKMFK
1266. H13.C.G.Sly.Vsl.
Am. 1218

MKMF
1267. H13.Svy.Vsl.
Ru. 1217

MKMF
1268. H13.O. Ru. 1189

1269. H13.O. Ge. 1192

MKMF
1270. H13.O. Ru. 1194

1271. H13.O. Br. 1188

MKMF
1272. H13.O. Br. 1191

1273. H13.Wr.C.
Ir. 1199

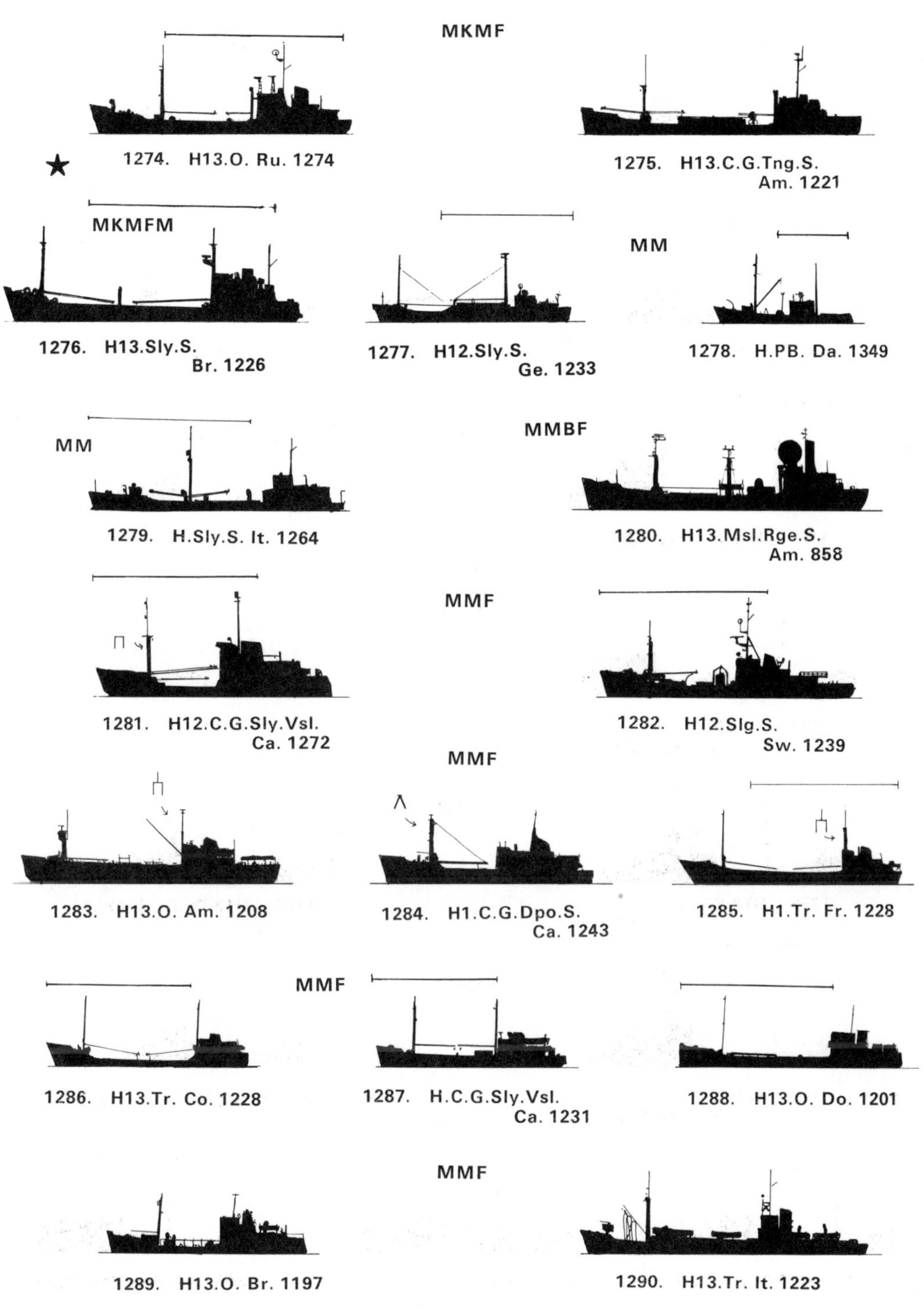

MKMF

1274. H13.O. Ru. 1274

1275. H13.C.G.Tng.S.
Am. 1221

MKMFM

1276. H13.Sly.S.
Br. 1226

1277. H12.Sly.S.
Ge. 1233

MM

1278. H.PB. Da. 1349

MM

1279. H.Sly.S. It. 1264

MMBF

1280. H13.Msl.Rge.S.
Am. 858

MMF

1281. H12.C.G.Sly.Vsl.
Ca. 1272

1282. H12.Slg.S.
Sw. 1239

MMF

1283. H13.O. Am. 1208

1284. H1.C.G.Dpo.S.
Ca. 1243

1285. H1.Tr. Fr. 1228

MMF

1286. H13.Tr. Co. 1228

1287. H.C.G.Sly.Vsl.
Ca. 1231

1288. H13.O. Do. 1201

MMF

1289. H13.O. Br. 1197

1290. H13.Tr. It. 1223

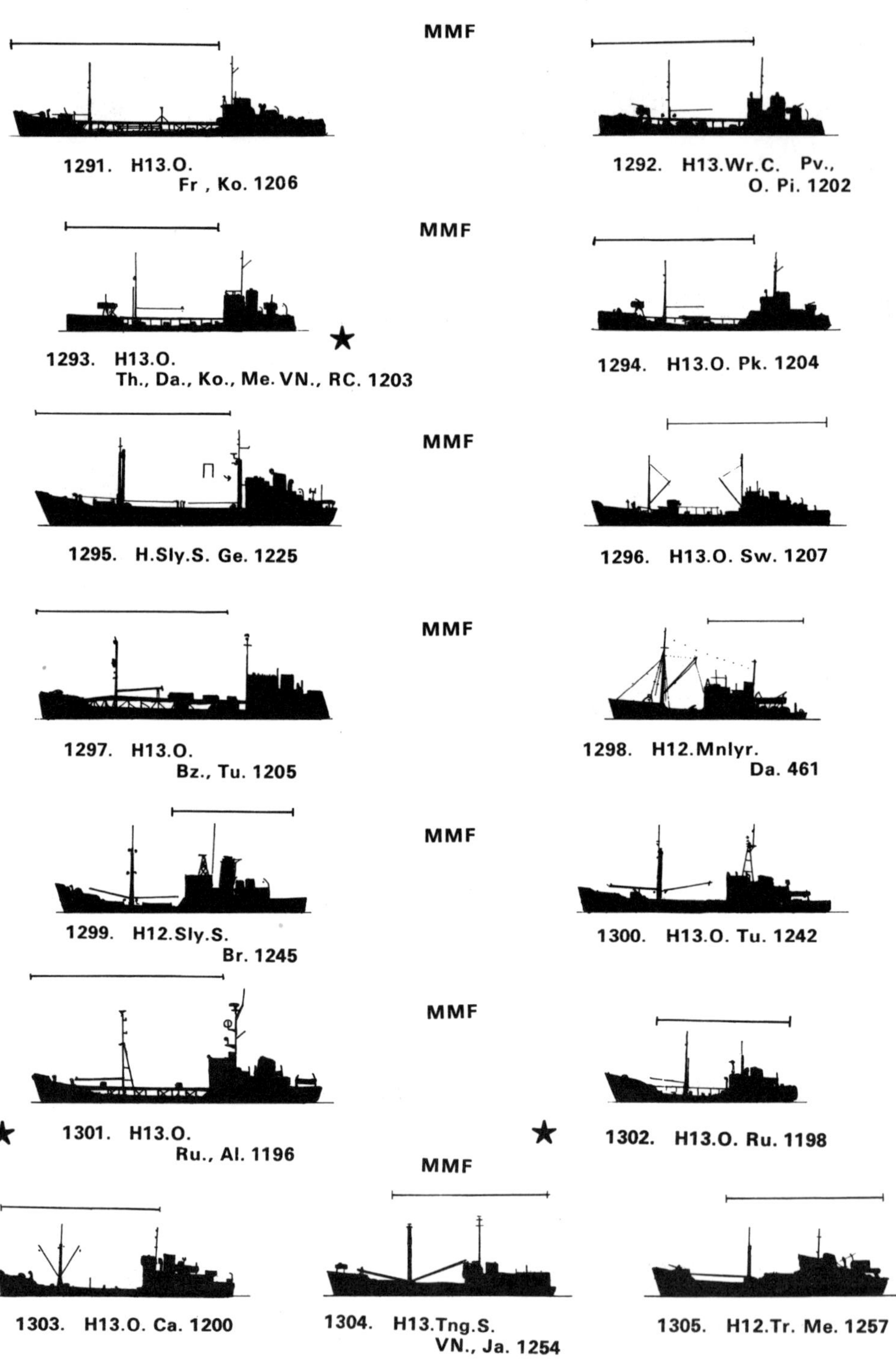


MMF

1291.  H13.O.
Fr , Ko. 1206

1292.  H13.Wr.C.  Pv.,
O. Pi. 1202

MMF

1293.  H13.O.
Th., Da., Ko., Me. VN., RC. 1203

1294.  H13.O. Pk. 1204

MMF

1295.  H.Sly.S. Ge. 1225

1296.  H13.O. Sw. 1207

MMF

1297.  H13.O.
Bz., Tu. 1205

1298.  H12.Mnlyr.
Da. 461

MMF

1299.  H12.Sly.S.
Br. 1245

1300.  H13.O. Tu. 1242

MMF

1301.  H13.O.
Ru., Al. 1196

1302.  H13.O. Ru. 1198

MMF

1303.  H13.O. Ca. 1200

1304.  H13.Tng.S.
VN., Ja. 1254

1305.  H12.Tr. Me. 1257

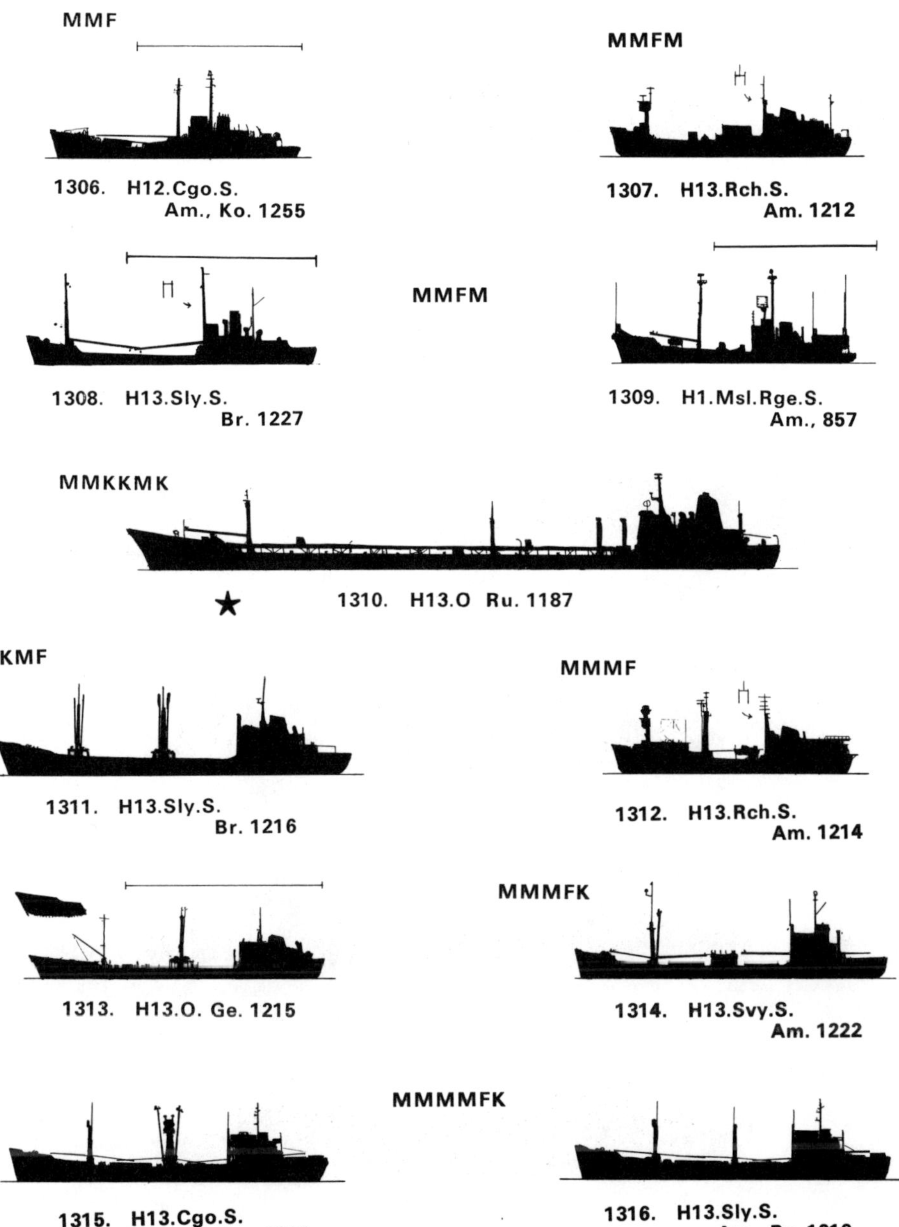


MMF
MMFM
1306.   H12.Cgo.S.
Am., Ko. 1255
1307.   H13.Rch.S.
Am. 1212
MMFM
1308.   H13.Sly.S.
Br. 1227
1309.   H1.Msl.Rge.S.
Am., 857
MMKKMK
1310.   H13.O  Ru. 1187
MMKMF
MMMF
1311.   H13.Sly.S.
Br. 1216
1312.   H13.Rch.S.
Am. 1214
MMMF
MMMFK
1313.   H13.O. Ge. 1215
1314.   H13.Svy.S.
Am. 1222
MMMMFK
1315.   H13.Cgo.S.
Am. 1220
1316.   H13.Sly.S.
Am., Pv. 1219

# P5

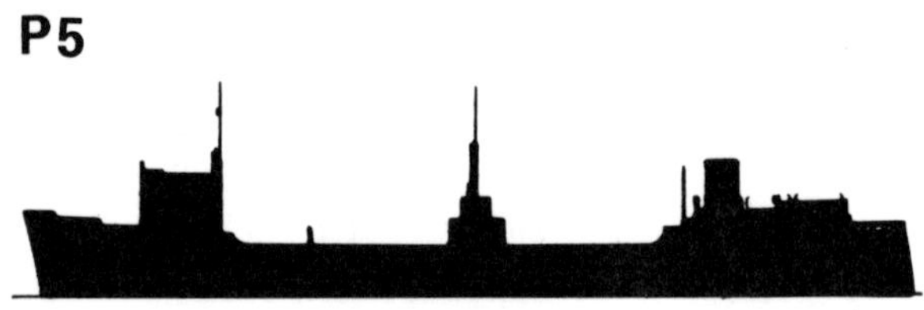

P5 (Bridge Foreward)

**BBMBMF**

1317.  H.Msl.Rge.S.
Ru. 866

**DMCFG**

1318.  H1.Mnlyr./Cbl.S.,
Ja. 813

**DMDDDDMFM**

1319.  H.Msl.Rge.S.    Am. 863

**DMKKKMKKKF**

1320.  H13.RO
Am. 1278

**GDMKKKMFDG**

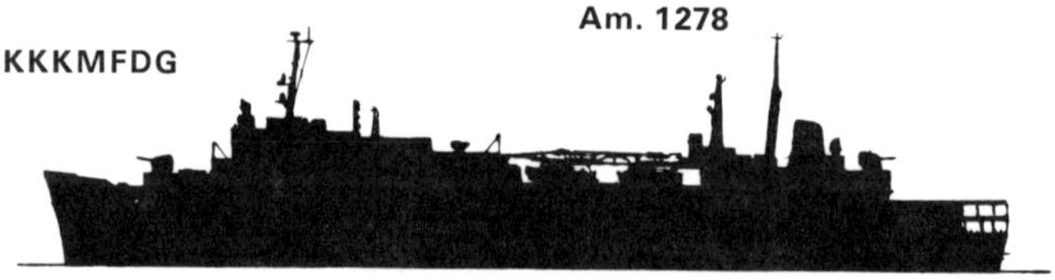

1321.  H1.Sub.Tdr.
Am. 861

**GMKKKKKKMFM**

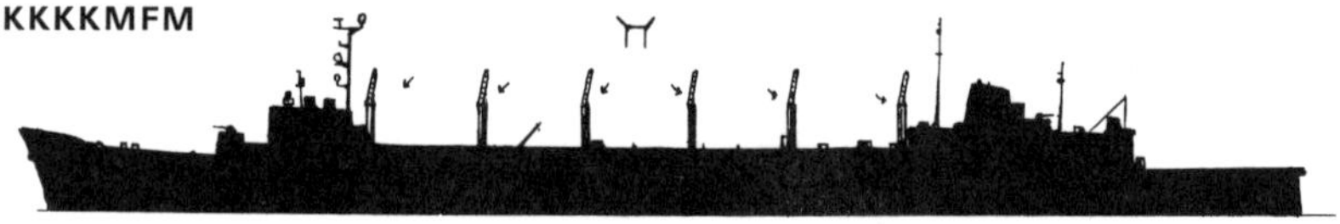

1322.  H.Spt.S.
Am. 1277

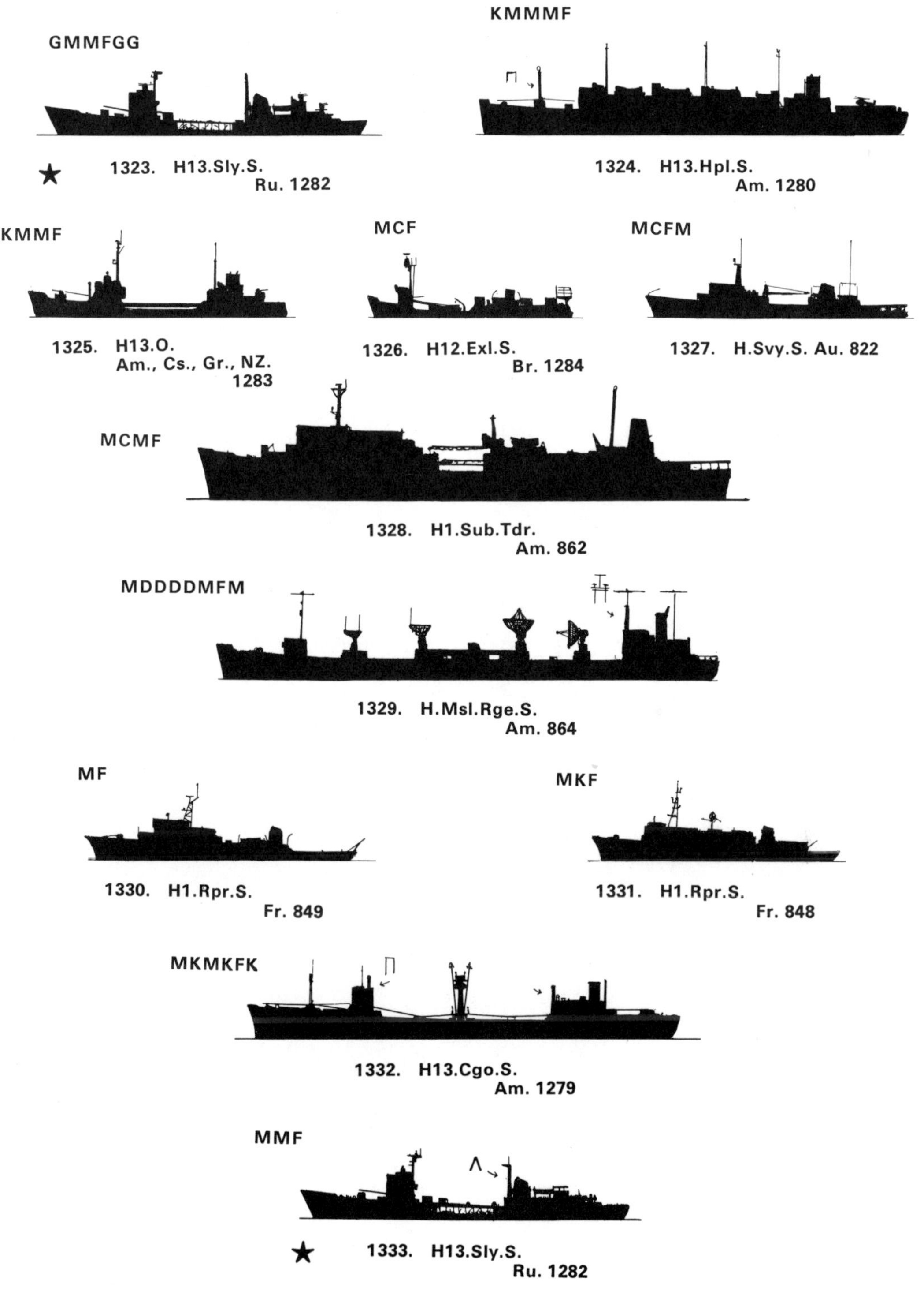


GMMFGG
1323.   H13.Sly.S.
Ru. 1282

KMMMF
1324.   H13.Hpl.S.
Am. 1280

KMMF
1325.   H13.O.
Am., Cs., Gr., NZ.
1283

MCF
1326.   H12.Exl.S.
Br. 1284

MCFM
1327.   H.Svy.S. Au. 822

MCMF
1328.   H1.Sub.Tdr.
Am. 862

MDDDDMFM
1329.   H.Msl.Rge.S.
Am. 864

MF
1330.   H1.Rpr.S.
Fr. 849

MKF
1331.   H1.Rpr.S.
Fr. 848

MKMKFK
1332.   H13.Cgo.S.
Am. 1279

MMF
1333.   H13.Sly.S.
Ru. 1282

# SECTION THREE

# Grey Outlines

# Arrangement of Grey Outline Section

Strict sequence is ignored and drawings are arranged according to appearance. Types are more or less kept together but it must be remembered that it is what ships *look like* rather than what their *function* may be.

For example, all vessels of the *Loch* Class Frigates are together even if some have been converted to other functions provided that the original appearance remains basically the same.

All *Fletcher* or former *Fletcher* Class Destroyers are together whether they are of the 4, 3 or 5 gun variety and irrespective of their present nationality.

The main divisions are as below:

**COMBAT SHIPS** (or vessels that look unmistakably like warships).

1 **Carrier Types**
2 **2-Funnelled Ships** Cruisers, Destroyers, Escorts, Frigates, Corvettes, River Gunboats etc.
3 **1-Funnelled or No Funnelled Ships** Cruisers, Destroyers, Escorts, Frigates, Corvettes, Patrol Craft, Coast Guard Vessels, Gunboats, Hydrofoils, Minelayers.
4 **Assault Craft** Dock Landing Ships, Amphibious Assault Ships, Landing ships, Landing craft etc.
5 **Minesweepers** Minehunters etc.
6 **Auxiliaries, 2-Funnelled Depot Ships, Support Ships etc.**
7 **Auxiliaries** 1-Funnelled. Maintenance Ships, Support Ships, Boom Defence Vessels, Survey Ships, Cable Ships, Experimental Vessels, Oilers, Replenishments Ships.
8 **Submarines.**

**MERCHANT SHIP TYPES** Similar to Numbers 6 and 7 but not *obviously* Naval ships.

9 **2-Funnelled Ships** Transports, Icebreakers.
10 **1-Funnelled Ships** Profiles 1 and 2— Engines amidships.
Icebreakers, Maintenance Ships, Cargo Vessels, Store Ships, Coast Guard Vessels, Japanese Maritime Safety Agency Ships, Yacht types, etc.
11 **Profile 3** Engines aft and bridge amidships.
Replenishment Oilers, Tankers, Water Carriers, Stores Ships etc.
12 **Profile 4** Engines aft and all superstructure aft.
Oilers, Armament Carriers, Supply Ships etc.
13 **Profile 5** Engines aft and bridge well foreward.
Support Ships, Hospital Ships, Missile Range Ships etc.
14 **Tug and Trawler Types**

# DATA BENEATH GREY OUTLINE DRAWINGS

**Scale** 150 feet to 1 inch except for smaller craft which are drawn larger. In these cases the 150 foot scale is indicated by the horizontal line above each.

1 Consecutive Number.
2 Name or Class Name.
3 Nationality with addition of black star in case of Communist block countries.
4 Pendant number if *actually appearing* on the ship.
5 Date of completion. Date of alteration, conversion or modernisation if any.
6 Type of ship.
7 Standard displacement to nearest 100 tons except in vessels of under 1,000 tons where it is to the nearest ton. In some cases gross or full load displacement is given.
8 Overall length, beam and draught—all to the nearest foot. All this repeated in Metres.
9 Number of screws if more than one. Type of engine and speed.
10 Armament. Guns, Launchers, Torpedo Tubes, Mortars, anti-submarine weapons, helicopters, mines etc.
11 Any remarks.
12 Similar ships or other ships in the Class.

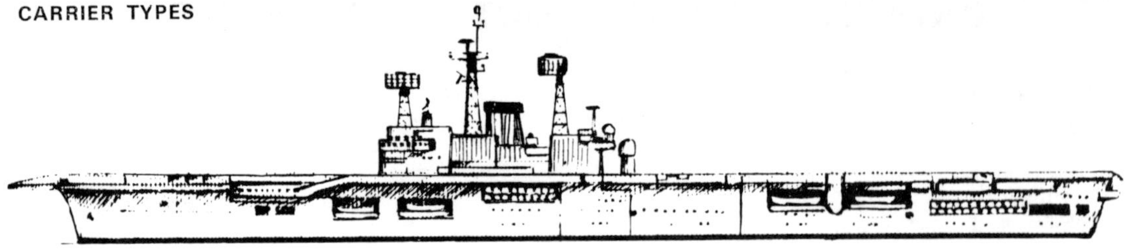

**1.** Br. **ARK ROYAL.** *R09.* 1955. Modernised 1967-70. Aircraft Carrier. 43,000 tons. 845 x 166 x 36. (259 x 51 x 11). 4 screws; turbines. 31.5 knots. 4 surface-to-air "Seacat" launchers (quadruple). Differs from "Eagle" principally by absence of "headlamp" radar on front of super-structure.

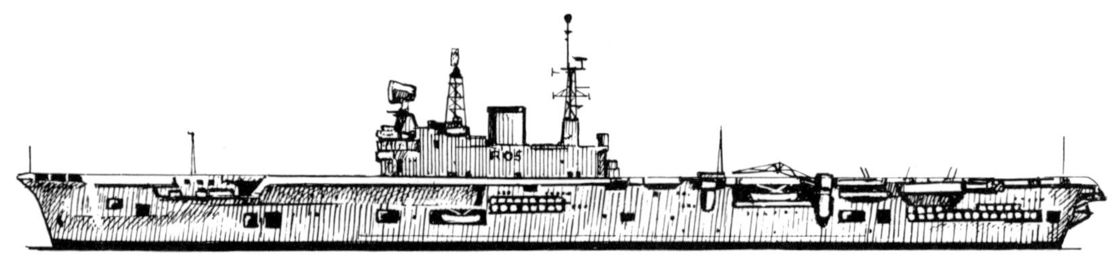

**2.** Br. **EAGLE.** *R05.* 1951. Modernised 1959-64. Aircraft Carrier. 43,000 tons. 812 x 171 x 36. (244 x 52.1 x 11). 4 screws; turbines. 31.5 knots. 6 surface-to-air "Seacat" launchers (quadruple). Distinguished from "Hermes" by her foremast and much larger funnel.

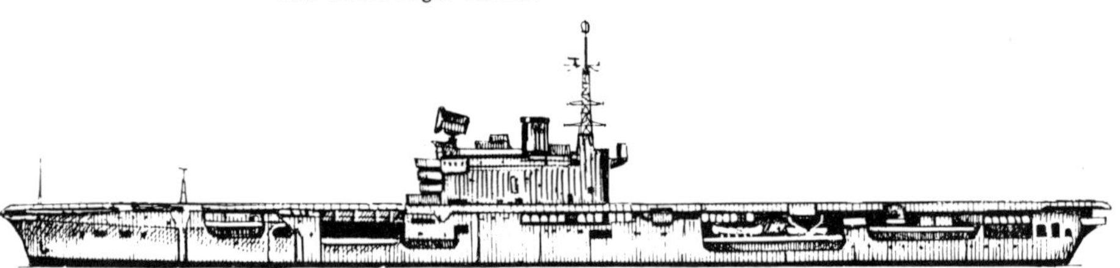

**3.** Br. **HERMES.** *R12.* 1959. Modernised 1964-66. Aircraft Carrier. 23,900 tons. 744 x 160 x 29. (227 x 49 x 9). 2 screws; turbines. 28 knots. 2 surface-to-air "Seacat" launchers (quadruple).

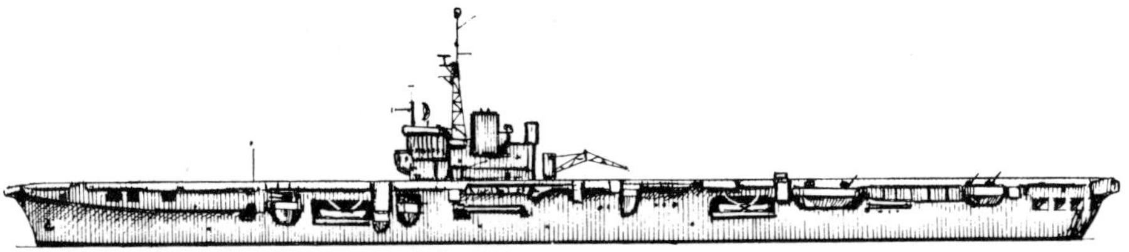

**5.** In. **VIKRANT.** *R11.* 1961. Aircraft Carrier. 16,000 tons. 700 x 128 x 24. (213 x 39 x 7.3). 2 screws; turbines. 24 knots. 15 A.A. guns. Ex-British "Majestic" class.

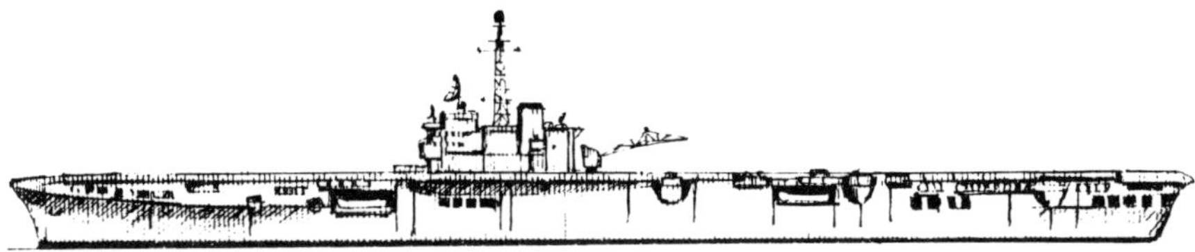

**6.** Au. **MELBOURNE.** *21.* 1955. Modernised 1965-66. Aircraft Carrier. 16,000 tons. 702 x 126 x 25. (213 x 38 x 7.7). 2 screws; turbines. 23 knots. 12 A.A. guns. Ex-British "Majestic" class.

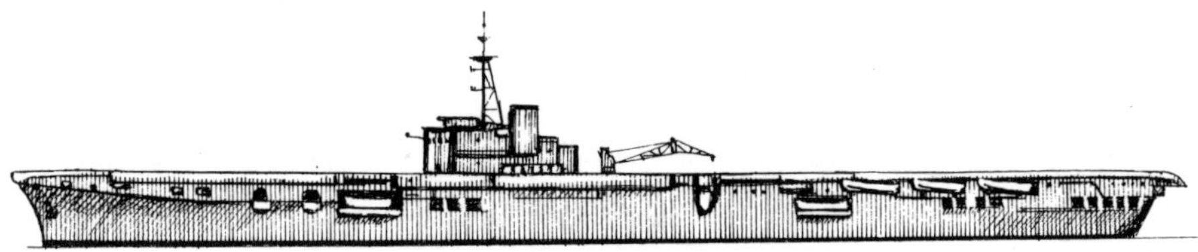

**7.** Au. **SYDNEY.** *214.* 1949. Converted 1962. Transport/Training Ship. 12,600 tons. 698 x 113 x 18. (213 x 34 x 5.5). 2 screws; turbines. 24 knots. Ex-British "Majestic" class.

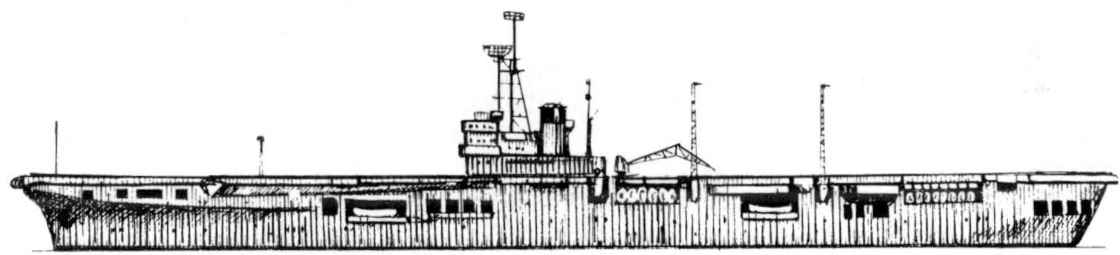

**8.** Fr. **ARROMANCHES.** *R95.* 1944. Modernised 1957-58. Aircraft Carrier. 14,000 tons. 695 x 118 x 23 (212 x 36 x 7) 2 screws; turbines. 23 knots. Ex-British "Colossus" class. Distinguished by light pole mast before the tripod, and black top to funnel.

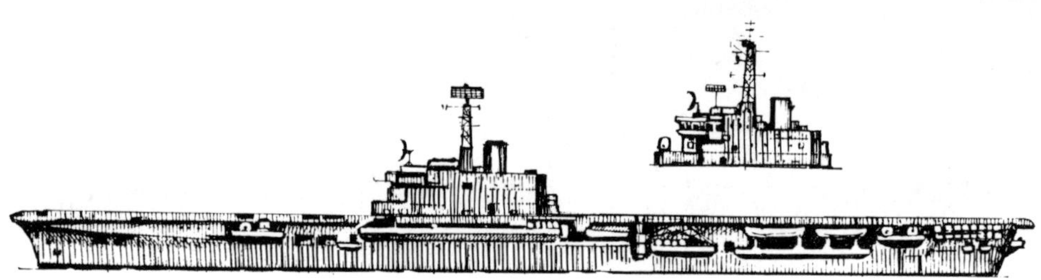

**9.** Br. **ALBION.** *R07.* 1954. Converted 1961-62.
Commando Carrier. 23,300 tons. 738 x 124 x 28.
(225 x 38 x 8.6). 2 screws; turbines. 28 knots.
8 A.A. guns. 4 landing craft. 16 helicopters.
Similar; **BULWARK** (See inset). Modified
"Centaur" class.

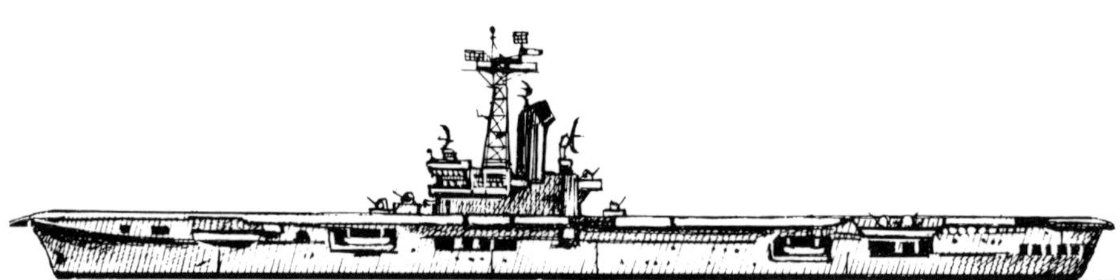

**11.** Ar. **VEINTICINO DE MAYO.** 1945. Modernised 1968. Aircraft Carrier. 15,900 tons. 693 x
121 x 25. (211 x 37 x 7.6). 2 screws; turbines.
24 knots. 10 A.A. guns. Ex-British "Colossus"
class. Distinguished by the unusual funnel and
tall mast which were added while she was under
the Dutch flag (1948-68).

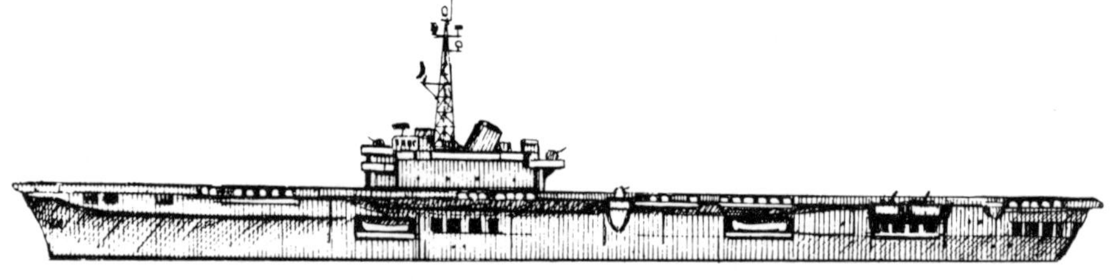

**12.** Bz. **MINAS GERAIS.** *A11.* 1945. Modernised 1957-60. Aircraft Carrier. 15,900 tons.
695 x 121 x 21. (212 x 37 x 6.6). 2 screws;
turbines. 25 knots. 10 A.A. guns. Ex-British
"Colossus" class. Very small, raking funnel and
tall mast.

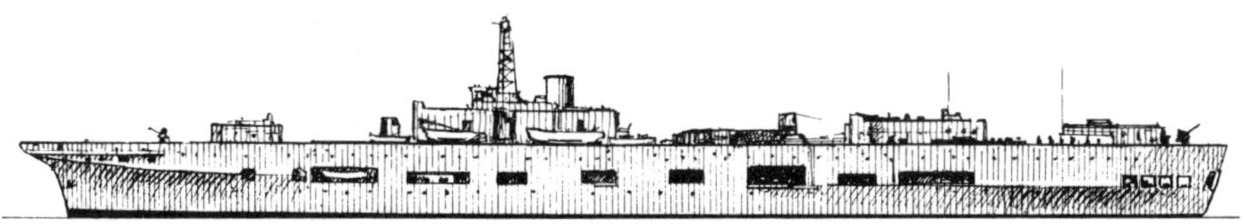

**13.** Br. **TRIUMPH.** *A108.* 1946. Converted 1958
65. Heavy Repair Ship. 13,400 tons. 699 x 114
x 23. (213 x 34 x 7.2). 2 screws; turbines.
24 knots. 4 A.A. guns. 3 helicopters. Originally a
"Colossus" class aircraft carrier.

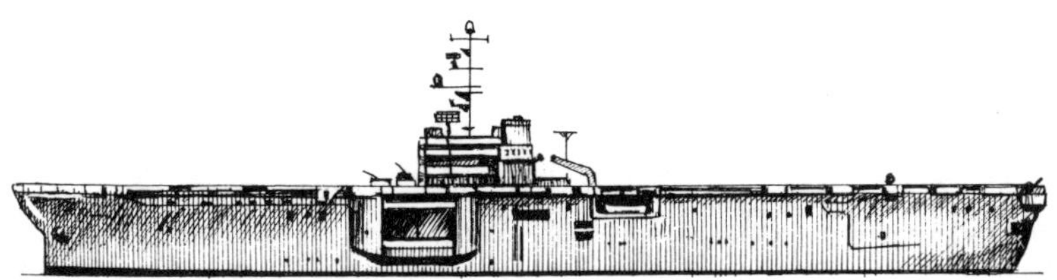

**14.** Am. **IWO JIMA** class. 1961-69. Amphibious
Assault Ships. 17,000 tons (light). 592 x 84 x 26
(180 x 25.6 x 7.9). Turbines. 20 knots. 8—3-inch
A.A. guns.
**GUADALCANAL.** *7,* **GUAM.** *9,* **INCHON.** *12,*
**IWO JIMA.** *2,* **NEW ORLEANS.** *11,* **TRIPOLI.**
*10.*

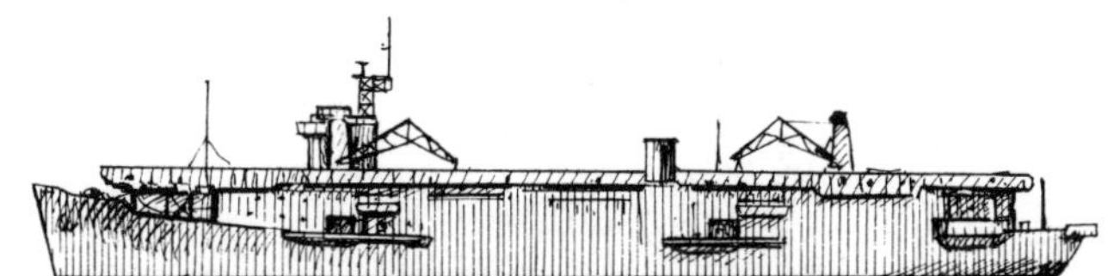

**15.** Am. **BOGUE** class. 1942-43. Cargo and
Aircraft Ferries. 9,800 tons. 496 x 112 x 26
(151 x 34 x 7.9). Turbines. 18 knots.
**BRETON.** *42,* **CORE.** *41,* **CROATAN.** *43.* Some
may be changed in appearance—see silhouette
No. 17.

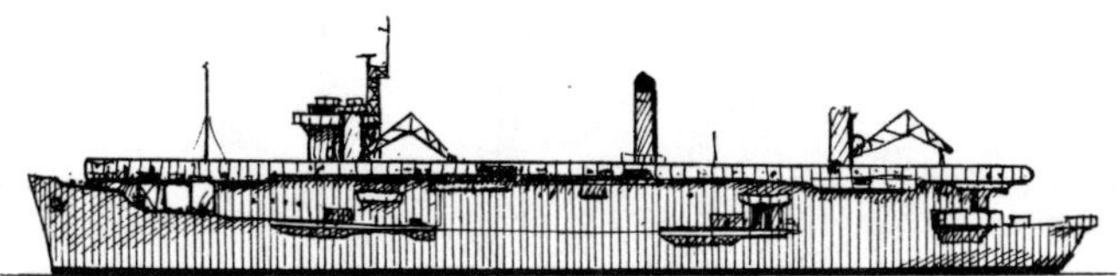

**16.** Am. **CARD** *40.* 1942. The fourth ship of the
Bogue class. All details the same as for No. 15.

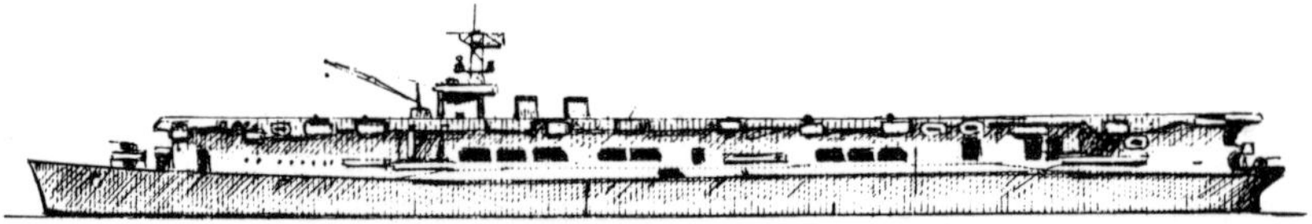

**17.** Am. **INDEPENDENCE** class. 1943. Aircraft Transports. 11,000 tons. 600 x 109 x 26 (183 x 33 x 7.9). 4 screws; turbines. 32 knots. **MONTEREY.** *2,* **SAN JACINTO.** *5.* May now be changed in appearance. Completed as aircraft carriers.

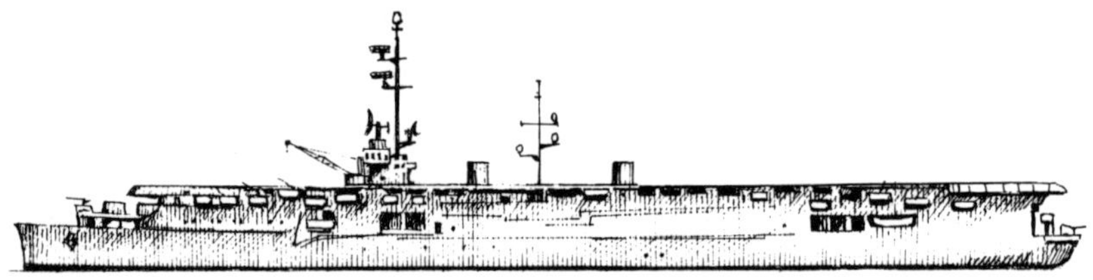

**18.** Sp. **DEDALO.** *01.* 1943. Helicopter Carrier. The third ship of "Independence" class and details as for No. 17.

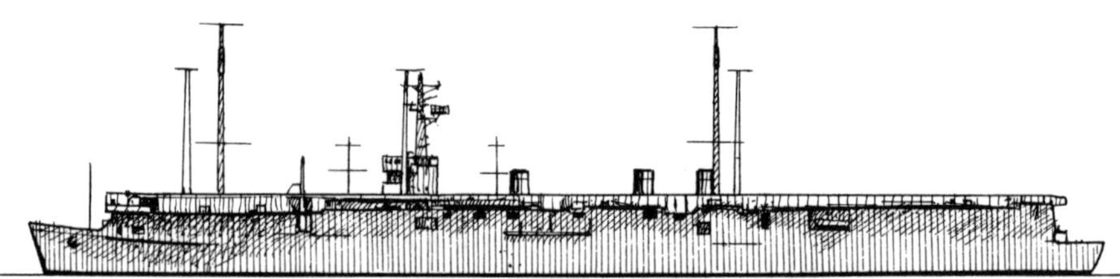

**19.** Am. **ARLINGTON.** *GMR 2.* 1945. Converted 1964-5. Major Communications Relay Ship. 14,500 tons. 684 x 109 x 28 (209 x 33 x 8.5). 4 screws; turbines. 33 knots. 8—3-inch guns (twin). Completed as aircraft carrier.

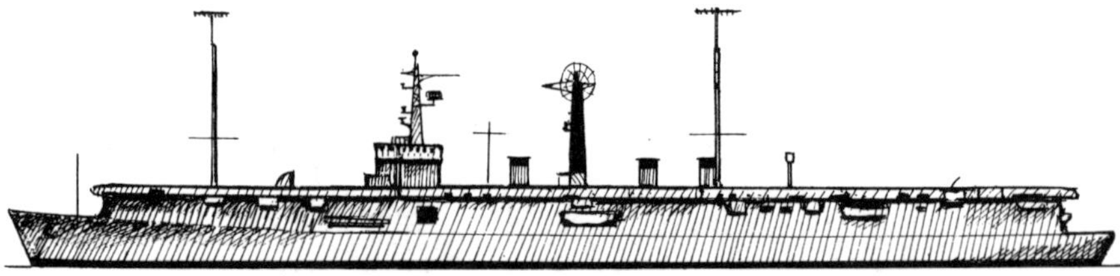

**20.** Am. **WRIGHT.** *2.* 1947. Converted 1962. Command Ship. 14,500 tons. 684 x 109 x 28. (209 x 33 x 8.5). 4 screws; turbines. 33 knots. 8 A.A. guns. Completed as aircraft carrier.

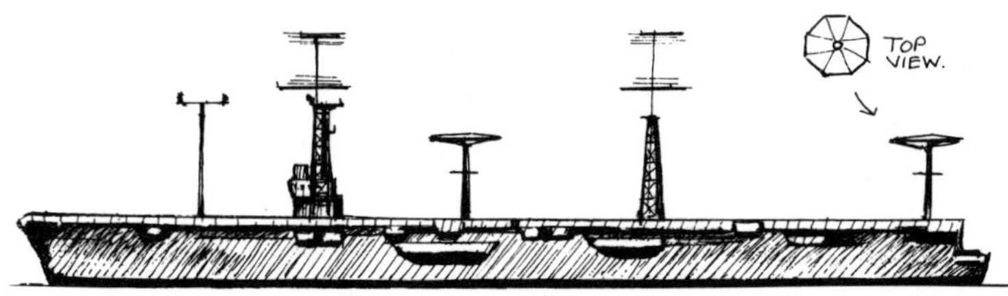

**21.** Am. **ANNAPOLIS.** *GMR 1.* 1945. Converted 1963. Major Communications Relay Ship. 11,500 tons. 563 x 106 x 31. (172 x 32 x 9.5). 2 screws; turbines. 18 knots. 8—3-inch A.A. guns (twin). Completed as escort carrier of "Commencement Bay" class.

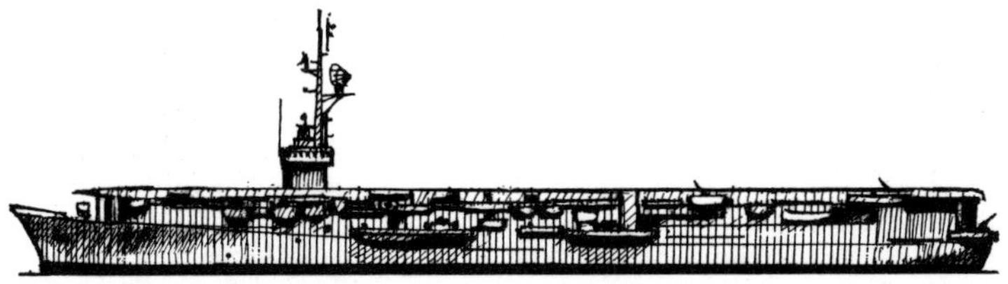

**22.** Am. **COMMENCEMENT BAY** class. 1944-46. Cargo and Aircraft Ferries. 11,500 tons. 557 x 105 x 31. (170 x 32 x 9.5). 2 screws; turbines. 18 knots. 1—5-inch gun, 24 A.A. guns (probably removed). Former escort carriers.

COMMENCEMENT BAY. *37,* BADOENG STRAIT. *16,* CAPE GLOUCESTER. *9,* KULA GULF. *8,* POINT CRUZ, RABAUL. *21,* RENDOVA. *14,* SAIDOR. *17,* TINIAN. *23,* SIBONEY, VELLA GULF.

**23.** Fr. **CLEMENCEAU.** *R98.* 1961. Aircraft Carrier. 22,000 tons. 865 x 168 x 26. (264 x 51 x 8). 2 screws; turbines. 31 knots.
**FOCH.** *R99.*

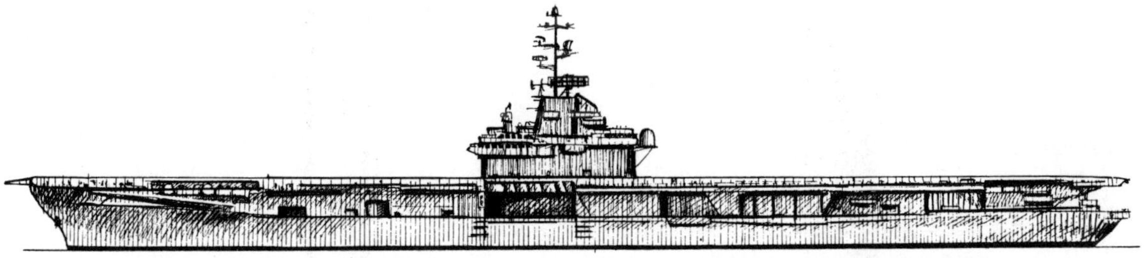

**24.** Am. **ESSEX** class & **HANCOCK** class. 1942-50. Aircraft Carriers. 33,000 tons (average). 890 x 196 x 31. (271 x 60 x 9.4). 4 screws; turbines. 33 knots. 4—5-inch guns. Ships vary slightly.

*Essex Class.* **ESSEX.** *9,* **ANTIETAM.** *36,* **BEN-NINGTON.** *20,* **HORNET.** *12,* **INTREPID.** *11,* **KEARSARGE.** *33,* **LEXINGTON.** *16,* **RAN-DOLPH.** *15,* **SHANGRI LA.** *38,* **WASP.** *18,* **YORKTOWN.** *10.*
*Hancock class.* **BON HOMME RICHARD.** *31,* **HANCOCK.** *19,* **ORISKANY.** *33,* **TICON-DEROGA.** *14.*

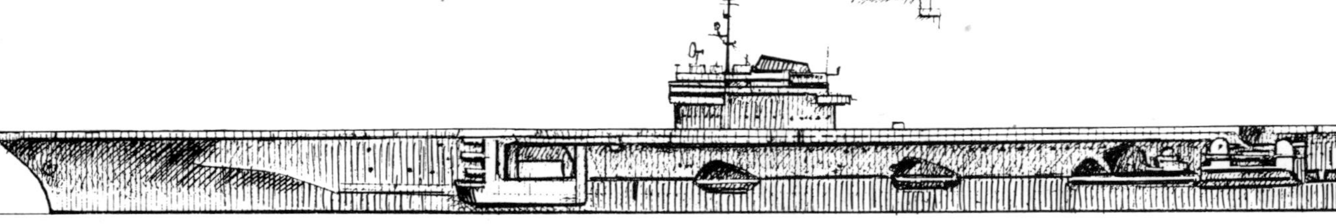

**25.** Am. **FORRESTAL** class. 1955-59. Aircraft Carriers. 60,000 tons. 1,040 x 252 x 37. (317 x 77 x 11.3). 4 screws; turbines. 35 knots. 4—5-inch D.P. guns (Except in "Forrestal"). 1 "Sea Sparrow" launcher (In "Forrestal" only).
**FORRESTAL.** *59,* **INDEPENDENCE.** *62* (see inset). **RANGER.** *61,* **SARATOGA.** *60.*

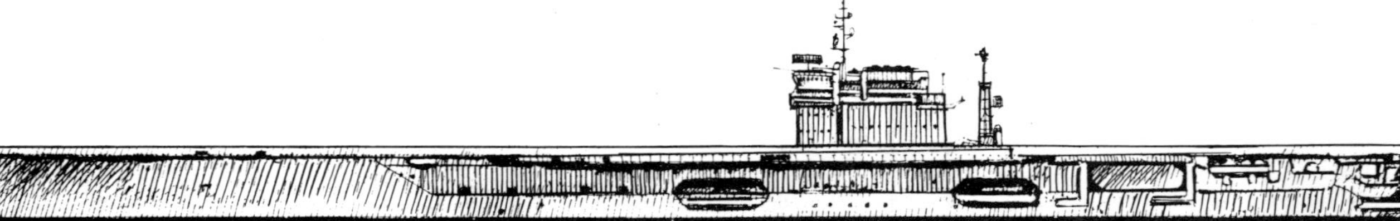

**26.** Am. **KITTY HAWK** class. 1961-68. Aircraft Carriers. 60,200 tons. 1,060 x 250 x 37. (323 x 76.8 x 11.3). 4 screws; turbines. 35 knots. 2 surface-to-air "Terrier" launchers (twin) and provision for "Sea Sparrow" launchers in "John F. Kennedy".
**CONSTELLATION.** *64,* **KITTY HAWK.** *63.*
Similar: **AMERICA.** *66,* **JOHN F. KENNEDY.** *67.*

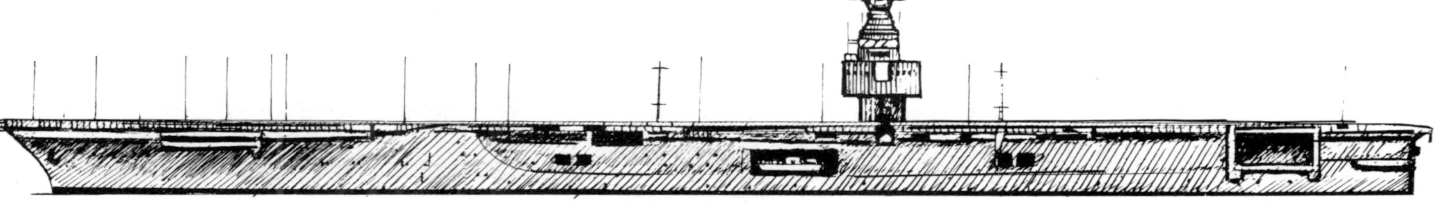

**27.** Am. **ENTERPRISE.** *65.* 1961. Aircraft
Carrier. 75,700 tons. 1,123 x 257 x 25. (341 x
78.3 x 7.6). 4 screws; nuclear powered turbines.
35 knots. 3 "Sea Sparrow" launchers.
Unique in appearance with tall, square superstructure.

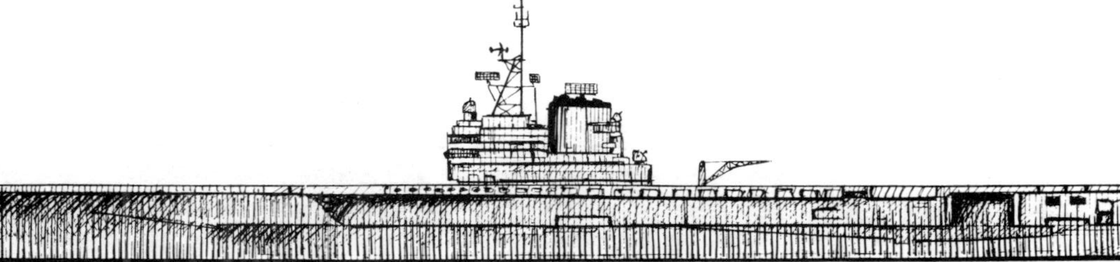

**28.** Am. **MIDWAY.** *41.* 1945. Modernised 1966-
71. Aircraft Carrier. 51,000 tons. 979 x 222 x 36.
(298 x 68 x 11). 4 screws; turbines. 33 knots.
3–5-inch D.P. guns. May be slightly different in
appearance after completion of current re-fit.
Distinguished from Nos. 29 & 30 by lattice-tripod
mast.

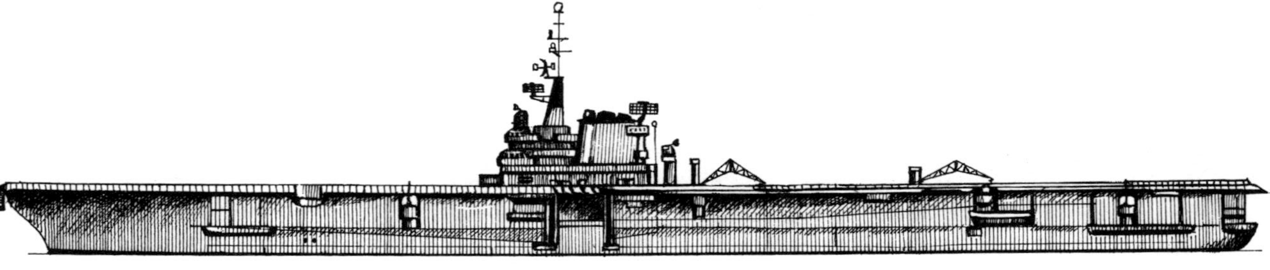

**29.** Am. **FRANKLIN D. ROOSEVELT.** *42.*
1945. Modernised 1953-56. Aircraft Carrier.
51,000 tons. 979 x 222 x 36. (298 x 68 x 11).
4 screws; turbines. 33 knots. 4—5-inch D.P. guns.
Distinguished from "Coral Sea" by absence of
light mast abaft funnel and by different stern.

**30.** Am. **CORAL SEA.** *43.* 1946. Modernised
1959-60. Aircraft Carrier. 52,500 tons. 979 x
222 x 36. (298 x 68 x 11). 4 screws; turbines.
33 knots. 3—5-inch D.P. guns.

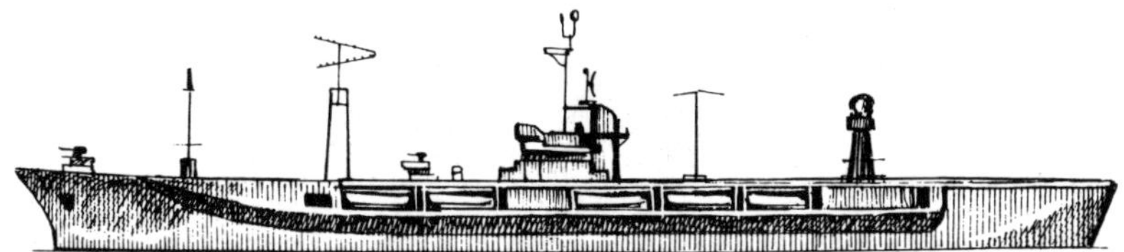

**31.** Am. **BLUE RIDGE** class. 1970-71. Amphibious Command Ships. 17,100 tons (Full). 620 x 82 x 27. (190 x 25.3 x 8.2). Turbines. 20 knots. 8—3-inch A.A. guns.
**BLUE RIDGE.** *19,* **MOUNT WHITNEY.** *20.*

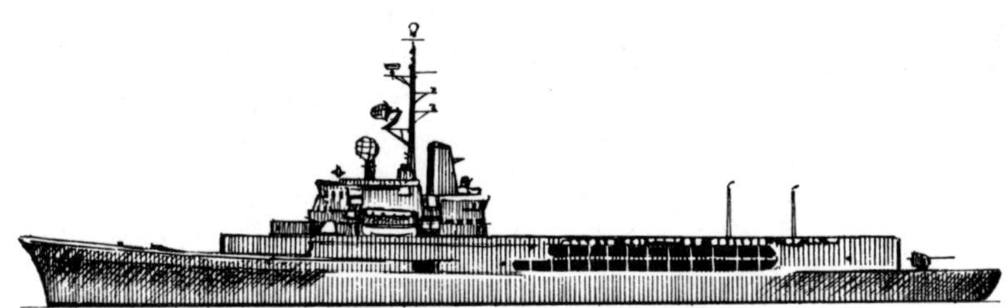

**32.** Fr. **JEANNE D'ARC.** *R97.* 1963. Helicopter Carrier. 10,000 tons. 597 x 85 x 21. (182 x 26 x 6.6). 2 screws; turbines. 26 knots. 4—3.9-inch A.A. guns.
Can also be employed as a commando ship.

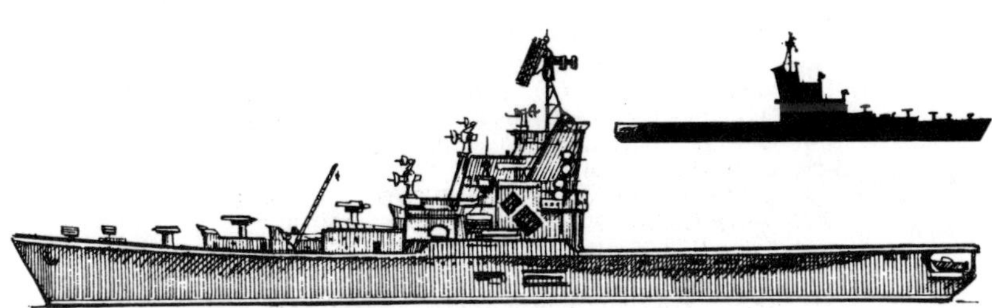

**33.** Ru. **MOSKVA** class. 1967-70. Cruiser/ Helicopter Ships. 15,000 tons. 645. (197). 30 knots. 4 A.A. guns (twin). 10 torpedo tubes. 2 surface-to-air launchers. 2 anti-submarine mortars.
**MOSKVA, LENINGRAD.**

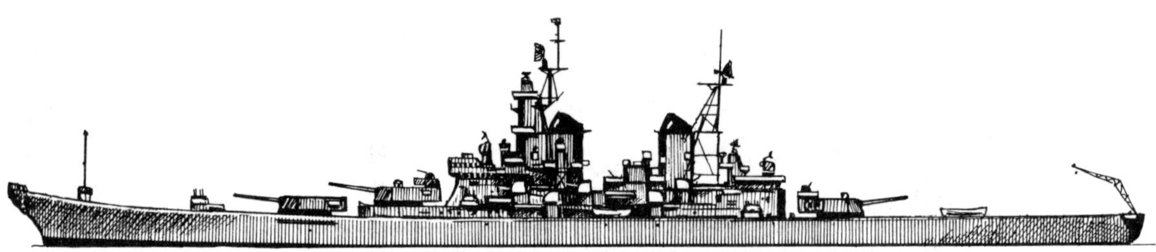

**34.** Am. **IOWA** class. 1943-44. Battleships.
45,000 tons. 887 x 108 x 38. (270 x 33 x 11.6).
4 screws; turbines. 33-35 knots. 9—16-inch guns
(triple). 20—5-inch D.P. guns.
**IOWA.** *61,* **MISSOURI.** *63,* **NEW JERSEY.** *62,*
**WISCONSIN.** *64.* "New Jersey" is the only
ship at present in commission. She was modernised in 1967-68.

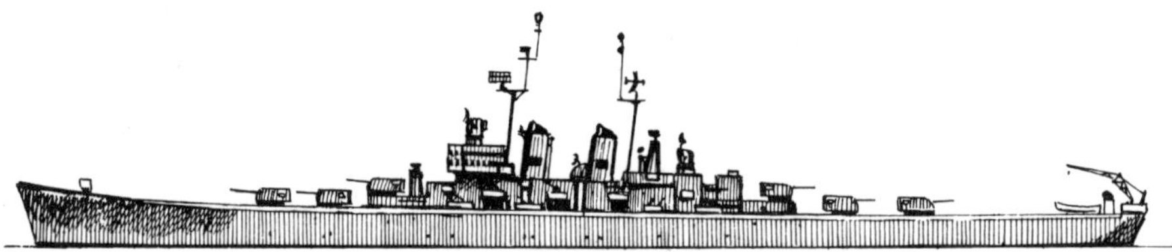

**35.** Am. **WORCESTER** class. 1948. Light
Cruisers. 14,700 tons. 680 x 71 x 25. (207 x
21.5 x 7.6). 4 screws; turbines. 32 knots. 12—
6-inch D.P. guns. 24—3-inch A.A. guns.
**ROANOKE.** *145,* **WORCESTER.** *144.* Laid up
since 1958.

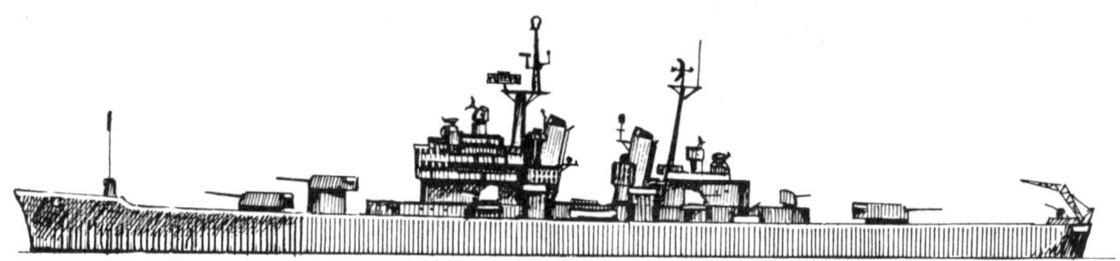

**36.** Am. **ST. PAUL.** *73.* Heavy Cruiser. 13,600
tons. 674 x 71 x 26. (205 x 21.6 x 7.9). 9—8-inch
guns (triple). 10—5-inch D.P. guns (twin).
12—3-inch guns. 4 screws; turbines. 33 knots.
The only ship of the "Baltimore" class in commission. The other ships are:
**BALTIMORE.** *68,* **BREMERTON.** *130,* **FALL
RIVER.** *131,* **HELENA.** *75,* **LOS ANGELES.**
*135,* **PITTSBURG.** *72,* **QUINCY.** *71,* **TOLEDO.**
*133.*
See silhouette number 199. "Helena" has a
heavy foremast like "St. Paul".

**37.** Am. **CLEVELAND** class. 1944-45. Light Cruisers. 10,500 tons. 610 x 66 x 25. (186 x 20 x 7.6). 4 screws; turbines. 33 knots. 12—6-inch guns (triple). 12—5-inch D.P. guns (twin). 28 A.A. guns. All out of commission.
**AMSTERDAM.** *101,* **PASADENA.** *65,* **PORTS-MOUTH.** *102,* **WILKES-BARRE.** *103.*

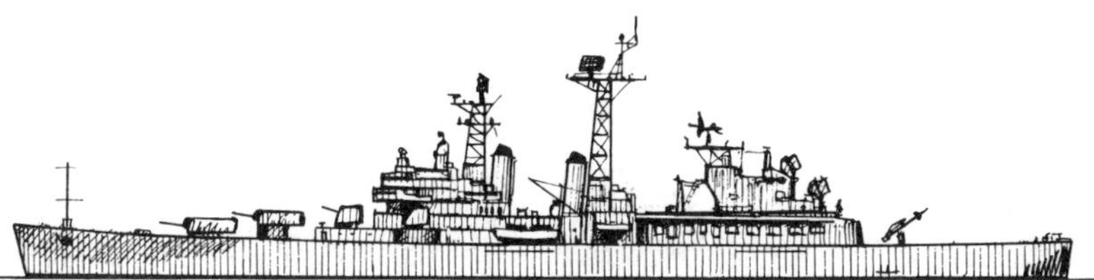

**38.** Am. Converted **CLEVELAND** class. 1946. Converted 1956-58. Guided Missile Light Cruiser. 10 700 tons. 610 x 66 x 25. (185.9 x 20 x 7.6). 4 screws; turbines. 31 knots. 6—6-inch guns (triple). 6—5-inch D.P. guns (twin). 1 "Talos" launcher (twin).
**GALVESTON.** *3.*

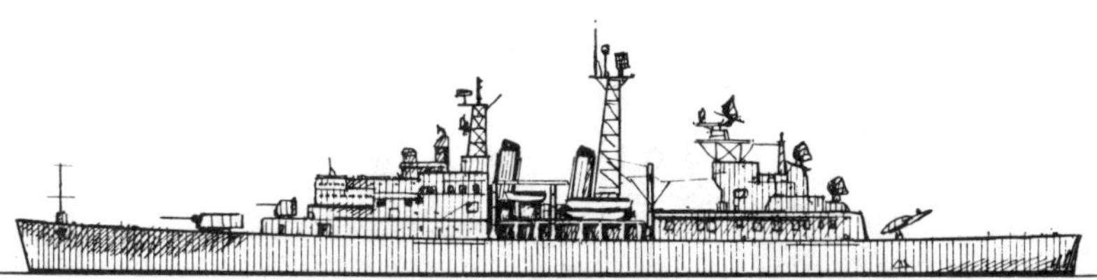

**39.** Am. Converted **CLEVELAND** class. 1944-45. Converted 1960. Guided Missile Light Cruisers. All particulars as for number 38 except that they only have 3—6-inch guns and 2—5-inch guns.
**LITTLE ROCK.** *4,* **OKHLAHOMA CITY.** *5.*

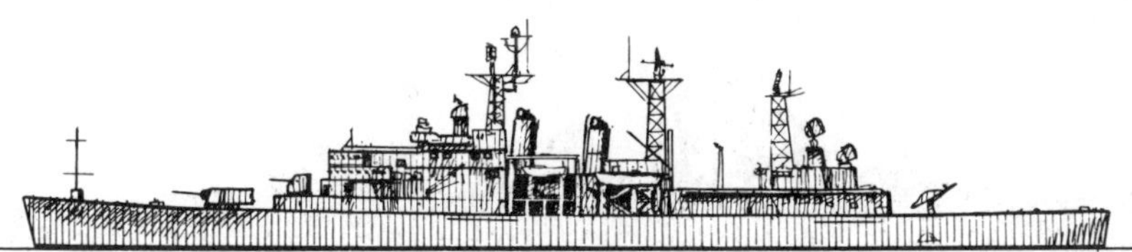

**40.** Am. Converted **CLEVELAND** class. 1944-45. Converted 1959-60. Guided Missile Light Cruisers. All particulars as for number 39 except that they carry 1 twin "Terrier" in place of the twin "Talos".
**PROVIDENCE.** *6,* **SPRINGFIELD.** *7.*

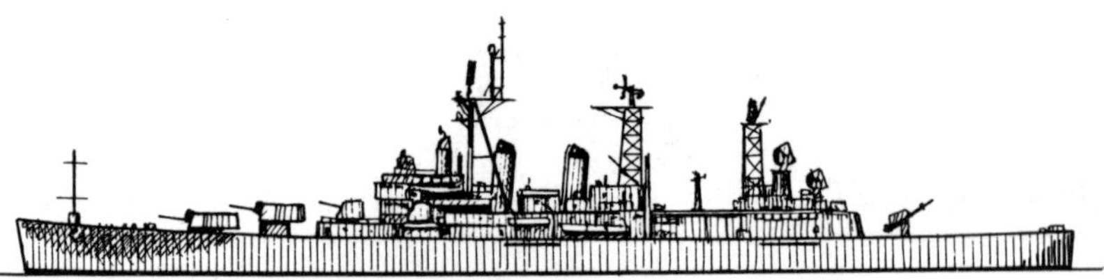

**41.** Am. Converted **CLEVELAND** class. 1944.
Converted 1960. Guided Missile Light Cruiser.
All particulars as for number 38 except that she
has a "Terrier" launcher in place of the "Talos".
**TOPEKA.** *8.*

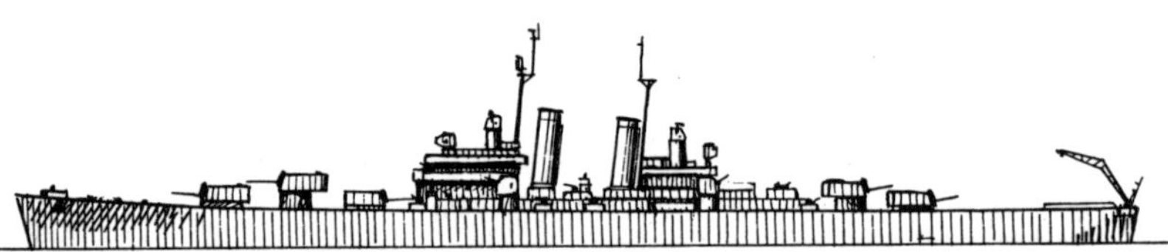

**42.** Bz. **TAMANDARE.** *C12.* 1939. Cruiser.
10,000 tons. 609 x 69 x 24. (186 x 21 x 7.3).
4 screws; turbines. 32 knots. 15—6-inch guns
(triple). 8—5-inch guns (twin). 36 A.A. guns.
1 helicopter. Formerly an American "St. Louis"
class cruiser.

**43.** Ar. **GENERAL BELGRANO.** 1939. Modernised 1951. Cruiser. 10,800 tons. 608 x 69 x
24. (185.4 x 21 x 7.3). 4 screws; turbines. 32
knots. 15—6-inch guns (triple). 8—5-inch guns
(twin). 42 A.A. guns. 2 surface-to-air "Seacat"
launchers (quadruple). Ex-US. "Brooklyn" class.

Sister (no launchers): **NUEVE DE JULIO.**
Similar (taller mainmast): Bz. **BARROSO.** *C11,*
Ch. **O'HIGGINS.** *02,* **PRAT.** *03.*

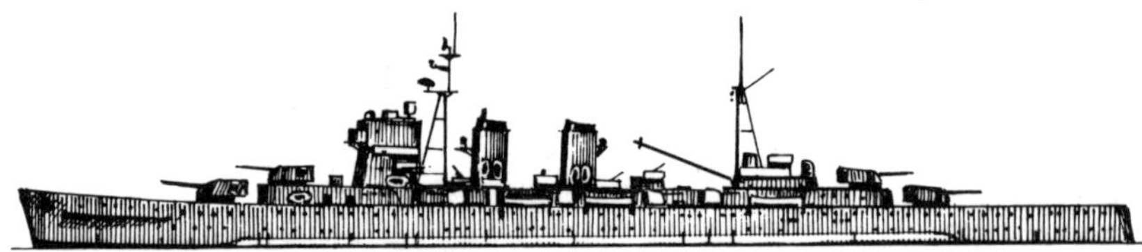

**44.** Sp. **CANARIAS.** *C21.* 1936. Modernised
1953. Cruiser. 10,700 tons. 637 x 64 x 21. (194 x
20 x 6.5). 2 screws; turbines. 30 knots. 8—8-inch
guns (twin). 8—4.7-inch guns. 10 A.A. guns.
May be modernised shortly.

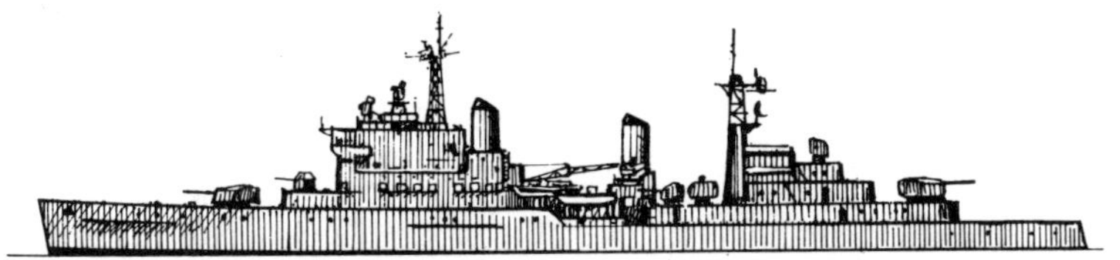

**45.** Br. **TIGER** class. 1959-61. Cruisers. 9,500 tons. 560 x 64 x 23. (170 x 19.5 x 7). 4 screws; turbines. 31 knots. 4—6-inch guns (twin). 6—3-inch guns (twin).
**LION.** *C34,*

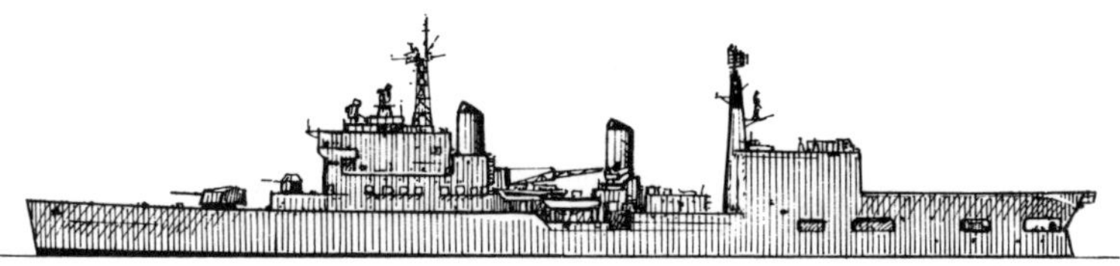

**46.** Br. **BLAKE.** *C99.* 1961. Converted 1965-69. Helicopter Cruiser. Dimensions as above. 2—6-inch guns (twin). 2—3-inch guns (twin). 2 Surface-to-air "Seacat" launchers (quadruple). 4 helicopters. **TIGER.** *C20.*

**47.** In. **MYSORE.** 1940. Modernised 1957. Cruiser. 8,700 tons. 556 x 62 x 21. (169 x 19 x 6.4). 4 screws; turbines. 31 knots. 9—6-inch guns (triple). 8—4-inch A.A. guns (twin). Ex-Br. "Colony" class.

Very similar: Pv. **ALMIRANTE GRAU.** *81,* **CORONEL BOLOGNESI.** *82.* Latter has tripod mainmast (see inset).

**48.** Ar. **LA ARGENTINA.** 1939. Training Cruiser. 6,000 tons. 541 x 57 x 17. (164.9 x 17 x 5). 4 screws; turbines. 25 knots. 9—6-inch guns (triple). 14 A.A. guns. 6 torpedo tubes (triple).

**49.** Pk. **BABUR.** *84.* 1944. Modernised 1957.
Light Cruiser/Training Ship. 5,900 tons. 512 x
52 x 19. (156 x 15.8 x 5.6). 4 screws; turbines.
32 knots. 8—5.25-inch guns (twin). 14 A.A. guns.
6 torpedo tubes (triple). Ex-Br. "Dido" class.

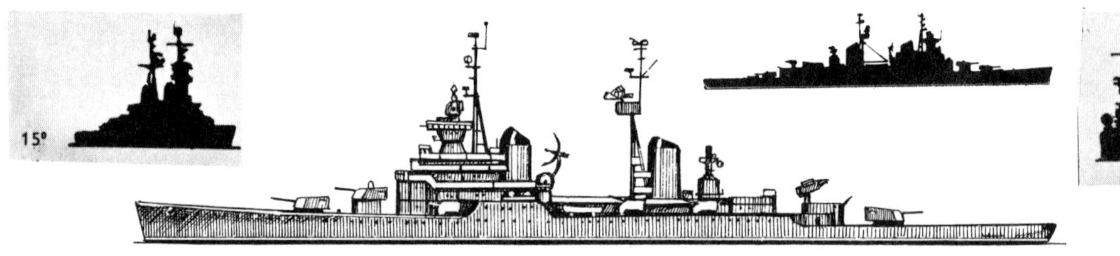

★ **51.** Ru. **DZERZHINSKI.** 1955 c. Modernised
1961-62. Guided Missile Cruiser. 15,500 tons.
689 x 70 x 24.5. (210 x 21.2 x 7.5). 2 screws;
turbines. 34 knots. 9—5.9-inch guns (triple).
12—3.9-inch D.P. guns (twin). 32 A.A. guns.
1 "Guideline" surface-to-surface missile (twin).
10 torpedo tubes (quintuple). Minelayer.
Unit of "Sverdlov" class with missile in place
of "X" turret.

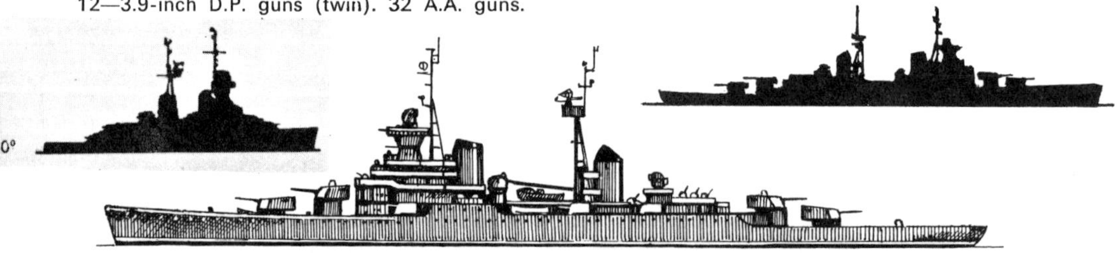

★ **52.** Ru. **SVERDLOV** class. 1951-60. Cruisers.
Details the same as for No. 51 except that they
carry 12—5.9-inch guns and some may have
torpedo tubes removed. Ships vary slightly in
appearance, some having taller bridges and variations in topmasts. Distinguished from No. 53
by longer forecastle.

**ADMIRAL LAZAREV, ADMIRAL SENJA-
VIN, ADMIRAL USHAKOV, ALEKSANDR
NEVSKII, ALEKSANDR SUVOROV, DMITRI
POZHARSKIY, MIKHAIL KUTUSOV, MUR-
MANSK, OKTYABRSKAYA REVOLUTSI-
YA, SVERDLOV, ZHDANOV.**
Ia. **IRIAN.** Formerly Russian "Ordzhonikidze".

**53.** Ru. **CHAPAEV** class. 1948-50. Cruisers.
11,500 tons. 656 x 65 x 21. (200 x 19.7 x 6.4).
Turbines and diesels. 34 knots. 12—5 9-inch guns
(triple). 8—3.9-inch guns (twin). 28 A.A. guns.
Minelayers.
**KOMSOMOLETS, ZHELEZNYAKOV.**

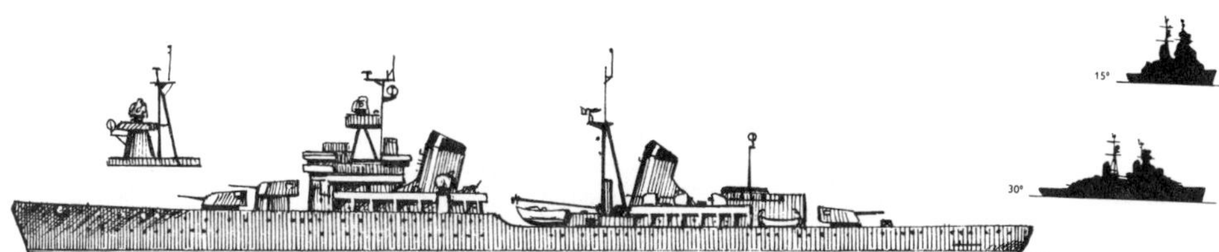

**54.** Ru. **KIROV** class. 1938-44. Cruisers. 8,800
tons. 627 x 59 x 20. (191 x 18 x 6.1). Turbines
and diesels. 34 knots. 9—7.1-inch guns (triple).
8—3.9-inch guns (twin). 22 A.A. guns. 6 torpedo
tubes (triple). Ships may vary slightly.
**KIROV, SLAVA.** A third ship may be in the
Chinese Communist navy.

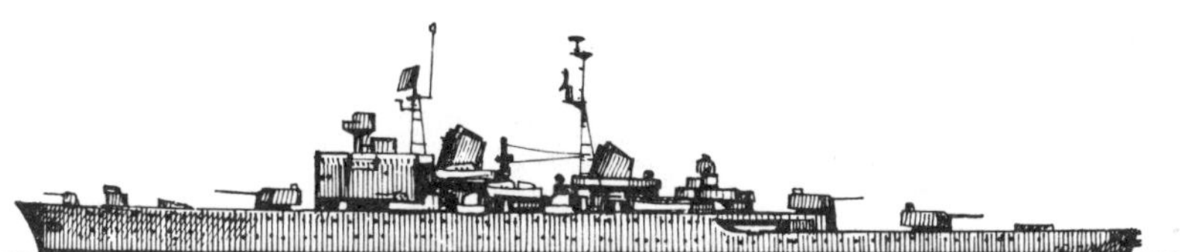

**55.** Sw. **GOTA LEJON.** 1947. Modernised 1958.
Cruiser. 8,200 tons. 597 x 54 x 19. (182 x 16.5 x
6). 2 screws; turbines. 33 knots. 7—6-inch guns
(1 triple and 2 twin). 15 A.A. guns. Minelayer.
Distinguished by short, heavily raking funnels
and by the space between "X" and "Y" turrets.

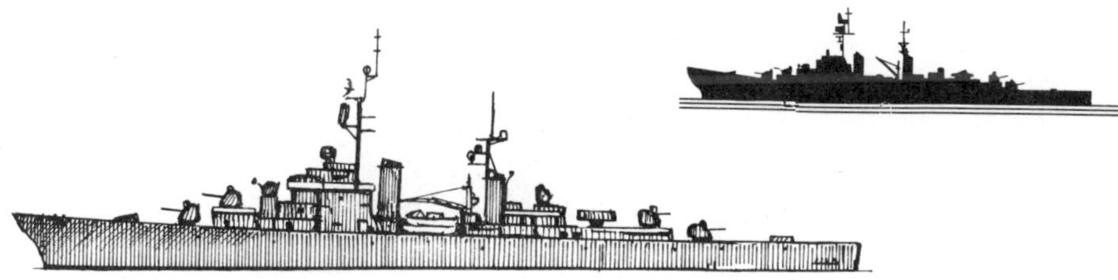

**56.** Am. **NORFOLK.** *1.* 1953. Frigate. 5,600 tons.
540 x 54 x 26. (164.6 x 16.5 x 7.9). 2 screws;
turbines. 32 knots. 8—3-inch D.P. guns. 1 anti-
submarine "Asroc" launcher (8 tubes). 2 anti-
submarine torpedo launchers (triple).

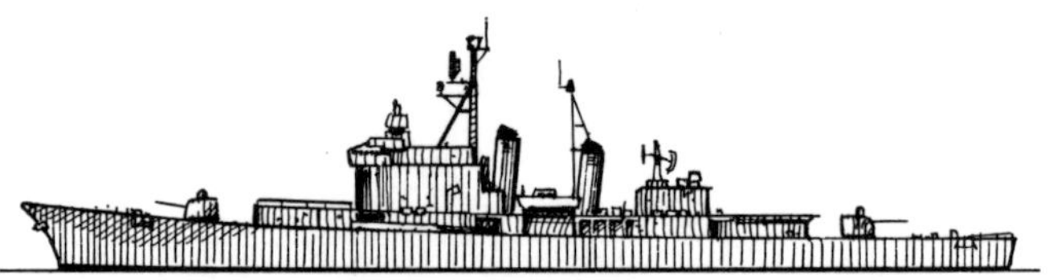

**57.** Am. **MITSCHER** class. 1953. Frigates.
3,700 tons. 493 x 50 x 26. (150.3 x 15.2 x 7.9).
2 screws; turbines. 35 knots. 2—5-inch D.P. guns.
4 torpedo tubes. 2 anti-submarine torpedo
launchers (triple). Facilities for helicopters.
**WILKINSON.** *5,* **WILLIS A. LEE.** *4.* Legs of
foremast tripod slope foreward.

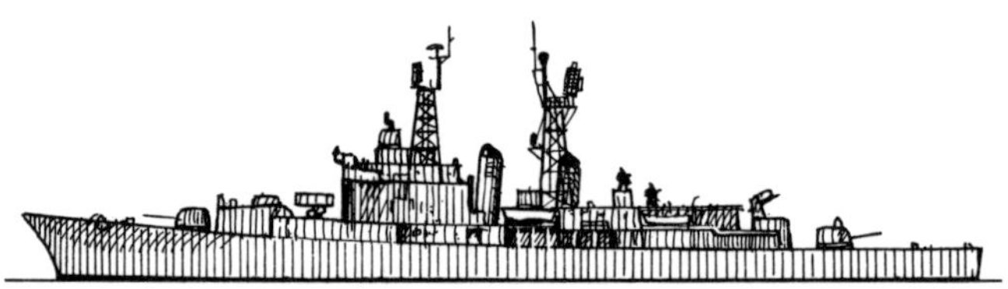

**58.** Am. **MITSCHER** class. 1953. Converted
1966-68. Guided Missile Destroyers. Details as
for No. 57 with following differences; 1 surface-
to-air "Tartar" launcher (single) and anti-
submarine "Asroc" launcher (8 tubes).
**JOHN S. MCCAIN.** *36,* **MITSCHER.** *35.*

**59.** Am. Converted **FORREST SHERMAN** class.
1956-59. Converted 1965-67. Guided Missile
Destroyers. 2,800 tons. 418 x 45 x 20. (127 x
14 x 6.1). 2 screws; turbines. 33 knots. 1—5-inch
D.P. gun. 1 surface-to-air "Tartar" launcher
(single), 1 anti-submarine "Asroc" launcher (8
tubes) 2 torpedo launchers (triple).
**DECATUR.** *31,* **JOHN PAUL JONES.** *32,*
**PARSONS.** *33,* **SOMERS.** *34.*

**60.** It. **IMPAVIDO** class. 1963-64. Guided
Missile Destroyers. 3,200 tons. 430 x 45 x 15.
(131 x 13.6 x 4.5). 2 screws; turbines. 33 knots.
2—5-inch (twin) 4—3-inch A.A. guns. 1 surface-
to-air "Tartar" launcher. Facilities for helicopters
**IMPAVIDO.** *D570,* **INTREPIDO.** *D571.*

**61.** Ge. **HAMBURG** or **STADT** class. 1964-68.
Destroyers. 3,300 tons. 440 x 44 x 17. (134 x
13.4 x 5.2). 2 screws; turbines. 35 knots. 4—3.9-
inch D.P. guns, 8 A.A. guns. 2 depth charge
mortars. (4 barrels), 5 torpedo tubes, 2 anti-
submarine torpedo tubes.
**BAYERN.** *D183,* **HAMBURG.** *D181,* **HES-
SEN.** *D184,* **SCHLESWIG-HOLSTEIN.** *D182.*

**62.** Br. **COUNTY** class. 1962-70. Guided Missile
Destroyers. 5,400 tons. 521 x 54 x 20. (159 x
16.5 x 6). 2 screws; gas and steam turbines.
32.5 knots. 4—4.5-inch D.P. guns (twin).
1 surface-to air "Seaslug" launcher (twin), 2
surface-to-air "Seacat" launchers (quadruple),
1 helicopter.

There are slight variations in the ships and they
are divided into 3 groups as under.
**DEVONSHIRE.** *D02,* **HAMPSHIRE.** *D06 —*
**KENT.** *D12,* **LONDON.** *D16 —* **ANTRIM.** *D18,*
**FIFE.** *D20,* **GLAMORGAN.** *D19,* **NORFOLK.**
*D21.*

**63.** Da. **PEDER SKRAM** class. 1966-67.
Frigates. 2,000 tons. 397 x 40 x 12. (112.6 x
12 x 3.6). 2 screws; gas turbines and diesels.
30 knots. 4—5-inch guns. 4 A.A. guns. Depth
charges.
**HERLUF TROLLE.** *F353,* **PEDER SKRAM.**
*F352.*

**64.** It. **SAN GIORGIO.** *D562.* 1943. Reconstruction 1963-65. Destroyer Leader. 4,500 tons
(full). 467 x 47 x 21. (142 x 14.4 x 6.4). 2 screws;
gas turbines and diesels. 28 knots. 4—5-inch
guns. 3—3-inch A.A. guns. 1 anti-submarine
mortar (3 barrels), 2 anti-submarine torpedo
tubes (triple). Formerly a light cruiser.

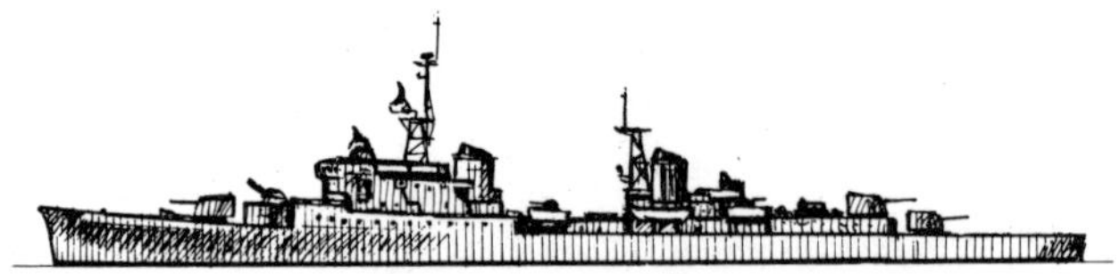

**65.** It. **SAN MARCO.** *D563.* 1956. Destroyer Leader. 5,300 tons (full). Dimensions as for No. 64. 2 screws; turbines. 38 knots. 6—5-inch (twin). 20 A.A. guns. 1 anti-submarine mortar (3 barrels). 4 depth charge throwers, 1 depth charge rack.

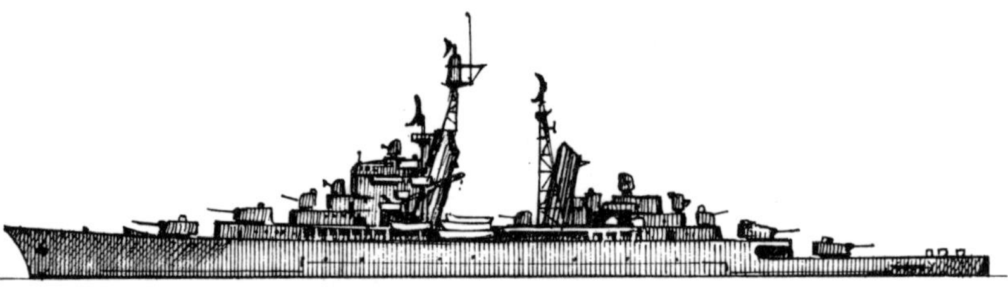

**66.** Du. **DE RUYTER.** *C801.* 1953. Cruiser. 9,500 tons. 614 x 57 x 22. (190 x 17.3 x 6.7). 2 screws; turbines. 32 knots. 8—6-inch guns (twin), 16 A.A. guns.

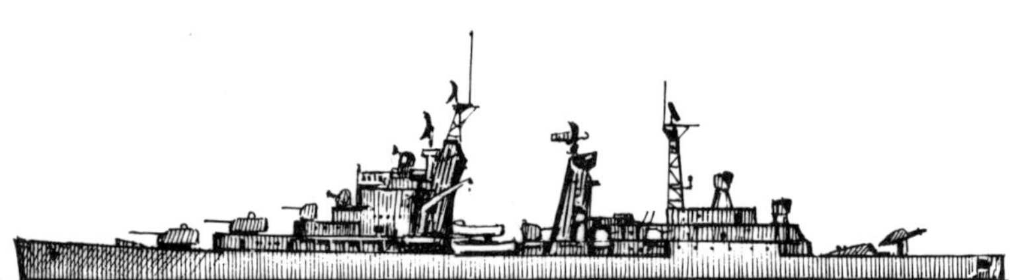

**67.** Du. **DE ZEVEN PROVINCIEN.** *C802.* 1953. Converted 1962-64. Guided Missile Cruiser. 9,900 tons. 609 x 57 x 22. (189 x 17.3 x 7). 2 screws; turbines. 32 knots. 4—6-inch guns (twin), 10 A.A. guns. 1 surface-to-air "Terrier" launcher (twin).

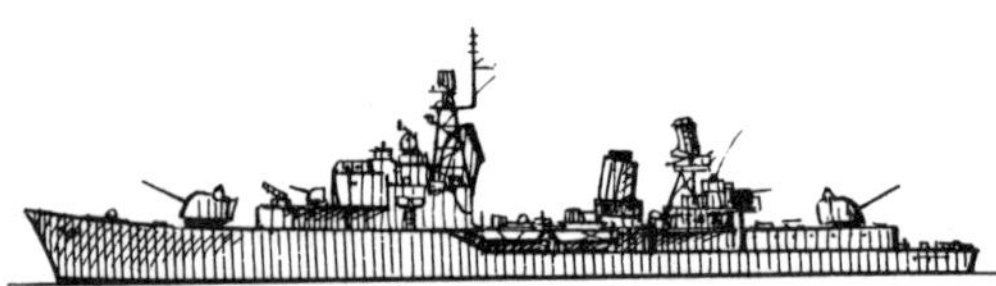

**68.** Du. **FRIESLAND** class. 1956-58. Destroyers. 2,500 tons. 381 x 39 x 17. (116 x 12 x 5.2). 2 screws; turbines. 36 knots. 4—4.7-inch guns (twin). 2 A.A. guns. 2 anti-submarine depth charge mortars (4 barrelled).
**AMSTERDAM.** *D819,* **DRENTHE.** *D816,* **FRIESLAND.** *D812,* **GRONINGEN.** *D813,* **LIMBURG.** *D814,* **OVERIJSSEL.** *D815,* **ROTTERDAM.** *D818,* **UTRECHT.** *D817.*

**69.** Du. **HOLLAND** class. 1954-55. Destroyers. 2,200 tons. 371 x 38 x 17. (113 x 11.4 x 5). 2 screws; turbines. 32 knots. 4—4.7-inch guns (twin). 2 anti-submarine depth charge mortars (4 barrelled).
**GELDERLAND.** *D811,* **HOLLAND.** *D808,* **NOORD BRABANT.** *D810,* **ZEELAND.** *D809,* Distinguished from No. 68 by absence of small gun before the bridge.

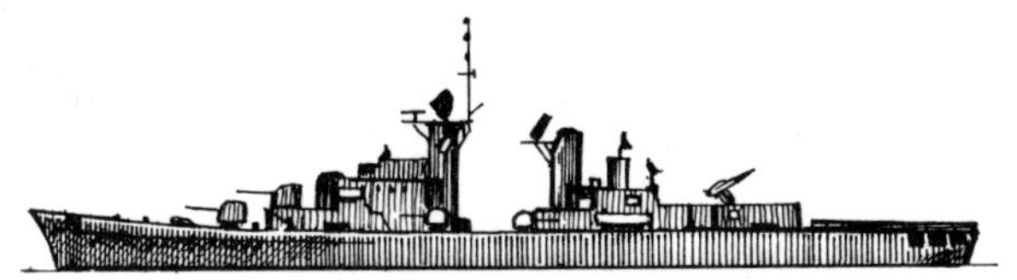

**70.** It. **AUDACE** class. Guided Missile Destroyers.
4,400 tons (full). 446 x 47 x 15. (136 x 14 x 4.6).
2 screws; turbines. 33 knots. 2—5-inch D.P. guns.
4—3-inch A.A. guns. 1 surface-to-air "Tartar"
launcher (single). 6 anti-submarine torpedo tubes
(triple). 2 helicopters.
**ARDITO, AUDACE.**

**71.** Ja. Improved **MOON** class. 1967-69.
Destroyers. 3,100 tons. 446 x 44 x 14.5. (136 x
13.4 x 4.4). 2 screws; turbines. 32 knots. 2—5-
inch D.P. guns. 2 anti-submarine homing torpedo
launchers (triple), 1 anti-submarine "Asroc"
launcher (8 tubes), 1 rocket launcher (4 barrels),
1 anti-submarine Drone helicopter.
**KIKUZUKI.** *165,* **MOCHIZUKI.** *166,* **NAGAT-
SUKI.** *167,* **TAKATSUKI.** *164.*

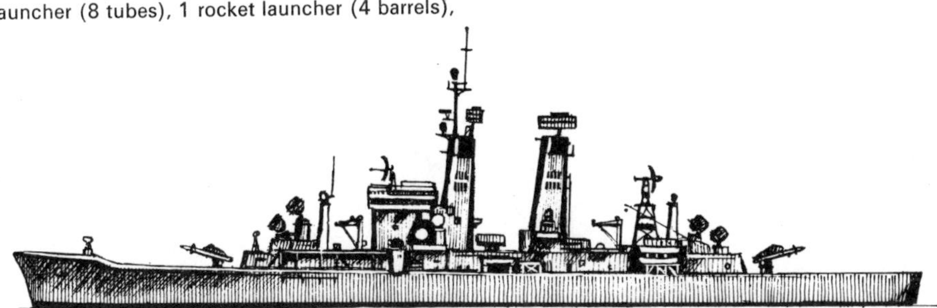

**72.** Am. **ALBANY** class. 1945-46. Converted
1959-64. Guided Missile Cruisers. 13,700 tons.
673 x 70 x 27. (205 x 21.6 x 8.2). 4 screws;
turbines. 33 knots. 2—5-inch D.P. guns. 2
surface-to-air "Talos" launchers (twin), 2
surface-to-air "Tartar" launchers (twin), 1 anti-
submarine "Asroc" launcher (8 tubes), 2 anti-
submarine torpedo launchers (triple). Converted
from heavy cruisers of "Oregon City" and
"Baltimore" classes.
**ALBANY.** *10,* **CHICAGO.** *11,* **COLUMBUS.**
*12.*

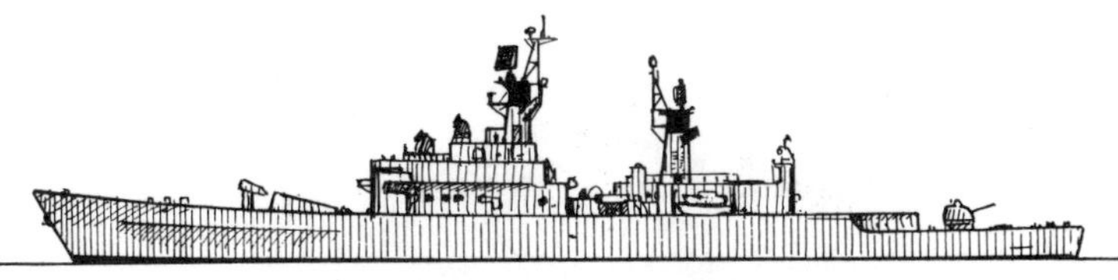

**73.** Am. **BELKNAP** class. 1964-67. Guided
Missile Frigates. 6,600 tons. 547 x 55 x 28.8.
(167 x 17 x 8.7). 2 screws; turbines. 34 knots.
1—5-inch D.P. gun. 2—3-inch A.A. guns. 1 twin
launcher for surface-to-air "Terrier" or anti-
submarine "Asroc" missiles. 2 anti-submarine
torpedo launchers (triple). Facilities for helicopters.
**BELKNAP.** *26,* **BIDDLE.** *34,* **FOX.** *33,* **HORNE.**
*30,* **JOSEPHUS DANIELS.** *27,* **JOUETT.** *29,*
**STERETT.** *31,* **WAINWRIGHT.** *28,* **WILLIAM.
H. STANDLEY.** *32.*
  Similar to "Leahy" class No. 74, but has gun
aft in place of launcher and no "Asroc" before
the bridge.

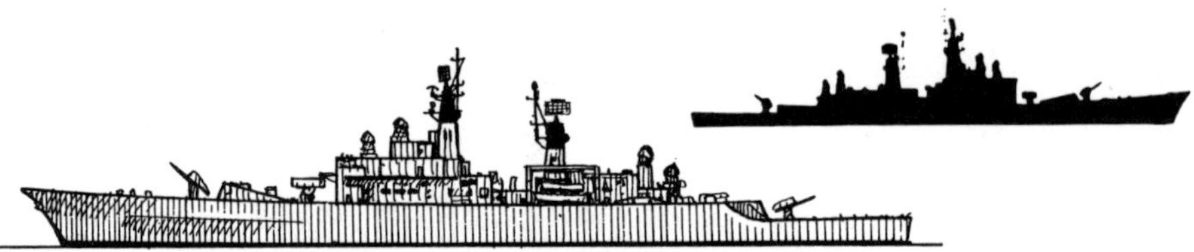

**74.** Am. **LEAHY** class. 1962-64. Guided Missile Frigates. 5.700 tons. 533 x 55 x 24.5. (163 x 17 x 7.4). 2 screws; turbines. 34 knots. 4—3-inch A.A. guns (twin), 2 surface-to-air "Terrier" launchers, (twin), 1 anti-submarine "Asroc" launcher (8 tubes), 2 triple torpedo launchers.

DALE. *19,* ENGLAND. *22,* GRIDLEY. *21,* HALSEY. *23,* HARRY E. YARNELL. *17,* LEAHY. *16,* REEVES. *24,* RICHMOND K. TURNER. *20.*
Similar; **WORDEN.** *18,* but has only 1 Director aft, see silhouette No. 644.

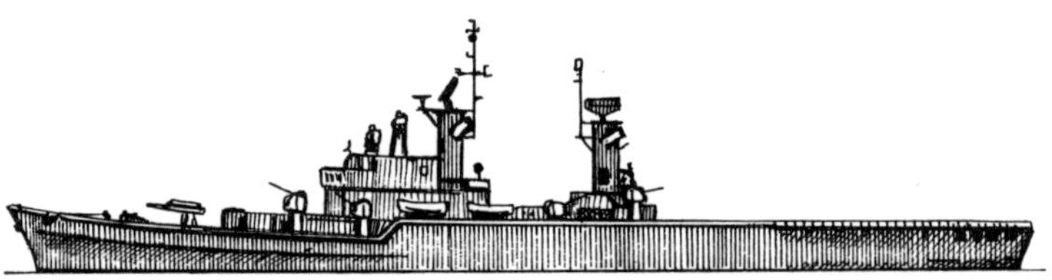

**75.** It. **VITTORIO VENETO.** *550.* 1969. Guided Missile Cruiser. 8,900 tons. 558 x 64 x 17. (170 x 19 x 5.2). 2 screws; turbines. 32 knots. 8—3-inch A.A. guns. 1 twin launcher for surface-to-air "Terrier" or anti-submarine "Asroc" missiles.

6 anti-submarine torpedo tubes (triple). Helicopters.
Recognized by unusual hull form and long deck aft.

**76.** It. **ANDREA DORIA** class. 1964. Guided Missile Escort Cruisers. 6,500 tons (full). 490 x 56 x 16. (149 x 17 x 5). 2 screws; turbines. 30 knots. 8—3-inch A.A. guns. 1 surface-to-air "Terrier" launcher (twin). 6 anti-submarine torpedo tubes (triple). 4 helicopters.
**ANDREA DORIA.** *553,* **CAIO DUILIO.** *554.*
Funnels are very small and tend to "disappear" from a distance.

**77.** Am. **CLAUD JONES** class. 1959-60. Escorts. 1,500 tons. 310 x 37 x 18. (95 x 11.3 x 5.5). Diesels. 22 knots. 1— or 2—3-inch guns. 6 anti-submarine torpedo tubes (triple).
**CHARLES BERRY.** *1035,* **CLAUD JONES.** *1033,* **JOHN R. PERRY.** *1034,* **McMORRIS.** *1036.* Very tiny funnels and foreward one tends to merge into superstructure.

**78.** Am. **COONTZ** class. 1960-66. Guided Missile Frigates. 4,700 tons. 513 x 53 x 25. (156 x 16 x 7.6). 2 screws; turbines. 34 knots. 1—5-inch D.P. gun. 4—3-inch A.A. guns (twin). 1 surface-to-air "Terrier" launcher (twin). 1 anti-submarine "Asroc" launcher (8 tubes). 6 anti-submarine torpedo launchers (triple).

COONTZ. *9,* DAHLGREN. *12,* DEWEY. *14,* FARRAGUT. *6,* KING. *10,* LUCE. *7,* MAHAN. *11,* MACDONOUGH. *8,* PREBBLE. *15,* WILLIAM V. PRATT. *13.*
Second mast is quite distinctive. "Asroc" before the bridge.

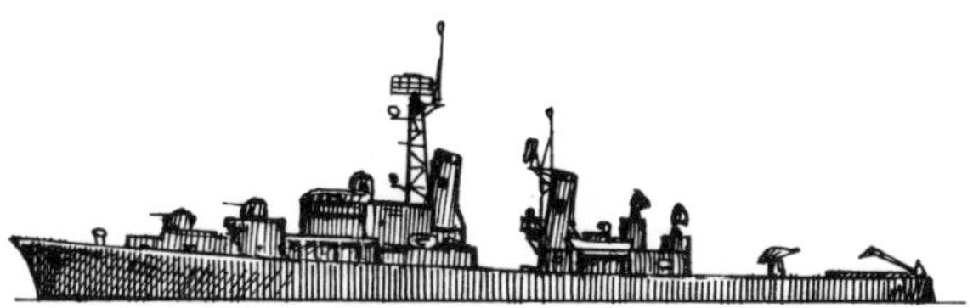

**79.** Ja. **AMATSUKAZE.** *163.* 1965. Guided Missile Destroyer. 3,100 tons. 430 x 44 x 14. (131 x 13.4 x 4.2). 2 screws; turbines. 33 knots. 4—3-inch A.A. guns (twin). 1 surface-to-air "Tartar" launcher (single). 2 anti-submarine "Hedgehogs". Anti-submarine torpedo dropping gear. 1 helicopter. Similar to "Charles F. Adams" class but has 2 guns mounted on superstructure foreward.

**80.** Am. **CHARLES F. ADAMS** class. 1960-64. Guided Missile Destroyers. 3,400 tons. 437 x 47 x 20. (133 x 14.3 x 6.1). 2 screws; turbines. 35 knots. 2—5-inch D.P. guns. 1 surface-to-air "Tartar" launcher (single or twin). 1 anti-submarine "Asroc" launcher (8 tubes). 6 torpedo tubes (anti-submarine) (triple).
BARNEY. *6,* BERKELEY. *15,* BUCHANAN. *14,* CHARLES F. ADAMS. *2,* CLAUDE V. RICKETTS. *5,* CONYNGHAM. *17,* HENRY B. WILSON. *7,* HOEL. *13,* JOHN KING. *3,* JOSEPH STRAUSS. *16,* LAWRENCE. *4,* LYNDE McCORMICK. *8,* ROBISON. *12,* SAMPSON. *10,* SEMMES. *18,* SELLERS. *11,* TATTNALL. *19,* TOWERS. *9.* The following have stem anchors: BENJAMIN STODDERT. *22,* COCHRANE. *21,* GOLDSBOROUGH. *20,* RICHARD E. BYRD. *23,* WADDELL. *24.*

**81.** Au. **CHARLES F. ADAMS** class. 1965-68. Guided Missile Destroyers. Particulars as for No. 80 except that they have 2 anti-submarine "Ikara" launchers in place of the "Asroc" launchers.
BRISBANE. *41,* HOBART. *39,* PERTH. *38.*
Distinguished from No. 80 by superstructure between funnels.

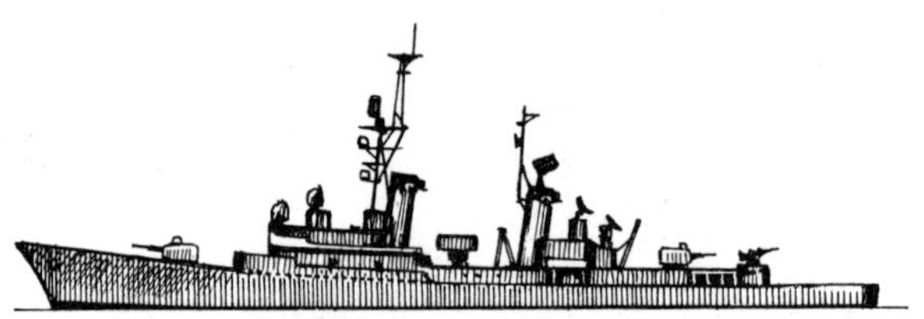

**82.** Ge. **CHARLES F. ADAMS** class. 1969-70.
Guided Missile Destroyers. Particulars as for
No. 80 with addition of 1 depth charge thrower.
**LUTJENS.** *D185,* **MOLDERS.** *D186,* **ROM-
MEL.** *D187.*
Distinguished by light mast from second funnel.

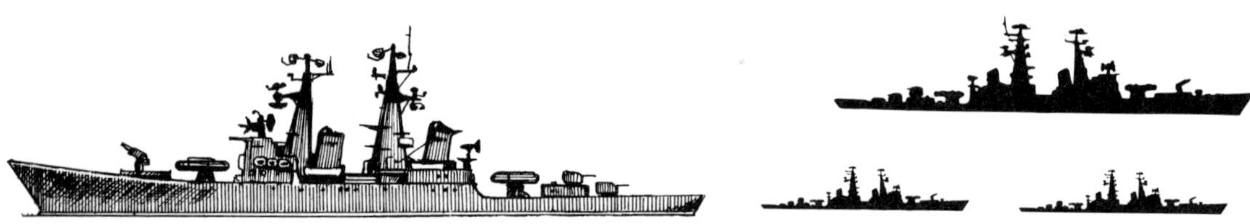

★ **83.** Ru. **KYNDA** class. 1962 and onwards.
Guided Missile Destroyer Leaders. 4,800 tons.
465 x 51 x 19. (142 x 15.5 x 5.8). 2 screws;
steam and gas turbines. 35 knots. 4—3-inch A.A.
guns (twin). 2 surface-to-surface "Shaddock"
launchers (quadruple). 1 surface-to-air "Goa"
launcher (twin). 2 anti-submarine rocket launchers (12 barrels). 6 torpedo tubes (triple).
**ADMIRAL GOLOVKO, GROM, GROZNY,
VARYAG.**
Very distinctive pyramidal tower masts and
prominent launchers.

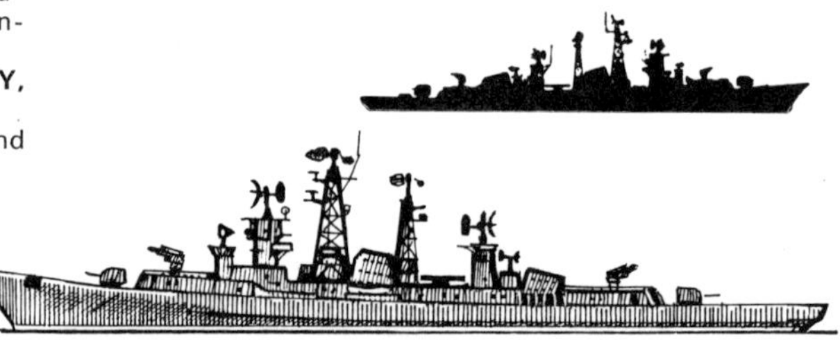

★ **84.** Ru. **KASHIN** class. 1964 and onwards.
Guided Missile Destroyers. 4,300 tons. 475 x
53 x 19. (145 x 16 x 5.8). Gas turbines. 35 knots.
4—3-inch A.A. guns (twin). 2 surface-to-air
"Goa" launchers (twin). 5 torpedo tubes (quintuple). Unmistakable in appearance with two
(paired) very short funnels and 4 masts or towers.
10 ships in class among which are:—
**BOIKI, OBRAZTSOVYI, PROVORNYI, SLA-
VNY, SOOBRAZITELNYI, STEREGUSHCH-
YI.**

★ **85.** Ru. **TALLIN.** 1950 c. Destroyer. 3,200 tons.
430 x 44 x 16. (131 x 13.4 x 4.9). 2 screws;
turbines. 35 knots. 4—5.1-inch D.P. guns (twin).
16 A.A. guns. 10 torpedo tubes (quintuple). 2
depth charge rocket launchers. Mines. Very
widely spaced funnels; very large bridge director
tower.
Sometimes known as **NEUSTRASHIMYI.**

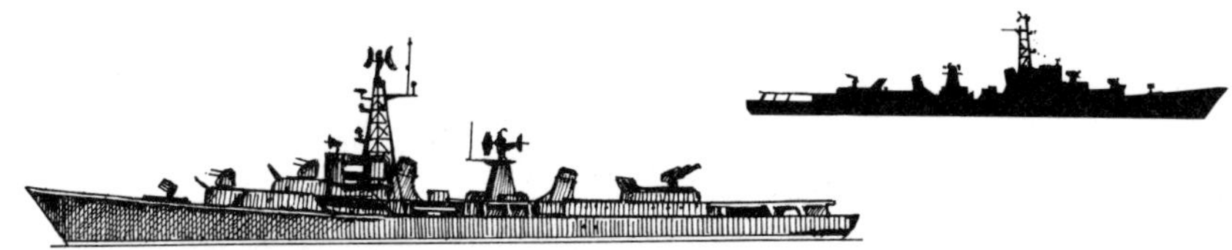

**86.** Ru. **KANIN** class. 1958 c. Converted 1967-onwards. Guided Missile Destroyers. 3,600 tons. 456 x 49 x 18. (139 x 14.9 x 5.5). 2 screws; turbines. 34 knots. 8—57 m.m.-guns (quadruple). 1 surface-to-air "SA-N-I" launcher (twin). 3 anti-submarine rocket launchers (12 barrel). 10 anti-submarine torpedo tubes (quintuple). Facilities for helicopter with platform. Converted from "Krupny" class; see No. 88. At least 2 ships in class. Pyramidal structure between funnels.

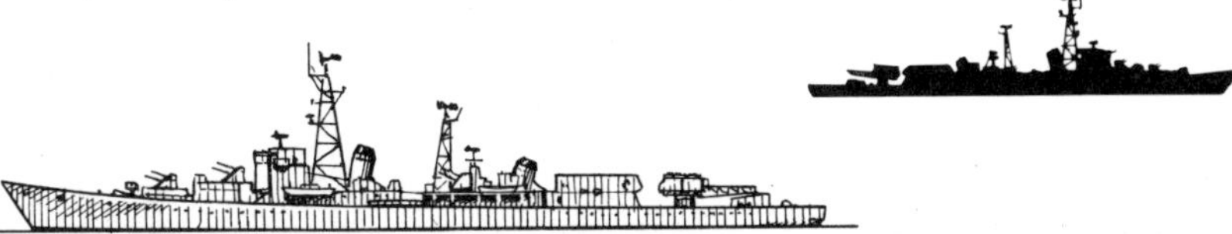

**87.** Ru. **KILDIN** class. 1958 c. Guided Missile Destroyers. 3,000 tons. 415 x 43.7 x 16. (126.5 x 13 x 4.9). 2 screws; turbines. 35 knots. 16—57-m.m. A.A. guns (quadruple). 1 surface-to-surface "Strela" launcher. 2 anti-submarine rocket launchers (16 barrel). 4 ships in class. Very similar to "Krupny" class, No. 88 but has no launcher foreward.

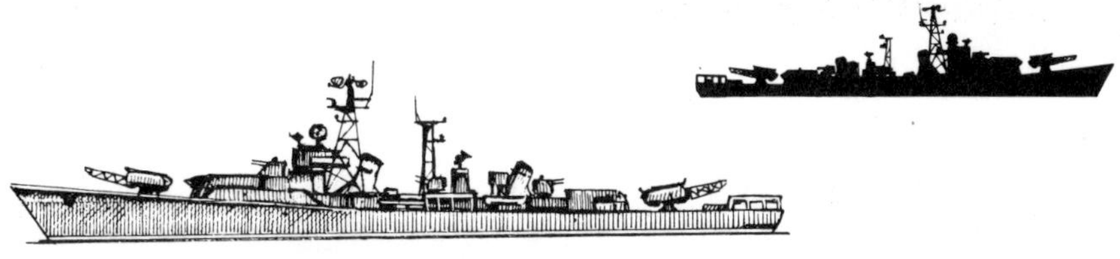

**88.** Ru. **KRUPNY** class. 1958 c. Guided Missile Destroyers. 3,700 tons. 453 x 44 x 17. (138 x 13.4 x 5.2). 2 screws; turbines. 34 knots. 16—57-m.m. A.A. guns (quadruple). 2 surface-to-surface "Strela" launchers. 6 anti-submarine torpedo launchers (triple). 6 in class including :— **GNEVNYI, GORDYI, GREMYASHCHYI, PLAMYONNY.**

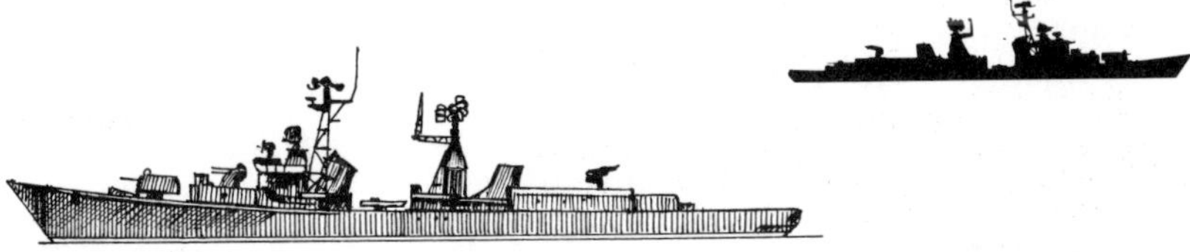

**89.** Ru. **KOTLIN SAM** class. 1954-57. Converted 1960 onwards. Guided Missile Destroyers. 2,900 tons. 415 x 42 x 16. (126.5 x 12.8 x 4.9). 2 screws; turbine. 36 knots. 4—57-m.m. A.A. guns (quadruple). 2—3.9-inch D.P. guns (twin). 1 surface-to-air "Goa" launchers (twin). 6 depth charge throwers. 5 ships in class. Pyramidal structure between funnels. In later ships the second funnel conforms more to that of the conventional vessels. (See No. 90.)

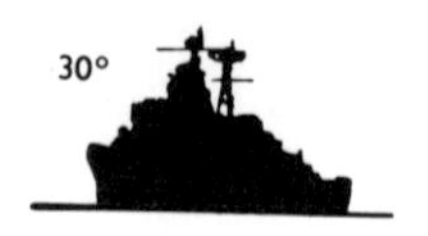

**90.** Ru. **KOTLIN** class. 1954-57. Particulars as for No. 89 except for weapons etc. 4—5.1-inch D.P. guns (twin). 16 A.A. guns (quadruple). 10 torpedo tubes. 6 depth charge throwers. Mines. Differs from modified "Kotlin" class (No. 91) by having torpedo tubes abaft second funnel. Some have helicopter platform aft. There are about 25 ships in the two classes among which are :—
**BESSLEDNYI, BURLIVYI, NASTOYCHIVYI, PLAMENNYI, SPRAVETLIVYI, SVETLIVYI-ARE, SVETLYI, VDOKHNOVENNYII, VOZ-MUSHCHENNY, NAPORISTYI.**

**91.** Ru. Modified **KOTLIN** class. All particulars as for No. 90 except for absence of torpedo tubes abaft second funnel. For possible names see No. 90.

**92.** Ru. **KOLA** class. Destroyer Escorts. 1,500 tons. 315 x 33 x 11.5. (96 x 10 x 3.5). 2 screws; turbines. 31 knots. 4—3.9-inch D.P. guns. 4 A.A. guns. 3 torpedo tubes (triple). Depth charge throwers and racks. Mines.
Six ships in the class. The only Soviet Destroyer type with guns in A, B, X & Y positions.

**93.** Ru. **SKORY** class. 1953 and onwards. Destroyers. 2,600 tons. 420 x 41 x 15. (128 x 12.5 x 4.6). 2 screws; turbines. 36 knots. 4—5.1-inch (twin). 2—3-inch A.A. guns. 7 or 8 smaller A.A. guns. 10 torpedo tubes (quintuple). 4 depth charge throwers. Mines.
About 50 of this class and of modified type (see No. 94) are in Soviet fleet among which are :—
**BESMENNYI, BEZUKORIZNENNYI, OT-CHAYANNYI, OTVETSTVENNYI, OZHES-TOCHENNYI, OZHIVLENNYI, SERIDTYI, SERIOZNYI, SMELNYI, SMOTRYASH-CHYI, SOKRUSHITELNYI, SOLIDNYI, SO-VERSHENNYI, SPOSOBNYI, STATNYI, STEPENNYI, STOJKYI, STREMITELNYI, SUROVYI, SVOBODNYI, VDUMCHIVYI, VRAZUMITELNYI.**

Also *Ph.* **GROM, WICHER.**
Also *Eg.* **AL NASSER, AL ZAFR, DUMYAT, SUEZ.**
Also *Ia.* **BRAWIDJAJA, DIPONEGORO, IS-KANDARMUDA, SANDJAJA, SAWUNG-GALING, SILIWANGI, SINGAMANGAR-ADJA.**

**94.** Ru. Modified **SKORY** class. Some of the original "Skory" class ships were modified and there are variations in masts.
The principal appearance differences are that the modified ships have the Torpedo Tubes between the funnels suppressed, no large director on bridge, and larger funnel cowls. Both these types are the only short-forecastle destroyers in the Soviet fleet.

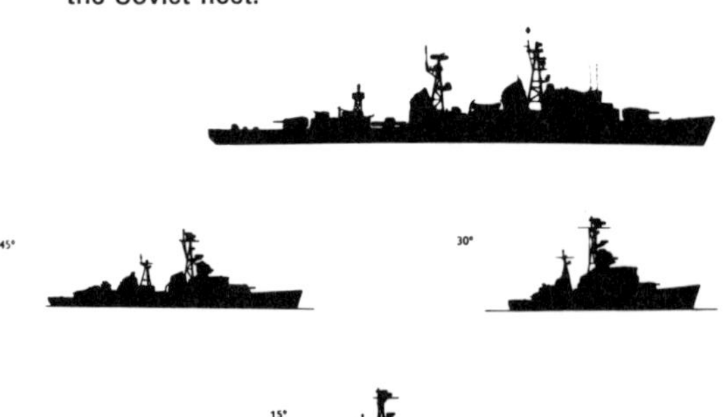

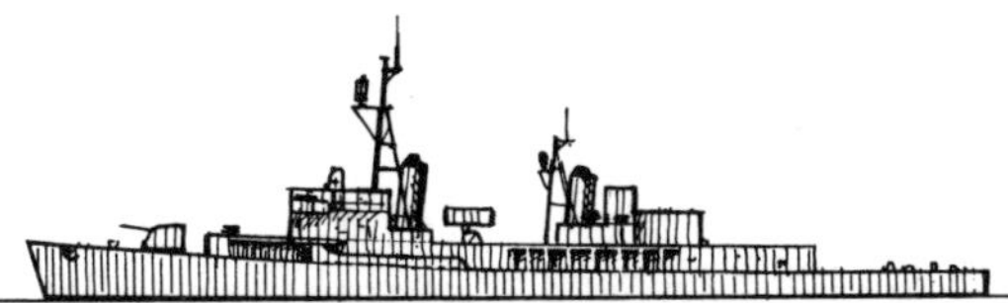

**95.** Am. **CARPENTER** class. 1946-49. Modernised 1962. Destroyers. 2,400 tons 390 x 41 x 19. (119 x 12.4 x 5.8). 2 screws; turbines. 34 knots. 2—5-inch D.P. guns. 1 "Asroc" anti-submarine launcher (8 tubes). 2 triple torpedo launchers. Laid down as units of the "Gearing" class.
**CARPENTER.** *825,* **ROBERT A. OWENS,** *827.*
Distinguished from No. 96 by mainmast and absence of gun aft.

**97.** Am. Modernised **GEARING** class (FRAM 11). 1945-47. Modernised 1962. Destroyers. Tonnage etc. as for number 96. 6—5-inch D.P. guns. 2 anti-submarine torpedo launchers (triple). 2 fixed anti-submarine torpedo tubes. 2 drone anti-submarine helicopters.
**FRANK KNOX.** *742,* **KENNETH D. BAILEY.** *713,* **DUNCAN.** *874,* **ERNEST G. SMALL.** *838,* **GOODRICH.** *831.*

*Similar* but with mast abaft second funnel as number 96: **BENNER.** *807,* **CHEVALIER.** *805,* **EVERETT F. LARSON.** *830,* **PERKINS.** *877.*
*See silhouette number 156.*

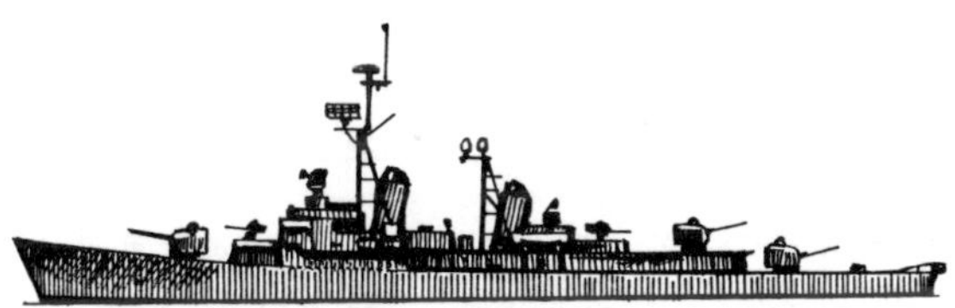

**98.** Am. **FORREST SHERMAN** class. 1955-59. Destroyers. 2,800 tons. 418 x 45 x 20. (127.5 x 13.7 x 6.1). 2 screws; turbines. 32 knots. 2—5-inch D.P. guns. 4—3-inch A.A. guns (twin). 2 "Hedgehogs". 2 anti-submarine torpedo launchers (triple).
**BIGELOW.** *942,* **EDSON.** *946,* **FORREST SHERMAN.** *931,* **MULLINIX.** *944,* **RICHARD S. EDWARDS.** *950,* **TURNER JOY.** *951.*

**96.** Am. Modernised **GEARING** class (FRAM 1). 1945-47. Modernised 1959 onwards. Destroyers. 2,400 tons. 391 x 41 x 19. (119 x 12.4 x 5.8). 2 screws; turbines. 34 knots. 4—5-inch D.P. guns. 1 anti-submarine "Asroc" launcher (8 tubes). 2 anti-submarine torpedo launchers (triple). Facilities for drone anti-submarine helicopter (DASH).

Some of the ships listed below have turrets in "A" and "B" positions. *See silhouette number 174.*
**AGERHOLM.** *826,* **ARNOLD J. ISBELL.** *869,* **BAUSELL.** *845,* **BORDELON.** *881,* **BRINKLEY BASS.** *887,* **CHARLES H. ROAN.** *853,* **CHARLES P. CECIL.** *835,* **CHARLES R. WARE.** *865,* **CONE.** *866,* **CORRY.** *817,* **DAMATO.** *871,* **DENNIS J. BUCKLEY.** *808,* **DYESS.** *880,* **EUGENE A. GREENE.** *711,* **EVERSOLE.** *789,* **FECHTELER.** *870,* **FISKE.** *842,* **FLOYD B. PARKS.** *884,* **FORREST ROYAL.** *872,* **FURSE.** *882,* **GEARING.** *710,* **GEORGE K. MacKENZIE.** *836,* **GLENNON.** *840,* **GURKE.** *783,* **HAMNER.** *718,* **HANSON.** *832,* **HAROLD J. ELLISON.** *864,* **HAWKINS.** *873,* **HENDERSON.** *785,* **HENRY W. TUCKER.** *875,* **HIGSBEE.** *806,* **HOLDER.** *819,* **HOLLISTER.** *788,* **JAMES E. KYES.** *787,* **JOHN R. CRAIG.** *885,* **JOHNSTON.** *821,* **JOSEPH P. KENNEDY Jr.** *850,* **LEARY.** *879,* **LEONARD F. MASON.** *852,* **McKEAN.** *784,* **MEREDITH.** *890,* **MYLES C. FOX.** *829,* **NEW.** *818,* **NEWMAN K. PERRY.** *883,* **NOA.** *841,* **O'HARE.** *889,* **ORLECK.** *886,* **OZBOURN.** *846,* **PERRY.** *844,* **POWER.** *839,* **RICH.** *820,* **RICHARD B. ANDERSON.** *786,* **RICHARD E. KRAUS.** *849,* **ROBERT H. McCARD.** *822,* **ROBERT L. WILSON.** *847,* **ROGERS.** *876,* **ROWAN.** *782,* **RUPERTUS.** *851,* **SAMUEL B. ROBERTS.** *823,* **SARSFIELD.** *837,* **SOUTHERLAND.** *743,* **STEINAKER.** *863,* **STICKELL.** *888,* **STRIBLING.** *867,* **THEODORE E. CHANDLER.** *717,* **VESOLE.** *878,* **VOGELGESANG.** *862,* **WARRINGTON.** *843,* **WILLIAM C. LAWE.** *763,* **WILLIAM M. WOOD.** *715,* **WILLIAM R. RUSH.** *714,* **WILTSIE.** *716.*

*Known* to have "A" and "B" turret: **SHELTON.** *790.*
*Similar* but bridge and superstructure more enclosed, used as a test ship for ABC warfare: **HERBERT A. THOMAS.** *833.*
*Also similar:* **BASILONE.** *824,* **EPPERSON.** *719.*
*Similar* (no "Asroc"); **FRED T. BERRY.** *764,* **HARWOOD.** *861,* **KEPPLER.** *765,* **LLOYD THOMAS.** *764,* **McCAFFERY.** *860,* **NORRIS.** *859. See silhouette number 68.*

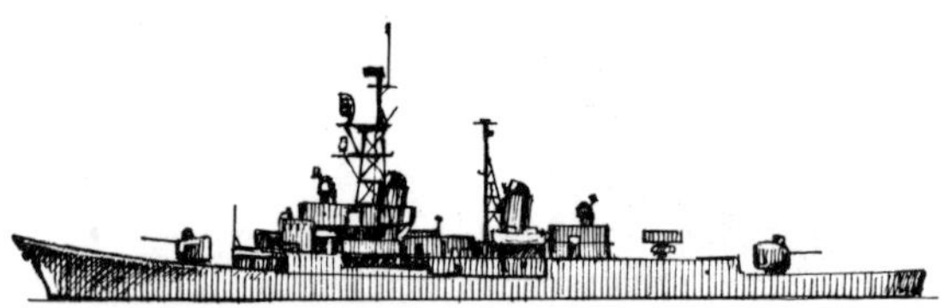

**99.** Am. **FORREST SHERMAN** class. 1955-59. Modernised 1964-71. Details as number 98 except for the armament. 2—5-inch D.P. guns. 1 anti-submarine "Asroc" launcher (8 tubes). 2 anti-submarine torpedo launchers (triple). **BARRY.** *933,* **BLANDY.** *943,* **DAVIS.** *937,* **DU PONT.** *941,* **HULL.** *945,* **JONAS INGRAM.** *938,* **MANLEY.** *940,* **MORTON.** *948.*

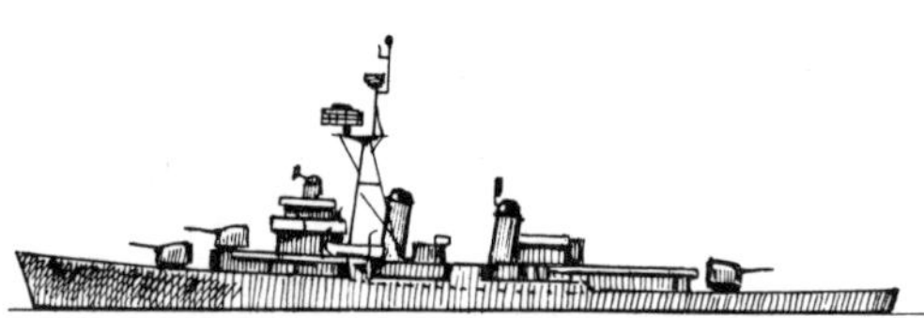

**101.** Am. **HAZELWOOD.** *531.* 1943. Modernised. Destroyer. 2,100 tons. 377 x 40 x 18. (115 x 11.9 x 5.5). 2 screws; turbines. 35 knots 3—5-inch D.P. guns. 2 anti-submarine torpedo launchers (triple). Modified unit of the "Fletcher" class as test ship for "DASH".

**103.** It. Ex-**FLETCHER** class. 1942-43. Modernised c.1960. Destroyers. 2,100 tons. 377 x 40 x 18. (114.3 x 12 x 5.5). 2 screws; turbines. 35 knots. 2—5-inch D.P. guns. 4—3-inch A.A. guns (twin). 1 anti-submarine "Alpha" weapon. 2 torpedo launchers (triple). 2 "Hedgehogs". Transferred from U.S.A. to Italy in 1970. **FANTE. LANCIERE.** *See No. 107.*

**100.** Am. Modernised **ALLEN M. SUMNER** class (FRAM 11). 1944-46. Destroyers. 2,200 tons. 377 x 41 x 19. (114.8 x 12.4 x 5.8). 2 screws; turbines. 34 knots. 6—5-inch D.P. guns (twin). 2 anti-submarine torpedo launchers (triple). 2 anti-submarine torpedo tubes (fixed). 2 "Hedgehogs". 2 drone anti-submarine helicopters "DASH".
**ALLEN M. SUMNER.** *692,* **ALFRED A. CUNNINGHAM.** *752,* **AULT.** *698,* **BLUE.** *744,* **BORIE.** *709,* **BUCK.** *761,* **CHARLES S. SPERRY.** *697,* **COLLETT.** *730,* **DE HAVEN.** *727,* **DOUGLAS H. FOX.** *779,* **HUGH PURVIS.** *709,* **INGRAHAM.** *697,* **JAMES C. OWENS.** *776,* **JOHN W. THOMASON.** *760,* **JOHN A. BOLE.** *755,* **LAFFEY.** *724,* **LYMAN K. SWENSON.** *729,* **LOFBERG.** *759,* **LOWRY.** *770,* **MANSFIELD.** *728,* **MASSEY.** *779,* **MOALE.** *693,* **O'BRIEN.** *725,* **PUTNAM.** *757,* **ROBERT K. HUNTINGTON.** *781,* **STORMES.** *780,* **TAUSSIG.** *746,* **WALDRON.** *699,* **WALKE.** *723,* **WALLACE L. LIND.** *703,* **ZELLARS.** *777.*

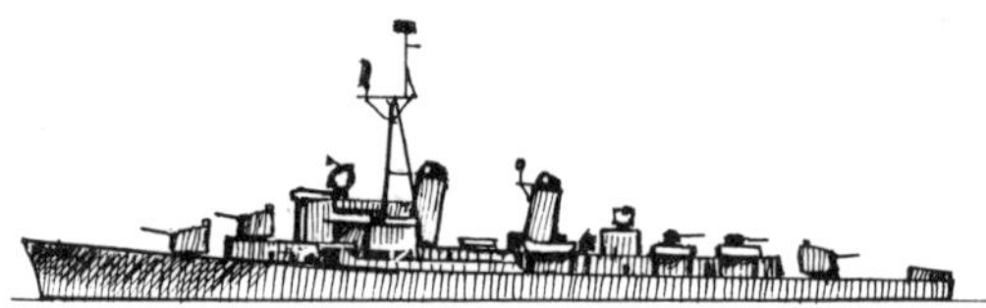

**104.** Am. **ALLEN M. SUMNER** class. 1944-45. Destroyers. 2,200 tons. 377 x 41 x 19. (114.8 x 12.4 x 5.8). 2 screws; turbines. 34 knots. 6—5-inch D.P. guns (twin). 4—3-inch A.A. guns (twin). 2 anti-submarine torpedo launchers (triple). 2 "Hedgehogs". Depth charges.
**BARTON.** *722,* **BEATTY.** *762,* **COMPTON.** *706,* **GAINARD.** *706,* **HANK.** *702,* **HARLAN R. DICKSON.** *708,* **HENLEY.** *762,* **JOHN R. PIERCE.** *753,* **JOHN W. WEEKS.** *701,* **MADDOX.** *731,* **PURDY.** *734,* **SOLEY.** *707,* **WILLARD KEITH.** *775.*

10 ships of this class were converted to minelayers and called the "Smith" class: **ADAMS.** *27,* **GWIN.** *33,* **HARRY F. BAUER.** *26,* **HENRY A. WILEY.** *29,* **LINDSEY.** *32,* **ROBERT H. SMITH.** *23,* **SHANNON.** *25,* **SHEA.** *30,* **THOMAS E. FRASER.** *24,* **TOLMAN.** *28.*

*China:* 2 transferred from the U.S.A. in 1970.

**105.** Am. **FLETCHER** and **LATER FLETCHER** classes (4 guns). 1943-45. Destroyers. 2,100 tons. 376 x 40 x 18. (114.7 x 11.9 x 5.5). 2 screws; turbines. 35 knots. 4—5-inch D.P. guns. 6 A.A. guns. 2 anti-submarine torpedo launchers (triple). (Not in all ships). 2 "Hedgehogs".
**ABBOT.** *629,* **BRAINE.** *630,* **COWELL.** *547,* **DALEY.** *519,* **MULLANY.** *528,* **ROSS.** *563,* **ROWE.** *564,* **STODDARD.** *566,* **TRATHEN.** *530.*

*Later* Fletcher: **BLACK.** *666,* **DASHIELL.** *659,* **HUNT.** *674,* **McNAIR.** *679,* **PICKING.** *685,* **UHLMANN.** *687.*

Ar.: **BROWN.** *20,* **ESPORA.** *21,* **ROSALES.** *22.*
Bz.: **PERNAMBUCO.** *D30.*
Ch.: **BLANCO ENCALADA.** *14,* **COCHRANE.** *15.*
Co.: **ANTIOQUIA.** *01.*
Cs.: **AN YANG.** *18,* **KUN YANG.** *19.*
Ge. (very large director on bridge): **Z1.** *D170,* **Z2.** *D171,* **Z3.** *D172,* **Z4.** *D178,* **Z5.** *D179.*
Gr.: **ASPIS.** *06,* **LONCHI.** *56,* **SFENDONI.** *85,* **VELOS.** *16.*
It.: **GENIERE.** Ja.: **YUGURE.** *184.*
Pv.: **GUISE.** *72,* **VILLAR.** *71.*
Sp.: **ALCALA GALIANO.** *D24,* **ALMIRANTE VALDES.** *D23* (pole mast), **JORGE JUAN.** *D25.*
Tu.: **ICEL.** **ISKENDERUN.** **IZMIT.**

Most of the transferred ships have 5 torpedo tubes (quintuple).

**106.** Am. **FLETCHER** and **LATER FLETCHER** classes (5 guns). 1943-44. Destroyers. 2,100 tons. 377 x 40 x 18. (115 x 11.9 x 5.5). 2 screws; turbines. 35 knots. 5—5-inch D.P. guns. 6—10-inch A.A. guns. 2 anti-submarine torpedo launchers (triple). (In some ships). 2 "Hedgehogs". Depth charges. 5-10 torpedo tubes (quintuple). (Removed from some ships). Later "Fletcher" class.

**ALBERT W. GRANT.** *649,* **BEARSS.** *654,* **BENNION.** *662,* **BRYANT.** *665,* **BULLARD.** *660,* **CAPERTON.** *650,* **CASSIN YOUNG.** *793,* **CHAUNCEY.** *667,* **COTTEN.** *669,* **HALSEY POWELL.** *686,* **HEALY.** *672,* **JOHN HOOD.** *655,* **KIDD.** *661,* **KNAPP.** *653,* **MELVIN.** *680,* **MERTZ.** *691,* **NORMAN SCOTT.** *690,* **POR-TER.** *800,* **PORTERFIELD.** *682,* **REMEY.** *688,* **STOCKHAM.** *683.*

"Fletcher" class. **BELL.** *587,* **BURNS.** *588,* **FOOTE.** *511,* **FRANKS.** *554,* **HARADEN.** *585,* **HART.** *594,* **HUDSON.** *475,* **IZARD.** *589,* **LA VALLETTE.** *448,* **LAWS.** *558,* **METCALF.** *595,* **MILLER.** *535,* **McCORD.** *534,* **McKEE.** *575,* **OWEN.** *546,* **ROBINSON.** *562,* **SCHROE-DER.** *501,* **SHIELDS.** *596,* **SIGOURNEY.** *643,* **SIGSBEE.** *502,* **STANLY.** *478,* **STEPHEN POTTER.** *538,* **STEVENS.** *479,* **TERRY.** *513,* **THE SULLIVANS.** *537,* **TWINING.** *540,* **WATTS.** *567,* **WICKES.** *578,* **WREN.** *568.*

Bz.: **PARA.** *D27,* **PARAIBA.** *D28,* **PARANA.** *D29,* **PIAUI.** *D31,* **SANTA CATERINA.** *D32.*
Gr.: **NAVARINON.** *63,* **THYELLA.** *28.*
Ko.: **CHUNG MU.** *91,* **PUSAN.** *93,* **SEOUL.** *92.*
Sp.: **ALMIRANTE FERRANDIZ.** *D22,* **LEP-ANTO.** *D21* (Pole mast).

**107.** It. Ex-**FLETCHER** class. *Particulars as for Number 103 but ships may actually look like 107.*
**FANTE. LANCIERE.**

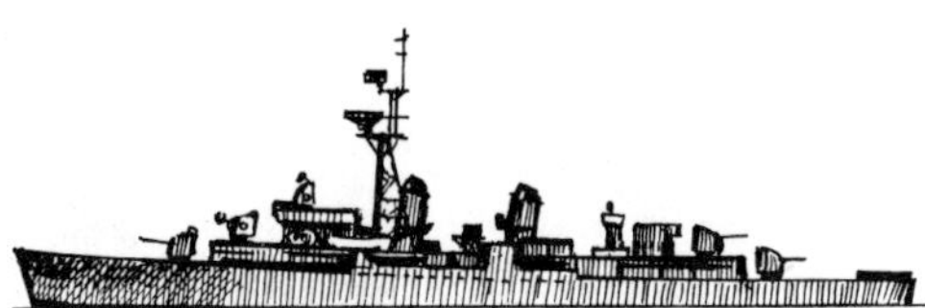

**108.** Ja. Ex-**FLETCHER** class. (Japanese "Twilight" class). 1944. Modernised 1960-62. *Details as for No. 103* except for armament which is: 3—5-inch D.P. guns. 10 A.A. guns. 1 anti-submarine "Alpha" Rocket launcher, dropping gear for anti-submarine homing torpedoes.
**ARIAKE.** *183.*

**109.** Fr. Modified **SURCOUF** class. 1958. Radar Picket Destroyers. 2,800 tons. 422 x 42 x 15. (129 x 12.7 x 4.6). 2 screws; turbines. 34 knots. 6—5-inch D.P. guns (twin). 6—2.25-inch A.A. guns. 1 anti-submarine rocket launcher (sextuple). 6 torpedo tubes (triple). *Similar to No. 110 but have extra gun before the bridge.*
**FORBIN.** *D635,* **JAUREGUIBERRY.** *D637,* **LA BOURDONNAIS.** *D634,* **TARTU.** *D636.*

**110.** Fr. **SURCOUF** class. 1955-56. Command Ships/Destroyers. *Particulars as for No. 109* except for armament which is: 6—5-inch D.P. guns (twin). 4 A.A. guns. 6 anti-submarine torpedo tubes (triple).
**CASSARD.** *D623,* **CHEVALIER PAUL.** *D626,* **SURCOUF.** *D621.*

**111.** Fr. **SURCOUF** class. 1956-57. Guided Missile Destroyers. *Particulars as for No. 109* except for armament which is: 6—57-m.m. A.A. guns. 6 smaller A.A. guns. 6 anti-submarine torpedo tubes (triple). 1 surface-to-air "Tartar" anti-submarine launcher.
**BOUVET.** *D624,* **DU CHAYLA.** *D630,* **DUPE-TIT THOUARS.** *D625,* **KERSAINT.** *D622.* Taller funnels than previo ships in class. *Very similar to No. 113.*

**112.** Fr. **LA GALISSONNIERE.** *D638.* 1962. Destroyer. 2,800 tons. 436 x 42 x 15.5. (133 x 12.8 x 4.7). 2 screws; turbines. 35 knots. 2—3.9-inch A.A. guns. 1 anti-submarine "Malafon" launcher for rockets/homing torpedoes. 6 anti-submarine torpedo tubes (triple). 1 helicopter. Built up aft.

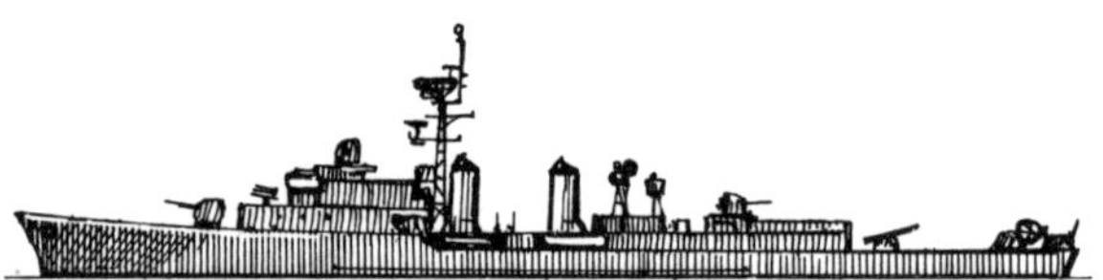

**113.** Fr. **SURCOUF** class. 1956-57. Destroyers. Converted 1966-69. Particulars as for No. 109 except for armament which is: 2—3.9-inch A.A. guns. 1 anti-submarine "Malafon" rocket for homing torpedo. 6 anti-submarine torpedo tubes (triple). 1 Bofors anti-submarine rocket launcher. Tall funnels.
**CASABIANCA.** *D631,* **D'ESTREES.** *D629,* **GUEPRATTE.** *D632,* **MAILLE BREZE.** *D627,* **VAUQUELIN.** *D628.*

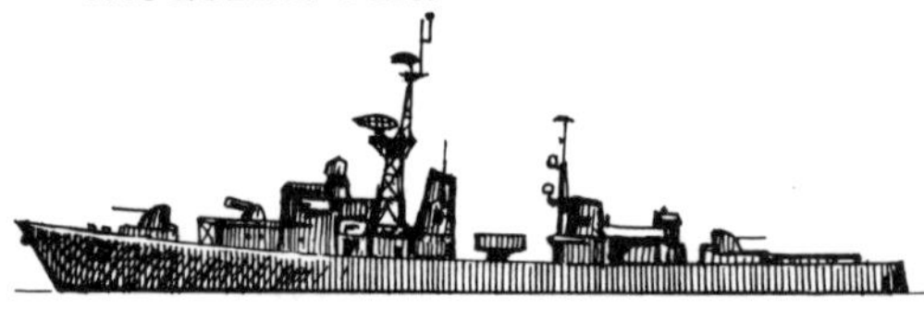

**114.** Ja. **CLOUD** class. 1966-67. Destroyers. 2,100 tons. 374 x 39 x 13. (114 x 11.8 x 3.9). 2 screws; diesel. 27 knots. 4—3-inch A.A. guns (twin). 1 anti-submarine "Asroc" launcher (8 tubes). 1 anti-submarine rocket launcher (4 barrels). 2 anti-submarine torpedo launchers (triple).

**ASAZUMO.** *115,* **MAKIZUMO.** *114,* **YAMA-ZUMO.** *113.*
A fourth ship of the class, "Minezumo" is completely different in appearance

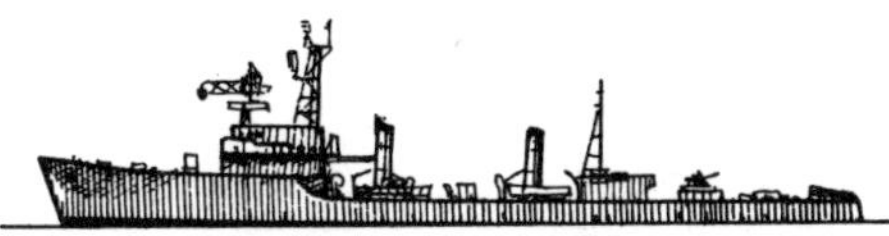

**115.** Ja. **WAKABA.** *261.* 1945. Experimental Ship (Destroyer). 1,300 tons. 330 x 31 x 11. (101 x 9.5 x 3.3). 2 screws; turbines. 24 knots. 2.3-inch A.A. guns. 1 "Hedgehog". 2 depth charge throwers. Very widely spaced funnels and large radar on bridge.

**116.** Ch. **ALMIRANTE** class. 1960. Destroyers. 2,700 tons. 402 x 43 x 13. (122.5 x 13 x 4). 2 screws; turbines. 34 knots. 4—4-inch A.A. guns. 6 small A.A. guns. 1 surface-to-air "Seacat" launcher (quadruple). 2 anti-submarine "Squids". 5 torpedo tubes (quintuple).
**RIVEROS.** *18,* **WILLIAMS.** *19.*

**117.** Ja. **AKEBONO.** *201.* 1956. Frigate. 1,100 tons. 295 x 29 x 11. (90 x 8.7 x 3.4). 2 screws; turbines. 28 knots. 2—3-inch A.A. guns.

**118.** Ja. **MOON** class. 1960. Destroyers. 2,400 tons. 387 x 39 x 13. (118 x 12 x 4). 2 screws; turbines. 32 knots. 3—5-inch D.P. guns. 4—3-inch A.A. guns (twin). 4 torpedo tubes (quadruple). 1 anti-submarine rocket launcher. 2 "Hedgehogs". 2 "Y" mortars. 2 depth charge throwers.
Distinguished from "Wave" class, No. 120, by mast before second funnel.
**AKIZUKI.** *161,* **TERUZUKI.** *162.*

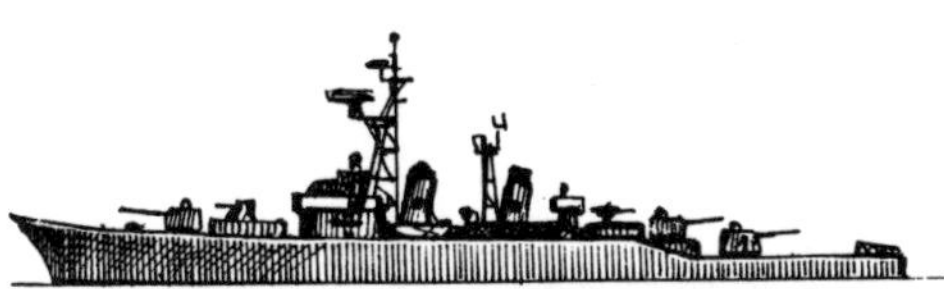

**119.** Ja. **RAIN** class. 1959. Destroyers. 1,800 tons. 354 x 36 x 12. (108 x 11 x 3.7). 2 screws; turbines. 30 knots. 3—5-inch D.P. guns. 4—3-inch A.A. guns (twin). 8 anti-submarine torpedoes. 1 "Hedgehog". 1 depth charge rack. 1 "Y" gun.
**HARUSAME.** *109,* **MURASAME.** *107,* **YU-DACHI.** *108.*
Distinguished from "Moon" class No. 118 by closer funnels and absence of rocket launcher foreward.

**120.** Ja. **WAVE** class. 1958-60. Destroyers. 1,700 tons. 358 x 35 x 12. (109 x 10.7 x 3.7). 2 screws; turbines. 32 knots. 6—3-inch A.A. guns. 2 "Hedgehogs". 2 "Y" anti-submarine mortars. 4 torpedo tubes (quadruple). 4 anti-submarine (fixed) torpedo launchers.
**AYANAMI.** *103,* **ISONAMI.** *104,* **MAKI-NAMI.** *112,* **ONAMI.** *111,* **SHIKANAMI.** *106,* **TAKANAMI.** *110,* **URANAMI.** *105.*

**121.** It. **IMPETUOSO** class. 1958. Destroyers. 2,800 tons. 419 x 44 x 17.5. (127.6 x 13.3 x 5.3). 2 screws; turbines. 34 knots. 4—5-inch A.A. and 16 smaller A.A. guns. 1 anti-submarine mortar (3 barrels). 4 depth charge throwers. 1 depth charge rack. 2 anti-submarine torpedo tubes (triple).
**IMPETUOSO.** *D558,* **INDOMITO.** *D559.*

**122.** It. **CENTAURO** class. 1957-58. Conversion 1966 and onwards. Frigates. 1,800 tons. 338 x 40 x 12.6. (103 x 12 x 3.8). 2 screws; turbines. 26 knots. 3—3-inch A.A. guns. 1 anti-submarine depth charge mortar (3 barrels). 6 torpedo launchers (triple).
**CANOPO.** *F552,* **CENTAURO.** *F554,* **CASTORE.** *F553,* **CIGNO.** *F553.* Distinctive stems.

**123.** Ja. **WIND** class. 1956. Destroyers. 1,700 tons. 359 x 35 x 12. (109.3 x 10.5 x 3.7). 2 screws; turbines. 30 knots. 3—5-inch D.P. guns. 8 A.A. guns (quadruple). 2 "Hedgehogs". Anti-submarine torpedo tubes. 1 depth charge rack.
**HARUKAZE.** *101,* **YUKIKAZE.** *102.*

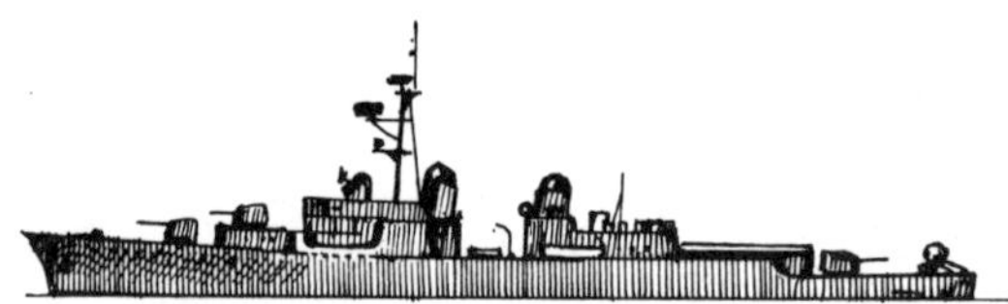

**124.** Sp. Modified **OQUENDO** class. 1969. Destroyers. 3,000 tons. 392 x 43 x 18. (119.3 x 13 x 5.6). 2 screws; turbines. 31 knots. 6—5-inch guns (twin). 6 anti-submarine torpedo tubes (triple). 2 single tubes. 1 helicopter.
**MARQUES DE LA ENSENADA.** *D43,* **ROGER DE LAURIA.** *D42.* Distinctive funnels.

**125.** Sp. **OQUENDO.** *D41.* 1964. Destroyer. 2,600 tons. 382 x 37 x 13. (116.4 x 11.1 x 3.8). 2 screws; turbines. 32 knots. 4—4.7-inch guns (twin). 6 A.A. guns. 2 "Hedgehogs".

**126.** Co. **SIETE DE AGOSTO.** *06.* 1958. Destroyers. 2,700 tons. 405 x 41 x 13. (122 x 12.4 x 3.8). 2 screws; turbines. 35 knots. 6—4.7-inch guns (twin). 4 A.A. guns. 4 torpedo tubes. 1 anti-submarine depth charge launcher (quadruple).

**VEINTE DE JULIO.** *05.* Modified Swedish "Halland" type. *See number 127,* from which they are immediately distinguished by lattice foremast and large funnels.

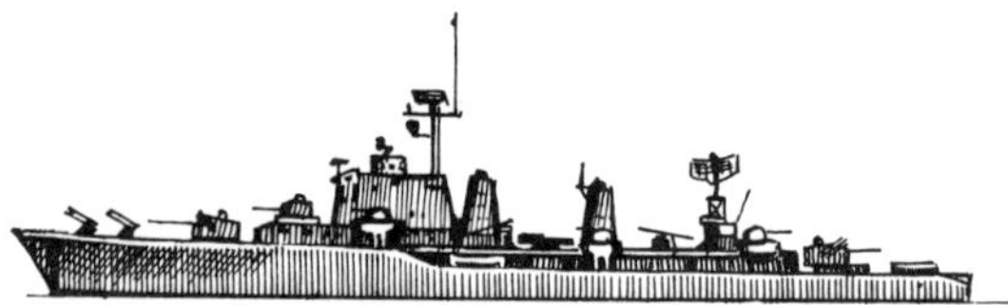

**127.** Sw. **HALLAND** class. 1955-56. Destroyers. 2,700 tons. 397 x 41 x 15. (121 x 12.6 x 4.5). 2 screws; turbines. 35 knots. 4—4.7-inch D.P. guns (twin). 8 A.A. guns. 8 torpedo tubes. 1 rocket launcher. 2 depth charge mortars (four barrelled). Equipped for minelaying.
**HALLAND.** *J18,* **SMALAND.** *J19.*

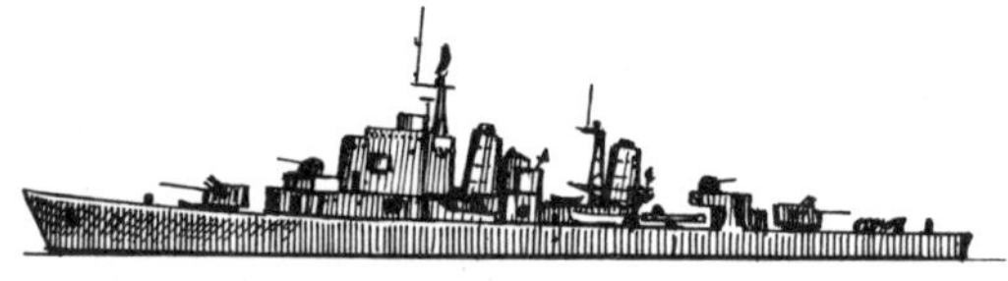

**128.** Sw. **OSTERGOTLAND** class. 1958-59. Modernised 1962-63. Destroyers. 2,200 tons. 380 x 37 x 12. (115.8 x 11.2 x 3.7). 2 screws; turbines. 35 knots. 4—4.7-inch guns (twin). 4- to 7-inch A.A. guns. 6 torpedo tubes. 1 depth charge mortar (triple). 1 surface-to-air "Seacat" launcher.
**GASTRIKLAND.** *J22,* **HALSINGLAND.** *J23,* **OSTERGOTLAND.** *J20,* **SODERMANLAND.** *J21.*

**129.** Br. **TRIBAL** class. 1961-64. Frigates. 2,300 tons. 360 x 42 x 18. (109.7 x 12.9 x 5.3). Combined steam and gas turbines. 28 knots. 2—4.5-inch guns. 2 A.A. guns. 1 "Limbo" depth charge mortar (triple). 1 helicopter. 2 surface-to-air "Seacat" launchers (in Zulu only).
**ASHANTI.** *F117,* **ESKIMO.** *F119,* **GURHKA.** *F122,* **NUBIAN.** *F131,* **TARTAR.** *F133,* **ZULU.** *F124.*
*Similar* (after gun removed): **MOHAWK.** *F125.*
*See silhouette No. 61.*

**131.** Sw. **KALMAR.** *14.* 1944. Frigate. Dimensions and engines as for number 130. 3—4.7-inch D.P. guns. 3 A.A. guns. 5 torpedo tubes. 1 depth charge mortar.

**133.** Sp. **AUDAZ** class. 1953-65. Earlier ships modernised 1961-63. Destroyers. 1,200 tons. 308 x 31 x 17. (94 x 9.3 x 5.2). 2 screws; turbines. 31 knots. 2—3-inch A.A. guns. 2 small A.A. guns. 2 anti-submarine torpedo racks (triple). 2 "Hedgehogs". 8 depth charge mortars. 2 depth charge racks.
**AUDAZ.** *D31,* **FUROR.** *D34,* **INTREPIDO.** *D38,* **METEORO.** *D33,* **OSADO.** *D32,* **RAYO.** *D35,* **RELAMPAGO.** *D39,* **TEMERARIO.** *D37.*

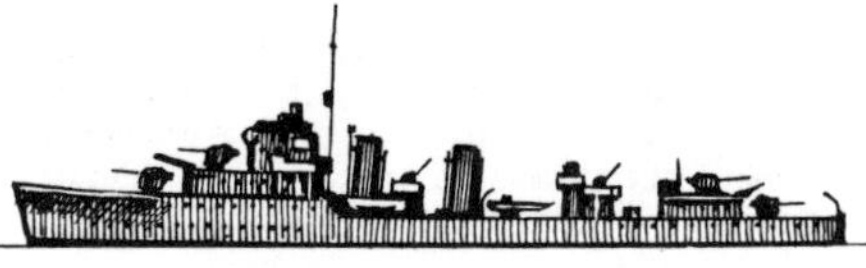

**135.** Ar. **BUENOS AIRES** class. 1937. Destroyers. 1,400 tons. 323 x 35 x 11. (98.5 x 10.6 x 3.3). 2 screws; turbines. 35 knots. 4—4.7-inch guns. 6 A.A. guns. 4 torpedo tubes (quadruple). 4 depth charge throwers.
**BUENOS AIRES.** *6,* **ENTRE RIOS.** *7,* **MISIONES.** *11,* **SAN JUAN.** *9,* **SAN LUIS.** *10,* **SANTA CRUZ.** *12.*

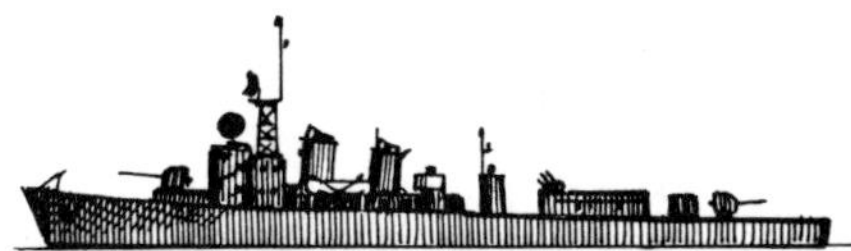

**130.** Sw. **VISBY** class. 1943. Frigates. 1,200 tons. 320 x 30 x 13. (97.5 x 9.1 x 3.8). 2 screws; turbines. 39 knots. Armament varies in these ships. "Halsingborg": 3—4.7-inch D.P. guns. 3 A.A. guns. 5 torpedo tubes (quintuple). 1 depth charge mortar. Other ships: 2 A.A. guns. 1 depth charge mortar. 1 helicopter.
**HALSINGBORG.** *F13,* **SUNDSVALL.** *F12,* **VISBY.** *F11.*

**132.** Sw. **KARLSKRONA.** *F79.* 1940. Converted 1963. Frigate. 1,300 tons. 311 x 30 x 13. (94.6 x 9 x 3.8). 3—4.7-inch D.P. guns. 4 A.A. guns. 2 depth charge mortars (triple). 2 screws; turbines. 39 knots.

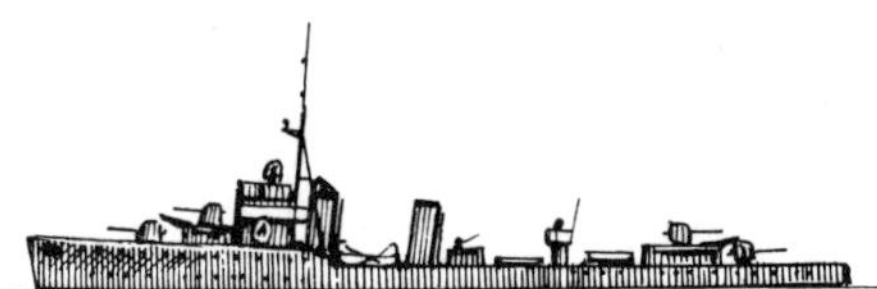

**134.** Sp. **ALMIRANTE ANTEQUERA** class. 1935. Destroyers. 1,600 tons. 333 x 32 x 20. (101.5 x 9.7 x 6). 2 screws; turbines. 27 knots. 4—4.7-inch guns. 2 A.A. guns. Anti-submarine torpedo racks. 4 depth charge throwers.
**ALMIRANTE ANTEQUERA.** *D14,* **ALMIR--ANTE MIRANDA.** *D15.*

**136.** Do. **DUARTE.,** *501.* 1936. Destroyer. 1,300 tons. 323 x 33 x 15. (98.5 x 10 x 4.6). 2 screws; turbines. 36 knots. 3—4.7-inch guns. 4 A.A. guns. 4 torpedo tubes (quadruple). 4 depth charge throwers. Ex-British "H" class destroyer.

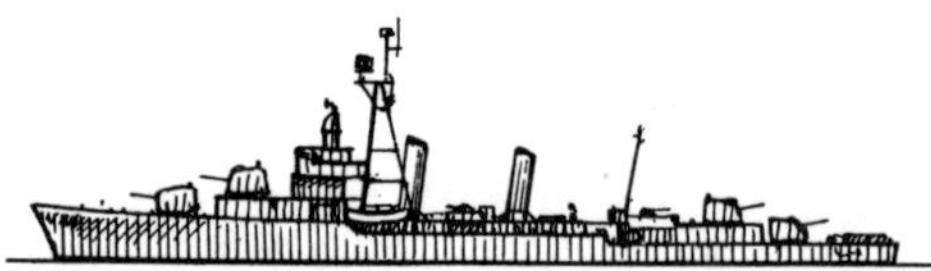

**137.** Ex-**U.S. GLEAVES** and **MAYO** classes. 1940-41. Destroyers. 1,600 tons. 348 x 36 x 18. (106 x 11 x 5.5). 2 screws; turbines. 35 knots. Gr.: **DOXA.** *20,* **NIKI.** *65.* 4—5-inch guns. 12 A.A. guns. Anti-submarine torpedo racks. "Hedgehogs". Depth charges.

It.: **ARTIGLIERE.** *D553.* 4—5-inch guns. 18 A.A. guns. 4 depth charge throwers. 2 depth charge racks.
Tu.: **GAZIANTEP.** *D344,* **GEMLIK.** *D347.* 4—5-inch guns. 4 A.A. guns. 5 torpedo tubes (quintuple). Homing torpedoes. 2 "Hedgehogs". 4 depth charge throwers.

**138.** Ex-**U.S. GLEAVES** class. 1942. Destroyer. 1,600 tons. 348 x 36 x 18. (106.2 x 11 x 5.5). 2 screws; turbines. 34 knots. 3—5-inch guns. 8 A.A. guns.
Cs.: **HSUEN YANG.** *16.*

Similar American ships, "Gleaves/Livermore" class (minesweeping gear aft): **CARMICK.** *493,* **COWIE.** *632,* **DAVISON.** *618,* **DORAN.** *634,* **DOYLE.** *493,* **FITCH.** *462,* **GHERARDI.** *637,* **HAMBLETON.** *455,* **JEFFERS.** *621,* **McCOOK.** *496,* **QUICK.** *490,* **THOMPSON.** *627.*

**139.** It. Ex-**U.S. GLEAVES** class. 1941. Destroyer. 2,600 tons. 348 x 36 x 18. (106 x 11 x 5.5). 2 screws; turbines. 31 knots. 4—5-inch guns. 18 A.A. guns. 4 depth charge throwers. 2 depth charge racks.
**AVIERE.** *D554.*

**140.** Ex-**U.S. GLEAVES** class. 1940. Destroyer. Dimensions and engines as for number 138. 4—5-inch guns. 8 A.A. guns. 5 torpedo tubes. Cs.: **NAN YANG.** *17.*

*Similar:* the following American ships of the "Benson - Mayo" class: **BANCROFT.** *598,* **BOYLE.** *600,* **CHAMPLIN.** *601,* **COGHLAN.** *606,* **FARENHOLT.** *491,* **FRAZIER.** *607,* **GANSEVOORT.** *608,* **GILLESPIE.** *609,* **HOBBY.** *610,* **LAUB.** *613,* **McLANAHAN.** *615,* **MacKENZIE.** *614,* **MAYO.** *422,* **MEADE.** *602,* **MURPHY.** *603,* **NIELDS.** *616,* **ORDRONAUX.** *617,* **PARKER.** *604.*

**141.** Ex-**U.S. MAYO** class. 1940. Destroyer. 1,600 tons. 348 x 35 x 18. (106.2 x 10.8 x 5.5). 2 screws; turbines. 34 knots. 4—5-inch guns. 10 A.A. guns. 1 depth charge mortar. Depth charge throwers.
Cs.: **HAN YANG.** *15,* **LO YANG.** *14.*

*Similar:* American ships of the "Gleaves/Livermore" class. Details as above but have 5 torpedo tubes: **EDWARDS.** *619,* **ERICSSON.** *440,* **FRANKFORD.** *497,* **GRAYSON.** *435,* **HERNDON.** *638,* **KEARNY.** *432,* **SATTERLEE.** *626,* **STOCKTON.** *646,* **SWANSON.** *443,* **THORN.** *647,* **TILLMAN.** *641,* **WOOLSEY.** *437.*

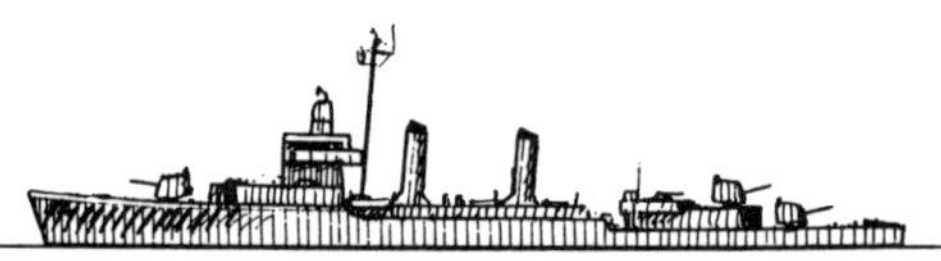

**142.** Ex-**U.S. GLEAVES** class. 1941-42. Destroyers. All details including armament *as No. 138.* Two ships lent to Japan in 1954, returned in 1970 and probably scrapped. U.S. names: **ELLYSON.** *454,* **MACOMB.** *458.*

**143.** Bz. **MARIZ E BARROS.** *D26.* 1944.
Modernised 1969 c. Destroyer. 1,500 tons.
360 x 35 x 12. (109.7 x 10.7 x 3.7). 2 screws;
turbines. 36 knots. 2—5-inch guns 4 A A guns.
4 torpedo tubes (quadrupled). 1 surface-to-air
"Seacat" launcher (quadruple). 2 "Hedgehogs".

**145.** Th. **SATTAHIB** class. 1937 and 58. Patrol
vessels. 110 tons. 132 x 16 x 4. (40 x 5 x 1.2).
2 screws; turbines. 19 knots. 1—3-inch gun.
1—20-m.m. gun. 2 torpedo tubes.
**KANTANG.** *7,* **KLONGYAI.** *5,* **SATTAHIB.**
*8,* **TAKBAI.** *6.*

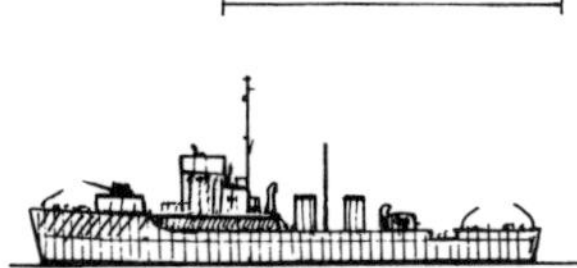

**147.** Pv. Ex-U.S. **ALBATROSS** class. 1943.
Coastal minesweepers. 300 tons. 136 x 25 x 6.
(41.4 x 7.6 x 1.8). Diesels. 13 knots. 1—3-inch
gun. 2 A.A. guns. Ex-U.S. YMS. type.
**BONDY.** *137,* **SAN MARTIN.** *138.*

**JASMINE** of Malagasy may be similar but with
a tripod mast.

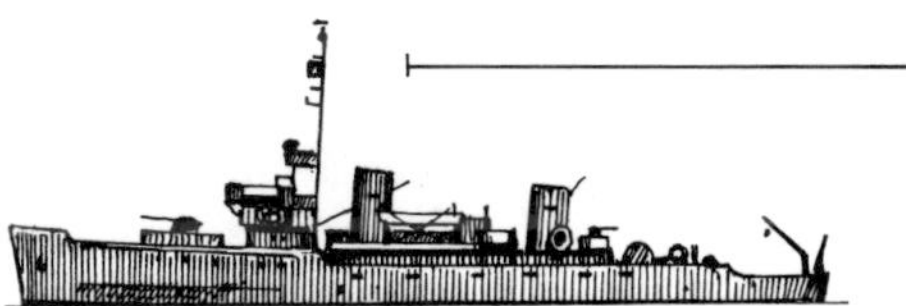

**149.** Tu. **CANDARLI** class (Ex-U.S. AUK class).
1942-43. Minesweepers (with various other
functions). 1,000 tons. 221 x 32 x 11. (67.4 x
9.8 x 3.3). 2 screws; diesel-electric. 18 knots.
1—3-inch gun. 6 A A. guns. 4 depth charge
throwers.
**CANDARLI.** *AGS2,* **CARDAK.** *A596,* **CAR-
SAMBA.** *AGS1,* **CESME.** *A595,* **EDINCIK.**
*A598,* **EREGLI.** *A592.*

*Similar* American surveying ship (*see silhouette
No. 721*): **SHELDRAKE.** *GS19,* and U.S.
Degaussing vessel: **SURFBIRD.** *DG383.*

**144.** Sp. **ALAVA** class. 1950-51. Modernised
1962. Destroyers. 1,800 tons. 340 x 32 x 20.
(103.6 x 9.6 x 6). 2 screws; turbines. 29 knots.
3—3-inch A.A. guns. 3 smaller A.A. guns. 2 anti-
submarine torpedo tubes (triple). 2 "Hedgehogs".
8 depth charge mortars. 6 depth charge racks.
**ALAVA.** *D52,* **LINIERS.** *D51.*

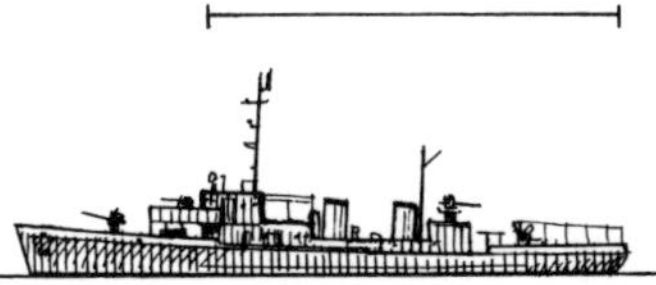

**146.** Do. **INDEPENDENCIA.** *204.* 1931. Patrol
vessel. 337 tons. 165 x 25 x 10. (50.3 x 7.6 x
2.8). Diesels. 15 knots. 1—3-inch gun. 2 smaller
guns. Ex-U.S. Coast Guard cutters.
**LIBERTAD.** *205,* **RESTAURACION.** *203.*

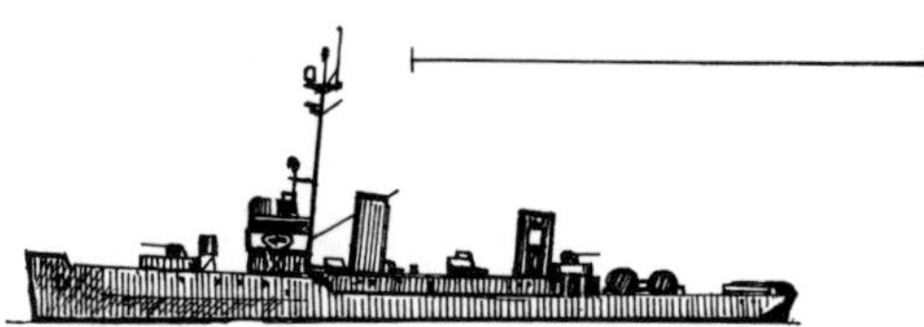

**148.** Am. **AUK** class. 1942-45. Fleet Minesweepers. 890 tons. 221 x 32 x 11. (67.3 x
9.7 x 3.3). 2 screws; diesel-electric. 18 knots.
1—3-inch gun. 2 or 4 A.A. guns.
**ARDENT.** *340,* **BROADBILL.** *58,* **CHAM-
PION.** *314,* **CHIEF.** *315,* **COMPETENT.** *316,*
**DEFENSE.** *317,* **DEVASTATOR.** *318,* **GLADI-
ATOR.** *319,* **HERALD.** *101,* **IMPECCABLE.**
*320,* **ROSELLE.** *379,* **SAGE.** *111,* **SCOTER.**
*381,* **SPEAR.** *322,* **SPRIG.** *384,* **STARLING.**
*64,* **SWAY.** *120,* **SWIFT.** *122,* **SYMBOL.** *123,*
**TERCEL.** *386,* **THREAT.** *124,* **VELOCITY.** *128,*
**WHEATEAR.** *390,* **PILOT.** *104,* **PIONEER.** *105.*

Pv. (patrol vessels, minesweeping gear removed
etc.): **DIEZ CANSECO.** *69,* **GALVEZ.** *68.*
Ur. (Escort): **COMMANDANTE PEDRO
CAMPBELL.** *MSF1.*

*Similar* in appearance but used as Escort ships
with the following armament: 2—3-inch D.P.
guns. 8 A.A. guns. 3 torpedo tubes. 1 "Hedgehog".
4 depth charge throwers. 2 depth charge racks.
*See silhouette No. 396.*
Cs.: **CHU YUNG.** *67,* **MO LING.** *68,* **PING
CHING.** *70,* **WU SHENG.** *66.*
Ko.: **KOJE.** *1003,* **SHIN SONG.** *1001,* **SUN-
CHON.** *1002.*
Pi.: **QUEZON.** *70,* **RIZAL.** *69.*

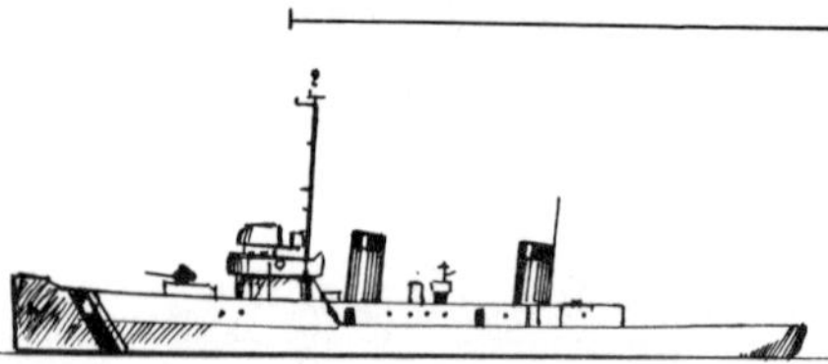

**150.** Am. **AUK** class. 1944. Converted 1964. Coast Guard training ship. *Details as No. 148* but carries no armament. Former minesweeper of the U.S. navy.
**TANAGER.** *385.*

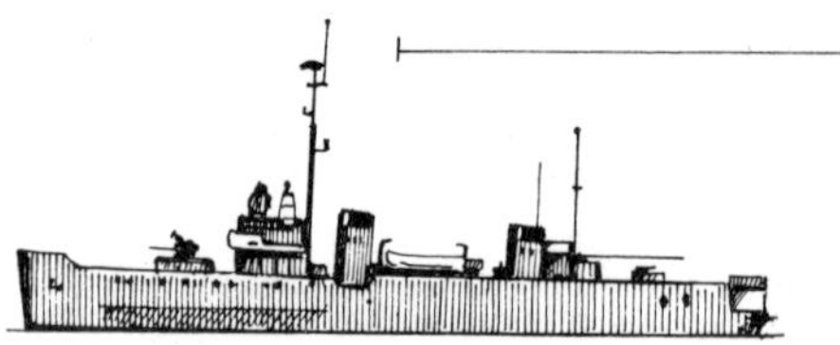

**151.** No. **GOR** class (Ex-U.S. AUK class). 1942-44. Converted 1959-60. Coastal minelayers. Dimensions etc. as for number 148. 1—3-inch gun. 1 or 4 A.A. guns. "Uller" has "Terne" anti-submarine system and one depth charge thrower. Other ships have two "Hedgehogs" and three depth charge throwers.
**BRAGE.** *N49,* **GOR.** *N48,* **TYR.** *N47,* **ULLER.** *N50.*

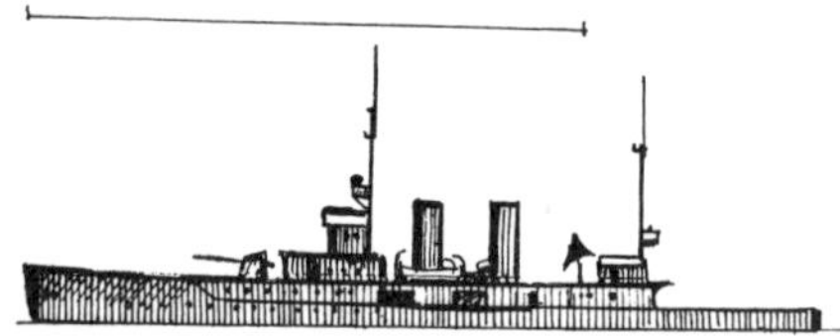

★ **152.** RC. Ex-**YUN SUI.** 1929. Coast defence vessel. 700 tons. 225 x 30 x 7. (68.6 x 9.2 x 2.2). 2 screws; reciprocating. 12 knots. 1—3-inch A.A. gun. 1 smaller A.A.
Ex-Nationalist Chinese.

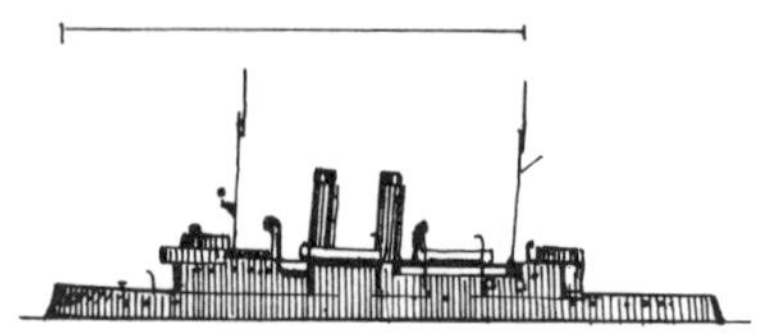

★ **153.** RC. **CHIANG YUAN.** 1905. Coast defence vessel. 600 tons. 180 x 28 x 7. (55 x 8.5 x 2.2). 2 screws; reciprocating. 12 knots. 1 A.A. gun.

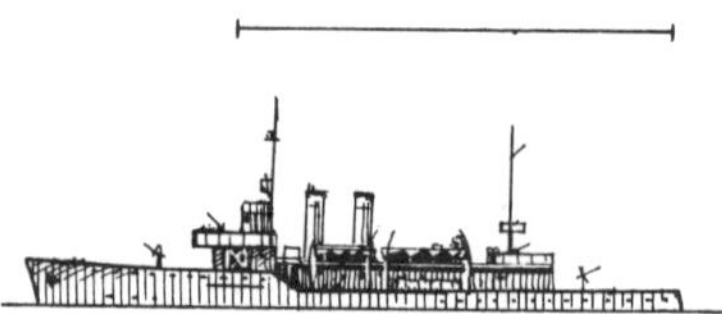

★ **154.** RC. **CH'ANG CHIANG.** 1929. Coast defence vessel. 500 tons. 177 x 26 x 7. (54 x 8 x 2.2). 2 screws; reciprocating. 12 knots. 3 light guns.
Ex-Nationalist Chinese.

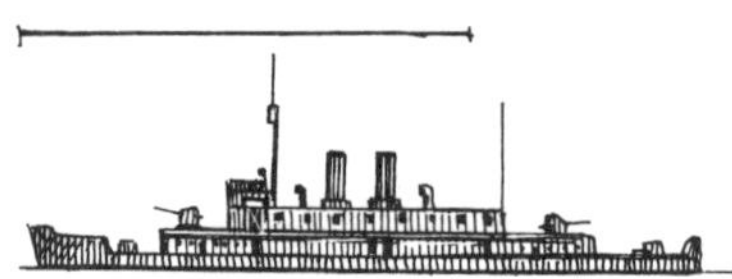

★ **155.** RC. Ex-**CHAN TEH.** 1923. River defence vessel. 1923. 180 x 27 x 3. (54.9 x 8.2 x 1). 2 screws; reciprocating. 14 knots. 2—3-inch guns. 6 smaller guns.
Former Japanese vessel.

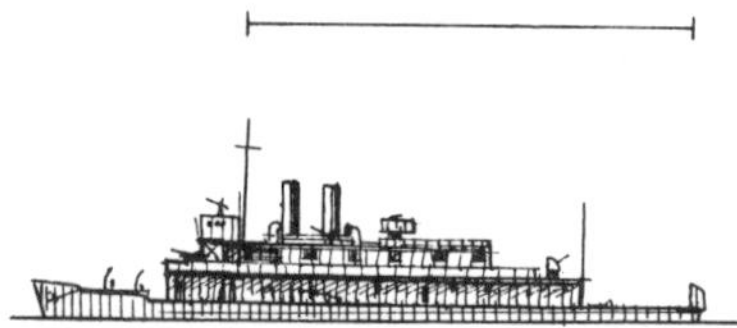

★ **156.** RC. Ex-**HO HSEUH.** 1911. River defence vessel. 200 tons. 180 x 27 x 2.5. (54.9 x 8.2 x 9). 2 screws; reciprocating. 9 knots. 3—3-inch guns. 3 A.A. guns.
Former Japanese ship.

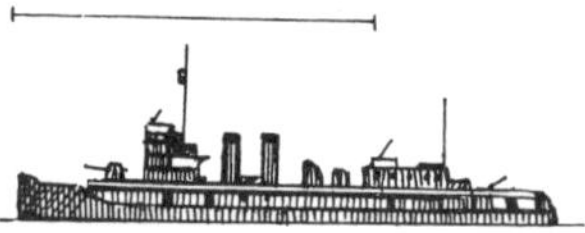

★ **157.** RC. Ex-**YUNG AN,** Ex-**YUNG PING.** River defence vessels. 1929. 170 tons. 149 x 22 x 4.7. (45.4 x 6.7 x 1.2). 2 screws; reciprocating. 12 knots. 6 A.A. guns.
Former Japanese craft.

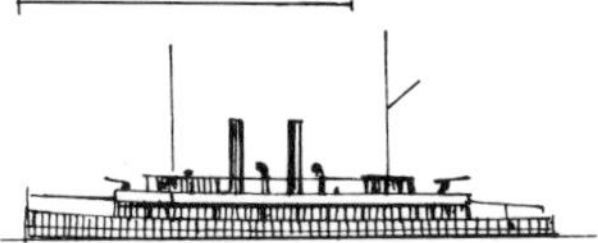

**158.** Pv. **AMERICA.**. 1904. River Gunboat. 240 tons. 133 x 20 x 4.5. (40.5 x 6.1 x 1.3). Reciprocating. 14 knots. 6 A.A. guns.

★ **159.** RC. Ex-**MEI YUAN.** 1927. River Defence Vessels. 400 tons. 160 x 27 x 5. (48.8 x 8.2 x 1.5). Reciprocating. 12 knots. 2—3-inch guns. Ex-**TAI YUAN.**

## SINGLE FUNNEL COMBAT SHIPS

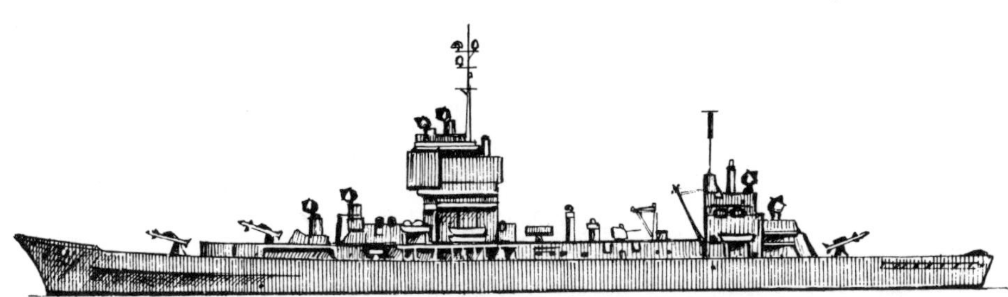

**160.** Am. **LONG BEACH.** *9.* 1961. Guided Missile Cruiser. 14,200 tons. 721 x 73 x 29. (220 x 22.3 x 8.8). Twin screw; nuclear powered turbines. 35 knots. 2—5-inch D.P. guns. 1 surface-to-air "Talos" launcher (twin). 2 surface-to-air "Terrier" launchers (twin). 1 "Asroc" anti-submarine launcher (8 tubes). 2 anti-submarine torpedo launchers (triple).

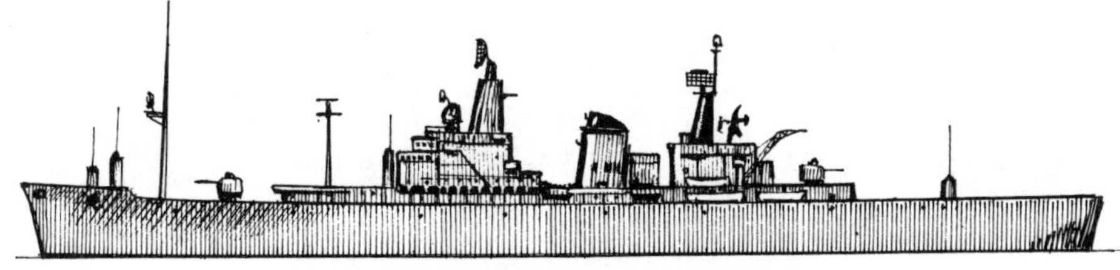

**161.** Am. **NORTHAMPTON.** *1.* 1953. Cruiser/Command Ship. Converted 1961. 14,700 tons. 676 x 71 x 29. (202.4 x 21.6 x 8.8). 4 screws; turbines. 33 knots. 2—5-inch D.P. guns. 2 helicopters. Converted from cruiser of "Oregon City" class.

**162.** Am. **BOSTON.** *69.* 1955. Converted 1968.
Heavy Cruiser. 13,300 tons. 674 x 71 x 26.
(205.3 x 21.6 x 7.9). 4 screws; turbines. 33 knots.
6—8-inch guns (triple). 10—5-inch D.P. guns.
8—3-inch A.A. guns. 2 "Terrier" launchers (twin).
Sister; **CANBERRA** *70.*

**163.** Am. **SALEM** class. 1948-49. Modernised.
Heavy Cruisers. 17,000 tons. 717 x 76 x 26.
(218.4 x 23.9 x 7.9). 4 screws; turbines. 33 knots.
9—8-inch (triple). 12—5-inch D.P. guns (twin).
8—3-inch A.A. guns.
**DES MOINES.** *134,* **NEWPORT NEWS.** *148,*
**SALEM.** *139.*

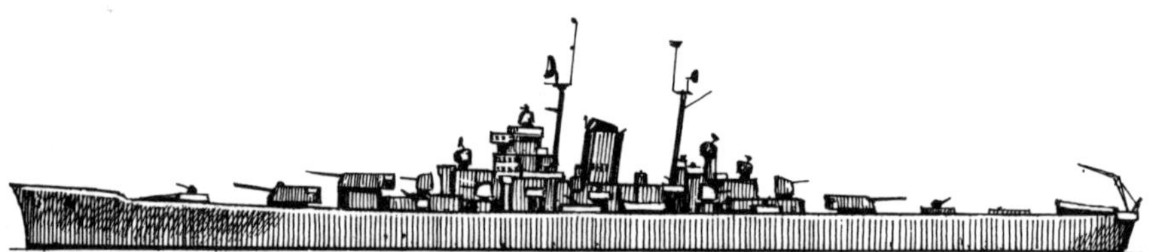

**164.** Am. **OREGON CITY** class. 1946. Heavy
Cruisers. 17,300 tons. 674 x 71 x 26. (205.3 x
21.6 x 7.9). 4 screws; turbines. 33 knots. 9—
8-inch (triple). 12—5-inch D.P. guns (twin).
20 to 40 A.A. guns.
**OREGON CITY.** *122,* **ROCHESTER.** *124.*

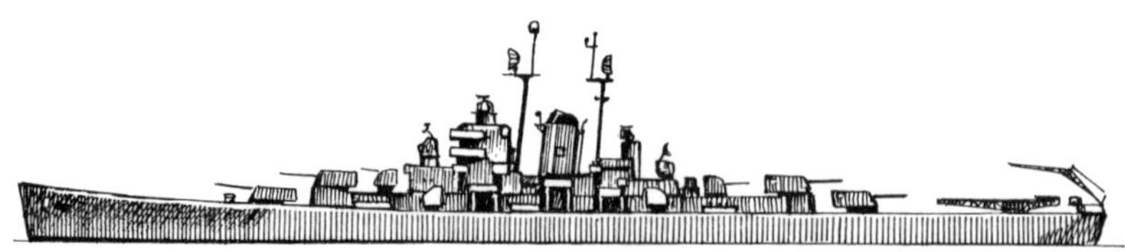

**165.** Am. **FARGO.** 1945. Light Cruiser. 10,500
tons. 610 x 66 x 25. (186 x 20.2 x 7.6). 4 screws;
turbines. 32 knots. 12—6-inch (triple). 12—5-inch
D.P. guns (twin). 28 A.A. guns.

**166.** It. **GIUSEPPE GARIBALDI.** *551.* 1937.
Converted 1957-62. Guided Missile Light Cruiser.
9,800 tons. 614 x 62 x 22. (187 x 18.8 x 6.7).
Twin screw; turbines. 30 knots. 4—5.3 inch guns
(twin) D.P. 8—3-inch A.A. guns (single).
1 surface-to-air "Terrier" launcher (twin). 4
Missile tubes.

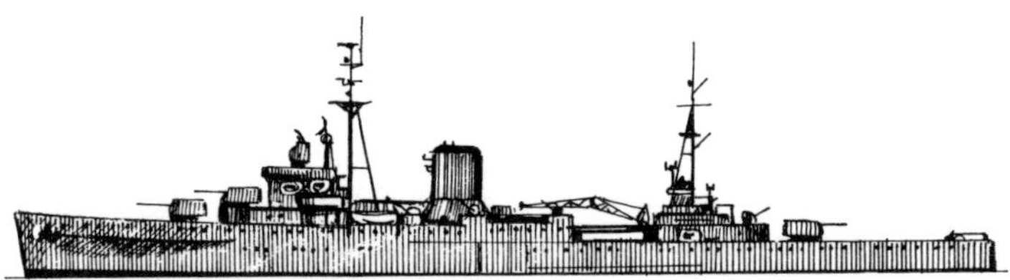

**167.** In. **DELHI.** 1933. Modernised 1958.
Cruiser. 7,100 tons. 545 x 55 x 20. (166 x 16.7 x
6.1). 4 screws; turbines. 32 knots. 6—6-inch
guns (twin). 8—4-inch A.A. guns.
Ex-"Leander" class of Great Britain.

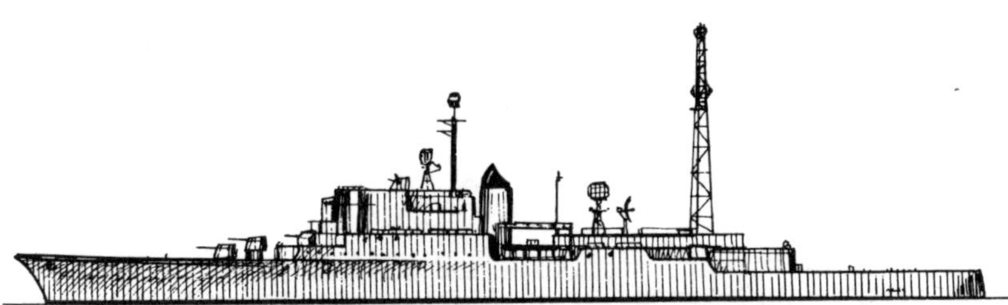

**168.** Fr. **DE GRASSE.** *C610.* 1956. Refitted
1966. Cruiser. 10,200 tons. 618 x 70 x 21.
(188.3 x 21.3 x 6.5). 2 screws; turbines. 33 knots.
12—5-inch guns (twin).
Serves also as Command ship.

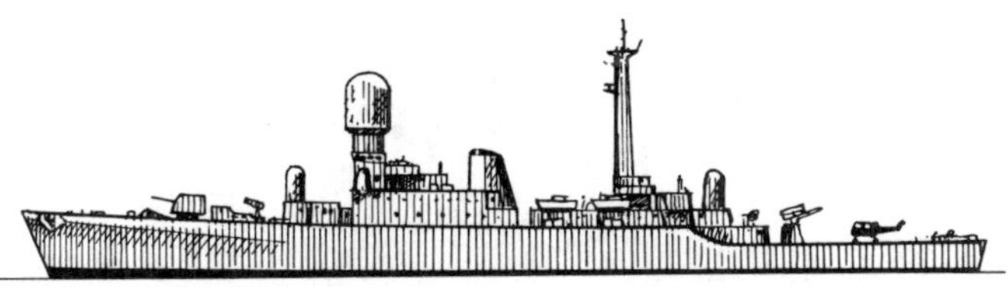

**169.** Br. **BRISTOL.** Under construction. Guided
Missile Destroyer. 5,700 tons. 507 x 55 x 23.
(154.5 x 16.8 x 6.9). 2 screws; steam and gas
turbines. 30 knots. 1—4.5-inch D.P. gun. 2 A.A.
guns. 1 "Ikara" anti-submarine launcher. 1
surface-to-air "Seadart" launcher (twin). 1
Limbo D.C. Mortar. (3 barrels). Helicopter.

**170.** Fr. **SUFFREN** class. 1968-69. Guided Missile Frigates. 4,700 tons. 518 x 51 x 20. (158 x 15.5 x 5.9). 2 screws; turbines. 34 knots. 2—3.9-inch A.A. guns. 2 smaller A.A. guns. 1 surface-to-air "Masurca" launcher (twin). 1 anti-submarine "Malafon" launcher. 4 anti-submarine homing torpedo launchers.
**DUQUESNE.** *D603,* **SUFFREN.** *D602.*

**171.** Fr. **ACONIT.** 1971. Guided Missile Frigate. 3,200 tons. Turbines. 26 knots. 2—3.9-inch A.A. guns. 1 anti-submarine "Malafon" launcher. 1 anti-submarine mortar. Torpedo tubes.
An enlarged version is also being built.

**172.** Ge. **DEUTSCHLAND.** *A59.* 1963. Light Cruiser/Training Ship. 4,800 tons. 476 x 59 x 15. (145 x 18 x 4.5). 3 screws; diesel and turbine. 21 knots. 4—3.9-inch D.P. guns. 6 A.A. guns. 2 anti-submarine rocket launchers (quadruple). 4 anti-submarine torpedo tubes. 2 surface torpedo tubes.

**173.** Ru. **KRESTA** class. 1967. Guided Missile Light Cruiser. 6,000 tons. 509 x 56 x 20. (155 x 17 x 6). Combined diesel and gas turbine. 34 knots. 4—57-m.m. guns (twin). 10 torpedo tubes (quintuple). 2 surface-to-surface "Shaddock" launchers (twin). 2 surface-to-air "Goa" launchers (twin). 2 anti-submarine rocket launchers (12 barrelled). 2 anti-submarine rocket launchers (6 barrelled). 1 helicopter.

★ **174.** Ru. **KRESTA II** class. An improved version of number 173 with different armament etc. The hull plating is carried further aft. The funnel stands clear of the mast which itself is different from the earlier version.

**175.** Ge. **KOLN** class, 1961-64. Refitted 1967 onwards. Frigates. 2,100 tons. 361 x 36 x 11. (110 x 11 x 3.4). 2 screws; combined diesel and gas turbines. 30 knots. 2—3.9-inch D.P. guns. 6 A.A. guns. 2 anti-submarine rocket launchers (4 barrelled). 2 anti-submarine torpedo tubes.
**AUGSBURG.** *F222,* **BRAUNSCHWEIG.** *F225,* **EMDEN.** *F221,* **KARLSRUHE.** *F223,* **KOLN.** *F220,* **LUBECK.** *F224.*

**176.** It. **ALPINO** class. 1968. Frigates. 2,700 tons. 372 x 43 x 13. (113.3 x 13 x 3.9). 2 screws; combined diesel and gas turbines. 28 knots. 6—3-inch D.P. guns. 2 anti-submarine torpedo launchers. 1 anti-submarine depth charge mortar. 2 helicopters.
**ALPINO.** *F580,* **CARABINIERE.** *F581.*

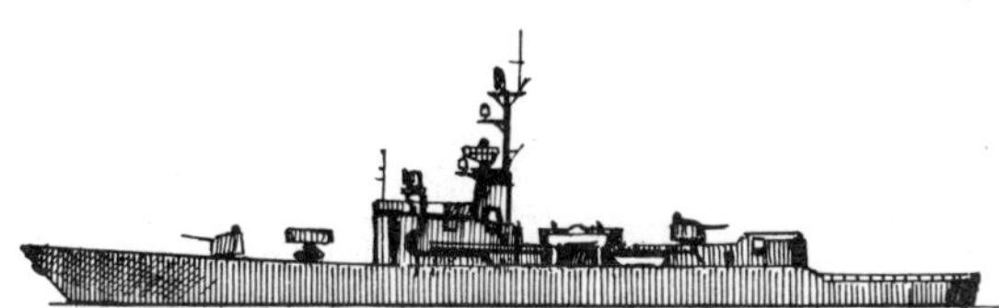

**177.** Am. **GARCIA** class. 1964-68. Escorts. 2,600 tons. 415 x 44 x 24. (126.3 x 13.5 x 7.3). Turbines. 27 knots. 2—5-inch D.P. guns. 1 anti-submarine "Asroc" launcher (8 tubes). 2 anti-submarine torpedo launchers (triple). 2 anti-submarine torpedo tubes (fixed). Differs from number 178 by the gun turret aft.
**ALBERT DAVID.** *1050,* **BRADLEY.** *1041,* **BRUMBY.** *1044,* **DAVIDSON.** *1045,* **EDWARD McDONNELL.** *1043,* **GARCIA.** *1040,* **KOELSCH.** *1049,* **O'CALLAHAN.** *1051,* **SAMPLE.** *1048,* **VOGE.** *1047.*

**178.** Am. **BROOKE** class. 1966-67. Guided Missile Escorts. Particulars as for number 177 but these ships have only 1—5-inch gun and in addition have one surface-to-air "Tartar" launcher (single).
**BROOKE.** *1,* **JULIUS A. FURER.** *6,* **RAMSEY.** *2,* **RICHARD L. PAGE.** *5,* **SCHOFIELD.** *3,* **TALBOT.** *4.*

The following ships are under construction in Spain for the Spanish Navy: **ANDALUCIA. ASTURIAS. BALEARES. CATALUNA. ESTREMADURA.**

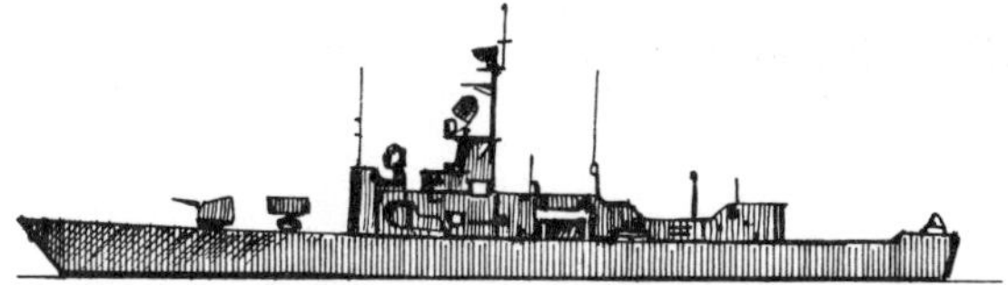

**179.** Am. **GLOVER.** *1.* 1965. Escort. All details as for number 178 but has no missile launcher aft.

**180.** Am. **BRONSTEIN** class. 1963. Escorts.
2,400 tons. 372 x 41 x 23. (113.2 x 12.3 x 7).
Turbine. 26 knots. 3—3-inch A.A. guns. 1 anti-
submarine "Asroc" launcher (8 tubes). 2 anti-
submarine torpedo launchers (triple). 2 drone
anti-submarine helicopters "Dash".
**BRONSTEIN.** *1037* **McCLOY.** *1038.*

**181.** Am. **KNOX** class 1969 onwards. Escorts.
3,000 tons. 438 x 47 x 25. (133.5 x 14.2 x 7.5).
Turbine. 27 knots. 1—5-inch D.P. gun. 1 anti-
submarine "Asroc" launcher (8 tubes). 4 fixed
anti-submarine torpedo launchers. Space reserved
for a surface-to-air missile system.
**AYLWIN.** *1081,* **BADGER.** *1071,* **BLAKELY.**
*1072,* **BOWEN.** *1079,* **CONNOLE.** *1056,*
**DOWNES.** *1070,* **FANNING.** *1076,* **FRANCIS
HAMMOND.** *1067,* **GRAY.** *1054,* **HAROLD**
**E. HOLT.** *1074,* **HEPBURN.** *1055,* **JOSEPH
HEWES.** *1078,* **KNOX.** *1052,* **LANG.** *1060,*
**LOCKWOOD.** *1064,* **MARVIN SHIELDS.**
*1066,* **MEYERKORD.** *1058,* **OUELLET.** *1077,*
**PATTERSON.** *1061,* **PAUL.** *1080,* **REASONER.**
*1063,* **ROARK.** *1053,* **RATHBURNE.** *1057,*
**STEIN.** *1065,* **TRIPPE.** *1075,* **VREELAND.**
*1068,* **W. S. SIMS.** *1059,* **WHIPPLE.** *1062.*
18 more under construction making **46** in the
class.

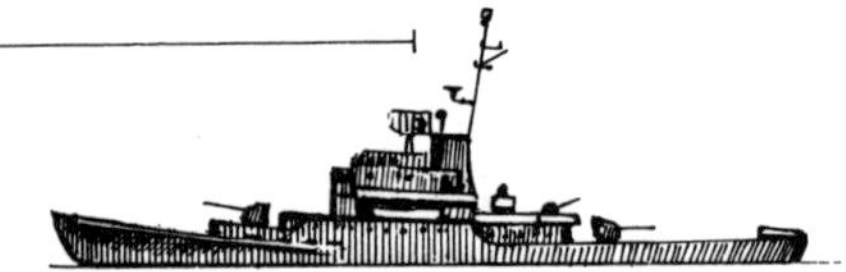

**182.** Da. **TRITON** class. 1955-57. Corvettes.
800 tons. 250 x 32 x 9. (76.3 x 9.6 x 2.7).
2 screws; diesels. 20 knots. 2—3-inch guns.
1 A.A. gun. 2 "Hedgehogs". 4 depth charge
throwers.
**BELLONA.** *F344,* **DIANA.** *F345,* **FLORA.**
*F346,* **TRITON.** *F347.*

Similar: It. **ALBATROS** class. Armament is
being modified.
**AIRONE.** *F545,* **ALBATROS.** *F543,* **ALCIONE.**
*F544,* **AQUILA.** *F542.*

Also: Ia. **PATTIMURA** class. Frigates. **PATTI-
MURA.** *252,* **SULTAN HASANUDIN.** *253.*
These ships have 3 screws and a speed of 22
knots.

**183.** It. **BERGAMINI** class. 1961-62. Frigates.
1,700 tons. 308 x 37 x 10. (94 x 11.4 x 3.1).
2 screws; diesels. 26 knots. 3—3-inch A.A. guns.
1 anti-submarine depth charge mortar. 2 anti-
submarine torpedo launchers (triple). 1 helicopter.
Very similar to number 182 but distinguished by
two turrets and a launcher forward.
**CARLO BERGAMINI.** *F593,* **CARLO MAR-
GOTTINI.** *F595,* **LUIGI RIZZO.** *F596,* **VIRGIN-
IO FASAN.** *F594.*

**184.** Am. **BAINBRIDGE.** *25.* 1962. Guided Missile Frigate. 7,600 tons. 565 x 58 x 29. (172.5 x 17.6 x 7.9). 2 screws; nuclear-powered turbines. 30 knots. 4—3-inch A.A. guns (twin). 2 surface-to-air "Terrier" launchers (twin). 1 anti-submarine "Asroc" launcher (8 tubes). 2 torpedo launchers (triple).

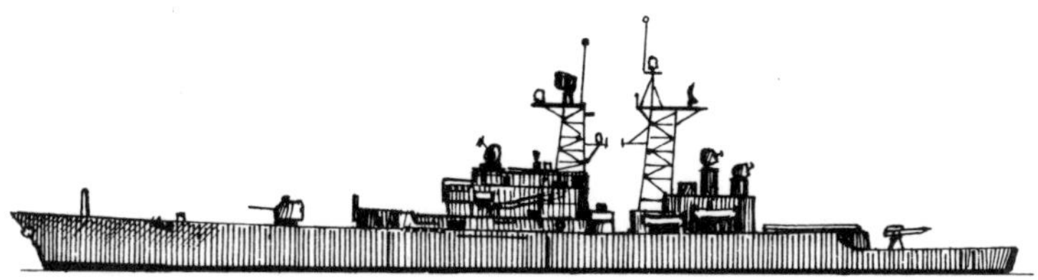

**185.** Am. **TRUXTON.** *35.* 1967. Guided Missile Frigate. 8,200 tons. 564 x 58 x 31. (172 x 17.7 x 9.4). 2 screws; nuclear-powered turbines. 30 knots. 1—5-inch D.P. gun. 2—3-inch A.A. guns. 1 twin launcher for surface-to-air "Terrier" or anti-submarine "Asroc" missiles. 2 anti-submarine torpedo launchers (triple). 2 fixed anti-submarine torpedo tubes. Facilities for helicopters.

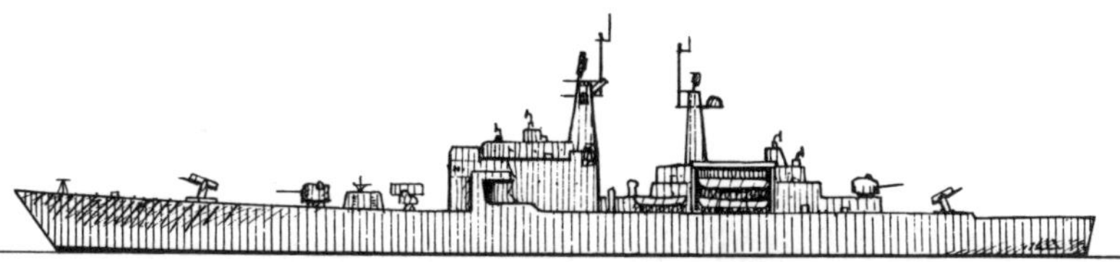

**186.** Am. **CALIFORNIA.** *36.* 1972. Guided Missile Frigate. 10,200 tons. 596 x 61. (181.7 x 18.6). 2 screws; nuclear-powered turbines. 30 knots. 2—5-inch D.P. guns. Surface-to-air "Tartar" and other launchers. 1 anti-submarine "Asroc" launcher (8 tubes). Anti-submarine torpedo launchers.
Sisterships **DLGN** *37* is in course of construction.

**187.** Br. **SALISBURY** class. 1957-60. Refitted 1962-68. Frigates. 2,200 tons. 340 x 40 x 16. (103.6 x 12.2 x 4.7). 2 screws; diesels. 25 knots. 2—4.5-inch guns. 1 surface-to-air "Seacat" launcher (quadruple). 1 "Squid" depth charge mortar (3 barrelled).
**LINCOLN.** *F99,* **SALISBURY.** *F32.* See number 188 for the other two units of this class.

**188.** Br. **SALISBURY** class. 1958. Refitted 1964 and 1966. Tonnage and dimensions as number 187. 2—4.5-inch D.P. guns. 2 A.A. guns. 1 "Squid" depth charge mortar (3 barrelled).
**CHICHESTER.** *F59,* **LLANDAFF.** *F61.*
Distinguished from number 187 by A.A. gun aft in place of launcher.

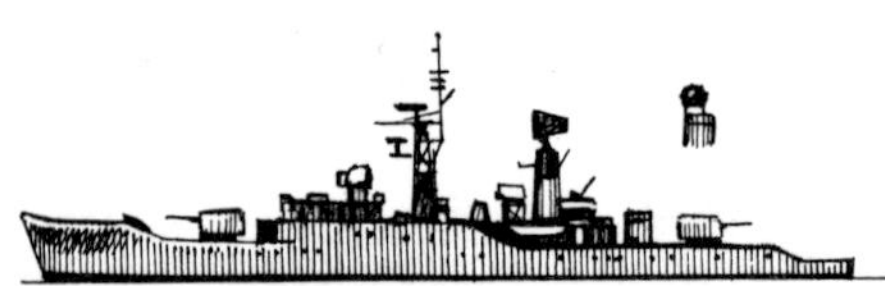

**189.** Br. **LEOPARD** class. 1957-59. Refitted 1963-66. Frigates. 2,300 tons. 340 x 40 x 16. (103.6 x 12.2 x 4.9). 2 screws; diesels. 25 knots. 4—4.5-inch D.P. guns (twin). 1 A.A. gun. 1 "Squid" depth charge mortar. Distinguished from the Salisbury class by the two gun turrets and the lattice foremast.
**JAGUAR.** *F37,* **LEOPARD.** *F14,* **LYNX.** *F27* (*see silhouette 122*), **PUMA.** *F34.*

Similar: Indian ships with both masts lattice: **BEAS.** *F137,* **BETWA.** *F139,* **BRAHMAPU-TRA.** *F31. See silhouette No. 122.*

**190.** Du. **VAN SPEIJK** class (LEANDER type). 1967-68. Frigates. 2,200 tons. 372 x 41 x 18. (113.3 x 12.5 x 5.5). 2 screws; turbines. 28 knots. 2—4.5-inch guns (twin). 1 anti-submarine depth charge mortar (3 barrelled). 2 surface-to-air "Seacat" launchers (quadruple). 1 helicopter. Basically similar to the British Leander class but with a slightly different bridge and smaller director forward. Smaller directors for launchers are abreast the mainmast. Radar aerial on the mainmast is different from the British type.
**EVERTSEN.** *F815,* **ISAAC SWEERS.** *F814,* **TJERK HIDDES.** *F804,* **VAN GALEN.** *F803,* **VAN NES.** *F805,* **VAN SPEIJK.** *F802.*

**191.** Br. **LEANDER** class. 1963-71. Frigates. 2,500 tons. 372 x 41 or 43 x 18. (113.4 x 12.5 or 13.1 x 5.5). 2 screws; turbines. 30 knots. 2—4.5-inch D.P. guns (twin). 2 A.A. guns. 1 anti-submarine "Limbo" depth charge mortar. 1 helicopter.

The following ships are of the later Leander type and were completed with the "Seacat" launcher: **ACHILLES.** *F12,* **ARGONAUT.** *F56,* **ANDRO-MEDA.** *F57,* **APOLLO, ARETHUSA.** *F38,* **ARIADNE, BACCHANTE.** *F69,* **CHARYBDIS.** *F75,* **CLEOPATRA.** *F28* **DANAE.** *F47,* **DIO-MEDE.** *F16,* **HERMIONE.** *F58,* **JUNO.** *F52,* **JUPITER.** *F60,* **MINERVA.** *F45,* **NAIAD.** *F39,* **PHOEBE.** *F42,* **SCYLLA.** *F71,* **SIRIUS.** *F40.*

The following are Commonwealth ships of the later type:
In.: **HIMGIRI, NILGIRI.**
NZ.: **CANTERBURY, WAIKATO.** *F55.*

The following British ships were the early ones which were completed with A.A. guns aft (see inset). In some of these ships these guns may now be replaced by a "Seacat" launcher:
**AJAX.** *F12,* **AURORA.** *F10,* **DIDO.** *F104,* **EURYALUS.** *F15,* **GALATEA.** *F18,* **LEANDER.** *F109.*
Also of the early type but with all A.A. guns removed as well as the "hayrake" aerial from the mainmast is the **PENELOPE.** *F127.* Now used as a trials ship.

**192.** Au. **RIVER** class. 1963-64. Escorts. 2,100 tons. 370 x 41 x 13. (113 x 12.5 x 3.9). 2 screws; turbines. 30 knots. 2—4.5-inch D.P. guns. 1 surface-to-air "Seacat" launcher (quadruple). 1 anti-submarine "Ikara" launcher. 1 "Limbo" depth charge mortar (3 barrels). Differs from other ships in class by not having drop in hull right aft.
**DERWENT.** *49,* **STUART.** *48.* The following ships, recently completed, probably have this appearance. **SWAN, TORRENS.**

**193.** Au. **RIVER** class. 1961. Escort. All details as for No. 192. Hull form different; slightly shorter mainmast and more built-up super-structure around mainmast.
**PARRAMATTA.** *46,* **YARRA.** *45.*

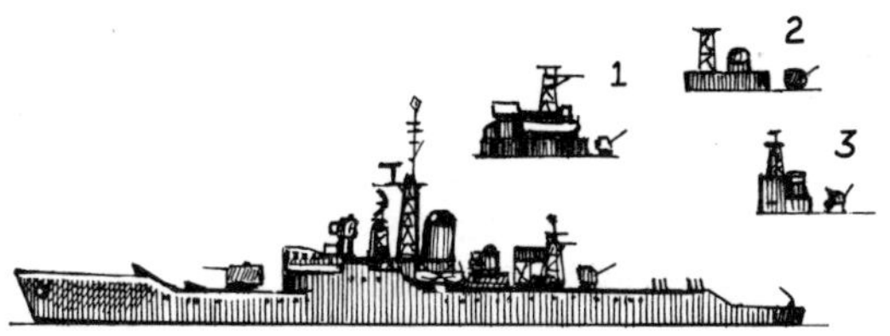

**194.** Br. **WHITBY** class. 1956-58. Frigates. 2,200 tons. 370 x 41 x 17. (113 x 12.5 x 5.2). 2 screws; turbines. 30 knots. 2—4.5-inch D.P. guns (twin). 2 A.A. guns. 2 anti-submarine "Limbo" depth charge mortars (3 barrels). **TORQUAY.** *F43,* **WHITBY.** *F36,* **BLACK-POOL.** *F77* (lent to R.N.Z.N.).

Similar: **EASTBOURNE.** *F73,* **TENBY.** *F65.* (See inset No. 1 and silhouette No. 112).

Similar but possibly, retains original small vertical funnel: **SCARBOROUGH.** *F63.* (See silhouette No. 110).

In. **TALWAR.** *F140,* **TRISHUL.** *F143.* (See inset No. 2 and silhouette No. 109).

SA. **PRESIDENT KRUGER.** *F150,* **PRESIDENT PRETORIUS.** *F145,* **PRESIDENT STEYN.** *F147.* (See inset No. 3 and silhouette No. 111).

**195.** Br. Modified **ROTHESAY** class. 1960-61. Modified 1966 and onwards. Frigates. 2,400 tons. 370 x 41 x 17. (113 x 12.5 x 5.3). 2 screws; turbines. 30 knots. 2—4.5-inch D.P. guns. 1 surface-to-air "Seacat" launcher (quadruple). 1 anti-submarine "Limbo" depth charge mortar (triple). 1 helicopter. **LONDONDERRY.** *F108,* **PLYMOUTH.** *F126,* **RHYL.** *F129,* **ROTHESAY.** *F107,* **YAR-MOUTH.** *F101.* The remaining ships of this class (see No. 196) are probably in course of conversion to this configuration.

**196.** Br. **ROTHESAY** class. 1960-1961. Dimensions and engines as for No. 195. 2—4.5-inch D.P. guns (twin). 1 A.A. gun. 2 anti-submarine "Limbo" depth charge mortars (triple). **BERWICK.** *F115,* **BRIGHTON.** *F106,* **FAL-MOUTH.** *F113,* **LOWESTOFT.** *F103.*

NZ. Similar with "Seacat" launcher aft (see inset) and silhouette No. 94. **OTAGO.** *F111,* **TARANAKI.** *F148.*

**197.** My. **RAMAT.** *F24.* 1969. Frigate. 1,600 tons. 308 x 34 x 15. (94 x 10.4 x 4.5). 2 screws; diesel and gas turbine. 27 knots. 1—4.5-inch D.P. gun. 2 A.A. guns. 1 surface-to-air "Seacat" launcher (quadruple). 1 anti-submarine "Limbo" depth charge mortar (3 barrels). 1 helicopter. Yarrow type. Ex-**HANG JEBAT** (1970).

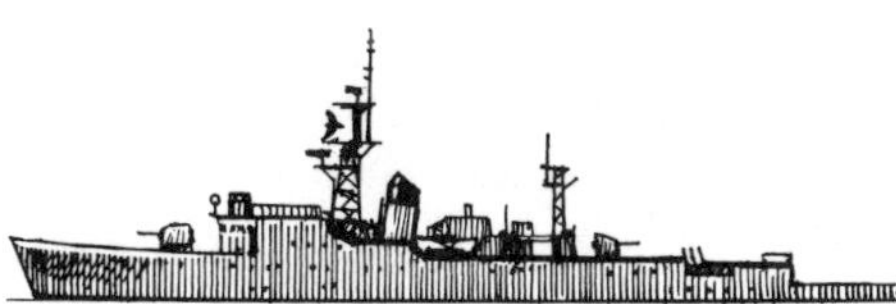

**198.** Ca. **ALGONQUIN** class. 1944-45. Converted 1956. Re-fitted 1958. Destroyer Escort. 2,100 tons. 363 x 36 x 13. (110.8 x 10.8 x 4). 2 screws; turbines. 31 knots. 2—4-inch guns (twin). 2—3-inch guns (twin). 2 A.A. guns. 1 anti-submarine "Limbo" depth charge mortar (triple). 3 anti-submarine torpedo launchers. **CRESCENT.** *226.* Similar; **ALGONQUIN.** *224.*

**199.** Br. **UNDAUNTED.** *F53.* 1944. Converted 1952-54. Frigate. 2,200 tons. 363 x 36 x 17. (110.8 x 10.9 x 5.2). 2 screws; turbines. 32 knots. 2—4-inch guns (twin). 2 A.A. guns. 2 anti-submarine "Limbo" depth charge mortars (triple). Helicopter deck.

**200.** Br. **GRENVILLE.** *F197.* 1943. Converted 1953-54. Frigate. Re-fitted 1969-70. Tonnage and dimensions etc., as for No. 199. 2—4-inch A.A. guns. 1 "Limbo" anti-submarine depth charge mortar (triple). Trials Ship and Training Ship. Distinguished by enclosed foremast.

**201.** SA. **VRYSTAAT.** *F157.* 1944. Converted 1951-52. Frigate. Particulars as for No. 199. Speed 36 knots. 2—4-inch guns. 2 A.A. guns. 1 "Squid" anti-submarine depth charge mortar (triple). Originally British "W" class Destroyer. Recognized by gun house aft.

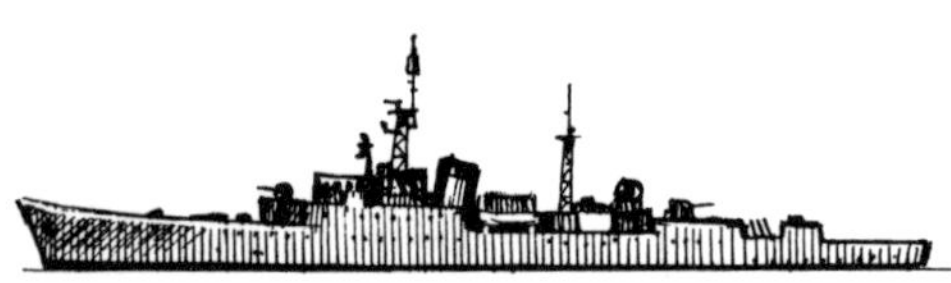

**202.** Au. **QUEENBOROUGH** class. 1942. Converted 1954-57. Frigates. All particulars as for No. 199 but no helicopter deck.
**QUEENBOROUGH.** *02,* **QUIBERON.** *03,* **QUICKMATCH.** *04.*
Originally British "Q" class Destroyers. Similar to "Vrystaat" but different bridge.

**203.** Br. **RAPID.** *F138.* 1943. Converted 1952-53. Frigate. Dimensions etc. same as for No. 200. 2—4-inch guns. 2 A.A. guns. 2 anti-submarine "Limbo" depth charge mortars (triple). Similar in appearance to No. 200 but has both mast lattice.

**204.** Br. **ULSTER.** *F83.* 1943. Converted 1952-54. Frigate. Particulars as for No. 203. Distinguished by her "Leopard" type bridge.

**205.** Br. **BLACKWOOD** class. 1955-58. Frigates. 1,200 tons. 310 x 33 x 152. (94.5 x 10.1 x 4.7). Turbines. 27 knots. 2 A.A. guns. 2 anti-submarine "Limbo" depth charge mortars (triple).
**DUNCAN.** *F80,* **DUNDAS.** *F48,* **HARDY.** *F54,* **KEPPEL.** *F85,* **MALCOLM.** *F88,* **MURRAY.** *F91,* **PALLISER.** *F94,* **RUSSELL.** *F97.*
**BLACKWOOD.** *F78* serves as part of shore training establishment at Portsmouth.

Readily distinguished by large vertical funnel set about amidships.

In. Practically identical to the British ships are the following.
**KHUKRI.** *F149,* **KIRPAN.** *F144,* **KUTHAR.** *F146.*

**206.** Br. **EXMOUTH.** *F84.* The remaining ship of "Blackwood" class was converted in 1966-70 to gas turbine propulsion. She is quite distinctive in appearance.

**207.** Fr. **COMMANDANT RIVIERE** class. 1962-65. Frigates. 1,800 tons. 338 x 38 x 14. (103 x 11.5 x 4.3). 2 screws; diesels. 25 knots. 3—3.9 inch A.A. guns. 2 smaller A.A. guns. 1 anti-submarine mortar (quadruple). 6 anti-submarine torpedo tubes. Can land helicopter aft.
**AMIRAL CHARNER.** *F727,* **COMMANDANT BORY.** *F726,* **COMMANDANT BOURDAIS.** *F740,* **COMMANDANT RIVIERE.** *F733,* **DOUDART DE LA GREE.** *F728,* **ENSEIGNE DE VAISSEAU HENRY.** *F749,* **PROTET.** *F748,* **VICTOR SCHOELCHER.** *F725.* "Bory" has gas turbines.

Po. **COMANDANTE HERMENEGILDO CAPELO.** *F481,* **COMANDANTE JOAO BELO.** *F480,* **COMANDANTE ROBERTO IVENS.** *F482,* **COMANDANTE SACADURA CABRAL.** *F483.*

**208.** Fr. **BALNY.** *F729.* 1969. Frigate. Dimensions the same as No. 207 but gas turbine engines and only one gunhouse aft.

**209.** Ja. **THUNDER** class. 1956. Escorts. 1,100 tons. 289 x 29 x 10. (87.5 x 8.7 x 3.1). 2 screws; diesels. 25 knots. 2—3-inch guns. 2 A.A. guns. 1 anti-submarine "Hedgehog" 8 K guns. 2 depth charge racks.
**IKAZUCHI.** *202,* **INAZUMA.** *203.*

**210.** Ja. **ERIMO.** *491.* 1955. Minelayer and Minesweeper. 630 tons. 210 x 26 x 8. (64 x 7.9 x 2.4). 4 A.A. guns. 1 "Hedgehog". 2 K guns. 2 depth charge racks.

**211.** Am. **HAMILTON** class. 1967-69. Coast Guard Cutters. 2,700 tons. 378 x 42 x 20. (115.2 x 12.8 x 6.1) 2 screws; diesel and gas turbines. 29 knots. 1—5-inch gun. 2 mortars. 2 "Hedgehogs". 2 anti-submarine torpedo launchers (triple). 1 helicopter. Funnels abreast.
**BOUTWELL.** *719,* **CHASE.** *718,* **DALLAS.** *716,* **GALLATIN.** *721,* **HAMILTON.** *715,* **JARVIS.** *724,* **MELLON.** *717,* **MORGENTHAU.** *722,* **MUNTO.** *725,* **RUSH.** *723,* **SHERMAN.** *720.*

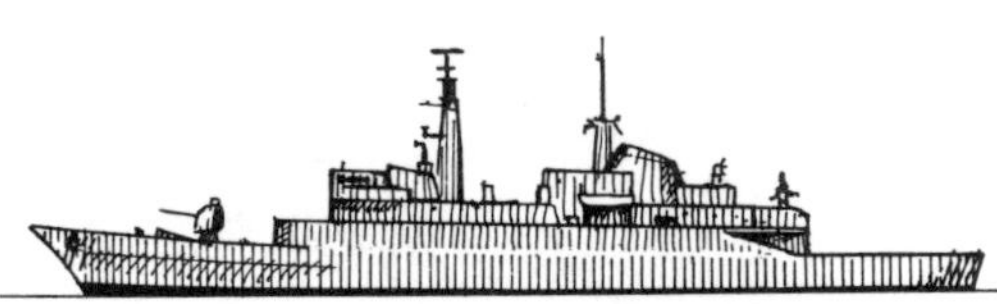

**212.** Br. **AMAZON.** Type 21. Building. Frigate. 2,500 tons. 384 ft. o.a. Gas turbines. 1—4.5-inch gun. 1 surface-to-air "Seacat" launcher. Helicopter. 4 ships in class. Vosper Thornycroft Type

**213.** Ly. Vosper Thornycroft Mark 7 type. Frigate. 1,500 tons. 330 x 36 x 11. (100.5 x 10.9 x 3.3). Gas turbines. 37 knots. 1—4.5-inch gun. 2 surface-to-air "Seacat" launchers (quadruple). 1 helicopter.

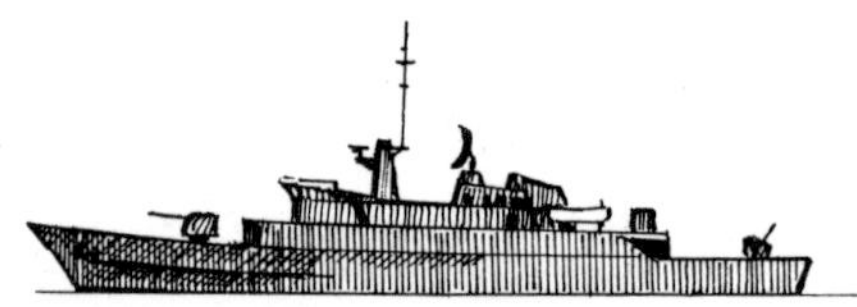

**214.** Ir. **SAAM** class. 1969 and onwards. Frigates. 1,200 tons. 310 (94.4). 2 screws; gas turbines. 35 knots. 1—4.5-inch gun. 1 surface-to-air "Seacat" launcher (quadruple). 1 anti-submarine depth charge launcher. Vosper Thornycroft Mark 5 type.
**FARAMAZ, ROSTAM, SAAM, ZAAL.**

**215.** No. **SLEIPNER** class. 1965-67. Patrol Vessels. 600 tons. 228 x 62. (69.5 x 18.9). 2 screws; diesel. 20 knots. 1—3-inch gun. 1 A.A. gun. "Terne" anti-submarine system.
**AEGER.** *P951,* **SLEIPNER.** *P950.*

**216.** No. **OSLO** class. 1966-67. Frigates. 1,500 tons. 317 x 37 x 17. (96.6 x 11.2 x 5 3). Turbines. 25 knots. 4—3-inch guns (twin). "Terne" anti-submarine system.
**BERGEN.** *F301,* **NARVIK.** *F304,* **OSLO.** *F300,* **STAVANGER.** *F303,* **TRONDHEIM.** *F302.*

Distinguished from No. 215 by smaller raking funnel and raking topmast.

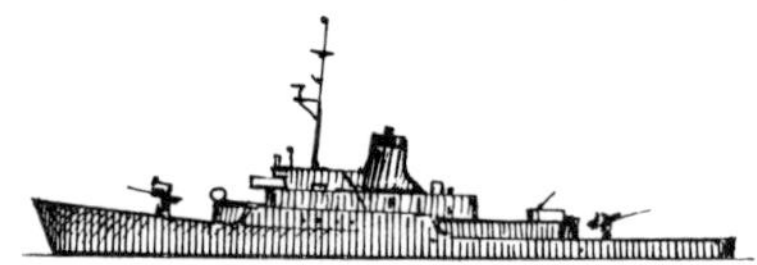

**217.** Ir. **BAYANDOR.** *F25.* 1963-68. Corvettes. 900 tons. 275 x 33 x 10. (83.8 x 10 x 3). Diesels. 20 knots. 2—3-inch guns. 2 A.A. guns. "Hedgehog" anti-submarine weapon. Built in U.S. as PF Type.
**KAHNAMUIE.** *F28,* **MILANIAN.** *F27,* **NAGHDI.** *F26.*

**218.** Po. NATO Type. **PERO ESCOBAR.** *F335.* 1957. Modernised 1968-69. Frigates. 1,300 tons. 322 x 36 x 10. (98 x 10.8 x 3). 2 screws; turbines. 32 knots. 4—3-inch guns. 2 anti-submarine torpedo tubes (triple). 2 "Squid" anti-submarine depth charge mortars. Distinguished by launcher before bridge.

Ve.

**ALMIRANTE CLEMENTE.** *D12,* **GENERAL JOSE TRINIDAD MORAN.** *D22,* **GENERAL JUAN JOSE FLORES.** *D13.*

**219.** Ve. Modified **ALMIRANTE CLEMENTE** class. 1956-57. Modernised 1962-69. Dimensions like No. 218. 4—4-inch guns (twin). 4—8-inch A.A. guns. 2 anti-submarine "Squid" depth charge mortars. 4 depth charge racks or 1 "Lanciabas". 4 depth charge mortars and 2 racks.
**ALMIRANTE JOSE GARCIA.** *D33,* **ALMIRANTE BRION.** *D23,* **GENERAL JOSE DE AUSTRIA.** *D32.*

Distinguished by elimination of deck tubes and longer superstructure. Three guns aft.

**220.** Ia. **SURAPATI** class. 1958. Frigates. Dimensions as No. 218. 4—4-inch guns (twin). 12 A.A. guns (twin). 3 torpedo tubes. 2 anti-submarine "Hedgehogs"; 4 depth charge throwers.
**IMAN BONDJOL.** *250,* **SURAPATI.** *251.*

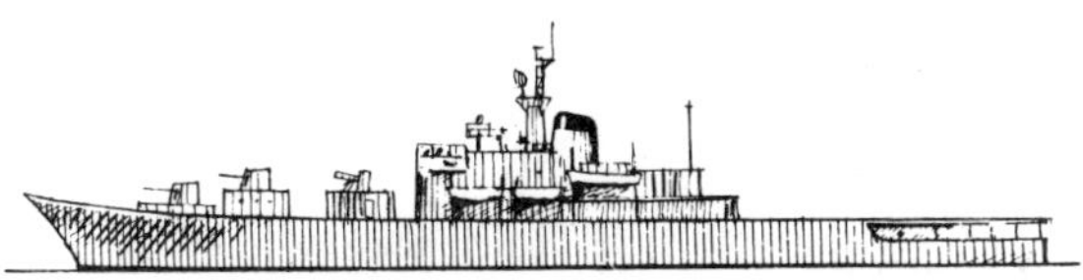

**223.** Ja. **KATORI.** *3501.* 1970. Training Ship. 3,400 tons. 419 x 49 x 15. (127.7 x 14.9 x 4 6). Turbines. 25 knots. 2—3-inch guns (twin). 1 anti-submarine rocket launcher (triple). 2 anti-submarine torpedo launchers (triple). Helicopter.

**224.** Au. **VAMPIRE.** *11.* 1959. Modernised. Destroyer 2,800 tons. 389 x 43 x 13. (118.4 x 13.1 x 3.9). 2 screws; turbines. 30 knots. 4—4.5-inch guns (twin). 6 A.A. guns. 5 torpedo tubes (quintuple). 1 anti-submarine "Limbo" depth charge mortar (triple). Modified "Daring" class. Distinguished from No. 225 by having only one turret foreward.

**225.** Au. **VENDETTA.** *08.* Identical with No. 224 but has turret in "B" position in addition.

**226.** Br. **DARING** class. 1952-54. Re-fitted 1963-64. Destroyers. Dimensions as for No. 224. 6—4.5-inch guns. 2 to 6 A.A. guns. 5 torpedo tubes (quintuple) in "Diamond" and "Duchess" only. 1 anti-submarine "Squid" depth charge mortar (triple).

The British ships are much less "built up" around second funnel, (first is within the lattice foremast), than Australian ships.

**DAINTY.** *D108,* **DEFENDER.** *D114,* **DIAMOND.** *D35.*
**RAN.**

Au. **DUCHESS.** *154,*

Pv. **DECOY** and **DIANA** sold to Peru in 1970

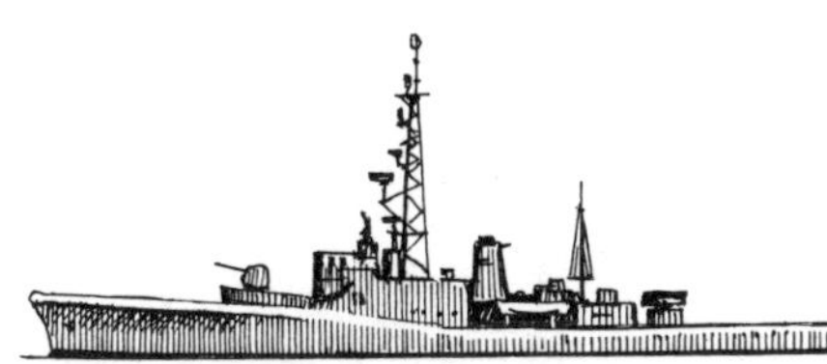

**227.** Ca. **TERRA NOVA.** 1959. Modernised 1967. Destroyer Escorts. 2,400 tons. 371 (after conversion) x 42 x 14. (113 x 12.8 x 4.1). 2 screws; turbines. 28 knots. 2—3-inch A.A. guns (twin). 1 anti-submarine "Asroc" launcher.

**228.** Ca. **RESTIGOUCHE** class. 1959-64. To be modernised like No. 227. Destroyer Escorts. Dimensions as for No. 227. 4—3-inch A.A. guns. 2 anti-submarine "Limbo" depth charge mortar (3 barrels).
**CHAUDIERE.** *235,* **COLUMBIA.** *260,* **GATINEAU.** *236,* **KOOTENAY.** *258,* **RESTIGOUCHE.** *257,* **ST. CROIX.** *256.*
Very similar are the ships of **MACKENZIE** class:
**MACKENZIE.** *261,* **QU'APPELLE.** *264,* **SASKATCHEWAN.** *262,* **YUKON.** *263.*

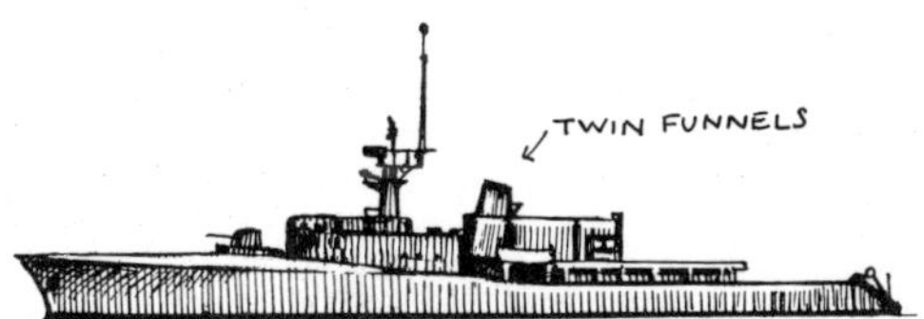


**229.** Ca. **ANNAPOLIS** class. 1959. Particulars the same as for No. 227 but 2—3-inch guns foreward only and 1 anti-submarine "Limbo" depth charge mortar. Helicopter.
**ANNAPOLIS.** *265,* **NIPIGON.** *266.*
Similar in appearance are ships of **ST. LAURENT** class:
**ASSINIBOINE.** *234,* **FRASER.** *233,* **MARGAREE.** *230,* **OTTAWA.** *229,* **SAGUENAY.** *206,* **ST. LAURENT.** *205,* **SKEENA.** *207.*

**230.** It. **DE CRISTOFARO** class. 1965-66. Corvettes. 850 tons. 263 x 34 x 9. (80.2 x 10.3 x 2.7). 2 screws; diesels. 23 knots. 2—3-inch D.P. guns. 1 anti-submarine depth charge mortar. 2 anti-submarine torpedo tubes (triple).
**LICIO VISINTINI.** *F546,* **PIETRO DE CRISTO-FARO.** *F540,* **SALVATORE TODARO.** *F550,* **UMBERTO GROSSO.** *F541.*

**231.** Ve. **NUEVA ESPARTA** class. 1953-56. Refitted 1959-60. Refitted 1964-69. 2,600 tons. 402 x 43 x 19. (122.5 x 13.1 x 5.8). 2 screws; turbines. 34 knots. 6—4.5-inch guns (twir). 16 A.A. guns. 2 anti-submarine "Squid" depth charge mortars, or 1 surface-to-air "Seacat" launcher. 2 depth charge racks.
**ARAGUA.** *D31,* **NUEVA ESPARTA.** *D11,* **ZULIA.** *D21.*

**232.** Au. **BATTLE** class. 1951. Modernised 1966. Destroyer. 2,400 tons. 379 x 41 x 14. (115.5 x 12.5 x 4.1). 2 screws; turbines. 31 knots. 4—4.5-inch guns (twin). 6 A.A. guns. 10 torpedo tubes (quintuple). 1 anti-submarine "Squid" depth charge mortar.
**TOBRUK.** *37.* Distinguished from No. 233 by gun in "B" position.

**233.** Au. **BATTLE** class. 1951. Modernised 1966. Destroyer. Tonnage and dimensions as No. 232. 2—4.5-inch guns (twin). 6 A.A. guns. 1 anti-submarine "Squid" depth charge mortar.
**ANZAC.** *59.*

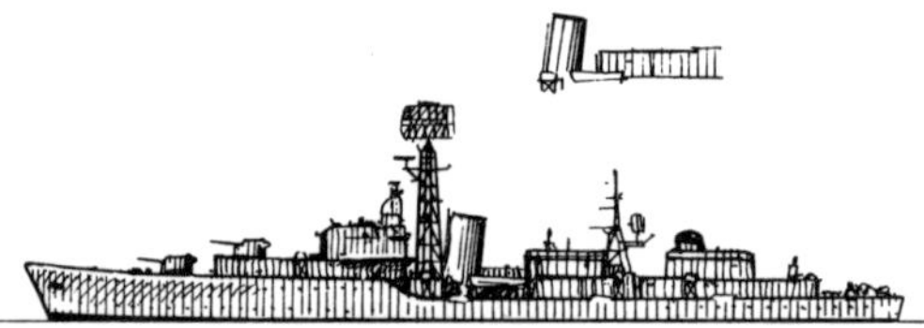

**234.** Br. **LATER BATTLE** class. 1947. Converted 1962. Radar Picket Destroyers. 2,800 tons. 379 x 41 x 18. (115.5 x 12.3 x 5.3). 2 screws; turbines. 35 knots. 4—4.5-inch D.P. guns. 1 anti-submarine "Squid" depth charge mortar. Distinguished by large "hayrake" on foremast.
**AGINCOURT.** *D86,* **BARROSA.** *D68,* **CO-RUNNA.** *D97.* Inset shows superstructure variation in Agincourt.

**235.** Pk. **BATTLE** class. 1946. Modernised 1957. Destroyers. 2,300 tons. 379 x 40 x 17. (115.5 x 12.3 x 5.2). 2 screws; turbines. 36 knots. 4—4.5-inch guns (twin). 10 A.A. guns. 8 torpedo tubes (quadruple). 1 anti-submarine "Squid" depth charge mortar.
**BADR.** *161,* (see inset), **KHAIBAR.** *163.*

**236.** Ir. **ARTEMIZ.** 1946. Modernised 1965-67. Dimensions, tonnage and engines as No. 235. 4—4.5-inch guns (twin). 8 A.A. guns. 1 surface-to-air "Seacat" launcher (quadruple). Ex-British "Battle" class Destroyer. Distinguished by the enclosed masts.

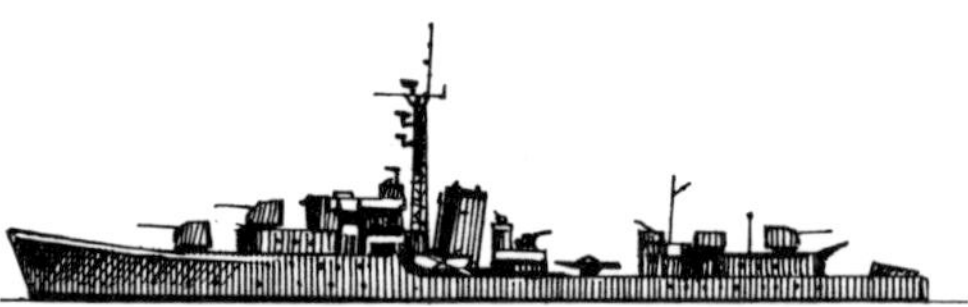

**237.** Tu. **ALP ARSLAN** class (Ex-Br. **MILNE** class). 1941-42. Refitted 1959. Destroyers. 2,100 tons. 363 x 37 x 16. (110.5 x 11.2 x 5). 2 screws; turbines. 36 knots. 6—4.7-inch guns (twin). 6 A.A. guns. 4 torpedo tubes (quadruple). 1 "Squid" depth charge mortar.
**ALP ARSLAN.** *D348,* **KILIC ALI PASA.** *D350,* **MARESAL FEVZI CAKMAK.** *D349,* **PIYALE PASA.** *D351.*

**238.** Is. Ex-Br. **Z** class. 1944. Refitted 1956. Destroyer. 1,700 tons. 362 x 36 x 17. (110.4 x 10.8 x 5.2). 2 screws; turbines. 31 knots. 4—4.5-inch D.P. guns (twin). 6 A.A. guns. 8 torpedo tubes (quadruple). 4 depth charge throwers.
**YAFFO.** *42.*

**239.** Eg. Ex-Br. **Z** class. 1942-44. Refitted 1956. Modernised 1963-64. Destroyers. Tonnage, dimensions, engines and armament as No. 238. Distinguished by tall mast aft.
**EL FATEH. EL QAHER.**

★ **240.** Ys. Ex-Br. **W** class. 1943-44. Refitted 1959. Destroyers. Tonnage and dimensions as No. 239. 2 screws; turbines. 36 knots. 4—4.7-inch guns. 4 A.A. guns. 8 torpedo tubes (quadruple). 4 depth charge throwers.
**KOTOR.** *21,* **PULA.** *22.*

**241.** SA. Ex-Br. **W** class. 1944. Modernised 1962-66. 2,100 tons. 363 x 36 x 17. (110.6 x 10.9 x 5.2). 2 screws; turbines. 36 knots. 4—4-inch guns (twin). 4 A.A. guns. 4 torpedo tubes (quadruple). 2 depth charge throwers. 2 depth charge racks. 2 helicopters.
**JAN VAN RIEBEECK.** *D278,* **SIMON VAN DER STEL.** *D237.*

**242.** In. Ex-Br. **R** class. 1942. Refitted 1949. Destroyers. Tonnage, dimensions and engines as No. 238. 4—4.7-inch guns (twin). 4 A.A. guns. 8 torpedo tubes (quadruple). In Rana only. 4 depth charge throwers.
**RANA.** *D115,* **RAJPUT.** *D209,* **RANJIT.** *D141.*

**243.** Pk. Ex-Br. **O** class. 1941-42. Refitted 1957. Destroyers. 1,800 tons. 345 x 35 x 16. (105.2 x 10.7 x 4.8). 2 screws; turbines. 34 knots. 2—4-inch D.P. guns (twin). 5 A.A. guns. 4 torpedo tubes (quadruple). 2 "Squid" depth charge mortars.
**TIPPU SULTAN.** *260,* **TUGHRIL.** *261.*

**244.** Br. **CA** class. 1944-45. Reconstructed. Destroyers. 2,100 tons. 363 x 36 x 17. (110.6 x 10.9 x 5.2). 2 screws; turbines. 36 knots. 3—4.5-inch D.P. guns. 4 A.A. guns. 4 torpedo tubes (quadruple). 1 surface-to-air "Seacat" launcher (quadruple). 2 "Squid" depth charge mortars (3 barrelled).
**CAPRICE.** *D01,* (see inset of bridge), **CAVALIER.** *D73.*

**245.** Pk. Ex-Br. **CR** class. 1946. Modernised 1957-58. Destroyers. Tonnage, dimensions and engines as No. 244. 3—4.5-inch guns. 6 A.A. guns. 4 torpedo tubes (quadruple). 2 "Squid" depth charge mortars.
**ALAMGIR.** *160,* **JAHANGIR.** *162.*
Similar: (Ex-"Ch" class). **SHAH JAHAN.** *164.*

**246.** Ys. **SPLIT.** *11.* 1958. Destroyer. 2,400 tons. 376 x 37 x 12. (114.7 x 11.1 x 3.8). 2 screws; turbines. 31 knots. 4—5-inch guns. 12 A.A. guns. 5 torpedo tubes (quintuple). 2 "Squid" depth charge mortars (3 barrelled). 6 depth charge throwers. 2 depth charge racks. Mines.
Easily distinguished by torpedo tubes being placed on superstructure.

**247.** Ph. **BLYSKAWICA.** *271.* 1937. Reconstructed 1959-60. Destroyer. 2,100 tons. 374 x 37 x 10. (114 x 11.3 x 3.1). 2 screws; turbines. 39 knots. 8—4-inch D.P. guns. 10 A.A. guns. 3 torpedo tubes (triple). 4 depth charge throwers and racks.

**248.** RC. Ex-U.S.S.R. **GORDY** class. 1941. Destroyers. 1,600 tons. 377 x 34 x 13. (114.9 x 10.2 x 4). 2 screws; turbines. 36 knots. 4—5.1-inch guns (twin). 8 A.A. guns. 6 torpedo tubes (triple). 8 depth charge throwers.
**ANSHAM, CHANG CHUN, FU CHUN.** Fourth ship un-named.

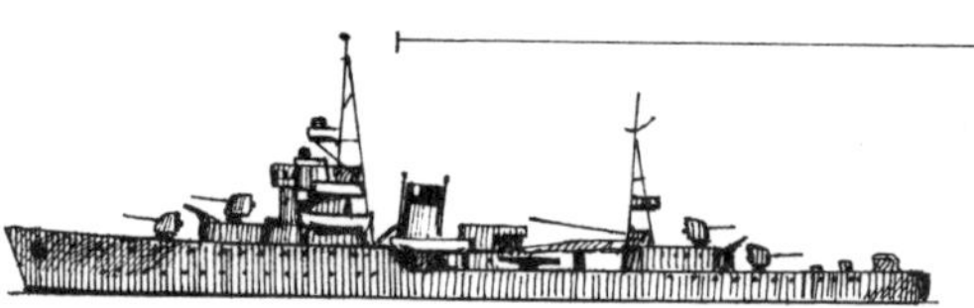

**249.** Th. **MAEKLONG.** *3.* 1937. Refitted 1969. Frigate. 1,400 tons. 270 x 34 x 11. (82 x 10.4 x 3.2). 2 screws; turbines. 14 knots. 4—3-inch guns. 3 A.A. guns.

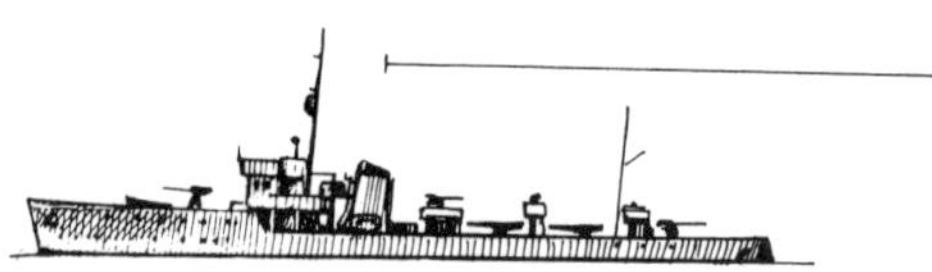

**250.** Th. **TRAD** class. 1935-37. Modified. Patrol Vessels. 318 tons. 223 x 21 x 27. (67.9 x 6.4 x 2.1). 2 screws; turbines. 31 knots. 2—3-inch A.A. guns. 1 or 2 smaller A.A. guns. 2 or 4 torpedo tubes (twin).
**CHANDHABURI.** *22,* **CHUMPORN.** *31,* **PATTANI.** *13,* **PUKET.** *12,* **RAYONG.** *23,* **SURASDRA.** *21,* **TRAD.** *11.*

**251.** Sw. **OLAND** class. 1947-49. Modernised 1960-63. Destroyers. 2,000 tons. 364 x 37 x 11. (111 x 11.2 x 3.4). 2 screws; turbines. 35 knots. 4—4.7-inch D.P. guns (twin). 6 A.A. guns. 6 torpedo tubes (triple). 1 depth charge mortar (triple). Mines. Helicopter platform. Ships differ slightly in appearance.
**OLAND.** *J16,* **UPPLAND.** *J17.*

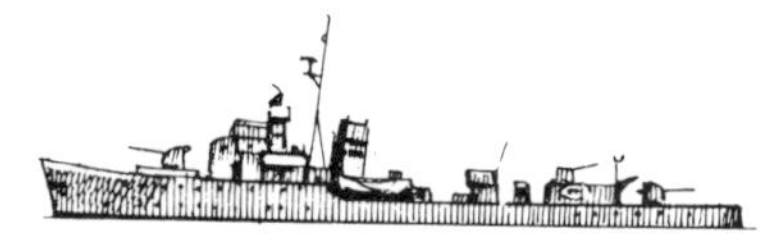

**252.** Eg. Ex-Br. **HUNT** class. 1940. Refitted 1951. Escort. 1,000 tons. 280 x 29 x 14. (85.3 x 8.8 x 4.3). 2 screws; turbines. 25 knots. 4—4-inch guns. 4 A.A. guns. 2 depth charge throwers.
**PORT SAID.** *11.*

**253.** In. Ex-Br. **HUNT** class. 1941-44. Refitted 1953. Escort Destroyers. Tonnage, dimensions and engines as No. 252. 6—4-inch guns (twin). 4 A.A. guns.
**GANGA.** *D94,* **GODAVARI.** *D92,* **GOMATI.** *D93.*

**254.** Ec. Ex-Br. **HUNT** class. 1940-41. Refitted 1955. Escort Destroyers. Tonnage and dimensions as No. 252. 2 screws; turbines. 23 knots. 4—4-inch guns (twin). 2 A.A. guns. 2 depth charge throwers. 2 depth charge racks.
**PRESIDENTE ALFARO.** *D01,* **PRESIDENTE VELASCO IBARRA.** *D02.*

**255.** Ge. Ex-Br. **HUNT** class. 1942. Reconstructed 1962-64. Frigate. Tonnage, dimensions and engines as No. 252. 1—3.9-inch D.P. gun. 4 A.A. guns.
**GNEISENAU.** *F212.*

★ **256.** Ys. **TRIGLAV.** *51.* 1941. Frigate. 1,200 tons. 293 x 33 x 10. (89 x 9.9 x 2.9). 2 screws; turbines. 26 knots. 3—3.9-inch D.P. guns. 11 A.A. guns. 4 torpedo tubes (twin). 4 depth charge throwers.
Differs from No. 257 by extra 3-inch gun aft, shorter forecastle plating and pole mast.

★ **257.** Ys. **BIOKOVO.** *52.* 1943. Tonnage, dimensions and engines as No. 256. 2—3.9-inch D.P. guns. 10 A.A. guns. 4 torpedo tubes (twin). 4 depth charge throwers.

**258.** Sw. **MJOLNER** class. 1955. Frigates. 800 tons. 256 x 26 x 8. (78 x 8 x 2.3). 2 screws; turbines. 30 knots. 2—4.1-inch D.P. guns. 2 A.A. guns.
**MODE.** *73,* **MUNIN.** *75.*

60°

30°

★ **259.** Ru. **RIGA** class. Escorts. 1,200 tons. 295 x 32 x 11. (90 x 9.6 x 3.4). 2 screws; turbines. 28 knots. 3—3.9-inch D.P. guns. 3 A.A. guns. 3 torpedo tubes (triple). 2 anti-submarine rocket launchers (16 barrels). 4 depth charge projectors. Ships vary in appearance some having larger directors etc. Approximately 50 in Soviet navy.

Bu. **DRUZKI, SMELI.**
EG. **ERNST THALMANN, FRIEDRICH ENGELS, KARL LIEBKNECHT, KARL MARX.**
RC. **KAINGNAN** class; similar to "Riga" class. **CH'ENG TU, KUEI LIN, KUEI YANG, K'UN MING.**

*Also* Fi. **HAMEENMAA, UUSIMAA.**
Ia. 7 vessels.

**260.** Fr. **LE NORMAND** class. 1956-60.
Frigates. 1,300 tons. 326 x 34 x 11. (99 x 10.3 x
3.4). Turbines. 28 knots. 6—2.25-inch A.A. guns
(twin). 2 smaller A.A. guns. 12 anti-submarine
torpedo tubes (triple). 1 anti-submarine mortar
(6 barrels). 2 depth charge mortars. 1 depth
charge rack. There are slight variations in the
bridges (see inset).

**LE BASQUE.** *F773,* **LE BOURGUIGNON.**
*F769,* **LE CHAMPENOIS.** *F770,* **LE GASCON.**
*F767,* **LE LORRAIN.** *F768,* **LE NORMAND.**
*F765,* **LE PICARD.** *F766,* **LE SAVOYARD.**
*F771.* Differ from No. 261 by the lighter bridges.

**261.** Fr. **LE NORMAND** class. 1957-58.
Particulars the same as for No. 260.
**L'AGENAIS.** *F774,* **LE BEARNAIS.** *F775,*
**LE BRETON.** *F772.*
Differ from No. 262 by armament and cowl on
funnel.

**262.** Fr. **LE NORMAND** class. 1959-60. Tonnage, dimensions and engines as for No. 261.
4—2.25-inch A.A. guns (twin). 2 smaller A.A.
guns. 12 anti-submarine torpedo tubes (triple).
1 anti-submarine mortar (quadruple). 2 depth
charge mortars. 1 depth charge rack.
**L'ALSACIEN.** *F776,* **LE PROVENCAL.** *F777,*
**LE VENDEEN.** *F778.*

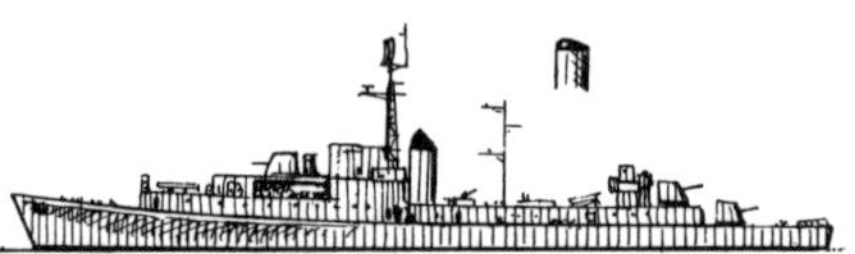

**263.** Fr. **LE CORSE** class. 1955-56. Frigates.
1,300 tons. 326 x 34 x 11. (99 x 10.3 x 3.4).
Turbines. 28 knots. 6—2.25-inch A.A. guns (twin).
2 smaller A.A. guns. 12 anti-submarine torpedo
tubes (triple). 2 anti-submarine mortars. 1 depth
charge rack. 1 rocket launcher (sextuple).
**LE BOULONNAIS.** *F763,* **LE BRESTOIS.** *F762,*
**LE CORSE.** *F761.*

Similar—modified funnel cowl (see inset), **LE
BORDELAIS.** *F764.*
Ships differ from "Le Normand" class by position
of foreward gun.

**264.** Ja. **RIVER** class. 1961-64. Frigates.
1,500 tons. 309 x 34 x 12. (94 x 10.4 x 3.5).
2 screws; diesels. 25 knots. 4—3-inch D.P. guns
(twin). 4 torpedo tubes (quadruple). 2 anti-
submarine torpedo launchers (triple). 1 anti-
submarine rocket launcher (4 barrels). 1 depth
charge thrower. 1 depth charge rack.
**KITAKAMI.** *213,* **OI.** *214.* Possibly also
**CHIKUGO.** *215.*
Similar—see silhouette No. 297—**ISUZU.** *211,*
**MOGAMI.** *212.*

**265.** Tn. **DUSTUR.** *E71.* 1939. Corvette. 650
tons. 257 x 28 x 11. (78.3 x 8.7 x 3.3). 2 screws;
diesels. 20 knots. 1—4.1-inch gun. 5 A.A. guns.
4 depth charge throwers. 2 depth charge racks.
Ex-French ship.

**266.** Am. **BOSTWICK** class. 1943-44. Escorts or Frigates. 1,200 tons. 306 x 37 x 14. (93 x 11.3 x 4.3). Twin screw; diesel-electric. 21 knots. 3—3-inch A.A. guns. 2 smaller A.A. guns. "Hedgehogs" and depth charges.
**ACREE.** *167,* **COFFMAN.** *191,* **COONER.** *172,* **EARL K. OLSEN.** *765,* **HILBERT.** *742,* **KYNE.** *744,* **LAMONS.** *743,* **LEVY.** *162,* **McCLELLAND.** *750,* **McDONNELL.** *163,* **OS-TERHOUS.** *164,* **OSWALD.** *767,* **PARKS.** *165,* **SNYDER.** *745,* **STRAUB.** *181,* **THUMPETER.** *180.*

Bz. Frigates. "Bertioga" class. **BAEPENDI.** *U27,* **BAURU.** *U28,* **BENEVENTE.** *U30,* **BOCAINA.** *U32,* **BRACUI.** *U31.*
Cs. Frigates. **TAI CHAO.** *26,* **TAI HO.** *23,* **TAI HU.** *25,* **TAI TSANG.** *24.*
Gr. Frigates. **AETOS.** *01,* **PANTHIR.** *67.* Two other ships are shown under No. 267.
It. Frigates. "Altair" class. Have tripod mast (see inset) and built up bridge. **ALDEBARAN.** *F590,* **ALTAIR.** *F591,* **ANDROMEDA.** *F592.*
Ja. Frigates. "Sun" class. **ASAHI.** *262,* **HAT-SUHI.** *263.*
Ko. Frigates. **KANG WON.** *72,* **KYONG KI.** *71,*
Pv. Destroyer Escorts. "Castilla" class. **AGUIRRE.** *62,* **CASTILLA.** *61.* **RODRIGUEZ.** *63.*
Th. Destroyer Escort. **PIN KLAO.** *3.*
Ur. Destroyer Escort. **URUGUAY.** *DE1.* For sister see No. 267.

**270.** Bz. **AMAZONAS** class. 1949-51. Destroyers. 1,500 tons. 323 x 35 x 9. (98.5 x 10.7 x 2.7). 2 screws; turbines. 34 knots. 3—5-inch guns. 6 A.A. guns. 6 torpedo tubes (triple). 4 depth charge throwers.
**ACRE.** *D10,* **AMAZONAS.** *D12,* **ARAGUAIA.** *D14,* **ARAGUARI.** *D15.*

**267.** Ex-American **BOSTWICK** class. All details as for No. 266 but they have a mainmast.
Gr. Frigates. **IERAX.** *31,* **LEON.** *54.*
Ur. Destroyer Escort. **ARTIGAS.** *DE2.*

**268.** Fr. **ARABE** class. (Ex-U.S. "Bostwick" class). 1944. Converted 1956. Experimental vessel. 1,300 tons. 306 x 37 x 11. (93 x 11.3 x 3.3). 2 screws; diesel-electric. 19 knots. All armament removed.
**ARAGO.** *A607.*

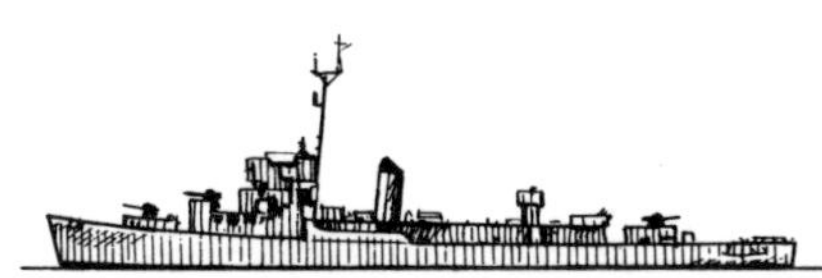

**269.** Am. **EDSALL** class. 1943-44. Escorts. 1,200 tons. 306 x 37 x 11. (93.3 x 11.3 x 3). 2 screws; diesel. 21 knots. 3—3-inch A.A. guns. Up to 8 smaller A.A. guns (removed from some ships). "Hedgehogs" and depth charges.
**CHATELAIN.** *149,* **COCKRILL.** *398,* **DALE W. PETERSEN.** *337,* **DANIEL.** *335,* **DOUGLAS L. HOWARD.** *138,* **EDSALL.** *129,* **FARQU-HAR.** *139,* **HAMMANN.** *131,* **HERBERT C. JONES.** *137,* **HILL.** *141,* **HURST.** *250,* **HUSE.** *146,* **INCH.** *146,* **JACOB JONES.** *130,* **JANS-SEN.** *396,* **J. R. Y. BLAKELEY.** *140,* **KEITH.** *241,* **MARCHAND.** *249,* **MENGES.** *320,* **MERRILL.** *392,* **MOORE.** *240,* **MOSLEY.** *321,* **NEUNZER.** *150* **O'REILLY.** *330,* **PETTIT.** *253,* **POOLE.** *151,* **POPE.** *134,* **PRIDE.** *323,* **RICK-ETTS.** *254,* **SLOAT.** *245,* **STANTON.** *247,* **STEWART.** *238,* **STOCKDALE.** *399,* **SWA-SEY.** *248,* **SWENNING.** *394,* **TOMICH.** *242,* **WILLIS.** *395.* See also No. 273.

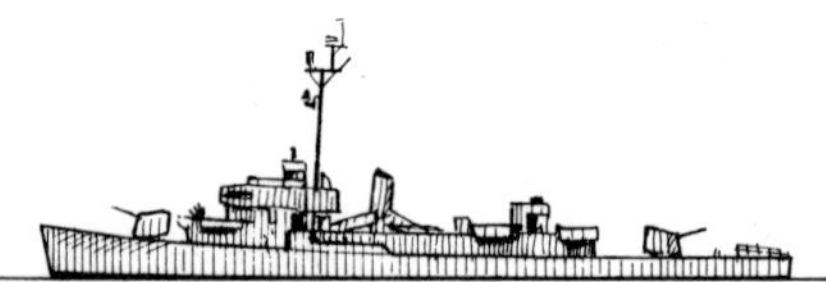

**271.** Am. **BUCKLEY** class. 1943-44. Escorts. 1,400 tons. 306 x 37 x 14. (93.3 x 11.3 x 4.3). 2 screws; turbo-electric. 23 knots. 2—5-inch D.P. guns. Up to 8 A.A. guns (removed from some ships). "Hedgehogs" and depth charges. 11 ships of this class have this appearance, others are like No. 272 or silhouette No. 516.

As the present appearance of all ships is not known, all ships of the class are listed below: **ALEXANDER J. LUKE.** *577,* **COOLBAUGH.** *217,* **CRONIN.** *704,* **DAMON M. CUMMINGS.** *643,* **EICHENBERGER.** *202,* **FIEBERLUNG.** *640,* **FRANCIS M. ROBINSON.** *220,* **FRYBARGER.** *705,* **GENDREAU.** *639,* **GILLETTE.** *681,* **GUNASON.** *793,* **HOLTUM.** *703,* **JACK W. WILKE.** *800,* **MAJOR.** *796,* **MARSH.** *699,* **OSMUS.** *701,* **ROBERT I. PAINE.** *578,* **SPANGLER.** *696,* **VARIAN.** *798,* **WILLIAM C. COLE.** *641,* **WISEMAN.** *667.*

**272.** Am. **BUCKLEY** class. Escorts. Details as above but they have 2 or 3—3-inch guns. Some have mainmasts. See silhouette No. 516. For names see No. 271.

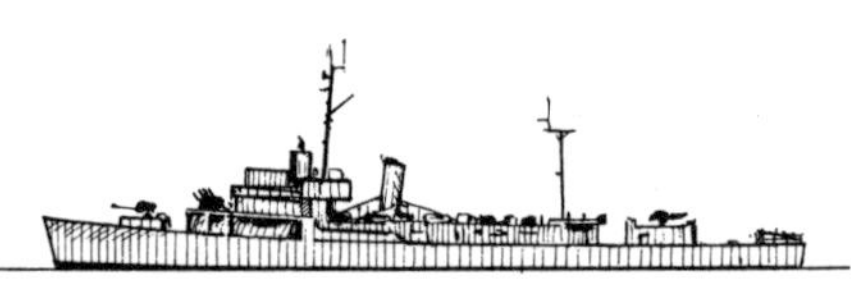

**273.** Am. Modified **BUCKLEY/EDSALL** classes. 1943-44. Escorts.
**VAMMEN.** *644.* ("Buckley" class). 1,400 tons. 306 x 37 x 14. (93.3 x 11.3 x 4.3). 2 screws; turbo-electric. 23 knots. 2—3-inch A.A. guns. 2 "Hedgehogs". Depth charges.
**PETERSON.** *152.* ("Edsall" class). 1,200 tons. 306 x 37 x 111. (93.3 x 11.3 x 3.4). 2 screws; diesel. 21 knots. Armament same as "Vammen".

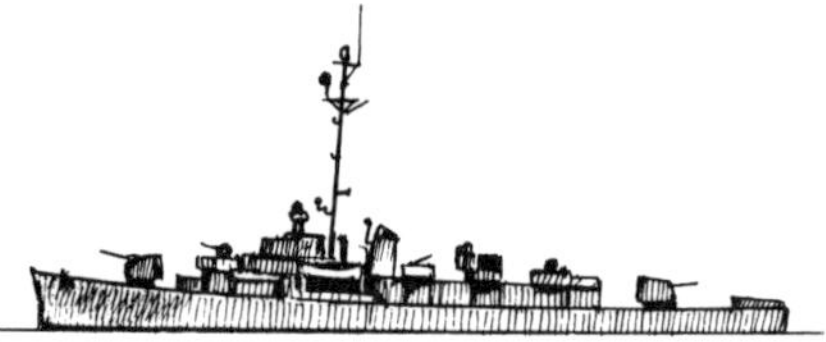

**274.** Am. **JOHN C. BUTLER** class. 1944-45. Escorts. 1,400 tons. 306 x 37 x 11. (93.3 x 11.3 x 3.4). 2 screws; turbines. 24 knots. 2—5-inch D.P. guns. 2 A.A. guns. "Hedgehogs". Depth charges.

**CHESTER T. O'BRIEN.** *421,* **CONKLIN.** *321,* **CORBESIER.** *438,* **DENNIS.** *405,* **DOYLE C. BARNES.** *353,* **DUFILHO.** *423,* **EDMONDS.** *406,* **EDWARD H. ALLEN.** *531,* **EDWIN A. HOWARD.** *346,* **FRENCH.** *367,* **GENTRY.** *349,* **GEORGE E. DAVIS.** *357,* **GILLIGAN.** *508,* **GOSS.** *444,* **HANNA.** *449,* **HOWARD F. CLARK.** *533,* **JOHN C. BUTLER.** *339,* **JOHN L. WILLIAMSON.** *370,* **JOHNNIE HUTCHINS.** *360,* **JOSEPH E. CONNOLLY.** *450,* **KENDALL C. CAMPBELL.** *443,* **KENNETH M. WILLETT.** *354,* **KEY.** *348,* **LA PRADE.** *409,* **LAWRENCE C. TAYLOR.** *415,* **LE RAY WILSON.** *414,* **LELAND E. THOMAS.** *420,* **LLOYD E. ACREE.** *356,* **MACK.** *350,* **MELVIN R. NAWMAN.** *416,* **O'FLAHERTY.** *340,* **OLIVER MITCHELL.** *417,* **OSBERG.** *538,* **PRATT.** *363,* **RAYMOND.** *341,* **RICHARD W. SUESENS.** *342,* **RIZZI.** *537,* **ROBERT BRAZIER.** *345,* **ROBERT F. KELLER.** *419,* **ROLF.** *362,* **ROMBACH.** *364,* **SILVERSTEIN.** *534,* **STAFFORD.** *411,* **TABBERER.** *418,* **WILLIAM SEIVERLING.** *441.*

Similar—**RUDDEROW** class.
Am. **HODGES.** *231,* **LESLIE L. B. KNOX.** *580,* **McNULTY.** *581,* **THOMAS F. NICKEL.** *587,* **TINSMAN.** *589.*

Cs. **TAIYUAN.**
Ko. **CHUNG NAM.** *73.*

**275.** Po. **ALMIRANTE PEREIRA DA SILVA** class. (U.S. "Dealey" class). 1966-67. Frigates. 1,500 tons. 315 x 37 x 14. (96 x 11.3 x 4.3). Turbines. 26 knots. 4—3-inch D.P. guns. 6 anti-submarine torpedo tubes (triple). 2 anti-submarine mortars (4 barrels). 2 depth charge throwers. Distinguished from American ships, Nos. 276 and 277 by smaller launcher before the bridge.
**ALMIRANTE GAGO COUTINHO.** *F473,* **ALMIRANTE MAGALHAES CORREIA.** *F474,* **ALMIRANTE PEREIRA DA SILVA.** *F472.*

**277.** Am. **DEALEY** class. 1954-58. Modified. Dimensions and enginés as No. 275. 2—3-inch guns (twin). 1 anti-submarine "Alpha" launcher. 2 anti-submarine torpedo launchers (triple). 2-Drone anti-submarine helicopters "Dash."
**BAUER.** *1025,* **BRIDGET.** *1024,* **COURTNEY.** *1021,* **CROMWELL.** *1014,* **EVANS.** *1023,* **HAMMERBERG.** *1015,* **HARTLEY.** *1029,* **HOOPER.** *1026,* **JOHN WILLIS.** *1027,* **JOSEPH K. TAUSSIG.** *1030,* **LESTER.** *1022,* **VAN VOORHIS.** *1028.*

**276.** Am. **DEALEY** class. 1954. Escort. 1,500 tons. Dimensions as No. 255 Engines as No. 275. 4—3-inch guns. 1 anti-submarine "Alpha" launcher. 2 anti-submarine torpedo launchers (triple).
Only ship of the class not modernised as No. 277.
**DEALEY.** *1006.*

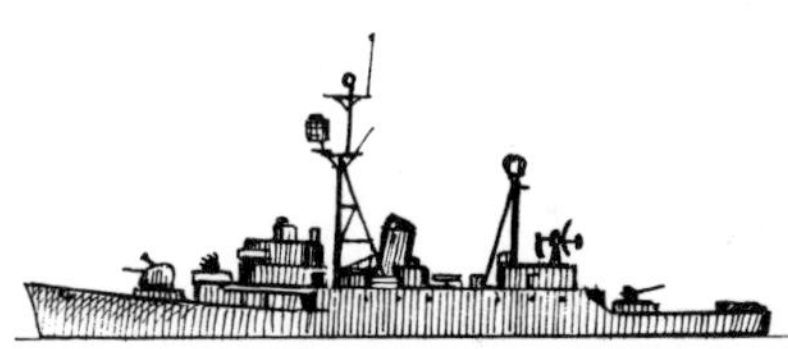

**278.** Am. Converted **EDSALL** class. 1943-44. Converted 1951-58. Radar Picket Escorts. 1,600 tons. 306 x 37 x 14. (93.3 x 11.1 x 4.3). 2 screws; diesels. 21 knots. 2—3-inch A.A. guns. 2 anti-submarine torpedo launchers (triple). 1 "Hedgehog". Depth charges.

These drawings represent those ships with the uncovered gun aft. Other ships have an enclosed gun aft. See silhouette No. 524.
**BLAIR.** *147,* **CALCATERRA.** *390,* **CAMP.** *251* (As No. 278), **CHAMBERS.** *391,* **DURANT.** *389,* **FALGOUT.** *324,* **FINCH.** *328,* **FORSTER.** *334* (Silhouette No. 524), **HISSEM.** *400,* **JOYCE.** *317,* **KIRKPATRICK.** *318,* **LANSING.** *388,* **MILLS.** *383,* **OTTERSTETTER.** *244,* **PRICE.** *332,* **RAMSDEN.** *382,* **RHODES.** *384,* **ROY O. HALE.** *336,* **SAVAGE.** *386* (See No. 278), **STRICKLAND.** *333,* **STURTEVANT.** *239,* **THOMAS J. GARY.** *326,* **VANCE.** *387.*

Similar but with extra mast aft (see silhouette No. 539), **KRETCHMER.** *329.*

**279.** Am Converted **JOHN C. BUTLER** class. 1955. Radar Picket Escorts. 1,700 tons. 306 x 37 x 11. (93.3 x 11.2 x 3.4). 2 screws; turbines. 24 knots. 2—5-inch D.P. guns. 1 anti-submarine "Hedgehog". Depth charges.
**VANDIVIER.** *540,* **WAGNER.** *549.*

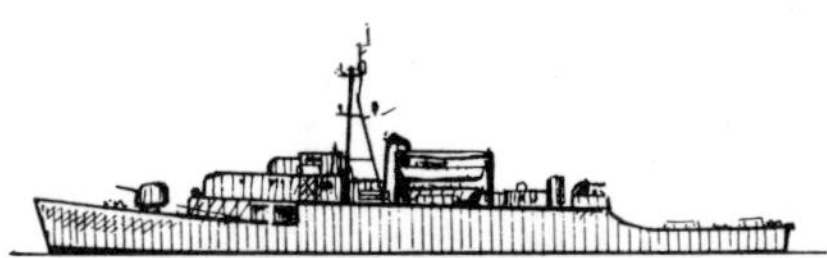

**280.** Am. Amphibious **TRANSPORTS.** 1943-45. All particulars as No. 282.
**BEVERLEY W. REID.** *119,* **DIACHENKO.** *123,* **WEISS.** *135.*

Co. **CORDOBA.**

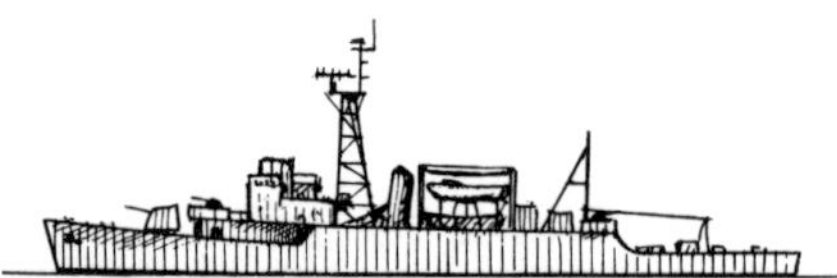

**281.** Ec. **DE JULIO.** *25.* Escort. All particulars as for No. 282.

Similar; Pole foremast. Lattice mainmast. See silhouette No. 252.
Ch. **ORELLA.** *27,* **RIQUELME.** *28,* **SERRANO.** *26,* **URIBE.** *29.*

Tripod foremast and Tripod mainmast.
Co. **ALMIRANTE BRION, ALMIRANTE PADILLA, ALMIRANTE TONO.**

Pole foremast, Tripod mainmast.
Cs. **CHUNG SHAN, FU SHAN.** *35,* **HENG SHAN.** *39,* **HWA SHAN.** *33,* **KANG SHAN.** *43,* **LU SHAN.** *36,* **SHOA SHAN.** *37,* **TAI SHAN.** *38,* **TIEN SHAN.** *315,* **WEN SHAN.** *34,* **YO SHAN.**

Ko. **ASAN.** *82,* **CHR JU.** *87,* **CHUN NAM.** *86,* **KYONG BUK.** *85,* **KYONG NAM.** *81,* **UNG PO.** *83.*

**282.** Am. Amphibious **TRANSPORTS.** Converted P.E. Type. 1943-45. 1,400 tons. 306 x 37 x 13. (93.3 x 11.2 x 3.9). 2 screws; turbo-electric. 23 knots. 1—5-inch gun. 8 A.A. guns. 2 anti-submarine torpedo launchers (triple) or depth charges.
**BALDUCK.** *132,* **BEGOR.** *127,* **HOLLIS.** *86,* **HORACE A. BASS.** *124,* **KIRWIN.** *90,* **KNUDSON.** *101,* **LANING.** *55,* **RINGNESS.** *100.*

Similar; Me. Frigates. **CALIFORNIA.** *B3,* **PAPALOAPAN.** *B4,* **TEHUANTEPEC.** *B5,* **USUMACINTA.** *B6.*

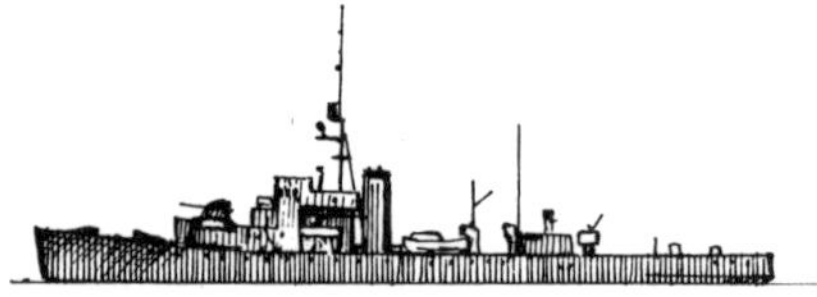

**282A.** Ca. **GRANBY.** *180.* 1944. Reconstructed 1953-58. Escort/Diving Support Ship. 1,600 tons. 310 x 37 x 16. (91.9 x 11.1 x 4.9). 2—4-inch guns. 6 A.A. guns. 2 anti-submarine "Squid" depth charge mortars (triple). 2 screws; reciprocating. 19 knots. Originally a Canadian built "River" class Frigate. Re-built as a flush decker.

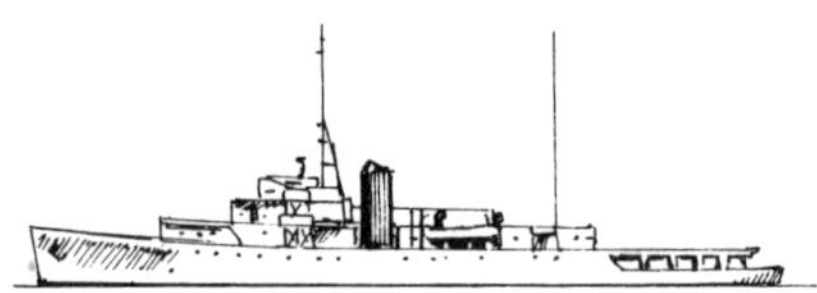

**283.** NZ. **LACHLAN.** A former Australian built "River" class Frigate, now a Survey Ship. All dimensions as for No. 282. No armament. but has large helicoper deck.

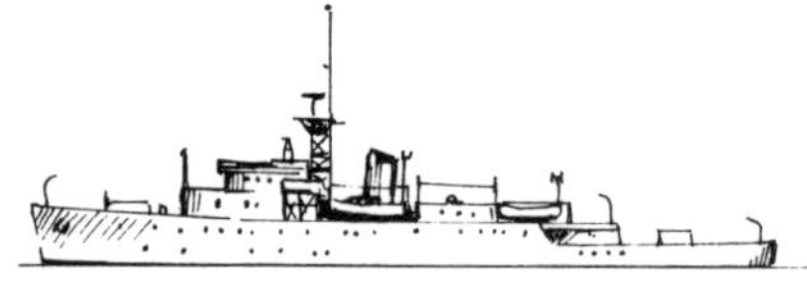

**284.** In. "River" class. **INVESTIGATOR.** Particulars the same as for No. 282 but no armament and 18 knots speed. Survey Ship. Distinguished by short king posts before the bridge, short funnel and short lattice mast.

**285.** No. Canadian "River" class 1944. Converted 1956. Depot Ships. Dimensions and tonnage and machinery as No. 282. 2 or 3 small guns.
**HORTEN.** *A530,* is Submarine Support Ship.
**VALKYRIEN.** *A535,* is Depot Ship for torpedo craft.

**286.** Bm. "River" class. **MAYU.** Frigate. Tonnage, dimensions and engines as for No. 282. 1—4-inch guns D.P. 4 A.A. guns.

**287.** Pk. "River" class. **ZULFIQUAR.** *262.* 1943. Converted 1963. Survey Ship. 1—4-inch gun. 12 A.A. guns.

**288.** Ce Canadian "River" class **GAJABAHU.** 1944. Frigate. 1,400 tons. Dimensions as for No. 282. 20 knots. 1—4-inch gun. 3 A.A. guns.

**289.** In "River" class. **TIR.** *F256.* 1943. Converted 1948. Training Frigate. Particulars similar to No. 282 but 1—4-inch gun and 3 A.A. guns.

**290.** Po. **DIOGO GOMES** class (Ex-"River" class). 1943-44. Refitted 1959. Dimensions as for No. 282. 18 knots. 2—4-inch guns. 6 A.A. guns. 2 "Squid" depth charge mortars. 2 depth charge racks.
**NUNO TRISTAO.** *F332.* Frigate.
**D. FERNANDO.** *F331.* Training Ship with main armament removed.

**291.** Eg. "River" class. **RASHID.** Details as for No. 282. Escort. 1942. Re-fitted 1959. 1—4-inch gun. 8 A.A. guns. 4 depth charge throwers.

**292.** Mo. "River" class. **AL MAOUNA.** 1944 Converted 1964. Frigate. Dimensions etc. as for No. 282. 2—4.1-inch gun. 3 A.A. guns. 1 "Hedgehog". 4 depth charge throwers. 2 depth charge racks. Helicopter deck and helicopter.

**293.** Do. **MELLA** (Ex-Canadian "River" class). Frigate. 1941. Modernised. 1,400 tons. 310 x 37 x 12. (91.9 x 11.2 x 12). 2 screws; reciprocating. 20 knots. Now carries no armament as employed as a Training Ship.

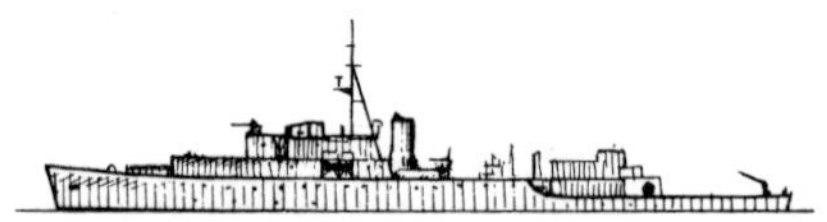

**294.** Au. "River" class. 1943-45. Converted 1959-60. Oceanographic Research Ships. 1,300 tons. 301 x 37 x 13. (91.8 x 11.2 x 3.8). 2 screws; reciprocating. 19 knots. 1—40-m.m. gun. **DIAMANTINA.** *A266,* **GASCOYNE.** *A276.* See also silhouette No. 347.

**295.** SA. "Loch" class. **GOOD HOPE.** *F432.* 1944. Converted 1955. Re-fitted 1961. Frigate. 1,600 tons. 307 x 39 x 15. (93.6 x 11.7 x 4.6). 2 screws; reciprocating. 19 knots. 2—4-inch guns. 2 A.A. guns. 2 "Squid" depth charge mortars.

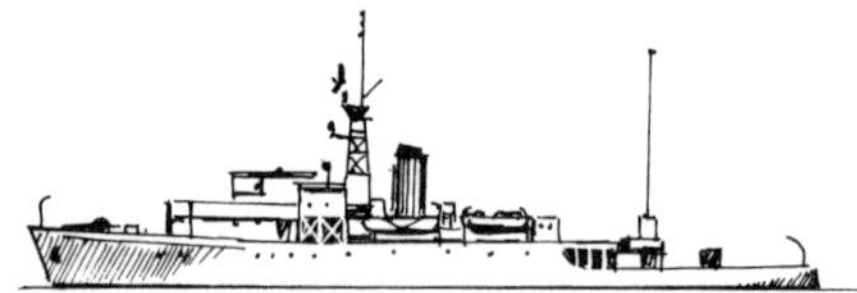

**296.** SA. "Loch" class. **NATAL.** 1945. Converted 1957. Survey Ship. 1,400 tons. Dimensions and engines as No. 295. No armament.

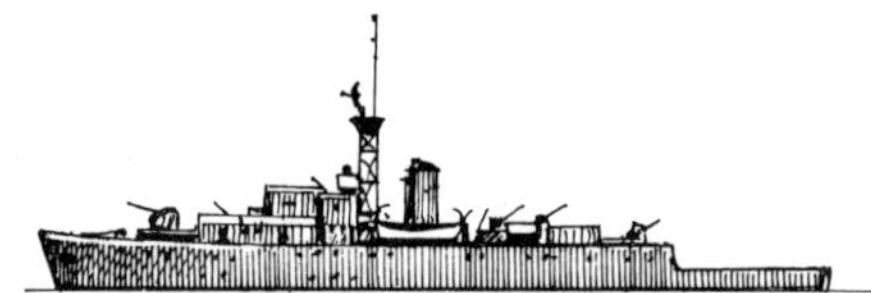

**297.** SA. "Loch" class. **TRANSVAAL.** 1945. Modernised. Frigate. Particulars as for No. 295. 6 A.A. guns. 2 "Squid" depth charge mortars.

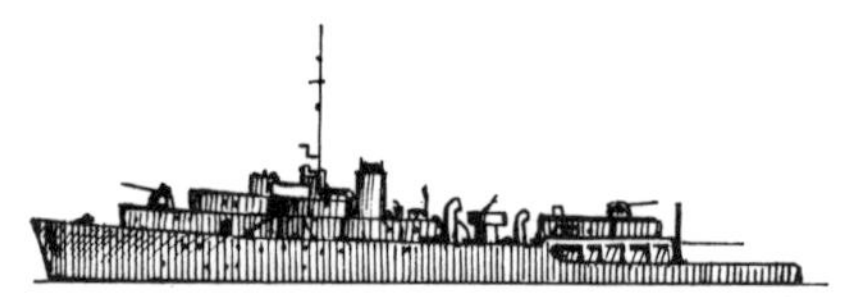

**298.** Ir. "Loch" class. **BABR.** Frigate. Dimensions and engines as for No. 295. 2—4-inch guns. 4 A.A. guns.

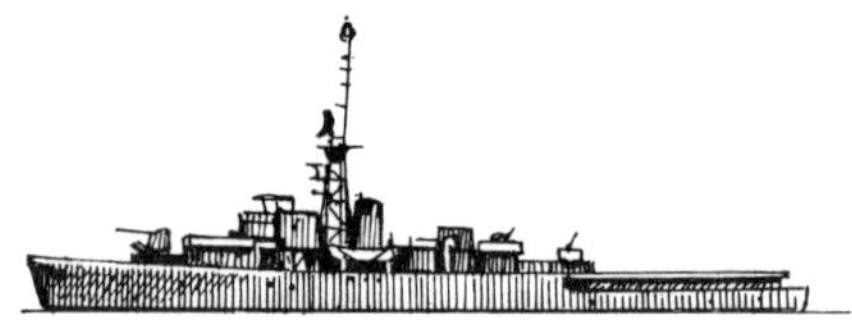

**299.** My. "Loch" class. **HANG TUAH.** *F433.* 1944. Modernised 1964. Frigate. All details as for No. 295.

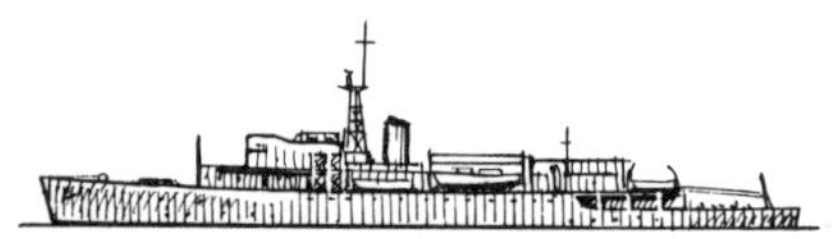

**300.** Po. "Bay" class. **AFONSO DU ALBU-QUERQUE.** *A526.* 1949. Modernised 1966. Survey Ship. Details as for No. 295 but no armament.

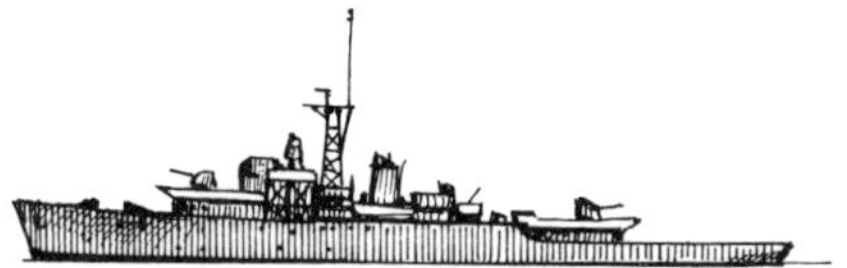

**301.** Fi. "Bay" class. **MATTI KURKI.** 1946. Modernised 1962. Training Frigate. Dimensions and engines as for No. 295. 4—4-inch guns. 6 A.A. guns.

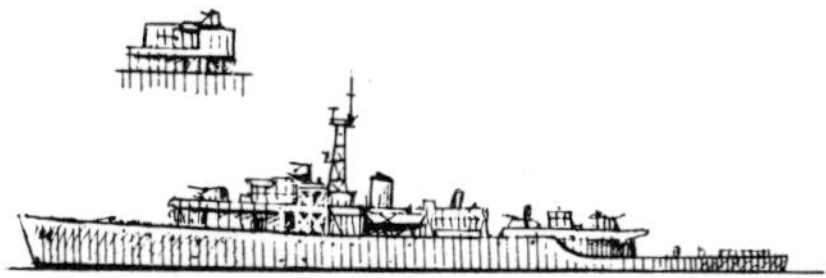

**302.** Po. Ex "Bay" class—"Alvares Cabral" class. 1945-49. Frigates. Modernised 1961. Dimensions and engines as for No. 295. 4—4-inch guns (twin). 6 A.A. guns. 1 "Hedgehog". 4 depth charge throwers. 2 depth charge racks.
**ALVARES CABRAL.** *F336,* **D. FRANCISCO DE ALMEIDA.** *F479,* **PACHECO PEREIRA.** *F337,* **VASCO DA GAMA.** *F478.*

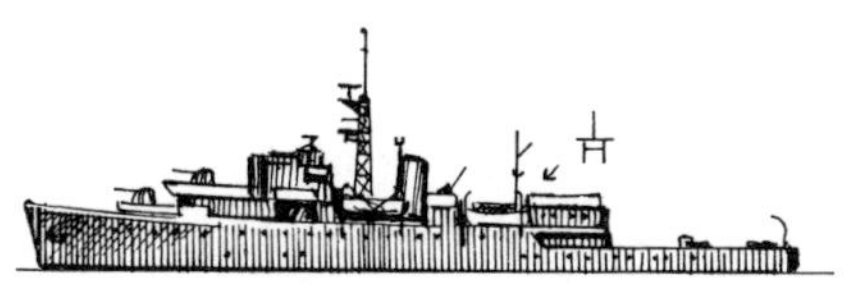

**304.** In. "Black Swan" class. 1943. Modified. Frigates. All particulars as for No. 303.
**KAVERI.** *F110,* **KISTNA.** *F46.*

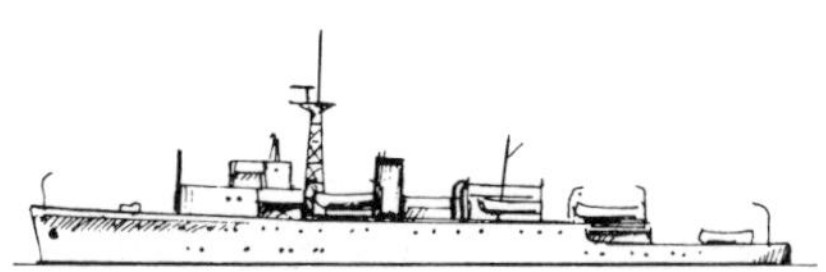

**306.** In. **SUTLEJ** class. 1941. Converted 1957. Survey Ships. 1,300 tons. 293 x 38 x 12. (89.2 x 11.4 x 3.5). 2 screws; turbines. 18 knots. No armament. Similar to British "Egret" class.
**JUMNA. SUTLEJ.**

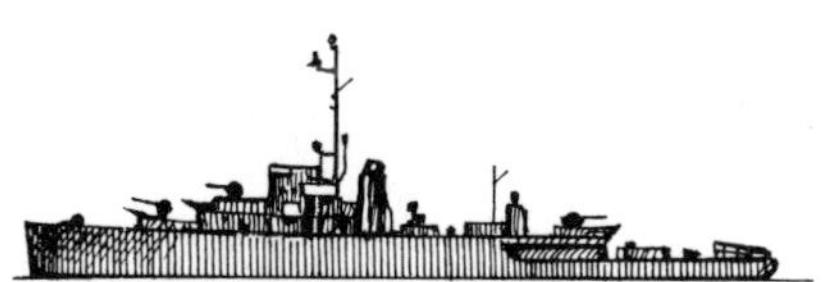

**308.** Ja. **TREE** class. Ex-U.S. "Tacoma" type. 1944. Frigates. 1,500 tons. Particulars as for No. 307 except armament. 3—3-inch guns. 11 A.A. guns. 1 "Hedgehog". 8 K guns. Depth charge racks.
**KAYA.** *288,* **KEYAKI.** *295,* **NIRE.** *287,* **SUGI.** *285.*
Similar—Drone Target Carrier—**KUSU.** *281.* See silhouette No. 263.

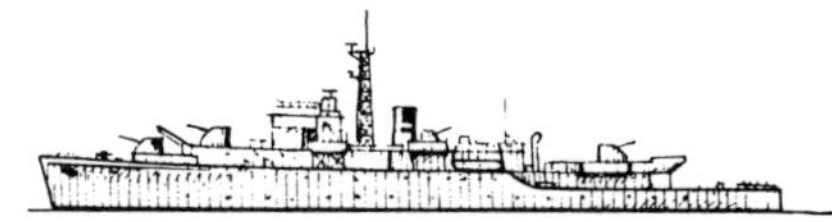

**303.** Eg. "Black Swan" class. **TARIK.** 1943. Escort. 1,500 tons. 300 x 39 x 12. (91.3 x 11.7 x 3.5). 2 screws; turbines. 18 knots. 6—4-inch guns. 6 A.A. guns. 4 depth charge throwers.

**305.** Ge. "Black Swan" class. **SCHARN-HORST.** *F213.* 1944. Converted 1962. Particulars as for No. 303 except armament which is: 2—3.9-inch guns. 4 A.A. guns. 1 depth charge thrower. 1 depth charge rack.

**307.** Cu. Ex-U.S. **RIVER** class. P.F. Type. 1944. Refitted 1956. Frigates. 1,400 tons. 304 x 38 x 14. (92.7 x 11.4 x 4.2). 2 screws; reciprocating. 18 knots. 3—3-inch D.P. guns. 4 to 12 A.A. guns. 1 "Hedgehog". Depth charge throwers. Depth charge racks.
**ANTONIO MACEO.** *F302,* **JOSE MARTI.** *F301,* **MAXIMO GOMEZ.** *F303.*

Do. **CAP. GENERAL PEDRO SANTANA.** *453,* **GREGORIO LUPERON.** *452.* (See silhouettes No. 262 and 264).
Ec. **GUAYAS.** See silhouette No. 262.
Ko. **DUMAN.** *61,* **IMCHIN.** *66,* **NAKTONG.** *65,* **TAE DONG.** *63.*

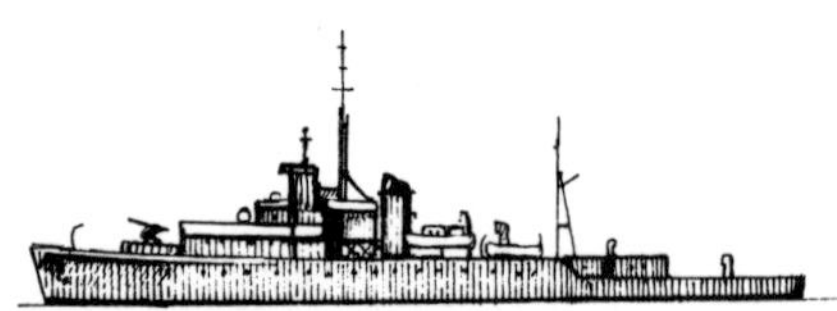

**309.** Ar. Ex-U.S. "Tacoma" Type. **JUAN B. AZOPARDO.** *GC11.* 1942. Converted 1963. Survey Ship. Details as for No. 308 but no armament.

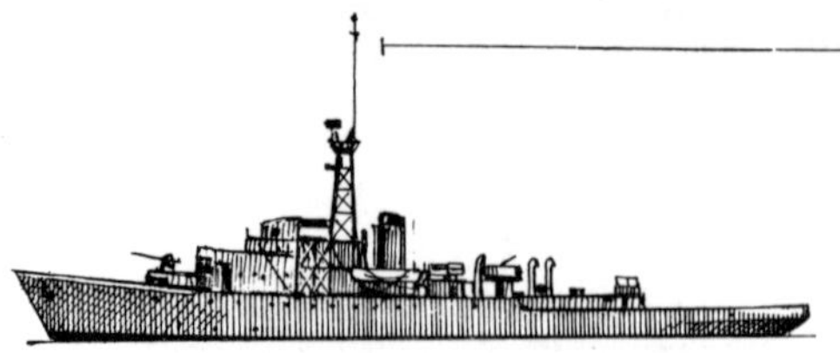

**310.** Ur. "Castle" class. **MONTEVIDEO.** *PF1.* 1944. Training Frigate. 1,000 tons. 252 x 37 x 10. (76.7 x 11.2 x 3). Reciprocating engines. 17 knots. 1—3-inch gun. 6 A.A. guns. 1 "Hedgehog". 4 depth charge throwers. 1 depth charge rack.

**311.** Am. "Barnegat" class. **VALCOUR.** *1.* 1946. Converted 1950. Miscellaneous Flagship and Communications Ship. 1,800 tons. 311 x 41 x 13. (94.7 x 12.5 x 4). 2 screws; diesels. 18 knots. 8 A.A. guns.
One of 35 seaplane tenders of this class built.

**312.** No. "Barnegat" class. **HAAKON VII.** *A537.* 1945. Converted 1957. Training Frigate. Details as for No. 311 but carries 1—5-inch gun and 12 A.A. guns.

**313.** Et. "Barnegat" class. **ETHIOPIA.** 1944. Converted 1962. Training Ship. All details as for No. 311 but carries 1—5-inch gun.

**314.** It. "Barnegat" class. **PIETRO CAVEZZALE.** *A5301.* 1944. Converted 1957. Support Ship. Details as for No. 311 but has a speed of 16 knots and an armament of 2 A.A. guns.

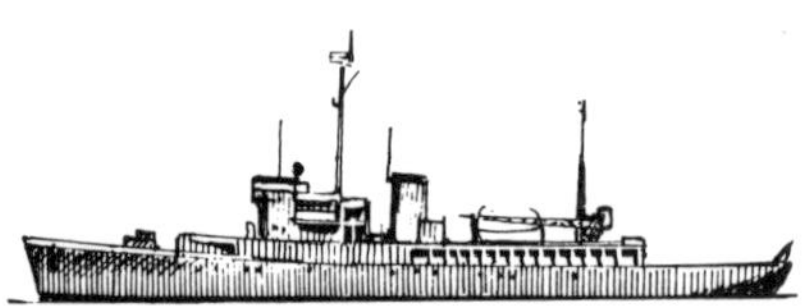

**315.** Am. "Barnegat" class. **JOSIAH WILLARD GIBBS.** *AGOR 1.* 1944. Converted 1958. Oceanographic Research Ship. Details as for No. 311 but no armament.

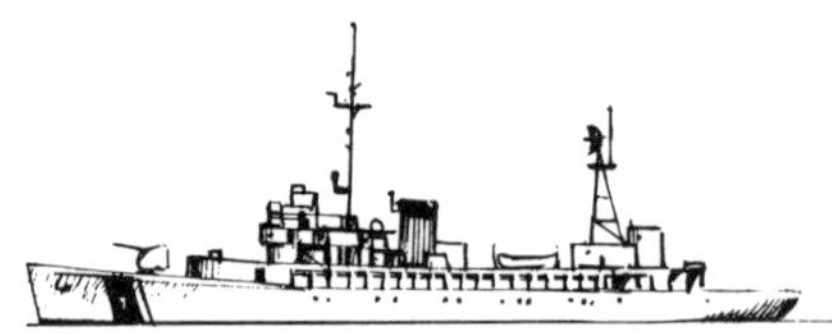

**316.** Am. "Barnegat" Type—**CASCO** class. 1943-44. U.S. Coastguard Cutter. Dimensions etc. as for No. 311. 1—5-inch gun D.P. 2 torpedo launchers (triple) and some ships have "Hedgehog".
**ABESECON.** *374,* **BARATARIA.** *381,* **CASTLE ROCK.** *383,* **CHINCOTEAGUE.** *375,* **COOK INLET.** *384,* **GRESHAM.** *387,* **McCULLOCH.** *386,* **UNIMAK.** *379.*
Similar; **ROCKAWAY.** *377.* Oceanographic Research Ship. No armament. See silhouette No. 477.

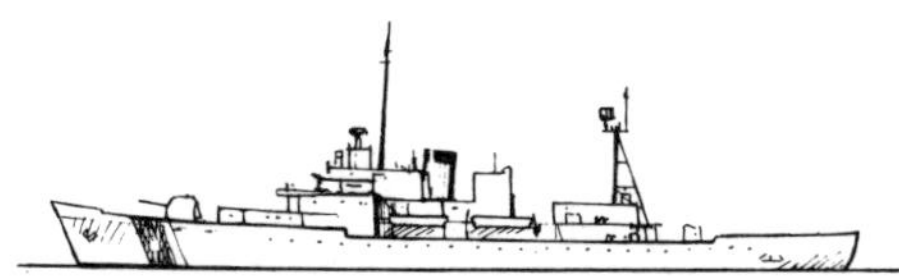

**317.** Am. **CAMPBELL** class. 1936-37. Coast Guard Cutters. 2,200 tons. 327 x 41 x 15. (99.6 x 12.5 x 4.5). 2 screws; turbines. 19 knots. 1—5-inch D.P. gun. 2 torpedo launchers (triple). "Hedgehog".
**BIBB.** *31,* **CAMPBELL.** *32,* **DUANE.** *33,* **INGHAM.** *35,* **SPENCER.** *36,* **TANEY.** *37.* Very small funnel and raised plating aft.

**318.** Ru. **PURGA.** Support Ship/Frigate. 2,300 tons. 325 x 40 x 17. (99 x 12 x 5.2). Diesel. 18 knots. 4—3.9-inch D.P. guns. 12 A.A. guns. Mines. Icebreaking stem.

**319.** Ng. **NIGERIA.** *F87.* 1965. Frigate. 1,700 tons. 360 x 37 x 11. (109.8 x 11.3 x 3.3). 2 screws; diesels. 26 knots. 2—4-inch D.P. guns (twin). 5 A.A. guns. 1 depth charge mortar (triple).

**320.** Ge. **RHEIN** class. 1961-64. Escort and Support Ships/Frigates. 2,400 tons. 324 x 39 x 11. (98.6 x 11.8 x 3.4). 2 screws; diesel or diesel-electric. 21 knots. 2—3.9-inch A.A. guns.
**DONAU.** *A69,* **ELBE.** *61,* **ISAR.** *64,* **MAIN.** *63,* **MOSEL.** *67,* **NECKAR.** *66,* **RHEIN.** *58,* **RUHR.** *64,* **SAAR.** *65,* **WERRA.** *68,* **WESER.** *62.* "Mosel" and "Saar" probably have helicopter deck.

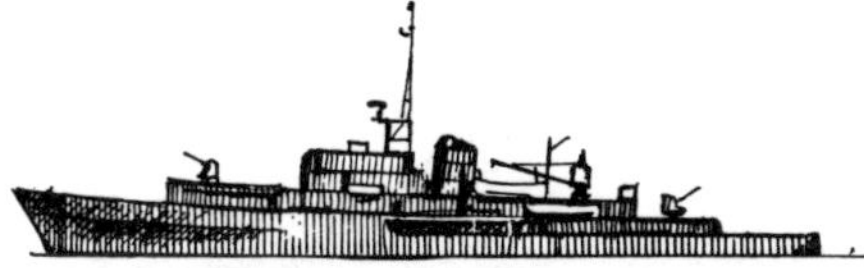

**321.** Ge. **RHEIN** class. Similar to No. 320 but armament may differ. Distinguished by long superstructure before bridge, different mast and lighter guns.
**LAHN.** *55,* **LECH.** *56.*

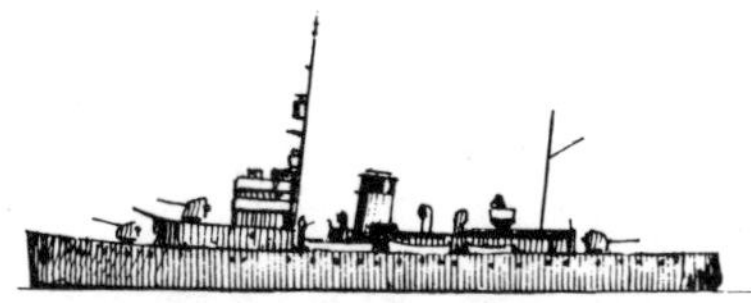

**322.** Me. **GUANJUATO** class. 1934. Modernised 1958-64. Gunboats. 1,300 tons. 264 x 38 x 10. (80.5 x 11.5 x 3). 2 screws; diesels. 14 knots. 3—4-inch guns. 6 A.A. guns.
**GUANJUATO.** *C7,* **POTOSI.** *C9,* **QUERETARO.** *C8.*

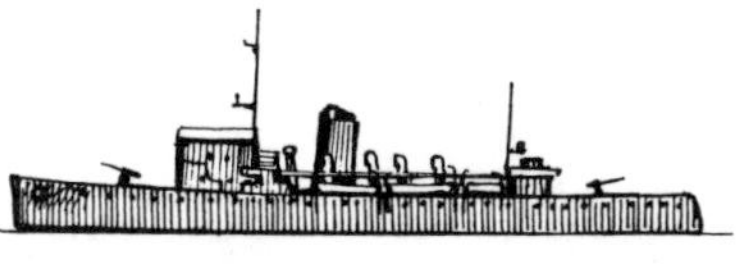

**323.** Cu. **CUBA.** 1911. Re-constructed 1936-37 and 1956. Gunboat. 2,100 tons. 270 x 39 x 14. (82.2 x 11.9 x 4.3). Reciprocating. 14 knots. 2—4-inch guns. 2—3-inch guns. 10 A.A. guns.

**324.** Sp. **JUPITER** class. 1937-39. Modernised 1960-61. Frigate Minelayers. 2,100 tons. 328 x 42 x 12. (100 x 12.6 x 3.5). 2 screws; turbines. 17 knots. 4—4.7-inch A.A. and 8 smaller A.A. guns. 2 "Hedgehogs". 8 anti-submarine mortars. 2 depth charge racks.
**MARTE.** *F01,* **NEPTUNO.** *F02.*

**325.** Sp. **JUPITER** class. The other two units differing slightly in armament.
**JUPITER.** *F11,* **VULCANO.** *F12.*

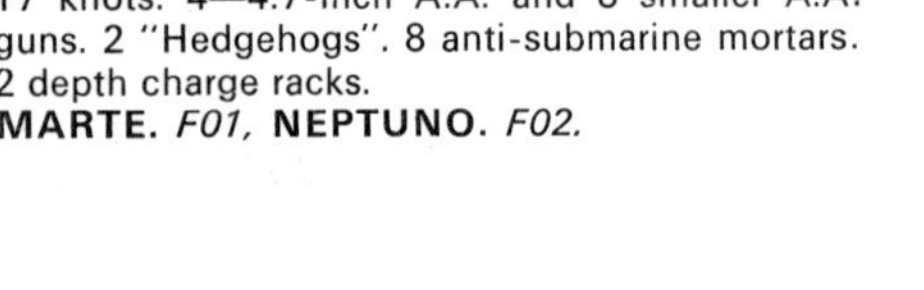

**326.** Po. **S. CRISTOVAO.** *A5208.* 1935. Converted 1967 from Frigate. Depot Ship. 1,800 tons. 339 x 44 x 13. (103.2 x 13.5 x 3.8). Turbines. 21 knots. 2—4.7-inch guns.

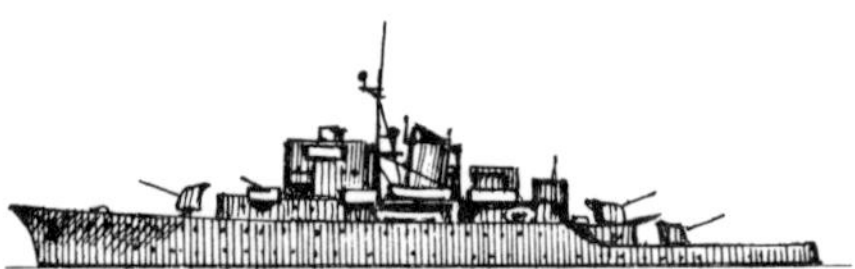

**327.** Sp. **PIZARRO** class. 1947-51. Modernised c. 1961. Frigates. 1,900 tons. 313 x 40 x 18. (95.3 x 12 x 5.4). 2 screws; turbines. 18 knots. 6—4.7-inch guns (twin). 14 A.A. guns. 4 depth charge throwers. 30 mines.
**HERNAN CORTES.** *F32,* **MAGALLANES.** *F35,* **SARMIENTO DE GAMBOA.** *F36,* **VASCO NUNEZ PINZON.** *F41.*

**328.** Sp. **PIZARRO** class. The other ships of this class, identical with No. 327 except that they have 2—5-inch guns. Distinguished by lattice mast and thinner funnel.
**LEGAZPI.** *F42,* **VICENTE YANEZ PINZON.** *F41.*

**329.** Sp. **EOLO** class. 1942-43. Frigate Minelayers. 1,700 tons. 292 x 39 x 17. (88.9 x 11.7 x 5.4). 2 screws; turbines. 19 knots. 4—4.1-inch guns. 4 A.A. guns. 4 depth charge throwers. Mines.
**EOLO.** *F21,* **TRITON.** *F22.*

**330.** Ar. **KING** class. 1946. Corvettes. 99 tons. 253 x 29 x 8. (77 x 8.8 x 2.3). 2 screws; diesels. 18 knots. 3—4.1-inch guns. 4 A.A. guns. 4 depth charge throwers.
**KING.** *P21,* **MURATURE.** *P20.*

**331.** Ar. **AZOPARDO** class. 1957-58. Frigates. 1,200 tons. 279 x 32 x 10. (85.1 x 9.6 x 3). 2 screws; turbines. 20 knots. 1—4.1-inch gun. 6 A.A. guns. 1 "Hedgehog". 4 depth charge mortars.
**AZOPARDO.** *35,* **PIEDRABUENA.** *36.*

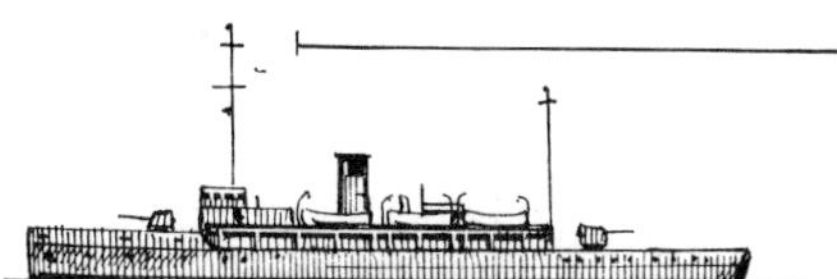

**332.** Th. **CHOW PRAYA**. 1918. Reconstructed. Training Ship. 680 tons. 220 x 28 x 8. (67 x 8.5 x 2.4). 2 screws; reciprocating. 16 knots. 3 A.A. guns. Former British "Racecourse" class.

**333.** Fr. **GUSTAVE ZEDE**. *A641*. 1934. Modernised 1952. Command Ship. 2,900 tons. 308 x 45 x 14. (93.9 x 13.5 x 4.3). 2 screws; diesels. 16 knots. 3—4.1-inch guns. 12 A.A. guns.

**334.** Po. **PEDRO NUNES**. *A528*. 1931. Converted 1956. Survey Ship. 1,100 tons. 235 x 33 x 10. (71.6 x 10 x 3). Diesels. 16 knots. 1—4.7-inch gun. 4 A.A. guns.

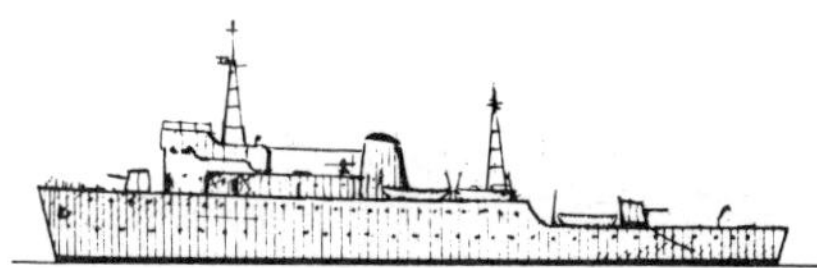

**335.** Me. **DURANGO**. *B1*. 1936. Modernised 1967. Frigate. 1,600 tons. 303 x 40 x 10. (92.4 x 12.2 x 3.1). 2 screws; diesel-electric. 18 knots. 2—4-inch guns. 2—2.4-inch guns. 6 A.A. guns.

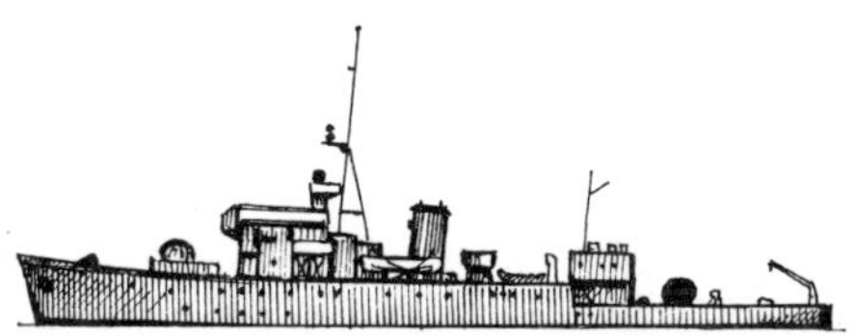

**336.** Be. "Algerine" class. **ADRIEN DE GER-LACHE**. *A954*. Minesweeper Support Ship. 1945. Refitted 1960. 1,000 tons. 225 x 36 x 11. (68.5 x 10.9 x 3.3). 2 screws; turbines. 16 knots. 2 A.A. guns.

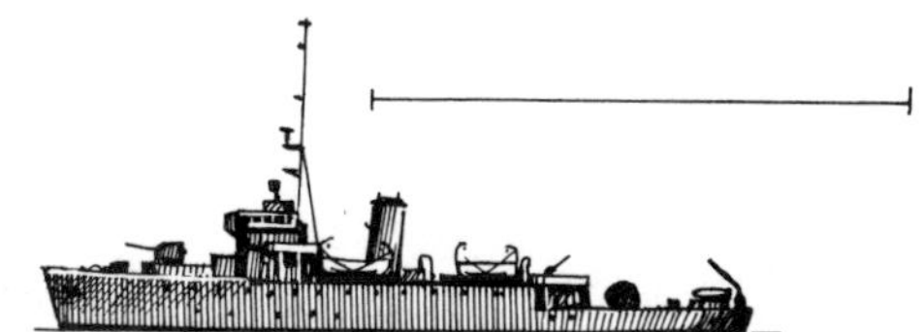

**337.** Th. "Algerine" class. **PHOSAMTON**. 1945. Refitted 1966. Dimensions etc. as No. 336. 1—4-inch gun. 6 A.A. guns. 4 depth charge throwers.

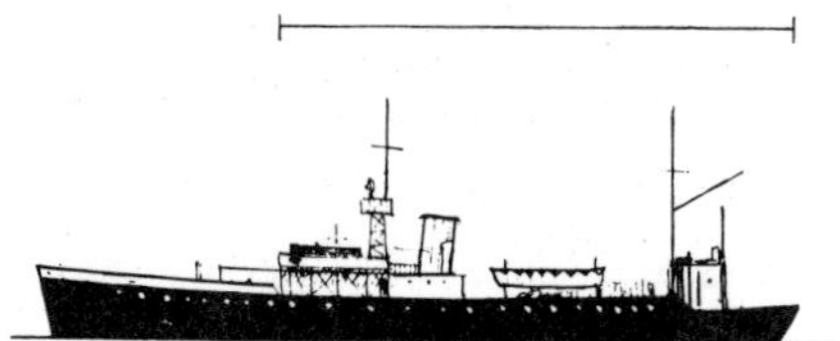

**338.** No. "Flower" class. 1944. Weather Ships. 1,100 tons. 208 x 33 x 15. (63.3 x 10 x 4.5). Reciprocating. 16 knots. Former British Corvettes. **POLARFRONT**. *1*, **POLARFRONT**. *11*.

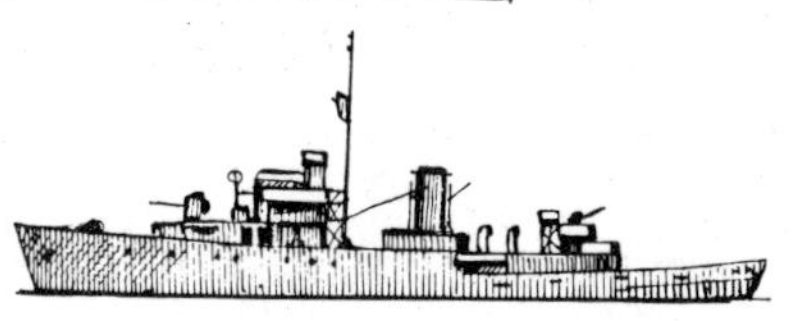

**339.** Do. "Flower" class. 1943-44. Corvettes. Dimensions as No. 338. 1—3-inch or 1—4-inch gun. 9 to 12 A.A. guns.
**CRISTOBAL COLON**. *401*, **GERARDO JANSEN**. *404*, **JUAN ALEJANDRO ACOSTA**. *402*, **JUAN BAUTISTA CAMBIASO**. *403*, **JUAN BAUTISTA MAGGIOLO**. *405*.

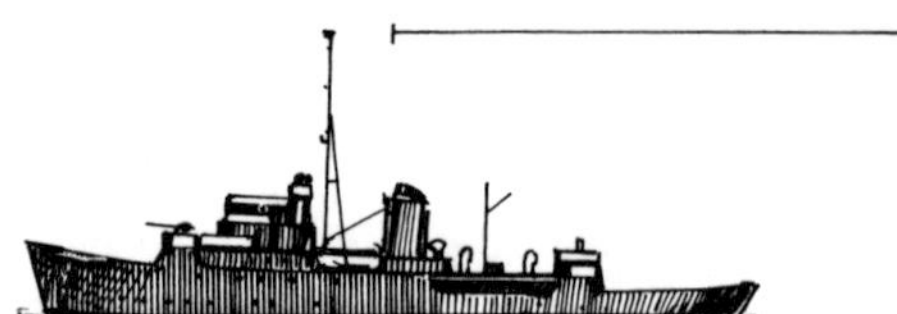

**340.** Th. "Flower" class. **BANGPAKONG.** 1943. Frigate. Modernised 1966. Dimensions as for No. 338. 1—3-inch gun. 7 A.A. guns. 4 depth charge throwers.

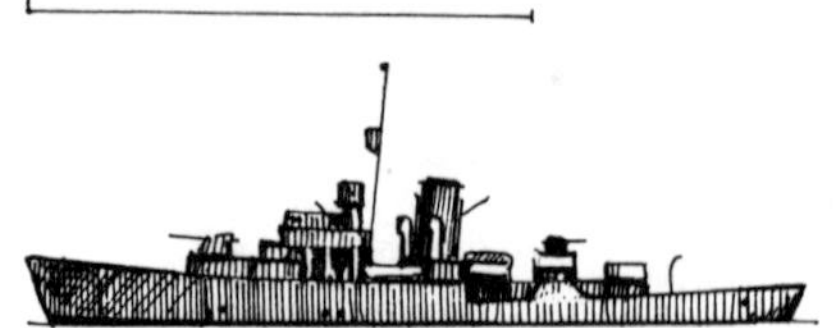

**341.** Eg. "Flower" class. **EL SUDAN.** 1940. Escort. Dimensions as for No. 338. 1—4-inch gun. 2 A.A. guns.

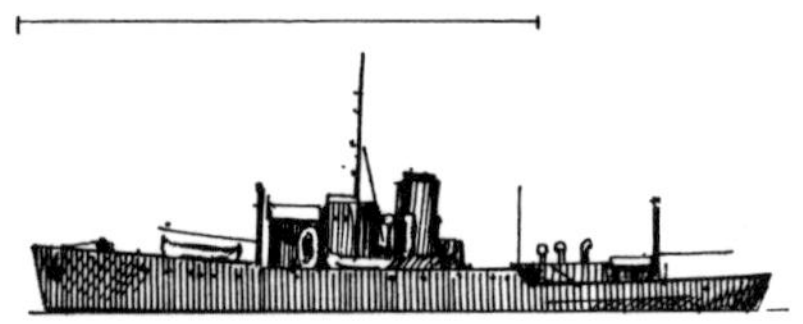

**342.** Gr. "Flower" class. **ST. LYKOUDIS.** *A481.* 1941. Lighthouse Tender. Dimensions as for No. 338. 14 knots. No armament.

**343.** Po. "Flower" class. **CARVALHO ARAUJO.** *A524.* 1942. Converted 1959. Survey Ship. Dimensions as for No. 338. 1—3-inch gun. 4 A.A. guns.

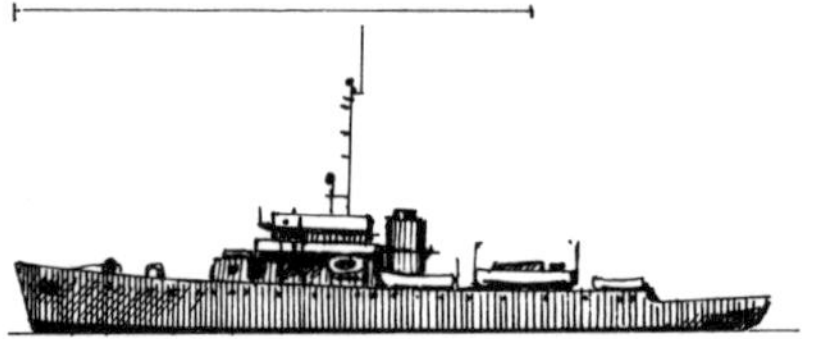

**344.** It. "Flower" class. **STAFFETTA.** 1943. Converted 1953. Survey Ship. Dimensions as for No. 338. 15 knots. 2 A.A. guns.

**345.** It. **APE** class. 1942-48. Modified. Corvettes. 700 tons. 213 x 29 x 9. (64.8 x 8.7 x 2.7). 2 screws; diesels. 15 knots. Armament varies and is changeable. 2 to 4 A.A. guns. "Hedgehogs". Depth charge throwers. Depth charge racks. 2 torpedo tubes in some ships.
**BAIONETTA.** *F578,* **BOMBARDA.** *F549,* **CHIMERA.** *F569,* **CORMORANO.** *F575,* **CRISALIDE.** *F547,* **FARFALIA.** *F548,* **FLORA.** *F572,* **GABBIANO.** *F571,* **GRU.** *F566,* **IBIS.** *F561,* **PELLICANO.** *F574,* **SCIMITARRA.** *F564,* **SFINGE.** *F579,* **SIBILLA.** *F565,* **URANIA.** *F570.* See also silhouette No. 356a.

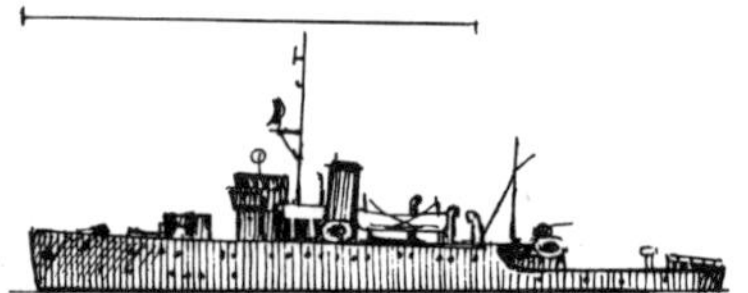

**346.** Tu. Ex-"Bangor" class. ("Bafra" class). 1940-42. Escorts. 670 tons. 180 x 29 x 13. (54.8 x 8.7 x 3.8). 2 screws; reciprocating. 16 knots. 7 A.A. guns. 1 "Hedgehog". 4 depth charge throwers.
**BAFRA.** *P121,* **BANDIRMA.** *P129,* **BARTIN.** *P130,* **BEYLERBEYI.** *P123,* **BODREM.** *P125,* **BORNOVA.** *P126,* **BOZCAADA.** *P127,* **BUYUKDERE.** *P128.*
Similar with very short mainmast. **BEYKOZ.** *P122.* See silhouette No. 755.

**347.** In. Ex-"Bangor" class. **KONKAN.** *M228.* Ocean Minesweeper. Details very similar to No. 346.

**348.** Po. Ex-"Bangor" class. **ALMIRANTE LACERDA.** *A525.* Survey Ship. Details as for No. 346 but carries 1—3-inch gun and 2 A.A. guns.

**349.** Po. Ex-"Bangor" class. **CACHEU.** *F470.* Corvette. Details as for No. 348.

**350.** Eg. Ex-"Bangor" class. Corvettes. Dimensions etc. as for No. 348. 1—4-inch gun. 1—3-inch gun. 2 to 4 A.A. guns. 2 depth charge throwers. **MATROUH, NASR.**

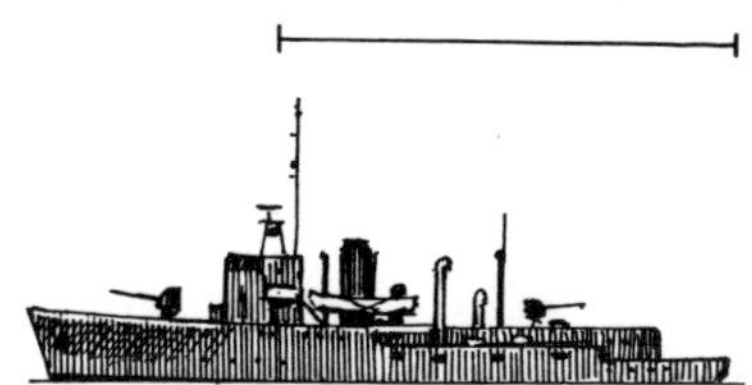

**351.** NZ. **BATHURST** class. 1943-44. Modernised 1965-66. Escort Minesweepers. 186 x 31 x 10. (56.7 x 9.4 x 2.9). 2 screws; reciprocating. 15 knots. 2 A.A. guns. **INVERELL.** *M233,* **KIAMA.** *M353.*

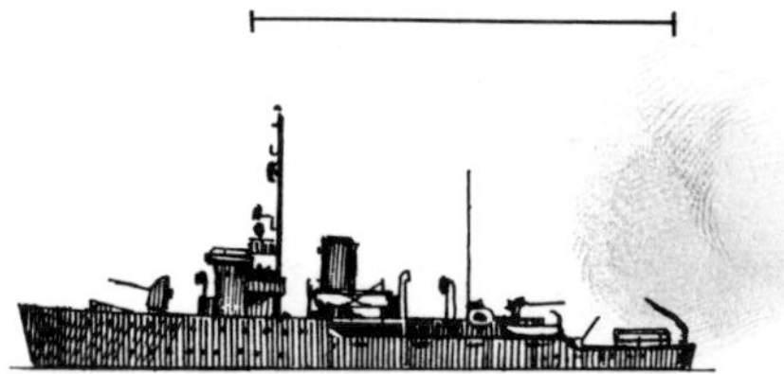

**352.** Tu. Ex-**BATHURST** class. ("Alanya" class). 1941. Minesweepers Support Ships. Dimensions etc. as for No. 351 but carry 1—4-inch gun. 5 A.A. guns. 2 depth charge throwers. **ALANYA.** *M501,* **AMASRA.** *M502.* **AYVALIK.** *M500.* Very short mainmast. See silhouette No. 534.

**353.** Ia. Ex-"Banteng" class. **PATI UNUS.** *256.* 1942. Training Ship. 800 tons. 186 x 31 x 8. 2 screws; reciprocating. 15 knots. 1—4-inch gun. 5 A.A. guns.

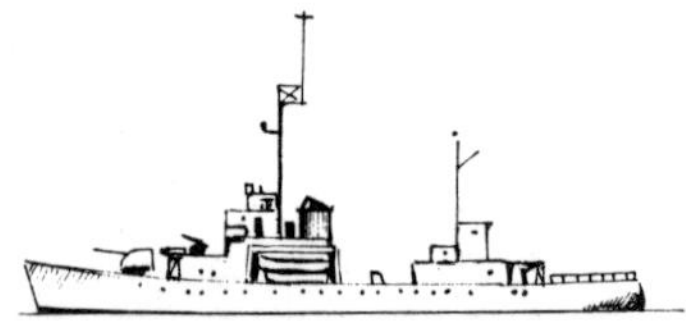

**354.** Am. **OWASCO** class. 1945-46. Coast Guard Cutters. 1,600 tons. 254 x 43 x 17. (77.4 x 13.1 x 5.1). Turbines. 18 knots. 1—5-inch D.P. gun. 2 A.A. guns. 2 "Hedgehogs". 2 anti-submarine torpedo launchers (triple).
**ANDROSCOGGIN.** *68,* **CHAUTAUQUA.** *41,* **ESCANABA.** *64,* **KLAMATH.** *69,* **MENDOTA.** *69,* **MINNETONKA.** *67,* **OWASCO.** *39,* **PONTCHARTRAIN.** *70,* **SEBAGO.** *42,* **WACHUSETT.** *44,* **WINNEBAGO.** *40,* **WINONA.** *65.*

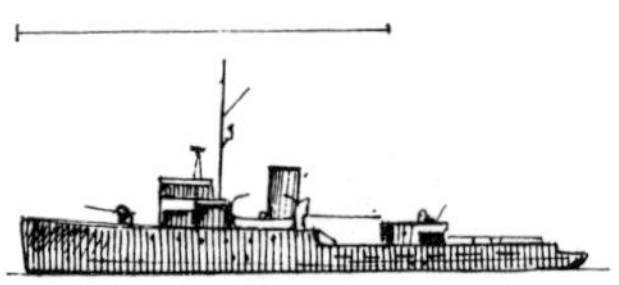

**355.** Fi. **RUOTSINSALMI.** 1941. Coastal Mine-layer. 150 x 23 x 5. (45.7 x 7 x 1.5). 2 screws; diesel. 15 knots. 4 A.A. guns. Mines.

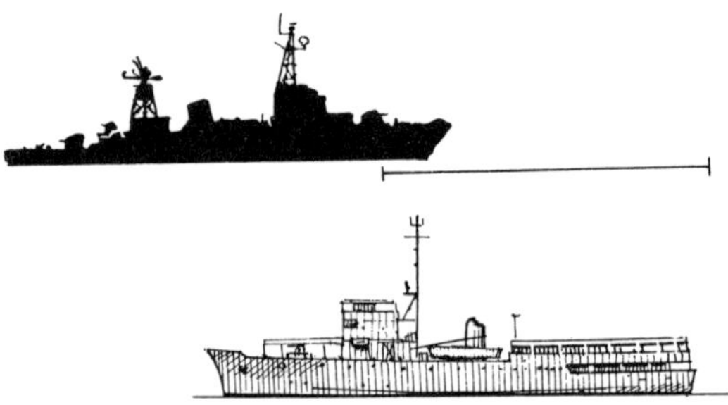

**356.** Ru. **T43** class. 1948-57. Radar Pickets. 500 tons. 200 x 27.5 x 9. (60.9 x 8.2 x 2.7). 2 screws; diesel. 17 knots. 4—37-m.m. A.A. guns (twin). 4 smaller A.A. guns. Converted from "T43" type minesweepers.

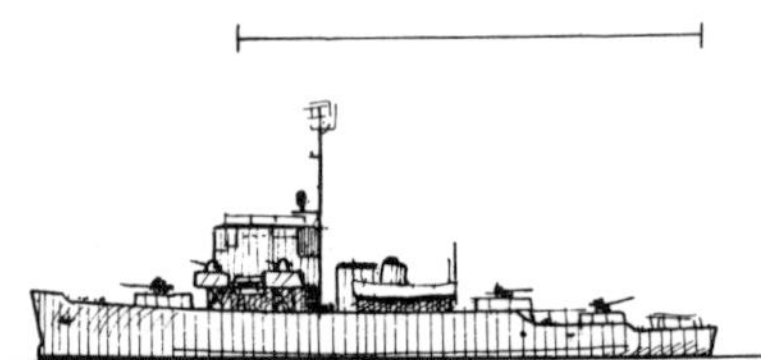

**357.** Pi. **MOUNT SAMAT.** *21.* 1944. Converted. Command Ship and President Yacht. 650 tons. 185 x 33 x 10. (56.3 x 10 x 3). 2 screws; diesel. 14 knots. 1—3-inch gun. 4 A.A. guns. Converted from Am. Fleet minesweeper.

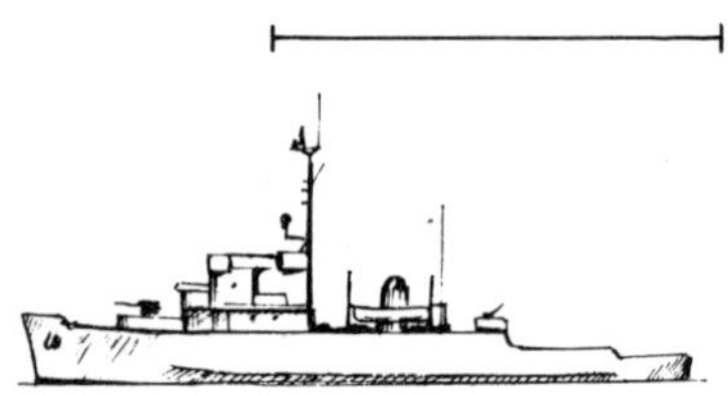

**358.** Am. "PCE" Type. **LAMAR.** *899.* Dimensions as for No. 357. No armament. Coast Guard Training Ship.

**359.** Pi. Ex-**PCE** Type. Escorts. Dimensions as for No. 357. 1—3-inch gun. 5 A.A. guns.
**CEBU.** *28,* **ILOILO.** *32,* **LEYTE.** *30,* **NEGROS OCCIDENTAL.** *29,* **PANGASINAN.** *31.*

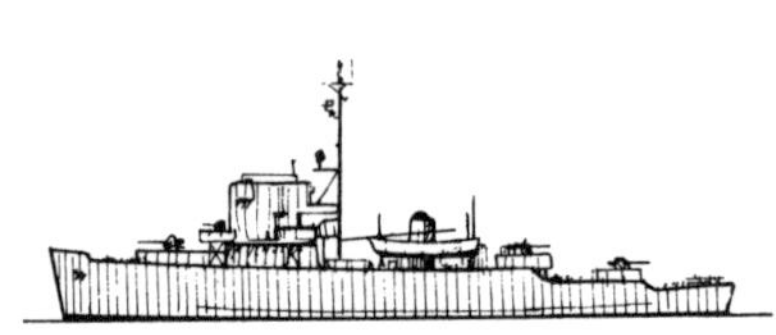

**360.** Ex-**PCE** Type. Dimensions as for No. 357. Armament varies.
Cs. **WEI YUAN.** *42.* Escort.
Cu. **CARIBE.** *PE201,* **SIBONEY.** *PE302.* Refitted 1956.
EC. **ESMERALDAS.** *E22,* **MANABI.** *E23.*
Ko. **HAN SAN.** *53,* **KOJIN.** *50,* **MYONG RYANG.** *52,* **OK PO.** *55,* **PYOK PA.** *47,* **RO RYANG.** *51,* **RYUL PO.** *58,* **SA CHON.** *59.*
Me. **TOMAS MARIN.** *C3.*
VN. **DONG DA II.** *07,* **NGOC HOI.** *012.*

**361.** Am. Ex-"PCE" Type. **LODESTONE.** *DG8.* Dimensions as for No. 357. Degaussing Ship. No armament.

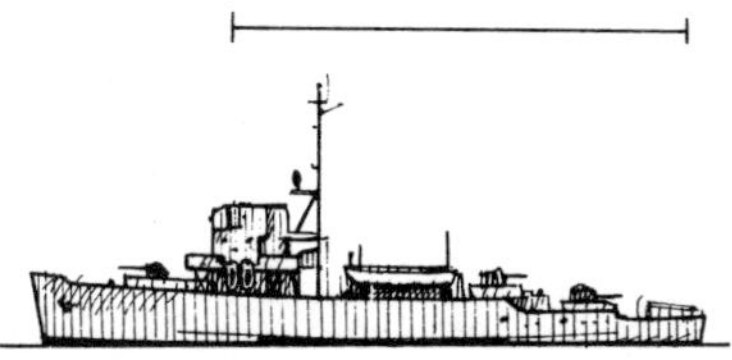

**362.** Du. Ex-"PCE" Type. **WOLF** class. 1954. Corvettes. Dimensions as for No. 357. Armament varies. 1—3-inch gun. 4 to 8 A.A. guns. 1 "Hedgehog". 2 depth charge throwers in some ships. 2 depth charge racks in some ships.
**FRET.** *F818,* **HERMELIJN.** *F819,* **JAGUAR.** *F822,* **PANTER.** *F821,* **VOS.** *F820,* **WOLF.** *F817.*

**363.** Sp. **ATREVIDA** class. 1954-60. Modernised 1959-60. Corvettes. 1,000 tons. 248 x 34 x 9. (75.5 x 10.2 x 2.7). 2 screws; diesels. 18 knots. 1—3-inch gun. 3 A.A. guns. 2 "Hedgehogs". 8 anti-submarine mortars. 2 depth charge racks.
**ATREVIDA.** *F61,* **DIANA.** *F63,* **NAUTILUS.** *F64,* **PRINCESA.** *F62,* **VILLA DE BILBAO.** *F65.*

**363A.** Sp. **DESCUBIERTA.** *F51.* The remaining vessel of the "Atrevida" class (see No. 363). She was not modernised and her armament comprises: 1—4.1-inch gun; 4 A.A. guns and 4 depth charge throwers.

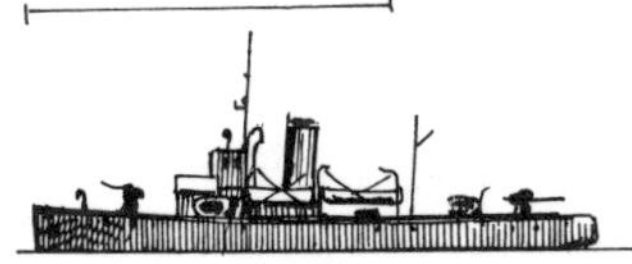

**364.** Po. **DIO.** *A5205.* 1929. Training Ship. 150 x 27 x 7. (45.7 x 8.2 x 2.1). 2 screws; reciprocating. 13 knots. 2—3-inch guns.

**365.** RC. Ex-**AN TUNG.** 1922. Coast Defence Vessel. 222 x 32 x 7.5 (67.6 x 9.7 x 2.2). Reciprocating. 11 knots. 2—3-inch guns. Ex-Japanese ship.

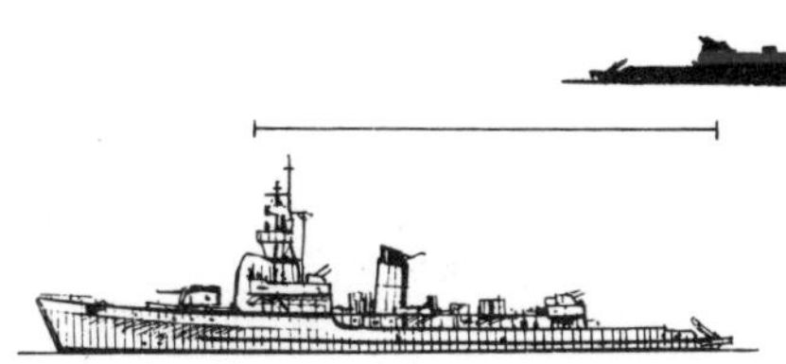

**366.** EG. **HABICHT I** class. 1952-54. Minesweepers. 500 tons. 194 x 26 x 12. (59.1 x 7.9 x 3.6). 2 screws; diesel. 17 knots. 1—3.4-inch gun. 10 A.A. guns. 4 depth charge throwers. Mines. *213, 214, 215, 216.*

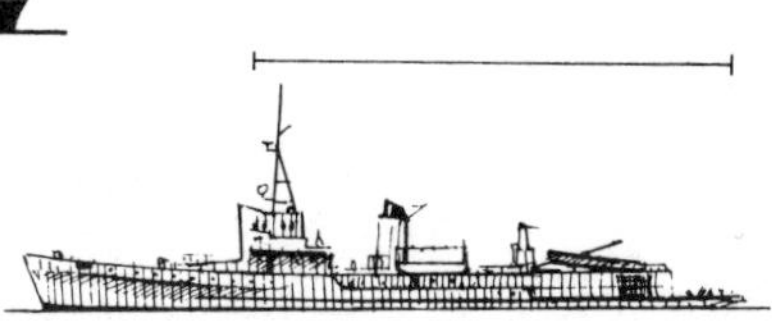

**367.** EG. **HABICHT I** class. As for No. 366 but no armament and converted to Rescue Ships in 1961

**368.** EG. **HABICHT II**, class. 1955-56. Minesweepers. 600 tons. 213 x 27 x 12. (64.9 x 8.2 x 3.6). 2 screws; diesel. 18 knots. 1—3.4-inch gun. 8 A.A. guns (twin—vertically). 4 depth charge throwers.

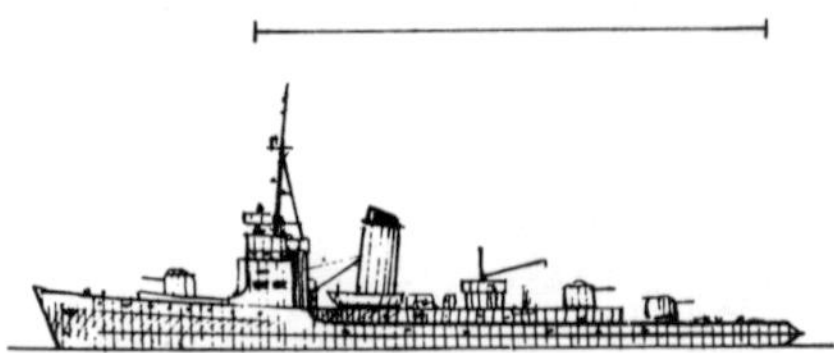

**369.** Rm. Ex-**M40** Type. 1943. Minesweepers. 500 tons. 204 x 28 x 8. (62.1 x 8.5 x 2.4). 2 screws; reciprocating. 17 knots. 6 A.A. guns (twin). 2 depth charge throwers.
**DESCATUSARIA, DESROBEIRA, DEMOCRATIA, DREPTATEA.**

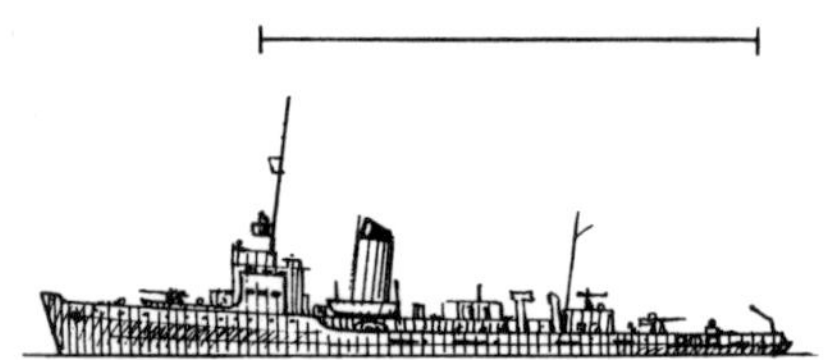

**370.** Sp. **BIDASOA** class. 1946-48. Minesweepers. 600 tons. 201 x 28 x 12. (61.2 x 8.5 x 3.6). 2 screws; reciprocating and exhaust turbines. 16 knots. 1—4-inch gun. 3 A.A. guns.
**BIDASOA.** *M01,* **LEREZ.** *M03,* **NERVION.** *M02,* **SEGURA.** *M05,* **TAMBRE.** *M04,* **TER.** *M06.*

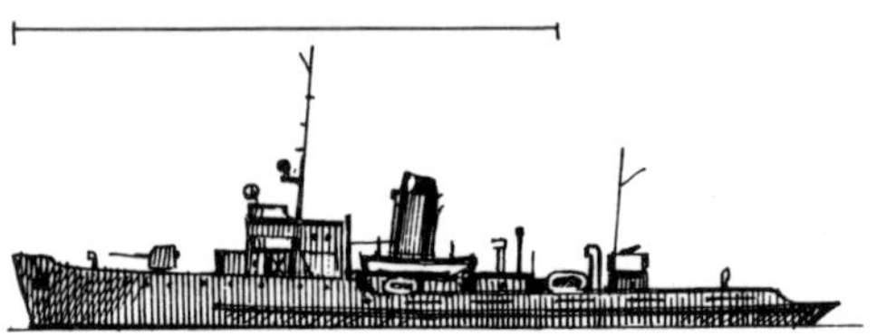

**371.** Sp. **ALMANZORA** class. 1959-61. Minesweepers. 700 tons. 244 x 34 x 12. (74.3 x 10.3 x 3.6). 2 screws; reciprocating and exhaust turbines. 16 knots. 2 A.A. guns.
**ALMANZORA.** *M14,* **EO.** *M17,* **EUME.** *M13,* **GUADALHORCE.** *M16,* **GUARDIARO.** *M11,* **NAVIA.** *M15,* **TINTO.** *M12.*

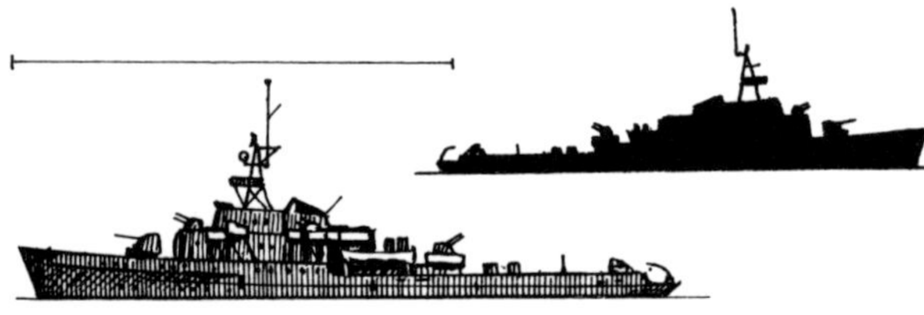

**372.** EG. **KRAKE** class. 1956-58. Minesweepers. 700 tons. 230 x 27 x 12. (70 x 8.2 x 3.6). 2 screws; diesels. 18 knots. 1—3.4-inch gun. 10 A.A. guns. 4 depth charge throwers. Ships differ in appearance.
**BERLIN, ERFURT, GERA, HALLE, LEIPZIG, MAGDEBURG, POTSDAM, ROSTOCK, KARL MARX-STADT, SASSNITZ.**

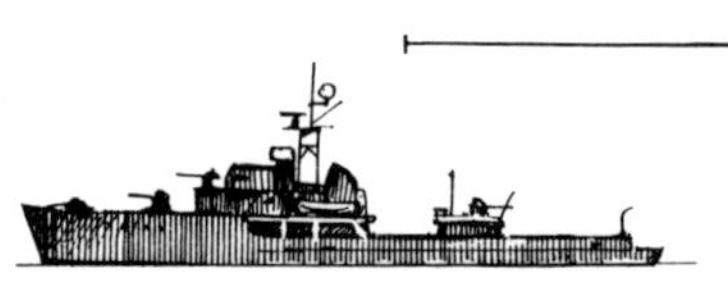

**373.** Fi. **KEIHASSALMI.** 1957. Coastal Minelayer. 400 tons. 168 x 23 x 6. (51.2 x 7 x 1.8). 2 screws; diesels. 15 knots. 4 A.A. guns.

**374.** Ge. **THETIS** class. 1961-63. Corvettes. 600 tons. 230 x 27 x 8. (70 x 8.2 x 2.3). 2 screws; diesels. 24 knots. 2 A.A. guns (twin). 1 depth charge mortar (quadruple) except "Hermes" which has twin mortars.
**HERMES.** *P6112,* **THESEUS.** *P6115,* **THETIS.** *P6111,* **TRITON.** *P6114.* Similar with bridge extension (see inset), **NAJADE.** *P6113.*

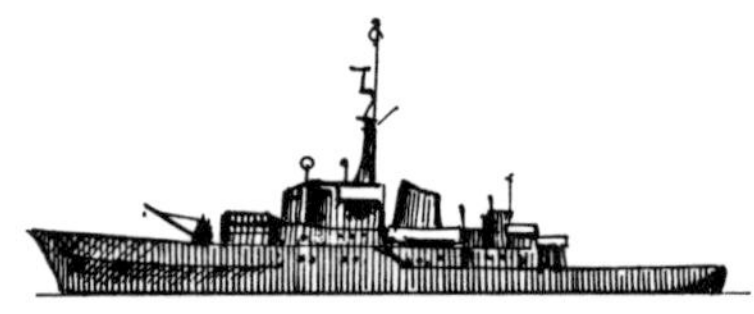

**375.** Ia. **BURUDJULASAD.** *1006.* 1966. Survey Ship. 2,200 tons (top). 270 x 38. (82.3 x 11.6). Diesels. 19 knots. No armament. 1 helicopter.

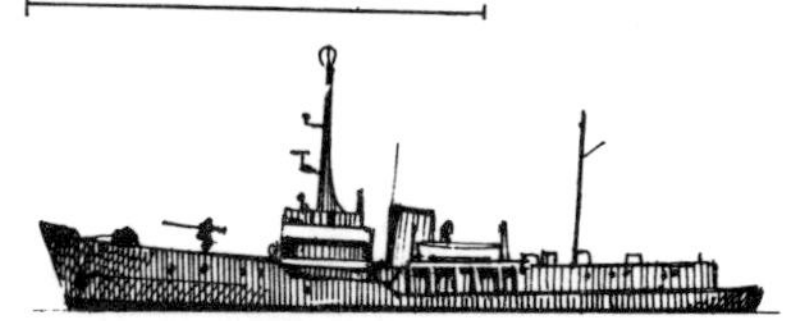

**376.** No. **ANDENES.** 1957. Fishery Protection Vessel. 500 tons (gross). 186 x 31 x 16. (56.7 x 9.5 x 4.9). Diesel. 16 knots. 1—3-inch gun. Converted from whalers.
**NORDKAPP, SENJA.**

**377.** Ge. **HANS BURKNER.** *Y879.* 1963. Corvette. 1,000 tons. 265 x 31 x 10. (80.8 x 9.5 x 3.1). 2 screws; diesels. 25 knots. 2 A.A. guns (twin). 2 anti-submarine torpedo tubes. 1 depth charge mortar (4 barrels). 2 depth charge racks.

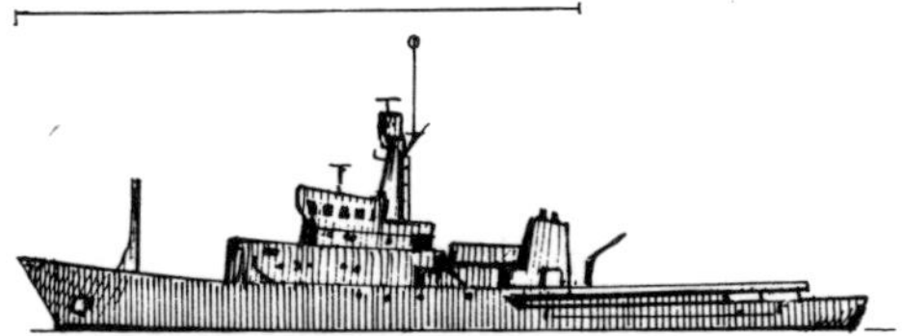

**378.** Ic. **AEGIR.** 1968. Patrol Vessel. 1,200 tons. 229 x 33 x 16. (69.7 x 10 x 4.7). 2 screws; diesels. 19 knots. 1—57-m.m. gun. 1 helicopter.

**379.** Th. **CHARTTRAKARN KOSOL.** 1956. Police Patrol Vessel. 400 tons (gross). 184 x 25 x 9. (56 x 7.6 x 2.6). Diesel. 12 knots.

**380.** RC. **NAN CHANG.** 1941. Modernised 1955. Frigate. 1,000 tons. 264 x 31 x 9. (80.5 x 9.4 x 2.6). 2 screws; turbines. 20 knots. 2—3.9-inch guns. 2—3-inch A.A. guns. 4 smaller A.A. guns. Former Japanese ship.

**381.** RC. **CHANG PAI.** 1943 Modernised 1955. Frigate. 900 tons. 255 x 30 x 10. (77.7 x 9.1 x 4). 2 screws; diesel. 20 knots. 2—3.9-inch guns. 2 A.A. guns. Former Japanese ship of "Etorofu" class.

**382.** RC. **CHANG SHA.** 1944. Frigate. 700 tons. 228 x 28 x 10. (58 x 8.6 x 3). Turbine. 17 knots. 2—3.9-inch guns. 3—3-inch A.A. guns. Former Japanese ship.

**383.** RC. **CHI NAN.** 1945. Very similar to No. 382. Armament probably the same as No. 382 or may comprise 2—4.7-inch guns. 3 to 6 A.A. guns.
Possibly similar are **HSI AN, WU CHANG.**

**384.** Ur. **PAYSANDU** class. 1935. Patrol Vessels. 150 tons. 137 x 18 x 10. (41.8 x 5.5 x 3.1). Diesel. 17 knots. 1 A.A. gun.
**SALTO.** *PR2,* and probably out of commission, **RIO NEGRO.** *PR3.*

**385.** Sw. **V57.** 1953. Patrol Vessel/Minelayer. 100 tons. 105 x 17 x 8). (32 x 5.2 x 2.3). Diesel. 13 knots. 2 A.A. guns.

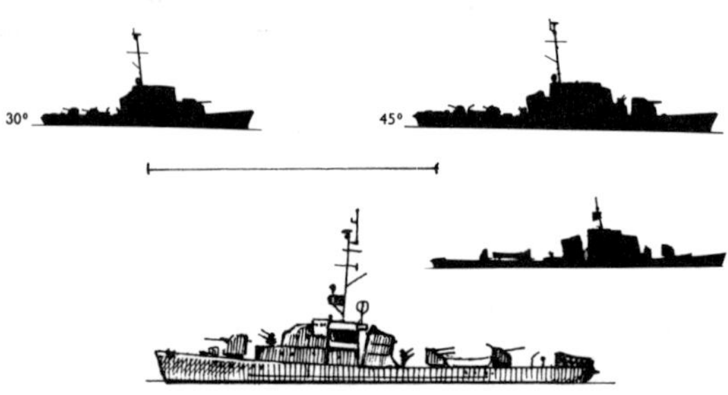

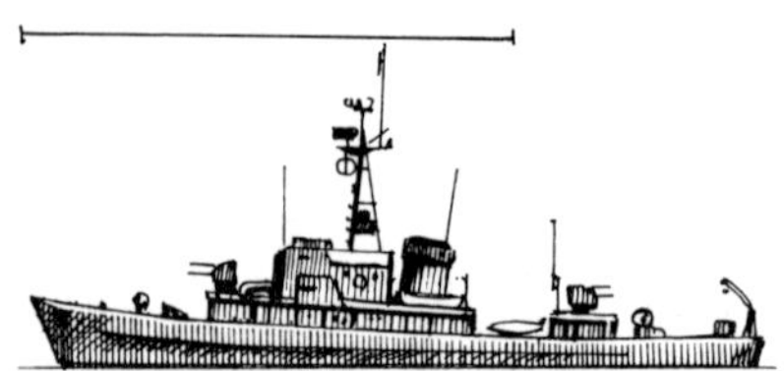

★ **386.** Ph. **KROGULEC** class. 1963-64. Fleet Minesweepers. 500 tons. 190 x 25 x 8. (57.9 x 7.6 x 2.5). Diesel. 16 knots. 6 A.A. guns.
There are at least 12 vessels in the class including the following:
**ALBATROS, CZAPLA, JASTRAB, KORMORAN, KROGULEC, ORLIK, TUKAN.**

★ **387.** Ru. **KRONSTADT,** class. 1948-56. Escorts. 300 tons. 167 x 19 x 9. (50.9 x 5.8 x 2.7). 2 screws; diesels. 18 knots. 1—3.9-inch gun. 5 A.A. guns. Depth charge throwers.
There were originally about 100 in the class but the Russian ships are gradually being taken out of service.

Al. 4 ships.
Bu. 2 ships.
Cu. 6 ships. (Designated Patrol Vessels and carry mines. Probably modernised.)
Ph. 8 ships. **CZUINY, GROZNY, NIEUGIETY, WYTRWALY, ZAWZIETY, ZRECZNY, ZWINNY, ZWROTNY.**
Rm. 3 ships. **V1, V2, V3.** Modernised with considerable anti-submarine gear.
RC. 24 ships.

*also:*
1a. 8 ships: **KATULA, LADJURA, LAPAI, LUMBA - LUMBA, MADIDIHANG, MO - MARE, TJUTTJUT, TONGKOL.**

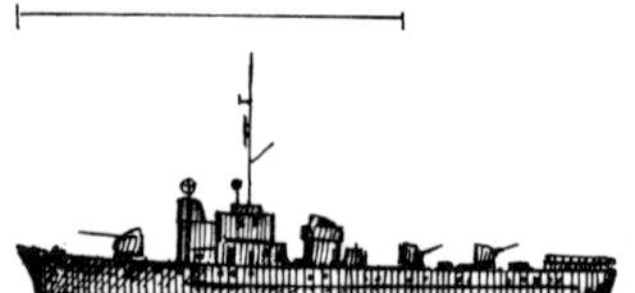

★ **388.** RK. **ARTILLERIST** class. Ex-U.S.S.R. 1943. Patrol Vessels. 240 tons. 161 x 19 x 7. (49 x 5.8 x 2.1). 2 screws; diesels. 20 knots. 1—3.9-inch gun. 2 A.A. guns. 2 depth charge throwers. 2 ships in service.

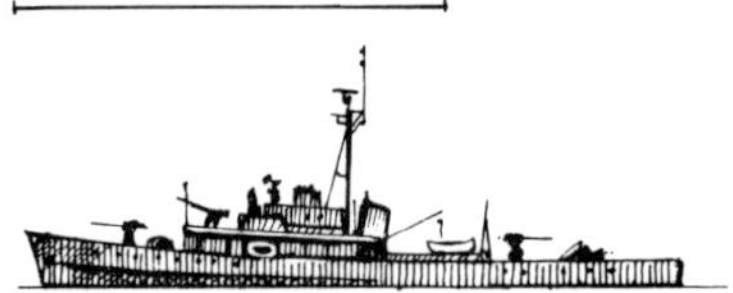

★ **389.** Ys. **MORNAR.** *551.* 1959. Patrol Vessel. 300 tons. 170 x 23 x 7. (51.8 x 7 x 2). Diesels. 24 knots. 2—3-inch guns. 4 A.A. guns. 2 depth charge throwers. 2 depth charge racks.

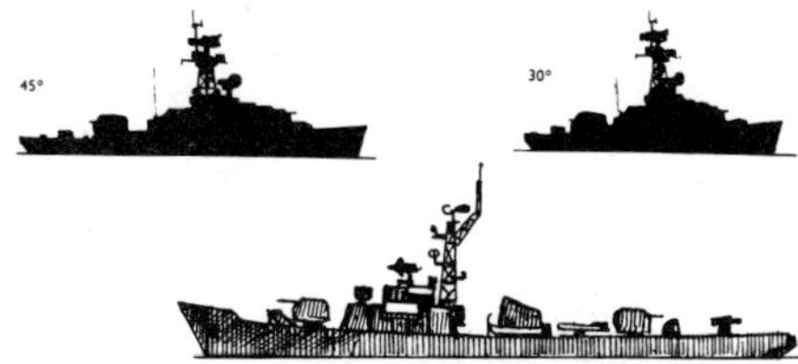

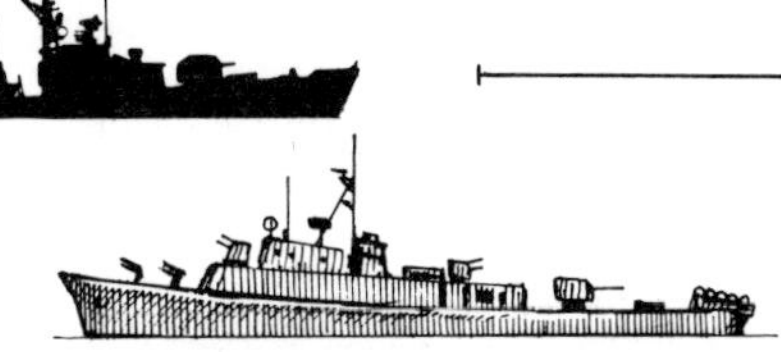

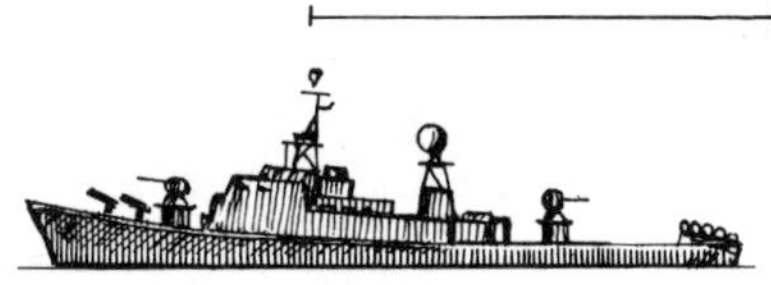

★ **390.** Ru. **PETYA** class. 1961 onwards. Escorts. 1,100 tons. 263 x 32 x 10. (80.2 x 9.8 x 3.1). 2 screws; diesel and gas turbines. 30 knots. 4—3-inch D.P. guns (twin). 5 torpedo tubes (quintuple). 4 anti-submarine rocket launchers (16 barrels).
A modified and later type has an extra set of torpedo tubes and 2 rocket launchers (12 barrels). About 35 vessels in the Russian fleet.

In. **KADMATH, KAMORTA, KATCHALL, KAVRATI, KILTON.** *P179.*

★ **391.** EG. **HAI** class—Type 1. 1963 onwards. Patrol Vessels. 300 tons. 187 x 19 x 10. (57 x 5.8 x 3.1). Diesel and gas turbine. 25 knots. 4 A.A. guns (twin). 4 anti-submarine rocket launchers (5 barrels).
There are about 12 vessels in Types 1 and 111.

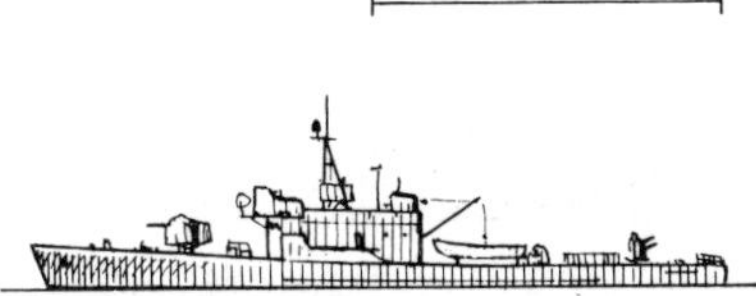

★ **392.** EG. **HAI** class. Type III. Particulars practically the same as for No. 391. Do not all have the Radar on after mast.

★ **393.** Ph. **BIRD** class. 1935-38. Patrol Vessels. 140 tons. 140 x 21 x 5.5. (42.7 x 6.4 x 1.5). Diesel. 15 knots.
**CZAIKA, MEWA, RYBITWA.**
**KOMPAS** is employed as a Survey Ship and may be different in appearance.

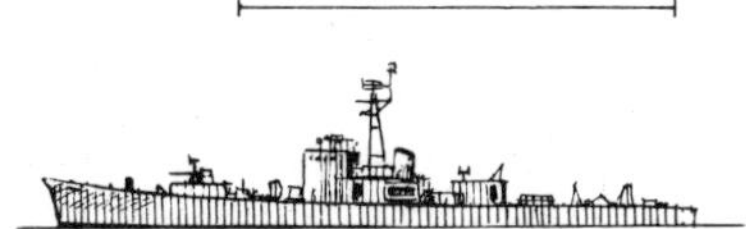

**394.** Ja. **KAMOME.** *305.* 1957. Patrol Vessels. 300 tons. 173 x 22 x 7. (52.7 x 6.7 x 2.1). 2 screws; diesels. 20 knots. 2—40-m.m. guns (twin). 1 "Hedgehog". 2 Y guns. 2 depth charge racks.
**MISAGO.** *307.*
The following vessels may have no funnel; see No. 469.
**KIJI.** *302,* **TAKA.** *303,* **TSUBAME.** *306,* **WASHI.** *304.*

**395.** Jap. **MIZUTORI** class. 1962-66. Patrol Vessels. 450 tons. 197 x 23 x 7.5. (60 x 7 x 2.3). 2 screws; diesels. 20 knots. 2—40-m.m. guns (twin). 1 "Hedgehog". 1 depth charge rack. 2 anti-submarine torpedo launchers (twin).
**MIZUTORI.** *311,* **HATSUKARI.** *315,* **HIYODORI.** *320,* **KASASAGI.** *314,* **KUMATAKA.** *318,* **OTORI.** *313,* **SHIRATORI.** *319,* **UMIDORI.** *316,* **WAKATAKA.** *317,* **YAMADORI.** *312.*
Very similar—no mainmast. See silhouette No. 350.
**UMITAKA.** *309,* **OTAKA.** *310.*

**396.** Ja. **HAYABUSA.** *308.* 1957. Patrol Vessel. 400 tons. 190 x 26 x 7. (57.9 x 7.8 x 2.1). 3 screws; gas turbines. 26 knots. 2 A.A. guns. 1 "Hedgehog". 2 depth charge throwers. 2 depth charge racks. Funnel is very low and raking, scarcely distinguishable from the bridge but thin tower on after superstructure may be mistaken for a funnel.

**397. RC. KAN TANG.** Coast Defence Vessel. 300 tons. 173 x 23 x 11. (52.7 x 7 x 3.3). 2 screws; diesel. 20 knots. 1—3-inch D.P. gun. 2 A.A. guns (twin). Ex-U.S. PGM type. There are two other ships in the class but their Chinese names are not known.

**398. Sy. AKABA BEN NASEH.** 1940. Patrol Vessel. 100 tons. 122 x 18 x 7. (37.1 x 5.3 x 2). 2 screws; diesels. 16 knots. 1—3-inch gun. 2 A.A. guns. Depth charges. Ex-Fr. "Ch" type. **AL HARISSI, TAREK BEN SAID.**

**399. It. LAMPO** class. 1963. Converted 1965. Convertible Gunboats. 170 tons. 132 x 21 x 5. (40.2 x 6.4 x 1.5). 3 screws; combined diesel and gas turbines. 39 knots. As gunboat; 2 or 3—40-m.m. guns. As torpedo boat; 1—40-m.m. gun. 2 torpedo tubes.
**BALENO.** *492,* **LAMPO.** *491.*

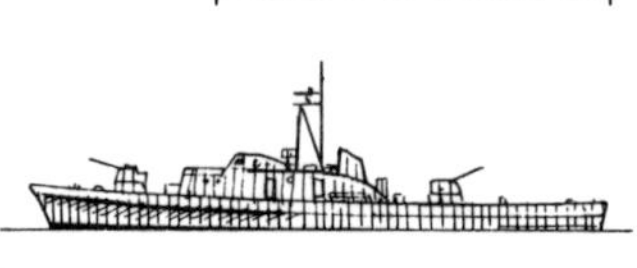

**400. Ge. SCHUTZE** class. 1959-64. Fast Minesweepers. 200 tons. 155 x 22 x 7. (47.2 x 6.8 x 2.1). 2 screws; diesels. 24 knots. 1 or 2 A.A. guns.

Some of the ships listed below are represented by drawings Nos. 401 and 402.
**ALGOL.** *M1068,* **ALTAIR.** *M1067,* **CAPELLA.** *M1098,* **CASTOR.** *M1051* **DENEB.** *M1064,* **FISCHE.** *M1096,* **GEMMA.** *M1097,* **HERKULES.** *M1095,* **JUPITER.** *M1065,* **KREBS.** *M1055,* **MARS.** *M1058,* **NEPTUN.** *M1093,* **ORION.** *M1053,* **PEGASUS.** *M1066,* **PERSEUS.** *M1090,* **POLLUX.** *M1054,* **PLUTO.** *M1092,* **REGULUS.** *M1057,* **RIGEL.** *M1056,* **SCHUTZE.** *M1062,* **SIRIUS.** *M1055,* **SKORPION.** *M1060,* **SPICA.** *M1059,* **STEINBACK.** *M1091,* **URANUS.** *M1099,* **WAAGE.** *M1063,* **WEGA.** *M1069,* **WIDDER.** *M1094.*

**401. Ge. SCHUTZE** class. This is a variation of No. 400. For list of names of entire class see drawing No. 400.

**402. Ge. SCHUTZE** class. A variation on the type illustrated in No. 400. See No. 400 for list of names of the entire class.

**403. Ge. SCHUTZE** class. Submarine Support Ship. All details as for No. 400 but has no armament. Note the decompression chamber erected on the after deck.
**STIER.** *M1061.*

**404.** It. **FRECCIA** class. 1965-66. Convertible Gunboats. 188 tons. 150 x 24 x 5.5. (45.7 x 7.2 x 1.6). Combined diesel and gas turbine. 40 knots. Armament as gunboat: 2 or 3—40-m.m. guns. As torpedo boat: 1—40-m.m. gun. A.A. guns. 2 torpedo tubes. As minelayer: 1 40-m.m. A.A. gun. 8 mines. As missile boat: 5 short range missiles. Drawing represents a gunboat. See silhouette No. 84 for appearance as a torpedo boat.
**DARDO.** *P495,* **FRECCIA.** *P493,* **SAETTA.** *P494,* **STRALE.** *P496.*

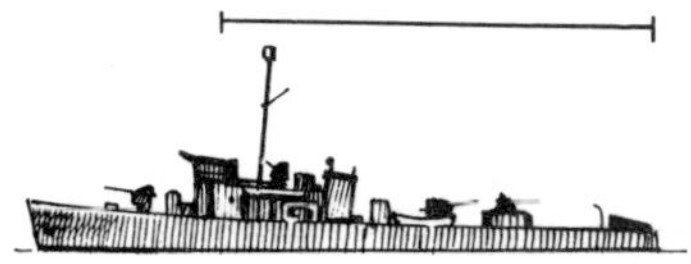

**405.** Ex-US. **PC** type. *C5.* 1941-43. 300 tons. 174 x 23 x 11. (53 x 7 x 3). Diesel. 20 knots. 1—3-inch gun. 6 A.A. guns.
(submarine    chasers).

Cs. **CHIH KIANG.** *109,* **CHING KIANG.** *116,* **CHUNG KIANG.** *115,* **FUKIANG.** *105,* **HAN KIANG.** *124,* **HSI KIANG.** *120,* **HSIANG KIANG.** *108,* **LI KIANG.** *111,* **LIU KIANG.** *123,* **KUNG KIANG.** *113,* **PEI KIANG.** *122,* **PO KIANG.** *114,* **TO KIANG.** *125,* **TUNG KIANG.** *119.*

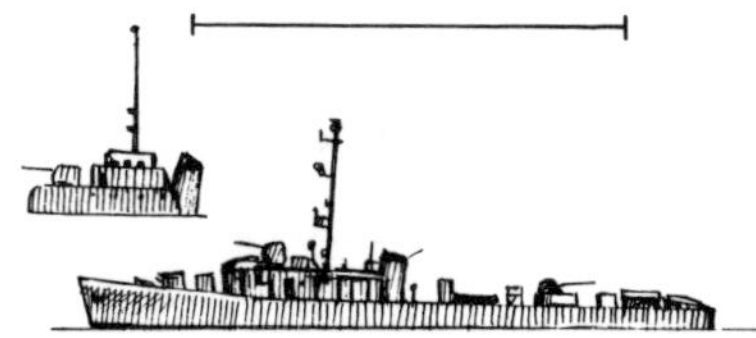

**406.** Fr. **LE FOUGUEUX** class. 1954-59. Patrol Vessels. 300 tons. 174 x 23 x 7. (53 x 7 x 2). Diesels. 19 knots. 4 A.A. guns. 1 "Hedgehog". 4 depth charge mortars. 2 depth charge racks. Very similar to US. PC type.
**L'AGILE.** *P643,* **LE FOUGUEUX.** *P641,* **L'OPINIATRE.** *P642.*

Mo. (see inset of bridge): **LIEUTENANT RIFFI.** *32.*
Po.: **MAIO** class. **MAIO.** *P587,* **BOAVISTA.** *P592,* **BRAVA.** *P590,* **FOGO.** *P591,* **PORTO SANTO.** *P588,* **S. NICOLAU.** *P589,* **SANTA LUZIA.** *P594,* **SANTO ANTAO.** *P593.*

Ys.: **PBR.** *581.*
All these ships can be distinguished from Nos. 405, 407, 408, and 409 by having forward gun mounted on top of the bridge.

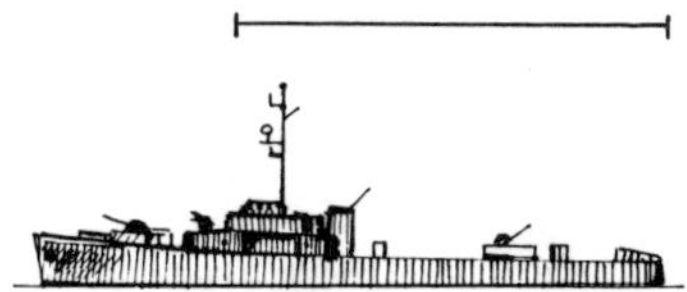

**407.** Fr. **LE FOUGUEUX** class. 1958-59. Patrol Vessels. Tonnage and dimensions as No. 406. 6 A.A. guns. 1 "Hedgehog". 4 depth charge mortars. 2 depth charge racks. 1 large anti-submarine mortar. In addition **L'INTREPIDE** has a stern mounted torpedo tube. These are the later units of the class.

**L'ADROIT.** *P644,* **L'ALERTE.** *P645,* **L'ATTENTIF.** *P646,* **L'ARDENT.** *P635,* **L'EFFRONTE.** *P638,* **L'ENJOUE.** *P647,* **L'ETOURDI.** *P637,* **LE FRINGANT.** *P640,* **LE HARDI.** *P648,* **L'INTREPIDE.** *P630.*

Similar: It. 1955. Refitted 1959. **VEDETTA.** *F597.* Distinguished by the large deck house abaft the funnel (see inset).

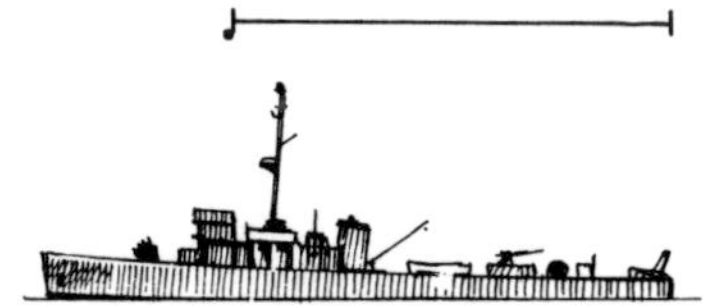

**408.** Tu. **AKHISAR** class. (Ex-US. "PC" type). 1964 c. Tonnage and dimensions as No. 405. 2 screws; diesels. 19 knots. 1—3-inch D.P. gun. 1 A.A. gun. 4 depth charge throwers.

Identified by mortar forward in place of gun.
**AKHISAR.** *P114,* **DEMIRHISAR.** *P112,* **KOCHISAR.** *P116,* **SIVRIHISAR.** *P115,* **SULTANHISAR.** *P111,* **YARHISAR.** *P113.*

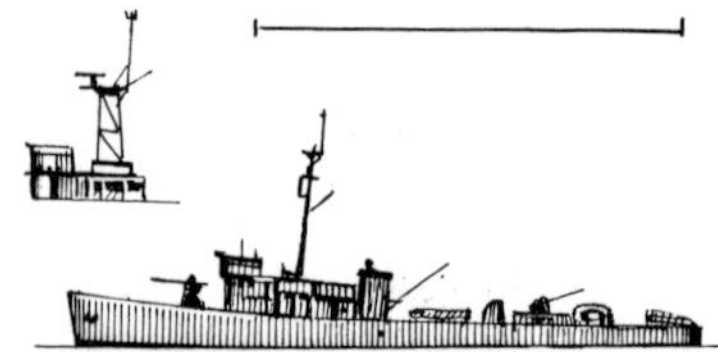

**409.** Ex-US. **PC** type. Patrol Vessels. Dimensions, tonnage and engines as No. 405. Armament is given under the individual countries.
Cambodia. 1—3-inch D.P. gun. 3 A.A. guns.
**E311, E312**.
Ia.: 1—3-inch D.P. gun. 3 A.A. guns. 4 depth charge throwers.
**HUI, TENGGIRI, TJAKALANG, TORANI.**
Is.: 1—4-inch gun. 4 A.A. guns. 4 depth charge throwers.
**NOGAH.**
Ko.: 1—3-inch D.P. gun. 5 A.A. guns. 2 anti-submarine rocket launchers. 1 "Mousetrap".
**KUM CHONG SAN.** *PC708,* **MYO HYANG SAN.** *PC706,* **O TAE SAN.** *PC707,* **SOL AK.** *PC709.*
Me.: 1—3-inch D.P. gun. 2 A.A. guns. 4 depth charge throwers.
*GC38, G8.*
Pi.: 1—3-inch D.P. gun. 6 A.A. guns.
**BATANGAS.** *24,* **BOHOL.** *22,* **CAPIZ.** *27,* **NUEVA ECIJA.** *25,* **NUEVA VISCAYA.** *80.*
Po.: **PRINCIPE** class. 4 A.A. guns. 1 "Hedgehog". 4 depth charge throwers. 2 depth charge racks.
**PRINCIPE.** *P581,* **MADEIRA.** *P582,* **S. TOME.** *P585,* **S. VICENTE.** *P586.*
Sp.: 2 37-m.m. A.A. guns. Has a very short mast from the back of the funnel.
**JAVIER QUIROGA.**
Th.: 7 A.A. guns. 2 anti-submarine torpedo tubes.
**LIULOM.** *7,* **LONGLOM.** *8,* **PHALI.** *4,* **SARASIN.** *1,* **SUKRIP.** *5,* **THAYANCHON.** *2,* **TONGPILU.** *6.*
Ur.: 1—3-inch D.P. gun. 4 A.A. guns. 1 anti-submarine mortar. 4 depth charge mortars.
**MALDONADO.** *PC1.*
Ve.: (see inset). 1—3-inch D.P. gun. 4 A.A. guns. 4 depth charge throwers.
**ALBATROS.** *P04,* **ALCATRAZ.** *P03,* **CALAMAR.** *P02,* **CAMARON.** *P08,* **CARACOL.** *P06.* **GAVIOTA.** *P10.* **PETREL.** *P05,* **PULPO.** *P07.* **MEJILLON.** *P01,* **TOGOGO.** *P09.*
VN.: 1—3-inch D.P. gun. 5 A.A. guns. 2 depth charge throwers. 2 anti-submarine rocket launchers.
**TUY DONG.** *HQ04,* **VAN DON.** *HQ06.*

**410.** Tu. Br. "Fairmile" B type. 1940-42. Patrol Launches. 85 tons. 112 x 18 x 4. (34.1 x 5.4 x 1.2). Oil engines. 21 knots. 1—3-pdr. gun. 2 A.A. guns.
**AB1.** *P321,* **AB2.** *P322,* **AB3.** *P323,* **AB4.** *P324,* **AB6.** *P326,* **AB7.** *P327.*

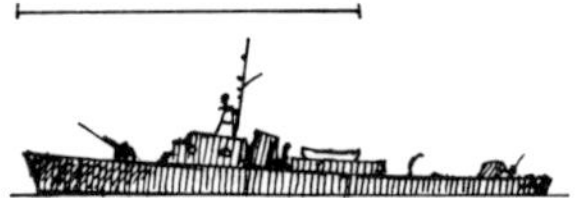

**411.** Ia. **MAWER** class, 1968 onwards. Patrol Boats. 150 tons. Dimensions not known. Diesel. 21 knots. 40 m.m. A.A. guns.
**KELABANG, KELALANG, KALAHITAM.**
Others under construction.

**412.** Bz. **P** class. 1947-48. Seaward Defence Boats. 130 tons. 128 x 20 x 6. (39 x 6.1 x 1.8). 3 screws; diesels. 20 knots. 1—3-inch gun. 2 A.A. guns. Depth charges.
**PIRAJU.** *J28,* **PIRANHA.** *J30,* **PIRAQUE.** *J32.*
Bear a superficial resemblance to the Soviet "Kronstadt" class. See No. 387.

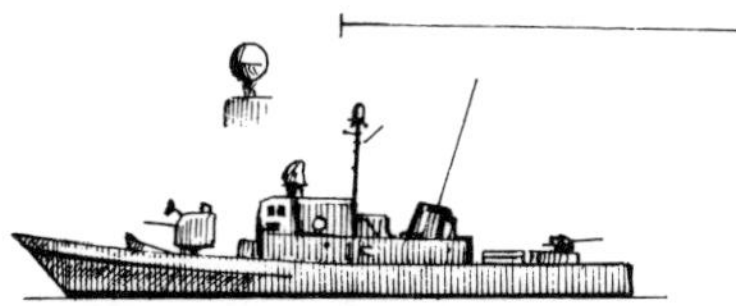

**413.** Am. **ASHEVILLE** class. 1966-70. Patrol Gunboats. 225 tons. 165 x 24 x 10. (50.2 x 7.3 x 3). Diesel and gas turbines. 2 screws. 40 knots. 1—3-inch D.P. gun. 1 A.A. gun.
**ASHEVILLE.** *84,* **CANON.** *90,* **CROCKET.** *88,* **CHEHALIS.** *94,* **DEFIANCE.** *95,* **DOUGLAS.** *100,* **BENICIA.** *96,* **BEACON.** *99,* **GALLUP.** *85,* **GRAND RAPIDS.** *98,* **GREEN BAY.** *101,* **MARATHON.** *89,* **SURPRISE.** *97,* **TACOMA.** *92,* **WELCH.** *93.*
Similar but with large sphere on bridge (see inset) and silhouette No. 48.
**ANTELOPE.** *86,* **READY.** *87.*
Other units are building and three were transferred to Thailand.

**414.** Ph. **OKSYWIE** class. 1967 c. Patrol Boats. 170 tons. 135 x 19 x 7. (41.1 x 5.7 x 2.1). Diesels. 20 knots. 2—37-m.m. guns (twin). Depth charge racks.
**OP301, OP302, OP303, OP304.**

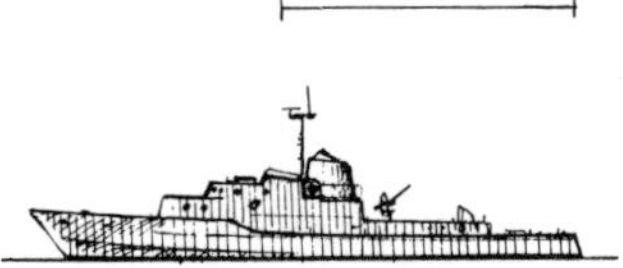

**415.** Co. **CARLOS E. RESTREPO.** 1964. Coast Guard Vessels. 124 tons. 108 x 18 x 6, (32.9 x 5.4 x 1.8). Diesels 26 knots. 1 A.A. gun.
**ESTEBAN JARAMILLO, PEDRO GUAL.**

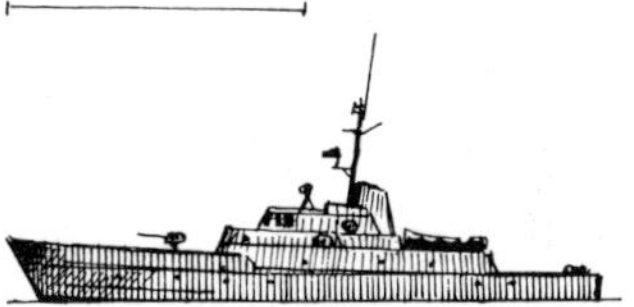

**416.** Fi. **VIIMA.** 1964, Patrol Boat. 135 tons. 118 x 22 x 8. (35.9 x 6.7 x 2.4). Diesels. 24 knots. 1 A.A. gun.

**417.** Gh. **KROMANTSE** class. 1964-65. Corvettes. 400 tons. 177 x 28 x 13. (53.9 x 8.5 x 3.9). 2 screws; diesels. 20 knots. 1—4-inch D.P. gun. 1 A.A. gun. 1 "Squid" depth charge mortar.
**KROMANTSE.** *F17,* **KETA.** *F18.*
Distinguished from No. 418 by lattice mast and a single gun house aft.

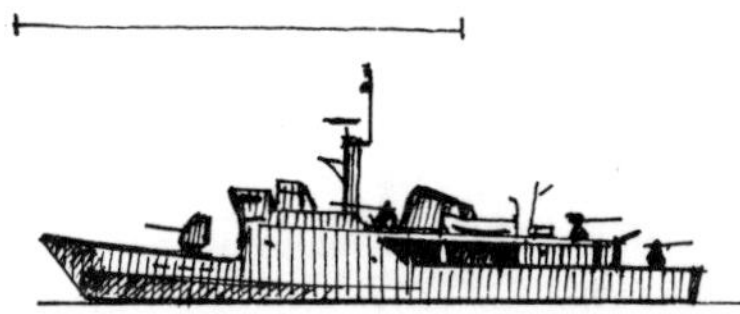

**418.** Ly. **TOBRUK.** 1966. Corvette. 450 tons. 177 x 29 x 10. (53.9 x 8.8 x 3). 2 screws; diesels. 18 knots. 1—4-inch gun. 4 A.A. guns.

**419.** Ly. **AR-RAKIB.** 1967. Coast Guard Vessel. 100 tons. 100 x 21 x 6. (30.4 x 6.4 x 1.8). Diesels. 18 knots. 1—20-m.m. gun.
**FARWA.**

**420.** Ku. "78 ft. type" 1966-69. Patrol Boats. tons. 78 x 16 x 5. (23.7 x 4.8 x 1.5). 2 screws; diesels. 20 knots.
**AL-SALEMI, AL-MUBARAKI, AMAN, MAR-ZOOK, MASHHOOR, MAYMOON, MUR-SHED, WATHAH.**

**421.** Pv. **DE LOS HEROS.** *23.* 1964-66. Patrol Boats. 100 tons. 110 x 21 x 6. (33.5 x 6.5 x 1.8). Turbo-charged diesels. 30 knots. 2 A.A. guns.
**HERRERA.** *24,* **LARREA.** *25,* **SANCHEZ CARRION.** *26,* **SANTILLANA.** *22,* **VELARDE.** *21.*

**422.** Au. **ACUTE.** 1966 and onwards. Fast Patrol Boats. 150 tons. 108 x 20 x 7. (32.9 x 6.1 x 3.1). 2 screws; diesels. 24 knots. 1—40-m.m. gun.
**ADROIT, ADVANCE, AITAPE, ARCHER, ARDENT, ARROW, ASSAIL, ATTACK, A-WARE, BANDOLIER, BARBETTE, BARRI-CADE, BAYONET, BOMBARD, BUCCAN-EER, LADAVA, LAE, MADANG, SAMARAI.**

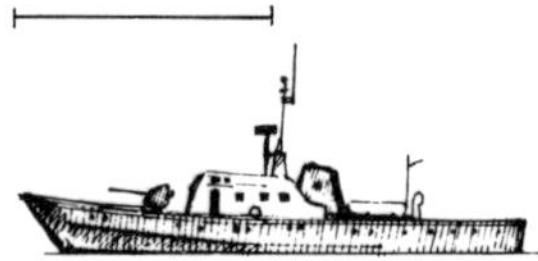

**423.** Tr. **COURLAND BAY.** *CG2.* 1965. Patrol Craft. 100 tons. 103 x 20 x 5.5. (31.4 x 6.1 x 1.6). Diesels. 25 knots. 1—40-m.m. A.A. gun.
**TRINITY.** *CG1.*

**424.** My. **SRI** class. 1963-68. Patrol Boats. 100 tons. 103 x 20 x 5.5. (31.4 x 6.1 x 1.6). Diesels. 27 knots. 2—40-m.m. guns. (Some may have only 1 gun). There are 3 variations as below :

**KEDAH** class: **SRI KEDAH.** *P3138,* **SRI KELANTAN.** *P3142,* **SRI PAHANG.** *P3141,* **SRI PERAK.** *P3140,* **SRI SELANGOR.** *P3139,* **SRI TRENGGANU.** *P3143.*

**SABAH** class: **SRI MELAKA.** *P3147,* **SRI NEGRI SEMBILAN.** *P3144,* **SRI SARAWAK.** *P3143.*

**KRIS** class: **BADEK.** *P37,* **BELADAU.** *P44,* **KELEWANG.** *P45,* **KERAMBIT.** *P43,* **KRIS.** *P34,* **LEMBING.** *P40,* **PANAH.** *P42,* **REN-CHONG.** *P38,* **RENTAKA.** *P46,* **SERAM-PANG.** *P41,* **SRI JOHOR.** *P49,* **SRI PERLIS.** *P47,* **SUNDANG.** *P36,* **TOMBAK.** *P39.*

**425.** Ke. **CHUI.** *P3112.* 1966. Patrol Boats. Dimensions and tonnage as No. 423. Diesels. 24 knots. 2—40-m.m. A.A. guns.
**NDOVU.** *P3117,* **SIMBA.** *P3110.*

**426.** Po. **AZEVIA** class. 1941-42. Fishery Protection Craft. 230 tons. 140 x 21 x 7. (42.6 x 6.4 x 2.1). 2 screws; diesels. 17 knots. 2—20-m.m. A.A. guns.
**AZEVIA.** *P595,* **BICUDA.** *P596,* **CORVINA.** *P597,* **DOURADA.** *P598,* **ESPADILHA.** *P599.*

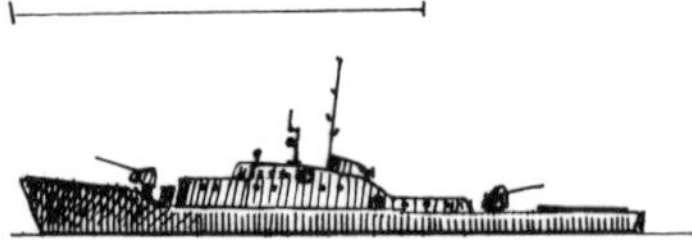

**427.** Mg. **MALAIKA,** 1967. Patrol Vessel. 250 tons. 156 x 24 x 8. (47.5 x 7.3 x 2.4) Diesels. 18 knots. 2—40-m.m. A.A. guns. Similar. Iv. **LE VIGILANT.**

**428.** Li. **PGM. 69.** 1969 and onwards. Gunboats. 100 tons. 95 x 19 x 5. (28.9 x 5.7 x 1.5). 2 screws; diesels. 21 knots. 1—40-m.m. A.A. gun, and may also have smaller guns.
**PGM. 102.** (U.S. number).

Do. **BETELGEUSE.** *GC102.*
Ec. **GUAYAQUIL.** *LC72,* **QUITO.** *LC71*
Th. **T11** (*11*), **T12** (*12*), **T13** (*13*).
Tu. **PGM. 72, PGM. 104, PGM. 105, PGM. 106, PGM. 108.** (These may be U.S. numbers).
VN. **DINH HAI.** *610,* **HOA LU.** *608,* **KEO NGUA.** *604,* **KIEN VANG.** *603,* **KIM QUI.** *605,* **MAY RUT.** *606,* **MINH HOA.** *602,* **NAM DU.** *607,* **PHU DU.** *600,* **THAI BINH.** *612,* **THI TU.** *613,* **TIEN MOI.** *601,* **TO YEN.** *609,* **TRUONG SA.** *611,* and No. 614.

**429.** Bm. **PGM** Type. Dimensions and tonnage as for No. 428. 2 screws; diesels. 16 knots. 1—40-m.m. A.A. gun.
**PGM. 401, PGM. 402, PGM. 403, PGM. 404, PGM. 405, PGM. 406.**
Similar:
Pi. **AGUSAN.** *61,* **CATAN DUANES.** *62,* **PALAWAN.** *64,* **ROMBLON.** *63.*
(There may be others with this appearance).

**430.** Am. **95 Foot** class—"C" type. 1958-59. Coast Guard Patrol Boats. 100 tons. 95 x 19 x 6. (28.9 x 5.7 x 1.8). 2 screws; diesels. 21 knots. 1—40-m.m. or 1—20-m.m. gun.
**CAPE CORWIN.** *95326,* **CAPE CROSS.** *95321,* **CAPE HENLOPEN.** *95328,* **CAPE HORN.** *95322,* **CAPE SHOALWATER.** *95324,* **CAPE YORK.** *95332.*

**431.** Am. **95 Foot** class—"A" type. 1953. Coast Guard Patrol Boats. Different superstructure from No. 430.
**CAPE CARTER.** *95309,* **CAPE CORAL.** *95301,* **CAPE CURRENT.** *95307,* **CAPE GEORGE.** *95306,* **CAPE GULL.** *95304,* **CAPE HATTERAS.** *95305,* **CAPE HIGGON.** *95302,* **CAPE SMALL.** *95300,* **CAPE STRAIT.** *95308,* **CAPE UPRIGHT.** *95303,* **CAPE WASH.** *95310,* **CAPE HEDGE.** *95311.*

**432.** Am. **95 Foot** class—"B" Type. 1955-56. Coast Guard Patrol Boats. 106 tons. All other details as for No. 430.
Recognised by having gun aft instead of foreward.
**CAPE FAIRWEATHER.** *95314,* **CAPE FOX.** *95316,* **CAPE JELLISON.** *95317,* **CAPE KNOX.** *95312,* **CAPE MORGAN.** *95313,* **CAPE NEWAGEN.** *95318,* **CAPE ROMAIN.** *95319,* **CAPE STARR.** *95320.*

Very similar.
Et. **PC11, PC12, PC13, PC14, PC15.**
Ha. **LA CRETE A PIERROT.** *GC8,* **VERTIERES.** *GC9.*
Ir. (These have a depth charge projector foreward.)
**KEYVAN, MAHAN, MEHRAN, TIRAN.**
Si. **RIYADH.**

**433.** Ca. **RACER.** 1963. Coast Guard Search and Rescue Cutters. 153 tons. 95 x 20 x 6.5. (28.9 x 6.1 x 1.6). 2 screws; diesel. 20 knots.
Similar to previous U.S. ships.
**RALLY, RAPID, READY, RELAY.**

**434.** Th. **CGC. 13,** 1953-54. Coast Guard Patrol Boats. 95 tons. 95 x 20 x 5. (28.9 x 6.1 x 1.8). 2 screws; diesel. 21 knots. 1—20-m.m. gun. Similar to previous U.S. ships. No. 431. **CGC. 14, CGC. 15, CGC. 16.**

**435.** Ar. **LYNCH** class. Patrol Boats. 100 tons. 90 x 19 x 6. (27.4 x 5.7 x 1.8). Diesels. 22 knots. 1—20-m.m. gun. **EREZCANO.** *GC23,* **LYNCH.** *GC21,* **TOLL.** *GC22.*

**436.** Bm. U.S. Coast Guard Cutter type. 1960. 50 tons. 83 x 16 x 5.5. (25.3 x 4.8 x 1.6). 2 screws; diesels. 11 knots. 1—40-m.m. gun (A.A.). 1—20-m.m. A.A. gun. **MGB. 101, MGB. 102, MGB. 104, MGB. 105, MGB. 106, MGB. 108, MGB. 110.**

★ **437.** Ys. **PC. 134.** Recently completed. Patrol Vessel. 85 tons. 92 x 15 x 8. (28 x 4.5 x 2.4). Diesels. 13 knots. 1—20-m.m. A.A. gun.

**438.** Th. **CGC. 11.** Coast Guard Patrol Vessel. 44 tons. 83 x 16 x 4.5. (25 x 4.8 x 1.3). Petrol engines. 20 knots. 1—20-m.m. A.A. gun. Ex-U.S. Coast Guard YP class.

**439.** Tu. **LS. 9,** (*P339*). Launches. 63 tons. 83 x 14 x 5. (25 x 4.2 x 1.5). Motor vessels. 1—20-m.m. A.A. guns. Ex-U.S. type. **LS. 10,** (*P308*), **LS. 11,** (*P309*), **LS. 12,** (*P310*).

**440.** Br. **FORD** class. 1953-57. Seaward Defence Boats. 120 tons. 117 x 20 x 7. (35.6 x 6.1 x 2.1). 2 screws; diesels. 15 knots. 1—40-m.m. A.A. gun. Depth charge rails. Funnels abreast. **DEE.** *P3104* (R.N.R. Training Ship). **KINGSFORD.** *P3117.*

Similar: (Mine rails at stern and Black star on funnels). Ga. **ELMINA.** *P13,* **KOMENDA.** *P14.*

Ke. (Raised plating foreward); no crane aft. **NYATI.** *P3102.* Ng. **BENIN, BONNY,** *P3111,* **ENUGU.** *P3137,* **IBADAN, KADUNA, SAPELE.** *P3119,* **IBADAN II.** *P3106.* In. **ABHAY, AJAY, AKSHAY.** SA. **GELDERLAND.** *P3105,* **NAUTILUS.** *P3120.* **OOSTERLAND.** *P3127,* **RIJGER.** *P3125* (Both these ships have 2-depth charge throwers).

**441**. SA. **FORD** class. Survey Vessel. Details as for No. 440 except for armament which comprises: 1—40-m.m. A.A. gun, 2 depth charge throwers.
**HAERLEM.** *P3126.* Has a chart room added abaft funnels.

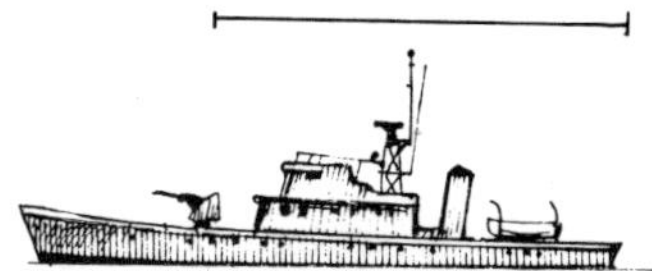

**442**. Sg. **FORD** class. 1956. Seaward Defence Boat. Tonnage and dimensions as for No. 440. Diesels; 14 knots. 1—40-m.m. gun. Distinguished by large bridge and thin funnels.
**PANGLIMA.** *P48.*

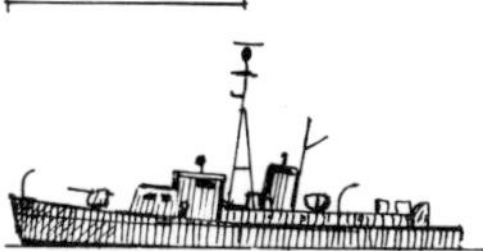

**443**. Ca. **BIRD** class. 1955. Patrol Boats. 66 tons. (Full). 92 x 17 x 5. (28 x 5.1 x 1.5). Diesels. 14 knots. 1—20-m.m. A.A. gun.
**BLUE HERON, CORMORANT.** *781,* **LOON.** *780,* **MALLARD.** *783.*
Similar—R.C.M.P.—**VICTORIA.**

**444**. Fi. **VMV II.** *1935.* Coast Guard Patrol Boat. 35 tons. 82 x 14 x 3. (24.9 x 4.2 x 9). Diesel. 25 knots. 1—20-m.m. gun.
**VMV 13.**

**445**. Ec. **LSP I.** 1954-55. Patrol Boats. 45 tons. 77 x 14 x 6. (23.4 x 4.2 x 1.8). 2 screws; diesel. 22 knots. 1 light A.A. gun.
**LSP 2, LSP 3, LSP 4, LSP 5, LSP 6.**

**446**. Abu Dhabi. **KAWKAB** class. 1968-69. Patrol Boats. 25 tons. 58 x 16 x 4.5. (17.6 x 4.8 x 1.3). 2 screws; diesel. 16 knots. 2—20-m.m. guns.
**KAWKAB, BANI YAS, THOABAN.**

**447**. Me. **POLIMAR** Type. 1962-66. Patrol Boats. 37 tons. 60 x 15 x 4. (18.2 x 4.5 x 1.2). Diesels. 16 knots. Guns.
**POLIMAR. 1, POLIMAR. 2, POLIMAR, 3.**

**448**. Co. **GENERAL RAFAEL REYES.** *AN01.* 1956. Coast Guard Patrol Boats. 150 tons. 125 x 23 x 5. (38 x 7 x 1.5). Diesels. 18 knots. 1—40-m.m. gun.
**GENERAL VASQUES COBO.** *AN02.*

**449.** Co. **CAPITAN BINNEY.** *GC101.* 1947. Coast Guard Buoy Inspection Vessel. 23 tons. 67 x 11 x 3.5. (20 x 3.3 x 1.1). Diesels. 13 knots.

**450.** Ru. **P8** class. Torpedo Boats. 66 tons. 83 x 20 x 6. (25.3 x 6.1 x 1.8). Diesels. 45 knots. 4—25-m.m. A.A. guns (twin). 2 torpedo tubes.

Similar: **P10** class.
Both classes are later versions of P6 type (see No. 515).

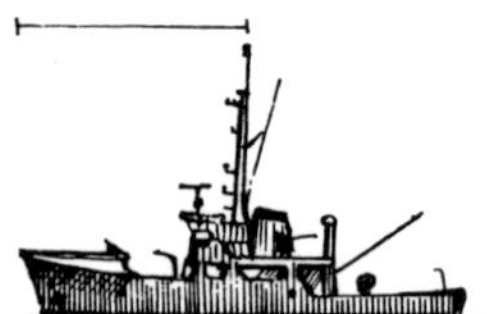

**451.** Da. **BARSO.** 1970. Coastal Minelayer. 155 tons. 97 x 20 x 9. (25.5 x 6 x 2.7). Diesels.

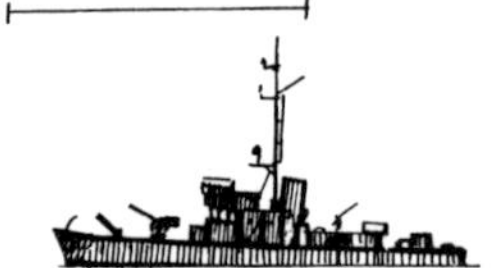

**452.** Du. **US—SC** type. 1954-55. Patrol Vessels. 150 tons. 119 x 20 x 6. (36.2 x 6.1 x 1.8). 2 screws; diesels. 15 knots. 1—40-m.m. gun. 3—20-m.m. guns. 2 depth charge throwers. "Mousetrap".
**BALDER.** *P802,* **BULGIA.** *P803,* **FREYR.** *P804,* **HADDA.** *P805,* **HEFRING.** *P806.*

**453.** Fi. **KOSKELO** class. 1956. Patrol Boats. 75 tons. 95 x 16 x 5. (28.9 x 4.8 x 1.5). 2 screws; diesel. 16 knots. 2—20-m.m. A.A. guns.
**KAAKKURI, KIILSA, KUOVI, KURKI, TAVI, TELKKA.** For the other ships in this class see drawing No. 536.

**454.** Me. **AZUETA** class. 1959-60. Patrol Boats. 80 tons. 85 x 16 x 7. (25.9 x 4.8 x 2.1). Motor. 12 knots. 2 A.A. guns.
**AZUETA.** *G9,* **VILLAPANDO.** *G6.*

**455.** RC. Ex-**KWANG KUO.** 1942. Patrol Craft. 135 tons. 96 x 19 x 9. (29.2 x 5.7 x 2.7). Diesel. 11 knots. Ex-Japanese.
Ex-**HSIEN FENG.** Names given are the old Nationalist ones.

**456.** Da. **ASKO** class. 1941. Coast Guard Cutters. 74 tons. 79 x 21 x 5. (24 x 6.4 x 1.5). Diesel. 11 knots. 1—20-m.m. gun. Ex-Inshore Minesweepers.
**ASKO.** *MHV81,* **ENO.** *MHV82,* **FAENO.** *MHV69,* **MANO.** *MHV83.*

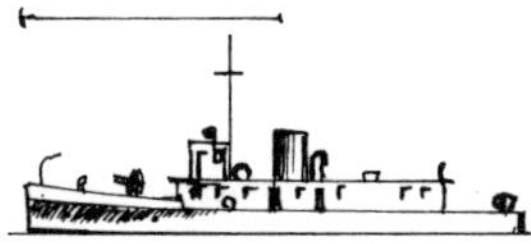

**456a**. Iq. Patrol Boats. 1937. 67 tons. 100 x 17 x 3. (30.4 x 5.1 x .9). 2 screws; diesels. 12 knots. 1—3.7-inch gun. 2—3-inch mortars. **No. 1, No. 2, No. 3, No. 4.**

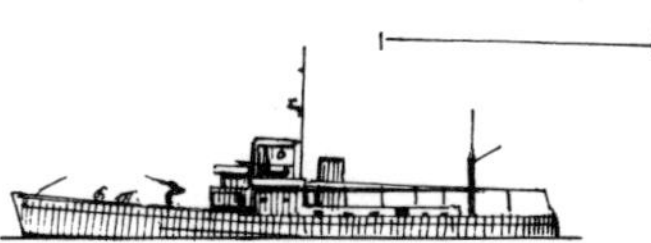

**457**. Cu. **LEONCIO PRADO.** *GC101.* 1946. Coast Guard Cutter. 80 tons. 110 x 18 x 6. (33.5 x 5.5 x 1.8). Diesels. 15 knots. 1—20-m.m. A.A. gun.

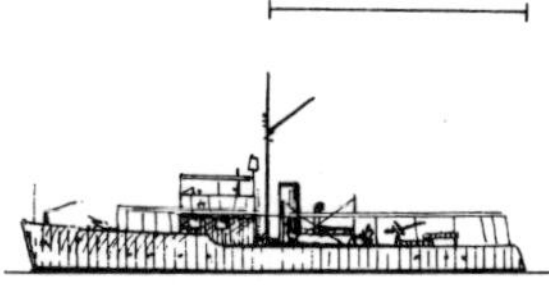

**458**. Cu. **DONATIVO.** *GC102.* 1932. Coast Guard Cutter. 130 tons. 101 x 18 x 7. (30.7 x 5.5 x 2.1). Diesels. 12 knots.

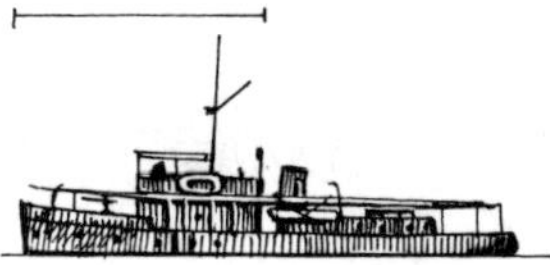

**458a**. Cu. **MATANZAS.** *GC103.* 1912. Coast Guard Cutter. 80 tons. 100 x 18 x 6. (30.4 x 5.4 x 1.8). Diesels. 12 knots. 1 small gun.

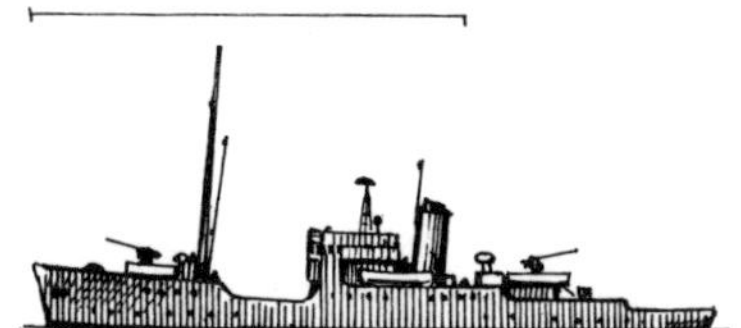

**459**. Da. **LINDORMEN.** *N39.* 1940. Coastal Minelayer. 600 tons. 176 x 29 x 8. (53.6 x 8.8 x 2.4). 2 screws; reciprocating. 12 knots. 2—40-m.m. A.A. guns.

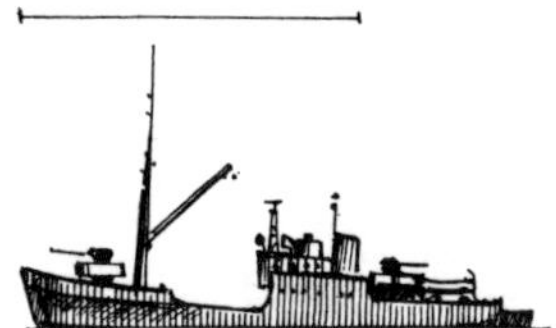

**460**. Da. **LANGELAND.** *N42.* 1951. Coastal Minelayer. 300 tons. 134 x 24 x 7. (40.8 x 7.3 x 2.1). 2 screws; diesel. 11 knots. 2—40-m.m. guns.

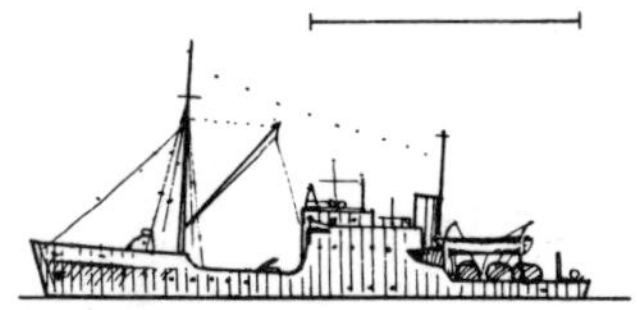

**461**. Da. **LOUGEN** class. 1946. Coastal Minelayer. 240 tons. 106 x 21 x 7. (32.3 x 6.4 x 2.1). 2 screws; diesels. 10 knots. 2—20-m.m. A.A. guns.
**LAALAND.** *N40,* **LOUGEN.** *N41.*

**462**. Da. **MAAGEN** class. 1960. Patrol Craft. 190 tons. 89 x 22 x 10. (27.1 x 6.5 x 2.8). Diesels. 11 knots. 1—40-m.m. A.A. gun.
**MAAGEN.** *Y384,* **MALLEMUKKEN.** *Y385.*

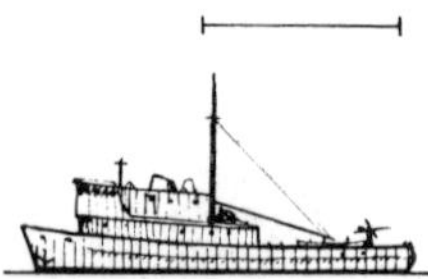

**463.** Ch. **FUENTEALBA.** *PC75.* 1966. Patrol Vessel. 200 tons. 80 x 21 x 9. (24.3 x 6.4 x 2.7). Diesels. 9 knots. 1—20-m.m. A.A. gun.
**ODGER.** *PC76.*

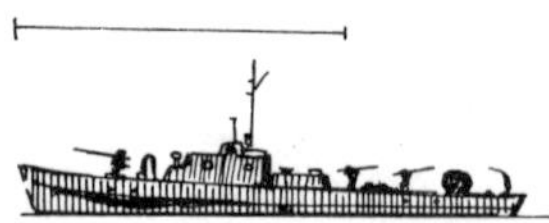

**464.** la. **R** class. 1945-57. Coastal Minesweepers. 140 tons. 129 x 19 x 5. (39.3 x 5.7 x 1.5). Diesels. 24 knots. 1—40-m.m. A.A. gun. 2—20-m.m. A.A. guns.
**PALAU RASS, PALAU RANGSANG, PALAU RAU, PALAU REMPANG, PALAU RENGAT, PALAU RINDJA, PALAU ROMA, PALAU ROTI, PALAU RUPAT, PALAU RUSA.**

**465.** Fi. **KARJALA.** 1968. Corvette. 650 tons. 243 x 26 x 8. (74 x 7.9 x 2.4). 3 screws; combined diesel and gas turbine. 35 knots. 1—4.7-inch D.P. gun. 2—40-m.m. A.A. guns. 2—30-m.m. A.A. guns (twin). Depth charge throwers.
**TURUNMAA.**

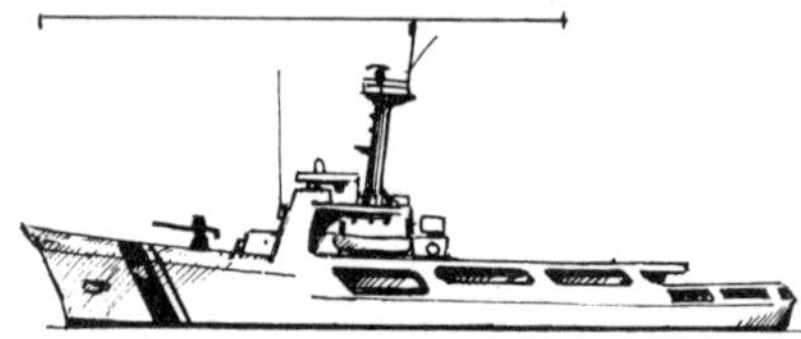

**465a.** Am. **RELIANCE** class. 1963-68. Coast Guard Cutters. 950 tons. 211 x 34 x 11. (64 x 10.3 x 3.3). 2 screws; combined diesel and gas turbine. 18 knots. 1—3-inch gun. Flight deck for helicopter.
**ACTIVE.** *618,* **ALERT.** *630,* **CONFIDENCE.** *619,* **COURAGEOUS.** *622,* **DAUNTLESS.** *624,* **DECISIVE.** *629,* **DEPENDABLE.** *626,* **DILI-GENCE.** *616,* **DURABLE.** *628,* **RELIANCE.** *615,* **RESOLUTE.** *620,* **STEADFAST.** *623,* **VALIANT.** *621,* **VENTUROUS.** *625,* **VIGI-LANT.** *617,* **VIGOROUS.** *627.*

★ **466.** Ru. **POTI** class. 1961 onwards. Coastal Escorts. 650 tons. 200 x 28 x 10. (60.9 x 8.5 x 3). Gas turbines. 28 knots. 2—57-m.m. A.A. guns (twin). 2 anti-submarine rocket launchers (12 barrelled). 4 anti-submarine torpedo tubes. Approximately 70 ships in the Russian Navy. A distinguishing feature is the raised hull aft.

★ **467.** Ru. **MIRKA** class. 1964 c. Escorts. 1,100 tons. 262 x 30 x 9. (79.8 x 9.1 x 2.7). Gas turbines. 28 knots. 2 or 4—3-inch A.A. guns. 5 or 10 anti-submarine torpedo tubes (quintuple). 2 or 4 rocket launchers (12 barrelled). Approximately 15 ships in this class. Hull is raised aft like No. 466 but tall mast amidships and gun houses in place of the rocket launchers distinguish this ship.

**468.** Ru. **SO I** class. Around 1957. Coastal Escorts. 250 tons. 147 x 20 x 10. (44.8 x 6.1 x 3). Diesels. 28 knots. 4—25-m.m. guns (twin). 4 anti-submarine rocket launchers (5 barrelled). Have a superficial resemblance to the Kronstadt class. The box-like structure amidships might be mistaken for a funnel. Approximately 100 in the Soviet Navy.

The armament of some of the vessels transferred to other countries (listed below) may vary from the above.
Ag. : 2 ships.    Bu. : 6 ships.    Cu. : 12 ships.
Eg. : 8 ships.
EG. : (Fitted with mine rails). **ADLER, BUSSARD, FALKE, HABICHT, KRANICH. MOWE. REIHER. WEIHE.**
and four others whose names are not known.
RC. : 2 ships.    North Vietnam : 3 ships.

Iq. : 3 ships.

**469.** Ja. **KAMOME** class. 1957. Patrol Vessels. 330 tons. 173 x 22 x 7. (52.7 x 6.5 x 2.1). 2 screws; diesels. 20 knots. 2—40-m.m. guns (twin), 1 "Hedgehog". 2 "Y" guns. 2 depth charge racks.
**KARI.** *301.* There are six other ships in this class which may have this appearance or may be like drawing No. 351 q.v.

**470.** Pi. Ex-U.S. **PGM** type. 1955. Patrol Boats. 95 tons. 110 x 17 x 6.5. (33.5 x 5.1 x 1.8). 2 screws; diesel. 18 knots. 1—60-m.m. mortar. 2—40-m.m. A.A. guns.
**CAMARINES SUR.** *48,* **LA UNION.** *50,* **ANTIQUE.** *51,* **MASBATE.** *52,* **SULU.** *49,* **MISAMIS OCCIDENTAL.** *59.*

**471.** Gr. **ANTIPLOIARKHOS LASKOS.** *P53,* 1943-44. Patrol Vessels. 335 tons. 175 x 23 x 11. (53.3 x 7 x 3.3) 2 screws; diesel. 19 knots. 1—3-inch gun. 6—20-m.m. A.A. guns. 1 "Hedgehog". Side launching torpedo racks. Depth charges. Ex-U.S.
**ANTIPLOIARKHOS PEZOPOULOS.** *P70,* **PLOIARKHOS MELETOPOULUS.** *P57,* **PLOTARKHIS ARSLANOGLOU.** *P14,* **PLOTARKHIS CHANTZIKONSTANDIS.** *P96.*
Similar. Cs. : **CHU KIANG.** *117.*

**472.** Da. **FALKEN** class. 1962-63. Torpedo Boats. 119 tons. 118 x 18 x 6. (35.9 x 5.3 x 1.8). 3 screws; diesel. 40 knots. 1—40-m.m. A.A. gun. 1—20-m.m. A.A. gun. 4 torpedo tubes.
**FALKEN.** *P506,* **GLENTEN.** *P507,* **GRIBBEN,** *P508,* **HOGEN.** *P509.*

**473.** Da. **FLYVEFISKEN** class. 1954-55. Torpedo Boats. 110 tons. 120 x 18 x 6. (36.5 x 5.4 x 1.8). 3 screws; diesel. 40 knots. 1—40-m.m. A.A. gun. 1—20-m.m. A.A. gun. 2 torpedo tubes.
**FLYVEFISKEN.** *P500,* **HAJEN.** *P501,* **HAVKATTEN.** *P502,* **LAXEN.** *P503,* **MAKRELEN.** *P504,* **SVAERDFISKEN.** *P505.*

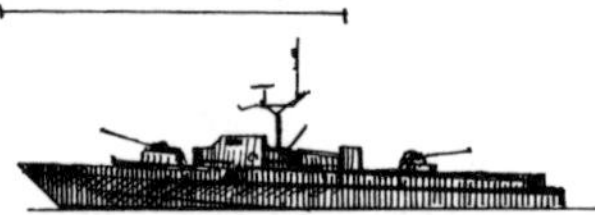

**474.** Ge. **JAGUAR** class. 1957-64. Torpedo Boats. 160 tons. 138 x 22 x 5. (42 x 6.7 x 1.5). 4 screws; diesels. 42 knots. 2—40-m.m. A.A. guns. 4 torpedo tubes or 2 tubes and mines. Ships vary slightly in appearance and tubes concealed by side plating.
**ALBATROS.** *P6069,* **ALK.** *P6084,* **BUSSARD.** *P6074,* **DACHS.** *P6094,* **DOMMEL.** *P6091,* **ELSTER.** *P6088,* **FALKE.** *P6072,* **FRETTCHEN.** *P6100,* **FUCHS.** *P6066,* **GEIER.** *P6073,* **GEPARD.** *P6098,* **GREIF.** *P6071,* **HABICHT.** *P6075,* **HAHER.** *P6087,* **HERMELIN.** *P6095,* **HYANE.** *P6099,* **ILTIS.** *P6058,* **JAGUAR.** *P6059,* **KONDOR.** *P6070,* **KORMORAN.** *P6077,* **KRANICH.** *P6083,* **LEOPARD.** *P6060,* **LOWE.** *P6065,* **LUCHS.** *P6061,* **MARDER.** *P6067,* **NERZ.** *P6069,* **OZELOT.** *P6101,* **PANTHER.** *P6064,* **PELIKAN.** *P6086,* **PINGUIN.** *P6090,* **PUMA.** *P6097,* **REIHER.** *P6089,* **SEEADLER.** *P6068,* **SPERBER.** *P6076,* **STORCH.** *P6085,* **TIGER.** *P6063,* **WEIHE.** *P6082,* **WIESEL.** *P6093,* **WOLF.** *P6062,* **ZOBEL.** *P6092.*

Tu.: **KARTAL** class (slightly longer superstructure).
**ATMACA.** *P335,* **DENIZKUSU.** *P336,* **KARTAL.** *P333,* **KASIRGA.** *P338,* **MELTEM.** *P337,* **SAHIN.** *P334.*

Similar. Ia.: **ADJAK.** *601,* **ANOA.** *602,* **BIRUANG.** *603,* **HARIMAU.** *604,* **MADJAN KUMBANG.** *605,* **SERIGALA.** *607,* **SINGA.** *608.*

**475.** Sw. **ALDEBARAN** class. 1954-60. Convertible Torpedo Boats/Gunboats. 155 tons. 158 x 18. (48.1 x 5.4). 3 screws; diesels. 37 knots. 2—40-m.m. A.A. guns. 6 torpedo tubes.
**ALDEBARAN.** *T107,* **ALTAIR.** *T108,* **ANTARES.** *T109,* **ARCTURUS.** *T110,* **ARGO.** *T111,* **ASTREA.** *T112,* **PLEJAD.** *T102,* **POLARIS.** *T103,* **POLLUX.** *T104,* **REGULUS.** *T105,* **RIGEL.** *T106.*

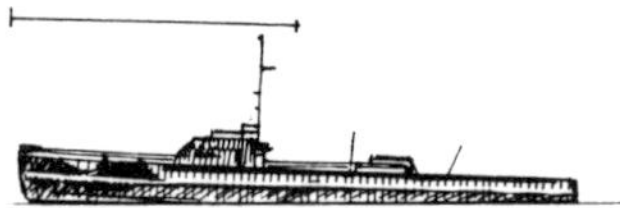

**476.** Sp. **LT 30.** 1956. Torpedo Boats. 100 tons. 114 x 17 x 5. (34.7 x 5.1 x 1.5). 3 screws; diesels. 41 knots. 1—20-m.m. A.A. gun. 2 torpedo tubes. German design.
**LT** *31,* **LT** *32.*

**477.** Fi. **R** class. 1957. Inshore Minesweepers. 110 tons. 109 x 18 x 6. (33.2 x 5.4 x 1.8). Diesels. 15 knots. 1—40-m.m. gun. 1—20-m.m. gun.
**RIHTNIEMI.** *1,* **RYMATTYLA.** *2.*

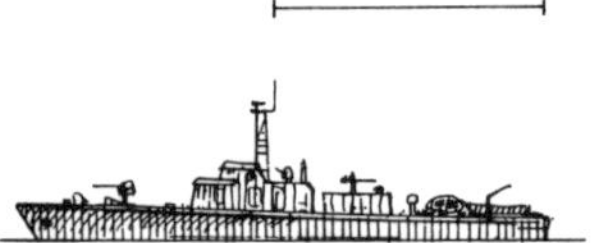

**478.** Fi. **R** class. All details as No. 477. These ships differ principally from 477 by the bridge fronts.
**RAISIO.** *4,* **ROYTTA.** *5,* **RUISSALO.** *3.*

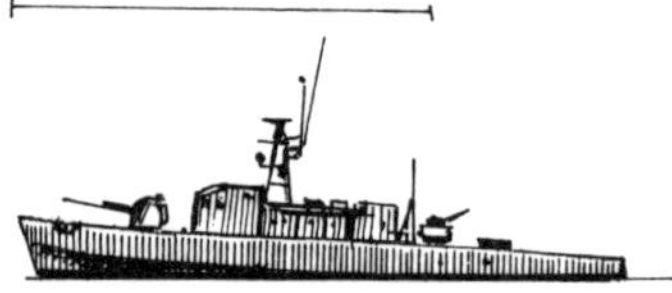

**479.** It. **FULMINE.** *499.* 1956. Gunboat. 300 tons. 163 x 22 x 7. (49.7 x 6.7 x 2.1). 2 screws; diesels. 30 knots. 1—3-inch gun. 2—40-m.m. A.A. guns.

**480.** Sp. Ex-U.S. **Sc** Type. **CANDIDO PEREZ.**
1942. Patrol Vessel. 108 tons. 111 x 19 x 7.
(33.8 x 5.7 x 2.1). 2 screws; diesels. 15 knots.
4 A.A. guns. 2 depth charge throwers.
Se. **SENEGAL.** All details as above.

**480B.** Ys. **KRALJAVICA** class. 1957-59.
Patrol Boats. 190 tons. 135 x 21 x 7. (40.8 x
6.4 x 2.1). 2 screws; diesels. 20 knots. 1—3-inch
gun. 3 A.A. guns. Depth charges. Distinguished
from Nos. 480 etc. by sloping mast and raised
plating foreward.
**509, 510, 511, 512, 513, 514, 515, 516.**
Practically identical but slightly earlier vessels:
**501, 502, 503, 504, 505, 506, 507, 508.**

Ia. **BUBARA, DORANG, JAJANG, KRAPU,
LEMADANG, TODAK.**

**482.** EG. **SCHWALBE II** class. 1955-57. Inshore
Minesweepers and various harbour duties. 100
tons. 105 x 18 x 4. (32 x 5.4 x 1.2). 2 screws;
diesels. 14 knots. 2 small guns. (Some may
have 4 A.A. guns.)
About 24 units among which are: **EISLEBEN,
ILMENAU, SONNEBERG, HAGENOW.**

**484.** Is. **YARDEN.** 1957 Patrol Boat. 100 tons.
100 x 20 x 6. (30.4 x 6.1 x 1.8). 2 screws;
diesels. 22 knots. 2 A.A. guns.
**YARKON.** *44.*

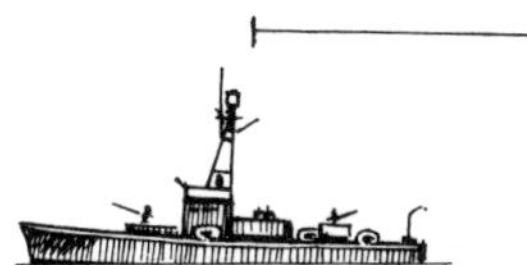

**480A.** Cu. Ex-U.S. **SC** type. Coast Guard
Cutters. Details as for No. 480 but only 2 A.A.
guns and no depth charge throwers.
**HABANA.** *GC107,* **LAS VILLAS.** *GC106,*
**ORIENTE.** *GC104,* **PINAR DEL RIO.** *GC108.*
Distinguished from No. 480 by having only one
gun aft.

Ha. Coast Guard Vessel. **16 AOUT.** *GC2.*
Ia. Patrol Craft. **BHAYAMAKARA I, BHAYA-
MAKARA II, BHAYAMAKARA III.**
Iv. Patrol Craft. **PATIENCE.**
Cs. Submarine Chasers, **SC502, SC503** and
about 7 other units whose numbers are unknown.

**481.** Su. 1961-62. Patrol Boats. 100 tons. 115 x
17 x 5. (35 x 5.1 x 1.5). 2 screws; diesels.
20 knots. 3 A.A. guns.
**GIHAD, HORRIYA, ISTIGLAL, SHAAB.** Built
in Yugoslavia and very similar to No. 480B but
larger bridges.

**483.** Ex-French **VC** Type. 1958. Patrol Boats.
75 tons. 104 x 16 x 5.5. (31.7 x 4.8 x 1.7).
2 screws; diesels. 28 knots. 2 A.A. guns.
Cameroons. **VIGILANTE.**
Iv. **PERSEVERANCE.**
Mt. **IM RAQ'NI.**
Se. **CASAMANCE, SINE-SALOUM.**

**485.** Pk. **TOWN** class. 1965. Patrol Craft.
115 tons. 107 x 20 x 5. (32.6 x 6.1 x 1.5).
Diesels. 24 knots. 2 A.A. guns.
**COMILLA.** *P142,* **JESSORE.** *P141,* **RAJSHA-
HI.** *P140,* **SYLHET.** *P143.*

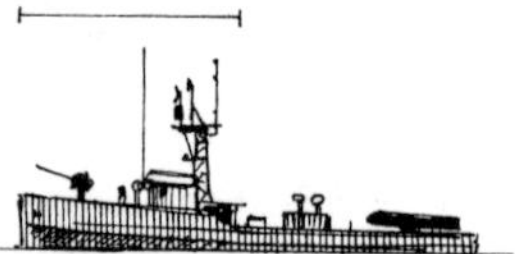

**486.** It. **MS472.** 1942-43. Refitted 1960. Convertible TB/MGB. 70 tons. 92 x 15 x 5. (28 x 4.5 x 1.5). 3 screws; motor vessel. 27 knots. 1 or 2—40-m.m. guns. 2 torpedo tubes.
**MS473, MS474, MS481**.

**487.** No. **STORM** class. 1963-66. Gunboats. 100 tons. 118 x 20 x 5. (35.9 x 6.1 x 1.5). Diesels. 30 knots. 1—3-inch gun. 1 A.A. rocket thrower.
**ARG.** *P968,* **BLINK.** *P961,* **BRANN.** *P970,* **BRASK.** *P977,* **BROTT.** *P974,* **DJERV.** *P966,* **GLIMT.** *P962,* **GNIST.** *P979,* **HVASS.** *P972,* **KJEKK.** *P965,* **LYN.** *P980,* **ODD.** *P975,* **PIL.** *P976,* **ROKK.** *P978,* **SKJOLD.** *P963,* **SKUDD.** *P967,* **STEIL.** *P969,* **STORM.** *P960,* **TRAUST.** *P973,* **TROSS.** *P971,* **TRYGG.** *P964.*

**489.** Fr. **LA COMBATTANTE.** *P730.* 1964. Patrol Vessel. 180 tons. 148 x 24 x 6.5. (45.1 x 7.3 x 1.9). 2 screws; diesels. 23 knots. 1—40-m.m. A.A. gun. 1 "SS" II missile launcher.

★ **491.** Ru. **SHERSHEN** class. Torpedo Boats. 150 tons. 130 x 23 x 6.5. (39.6 x 9.7 x 2). Diesels. 40 knots. 4—25-m.m. A.A. guns (twin). 4 torpedo tubes.
About 20 vessels in the class.
Eg. 3 vessels.

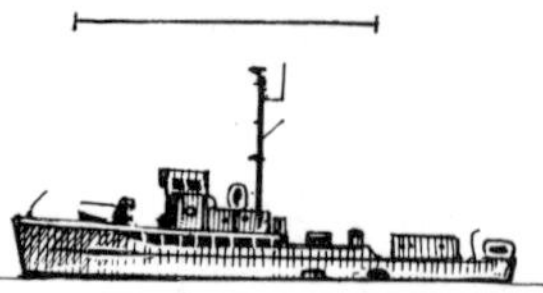

**486A.** Pi. **LAGUNA.** *12,* 1943-44. Patrol Vessels. 230 tons. 136 x 24 x 8.5. (41.4 x 7.3 x 2.6). 2 screws; diesels. 14 knots. 1—3-inch gun. 4 A.A. guns. Ex-U.S. PCS type.
**TARLAC.** *11.*

Similar. Am. Naval Reserve Training craft; no guns.
**HOLLIDAYSBURG.** *1385.*

**488.** Ja. **PT7.** 1957. Torpedo Boats. 100 tons. 112 x 25 x 4 (34.1 x 7.6 x 1.2). 3 screws; diesels. 33 knots. 2 A.A. guns. 4 torpedo tubes. *PT8.*

**490.** It. **FOLGORE.** *490.* 1955. Torpedo Boat. 160 tons. 130 x 20 x 5. (39.6 x 6.1 x 1.5). 4 screws; diesel. 38 knots. 2—40-m.m. A.A. guns. 2 torpedo tubes.

★ **492.** Ru. **STENKA** class. 1967 onwards. Coastal Escorts. 170 tons. 131 x 23 x 6.5. (39.6 x 7 x 2). Diesels. 40 knots. 4—30-m.m. A.A. guns. 4 anti-submarine torpedo tubes. Depth charge racks. At least 6 vessels in service.

**493.** Br. **TENACITY.** 1969. Missile Boat. 165 tons. 145 x 27 x 8. (44.1 x 8.2 x 2.4). 3 screws; diesels and gas turbines. 39 knots. 2—35-m.m. D.P. guns (twin). 2 "Seakiller" surface-to-surface launchers (twin). Prototype of new class.

**494.** Ru. **OSA** class. 1959 and onwards. Missile Boats. 160 tons. 132 x 23 x 6.5. (40 x 7 x 2). Diesels. 35 knots. 4—25-m.m. guns (twin). 4 "Styx" surface-to-surface launchers. Later versions have cylindrical launchers.
At least 75 vessels in Soviet fleet.

Ag. 1 vessel.
Eg. At least 12 units.
EG. 12 vessels among which are:
ALBERT GAST, ALBIN KOBIS, FRITZ GAST, KARL MESEBERGER, MAX REICHPIETSCH, PAUL WIECZOREK, RICHARD SORGE, RUDOLF EGELHUFER.
Ph. 12 units.
RC. At least 7 units.

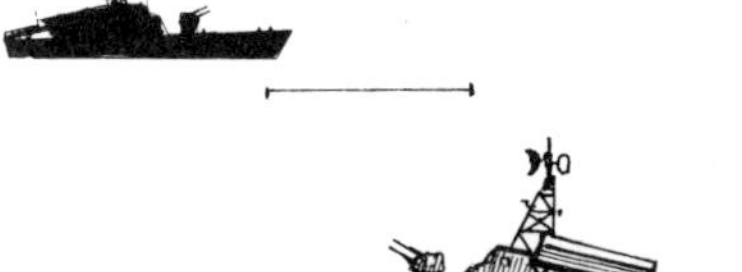

**495.** Ru. **KOMAR** class. 1960-61. Missile Boats. 75 tons. 82 x 20 x 6. (24.9 x 6.1 x 1.8). 2 screws. 40 knots. 2—25-m.m. A.A. guns (twin). 2 surface-to-surface "Styx" launchers.
At least 50 vessels in Soviet fleet.

| | |
|---|---|
| Ag. 8 units. | Ia. 12 units. |
| Cu. 18 units. | RC. 3 units. |
| Eg. 8 units. | Sy. 10 units. |

**496.** Is. **SAAR** class. 1968-69. Gunboats. 220 tons. 148 x 23 x 6. (45.1 x 7 x 1.8). Diesels. 45 knots. 3—40-m.m. A.A. guns. 4 surface-to-surface launchers.
There are 7 vessels in the class.

**497.** Sw. **SPICA** class. 1966-70. Torpedo Boats. 190 tons. 140 x 23 x 00. (42.6 x 7 x 00). 3 screws; gas turbines. 40 knots. 1—57-m.m. A.A. gun. 6 torpedo tubes. Rocket launchers. Distinguished by the weather dome on the bridge.
**CAPELLA.** *T123,* **CASTOR.** *T124,* **SIRIUS.** *T122,* **SPICA.** *T121,* **VEGA.** *T125,* **VIRGO.** *T126.*
With probably 12 more units under construction, among which are:
*T127, T128, T129, T130, T131* and *T132.*

**500.** Gr. **AIOLOS.** *P19.* 1962. Torpedo Boat. 75 tons. 95 x 24 x 6.5. (28.9 x 7.3 x 2). 2 screws; gas turbines. 50 knots. 2—40-m.m. A.A. guns. 4 torpedo tubes (side launching). Vosper type.

**501.** Gr. **ASTRAPI.** *P20.* 1962. Torpedo Boat. 95 tons. 99 x 25 x 7. (30.1 x 7.6 x 2.1). 3 screws; gas turbines. 55 knots. 2—40-m.m. A.A. guns. 4 torpedo tubes.
Vosper type similar to British "Brave" class.

**502.** Da. **SOLOVEN** class. 1964-67. Torpedo Boats. 95 tons. 99 x 26 x 7. (30.1 x 7.9 x 2.1). 3 screws; diesels and gas turbines. 54 knots. 2—40-m.m. A.A. guns. 4 torpedo tubes.
**SOLOVEN.** *P510,* **SOBJORNEN.** *P512,* **SO-HUNDEN.** *P514,* **SORIDDEREN.** *P511,* **SOU-LVEN.** *P515.*
Some may be employed as Gunboats; see **SOHESTEN**—Silhouette No. 570.

**503.** Brunei. **PAHLAWAN.** 1967. Patrol Boat. 95 tons. 99 x 25 x 7. (30.1 x 7.6 x 2.1). 3 screws; diesels and gas turbines. 57 knots. 1—40-m.m. gun and 2—20-m.m. guns. Vosper type.

My. **PERKASA** class. Same as above with addition of 4 torpedo tubes.
**GEMPITA.** *P152,* **HANDALAN.** *P151,* **PEN-DEKAR.** *P153,* **PERKASA.** *P150.*

Ly. Same dimensions etc. but armament comprises: Guns and 2 surface-to-surface "S S 12" launchers (quadruple).
**SEBHA, SIRTE, SUSA.**

**504.** Br. **SCIMITAR.** *P271.* 1970. Training Boat. 100 tons. 100 x 27 x 0. (30.4 x 8.2 x 0). Diesel and gas turbine. 40 knots. Could be modified to produce a speed of 60 knots. No armament.
**CUTLASS, SABRE.**

**505.** Sw. **T42** type. 1959-60 Torpedo Boats. 40 tons. 76 x 19 x 4.5. (1.9 x 5.7 x 1.4). Diesels. 45 knots. 1—40-m.m. A.A. gun. 2 torpedo tubes. Rocket launcher.
15 units numbered from **T42 to T56** inclusive.

**506.** Sw. **T32** type. 1953-62. Torpedo Boats. 40 tons. 76 x 18 x 4. (23.1 x 5.4 x 1.4). Diesels. 40 knots. 1—40-m.m. A.A. gun. 2 torpedo tubes. Rocket launchers.
10 units numbered from **T32 to T41** inclusive.

**507.** Tu. **NASTY** Type. 1959-60. Torpedo Boats. 70 tons. 80 x 25 x 7. (2 x 7.6 x 2.1). Diesels. 43 knots. 1—40-m.m. A.A. gun. 2 torpedo tubes.
**DOGAN, MARTI.**

**508.** Br. **DARK** class. 1957. Convertible TB/GB. 50 tons. 72 x 20 x 6. (21.9 x 6.1 x 1.8) 2 screws; diesels. 36 knots.
As MGB; 1—4.5-inch gun and 1 or 2 40-m.m. A.A. guns.
As MTB; 1—40-m.m. A.A. gun and 4 torpedo tubes.
**DARK GLADIATOR.** *P1114.*

**509.** Bm. **DARK** class. 1956-57. Convertible TB/GB. Dimensions etc. as No. 508. 2 screws; diesels. 42 knots.
As MGB: 1—4.5-inch gun. 1—40-m.m. A.A. gun.
As MTB: 2—20-m.m. A.A. guns and 4 torpedo tubes.
5 units numbered **T201 to T205** inclusive.

**510**. Ja. **PT 9**. 1957. Torpedo Boat. 55 tons. 71 x 20 x 6. (21.6 x 6.1 x 1.8). 2 screws; diesels. 40 knots. 2 torpedo tubes. Mounting for 1—40-m.m. gun.
Basically of British "Dark" class.

**511**. Fi. **VASAMA** class ("Dark" class). 1955-57. Convertible TB/GB. 70 tons. 72 x 20 x 6. (21.9 x 6.1 x 1.8). 2 screws; diesels. 42 knots. 2—40-m.m. A.A. guns.
As Torpedo Boat see No. 512.
**VASAMA. 1, VASAMA. 2.**

**512**. Fi. **VASAMA** class as torpedo boat. For details see No. 511.

**513**. No. **TJELD** class ("Nasty" type). 1960-66. Torpedo Boats. 70 tons. 80 x 25 x 7. (24.3 x 7.6 x 2.1). 2 screws; diesels. 45 knots. 1—40-m.m. A.A. gun. 1—20-m.m. A.A. gun. 4 torpedo tubes.
**DELFIN.** *P386,* **ERLE.** *P390,* **FALK.** *P350,* **GEIR.** *P389,* **GRIBB.** *P388,* **HAI.** *P381,* **HAUK.** *P349,* **HVAL.** *P383,* **JO.** *P346,* **KNURR.** *P385,* **LAKS.** *P384,* **LOM.** *P347,* **LYR.** *P387,* **RAVN.** *P357,* **SEL.** *P382,* **SKARV.** *P344,* **SKREI.** *P380,* **STEGG.** *P348,* **TEIST.** *P345,* **TJELD.** *P343.*

Gr. Larger gun foreward.
**ANDROMEDA.** *P21,* **KASTOR.** *P23,* **KYKONOS.** *P24,* **PIGASSOS.** *P25,* **TOXOTIS.** *P26.*

Am. Similar to above ships. No torpedo tubes. 4 single mountings.
**PTF3, PTF5, PTF6, PTF7, PTF10, PTF11, PTF12, PTF13.** Possibly also
**PTF17, PTF18, PTF19, PTF20, PTF21, PTF22, PTF23, PTF24, PTF25, PTF26.**

**514**. Ar. Ex-U.S. **HIGGINS** Type. 1946. Torpedo Boats. 45 tons. 79 x 20 x 4.5. (24 x 6.1 x 1.4). Motor vessels. 40 knots. 2—40-m.m. A.A. guns. 4 torpedo cradles. 2 rocket launchers.
**P82, P84.**

**515**. Ru. **P6** class. 1951-60. Torpedo Boats. 66 tons. 85 x 20 x 6. (26 x 6.1 x 1.8). 2 screws; diesels. 42-45 knots. 4—25-m.m. A.A. guns (twin-vertical). 2 torpedo tubes.
Later developments were the "P8" and "P10" classes. See No. 450. 200 or more units in the Soviet fleet.

Cu. 12 units.
Eg. 36 units.
EG. Known as "Forelle" class and about 30 units among which are:
**ANTON SAEFKOW, BERNHARD BAST-** **LEIN, HANS COPPI, HANS BEIMLER, JOSEF ROMER, FRITH RIEDEL, ARVID, HARNACK.**
RC. About 80 units. (Built in China.)
Ph. 20 units. Possibly numbered 401-420.
NV. 3 units. (Built in China.)

Also in non-Communist countries.
Iq. 12 units.
Ia. 24 units including **ANGIN KUMBANG.**
Guinea. About 8 units.
So. 12 units. (Probably more.)
Sy. Probably 6 or 7.

**516.** Ru. **MO-VI** type. A gunboat version of the P6 type shown in No. 515. All details are the same but they have no torpedo tubes and carry depth charges or mines. Several in the Soviet Navy plus the following

Ng.: 3 ships. **EKPEN, EKUN, ELOLE.**
The Republic of China also have their own gunboat version of the P6 known as the **SWA-TOW** class. She has about 45 in her own Navy and has transferred about 20 to North Vietnam.

**517.** Ja. **PT1** type. 1953. Torpedo Boats. 75 tons. 82 x 20 x 6. (24.9 x 6.1 x 1.8). 2 screws; diesels. 31 knots. 1—40-m.m. A.A. gun. 2 torpedo launchers.
**PT1, PT2, PT3, PT4, PT5, PT6.**

**518.** Ru. **P4** type. 1951-58. Torpedo Boats. 25 tons. 82 x 17 x 6. (24.9 x 5.1 x 1.8). Diesels. 42 knots. 2—25-m.m. A.A. guns. 2 torpedo tubes. About 50 in the Soviet Navy but this figure probably includes the type represented by drawing No. 519. Some of the 70 vessels of the P4 type in the Chinese Navy may be of this type 1.

**519.** Ru. **P4** type. 1951-58. Type 2 of the P4 class torpedo boats as represented by No. 518. All details are as under No. 518, but has an extra turret aft. Probably a few of this type in the Soviet Navy.

| | |
|---|---|
| Al. : 12 ships. | Bu. : 8 ships. |
| Cu. : 12 ships. | RC. : 70 ships (some are type 1) |
| RK. : 39 ships. | Rm. : 8 ships. |
| NV. : 12 ships. | |

**520.** Ys. Type **108.** 1951-52. Torpedo Boats. 55 tons. 78 x 21 x 8. (23.7 x 6.4 x 2.4). 3 screws; motors. 36 knots. 1—40-m.m. A.A. gun. 2 torpedo tubes. Some of the Yugoslavian ships have no mast, see silhouette No. 129.
Ys. : Total of 90 vessels most numbers in 100 and 200 series.

Cambodia: **VR1, VR11.**
Eg. : 6 vessels.
Et. : **BARRACUDA.** *P22,* **SHARK.** *P21.*

**521.** No. **RAPP** class. 1952-56. Torpedo Boats. 73 tons. 87 x 23 x 5. (26.5 x 7 x 1.5). 2 screws; motors. 32 knots. 1—40-m.m. gun. 1—20-m.m. A.A. gun. 4 torpedo tubes.
**KJAPP.** *P344,* **KVIKK.** *P353,* **RAPP.** *P351,* **RASK.** *P352,* **SNAR.** *P355,* **SNOGG.** *P356.*

**522.** EG. **ILTIS** class. Around 1964. Torpedo Boats. 30 tons. 60 x 17 x 4. (18.2 x 5 x 1.2). Motor. 48 knots. 2 torpedo tubes (over the stern). Approximately 33 vessels in the East German Navy.

**523.** is. **OPHIR.** *150.* 1956-57. Torpedo Boats. 40 tons. 70 x 17 x 5. (21.3 x 5.1 x 1.5). Petrol engines. 40 knots. 5 A.A. guns. 2 torpedoes.
**SHVA.** *151,* **TARSHISH.** *152.*

**524.** Fi. **NUOLI** class. 1961-63. Patrol Boats.
40 tons. 72 x 22 x 5. (21.9 x 6.7 x 1.5). Diesels.
40 knots. 1—40-m.m. gun. 1—20-m.m. A.A. gun.
**NUOLI 1—NUOLI 13** (inclusive).

**525.** Po. **ALVOR** class. 1967-68. Patrol Boats.
36 tons. 68 x 18 x 5. (20.7 x 5.4 x 1.5). Diesels.
12 knots. 1—20-m.m. A.A. gun.
**ALBUFEIRA.** *P1157,* **ALJEZUR.** *P1158,* **AL-
VOR.** *P1156.*

Similar: (slightly smaller). **BELLATRIX** class.
**ALDEBARAN, ALTAIR.** *P377,* **ARCTURUS,
BELLATRIX.** *P363,* **CANOPUS.** *P364,* **DE-
NEB.** *P365,* **ESPIGA.** *P366,* **FOMALHAUT.**
*P367,* **POLLUX.** *P368,* **PROCION, RIGEL.**
*P378,* **SIRIUS, VEGA.**

**526.** Po. **JUPITER** class. 1964-65. Patrols.
Boats. 32 tons. 69 x 17 x 4. (21 x 5 x 1.2). Diesels.
20 knots. 1 A.A. gun.
**JUPITER.** *P1132,* **MARTE.** *P1134,* **MERCU-
RIO.** *P1135,* **SATURNO.** *P1136,* **URANO.**
*P1137,* **VENUS.** *P1133.*

**527.** Ch. **FRESIA.** *81.* 1965-66. Torpedo Boats.
134 tons. 118 x 18 x 7. (35.9 x 5.4 x 2.1).
2 screws; diesels. 32 knots. 2—40-m.m. A.A.
guns. 4 torpedo tubes. German "Lurssen" type.
**GUACOLDA.** *80,* **QUIDORA.** *82,* **TEGUALDA.**
*83.*

**528.** Ja. **PT10.** 1962. Torpedo Boat. 90 tons.
105 x 28 x 4. (32 x 8.5 x 1.2). Diesels. 40 knots.
2—40-m.m. A.A. guns. 4 torpedo tubes.

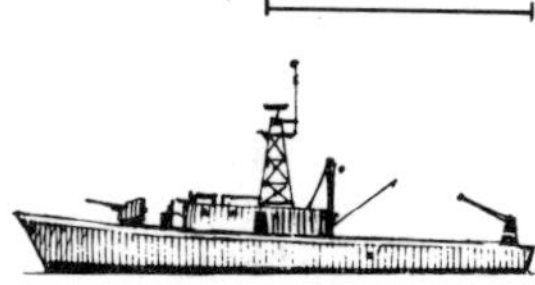

**529.** Is. **AYAH.** *200.* 1951-57. Torpedo Boats.
62 tons. 85 x 21 x 5. (25.9 x 6.4 x 1.5). 2 screws;
diesels. 42 knots. 1—40-m.m. gun. 4—20-m.m.
A.A. guns. 2 torpedoes.
**BAZ.** *201,* **DAYA.** *202,* **PERESS.** *203,* **TAH-
MASS.** *204,* **YASOOR.** *205.*

**530.** Ir. **AZAR** class. 1955-56. Coast Guard
Cutters. 65 tons. 90 x 16 x 9. (27.4 x 4.8 x 2.7).
Diesels. 22 knots.
**AZAR, CHAHAB, DARAKHSH, NAVAK,
PEYKAN, TONDBAD, TONDAR, TOUFAN,
TOUSAN.**

**531.** Br. **AVELEY.** 1953. Minehunter. 120 tons.
107 x 22 x 6. (32.6 x 6.7 x 1.8). 2 screws;
diesels. 13 knots. 1 A.A. gun. "Ley" class.

**532.** In. **SHARADA** class. 1959. Seaward Defence Boats. 86 tons. 103 x 00 x 00. (31 x 00 x 00). Diesels. 00 knots. Built in Yugoslavia and similar to the **KRALJAVICA** class; see No. 480a. **SHARADA, SUKANYA.**

**533.** In. **SAVITRI** class. 1957. Seaward Defence Boats. 63 tons. 90 x 20 x 5. (27.4 x 6.1 x 1.5). 2 screws; diesels. 21 knots. **SAVITRI, SHARYU, SUBHADRA, SUVARNA.**

**534.** Sw. **200** series. 1957 onwards. Landing Craft. 31 tons. 69 x 14 x 4. (21 x 4.2 x 1.2). 18 knots. 43 craft in this series, numbering **201-243** inclusive.

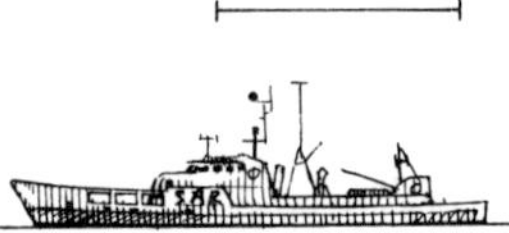

**535.** Ge. **KW** type. 1951-52. Rescue Launches. 45 tons. 94 x 16 x 4. (28.6 x 4.8 x 1.2). 2 screws; diesels. 25 knots. **FL5, FL6, FL7, FL8.**

**536.** Fi. **KOSKELO** class. 1956. Patrol Boats. 75 tons. 95 x 16 x 5. (28.9 x 4.8 x 1.5). 2 screws; diesels. 16 knots. **KOSKELO, KUIKKA.** For the other six ships in this class see No. 453.

**537.** Le. **TARABLOUS.** *31.* 1959. Patrol Boat. 105 tons. 125 x 18 x 6. (38.1 x 5.4 x 1.8). 2 screws; diesels. 27 knots. 2—40-m.m. guns. Similar to French "VC" type.

**538.** Fr. **VC** type. 1959. Seaward Patrol Craft. 75 tons. 104 x 16 x 6. (31.7 x 4.8 x 1.8). 2 screws; diesels. 28 knots. 2—20-m.m. A.A. guns. **VC1.** *P751,* **VC2.** *P752,* **VC3.** *P753,* **VC10.** *P760.*

**539.** Tn. **VC** type. 1958. Patrol Craft. All details as No. 538. **AL JALA, ISTIQLAL, JOUMOURIA, REMADA.**

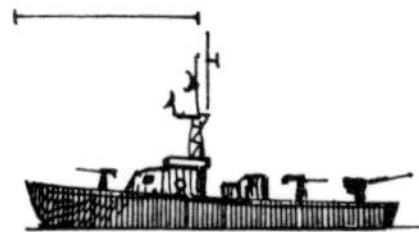

**540.** It. Ex-U.S. **HIGGINS** type. Around 1946. Refitted 1953. Torpedo Boats. 64 tons. 78 x 20 x 6. (23.7 x 6.1 x 1.8). 3 screws; motors. 34 knots. 3 or 4 small guns. 2 torpedoes. **MS441, MS443, MS453.**

**541.** EG. **PARTISAN.** 1957. Coast Guard Boat. 79 tons. 13 knots. **PIONIER.**

**542.** EG. **TUMMLER** class. 1954-56. Coast Guard Boats. 50 tons. 77 x 17 x 4.5. (23 x 5 x 1.3). Diesels. 15 knots. 4 A.A. guns (twin). Between 15 and 20 were built. Some have an uncovered bridge; see No. 543.

**543.** EG. **TUMMLER** class. Others in this class have covered bridges; see No. 542. For all particulars see No. 542.

**544.** EG. **DELPHIN** class. 1953-55. Coast Guard Vessels. 70 tons. 73 x 16 x 5. (22 x 4.9 x 1.5). 2 screws; diesels. 20 knots. 1 light gun. About 20 ships in the class. Some have a pole mast.

**545.** Cu. **R41.** 1945. Air-sea Rescue Craft. 35 tons. 71 x 19 x 5. (21.6 x 5.7 x 1.5). 3 screws; gas engines. 35 knots. 2 light guns. **R42.**

**545A.** Am. **82 Foot** class. 1960-70. Coast Guard
Patrol Boats. 64 tons. 83 x 17 x 6. (25.3 x 5.2 x
1). 2 screws; diesels. 16 knots. "A" and "B"
classes; 22 knots. "C" and "D" classes. 2 to 4
guns.
"A" class Nos. CG 82301-82317. "B" class Nos.
82318-82331. "C" class Nos. 82332-82370.
"D" class Nos. 82371-82379.
**POINT ARDEN.** *82309,* **POINT ARENA.**
*92346,* **POINT BAKER.** *82342,* **POINT BANKS.**
*82327,* **POINTBARNES.** *82371,* **POINT BAR-
ROW.** *82348,* **POINT BATAN.** *82340,* **POINT
BENNETT.** *82351,* **POINT BONITA.** *82347,*
**POINT BRIDGE.** *82338,* **POINT BROWER.**
*82372,* **POINT BROWN.** *82362,* **POINT CAM-
DEN.** *82372,* **POINT CARREW.** *82374,*
**POINT CAUTION.** *82301,* **POINT CHARLES.**
*92361,* **POINT CHICO.** *82339,* **POINT COM-
FORT.** *82317,* **POINT COUNTESS.** *82335,*
**POINT CYPRESS.** *82326,* **POINT DIVIDE.**
*82337,* **POINT DURAN.** *82375,* **POINT DUME.**
*82325,* **POINT ELLIS.** *82330,* **POINT ESTERO.**
*82344,* **POINT EVANS.** *82354,* **POINT FRAN-
CIS.** *82356,* **POINT FRANKLIN.** *82350,*
**POINT GAMMON.** *82328,* **POINT GLASS.**
*82336, .* **POINT GLOVER.** *82307,* **POINT
GRACE.** *82323,* **POINT GREY.** *82324,* **POINT
HANNON.** *82355,* **POINT HARRIS.** *82376,*
**POINT HERRON.** *82318,* **POINT HEYER.**
*82369,* **POINT HIGHLAND.** *82333,* **POINT
HOBART.** *82377,* **POINT HOPE.** *82302,*
**POINT HUDSON.** *82322,* **POINT HUDSON.**
*72322,* **POINT HURON.** *82357,* **POINT JACK-
SON.** *82378,* **POINT JEFFERSON.** *82306,*
**POINT JUDITH.** *82345,* **POINT KENNEDY.**
*82320,* **POINT KNOLL.** *82367,* **POINT LEDGE.**
*82324,* **POINT LOBOS.** *82366,* **POINT LO-
MAS.** *82321,* **POINT LOOKOUT.** *82341,*
**POINT MARTIN.** *82379,* **POINT MAST.** *92316,*
**POINT MONROE.** *82353,* **POINT MORONE.**
*82331,* **POINT NOWELL.** *82363,* **POINT
ORIENT.** *82319,* **POINT PARTRIDGE.** *82305,*
**POINT RICHMOND.** *82370,* **POINT RO-
BERTS.** *82332,* **POINT SAL.** *82352,* **POINT
SLOCUM.** *82313,* **POINT SPENCER.** *82349,*
**POINT STEELE.** *82359,* **POINT STUART.**
*82358,* **POINT SWIFT.** *82312,* **POINT THAT-
CHER.** *82314,* **POINT TURNER.** *82365,*
**POINT VERDE.** *82311,* **POINT WELCOME.**
*82329,* **POINT WELLS.** *82343,* **POINT WHITE.**
*82308,* **POINT WHITEHORN.** *82364,* **POINT
WINSLOW.** *82360,* **POINT YOUNG.** *82303.*

**546.** Co. **ESPARTANA.** 1950. Coast Guard
Vessel. 50 tons. 96 x 14 x 4. (29.3 x 4.3 x 1.2).
Diesels. 13 knots. 1—20-m.m. A.A. gun.

**547.** Sp. **V21.** Coastal Launch. 16 tons. 1 small
gun. 17 knots.

★ **548.** Cu. **BERTHA.** 1944. Lighthouse Tender.
98 tons. 104 x 19 x 11. (31.7 x 5.8 x 3.4).
Diesels. 10 knots.

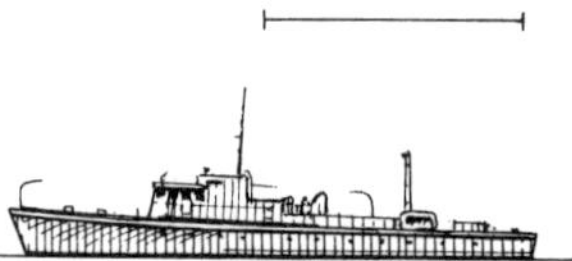

**549.** Do. **CAPITAN ALSINA.** *105.* 1944.
Rescue Launch. 100 tons. 105 x 19 x 6. (32 x
5.8 x 1.8). 2 screws; diesels. 17 knots. 2 A.A.
guns.

**550**. Ja. **MUTSUKI**. *PC25*. Patrol Craft. 55 tons. 84 x 16 x 3. (25.6 x 4.9 x 9). Diesels. 15 knots. Operated by Maritime Safety Agency.

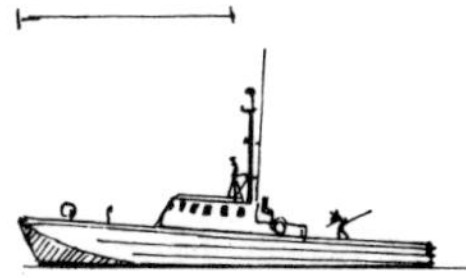

**551**. Ja. **BIZAN**. *PS42*. 1966. Rescue Vessel. 40 tons. 81 x 18 x 3. (24.7 x 5.5 x 9). Diesels. 21 knots. 1 light gun. Operated by Maritime Safety Agency.

**552**. Jm. **DISCOVERY BAY**. *P4*. 1966. Patrol Boat. 60 tons. 85 x 19 x 6. (25.9 x 5.8 x 1.8). 2 screws; diesels. 21 knots. 3 light guns. **HOLLAND BAY**. *P5*, **MANATEE BAY**. *P6*.

★ **553**. Cu. **GC. 11**. 1942-43. Coast Guard Cutter. 45 tons. 83 x 16 x 4.5. (25.3 x 4.9 x 1.3). Petrol motors. 18 knots. 1—20-m.m. A.A. gun. Ex-U.S. Coastguard cutters.
**GC. 13, GC. 14**.
Similar: **GC. 32, GC. 33, GC. 34**.

**554**. Ja. **HATSUNAMI** class. Patrol Craft. 45 tons. 76 x 15 x 3. (23.2 x 4.6 x 1). Diesels. 14 knots. Maritime Safety Agency.
**AKIZUKI**. *PC23*, **AYANAMI**. *PC02*, **CHIYO-NAMI**. *PC09*, **FUYUZUKI**. *PC24*, **HARUZUKI**. *PC21*, **HATSUNAMI**. *PC01*, **HATSUZUKI**. *PC11*, **HAYANAMI**. *PC10*, **ISONAMI**. *PC03*, **KIYOZUKI**. *PC13*, **KYONAMI**. *PC05*, **MOCHI-ZUKI**. *PC14*, **NATSUZUKI**. *PC22*, **NIIZUKI**. *PC15*, **OKINAMI**. *PC06*, **SUZUNAMI**. *PC08*, **SUZUTSUKI**. *PC16*, **TERUZUKI**. *PC17*, **URA-NAMI**. *PC04*, **URAZUKI**. *PC18*, **WAKAZUKI**. *PC19*, **TAMANAMI**. *PC07*, **YAMAZUKI** *PC20*, **HANAZUKI**. *PC12*.

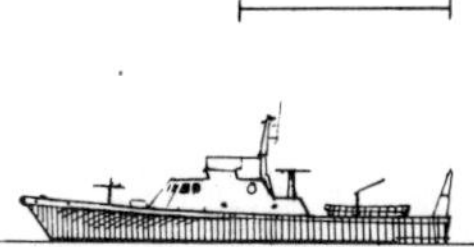

**555**. Do. **BELLATRIX**. *106*. 1969. Coast Guard Vessel. 60 tons. 85 x 18 x 5. (25.9 x 5.5 x 1.5). Diesels. 19 knots. 3 small guns.
**CAPELLA**. *108*, **PROCION**. *103*.

**556**. Ce. **HANSAYA** class. Patrol Boats. 36 tons. 66 x 14 x 4. (20.1 x 4.3 x 1.2). Diesels. 16 knots.
**HANSAYA, LIHINIYA**.

**557.** Ca. **SPINDRIFT.** 1964. Coast Guard Search and Rescue Cutter. 57 tons. (gross) 70 x 17 x 5. (21.3 x 5.2 x 1.4). Diesels. 19 knots. **SPRAY, SPUME.**

**558.** Ja. **HANAYUKI** class. 1959-60. Patrol Craft. 37-40 tons. 69 x 17 x 3. (21 x 5.2 x 1). Diesels. 21 knots. Maritime Safety Agency. **HANAYUKI.** *PC37,* **MINEYUKI.** *PC38,* **ISO-YUKI.** *PC39.*

**559.** Ja. **SHINONOME** class. 1954-55. Patrol Craft. 43-46 tons. 69 x 17 x 3. (21 x 5.2 x 1). Diesels. 18-25 knots. Maritime Safety Agency. **ASAGUMO.** *PC34,* **HATAGUMO.** *PC31,* **MAKIGUMO.** *PC32,* **NATSUGUMO.** *PC35,* **SHINONOME.** *PC30,* **TATSUGUMO.** *PC36,* **YAEGUMO.** *PC33.*

**560.** Ja. **TSUKUBA.** *PS31.* 1962. Rescue Launch. 65 tons. 80 x 22 x 4. (24.4 x 6.5 x 1.1). Diesels. 18 knots. Maritime Safety Agency. Similar: **AKAGI.** *PS40.* .

**561.** Is. **DROR.** 1943. Patrol Boat. 46 tons. 72 x 16 x 5.5. (21.9 x 4.9 x 1.7). 2 screws; diesels. 12 knots. 2—20-m.m. A.A. guns. 8 depth charges. **TIRTSA.** Ex-British H.D.M.L. type.

**562.** Ex-British **H.D.M.L.** type. Details as No. 561 but no depth charges.
Cambodia. **VP.** *212.*
Cameroon. **PATRIE DU CAMEROUN.**
In. **SPC. 3110** *(P3110),* **SPC. 3111** *(P3112),* **SPC. 3117** *(P3117).* **SPC. 3118** *(P3118).*
Ia. **PP. 01** to **PP. 025** (25 craft).
My. **SDML.** *3502.*
Cs. **FANG I.** *681,* **FANG CHI.** *685,* **FANG LIU.** *686,* **FANG PA.** *687,* **FANG SAN.** *682,* **FANG SEU.** *684.*
Pk. **SDML. 3517** *(P3517),* **SDML. 3520** *(P3520).* May have no guns—see No. 563.

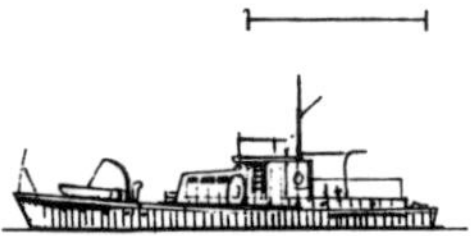

**563.** Pk. **SDML. 3517** *(P3517),* **SDML. 3520** *(P3520).* Details as No 561. This drawing shows the ships without guns.

**564.** Au. Ex-British **H.D.M.L.** type. Seaward Defence Boats. 59 tons. 80 x 16 x 5.5. (24.4 x 4.9 x 1.7). 2 screws; diesels. 11 knots. 1—40-m.m. A.A. gun.
**SDB. 1321, SDB. 1324, SDB. 1325.**

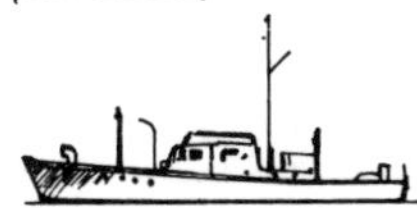

**564A.** Ir. Ex-British **H.D.M.L.** type. Details as No 561 **ABSALON; TAHMADGU.**

**565.** NZ. **D.H.M.L.** type. Seaward Patrol Craft. 46 tons. 72 x 16 x 5. (21.9 x 4.9 x 1.7). 2 screws; diesels. 12 knots. 1—20-m.m. A.A. gun (removed from some craft).
Appearance and function varies throughout the class. See silhouette No. 759.
**MAKO.** *P3551,* **MANGA.** *P3567,* **PAEA.** *P3552.*
Similar: **HAKU.** *P3565,* **KAHAWAI.** *P3553,*
**KOURA.** *P3563,* **KUPARU.** *P3563,* **MARORO.**
*P3554,* **PARORE.** *P3562,* **TAKAPU.** *P3556,*
**TAMURE.** *P3555,* **TARAPUNGA.** *P3566.*

**566.** Ce. **SERUWA** class. Patrol Boats. 13 tons. 48 x 12 x 3. (14.6 x 3.7 x .9). Diesels; 15 knots.
**DIYAKAWA, KORAWAKKA, SERUWA, TARAWA.**

**567.** Pi. U.S. **PCF** Type. 1965-66. Patrol Boats. 22 tons. 50 x 13 x 3.5. (15.2 x 4 x 1). 2 screws; diesels. 25 knots. 2 light guns.
306 to 311 inclusive (6 craft).
Am. Many similar craft and others transferred to Thailand, South Korea and South Vietnam.

**568.** Pv. **RIO** class. 1960. Patrol Launches. 37 tons. 66 x 17 x 3. (20.1 x 5.2 x 1). 2 screws; diesels. 18 knots. 2—40-m.m. guns.
**RIO PIURA, RIO TUMBES, RIO ZARU-MILLA.**

**569.** Le. **BYBLOS** class. 1955. Patrol Boats. 28 tons. 66 x 14 x 4. (20.1 x 4 x 1.2). 2 screws; diesels. 18 knots. 1—20-m.m. A.A. gun.
**BYBLOS.** *11,* **SIDON.** *12,* **BEYROUTH.** *13.*

**570.** Do. **RIGEL.** *101.* Coast Guard Vessel. About 75 feet long. Diesel. 18 knots.

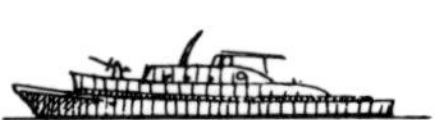

**571.** Co. **FRITZ HAGALE.** *124.* 1952. Patrol Launch. 33 tons. 76 x 12 x 3. (23.2 x 3.7 x 1). Diesels. 13 knots. 1—20-m.m. A.A. gun.
**ALFONSO VARGAS.** *123.*

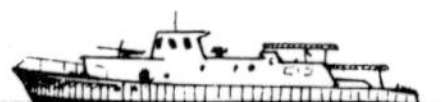

**572.** Co. **ALBERTO RESTREPO.** *125.* 1953.
Patrol Launch. 35 tons. 82 x 12 x 3. (25 x 3.7 x
1). Diesels. 13 knots. 1—20-m.m. A.A. gun and
4 lighter guns.
**CARLOS GALINDO.** *128,* **HUMBERTO COR-
TES.** *126,* **JUAN LUCIO.** *122.*

**573.** Ce. **THORNYCROFT** Type. 1966-68.
Patrol Launches. 15 tons. 46 x 12 x 3. (14 x
3.7 x 1). Motor vessels. 25 knots.
The drawing represents **PC.** *97* and there are
about 20 other vessels in the class.

**574.** Po. **DOM ALEIXO** class. 1967. Patrol
Launches. 60 tons (full). 82 x 17 x 5. (25 x 5.2 x
1.6). Diesel. 16 knots. 1—20-m.m. A.A. gun.
**DOM ALEIXO.** *P1148,* **DOM JEREMIAS.**

**575.** Sw. **61** Type. 1960-61. Patrol Boats.
30 tons. 62 x 15 x 4. (18.9 x 4.6 x 1.2). Diesel.
19 knots. 1—20-m.m. gun.
**61** to **70** inclusive (10 craft).

**576.** Ja. **HIRYU.** *PC109.* 1943. Converted 1957.
Inshore Patrol Boat. 34 tons. 73 x 18 x 5. (22.3 x
5.5 x 1.5). Petrol engines. 15 knots. Ex-U.S.
Motor Torpedo Boat.

**577.** Li. **ML. 4001,** Patrol Boat. 11 tons. 41 x
12 x 3.5. (12.5 x 3.5 x 1). 2 screws; diesels.
23 knots. 2 light guns. U.S. Coastguard Cutter
type.
**ML. 4002.**

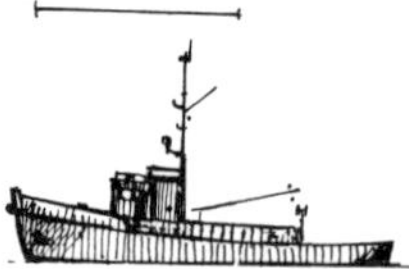

**578.** Da. **MHV** Type. 1958. Naval Home Guard
Training Craft 76 tons. 10 knots. 1—20-m.m.
A.A. gun.
**MHV. 70, MHV. 71, MHV. 72.**

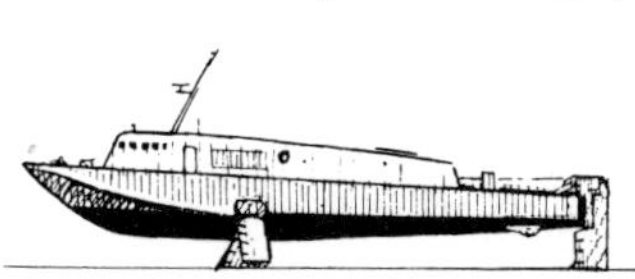

**579.** Am. **DENISON**. 1962. Experimental Hydrofoil. 90 tons. 117 x 45. (35.6 x 13.7). Gas turbine. 62 knots.

**580.** Am. **PLAINVIEW**. *GEH1*. 1968. Hydrofoil Research Craft. 310 tons (full). 212 x 40. (64.6 x 12.1). Gas turbine. (Diesel auxiliary). 50 knots. (Reported to be capable of 80 knots.) 2 anti submarine torpedo launchers (triple).

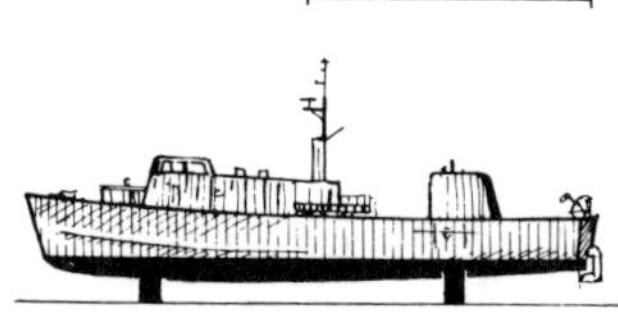

**581.** Am. **HIGH POINT**. *PCH1*. 1963. Experimental Hydrofoil Submarine Chaser. 110 tons. 117 x 32. (35.6 x 9.7). Gas turbine. 2 screws. (Diesel auxiliary.) 48 knots. 2 anti-submarine torpedo launchers (twin). Depth charge thrower. 2 light guns.

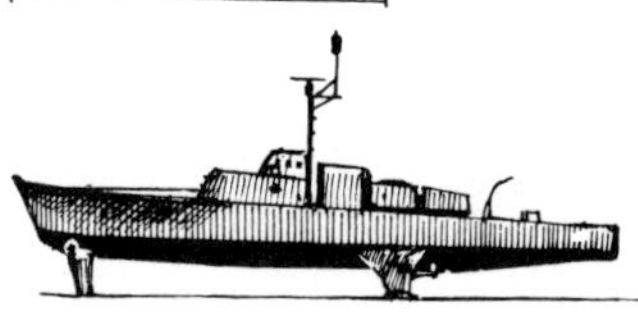

**582.** Ca. **BRAS D'OR**. *400*. 1966. Anti-submarine Hydrofoil. 180 tons. 151 x 21. (46 x 6.4). Gas turbine. 50-60 knots. (Diesel auxiliary.)

**583.** Am. **TUCUMCARI**. *2*. 1968. Hydrofoil Gunboat. 58 tons. 72 x 20. (21.9 x 6.1). Gas turbine. 40 knots. (Diesel auxiliary.) 1—40-m.m. gun. 4 light guns. 1 anti-submarine mortar.

**584.** Pi. **BALER**. *75*. 1966. Hydrofoil Patrol Boat. 32 tons. 69 x 16. (21 x 4.8). Diesel. 38 knots. Light guns. Japanese built *PT32* type. **BONTOC**. *74*.

**585.** Am. **FLAGSTAFF**. *1*. 1968. Hydrofoil Gunboat. 57 tons. 74 x 22. (22.5 x 6.7). Gas turbine. 40 knots. (Diesel auxiliary.) 1—40-m.m. gun. 4 lighter guns. 1 anti-submarine mortar.

**586.** Pi. **CAMIGUIN**. *72*. 1965. Hydrofoil Patrol Boat. 28 tons. 69 x 25. (21 x 7.6). Diesel. 2 screws. 38 knots. 1—20-m.m. A.A. gun. 1 anti-submarine torpedo launcher. Pt 20 type. **SIQUIJOR**. *73*.

★ **587.** RC. Ex-**YING SHAN**. 1927. River Gunboat. 310 tons. 185 x 29 x 3. (56.3 x 8.8 x .9). Turbines. 16 knots. 2—3-inch A.A. guns. 8 light guns. Ex-H.M.S. "Gannet".

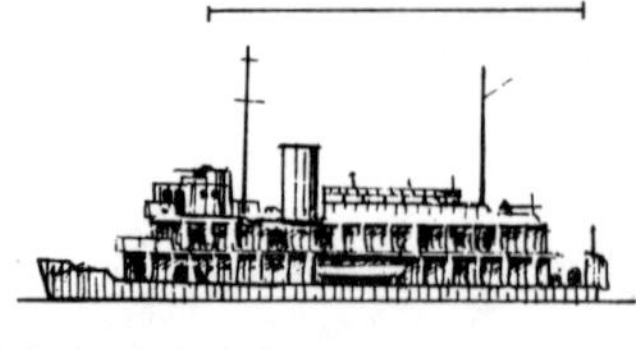

★ **588.** RC. Ex-**NAN CHIANG**. 1931. River Gunboat. 370 tons. 150 x 29 x 5. (45.7 x 8.8 x 1.5). Turbines. 15 knots. 1—3.7-inch gun. 10 light guns. Ex-H.M.S. "Falcon".

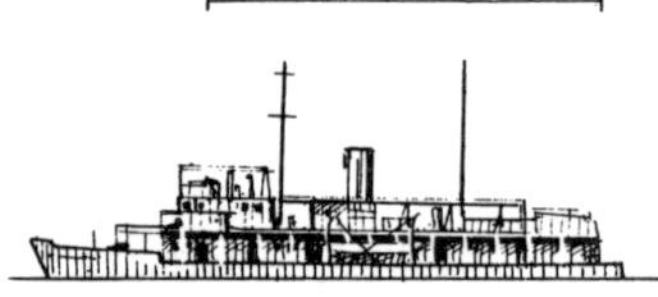

★ **589.** RC. Ex-**YING HAO**. 1933. River Gunboat. 185 tons. 160 x 31 x 2. (48.7 x 9.4 x .6). 2 screws; reciprocating. 11 knots. 1—3.7-inch gun. 9 light guns. Ex-H.M.S. "Sandpiper".

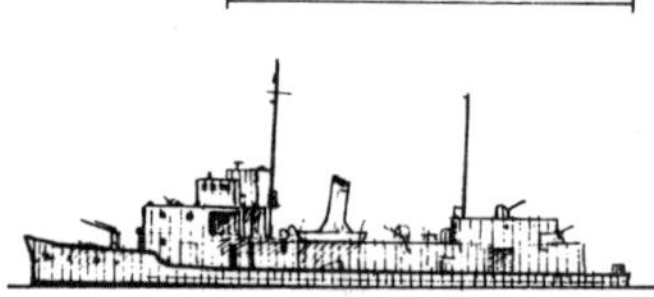

★ **590.** RC. **FU CHIANG**. 1939. River Gunboat. 320 tons. 165 x 32 x 4. (50.2 x 9.7 x 1.2). Turbines. 2 screws. 16 knots. 1—3.1-inch gun. (HA). 8 light guns. Ex-Japanese and Ex-**CHIANG HSI.**

**591.** Bm. **SAGU**. River Gunboats. 100 tons. 95 x 22 x 5. (28.9 x 6.7 x 1.5). Diesel. 12 knots. 1—40-m.m. gun and 2 lighter guns. Possibly similar: **HINTHA, SABAN, SEINDA, SETKAYA, SETYAHAT, SHWEPAZUN, SH-WETHIDA, SINMIN.**

**592.** Bm. "Y" Type. 1958. River Gunboats. 120 tons. 105 x 24 x 3. (32 x 7.3 x .9). 2 screws; diesels. 13 knots. 2—40-m.m. A.A. guns. 1 small gun. 10 in class—**Y. 301** to **Y. 310** (inclusive).

**593.** Bm. **NAGAKYAY**. 1960. River Gunboat. 400 tons. 163 x 27 x 6. (49.6 x 8.2 x 1.8). 2 screws; diesels. 12 knots. 2—25-pdr. guns. 2 lighter guns. **NAWARAT.**

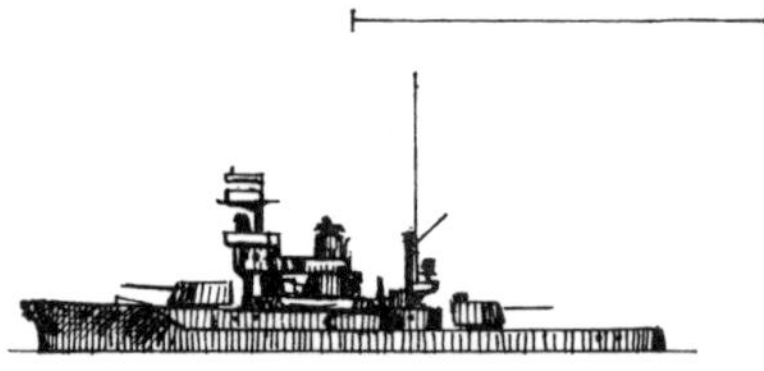

**594.** Th. **SUKOTHAI**. 2. 1930. Coast Defence Vessel. 900 tons. 173 x 37 x 11. (52.7 x 11.2 x 3.3). 2 screws; reciprocating. 12 knots. 2—6-inch guns. 4—3-inch D.P. guns. 5 A.A. guns.

**595**. Po. **TETE.** *P371.* 1919. River Gunboat.
100 tons. 80 x 20 x 2. (23.5 x 6.1 x .6). Stern
Wheeler. 8 knots. 2—47-m.m. guns. 2 smaller
guns. Service on Zambesi River.

**596**. Bz. **PARNAIBA.** *U17.* 1937. River Monitor.
620 tons. 180 x 33 x 5. (54.8 x 10 x 1.5). 2 screws;
reciprocating. 12 knots. 1—3-inch gun. 2—
47-m.m. guns. 8 A.A. guns.
Matto Grosso Flotilla.

**597**. Bz. **PARAGUACO.** *U16.* 1939. River
Monitor. 430 tons. 150 x 35 x 5. (45.7 x 10.7 x
1.5). Reciprocating. 13 knots. 1—3-inch gun.
2—47-m.m. guns. 8 A.A. guns.
Matto Grosso Flotilla.

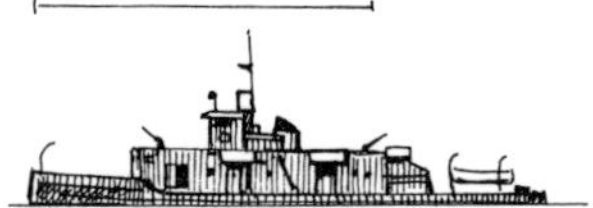

**598**. Co. **BARRANQUILLA.** *31.* 1930. Modernised. River Gunboat. 140 tons. 138 x 24 x 3.
(42 x 7.3 x .9). 2 screws; semi-diesels in tunnels.
15 knots. 2—3-inch guns. 1 A.A. gun. 4 small
guns.

**599**. Co. **CARTAGENA.** *33.* 1930. River Gunboat. All details as for No. 598.
May be modernised as "Barranquilla".

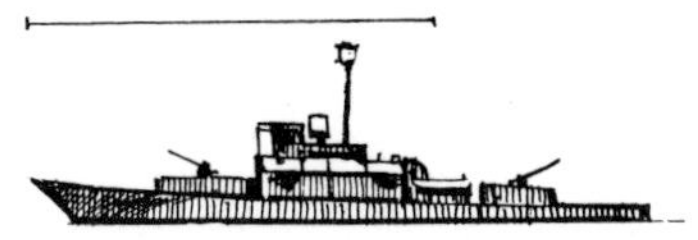

**600**. Co. **ARAUCA** class. 1956. River Gunboats.
180 tons. 164 x 24 x 3. (49.9 x 7.3 x .9). 2 Cater-
pillar engines. 13 knots. 2—3-inch D.P. guns.
4 smaller guns. Some of these vessels may now
have been disarmed.
**ARAUCA.** *37,* **LETICIA.** *36,* **RIOHACHA.** *35.*

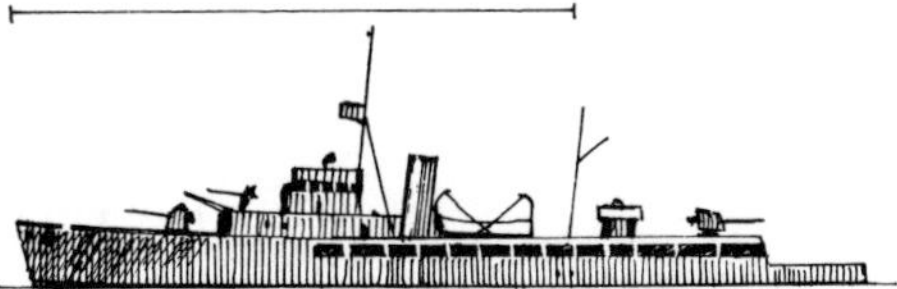

**601**. Py. **HUMAITA.** 1931. River Gunboat.
640 tons. 231 x 35 x 5. (70 4 x 10 6 x 1.5).
2 screws; turbines. 17 knots. 4—4.7-inch guns.
4—3-inch A.A. guns. 2 smaller guns. 6 mines.
**PARAGUAY.**

**602.** Py. **CAPITAN CABRAL.** 1907. River Patrol Boat. 180 tons. 107 x 24 x 10. (32.6 x 7.3 x 3). Reciprocating. 9 knots. 1—3-inch gun. 2 smaller guns. Built as a tug.

**603.** Pv. **MARANON** class. 1951. River Gunboats. 360 (Full). 157 x 32 x 4. (47.8 x 9.7 x 1.2). Diesel. 12 knots. 2—3-inch D.P. guns. 7 A.A. guns. Upper Amazon service.
**MARANON.** *13,* **UCAYALI.** *14.*

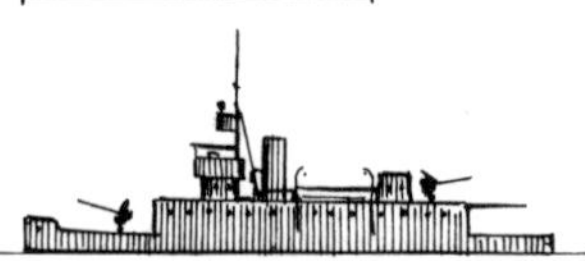

**604.** Pv. **LORETO** class. 1934. River Gunboats. 250 tons. 154 x 22 x 4. (46.9 x 6.7 x 1.2). Diesel. 15 knots. 2—3-inch guns. 1—47-m.m. gun. 2 A.A. guns.
**AMAZONAS.** *11,* **LORETO.** *12.*

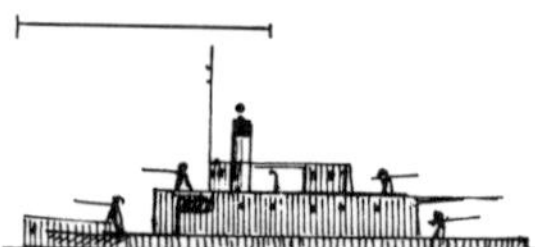

**605.** Pv. **NAPO.** *301.* 1920. River Gunboat. 100 tons. 102 x 18 x 3. (31 x 5.4 x .9). Reciprocating. 12 knots. 3—47-m.m. guns. 2 light A.A. guns.

## ASSAULT SHIPS AND LANDING CRAFT

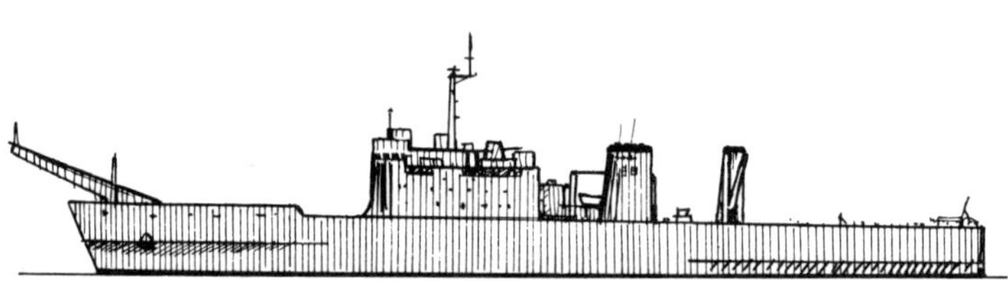

**606.** Am. **NEWPORT** class. 1969 onwards. Tank Landing Ships. 8,300 tons. (Full). 522 x 70 x 15. (158.7 x 21 x 4.5). 2 screws; diesels. 20 knots. 4—3-inch A.A. guns (twin). Helicopter Platform. Bow gantry for lowering ramp.
**BOULDER.** *1190,* **CAYUGA.** *1186,* **FREDER-ICK.** *1184,* **FRESNO.** *1182,* **MANITOWOC.** *1180,* **NEWPORT.** *1179,* **PEORIA.** *1183,* **SAGINAW.** *1188,* **SAN BERNADINO.** *1189,* **SCHENECTADY.** *1185,* **SUMTER.** *1181,* **TUSCALOOSA.** *1187.*
There are to be 27 ships in the class.

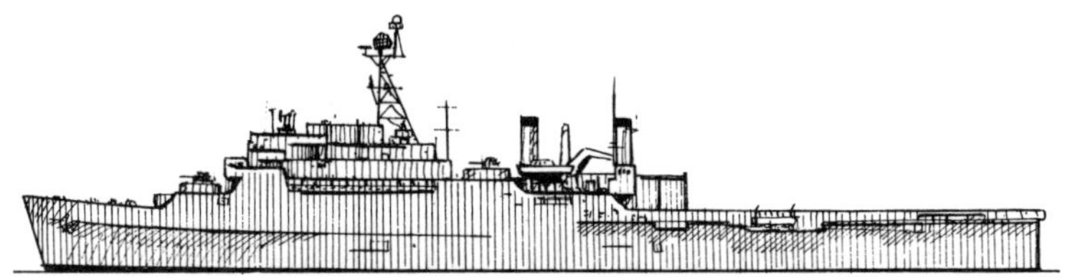

**607.** Am. **CLEVELAND** class. 1967-69. Amphibious Transport Docks. 17,000 tons (full). 570 x 84 x 23. (173.3 x 25.6 x 7). 2 screws; turbines. 20 knots. 8—3-inch A.A. guns (twin). 6 helicopters. Telescopic Hangar. (Shown extended in drawing.)

Differs from No. 608 by having higher bridge. (Flagships.)
**CLEVELAND.** *7,* **CORONADO.** *11,* **DENVER.** *9,* **DUBUQUE.** *8,* **JUNEAU.** *10,* **SHREVEPORT.** *12,* **NASHVILLE.** *13.*

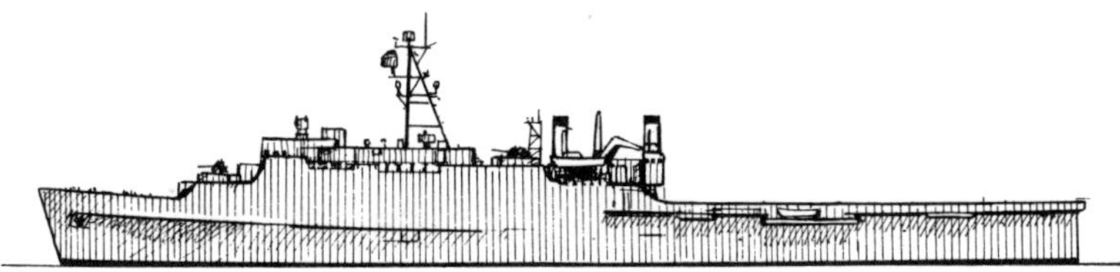

**608.** Am. **AUSTIN** class. 1965-70. All details as for No. 607 but lower bridge structure.
**AUSTIN.** *4,* **DULUTH.** *6,* **OGDEN.** *5,* **PONCE.** *15,* **TRENTON.** *14.*

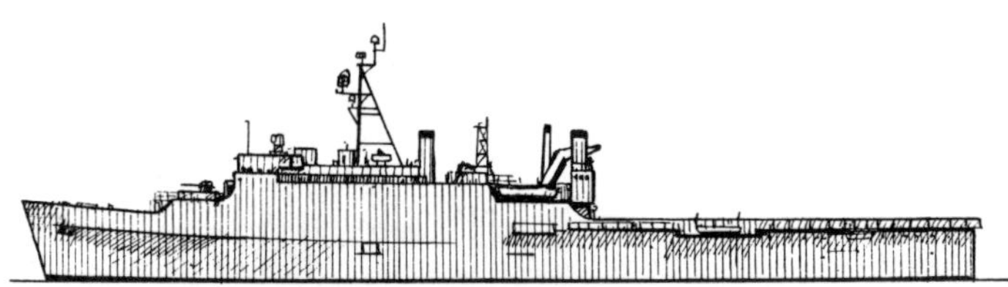

**609.** Am. **RALEIGH** class. 1962-64. Amphibious Transport Docks. 14,000 tons (full). 522 x 84 x 21. (158.4 x 25.6 x 6.4). 2 screws; turbines. 20 knots. 8—3-inch A.A. guns. 6 helicopters. Telescopic Hangars.
**RALEIGH.** *1,* **VANCOUVER.** *2.*
Similar with additional superstructure level. (Command Ship.)
**LA SALLE.** *3.*

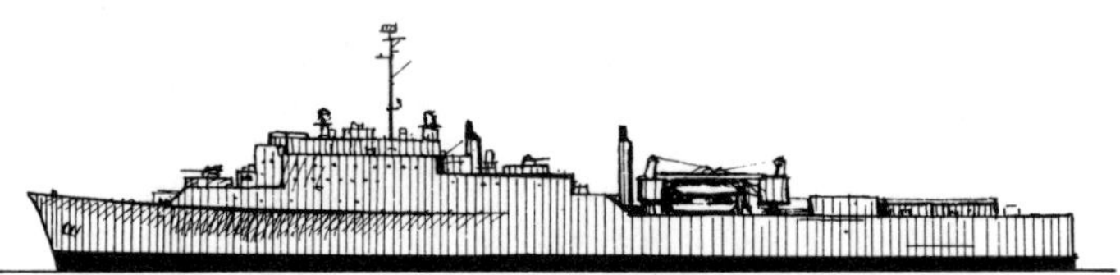

**610.** Am. **THOMASTON** class. 1954-57. Dock Landing Ships. 11,300 tons (full). 510 x 84 x 19. (155.4 x 25.6 x 5.7). 2 screws; turbines. 24 knots. 12—3-inch A.A. guns (twin). Helicopter landing platform.

**ALAMO.** *33,* **FORT SNELLING.** *30,* **HERMITAGE.** *34,* **MONTICELLO.** *35,* **PLYMOUTH ROCK.** *29,* **POINT DEFIANCE.** *31,* **SPIEGEL GROVE.** *32,* **THOMASTON.** *28.*

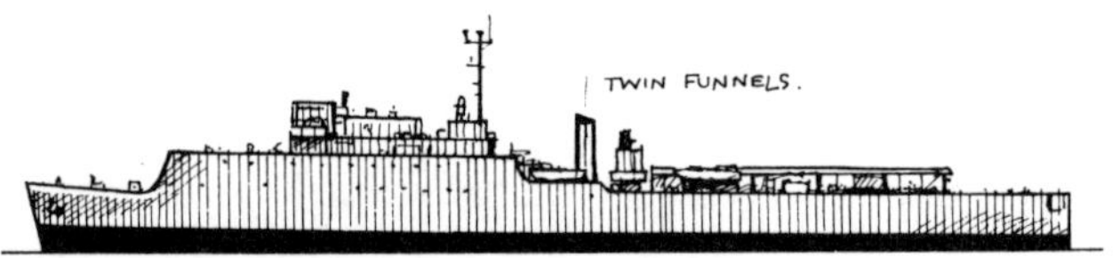


**611.** Am. **CASA GRANDE** class. 1944-46.
Dock Landing Ships. 4,800 tons. 475 x 76 x 18.
(144.7 x 23.1 x 5.5). 2 screws; turbines. 15 knots.
8 or 12—40-m.m. A.A. guns.
**CABILDO.** *16,* **CASA GRANDE.** *13,* **CATA-
MOUNT.** *17,* **COMSTOCK.** *19,* **COLONIAL.**
*18,* **DONNER.** *20,* **FORT MANDAN.** *21,*
**FORT MARION.** *22,* **RUSHMORE.** *14,* **SAN
MARCOS.** *25,* **SHADWELL.** *15,* **TORTUGA.**
*26,* **WHETSTONE.** *27.*

Similar: **ASHLAND** class. Am. **GUNSTON
HALL.** *5.* Cs. **TUNG HAI.** *191.* Gr. **NAFKRA-
TOUSSA.** *L153.*

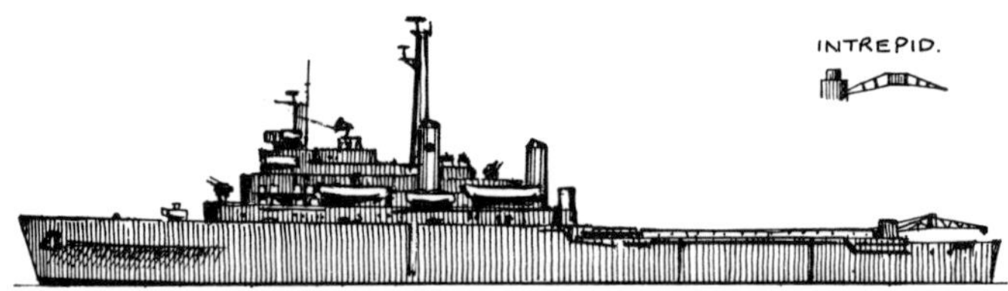


**612.** Br. **FEARLESS.** *L10.* 1965. Assault Ship.
11,100 tons. 520 x 80 x 21. (158.5 x 24.4.x 6.2).
2 screws; turbines. 21 knots. 2—40-m.m. A.A.
guns. 4 surface-to-air "Seacat" missile launchers
(quadruple). Facilities for 5 helicopters. The fore
funnel is alongside the mast and cannot be seen
when broadside.
**INTREPID.** *L11.*

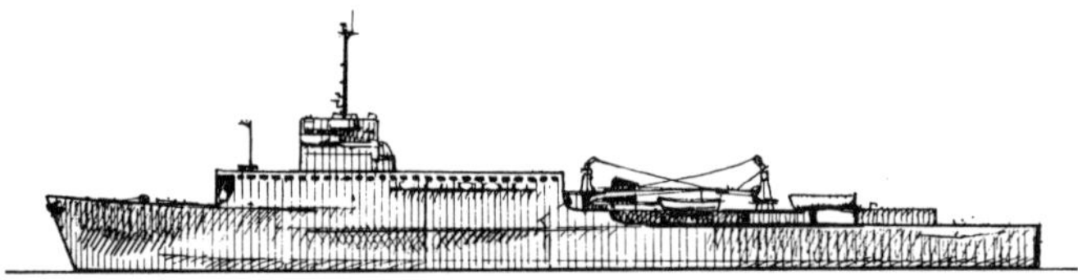

**613.** Fr. **ORAGE.** *L9022.* 1968. Assault Landing
Ships. 8,500 tons (full). 489 x 71 x 29. (149 x
21.5 x 8.7). 2 screws; diesels. 17 knots. 2—
4.7-inch mortars. 6 A.A. guns. Facilities for 3
helicopters.
**OURAGAN.** *L9021.*

**614.** Br. **SIR LANCELOT** class. 1964-68.
Logistics Ships. 6,400 tons gross (average).
415 x 59 x 13. (126.5 x 18 x 4). 2 screws;
diesels. 17 knots. Facilities for helicopters.
Operated by the Royal Fleet Auxiliary. Vary
slightly in appearance.
**SIR BEDEVERE.** *L3004,* **SIR GALAHAD.**
*L3005,* **SIR GERAINT, SIR LANCELOT.**
*L3009,* **SIR PERCIVALE, SIR TRISTRAM.**

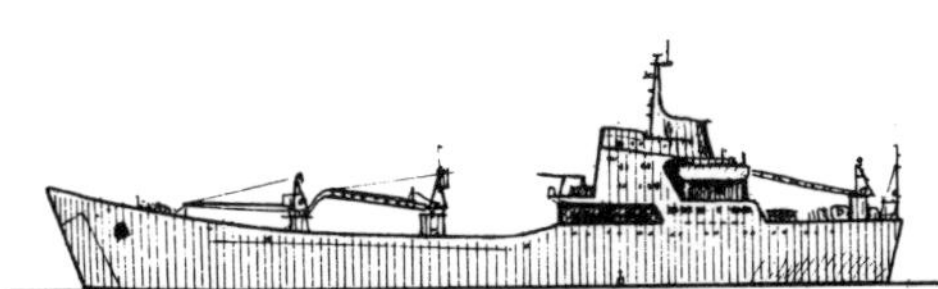

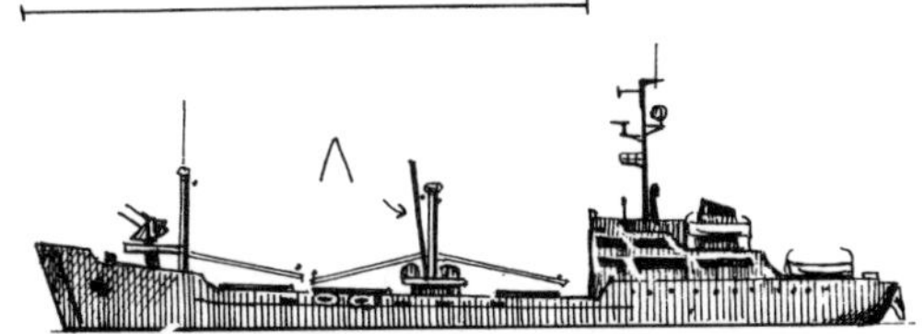

**615.** Ru. **ALLIGATOR** class. 1966 onwards. Landing Ships. 4,000 tons. 328 x 15 x 14. (100 x 15.2 x 4.2). 15 knots. 2—57-m.m. A.A. guns (twin). Bow and stern ramps. Some vessels have only one crane on the foredeck; see silhouette No. 1191. At least seven in the Soviet Navy.

**616.** Ru. **MP. 6** class. Landing Ships. 1,800 tons. 246 x 40 x 10.5. (74.9 x 12.1 x 3.2). Diesels. 10 knots. 4—47-m.m. guns (quadruple). 8 to 10 tanks. Similar to the Beira class in the Soviet merchant fleet.

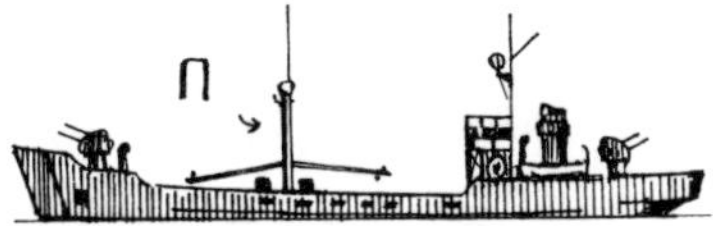

**617.** Ru. **MP. 4** class. Landing Craft. 800 tons. 181 x 23 x 9. (55.1 x 7 x 2.7). 4—25-m.m. guns (twin). 6 to 8 tanks. 30 units in the Soviet Navy.

**618.** Am. **SUFFOLK COUNTY** class. 1956-57. Tank Landing Ships. 8,000 tons full load. 445 x 62 x 17. (135.6 x 18.9 x 5.1). 2 screws; diesels. 17 knots. 6—3-inch guns (twin).
**DE SOTO COUNTY.** *1171,* **GRAHAM COUNTY.** *1176,* **GRANT COUNTY.** *1174,* **LORAIN COUNTY.** *1177,* **SUFFOLK COUNTY.** *1173,* **WOOD COUNTY.** *1178,* **YORK COUNTY.** *1175.*

**619.** Am. **TALBOT COUNTY.** *1153.* Tank Landing Ship. 6,000 tons. 382 x 54 x 17. (116.4 x 16.4 x 5.1). 2 screws; turbines. 14 knots.

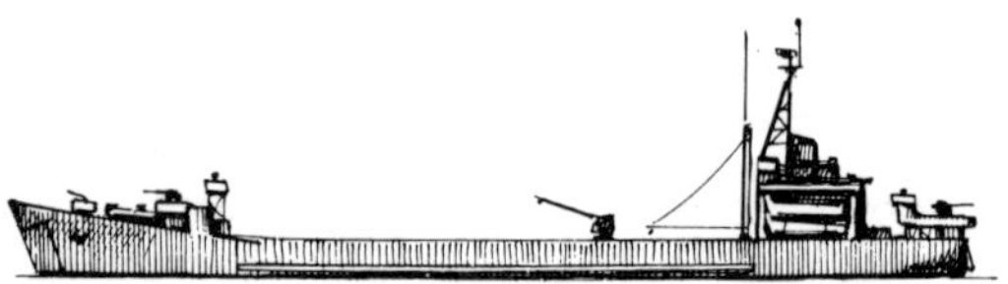

**620.** Am. **TERREBONNE PARISH** class. 1952-54. Tank Landing Ships. 5,800 tons full load. 384 x 55 x 17. (117 x 16.7 x 5.1). 2 screws; diesels. 15 knots. 6—3-inch guns (twin).
**TERREBONNE PARISH.** *1156,* **TERRELL COUNTY.** *1157,* **TIOGA COUNTY.** *1158,* **TOM GREEN COUNTY.** *1159,* **TRAVERSE COUNTY.** *1160,* **VERNON COUNTY.** *1161,* **WAHKIAKUM COUNTY.** *1162,* **WALDO COUNTY.** *1163,* **WALWORTH COUNTY.** *1164,* **WASHOE COUNTY.** *1165,* **WASHTE-NAW COUNTY.** *1166,* **WESTCHESTER COUNTY.** *1167,* **WEXFORD COUNTY.** *1168,* **WHITFIELD COUNTY.** *1169,* **WINDHAM COUNTY.** *1170.*
Some ships have pole masts.

40 American ships of this class are employed in cargo carrying including the following:
**CHASE COUNTY, CHESTERFIELD COUNTY, DAVIESS COUNTY, DE KALB COUNTY, HARRIS COUNTY, NEW LONDON COUNTY, NYE COUNTY, ORLEANS COUNTY, PLUMAS COUNTY, PULASKI COUNTY.**
Similar.: Am. Tank Landing Ships. **BLANCO COUNTY.** *LST344,* **BULLOCH COUNTY.** *LST509.*

Similar: .
Gr.: **CHIOS.** *L195,* **LIMNOS.** *L158,* **SAMOS.** *L179.*
Po.: (pole masts). **ALBAY.** *39,* **BULACAN.** *38,* **MISAMIS ORIENTAL.** *40.*
Th.: (light lattice tripod). **ANGTHONG, CHANG, PANGAN.**
VN.: (pole masts). **CAM RANH.** *500,* **DA NANG.** *501,* **THI NAI.** *502,* **VUNG TAU.** *503.*

**621.** Fr. **EDIC** class. 1958-67. Landing Craft. 290 tons. 194 x 39 x 5. (59.1 x 11.8 x 1.5). 2 screws; diesels. 8 knots. 2 A.A. guns. 9 ships numbering **Edic 1—Edic 9** (inclusive).

Mo.: **LIEUTENANT MALGHAGH.**

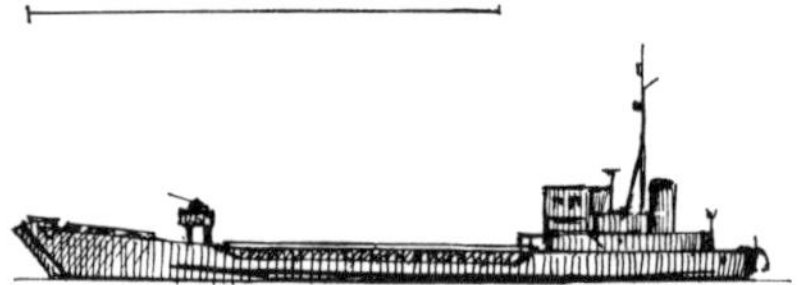

**622.** Ng. **LOKOJA.** *L1312.* 1944. Refitted 1966-67. 350 tons. 188 x 39 x 5. (42 x 11.8 x 1.5). 2 screws; diesels. 10 knots. 2—20-m.m. A.A. guns. Ex-British LCT(4) type.

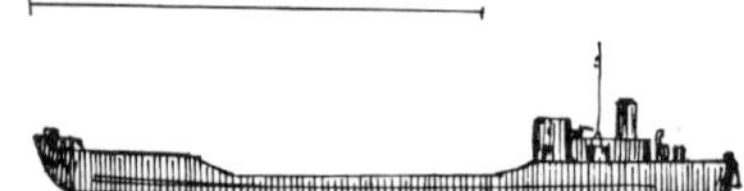

**623.** Po. **ALFANGE.** *LDG101.* 1965-69. Landing Craft. 500 tons. 187 x 39 x 4. (56.9 x 11.8 x 1.5). 2 screws; diesels. Similar to British LCT(4) type.
**ARIETE, BOMBARDA, CIMITARRA, MONTANTE.**

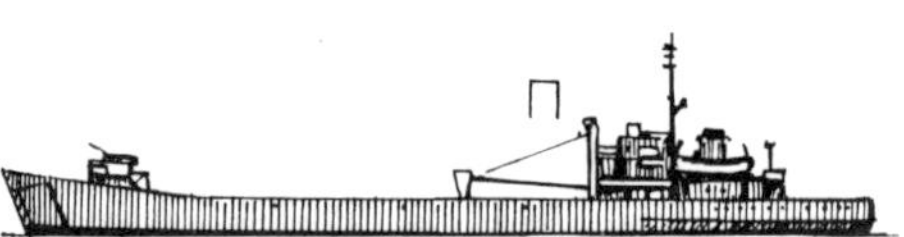

**624.** In. **MAGAR.** *L3011.* 1945. Landing Ship. 4,500 tons full load. 348 x 55 x 11. (106 x 16.7 x 3.3). 2 screws; reciprocating. 13 knots. 2—40-m.m. A.A. guns. 6—20-m.m. A.A. guns. Ex-British LST(3) type.
Similar: Br. **STALKER.** *L3515,* **TRACKER.** *L3522.* (Depot Ships). Gr. **PINIOS.** *L171.*

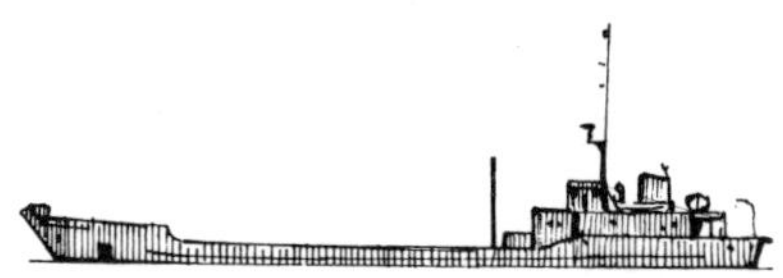

**625.** Ca. **MARMOT.** 1944. Supply Ships. 590 tons. 188 x 34 x 4. (57.3 x 10.2 x 1.2). Diesels. 8 knots. Canadian Coast Guard. Converted British LCT(4) type.
Very similar with light, tall masts between the kingposts: **MINK.**

**626.** Fr. **ARGENS.** *L9003.* 1958-60. Landing Ship. 1,400 tons. 328 x 50 x 14. (99.9 x 15.2 x 4.2). 2 screws; diesels. 11 knots. 2—40-m.m. A.A. guns. Some ships have 1—4.7-inch mortar and 3—40-m.m. guns.
**BIDASSOA.** *L9004,* **BLAVET.** *L9009,* **DIVES.** *L9008,* **TRIEUX.** *L9007.*

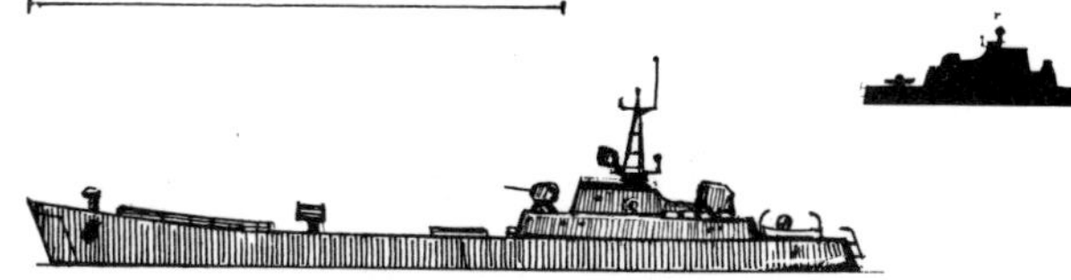

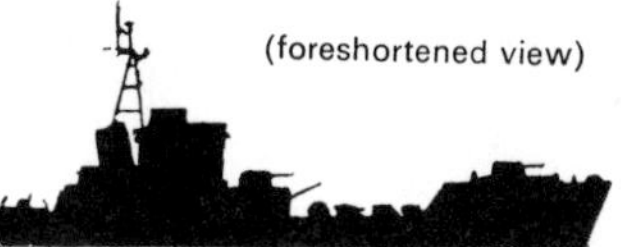

**627.** Ru. **POLNOCNY II** class. Landing Ships. 720 tons. 235 x 39 x 10. (71.6 x 11.8 x 3). Diesels. 15 knots. 1—30-m.m. A.A. gun. 2 anti-submarine rocket projectors. 8 to 10 tanks.

Similar but without rocket launchers and different mast is **POLNOCNY I** type, see silhouette No. 651. At least 25 in the Soviet Navy.

The following countries have Polnocny I type:
Eg.: May have both types.
In.: At least 2.    Ph.: At least 16.

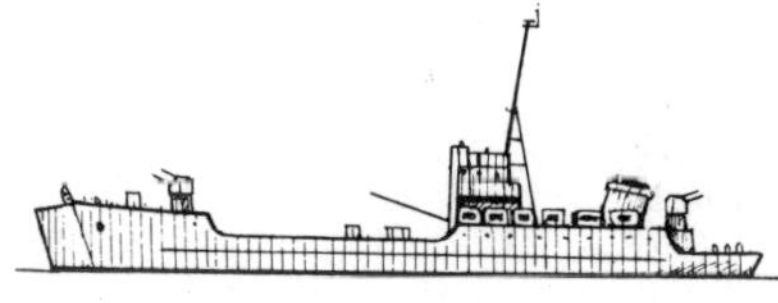

(foreshortened view)

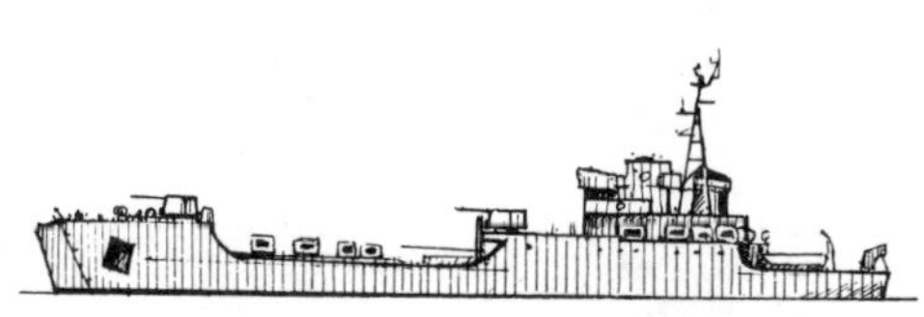

**628.** Ru. **MP. 8** class. Landing Ships. 800 tons. 236 x 36 x 13. (71.9 x 10.9 x 3.9). Diesels. 15 knots. 4—57-m.m. guns (twin). 8 or more tanks. At least 20 in the Soviet Navy.

**629.** Ru. **MP. 2** class. Landing Craft. 600 tons. 190 x 25 x 8. (57.9 x 7.6 x 2.4). Diesels. 16 knots. 4—25-m.m. guns (twin). 4 tanks. About 15 in the Soviety Navy.

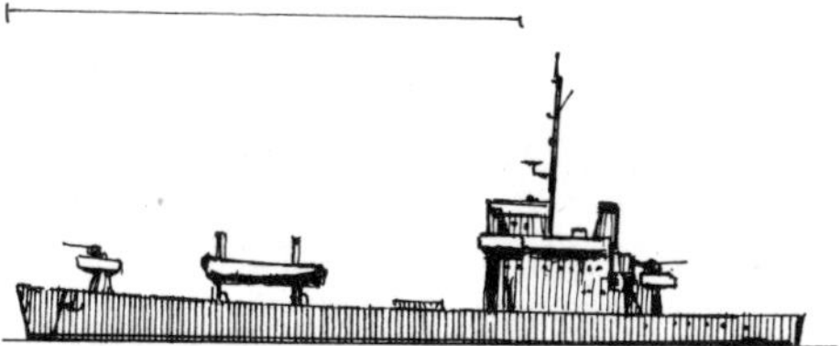

**630.** It. **CAPRERA.** 1966. Landing Ship. 760 tons. 226 x 31 x 6. (68.8 x 9.4 x 1.8). Diesels. 13 knots. 4—40-m.m. A.A. guns (twin).
**MARSALA, QUARTO.** *A5302.*

**632.** Fr. **CHELIFF.** *L9006.* Water Carrier. 1,600 tons. 328 x 50 x 14. (99.9 x 15.2 x 4.2). 2 screws; diesels. 11 knots. Ex-U.S. LST.

**633.** Ar. **CABO SAN BARTOLOME.** *BDT1.* 1944. Tank Landing Ship. 4,000 tons full load. 328 x 50 x 14. (99.9 x 15.2 x 4.2). 2 screws; diesels. 11 knots. Ex-U.S. LST type.
**CABO SAN GONZALO.** *BDT4,* **CABO SAN ISIDRO.** *BDT6,* **CABO SAN PIO.** *BDT10,* **CABO SAN VICENTE.** *BDT14.*

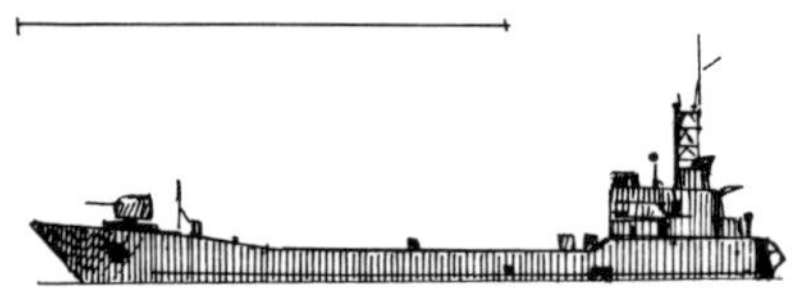

★ **634.** EG. **ROBBE** class. 1964. Landing Craft. 600 tons. 197 x 33 x 7. (60 x 10 x 2.1). Diesels. 12 knots. 6 A.A. guns (twin). At least 6 vessels including the following:
**EISENHUTTENSTADT, GRIMMEN, HOY-ERSWERDA, LUBBENAU, SCHWEDT.**

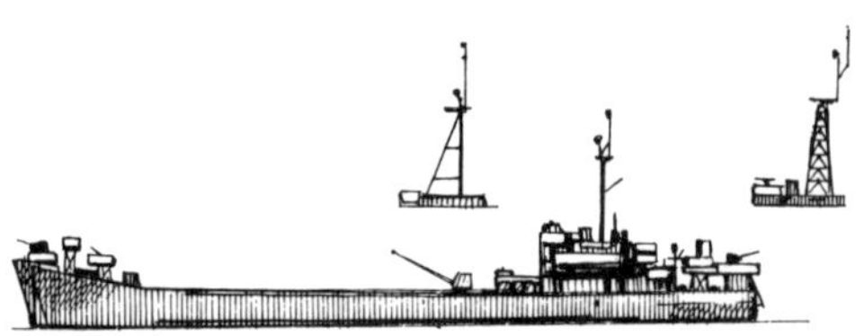

**635.** Am. **LST.** *511-1152* series. Around 1944. Tank Landing Ships. 1,650 tons. 328 x 50 x 14. (99.9 x 15.2 x 4.2). 2 screws; diesels. 11 knots. 8—40-m.m. A.A. guns. Three different types of mast as shown in the insets.
Am. **CAROLINE COUNTY.** *525,* **CHEBOY-GAN COUNTY.** *533,* **CHURCHILL COUNTY.** *583,* **CLARKE COUNTY.** *601,* **DODGE COUN-TY.** *722,* **DUVAL COUNTY.** *758,* **FLOYD COUNTY.** *762,* **GARRETT COUNTY.** *786,* **HAMPSHIRE COUNTY.** *819,* **HENRY COUN-TY.** *824,* **HOLMES COUNTY.** *836,* **HUNTER-DON COUNTY.** *838,* **IREDELL COUNTY.** *839,* **JENNINGS COUNTY.** *846,* **JEROME COUNTY.** *848,* **KEMPER COUNTY.** *854,* **LITCHFIELD COUNTY.** *901,* **LUZERNE COUNTY.** *902,* **MADERA COUNTY.** *905,* **MEEKER COUNTY.** *980,* **MIDDLESEX COUN-TY.** *983,* **MONMOUTH COUNTY.** *1032,* **OUTAGAMIE COUNTY.** *1073,* **PAGE COUN-TY.** *1076,* **PARK COUNTY.** *1077,* **PITKIN COUNTY.** *1082,* **POLK COUNTY.** *1084,* **ST. CLAIR COUNTY.** *1096,* **SAN JOAQUIN COUNTY.** *1122,* **SEDGWICK COUNTY.** *1123,* **SNOHOMISH COUNTY.** *1126,* **STONE COUNTY.** *1141,* **SUMMIT COUNTY.** *1146,* **SUMNER COUNTY.** *1148,* **SUTTER COUN-TY.** *1150.*

Cs.: **CHUNG KUANG.** *216,* **CHUNG MING.** *227,* **CHUNG YEA.** *231,* **CHUNG CHIH.** *218,* **CHUNG CH'UAN.** *221,* **CHUNG CHENG.** *224,* **CHUNG CHI.** *206,* **CHUNG CHIEN.** *205,* **CHUNG CHIANG.** *225,* **CHUNG BANG.** *230,* **CHUNG FU.** *223,* **CHUNG HAI.** *201,* **CHUNG HSING.** *204,* **CHUNG SHUN.** *208,* **CHUNG LIEN.** *209,* **CHUNG SHENG.** *222,* **CHUNG SUO.** *228,* **CHUNG TING.** *203,* **CHUNG WAN.** *229,* **CHUNG YU.** *215,* **CHUNG YUNG.** *210.*
Gr.: **IKARIA.** *L154,* **LESBOS.** *L172,* **RODOS.** *L157,* **SYROS.** *L144.*
Ia.: **TANDJUNG NUSANIE.** *1,* **TELUK BAY-UR.** *870,* **TELUK KAU.** *871,* **TELUK LANGSA.** *868,* **TELUK MENADO.** *872.* All have nine A.A. guns.
Ja.: **OOSUMI.** *4001,* **SHIMOKITA.** *4002,* **SHIRETOKO.** *4003.*
Ko.: **BI BONG.** *809,* **BUK HAN.** *815,* **DUK BONG.** *808,* **HWA SAN.** *816,* **KAE BONG.** *810,* **SU YONG.** *813,* **UN BONG.** *807,* **WEE BONG.** *812.*
Pv.: (pole mast). **PAITA.** *35.*
Pi.: **BATAAN.** *LT85,* Ex-U.S.S. **HICKMAN COUNTY.** New name not known.

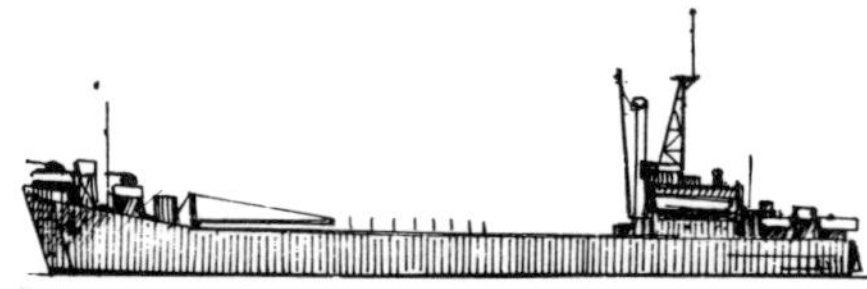

**636.** Am. **HARNETT COUNTY.** *821.* All details as for No. 635. Differs by the large kingposts before the bridge. Serving as base ship for LST's and helicopters.

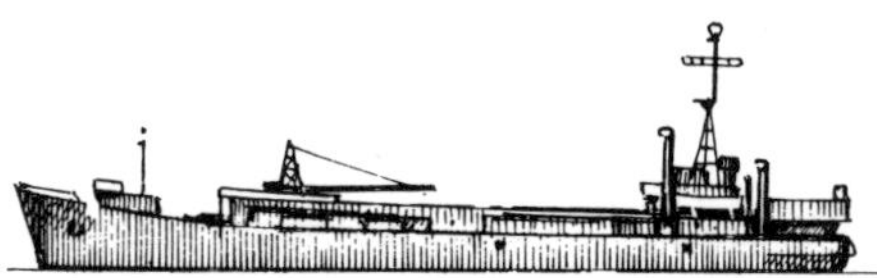

**637.** Ge. **ODIN.** *A512.* 1944. Converted 1965-66. Repair Ships Ex-U.S. Landing Ships. 1,600 tons. 328 x 50 x 11. (99.9 x 15.2 x 3.3). 2 screws; diesels. 11 knots.
**WOTAN.** *A513.*

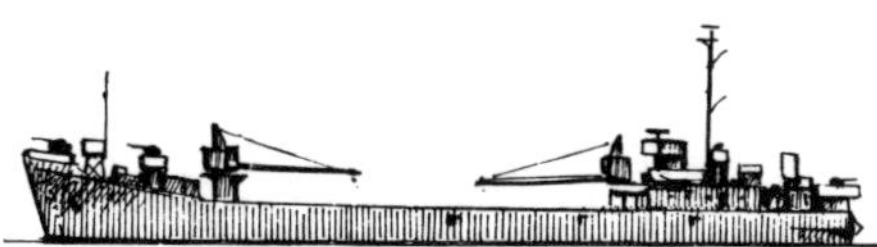

**638.** Ge. **BOCHUM.** *N120.* 1944 c. Converted 1961. Minelayers Ex-U.S. LST. All particulars as for No. 637.
**BOTTORP.** *N121.*

**639.** Pv. **CHIMBOTE.** *34.* 1943. Landing Ship; Ex-U.S. Particulars as for No. 637 but 10 knots speed and armed with 1—3-inch gun.

**640.** Am. Ex-**LST** Type. 1944. Converted. Repair Ships. All details as for No. 637.
**ACHELOUS.** *1,* **AMYCUS.** *2,* **ASKARI.** *30,* **ATLAS.** *7,* **BELLEROPHON.** *31,* **EGERIA.** *8,* **ENDYMION.** *9,* **INDRA.** *37,* **KRISHNA.** *38,* **SATYR.** *23,* **SPHINX.** *.24.*

Similar: Battle Damage Repair Craft:
**MIDAS.** *5,* **SARPEDON.** *7,* **TELAMON.** *8,* **ZEUS.** *4.*
Aircraft Repairs (Engines). **CHLORIS.** *4.*
Aircraft Repairs (Aircraft). **FABIUS.** *5.*
                        **MEGARA.** *6.*

Also similar: repair ships:
**SORAB.** Ir. Pole mast and large dome foreward.

**AKLAN.** Pi. Pole mast.

**641.** Br. Tank Landing Craft; Type 8. 650 tons. 231 x 39 x 5. (70 x 11.8 x 1.5). Diesels. 12 knots. Operated by British Army and there may be others.
**AGHEILA.** *L4002,* **ANDALNES.** *L4097.*

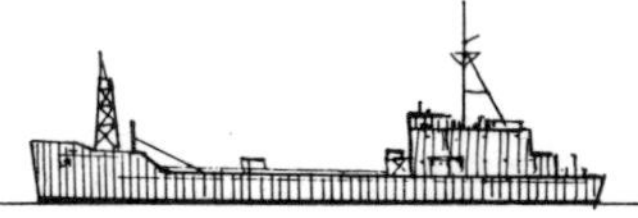

**642.** Br **ARROMANCHES.** *L4086.* All details as for No. 641.

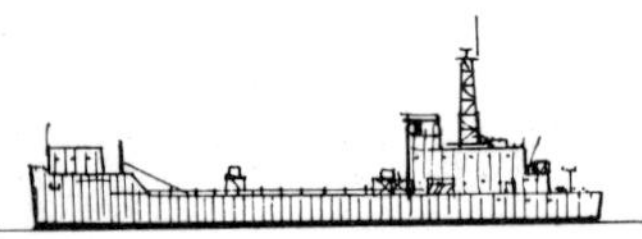

**643**. Br. **AKYAB**. *L4037*. All details as for No. 641.

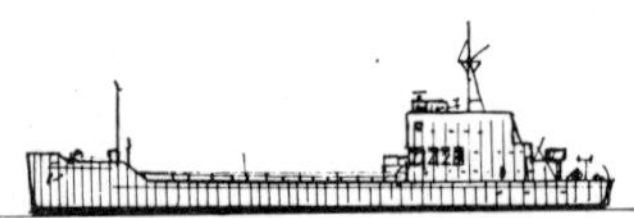

**644**. Br. **AUDEMER**. *L4061*. All details as for No. 641.

**645**. Am. **CARRONADE**. *IFS.1*. 1956. Inshore Fire Support Ship. 1,000 tons. 245 x 29 x 10. (74.6 x 11.8 x 3). 2 screws; diesels. 15 knots. 1—5-inch D.P. gun. 4 A.A. guns (twin). 8—5-inch rocket launchers.

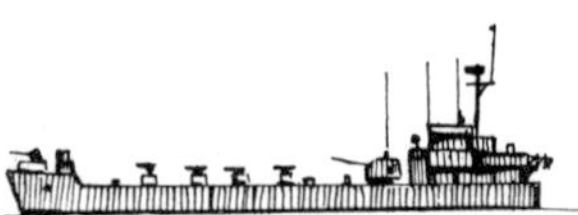

**646**. Am. **RIVER** class. 1945. Rocket Landing Ships. 1,000 tons. 205 x 35 x 10. (62.4 x 10.6 x 3). 2 screws. 12 knots. 1—5-inch D.P. guns. 4 A.A. guns (twin). 8—5-inch rocket launchers. **BIG BLACK RIVER**. *401*, **BROADKILL RIVER**. *405*, **CLARION RIVER**. *409*, **DES PLAINES RIVER**. *412*, **LAMOILLE RIVER**. *512*, **LARA-MIE RIVER**. *513*, **OWYHEE RIVER**. *515*, **RED RIVER**. *522*, **SMOKY HILL RIVER**. *531*. **WHITE RIVER**. *536*. Similar: Ko. **SI HUNG**.

**647**. Bm. **INLAY** class. Support Gunboats. Ex-British LCG(M) Type. 380 tons. 155 x 23 x 8. (47.2 x 7 x 2.4). 2 screws; diesels. 13 knots. 2—25-pdr. guns. (In gun houses abreast or "en echelon".) 2 smaller guns. **INDAW, INLAY, INMA, INYA**.

**648**. EG. **LABO** class. 1961-63. Landing Craft. 150 tons. 130 x 28 x 6. (39.6 x 8.5 x 1.8). Diesel. 10 knots. 4—25-m.m. A.A. guns (twin-abreast).

**649**. Ys. **D. 230**, Landing Craft.

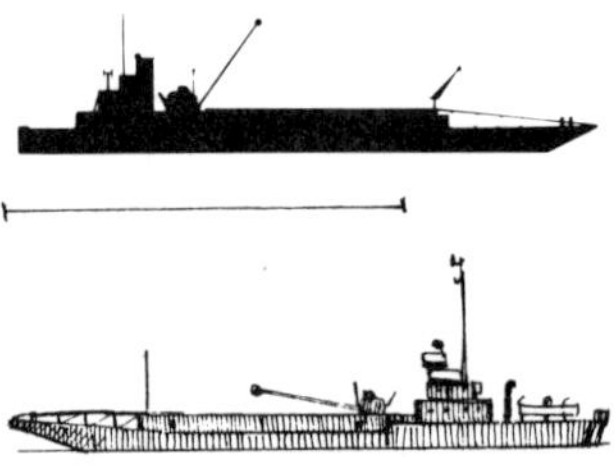

**650**. Ru. **MP. 10** Type. Landing Craft. 200 tons. 158 x 20 x 7. (48.1 x 6.1 x 2.1). Diesel. 10 knots. Capacity for 4 tanks. About 40 craft believed to exist. Similar to British LCT Type 4.

**651.** It. **MTC** Type. (Ex-German MFP type). Motor Transports. 240 tons. 164 x 21 x 6. (49.9 x 6.4 x 1.8). Diesel. 10 knots. 2 or 3 small A.A. guns. 13 vessels; **MTC. 1001** to **MTC. 1104** (excluding **MTC. 1002**).
See also silhouette No. 614.

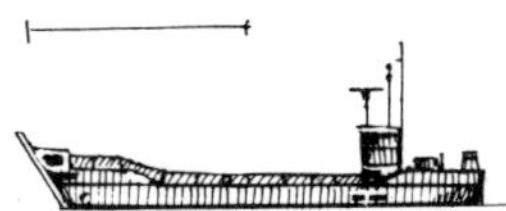

**652.** Br. **LCM** Type *9*. 1962-66. Landing Craft. 75 tons. 85 x 22 x 6. (25.9 x 6.7 x 1.8). 2 screws; diesels. 10 knots. 2 tanks or 100 tons of supplies. **LCM. 700, LCM. 711, LCM. 3507, LCM. 3508.**

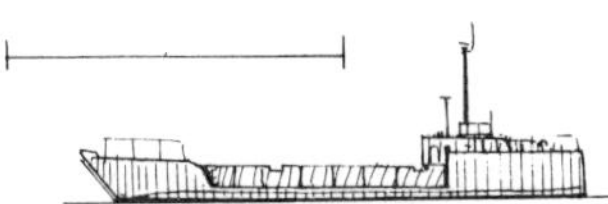

**653.** Am. **LCU.** 1610 series. Utility Landing Craft. 200 tons. 135 x 29 x 6. (41.1 x 8.8 x 1.8). 2 screws; diesels. 11 knots. 2—20-m.m. A.A. guns.
**LCU. 1625.**
Bm. **LCU. 1626.**
These 2 ships have superstructure aft as do others in the series. There is however no information as to which have this appearance so all other craft in the series are listed under No. 667.

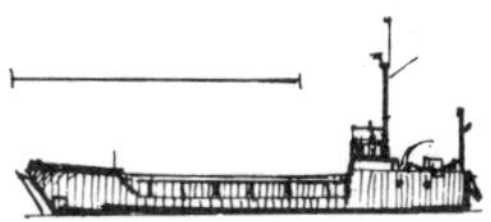

**655.** Le. **SOUR.** Ex-U.S. **LCU.** Landing Craft. Details as for No. 654.

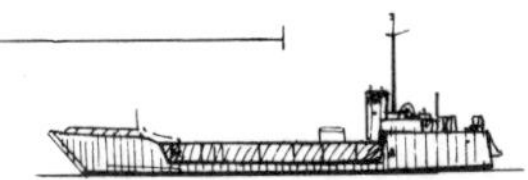

**654.** Am. **LCU.** *1466* series. Utility Landing Craft. 180 tons. 119 x 34 x 6. (36.3 x 10.3 x 1.8). 3 screws; diesels. 10 knots. 2—20-m.m. guns.
**LCU. 1466, LCU. 1467, LCU. 1468, LCY. 1469, LCU. 1470, LCU. 1471, LCU. 1472, LCU. 1473, LCU. 1475, LCU. 1476, LCU. 1477, LCU. 1481, LCU. 1482, LCU. 1483, LCU. 1484, LCU. 1485, LCU. 1486, LCU. 1487, LCU. 1488, LCU. 1489, LCU. 1490, LCU. 1491, LCU. 1492, LCU. 1493, LCU. 1494, LCU. 1495, LCU. 1497, LCU. 1498, LCU. 1499, LCU. 1500, LCU. 1525, LCU. 1535, LCU. 1536, LCU. 1537, LCU. 1539, LCU. 1547, LCU. 1548, LCU. 1559, LCU. 1576, LCU. 1582, LCU. 1608, LCU. 1609.**

Cs. **LCU. 1596, LCU. 1597, LCU. 1598, LCU. 1600, LCU. 1601.**
Do. **ENRIQUILLO, SAMANA.** Built 1957-58.
Ja. **LCU. 2001—LCU. 2006** (6 vessels).
VN. **HQ. 533—HQ. 539** (7 vessels).

**656.** Am. **LCU. 501** series. Utility Landing Craft. 143 tons. Details as for No. 654. Formerly **LSU.** (1949) and **LCU.** (1952).
**LCU. 539, LCU. 588, LCU. 599, LCU. 608, LCU. 654, LCU. 660, LCU. 666, LCU. 667, LCU. 674, LCU. 742, LCU. 768, LCU. 780, LCU. 803, LCU. 871, LCU. 893, LCU. 1045, LCU. 1124, LCU. 1241, LCU. 1348, LCU. 1387, LCU. 1430, LCU. 1451, LCU. 1459, LCU. 1462,**
Cs. **HO CHANG, HO CHEN, HO CHENG, HO CHIH, HO CHUN, HO CHUNG, HO CH'UNG.**

Cambodia. **T. 914, T. 915.**
Ch. **GRUMETE BOLADOS, GRUMETE DIAZ, GRUMETE TELLEZ.**
Gr. **LCU. 763, LCU. 766, LCU. 827, LCU. 852, LCU. 971, LCU. 1229, LCU. 1379, LCU. 1382.**
Th. **ARDANG, KOLUM, MATAPHON, PHE-TRA, RAWI, TALIBONG.**

RC. Ex-**HO CHEN**, Ex-**HO YUNG.** 

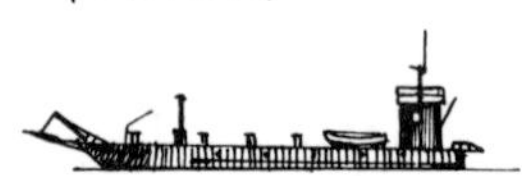

**657.** Fi. **KALA** class. 1959. Utility Landing Craft.
60 tons. 82 x 26 x 6. (24.9 x 7.9 x 1.8). Diesel.
9 knots.
**KALA. 1, KALA. 2, KALA. 3, KALA. 4, KALA.
5, KALA. 6.**

**658.** Sw. **L** Type. 1948. Landing Craft. 32 tons.
51 x 16 x 3. (15.5 x 4.8 x .9). Diesel. 8 knots.
**L. 51, L. 52, L. 53, L. 54, L. 55.**

**659.** Ex-U.S. Landing Craft **LSM** Type. 740 tons.
204 x 35 x 8. (62.1 x 10.6 x 2.4). 2 screws;
diesels. 12 knots. 1—40-m.m. A.A. gun (twin).
4—20-m.m. A.A. guns. (Armament may vary.)
Ar. **BDM. 1.**
Ch. **ASPIRANTE MOREL.**
Cs. 13 craft. **MEI CHIN, MEI HENG, MEI HO,
MEI PENG, MEI HUNG, MEI CHIEN, MEI
CHEN, MEI HWA, MEI HAN, MEI I, MEI
KUN, MEI LO, MEI SUNG, MEI WEN.**
Do. **SIRIO.**
Ec. **JAMBELI, TARQUI.**
Ge. (Mast slightly different and helicopter deck
aft.)
**EIDECHSE, KROKODIL, SALAMANDER,
VIPER.**
Gr. **IPOPLIARKHOS CRYSTALIDIS, IPOP-
LIARKHOS DANIOLOS, IPOPLIARKHOS
GRIGOROPOULOS, IPOPLIARKHOS MER-
LIN, IPOPLIARKHOS ROUSSEN, IPOPLIAR-
KHOS TOURNAS.**
Ja. (Slight forward extension of bridge and taller
topmast). **LSM. 3001.**
Pv. **ATICO, LOMAS.**
Pi. **BATANES, ISABELA, ORIENTAL MIN-
DORO.**
Sp. **LSM. 1, LSM. 2, LSM. 3.**
Th. **KRAM, KUT, PAI.**
Ve. **LOS FRAILES.** *T15,* **LOS MONJES.** *T13,*
**LOS ROQUES.** *T14,* **LOS TESTIGOSI.** *T16.*
VN. **HAU GIANG, HAN GIANG, HAT GIANG,
HUON GIANG, LAM GUANG, NINH GIANG,
TIEN GIANG.**

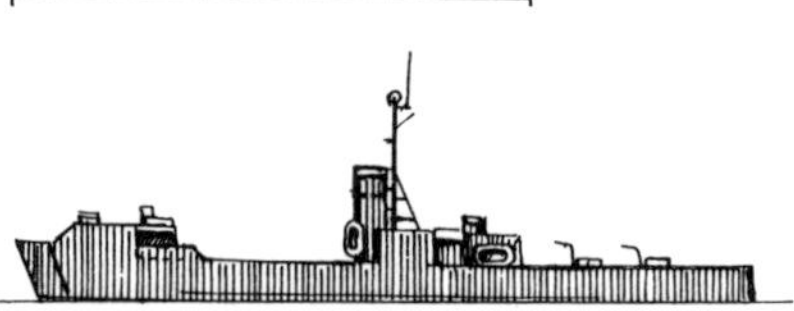

**660.** Ko. **LSM's.** All details as for No. 659.
**BIYOUP.** *602,* **KA DUK.** *605,* **KI RIN.** *610,*
**KU MOON.** *606,* **NEUNG RA.** *611,* **PUNG DO.**
*608,* **SIN MI.** *612,* **TAE CHO.** *601,* **ULRYUNG.**
*613,* **WOLMI.** *609,* **YEU DO.** *602.*

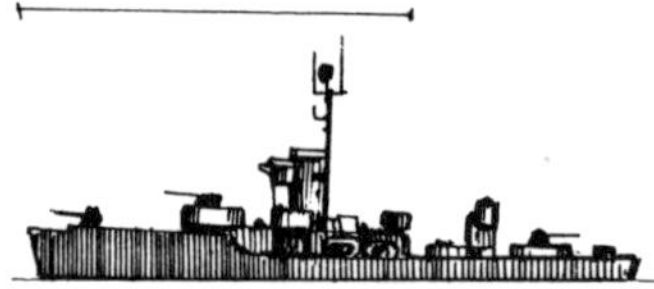

**661.** Gr. **PLOTARKHIS MARIDAKIS.** *94.*
Patrol Vessel Ex-U.S. **LSM** Type. 260 tons.
157 x 23 x 6. (47.8 x 6.7 x 1.8). 2 screws;
diesels. 14 knots. 1—3-inch gun. 8 A.A. guns.
**PLOTARKHIS VLACHAVAS.**
It. (Classes as Support Gunboats and have a
speed of 12 knots.)
**ALANO, BRACO, MASTINO, MOLOSSO,
SEGUGIO, SPINONE.**

**662.** VN. Ex-U.S. **LSSL** Type. Landing Ships.
227 tons. 158 x 24 x 6. (48.1 x 7.3 x 1.8).
2 screws; diesels. 14 knots. 1—3-inch gun. 4—
40-m.m. guns. 4—20-m.m. guns.
**DOAN NGOC TANG, LE VAN BINH, LINH
KIEM, LUO PHU THO, NO THAN, NGUYEN
DUC BONG, NGUEN NGOC LONG.**
Also probably
Th. **NAKA.** *LSSL3.*

**663.** Ex-U.S. **LSIL** Type. Landing Craft. Cs. 227 tons. 159 x 24 x 6. (48.4 x 7.3 x 1.6). 2 screws. 14 knots. 2—20-m.m. A.A. guns( varies). **LIEN CHENG, LIEN CHU, LIEN HUA, LIEN LI, LIEN SHENG.**

**664.** Ar. Infantry **LANDING CRAFT.** Ex-U.S. Type. All details as for No. 663. **BDI. 1, BDI. 4, BDI. 15.**

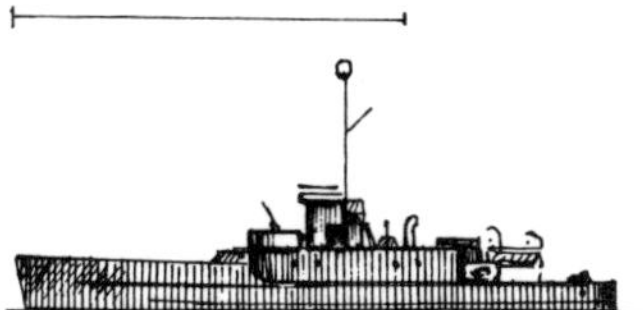

**665.** Th. **PRAB.** *1.* Landing Craft. Ex-U.S. LCI Type. (LSIL). Details as for No. 663. **SATAKUT.** *2.*
Ir. **GHASM, HENGAM, LARAK.**

**666.** Ge. **LACHS** class. 1965-66. Landing Craft. 200 tons. 137 x 29 x 5. (41.7 x 8.8 x 1.5). 2 screws; diesels. 12 knots. 1—20-m.m. A.A. gun. **BARBE.** *L790,* **BRASSE.** *L789,* **BUTT.** *L788,* **DELPHIN.** *L791,* **DORSCH.** *L792,* **FELCHEN.** *L793,* **FLUNDER.** *L760,* **FORELLE.** *L794,* **INGER.** *L759,* **KARPFEN.** *L761,* **LACHS.** *L762,* **MAKRELE.** *L796,* **MURANE.** *L797,* **PLOTZE.** *L763,* **REMKE.** *L798,* **ROCHEN.** *L764,* **SALM.** *L799,* **SCHLEIE.** *L765,* **STOR.** *L766,* **TUMM-LER.** *L767,* **WELS.** *L768,* **ZANDER.** *L769.*

**667.** Am. **LCU. 1610** Series. Utility Landing Craft. 200 tons. 135 x 29 x 6. (41.1 x 8.8 x 1.8). 2 screws; diesels. 11 knots. 2—20-m.m. A.A. guns.
See No. 653 for ships with different appearance. **LCU. 1610—1624, LCU. 1627—1636.**

**668.** Co. **ALBERTO GOMEZ.** *TF53.* 1953-55. Transports. 70 tons. 82 x 18 x 3. (24.9 x 5.4 x .9). Diesels. 9 knots. **HERNANDO GUTIERREZ.** *TF52,* **MARIO SERPA.** *TF51.*

**669.** Sw. **SKAGUL.** *A333.* 1960. Landing Craft. 355 tons. 188 x 28 x 9. (57.3 x 8.5 x 2.7). Motor. 12 knots. Double-ended ferry type. **SLEIPNER.** *A335.*

**670.** Sw. **BORE.** 1961-66. Landing Craft. 380 tons. 117 x 28 x 9. (35.6 x 8.5 x 2.7). Diesels. 12 knots. All vessels may not be the same in appearance. **GRIM** (May have funnels), **HEIMDAL.**

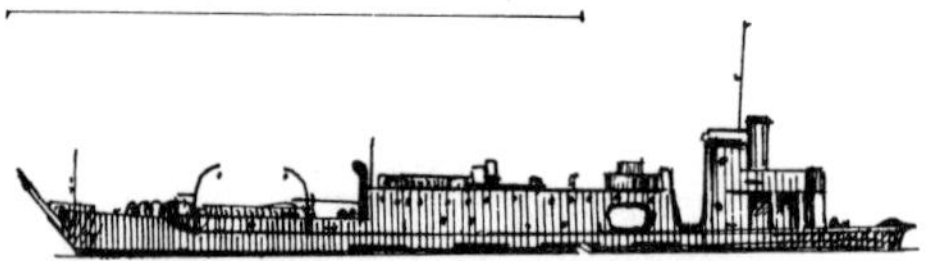

**671** *Gh.* **ASUANTSI.** Repair Craft. Ex-British Landing Craft. 660 tons. 231 x 39 x 5. (68.5 x 11.8 x 1.5). Motor vessel. 9 knots.

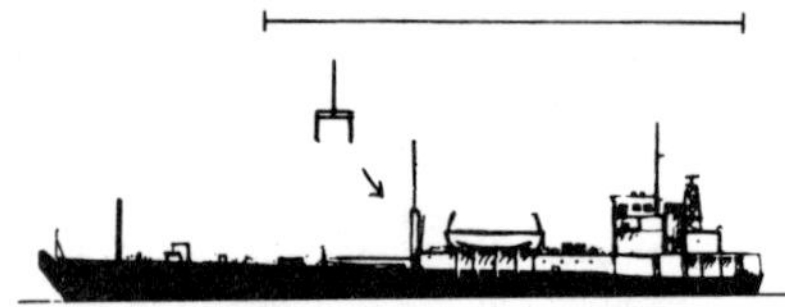

**672.** Br. **WHIMBREL.** Experimental Vessel. 300 tons. 190 x 30 x 5. (57.9 x 9.1 x 1.5). Originally a basic Tank Landing Craft—Type 3.

## MINESWEEPER TYPES

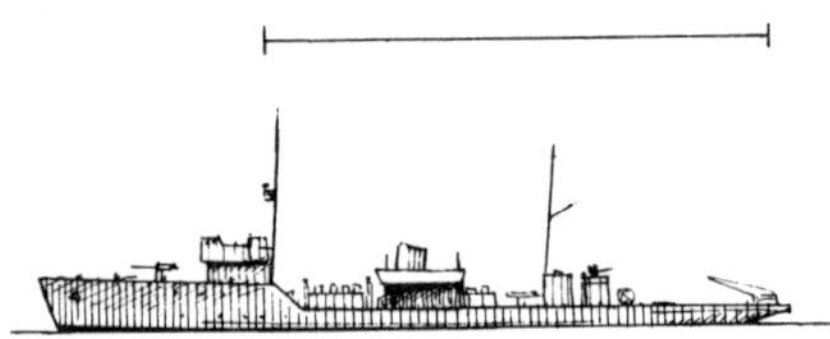

★ **673.** RK. **FUGAS** Type. Fleet Minesweepers. 440 tons. 204 x 24 x 8. (62.1 x 7.3 x 2.4). 2 screws. 18 knots. 1—3.9-inch gun. 1—37-m.m. A.A. gun.
Also serve as minelayers.

★ **674.** Ru. **T. 58** class. 1959 onwards. Fleet Mine-sweepers. 900 tons. 230 x 30 x 9. (70.1 x 9.1 x 2.7). 2 screws; diesels. 18 knots. 4—57-m.m. A.A. guns.
About 20 units in the Soviet Fleet but some have been converted into submarine rescue ships without armament or mine-sweeping gear. See No. 675.

★ **675.** Ru. **T. 58** class. Submarine Rescue Vessels. See No. 674.

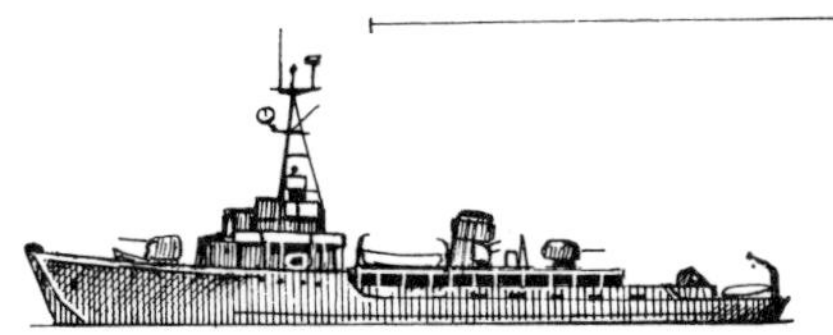

**676.** Ru. **T. 43** class. 1948-57. Fleet Minesweepers. 500 tons. 190 x 28 x 9. (57.9 x 8.5 x 2.7). 2 screws; diesels. 17 knots. 4—37-m.m. A.A. guns and smaller A.A. guns.

Principally distinguished from **T.** *58* type by having funnel further aft; some ships have a pole mast and others have been converted into radar pickets. See No. 356. About 120 units in the Soviet Fleet.

Al. 2 ships.

Bu. 3 ships.

Eg. **BAHAIRA, CHARKIEH, GHARBIA, MINIYA.**

Po. **BIZON, BOBR, DELFIN, DZIK, FOKA, LOS, MORS, ROSOMAIL, TUR, ZBIK, ZUBR.**

RK. 2 ships.

Sy. **HITTINE, YARMOUK.**

RC. 20 ships.

Ia. 2 ships.

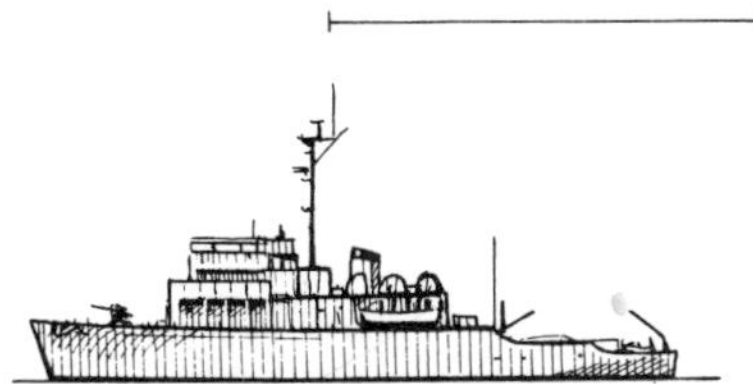

**679.** Am. **ACME** class. 1956-57. Ocean Minesweepers. 720 tons. 173 x 35 x 10. (52.7 x 10.6 x 3). 2 screws; diesel. 14 knots. 2—20-m.m. A.A. guns.

**ACME.** *508,* **ADROIT.** *509,* **ADVANCE.** *510,* **AFFRAY.** *511.*

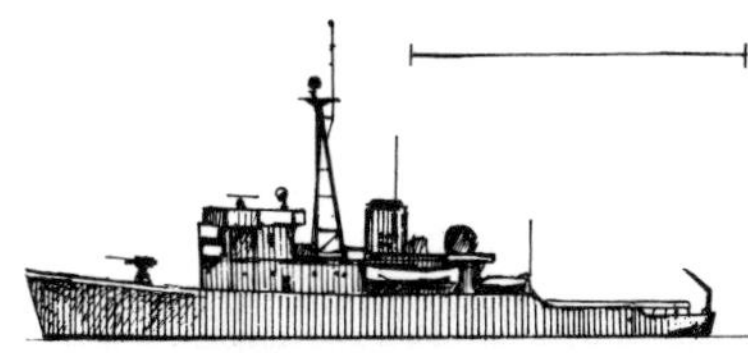

**677.** Am. **ABILITY** class. 1957. Ocean Minesweepers. 810 tons. 190 x 36 x 15. (57.9 x 10.9 x· 4.5). 2 screws; diesels. 15 knots. 1—40-m.m. A.A. gun.

**ABILITY,** *519,* **ALACRITY.** *520,* **ASSURANCE.** *521.*

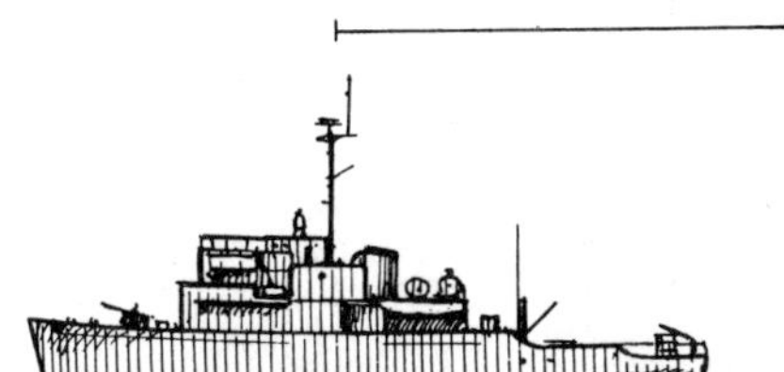

**678.** Am. **AGILE** class. 1952-55. Ocean Minesweepers. 650 tons. 173 x 35 x 10. (52.7 x 10.7 x 2). 2 screws; diesels. 15 knots. 2—20-m.m. A.A. guns.

Some ships have very small funnel like those serving in some NATO Navies.

**AGILE.** *421,* **AGGRESSIVE.** *422,* **BOLD.** *424,* **BULWARK.** *425,* **CONFLICT.** *426,* **CONQUEST.** *488,* **CONSTANT.** *427,* **DASH.** *428,* **DETECTOR.** *429,* **DIRECT.** *430,* **DOMINANT.** *431,* **DYNAMIC.** *432,* **ENBATTLE.** *433,* **ENDURANCE.** *435,* **ENERGY.** *436,* **ENGAGE.** *433,* **ENHANCE.** *437,* **ESTEEM.** *438,* **EXCEL.** *439,* **EXPLOIT.** *440,* **EXULTANT.** *441,* **FEARLESS.** *442,* **FIDELITY.** *443,* **FIRM.** *444,* **FORCE.** *445,* **FORTIFY.** *446,* **GALLANT.** *489,* **GUIDE.** *447,* **ILLUSIVE.** *448,* **IMPERVIOUS.** *449,* **IMPLICIT.** *455,* **INFLICT.** *456,* **LEADER.** *490,* **LOYALTY.** *457,* **LUCID.** *458,* **NIMBLE.** *459,* **NOTABLE.** *460,* **OBSERVER.** *461,* **PERSISTANT.** *491,* **PINNACLE.** *462,* **PIVOT.** *463,* **PLEDGE.** *492,* **PLUCK.** *464,* **PRIME.** *466,* **REAPER.** *467,* **RIVAL.** *468,* **SAGACITY.** *469,* **SALUTE.** *470,* **SKILL.** *471,* **STURDY.** *494,* **SWERVE.** *495,* **VALOR.** *472,* **VIGOR.** *473,* **VENTURE.** *496,* **VITAL.** *474.*

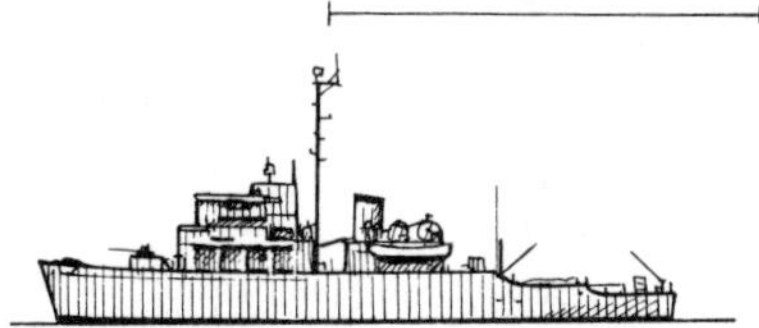

**680.** Be. Ex-U.S. MSO **ACME** Type 498. Ocean Minesweepers. 1956-60. Dimensions as for No. 679. 1—40-m.m. gun.

**A. F. DUFOUR.** *M903,* **ARTEVELDE.** *M907,* **BREYDEL.** *M906,* **DE BROUWER.** *M904,* **F. BOVESSE.** *M909,* **G. TRUFFAUT.** *M908,* **VAN HAVERBEKE.** *M902.*

Fr. **AUTUN.** *M622,* **BACCARAT.** *M623,* **BERLAIMONT.** *M620,* **COLMAR.** *M624,* **NARVIK.** *M609,* **ORIGNY.** *M621,* **OUISTREHAM.** *M610.*

It. **SALMONE.** *M5430,* **SGOMBRO.** *M5432,* **SQUALO.** *M5433,* **STORIONE.** *M5431.*

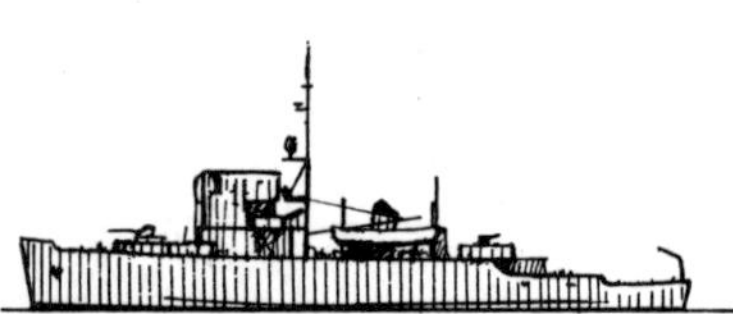

**681.** Am. **ADMIRABLE** class. 1943-44. Fleet Minesweepers. 650 tons. 185 x 33 x 10. (56 x 10 x 3). 2 screws; diesels. 15 knots. 1—3-inch D.P. gun. 4—40-m.m. A.A. guns.
**COUNSEL.** *165,* **CRUISE.** *215,* **SPECTRE.** *306,* **SUPERIOR.** *311.*
Bm. **YAN GYI AUNG.** (Patrol vessel). May have no funnel.
Cs. **YUNG CHIA.** *47,* **YUNG FENG.** *50,* **YUNG HSIU.** *48.*
Do. **SEPARACION.** *454,* **TORTUGUERO.** *455.*
ME. **DM. 02, DM. 11** and the following, some of which may not have funnels.
**DM. 01, DM. 03, DM. 04, DM. 05, DM. 06, DM. 07, DM. 08, DM. 09, DM. 10, DM. 12, DM. 13, DM. 14, DM. 15, DM. 17, DM. 18, DM. 20.**
VN. **CHI LANG II.** *HQ08,* **CHI LINH.** *HQ11,* **KU HOA.** *HQ09,* **NHUT TAO.** *HQ10.*

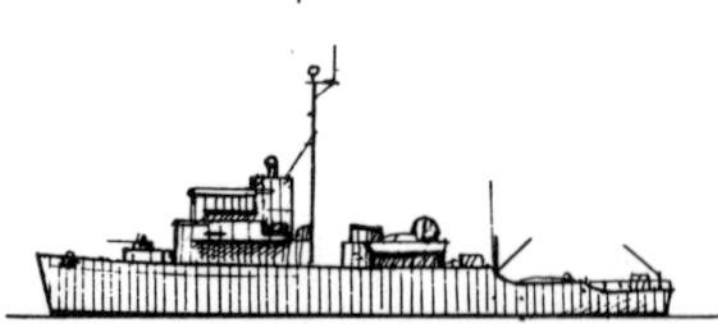

**682.** Ex-U.S. **AGILE** class. 1953. Coastal Minesweepers. 700 tons. 171 x 35 x 10. (52.1 x 10.6 x 3). 2 screws; diesels. 10 to 14 knots. 1—40-m.m. A.A. gun. Have very small funnels.
Fr. **ALENCON.** *M612,* **BERNEVAL.** *M613,* **BIR HACHEIM.** *M614,* **CANTHO.** *M615,* **DOMPAIRE.** *M616,* **GARGLIANO.** *M617,* **MYTHO.** *M618,* **VINH LONG.** *M619.*
Du. **ONVERSAAGD.** *A854,* **ONBEVREESD.** *A855,* **ONVERSCHROKKEN.** *A856,* **ONVER-MOEID.** *A857,* **ONVERVAAED.** *A858,* **ON-VERDROTEN.** *A859.*
Po. **CORVO.** *M418,* **PICO.** *M416,* **GRACIOSA.** *M417,* **S. JORGE.** *M415.*

**683.** Ru. **YURKA** class. 1964. Fleet Minesweepers. 500 tons. 165 x 28 x 7. (50.2 x 8.5 x 2.1). 2 screws; diesels. 15 knots. 4—25-m.m. A.A. guns.
There are some 30 in the Soviet Navy.

**684.** Ge. **LINDAU** class. 1957. Coastal Minesweepers. 370 tons. 148 x 27 x 9. (45.1 x 8.2 x 2.7). 2 screws; diesel. 17 knots. 1—40-m.m. A.A. gun.
Some ships have been converted into minehunters with armament removed and they retain the high bridge. See No. 685.
**CUXHAVEN.** *M1078,* **DUREN.** *M1079,* **GOTTINGEN.** *M1070,* **KOBLENZ.** *M1071,* **KONSTANZ.** *M1081,* **LINDAU.** *M1072,* **MARBURG.** *M1080,* **MINDEN.** *M1085,* **PADERBORN.** *M1076,* **SCHLESWIG.** *M1073,* **TUBINGEN.** *M1074,* **ULM.** *M1083,* **VOLKLINGEN.** *M1087,* **WEILHEIM.** *M1077,* **WETZLAR.** *M1075,* **WOLFSBURG.** *'M1082.*

**685.** Ge. **LINDAU** class. 1957. Minhunters. Details as for No. 684 but armament removed. There may be others converted.
**FLENSBURG.** *M1084,* . **FULDA.** *M1068.*

**686.** Ru. **T.** *301* class. 1943-56. Coastal Mine-sweepers etc. 130 tons. 125 x 16 x 5. (38.1 x 4.8 x 1.5). 2 screws; diesels. 10 knots. 2—37-m.m. A.A. guns. 2—25-m.m. A.A. guns.
Some ships may have vertical mast and funnel. Being withdrawn from service in Russian Fleet and many converted to coastal survey ships or auxiliary services. Probably 60 still in service.

Al. 6 ships.
Bu. 4 ships.

Rm. 22 ships.

Eg. **EL FAYUH, EL HANUFIEH.**

Ia. At least 1 unit.

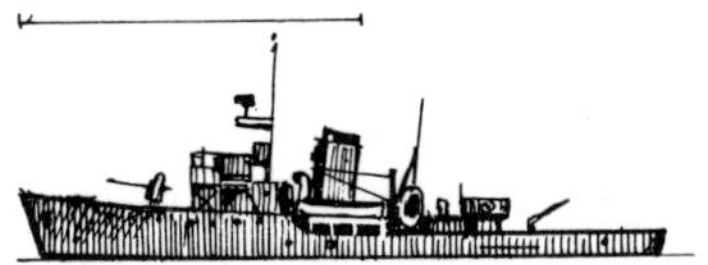

**687.** Sp. **PEGASO.** 1951. Patrol Vessels. 440 tons. 138 x 27 x 10. (42 x 8.2 x 2). Diesel. 12 knots. 2—20-m.m. A.A. guns.
**PROCYON.**

**688.** Ge. **VEGESACK** class. 1958. Coastal Minesweepers. 333 tons. 146 x 27 x 9. (44.5 x 8.2 x 2.7). 2 screws; diesels. 15 knots. 2—20-m.m. A.A. guns.
**DETMOLD.** *M1252,* **HAMELN.** *M1251,* **PAS-SAU.** *M1255,* **SIEGEN.** *M1254.* **VEGESACK.** *M1250,* **WORMS.** *M1253.*
Fr. **MERCURE.** *M765.*

**689.** Br. **TON** class. 1954. Ocean Minesweepers. 360 tons. 152 x 29 x 8. (46.3 x 8.8 x 2.4). 2 screws; diesels. 15 knots.
There are two main types—1. With light tripod mast and frigate bridge. 2. With lattice mast.
Ships also vary slightly in appearance in other ways and some have an A.A. gun foreward. Conversions to minehunters have kingpost removed; see No. 691. Others serve as R.N.R. Training ships.

The following vessels have a lattice foremast:
**ALVERTON.** *M1104,* **BELTON.** *M1199,* **BIL-DESTON.** *M1110,* **BOSSINGTON.** *M1133,* **CURZON.** *M1136,* **GLASSERTON.** *M1141,* **HIGHBURTON.** *M1130,* **KILLIECRANKIE.** *M1109,* **MONKTON.** *M1155,* **STUBBING-TON.** *M1204,* **SHAVINGTON.** *M1180,* **UP-TON.** *M1187,* **VENTURER.** *M1146,* **WASPER-TON.** *M1189,* **WOTTON.** *M1195,* **YARNTON.** *M1196.*

Appearance of following British ships doubtful:
**BLAXTON.** *M1132,* **BRERETON.** *M1113,* **BRINTON.** *M1114,* **CLYDE.** *M1105,* **CUXTON.** *M1125,* **HUBBERSTON.** *M1147,* **KEDLES-TON.** *M1153,* **KELLINGTON.** *M1154,* **KIL-MOREY.** *M1103,* **LEVERTON.** *M1161,* **MAD-DISTON.** *M1164,* **MAXTON.** *M1165,* **OUL-STON.** *M1129,* **ST. DAVID.** *M1124.*

Gh. **EJURA.** *M16.* (Lattice foremast and Black Star on funnel.)
My. (Lattice foremast.)
**BRINCHANG.** *M1168,* **JERAI.** *M1168,* **KINA-BALU.** *M1134,* **LEDANG.** *M1143,* **MAHAM-IRU.** *M1127,* **TAHAN.** *M1163.*
Po. (Lattice foremast.)
**LAGOA.** *M403,* **RIBEIRA GRANDE.** *M402,* **ROSARIO.** *M404,* **S. ROQUE.** *M401.*
SA. (Lattice mast.)
**PRETORIA.** *M1144.*

The following vessels have lattice mast but no gun; see silhouette No. 776.
Br. **BEACHAMPTON.** *M1107,* **LALESTON.** *M1158,* **SHOULTON.** *M1182.*
In. **CANNANORE.** *M1191,* **CUDDALORE.** *M1190,* **KAKINDA.** *M1201,* **KARWAR.** *M1197.*

Br. **TON** class

**690.** Ships with Tripod foremast.
Br. **ASHTON.** *M1198,* **BRONINGTON.** *M1115,*
**CHAWTON.** *M1209,* **GAVINGTON.** *M1140,*
**HOUGHTON.** *M1211,* **IVESTON.** *M1151,*
**KIRKLISTON.** *M1157,* **LEWISTON.** *M1208,*
**MONTROSE.** *M1126,* **NORTHUMBRIA.**
*M1175,* **NURTON.** *M1166,* **MERSEY.** *M1173,*
**PUNCHESTON** *M1174,* **SHERATON.** *M1181*
**SOBERTON.** *M1200,* **WALKERTON.** *M1188,*
**WILKIESTON.** *M1192,* **WOLVERTON.** *M1193,*
Ar. **CHUBUT.** *3,* **NEUQUEN.** *1,* **RIO NEGRO.**
*2,* **TIERRA DEL FUEGO.** *4.*
SA. **DURBAN.** *M1499,* **EAST LONDON.**
*M1215,* **JOHANNESBURG.** *M1207,* **KAAP-
STAD.** *M1142,* **KIMBERLEY.** *M1210,* **MOS-
SELBAU.** *M1213,* **PORT ELIZABETH.** *M1212,*
**WALVISBAI.** *M1214,* **WINDHOEK.** *M1498.*

The following vessels have tripod mast but no
gun; see silhouette No. 776.
Au. **CURLEW, GULL, HAWK, IBIS, SNIPE,
TEAL.**

**691.** Br. **TON** class but converted in 1968,
kingpost removed and serving as minehunters.
**BOSSINGTON.** *M1133,* **BRERETON.** *M1113,*
**DERRITON.** *M1128,* **GLASSERTON.** *M1141,*
**HIGHBURTON.** *M1130,* **KELLINGTON.**
*M1154,* **KIRKLISTON.** *M1157,* **IVESTON.**
*M1151,* **SHERATON.** *M1181.*

Ar. **CHACO.** *5,* **FORMOSA.** *6.*

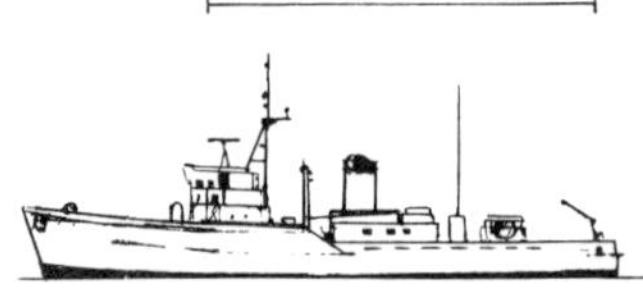

**692.** My. **PERANTAU.** Ex-"Ton" class minesweepers. Coastal Survey Craft. No armament.

**693.** Fr. **SIRIUS** class. 1953-56. Coastal Mine-
sweepers. 365 tons. 152 x 28 x 8. (46.3 x 8.5 x
2.4). 2 screws; gas turbine or diesel. 15 knots.
1—40-m.m. A.A. gun. Practically the same as
British "Ton" class.
**ACHERNAR.** *M744,* **ALDEBARAN.** *M705,*
**ALGOL.** *M704,* **ALTAIR.** *M736,* **ANTARES.**
*M703,* **ARCTURUS.** *M746,* **ARIES.** *M758,*
**BELLATRIX.** *M750,* **BETELGEUSE.** *M747,*
**CANOPUS.** *M754,* **CAPELLA.** *M755,* **CAPRI-
CORNE.** *M737,* **CASSIOPE.** *M740,* **CASTOR.**
*M708,* **CENTAURE.** *M752,* **CEPHEE.** *M756,*
**CROIX DU SUD.** *M734,* **DENEBOLA.** *M751,*
**ERIDAN.** *M741,* **ETOILE POLAIRE.** *M755,*
**FOMALHAUT.** *M753,* **LYRE.** *M759,* **ORION.**
*M742,* **PEGASE.** *M710,* **PERSEE.** *M748,*
**PHENIX.** *M749,* **POLLUX.** *M709,* **PROCYON.**
*M745,* **REGULUS.** *M706,* **RIGEL.** *M702,*
**SAGITTAIRE.** *M743,* **SIRIUS.** *M701,* **VEGA.**
*M707,* **VERSEAU.** *M757.*

Similar. (Light tripod mast.)
Du. **ABCOUDE.** *M810,* **DOKKUM.** *M801,*
**DRACHTEN.** *M812,* **DRUNEN.** *M818,* **GEM-
ERT.** *M841,* **GIETHOORN.** *M815,* **HOOGE-
ZAND.** *M802,* **HOOGEVEEN.** *M827,* **NAALD-
WIJK.** *M809,* **NAARDEN.** *M823,* **OMMEN.**
*M813,* **RHENEN.** *M844,* **ROERMOND.** *M806,*
**SITTARD.** *M830,* **STAPHORST.** *M828,*
**VEERE.** *M842,* **VENLO.** *M817,* **WOERDEN.**
*M820.*

Ys. **HRABRY, SLOBODNI, SMELI, SNAZNI.** ★

**694.** Fr. **DUNKERQUOISE** class Ex-Canadian "Bay" class. 1952-53. Coastal Minesweepers. 390 tons. 152 x 28 x 9. (46.3 x 8.5 x 2.7). 2 screws; diesels. 16 knots. 1—40-m.m. A.A. gun.
**LA BAYONNAISE.** *M728,* **LA DIEPPOISE.** *M730,* **LA DUNKERQUOISE.** *M726,* **LA LORIENTAISE.** *M731,* **LA MALOUINE.** *M727,* **LA PAIMPOLAISE.** *M729.*

Tu. **TIREBOLU.** *M524,* **TEKIRDAG.** *M525,* **TERME.** *M523,* **TRABZON.** *M522.*

**695.** Ca. **BAY** class. 1955-57. Coastal Minesweepers. All details as for No. 694. Have a much smaller funnel than the French and Turkish vessels.
**CHALEUR.** *164,* **CHIGNECTO.** *160,* **COWICHAN.** *162,* **FUNDY.** *159,* **MIRAMICHI.** *163,* **THUNDER.** *161.*

**696.** Am. **ALBATROSS** class Ex-YMS. 1941-43. Coastal Minesweepers. 270 tons. 136 x 25 x 8. (41.4 x 7.6 x 2.4). 2 screws; diesels. 15 knots. 1—40-m.m. A.A. gun. 1—3-inch A.A. gun.
**FULMAR.** *47,* **PLOVER.** *33,* **SISKIN.** *58,* **TURKEY.** *56.*
Ag. **SIDI FRADJ.**
Gr. **AFROESSA.** *M209,* **KALYMNOS.** *M201,* **KARTERIA.** *M203,* **KERKYRA.** *M208,* **PARALOS.** *M204,* **ZAKYNTHOS.** *M212.*
Ja. **YAKUSHIMA.** (Used only for training purposes.)
Ko.**KIMCHON.** *513,* **KIMPO.** *520,* **KOCHANG.** *521,* **KUM HWA.** *519,,* **KWANG CHE.** *503.*

★ RC. Possibly 4 vessels.

**697.** Am. **BITTERN.** 1957. Coastal Minehunter. 300 tons. 145 x 28 x 8. (44.1 x 8.5 x 2.4). 2 screws; diesels. 14 knots.
This vessel remains on the Navy List although temporary on charter to.a commercial firm.

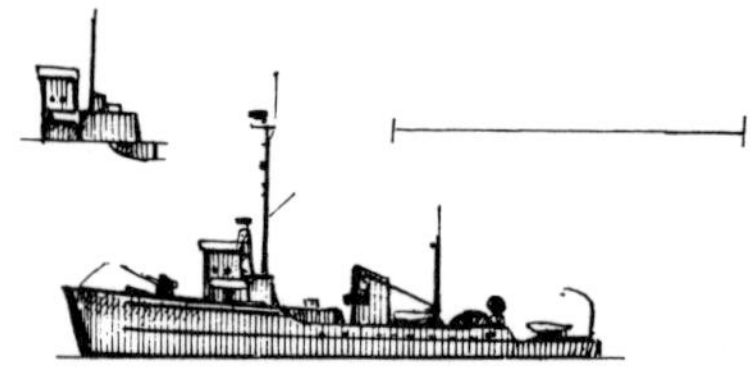

**698.** Am. **BLUEBIRD** class. 1950 and onwards. Coastal Minesweepers. 320 tons. 144 x 28 x 8. (43.8 x 8.5 x 2.4). 2 screws; diesels. 14 knots. 2 A.A. guns (twin).
**BLUEBIRD.** *121,* **CORMORANT.** *122,* **FALCON.** *190,* **FRIGATE BIRD.** *191,* **HUMMING BIRD.** *192,* **JACANA.** *193,* **KING BIRD.** *194,* **LIMPKIN.** *195,* **MEADOW LARK.** *196,* **PARROT.** *197,* **PEACOCK.** *198,* **PHOEBE.** *199,* **SHRIKE.** *201,* **THRASHER.** *203,* **THRUSH.** *204,* **VIREO.** *205,* **WARBLER.** *206,* **WHIPPORWILL.** *207,* **WIDGEON.** *208,* **WOODPECKER.** *209.*

Be. **BLANKENBERGE.** *M923,* **CHARLEROI.** *M917,* **DE PANNE.** *M925,* **DIEST.** *M910,* **DIKSMUIDE.** *M920,* **EEKLO.** *M911,* **HEIST.** *M929,* **HERVE.** *M921,* **KNOKKE.** *M931,* **KOKSIJDE.** *M923,* **LAROCHE.** *M924,* **LIER.** *M912,* **MAASEIK.** *M913,* **MALMEDY.** *M922,* **NIEUWPORT.** *M932,* **ROCHEFORT.** *M930,* **ST. NIKLAAS.** *M918,* **ST. TRUIDEN.** *M919,* **SPA.** *M927,* **STAVELOT.** *M928,* **VERVIERS.** *M934,* **VEURNE.** *M935.*

Da. **AAROSUND.** *M571,* **ALSSUND.** *M572,* **EGERNSUND.** *M573,* **GRONSUND.** *M574,* **GULDBORGSUND.** *M575,* **OMOSUND.** *M576,* **ULVSUND.** *M577,* **VILSUND.** *M578.*

Fr. **ACACIA.** *M638,* **ACANTHE.** *M639,* **AJONC.** *M667,* **AZELEE.** *M668,* **BEGONIA.** *M669,* **BLEUET.** *M670,* **CAMELIA.** *M671,* **CHRYSABTHEME.** *M672,* **COQUELICOT.** *M673,* **CYCLAMEN.** *M674,* **EGLANTINE.** *M675,* **GARDENIA.** *M676,* **GIROFLEE.** *M671,* **GLAIEUL.** *M678,* **GLYCINE.** *M679,* **JACINTHE.** *M680,* **LAURIER.** *M681,* **LILAS.** *M682,* **LISERON.** *M683,* **LOBELIA.** *M684,* **MAGNOLIA.** *M685,* **MARJOLAINE.** *M000,* **MIMOSA.** *M687,* **MUGUET.** *M688,* **PERVENCHE.** *M632,* **PIOVINE.** *M633,* **RESEDA.** *M635.*

It. **AGAVE** class. **AGAVE.** *M5331,* **ALLORO.** *M5532,* **EDERA.** *M5533,* **GAGGIA.** *M5534,* **GEISOMINO.** *M5535,* **GIAGGIOLO.** *M5536,* **GLICINE.** *M5537,* **LOTO.** *M5538,* **MIRTO.** *M5539,* **TIMO.** *M5540,* **TRIFOGLIO.** *M5541,* **VISCHIO.** *M5542,* **BAMBO.** *M5521,* **EBANO.** *M5522,* **MANGO.** *M5523,* **MOGANO.** *M5524,* **PALMA.** *M5525,* **ROVERE.** *M5526,* **SANDALO.** *M5527.*

**ABETE** class. **ABETE.** *M5501,* **ACACIA.** *M5502,* **BETULLA.** *M5503,* **CASTAGNO.** *M5504,* **CEDRO.** *M5505,* **CILIEGIO.** *M5506,* **FAGGIO.** *M5507,* **FRASSINO.** *M5508,* **GELSO.** *M5509,* **LARICE.** *M5510,* **MANDORLO.** *M5519,* **NOCE.** *M5511,* **OLMO.** *M5512,* **ONTANO.** *M5513,* **PINO.** *M5514,* **PIOPPO.** *M5515,* **PLATANO.** *M5516,* **QUERCIA.** *M5517*

Du. **BEEMSTER.** *M845,* **BEDUM.** *M847,* **BEILEN.** *M848,* **BLARICUM.** *M853,* **BOLSWARD.** *M846,* **BORCULO.** *M849,* **BORNE.** *M850,* **BREUKELEN.** *M852,* **BRIELLE.** *M854,* **BRESKENS.** *M855,* **BOXTEL.** *M857,* **BROUWERSHAVEN.** *M858,* **BRUINISSE.** *M856,* **BRUMMEN.** *M851.*

Ja. **HASHIMA, TOSHIMA, TSUSHIMA, YASHIMA.**

No. **ALTA.** *M314,* **GLOMMA.** *M317,* **KVINA.** *M332,* **OGNA.** *M315,* **SAUDA.** *M311,* **SIRA.** *M312,* **TANA.** *M313,* **TISTA.** *M331,* **UTLA.** *M334,* **VOSSO.** *M316.*

Pi. **ZAMBALES.** *55,* **ZAMBOANGA DEL NORTE.** *56.*

Po. **ANGRA DO HEROISMO.** *M407,* **HORTA.** *M406,* **LAJES.** *M411,* **PONTA DELGADA.** *M405,* **SANTA CRUZ.** *M409,* **S. PEDRO.** *M412,* **VELAS.** *M410,* **VILA DO PORTO.** *M408.*

Sp. **ULLA.** *M24.*

Tu. **PAVOT, RENONCULE.** Transferred from France. New names not known.

Ur. **RIO NEGRO.**

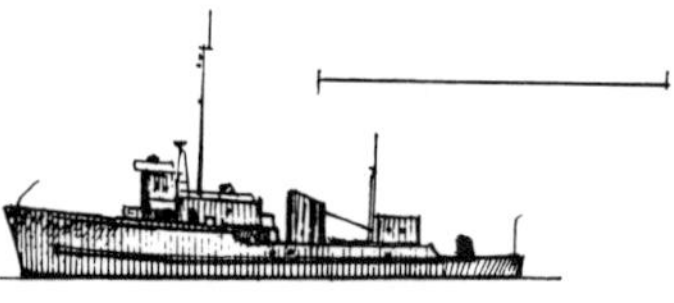

**699.** Be. **MECHELEN.** *A962.* Ex-"Bluebird" class. Research Ship. 330 tons. 144 x 28 x 8. (43.8 x 8.5 x 2.4). 2 screws; diesel. 13 knots.

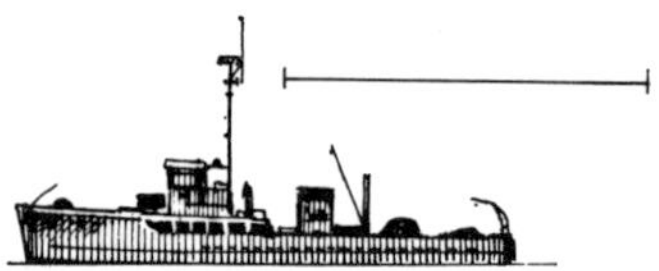

**700.** Bz. **JURUENA.** *M14.* "Albatross" class. Coastal Minesweeper. 270 tons. 136 x 25 x 8. (41.4 x 7.6 x 2.4). 2 screws; diesel. 15 knots. 4—20-m.m. guns. 2 depth charge throwers. **JURUA.** *M13.*

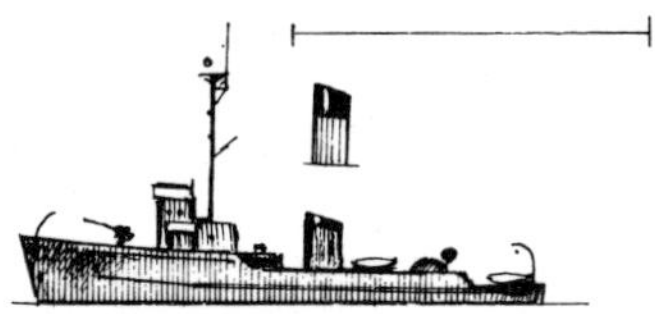

**701. Cs. Ex-BLUEBIRD** class. Coastal Mine-sweepers. No mainmast. 320 tons. 144 x 28 x 8. (43.8 x 8.5 x 2.4). 2 screws; diesels. 14 knots. 2 A.A. guns. The vessels vary slightly.
YUNG AN. *56,* YUNG CHI. *160,* YUNG CHUAN. *58,* YUNG HSIN. *59,* YUNG LO. *161,* YUNG NIEN. *57,* YUNG PING. *55.*

Gr. ARGO. *M213,* AVRA. *M214,* AIDON. *M248,* AIGLI. *M246,* DAPHNI. *M247,* DORIS. *M245,* KICHLI. *M241,* KISSA. *M242.*
These vessels have a very tall funnel (see inset).

Ir. KARKAS, SHAHBAS, SHAHROKH, SI-MORGH.
Ko. HA DONG. *527,* KO HUNG. *523,* KUM KOK. *525,* KUM SAN. *522,* NAM YANG. *526,* SAM CHOK.
Pk. MAHMOOD, MOMIN, MOSHAL, MU-BARAK, MUHAFIZ, MUJAHID, MUKHTAR, MUNSIF.
Sp. DUERO. *M28,* EBRO. *M26,* GENIL. *M31,* JUCAR. *M23,* LLOBREGAT. *M22,* MINO. *M25,* NALON. *M21,* ODIEL. *M32,* SIL. *M29,* TAJO. *M30,* TURIA. *M27.*
Th. BANGKEO. *6,* DONCHEDI. *8,* LADYA. *5,* TADINENG. *7.*
Tu. SAMSUN. *M257,* SAPANCA. *M266,* SARIYER. *M267,* SAROS. *M264,* SEDDUL-BAHIR. *M260,* SIGACIK. *M265,* SILIFKE. *M263,* SINOP. *M258,* SURMENE. *M259.*
VN. CHU'O'NG - DU'O'NG II, BACH DANG II, HAM TU II.

**704. Ge. FRAUENLOB** class. 1965-68. Inshore Minesweepers. 200 tons. 125 x 27 x 7. (38.1 x 8.2 x 2.1). Diesels. 14 knots. 1—40-m.m. A.A. gun.
ACHERON. *M2680,* ATLANTIS. *M2679,* DI-ANA. *M2677,* FRAUENLOB. *M2671,* GEFION. *M2673,* LORELEY. *M2678,* MEDUSA. *M2674,* MINERVA. *M2676,* NAUTILUS. *M2672,* UN-DINE. *M2675.*

Very similar but slightly smaller: ARIADNE class. ARIADNE. *W23,* AMAZONE. *W29,* FREYA. *W24,* GAZELLE. *W30,* HERTHA. *W26,* NIXE. *W28,* NYMPHE. *W27,* VNETA. *W25.*

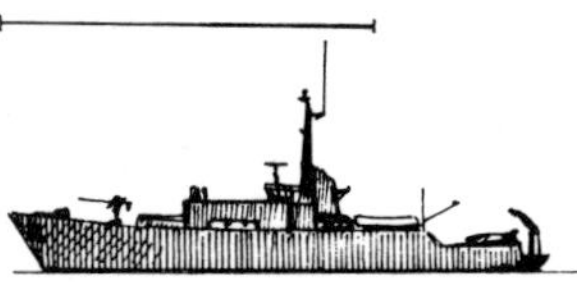

**702. Fr. CIRCE** class. 1970. Minehunters. 460 tons. 150. (45.7). Diesel. 15 knots.
CALLIOPE, CIRCE, CLIO, CYBELE.

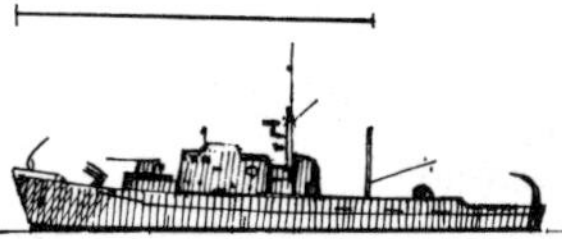

**703. Sw. ARKO** class. 1957-64. Coastal Mine-sweepers. 300 tons. 146 x 25 x 8. (44.5 x 7.6 x 2.4). 2 screws; diesels. 14 knots. 1—40-m.m. A.A. gun.
ARKO. *M57,* ASPO. *M63,* BLIDO. *M68,* HASSLO. *M64,* IGGO. *M60,* KARLSO. *M59,* NAMDO. *M67,* SKAFTO. *M62,* SPARO. *M58,* STYRSO. *M61,* VALLO. *M66,* VINO. *M65.*

**705. Am. COVE** class. 1958-59. Inshore Mine-sweepers. 120 tons. 112 x 22 x 10. (34.1 x 6.7 x 3). Diesels. 12 knots. 1 light gun.
CAPE. *2,* COVE. *1.*

Iran: HARISCHI. *301,* RIAZI. *302.*
Tu.: FETHIYE. *M000,* FINIKE. *M503,* FOKA. *M000.*

**706. Da. VIG** class. 1961-62. Inshore Mine-sweepers. 180 tons. 114 x 23 x 6. (34.7 x 7 x 1.8). 2 screws; diesels. 13 knots. 2—20-m.m. A.A. guns. Very similar to U.S. "Cove" class.
ASVIG. *M579,* MOSVIG. *M580,* SANDVIG. *M581,* SAELVIG. *M582.*

**707.** Du. **VAN STRAELEN** class. 1960. Inshore Minesweepers. 150 tons. 99 x 18 x 5. (30.1 x 5.4 x 1.5). 2 screws; diesels. 13 knots. 1—20-m.m. A.A. gun.
**ALBLAS.** *M868,* **BUSSEMAKER.** *M869,* **CHOMPFF.** *M874,* **HOUTEPEN.** *M882,* **LA-COMBLE.** *M870,* **MAHU.** *M880,* **SCHUILING.** *M876,* **STAVERMAN.** *M881,* **VAN DER WEL.** *M878,* **VAN HAMEL.** *M871,* **VAN 'T HOFF.** *M879,* **VAN MOPPES.** *M873,* **VAN STRAE-LEN.** *M872,* **VAN VERSENDAAL.** *M877,* **VAN WELL GROENEVALD.** *M875,* **ZOMER.** *M883.*

**708.** Sw. **M.** *7.* Patrol Vessels. 50 tons. 56 x 17 x 5. (17 x 5.1 x 1.5) Diesels. 13 knots. 1 20-m.m. gun. Former Inshore Minesweepers. Sister: **M.** *8.*

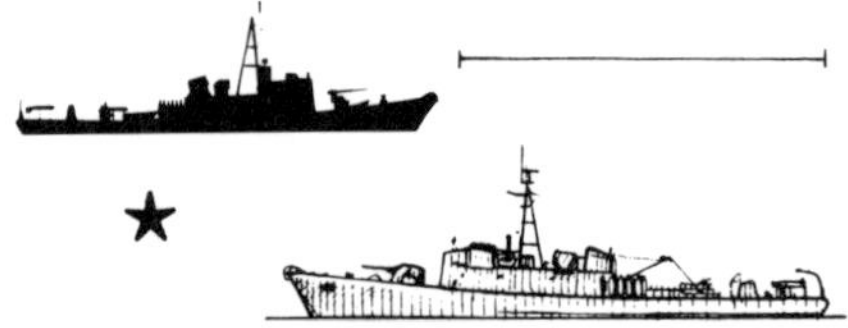

★

**709.** Ru. **SASHA** class. Coastal Minesweepers. 180 tons. 147 x 20 x 7. (44.8 x 6.1 x 2.1). Diesels. 18 knots. 1—57-m.m. D.P. gun. 4—25-m.m. A.A. guns (twin). 35 vessels in the Soviet Navy.

**710.** Ja. **ATADA** class. 1956. Coastal Mine-sweepers. 240 tons. 123 x 21 x 7. (37.4 x 6.4 x 2.1). 2 screws; diesel. 13 knots. 1—20-m.m. A.A. gun.
**ATADA.** *601,* **ITSUKI.** *602.*

**711.** Sw. **M. 15.** 1941. Inshore Minesweepers. 70 tons. 85 x 17 x 5. (25.9 x 5.1 x 1.5). Diesel. 13 knots. 1—20-m.m. gun.
**M. 16, M. 21—M. 26** inclusive. Two other vessels of this are converted into tenders as **LOMMEN** and **SPOVEN**; see silhouette No. 814.

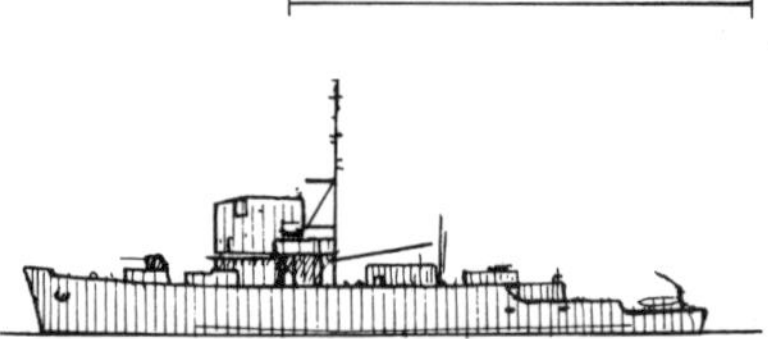

**712.** Am. **ADMIRABLE** class. 1943-44. Coastal Minesweepers. 650 tons. 185 x 33 x 10. (56.3 x 10 x 3). 2 screws; diesels. 15 knots. 1—3-inch D.P. gun. 4—40-m.m. A.A. guns.
Some "Admirable" class have funnels see drawing No. 681. The following American ships may or may not have funnels:
**COUNSEL.** *165,* **CRUISE.** *215,* **SPECTRE.** *306,* **SUPERIOR.** *311.*

Mexico: **DM.** *16,* **DM.** *19.* The following Mexicans may or may not have funnels:
**DM.** *01,* **DM.** *03,* **DM.** *04,* **DM.** *05,* **DM.** *06,* **DM.** *07,* **DM.** *08,* **DM.** *09,* **DM.** *10,* **DM.** *12,* **DM.** *13,* **DM.** *14,* **DM.** *15,* **DM.** *17,* **DM.** *18,* **DM.** *20.*

★ **713.** Ru. **VANYA** class. 1969 onwards. Coastal Minesweepers. 250 tons. 130 x 20 x 7. (39.6 x 6.1 x 2.1). Diesels. 15 knots. 2—25-m.m. A.A. guns (twin). About 40 ships in the Soviet Navy.

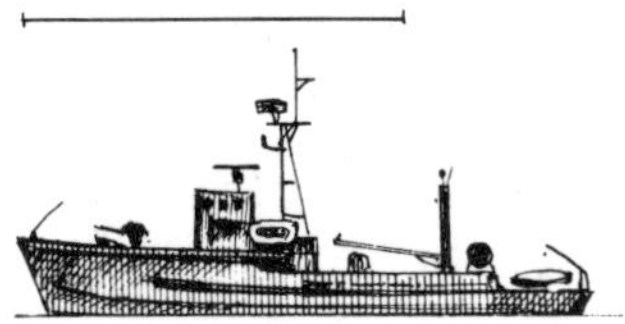

**714.** Ja. **KASADO** class. 1958-68. Coastal Minesweepers. 340 tons. 151 x 28 x 18. (46 x 8.5 x 5.4). 2 screws; diesels. 14 knots. 1—20-m.m. A.A. gun.
In some ships the legs of the tripod slope forward. These ships might be confused with the Russian "Vanya" class. The principal distinguishing feature is the tall kingpost.

**AMAMI.** *625,* **CHIBURI.** *620,* **HIRADO.** *614,* **HARIO.** *618,* **HABUSHI.** *608,* **IBUKI.** *628,* **KANAWA.** *606,* **KARATO.** *617,* **KASADO.** *604,* **KATSURA.** *629,* **KUDAKO.** *622,* **KOOZU.** *609,* **KOSHIKI.** *615,* **HOTAKA.** *616,* **MIKURA.** *612,* **MINASE.** *627,* **MUTSURE.** *619,* **OOTSU.** *621,* **REBUN.** *624,* **RISHIRI.** *623,* **SAKITO.** *607,* **SHIKINE.** *613,* **SHISAKA.** *605,* **TATARA.** *610,* **TSUKUMI.** *611,* **URUME.** *626,* and possibly **IOU.** *631,* **TAKAMI.** *630.*

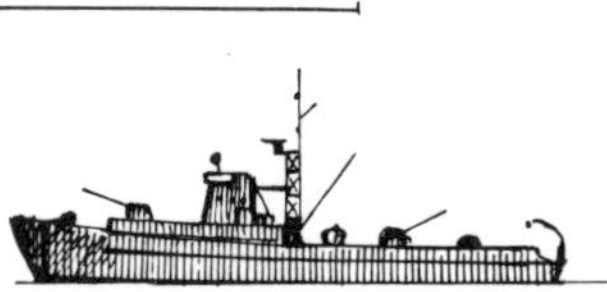

**715.** Sw. **HANO** class. 1953. Coastal Minesweepers. 270 tons. 131 x 23 x 8. (39.9 x 7 x 2.4). 2 screws; diesels. 14 knots. 2—40-m.m. A.A. guns.
**ORNO.** *M55,* **STURKO.** *M54,* **TARNO.** *M52,* **TJURKO.** *M53,* **UTO.** *M56.*
Similar but with no guns (see silhouette No. 687):
**HANO.** *M51.*

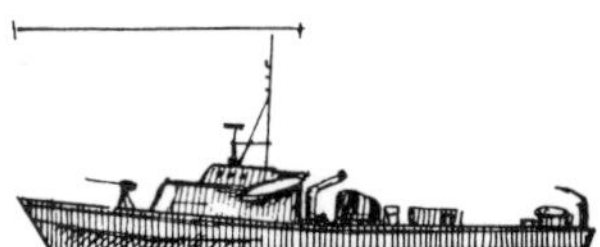

**716.** Ge. **HOLNIS.** *M2651.* 1966. Inshore Minesweeper. 180 tons. 117 x 24 x 7. (35.6 x 7.3 x 2.1). 2 screws; diesels. 14 knots. 1—20-m.m. A.A. gun.

**717.** Ge. **HANSA.** *W22.* 1958. Inshore Minesweeper. 150 tons. 115 x 21 x 6. (35 x 6.4 x 1.8). Diesel. 14 knots. 1—40-m.m. A.A. gun.
Identical appearance but with 2 screws (16 knots): **NIOBE.** *W21.*

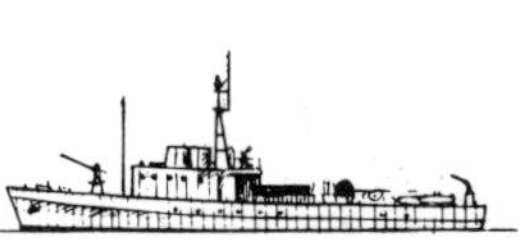

★ **718.** Ys. **ML. 117.** Inshore Minesweepers. 120 tons. 98 x 18 x 5. (29.8 x 5.4 x 1.5). Diesels. 12 knots. 1—40-m.m. A.A. gun.
**ML118.** *M118,* **ML119.** *M119,* **ML121.** *M121.*

**719.** Ja. **YASHIRO.** *603.* 1956. Coastal Mine-sweeper. 230 tons. 120 x 23 x 6. (36.5 x 7 x 1.8). 2 screws; diesel. 13 knots. 1—20-m.m. A.A. gun.

**721.** Br. **ISIS.** *M2010.* All details as No. 720. Attached to the R.N.R. London division. Distinguished by the large superstructure.

**722.** Br. **HAM** class. Torpedo Recovery Vessels. All details as No. 720 but sweeping gear removed.
**BUCKLESHAM.** *M2614,* **DITTISHAM.** *M2621,* **DOWNHAM.** *M2622,* **FLINTHAM.** *M2628,* **FRITHAM.** *M2630,* **HAVERSHAM.** *M2635,* **LASHAM.** *M2636.*
Malaysia: **JERONG.** *M2627,* **TODAK.** *M2610.*

**723.** Br. **HAM** class. All details as No. 720 but serve with the Port Auxiliary Service and have the gun removed.
**ARLINGHAM.** *M2603,* **EVERINGHAM.** *M2626,* **TONGHAM.** *M2735,* **WOLDING-HAM.** *M2778.*

**724.** Au. Ex-Br. **HAM** class. Diving Tenders. All details as No. 720 but have no armament. Distinguished by large deckhouse amidships.
**SEAL,** and possibly similar: **OTTER.**

**720.** Br. **HAM** class. Around 1952. Inshore Minesweepers. 120 tons. 107 x 21 x 6. (32.6 x 6.4 x 1.8). Diesel. 9-14 knots. 1 A.A. gun.
The following ships are operated by the R.N.R. and the R.N.X.S.:
**BIRDHAM.** *M2785,* **ODIHAM.** *M2783,* **PAG-HAM.** *M2716,* **PORTISHAM.** *M2781,* **PUT-TENHAM.** *M2784,* . **SHIPHAM.** *M2726,* **THAKEHAM.** *M2733.* .

France: **ARMOISE.** *M772,* **AUBEPINE.** *M781,* **CAPUCINE.** *M782,* **DAHLIA.** *M786,* **GERA-NIUM.** *M784,* **HIBISCUS.** *M785,* **HORTEN-SIA.** *M783,* **JASMIN.** *M776,* **JONQUILLE.** *M787,* **MYOSOTIS.** *M788,* **OEILLET.** *M774,* **PAQUERETTE.** *M775,* **PETUNIA.** *M889,* **TU-LIPE.** *M771,* **VIOLETTE.** *M773.*

India: **BASSEIN.** *M2707,* **BIMLIPTAN.** *M2705.*
Italy: (no gun). **ARAGOSTA.** *5450,* **ARSELLA.** *5451,* **ASTICE.** *5452,* **ATTINA.** *5453,* **CALA-MARO.** *5454,* **CONCHIGLIA.** *5455,* **DRO-MIA.** *5456,* **GAMBERO.** *5457,* **GRANCHIO.** *5458,* **MITILO.** *5459,* **OSTRICA.** *5460,* **PAG-URA.** *5461,* **PINNA.** *5462,* **POLIPO.** *5463,* **PORPORA.** *5464,* **RICCIO.** *5465,* **SCAMPO.** *5466,* **SEPPIA.** *5467,* **TELLINA.** *5468,* **TOT-ANO.** *5469.*
Libya: **BRAK, ZUARA.**
South Arabia: 3 ships transferred from Britain, new names not known.

★ Very similar. Ex-U.S. "Yugoslavia": **M.** *141,* **M.** *142,* **M.** *143,* **M.** *144.*

Similar. Built in Belgium and slightly larger. Belgian: **ANDENNE.** *M485,* **DINANT.** *M484,* **HASSEL.** *M471,* **HERSTAL.** *M478,* **HUY.** *M479,* **KORTRIJK.** *M472,* **LOKEREN.** *M473,* **MER-KSEM.** *M476,* **OUDENAERDE.** *M477,* **OU-GREE.** *M483,* **SERAING.** *M480,* **TEMSE.** *M470,* **TONGEREN.** *M475,* **TOURNAI.** *M481,* **TURN-HOUT.** *M474,* **VISE.** *M482.*

**725.** Ja. **No. 1—No. 6** (inclusive). 1957-59. Minesweeping Boats. 40 tons. 62 x 16 x 4. (18.9 x 4.8 x 1.2). 2 screws; diesel. 10 knots.

**726.** Am. **AEOLUS.** *3.* 1946. Cable Ship. 7,000 tons. 438 x 64 x 16. (133.5 x 19.5 x 4.8). Turbo-electric. 16 knots. Helicopter platform aft. **THOR.** *4.*

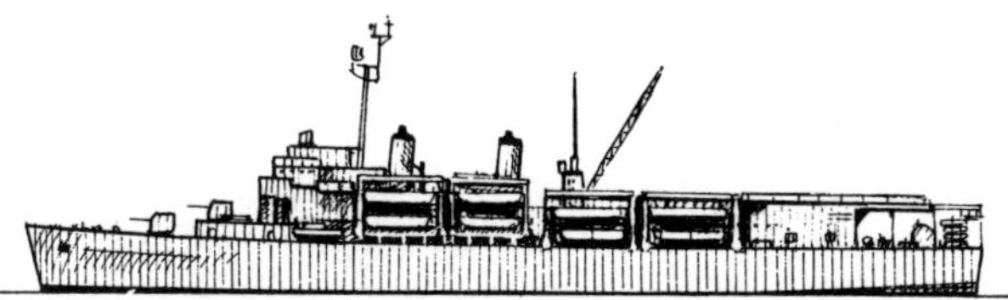

**727.** Am. **CATSKILL.** *1.* 1944. Mine Counter-measures Ship. 5,900 tons. 456 x 60 x 20. (138.9 x 18.2 x 6.1). 2 screws; turbines. 20 knots. 2—5-inch guns. 8—40-m.m. A.A. guns. Helicopter deck. 2 helicopters. Minelaying capabilities. **OZARK.** *2.*

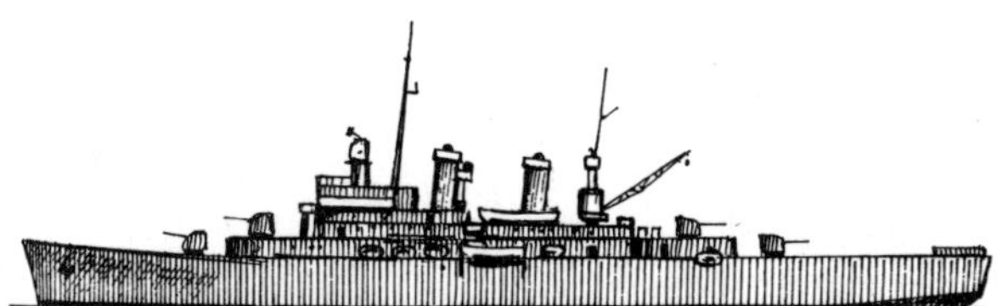

**728.** Am. **TERROR.** 1942. Fleet Minelayer. 5,900 tons. 455 x 60 x 20. (138 x 18.2 x 6.1). 2 screws; turbines. 20 knots. 4—5-inch guns. 24—40-m.m. A.A. guns. 20 smaller A.A. guns. 900 mines capacity.

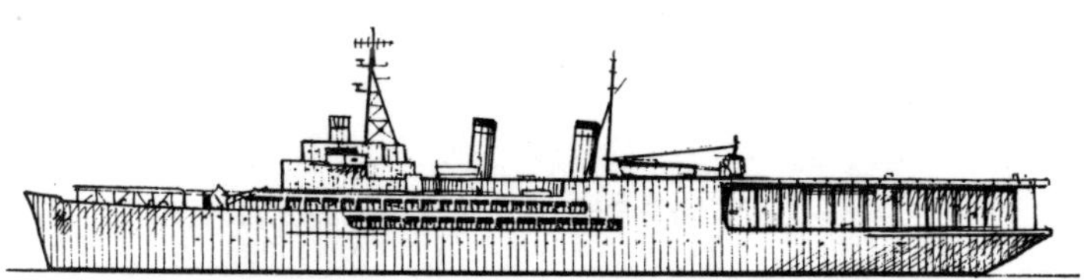

**729.** Am. **CORPUS CHRISTI BAY.** 1940. Modernised 1956-57. Converted to Helicopter Repair Ship. 1964-65. 8,700 tons. 536 x 69 x 21. (163.7 x 21.1 x 6.5). 2 screws; turbines. 19 knots. Operated by Military Sea Transportation Service.

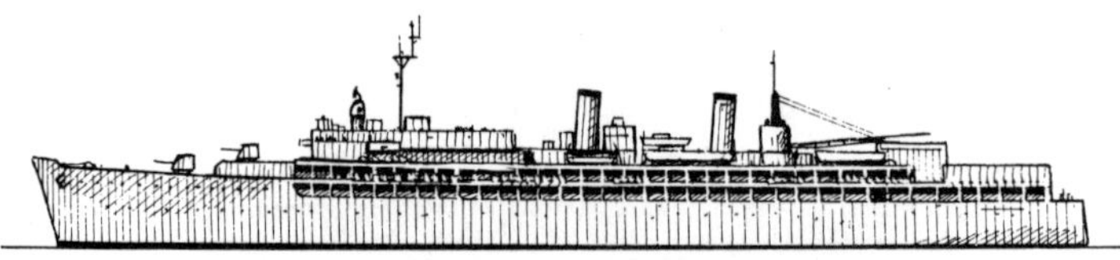

**730.** Am. **DIXIE** class. 1940-44. Modernised. Destroyer Tenders. 9,500 tons. 531 x 73 x 25. (161.8 x 22.2 x 7.6). 2 screws; turbines. 19 knots. 1 or 2—5-inch D.P. guns. Helicopters. **DIXIE.** *D14,* **PIEDMONT.** *D17,* **PRAIRIE.** *D15,* **SIERRA.** *D18,* **YOSEMITE.** *D19.* Distinguished from following ships by taller funnels.

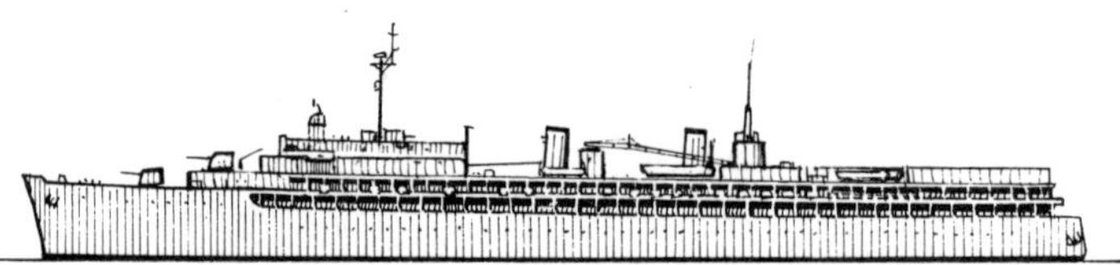

**731.** Am. **FULTON** class. 1941-45. Submarine Tenders. Modernised. 531 x 73 x 25. (161.8 x 22.2 x 7.6). 2 screws; turbines. 15 knots. 2—5-inch guns.
**BUSHNELL.** *S15,* **FULTON.** *S11,* **HOWARD W. GILMORE** *.S16,* **NEREUS.** *S17,* **ORION.** *S18,* **SPERRY.** *S12.*

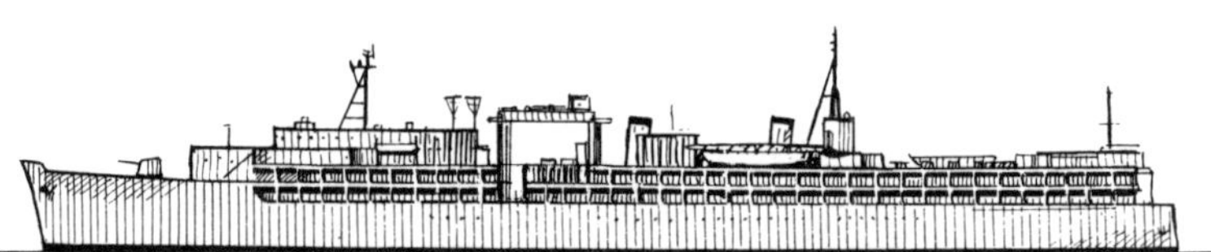

**732.** Am. **PROTEUS.** *S19.* 1944. Tender for Nuclear Powered Submarines. Converted from "Fulton" class ship 1960. 10,200 tons. 574 x 73 x 26. (177.8 x 22.2 x 7.9). 2 screws: turbines. 15 knots. 1—5-inch gun. Distinguished by large gantry amidships.

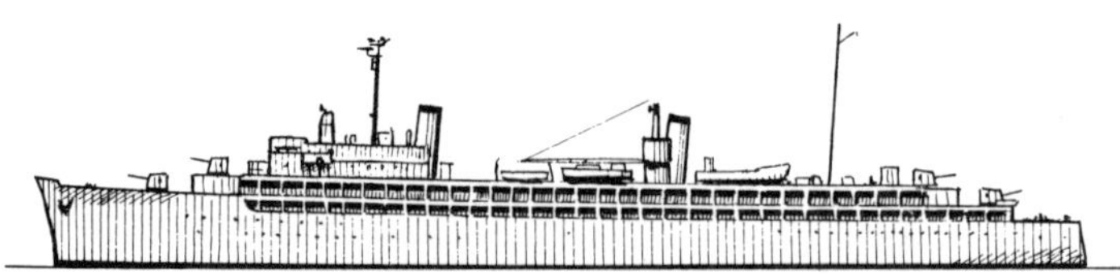

**733.** Am. **VULCAN** class. 1941-44. Modernised 1957. Heavy Repair Ships. 9,100 tons. 529 x 73 x 25. (161.1 x 22.2 x 7.6). 2 screws; turbines. 19 knots. 4—5-inch D.P. guns.
**AJAX.** *R6,* **HECTOR.** *R7,* **JASON.** *R8,* **VULCAN.** *R5.* Distinguished by widely spaced funnels.

**734.** Ru. **TOVDA** class. Repair Ships. Converted from merchant ships 1958-60. 3,000 tons. 282 x 39 x 16. (85.9 x 11.8 x 4.8). Diesel. 16 knots. 6 A.A. guns.
**INZA, TOVDA, VYTEGRA** and possibly others. Short, thick, widely spaced funnels.

**735.** Br. **TYNE.** *A194*. 1942. Rebuilt 1956-58. Destroyer Depot Ship. 11,000 tons. 621 x 66 x 21. (189.3 x 20.1 x 6.3). 2 screws; turbines. 17 knots. 8—4.5-inch guns. Now an accommodation ship.

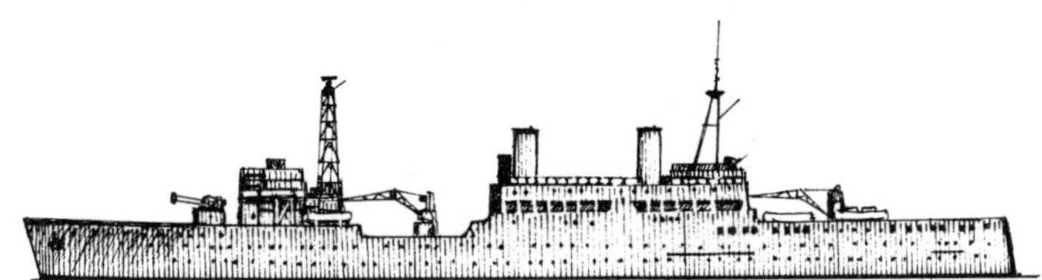

**736.** Br. **MAIDSTONE.** 1938. Rebuilt 1958-62. Support Ships for nuclear powered submarines. 10,000 tons, 531 x 73 x 21. (161.8 x 22.3 x 6.5). 2 screws; turbines. 16 knots. 5 A.A. guns. Now employed as accommodation ship at Belfast and known as "Maidstone Barracks".

**738.** Am. **HUNLEY** class. 1962. Submarine Tenders. 10,500 tons. 599 x 83 x 24 (182 x 25.3 x 7.3). Diesel electric. 19 knots. 4—3-inch A.A. guns (twin). Helicopter platform.
**HOLLAND.** *S32*, **HUNLEY.** *S31*.

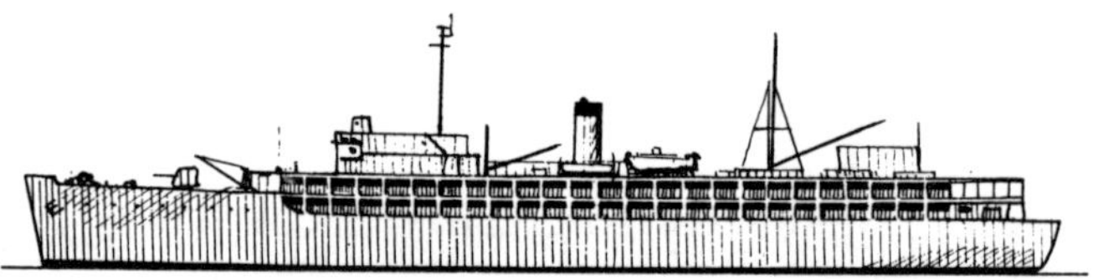

**739.** Am. **CASCADE.** *D16*. 1943. Destroyer
Tender. Modernised. 9,800 tons. 493 x 70 x 27.
(150.2 x 21.3 x 8.2). Turbine. 18 knots. 1—5-
inch D.P. gun.

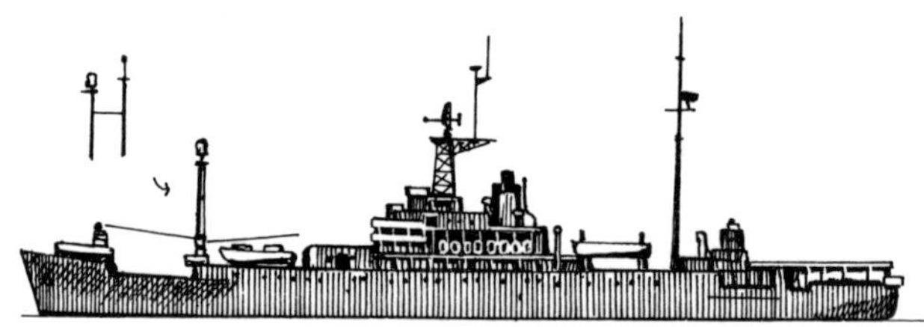

**740.** Am. **MOUNT MCKINLEY** class. 1945-46.
Modernised. Amphibious Command Ship. 7,500
tons. 459 x 63 x 28. (139.9 x 19.2 x 8.5). Turbine.
16 knots. 1—5-inch D.P. gun. 4 A.A. guns (twin).
**POCONO.** *CC16*, **TACONIC.** *CC*17.
Three other units in the class have a different
appearance; see silhouette number 836:
**ELDORADO.** *CC11*, **ESTES.** *12*, **MOUNT
MCKINLEY.** *CC7*.

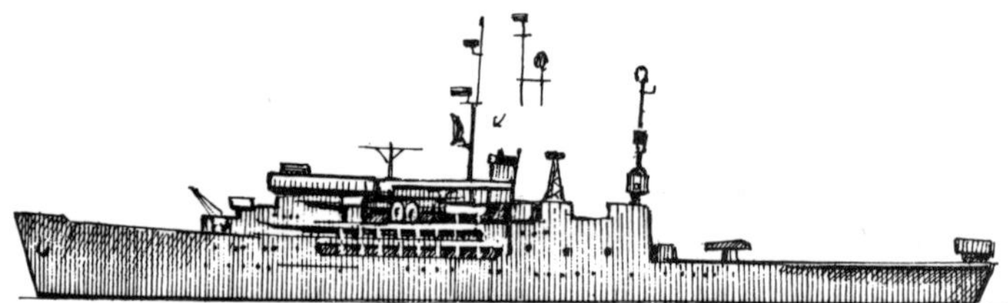

**741.** Am. **NORTON SOUND.** *VM1*. 1945. Converted 1963-64. Guided Missile Test Ship. 9,100
tons. 543 x 72 x 24. (165.2 x 21.5 x 7.3). Turbine.
19 knots. 1—5-inch gun. 1 missile launcher
(twin) for "Sparrow" missile. 1 other testing
launcher. Distinguished from No. 742 by absence
of crane aft and by having foremast close to
funnel, amidships. The 4th unit of "Currituck"
class.

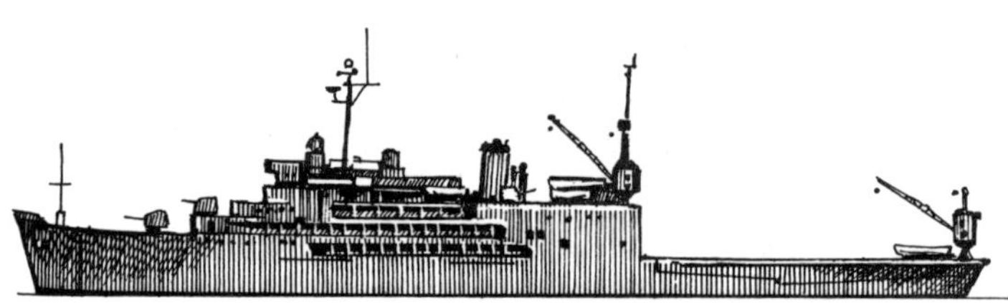

**742.** Am. **CURRITUCK** class. 1944-45. Converted 1957. Seaplane Tenders. 9,100 tons. 540 x
69 x 26. (164.7 x 21.1 x 7.9). 2 screws; turbines.
19 knots. 4—5-inch D.P. guns.

**CURRITUCK.** *V7*, **PINE ISLAND.** *V12*, **SALIS-
BURY SOUND.** *V13*.

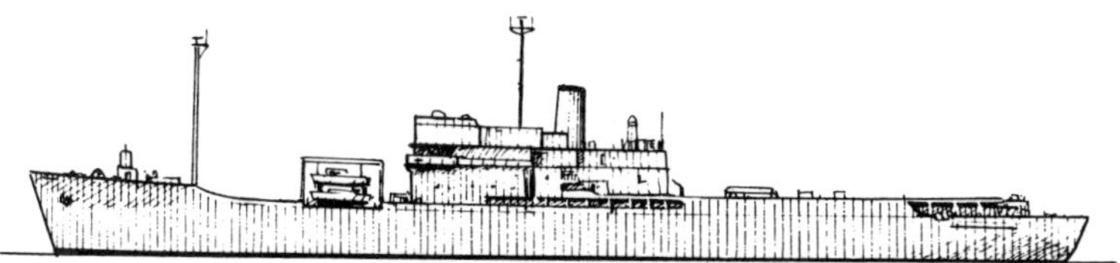

**743.** Am. **OBSERVATION ISLAND.** *EAG154.*
1958. Missile Test Ship. 17,600 tons (full). 563 x
76 x 29. (171.6 x 23.2 x 8.8). Turbine. 20 knots.
Former "Mariner" type merchant ship.

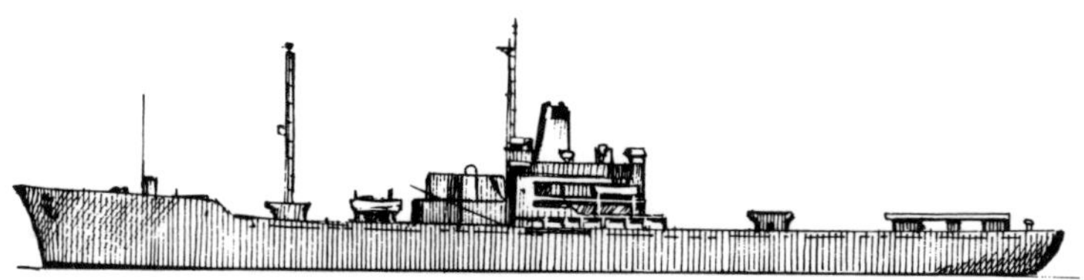

**744.** Am. **COMPASS ISLAND.** *EAG153.* Experimental Navigation Ship. 16,100 tons (full).
Other details as for No. 743.

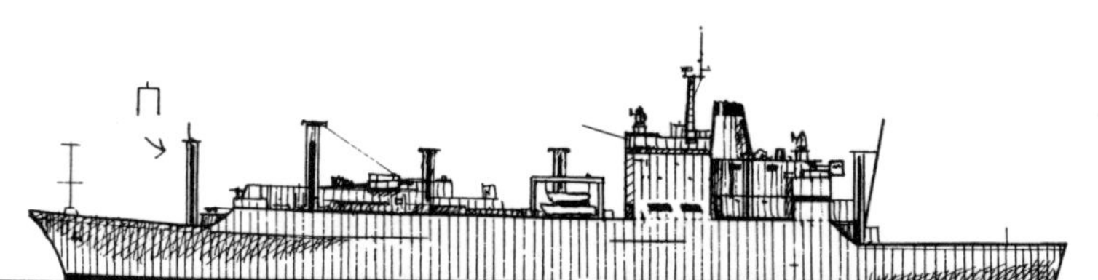

**745.** Am. **BUTTE** class. 1968-71. Ammunition
Ships. 20,500 tons full load. 565 x 81 x 26. (172.1
x 24.6 x 7.9). Turbines. 20 knots. 8—3-inch guns.
Helicopters.
**BUTTE.** *E27,* **FLINT.** *E32,* **KILAUEA.** *E26,*
**MOUNT HOOD.** *E29,* **SANTA BARBARA.**
*E28,* 3 other ships building.

**746.** Br. **LYNESS.** *A339.* 1966. Stores Support
Ship. 16,500 tons full load. 524 x 72 x 26. (159.6 x
21.9 x 7.9). Diesels. 17 knots. Facilities for helicopters. Operated by the Royal Fleet Auxiliary.
**STROMNESS.** *A344* **TARBATNESS.** *A345.*

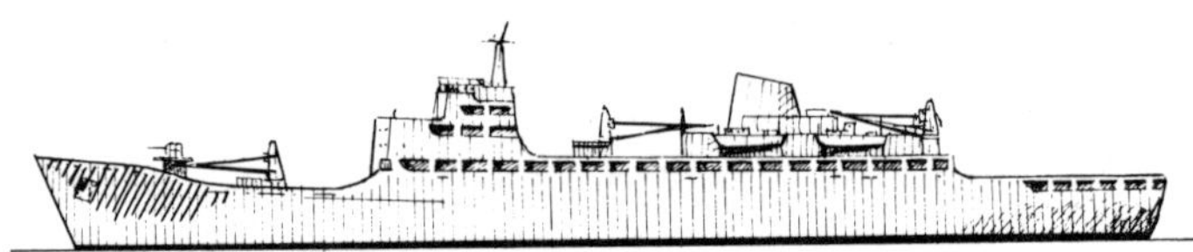

**747.** Au. **STALWART.** *A215*. 1968. Destroyer Tender. 15,500 tons. 516 x 68 x 30. (156.8 x 20.7 x 9.1). 2 screws; turbo-diesels. 18 knots. 2—40-m.m. A.A. guns (twin). Helicopter deck.

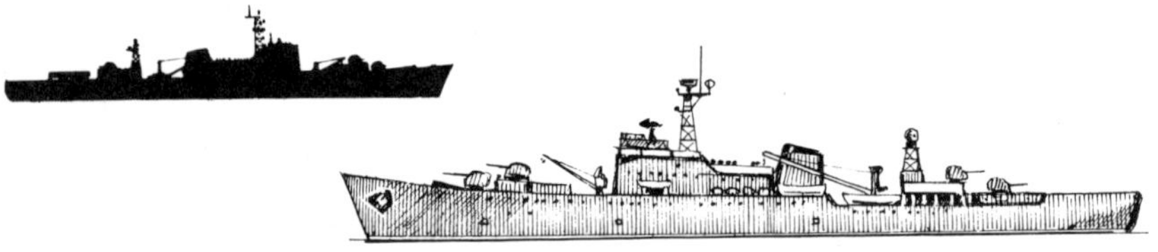

★ **748.** Ru. **OUGRA** class. About 1964. Nuclear Submarine Depot Ship. 7,500 tons. 460 x 65 x 20. (140.2 x 19.8 x 6.1). 2 screws; diesels. 17 knots. 8—2.3-inch D.P. guns (twin). Helicopter platform. At least 3 ships in the Soviet Navy.

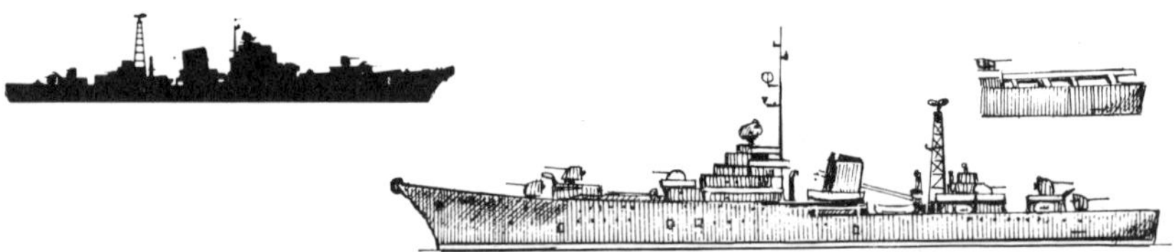

★ **749.** Ru. **DON** class. 1957-60. Submarine Support Ships. 4,800 tons. 427 x 49 x 17. (130.1 x 14.9 x 5.1). Diesels. 20 knots. 4—3.9-inch D.P. guns. 8—45-m.m. A.A. guns. Capacity for 80 mines.
At least 6 ships in the Soviet Navy, including the following names:
**DMITRI GALKIN, FEDOR VIDYAEV, MAG-OMET GADZHIEV, NIKOLAI STOLBOV, VASILII VERESOVOI.** Similar (with helicopter deck, see inset): **VIKTOR KOTELNIKOV.**
Some ships may vary in appearance; see silhouette No. 829.

Indonesia: **RATULANGI.**

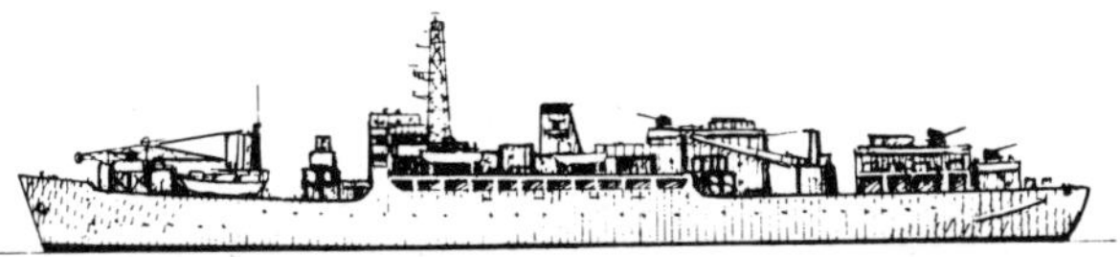

**750.** Br. **HARTLAND POINT.** *A262*. 1945.
Modernised 1959-60. Maintenance Ship. 8,600
tons. 442 x 58 x 21. (134.6 x 17.5 x 6.4). Reciprocating. 10 knots. 11—40-m.m. A.A. guns.

**751.** Br. **HEAD** class. 1945. Refitted 1960-63,
1968-69. Maintenance ships. 9,000 tons. 442 x
58 x 23. (134.6 x 17.5 x 7), Reciprocating. 10
knots. 11—40-m.m. A.A. guns.
**BERRY HEAD.** *A191*, **RAME HEAD.** *A134*.

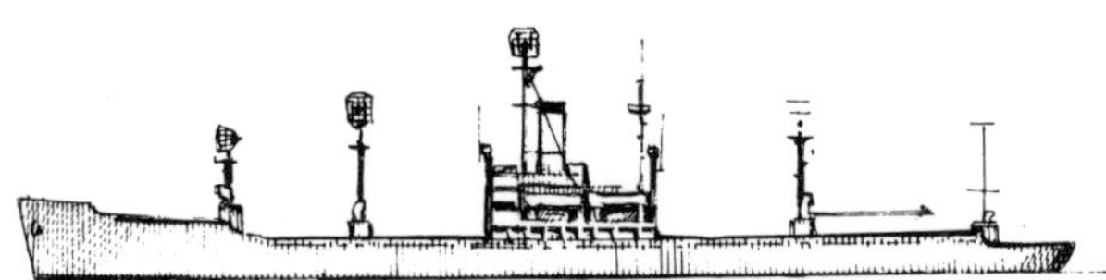

**752.** Am. **WATERTOWN.** *AGM6*. 1944. Converted 1960c. Range Instrumentation Ship.
10,700 tons full load. 456 x 62 x 29. (138.9 x
18.9 x 8.5). Turbines. About 15 knots. Former
"Victory" type ship.

**753.** Am. **LONGVIEW.** *AGM3*. All details as
No. 752 but has a helicopter platform aft.

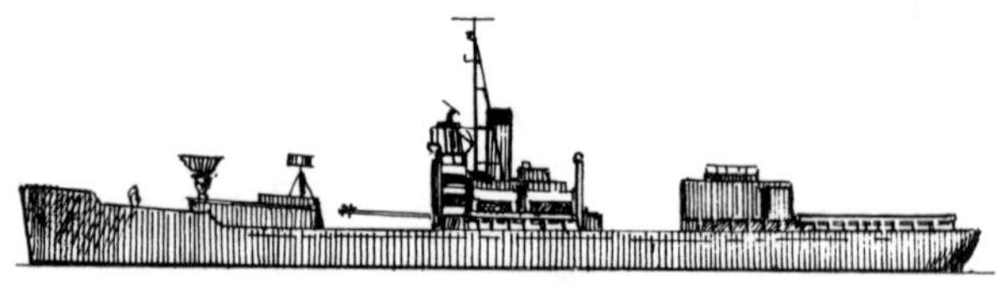

**754.** Am. **WHEELING.** *AGM8.* All details as No. 752. Has a helicopter platform aft.

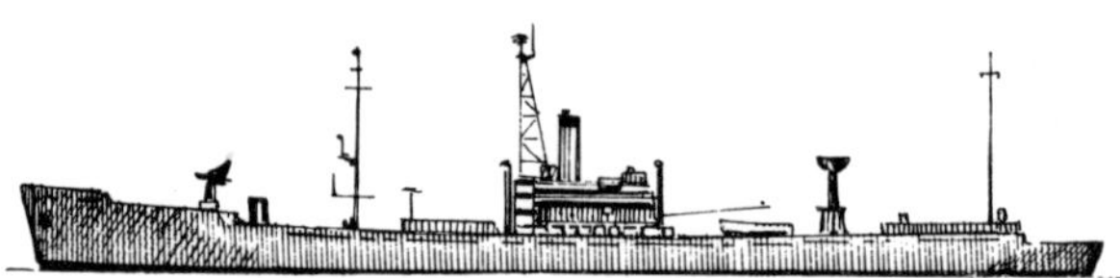

**755.** Am. **LIBERTY.** *GTR5.* 1944. Converted 1964c. Technical Research Ship. All details as for No. 752.

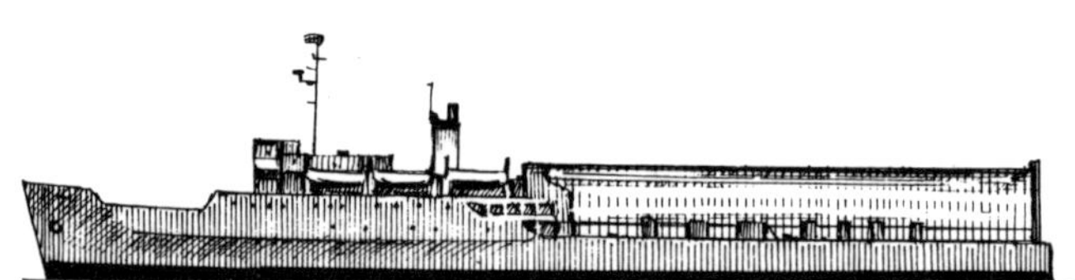

**756.** Am. **POINT BARROW.** *AKD1.* 1958. Dock Cargo Ship. 9,400 tons. 492 x 78 x 22. (149.9 x 23.7 x 6.7). 2 screws ; turbines. 18 knots. Large hangar aft. Used to carry sections of large rockets.

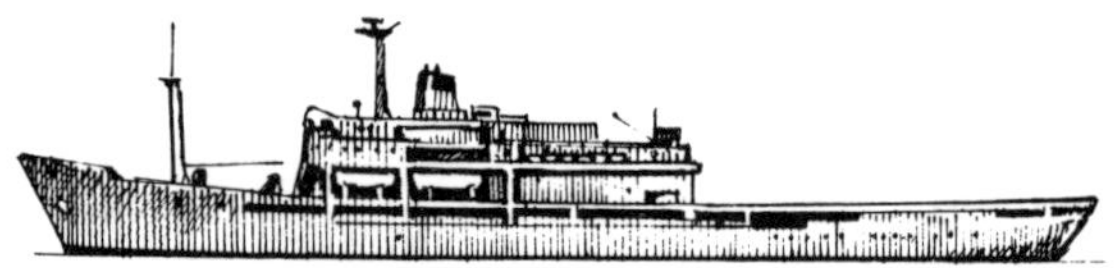

**757.** Br. **ENGADINE.** *K08.* 1967. Helicopter Support Ship. 8,000 tons deadweight. 424 x 58 x 22. (129.2 x 17.6 x 6.7). Diesel. 16 knots. Helicopter deck and hangar. Operated by the Royal Fleet Auxiliary.

**758.** Ly. **ZELTIN.** 1969. Logistics Support Ship. 2,200 tons. 324 x 48 x 10. (98.7 x 14.6 x 3). Diesels. 15 knots. 2—40-m.m. A.A. guns. Docking facilities aft for fast patrol boats.

**759.** Ic. **ODINN.** 1960 Coast Guard Patrol Vessel. 1,000 tons. 210 x 33 x 13. (64 x 10 x 3.9). 2 screws; diesels. 18 knots. 1—57-m.m. gun. Helicopter deck aft.

**760.** Ch. **PILOTO PARDO.** *45.* 1959. Antarctic Patrol Ship/Transport. 2,000 tons. 270 x 39 x 15. (82.2 x 11.5 x 4.5). Diesel-electric. 14 knots. 1 helicopter. Also used as a research ship.

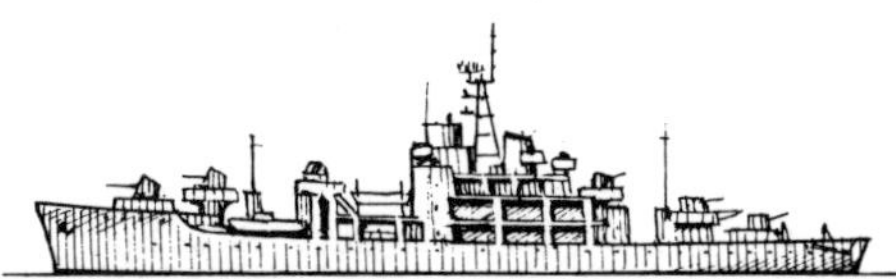

**761.** Sw. **ALVSNABBEN.** *M01.* 1943. Refitted 1959. Minelayer/Training Ship. 4,300 tons. 335 x 45 x 16. (120 x 13.5 x 4.9). Diesel. 14 knots. 2—6-inch guns. 2—57-m.m. A.A. guns. 2 or 4 smaller A.A. guns.

**762.** Ru. **ALESHA** class. Around 1965 onwards. Minelayer. 3,600 tons. 322 x 46 x 15. (98.1 x 14 x 4.5). Diesels. 20 knots. 4—57 m.m. A.A. guns (quadruple).

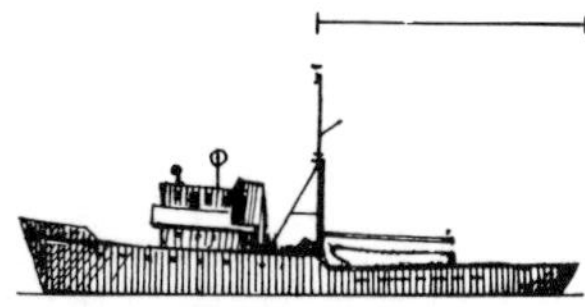

**763.** Ic. **ARVAKUR.** 1962. Coast Guard Patrol Vessel. 700 tons. 106 x 33 x 18. (32.3 x 10 x 3.9). Diesel. 12 knots. No guns at present.

**764.** Sw. **MUL 12.** class 1952. Mining Tender. 250 tons. 102 x 25 x 10. (31 x 7.6 x 3). Diesel-electric. 10 knots. 1—40-m.m. gun. **MUL 12, MUL 19** (inclusive).

**765.** Ja. **CHIHAYA**. *401*. 1961. Submarine Rescue Vessel. 1,300 tons. 240 x 39 x 13. (72.8 x 11.8 x 3.9). Diesels. 15 knots.

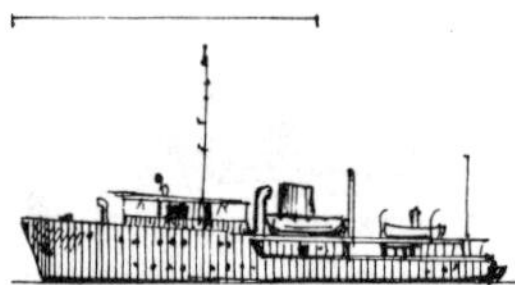

**766.** Ia. **BANGO** class. 1952. Patrol Craft. 200 tons. 125 x 21 x 7. (38.1 x 6.4 x 2.1). Diesels. 11 knots.
**BABUT, BANGO, BEO, BETTET, BIDO, BLEKOK, BLIBIS.**
Very similar: **SAMUDERA**. (Surveying ship.)

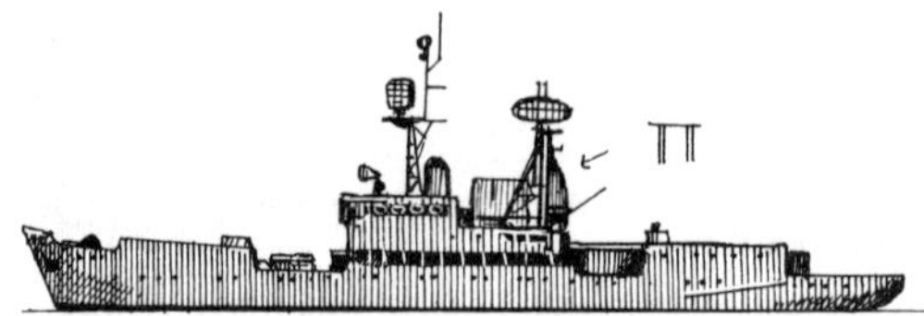

**767.** Fr. **ILE d'OLERON**. *A610*. 1939. Converted 1957-58. Experimental Guided Missile Ship. 3,300 tons. 378 x 50 x 21. (115.2 x 15.2 x 6.5). Diesels. 14 knots.

**768.** Ru. **SIBIR**. 1959. Missile Range Ship. 4,000 tons. 355 approx. (108.2 approx.). 2 screws; reciprocating. 15 knots. Helicopter. Converted from a cargo ship.

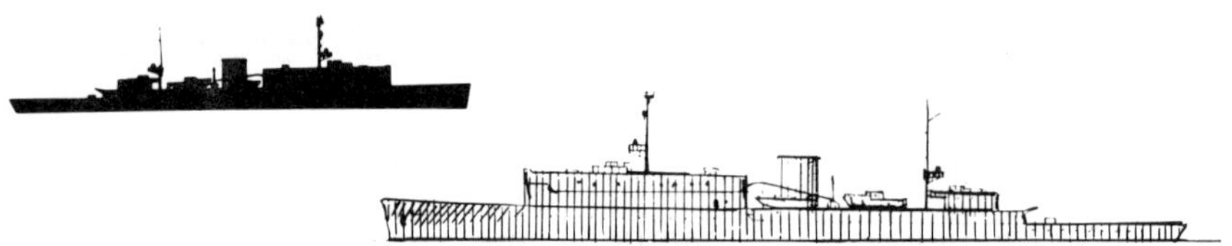

**769.** Ru. **KUBAN**. 1939. Refitted 1951-57. Submarine Depot Ship. 4,700 tons. 446 x 53 x 15. (135.9 x 16.1 x 4.5). 2 screws; diesels. 20 knots. 2—4.1-inch guns. 2—37-m.m. A.A. guns.

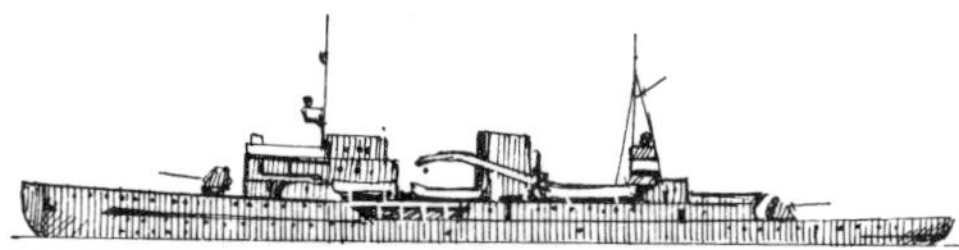

**★ 770. Ru. Ex-ADOLF LUDERITZ.** Depot Ship. 3,600 tons. 374 approx. (114 approx.). 2 screws; diesels. 20 knots. 4—4.1-inch guns. 12 A.A. guns. Probably no longer in service.

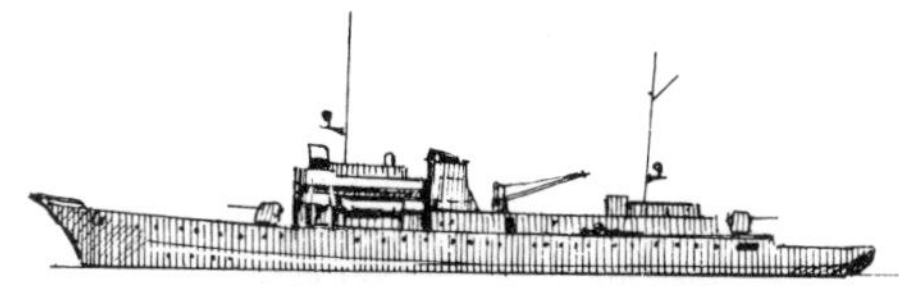

**★ 771. Ru. ANGARA.** 1939. Depot Ship. 2,100 tons. 323 x 43 x 11. (98.4 x 13.1 x 3.3). 2 screws; diesels. 18 knots. 2—4.1-inch guns. 3 A.A. guns. Probably no longer in service.

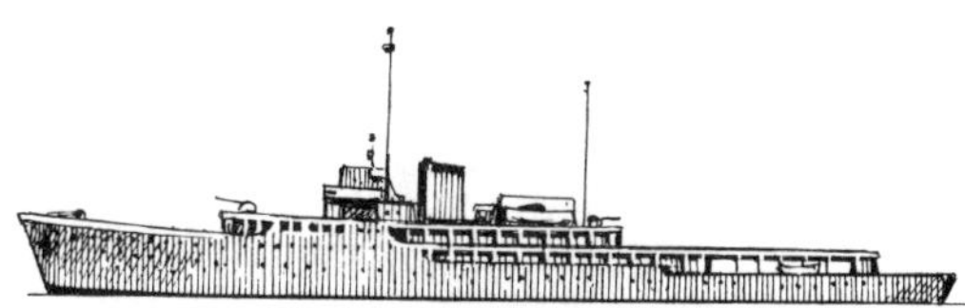

**★ 772. Ys. GALEB.** 1952. Minelayer/Training Ship. 5,200 tons. 385 x 51 x 18. (117.3 x 15.2 x 5.5). 2 screws; diesels. 17 knots. 6—40-m.m. A.A. guns. Helicopter deck.

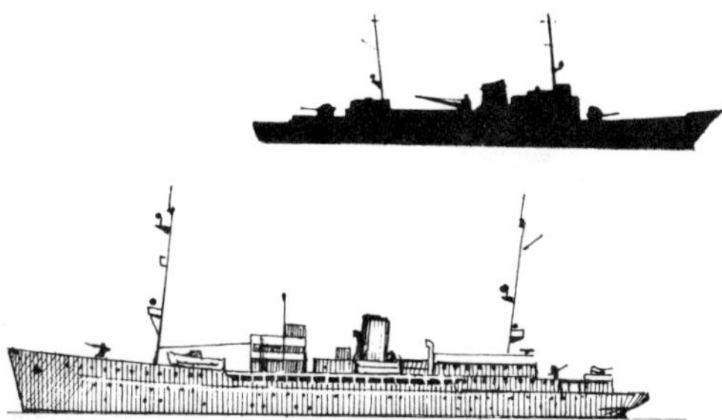

**★ 773. Ru. NYEMAN.** 1930. Training Ship. 3.900 tons, 320 x 46 x 13. (97.5 x 13.7 x 3.9). 2 screws; reciprocating. 12 knots. 4 A.A. guns. Probably no longer in service.

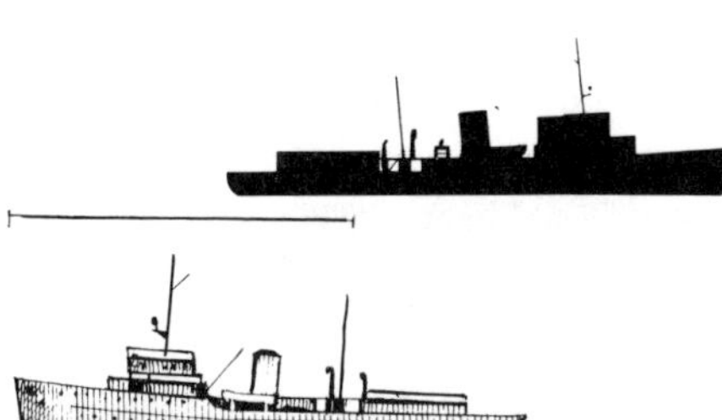

**★ 774. Ru. Ex-TEREK.** 1931. Submarine Supply Ship. 800 tons. 158 x 28 x 11. (48.1 x 8.5 x 3.3). 2 screws; diesels. 15 knots. 1—3.5-inch gun. 1—20-m.m. A.A. gun.

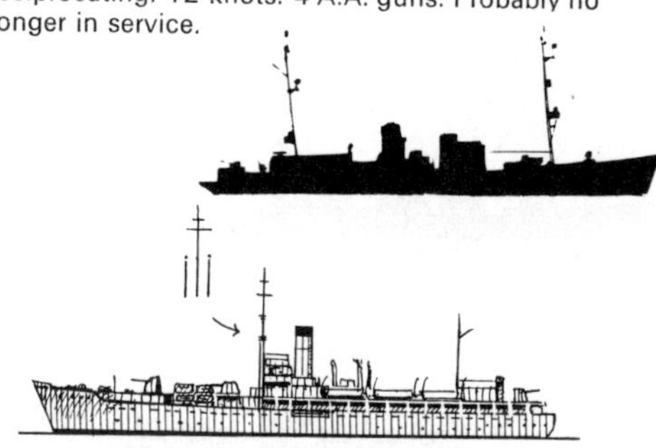

**775. Ph. GRYF** 1947. Training Ship. 2,000 tons. 282 x 44 x 19. (85.9 x 13.4 x 5.7). Reciprocating. 10 knots. 2—3.9-inch guns. 4—37-m.m. A.A. guns.

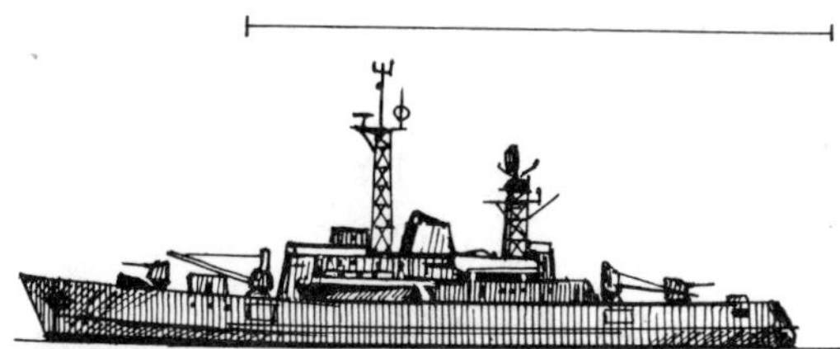

**776. Da. FALSTER** class. 1963-64. Minelayers. 1,900 tons. 253 x 41 x 10. (77 x 12.5 x 3). 2 screws; diesels. 17 knots. 4—3-inch guns (twin). **FALSTER.** *N80,* **FYEN.** *N81.* **MOEN.** *N82,* **SJAELLAND.** *N83.*

Turkey: **NUSRET.** *N108.*

**777 Da. HVIDBJORNEN** class. 1962-63 Frigates. 1,300 tons. 238 x 38 x 16. (72.6 x 11.6 x 4.9). Diesels. 18 knots. 1—3-inch D.P. gun. 1 helicopter and helicopter deck.

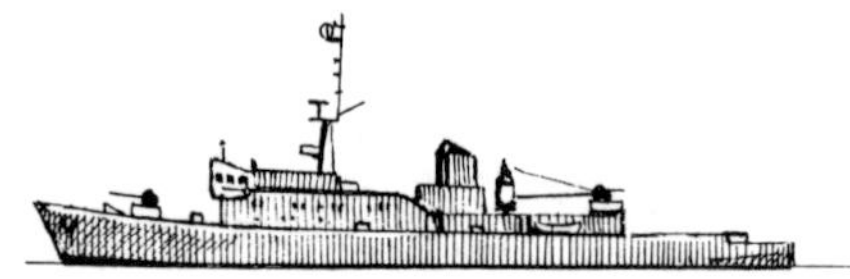

**778.** Be. **GODETIA.** *A960.* 1966. Support Ship. 2,000 tons. 301 x 46 x 12. (91.7 x 14 x 3.4). 2 screws; diesels. 19 knots. 4—40-m.m. A.A. guns (twin). Provision for helicopter.

**779.** Be. **ZINNIA.** *A961.* 1967. Support Ship. 2,000 tons. 326 x 46 x 12. (99.3 x 14 x 3.6). Diesels. 18 knots. 3—40-m.m. A.A. guns. 1 helicopter.

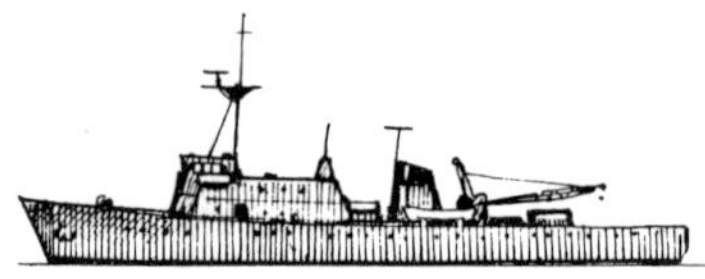

**780.** Br. **ABDIEL.** *N21.* 1967. Minelayer. 1,400 tons. 265 x 39 x 10. (80.7 x 11.8 x 3). Diesels. 16 knots.

**781.** Co. **GORGONA.** *161.* 1955. Tender. 600 tons. 135 x 30 x 9 (41.1 x 9.1 x 2.8). Diesels. 13 knots.

**782.** Sw. **MUL** type. 1946. Mining Tender. 200 tons. 100 x 24 x 11. (30.4 x 7.3 x 3.3). Diesel. 10 knots. 2—20-m.m. guns. Probably **MUL 11.**

**783.** Tu. Ex-U.S. **LSM** type. 1945. Converted 1952. Coastal Minelayers. 750 tons. 203 x 35 x 9. (61.8 x 10.6 x 2.6). 2 screws; diesels. 12 knots. 2—40-m.m. A.A. guns. 2—20-m.m. A.A. guns. **MARMARIS.** *N100,* **MERIC.** *N102,* **MERSIN.** *N103,* **MORDOGAN.** *N101,* **MUREFTE.** *N104.*

**784.** Gr. **AKTION.** *N04.* 1945. Converted 1953. Minelayers. 700 tons. 204 x 35 x 8. (62.1 x 10.6 x 2.4). 2 screws; diesel. 12 knots. 8—40-m.m. D.P. guns. 6—20-m.m. A.A. guns. Ex-U.S. LSM type. **AMVRAKIA.** *N05.*

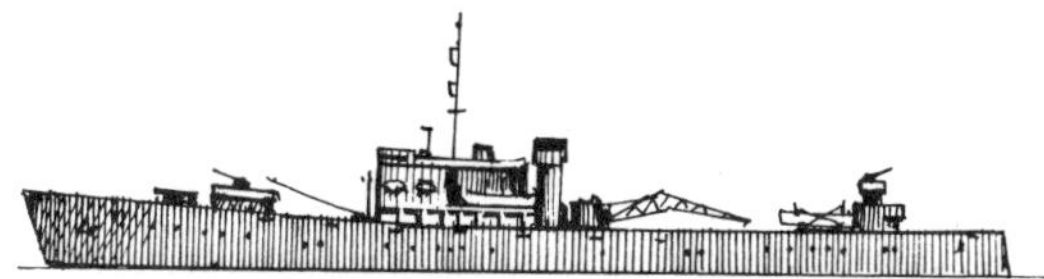

**785.** Du. **PELIKAAN.** *A830,* 1943. Converted 1947. Supply Ship. 4,300 tons. 390 x 49 x 14. (118.8 x 14.9 x 3.9). Turbine. 17 knots. 2—40-m.m. A.A. guns. 10—20-m.m. A.A. guns. Ex-British LST.

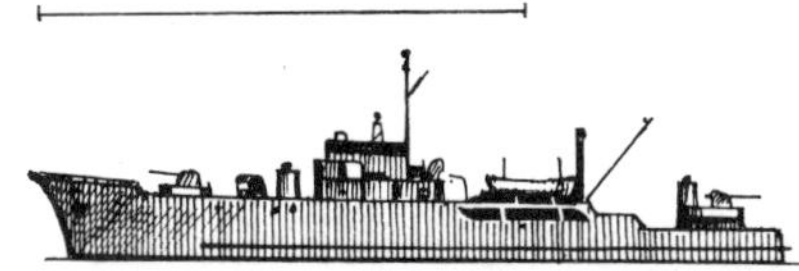

**786.** Da. **HJAELPEREN.** *A563.* 1945. Converted 1953. Depot Ship. 1,000 tons. 204 x 35 x 8. (62.1 x 10.4 x 2.4). 2 screws; diesesl. 12 knots. 2—40-m.m. guns. Ex-U.S. LSM.

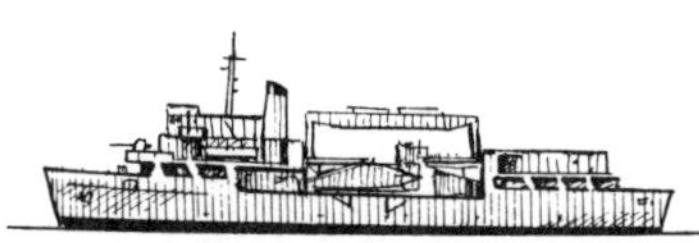

**787.** Am. **PIGEON.** 1970. Submarine Rescue Ship. 3,400 tons full load. 250 x 86. (76.1 x 26.2). 2 screws; diesels. 15 knots. 2—3-inch A.A. guns. Catamaran hulls.
**ORTOLAN.**

**788.** Am. **ELK RIVER.** *IX501.* 1945. Converted 1967-68. Range Support Ship. 1,100 tons full load. 225 x 50 x 9. (68.5 x 15.2 x 2.7). 2 screws; diesel. 11 knots. Ex-LSM.

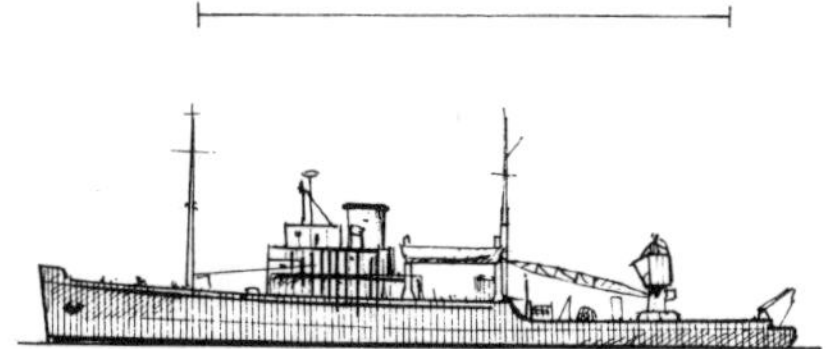

**789.** Am. **ARGO.** 1944. Converted 1958. Oceanographic Research Ships. 2,100 tons full load. 214 x 39 x 15. (65.2 x 11.8 x 4.5). 2 screws; disel-electric, 14 knots. Former "Escape" class salvage ship
**CHAIN.**

**790.** Ru. **PRUT** class. Built since 1960. Salvage Vessels. 2,000 tons. 345 approx. (105 approx.). 18 knots. 4—57-m.m. guns (quadruple). At least 6 ships in the Soviety Navy including **VLADIMIR TREFOLEV.**

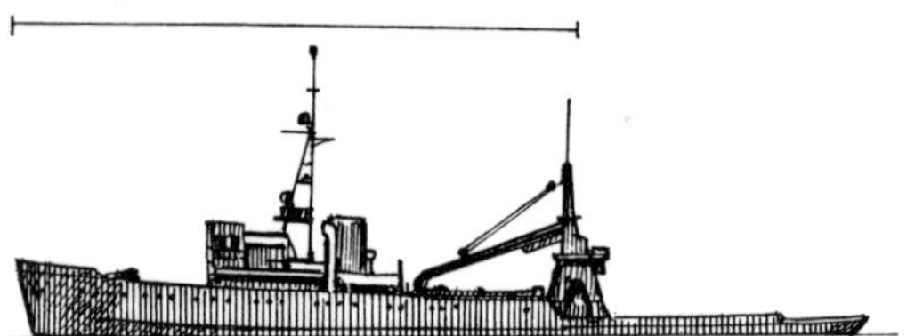

**791.** Fr. **COMMANDANT ROBERT GIRAUD.**
*A755*. 1944. Research Ship. 1,000 tons. 256 x 36
x 12. (78 x 11 x 3.7). 2 screws; diesels. 20 knots.
Built as a German aircraft tender.

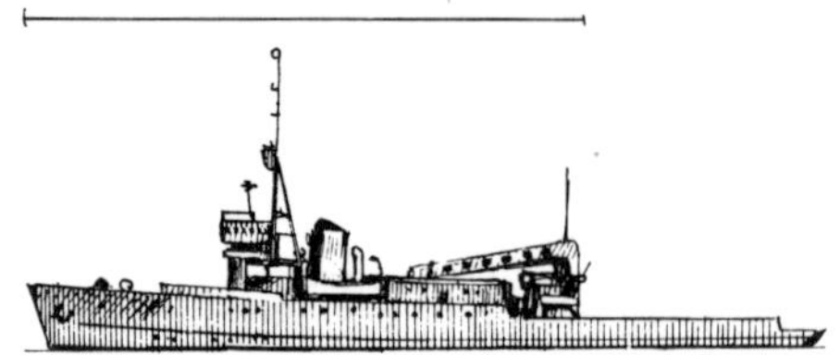

**792.** Fr. **MARCEL LE BIHAN**. *A759*. 1937.
Tender. 800 tons. 236 x 35 x 11. (71.9 x 10.7 x
3.4). 2 screws; diesel. 16 knots. 4—20-m.m.
A.A. guns. Former German aircraft tender.

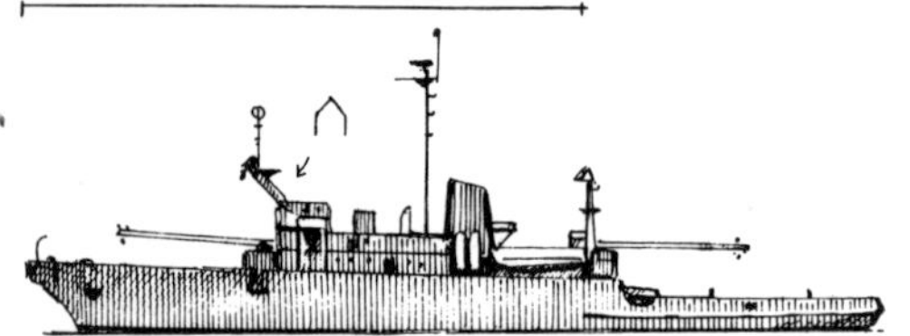

**793.** Am. **EDENTON** class. 1969-70. Salvage
tugs. 2,700 tons (full). 233 x 50 x 15. (71 x 15.2 x
4.6). 2 screws; diesels. 16 knots.
**EDENTON.** *TS1*, **BEAUFORT.** *TS2*, **BRUNS-
WICK.** *TS3*.

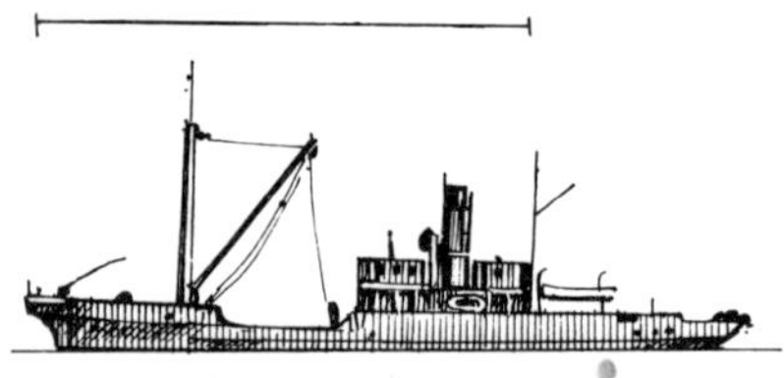

**794.** Tu. **KALDIRAY.** *P305* 1938. Boom Defence
Vessel. 700 tons (gross). Reciprocating. 10
knots. Acquired from France. 1964.

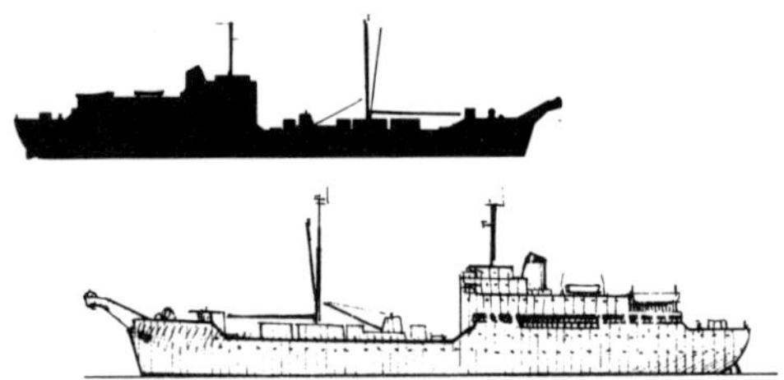

**795.** Ru. **DNEPR** class. 1957-66. Repair and
Depot Ships. 3,000 tons. 325 x 45 x 14. (100 x
13.7 x 4.3). Diesels. 12 knots.
At least 5 ships in the class.

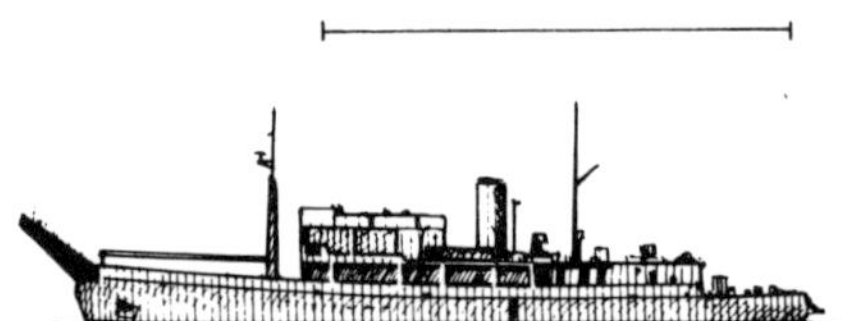

**796.** Br. **LAY** class. 1959-60. Boom Defence
Vessels. 800 tons. 193 x 35 x 12. (58.8 x 10.5 x
3.5). 2 screws; reciprocating. 14 knots.
**LAYBURN.** *P191*, **LAYMOOR.** *P190*.

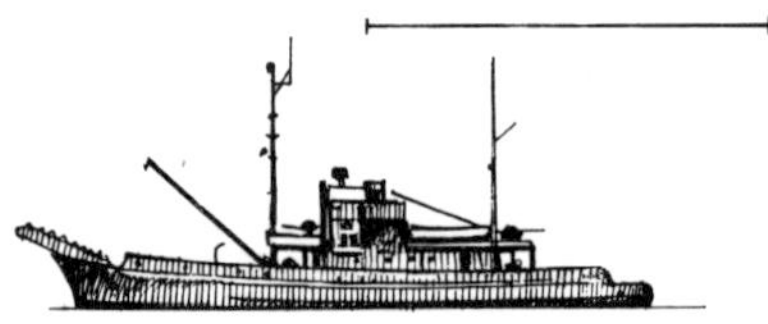

**797.** Am. **TREE** class. 1941. Net Layers. 600
tons. 163 x 31 x 12. (49.7 x 9.5 x 3.7). Diesel-
electric. 11 knots. 4—20-m.m. A.A. guns.
**BUTTERNUT.** 9.

Ec. **ORION.** Survey Ship.

Fr. **ARAIGNEE.** *A727*, **LOCUSTE.** *A765*,
**SCORPION.** *A728*, **LUCIOLE.** *A777*, **TAREN-
TULE.** *A729*.
Tu. **AG4.** *P304*. (Tall radar mast from bridge).
See silhouette No. 1126.

RC. Possibly at least 5 ships. 

**798.** Br. **WILD DUCK** class. 1963-67. Boom Defence Vessels. 1,000 tons. 168 (over horns) x 37 x 11. (51.2 x 11.3 x 3.5). Diesels. 14 knots. Funnel very short.
**GARGANEY.** *P194,* **GOLDENEYE.** *P195,* **MANDARIN.** *P192* **PINTAIL.** *P193.*

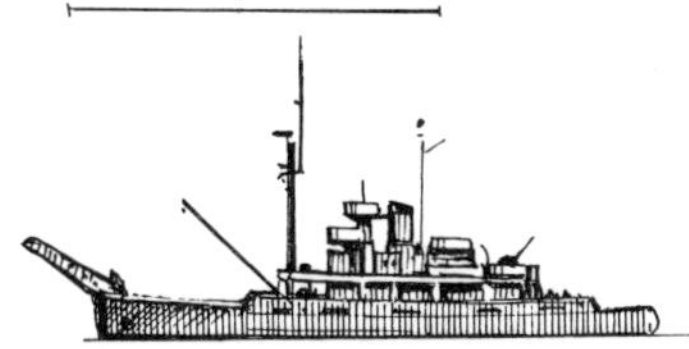

**800.** Fr. **GRILLON** class. 1954. Boom Defence Vessels. 600 tons. 165 x 34 x 11. (50.3 x 10.4 x 3.2). Diesels. 12 knots. 5 A.A. guns.
U.S. Netlayer type.
**CIGALE.** *A760,* **CRIQUET.** *A761,* **FOURMI.** *A762,* **GRILLON.** *A763,* **SCARABEE.** *A764.*
Sp. **CR1.**
Similar:
It. **ALICUDI.** *A5304,* **FILICUDI.** *A5305.*
Du. **CERBERUS.** *A895.* (Diving Tender).

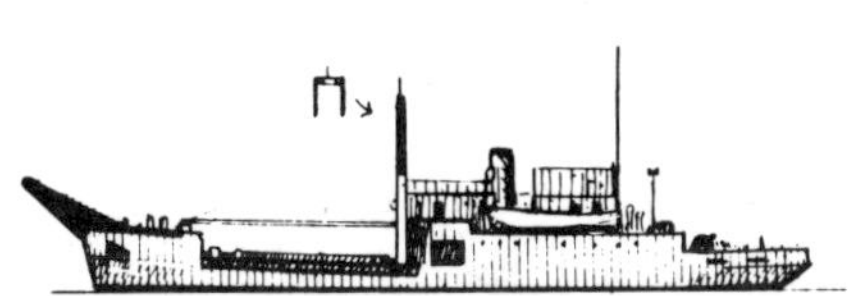

**800B.** Br. **KIN** class. 1943-45. Coastal Salvage Vessels. 950 tons. 179 x 35 x 10. (54.6 x 10.7 x 3.1). Reciprocating. 9 knots. May vary in appearance; see "Kinloss" No. 800C.
**KINBRACE, KINGARTH, SUCCOUR, SWIN, UPLIFTER.**

**799.** Gr. **THETIS.** *A307.* 1959. Boom Defence Vessel. 680 tons. 170 x 34 x 12. (51.8 x 10.4 x 3.7). Diesels. 12 knots. 1—40-m.m. A.A. gun. 4—20-m.m. A.A. Guns.
U.S. type Netlayer.
Tu. **AG5.** *P306.*

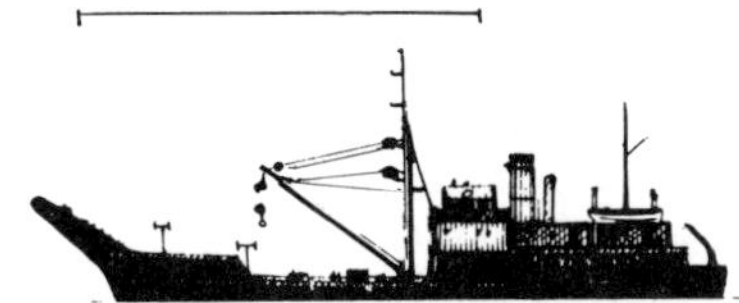

**800A.** Br. **MOOR** class .1938-46. Boom Defence Vessels. 600-650 tons. 145-160 x 30 x 12. (44.2-48.5 x 9.1 x 3.7). Reciprocating. 9 knots.
**MOORHEN.** *A489,* **MOORLAND.** *A491,* **MOORSMAN.** *P284,* **MOORPOUT.** *P223.*

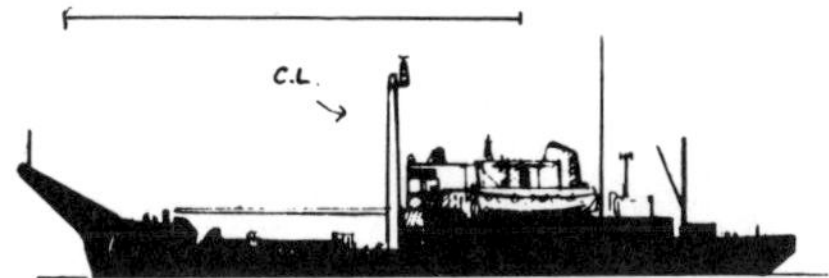

**800C** Br. **KINLOSS.** All details as for No. 800B. Some other "Kin" class vessels may have this appearance.

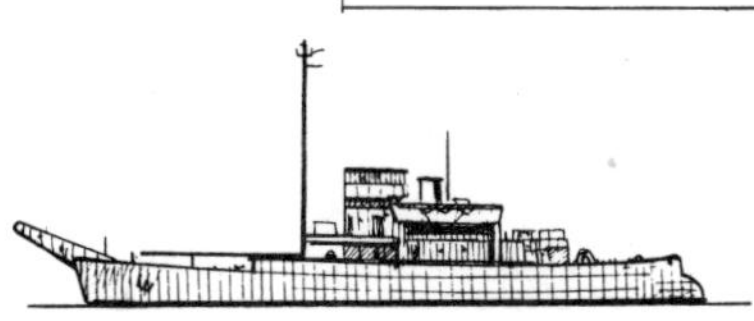

**801.** Am. **COHOES** class. 1945. Netlayer. 650 tons. 169 x 34 x 12. (51.5 x 10.4 x 3.7). Diesel electric. 12 knots. 3—20-m.m. A.A. guns.
**COHOES.** *78.*

Haiti. **DESSALINES.** (Coastguard Patrol Vessel.)
Ve. **PUERTO** class Survey Vessels.
**PUERTO DE NUTRIAS, PUERTO MIRANDA, PUERTO SANTO.**

**802.** Br. **BAR** class. 1939-44. Boom Defence Vessels. 750 tons. 182 x 32 x 12. (55.5 x 9.8 x 3.7). Reciprocating. 9 knots. Vary in details. **BARBECUE.** *P214*, **BARBAIN.** *P201*, **BARFOIL.** *P294*, **BARFOOT.** *P202*, **BARGLOW.** *P216*, **BARHILL.** *P204*, **BARMOND.** *P232*, **BARNARD.** *P241*, **BARNDALE.** *P215*, **BARRINGTON.** *P259*.

Ceylon. **BARON.** Name probably now changed. Tu. **AG1.** *P301*, **AG2.** *P302*, **AG3.** *P303*.

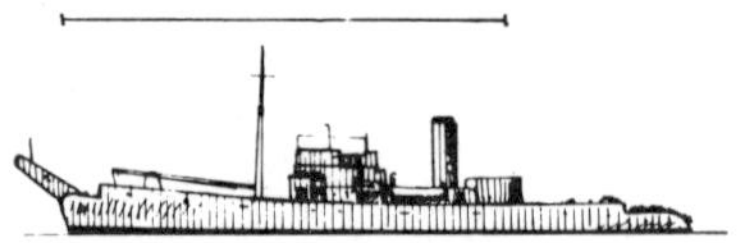

**803.** SA. **SOMERSET.** 1942. Boom Defence Vessel. Details as for No. 802. Ex-British "Bar" class but differs in superstructure and large funnel.

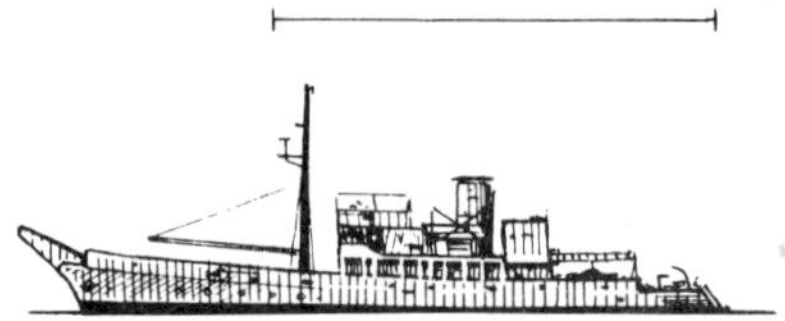

**804.** Au. **KIMBLA.** *GOR314*. 1956. Oceanographic Research Ship. 760 tons. 179 x 32 x 12. (54.6 x 9.8 x 3.7). Reciprocating. 12 knots. 3 A.A. guns. Former Boom Defence Vessel of British "Bar" type.

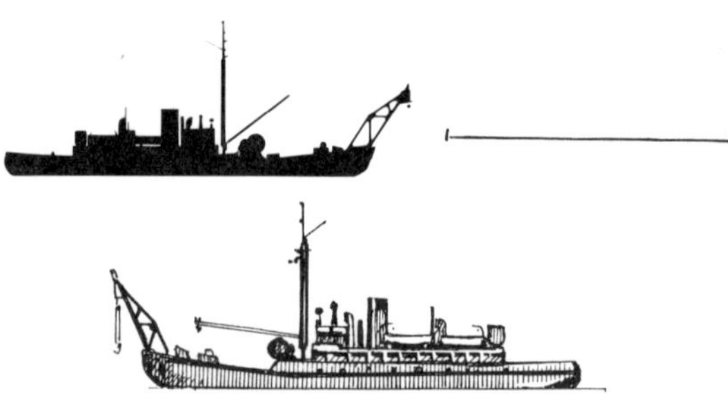

★ **805.** Ru. **NEPTUN** class. 1957-60. Boom Defence Vessels. 700 tons. 170 x 36 x 13. (51.8 x 11 x 4). Motor vessels. 12 knots. 18 vessels in the class.

**806.** Am. **NEPTUNE.** *RC2*. 1946. Cable Ship. 7,400 tons (full). 370 x 47 x 18 (112.7 x 14.3 x 5.4). 2 screws; reciprocating. 14 knots.

**807.** Am. **ALBERT J. MYER.** *RC6*. Cable and Research Ship. 362 x 47 x 18. (110.3 x 14.3 x 5.4). 2 screws; reciprocating. 14 knots. Operated by Military Sea Transport Service.

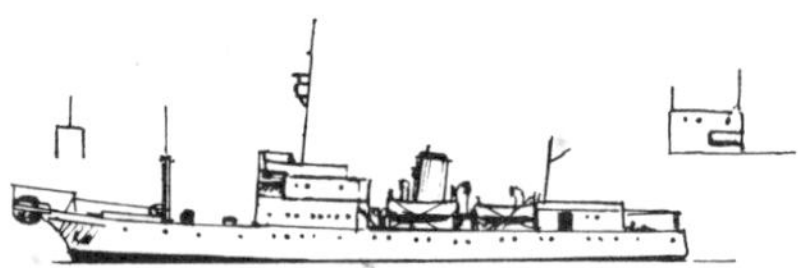

**808.** Br. **BULL** class. 1940-43. Cable Ships. 1,300 tons. 252 x 37 x 16. (76.8 x 11.2 x 4.8). 2 screws; reciprocating. 12 knots. **BULLFINCH, ST. MARGARET'S.** Royal Fleet Auxiliaries. 2 similar ships in commercial service.

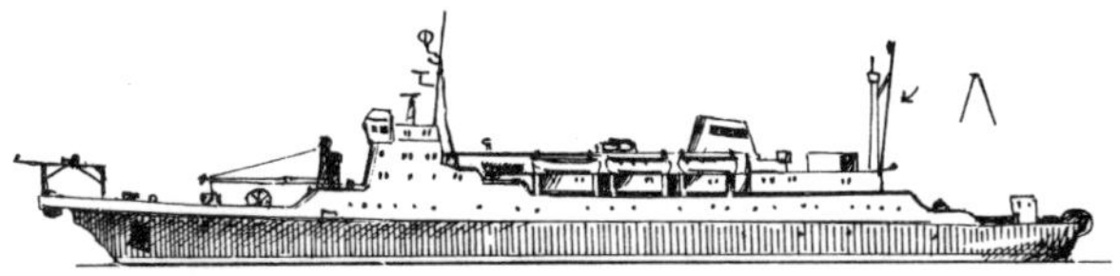

**809.** Ru. **INGUL.** 1962. Cable Ship. 7,000 tons.
428 x 53 x 17  (130.4 x 16.1 x 5.1) Diesels. 14
knots.
**JANA.**
Very similar to No. 810 but shorter bridge deck.

**810.** Ru. **DONETS.** All particulars as for No. 809.

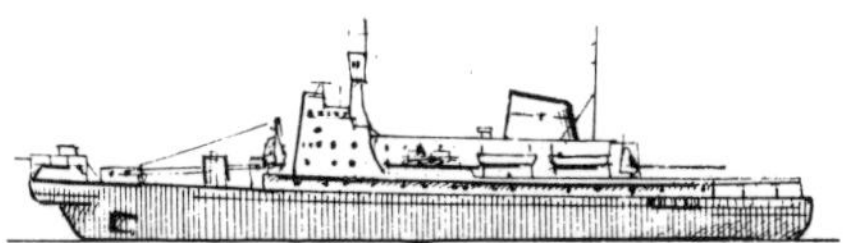

**811.** Ca. **JOHN CABOT.** 1965. Ice Breaking
Cable Repair Ship of Canadian Coast Guard.
6,400 tons (full). 313 x 60 x 22. (95.4 x 18.2 x
6.7). 2 screws; diesel-electric. 15 knots. Facilities
for helicopters.

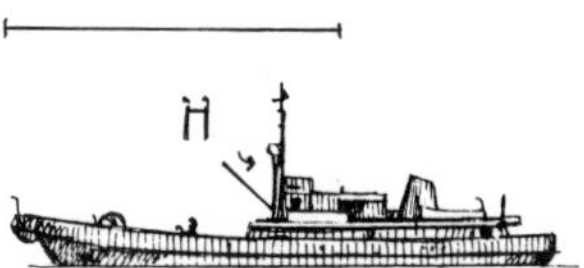

**812.** Fi. **PUTSAARI.** 1965. Cable Ship. 430 tons.
148 x 39 x 10 (45.1 x 11.8 x 3). Diesel. 10 knots.

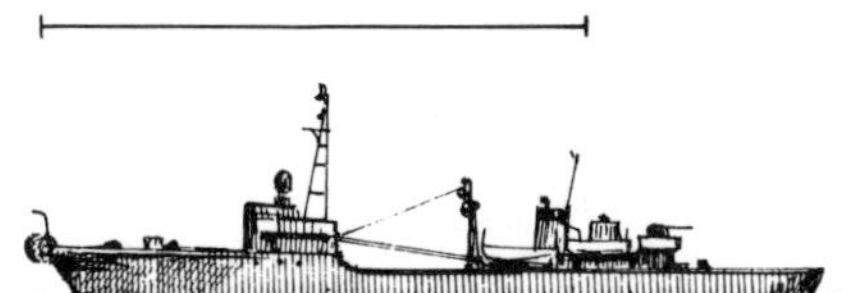

**813.** Ja. **TSUGARU.** *481*. Cable Ship and Minelayer. 1,955.950 tons. 206 x 34 x 11. (62.7 x 10.3
x 3.3). 2 screws; diesel. 16 knots. 1—3-inch D.P.
gun. 2—20-m.m. A.A. guns. 4 depth charge
mortars. 4 mine launchers.

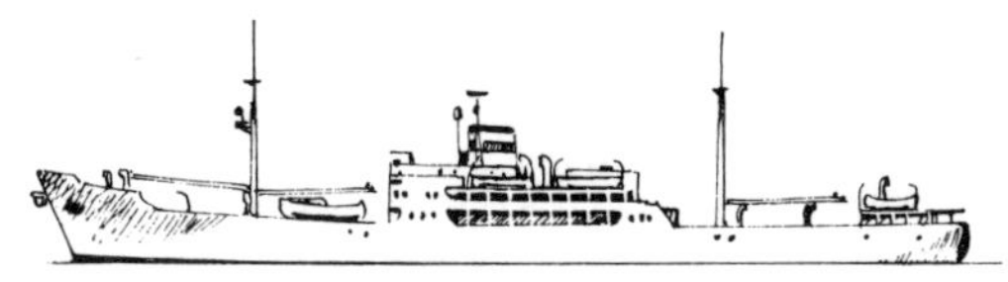

**814.** Ru. **VITYAZ.** 1965. Oceanographic Ship.
6,000 tons. 380 (approx.). (115.8) Diesels. 14
knots.

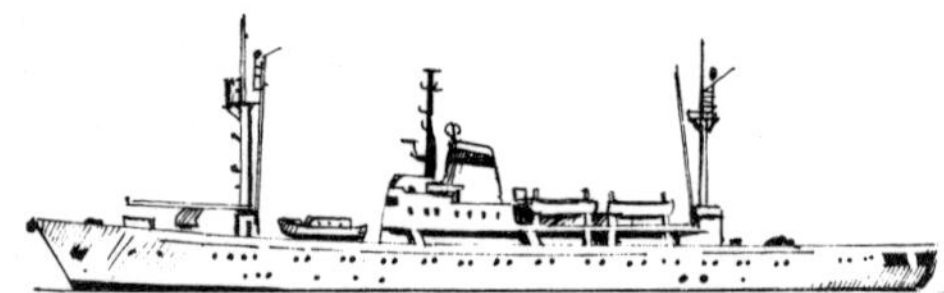

**★ 815.** Ru. **POLYUS** class. 1962-64. Survey ships. 4,000 tons. 366 x 45 x 20. (111.5 x 13.7 x 6.1). Diesels. 15 knots.
**BAIKAL, BALKHASH, POLYUS.**

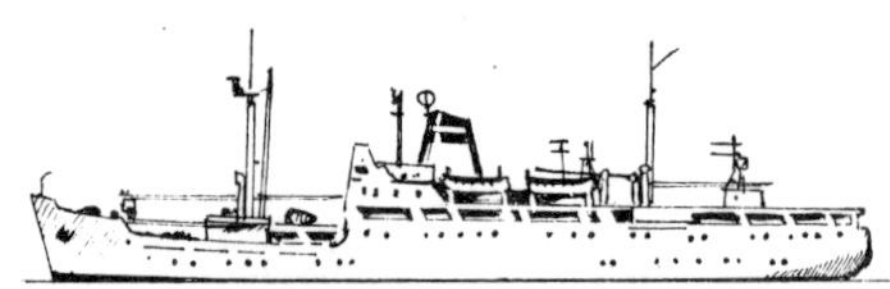

**★ 816.** Ru. **MIKHAIL LOMONOSOV.** 1957. Survey and Research Ship. 6,000 tons. 335 (approx.). (102.1). Diesels. 13 knots.

**817.** Bz. **CANOPUS.** *H22.* 1958. Survey Ship. 1,500 tons. 256 x 39 x 12. (78 x 11.8 x 3.6). 2 screws; diesels. 15 knots. 1—3-inch A.A. gun. Helicopter deck.
**SIRIUS.** *H21.*

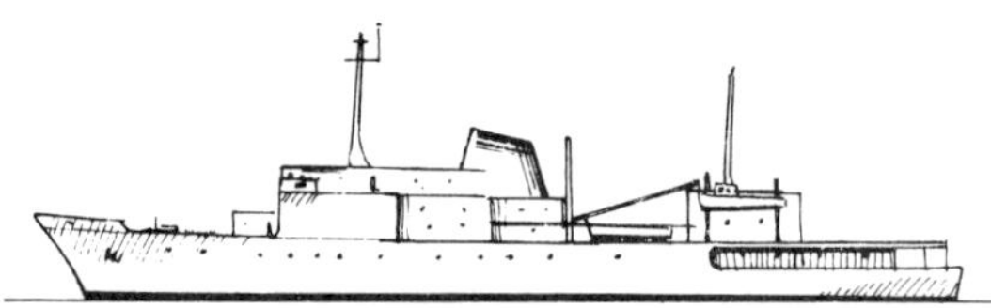

**818.** Am. **CHAUVENET** class. 1969. Survey Ships. 4,200 tons ;full). 393 x 54 x 16. (119.7 x 16.4 x 4.8). Diesel. 15 knots. Operated by M.S.T.S.
**CHAUVENET.** *AGS29.* **HARKNESS.** *AGS32.*

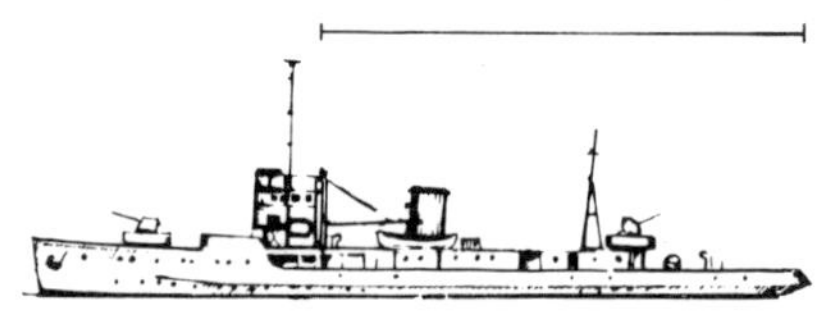

**819.** Ar. **SPIRO.** *GC12,* 1937. Survey Ship. 600 tons. 197 x 24 x 12. (59.7 x 7.3 x 3.6). Diesel. 13 knots. 4—40-m.m. guns. Formerly minesweeper of "Bouchard" class.

Py. 2 ships of this class employed as river gunboats.
**BOUCHARD.** *M7,* **PARKER.** *M11.*

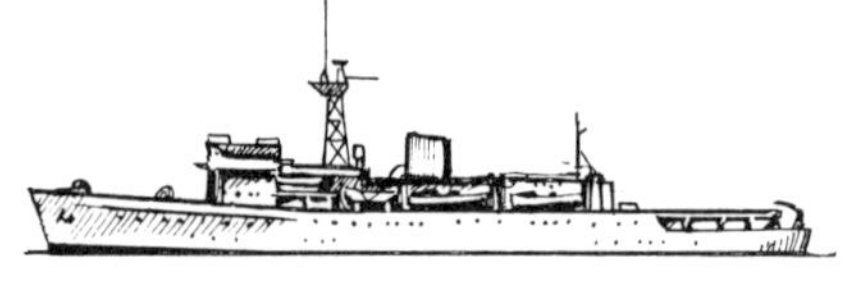

**820.** Br. **VIDAL.** 1954. Survey Ship. 1,900 tons. 315 x 40 x 12. (96 x 12.1 x 3.6). 2 screws; diesels. 15 knots. 1 helicopter and platform.

**821.** In. **DARSHAK.** 1964. Survey Ship. 2,800 tons. 319 x 49 x 29. (97.2 x 14.9 x 8.8). Diesel-electric. 16 knots. 1 helicopter.

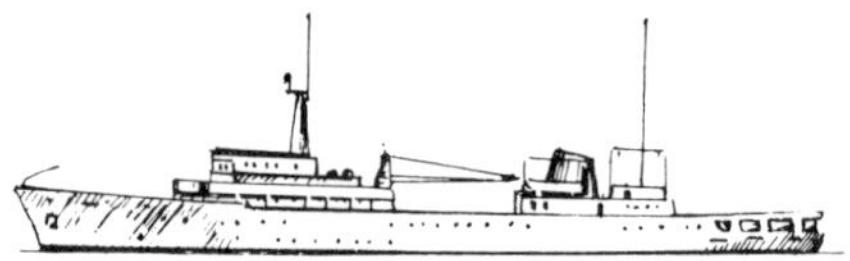

**822.** Au. **MORESBY.** 1964. Survey Ship. 1,700 tons. 314 x 42 x 13. (95.7 x 12.8 x 3.9). 2 screws; diesel-electric. 19 knots. 2—40-m.m. A.A. guns. 1 helicopter.

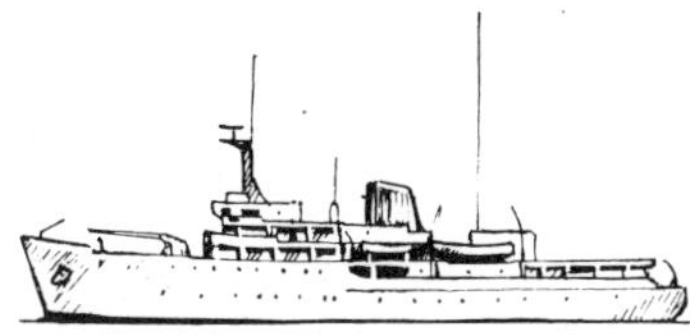

**823.** Br. **HECA** class. 1965-66. Survey Ships.
2,300 tons. 260 x 49 x 16 (79.3 x 15 x 4.8).
Diesel-electric. 14 knots. 1 helicopter.
**HECATE, HECLA, HYDRA.**

**824.** Br. **FAWN** class. 1968-70. Coastal Survey
Ships. 800 tons. 190 x 38 x 12. (58.2 x 11.5 x 3.6).
2 screws; diesels. 15 knots.
**BEAGLE, BULLDOG, FAWN, FOX.**

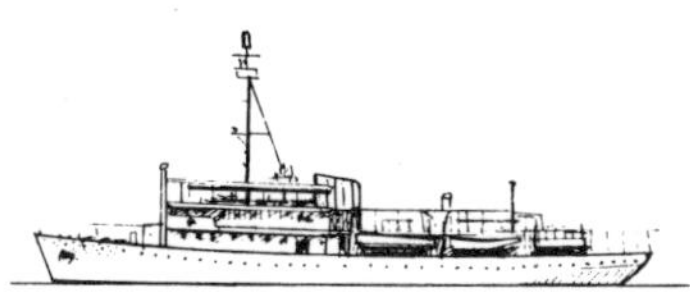

**825.** Du. **LUYMES.** *A902.* 1952. Survey Ship.
1,100 tons. 234 x 36 x 7. (71.3 x 10.9 x 2.1). 2
screws; diesels. 15 knots. 1—40-m.m. A.A. gun.
2—20-m.m. A.A. guns. 2 depth charge throwers.
1 mousetrap.
**SNELLIUS.** *A907.*

**826.** Du. **ZEEFAKKEL.** *A903.* 360 tons. 149 x
25 x 7. (45 4 x 7.6 x 2.1). 2 screws; diesels. 12
knots. 1—3-inch A.A. gun. 1—40-m.m. A.A. gun.

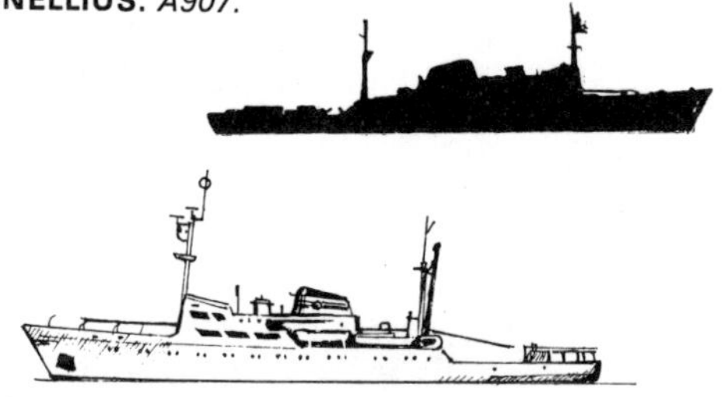

**827.** Ru. **NIKOLAI ZUBOV** class. 1964c.
Survey Ships. 2,700 tons. 295 x 43 x 15. (89.9 x
13.1 x 4.5). Diesels. 16 knots.
**A. CHIRIKOV, A. VILKITSKIJ, BORIS
DAVIDOV, F. BELLINGSGAUSEN, F. LITKE,
GAVRIL SARITSHEV, KHARITON LAPTEV,
NIKOLAI ZUBOV, S. CHELYUSKIN, S.
DEZHNEV, V. GOLOVNIN.**

**828.** Ca. **ENDEAVOUR.** *171.* 1963. Oceanographic Research Ship. 1,600 tons. 236 x 39 x 13.
(71.9 x 11.8 x 3.9). 2 screws; diesel-electric. 16
knots. 1 helicopter.

**829.** Am. **CONRAD** class. 1962-69. Oceanographic Research Ships. 1,200 tons. 209 x 37 x
15. (63.7 x 11.2 x 4.5). Diesel-electric. 13 knots.
Ships vary in appearance and some may be like
No. 830.

**ROBERT D. CONRAD, JAMES M. GILLISS,
SANDS, LYNCH, DE STEIGUER, BARTLETT,
THOMAS G. THOMPSON,**
Also similar:
**KELLAR, S. P. LEE.**

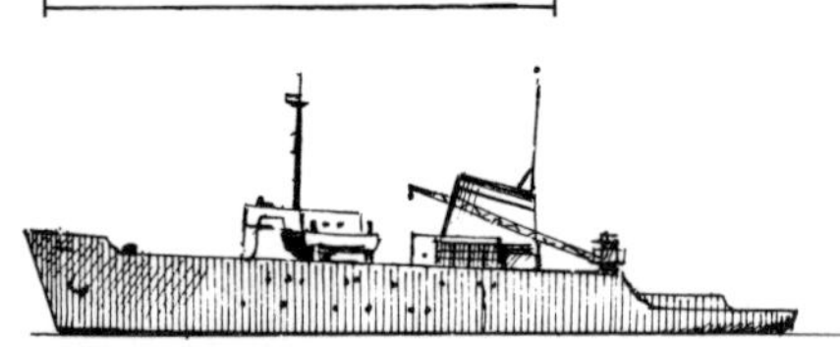

**830.** Am. **CONRAD** class. Remaining ships, but others under No. 829 may have this appearance. **CHARLES H. DAVIS** (temporarily under New Zealand flag), **THOMAS WASHINGTON**.

**831.** Ja. **FUJI.** *5001*. Icebreaker. 5,300 tons. 328 x 72 x 29. (100 x 21.9 x 8.8) ; 2 screws ; diesel-electric. 16 knots. 3 helicopters. Also serves as Antarctic Support Ship.

**832.** Br. **ENDURANCE.** *A171*. Ice Patrol Ship. 3,600 tons. 305 x 46 x 18 (92.9 x 14 x 5.4). Diesel. 14 knots. 2 helicopters and platform. Former Danish merchant ship.

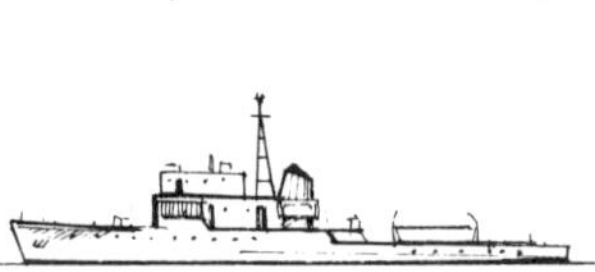

**833.** Bz **ARGUS.** *H31*. 1959. Coastal Survey Ship. 250 tons. 148 x 20 x 7. (45.1 x 6.1 x 2.1). 2 screws ; diesels. 15 knots. **ORION.** *H32*, **TAURUS.** *H33*.

★ **834.** Ru. **MOMA** class. 1969c. Survey Ships. 1,200 tons. 215 (approx.). Similar to No. 835. Numbers in service not known but they include the following : **ARKTIKA, MOMA, TAMYR**.

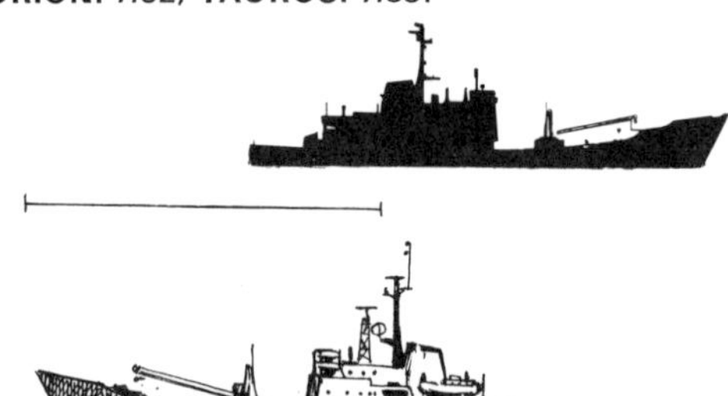

★ **835.** Ru. **SAMARA** class. 1962. Survey Ships. 800 tons. 180 (approx.). At least 16-20 ships in class including : **AZIMUT, GIGROMETR, GLOBUS, GORIZONT, HIGROMETR, KOMPAS, P. MERKURYA, TROPIK, ZENIT**.

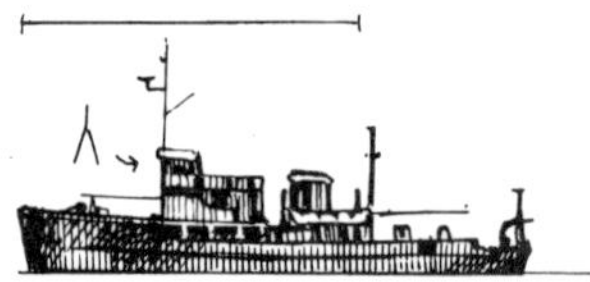

**836.** Ge. **ADOLF BESTELMEYER.** 1943. Experimental Vessel. 300 tons. 136 x 25 x 8 (41.5 x 7.6 x 2.4). 2 screws ; diesel. 15 knots. Former U.S. "YMS" type minesweeper. **RUDOLF DIESEL.** May be similar.

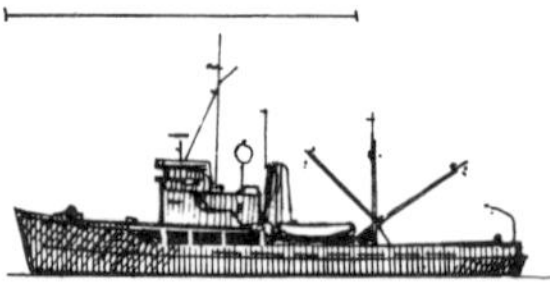

**837.** Ge. **H. C. OERSTED.** All particulars as for No. 836.

**838.** Du. **CUMULUS.** 1963. Weather Ship. 1,900 tons (gross). 234 x 41 x 15. (71.3 x 12.5 x 4.6). Diesel. 12 knots.

**839.** Am. **T-AGOR 16.** 1971. Oceanographic Research Ship. 3,000 tons (full). 247 x 75 x 19. (75.3-75.3 x 22.9 x 5.7). 2 screws; diesels. 15 knots. Catamaran hull.

**840.** Sw. **JOHAN MANSSON.** 1966. Survey Ship. 900 tons. 184 x 36 x 9. (56.1 x 11 x 2.5). Diesel. 15 knots. Small funnels abreast.

**841.** Am. **MELVILLE.** 1969. Oceanographic Research Ship. 1,900 tons. 244 x 46 x 15. (74.4 x 14 x 4.5). 2 screws; diesel. 12 knots. **KNORR.**

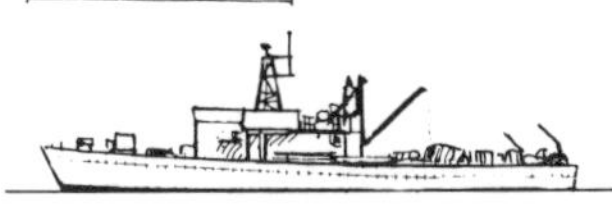

**842.** Br. **E** class. 1957-58. Inshore Survey Vessels. 160 tons. 107 x 22 x 6 (32.6 x 6.7 x 1.8). 2 screws; diesel. 14 knots. **ECHO, EGERIA, ENTERPRISE.**

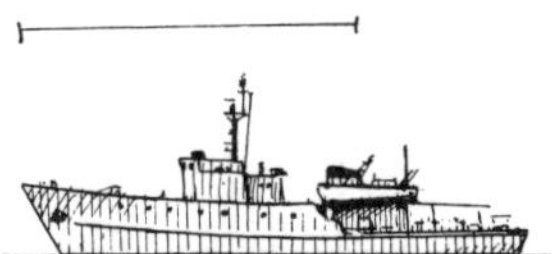

**843.** Fr. **ASTROLABE.** *A780*. 1963. Survey Ship. 350 tons. 138 x 27 x 8 (42.1 x 8.2 x 2.5). Diesels. 13 knots. **BOUSSOLE.** *A781*.

**844.** Fr. **ALIDADE.** *A682*. 1962. Survey vessel. 120 tons. 78 (23.7). Diesels. 9 knots. **OCTANT.** *A683*.

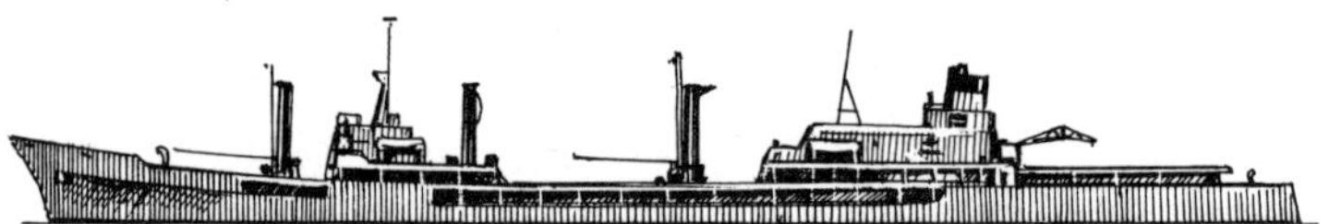

**845.** Ca. **PROVIDER.** *508*. 1963. Helicopter Carrier and Supply Ship. 22,700 tons full load. 555 x 76 x 32. (169.2 x 23.2 x 9.8). Turbine. 20 knots. 3 helicopters and flight deck. 2 funnels abreast.

**846.** Du. **POOLSTER.** *A835*. 1964. Combat Support Ship. 16,800 tons full load. 552 x 67 x 27. (168.1 x 20.4 x 8.2). Turbines. 21 knots. 2—40-m.m. A.A. guns. 5 helicopters and helicopter deck.

**847.** Ge. **LUNEBURG** class. 1968. Supply Ships. 3,300 tons. 341 x 43 x 14. (103.9 x 13.1 x 4.2). 2 screws. Diesels. 17 knots. 4—40-m.m. A.A. guns (twin).

**COBURG.** *A1412,* **FREIBURG.** *A1413,* **GLUCKSBURG.** *A1415,* **LUNEBURG.** *A1411,* **MEERSBURG.** *A1418,* **NIENBURG.** *A1416,* **OFFENBURG.** *A1417,* **SAARBURG.** *A1415.*

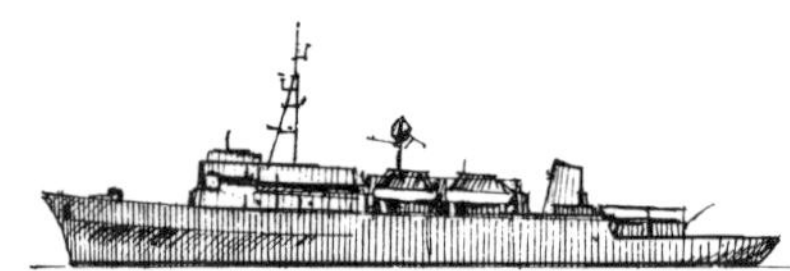

**848.** Fr. **RANCE.** *A618*. 1966. Maintenance Ship (damage control). 2,100 tons. 300 x 43 x 12. (91.4 x 13.1 x 3.6). Diesels. 16 knots. Hangar for three helicopters.
For other ships in class see Nos. 849 and 855.

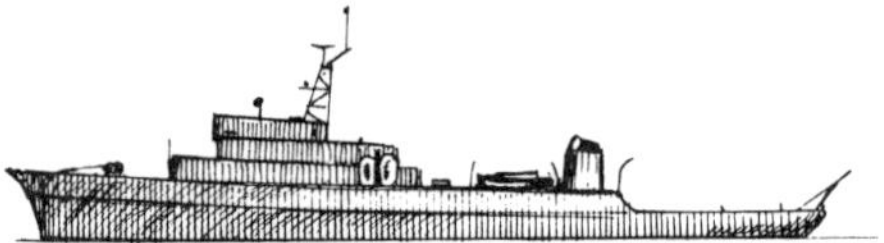

**849.** Fr. **GARONNE.** *A617*. 1965. Repair Ship. 2,100 tons. 333 x 45 x 13. (101.4 x 13.7 x 3.9). Diesels. 16 knots. 3—40-m.m. A.A. guns. 2 helicopters.
For others in class see Nos. 848 and 855.

★ **850.** Ru. **DESNA** class. 1963. Missile Range Instrumentation Ships. 5,300 tons. 436 x 57 x 20. (132.8 x 17.3 x 6.1). Reciprocating. 18 knots. 1 helicopter.
**CHAZHMA, CHUMIKAN.**

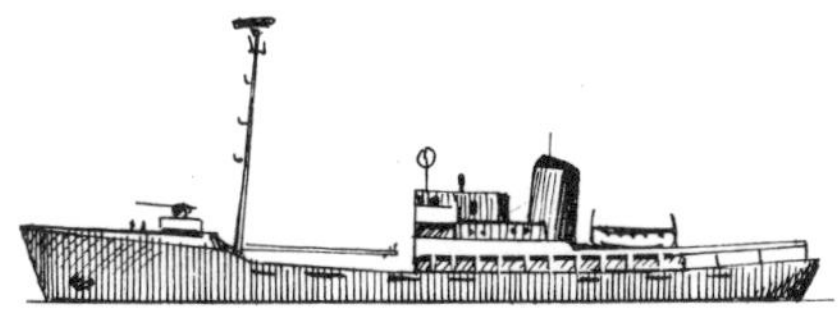

**851.** Ic. **THOR.** 1951. Coast Guard Patrol Vessel. 900 tons. 206 x 31 x 13. (62.7 x 9.4 x 3.9). Diesels. 17 knots. 1—57-m.m. gun.

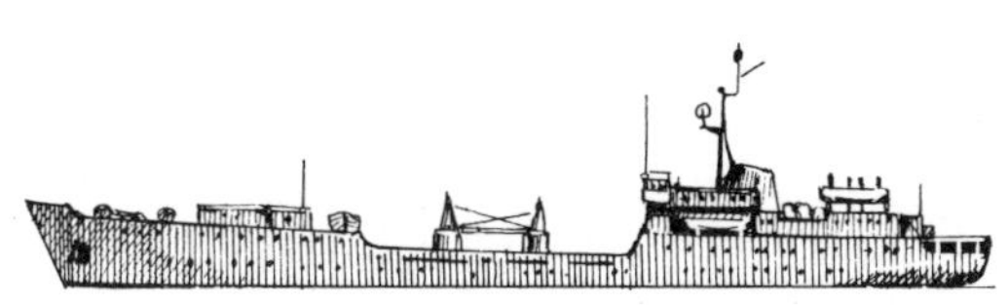

★ **852.** Ru. **OSKOL** class. Support Ship. Approx. 380 feet. No other information available.

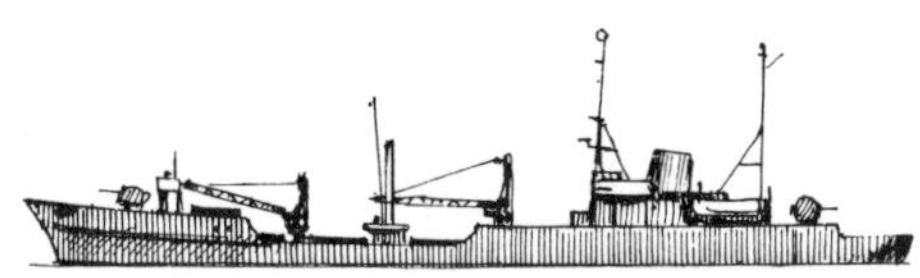

**853.** Ge. **ODENWALD.** *A1436.* 1966. Supply Ship. 3,500 tons. 348 x 46 x 12. (106 x 14 x 3.6). Diesels. 17 knots. 4—40-m.m. A.A. guns.
**WESTERWALD.** *A1435.*

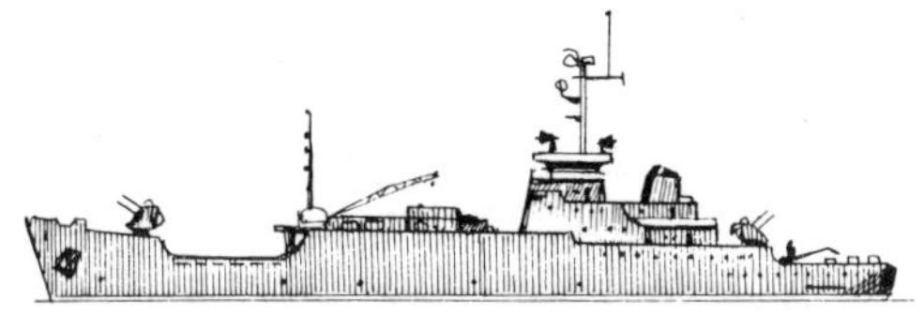

★ **854.** Ru. **LAMA** class. 1964c. Missile Supply Ships. 7,000 tons full load. 370 x 60 x 19. (112.8 x 18.3 x 5.8). 2 screws. Disels. 15 knots. 8—57-m.m. guns (quadruple). At least 3 in the Soviet Navy.

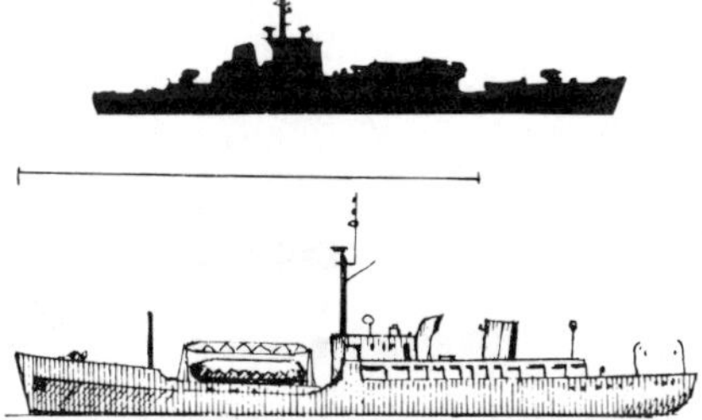

**855.** Fr. **RHIN.** *A621.* 1964. Maintenance Support Ship. 2,100 tons. 300 x 43 x 12. (91.4 x 13.1 x 3.6). Diesel. 16 knots. 3—40-m.m. A.A. guns. 2 helicopters.
For other ships in class see drawings Nos. 848 and 849. These ships are sometimes prefixed with "Le" or "La".
**RHONE.** *A622,* **LOIRE.** *A615.*

**856.** Fr. **LA RECHERCHE.** *A758.* 1951. Converted 1960. Research Ship. 780 tons. 222 x 34 x 13. (67.7 x 10.4 x 4). Diesel. 13½ knots. Former passenger vessel.

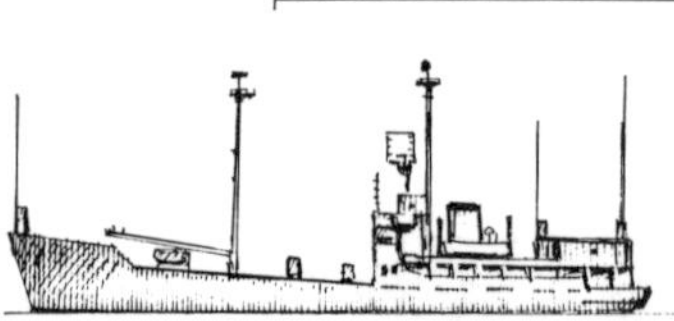

**857.** Am. **RANGE RECOVERER.** 1944. Converted 1959-60. Range Instrumentation Ship. 550 tons. 177 x 32 x 11. (53.9 x 9.7 x 3.4). Diesel. 14 knots. Former small cargo ship.

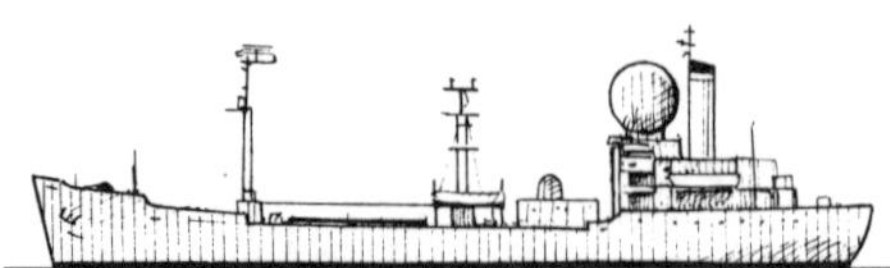

**858.** Am. **COASTAL CRUSADER.** 1945. Converted 1963-64. Range Instrumentation Ship. 339 x 50 x 12. (103.3 x 15.2 x 3.7). Diesel. 10 knots. Former CI-M-AVI type merchant ships. **SWORD KNOT.**

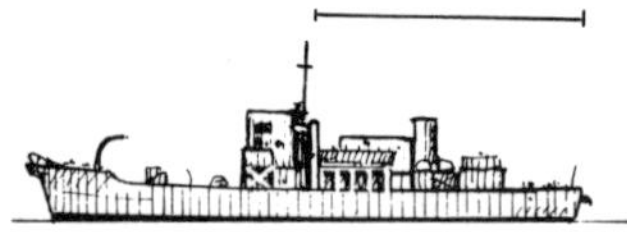

**859.** Br. **MINER III.** *N13.* 1940. Tender. (Controlled Minelayer). 300 tons. 110 x 27 x 8. (33.5 x 8.2 x 2.4). 2 screws ; diesels. 10 knots.

**860.** Br. **BRITANNIC.** 1941. Store Carrier. Tonnage etc. as No. 859. "Miner" class. **STEADY** may be similar.

**861.** Am. **L. Y. SPEAR.** *S36.* 1969. Submarine Tender. 13,000 tons. 643 x 85. (195.7 x 25.9). Turbines. 2—5-inch guns. **DIXON.** *S37.*

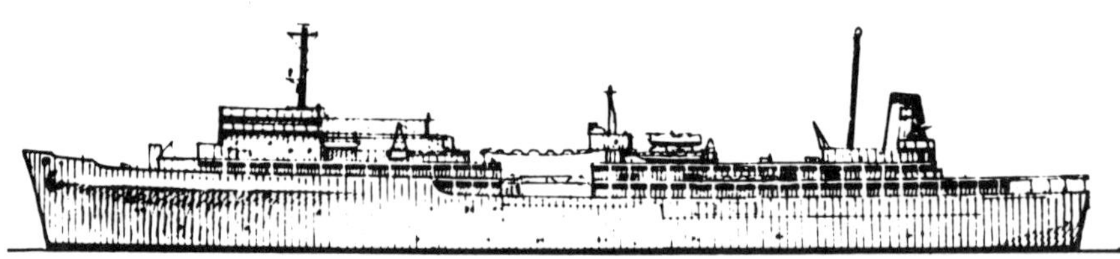

**862.** Am. **SIMON LAKE** class. 1964-65. Submarine Tenders. 22,000 tons (full load). 644 x 85 x 30. (195.8 x 25.9 x 9.1). Turbines. 18 knots. 4—3-inch A.A. guns. Very large cranes amidships.
**SIMON LAKE.** *S33,* **CANOPUS.** *S34.*

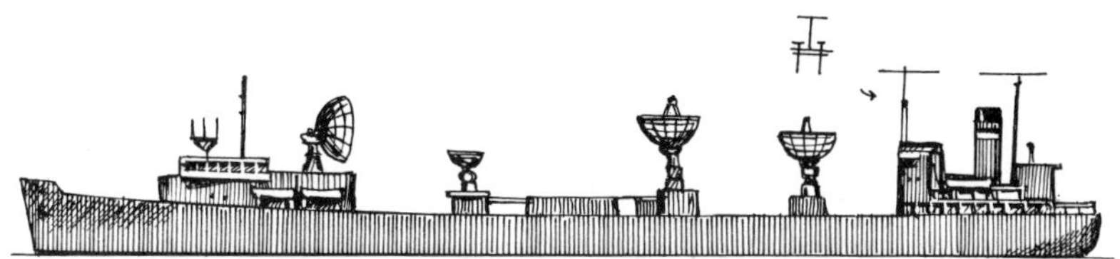

**863.** Am. **REDSTONE.** 1944. Converted 1964-65. Range Instrumentation Ship. 21,626 tons full load. 595 x 75 x 25. (181 x 22.9 x 7.6). Turbo-electric. 16 knots. Former T-2 type tanker.

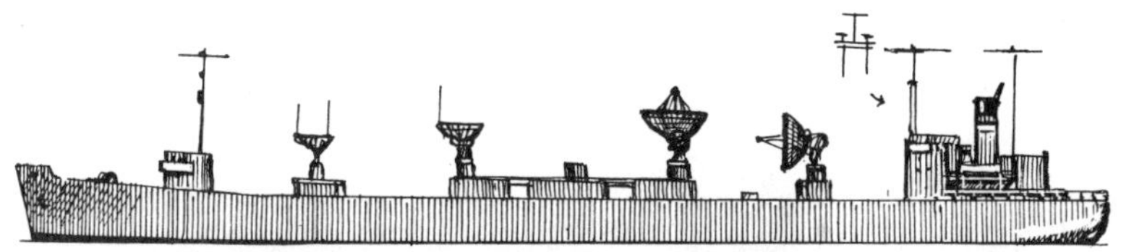

**864.** Am. **VANGUARD.** 1944. Converted 1965-66. Range Instrumentation Ship. All details as for number 863. Principally distinguished from Redstone by lighter structure forward.

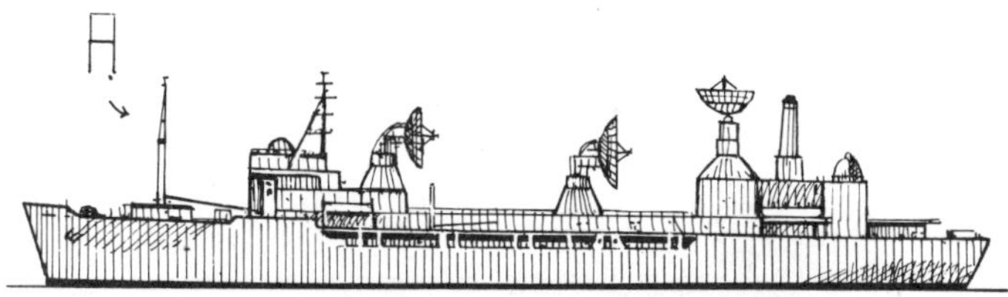

**865.** Am. **GENERAL H. H. ARNOLD.** 1944. Converted 1962-63. Range Instrumentation Ship. 16,600 tons (full load). 553 x 72 x 26. (168.6 x 21.9 x 7.9). Turbines. 15 knots. Former C-4 type transport.
**GENERAL HOYT S. VANDENBERG.**

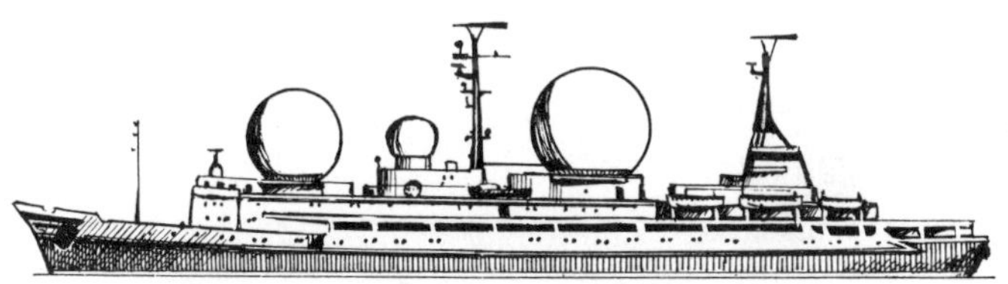

**866.** Ru. **KOSMONAUT VLADIMIR KOMAROV.** 1967. Missile Detection Ship. Approx. 8,000 tons. Approx. dimensions 511 x 68 x 30. (156.8 x 20.7 x 9.1). Diesel. Approx. 17 knots. Merchant ship hull.

**867.** Ru. **E-I** class. Nuclear-powered Missile Submarines. 4,600/5,000 tons. 385 x 33 x 27. (117.3 x 10 x 8.2). Nuclear-powered turbines. 20 knots. 6 surface-to-surface "Shaddock" launchers. 2 torpedo tubes.
At least five ships in service with the Soviet Navy.

**868.** Ru. **E-II** class. Nuclear-powered Missile Submarines. 5,000/5,600 tons. 394 x 33 x 27. (120 x 10 x 8.2). Nuclear-powered turbines. 22 knots. 8 surface-to-surface "Shaddock" launchers. 6 torpedo tubes (bow).
At least 25 in service.

**869.** Am. **TRITON.** *586.* 1959. Nuclear-powered Attack Submarine. 5,900/7,800 tons. 448 x 37 x 24. (136.3 x 11.3 x 7.3). 2 screws; nuclear-powered turbines. 27/20 knots. Anti-submarine torpedoes and 6 torpedo tubes (4 forward, 2 aft).
Longest submarine in the world.

**870.** Am. **ETHAN ALLEN** class. 1961-63. Nuclear-powered Missile Submarines. 6,900/7,900 tons. 410 x 33 x 30. (125 x 10.1 x 9.4). Nuclear-powered turbines. 20/30 knots. 16 launching tubes for surface-to-surface "Polaris" missiles. 4 torpedo tubes (bow).
**ETHAN ALLEN.** *608,* **JOHN MARSHALL.** *611,* **SAM HOUSTON.** *609,* **THOMAS A. EDISON.** *610,* **THOMAS JEFFERSON.** *618.*

**871.** Am. **LAFAYETTE** class. 1963-67. Nuclear-powered Missile Submarines. 7,300/8,300 tons. 425 x 33 x 31. (129.5 x 10.1 x 9.4). Nuclear-powered turbines. 20/30 knots. 16 launching tubes for surface-to-surface "Polaris" missiles. Being converted to operate the "Poseidon" missile. 4 torpedo tubes (bow).
**ALEXANDER HAMILTON.** *617,* **ANDREW JACKSON.** *619,* **BENJAMIN FRANKLIN.** *640,* **CASIMIR PULASKI.** *633,* **DANIEL WEBSTER** (see inset). *626,* **DANIEL BOONE.** *629,* **FRANCIS SCOTT KEY.** *657,* **GEORGE BANCROFT.** *643,* **GEORGE C. MARSHALL.** *654,* **GEORGE WASHINGTON CARVER.** *656,* **HENRY CLAY.** *625,* **HENRY L. STIMSON.** *655,* **JAMES MONROE.** *622,* **JAMES MADISON.** *627,* **JAMES K. POLK.** *645,* **JOHN ADAMS.** *620,* **JOHN C. CALHOUN.** *630,* **LAFAYETTE.** *616,* **LEWIS AND CLARK.** *644,* **KAMEHAMEHA.** *642,* **MARIANO G. VALLEJO.** *658,* **NATHAN HALE.** *623,* **NATHANEAL GREENE.** *636,* **STONEWALL JACKSON.** *634,* **SAM RAYBURN.** *635,* **SIMON BOLIVAR.** *641,* **TECUMSEH.** *628,* **ULYSEES S. GRANT.** *631,* **VON STEUBEN.** *632,* **WILL ROGERS.** *659,* **WOODROW WILSON.** *624.*

**872.** Am. **GEORGE WASHINGTON** class. 1959-61. Nuclear-powered Missile Submarines. 5,900/6,700 tons. 382 x 33 x 29. (116.4 x 10.1 x 8.8). Nuclear-powered turbines. 20/30 knots. 16 launching tubes for surface-to-surface "Polaris" missiles. 6 torpedo tubes (bow)
**ABRAHAM LINCOLN.** *602,* **GEORGE WASHINGTON.** *598,* **PATRICK HENRY.** *599,* **ROBERT E. LEE.** *601,* **THEODORE ROOSEVELT.** *600.*

**873.** Fr. **LE REDOUBTABLE** class. 1970-75. Nuclear-powered Missile Submarines. 7,900/9,000 tons. 420 x 34.8 x 32.8. (128 x 10.6 x 10). Nuclear-powered turbo-electric. 20/25 knots. 16 launching tubes for surface-to-surface "Polaris" missiles. 4 torpedo tubes.
**LE FOUDROYANT.** *S610,* **LE REDOUBTABLE.** *S611,* **LE TERRIBLE.** *S612.*

**874.** Br. **RESOLUTION** class. 1967-70. Nuclear-powered Missile Submarines. 7,500/8,400 tons. 425 x 33 x 30. (129.5 x 10.1 x 9.1). Nuclear-powered turbines. 20/25 knots. 16 launching tubes for surface-to-surface "Polaris" missiles. 6 torpedo tubes (bow).

Differ principally from the U.S. boats by having the diving planes on the bows rather than on the fin.
**RENOWN, REPULSE, RESOLUTION, REVENGE.**

**875.** Am. **TULLIBEE.** *597.* 1960. Nuclear-powered Attack Submarine. 2,300/2,600 tons 273 x 23 x 21. (83.2 x 7 x 6.4). Nuclear-powered turbo-electric. 15 20 knots. Anti-submarine torpedoes. 4 torpedo tubes (amidships).

**876.** Am. **NARWHAL.** *671.* 1969. Nuclear-powered Attack Submarine. 4,600 tons full load. 314 x 38 x 26. (95.7 x 11.5 x 7.9). Nuclear-powered turbines. 20/30 knots. "Subroc" (anti-submarine missile) and anti-submarine torpedo tubes. 4 torpedo tubes (amidships).

Similar in appearance but slightly smaller:
**STURGEON** class.
**ASPRO.** *648,* **ARCHERFISH.** *678,* **BATFISH.** *681,* **BERGALL.** *667,* **BILLFISH.** *676,* **BLUEFISH.** *675,* **CAVALLA.** *684,* **DRUM.** *677,* **FLYINGFISH.** *673,* **GRAYLING,** *646,* **GUITARRO.** *665,* **GURNARD.** *662,* **FINBACK.** *670,* **HAWKBILL.** *666,* **HAMMERHEAD.** *663,* **PARCHE.** *683,* **PINTADO.** *672,* **PUFFER.** *652,* **POGY.** *647,* **PARGO.** *650,* **QUEENFISH.** *651,* **LAPON.** *661,* **RAY.** *653,* **REDFISH.** *680,* **SAND LANCE.** *660,* **SEA DEVIL.** *664,* **SEAHORSE.** *669,* **SILVERSIDES.** *679,* **SPADEFISH.** *668,* **STURGEON.** *637,* **SUNFISH.** *649,* **TAUTOG.** *639,* **TREPANG.** *674,* **TUNNY.** *682,* **WHALE.** *638.*

**877.** Am. **PERMIT** class. 1962-68. Nuclear-powered Attack Submarines. 3,700/4,600 tons. 279 or 296 x 32 x 25. (84.9 or 90.2 x 9.6 x 7.6). Nuclear-powered turbines. 20/30 knots. "Subroc" (anti-submarine missile) and anti-submarine torpedo tubes. 4 torpedo tubes (amidships). Originally known as the Thresher class.
**BARB.** *596,* **DACE.** *607,* **FLASHER.** *613,* **GATO.** *615,* **GREENLING.** *614,* **GUARDFISH.** *612,* **HADDO.** *604,* **HADDOCK.** *621,* **JACK.** *605,* **PERMIT.** *594,* **POLLACK.** *603,* **PLUNGER.** *595.* **TINOSA.** *606.*

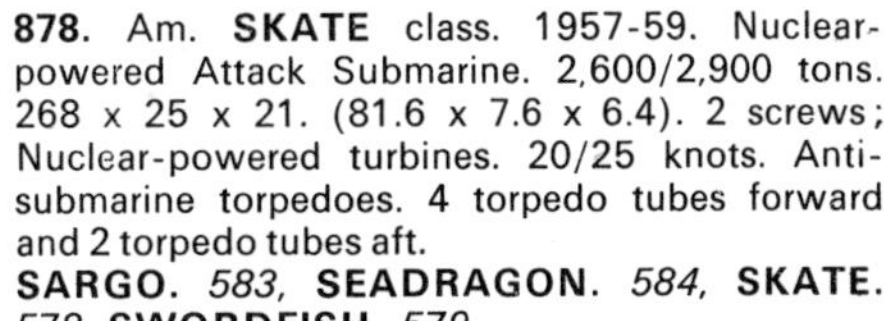

**878.** Am. **SKATE** class. 1957-59. Nuclear-powered Attack Submarine. 2,600/2,900 tons. 268 x 25 x 21. (81.6 x 7.6 x 6.4). 2 screws; Nuclear-powered turbines. 20/25 knots. Anti-submarine torpedoes. 4 torpedo tubes forward and 2 torpedo tubes aft.
**SARGO.** *583,* **SEADRAGON.** *584,* **SKATE.** *578,* **SWORDFISH.** *579.*

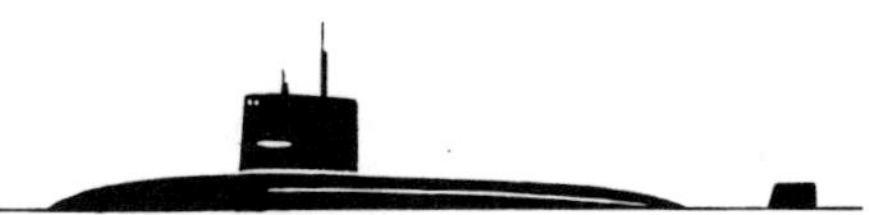

**879.** Am. **SKIPJACK** class. 1959-61. Nuclear-powered Attack Submarines. 3,100/3,500 tons. 252 x 32 x 28. (76.8 x 9.7 x 8.5). Nuclear-powered turbines. 20/30 knots. Anti-submarine torpedoes. 6 torpedo tubes (forward).
**SCAMP.** *588,* **SCULPIN.** *590,* **SHARK.** *591,* **SNOOK.** *592.*

**800.** Am. **BARBEL** class. 1959. Attack submarines. 2,200/2,900 tons. 200 x 29 x 28. (67 x 8.8 x 8.5). Diesel/electric. 15/25 knots. 6 torpedo tubes (forward).
**BARBEL.** *580,* **BONEFISH.** *582,* **BLUEBACK.** *581.*

**881.** Am. **ALBACORE.** *569.* 1953. Experimental Submarine. 1,500/1,900 tons. 204 x 28 x 19. (62.2 x 8.5 x 5.7). Diesel/electric. 25/33 knots.

**882.** Sw. **SJOORMEN** class. 1967-69. 700/1,100 tons. 167 x 20 x 20. (51 x 6.1 x 6.1). Diesel/electric. Torpedo tubes and mines.
**SJOBJORNEN.** *Sbj,* **SJOHASTEN.** *She,* **SJOHUNDEN.** *Shu,* **SJOLEJONET.** *Sle,* **SJOORMEN.** *Sor.*

**883.** Am. **NR-1.** 1969. Nuclear-powered Research Vessel. 400 tons submerged. 140 x 12. (42.6 x 3.6). 2 screws; nuclear-powered electric motors.

**884.** Br. **DREADNOUGHT.** 1963. Nuclear-powered Fleet Submarine. 3,000/4,000 tons. 266 x 32 x 26. (81 x 9.8 x 7.9). Nuclear-powered turbines. 30 knots. 6 torpedo tubes (bow).

**885.** Br. **VALIANT** class. 1966-1971. Nuclear-powered Fleet Submarines. 3,500/4 500 tons. 285 x 33 x 27. (86.9 x 10.1 x 8.2). Nuclear-powered turbines. 30 knots. 6 torpedo tubes homing).
**CHURCHILL, CONQUEROR, COURAGEOUS, VALIANT, WARSPITE.**
Differ from Dreadnought principally by the diving planes being at a higher level.

**886.** Ru. **G** class. 1958 et seq. Ballistic Missile Submarines. 2,400/2,800 tons. 320 x 28 x 22. (97.5 x 8.5 x 6.7). Diesel/electric. 17 knots. 3 missile launching tubes (fin). 6 torpedo tubes (bow). About 25 vessels in the class.

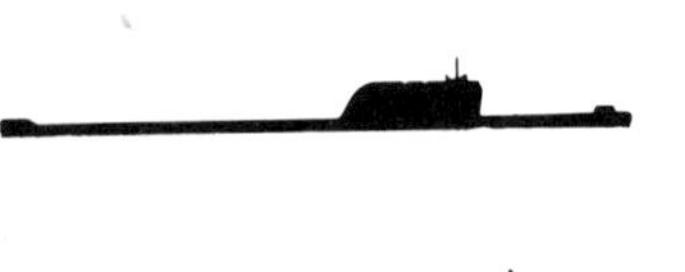

**887.** Ru. **H** class. 1959-64. Ballistic Missile Submarines. 3,700/4,100 tons. 344 x 33 x 25. (104.8 x 10.1 x 8.2). Nuclear-powered turbines. 25 knots. 3 missile launching tubes (fin). 6 torpedo tubes. 15 in class in 2 types.

**888.** Ru. **J** class. 1963 et seq. Ballistic Missile Submarines. 1,800/2,500 tons. 328 x 27 x 20. (100 x 8.2 x 6.1). Diesel/electric. 19/15 knots. 4 surface to surface "Shaddock" launchers from deck. 6 torpedo tubes. Distinguished by high freeboard and long, low sail.
At least 10 vessels in the class.

**889**. Am. **SAILFISH**. 572. 1956. Attack Submarine. 2,600/3,200 tons. 351 x 29 x 18. (107 x 8.8 x 5.5). Diesel/electric; 2 screws; 20/15 knots. 6 torpedo tubes.

Similar: (Sonar antennaes may be temporarily removed).
**SALMON**. *573*.

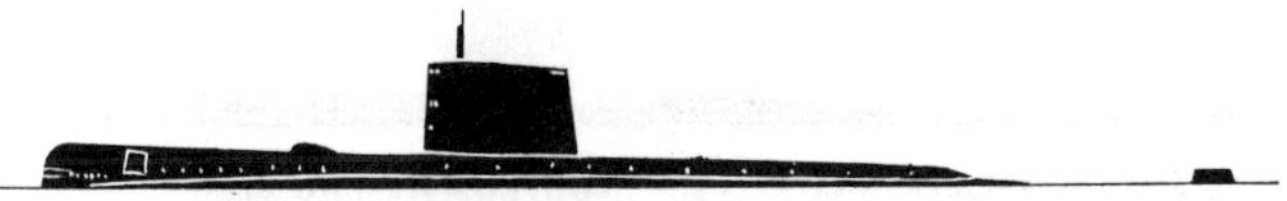

**890**. Du. **POTVIS** and **DOLFIJN** classes. 1960-65. 1,500/1,800 tons. 261 x 26 x 16. (79.4 x 7.8 x 4.6). Diesel/electric; 2 screws. 14/17 knots. 8 torpedo tubes.

**POTVIS** class. **POTVIS**. *S804*, **TONIJN**. *S*805.

**DOLFIJN** class (Sonar on bows—see inset).
**DOLFIJN**. *S808*, **ZEEHOND**. *S*809.

**891**. Am. **NAUTILUS**. *571*. 1954. Nuclear-powered Submarine. 3,500/4,000 tons. 324 x 28 x 22. (98.5 x 8.3 x 6.7). Nuclear-powered turbines. 20 knots. Anti-submarine torpedoes. 6 torpedo tubes (foreward). First nuclear-propelled submarine.

**892**. Ja. **OYASHIO**. *511*. 1960. 1,100/1,400 tons. 259 x 23 x 15. (78.8 x 7 x 4.6). Diesel/electric. 13/19 knots. 4 torpedo tubes.

★ **893**. Ru. **Z** class. 1952-55. Converted 1960-61. Ballistic Missile Submarines. 2,100/2,600 tons. 295 x 29 x 19. (89.9 x 8.8 x 5.8). Diesel/electric; 2 screws. 22-16 knots. 2 missile launching tubes. 6 torpedo tubes. Possibly mines. Converted from conventional "Z" class.

★ **894**. Ru. **Z** class. Details as for No. 893 but no missiles and a radar on the fin. 20 in class.

**895**. Ve. **CARITE**. *S11*. 1943. Modernised 1960-62. 1.800/2,400 tons. 312 x 27 x 17. (91.8 x 8.2 x 5.2). Diesel/electric; 2 screws. 20/10 knots. 10 torpedo tubes. (6 bow and 4 aft). Ex-U.S. "Balao" class.

Bz. **BAHIA**. *S12*. **RIO GRANDE DO SUL**. *S11*.

Ch. **THOMSON**. *20*. Sister **SIMPSON** has open fin; see No. 920.

**896**. Am. **GRAYBACK**. *574*. 1958. Converted 1968-69. Amphibious Transport Submarine. 2,700/3,700 tons. 334 x 30 x 19. (101.8 x 9 x 5.8). Diesel/electric; 2 screws. 20/17 knots. 8 torpedo tubes (6 forward, 2 aft). Carries frogmen and commandos.

Similar—slightly smaller—Attack Submarine **GROWLER**. *577*.

**897.** Am. **GUPPY II, IIA, IA** types. 1943-51 Attack Submarines. 1,100/2,400 tons. 308 x 27 x 18 (93.6 x 8.3 x 5.5). Diesel/electric; 2 screws. 18/15 knots. 10 torpedo tubes (6 forward, 4 aft). Modernised "Balao" and "Tench" classes. (Greater Underwater Propulsion Programme.) Some have stepped fins; see No. 926.

Type II: **CATFISH,** *339,* **CUBERA.** *347,* **DIODON.** *349,* **HALFBEAK.** *352,* **TUSK.** *426,* **CUTLASS.** *478,* **SEA LEOPARD.** *483,* **ODAX.** *584,* **SIRAGO.** *485,* **POMODON.** *486,* **AM-BERJACK** *522,* **GRAMPUS.** *523,* **GRENA-DIER.** *525.*

Type IIA: **ENTEMEDOR.** *340,* **HARDHEAD.** *365,* **JALLAO.** *368,* **MENHADEN.** *377,* **PIC-UDA.** *382,* **BANG.** *385,* **POMFRET.** *391,* **RAZORBACK.** *394,* **RONQUIL.** *396,* **SEA FOX.** *402,* **THREADFIN.** *410,* **THORNBACK.** *418,* **TRUTTA.** *421,* **QUILLBACK.** *424.*

Type IA: **BECUNA.** *319,* **BLACKFIN.** *322,* **CAIMAN.** *323,* **CHIVO.** *341,* **CHOPPER.** *342,* **ATULE.** *403,* **SEA POACHER.** *406,* **SEA ROBIN.** *407,* **TENCH.** *417.*

Similar: With Sonar Antennas (see No. 899). **BLENNY.** *324.*

**898.** Fr. **NARVAL** class. 1957-60. Reconstructed 1966 onwards. 1,200/1,900 tons. 256 x 24 x 18. (78 x 7.3 x 5.5). 2 screws; diesel/electric. 16/18 knots. 8 torpedo tubes (6 bow, 2 stern). Also shown as their old appearance, see drawing No. 928.
**DAUPHIN.** *S633,* **ESPADON.** *S637,* **MAR-SOUIN.** *S632,* **MORSE.** *S638,* **NARVAL.** *S631,* **REQUIN.** *S634.*

**899.** Am. **GUPPY III** type. 1944-49. Modernised 1960-62. Attack Submarines. 2,000/2,500 tons. 327 x 27 x 17. (99.6 x 8.2 x 5.2). Diesel/electric; 2 screws. 20/15 knots. 10 torpedo tubes (6 forward, 4 aft).

"Balao" class: **CLAMAGORE.** *343,* **COBBLER.** *344,* **CORPORAL.** *346,* **GREENFISH.** *351,* **TIRU.** *416.*

"Tench" class: **TRUMPETFISH.** *425,* **PICK-EREL.** *524,* **REMORA.** *487,* **VOLADOR.** *490.*

**900.** Ru. F class. 1957-59. Fleet Submarines. 2,000/2,300 tons. 300 x 27 x 19. (91.4 x 8.2 x 5.7). 3 screws; diesels/electric. 15 knots. 8 tor-pedo tubes.
Improved Z class. At least 40 were built for the Soviet Navy. Some are fitted with ice-protector on bows (see No. 901.)

India: **KALVARI, KANDHERI, KANJAR, KARANJ, KHADERI.**

★ **901.** Ru. **F** class. All details as **900.** Fitted with ice-protector on the bows.

★ **902.** Ru. **Z** class. 1951-52c. Fleet Submarines. All details as for No. 894 but does not have the radar. Capacity for 40 mines. Original Z class design. See later design No. 937.

**903.** Sp. **D** class. 1951-54. 1.100/1.500 tons. 277 x 22 x 13. (84.4 x 6.7 x 4). Diesels/electric. 20/9 knots. 6 torpedo tubes (4 forward, 2 aft). **D2.** *S21*, **D3.** *S22*.

★ **904.** Ru. **R** class. 1959-60. Fleet Submarines. 1,100/1,600 tons. 246 x 24 x 15. (74.9 x 7.3 x 4.5). Diesels/electric. 18/15 knots. 6 torpedo tubes (bow).
About 15 in the Soviet Navy. Improved "W" class. Recognised by the funnel like structure on the fin.

The following have been transferred:
RC. At least 4 boats.
Eg. At least 8 boats.

**905.** Br. **OBERON** and **PORPOISE** classes. 1958-67. Patrol Submarines. 1,600/2,400 tons. 295 x 27 x 18. (90 x 8.2 x 5.5). 2 screws; diesels/electric. 12/17 knots. 8 torpedo tubes (homing torpedoes in the "O" class).
O class: **OBERON, OCELOT, ODIN, OLYMPUS, ONSLAUGHT, ONYX, OPOSSUM, OPPORTUNE, ORACLE, ORPHEUS, OSIRIS, OTTER, OTUS.**

Australia: **ONSLOW, OTWAY, OVENS, OXLEY.** 1967-69.

Canada: **OJIBWA.** *72,* **OKANAGAN.** *74,* **ONONDAGA.** *73.* 1965-68.

Also ordered for the Chilean Navy.

Porpoise class: **CACHALOT, FINWHALE, GRAMPUS, NARWHAL, PORPOISE, RORQUAL, SEALION, WALRUS.**

**906.** Pv. **ABTAO** class (modified U.S. "Mackerel" class). 1954-57. 800/1,400 tons. 243 x 22 x 14. (74.1 x 6.7 x 4.3). 2 screws; diesels/electric. 16/10 knots. 6 torpedo tubes (4 bow, 2 stern). 1—5-inch gun in "Abtao" and "Dos de Mayo" only.
**ABTAO.** *42,* **ANGAMOS.** *43,* **DOS DE MAYO.** *41,* **IQUIQUE.** *44.*

**907.** Fr. **DAPHNE** class. 1964 onwards. 805/1,000 tons. 190 x 22 x 15. (58 x 6.8 x 4.7). 2 screws; diesel/electric. 16/16 knots. 12 torpedo tubes (8 forward, 4 aft).
**DAPHNE.** *S641,* **DIANE.** *S642,* **DORIS.** *S643,* **FLORE.** *S645,* **GALATEE.** *S646,* **JUNON.** *S648,* **PSYCHE.** *S650,* **SIRENE.** *S751,* **VENUS.** *S649.*

Pakistan: **MANGRA, SHUSHUK.**
Portugal: **ALBACORA.** *S163,* **BARRACUDA.** *S164,* **CACHALOTE.** *S165,* **DELFIM.** *S166.*
South Africa: **EMILY HOBHOUSE, JOHANNA VAN DER MERWE, MARIA VAN RIEBEECK.**

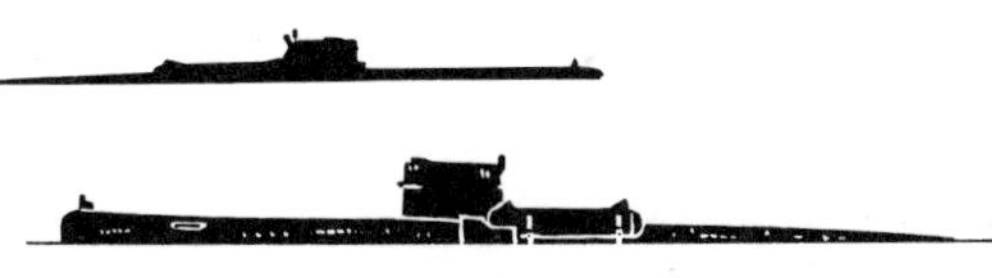

★ **908.** Ru. **W** class (missiles). About 1950-57. Converted around 1950-60. Guided Missile Submarines. 1,100/1,600 tons. 240 x 22 x 15. (73.1 x 6.7 x 4.5). Diesels/electric. 17/15 knots. 6 torpedo tubes (4 bow, 2 stern). 2 surface-to-surface "Shaddock" launchers. Launchers are on deck distinguishing them from the other "W" class missile submarine (No. 915).
About 15 in the Soviet Navy.

**909.** Da. **DELFINEN** class. 1958-64. 550/650 tons. 177 x 15 x 13. (54 x 4.7 x 4). Diesels/electric. 15/15 knots. 4 torpedo tubes.
**DELFINEN.** *S326,* **SPAEKHUGGEREN.** *S327,* **SPRINGEREN.** *S329,* **TUMLEREN.** *S328.*

**910.** Fr. **ARETHUSE** class. 1958-60. 400/650 tons. 164 x 19 x 12.8. (50 x 5.8 x 3.9). Diesel/electric. 16/18 knots. 4 torpedo tubes (bow).
**AMAZONE.** *S639,* **ARETHUSE.** *S635,* **ARGONAUTE.** *S636,* **ARIANE.** *S640.*

**911.** It. **TOTI** class. 1968-69. 460/580 tons. 153 x 15 x 13. (46.7 x 4.7 x 4). Diesel/electric. 9/14 knots. 4 torpedo tubes.
**BAGNOLINI.** *505,* **DANDOLO.** *513,* **MOCENIGO.** *514,* **TOTI.** *506.*

**912.** Is. Ex-British **T** class. 1944. Refitted 1967. 1,300/1,700 tons. 286 x 27 x 15. (87.1 x 8.2 x 4.5). Diesels/electric. 15/15 knots. 6 tubes for homing torpedoes.
**LEVIATHAN.** *75,* **DOLPHIN.**

**913.** Am. **HALIBUT.** *587*. 1960. Converted
1969-70. Nucelar-powered Support Submarine.
3,900/5,000 tons. 350 x 30 x 22. (106.6 x 9.1 x
6.7). 2 screws; nuclear-powered turbines. 15/20
knots. 6 torpedo tubes.
Originally a guided missile submarine but now
employed as a mother ship for small craft used
for submarine rescue.

**914.** Ru. **N** class. Around 1961-65. Nuclear-
powered Fleet Submarines (anti-submarine type).
3,500/4,000 tons. 360 x 32 x 24. (109.8 x 9.8 x
7.3). Nuclear-powered turbines. 25/30 knots.
6 torpedo tubes (bow).
15 units in the Soviet Navy, one having the name
**LENINSKY KOMSOMOL.**

**915.** Ru. **W** class (missiles). About 1950-57.
Converted about 1960-61. Guided Missile Submarines. 1,250/1,700 tons. 270 x 24 x 15. (82.5 x
7.3 x 4.7). 4 missile launchers (twin). May have
6 torpedo tubes.
Differs from the other type of "W" class missile
submarine (see No. 908) by having the missile
launchers in the fin. Converted and lengthened
from conventional "W" class submarines.

**916.** Ru. **C** class. Late 1960s onwards. Nuclear-
powered Missile Submarines. No details known.
Probably has 8 missile launchers (4 to port and
4 to starboard). Very similar to the "N" class
(No. 914). Large, bulbous bows are very prominent.

**917.** Ph. **SEP** *291*. 1939. Training Submarine.
1,100/1 450 tons. 276 x 22 x 13. (84.1 x 6.7 x 4).
Diesels/electric. 19/9 knots. 8 torpedo tubes.
1—4-inch gun. 2—40-m.m. A.A. guns. Mines.
Over-age and relegated to initial training.

**918.** Ia. Ex-Russian **W** class. Around 1950-51,
1,000/1,200 tons. 240 x 22 x 15. (73.1 x 6.7 x
4.6). 2 screws; diesels/electric. 17/15 knots.
6 torpedo tubes (4 foreward, 2 aft). 4 A.A. guns.
Mines.
Early "W IV" class distinguished by the fin being
stepped fore and aft.
**ALUGORO.** *512*, **NANGGALA.** *402*, **TJAKRA.**
*401*,
12 boats in all, of which only 6 are operational at
any one time.

**919.** Am. **BAYA.** *318*. 1944. Converted 1958-59.
Experimental Submarine. 1,900/2,600 tons.
335 x 27 x 17. (102.1 x 8.2 x 5.2). 2 screws;
diesels/electric. 10/8 knots. 4 torpedo tubes
(aft). Used as an electronics laboratory. Very
bluff bows. "Balao" class.

**920.** Ar. **SANTA FE.** (Ex-U.S. "Balao" class).
*11*. 1944. Refitted 1960. 1,500/2,400 tons. 312 x
27 x 17. (95 x 8.2 x 5.2). Diesels/electric. 20/10
knots. 10 torpedo tubes (6 bow, 4 stern). Note
open type fin.

Chile: **SIMPSON.** *21*, is similar.

Similar: American amphibious transport submarine. **SEALION.** *315*.

See No. 924 for vessels with the streamlined type
of fin.

**921.** Ge. **U9.** *S188*. 1966. Coastal Submarines.
370/450 tons. 143 x 15. (43.5 x 4.6). Diesels/
electric. 10/17 knots. 8 torpedo tubes (bow).
Probably similar are: **U10.** *S189*, **U11.** *S190*,
**U12.** *S191*.

**923.** Tu. **GUR** class (Ex-U.S. "Balao" class).
1944-45. Modernised 1950-54. 1,500/2,400
tons. 312 x 27 x 14. (95 x 8.2 x 4.2). Diesels/
electric. 20/10 knots. 10 torpedo tubes (6 bow,
4 stern). 1—5-inch gun (removed from most).
Not all of these boats have the second sonar
aerial.
**BIRINCI INONU.** *S330,* **CANAKKALE.** *S333,*
**CERBE.** *S341,* **GUR.** *S334,* **HIZIR REIS.** *S344,*
**IKINCI INONU.** *S331,* **PIRI REIS.** *S343,*
**PREVEZE.** *S340,* **SAKARYA.** *S332,* **TURGUT
REIS.** *S342.*

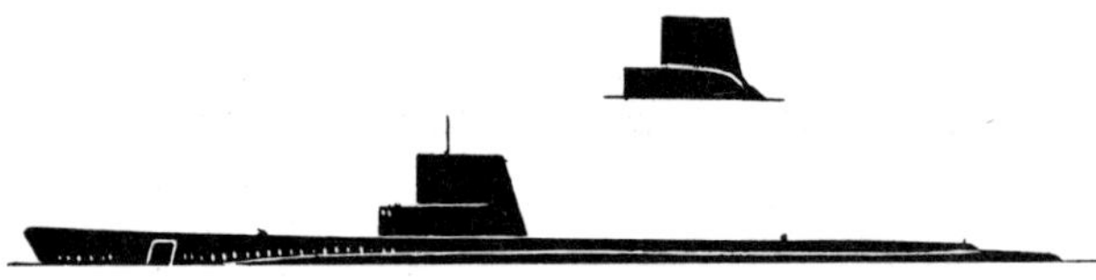

**924.** Ar. **SANTIAGO DEL ESTERO.** *12.* 1945.
Modernised 1960. All details as for No. 920
"Balao" class.

Similar: Am. (see inset). **SABALO.** *302,*
**SEGUNDO.** *398.* ("Balao" class.)

Greece: ("Balao" class) **TRIAINA.** *S86,* ("Gato"
class) **POSEIDON.** *S78.*

Spain: ("Balao" class) **ALMIRANTE GARCIA
DE LOS REYES.** *S31.*

**925.** Ca. **RAINBOW.** *75.* (Ex-U.S. "Tench"
class). 1945. Modernised. Tonnage etc. as
No. 920.

America: **MEDREGAL.** *480,* **TIGRONE.** *419.*

Pakistan. **GHAZI.** *130.*

**926.** Am. **GUPPY II, IIA,** and **IA** types. Most of
these ships have a fully streamlined fin and some
of these with the stepped fin are being converted.
For all details see No. 897.

Similar but not "Guppy" type:
Italy ("Gato" class). **ENRICO TAZZOLI.** *511,*
**LEONARDO DA VINCI.** *510.*

Netherlands: ("Balao" class). **WALRUS.** *S802,*
**ZEELEEUW.** *S803.*

**927.** Am. **BALAO** class. 1944-45. Experimental
Submarines. All details as No. 920. Note unusual
bows and large sonar.
**BUGARA.** *331.* **CARBONERO.** *337.* May be
others with this appearance.

**928.** Fr. **NARVAL** class. This drawing shows this
class before reconstruction. For drawing after
reconstruction and all details see No. 898.

**929.** Sw. **DRAKEN** class. 1961-62. 770/840
tons. 229 x 17 x 17. (70 x 5.1 x 5.1). Diesels/
electric. 17/25 knots. 4 torpedo tubes (bow).
**DELFINEN.** *De,* **DRAKEN.** *Dr,* **GRIPEN.** *Gr,*
**NORDKAPAREN.** *No,* **SPRINGAREN.** *Sp,*
**VARGEN.** *Vg.*

Similar: "Hajen" class 1957-60.
**BAVERN.** *Ba,* **HAJEN.** *Ha,* **ILLERN.** *Il,*
**SALEN.** *Sa,* **UTTERN.** *Ut,* **VALEN.** *Va.*

**930.** Am. **BARRACUDA.** *3,* 1951. Training
Submarine. 770/1,200 tons. 196 x 25 x 16.
(59.7 x 7.5 x 4.9). 2 screws; diesels/electric.
10/8 knots. 4 torpedo tubes. (2 bow and 2 stern).

**931.** Am. **SEAWOLF.** *575.* 1957. Nuclear-
powered Attack Submarine. 3,700/4,300 tons.
338 x 28 x 22. (102.9 x 8.4 x 6.7). Nuclear-
powered turbines; 2 screws. 20/20 knots.
6 tubes (foreward). Anti-submarine torpedoes.

**932.** Br. **A** class. 1945-48. Reconstructed 1955c. 1,400/1,600 tons. 283 x 22 x 17. (86.3 x 6.8 x 5.2). Diesels/electric. 19/8 knots. 6 torpedo tubes (4 bow, 2 aft).
Some may have a gun. Becoming obsolete.
**ACHERON, AENEAS, ALARIC, ALCIDE, ALLIANCE, AMBUSH, ANDREW, ARTEMIS, AURIGA, ASTUTE.** (In reserve.)

**933.** Ge. **WILHELM BAUER.** 1945. Experimental Submarine. 1,600/1,800 tons. 260 x 22 x 20. (79 x 6.6 x 6.2). Diesel/electric. 15/17 knots. Sunk during the war and not commissioned until 1960.

**934.** Ja. **HAYASHIO** class. 1962-63. 750 tons (Standard). 194-200 x 21 x 14. (59 or 61 x 6.5 x 4.3). 2 screws; diesels/electric. 11/14 knots. 3 torpedo tubes (bow).
**FUYUSHIO.** *524,* **HAYASHIO.** *521,* **NATSU-SHIO.** *523,* **WAKASHIO.** *522.*

**935.** Ja. **OSHIO** class. 1965-69. 1,600 tons (Standard). 289 x 27 x 15. (88 x 8.2 x 4.7). 2 screws; diesels/electric. 14/18 knots. 8 tubes (6 bow, 2 stern).
**ARASHIO.** *565,* **ASASHIO.** *562,* **HARUSHIO.** *563,* **OSHIO.** *561,* **MICHISHIO.** *564.*

**936.** It. **FLUTTO** class. 1957. Rebuilt 1961. 900/1,100 tons. 217 x 23 x 13. (66 x 7 x 4). Diesels/electric. 14/14 knots. 4 torpedo tubes. Launched in 1944 but sunk.
**PIETRO CALVI.** *503.*

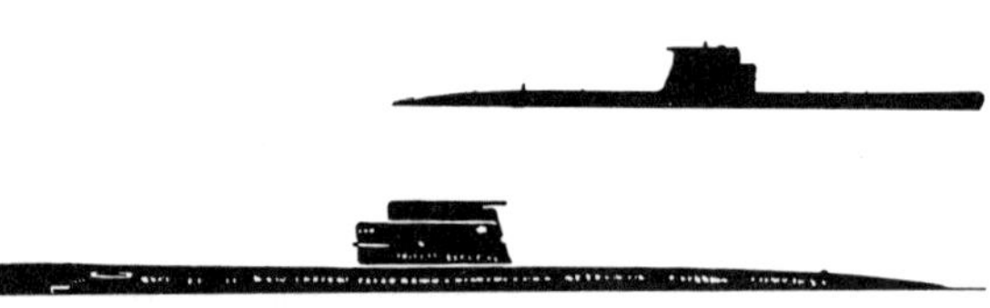

★ **937.** Ru. **Z** class. Later version of the conventional type. For tonnage etc. see No. 893.

**938.** Sp. **TIBURON** class. 1958. Small Attack Submarines. 78/81 tons. 71 x 9 x 9. (21.6 x 2.7 x 2.7). Diesels/electric. 10/14 x knots. 2 torpedo tubes.
**SA** *51,* **SA** *52.*

**939.** Ge. **U4.** *S183.* Coastal Submarines. All details as for No. 921.
**U5.** *S184,* **U6.** *S185,* **U7.** *S186,* **U8.** *S187.*
**U1** and **U2** (see No. 940) may now have rebuilt to this appearance.

Da.
Very similar in appearance but slightly smaller and with 8 torpedo tubes (bow).
"Narhvalen class" (1970).
**NARHVALEN.** *S320,* **NORDKAPEREN.** *S321.*

**940.** Ge. **U1.** *S180.* All details as for No. 939.
May be rebuilt like number U4 etc.
**U2.** *S181.*

**941.** No. **KOBBEN** class. 1964-67. 350/470
tons. 149 x 15 x 14. (55.4 x 4.6 x 4.3). Diesels/
electric. 17 knots. 8 torpedo tubes. Very similar
to the German coastal type.
**KAURA.** *S315,* **KINN.** *S316,* **KOBBEN.** *S318,*
**KUNNA.** *S319,* **KYA.** *S317.*
**SKLINNA.** *S305,* **SKOLPEN.** *S306,* **STADT.**
*S307,* **STORD.** *S308,* **SVENNER.** *S309.*
**ULA.** *S300,* **UTHAUG.** *S304,* **UTSIRA.** *S301,*
**UTSTEIN.** *S302,* **UTVAER.** *S303.*

**942.** It. Ex-U.S. **BALAO** class. All details as for
No. 924. May now have the same type of fin as
No. 924.
**ALFREDO CAPPELLINI.** *513,* **EVANGELISTA**
**TORRICELLI.** *512,* **FRANCESCO MOROSINI.**
*514.*

**943.** Am. **MACKEREL** type, 1953. Training
Submarines. 300/350 tons. 131 x 14 x 12. (40 x
4.2 x 3.7). Diesels/electric. 8/9 knots. 1 torpedo
tube.
**MACKEREL.** *1,* **MARLIN.** *2.*

**944.** Ru. **Q** class. 1954-60. Short-range Submarines. 650/740 tons. 185 x 18 x 13. (56.3 x
5.4 x 3.9). Diesels/electric. 18/16 knots. 4 torpedo
tubes. 25 boats in the Soviet Navy.

**945.** Ys. **SUTJESKA** class. 1958-60. 550/950
tons. 197 x 21 x 16. (56 x 6.5 x 4.9). Diesels/
electric. 14/9 knots. 6 torpedo tubes.
**HEROJ, NERETVA, SUTJESKA, ULJANIK.**

**946.** Am. **DOLPHIN.** *555.* 1968. Experimental
Submarine. 600/900 tons. 152 x 19. (46.3 x 5.8).
Diesel/electric. 1 experimental torpedo tube.

**947.** Sw. **ABBORREN** class. 1943-44. Reconstructed 1963-64. 420/460 tons. 164 x 18 x 18. (50 x 5.4 x 5.4). Diesels/electric. 14/9 knots. 4 torpedo tubes (3 bow, 1 stern).
**ABBORREN, FORELLEN, GADDAN, LAXEN, MAKRILLEN, SIKEN.**

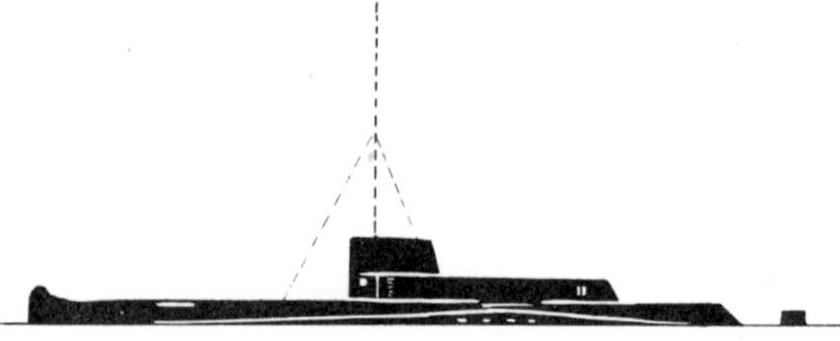

**948.** Fr. **GYMNOTE.** *S655.* 1966. Experimental Missile Submarine. 3,800 tons. 276 x 35 x 25. (84.1 x 10.6 x 7.6). 2 screws; diesels/electric. 11/10 knots. 4 tubes for surface-to-air "Polaris" missiles. The tall mast shown by dotted lines may be erected when trials are being undertaken.

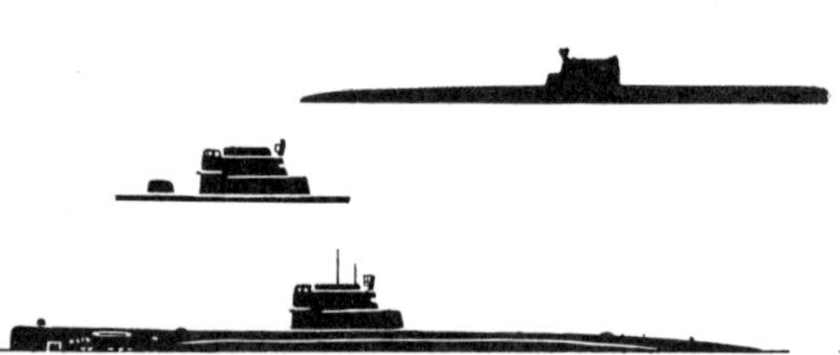

**949.** Ru. **W** class. 1950-57. Patrol Submarines. 1,030/1,180 tons. 240 x 22 x 15. (73.1 x 6.7 x 4.5). 2 screws; diesel/electric. 17/15 knots. 6 torpedo tubes (4 bow, 2 stern). Capacity for mines.
About 150 in the Soviet Navy.

Egypt: 7 boats.
Bulgaria: 2 boats.
Poland: 5 boats.
**BIELIK, KONDOR, ORZEL, SOKOL, WILK.**
Red China: 21 boats.
Albania: 4 boats.

**950.** Am. **TANG** class. 1951-52. Attack Submarines, 2,100/2,400 tons. 287 x 27 x 19. (87.4 x 8.3 x 6.2). Diesels/electric. 20/18 knots 8 torpedo tubes (6 bow, 2 stern). All were modernised in 1960.
**GUDGEON.** *567,* **HARDER.** *568,* **TANG.** *563,* **TRIGGER.** *564,* **TROUT.** *566,* **WAHOO.** *565.*

**951.** Sp. **G7.** *S01.* About 1940. 710/870 tons. 228 x 21 x 15. (69.4 x 6.4 x 4.5). Diesels/electric. 18/9 knots. 5 torpedo tubes (4 forward, 1 aft). 1—3.5-inch gun. Former German U-Boat.

**952.** RC. Ex-U.S.S.R. **S-I** type. 1937-40. 800/1,100 tons. 256 x 21 x 13. (78 x 6.4 x 4). Diesel/electric. 19/8 knots. 6 torpedo tubes. 1—3.9-inch gun. 1 A.A. gun. May vary in appearance (see inset).
**S 400, S 401, S 402, S 403.**

**953.** Is. Ex-British **S** class. 1945. Refitted 1959-60. 715/1,000 tons. 217 x 24 x 11. (66.2 x 7.3 x 3.3). Diesels/electric. 14/9 knots. 6 torpedo tubes. 1—4-inch gun.
**RAHAV.** *73,* **TANIN.** *71.*

**954.** Ex-U.S.S.R. **M-V** type. 1944-50. Coastal Submarines. 350/420 tons. 167 x 16 x 12. (51 x 4.8 x 3.6). Diesels/electric. 13/10 knots. 2 torpedo tubes. 1 A.A. gun.
Poland: **KASZUB, KRAKOWIAK, KUJA-WIAK, MAZOWSZE, MAZUR, SLAZAC.**

Egypt: 1 boat.
Syria: May have 2.
Red China: **M 201, M 202, M 203.**

**955**. Am. **X-I**. 1955. Experimental Midget Submarine. 31/36 tons. 50 x 7 x 7. (15.2 x 2.1 x 2.1).
Diesel/electric.

**956**. Sp. **FOCA** class. 1958. Midget Submarines.
16/20 tons. 45 x 6 x 5. (13.9 x 1.8 x 1.5). Diesel/
electric. 9/12 knots. 2 torpedo tubes.
**SA 41**. *F1*, **SA 42**. *F2*.

**957**. Sw. **SPIGGEN**. 1954. Refitted 1957-58.
Midget Submarine. 36/41 tons. 54 x 6 x 8.
(16.4 x 1.9 x 2.4). Diesel/electric. 7/6 knots.
Ex-British.

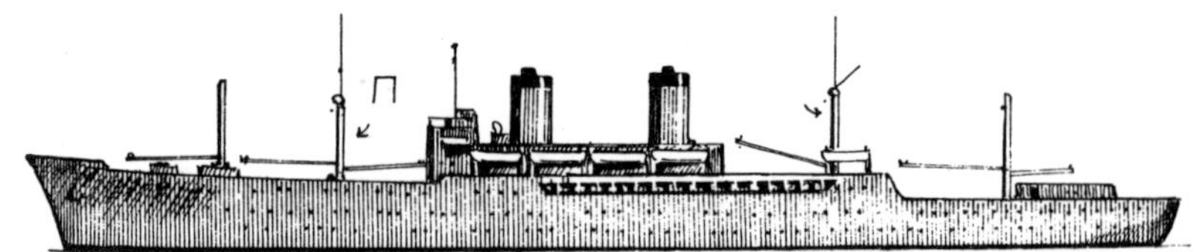

**958.** Am. **ADMIRAL** class. 1944-45. Transports.
9,700 tons. 609 x 76 x 28. (185.7 x 22.9 x 8.5).
2 screws; turbo-electric. 19 knots. P2-SES-RI
type.
**GENERAL ALEXANDER M. PATCH, GENERAL MAURICE ROSE, GENERAL NELSON M. WALKER, GENERAL WILLIAM O. DARBY.**

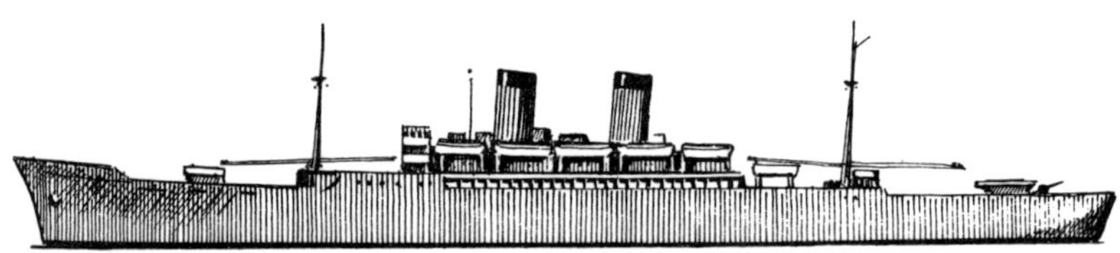

**959.** Am. **GENERAL** class. 1944-45. Transports.
11,800 tons. 623 x 76 x 26 (189.9 x 22.9 x 7.8).
2 screws; turbines. 20 knots.
**GENERAL JOHN POPE, GENERAL W. H. GORDON, GENERAL WILLIAM WEIGEL.**

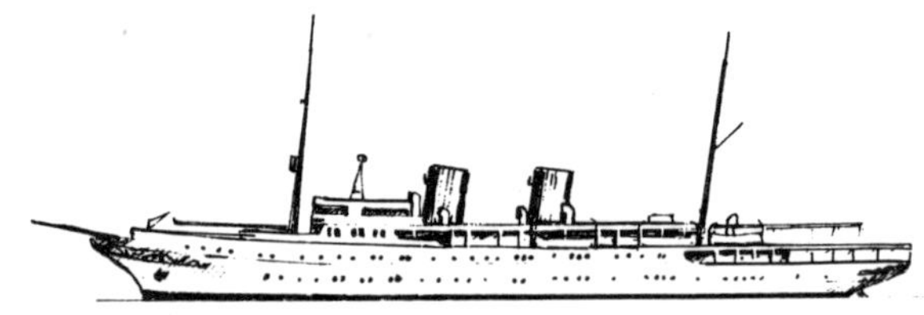

**960.** Tu. **SAVARONA.** 1931. Training Ship.
5,100 tons. 409 x 53 x 21. (124.5 x 16.2 x 6.2).
2 screws; turbines. 18 knots. 4—3-inch guns.
4 A.A. guns. Former yacht.

★ **961.** Ru. **MIKOYAN.** 1939. Icebreaker. 4,900
tons (gross). 351 x 76 x 32. (107 x 22.9 x 9.8).
3 screws; reciprocating and diesel/electric. 15
knots. Also known as "A. Mikoyan". 1 helicopter.
Similar: See silhouette 964.
**ADMIRAL LAZAREV, LAZAR KAGANOVICH.**

★ **962.** Ru. **SIBIRYAKOV.** 1926. Icebreaker.
4,800 tons. 246 x 63 x 21. (75 x 19.2 x 6.4). 3
screws; reciprocating. 15 knots. Ex-Finnish
"Jaakarhu".

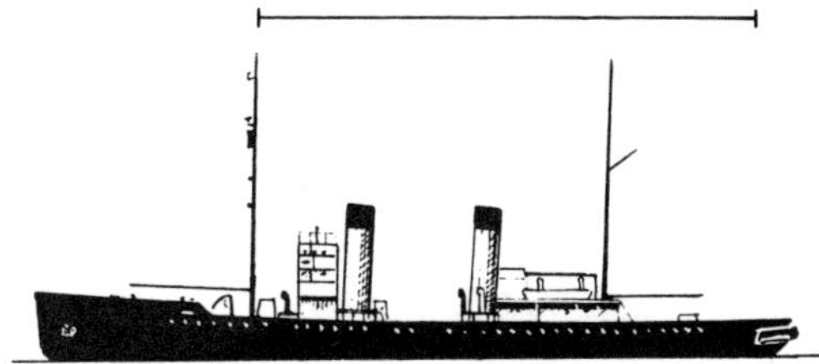

★ **963.** Ru. **VOLYNETS.** 1914. Icebreaker. 4,000 tons. 246 x 57 x 19. (75 x 17.4 x 5.8). 3 screws; reciprocating. 13 knots. Ex-Estonian ship.

★ **964.** Ru. **VLADIMIR ILYICH.** 1917. Icebreaker. Refitted 1946-47. 6,200 tons. 281 x 64 x 19. (85.6 x 19.5 x 5.8). 3 screws; reciprocating. 12 knots. Also may be known as "Lenin".

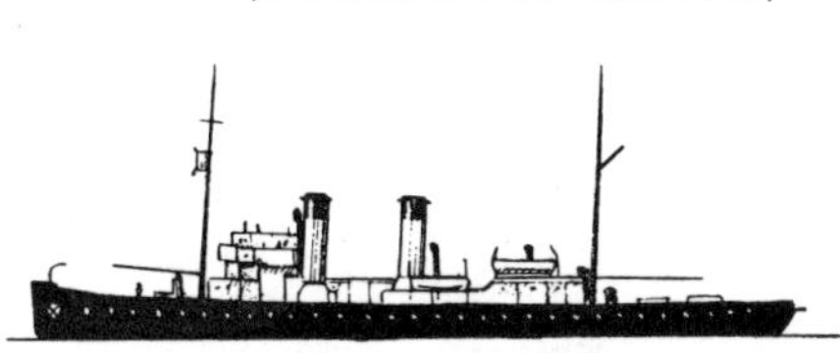

★ **965.** Ru. **MALYGIN.** 1917. Icebreaker. 2,100 tons. 211 x 47 x 17. (64.3 x 14.3 x 5.2). Reciprocating. 13 knots.
This ship may no longer be in service. Ex-Finnish ship "Voima".

**966.** Fi. **APU.** 1907. Icebreaker. 2,300 tons. 220 x 47 x 18. (67.1 x 14.3 x 5.5). 2 screws; reciprocating. 12 knots.
Probably no longer in service.

**967.** Ca. **N. B. McLEAN.** 1930. Icebreaker. 5,000 tons. 277 x 61 x 20. (84.4 x 18.4 x 5.9). 2 screws; reciprocating. 13 knots. Canadian Coast Guard.

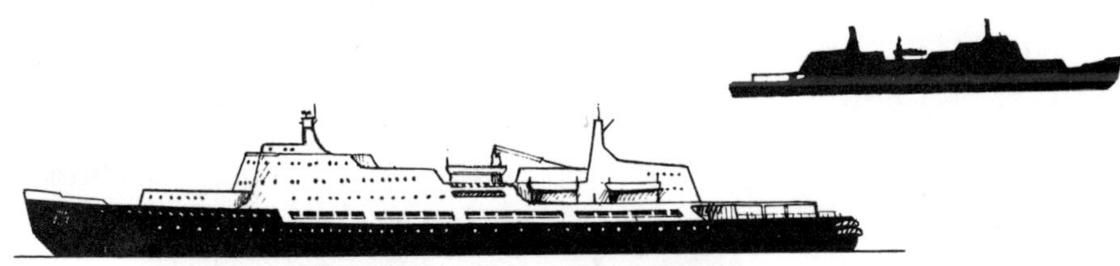

★ **968.** Ru. **ARKTIKA.** 1971. Icebreaker. 25,000 tons. 525 x 82 x 29. (160 x 25 x 8.8). Nuclear-powered turbines. 25 knots. 10 helicopters. Equipped with hangar. Largest icebreaker ever designed. Another ship is under construction.

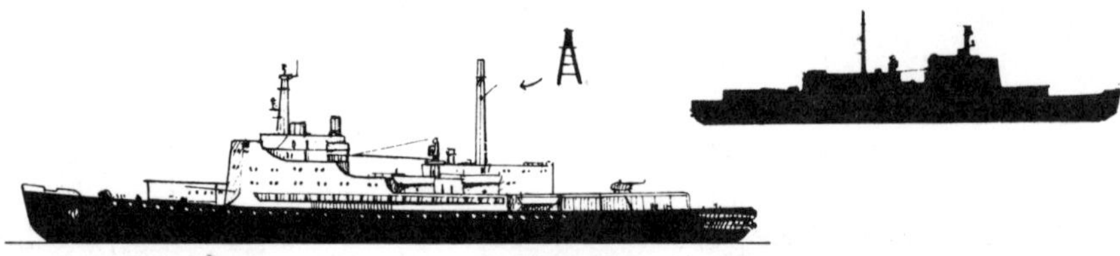

**969.** Ru. **LENIN.** 1958. Icebreaker. 16,000 tons. 440 x 91 x 30. (134.1 x 27.7 x 9.1). 3 screws; nuclear-powered turbines. 18 knots. 2 helicopters and hangar. No visible funnel.

**970.** Ru. **ILYA MUROMETS.** 1941. Icebreaker. 1,900 tons. 184 x 49 x 22. (56.1 x 14.9 x 6.7). Reciprocating. 15 knots. Former German "Eisbar".

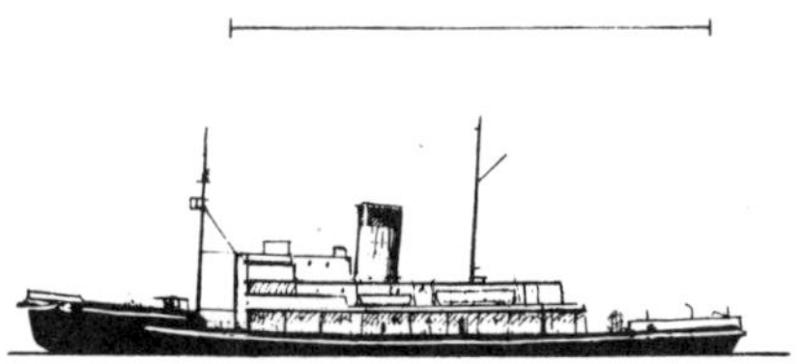

**971.** Ru. **ALIOSHA POPOVICH.** 1941. Icebreaker. 2,100 tons. 200 x 49 x 22. (61. x 14.9 x 6.7). Reciprocating. 13 knots. Former German "Eisvogel".

**972.** Ru. **SADKO.** 1913. Icebreaker. 2,000 tons. 255 x 38 x 21. (77.7 x 11.6 x 6.4). Reciprocating. 14 knots. Former Canadian "Lintrose".

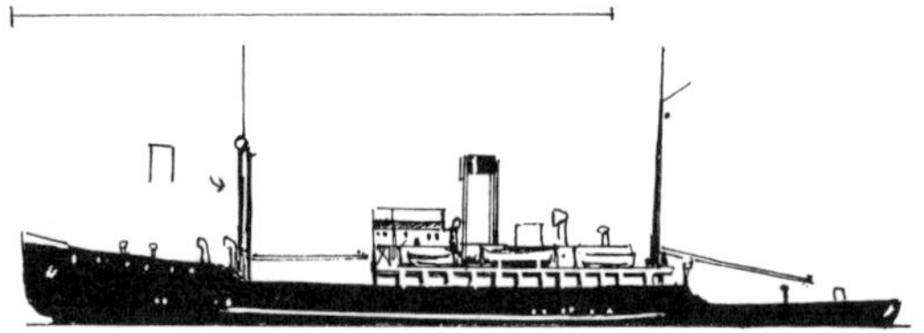

**973.** Ru. **MURMAN** class. 1937-38. Survey Ships with Icebreaking Stems. 1,500 tons. 266 x 43 x 18. (81.1 x 13.1 x 5.5). 2 screws; reciprocating. 14 knots. Originally minelayers. **MURMAN, OKEAN, OKHOTSK.**

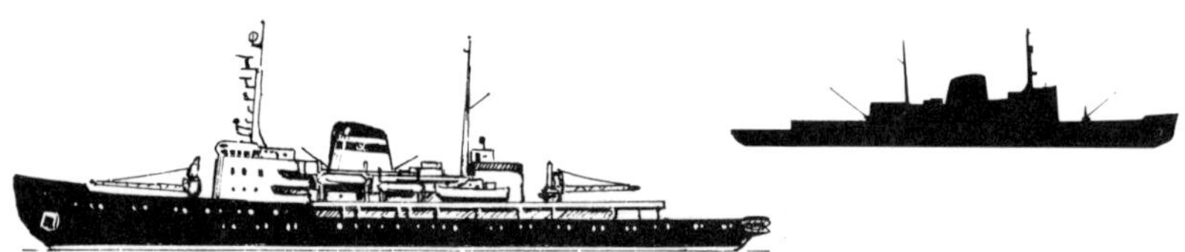

**974.** Ru. **MOSKVA** class. 1960-67. Icebreakers. 1,800 tons. 401 x 80 x 35. (122.2 x 24.4 x 10.5). 3 screws; diesel/electric. 18 knots. 2 helicopters. **KIEV, LENINGRAD, MOSKVA, MURMANSK, VLADIVOSTOCK.**

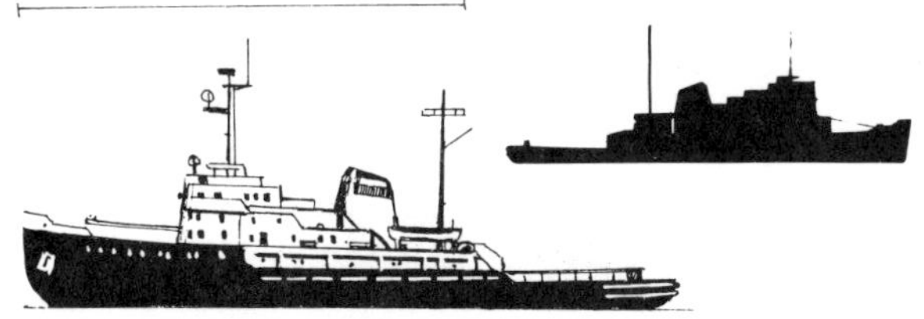

★ **975.** Ru. **DOBRYNA NIKITCH** class. 1961-65. Icebreakers. 2,500tons. 222 x 59 x 18. (67.6 x 18 x 5.5). 3 screws; diesel/electric. 13 knots. Large bridge and funnel well aft.
**AFANASY NIKITIN, EROFEY KHABAROV, IVAN KRUZENSHTERN, KHARITON LAPTEV, DOBRYNA NIKITCH, SEMYON CHELYUSKIN, VASILY POYARKOV, VASILY PRONCHISCHEV, VLADIMIR RUSANOV, VYUGA, YURI LISYANSKY** and possibly **PURGA.**

★ **976.** Ru. **KAPITAN** class. 1955-57. Icebreakers. 4,400 tons. 273 x 64 x 23 (83.2 x 19.5 x 7) 4 screws; diesel/electric. 15 knots. (2 screws forward and 2 aft.)
**KAPITAN BELOUSOV, KAPITAN MELEKHOV, KAPITAN VORONIN.**

★ **977.** Ru. **KRASIN**. 1917. Icebreaker. 9,300 tons. 323 x 71 x 26 (98.4 x 21.6 x 7.9). 3 screws; reciprocating. 15 knots.
Ship was completely rebuilt and is probably no longer in service. Name may be spelt "Krassin"

**978.** Sw. **ODEN**. 1958. Icebreaker. 4,900 tons. 274 x 64 x 23. (83.5 x 19.5 x 7). 4 screws (2 forward and 2 aft); diesel/electric. 17 knots. Similar to Finnish "Voima" class; see No. 983.

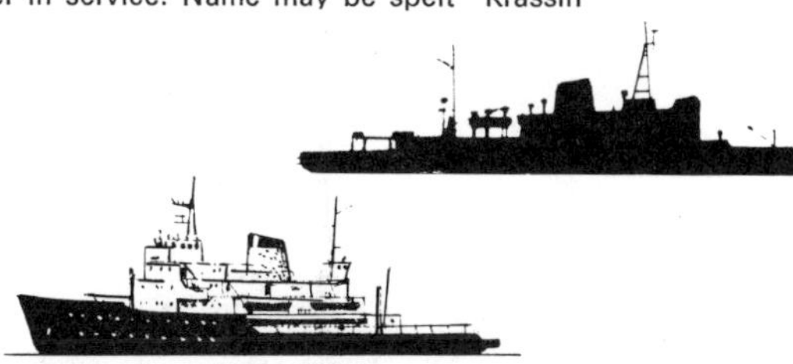

**979.** Ge. **HANSE**. 1966. Icebreaker. 3.700 tons. 245 x 57 x 20. (74.7 x 17.4 x 6.1). 4 screws (2 forward and 2 aft); diesel/electric 16 knots. Sails under the Finnish flag.

**980.** Fi. **TARMO**. 1963. Icebreaker. 4,900 tons. 277 x 71 x 21. (84.4 x 21.6 x 6.4). 4 screws (2 forward, 2 aft); diesel/electric. 17 knots.
**VARMA.** And 2 ships building.
Similar: Sweden. **TOR.** See silhouette No. 1074.

**981.** Da. **DANBJORN**. 1965. Icebreaker. 3,700 tons. 252 x 56 x 20. (76.8 x 17 x 6.1). Diesel/electric. 14 knots.
**ISBJORN.**

**982.** Fi. **KARHU** class. 1958-60. Icebreakers. 3,500 tons. 243 x 57 x 20. (74 x 17.3 x 6.1). 4 screws; diesel/electric. 16 knots.
**KARHU, MURTAJA, SAMPO.**

**983.** Fi. **VOIMA.** 1953. Icebreaker. 4,400 tons. 274 x 64 x 20. (83.5 x 19.5 x 6.1). 4 screws (2 forward, 2 aft); diesel/electric. 16 knots.

**984.** Fi. **SISU.** 1939. Icebreaker. 2,100 tons. 210 x 47 x 17. (64 x 14.3 x 5.1). 2 screws; diesel/electric. 16 knots.

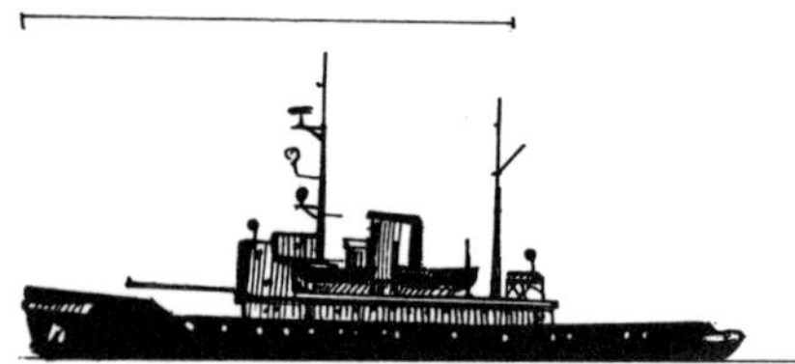

**985.** Sw. **THULE.** 1953. Icebreaker. 2,200 tons. 204 x 50 x 19. (62.1 x 15.2 x 5.7). 3 screws (1 forward, 2 aft); diesel/electric. 16 knots.

**986.** Fi. **OTSO.** 1936. Icebreaker. 900 tons. 144 x 38 x 17. (43.8 x 11.5 x 5.1). Reciprocating. 13 knots.

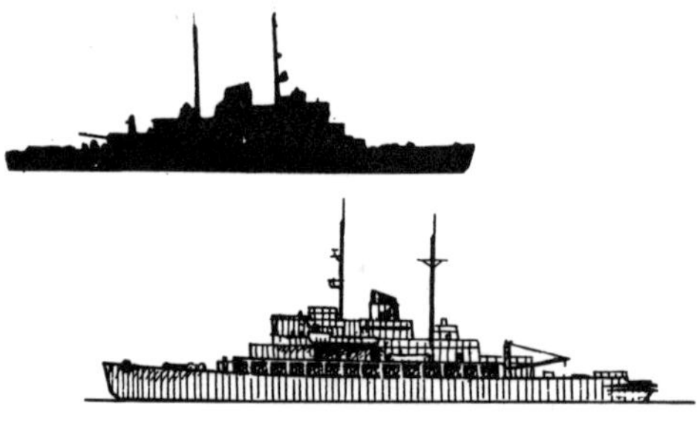

**987.** Ru. **PERESVET.** 1939. Icebreaker. 5,200 tons. 295 x 69 x 22. (89.9 x 21 x 6.7). 3 screws. Reciprocating. 15 knots. Ex-German. Distinguished by pyramidal silhouette with small funnel amidships and masts close together.

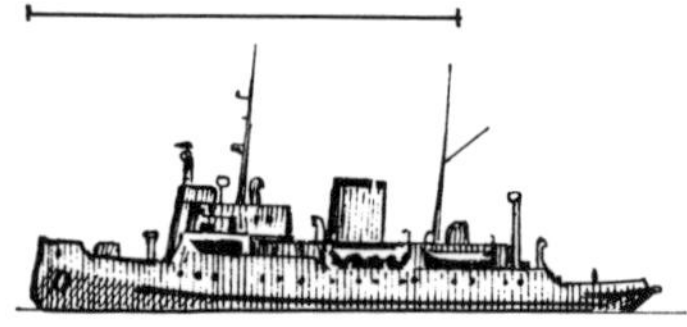

**988.** Da. **ELBJORN.** 1953. Icebreaker. 900 tons. 167 x 40 x 15. (50.9 x 12.1 x 4.5). Diesel/electric. 12 knots.

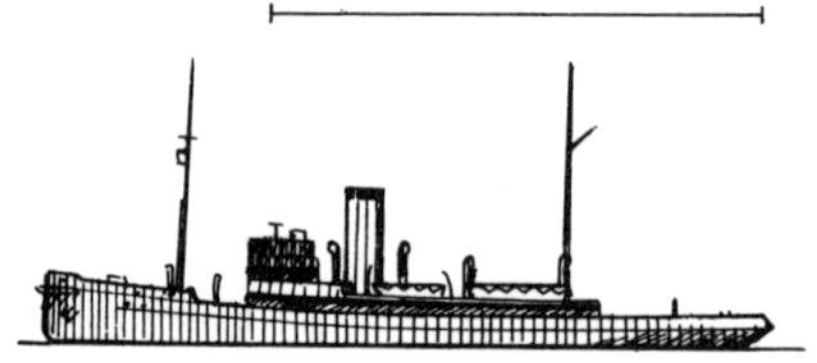

**989.** Da. **STOREBJORN.** 1931. Icebreaker. 2,500 tons. 197 x 49 x 19. (60 x 14.9 x 5.7). 3 screws (2 foreward, 1 aft). Reciprocating.

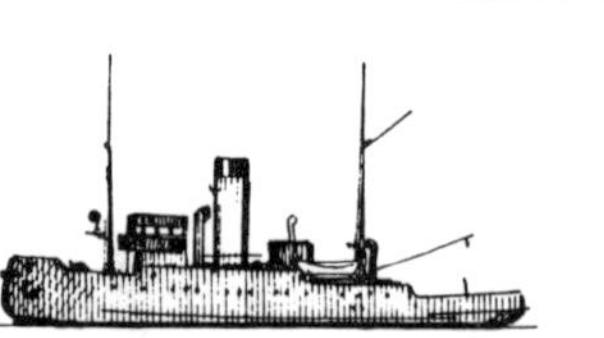

**990.** Da. **LILLEBJORN.** 1926. Icebreaker. 1,000 tons. 144 x 37 x 18. (43.8 x 11.2 x 5.4). Reciprocating.

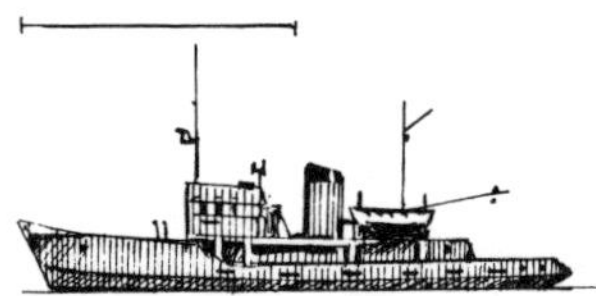

**991.** Fr. **INGENIEUR ELIE MONNIER.** *A647*. 1944. Diving Tender. 300 tons. 112 x 24 x 10. (34 x 7.3 x 3). Diesel. 12 knots. Former German trawler. .

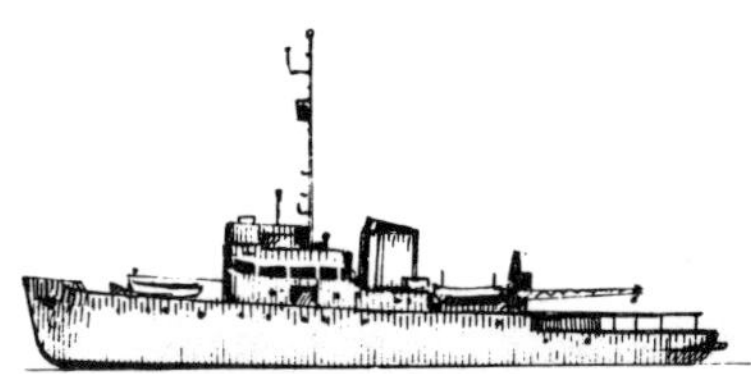

**992.** Ar. **GENERAL SAN MARTIN.** *Q4*. 1954. Icebreaker (Antarctica). 4,900 tons. 279 x 61 x 21. (85 x 18.5 x 6.4). 2 screws; diesel/electric. 16 knots. 1—4-inch gun. 2 A.A. guns. 1 reconnaissance aircraft. 1 helicopter.

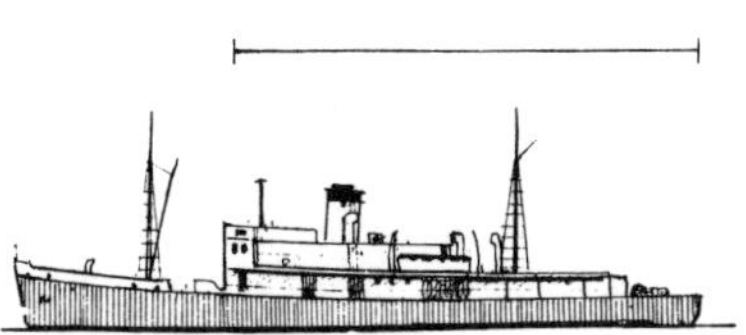

**993.** Ca. **ERNEST LAPOINTE.** 1941. Icebreaker. 1,700 tons. 184 x 36 x 16. (56 x 10.9 x 4.8). Reciprocating. 13 knots.

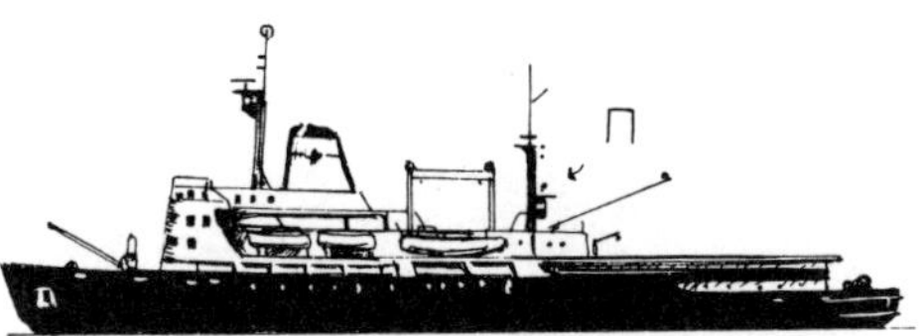

**994.** Ca. **LOUIS S. ST. LAURENT.** 1969. Icebreaker. 13,000 tons. 367 x 80 x 31. (111.8 x 24.3 x 9.4). 3 screws; turbo/electric. 17 knots. Hangar with 2 helicopters. Funnel very far forward and goalpost mainmast.

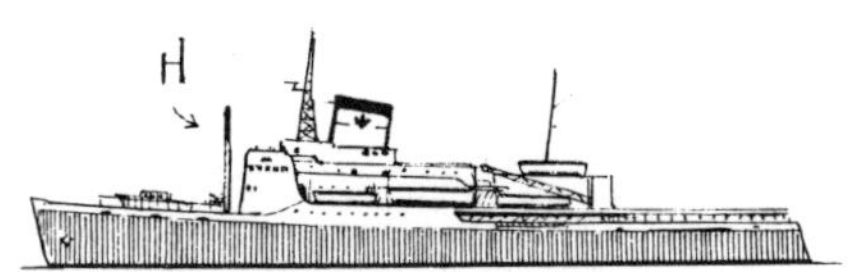

**995.** Ca. **D'IBERVILLE.** 1953. Icebreaker. 9,900 tons. 310 x 67 x 30. (94.4 x 20.4 x 9.1). Reciprocating. 15 knots.

**996.** Ca. **JOHN A. MACDONALD.** 1960. Icebreaker. 9,200 tons. 315 x 70 x 28. (96 x 21.3 x 8.5). Diesel/electric. 15 knots. Helicopter deck and hangar.

**997.** **NORMAN MCLEOD ROGERS.** 1969. Icebreaker. 6,300 tons. 295 x 63 x 20. (89.9 x 19.2 x 6.1). 2 screws; diesel/electric and gas turbines. 15 knots. 1 helicopter and hangar.

**998.** Ja. **SOYA.** *PL107*. Converted into an Antarctic Research Ship in 1957. 4,400 tons. 260 x 52 x 19. (79.2 x 15.8 x 5.7). Diesels. 12 knots. 4 helicopters and flight platform. Operated by the Maritime Safety Agency.

**999.** Ca **C. D. HOWE.** 1950 Arctic Supply Ship. 5,200 tons. 295 x 50 x 19. (89.9 x 15.2 x 5.7). Reciprocating. 13 knots. Icebreaking hull. May be out of service.

**1000.** Ca. **LABRADOR.** 1954. Coast Guard Icebreaker. 6,500 tons. 290 x 64 x 29. (88.3 x 19.5 x 8.8). Diesel/electric. 16 knots. 2 helicopters and hangar.

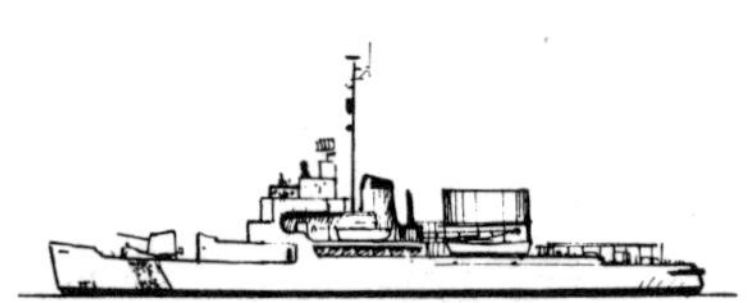

**1001.** Am. **WIND** class. 1942-46. Icebreakers. 3,500 tons. 269 x 64 x 29. (81.9 x 19.5 x 8.8). 2 screws; diesel/electric. 16 knots. 1 or 3—3-inch guns. 2 helicopters and hangar. U.S. Coast Guard. **BURTON ISLAND.** *283,* **EASTWIND.** *279,* **EDISTO.** *284,* **NORTHWIND.** *282,* **SOUTHWIND.** *280,* **STATEN ISLAND.** *278,* **WESTWIND.** *281.*

**1002.** Am. **GLACIER.** *4.* 1955. Icebreaker. 8,400 tons. 310 x 74 x 29. (94.4 x 22.5 x 8.8). 2 screws; diesel/electric. 18 knots. 2—5-inch guns (twin). 1 helicopter and hangar. U.S. Coast Guard.

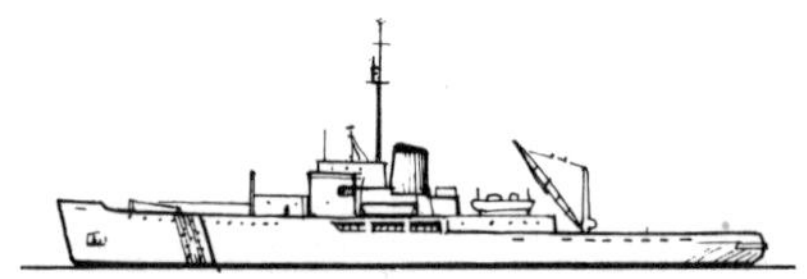

**1003.** Am. **MACKINAW.** *83.* 1945. Icebreaker. 5,300 tons. 290 x 74 x 19. (88.3 x 22.5 x 5.7). 3 screws (1 forward, 2 aft); diesel/electric. 18 knots. 1 helicopter. U.S. Coast Guard. On the Great Lakes.

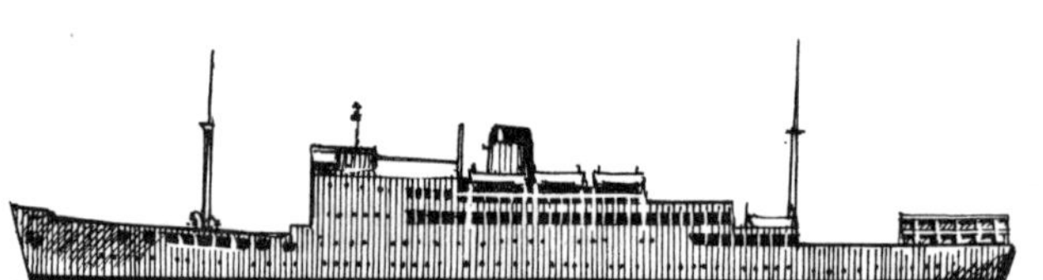

**1004.** Fr. **MAURIENNE.** *A637.* 1948. Maintenance ship. 8,700 tons. 480 x 62 x 22. (146.3 x 18.9 x 6.7). 2 screws; diesels. 17 knots. **MOSELLE.** *A608.*

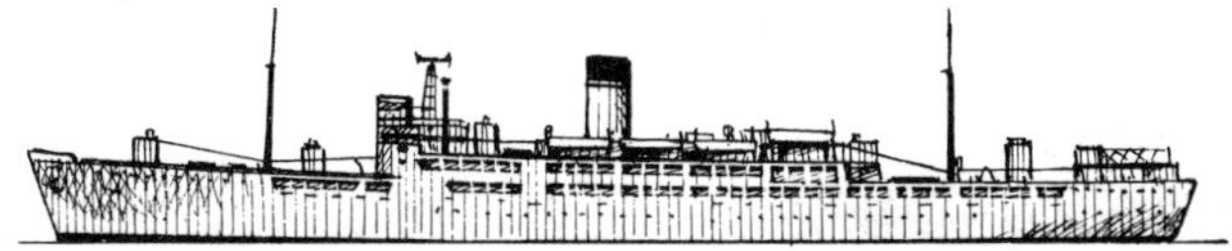

**1005.** Br. **RESURGENT.** *A280*. 1951. Fleet Replenishment Ship. 14,000 tons. 477 x 62 x 29. (145.3 x 18.9 x 8.8). Diesels. 15 knots. Royal Fleet Auxiliary.
**RETAINER.** *A329*.

**1006.** Am. **BARRETT** class. 1951-52. Transports. 17.600 tons. 533 x 73 x 27. (162.3 x 22.2 x 8.2). Turbines. 19 knots. Thin funnels amidships are abreast.
**BARRETT.** *AP196*, **GEIGER.** *AP197*, **UPSHUR.** *AP198*.

**1007.** Ca. **QUADRA.** 1967. Canadian Coast Guard Weather Ship. 5,600 tons. 404 x 50 x 18. (123.1 x 15.2 x 5.4). 2 screws; turbo/electric. 18 knots.
**VANCOUVER.**

**1008.** Fr. **MAINE.** *A611*. 1949. Maintenance Ship. 5,500 tons. 400 x 54 x 18. (121.9 x 16.4 x 5.4). 2 screws; turbines. 15 knots. Former passenger vessel "El Mansour".

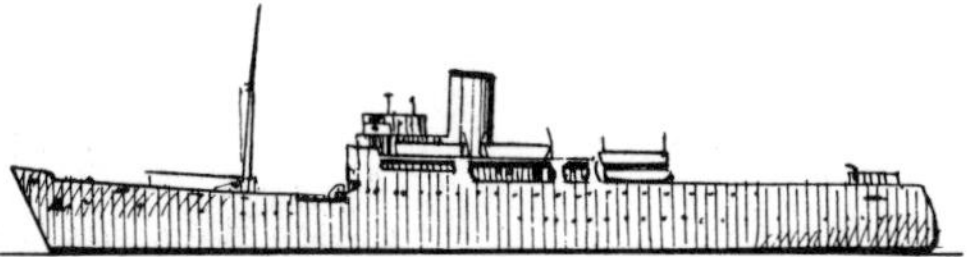

**1009.** Fr. **MEDOC.** *A612*. 1949. Maintenance Ship. 4,400 tons. 372 x 49 x 22. (113.3 x 14.9 x 6.7). 2 screws; turbines. 15 knots. Ex-merchant ship "Sidi Ferruch".
Similar: **MORVAN.** *A613*.

**1010.** Ar. **LA PATAIA.** 1950. Transport. 3,800 tons. 335 x 50 x 23 (102.1 x 15.2 x 7). 2 screws; diesels. 16 knots.

**1011.** Bm. **PYIDAWAYE.** 1955. Transport. 2,200 tons (gross). 287 x 47 x 15. (87.4 x 14.3 x 4.5). Reciprocating. Former passenger ship. Sister in commercial service is **PYIDAWNYUNT.**

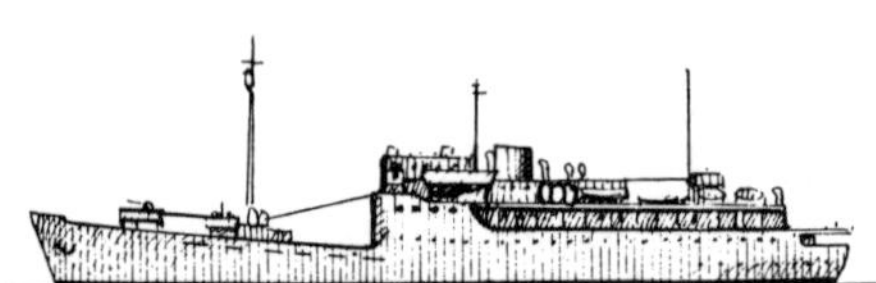

**1012.** Ar. **BAHIA AGUIRRE.** 1950. Transport. 3,100 tons. 336 x 47 x 14. (102.4 x 14.3 x 4.2). 2 screws; diesels. 16 knots. 2—4.1-inch guns. 4 A.A. guns.
**BAHIA BUEN SUCESO, BAHIA THETIS.**

**1013.** Sw. **PATRICIA.** *A206.* 1926. Submarine Depot Ship. 5,000 tons. 335 x 48 x 20. (102 x 14.5 x 6). 2 screws; reciprocating. 14 knots. 10 A.A. guns. Former liner "Patris II".

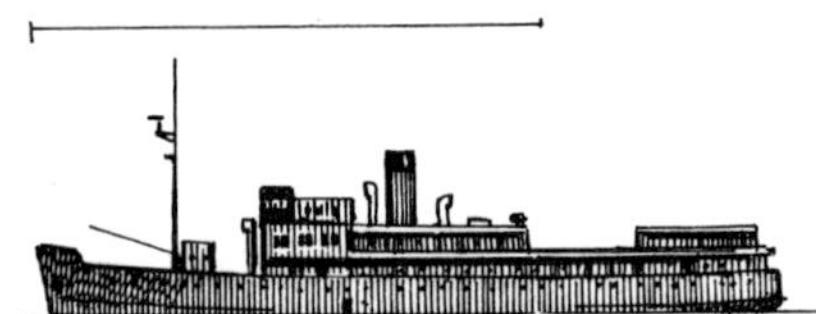

**1014.** Sw. **MARIEHOLM.** *A201.* 1934. Converted 1942. Staff Ship. 1,400 tons. 210 x 33 x 14. (64 x 10 x 4.2). Reciprocating. 12 knots. 1 helicopter. May have A.A. guns. Former passenger liner.

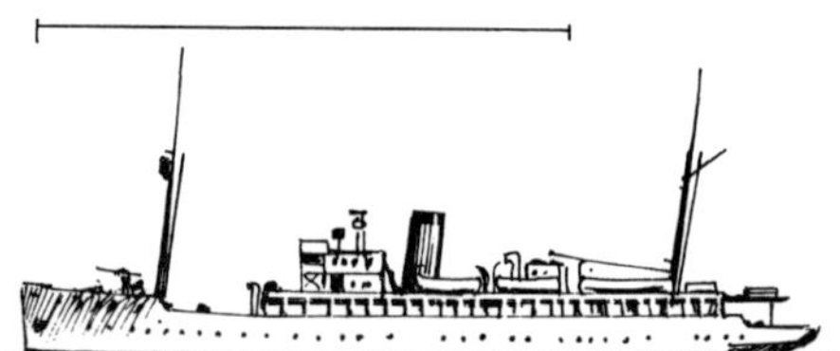

**1015.** Sp. **MALASPINA.** 1935. Survey Ship. 1,000 tons. 225 x 35 x 11 (68.5 x 10.6 x 3.3). 2 screws; reciprocating. 12 knots. 1—37-m.m. gun.
**TOFINO.**

**1016.** Br. **BRITANNIA.** 1954. H.M. Yacht. 5,000 tons (full). 412 x 55 x 17. (125.5 x 16.7 x 5.1). 2 screws; turbines. 21 knots. Converted to a hospital ship in times of emergency.

**1017.** Ch. **AQUILES.** *47.* 1953. Transport. 2,700 tons (gross). 288 x 44 x 17. (87.7 x 13.4 x 5.1). Diesel. 16 knots. Former merchant ship "Tjaldur"

**1018.** Da. **HENRIK GERNER.** 1936. Submarine Depot Ship. 2,200 tons. 252 x 40 x18. (76.8 x 12.1 x 5.4). Diesel. 15 knots. 6—40-m.m. A.A. guns. Former merchant ship "Hammershus".

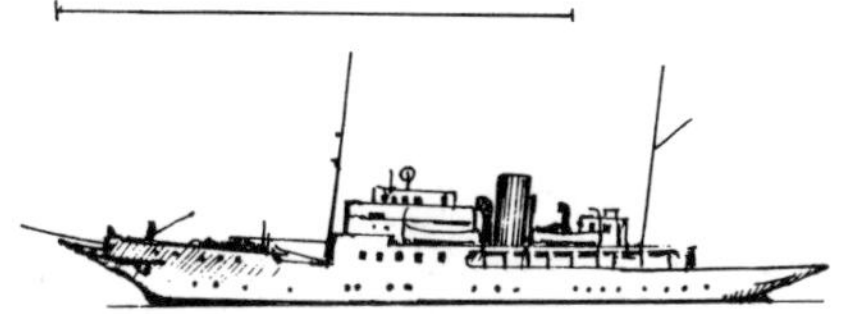

**1019.** Li. **LIBERIAN.** 1930. Presidential Yacht. 700 tons (gross). 209 x 30 x 13. (63.7 x 9.1 x 3.9). Formerly "Virginia" and acquired in 1957.

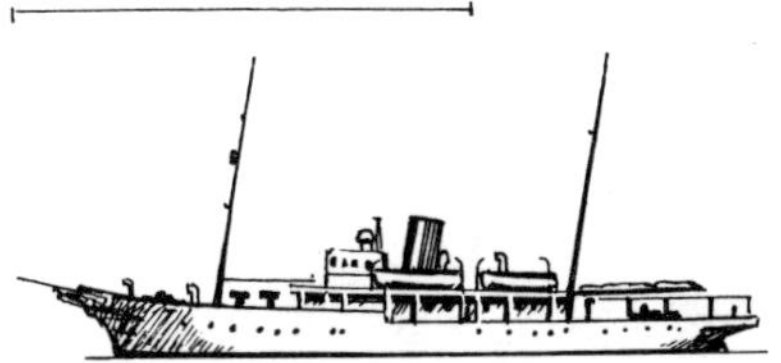

**1020.** Ur. **CAPITAN MIRANDA.** 1930. Survey Ship and Tender. 500 tons. 179 x 26 x 11 (54.5 x 7.9 x 3.3). Diesel. 11 knots.

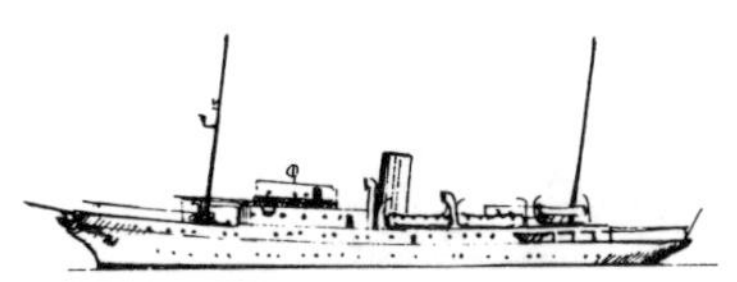

**1021.** Da. **DANNEBROG.** 1931. Royal Yacht. 1,100 tons. 246 x 34 x 11. (74.9 x 10.3 x 3.3). Diesels. 14 knots. 2—37-m.m. guns.

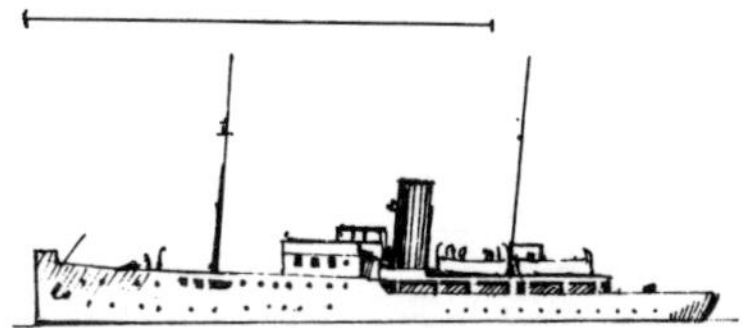

**1022.** Iq. **FAISAL I.** 1923. Lighthouse Tender. 1,000 tons. 186 x 30 x 14. (56.6 x 9.1 x 4.2). 2 screws; reciprocating. 13 knots.

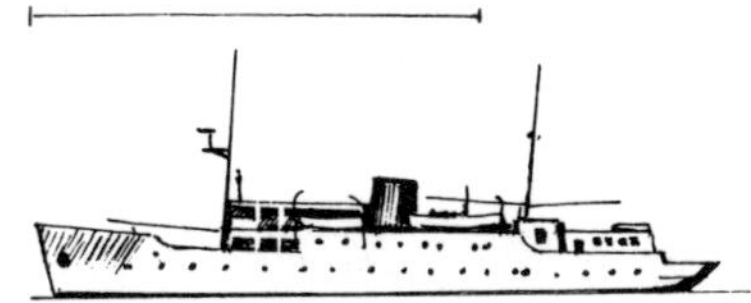

**1023.** Sp. **JUAN DE LA COSA.** 1935. Survey Ship. 800 tons. 188 x 36 x 9. (57.3 x 10.9 x 2.7). Diesel/electric. 9 knots.

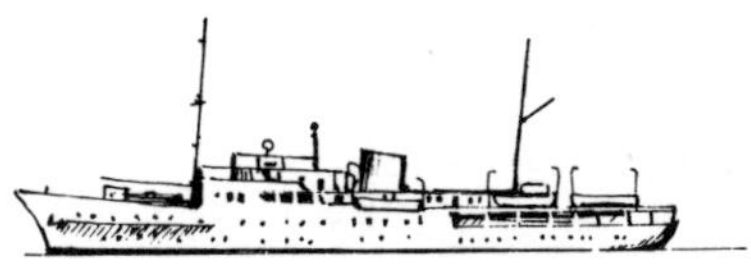

**1024.** No. **NORGE.** 1937. Royal Yacht. 1,700 tons (Thames). 263 x 28 x 15. (80.1 x 8.5 x 4.5). 2 screws; diesels. 17 knots. Former "Philante".

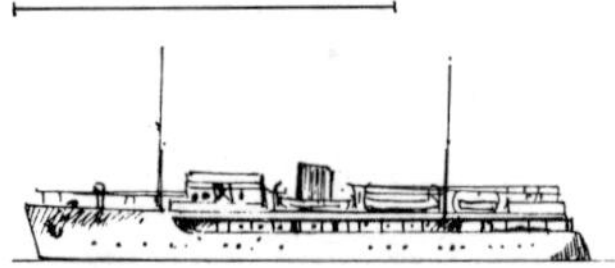

**1025.** Iq. **AL THAWRA**. Presidential Yacht. 750 tons. 2 screws; diesel. 14 knots.

**1026.** Ve. **LAS AVES**. 1955. Transport. 2 screws; diesels. 15 knots.

**1027.** Pi. **THE PRESIDENT**. *777*. 1959. Command Ship. 2,200 tons (gross). 250. (76.1). 2 screws; diesels. 16 knots. 2—40-m.m. guns. 2—20-m.m. A.A. guns. Originally "Lapu Lapu".

**1028.** Bz. **ALMIRANTE SALDANHA**. *U10*. 1934. Survey Ship. 3 300 tons. 307 x 52 x 18. (93.5 x 15.8 x 5.4). Diesel. 11 knots. Originally a sail training ship.

**1029.** Th. **CHANTHARA**. 1961. Survey Ship. 870 tons. 229 x 35 x 10. (69.7 x 10.6 x 3). 2 screws; diesels. 13 knots. 1—20-m.m. gun. Also employed as a training ship.

**1030.** Gh. **ACHIMOTA**. *A15*. 1927. Training Ship. 600 tons. 174 x 28 x 14. (53 x 8.5 x 4.2). 2 screws; diesels. 13 knots. Former "Radiance". Also serves as fleet flagship.

**1031.** Ys. **JADRANKA**. 1939. Despatch Vessel. 600 tons. 213 x 27 x 9. (64.9 x 8.2 x 2.7). Diesels. 18 knots. 2—40-m.m. A.A. guns.

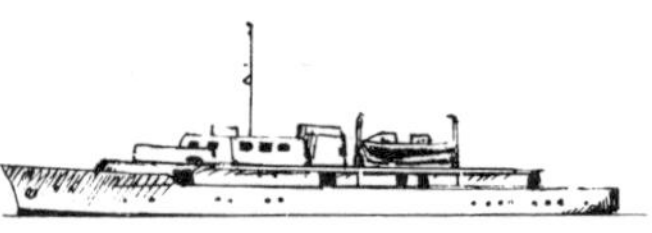

**1032.** Me. **SOTAVENTO**. 1947. Survey Ship. 300 tons. 166 x 28 x 10. (50.5 x 8.5 x 3). Diesels. 17 knots. Formerly Presidential Yacht.

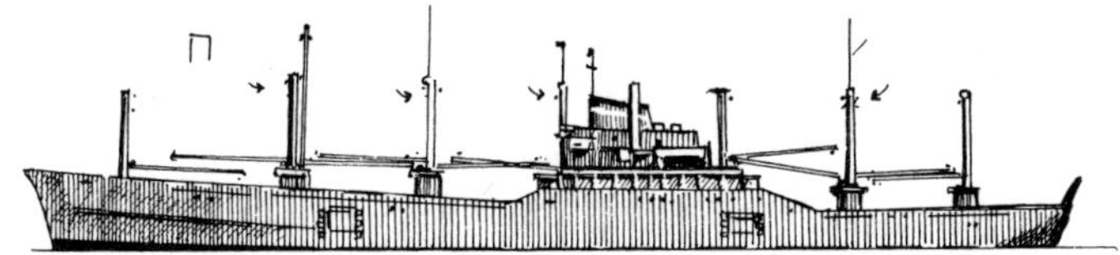

**1033.** Am. **COMET.** 1958. Roll on/Roll off Vehicle Cargo Ship. 18,200 tons full load. 499 x 78 x 29. (152 x 23.7 x 8.8). 2 screws; turbines. 18 knots. Has a stern ramp. Accommodation for 700 vehicles.

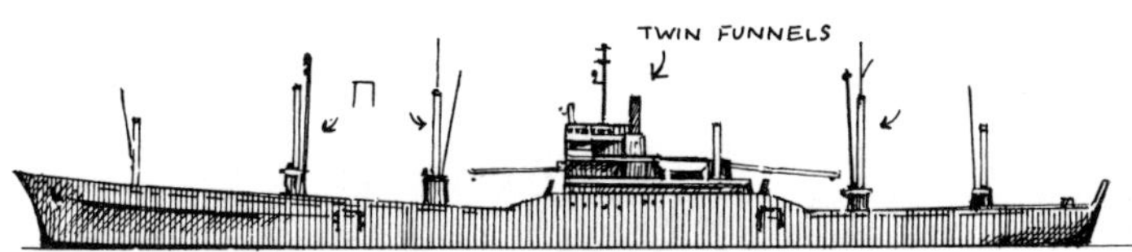


**1034.** Am. **SEA LIFT.** 1967. Roll on/Roll off Vehicle Cargo Ship. 16,900 tons. 540 x 83 x 29. (164.4 x 25.3 x 8.8). 2 screws; turbines. 20 knots. The two very thin funnels amidships are abreast. Has a stern ramp and side openings.

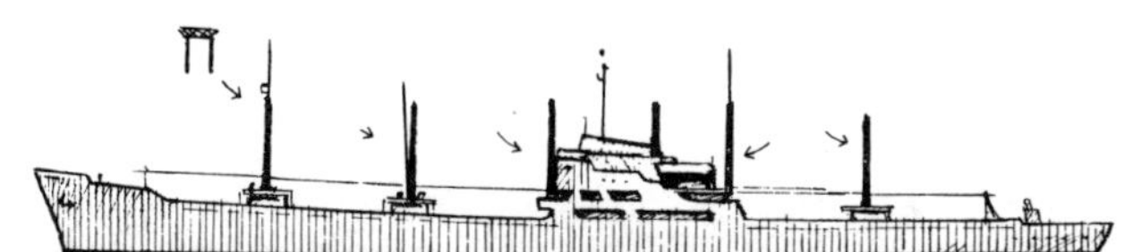

**1035.** Am. **SCHUYLER OTIS BLAND.** 1951. Cargo Ship. 15,900 tons. 478 x 66 x 29. (145.6 x 20.1 x 8.8). Turbine. 18 knots.

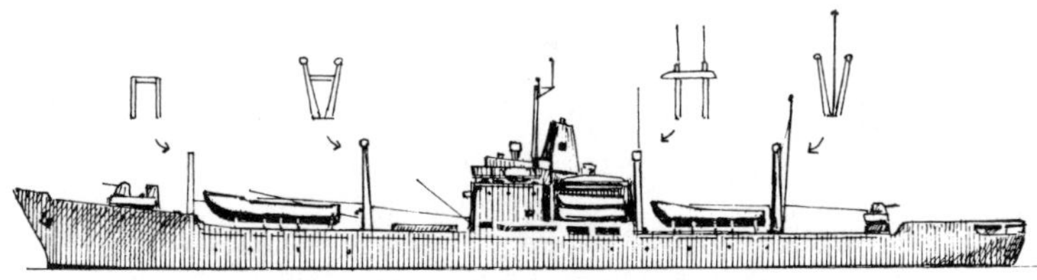

**1036.** Am. **CHARLESTON** class. 1968-70. Amphibious Cargo Ships. 20,700 tons full load. 576 x 82 x 26. (175.4 x 24.9 x 7.9). Turbines. 20 knots. 8—3-inch A.A. guns (twin). Helicopter deck.
**CHARLESTON.** *KA113,* **DURHAM.** *KA114* **EL PASO.** *KA117,* **MOBILE.** *KA115,* **ST. LOUIS.** *KA116.*

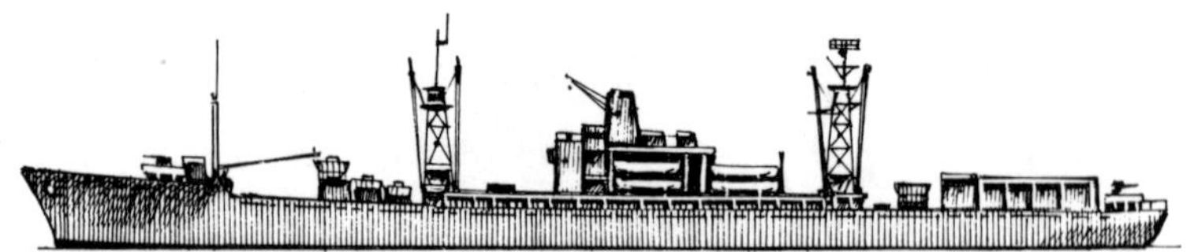

**1037.** Am. **FRANCIS MARION**. *PA249*. 1961. Amphibious Transport. 16,800 tons full load. 564 x 76 x 27. (171.8 x 23.1 x 8.2). Turbines. 20 knots. 8—3-inch A.A. guns (twin). Former "Mariner" type.
**PAUL REVERE.** *PA248*. (Goalpost foremast.)

Similar : **TULARE.** *KA112*. (Kingposts foreward).

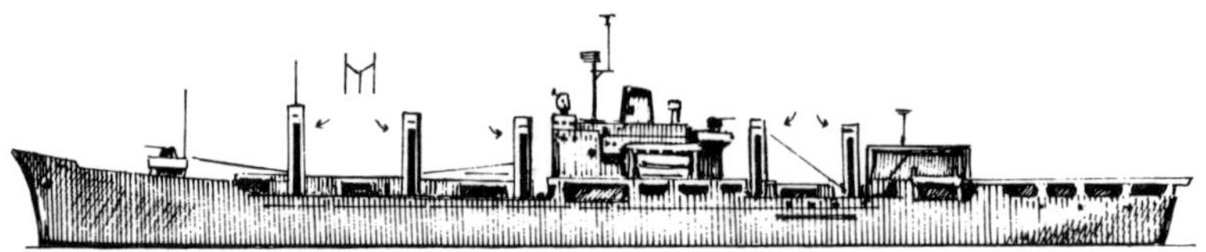

**1038.** Am. **MARS** class. 1963-70. Combat Store Ships. 16,500 tons full load. 581 x 79 x 24. (177 x 24 x 7.3). Turbines. 20 knots. 8—3-inch guns (twin). 2 helicopters.
**CONCORD.** *FS5*, **MARS.** *FS1*, **NIAGARA FALLS.** *FS3*, **SAN DIEGO.** *FS6*, **SAN JOSE.** *FS7*, **SYLVANIA.** *FS2*.

**1039.** Am. **DELTA** class. 1941-43 Repair Ships. 9,000 tons. 491 x 70 x 24. (149 x 21.3 x 7.3). Turbines. 17 knots. 4—3-inch A.A. guns.
**BRIAREUS.** *R12*, **DELTA.** *R9*. Former "C-3" type.

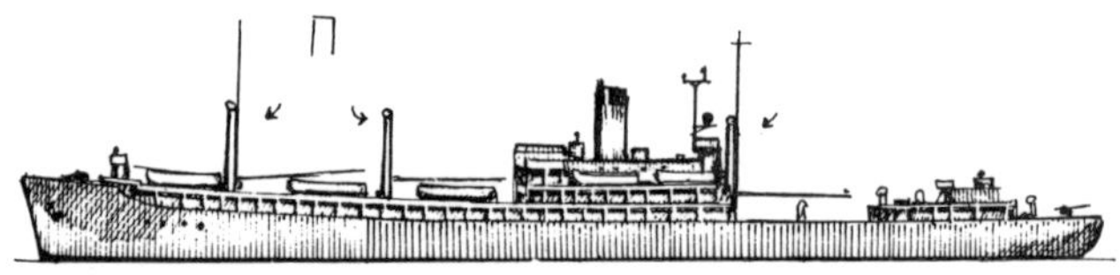

**1040.** Am. **MARKAB.** *R23*. 1941. Repair Ship. 8,600 tons. 493 x 70 x 25. (150.2 x 21.3 x 7.6). Turbines. 18 knots. 4—3-inch A.A. guns "C-3" type.

**1041.** Am. **KLONDIKE** class. 1945. Destroyer Tenders. All details as above but has one 5-inch D.P. gun.
**ARCADIA.** *D23*, **FRONTIER.** *D25*. For others of the class see No. 1042 and 1043.

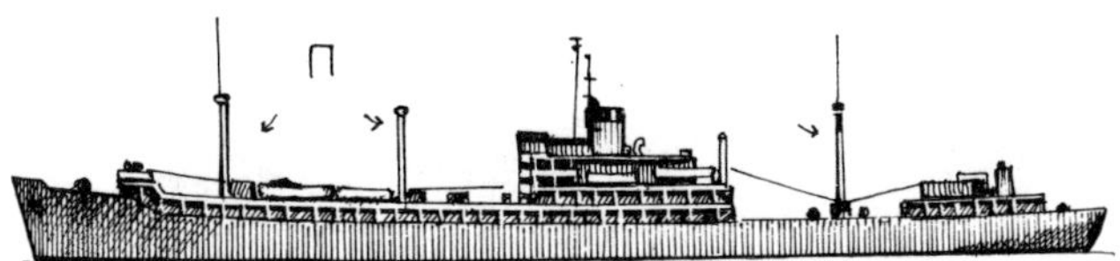

**1042.** Am. **KLONDIKE.** *R22*. 1945. Repair Ship. All details as No. 1041. 2—3-inch A.A. guns. "C-3" type.

**1043.** Am. **KLONDIKE** class. 1945-51. Destroyer Tenders. All details as No. 1041.
**GRAND CANYON.** *D28*, **SHENANDOAH.** *D26*.

Similar: **EVERGLADES.** *D24*, **BRYCE CANYON.** *D36*, **ISLE ROYALE.** *D29*, **YELLOWSTONE.** *D27*.

Similar but repair ship: **AMPHION.** *R13*, **CADMUS.** *R14*.  (See inset.)

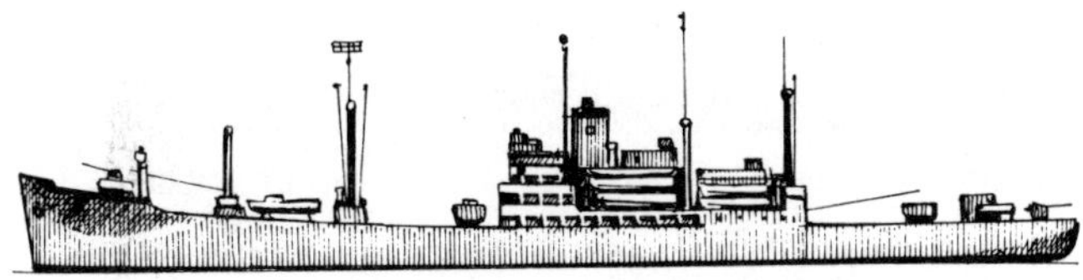

**1044.** Am. **BAYFIELD** class. 1943. Attack Transports. All details as No. 1041. "C-3" type.
**CAMBRIA.** *PA36*, **CHILTON.** *PA38*, **FREMONT.** *PA44*. (All goalpost masts.)

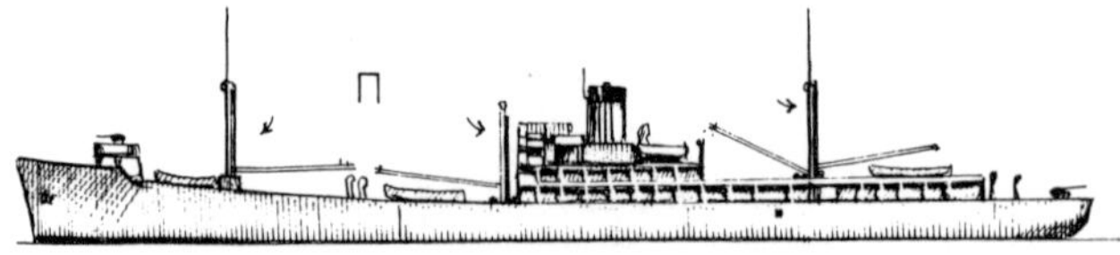

**1045.** Am. **GRIFFIN** class. 1941. Submarine Tenders. Tonnage and dimensions as No. 1041. Diesel. 16 knots. 4—3-inch A.A. guns. "C-3" type.
**GRIFFIN.** *S13*, **PELIAS.** *S14*.

Similar: **AEGIR, EURYALE.**

**1046.** Am. **HASKELL** class. 1944-45. Amphibious Transports. 10,500 tons full load. 455 x 62 x 24. (138.6 x 18.9 x 7.3). Turbines. 17 knots. 12—40-m.m. A.A. guns. "Victory" type.
**BEXAR.** *PA237*, **MOUNTRAIL.** *PA213*, **NAVARRO.** *PA215*, **OKANOGAN.** *PA220*. (Short kingposts and foremast.) **PICKAWAY.** *PA222*, **SANDOVAL.** *PA194*, **TALLADEGA.** *PA208*.
Similar but with tall kingpost foreward: Spanish **ARAGON.** *TA11*.

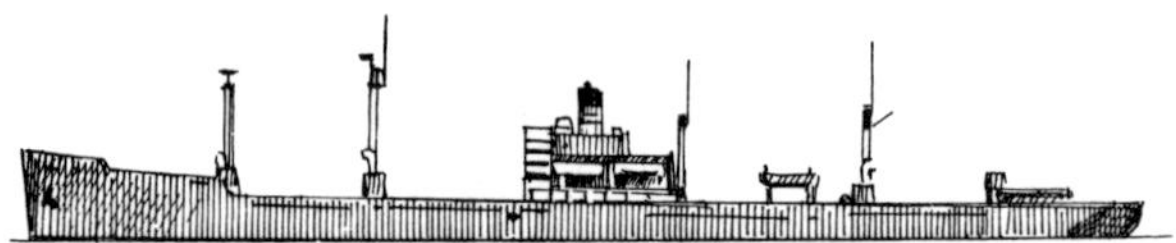

**1047.** Am. **BOWDITCH.** 1945. Converted 1957-58. Survey Ship. 4,500 tons. 455 x 62 x 25. (138.6 x 18.9 x 7.6). Turbine. 15 knots. "Victory" type. **DUTTON, MICHELSON.**

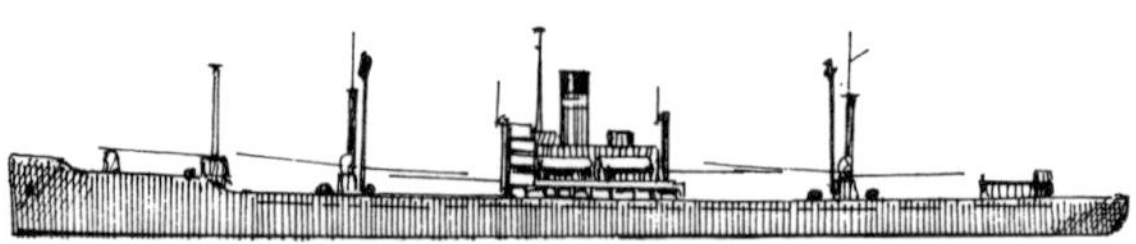

**1048.** Am. **VICTORY** type. 1944-45. All details as No. 1046.
Store ships: **ASTERION, PERSEUS.**
Cargo ships: **CHEYENNE, PHOENIX, PROVO.**
Cargo ships: **GREENVILLE VICTORY, LIEUTENANT JAMES E. ROBINSON, PRIVATE JOHN R. TOWLE, PRIVATE JOSEPH F. MERRELL, SERGEANT JACK J. PENDLETON.**

Cargo ships: **LT. GEORGE W. G. BOICE, LT. ROBERT CRAIG, PRIVATE FRANCIS X. McGRAW, SERGEANT ANDREW MILLER, SERGEANT ARCHER T. GAMMON, SERGEANT MORRIS E. CRAIN, SERGEANT TRUMAN KIMBRO.**
Similar with shorter funnel: **BETELGEUSE.**

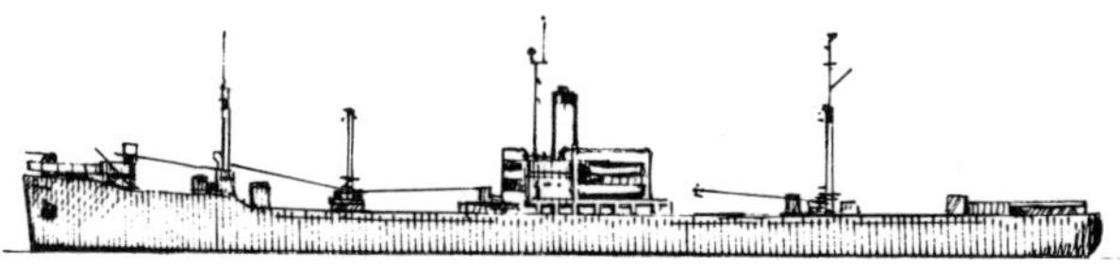

**1049**. Am. **DENEBOLA**. *F56*. 1954. Store Ships.
"Victory" type. All details as No. 1046. Helicopter
deck aft.
**REGULUS**. *F57*.

Similar (tripod mast against front of funnel):
**FURMAN, VICTORIA, NORWALK**

**1050**. Am. **KINGSPORT**. 1944. Converted
1961-62. Hydrographic Research Ship. 10,700
tons full load. All other details as No. 1046.
"Victory" type.

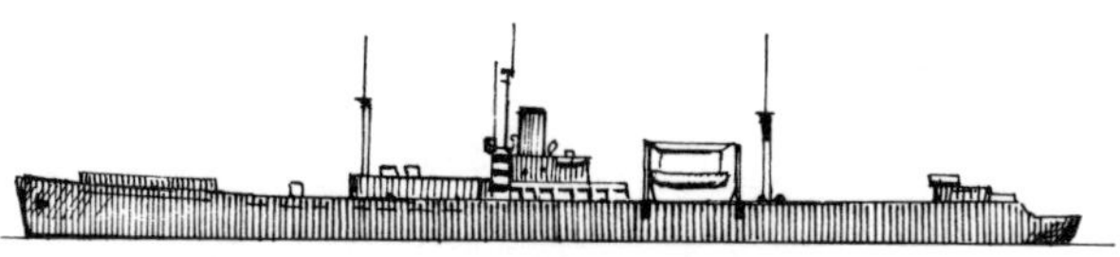

**1051**. Am. **GEORGE EASTMAN**. *AG*39. 1943-
44. Converted 1952-53. 11,600 tons full load.
423 x 57 x 23. (128.9 x 17.3 x 7). Reciprocating.
11 knots. Research Ship.
**GRANVILLE S. HALL**. *AG*40. Former minesweepers. "Liberty" type.

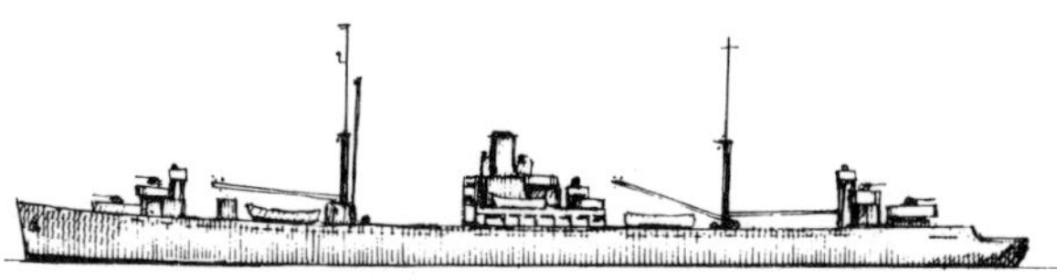

**1052**. Am. **TUTUILA**. *RG4*. 1944. Engine
Repair Ship. 5,800 tons. 442 x 57 x 23. (134.7 x
17.3 x 7). Reciprocating. 12 knots. 3—3-inch
A.A. guns. "Liberty" type.

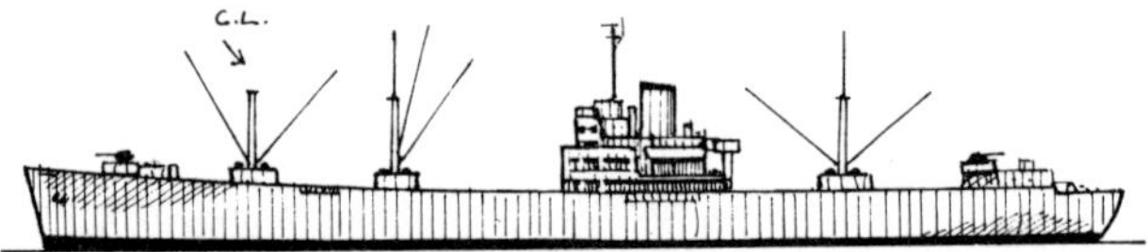

**1053**. Am. **HYADES**. F.28. 1943. Store Ship. 15,300 tons (full). 464 x 63 x 28. (141.4 x 19.2 x 8.5). Turbines. 15 knots. 4—3-inch guns. "C2-EI" type.

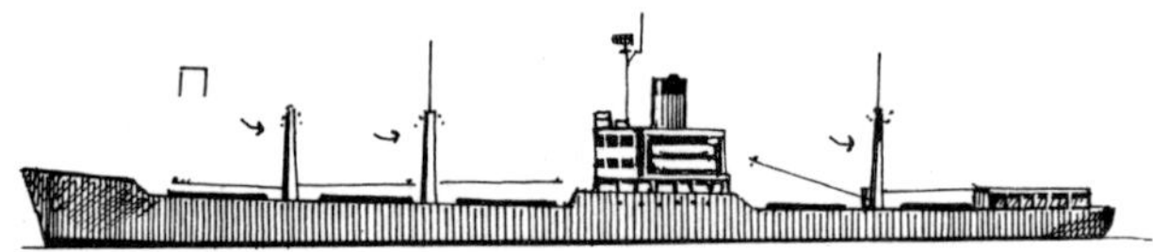

**1054**. Am. **ALUDRA**. *F55*. 1946-52. Dimensions as for No. 1053. 16 knots. 4—40-m.m. A.A. guns. Store Ships. "C2-S-BI" type. **ARCTURUS**. *F52*, **PICTOR**. *F54*, **PROCYON**. *F61*, **ZELIMA**. *F49*.

Similar: **SIRIUS**. Transferred to Maritime Administration Reserve Fleet.

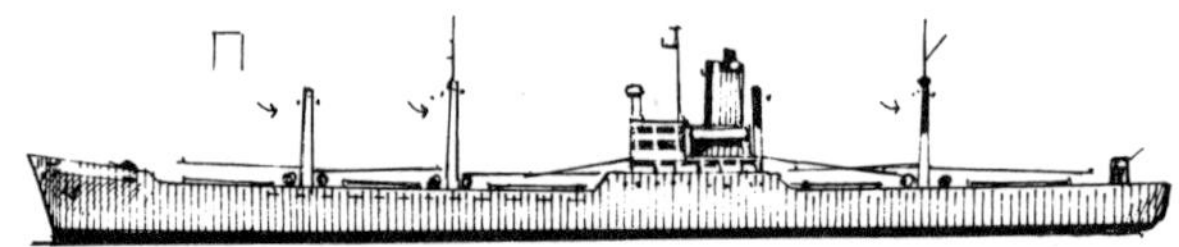

**1055**. Am. **BALD EAGLE**. *AF50*. 1942. Store Ship. Details as for No. 1053. C2-S-BI type. **BLUE JACKET**. *AF51*.

Similar: Hydrographic Research Ship. **FLYER**. *AG178*.

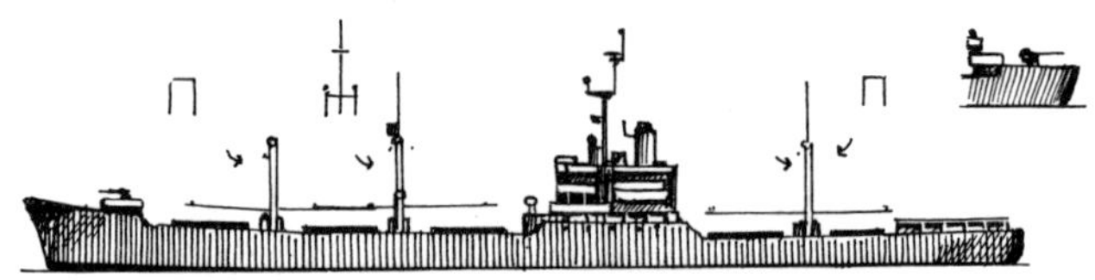

**1056**. Am. **WRANGELL** class. Ammunition Ships. All details as for No. 1053. Some ships do not have helicopter deck aft. (See inset.) **DIAMOND HEAD**. *E19*, **FIREDRAKE**. *E14*, **GREAT SITKIN**. *F17*, **MOUNT KATMAI**. *F16*, **PARICUTIN**. *E18* (plain, tall funnel), **VESU-VIUS**. *E15*, **WRANGELL**. *F12*.

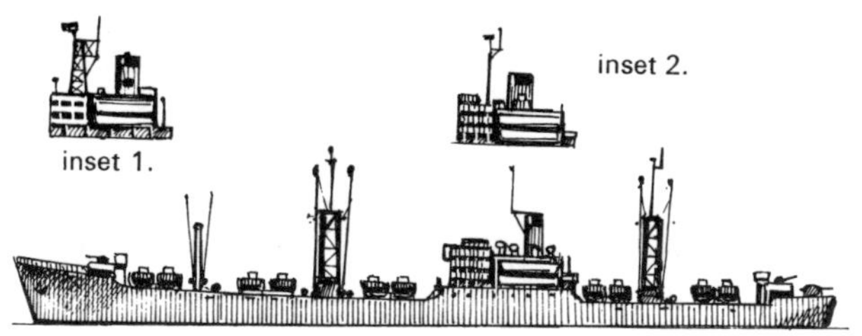


**1057.** Am. **RANKIN**. *KA103*. Attack Cargo Ship. All details as for No. 1053.
**SEMINOLE**. *KA104*, **UNION**. *KA106*, **VER-MILLION**. *KA107*, **WASHBURN**. *KA108*. "C2-S-AJ3" type.

Similar: Some with thicker short funnel more amidships and pole mast from bridge; see inset 2. "C2-S-B1" type.
**ALGOL**. *KA54*, **ARNEB**. *KA56*, **CAPRICOR-NUS**. *KA57*, **MERRICK**. *KA97*, **MULIPHEN**. *KA61*, **THUBAN**. *KA19*, **WINSTON**. *KA84*, **YANCEY**. *KA93*. Some may have lattice mast from bridge; see inset 1.

Also. **CHARA, VIRGO**. (Both tall pole masts from bridge.)
Sp. **CASTILLA**. *TA21*. (Pole mast from bridge, thick lattice masts.)
It. **ETNA**. *A5328*. (Lattice mast from bridge.)

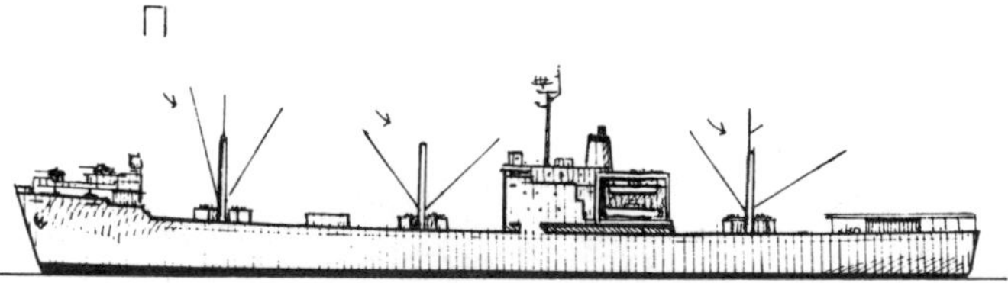

**1058.** Am. **RIGEL**. *F58*. 1955. Store Ship. 15,500 tons (full). 502 x 72 x 29 (153 x 21.9 x 8.8). Turbine. 18 knots. 4—3-inch A.A. guns (twin). "R3-S-4A" type. Helicopter platform.
**VEGA**. *F59*.

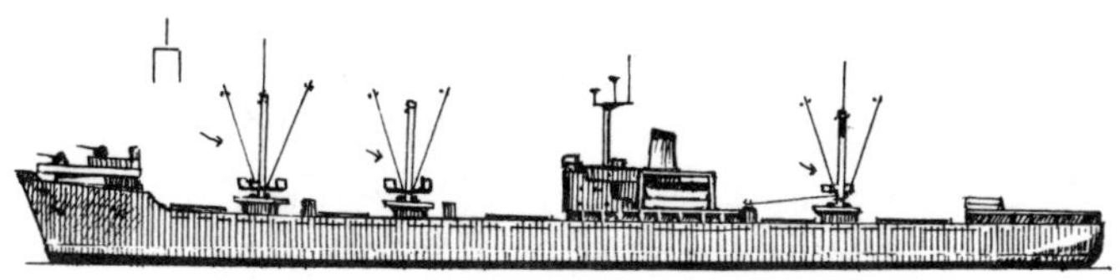

**1059.** Am. **SURIBACHI** class 1956-59. Ammu-nition Ships. 10,000 tons. 512 x 72 x 29. (156.2 x 21.9 x 8.8). Turbines. 21 knots. 4—3-inch A.A. guns (twin). Helicopter deck.
**HALEAKALA**. *E25*, **MAUNA KEA**. *E22*, **NITRO**. *E23*, **PYRO**. *E24*, **SURIBACHI**. *E21*.

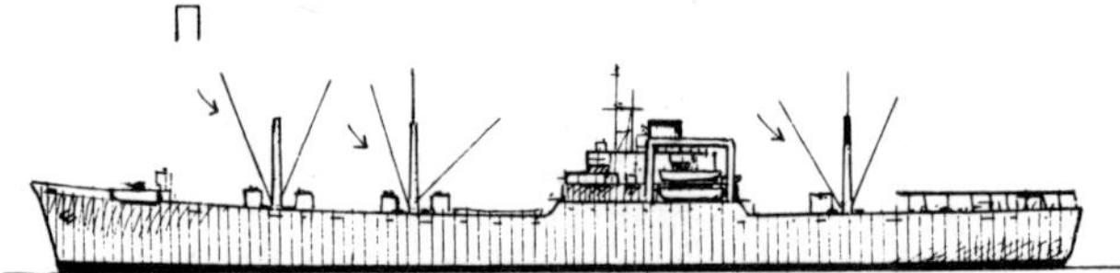

**1060.** Am. **LASSEN** class. 1941-44. Ammunition Ships. 14,200 tons (full). 459 x 63 x 27. (139.9 x 19.2 x 8). Diesels. 15 knots. 2 or 4—3-inch A.A. guns. Some have helicopter platform.
Modified "C2" type.
**MAUNA LOA.** *E8,* **MAZAMA.** *E9,* **RAINER.** *E5.*
**LASSEN** was transferred to Maritime Administration.

**1061.** Br. **RELIANT.** *A84.* 1954. Converted 1958. Air Stores Support Ship. Royal Fleet Auxiliary. 13,700 tons (full). 469 x 62 x 26. (142.9 x 18.9 x 7.9). Diesel. 18 knots. Helicopter platform. Former merchant ship "Somersby".

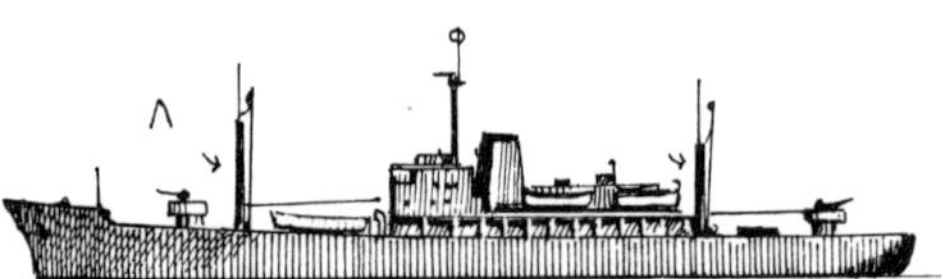

**1062.** Ia. **MULTATULI.** 1961. Submarine Support Ship. 3,200 tons. 365 x 53 x 23. (111.2 x 16.2 x 7). Diesel. 18 knots. 1—85-m.m. gun. 4—40-m.m. guns.

**1063.** Bz. **PEREIRA** class. 1956-57. Transports. 7,300 tons (full). 392 x 53 x 21. (119.5 x 16.2 x 6.1). 2 screws; turbines. 17 knots. 2—21-m.m. A.A. guns. Elevator helicopter deck.
**ARY PARREIRAS.** *G21,* **SOARES DUTRA.** *G22.*
For others in class see No. 1064.

**1064.** Bz. **PEREIRA** class. All details as for No. 1063. Have extra kingpost foreward and superstructure extends to poop.
**BARROSO PEREIRA.** *G16,* **CUSTODIO DE MELLO.** *U26.*

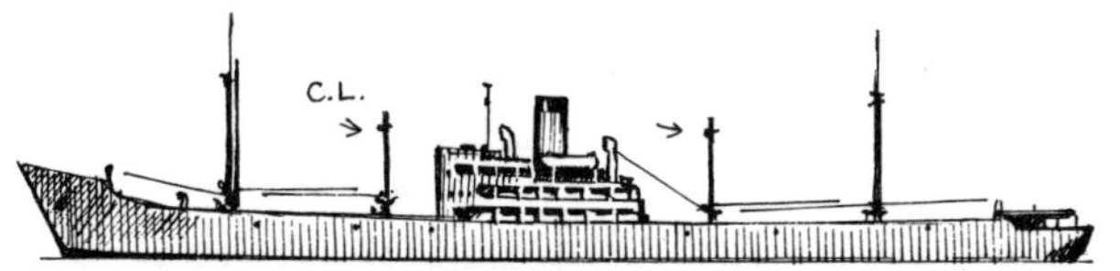


**1065.** Pv. **CALLAO.** *132*. 1939. Transport.
7,800 tons (full). 459 x 56 x 22. (139.9 x 17.1 x
6.7). Diesels. 14 knots.
Former German merchant ship "Monserrate".

**1066.** Ca. **CAPE** class. 1945. Maintenance Ships.
8,500 tons. 442 x 57 x 20. (134.7 x 17.4 x 6.1).
Reciprocating. 11 knots. Helicopter deck. Standard type; see also No. 1067.
**CAPE BRETON.** *100,* **CAPE SCOTT.** *101*.

**1067.** Br. **FORT** class. 1944. Armament Support
Ships. 9,800 tons. 442 x 57 x 27. (134.7 x 17.4 x
8.2). Reciprocating. 11 knots. Royal Fleet
Auxiliaries.
**FORT ROSALIE.** *A186,* **FORT SANDUSKY.**
*A316*.

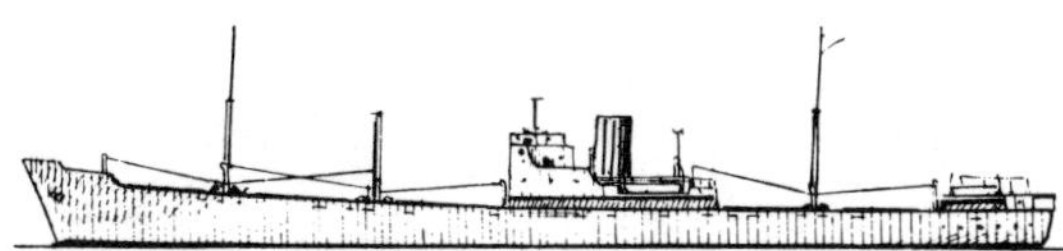

**1069.** Cs. **TIEN CHU.** 313. 1939 Transport.
5,100 tons (gross). 414 x 56 x 26 (126.3 x 16.8 x
7.9). Diesels. 12 knots. Former Polish ship
"Prezydent Gottwald."

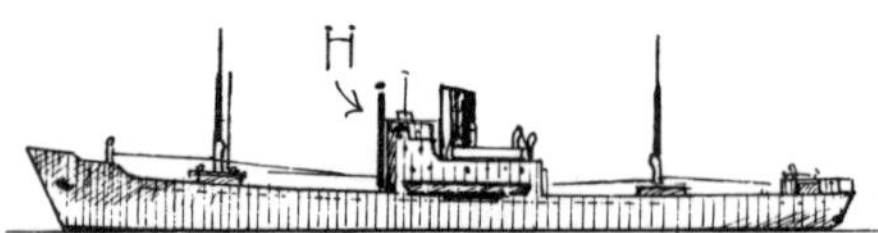

**1070.** Fr. **TARN.** *A771.* 1952. Converted 1965-66. Transport. 2,700 tons. 331 x 48 x 19. (100.9 x 14.6 x 6). Reciprocating and low pressure turbine. 12 knots. Former merchant ship "Colomb Bechar".
Sister ship still in commercial service, "Berkane".

**1071.** Sp. **ALMIRANTE LOBO.** 1954. Transport. 5,700 tons. 363 x 48 x 26. (110.6 x 14.6 x 7.8). Reciprocating. 12 knots. 2—37-m.m. guns. Former cargo vessel "Torre Laguna".

**1072.** Ia. **DHARINI.** 1944. Repair Ship. 4,600 tons. 328 x 46 x 19. (100 x 14 x 5.8). Reciprocating. Wartime "Scandinavian" type merchant ship, "La Petite Hermine".

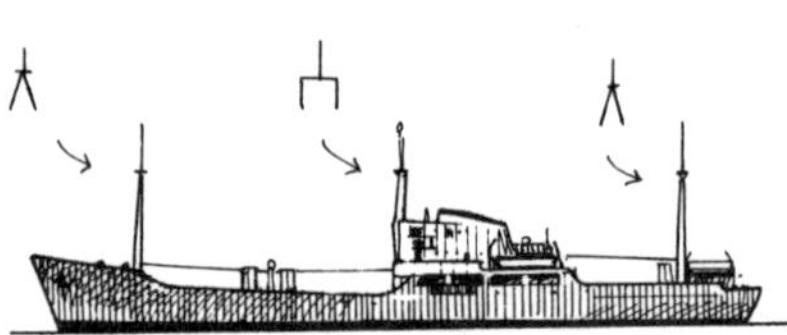

**1073.** Ge. **ANGELN** class. 1954-55. Supply Ships. 2,100 tons (gross). 297 x 44 x 20. (90.5 x 13.4 x 6.2). Diesels. 17 knots. Former French merchant ships.
**ANGELN.** *A1408,* **DITHMARSCHEN.** *A1409.*

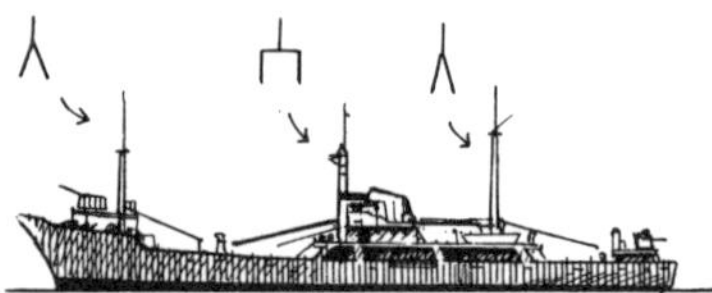

**1074.** Ge. **SCHWARZWALD.** *A1400.* 1956 Supply Ship. 1,100 tons (gross). 263 x 39 x 15. (80.2 x 11.9 x 4.6). Diesel. 17 knots. 4—40-m.m. A.A. guns.
Former French merchant ship "Amalthee".

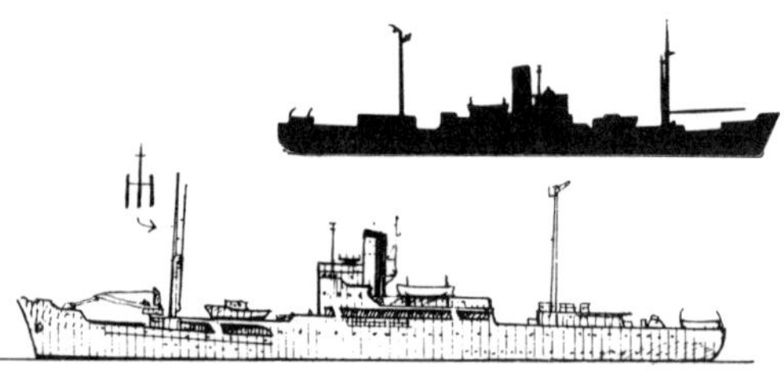

**1075.** Ru. **ATREK** class. 1956-58. Depot Ships. 3,500 tons. 336 x 49 x 20. (102.4 x 14.9 x 6.1). Turbine. 13 knots. Converted from merchant ships and a large number still in commercial service.
At least 6 ships including: **ATREK, AYAT, BAKHMUT.**

Ia. **THAMRIN.** (Submarine Parent Ship.)

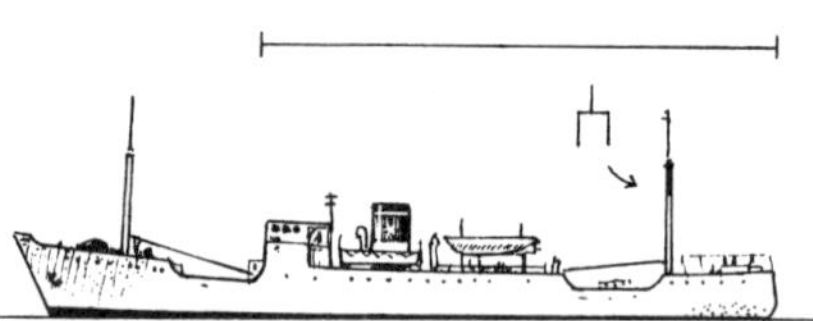

**1076.** Ja. **WAKAKUSA.** *LL01* 1946. Lighthouse Tender. 1,800 tons. 226 x 32 x 19. (68.9 x 9.8 x 5.8). Diesel. Former merchant ship.
Now operated by Maritime Safety Agency.

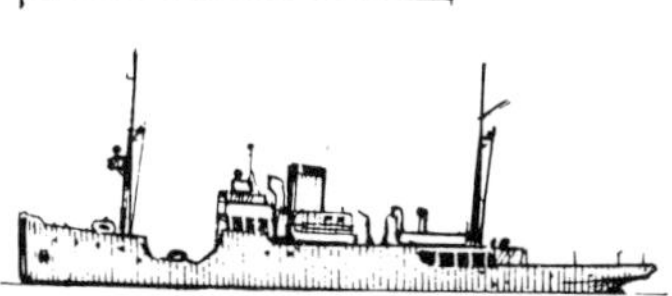

★ **1077.** Ys. **SPASILAC.** 1929. Salvage Vessel. 750 tons. 174 x 26 x 13. (53 x 7.9 x 4). Reciprocating. 15 knots.

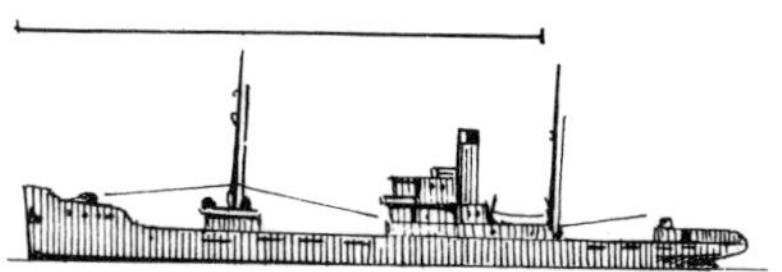

**1078.** Cu. **ENRIQUE COLLAZO.** 1906. Lighthouse Tender. 800 tons. 211 x 34 x 9. (64.3 x 10.4 x 2.7). 2 screws; reciprocating. 8 knots. Former merchant ship.

**1079.** Am. **IVY.** *329.* 1942. Coast Guard Seagoing Tender. 1,050 tons. 189 x 37 x 12. (57.6 x 11.3 x 3.7). 2 screws; reciprocating. 12 knots. Former army minelayer.
**MAGNOLIA.** *328,* **WILLOW.** *332.*

**1080.** Am. **JUNIPER.** *224.* 1940. Coast Guard Tender. 800 tons. 177 x 24 x 9. (53.9 x 7.3 x 2.7). 2 screws; diesel/electric. 11 knots.

**1081.** Ca. **EDWARD CORNWALLIS.** 1949. Light Icebreaker. Canadian Coast Guard. 3,700 tons full load. 259 x 44 x 18. (78.9 x 13.4 x 5.4). Reciprocating. 13 knots.

**1082.** Do. **CAPOTILLO.** *1.* 1911. Lighthouse and Buoy Tender. 300 tons. 117 x 24 x 8. (35.6 x 7.3 x 2.4). Diesels. 10 knots.

**1083.** Am. **WHITE** class. 1943. Coast Guard Tenders. 400 tons. 133 x 30 x 10. (40.5 x 9.1 x 3). Diesel. 10 knots.
**WHITE BUSH.** *542,* **WHITE HEATH.** *545,*
**WHITE HOLLY.** *543,* **WHITE LUPINE.** *546,*
**WHITE PINE.** *544,* **WHITE SAGE.** *544,*
**WHITE SUMAV.** *540.*

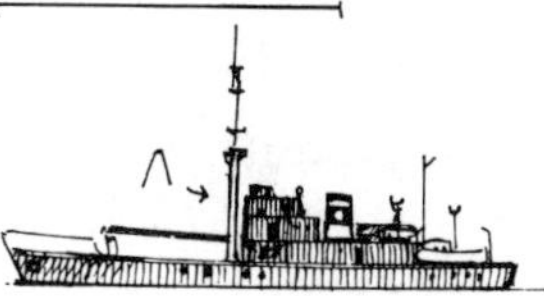

**1084.** Ja. **GINGA.** *LL12.* 1954. Tender. 500 tons. 129 x 31 x 14. (39.3 x 9.4 x 4.2). Diesels. 11 knots. Operated by the Maritime Safety Agency.

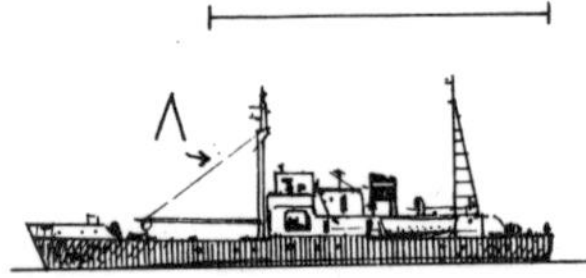

**1085.** Ja. **KAIO.** *LL13.* 1954. Tender. All details as No. 1084.

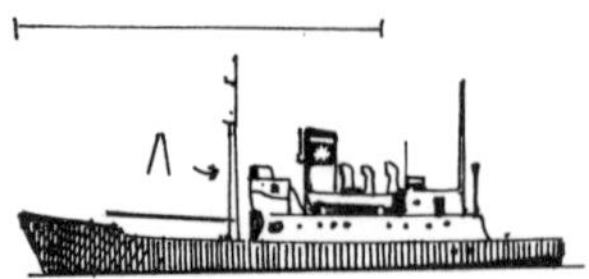

**1086.** Ja. **HOKUTO.** *LL11.* 1954. Tender. All details as No. 1084.

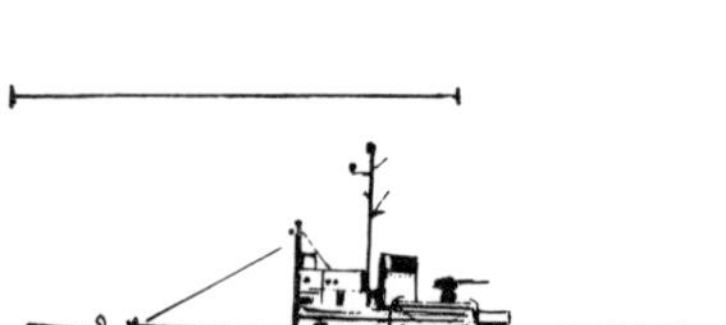

**1087.** Am. **CACTUS** and **IRIS** classes. 1942-44. Coast Guard Tenders. 950 tons. 180 x 37 x 14. (54.8 x 11.2 x 4.2). Diesel/electric. 11 or 12 knots. 1—3-inch gun or machine guns.
Ships vary in appearance,

Cactus class: **BASSWOOD.** *388,* **BLACK-HAW.** *390,* **BLACKTHORN.** *391,* **BUTTON-WOOD.** *306,* **CACTUS.** *270,* **CITRUS.** *300,* **CONIFER.** *301,* **COWSLIP.** *277,* **EVERGREEN.** *295,* **HORNBEAM.** *394,* **MESQUITE.** *305,* **PAPAW.** *308,* **PLANETREE.** *307,* **SASSA-FRAS.** *401,* **SEDGE.** *402,* **SPAR.** *403,* **SUN-DEW.** *404,* **SWEETBRIAR.** *405,* **SWEETGUM.** *309.*
(Cactus and Evergreen are used as Oceanographic cutters.)

Acacia class: **ACACIA.** *406,* **BALSAM.** *62,* **BRAMBLE.** *392,* **FIREBRUSH.** *393,* **GENTIAN.** *290,* **IRIS.** *395,* **IRONWOOD.** *297,* **LAUREL.** *291,* **MADRONA.** *302,* **MALLOW.** *396,* **SAGEBUSH.** *399,* **SALVIA.** *400,* **SORRELL.** *296,* **TUPELO.** *303* **WOODBINE.** *289,* **WOOD-BRUSH.** *407.*
See number 1089 for other ships of this class.

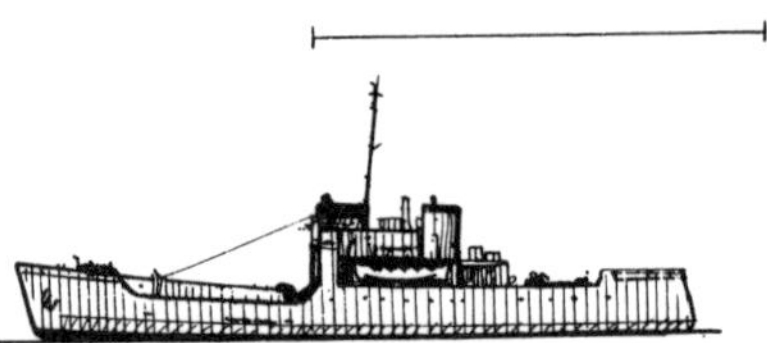

**1088.** Am. **REDBUD.** 1943. Light Cargo Ship. 700 tons. 180 x 37 x 14. (54.8 x 11.2 x 4.2). Diesel. 10 knots. Transferred from the U.S. Coast Guard. A unit of the Acacia class; see No. 1087.

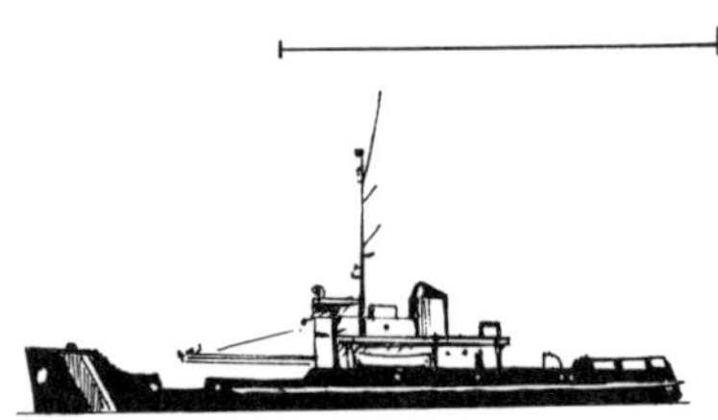

**1089.** Am. **IRIS** class. 1943-44. Coast Guard Tenders. All details as No. 1087.
**BITTERSWEET.** *389,* **MARIPOSA.** *397.*

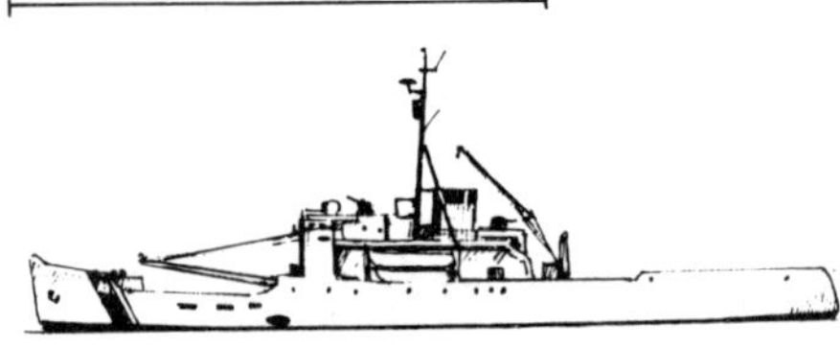

**1090.** Am. **STORIS.** *38.* 1942. Icebreaker. 1,700 tons. 230 x 43 x 15. (70.1 x 13.1 x 4.5). Diesel-electric. 1—3-inch gun. 1 helicopter. Helicopter deck aft.

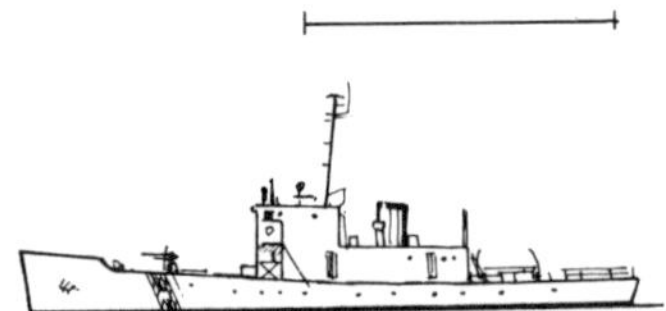

**1091.** Am. **MORRIS.** *147.* 1927. Re-engined 1942. Coast Guard Cutter. 220 tons. 125 x 24 x 9. (38.1 x 7.3 x 2.7). 2 screws; diesels. 13 knots. 1—40-m.m. A.A. gun. Only survivor of the large "Alert" class.

**1092.** Am. **RED** class. 1964-65. Coast Guard Coastal Tenders. 500 tons. 157 x 32 x 6. (47.8 x 9.7 x 1.8). 2 screws; diesels. 14 knots.
**RED BEECH.** *686*, **RED BIRCH.** *687*, **RED WOOD.** *685*.

**1093.** Am. **HOLLYHOCK** class. 1938. Coast Guard Coastal Tenders. 1,000 tons. 175 x 32 x 12. (53.3 x 9.7 x 3.6). 2 screws; diesel. 12 knots.
**FIR.** *212*, **HOLLYHOCK.** *220*, **WILLOW.** 252.

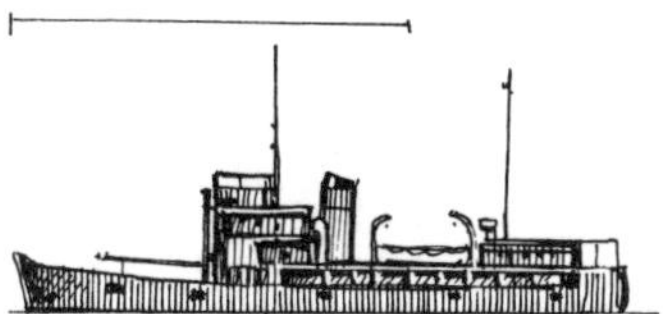

**1094.** Ng. **PATHFINDER.** *P06*, 1954. Survey Craft, 550 tons gross. 162 x 27 x 11. (49.3 x 8.2 x 3.3). Reciprocating. 8 knots.

**1095.** Du. **HENDRIK KARSSEN.** *Y8102.* 1939. Training Ship and Ferry. 170 tons. 138 x 21 x 6. (42 x 6.4 x 1.8). Diesels. 11 knots. 2—20-m.m. A.A. guns.

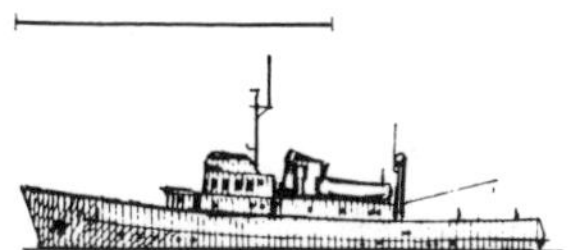

**1096.** Fi. **UISKO.** 1959. Coast Guard Patrol Vessel. 400 tons. 141 x 24 x 13. (42.9 x 7.3 x 3.9). Diesel. 15 knots.

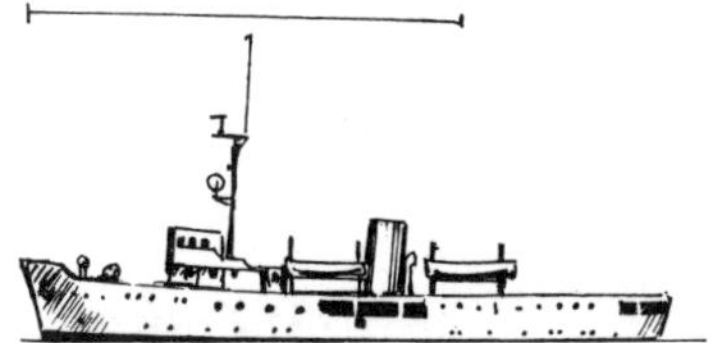

**1097.** Sw. **GUSTAV** af **KLINT.** 1941. Reconstructed 1963. Survey Ship. 750 tons. 171 x 29 x 16. (52.1 x 8.8 x 4.8). Diesels. 10 knots.

**1098.** Br. **ISLES** class. 1942-43. Tank-cleaning Vessels (trawlers). 560 tons. 164 x 28 x 14. (49.9 x 8.5 x 4.2). Reciprocating. 12 knots.
**BERN, CALDY, COLL, FOULNESS, GRAEM-SAY, LUNDY, SKOMER, SWITHA.**

**1099.** Po. **SANTA MARIA.** 1942. Minesweeper. 600 tons. 164 x 28 x 15. (49.9 x 8.5 x 4.5). Reciprocating. 12 knots. 1—3-inch gun. 2—20-m.m. A.A. guns. Depth charges. Ex-British "Isles" class trawler.

**1100.** Co. **ANDAGOYA**. 1928. Re-engined 1955. Fleet Tug. 100 tons. 65 x 00 x 00.( 19.8 x 00 x 00). Diesels. 8 knots.

**1101.** Br. **RECLAIM**. *A231*. 1948. Diving Trial Ship. 1,200 tons. 218 x 38 x 16. (66.4 x 11.5 x 4.8). 2 screws; reciprocating. 12 knots. Former salvage ship of the "Salv" class (see No. 1102).

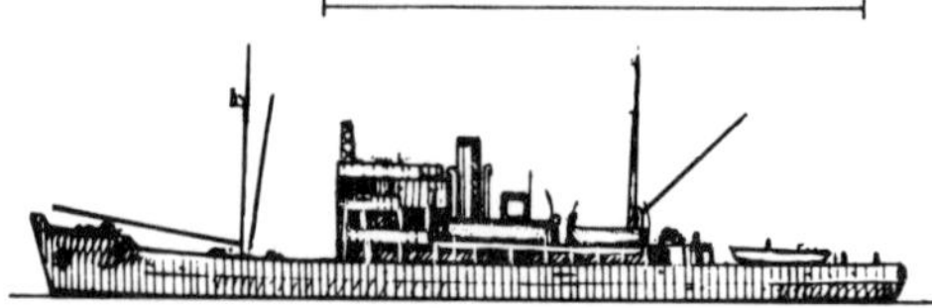

**1102.** Br. **SALV** class. 1943-44. Salvage Ships. Details as No. 1101.
**SALVALOUR, SEA SALVOR.** (Royal Fleet Auxiliary.)
Similar: Greece: **SOTIR**. *A384*.
Argentina. **GUARDIAMARINA ZICARI**. *Q81*.

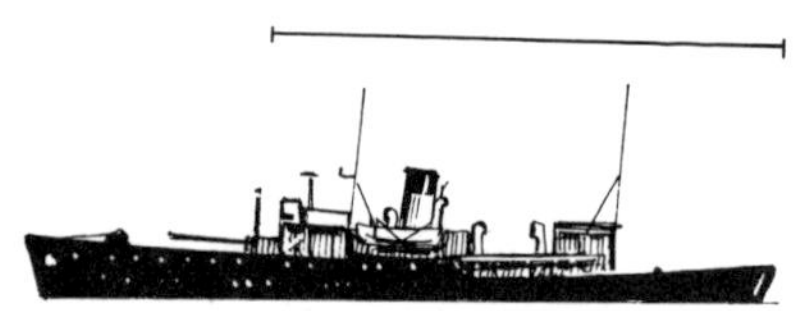

**1103.** Ca. **SACKVILLE**. *113*. 1941. Converted 1964. Research Vessel. 1,100 tons. 205 x 33 x 15. (62.4 x 10 x 4.5). Reciprocating. 16 knots. Former "Flower" class frigate. Similar to Norwegian weather ships; see No. 338.

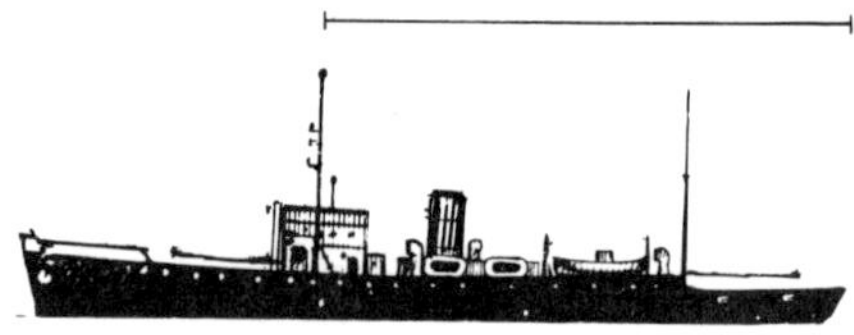

**1104.** Ar. **CAPITAN CANEPA**. *Q8*. 1941. Survey Ship. 1,000 tons. 208 x 34 x 16. (63.3 x 10.3 x 4.8). Reciprocating. 15 knots. Former Canadian "Flower" class corvette.

**1105.** Ar. **USHUAIA**. *Q10*. 1940. Survey Ship/Buoy Ship. 1,300 tons. 211 x 32 x 11. (4.3 x 9.7 x 3.3). 2 screws; diesels. 12 knots.

**1106.** Ca. **WOOD**. *MP17*. 1958. Patrol Craft. 600 tons. 178 x 29 x 9. (54.2 x 8.8 x 2.7). 2 screws; diesels. 16 knots.
Operated by Royal Canadian Mounted Police.

**1107.** Ic. **ALBERT.** 1957. Coast Guard Patrol
Vessel. 200 tons (gross). 111. (33.8). Diesel. 12
knots. 1—47-m.m. gun.

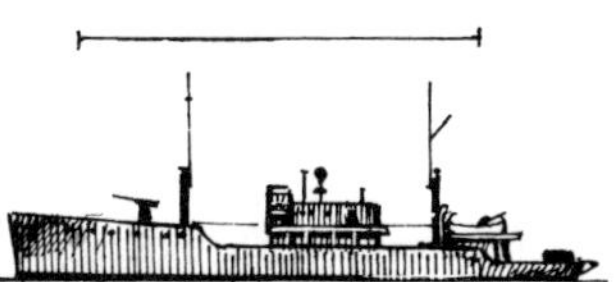

**1108.** Th. **BANGRACHAN** class. 1936. Coastal
Minelayers. 400 tons. 161 x 26 x 7. (49 x 7.9 x
2.1). 2 screws; diesels. 12 knots. 2—3-inch A.A.
guns. 2—20-m.m. A.A. guns. 140 mines.
**BANGRACHAN.** *1,* **NHONG SARHAI.** *2.*

**1109.** Ja. **IZU** class. 1967-69. Patrol Vessels and
Weather Ships. 2,100 tons. 300 x 38 x 18. (91.4 x
11.5 x 5.4). 2 screws; diesels. 21 knots.
Maritime Safety Agency.
**IZU.** *PL31,* **MIURA.** *PL32.*

**1110.** Ja. **KOJIMA.** *PL21.* 1964. Training Ship.
1,100 tons. 228 x 34 x 11. (69.4 x 10.3 x 3.3).
Diesels. 17 knots. 1—3-inch gun. 2 A.A. guns.
Maritime Safety Agency.

**1111.** Ja. **ERIMO.** *PL13.* 1965. Patrol Vessel.
1,000 tons. 242 x 30 x 10. (73.7 x 9.1 x 3). 2
screws; diesels. 20 knots. 1—3-inch gun. 1—20-
m.m. A.A. gun.
Maritime Safety Agency.
**SATSUMA.** *PL14.*

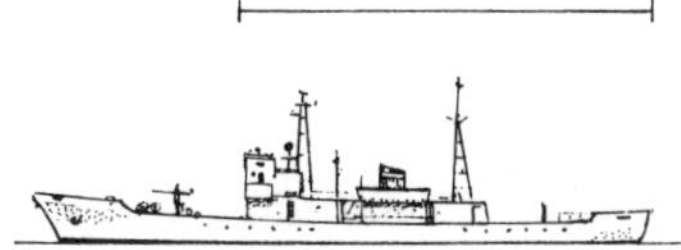

**1112.** Ja. **YAHAGI** class. 1956-61. Patrol
Vessels. 330 tons. 160 x 24 x 7. (48.7 x 7.3 x 21.).
Diesels. 15 knots. 1—40-m.m. A.A. gun.
Maritime Safety Agency.
**CHITOSE.** *PS56,* **HORONAI.** *PS59,* **SORACHI.**
*PS57,* **SUMIDA.** *PS55,* **YAHAGI.** *PS54,*
**YUBARI.** *PS58.*

**1113.** Ja. **MATSUURA** class. 1961-66. Patrol
Vessels. 400 tons. 182 x 23 x 7½. (55.4 x 7 x 2.4).
Diesels. 16 knots. 1—20-m.m. A.A. gun.
Maritime Safety Agency.
**AMAMI.** *PS62,* **KARATSU.** *PS64,* **MATSU-
URA.** *PS60,* **NATORI** *PS63,* **SENDAI.** *PS61.*

**1114.** Ja. **NOJIMA** class. 1962-63. Patrol
Vessels and Weather Ships. 950 tons. 227 x 30 x
10½. (69.1 x 9.1 x 3.1). Diesels. 17 knots.
Maritime Safety Agency.
**NOJIMA.** *PL11,* **OJIKA.** *PL12.*

**1115.** Ja. **TOKACHI** class. 1954. Patrol Vessels. 325 tons. 170 x 22 x 11. (51.8 x 6.7 x 3.3). Diesels. 12-15 knots. 1—40-m.m. A.A. gun. Maritime Safety Agency.
**TATSUTA.** *PS52,* **TOKACHI.** *PS51.*

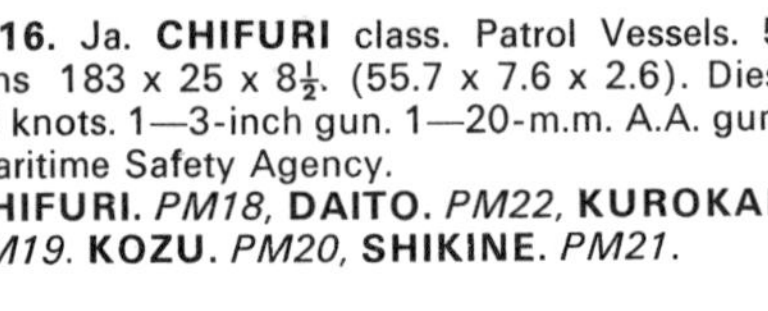

**1116.** Ja. **CHIFURI** class. Patrol Vessels. 500 tons 183 x 25 x 8½. (55.7 x 7.6 x 2.6). Diesels 16 knots. 1—3-inch gun. 1—20-m.m. A.A. gun. Maritime Safety Agency.
**CHIFURI.** *PM18,* **DAITO.** *PM22,* **KUROKAMI.** *PM19.* **KOZU.** *PM20,* **SHIKINE.** *PM21.*

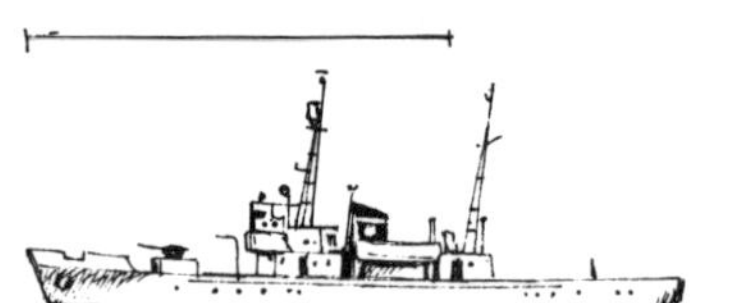

**1118.** Ja. **TESHIO.** *PS53,* 1955. Patrol Vessel. 420 tons. 164 x 23 x 8. (49.9 x 7 x 2.4). Diesels. 16 knots. 1—40-m.m. A.A. gun. Maritime Safety Agency.

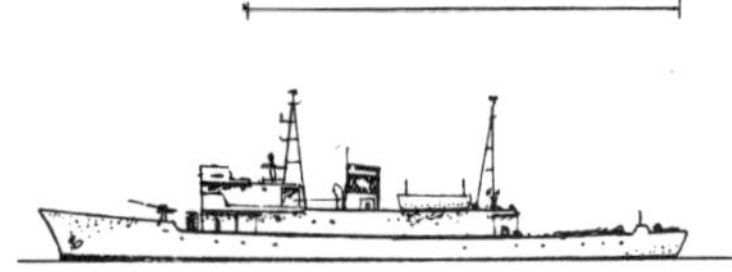

**1119.** Ja. **AWAJI.** class. 1950. Patrol Vessels. 500 tons. 172 x 27 x 9. (52.1 x 8.2 x 2.7). Diesels. 15 knots. 1—3-inch gun. 1—20-m.m. A.A. gun. Maritime Safety Agency.
**AWAJI.** *PM01,* **MIYAKE.** *PM02,* **SACO.** *PM03.*

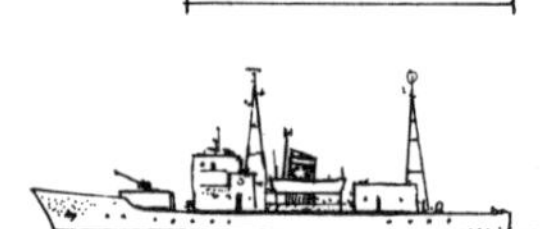

**1120.** Ja. **NAGARA** class. 1952. Patrol Vessels. 260 tons. 131 x 23 x 7. (39.9 x 7 x 2.1). 2 screws; 13 knots. 1—40-m.m. A.A. gun. Maritime Safety Agency.
**NAGARA.** *PS18,* **KITAKAMI.** *PS20,* **TONE.** *PS19.* (May have a short mainmast.)

**1121.** Ja. **KUMA** class. 1951. Patrol Vessels. 260 tons. 132 x 23 x 7½. (39.9 x 7 x 2.3). Diesels. 13 knots. 1—40-m.m. A.A. gun.
**ABUKUMA.** *PS08,* **CHIKUGO.** *PS16* **FUJI.** *PS02,* **ISHIKARI.** *PS05,* **ISUZU.** *PS04,* **KIKU-CHI.** *PS10,* **KUMANO.** *PS17,* **KUZURYU.** *PS09* **KUMA.** *PS01,* **MOGAMI.** *PA11,* **NOSH-IRO.** *PS13,* **OYODO.** *PS07,* **SAGAMI.** *PS06,* **SHINANO.** *PS15,* **TENRYU.** *PS03,* **YOSHINO.** *PS12.*

**1122.** Ja. **REBUN** class. 1951. Patrol Vessels. 450 tons. 170 x 27 x 8½. (51.8 x 8.2 x 2.5). Diesels. 15 knots. 1—3-inch gun. 1—20-m.m. A.A. gun.
Maritime Safety Agency.
Some ships have boat on deck aft only and shorter mainmast.

**AMAKUSA.** *PM09,* **GENKAI.** *PM07,* **HACH-IJO.** *PM08,* **HEKURA.** *PM14,* **HIRADO.** *PM17,* **IKI.** *PM05,* **KOSHIKI.** *PM16,* **KUSAKAKI.** *PM11,* **MIKURA.** *PM15,* **NOTO.** *PM13,* **OKI.** *PM06,* **OKUSHIRI.** *PM10,* **REBUN.** *PM04,* **RISHIRI.** *PM12.*

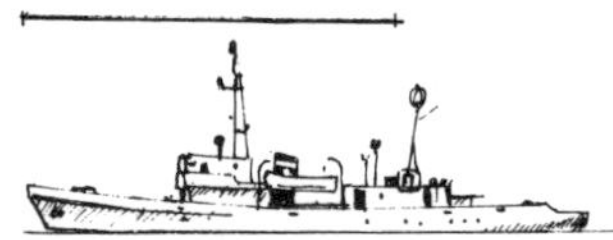

**1123.** Ja. **KAWACHIDORI** class. Patrol Vessels. 300 tons. 153 x 22 x 7½. (46.6 x 6.7 x 2.3). Diesels. 14 knots.
Maritime Safety Agency.
**ASACHIDORI.** *PS103* **HAMACHIDORI.** *PS-102,* **HARUCHIDORI.** *PS115,* **MIOCHIDORI.** *PS104,* **SAWACHIDORI.** *PS107,* **TOMO-CHIDORI.** *PS105.*

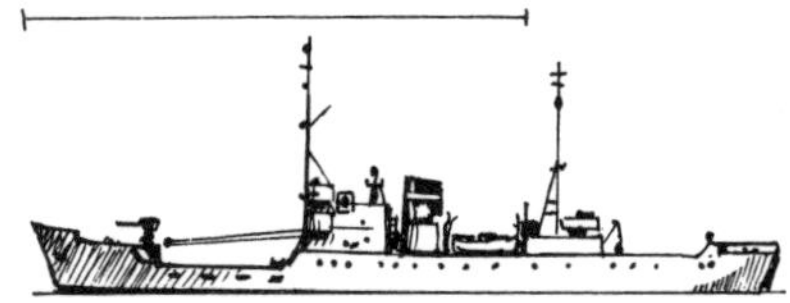

**1124.** Ja. **MUROTO** class. 1950. Patrol Vessels. 750 tons. 200 x 31 x 10. (60.9 x 9.4 x 3). Diesels. 15 knots. 1—3-inch gun. 2—20-m.m. A.A. guns. **DAIO.** *PL02,* **MUROTO.** *PL01.*

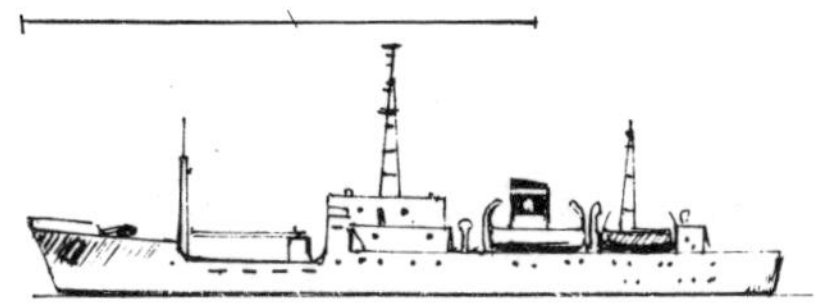

**1125.** Ja. **TAKUYO.** *HL03.* 1957. Survey Vessel. 900 tons. 200 x 31 x 11. (60.9 x 9.4 x 3.3). Diesels. 14 knots.

**1126.** Ja. **HIDAKA** class. 1962-68. Patrol Vessels. 170 tons. 111 x 22 x 5½. (33.8 x 6.7 x 1.7). Diesels. 13 knots.
Maritime Safety Agency.
**AKIYOSHI.** *PS37,* **ASHITAKA.** *PS43,* **HIDAKA.** *PS32,* **HIMAYA.** *PS33,* **IBUKI.** *PS45,* **KAMUI.** *PS41,* **KUNIMI.** *PS38,* **KURAMA.** *PS44,* **ROKKO.** *PS35,* **TAKANAWA.** *PS36,* **TAKA-TSUKI.** *PS39,* **TOUMI.** *PS46,* **TSURUGI.** *PS34.*

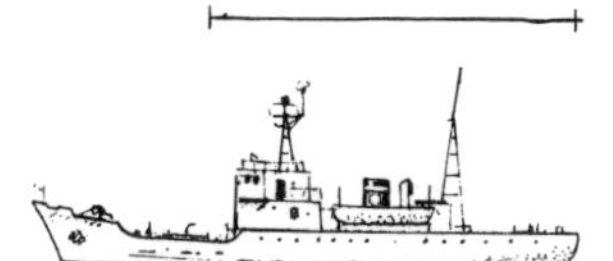

**1127.** Ja. **MEIYO.** *HL03,* 1963. Survey Vessel. 500 tons. 146 x 27 x 9½. (44.5 x 8.2 x 2.9). Diesel. 12 knots.

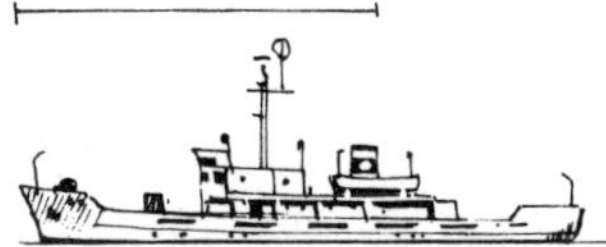

**1128.** Ja. **KAIYO.** *HM06.* 1964. Survey Vessel. 400 tons. 146 x 27 x 8. (44.5 x 8.2 x 2.4). Diesels. 12 knots.
Maritime Safety Agency.

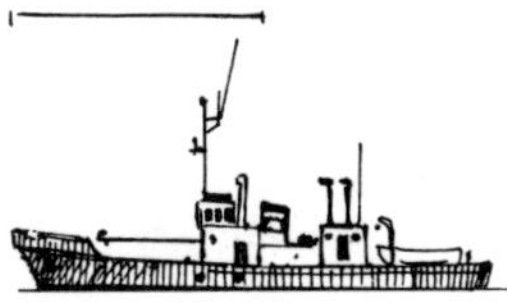

**1129.** Ja. **AKEBONO.** *LM106.* 1955. Buoy Tender. 80 (approx.).
Maritime Safety Agency.

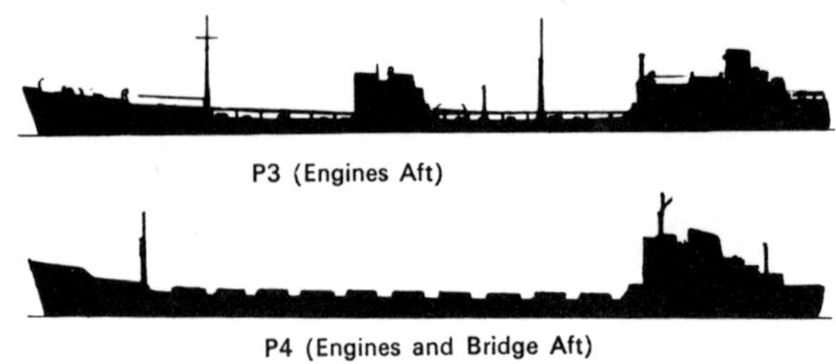


# P3

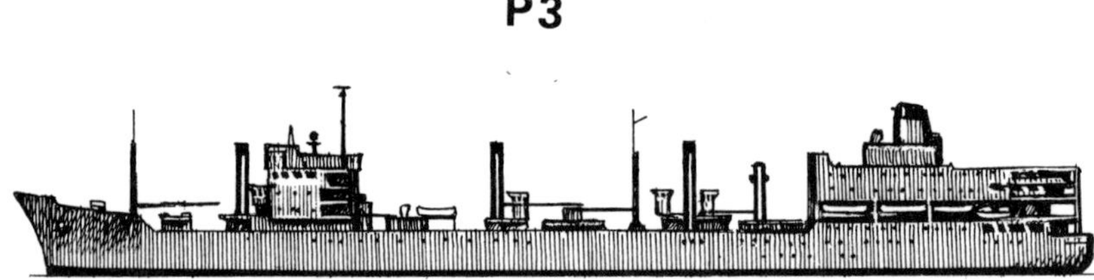

**1130.** Br. **REGENT.** *A486.* 1967. Replenishment
Ship. 19,000 tons full load. 640 x 77 x 26.
195 x 23.4 x 7.9). Turbines. 2—40-m.m. A.A.
guns. 1 helicopter with hangar.
Royal Fleet Auxiliaries.
**RESOURCE.** *A480.*

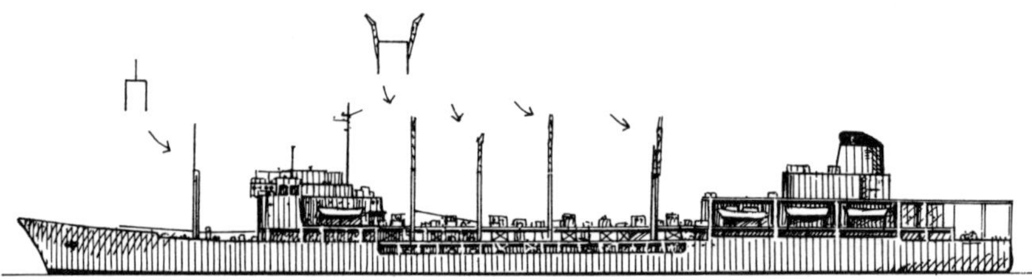

**1131.** Br. **OL** class. 1964-65. Fleet Replenish-
ment Oilers. 33,200 tons full load. 648 x 84 x 34.
(197.4 x 25.6 x 10.3). Turbines. 19 knots.
Capacity for 3 helicopters.
Royal Fleet Auxiliary.
**OLMEDA.** *A124,* **OLNA.** *A123* **OLWEN.** *A122.*

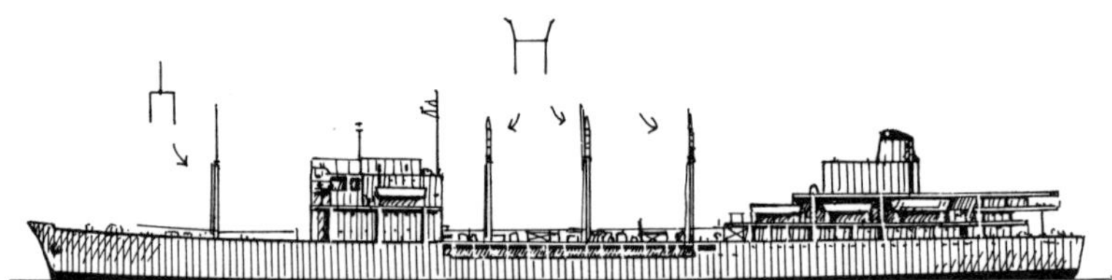

**1132.** Br. Later **TIDE** class. 1963. Fleet Replenishment Oilers. 25,900 tons full load. 583 x 71 x 32.
(177.6 x 21.6 x 9.7). Turbines. 17 knots. Helicopter landing platform and hangar.
Royal Fleet Auxiliary.
**TIDEPOOL.** *A76,* **TIDESPRING.** *A75.*

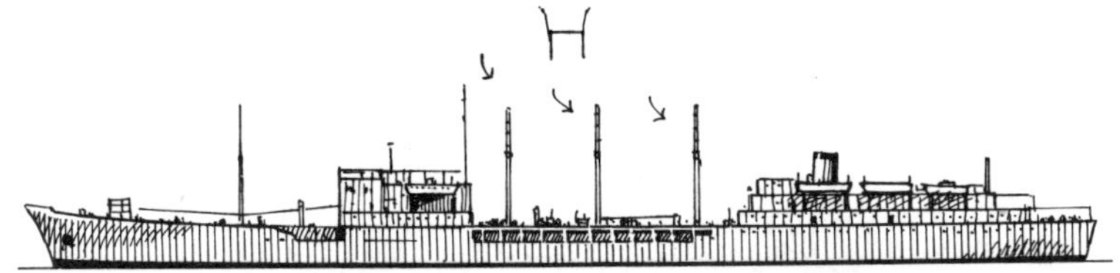

**1133.** Br. **TIDE** class. 1955. Fleet Replenishment Oilers. 25,900 tons full load. 583 x 71 x 32. (177.6 x 21.6 x 9.7). Turbines. 17 knots. Royal Fleet Auxiliary.
**TIDEFLOW.** *A97*, **TIDEREACH.** *A96*, **TIDE-SURGE.** *A96.*

Very similar: Australia. 15,000 tons standard. **SUPPLY.** *A195.*

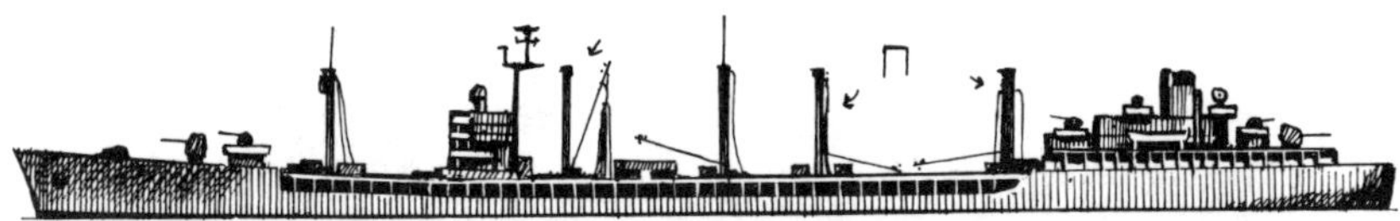

**1134.** Am. **NEOSHO** class. 1964-66. Underway Replenishment Ship (oiler). 40,000 tons full load. 655 x 86 x 35. (199.5 x 26.2 x 10.6). 2 screws. 20 knots. 12—3-inch guns (twin). Some ships have a helicopter deck and a kingpost replacing the after gun turret.

**HASSAYAMPA.** *145*, **KAWISHIWI.** *146*, **MISSISSINEWA.** *144*, **NEOSHO.** *143*, **PONCHATOULA.** *148*, **TRUCKEE.** *147.*

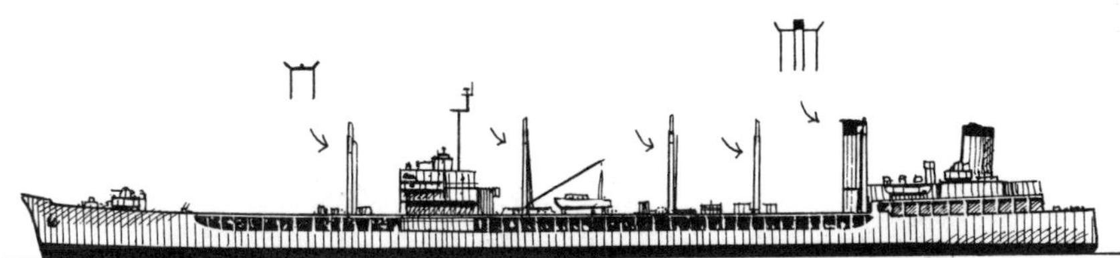

**1135.** Am. Lenghtened **T3** type. 1945-46. Rebuilt 1963-64. Replenishment Oilers. 34,800 tons full load. 646 x 75 x 36. (196.8 x 22.8 x 10.9). 2 screws; turbines. 16 knots. 4—3-inch A.A. guns. Helicopter deck foreward.

**MISPILLION.** *105*, **NAVASOTA.** *106*, **PASSUMPSIC.** *107*, **PAWCATUCK.** *108*, **WACCAMAW.** *109.*

Possibly similar are: **ASHTABULA.** *51*, **CALOOSAHATCHEE.** *88*, **CANISTEO.** *99.* (8—3-inch guns).

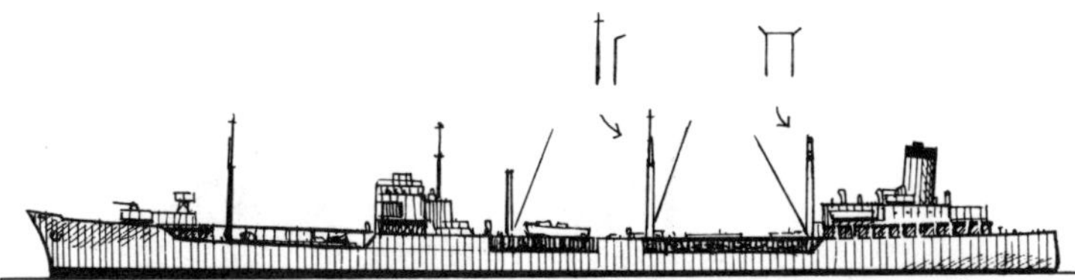

**1136.** Am. **T3** type. 1939-45. Replenishment Oilers. 25,500 tons full load. 553 x 75 x 32. (168.4 x 22.8 x 9.7). 2 screws; turbines. 18 knots. 1 to 3—5-inch guns. 2 to 4—3-inch guns.

**ALLAGASH.** *97*, **AUCILLA.** *55*, **CACAPON.** *52*, **CALIENTE.** *53*, **CHIKASKIA.** *54*, **CHIPOLA.** *63*, **CHUKAWAN.** *100*, **CHEMUNG.** *30*, **GUADALUPE.** *32*, **MANATEE.** *58*, **MARIAS.** *57*, **NANTAHALA.** *60*, **PLATTE.** *24*, **SABINE.** *25*, **SEVERN.** *61*, **TALUGA.** *62*, **TOLOVANA.** *64.*

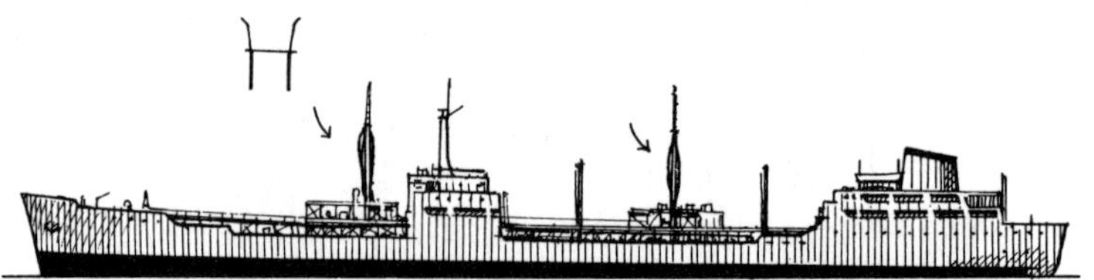

**1137.** SA. **TAFELBERG.** *A243.* 1958. Converted 1966. Replenishment Oiler. 18,400 tons deadweight. 560 x 72 x 30. (170.6 x 21.9 x 9.1). Diesels. 15 knots.
Former merchant ship "Annam".

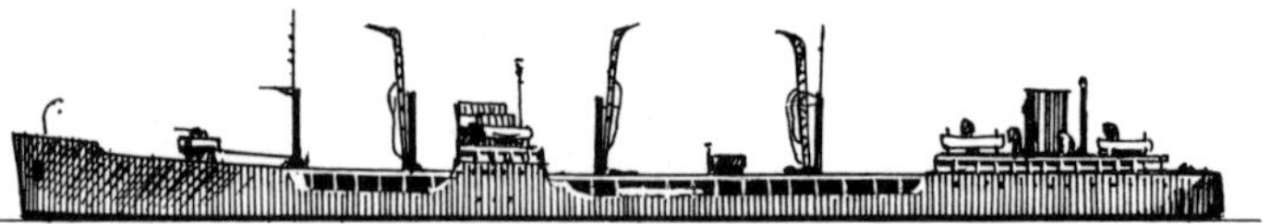

**1138.** Fr. **LA SAONE.** *A628.* 1964. Replenishment Oiler. 23,800 tons full load. 535 x 73 x 33. (159.9 x 22.2 x 10). 2 screws; turbines. 17 knots.
**LA SEINE.** *A627.*

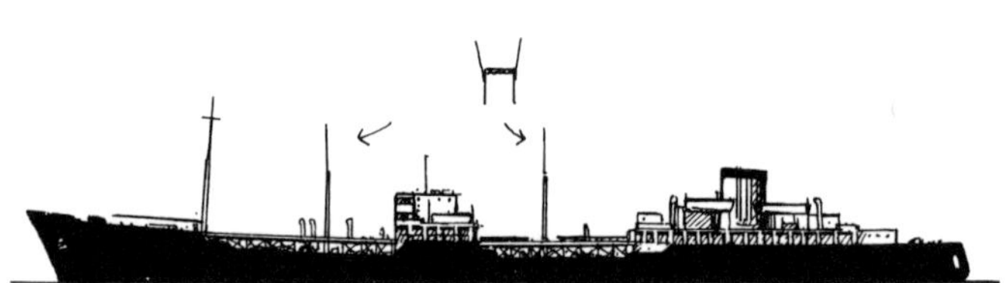

**1139.** Ar. **PUNTA MEDANOS.** 1950. Replenishment Oiler. 14,400 tons. 502 x 62 x 29. (152.9 x 18.9 x 8.8). 2 screws; turbines. 18 knots.

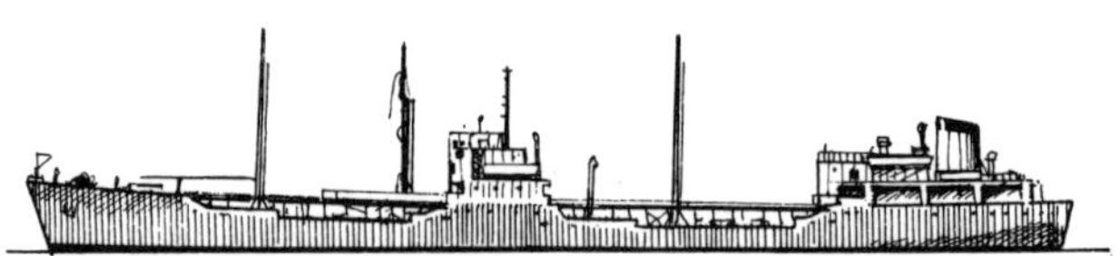

**1140.** Ge. **MUNSTERLAND.** *Y829.* 1946. Converted 1961. Replenishment Oiler. 6,200 tons gross. 461 x 54 x 26. (140.5 x 16.4 x 7.7). Diesel. 13 knots.
Former Italian merchant ship.
**EMSLAND** may also have this appearance. See drawing No. 1156.

**1141.** Po. **S. GABRIEL.** *A5206*. 1963. Replenishment Oiler. 9,000 tons. 479 x 60 x 26. (145.9 x 18.2 x 7.9). Turbine. 17 knots.

**1142.** Br. **ORANGELEAF.** *A80*. 1955. Refitted around 1959. Replenishment Oiler. 17,500 tons deadweight. 557 x 72 x 31. (169.6 x 21.9 x 9.4). Diesel. 15 knots. Former merchant ship. Royal Fleet Auxiliary.

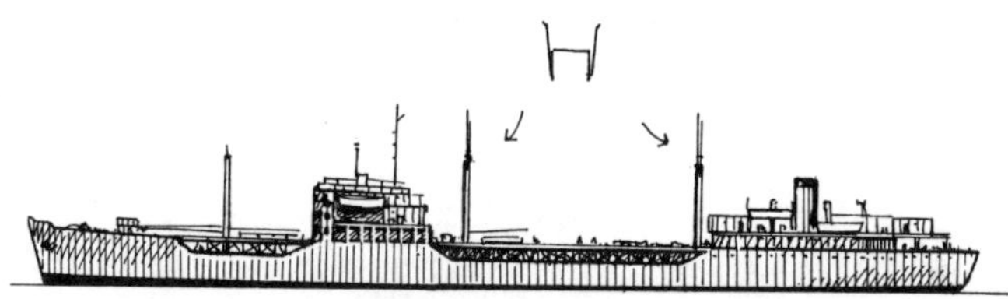

**1143.** Br. **WAVE** class. 1944-46. Modernised 1961-62. Replenishment Oilers. 8,200 tons. 493 x 65 x 29. (150.2 x 19.8 x 8.8). Turbines. 14 knots.
Royal Fleet Auxiliaries.
**WAVE BARON.** *A242* **WAVE CHIEF.** *A265,* **WAVE PRINCE.** *A207,* **WAVE RULER.** *A212.*

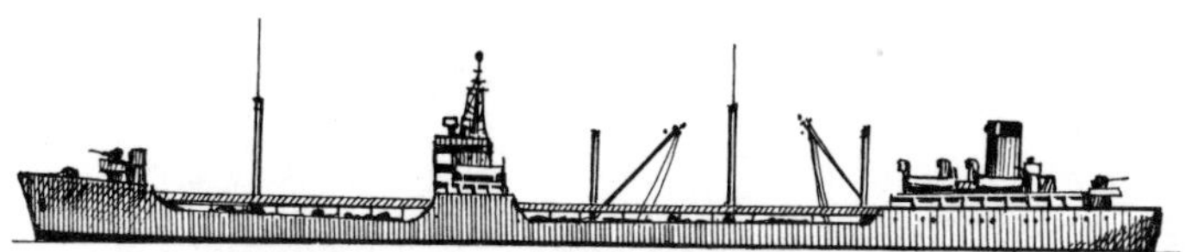

**1144.** Am. **T2-A** type. 1942. Replenishment Oilers. 21,900 tons full load. 502 x 68 x 31. (152.9 x 20.7 x 9.4). Turbo/electric. 2 to 4—3-inch A.A. guns.
**KENNEBEC.** *36,* **MATTAPONI.** *41,* **TAPPAHANNOCK.** *43,* **NECHES.** *47.*

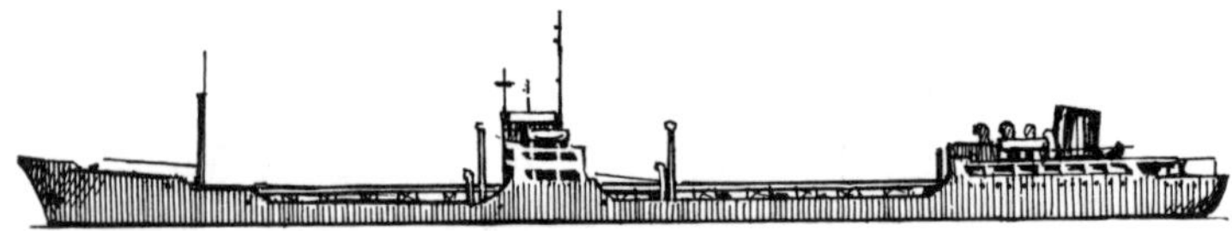

**1145.** Br. **BAYLEAF.** *A79*. 1955. Oilers. 18,000 tons deadweight. 557 x 71 x 30. (169.6 x 21.6 x 9.1). Diesel. 14 knots. Royal Fleet Auxiliary. Former merchant ship.
**BRAMBLELEAF.** *A81*.

**1146.** Br. **PEARLEAF.** *A77*. Oiler. 18,000 tons deadweight. 568 x 72 x 30. (173 x 21.9 x 9.1). Diesels. 15 knots. Royal Fleet Auxiliary. Former merchant ship.

**1147.** Br. **PLUMLEAF.** *A78*. 1960. Oiler. 24,900 tons. 560 x 72 x 30. (170.6 x 21.9 x 9.4). Diesels. 15 knots. Royal Fleet Auxiliary. Former merchant ship.

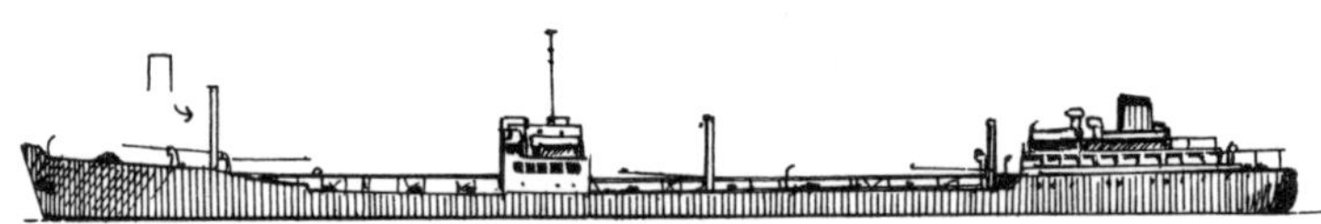

**1148.** Fr. **ISERE.** *A675*. 1959. Oiler. 18,000 tons deadweight. 559 x 71 x 30. (176.4 x 21.6 x 9.1). Turbine. 16 knots. Former merchant ship.

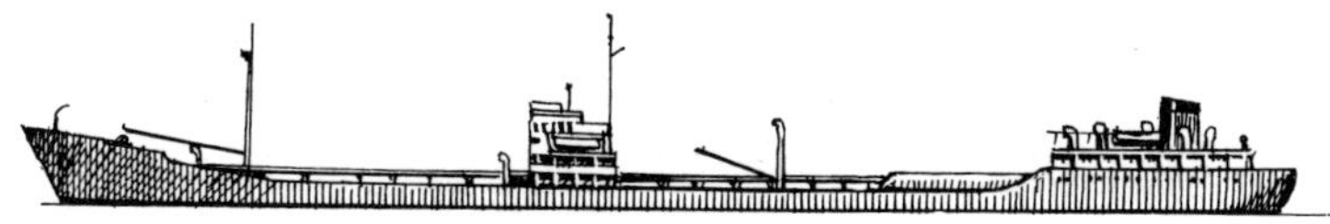

**1149**. Co. **ANTONIO DE AREVALO**. *64*. 1952.
Oiler. 16,700 tons deadweight. 550 x 68 x 30.
(167.5 x 20.7 x 9.1). Diesel. 15 knots. Former
merchant ship.

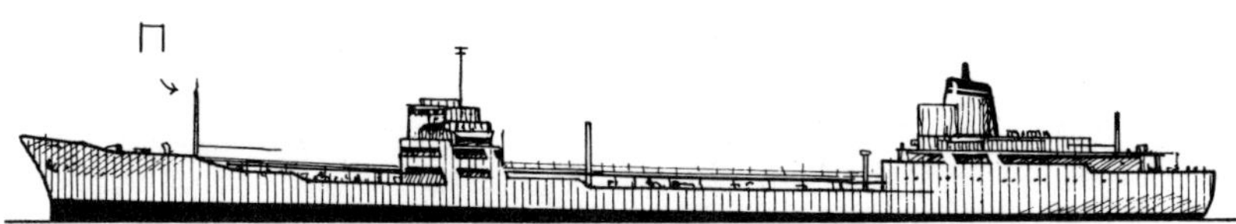

**1150**. Am. **MAUMEE** class. 1956-57. Oilers.
25,000 tons deadweight. 620 x 84 x 32. (188.9 x
25.6 x 9.7). Turbine. 18 knots.
**MAUMEE**. *149*, **SHOSHONE**. *151*, **YUKON**.
152.

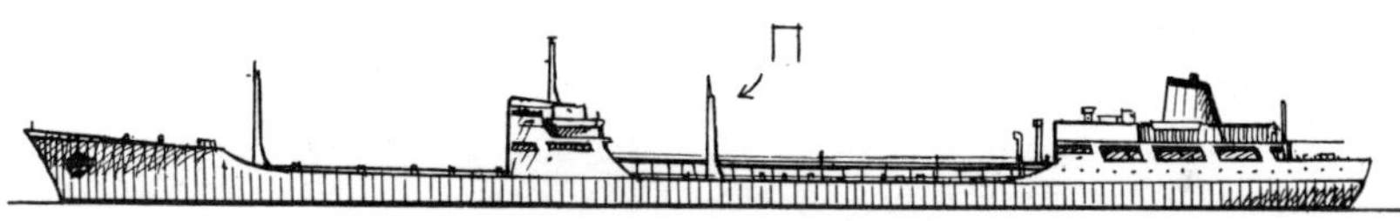

**1151**. Ur. **PRESIDENTE ORIBE**. *AO9*. 1962.
Oiler. 28,300 tons deadweight. 620 x 84 x 33.
(188.9 x 25.6 x 10). Turbine. 16 knots.

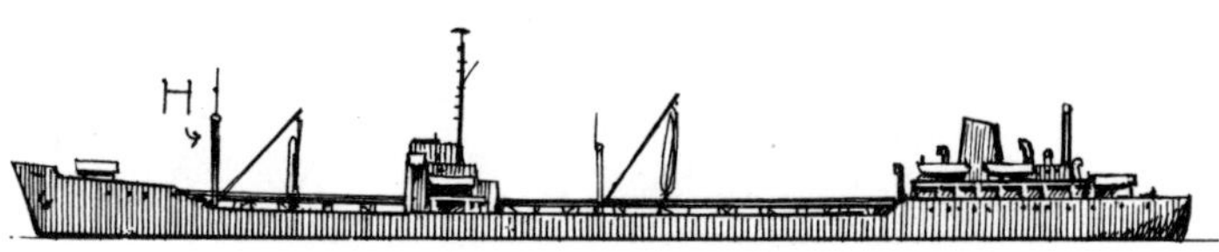

**1152**. Ch. **ALMIRANTE JORGE MONTT**.
*AO52*. 1966. 17,500 tons. 548 x 68 x 30.
(166.9 x 20.7 x 9.1). Replenishment Oiler.
Turbine. 14 knots.

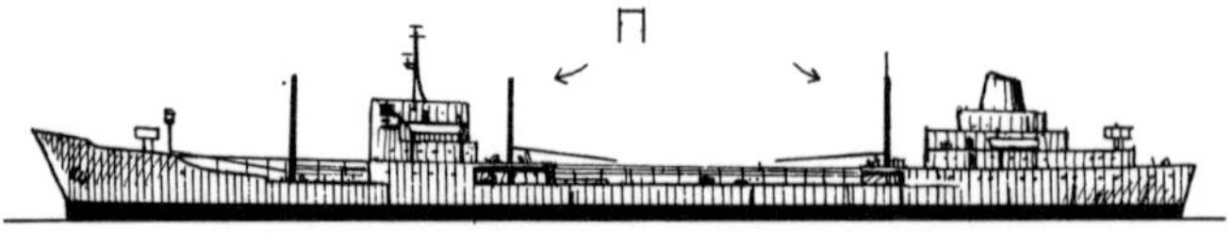

**1153.** Ch. **ARAUCANO.** *AO53.* 1967. Oiler.
18,000 tons deadweight. 497 x 75 x 29. (151.5 x
22.8 x 8.8). Diesels. 14 knots. 4—40-m.m. A.A.
guns.

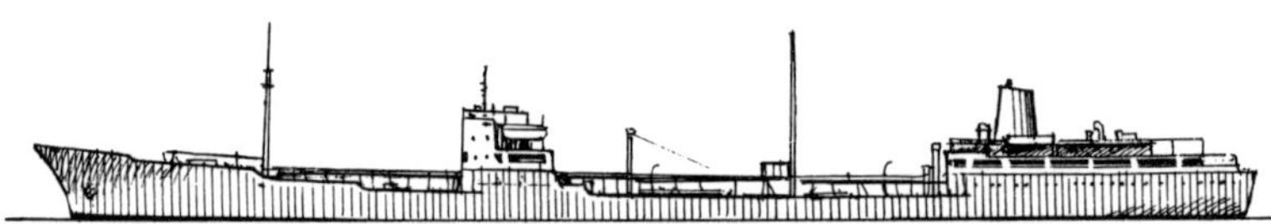

**1154.** Fr. **LA CHARENTE.** *A626.* 1957. Oiler.
26,000 tons full load. 587 x 72 x 30. (178.5 x 21.9
x 9.1). Turbine. Former merchant ship purchased
in 1965.

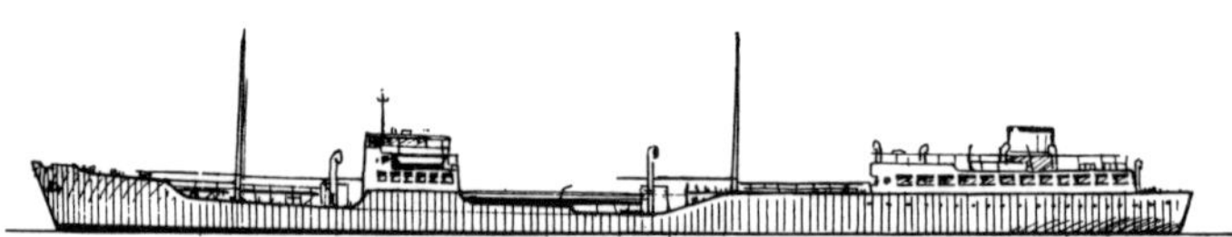

**1155.** Co. **COVENAS.** *65.* 1950. Oiler. 14,000
tons deadweight. 515 x 64 x 31. (156.7 x 19.5 x
9.4). Diesel. 14 knots. Former merchant ship
acquired in 1966. Very distinctive long poop.

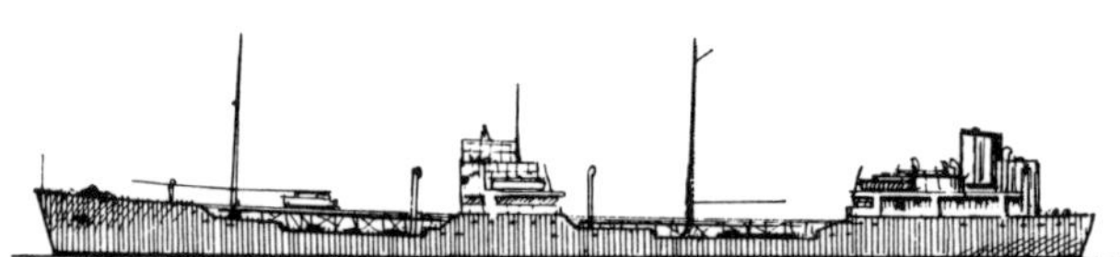

**1156.** Ge. **EMSLAND.** *Y828.* 1947. Converted
1960. Oiler. All details as No. 1140. May now
have the same appearance as Munsterland (see
No. 1140).

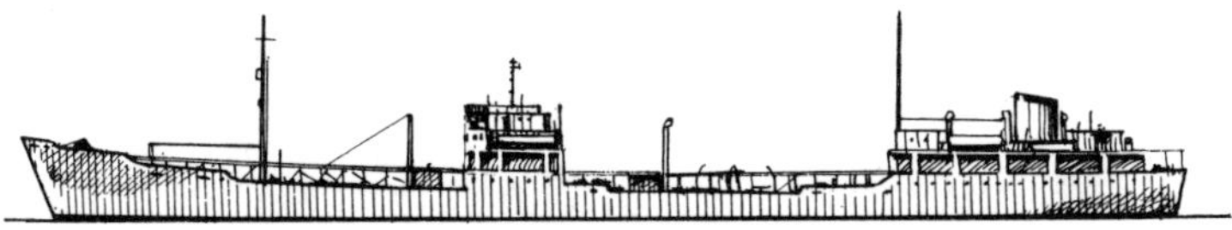

**1157.** Ge. **FRANKENLAND.** *Y827*. 1959. Oiler 16,300 tons. 522 x 70 x 38. (159 x 21.3 x 11.5) Diesels. 13 knots. Former merchant ship.

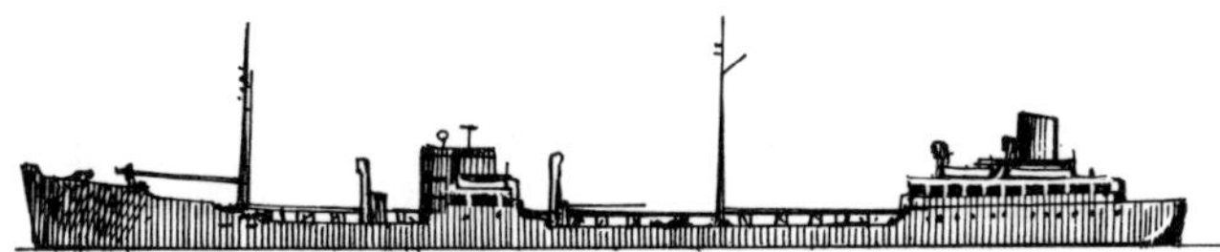

**1158.** Cs. **KUAI CHI.** *306*. 1954. Oiler. 8,800 tons gross. 486 x 63 x 35. (148.1 x 19.2 x 10.6). Diesel. Former Russian tanker "Tuapse".

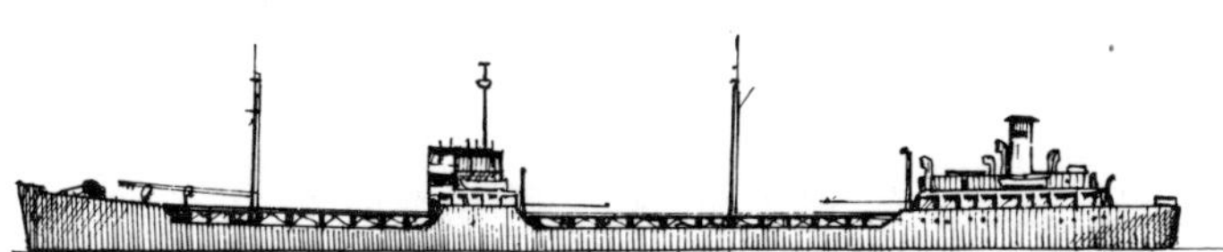

**1159.** Am. **MISSION SAN RAFAEL** (T2 type). Tanker. 22,300 tons full load. 524 x 68 x 31.). (159.3 x 20.7 x 9.4). Turbo/electric. 15 knots. May be other T2's with this appearance; see No. 1160.

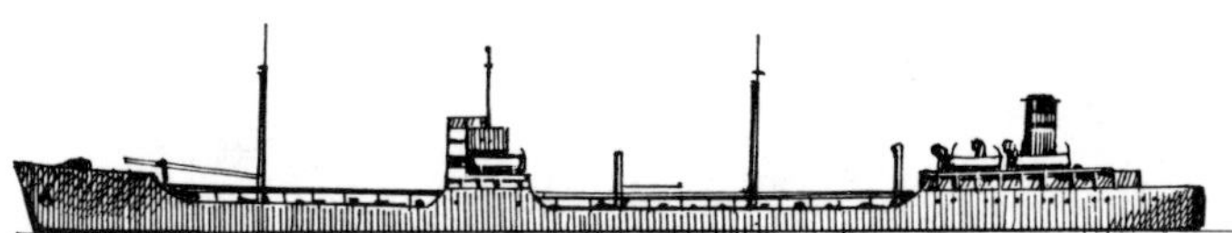

**1160.** Am. **T2** type. 1941-43. Tankers. All details as No. 1159. Engines may be turbo/electric or steam turbine. Some of these ships may have the same appearance as No. 1159. Operated for the Navy by commercial companies.

**CACHE, COSSATOT, COWANESQUE, MISSION SANTA CRUZ, MISSION SANTA YNEX, MISSION BUENAVENTURA, MILLICOMA, PECOS, PIONEER VALLEY, SAUGATUCK, SCHUYLKILL, SHAWNEE TRAIL, SUAMICO, TALLUAH, CHEPACHET.**

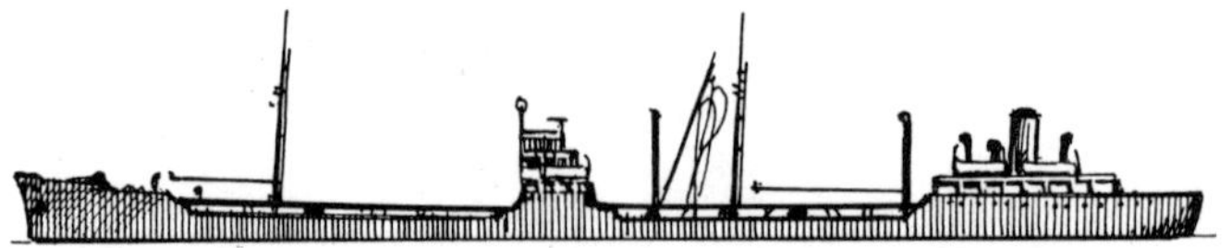

**1161.** It. **STEROPE** (Ex-U.S. T2 type). *A5368*.
1942c. Refitted 1959. Oiler. Tonnage etc. as
No. 1159.

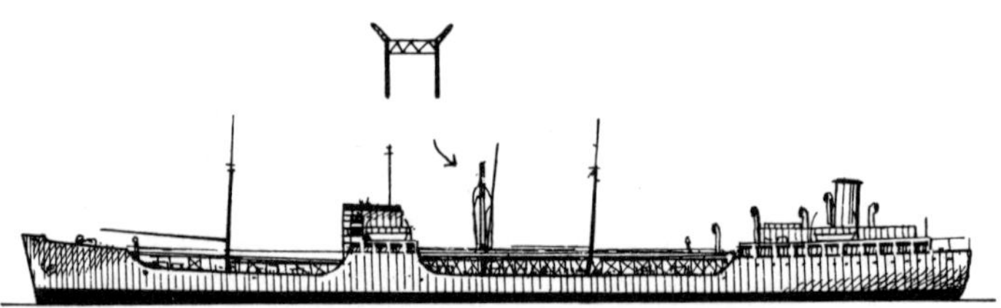

**1162.** Pk. **DACCA** (Ex-U.S. T2 type). *A41*.
1942c. Replenishment Oiler. Tonnage etc. as
No. 1159.

**1163.** Am. **MISSION CAPISTRANO.** 1944.
Converted. Sound Testing Ship. Former Mission
class, T2 type tanker. Tonnage etc. as No. 1159.

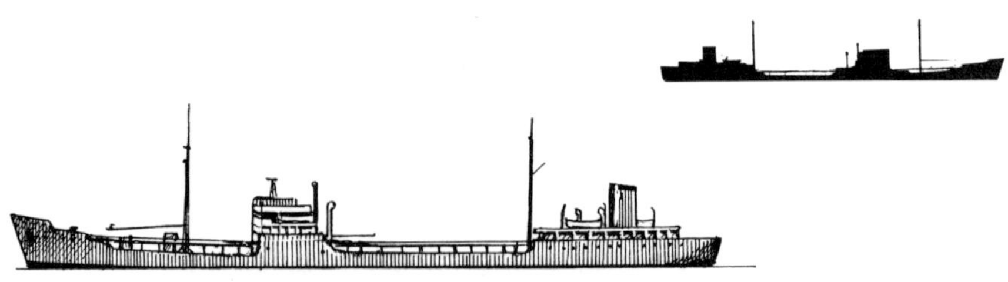

★ **1164.** Ru. **KAZBEK** class. 1953-57. Oilers.
11,800 tons deadweight. 498 x 63 x 34. (151.8 x
19.2 x 10.4). 2 screws; diesels. 12 knots.
A large class of about 70 vessels some of which
are in naval and some in commercial service.
"Volkhov" is known to be in Naval service.

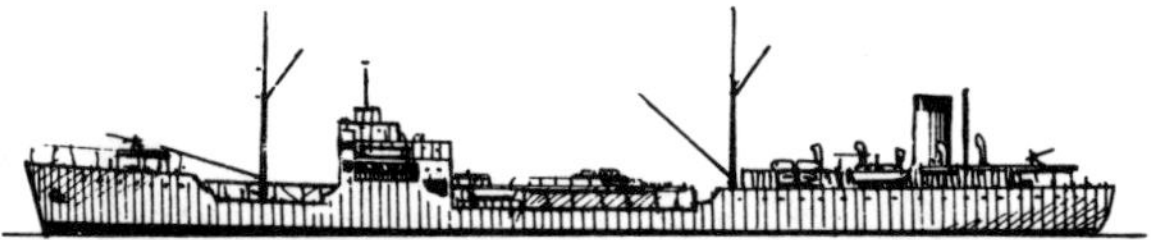

**1165.** Tu. **AKAR.** *A580*. Oiler. 13,200 tons full load. 433 x 53 x 27. (132 x 16.1 x 8.2). Turbines. 15 knots. Former merchant ship.

**1166.** Pv. **TALARA.** *153*. 1955. Oiler. 7,000 tons. 336 x 51 x 23. (102.4 x 15.5 x 7). Diesel. 12 knots.

**1167.** Am. **PECONIC** class. Gasoline Tankers. 6,000 tons full load. 325 x 48 x 19. (99 x 14.6 x 5.7). Diesel. 12 knots.
**PETALUMA, NODAWAY** and **PISCATAQUA** may have this appearance or may be like "Rincon" No. 1168.

Colombia: **MAMONAL.** *62*, **SANCHO JIM-ENO.** *63*.

**1168.** Am. **PECONIC** class. Gasoline Tankers. Tonnage etc. as No. 1167.
**RINCON,**

**NODAWAY** and **PISCATAQUA** may be like this or like "Petaluma" (see No. 1167).

**1169.** Ar. **PUNTA DELGADA.** 1945. Oiler. All details as No. 1167.

**1170.** Pv. **SECHURA** class. 1955-58. Oilers. 8,700 tons. 385 x 52 x 21. (117.3 x 15.8 x 6.4). Diesel. 12 knots.
**LOBITOS.** *159*, **SECHURA.** *154*, **ZORRITOS.** *158*.

**1171.** Sp. **PLUTON.** *BP01*. 1934. Oiler. 7,600 tons full load. 342 x 54 x 20. (104.2 x 16.4 x 6.1). Diesels. 13 knots.

**1172.** Po. **SAM BRAS.** *A523*. 1942. Logistics Ship. 5,600 tons. 357 x 51 x 18. (108.8 x 15.5 x 5.4). Diesel. 12 knots. 1—3-inch gun. 4 A.A. guns. Formerly an oil tanker.

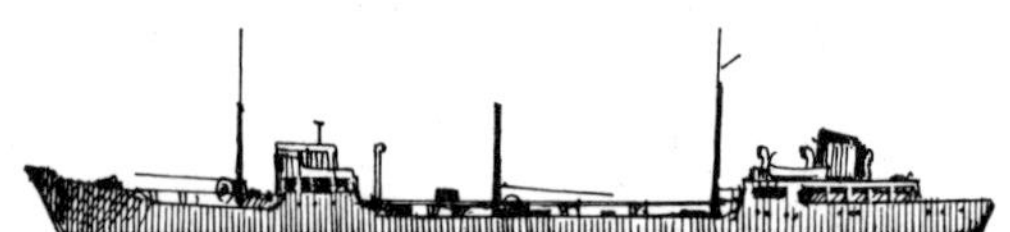

**1173.** Sp. **TEIDE.** 1956. Oiler. 8,000 tons full load. 386 x 49 x 20. (117.6 x 14.9 x 6.1). Diesels. 12 knots. 1—4-inch gun.

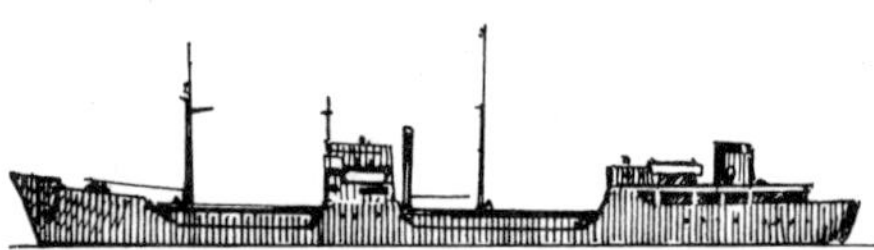

**1174.** Ia. **BUNJU.** *904*. Oiler. 6,200 tons full load. 351 x 49 x 20. (106.9 x 14.9 x 6.1). Diesel. 10 knots. 2—20-m.m. A.A. guns.
**SAMBU.** *903*.

Ex-Russian.
★ There are many similar ships in the Soviet naval and commercial fleets.

★ **1175.** Ru. **ABRENE** class. Around 1963. Oilers. 4,400 tons deadweight. 345 x 49 x 21. (104.8 x 14.9 x 6.1). Diesel. 13 knots.
**OLEKMA.** There are many ships in this class most of which serve with the Soviet commercial fleet.

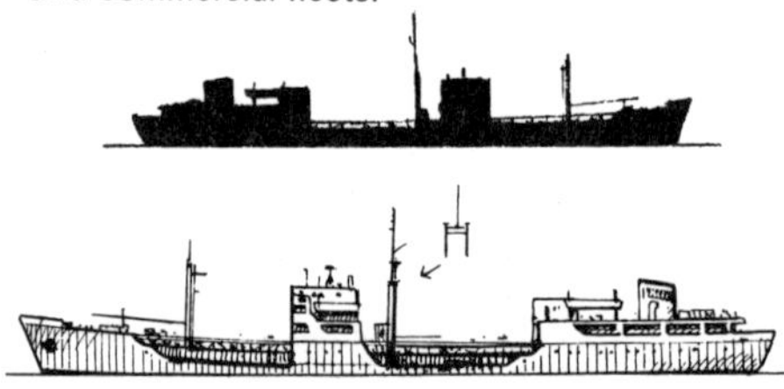

★ **1176.** Ru. **PEVEK** class. 1959c. Oilers. Tonnage etc. as No. 1175. A commercial type some of which serve with the Soviet Navy.
Names include: **ZOLOTAJ ROG, POLYARNIK.**

**1177.** Ge. **EIFEL.** *A1429*. 1958. Oiler. 4,700 tons full load. 334 x 47 x 23. (101.8 x 14.3 x 7). Diesel. 14 knots. Former merchant ship.

**1178.** Br. **EDDYFIRTH.** *A261*. 1954. Oiler. 4,200 tons full load. 286 x 44 x 17. (87.1 x 13.4 x 5.1). Reciprocating. 12 knots. Royal Fleet Auxiliary.

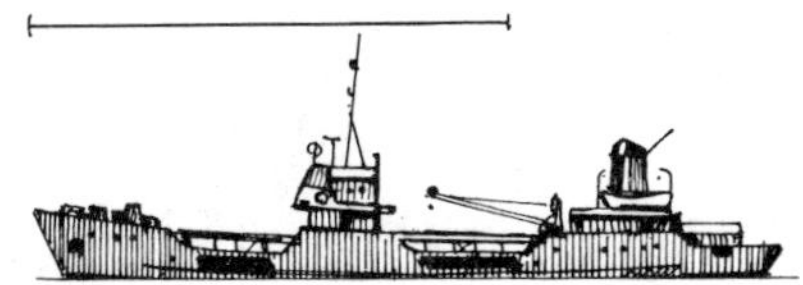

**1179.** EG. **RIEMS** class. 1960-61. Oilers. 1,000 tons. 195 x 30 x 13. (59.4 x 8.9 x 3.9). Diesels. 14 knots.
**HIDDENSEE, POEL, RIEMS.**

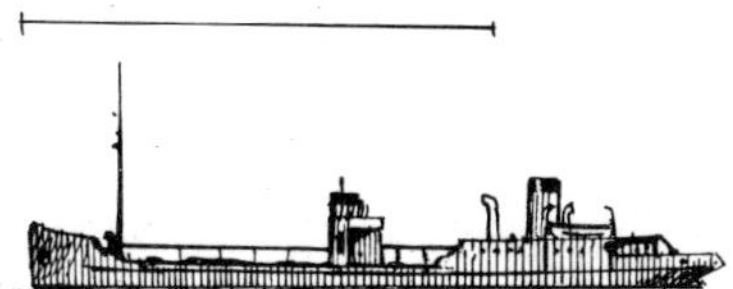

**1180.** Tu. **GOLCUK.** *A573*. 1935. Oiler. 1,300 tons. 185 x 31 x 10. (56.3 x 9.4 x 3). Diesel. 12 knots.

**1181.** It. **DALMAZIA.** *A5367*. 1922. Oiler. 3,200 tons. 260 x 33 x 15. (79.2 x 9.7 x 4.5). 2 screws; reciprocating. 10 knots. 1—4.7-inch gun. 2—20-m.m. A.A. guns.

**1182.** It. **VOLTURNO.** *A5366*. 1936. Rebuilt 1951. Water Carrier. 3,500 tons. 271 x 39 x 17. (82.6 x 11.8 x 5.1). Reciprocating. 11 knots. 1—4.7-inch gun. 2—40-m.m. guns. 2—20-m.m. A.A. guns.
**PO.** *A5365*.

**1183.** Th. **SICHANG.** 1937. Transport. 800 tons. 160 x 28 x 16. (48.7 x 8.5 x 4.8). 2 screws; diesel. 16 knots.

**1184.** Fr. **ANJOU.** *A645*. 1958. Refitted 1966. Transport. 2,700 tons. 285 x 38 x 15. (86.8 x 11.5 x 4.5). Diesels. 15 knots. Former merchant ship.
**BERRY.** *A644*.

Similar: **AUNIS.** *A643*.

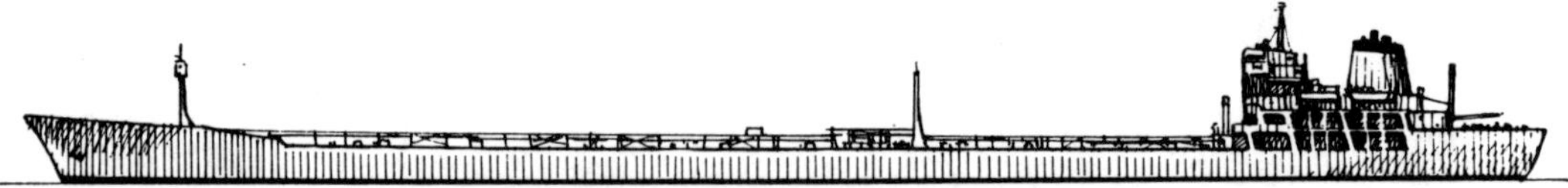

**1185.** Br. **DERWENTDALE.** *A221*. 1964. Oiler.
67,700 tons (deadweight). 799 x 118 x 42.
(243.6 x 36 x 12.8). Diesels. 15 knots.
Royal Fleet Auxiliary. Former merchant ship.

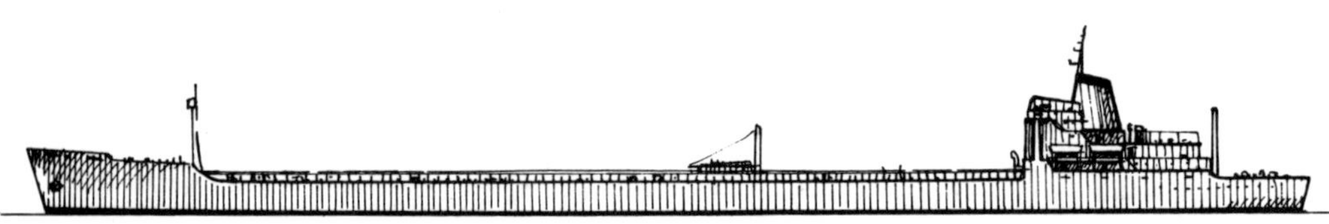

**1186.** Br. **DEWDALE.** *A219*. 1965. Oiler.
63,600 tons (deadweight). 775 x 108 x 42.
(233.4 x 32.9 x 12.8). Diesels.
Royal Fleet Auxiliary. Former merchant ship.

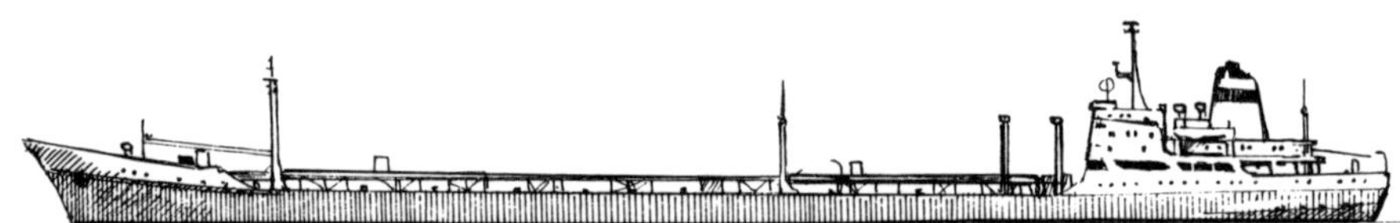

**1187.** Ru. **LENINAKAN.** 1964. Oiler. 35,300
tons (deadweight). 679 x 89 x 35. (207 x 27.1 x
10.8). Diesels. 16 knots.
Vessel of the "L" class, a large number of which
are in the commercial fleet and some of which
are serving in the Soviet Navy.

**1188.** Br. **ROVER** class. 1969-70. Replenishment
Oilers. 7,000 tons (deadweight). 461 x 63 x 00.
(140.5 x 19.2 x 00). Diesels. Helicopter landing
platform.
Royal Fleet Auxiliaries.
**BLUE ROVER.** *A270,* **GREEN ROVER.** *A268,*
**GREY ROVER.** *A269.*

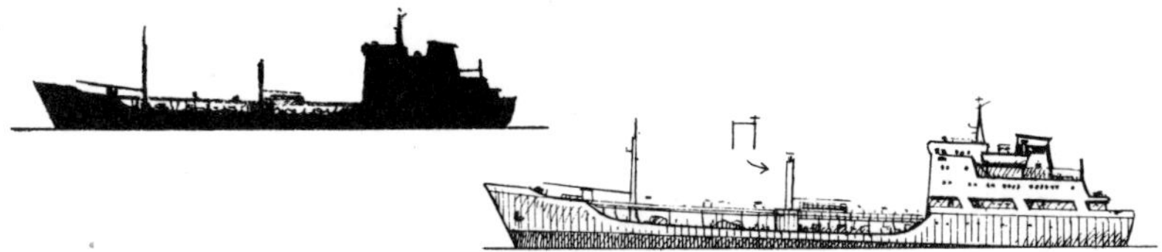

★ **1189.** Ru. **KOLA.** 1967. Oiler. 4,400 tons (deadweight). 348 x 51 x 21. (106.1 x 15.4 x 6.4). Diesels. 13 knots.
Others of this type are in commercial service and may also be employed as fleet oilers.

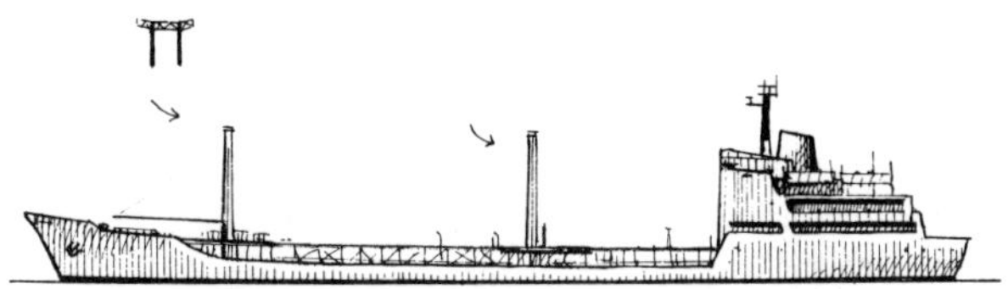

**1190.** Bz. **MARAJO.** *G27*. 1968. 10,500 tons (deadweight). 441 x 63 x 24. (134.4 x 19.3 x 7.3). Diesel. 13 knots.

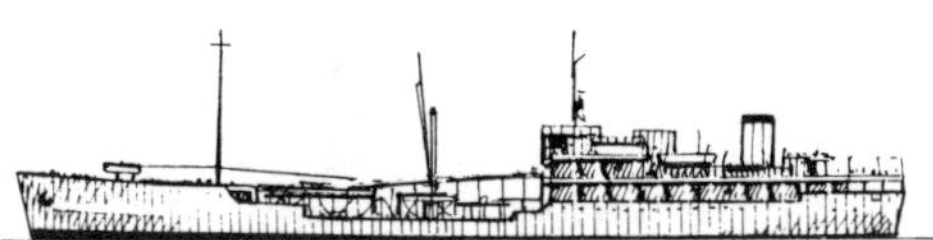

**1191.** Br. **BROWN RANGER.** *A169*. 1941. Oiler. 3,500 tons (deadweight). 366 x 47 x 20. (111.6 x 14.3 x 6.1). Diesels. 12 knots.
Royal Fleet Auxiliary.
Similar: **GOLD RANGER.** *A130*. 3,800 tons. 355 feet.

Similar: see silhouette No. 1265. **BLACK RANGER.** *A163*, in reserve, **BLUE RANGER.** *A157*.

**1192.** Ge. **HARZ.** *A1428*. 1953. Oiler. 3,700 tons (full). 303 x 44 x 22. (92.4 x 13.2 x 6.6) Diesel. 13 knots.
Former merchant ship. Acquired 1963.

**1193.** Tu. **ALBAY HAKKI BURAK.** *A572*. 1964. Oiler. 3,800 tons (full). 275 x 40 x 18. (83.8 x 12.2 x 5.5). Diesel/electric. 16 knots.

★ **1194.** Ru. **CRYPTON.** 1965. Oiler. 1,800 tons (gross). 275 x 40 x 15. (83.8 x 12.2 x 4.6). Diesels. 13 knots.
Name may be spelt **KRYPTON.**

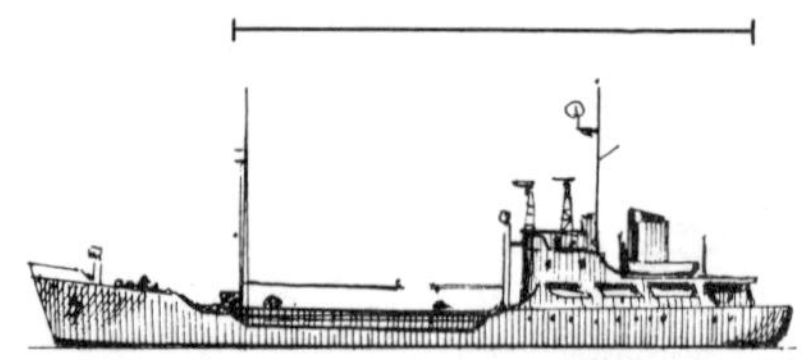

★ **1195.** Ru. **KONDA** class. 1955c. Oilers. 1,300 tons (deadweight). 209 x 33 x 15. (63.7 x 10 x 4.5). Diesels.
**KONDA, JAHROMA, ROSHOH.** Others are in commercial service.

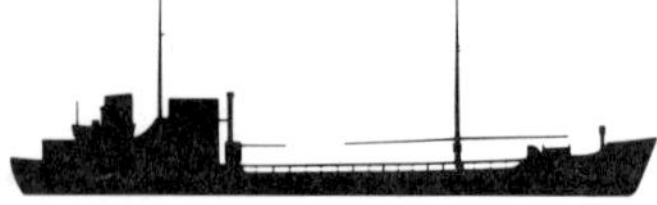

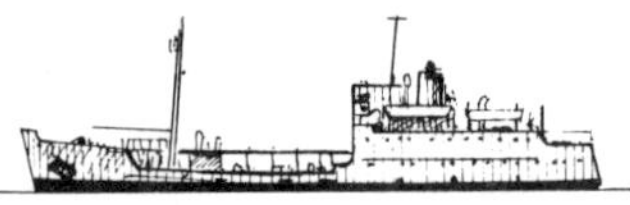

**1197.** Br. **ROWANOL.** *A284.* 1946. Oiler. 2,700 tons. 232 x 39 x 16. (707.7 x 11.8 x 4.8). Reciprocating. 11 knots.
Royal Fleet Auxiliary.

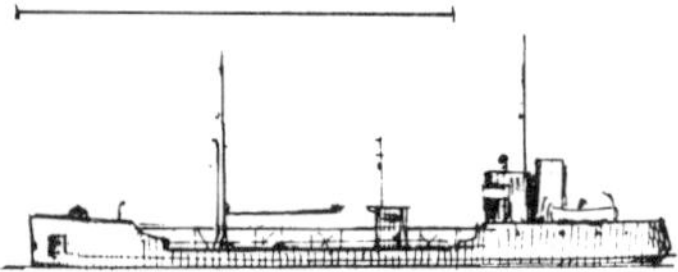

**1199.** Ir. **LENGEH.** *46.* 1940c. Water Carrier. 1,200 tons (full). 174 x 32 x 15. (53 x 9.7 x 4.5). Diesel. 9 knots. Ex-U.S. "YW" type. See also No. 1202.

**1201.** Do. **CAPITAN W. ARVELO.** Oilers. 1,100 tons (full). 175 x 30 x 13. (53.3 x 9.1 x 3.9). Diesel. 8 knots. 1—20-m.m gun. Ex-U.S. "Yo" type.
**CAPITAN BEOTEGUI.**

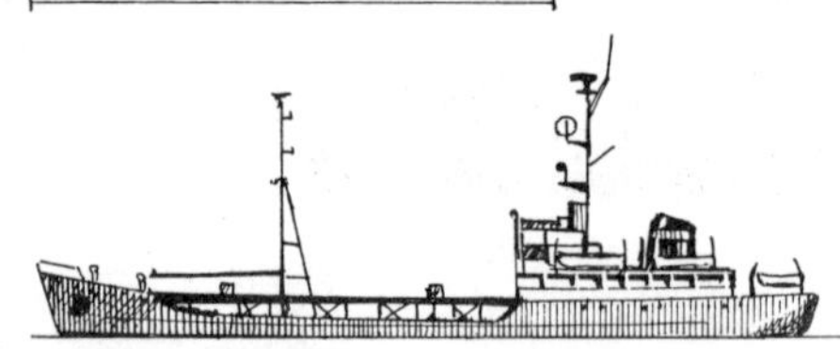

★ **1196.** Ru. **KHOBI** class. 1957-59. Oilers. 800 tons (gross). 221 x 33 x 15. (67.3 x 10 x 4.5). Diesels. 12 knots.
Many units in commercial service and those in naval service include **KHOBI, SEYMA.**

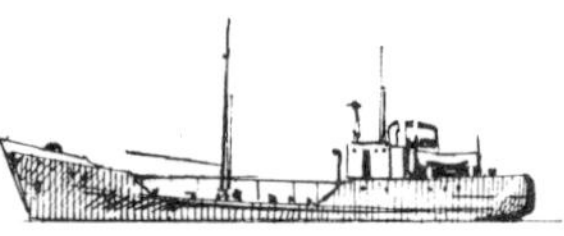

★ **1198.** Ru. **TM** type. 1957c. Oilers. 00 tons. 150 (approx.). (45.7).
There may be about 30 ships in the class.
**TM 41, TM 43. TM 40** etc. Some numbers may be in the "300" series.

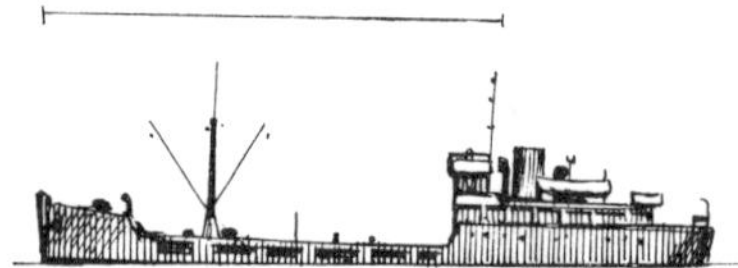

**1200.** Ca. **DUN** class. Oilers. 1,000 tons. 179 x 32 x 13. (54.5 x 9.7 x 3.9). Diesel. 10 knots.
**DUNDALK.** *AOC50,* **DUNDURN.** *AOC502.*

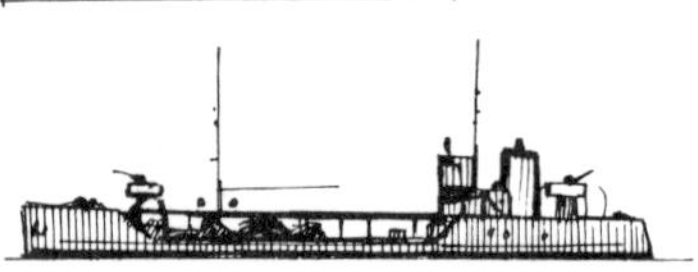

**1202.** Pv. **MANTILLA.** *141.* Water Carrier. Dimensions etc. as No. 1199. Ex-U.S. "YW" type.
Pi. **LAKE LANAO.** *Y42.*
Similar:

Pi. **LAKE NAUJAN** *43.* Oiler. Ex-U.S. "Yo" class.

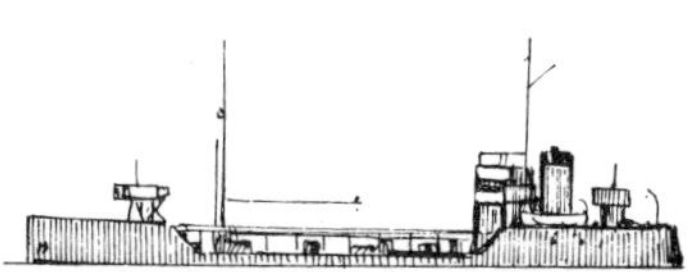

**1203.** Th. **SAMUI.** Oiler. Dimensions etc. as for No. 1201. U.S. "YOG" type.

Da. **RIMFAXE.** *A568,* **SKINFAXE.** *A569.* (no gun platform foreward).
Ko. **KU RYONG.**
Me. **AGUASCALIENTES.** *15,* **TLAXCALA.** *16.*
VN. *HQ470, HQ471.*

There may be some of this type in the navy of Communist China.

**1204.** Ir. **HORMUZ.** *43.* Oiler. 1,250 tons. 178 x 32 x 14. (54.2 x 9.7 x 4.2). Diesel. 8 knots. Similar to U.S. "YO" type but Italian built.

Pk. **ATTOCK.** *A298.*

**1205.** Bz. **RAZA.** *G19.* Oiler. 2,200 tons (full). 218 x 37 x 7. (66.4 x 11.2 x 2.1). Diesel. 9 knots. Ex-U.S. "T1-M-A2" type.
**RIJO.** *G20.*

Tu. **AKPINAR.** *A574.*

**1206.** Fr. **LAC** class. Oilers. 2,700 tons (full). 235 x 37 x 16. (71.6 x 11.2 x 4.8). Diesels. 11 knots. 3—20-m.m. A.A. guns. Ex-U.S. Oil barges.
**LAC CHAMBON.** *A629,* **LAC TCHAD.** *A631,* **LAC TONLE-SAP.** *A630.*

Probably similar:
KO. **HWA CHON.**

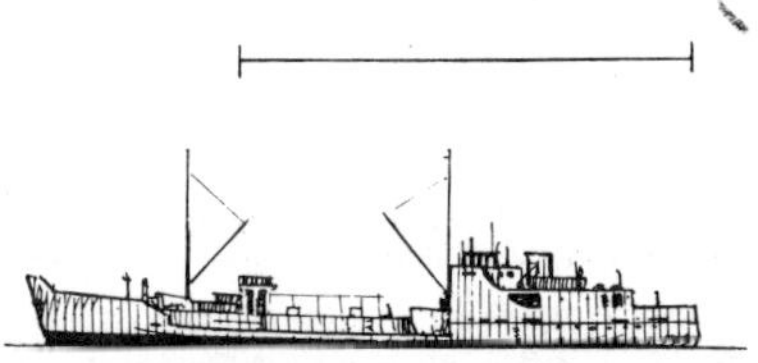

**1207.** Sw. **OLJAREN.** *A227.* 1939. Oiler. 1,100 tons. 179 x 28 x 11. (54.5 x 8.5 x 3.3). Diesel. 9 knots. 2—25-m.m. A.A. guns.

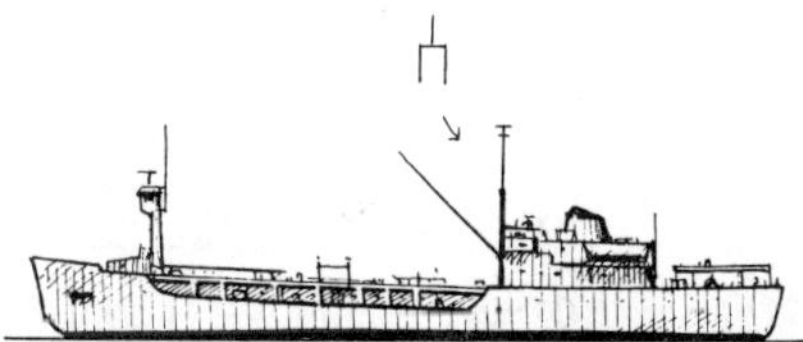

**1208** Am. **ALATNA** class. 1956. Gasoline Tankers. 5,700 tons. 302 x 61 x 19. (92 x 18.5 x 5.7). 2 screws; diesel/electric. 12 knots.
**TI-MET-24a** type. Helicopter flight deck. Ice-breaking stem.
**ALATNA, CHATTAHOOCHEE.**

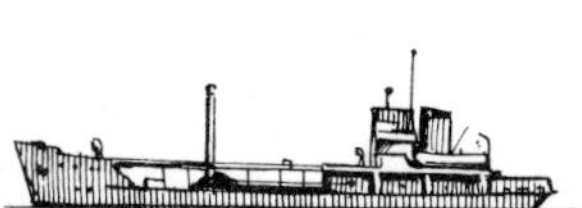

**1209.** Ys. **PN** *17.* Oiler. 420 tons. 142 x 23 x 13. (43.2 x 7 x 3.9). Diesel. 7 knots.

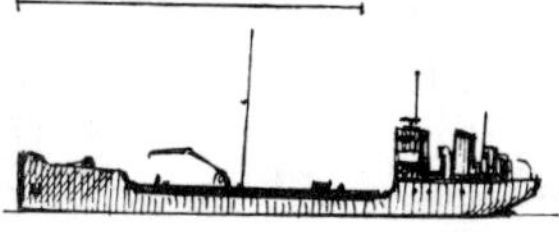

**1210.** Th. **CHAN.** Water Carrier. 360 tons. 140 x 24 x 10. (42.6 x 7.3 x 3). Diesel. 6 knots. Name may sometimes be spelt JARN.

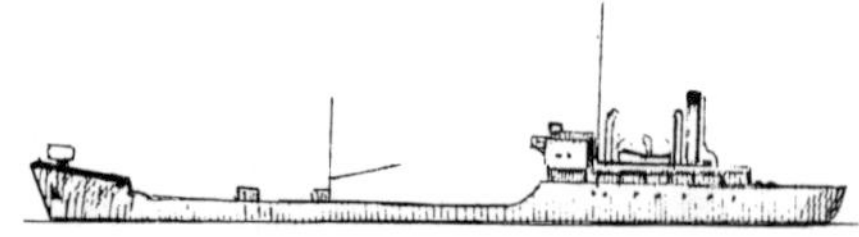

**1211.** Th. **CHULA.** Oiler. 2,400 tons. 328 x 43 x 25. (99.9 x 13.1 x 7.6). Turbine.
Similar: **MATRA.** (Fleet replenishment tanker).

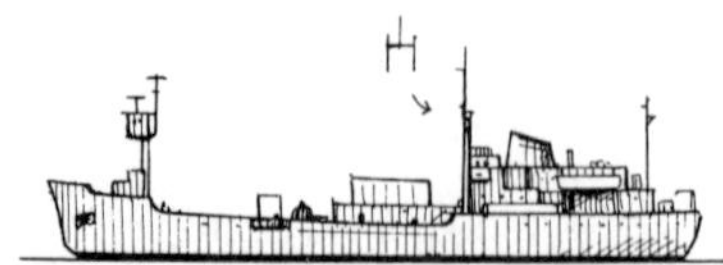

**1212.** Am. **MIZAR.** 1957. Oceanographic Research Ship. 5,000 tons (full). 262 x 52 x 23. (79.8 x 15.8 x 7). 2 screws; diesel/electric. 12 knots.
For similar ships see Nos. 1913, 1214.

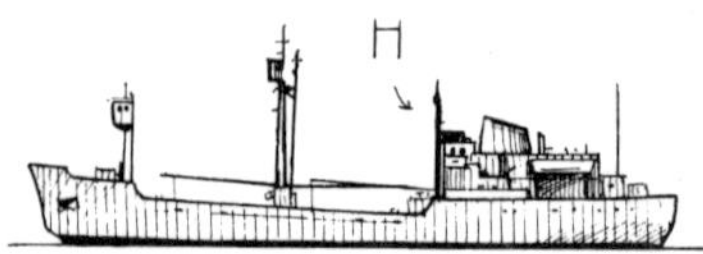

**1213.** Am. **MIRFAK.** 1957. Cargo Ship. Dimensions same as No. 1212 but 18 foot draught. Cl-M-E2-13a type. Icebreaking stem.

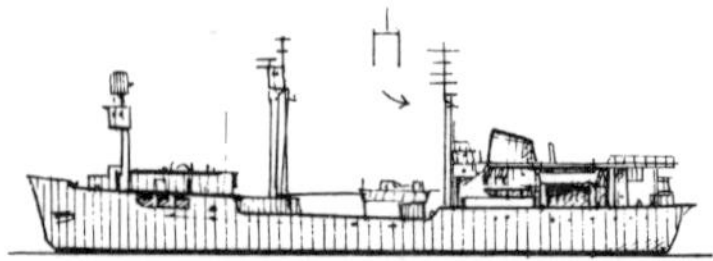

**1214.** Am. **ELTANIN.** 1957. Oceanographic Research Ship. Details as for No. 1212 (18 foot draught). Distinguished by having a mainmast in the well.

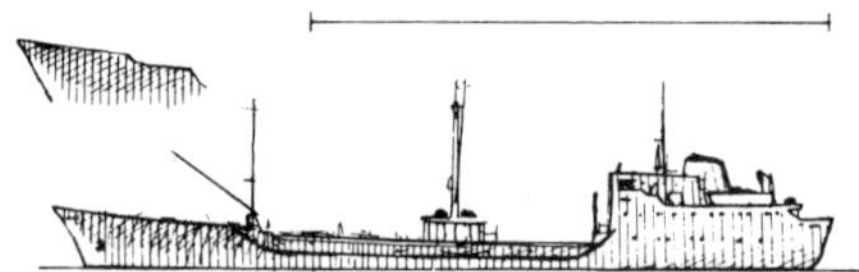

**1215.** Ge. **BODENSEE.** *A1406.* 1956. Oiler. 1,200 tons. 208 x 33 x 15. (63.3 x 10 x 4.5). Diesels. 12 knots.
Similar (inset of Forecastle): **WITTENSEE.** *A1407.*

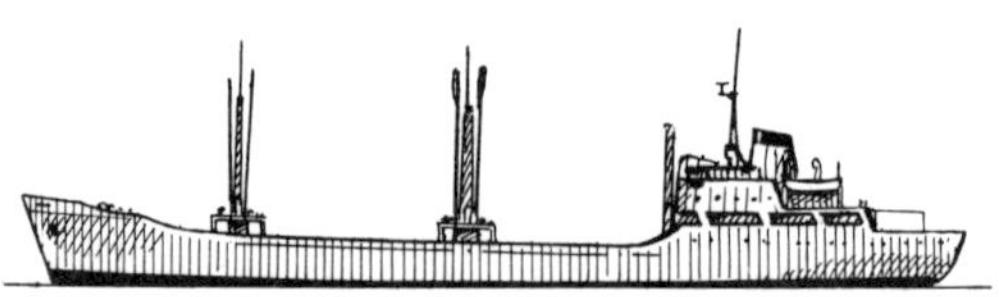

**1216.** Br. **BACCHUS** class. 1962. Store Carriers. 8,000 tons (full). 379 x 54 x 22. (115.5 x 16.7 x 6.7). Diesel. 15 knots. Royal Fleet Auxiliary. **BACCHUS.** *A404,* **HEBE.** *A406.*

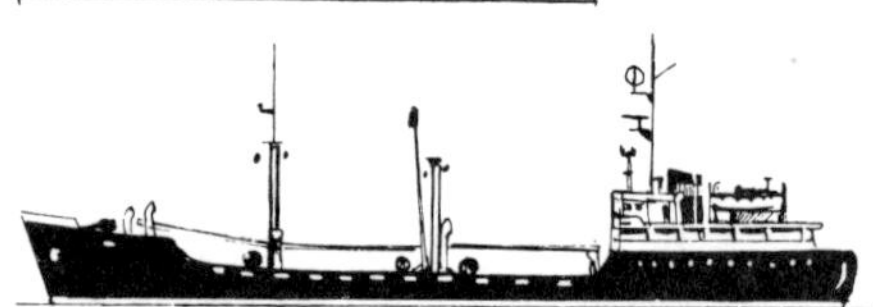

★ **1217.** Ru. **AYTODOR.** 1962. Survey Ship. 1,000 tons (gross). 207 x 31 x 11. (63 x 9.4 x 3.3). Diesel. 12 knots.
Former merchant ship and many of the same class in the commercial fleet. "Jan Kreuks" class.

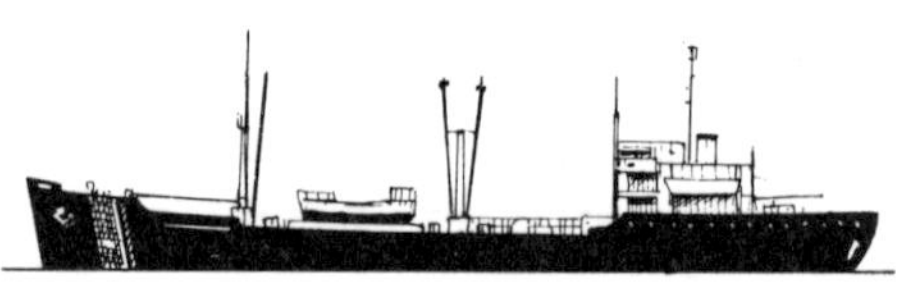

**1218.** Am. **KUKUI.** 1944. Supply Ship. Coast Guard. 7,500 tons (full). 339 x 50 x 21. (103.3 x 15.2 x 6.4). Diesel. 11 knots. Cl-MAV-I type.

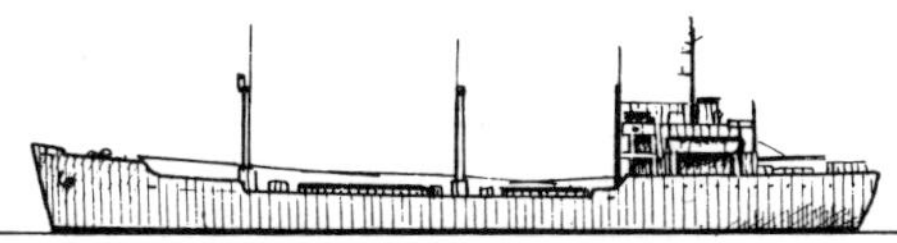

**1219.** Am. **ADRIA** and **O'BRIEN** classes. Details as for number 1218. CI-MAV-I type.
**ADRIA** class. Storeships.
**BONDIA.**
**O'BRIEN** class. Cargo Ships.
**FENTRESS, HERKIMER, MUSKINGUM, PRIVATE FRANK J. PETRARCA.**
Two of this class are now heavy lift ships; see No. 1220.

Pv. **ILO.** *133*.

**1220.** Am. **O'BRIEN** class. Details as for No. 1219. Heavy Lift cargo ships.
**COLONEL WILLIAM J. O'BRIEN, SHORT SPLICE.**

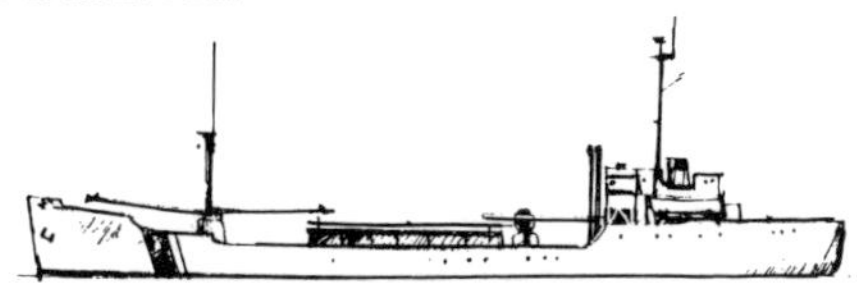

**1221.** Am. **COURIER.** 1945. Training Ship. Coastguard. Details as for No. 1219. Helicopter platform. CI-MAV-I type.

**1222.** Am. **PRIVATE JOSE E. VALDEZ.** Oceanographic Research and Survey Ship. 7,500 tons full load. All particulars as No. 1218. CI-M-AVI type.

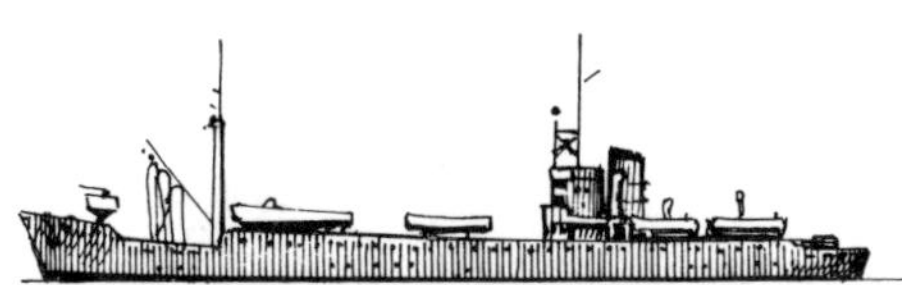

**1223.** It. **STROMBOLI.** *A5329*. 1948. Logistics Support Transport. 4,700 tons. 334 x 46 x 22. (101.8 x 14 x 6.7). Turbines. 15 knots. 1—3.9-inch gun. 4—40-m.m. guns.

**1224.** It. **VESUVIO.** *A5330*. 1954. Converted Helicopter Tender. All particulars as No. 1223 except for armament which consists of 2—40-m.m. guns. Helicopter flight deck and hangar.

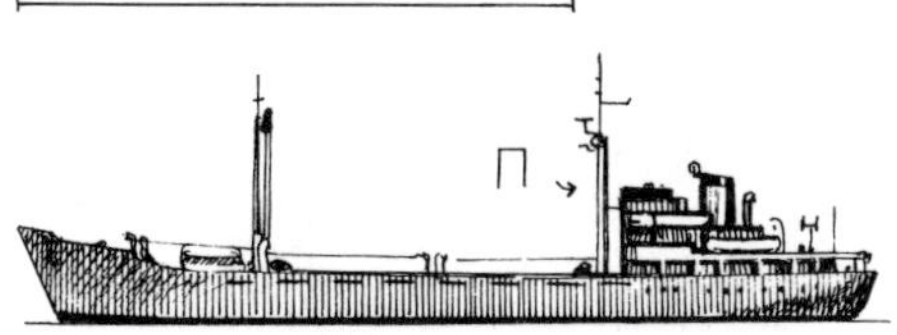

**1225.** Ge. **SAUERLAND.** *Y830*. 1953. Supply Ship. 1,800 tons deadweight. 233 x 36 x 17. (71 x 10.9 x 5.1). Diesel. 12 knots. Former merchant ship.

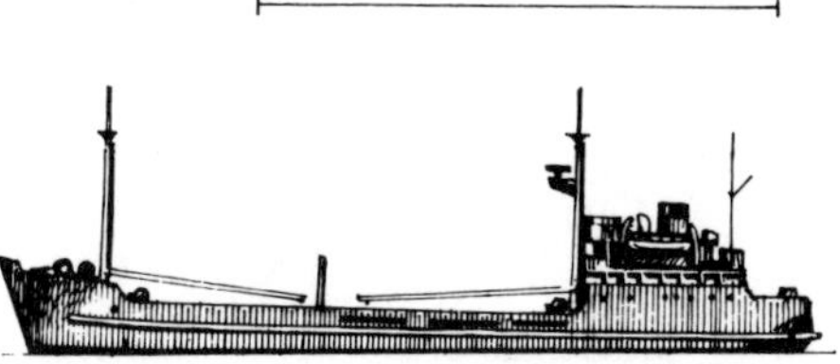

**1226.** Br. **ROBERT DUNDAS.** *A204*. 1938. Store Carrier. 1,900 tons full load. 223 x 35 x 14 (67.9 x 10.6 x 4.2). Diesel. 10 knots. Royal Fleet Auxiliary.
**ROBERT MIDDLETON.** *A241*.

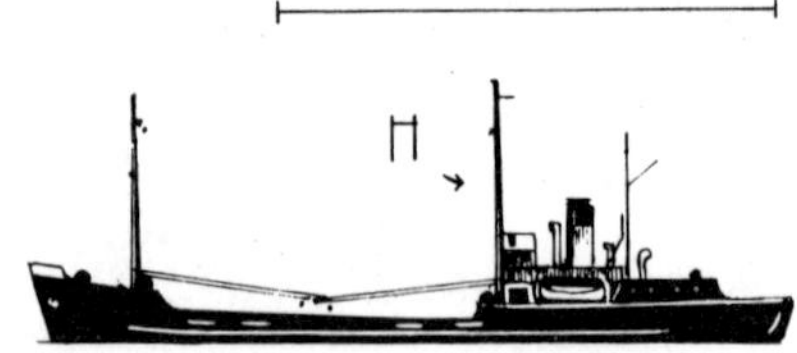

**1227.** Br. **THROSK.** 1944. Converted 1959. Armament Carrier, 1,500 tons. 200 x 34 x 13. (60.9 x 10.3 x 3.9). Reciprocating. 11 knots. **KINTERBURY.**

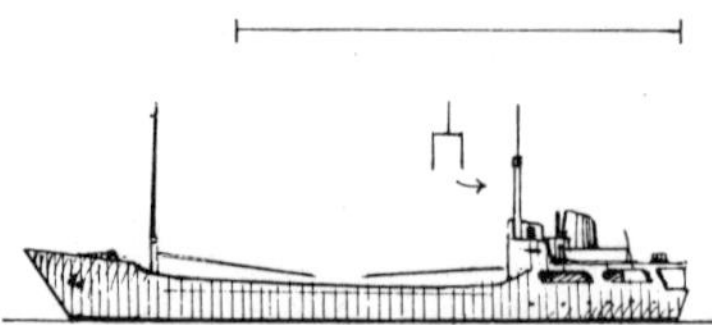

**1228.** Fr. **SAINTONGE.** *A733*. 1956. Converted 1965. Transport. 500 tons deadweight. 177 x 28 x 11. (53.9   8.5 x 3.3). Diesel. 10 knots. Former merchant ship.

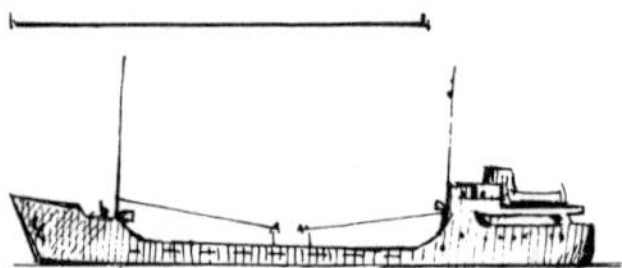

**1229.** Co. **CIUDAD DE QUIBDO.** Transport. 600 tons. 165 x 24 x 9. (50.2 x 7.3 x 2.7). Diesel. 11 knots.

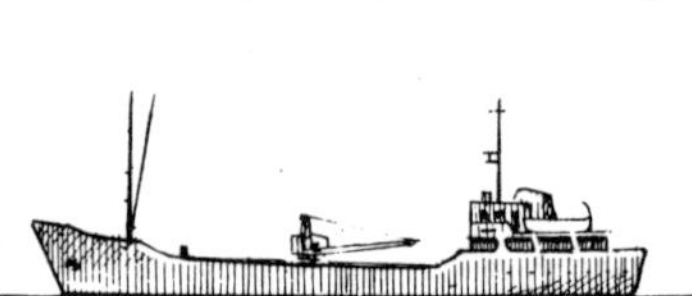

**1230.** Sw. **FREJA.** 1953. Supply Ship. 300 tons. 161 x 28 x 10. (49 x 8.5 x 3). Diesel. 10 knots.

**1231.** Ca. **C. P. EDWARDS.** 1946. Coast Guard Supply Vessel. 600 tons full load. 144 x 27 x 10. (43.8 x 8.2 x 3). Reciprocating.

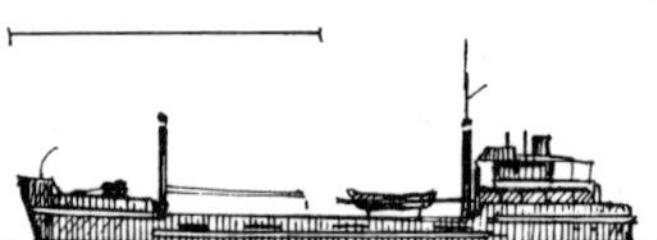

**1232.** Pi. **PEARL BANK.** *47.* Lighthouse Tender. 160 tons. 120 x 24 x 8. (36.5 x 10.3 x 2.4). 2 screws; diesel. 6 knots. 2—20-m.m. A.A. guns. Ex-U.S. "OL" type.

**1233.** Ge. **PFALZERLAND.** *Y831*. 1956. Supply Ship. 500 tons deadweight. 156 x 26 x 8. (47.5 x 7.9 x 2.4). 2 screws; diesel. 10 knots.

**1234.** Br. **WATER** class. 1966. Water Carriers. 300 tons gross. 132 x 25 x 8. (40.2 x 7.6 x 2.4). Diesels. 11 knots. Port Auxiliary Service. **WATERFALL, WATERSHED, WATERSIDE, WATERSPOUT.**

**1235.** Br. **FLINTOCK**. 1946. Armament Carrier. 170 tons deadweight. 103 x 21. (31.4 x 6.4). Diesel.
Probable sister: **MATCHLOCK**.

Possibly similar: **BALLISTA, BOWSTRING, CATAPAULT, SPEAR**.

**1236.** Br. **THOMAS GRANT**. 1953. Converted 1968. Torpedo Recovery Vessel. 500 tons full load. 114 x 26 x 9. (34.7 x 7.9 x 2.7). Diesels. 9 knots. Port Auxiliary Service. Former store ship.

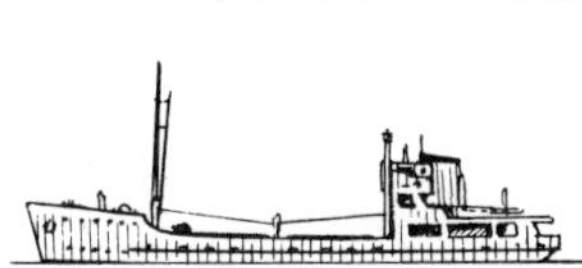

★ **1237.** Ys. **PT 71**. Transport. 300 tons. 142 x 22 x 16. (43.2 x 6.7 x 4.8). Diesels. 7 knots.
**PT 72**.

**1238.** Tu. **ISIN**. *A570*. 1941. Diving Tender. 400 tons full load. 110 x 24 x 7. (33.5 x 7.3 x 2.1). Diesel.

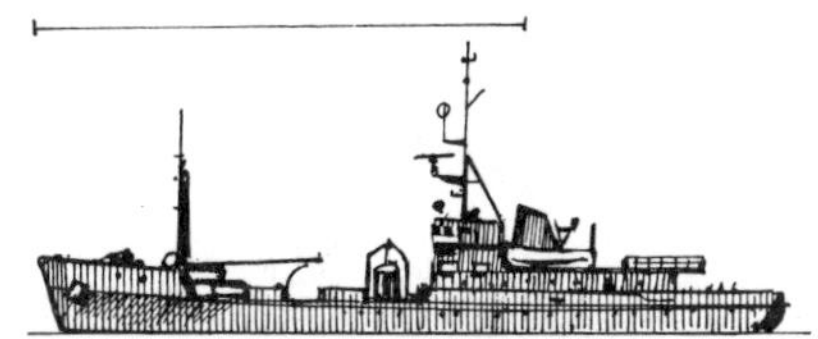

**1239.** Sw. **BELOS**. *A211*. 1863. Salvage Vessel. 1,000 tons. 204 x 27 x 12. (62.1 x 8.2 x 3.6). 2 screws. Diesels. 13 knots. 1 helicopter.

★ **1240.** Ph. **BALTYK**. 1944. 1,000 tons. Surveying Vessel. 194 x 30 x 14. (59.1 x 9.1 x 4.2). Reciprocating. 11 knots. Former B10 type trawler.

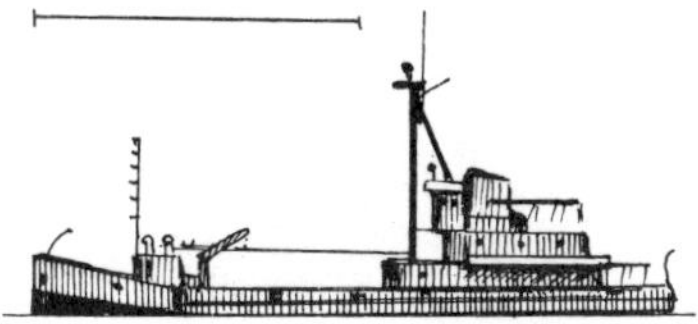

**1241.** Tu. **MEHMEDCIK**. *N105*. 1958. Coastal Minelayer. 500 tons full load. 130 x 35 x 6. (39.6 x 10.6 x 1.8). 2 screws; diesels. 10 knots. Ex-U.S. "YMP" type.

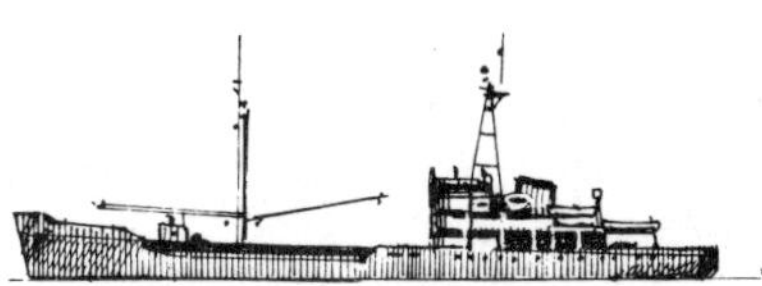

**1242.** Tu. **YUZBASI TOLUNAY**. *A586*. 1950. Oiler. 2,500 tons. 260 x 41 x 20. (79.2 x 12.5 x 6.1). 2 screws; diesels. 14 knots.

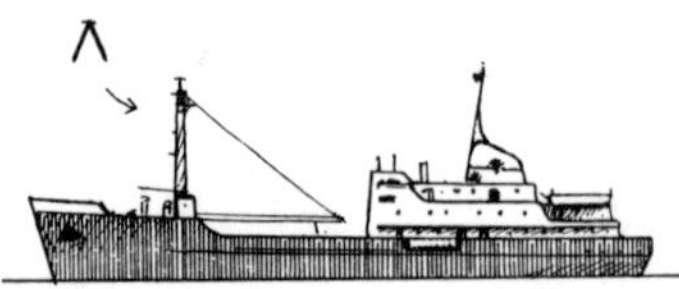

**1243.** Ca. **NARWHAL.** 1963. Coast Guard Depot Ship. 2,000 tons gross. 252 x 42 x 12. (76.8 x 12.8 x 3.6). Diesel.

**1244.** Br. **SPA** class. 1941-46. Water Carriers. 1,200 tons full load. 172 x 30 x 12. (52.4 x 9.1 x 3.6). Reciprocating. 9 knots. Ships may vary in appearance.
**SPABROOK, SPABURN, SPALAKE, SPAPOOL.**

**1245.** Br. **MAXIM.** Armament Carrier. 650 tons. 145 x 25 x 8. (44.1 x 7.6 x 2.4). Reciprocating. 9 knots.
**NORDENFELT.**

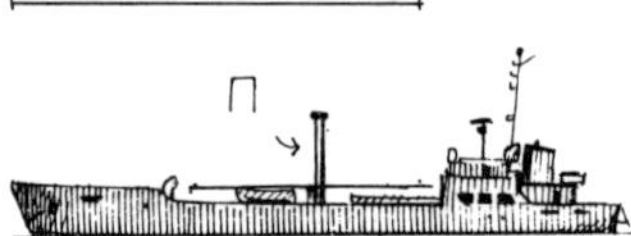

**1246.** Fr. **ISSOLE.** *L9097.* Landing Craft. 1958. 600 tons full load. 161 x 23 x 7. (49 x 7 x 2.1). Diesels. 12 knots. Bow doors and ramp.

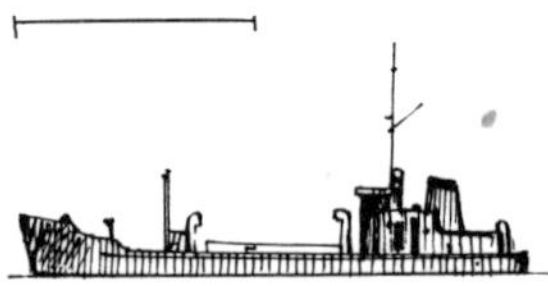

**1247.** Du. **VAN BOCHOVE.** *A923.* 1962. Torpedo Recovery Vessel. 150 tons. 97 x 18 x 6. (29.5 x 5.4 x 1.8). Diesel. 8 knots.

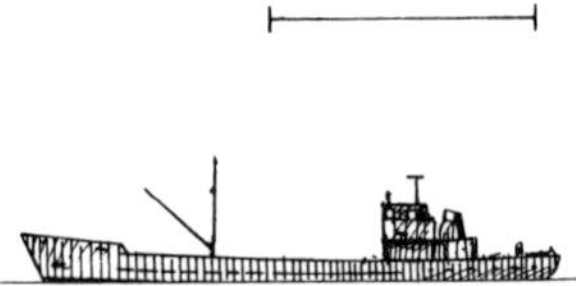

**1248.** Sw. **FRYKEN.** *A217.* 1960. Water Carrier. 300 tons. 105 x 19 x 9. (32 x 5.7 x 2.7). Motor. 10 knots.

**1249.** Br. **OIL** class. 1969-70. Oil Carriers. 250 tons. Diesel. 10 knots.
**OILBIRD, OILFIELD, OILMAN, OILPRESS, OILSTONE, OILWELL.**

**1250.** Br. **ABERDOVEY** class. 1963-65. Fleet Tenders. 70 tons gross. 79 x 18 x 6. (24 x 5.4 x 1.8). Diesel. 10 knots.
**ABERDOVEY, ABINGER, ALNESS, ALNMOUTH, APPLEBY, ASHCOTT, BEAULIEU, BEDDGELERT, BEMBRIDGE, BIBURY, BLAKENEY, BRODICK.** 8 more ships building.

**1251.** It. **METAURO.** *A5373*. 1933. Water Carrier. 600 tons. 133 x 27 x 11. (40.5 x 10 x 3.3). Diesels. 8 knots. 1—20-m.m. A.A. gun.

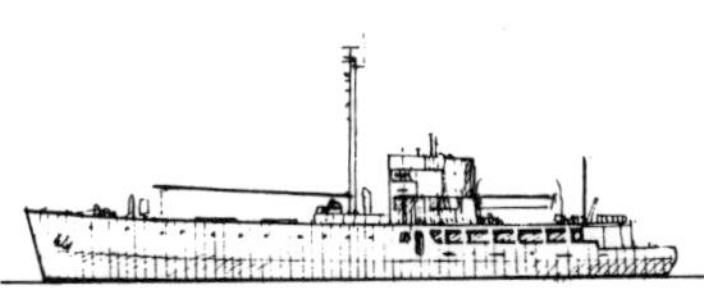

**1252.** Am. **MARK.** *KL12*. Light Cargo Ship. 700 tons. 177 x 33 x 10. (53.9 x 10 x 3). Diesel. 10 knots. 1—20-m.m. A.A. gun.

Probably similar: **BRAULE.** *KL28*.

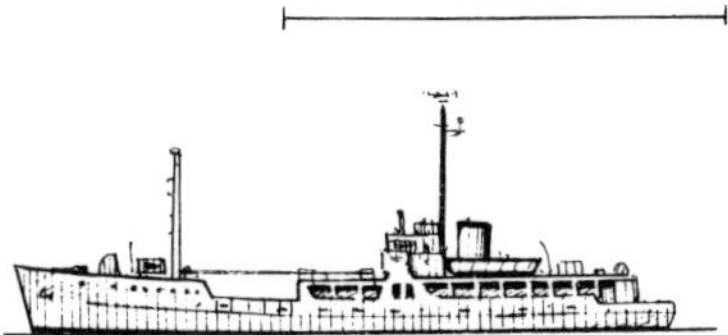

**1253.** Am. **AKL 31.** *KL31*. Light Cargo Ship. All details as No. 1252 but has no armament.

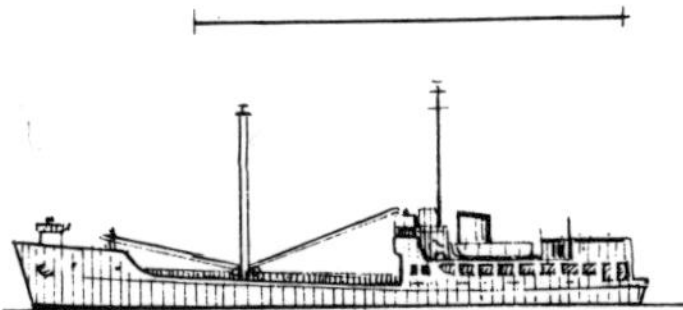

**1254.** VN. **HOA GIANG.** *451*. Training Ship. Former U.S. "AKL" type. All details as No. 1252 but has no armament.

Similar: Japan. **MIHO, NASAMI.** (Minesweeper tenders.)

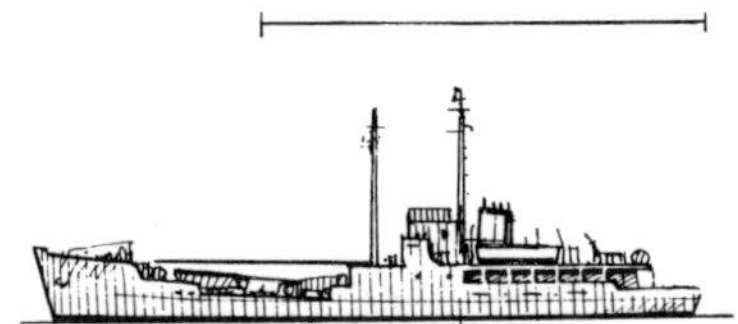

**1255.** Am. **AKL 17.** Light Cargo Ship. All details as for No. 1252 but has no armament.

**1256.** Pi. **BOJEADUR.** *46*. Lighthouse Tender. Ex-U.S. "FS" type. All details as for No. 1252 but has no armament.
**LAUIS LEDGE.** *45*.

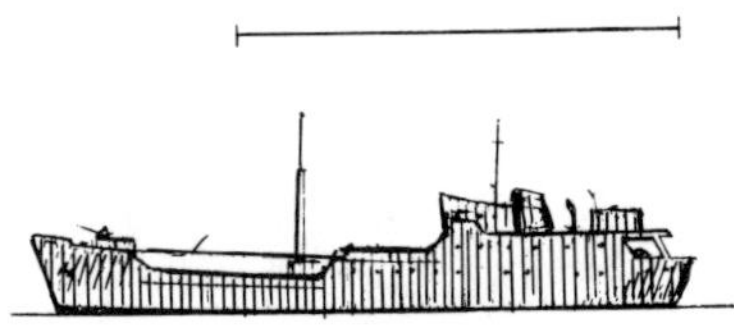

**1257.** Me. **ZACATECAS.** *60*. 1959. Transport. 800 tons. 158 x 27 x 9. (48.1 x 8.2 x 2.7). Diesel. 10 knots. 1—40-m.m. A.A. gun. 2—20-m.m. A.A. guns.

**1258.** Ca. **LAYMORE.** *516*. Research Vessel. 600 tons gross. 177 x 32 x 8. (53.9 x 9.7 x 2.4) Diesels. 10 knots. Former supply vessel converted in 1966.

**1259.** Ca. **BLUETHROAT.** *114*. 1955. Research Vessel. 870 tons full load. 157 x 33 x 10. (47.8 x 10 x 3) 2 screws; diesel. 13 knots. Built as a mine and loop-layer.

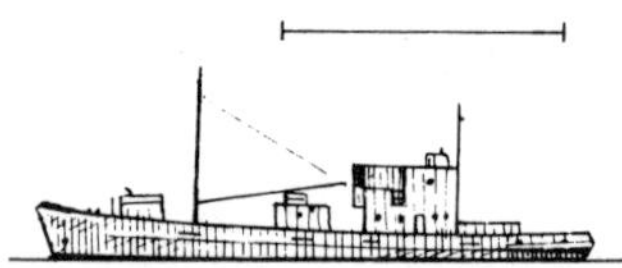

**1260.** Ge. **EUTIN.** *Y825*. 1943. Oiler. 400 tons. 6 knots.

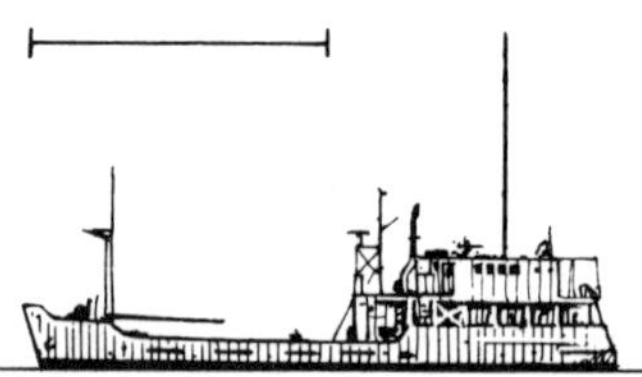

**1261.** Au. **PALUMA.** Survey Ship. Converted in 1958 from a stores lighter. Built during World War II. 350 tons. 120 x 24 x 7. (36.5 x 7.3 x 2.1). Diesel. 9 knots.

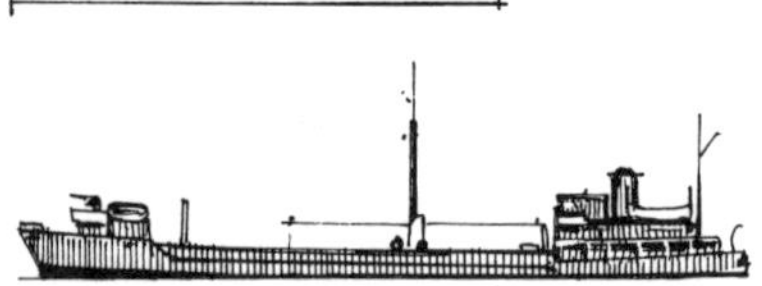

**1262.** It. **MOC 1202.** 1943-44c. Repair Craft. 350 tons. 192 x 31 x 7. (58.5 x 9.4 x 2.1), Diesel. 8 knots. 1 or 2 A.A. guns. Ex-British LCT(3) type.

Possibly similar: **MOC 1203. MOC 1204. MOC 1205**

**1263.** It. **MOC 1201.** Repair Craft. All details as No. 1262.

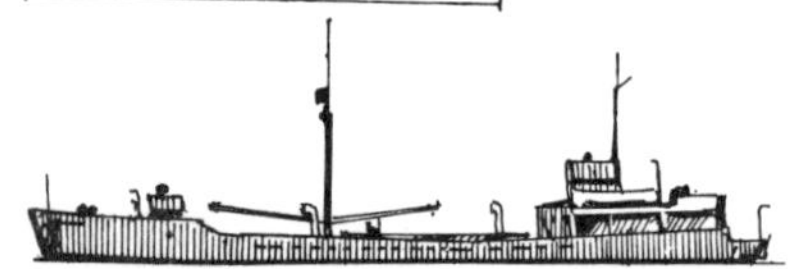

**1264.** It. **MOC 1207.** Ammunition Transport. All details as No. 1262. **MOC 1208.**

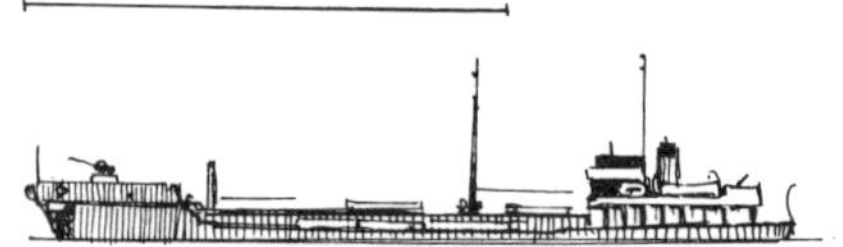

**1265.** It. **MTF 1301.** Lighthouse Tender. All details as No. 1262. **MTF 1302. MTF 1303.**

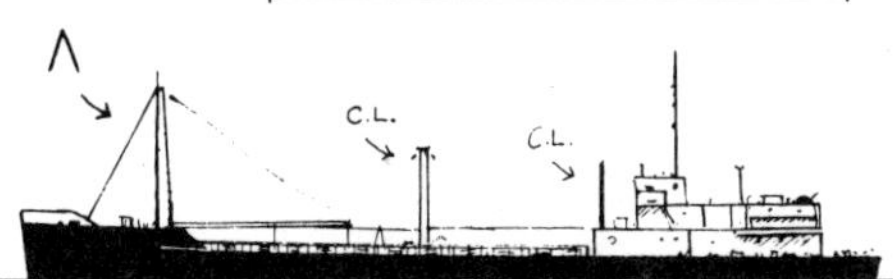

**1266.** Ca. **SKUA.** 1946. Coast Guard Supply Vessel. 1,100 tons gross. 231 x 38 x 3. (70.4 x 11.5 x 0.9). Diesel. 9 knots. Converted British LCT(8) type.

Possibly similar: **AUK, EIDER, PUFFIN, RAVEN.** These may be like Gannet (see No. 1267).

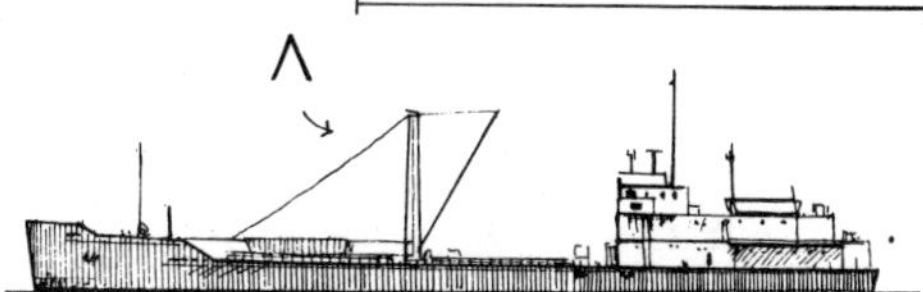

**1267.** Ca. **GANNET.** 1946. Coast Guard Supply Vessel. All details as No. 1266.

Possibly similar: **AUK, EIDER, PUFFIN, RAVEN.** These may be like "Skua" (see No. 1266).

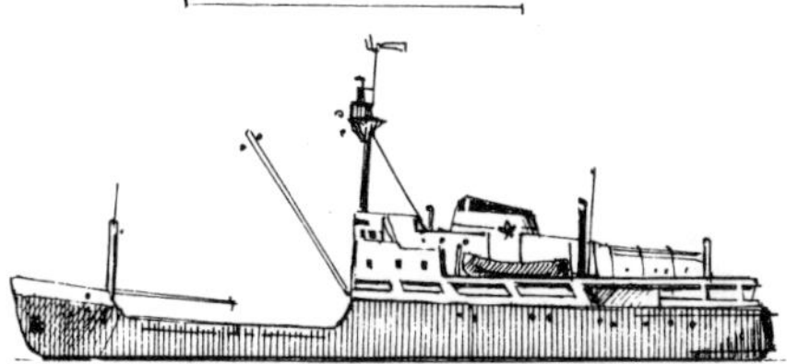

**1268.** Ca. **CAMSELL.** 1959. Coast Guard Icebreaker. 3.100 tons full load. 224 x 48 x 16. (68.2 x 14.6 x 4.8). Diesel/electric. 13 knots. Helicopter deck and telescopic hangar.

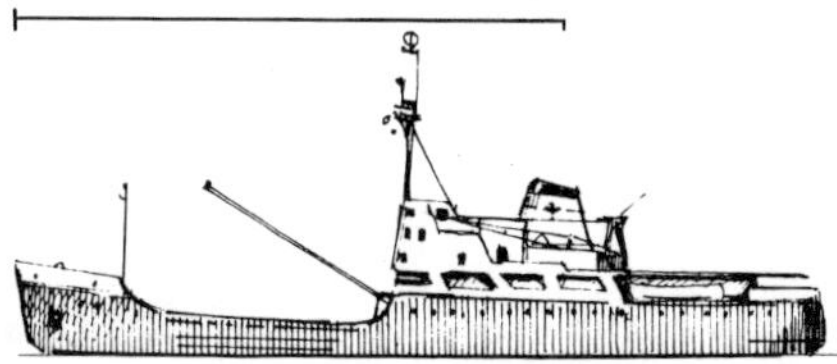

**1269.** Ca. **SIR HUMPHREY GILBERT.** 1959. Coast Guard Icebreaker. 3,000 tons full load. 220 x 48 x 16. (67 x 14.6 x 4.8). Diesel/electric. 13 knots. Helicopter deck and telescopic hangar.

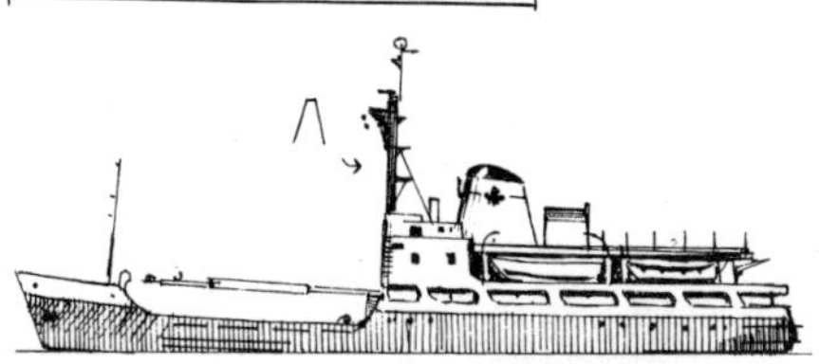

**1270.** Ca. **WOLFE.** 1959. Coast Guard Icebreaker. Tonnage and dimensions as No. 1268. Reciprocating. 13 knots. Helicopter deck and telescopic hangar.
Almost identical: **MONTCALM.** (1957).

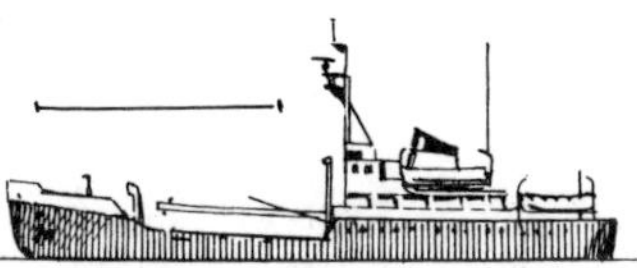

**1271.** Ca. **MONTMORENCY.** 1957. Coast Guard Supply Vessel. 1,000 tons full load. 163 x 34 x 11. (49.6 x 10.3 x 3.3). Diesel; 2 screws.

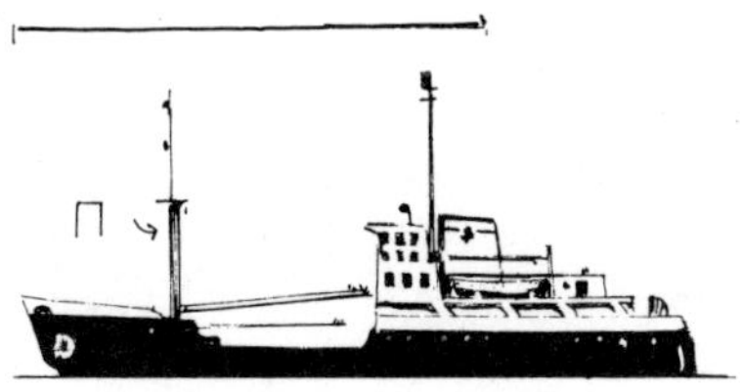

**1272.** Ca. **BARTLETT.** 1970. Coast Guard Supply Vessels. 189 x 43 x 12. (57.6 x 13 x 3.6). Diesel. **PROVO WALLACE.**

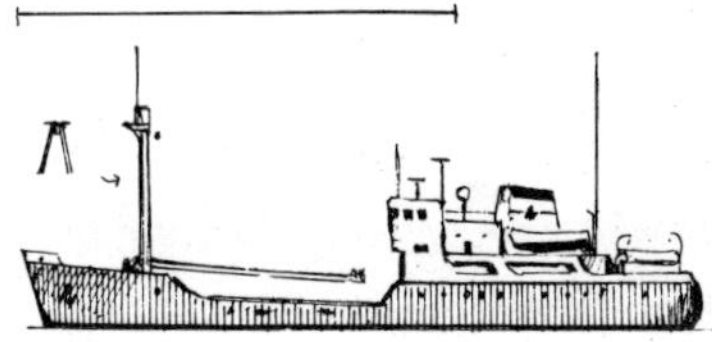

**1273.** Ca. **SIMCOE.** 1962. Coast Guard Light Icebreaker and Supply Vessel 1,300 tons full load. 180 x 38 x 12. (54.8 x 11.5 x 3.6). Diesel/electric. 12 knots.

**1274.** Ca. **SIR JAMES DOUGLAS.** 1956. Coast Guard Supply Vessel. 700 tons full load. 150 x 30 x 10. (45.7 x 9.1 x 3). Diesel. Similar: **ALEXANDER MACKENZIE.**

**1275.** Ca. **TRACY.** 1969. Coast Guard Icebreaker and Supply Vessel. 1,300 tons. 182 x 38 x 12. (55.4 x 11.5 x 3.6). Diesel/electric. 13 knots.

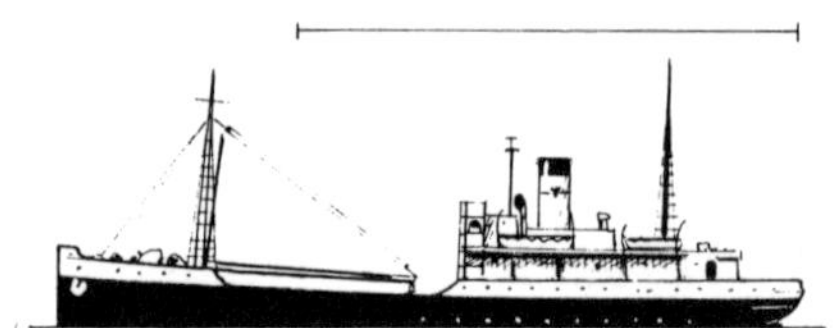

**1276.** Ca. **ESTEVAN.** 1912. Coast Guard Supply Vessel. 2,100 tons full load. 200 x 38 x 12. (60.9 x 11.5 x 3.6). Reciprocating.

## P5

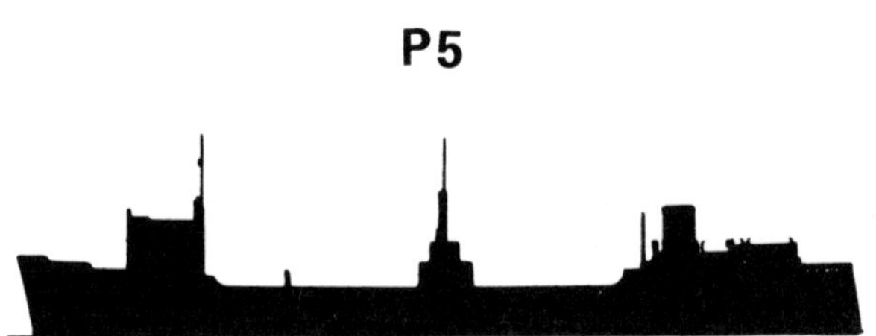

P5 (Bridge Foreward)

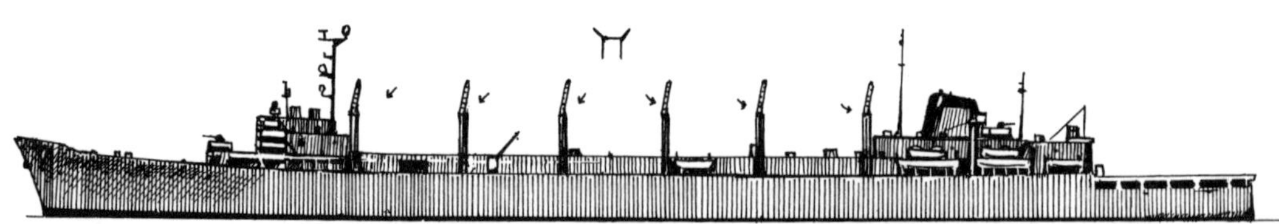

**1277.** Am. **SACRAMENTO** class. 1964-70. Combat Support Ships. 53,600 tons full load. 793 x 107 x 39. (241.6 x 32.6 x 11.8). 2 screws; turbines. 26 knots. 8—3-inch guns (twin). 2 cargo helicopters.
**CAMDEN.** *OE2*, **DETROIT.** *OE4*, **SACRA-MENTO.** *OE1*, **SEATTLE.** *OE3*. One more building.

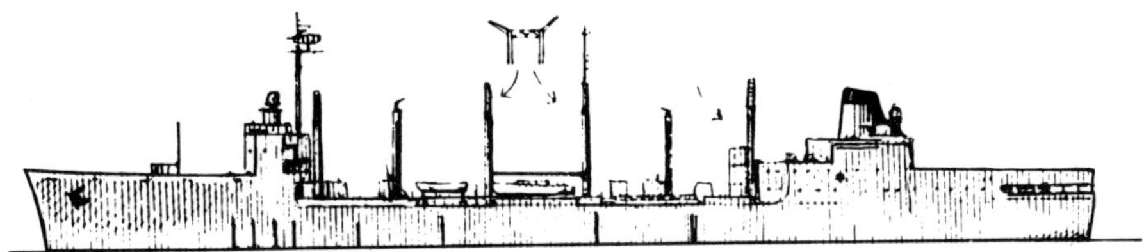

**1278.** Am. **WICHITA** class. 1969-71. Replenishment Oilers. 38,100 tons full load. 659 x 96 x 35. (200.7 x 29.2 x 10.6). 2 screws; turbines. 20 knots. 8—3-inch guns (twin). Helicopter platform.
**KANSAS CITY.** *OR3,* **MILWAUKEE.** *OR2,* **WABASH.** *OR5,* **WICHITA.** *OR1.* 2 ships building.

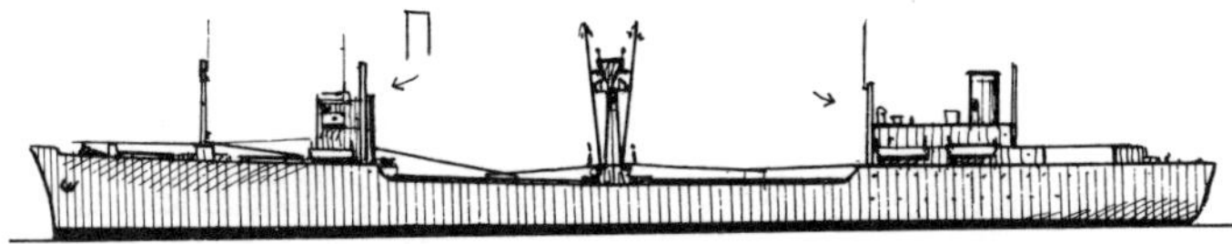

**1279.** Am. **MARINE FIDDLER.** 1945. Converted 1954. Heavy Lift Ship. 520 x 72 x 33. (158.4 x 21.9 x 10). Turbine. 15 knots. C4-S-B5 type.

Similar but with longer forecastle: **PVT, LEONARD C. BROSTROM.**

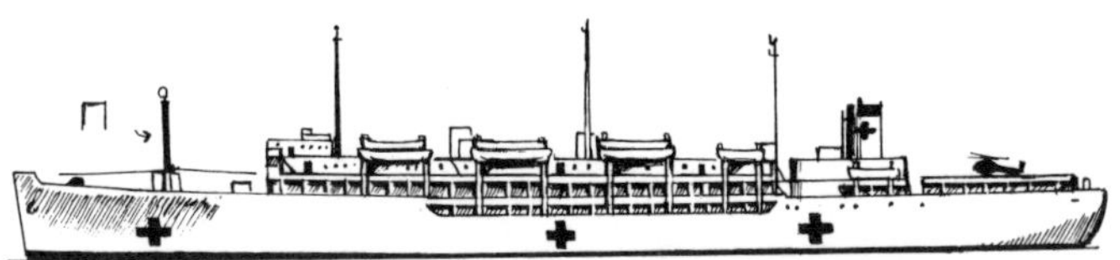

**1280.** Am. **HAVEN** class. 1945. Hospital ships. 15,400 tons full load. 520 x 72 x 24. (158.4 x 21.9 x 7.3). Turbine. 18 knots. C4-S-B2 type.
**REPOSE, SANCTUARY.**

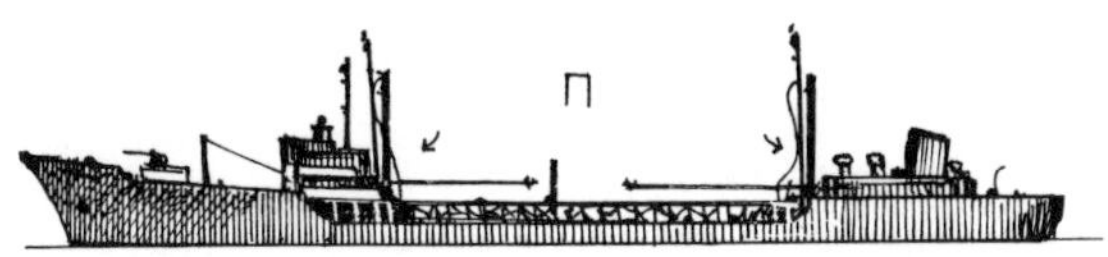

**1281.** Ja. **HAMANA.** *411.* 1962. Oiler. 7,600 tons full load. 420 x 52 x 21. (128 x 15.8 x 6.4). Diesel. 16 knots. 2—40-m.m. A.A. guns.

**1282.** Ru. **UDA** class. 1964-65. Supply Ship and Oilers. 3,500 tons. 380 x 47 x 13. (115.8 x 14.3 x 3.9). 2 screws; diesels. 13 knots.
4 ships in the Soviet Navy including the following:

**DUNAY, SVIR, TEREK.** These may be of a different appearance and armed with 6—25-m.m. A.A. guns (see silhouette No. 1323). They may also have a bipod mainmast.

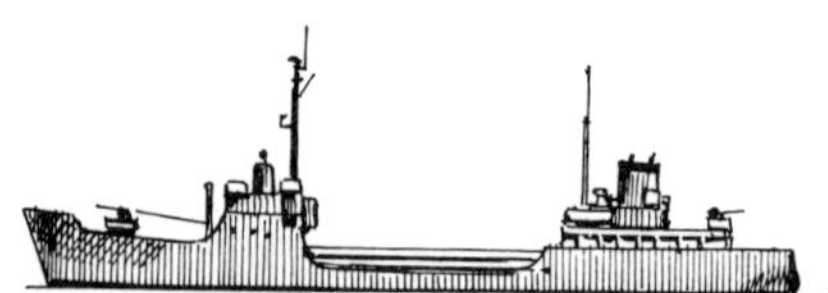

**1283.** Am. **PATAPSCO** class. 1944. Gasoline Tankers. 4,600 tons full load. 311 x 49 x 16. (94.7 x 14.7 x 4.8). 2 screws; diesel/electric. 14 knots. 3—3-inch guns.
**CHEWAUCAN.** *OG50,* **ELKHORN.** *OC7,* **GEN-ESEE.** *OG8,* **KISHWAUKEE.** *OG9,* **NESPELEN.** *OG55,* **NOXUBEE.** *OG56,* **PATAPSCO.** *OG1,* **TOMBIGBEE.** *OG11.*

Similar:
China. **CHANG PEI.** *307.*

Greece. **ARETHOUSA.** *A377.*

New Zealand. **ENDEAVOUR.** *A184.* Antarctic Support Ship. No guns. .

★ There may be two ships of this type in the Red Chinese Navy.

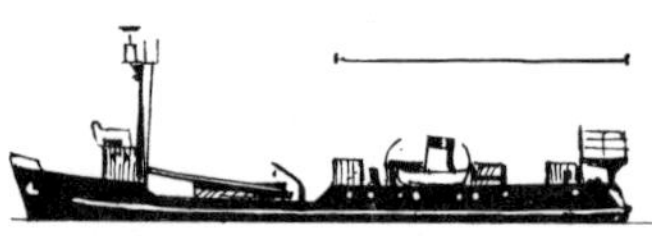

**1284.** Br. **ICEWHALE.** Experimental Trials Vessel. 300 tons. 120 x 24 x 9. (36.5 x 7.3 x 2.7). Diesel. 9 knots.

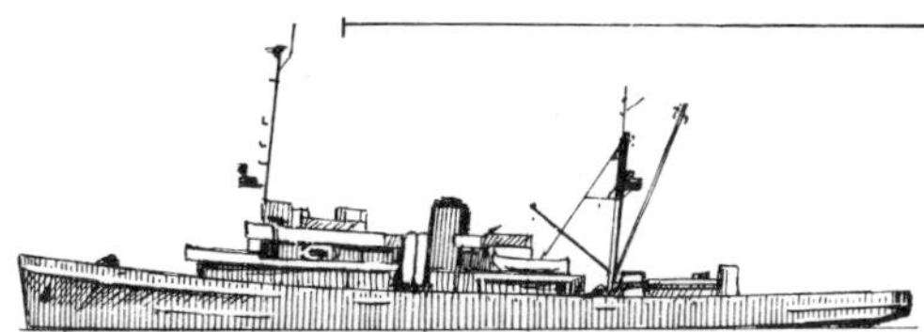

**1285.** Am. **CHANTICLEER** class. 1945-46.
Submarine Rescue Ships. 1,700 tons. 252 x 42 x
15. (76.7 x 12.8 x 4.4). Diesel/electric. 14 knots.
**CHANTICLEER,** *7,* **COUCAL.** *8,* **FLORIKAN.**
**GREENLET.** *10,* **KITTIWAKE.** *13,* **PETREL.**
*14,* **SUNBIRD,** *15,* **TRINGA.** *16.*

**1287.** Am. **APACHE** class. 1943-45. Fleet Tugs.
Dimensions and tonnage as No. 1286. Speed 15
knots. 1—3-inch gun. Salvage equipment.
**ABNAKI.** *96* **APACHE.** *67* **ARIKARA.** *98,*
**ATAKAPA.** *149* (has electronic equipment on
mainmast), **CHOWANOC.** *100,* **COCOPA.** *101,*
**CREE.** *84,* **HITCHITI.** *103,* **KIOWA.** *72,*
**LIPAN.** *85,* **LUISENO.** *156,* **MATACO.** *86,*
**MOCTOBI.** *105,* **MOSOSPELEA.** *158,* **NIT-**
**MUC.** *157,* **PAKANA.** *108,* **PAIUTE.** *159,*
**PAPAGO.** *160,* **QUAPAW.** *110,* **SALINAN.**
*161,* **SENECA.** *91,* **SHAKORI.** *162,* **SIOUX.** *75,*
**TAKELMA.** *113,* **TAWAKONI.** *114,* **TAWASA.**
*92,* **UTE.** *76,* **UTINA.** *163.*

Ch. (Survey Ship). **YELCHO.** *AGS64.* (Has
deck house alongside mainmast.)
Cs. **TA TUNG.**
Ec. **CAYAMBE.** *R51.*
Ia. **RAKATA.** *928.*
Pv. **RIOS.** *123.*

Some other ships in this class have no funnels;
see silhouette No. 868.
Am. **MOLALA.** *106.* (Possibly others.)
Ve. **FELIPE LARRAZABAL.** *R11.*

Similar—no guns; see silhouette No. 1046.
Co. **PEDRO DE HEREDIA.**

Similar: Am. Coast Guard. **AVOYEL, CHERO-**
**KEE, CHILULA, TAMAROA.**

**1286.** Ar. **COMMANDANTE GENERAL IRI-**
**GOYEN.** *1.* 1945. Patrol Vessels. 1,200 tons,
205 x 38 x 15. (62.5 x 11.6 x 4.6). Diesel/electric.
16 knots. 1—3-inch gun. 4—40-m.m. A.A. guns.
Former U.S. "Apache" class tugs.
**COMMANDANTE GENERAL ZAPIOLA.** *2.*

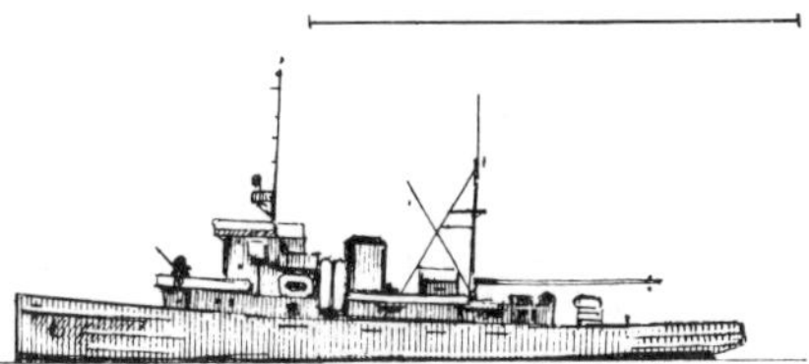

**1288.** Tu. **KURTARAN.** *A584.* Submarine
Rescue Ships. Tonnage and dimensions etc. as
for No. 1286. Ex-U.S. "Apache" class tugs.

Similar: U.S. **PENGUIN** class. See silhouette
No. 1047.
**PENGUIN.** *12,* **SKYLARK.** *20.*

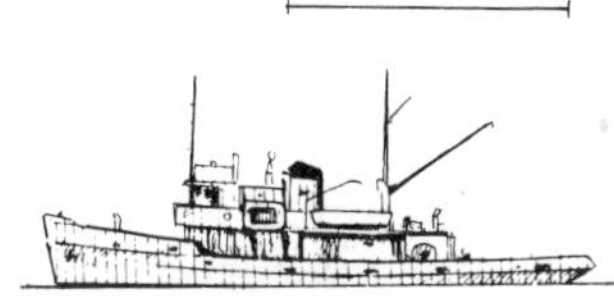

**1289.** Ca. **TON** class. 1944. Harbour Tugs. 470
tons. 111 x 28 x 11. (33.8 x 8.5 x 3.4). Diesel.
11 knots.
**CLIFTON, HEATHERTON, RIVERTON.**

**1290.** Ph. **PERKUN.** 1962. Icebreaker. 800 tons.
185 x 36 x 16. (56.4 x 14 x 4.9). 2 screws;
diesel/electric. 12 knots.
Commercial craft but employed frequently by
the Polish Navy.

**1291.** Pk. **RUSTOM.** 1956. Tug. 105 x 30 x 11. (32 x 9.1 x 3.4). Diesel. 9 knots.

**1292.** Br. **EXPELLER.** Harbour Tug. 100 tons. (approx.). Port Auxiliary Service.
Possibly similar: **EMINENT, ENERGY.**

**1293.** Th. **SAMAESAN.** Tug. 500 tons (full). 105 x 27 x 13. (32 x 8.2 x 3.9). Reciprocating. 10 knots.
Former British "Empire" type.

**1294.** Ec. **COTOPAXI.** 1944c. Tug. 150 tons. 82 x 21 x 8. (25 x 6.4 x 2.4). Diesel. 9 knots.

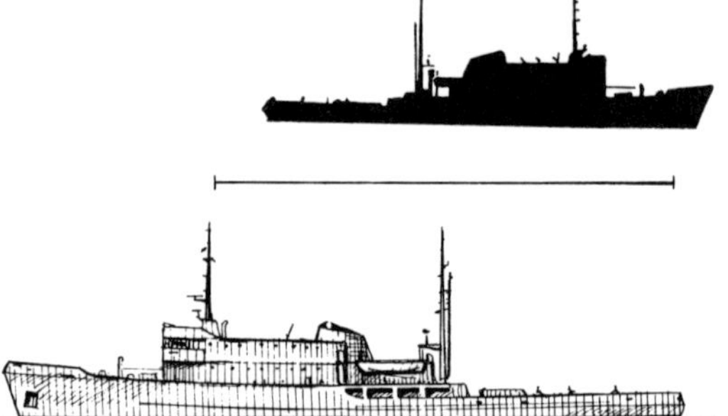

**1295.** Fi. **PIRTTISAARI** class. 1943-44. Tugs. 100 tons. 69 x 20 x 8½. (21 x 6.1 x 2.5). Diesel. 8 knots. 1—20-m.m. gun.
Former U.S. Army tugs.
**PURHA** and the following which are employed as coast artillery transports:
**PIRTTISAARI, PYHTAA.**

★ **1296.** Ru. **PAMIR** class. 1959-60. Salvage Tugs. 1,400 tons (gross). 256 x 42 x 13. (78 x 12.8 x 4). 2 screws; diesels. 17 knots.
At least 4 ships in the class.
**AGATAN, ALDAN, ARBAN, PAMIR.**

**1297.** It. **PROTEO.** *A5310.* 1950. Salvage Tug. 1,900 tons. 248 x 38 x 21. (75.6 x 11.6 x 6.4). Diesels. 16 knots.

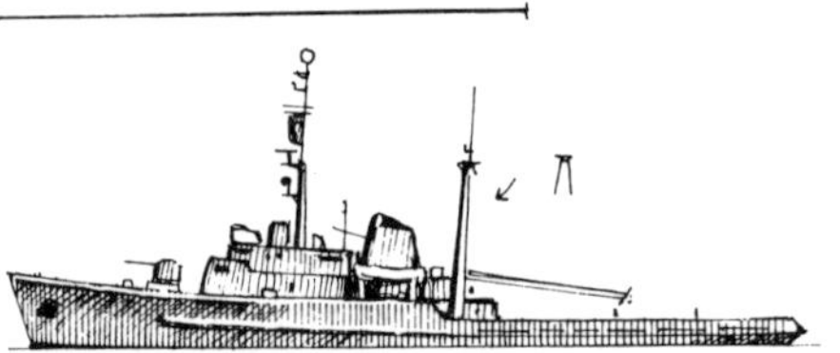

**1298.** Ge. **FEHRMARN.** *A1458.* 1967. Salvage Tug. 1,300 tons. 223 x 42 x 14½. (68 x 12.7 x 4.3). 2 screws diesel/electric. 16 knots. 1—40-m.m. A.A. gun.
**HELGOLAND.** *A1457.*

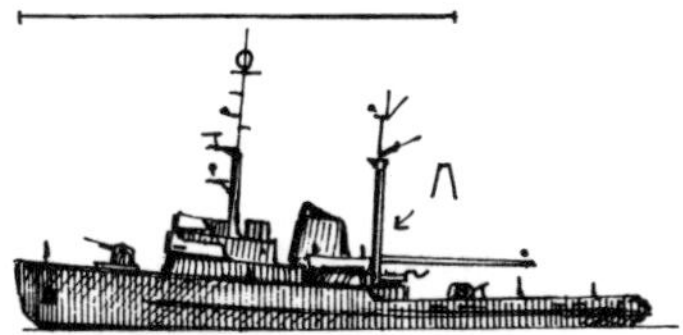

**1299.** Ge. **WANGEROOGE** class. 1968. Salvage Tugs. 900 tons. 170 x 39 x 13. (52 x 12.1 x 3.7). Diesel/electric. 13 knots. 1—40-m.m. A.A. gun.
**BALTRUM, JUIST, LANGEOOG, NORDERNEY, SPIEKEROOG, WANGEROOGE.**

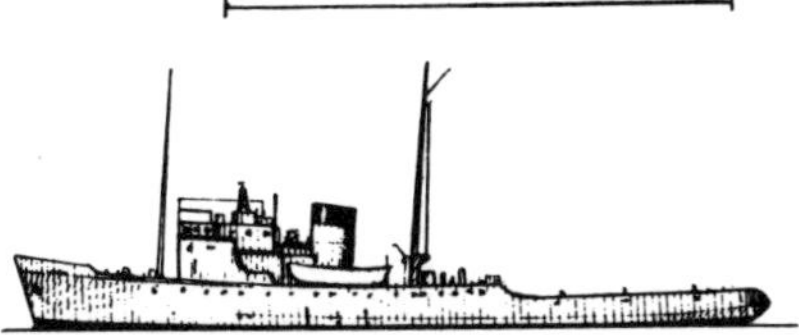

**1300.** Br. **BUSTLER** class. 1942-45. Fleet Tugs. 1,100 tons. 205 x 40 x 17. (62.5 x 12.2    5.2). Diesel. 16 knots.
**BUSTLER.** *A240,* **CYCLONE.** *A111,* **REWARD.** *A264,* **SAMSONIA.** *A218.*
Royal Fleet Auxiliary.
Others have been transferred or chartered to commercial firms.

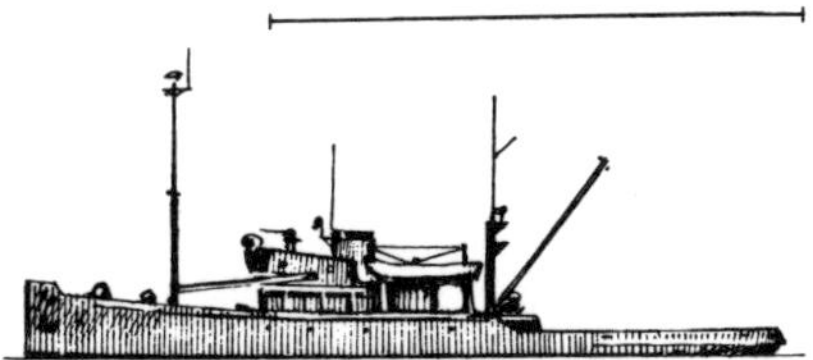

**1301.** Am. **DIVER** class. 1943-46. Salvage Ships. 1,500 tons. 214 x 39 x 13. (65.2 x 11.9 x 4). 2 screws; diesel/electric. 14 knots. 1—40-m.m. A.A. gun.
**BOLSTER.** *RS38,* **CONSERVER.** *RS39,* **CURRENT.** *RS22,* **DELIVER.** *RS23,* **ESCAPE.** *RS6,* **GRAPPLE.** *RS7,* **GRASP.** *RS24,* **HOIST.** *RS40,* **OPPORTUNE.** *RS41,* **PRESERVER.** *RS8* **RECLAIMER.** *RS42,* **RECOVERY.** *RS43,* **SAFEGUARD.** *RS25.*

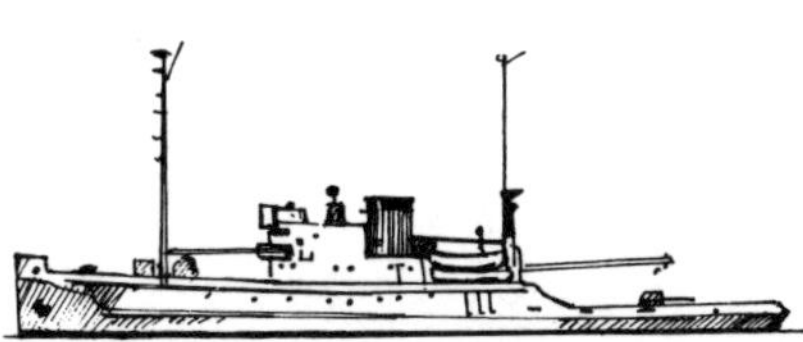

**1302.** Am. **ACUSHNET.** 1943. Fleet Tug. 1,600 tons. 214 x 39 x 16. (65.2 x 11.9 x 4). 2 screws; diesel-electric. 13 knots. "ARS" type.
**YOCONA.**

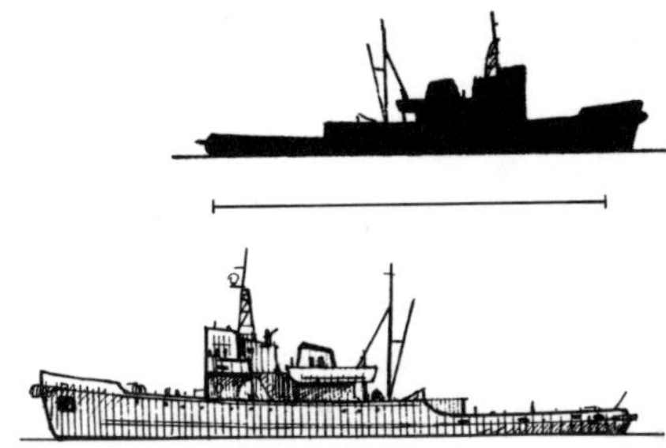

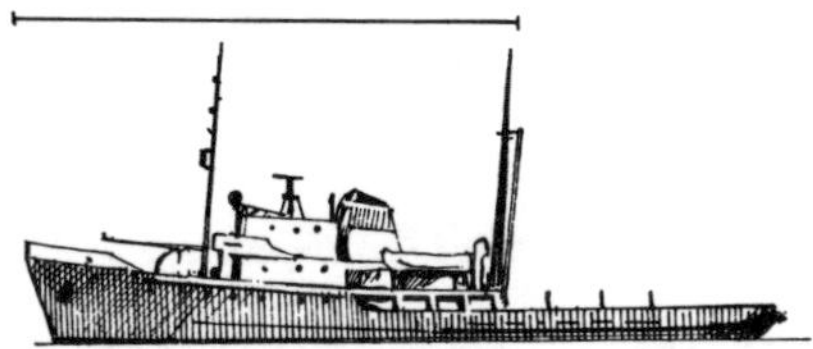

★ **1303.** Ru. **OREL** class. 1960c. Fleet Tugs. 1,100 tons (gross). 202 x 38 x 15. (61.7 x 11.6 x 4.4). Diesels. 13 knots.
A large commercial class and many serve with navy as required. Some may be modified "Orel" class with tripod mast.

★ **1304.** Ru. **SILNIJ** class. 1958c. Tugs. 1,000 tons (gross). 202 x 38 x 15. (61.7 x 11.6 x 4.4). Diesels.
A later modification have a lattice type foremast. A few are in commercial service.

**1305.** Br. **TYPHOON.** *A95.* Fleet Tug (Salvage). 800 tons. 200 x 40 x 14. (61 x 12.2 x 4). Diesels. 16 knots. Royal Fleet Auxiliary.

**1306.** Sp. **BS1.** Tug serving as base for frogmen. 950 tons. 184 x 33 x 16. (56.1 x 9.8 x 4.7) Diesels. 15 knots.
**RA4, RA5** (both fleet tugs).

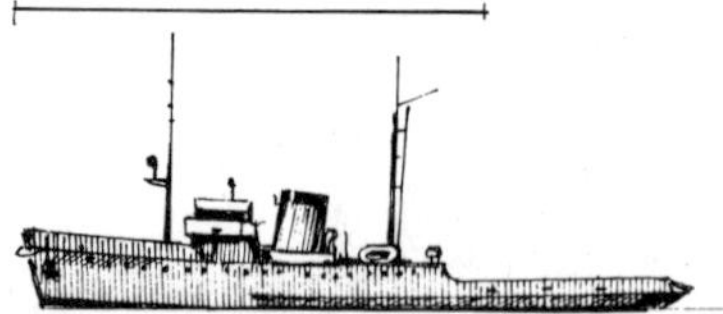

**1307.** Sp. **RA1.** 1955. Salvage Tug. 800 tons. 184 x 34 x 12. (56.1 x 10.2 x 3.7). Diesels. 15 knots. 2 light guns.
**RA2.**

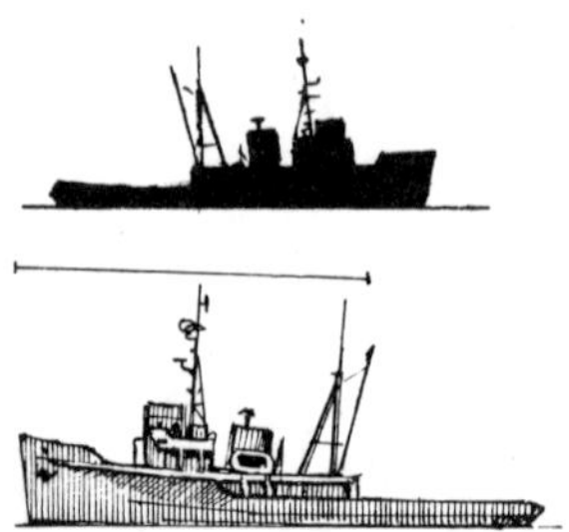

**1309.** Ru. **OKHTENSKY** class. Fleet Tugs. 835 tons. 143 x 34 x 15. (43.6 x 10.3 x 4.6). Diesel/electric. 13 knots. 1—3-inch gun. 2—20-m.m. A.A. guns.
Former American "ATA" type. May be numbered **MB 24**, **MB 25**, **MB 26**.

**1310.** Fr. **RHINOCEROS.** *A668.* Tug. 700 tons. 140 (approx.). Diesels. 12 knots. Similar to U.S. "ATA" type.

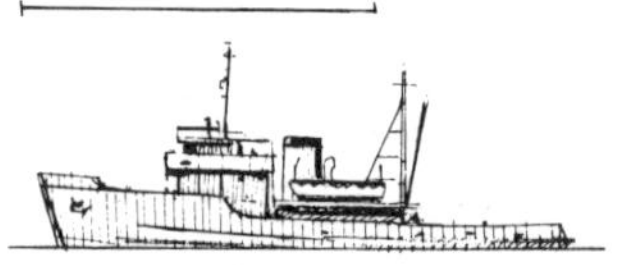

**1312.** Fr. **HIPPOPOTAME.** *A660.* 1943. Tug. 500 tons. Dimensions as No. 1308. Similar to U.S. "ATA" type.

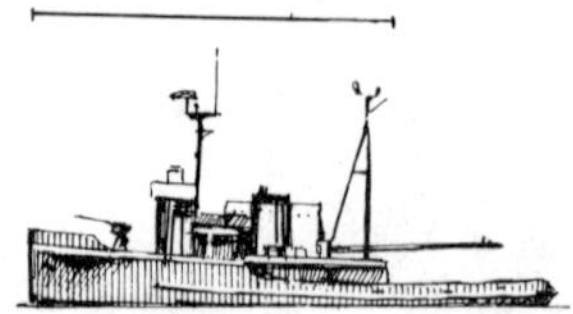

**1308.** Am. **MARICOPA** class. 1944-45. Tugs. 530 tons. 143 x 34 x 13. (43.6 x 10.3 x 4). Diesel/electric. 13 knots. 1—3-inch gun.
**ACCOKEEK.** *TA181,* **CAHOKIA.** *TA186,* **CATAWBA.** *TA210,* **KALMIA.** *TA184,* **KOKA.** *TA185,* **KEYWADIN.** *TA213,* **MAHOPAC.** *TA196,* **PENOBSCOT.** *TA188,* **SAGAMORE.** *TA208,* **SALISH.** *TA187,* **SAMOSET.** *TA190,* **STALLION.** *TA193,* **TATNUCK.** *TA195,* **TILLAMOOK.** *TA192,* **UMPQUA.** *TA209,* **WANDANK.** *TA206.*

Ch. Patrol Vessels. **LAUTARO.** *62,* **LIENTUR.** *60.*
Cs. **TA SHUEH.** *347.* (Sister without gun foreward).
**TA YU** *345.*
Ko. **DO BONG.** *TA3,* **YONG MUN.** *TA2.*
RC. Possibly 2 in Communist Chinese Navy.

The following have no gun forward; see silhouette No. 1052.
Am. Coast Guard. **COMANCHE, MODOC.**
Bz. **TRIDENTE.** *R22,* **TRITAO.** *R21,* **TRIUNFO.** *R23.*
Pv. **UNANUE.** *136.*
Pk. **MADADGAR.** *294.*

**1311.** Ar. **CHIRIGUANO.** *7.* 1945. Patrol Vessel. 700 tons. 143 x 34 x 12. (33.6 x 10.4 x 3.6). Diesel/electric. 12 knots. 2—20-m.m. A.A. guns. Former U.S. "Maricopa" class.
**DIAGUITA.** *5,* **SANAVIRON.** *4,* **YAMANA.** *6.*

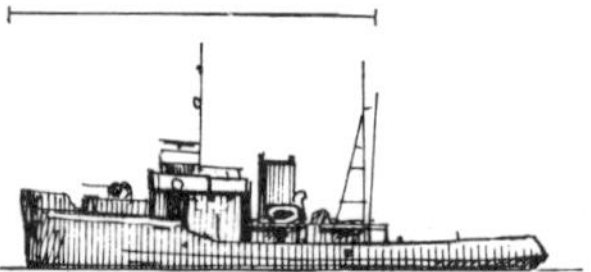

**1313.** Pi. **IFUGAO.** *R44.* 1944c. Rescue Tug. 500 tons. Dimensions as for No. 1308. 1—3-inch gun. 2—20-m.m. guns. Ex-U.S. "ATR" type.

**1314.** Au. **SPRIGHTLY.** 1942. Fleet Tug. 600 tons. 143 x 35 x 13. (43.6 x 10.7 x 3.8). Diesels. 12 knots. 3—40-m.m. A.A. guns. Similar to U.S. "ATR" type.

**1315.** Ca. **SAINT** class. 1956-57. Ocean Tugs. 840 tons (full). 152 x 33 x 17. (46.3 x 10.1 x 5.2). Diesel. 14 knots. 2—40-m.m. A.A. guns. **SAINT ANTHONY.** *ATA531,* **SAINT CHARLES.** *ATA533,* **SAINT JOHN.** *ATA535.*

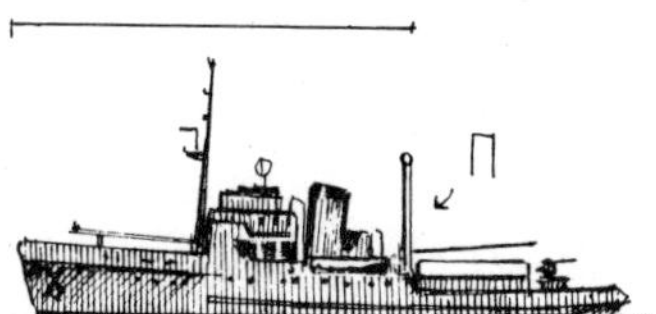

**1316.** Ge. **OSTE.** *A52.* 1943. Depot Ship; Tender. 600 tons (gross). 160 x 30 x 17. (48.8 x 9.1 x 5.2). Diesel. 14 knots. 2—20-m.m. A.A. guns. Former U.S. Navy.

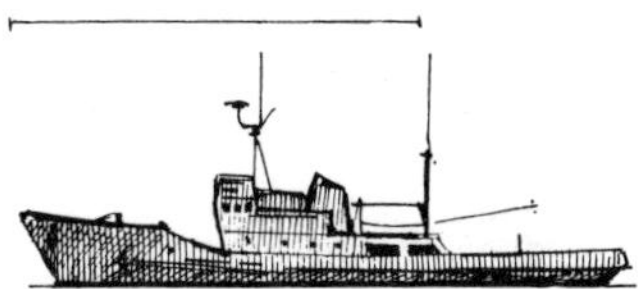

**1317.** Fi. **SILMA.** 1963. Patrol Vessel (Coast Guard). 500 tons. 161 x 27 x 12. (49 x 8.2 x 3.6). Diesel. 15 knots.

**1318.** Cu. **IO DE OCTUBRE.** 1943. Salvage Vessel. 850 tons. 166 x 33 x 16. (50.5 x 10 x 4.8). Reciprocating. 12 knots. Former U.S. rescue tug.

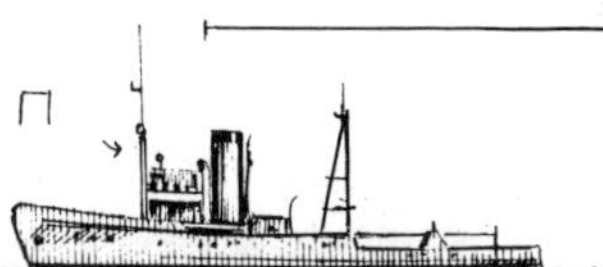

**1319.** Th. **RANG KWIEN.** Tug type Mine Countermeasures Support Ship. 600 tons. 162 x 31 x 13. (49.3 x 9.4 x 3.9). Reciprocating. 10 knots.

**1320.** Br. **NIMBLE** class. 1941-45. Tugs. 900 tons. 175 x 36 x 14. (53.3 x 10.9 x 4.2). 2 screws; reciprocating. 16 knots. **CAPABLE, CAREFUL, NIMBLE.**

**1321.** Br. **ANTIC.** *A141.* 1943. Tug. 700 tons. 157 x 33 x 15. (47.8 x 10 x 4.5). Reciprocating. 12 knots. Last survivor of the "Assurance" class.

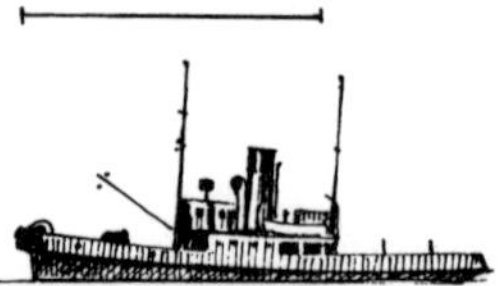

**1322.** Ch. **CABRALES.** *ATA71*. Tug. 800 tons. 1929-59. 127 x 27 x 12. (38.7 x 8.2 x 3.6). Reciprocating. 11 knots.
**COLOCOLO.** *ATA73*.

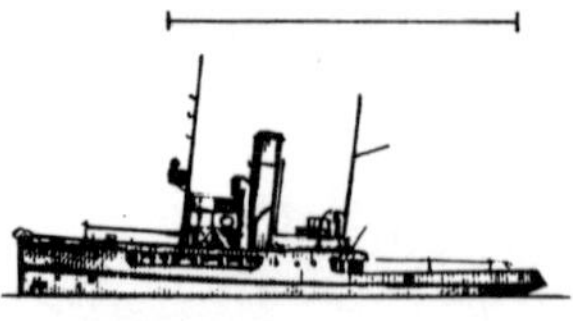

**1323.** Ar. **MATACO.** *R3*. 1928. Tug. 600 tons. 139 x 29 x 12. (43.3 x 8.8 x 3.6). 2 screws; reciprocating. 12 knots.
**TOBA.** *R4*.

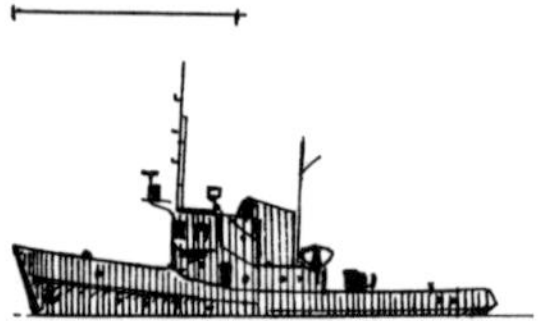

**1324.** Be. **SUB-LIEUTENANT VALCKE.** *A950*. 1951. Tug. 110 tons. 95 x 21 x 6. (28.9 x 6.4 x 1.8). Diesel. 12 knots.

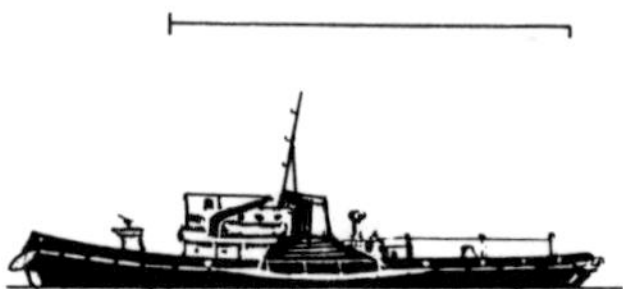

**1325.** Br. **DIRECTOR** class. 1956-58. Dockyard and Harbour Tugs. 157 x 30. (60 feet over sponsons). 10.2 Paddles. Diesel/electric. 13 knots. (47.8 x 9.1 (18.2 x 3).
**DEXTEROUS, DIRECTOR, FAITHFUL, FAV-OURITE, FORCEFUL, GRINDER, GRIPER.** Funnels abreast.

**1326.** Br. **DOG** class. 1961. Harbour Tugs. 94 x 24 x 12. (28.6 x 7.3 x 3.6). 2 screws; diesel/electric. Funnels abreast.
**AIREDALE, ALSATIAN, BEAGLE, BOXER, CAIRN, DALMATIAN, ELKHOUND, LAB-RADOR, POINTER.**
Similar: **GIRL** class. **AGATHA, AGNES, ALICE, AUDREY, BETTY.**

**1327.** Bz. **IMPERIAL MARINHEIRO** class. 1955. Fleet Tugs (Corvettes). 900 tons. 184 x 31 x 12. (56 x 9.4 x 3.6). Diesels. 16 knots.
**ANGOSTURA.** *V20*, **BAHIANA.** *V21*, **CAB-OCLO.** *V19*, **FORTE DE COMBRA.** *V18*, **IGUATEMI.** *V16*, **IMPERIAL MARINHEIRO.** *V15*, **IPIRANGA.** *V17*, **MEARIM.** *V22*, **PURUS.** *V23*, **SOLIMOES.** *V24*.

**1328.** Br. **CON** class. 1941-45. Tugs. 900 tons. 175 x 36 x 14. (53.3 x 10.9 x 4.2). 2 screws; diesels. 13 knots.
**CONFIANCE.** *A289*, **CONFIDENT.** *A290*.
Similar: **AGILE, ADEPT, ACCORD, ADVICE.** (Some may have a mainmast.).

**1329.** Br. **REGARD.** Tug. Port Auxiliary Service.

**1330.** Sp. **RR10.** 1941-42. Fleet Tugs and Auxiliary Patrol Vessel. 370 tons. 124 x 29 x 10. (37.7 x 8.8 x 3). Reciprocating. 11 knots. 1—47-m.m. gun. 1—20-m.m. A.A. gun.
**RR19, RR20, RR28, RR29.**

**1331.** Br. **SAMSON** class. Tugs. Port Auxiliary Service. 1,200 tons. 180 x 37 x 14. (54.8 x 11.2 x 4.2). 2 screws; reciprocating. 15 knots.
**SAMSON.** *A390,* **SEA GIANT.** *A288,* **SUPERMAN.** *A000.*

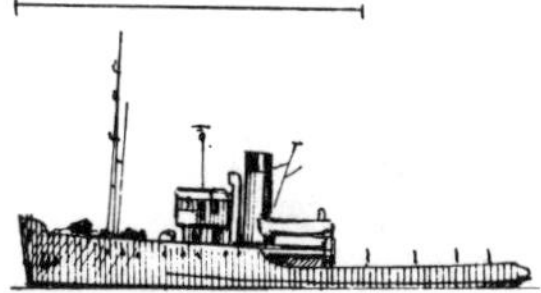

**1332.** Fr. **BELIER.** *A719.* 900 tons. Tug. 12 knots.
**PACHYDERME.** *A718.*

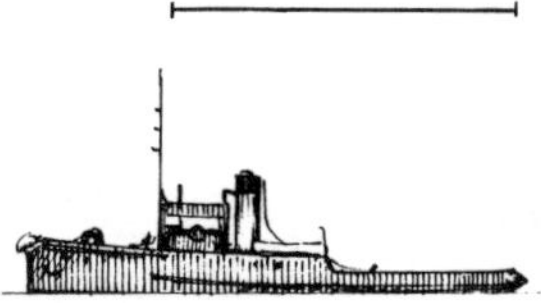

**1333.** Iq. **ALARM.** 1919. Tug. 570 tons. 135 x 20 x 15. (41.1 x 6.1 x 4.5). Reciprocating. 12 knots. Former British "Saint" class.

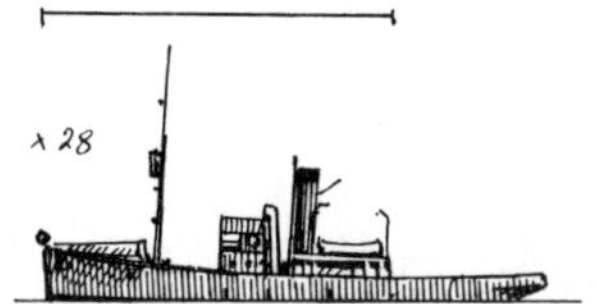

**1334** Sp. **RA3.** Tug. 800 tons. 137 x 33 x 16. (41.7 x 10 x 4.8). Reciprocating. 10 knots.

**1334.** Ge. **EISBAR.** *A1402.* 1961. Tug and Icebreaker. 600 tons. 125 x 31 x 8. (38.1 x 9.4 x 2.4). 2 screws; diesels. 13 knots. 1—40-m.m. A.A. gun.
**EISVOGEL.** *A1401.*

**1335.** Do. **ISABELA.** *20.* Tug. 40 tons. 65 x 14 x 9. (19.8 x 4.2 x 2.7). Diesels. 8 knots.

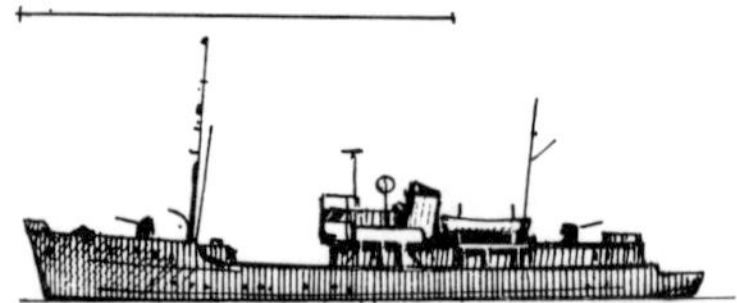

**1336.** Ge. **EIDER.** *A50.* 1942. Trawler type Training Vessel and Tender. 500 tons. 177 x 28 x 14. (53.9 x 8.5 x 4.2). Reciprocating .12 knots. 1—40-m.m. A.A. gun. 1—20-m.m. A.A. gun. Former British "Isles" class trawler.
**TRAVE.** *A51.* (Slightly different in appearance.)

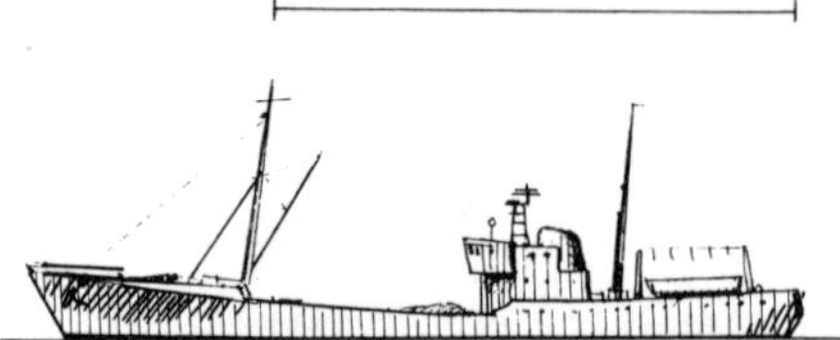

**1337.** Fr. **L'ESPERANCE.** Ex-Trawler type Survey Ship. 1962. 800 tons. Diesels. 15 knots. 208 x 33. (63.3 x 10).
Sister ship: Name not known. Former merchant ships—Polish built.

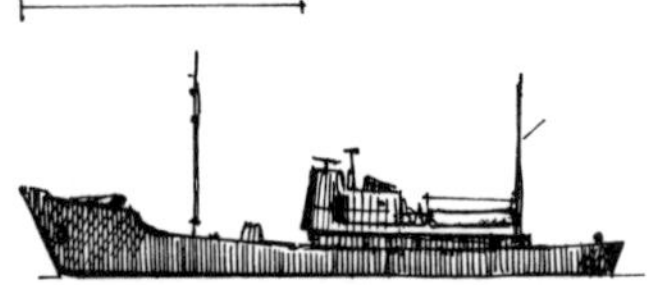

**1338.** Sp. **CENTINELA.** 1953. Fishery Protection Vessel. 250 tons. 118 x 23 x 10. (35.9 x 7 x 3). Diesel. 12 knots. 2—27-m.m. guns.
**SERVIOLA.**

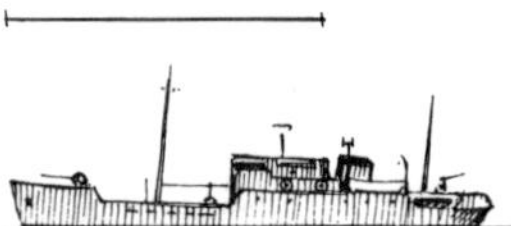

**1339.** Fi. **TURSAS.** 1933. Coast Guard Patrol Vessel. 400 tons. 131 x 24 x 14. (39.9 x 7.3 x 4.2). Diesel. 12 knots. 1—3-inch gun. 1—40-m.m. A.A. gun, 2—20-m.m. A.A. guns.

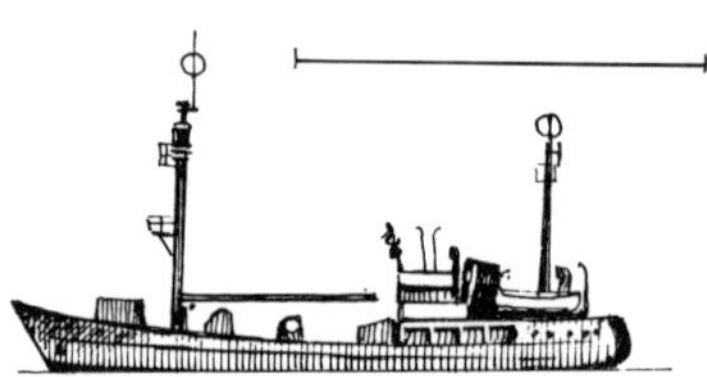

★ **1340.** Ru. **LENTRA** class. Intelligence Trawlers. 700 tons (gross, approx.). 165 feet long (approx.).

★ **1341.** Ru. Typical Soviet Trawler type of which there are large numbers in the fishing fleets. Drawing is similar to "Mayak" class.

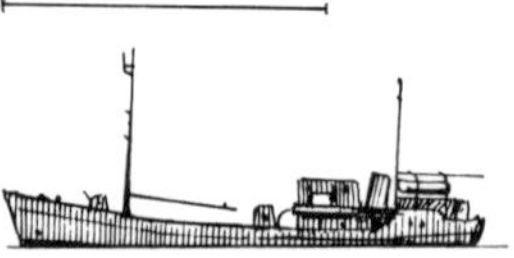

★ **1342.** EG. **JOHANN L. KRUGER.** 1951. Trawler type Survey Vessel. 500 tons. 128 x 24 x 11. (39 x 7.3 x 3.3). Diesel. 10 knots.
**HELMUT JUST.** Probably employed in intelligence survey as are a number of similar vessels in the navy.

**1343.** Sw. **ORUST** class. 1958-64. Inshore Minesweepers. Fishing cutter type. 140 tons. 76 x 21 x 5. (23.1 x 6.4 x 1.4). Diesels. 9 knots. 1—40-m.m. A.A. gun.
**BLACKAN.** *M44,* **DAMMAN.** *M45,* **GALTEN.** *M46,* **GILLOGA.** *M47,* **HISINGEN.** *M43,* **RODLOGA.** *M48,* **SVARTLOGA.** *M49.*
2 others of this class are shown in No. 1348.

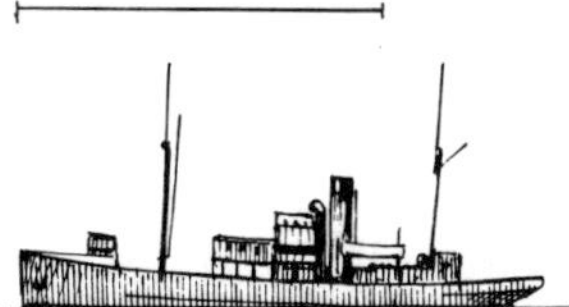

**1344.** Sp. **ARCILA.** 1918. Trawler/Patrol Vessel. 460 tons. 149 x 24 x 15. (45.4 x 7.3 x 4.5). Reciprocating. 10 knots. 2—3-inch guns. Ex-British "Mersey" type. Rated as oceanographic ship.
**XAUEN.** 1—3-inch gun. 1—47-m.m. A.A. gun.

**1345.** Gr. **HERMES.** *A324*. 1941. Trawler type Minesweeper Depot Ship. 550 tons. 133 x 28 x 11. (40.5 x 8.5 x 3.3). Diesel. 11 knots. Former British type.

**1346.** Br. **FRESH** class. Water Carriers. 600 tons. 126 x 26 x 11. (38.4 x 7.9 x 3.3). Reciprocating. 9 knots.
Some were converted to oil fuel 1961. Ships vary slightly in appearance.
**FRESHBURN, FRESHENER, FRESHLAKE, FRESHMERE, FRESHPOND, FRESHPOOL, FRESHSPRING.**

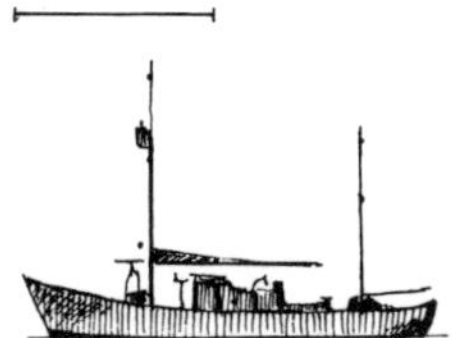

**1347.** Da. **TEJSTEN.** *Y383*. 1951. Patrol Craft/Fishing Vessel type. 130 tons. 82 x 21 x 9. (24.9 x 6.4 x 2.7). Diesel. 9 knots. 1—37-m.m. gun. Greenland waters. .

**1348.** Sw. **ORUST** class. 1948. Inshore Minesweepers; fishing craft type. 110 tons. 62 x 20 x 5. (18.9 x 6.1 x 1.5). Diesels. 9 knots. 1—20-m.m. A.A. gun.
**ORUST.** *M41*, **TJORN.** *M42*. Others in the class, see No. 1343.

**1349.** Da. **ALHOLM** class. 1945. Patrol Vessels. 70 tons. 69 x 17 x 9. (21 x 5.1 x 2.7). Diesel. 10 knots. 1—20-m.m. A.A. gun.
**ALHOLM.** *Y369*, **BIRKHOLM.** *Y370*, **ERTHOLM.** *Y371*.

**1350.** Ca. **PORTE** class. 1952. Gate Vessels; trawler type. 430 tons (full). 126 x 26 x 13. (38.4 x 7.9 x 3.9). Diesel/electric. 11 knots. 1—40-m.m. A.A. gun.
**PORTE DAUPHINE.** *186*, **PORTE DE LA REINE.** *184*, **PORTE QUEBEC.** *185*, **PORTE ST. JEAN.** *180*, **PORTE ST. LOUIS.** *183*.

**1351.** Da. **FYRHOLM** class. 1944-45. Patrol
Vessels. 70 tons. 66 x 17 x 8. (20.1 x 5.1 x 2.4).
Diesel. 9 knots.
**FYRHOLM.** *Y372,* **LINDHOLM.** *Y374.*

**1352.** Po. **ALMIRANTE SCHULTZ.** *A521.*
1929. Lighthouse Tender. 540 tons. 131 x 31 x
11. (39.9 x 9.4 x 3.3). 2 screws; diesels. 9 knots.
Unique stem.

# Hovercraft or Cushion Craft

These are likely to have an important role in future naval operations.

To date most of the military operators have only been evaluating them although the United States has used them operationally in Vietnam and in particular they have many ideas for a possible future development, principally for assault landing craft and fast patrol or anti-submarine craft.

The principal military organisations testing hovercraft in the United Kingdom are the *Interservice Hovercraft Trials Unit* (IHTU) and the *Royal Naval Hovercraft Unit* (RNHU).

In addition to the two British types illustrated below the *Saunders-Roe Mountbatten* Class SR 4 has also been considered as an assault landing craft.

The drawings are to a scale of 25 feet to 1 inch; lengths are overall and tonnage, the normal gross tons.

1 **British Hovercraft Corporation. BH7.** Fast attack craft. 40 tons. 76ft 7in long. 60 knots top speed. The first of two prototypes was completed for the Royal Navy as a fast patrol boat. It has a medium gun foreward and can be equipped with missiles.
Particularly useful for fishery protection duties.
Two of this type have been ordered by the Iranian Navy.

2 **British Hovercraft Corporation. SR.-N6.** General purpose type. 9 tons. 48ft 5in. 60 knots top speed. One of the most favoured types, used by the IHTU, the Royal Navy and the British Army. Extremely versatile and can be employed for logistics support and medical evacuation as well as a gun ship. The RNHU carried out particularly rugged tests with this craft in the Falkland Islands in 1969. The unit also operates a larger 37 ton SR.N3 and a smaller, SR.N5. (See drawing 3).
Iran and other foreign countries are operating craft of this type.

3 **Bell. SK.5.** A licence-built version of the British SR.N5. Patrol Craft. 8½ tons. 39ft. 60 knots top speed. Called Patrol Air Cushion Vehicles (PACV) in the U.S. Navy. Employed in Vietnam. Note radar and gun position on roof of cabin.

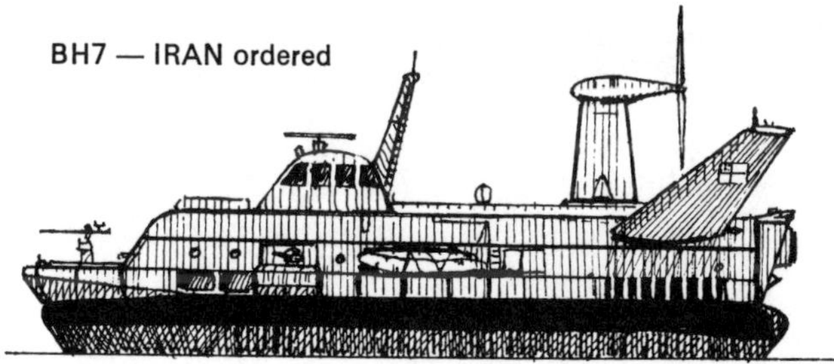

BH7 — IRAN ordered

BELL SK5  PACV  USA

SR-N6 — UK, IRAN ordered.

# Pendant Numbers

Most warships in the world are allotted a series of Flags for identification purposes. In times of peace these usually take the form of a number or numbers which are also painted prominently on some part of the ship such as on the bows, and/or quarters, across the transom or round the counter. Sometimes the markings are further aft from the bows, below the forebridge or again, and especially in aircraft carriers, on the superstructure. Submarines may have them on the fin or sail.

These numbers are usually in white, sometimes outlined or shadowed in black or occasionally, entirely in a dark colour on a light hull.

Most of the numbers are prefixed by a letter or letters known as a *Flag Superior* but this is not by any means universal and in some cases only a part of the prefix appears on the ship.

Most British Commonwealth countries and those in NATO employ a similar system, frequently self-evident, such as D for a Destroyer, F for a Frigate and so on. Again however this is not universal and sometimes the NATO number is entirely different from that displayed on the vessel.

Countries are sometimes allocated Blocks of numbers, for example, figures in an "800" block belong to the Netherlands.

Just as the designation for types of ships varies from country to country, so sometimes do the Pendant Numbers. For example while the prefix A usually denotes an auxiliary of some kind it is not always the case.

The United States and many countries friendly to it, Canada and recently Australia, employ no Flag Superior on the ship except in the case of auxiliaries and the latter may have it or part of it in *very small* letters before *very large* figures.

To make matters more difficult these and other countries repeat the same numbers in many Classes of ships. Thus the figure 3 may be the number allotted to a Destroyer, a Cruiser or any other type of ship at the same time. For this reason a knowledge of types *does* help although not foolproof.

It must be understood that Pendant Numbers may be periodically changed and if a ship is re-rated this is almost invariably the case. Sometimes this may mean that only the Flag Superior is changed but at other times it may involve both letter and figures. The Pendant Numbers given in the following list are only those which appeared *on the ships* themselves at the time of going to press.

Numbers on ships of the Communist bloc are not included as they are deliberately changed very frequently. The Flag Superior on ships may given an indication of whether she is in the Russian Black Sea or Baltic fleet but these ships are also switched very frequently and so little reliance may be placed upon them.

Submarine identification numbers appear at the end of those ships having numbers only (without flag superior).

Letter 'N' after type of vessel in a few cases indicates that she is nuclear powered.

A01 **ETHIOPIA** Training Ship. Et.
A7 **KLED KEO** Transport. Th.
A11 **MINAS GERAIS** Aircraft Carrier. Bz.
A15 **ACHIMOTA** Training Ship. Gh.
A41 **DACCA** Oiler. Pk.
A45 **AG 4** Boom Defence. Tu.
A48 **AKAR** Oiler. Tu.
(NATO Number *A 580*)
A50 **EIDER** Depot Ship. Ge.
A51 **TRAVE** Depot Ship. Ge.
A52 **OSTE** Depot Ship. Ge.
A54 **BODENSEE** Oiler. Ge.
(NATO Number *A 1406*)
A55 **LAHN** Escort and Submarine Support. Ge.
A56 **LECH** Escort and Submarine Support. Ge.
A58 **RHEIN** Escort and MTB Support. Ge.
A59 **DEUTSCHLAND** Training Ship Light Cruiser. Ge.
A62 **WESER** Escort and Support. Ge.
A63 **MAIN** Escort and Support. Ge.
A64 **RUHR** Escort and Support. Ge.
A65 **SAAR** Escort and Support. Ge.
A66 **NECKAR** Escort and Support. Ge.
A67 **MOSEL** Escort and Support. Ge.
A67 **KURTURAN** Submarine Rescue Ship. Tu.
(NATO Number *A 584*)
A68 **WERRA** Escort and Support. Ge.
A69 **DONAU** Escort and Support. Ge.
A75 **TIDESPRING** Fleet Replenishment Tanker. Br. (RFA)
A76 **TIDEPOOL** Fleet Replenishment Tanker. Br. (RFA)
A77 **PEARLEAF** Oiler. Br. (RFA)
A78 **PLUMLEAF** Oiler. Br. (RFA)
A79 **BAYLEAF** Oiler. Br. (RFA)
A80 **ORANGELEAF** Oiler. Br. (RFA)
A81 **BRAMBLELEAF** Oiler. Br. (RFA)
A82 **CHERRYLEAF** Oiler Br. (RFA)
A95 **TYPHOON** Fleet Tug. Br. (RFA)
A96 **TIDEREACH** Fleet Replenishment Tanker. Br. (RFA)
A97 **TIDEFLOW** Fleet Replenishment Tanker. Br. (RFA)
A98 **TIDESURGE** Fleet Replenishment Tanker. Br. (RFA)
A108 **TRIUMPH** Heavy Repair Ship. (Number on island superstructure)
A111 **CYCLONE** Fleet Tug. Br. (RFA)
A122 **OLWEN** Fleet Replenishment Tanker. Br. (RFA)
A123 **OLNA** Fleet Replenishment Tanker. Br. (RFA)
A124 **OLMEDA** Fleet Replenishment Tanker. Br. (RFA)
A130 **GOLD RANGER** Oiler. Br. (RFA)
A134 **RAME HEAD** Maintenance Ship. Br.
A135 **NORDENFELT** Armament Carrier. Br.
A141 **ANTIC** Fleet Tug. Br.
A157 **BLUE RANGER** Oiler. Br. (RFA)

A160 **FORT DUNVEGAN** Fleet Supply Ship. Br. (RFA)
A163 **BLACK RANGER** Oiler. Br. (RFA)
A169 **BROWN RANGER** Oiler. Br. (RFA)
A171 **ENDURANCE** Ice Patrol Ship. Br.
A184 **ENDEAVOUR** Antarctic Support Ship. NZ.
(Number on mid castle)
A186 **FORT ROSALIE** Fleet Supply Ship. (RFA)
A191 **BERRY HEAD** Maintenance Ship. Br. (RFA)
A194 **TYNE** Destroyer Depot. Br.
A201 **MARIEHOLM** Staff Ship. Sw.
A204 **ROBERT DUNDAS** Stores Carrier. Br. (RFA)
A206 **PATRICIA** Submarine Depot Ship. Sw.
(May *not* be on ship)
A207 **WAVE PRINCE** oiler. Br. (RFA)
A211 **WAVE SOVEREIGN** Oiler. Br. (RFA)
(May *not* be on ship)
A211 **BELOS** Salvage Vessel. Sw.
A212 **WAVE RULER** Oiler. Br. (RFA)
A216 **OLNA** Oiler. Br. (RFA)
A219 **DEWDALE** Oiler. Br. (RFA) Number amidships.
A221 **DERWENTDALE** Oiler. Br. (RFA)
A221 **FREJA** Supply Ship. Sw.
A222 **SPAPOOL** Water Carrier. Br. (RFA)
A223 **NIMBLE** Fleet Tug. Br.
A224 **SPABROOK** Water Carrier. Br. (RFA)
A226 **ELDAREN** Oiler. Sw.
A227 **OLJAREN** Oiler. Sw.
A231 **RECLAIM** Diving Tender. Br.
A231 **LOMMEN** Tender. Sw.
A232 **SPOVEN** Tender. Sw.
A236 **FALLEREN** Mine Transport. Sw.
A237 **MINOREN** Mine Transport. Sw.
A240 **BUSTLER** Fleet Tug. Br. (RFA)
A241 **ROBERT MIDDLETON** Stores Carrier. Br. (RFA)
A242 **WAVE BARON** Oiler. Br. (RFA)
A243 **TAFELBERG** Fleet Replenishment Ship. SA.
A245 **BARCOO** Survey Ship. Au.
A246 **HAGERN** Tender. Sw.
A247 **PELIKANEN** Tender. Sw.
A251 **ACHILLES** Tug. Sw.
A252 **AJAX** Tug. Sw.
A253 **HERMES** Tender. Sw.
A255 **PANJI** Auxiliary. My.
A256 **CULGOA** Minesweeper Depot. Au.
A256 **SIGRUN** Tender. Sw.
A257 **SPABURN** Water Carrier. Br. (RFA)
A260 **SPALAKE** Water Carrier. Br. (RFA)
A261 **EDDYFIRTH** Oiler. Br. (RFA).

A262 **HARTLAND POINT** Maintenance Ship. Br.
A264 **REWARD** Fleet Tug. Br. (RFA)
A265 **WAVE CHIEF.** Oiler. Br. (RFA)
A266 **DIAMANTINA** Survey Vessel. Au.
A268 **GREEN ROVER** Oiler. Br. (RFA)
A269 **GREY ROVER** Oiler. (RFA)
A270 **BLUE ROVER** Oiler. Br. (RFA)
A276 **GASCOYNE** Survey Vessel. Au.
A280 **RESURGENT** Fleet Replenishment Ship. Br. (RFA)
A284 **ROWANOL** Oiler. Br. (RFA)
A288 **SEA GIANT** Fleet Tug. Br.
A289 **CONFIANCE** Fleet Tug. Br.
A290 **CONFIDENT** Fleet Tug. Br.
A293 **CAREFUL** Fleet Tug. Br.
A298 **ATTOCK** Oiler. Pk.
A307 **THETIS** Boom Defence. Gr.
A316 **FORT SANDUSKY** Fleet Supply Ship. Br. (RFA)
A324 **HERMES** Minesweeper Depot. Gr.
A329 **RETAINER** Fleet Replenishment Ship. Br. (RFA)
A329 **SAKIPIS** Repair Ship. Gr.
A339 **LYNESS** Stores Support Ship. Br. (RFA)
A344 **STROMNESS** Stores Replenishment Ship. Br. (RFA)
A345 **TARBATNESS** Stores Support Ship. Br. (RFA)
A345 **SIRIOS** Oiler. Gr.
A354 **‘WHITEHEAD** Torpedo Trials Vessel. Br.
A372 **ZEUS** Oiler. Gr.
A373 **KRONOS** Oiler. Gr.
A374 **PROMETHEUS** Oiler. Gr.
A376 **ORION** Oiler. Gr.
A377 **MAXIM** Armament Carrier. Br.
A377 **ARETHOUSA** Oiler. Gr.
A378 **KINTERBURY** Armament Carrier. Br.
A379 **ENCORE** Fleet Tug. Br.
A384 **SOTIR** Salvage Vessel. Gr.
A390 **SAMSON** Fleet Tug. Br.
A404 **BACCHUS** Store Carrier. Br. (RFA)
A406 **HEBE** Supply Ship. Br. (RFA)
A410 **ATROMITOS** Fleet Tug. Gr.
A411 **ADAMASTOS** Fleet Tug. Gr.
A471 **VIVIIS** Oiler. Gr.
A480 **RESOURCE** Fleet Replenishment Tanker. Br. (RFA)
A481 **ST. LYKOUDIS** Lighthouse Tender. Gr.
A485 **SKYROS** Lighthouse Tender. Gr.
A486 **REGENT** Fleet Replenishment Ship. Br. (RFA)
A487 **SERRAM** Lighthouse Tender. Gr.
A489 **MOORHEN** Boom Defence. Br.
A491 **MOORLAND** Boom Defence. Br.
A508 **CAPABLE** Fleet Tug. Br.
A510 **LOYAL GOVERNOR** Tender. Br.
A512 **ODIN** Repair Ship. Ge.

*A513*  **WOTAN** Repair Ship. Ge.
*A520*  **SAGRES** Sail Training Ship. Po.
*A523*  **SAM BRAS** Oiler. Po.
*A524*  **CARVALHO ARAUJO** Survey Ship. Po.
*A525*  **ALMIRANTE LACERDA** Survey Ship. Po.
*A526*  **AFONSO DU ALBUQUERQUE** Survey Ship. Po.
*A528*  **PEDRO NUNEZ** Survey Ship. Po.
*A530*  **HORTEN** Depot Ship. No.
*A535*  **VALKYRIEN** Depot Ship. No.
*A537*  **HAAKON VII** Depot Ship. No.
*A541*  **FREJA** Survey Ship. Da.
*A542*  **HENRIK GERNER** Depot Ship. Da.
*A543*  **BALDER** Landing Craft. Da.
*A544*  **BRAGE** Landing Craft. Da.
*A545*  **HERMOD** Landing Craft. Da.
*A546*  **LOKE** Landing Craft. Da.
*A554*  **HOLLAENDERDYBET** Tender. Da.
*A555*  **KONGEDYBET** Tender. Da.
*A560*  **AEGIR** Depot Ship. Da.
*A561*  **ODIN** Landing Craft. Da.
*A562*  **THOR** Landing Craft. Da.
*A563*  **HJAELPEREN** Depot Ship. Da.
*A564*  **TYR** Landing Craft. Da.
*A565*  **ULLER** Landing Craft. Da.
*A566*  **VALE** Landing Craft. Da.
*A567*  **VIDAR** Landing Craft. Da.
*A568*  **RIMFAXE** Oiler. Da.
*A569*  **SKINFAXE** Oiler. Da.
*A570*  **ISIN** Tender. Tu.
*A572*  **ALBAY HAKKI BURAK** Oiler. Tu.
*A573*  **GOLCUK** Oiler. Tu
*A574*  **AKPINAR** Oiler. Tu.
*A580*  **AKAR** Oiler. Tu.
*A581*  **ONARAN** Repair Ship. Tu.
*A582*  **BASARAN** Repair Ship. Tu.
*A584*  **KURTARAN** Submarine Rescue Ship. Tu.
*A586*  **YUZBASI TOLUNAY** Oiler. Tu.
*A592*  **EREGLI** Escort Minesweeper. Tu.
*A595*  **CESME** Escort Minesweeper. Tu.
*A596*  **CARADAK** Escort Minesweeper. Tu.
*A598*  **EDINCIK** Escort Minesweeper. Tu.
*A603*  **HENRI POINCARE** Tracking ship. Fr.
*A607*  **ARAGO** Experimental Ship. Fr.
*A608*  **MOSELLE** Maintenance Ship. Fr.
*A610*  **ILE d'OLERON** Experimental Guided Missile Ship. Fr.
*A611*  **MAINE** Maintenance Ship. Fr.
*A612*  **MEDOC** Maintenance Ship. Fr.
*A613*  **MORVAN** Maintenance Ship. Fr.
*A614*  **FALLERON** Transport. Fr.
*A615*  **LA LOIRE** Maintenance Ship. Fr.
*A617*  **LA GARRONNE** Maintenance Ship. Fr.
*A618*  **LA RANCE** Maintenance Ship. Fr.

*A619*  **ABER-WRAC'H** Oiler. Fr.
*A620*  **ACHERON** Ammunition Ship. Fr.
*A621*  **LE RHIN** Maintenance Ship. Fr.
*A622*  **LA RHONE** Maintenance Ship. Fr.
*A625*  **LA BAISE** Oiler. Fr.
*A626*  **LA CHARENTE** Oiler. Fr.
*A627*  **LA SEINE** Oiler. Fr.
*A628*  **LA SAONE** Oiler. Fr.
*A629*  **LAC CHAMBON** Oiler. Fr.
*A630*  **LAC TONLE-SAP** Oiler. Fr.
*A631*  **LAC TCHAD** Oiler. Fr.
*A633*  **DUPERRE** Destroyer. Experimental Ship. Fr.
*A634*  **VERDON** Transport. Fr.
*A635*  **RUMMEL** Water Carrier. Fr.
*A637*  **MAURIENNE** Maintenance Ship. Fr.
*A638*  **SAHEL** Water Carrier. Fr.
*A641*  **GUSTAVE ZEDE** Command Ship. Fr.
*A643*  **AUNIS** Transport. Fr.
*A644*  **BERRY** Transport. Fr.
*A645*  **ANJOU** Transport. Fr.
*A646*  **TRITON** Diving Tender. Fr.
*A647*  **INGENIEUR ELIE MONNIER** Diving Tender. Fr.
*A649*  **L'ETOILE** Sail Training Ship. Fr.
*A650*  **LA BELLE POULE** Sail Training Ship.
*A652*  **MUTIN** Tender. Fr.
*A666*  **ELEPHANT** Tug. Fr.
*A667*  **HERCULE** Fleet Tug. Fr.
*A668*  **RHINOCEROS** Fleet Tug. Fr.
*A669*  **TENACE** Tug. Fr.
*A670*  **IMPLACABLE** Fleet Tug. Fr.
*A675*  **ISERE** Oiler. Fr.
*A778*  **LA COQUILLE** Survey Ship. Fr.
*A682*  **ALIDADE** Survey Ship. Fr.
*A684*  **COOLIE.** Fr.
*A685*  **ROBUSTE** Tug. Fr.
*A686*  **ACTIF** Tug. Fr.
*A687*  **LABORIEUX** Tug. Fr.
*A688*  **VALEUREUX** Tug. Fr.
*A692*  **TRAVEILLEUR** Tug. Fr.
*A700*  **BUFFLE** Tug. Fr.
*A702*  **UTILE** Tug. Fr.
*A706*  **COURAGEUX** Tug. Fr.
*A709*  **MALABAR** Tug. Fr.
*A718*  **PACHYDERME** Tug. Fr.
*A719*  **BELIER** Tug. Fr.
*A727*  **ARAIGNEE** Boom defence. Fr.
*A728*  **SCORPION** Boom Defence. Fr.
*A729*  **TARENTULE** Boom Defence. Fr.
*A731*  **PERSISTANTE** Boom Defence. Fr.
*A733*  **SAINTONGE** Oiler. Fr.
*A735*  **GUYENNE** Oiler. Fr.
*A737*  **PATIENTE** Boom Defence. Fr.
*A740*  **MANAP** Water Carrier. Fr.
*A750*  **LIAMONE** Water Carrier. Fr.
*A751*  **OASIS** Water Carrier. Fr.
*A755*  **COMMANDANT ROBERT GIRAUD** Survey Ship. Fr.
*A756*  **L'ESPERANCE** Survey Ship. Fr.
*A757*  **OCEANOGRAPHER D'ENTRECASTEAUX** Survey Ship. Fr.
*A758*  **LA RECHERCHE** Survey Ship. Fr.

*A759*  **MARCEL LE BIHAN** Boom Defence. Fr.
*A760*  **CIGALE** Boom Defence. Fr.
*A761*  **CRIQUET** Boom Defence. Fr.
*A762*  **FOURMI** Boom Defence. Fr.
*A763*  **GRILLON** Boom Defence. Fr.
*A764*  **SCARABEE** Boom Defence. Fr.
*A771*  **TARN** Transport. Fr.
*A780*  **ASTROLABE** Survey Ship. Fr.
*A781*  **BOUSSOLE** Survey Ship. Fr.
*A790*  **ENCLUME** Rhine Patrol Boat. Fr.
*A793*  **AMIRAL EXELMANS** Rhine Patrol Boat. Fr.
*A828*  **HERCULES** Tug. Du.
*A829*  **MERCUR** Tender. Du.
*A830*  **PELIKAAN** Supply Ship. Du.
*A832*  **WOENDI** Supply Ship. Du.
*A835*  **POOLSTER** Supply Ship. Du.
*A843*  **ARGUS** Diving Vessel. Du.
*A848*  **TRITON** Diving Vessel. Du.
*A849*  **NAUTILUS** Diving Vessel. Du.
*A850*  **HYDRA** Diving Vessel. Du.
*A854*  **ONVERSAAGD** Escort. Du.
*A855*  **ONBEVREESD** Escort. Du.
*A856*  **ONVERSCHROKKEN** Escort. Du.
*A857*  **ONVERMOEID** Escort. Du.
*A858*  **ONVERVAARD** Escort. Du.
*A859*  **ONVERDROTEN** Escort. Du.
*A870*  **WAMANDAI** Tug. Du.
*A871*  **WAMBRAU** Tug. Du.
*A872*  **WESTGAT** Tug. Du.
*A873*  **WIELINGEN** Tug. Du.
*A877*  Accommodation Ship. Du.
*A878*  **TROMP** Accommodation Ship. Du.
*A879*  **JACOB VAN HEEMSKERK** Accommodation Ship. Du.
*A880*  **WILLIAM VAN DER ZAAN** Accommodation Ship. Du.
*A881*  **NEPTUNUS** Accommodation Ship. Du.
*A882*  **SCHORPIOEN** Accommodation Ship. Du.
*A884*  **BUFFEL** Accommodation Ship. Du.
*A886*  **CORNELIS DREBBEL** Accommodation Ship. Du.
*A887*  **HAARLEMMERMEER** Accommodation Ship. Du.
*A888*  **HERTOG HENDRIK** Accommodation Ship. Du.
*A891*  **SOEMBA** Accommodation Ship. Du.
*A895*  **CERBERUS** Diving Tender. Du.
*A902*  **LUYMES** Survey Ship. Du.
*A903*  **ZEEFAKKEL** Survey Ship. Du.
*A907*  **SNELLIUS** Survey Ship. Du.
*A909*  **DREG I** Survey Ship. Du.
*A910*  **DREG II** Survey Ship. Du.
*A919*  **DREG III** Survey Ship. Du.
*A920*  **DREG IV** Survey Ship. Du.
*A923*  **VAN BOCHOVE** Tender. Du.
*A950*  **SUB-LIEUTENANT VALCKE** Fleet Tug. Be.
*A954*  **ADRIEN DE GERLACHE** Fleet Tug. Be.
*A958*  **ZENOBE GRAMME** Research Ship. Be.
*A960*  **GODETIA** Escort Support. Be.
*A961*  **ZINNIA** Escort Support. Be.

A962 **MECHELEN** Research Ship. Be.

A1400 **SCHWARZWALD** Supply Ship. Ge.

A1401 **EISVOGEL** Tug. Ge.

A1402 **EISBAR** Tug. Ge.

A1406 **BODENSEE** Oiler. Ge.

A1407 **WITTENSEE** Oiler. Ge.

A1407 **ANGELN** Support Ship. Ge.

A1409 **DITHMARSCHEN** Supply Ship. Ge.

A1411 **LUNEBURG** Supply Ship. Ge.

A1412 **COBURG** Supply Ship. Ge.

A1413 **FREIBURG** Supply Ship. Ge.

A1414 **GLUCKSBURG** Supply Ship. Ge.

A1415 **SAARBURG** Supply Ship. Ge.

A1416 **NIENBURG** Supply Ship. Ge.

A1417 **OFFENBURG** Supply Ship. Ge.

A1424 **WALCHENSEE** Oiler. Ge.

A1425 **AMMERSEE** Oiler. Ge.

A1426 **TEGERNSEE** Oiler. Ge.

A1427 **WESTERNSEE** Oiler. Ge.

A1428 **MARZ** Oiler. Ge.

A1429 **EIFEL** Oiler. Ge.

A1435 **WESTERWALD** Supply Ship. Ge.

A1436 **ODENWALD** Supply Ship. Ge.

A1437 **SACHSENWALD** Mine transport. Ge.

A1438 **STEIGERWALD** Mine transport. Ge.

A1457 **HELGOLAND** Salvage Tug. Ge.

A1458 **FEHMARN** Salvage Tug. Ge.

A5205 **DIO** Auxiliary Gun Boat. Po.

A5206 **S.GABRIEL** Oiler. Po.

A5207 **SANTO ANDRE** Depot Ship. Po.

A5208 **S.CRISTAVAO** Depot Ship. Po.

A5214 **S.RAFAEL** Diving Tender. Po.

A5301 **PIETRO CAVEZZALE** Support Ship. It.

A5302 **QUARTO** Landing Ship. It.

A5304 **ALICUDI** Netlayer. It.

A5305 **FILICUDI** Netlayer. It.

A5306 **ANTEO** Transport. It.

A5308 **GAZZELLA** Training Ship. It.

A5309 **RAMPINO** Lighthouse Tender. It.

A5310 **PROTEO** Rescue and Salvage Ship. It.

A5317 **ATLANTE** Tug. It.

A5318 **ATLETA** Tug. It.

A5319 **CICLOPE** Tug. It.

A5320 **TITANO** Tug. It. (Or **COLOSSO**, tug)

A5321 **FORTE** Tug. It.

A5322 **GAGLIARDO** Tug. It.

A5323 **ROBUSTO** Tug. It.

A5324 **TENACE** Tug. It.

A5327 **BUFFOLUTO** Lighthouse Tender. It.

A5328 **ETNA** Transport. It.

A5329 **STROMBOLI** Transport. It.

A5330 **VESUVIO** Transport. It. Helicopter ship.

A5365 **PO** Water Carrier. It.

A5366 **VOLTURNO** Water Carrier. It.

A5327 **DALMAZIA** Oiler. It.

A5368 **STEROPE** Oiler. It. (Number on mid-castle)

A5369 **ADIGE** Water Carrier. It.

A5370 **ARNO** Water Carrier. It.

A5371 **FLEGETONTE** Water Carrier. It.

A5372 **ISONZO** Water Carrier. It.

A5373 **METAURO** Water Carrier. It.

A5374 **MINCIO** Water Carrier. It.

A5375 **SESIA** Water Carrier. It.

A5376 **TICINO** Water Carrier. It.

A5377 **TANARO** Water Carrier. It.

AG1 Boom Defence Vessel. Tu.*

AG2 Boom Defence Vessel. Tu.*

AG3 Boom Defence Vessel. Tu.*

AG4 Boom Defence Vessel. Tu.*

AG5 Boom Defence Vessel. Tu.*

*May have numbers with letter "P" on the bows.

AG39 (YAG39) **GEORGE EASTMAN** Research Ship. Am.

AG40 (YAG40) **GRANVILLE S. HALL** Research Ship. Am.

AGS1 **CARSAMBA** Escort Minesweeper. Tu.

AGS2 **CANDARLI** Escort Minesweeper. Tu.

AGS25 **KELLAR** Survey Ship. Am.

AGS26 **SILAS BENT** Survey Ship. Am.

AGS27 **KANE** Survey Ship. Am.

AGS31 **S. P. LEE** Survey Ship. Am.

AGS33 **WILKES** Survey Ship. Am.

AGS34 **WYMAN** Survey Ship. Am.

AGS64 **YELCHO** Survey Ship. Am.

AKA41 **PRESIDENTE PINTO** Attack Transport. Ch.

AKL8 **SICHANG** Transport. Th.

AKL31 Light Cargo Ship. Am.

AN01 **GENERAL RAFAEL REYES** Coastguard Vessel. Co.

AN02 **GENERAL VASQUES** Coastguard Vessel. Co.

AN203 **OLAYA HERRERA** Coastguard Vessel. Co.

AN204 **PEDRO GUAL** Coastguard Vessel. Co.

AN205 **ESTEBAN JARAMILLO** Coastguard Vessel. Co.

AN206 **CARLOS E. RESTREPO** Coastguard Vessel. Co.

AO1 **ATAHUALPA** Water Carrier. Ec.

AO2 **CHULA** Oiler. Th.

AO3 **MATRA** Oiler. Th.

AO9 **PRESIDENTE ORIBE** Oiler. Ur.

AO52 **ALMIRANTE JORGE MONTT** Oiler. Ch.

AO53 **ARAUCANO** Oiler. Ch.

AO195 **SUPPLY** Fleet Replenishment Oiler. Au.

AOC50 **DUNDALK** Oiler. Ca.

AOC502 **DUNDURN** Oiler. Ca.

AP45 **PILOTO PARDO** Antarctic Patrol Ship. Ch.

AP47 **AQUILES** Transport. Ch.

AP48 **ANGAMOS** Transport. Ch.

ARB9 **ULYSSES** Repair Ship. Am.

ARB11 **DIOMEDES** Repair Ship. Am.

ARC5 **YAMACRAW** Cable Repair Ship. Am.

AS31 **HUNLEY** Submarine Tender. Am.

AS32 **HOLLAND** Submarine Tender. Am.

ASV92 **FERREL** Coastguard Survey Vessel. Am.

ATA71 **CABRALES** Tug. Ch.

ATA73 **COLOCOLO** Tug. Ch.

ATA527 **HEATHERTON** Tug. Ca.

ATA528 **RIVERTON** Tug. Ca.

ATA529 **CLIFTON** Tug. Ca.

ATA531 **SAINT ANTHONY** Tug. Ca.

ATA533 **SAINT CHARLES** Tug. Ca.

ATA535 **SAINT JOHN** Tug. Ca.

AV7 **CURRITUCK** Seaplane Tender. Am.

AV10 **CHANDELEUR** Seaplane Tender. Am.

AV12 **PINE ISLAND** Seaplane Tender. Am.

AV13 **SALISBURY SOUND** Seaplane Tender. Am.

B1 **DURANGO** Frigate. Me.

B3 **CALIFORNIA** Frigate. Me.

B4 **PAPALOAPAN** Frigate. Me.

B5 **TEHUANTEPEC** Frigate. Me.

B6 **USUMACINTA** Frigate. Me.

B7 **SAN JULIAN** Frigate. Me.

B10 **LA PATAIA** Frigate. Me.

B12 **PUNTA ALTA** Oiler. Ar.

B16 **PUNTA DELGADA** Oiler. Ar.

B18 **PUNTA MEDANOS** Oiler. Ar.

B20 **PUNTA RASA** Oiler. Ar.

BDC1 **TRIEUX** Landing Ship. Fr.

BDC2 **ARGENS** Landing Ship. Fr.

BDC3 **BLAVET** Landing Ship. Fr.

BDC4 **DIVES** Landing Ship. Fr.

BDC5 **BIDASSOA** Landing Ship. Fr.

BDM454 **SEPARACION** Patrol Vessel. Do.

BDM455 **TORTUGUERO** Patrol Vessel. Do.

BDT1 **CABO SAN BARTOLOME** Tank Landing Craft. Ar.

BDT4 **CABO SAN GONZALO** Tank Landing Craft. Ar.

BDT6 **CABO SAN ISIDRO** Tank Landing Craft. Ar.

BDT10 **CABO SAN PIO** Tank Landing Craft. Ar.

BDT14 **CABO SAN VICENTE** Tank Landing Craft. Ar.

BE43 **ESMERALDA** Sail Training Ship. Ch.

BG2 **BG2** Coastal Patrol Boat. Ge.

BP01 **PLUTON** Oiler. Sp.

BS1 Frogman Base. Sp.

BT4 **CAPITAN W. ARVELO** Oiler. Do.

BT5 **CAPITAN BEOTEGUI** Oiler. Do.

BT63 **SANCHO JIMENO** Oiler. Co.

BT64 **ANTONIO DE AREVALO** Oiler. Co.

C7 **GUANAJUATO** Frigate. Me.

C8 **QUERETARO** Frigate. Me.

C9 **POTOSI** Frigate. Me.

C11 **BARROSO** Cruiser. Bz.

C12 **TAMANDARE** Cruiser. Bz.

C20 **TIGER** Cruiser. Br.

*C21* **CANARIAS** Cruiser. Sp.
*C34* **LION** Cruiser. Br.
*C99* **BLAKE** Cruiser, Helicopter Carrier. Br.
*C551* **GIUSEPPE GARIBALDI** Cruiser. It.
*C610* **DE GRASSE** Cruiser. Fr.
*C611* **COLBERT** Cruiser. Fr.
*C801* **DE RUYTER** Cruiser. Du.
*C802* **DE ZEVEN PROVINCIEN** Cruiser. Du.
*CC7, CC11, CC12, 16, 17, 19, 20—* See *GC7* etc.
*CF01* Salvage Craft. Ja.
*CF02* Salvage Craft. Ja.
*CF03* Salvage Craft. Ja.
*CF04* Salvage Craft. Ja.
*CF05* Salvage Craft. Ja.
*CF06* Salvage Craft. Ja.
*CF07* Salvage Craft. Ja.
*CG1* **TRINIDAD** Coast Guard and Patrol Craft. Tr.
*CG2* **COURLAND BAY** Coast Guard and Patrol Craft. Tr.
*CG4* **SEA SCOUT** Coast Guard and Patrol Craft. Tr.
*CG82301* **POINT CAUTION** Coast Guard Patrol Vessel. Am.
*CG82302* **POINT HOPE** Coast Guard Patrol Vessel. Am.
*CG82303* **POINT YOUNG** Coast Guard Patrol Vessel. Am.
*CG82304* **POINT LEAGUE** Coast Guard Patrol Vessel. Am.
*CG82305* **POINT PARTRIDGE** Coast Guard Patrol Vessel. Am.
*CG82306* **POINT JEFFERSON** Coast Guard Patrol Vessel. Am.
*CG82307* **POINT GLOVER** Coast Guard Patrol Vessel. Am.
*CG82308* **POINT WHITE** Coast Guard Patrol Vessel. Am.
*CG82309* **POINT ARDEN** Coast Guard Patrol Vessel. Am.
*CG82310* **POINT GARNET** Coast Guard Patrol Vessel. Am.
*CG82311* **POINT VERDE** Coast Guard Patrol Vessel. Am.
*CG82312* **POINT SWIFT** Coast Guard Patrol Vessel. Am.
*CG82313* **POINT SLOCUM** Coast Guard Patrol Vessel. Am.
*CG82314* **POINT THATCHER** Coast Guard Patrol Vessel. Am.
*CG82315* **POINT CLEAR** Coast Guard Patrol Vessel. Am.
*CG82316* **POINT MAST** Coast Guard Patrol Vessel. Am.
*CG82317* **POINT COMFORT** Coast Guard Patrol Vessel. Am.
*CG82318* **POINT HERRON** Coast Guard Patrol Vessel. Am.
*CG82319* **POINT ORIENT** Coast Guard Patrol Vessel. Am.
*CG82320* **POINT KENNEDY** Coast Guard Patrol Vessel. Am.
*CG82321* **POINT LOMAS** Coast Guard Patrol Vessel. Am.
*CG92322* **POINT HUDSON** Coast Guard Patrol Vessel. Am.
*CG82323* **POINT GRACE** Coast Guard Patrol Vessel. Am.

*CG82324* **POINT GREY** Coast Guard Patrol Vessel. Am.
*CG82324* **POINT LEDGE** Coast Guard Patrol Vessel. Am.
*CG82325* **POINT DUME** Coast Guard Patrol Vessel. Am.
*CG82326* **POINT CYPRESS** Coast Guard Patrol Vessel. Am.
*CG82327* **POINT BANKS** Coast Guard Patrol Vessel. Am.
*CG82328* **POINT GAMMON** Coast Guard Patrol Vessel. Am.
*CG82329* **POINT WELCOME** Coast Guard Patrol Vessel. Am.
*CG82330* **POINT ELLIS** Coast Guard Patrol Vessel. Am.
*CG82331* **POINT MORONE** Coast Guard Patrol Vessel. Am.
*CG82332* **POINT ROBERTS** Coast Guard Patrol Vessel. Am.
*CG82333* **POINT HIGHLAND** Coast Guard Patrol Vessel. Am.
*CG82335* **POINT COUNTESS** Coast Guard Patrol Vessel. Am.
*CG82336* **POINT GLASS** Coast Guard Patrol Vessel. Am.
*CG82337* **POINT DIVIDE** Coast Guard Patrol Vessel. Am.
*CG82338* **POINT BRIDGE** Coast Guard Patrol Vessel. Am.
*CG82339* **POINT CHICO** Coast Guard Patrol Vessel. Am.
*CG82340* **POINT BATAN** Coast Guard Patrol Vessel. Am.
*CG82341* **POINT LOOKOUT** Coast Guard Patrol Vessel. Am.
*CG82342* **POINT BAKER** Coast Guard Patrol Vessel. Am.
*CG82343* **POINT WELLS** Coast Guard Patrol Vessel. Am.
*CG82344* **POINT ESTERO** Coast Guard Patrol Vessel. Am.
*CG82345* **POINT JUDITH** Coast Guard Patrol Vessel. Am.
*CG82346* **POINT ARENA** Coast Guard Patrol Vessel. Am.
*CG82347* **POINT BONITA** Coast Guard Patrol Vessel. Am.
*CG82348* **POINT BARROW** Coast Guard Patrol Vessel. Am.
*CG82349* **POINT SPENCER** Coast Guard Patrol Vessel. Am.
*CG82350* **POINT FRANKLIN** Coast Guard Patrol Vessel. Am.
*CG82351* **POINT BENNETT** Coast Guard Patrol Vessel. Am.
*CG82352* **POINT SAL** Coast Guard Patrol Vessel. Am.
*CG82353·* **POINT MONROE** Coast Guard Patrol Vessel. Am.
*CG82354* **POINT EVANS** Coast Guard Patrol Vessel. Am.
*CG82355* **POINT HANNON** Coast Guard Patrol Vessel. Am.
*CG82356* **POINT FRANCIS** Coast Guard Patrol Vessel. Am.
*CG82357* **POINT HURON** Coast Guard Patrol Vessel. Am.
*CG82358* **POINT STUART** Coast Guard Patrol Vessel. Am.
*CG82359* **POINT STEELE** Coast Guard Patrol Vessel. Am.

*CG82360* **POINT WINSLOW** Coast Guard Patrol Vessel. Am.
*CG82361* **POINT CHARLES** Coast Guard Patrol Vessel. Am.
*CG82362* **POINT BROWN** Coast Guard Patrol Vessel. Am.
*CG82363* **POINT NOWELL** Coast Guard Patrol Vessel. Am.
*CG82364* **POINT WHITEHORN** Coast Guard Patrol Vessel. Am.
*CG82365* **POINT TURNER** Coast Guard Patrol Vessel. Am.
*CG82366* **POINT LOBOS** Coast Guard Patrol Vessel. Am.
*CG82367* **POINT KNOLL** Coast Guard Patrol Vessel. Am.
*CG82368* **POINT WARDE** Coast Guard Patrol Vessel. Am.
*CG82369* **POINT HEYER** Coast Guard Patrol Vessel. Am.
*CG82370* **POINT RICHMOND** Coast Guard Patrol Vessel. Am.
*CG95300* **CAPE SMALL** Coast Guard Patrol Vessel. Am.
*CG95301* **CAPE CORAL** Coast Guard Patrol Vessel. Am.
*CG95302* **CAPE HIGGON** Coast Guard Patrol Vessel. Am.
*CG95303* **CAPE UPWRIGHT** Coast Guard Patrol Vessel. Am.
*CG95304* **CAPE GULL** Coast Guard Patrol Vessel. Am.
*CG95305* **CAPE HATTERAS** Coast Guard Patrol Vessel. Am.
*CG95306* **CAPE GEORGE** Coast Guard Patrol Vessel. Am.
*CG95307* **CAPE CURRENT** Coast Guard Patrol Vessel. Am.
*CG95308* **CAPE STRAIT** Coast Guard Patrol Vessel. Am.
*CG95309* **CAPE CARTER** Coast Guard Patrol Vessel. Am.
*CG95310* **CAPE WASH** Coast Guard Patrol Vessel. Am.
*CG95311* **CAPE HEDGE** Coast Guard Patrol Vessel. Am.
*CG95312* **CAPE KNOX** Coast Guard Patrol Vessel. Am.
*CG95313* **CAPE MORGAN** Coast Guard Patrol Vessel. Am.
*CG95314* **CAPE FAIRWEATHER** Coast Guard Patrol Vessel. Am.
*CG95316* **CAPE FOX** Coast Guard Patrol Vessel. Am.
*CG95317* **CAPE JELLISON** Coast Guard Patrol Vessel. Am.
*CG95318* **CAPE NEWAGEN** Coast Guard Patrol Vessel. Am.
*CG95319* **CAPE ROMAIN** Coast Guard Patrol Vessel. Am.
*CG95320* **CAPE STARR** Coast Guard Patrol Vessel. Am.
*CG95321* **CAPE CROSS** Coast Guard Patrol Vessel. Am.
*CG95322* **CAPE HORN** Coast Guard Patrol Vessel. Am.
*CG95323* **CAPE DARBY** Coast Guard Patrol Vessel. Am.
*CG95324* **CAPE SHOALWATER** Coast Guard Patrol Vessel. Am.
*CG95325* **CAPE FLORIDA** Coast Guard Patrol Vessel. Am.

*CG95326* **CAPE CORWIN** Coast Guard Patrol Vessel. Am.
*CG95327* **CAPE PORPOISE** Coast Guard Patrol Vessel. Am.
*CG95328* **CAPE HENLOPEN** Coast Guard Patrol Vessel. Am.
*CG95329* **CAPE KIWANDA** Coast Guard Patrol Vessel. Am.
*CG95332* **CAPE YORK** Coast Guard Patrol Vessel. Am.
*CL01* **HARUSAME** Coast Patrol Boat. Ja.
*CL02* **MURASAME** Coastal Patrol Boat. Ja.
*CL03* **SOYOKAZE** Coastal Patrol Boat. Ja.
*CL04* **SAWAKAZE** Coastal Patrol Boat. Ja.
*CL05* **OKIKAZE** Coastal Patrol Boat. Ja.
*CL06* **YAMAKAZE** Coastal Patrol Boat. Ja.
*CL07* **MINEKAZE** Coastal Patrol Boat. Ja.
*CL08* **UMIKAZE** Coastal Patrol Boat. Ja.
*CL09* **NOKAZE** Coastal Patrol Boat. Ja.
*CL10* **NUMAKAZE** Coastal Patrol Boat. Ja.
*CL11* **KAWAKAZE** Coastal Patrol Boat. Ja.
*CL12* **TANAKAZE** Coastal Patrol Boat. Ja.
*CL13* **FIATSUKAZE** Coastal Patrol Boat. Ja.
*CL14* **ARAKAZE** Coastal Patrol Boat. Ja.
*CL15* **HARUKAZE** Coastal Patrol Boat. Ja.
*CL16* **SACHIKAZE** Coastal Patrol Boat. Ja.
*CL17* **HATAKAZE** Coastal Patrol Boat. Ja.
*CL18* **MATSUKAZE** Coastal Patrol Boat. Ja.
*CL19* **IWAKAZE** Coastal Patrol Boat. Ja.
*CL20* **NATSUKAZE** Coastal Patrol Boat. Ja.
*CL21* **YUKEKAZE** Coastal Patrol Boat. Ja.
*CL22* **SHIMAKAZE** Coastal Patrol Boat. Ja.
*CL23* **YUKAZE** Coastal Patrol Boat. Ja.
*CL24* **YODOKAZE** Coastal Patrol Boat. Ja.
*CL25* **ASAKAZE** Coastal Patrol Craft. Ja.
*CL26* **YAKAZE** Coastal Patrol Craft. Ja.
*CL27* **KIYAKAZE** Coastal Patrol Craft. Ja.
*CL28* **IYOKAZE** Coastal Patrol Craft. Ja.
*CL29* **FUSAKAZE** Coastal Patrol Craft. Ja.
*CL30* **TACHIKAZE** Coastal Patrol Craft. Ja.
*CL31* **KOTOKAZE** Coastal Patrol Craft. Ja.

*CL32* **KITAKAZE** Coastal Patrol Craft. Ja.
*CL33* **ISOKAZE** Coastal Patrol Craft. Ja.
*CL34* **KISOKAZE** Coastal Patrol Craft. Ja.
*CL35* **MICHIKAZE** Coastal Patrol Craft. Ja.
*CL36* **TSURUKAZE** Coastal Patrol Craft. Ja.
*CL37* **AMATSUKAZE** Coastal Patrol Craft. Ja.
*CL38* **KUKIKAZE** Coastal Patrol Craft. Ja.
*CL39* **SAGIKAZE** Coastal Patrol Craft. Ja.
*CL40* **SHIOKAZE** Coastal Patrol Craft. Ja.
*CL41* **NIIKAZE** Coastal Patrol Craft. Ja.
*CL42* **TOMOKAZE** Coastal Patrol Craft. Ja.
*CL43* **WAKAKAZE** Coastal Patrol Craft. Ja.
*CR01* Rescue Service Craft. Ja.
*CR02* Rescue Service Craft. Ja.
*CR03* Rescue Service Craft. Ja.
*CR04* Rescue Service Craft. Ja.
*CR05* Rescue Service Craft. Ja.
*CR06* Rescue Service Craft. Ja.
*CR07* Rescue Service Craft. Ja.
*CR08* Rescue Service Craft. Ja.
*CR09* Rescue Service Craft. Ja.
*CR10* Rescue Service Craft. Ja.
*CR11* Rescue Service Craft. Ja.
*CR12* Rescue Service Craft. Ja.
*CR13* Rescue Service Craft. Ja.
*CR14* Rescue Service Craft. Ja.
*CR15* Rescue Service Craft. Ja.
*CR16* Rescue Service Craft. Ja.
*CR17* Rescue Service Craft. Ja.
*CR18* Rescue Service Craft. Ja.
*CR51* Rescue Service Craft. Ja.
*CS01* Harbour Patrol Craft. Ja.
*CS02* Harbour Patrol Craft. Ja.
*CS03* Harbour Patrol Craft. Ja.
*CS04* Harbour Patrol Craft. Ja.
*CS05* Harbour Patrol Craft. Ja.
*CS06* Harbour Patrol Craft. Ja.
*CS07* Harbour Patrol Craft. Ja.
*CS08* Harbour Patrol Craft. Ja.
*CS09* Harbour Patrol Craft. Ja.
*CS10* Harbour Patrol Craft. Ja.
*CS11* Harbour Patrol Craft. Ja.
*CS12* Harbour Patrol Craft. Ja.
*CS13* Harbour Patrol Craft. Ja.
*CS14* Harbour Patrol Craft. Ja.
*CS15* Harbour Patrol Craft. Ja.
*CS16* Harbour Patrol Craft. Ja.
*CS17* Harbour Patrol Craft. Ja.
*CS18* Harbour Patrol Craft. Ja.
*CS19* Harbour Patrol Craft. Ja.
*CS20* Harbour Patrol Craft. Ja.
*CS21* Harbour Patrol Craft. Ja.
*CS22* Harbour Patrol Craft. Ja.
*CS23* Harbour Patrol Craft. Ja.
*CS24* Harbour Patrol Craft. Ja.
*CS25* Harbour Patrol Craft. Ja.
*CS26* Harbour Patrol Craft. Ja.
*CS27* Harbour Patrol Craft. Ja.
*CS28* Harbour Patrol Craft. Ja.
*CS29* Harbour Patrol Craft. Ja.

*CS30* Harbour Patrol Craft. Ja.
*CS31* Harbour Patrol Craft. Ja.
*CS32* Harbour Patrol Craft. Ja.
*CS33* Harbour Patrol Craft. Ja.
*CS34* Harbour Patrol Craft. Ja.
*CS35* Harbour Patrol Craft. Ja.
*CS36* Harbour Patrol Craft. Ja.
*CS37* Harbour Patrol Craft. Ja.
*CS38* Harbour Patrol Craft. Ja.
*CS39* Harbour Patrol Craft. Ja.
*CS40* Harbour Patrol Craft. Ja.
*CS41* Harbour Patrol Craft. Ja.
*CS42* Harbour Patrol Craft. Ja.
*CS43* Harbour Patrol Craft. Ja.
*CS44* Harbour Patrol Craft. Ja.
*CS45* Harbour Patrol Craft. Ja.
*CS46* Harbour Patrol Craft. Ja.
*CS47* Harbour Patrol Craft. Ja.
*CS48* Harbour Patrol Craft. Ja.
*CS49* Harbour Patrol Craft. Ja.
*CS50* Harbour Patrol Craft. Ja.
*CS51* Harbour Patrol Craft. Ja.
*CS52* Harbour Patrol Craft. Ja.
*CS53* Harbour Patrol Craft. Ja.
*CS54* Harbour Patrol Craft. Ja.
*CS55* Harbour Patrol Craft. Ja.
*CS56* Harbour Patrol Craft. Ja.
*CS57* Harbour Patrol Craft. Ja.
*CS58* Harbour Patrol Craft. Ja.
*CS102* Harbour Patrol Craft. Ja.
*CS103* Harbour Patrol Craft. Ja.
*CS104* Harbour Patrol Craft. Ja.
*CS105* Harbour Patrol Craft. Ja.
*CS106* Harbour Patrol Craft. Ja.
*CS107* Harbour Patrol Craft. Ja.
*CS108* Harbour Patrol Craft. Ja.
*CS109* Harbour Patrol Craft. Ja.
*CS110* Harbour Patrol Craft. Ja.
*CS111* Harbour Patrol Craft. Ja.
*CS112* Harbour Patrol Craft. Ja.
*CS113* Harbour Patrol Craft. Ja.
*CS114* Harbour Patrol Craft. Ja.
*CS115* Harbour Patrol Craft. Ja.
*CS116* Harbour Patrol Craft. Ja.
*CS117* Harbour Patrol Craft. Ja.
*CS118* Harbour Patrol Craft. Ja.
*CS119* Harbour Patrol Craft. Ja.
*CS120* Harbour Patrol Craft. Ja.
*CS121* Harbour Patrol Craft. Ja.
*CS122* Harbour Patrol Craft. Ja.
*CS123* Harbour Patrol Craft. Ja.
*CS124* Harbour Patrol Craft. Ja.
*CS125* Harbour Patrol Craft. Ja.
*CS126* Harbour Patrol Craft. Ja.
*D01* **CAPRICE** Destroyer. Br.
*D01* **PRESIDENTE ALFARO** Destroyer. Ec.
*D02* **DEVONSHIRE** G.M. Destroyer. Br.
*D02* **PRESIDENTE VELASCO IBARRA** Destroyer. Ec.
*D06* **HAMPSHIRE** G.M. Destroyer. Br
*D-1* **(DM-01)** Minesweeper Escort. Me.
*D-2* **(DM-02)** Minesweeper Escort. Me.
*D-3* **(DM-3)** Minesweeper Escort. Me.
*D-4* **(DM-4)** Minesweeper Escort. Me.
*D5* **ARTEMIZ** Destroyer. Iran.

D-5 **(DM-05)** Minesweeper Escort. Me.

D-6 **(DM-06)** Minesweeper Escort. Me.

D-7 **(DM-07)** Minesweeper Escort. Me.

D-8 **(DM-08)** Minesweeper Escort. Me.

D-9 **(DM-09)** Minesweeper Escort. Me.

D10 **ACRE** Destroyer. Bz.

D10 **DM-10** Minesweeper Escort. Me.

D-11 **NUEVA ESPARTA** Destroyer. Ve.

D12 **KENT** G.M. Destroyer. Br.

D12 **AMAZONAS** G.M. Destroyer. Bz.

D12 **JOSE LUIS DIEZ** Destroyer. Sp.

D-12 **ALMIRANTE CLEMENTE** Frigate. Ve.

D-13 **GENERAL JUAN JOSE FLORES** Light Destroyer. Ve.

D14 **DIXIE** Destroyer Tender. Am.

D14 **ARAGUAIA** Destroyer. Bz.

D14 **ALMIRANTE ANTEQUERA** Destroyer. Sp.

D15 **PRAIRIE** Destroyer Tender. Am.

D15 **ARAGUARI** Destroyer. Bz.

D15 **ALMIRANTE MIRANDA** Destroyer. Sp.

D16 **LONDON** G.M. Destroyer. Br.

D16 **CASCADE** Destroyer Tender. Am.

D17 **PIEDMONT** Destroyer Tender. Am.

D18 **ANTRIM** G.M. Destroyer. Br.

D18 **SIERRA** Destroyer Tender. Am.

D19 **YOSEMITE** Destroyer Tender. Am.

D19 **GLAMORGAN** G.M. Destroyer. Br.

D19 **BEBERIBE** Frigate. Bz.

D20 **FIFE** G.M. Destroyer. Br.

D21 **NORFOLK** G.M. Destroyer. Br.

D21 **LEPANTO** G.M. Destroyer. Sp.

D-21 **ZULIA** G.M. Destroyer. Ve.

D22 **ALMIRANTE FERRANDIZ** Destroyer. Sp.

D-22 **GENERAL JOSE TRINIDAD MORAN** Frigate. Ve.

D23 **ALMIRANTE VALDES** Destroyer. Sp.

D23 **ARCADIA** Destroyer Tender. Am.

D-23 **ALMIRANTE BRION** Frigate. Ve.

D24 **EVERGLADES** Destroyer Tender. Am.

D24 **GREENHALGH** Destroyer. Bz.

D24 **ALCALA GALIANO** Destroyer. Sp.

D25 **FRONTIER** Destroyer Tender. Am.

D25 **MARCILIO DIAS** Destroyer. Bz.

D25 **JORGE JUAN** Destroyer. Sp.

D26 **SHENANDOAH** Destroyer Tender. Am.

D26 **MARIZ E. BARROS** Destroyer. Bz.

D27 **YELLOWSTONE** Destroyer Tender. Am.

D27 **PARA** Destroyer. Bz.

D28 **GRAND CANYON** Destroyer Tender. Am.

D28 **PARAIBA** Destroyer. Bz.

D29 **ISLE ROYALE** Destroyer Tender. Am.

D29 **PARANA** Destroyer. Bz.

D30 **PERNAMBUCO** Destroyer. Bz.

D31 **TIDEWATER** Destroyer Tender. Am.

D31 **PIAUI** Destroyer. Bz.

D31 **AUDAZ** Destroyer. Sp.

D-31 **ARAGUA** Destroyer. Ve.

D32 **SANTA CATERINA** Destroyer. Bz.

D32 **OSADO** Destroyer. Sp.

D-32 **GENERAL JOSE DE AUSTRIA** Frigate. Ve.

D33 **METEORO** Destroyer. Sp.

D-33 **ALMIRANTE JOSE GARCIA** Frigate. Ve.

D34 **FUROR** Destroyer. Sp.

D35 **DIAMOND** Destroyer. Br.

D35 **RAYO** Destroyer. Sp.

D36 **BRYCE CANYON** Destroyer Tender. Am.

D37 **TEMERARIO** Destroyer. Sp.

D37 **SAMUEL GOMPERS** Destroyer Tender. Am.

D38 **INTREPIDO** Destroyer. Sp.

D38 **PUGET SOUND** Destroyer Tender. Am.

D39 **RELAMPAGO** Destroyer. Sp.

D41 **OQUENDO** Destroyer. Sp.

D42 **ROGER DE LAURIA** Destroyer. Sp.

D43 **MATAPAN** Destroyer. Br.

D43 **MARQUES DE LA ENSENADA** Destroyer. Sp.

D45 **CZAIKA** Coastal Minesweeper. Ph.

D46 **RYBITWA** Coastal Minesweeper. Ph.

D50 **ARTEMIZ** Destroyer. Ir.

D51 **LINIERS** Destroyer. Sp.

D52 **ALAVA** Destroyer. Sp.

D68 **BARROSA** Destroyer. Br.

D73 **CAVALIER** Destroyer. Br.

D86 **AGINCOURT** Destroyer. Br.

D92 **GODAVARI** Frigate. In.

D93 **GIAMATI** Frigate. In.

D94 **GANGA** Frigate. In.

D97 **CORUNNA** Destroyer. Br.

D101 **DUARTE** Destroyer. Co.

D102 **SANCHEZ** Destroyer. Do.

D108 **DAINTY** Destroyer. Br.

D114 **DEFENDER** Destroyer. Br.

D170 **Z1** Destroyer. Ge.

D171 **Z2** Destroyer. Ge.

D172 **Z3** Destroyer. Ge

D178 **Z4** Destroyer. Ge.

D179 **Z5** Destroyer. Ge.

D181 **HAMBURG** Destroyer. Ge.

D182 **SCHLESWIG - HOLSTEIN** Destroyer. Ge.

D183 **BAYERN** Destroyer. Ge.

D184 **HESSEN** Destroyer. Ge.

D185 **LUTJENS** Destroyer. Ge.

D186 **MOLDERS** Destroyer. Ge.

D187 **ROMMEL** Destroyer. Ge.

D203 Landing Craft. Ys.

D204 Landing Craft. Ys.

D206 Landing Craft. Ys.

D219 Landing Craft. Ys.

D221 **(DTK 221)** Landing Craft. Ys.

D230 Landing Craft. Ys.

D237 **SIMON VAN DER STEL** Destroyer. SA.

D238 **JAN VAN RIEBEECK** Destroyer. SA.

D340 **ISTANBUL** Destroyer. Tu.

D341 **IZMIR** Destroyer. Tu.

D344 **GAZIANTEP** Destroyer. Tu.

D345 **GIRESUN** Destroyer. Tu.

D346 **GELIBOLU** Destroyer. Tu.

D347 **GEMLIK** Destroyer. Tu.

D348 **ALP ARSLAN** Destroyer. Tu.

D349 **MARESAL FEVZI CAKMAK** Destroyer. Tu.

D350 **KILIC ALI PASA** Destroyer. Tu.

D351 **PIYALE PASA** Destroyer. Tu.

D553 **ARTIGLIERE** Destroyer. It.

D554 **AVIERE** Destroyer. It.

D558 **IMPETUOSO** Destroyer. It.

D559 **INDOMITO** Destroyer. It.

D562 **SAN GIORGIO** Destroyer Leader. It.

D563 **SAN MARCO** Destroyer Leader. It.

D570 **IMPAVIDO** G.M. Destroyer. It.

D571 **INTREPIDO** G.M. Destroyer. It.

D602 **SUFFREN** G.M. Frigate. Fr.

D603 **DUQUESNE** G.M. Frigate. Fr.

D621 **SURCOUF** Destroyer. Fr.

D622 **KERSAINT** Destroyer. Fr.

D623 **CASSARD** Destroyer. Fr.

D624 **BOUVET** Destroyer. Fr.

D625 **DUPETIT THOUARS** Destroyer. Fr.

D626 **CHEVALIER PAUL** Destroyer. Fr.

D627 **MAILLE BREZE** Destroyer. Fr.

D628 **VAUQUELIN** Destroyer. Fr.

D629 **D'ESTREES** Destroyer. Fr.

D630 **DU CHAYLA** Destroyer. Fr.

D631 **CASABIANCA** Destroyer. Fr.

D632 **GUEPRATTE** Destroyer. Fr.

D634 **LA BOURDONNAIS** Destroyer. Fr.

D635 **FORBIN** Destroyer. Fr.

D636 **TARTU** Destroyer. Fr.

D637 **JAUREGUIBERRY** Destroyer. Fr.

D638 **LA GALISSONNIERE** Destroyer. Fr.

D808 **HOLLAND** Destroyer. Du.

D809 **ZEELAND** Destroyer. Du.

D810 **NOORD BRABANT** Destroyer. Du.

D811 **GELDERLAND** Destroyer. Du.

D812 **FRIESLAND** Destroyer. Du.

D813 **GRONINGEN** Destroyer. Du.

D814 **LIMBURG** Destroyer. Du.

D815 **OVERIJSSEL** Destroyer. Du.

D816 **DRENTHE** Destroyer. Du.

D817 **UTRECHT** Destroyer. Du.

D818 **ROTTERDAM** Destroyer. Du.

D819 **AMSTERDAM** Destroyer. Du.

DE1 **URUGUAY** Frigate. Ur.

DE2 **ARTIGAS** Frigate. Ur.

DE12 **SAAM** Frigate. Ir.

DG8 **LODESTONE** Degaussing Vessel. Am.

DG9 **MAGNET** Degaussing Vessel. Am.

*DG10* **DEPERM** Degaussing Vessel. Am.

*DG383* **SURFBIRD** Degaussing Vessel. Am.

*DM-01* **D1** Minesweeper Escort. Me.

*DM-02* **D2** Minesweeper Escort. Me.

*DM-03* **D3** Minesweeper Escort. Me.

*DM-04* **D4** Minesweeper Escort. Me.

*DM-05* **D5** Minesweeper Escort. Me.

*DM-06* **D6** Minesweeper Escort. Me.

*DM-07* **D7** Minesweeper Escort. Me.

*DM-08* **D8** Minesweeper Escort. Me.

*DM-09* **D9** Minesweeper Escort. Me.

*DM-10* **D-10** Minesweeper Escort. Me.

*DM-11* **E-1** Minesweeper Escort. Me.

*DM-12* **E-2** Minesweeper Escort. Me.

*DM-13* **E-3** Minesweeper Escort. Me.

*DM-14* **E-4** Minesweeper Escort. Me.

*DM-15* **E-5** Minesweeper Escort. Me.

*DM-16* **E-6** Minesweeper Escort. Me.

*DM-17* **E-7** Minesweeper Escort. Me.

*DM-18* **E-8** Minesweeper Escort. Me.

*DM-19* **E-9** Minesweeper Escort. Me.

*DM-20* **E-0** Minesweeper Escort. Me.

*E-1* **DM-11** Escort. Me.

*E-2* **DM-12** Escort. Me.

*E-3* **DM-13** Escort. Me.

*E4* **MOUNT BAKER** Ammunition Ship. Am.

*E5* **RAINER** Ammunition Ship. Am.

*E-5* **DM-15** Escort. Me.

*E-6* **DM-16** Escort. Me.

*E-7* **DM-17** Escort. Me.

*E8* **MAUNA LOA** Ammunition Ship. Am.

*E-8* **DM-18** Ammunition Ship. Am.

*E9* **MAZAMA** Ammunition Ship. Am.

*E-9* **DM-19** Escort. Me.

*E12* **WRANGELL** Ammunition Ship. Am.

*E12* **25 DE JULIO** Escort Destroyer. Ec.

*E14* **FIREDRAKE** Ammunition Ship. Am.

*E15* **VESUVIUS** Ammunition Ship. Am.

*E16* **MOUNT KATMAI** Ammunition Ship. Am.

*E17* **GREAT SITKIN** Ammunition Ship. Am.

*E18* **PARICUTIN** Ammunition Ship. Am.

*E19* **DIAMOND HEAD** Ammunition Ship. Am.

*E21* **SURIBACHI** Ammunition Ship. Am.

*E21* **GUAYAS** Frigate. Ec.

*E22* **MAUNA KEA** Ammunition Ship. Am.

*E22* **ESMERALDAS** Escort Patrol Vessel. Ec.

*E23* **NITRO** Ammunition Ship. Am.

*E23* **MANABI** Escort Patrol Vessel. Ec.

*E24* **PYRO** Ammunition Ship. Am.

*E25* **HALEAKALA** Ammunition Ship. Am.

*E26* **KILAUEA** Ammunition Ship. Am.

*E27* **BUTTE** Ammunition Ship. Am.

*E28* **SANTA BARBARA** Ammunition Ship. Am.

*E29* **MOUNT HOOD** Ammunition Ship. Am.

*E30* **VIRGO** Ammunition Ship. Am.

*E31* **CHARA** Ammunition Ship. Am.

*E32* **FLINT** Ammunition Ship. Am.

*E33* **SHASTA** Ammunition Ship. Am.

*E34* **MOUNT BAKER** Ammunition Ship. Am.

*E35* **KISKA** Ammunition Ship. Am.

*E71* **DUSTUR** Corvette. Tn.

*E311* — Patrol Vessel. Cambodia.

*E312* — Patrol Vessel. Cambodia.

*EAG153* **COMPASS ISLAND** Experimental Navigation Ship. Am.

*EAG154* **OBSERVATION ISLAND** Experimental Navigation Ship. Am.

*E0-2* **MANABI** Escort Patrol Vessel. Ec.

*E0-3* **ESMERALDAS** Escort Patrol Vessel. Ec.

*F01* **MARTE** Frigate. Sp.

*F02* **NEPTUNO** Frigate. Sp.

*F3* This is not a Pendant number (which is *L702*) but it appears in addition, on ramp and bows. One of H.M.S. "Fearless" Landing Craft.

*F10* **AURORA** Frigate. Br.

*F10* **ALDEBARAN** Store Ship. Am.

*F11* **JUPITER** Frigate. Sp.

*F11* **VISBY** Frigate. Sw.

*F12* **ACHILLES** Frigate. Br.

*F12* **VULCANO** Frigate. Sp.

*F12* **SUNDSVALL** Frigate. Sw.

*F14* **LEOPARD** Frigate. Br.

*F15* **EURYALUS** Frigate. Br.

*F16* **DIOMEDE** Frigate. Br.

*F17* **KROMANTSE** Corvette. Gh.

*F18* **GALATEA** Frigate. Br.

*F18* **KETA** Corvette. Gh.

*F21* **EOLO** Frigate. Sp.

*F22* **TRITON** Frigate. Sp.

*F24* **RAMAT.** Frigate. My.

*F25* **BAYANDOR** Corvette. Ir.

*F26* **NAGHDI** Corvette. Ir.

*F27* **LYNX** Frigate. Br.

*F27* **MILANIAN** Corvette. Ir.

*F28* **CLEOPATRA** Frigate. Br.

*F28* **KAHNAMUIE** Corvette. Ir.

*F28* **HYADES** Store Ship. Am.

*F31* **BRAHMAPUTRA** Frigate. In.

*F32* **SALISBURY** Frigate. Br.

*F32* **HERMAN CORTES** Frigate. Sp.

*F33* **VASCO NUNEZ DE BALBOA** Frigate. Sp.

*F34* **PUMA** Frigate. Br.

*F35* **MAGALLANES** Frigate. Sp.

*F36* **WHITBY** Frigate. Br.

*F36* **SARMIENTO DE GAMBOA** Frigate Sp.

*F37* **JAGUAR** Frigate. Br.

*F38* **ARETHUSA** Frigate. Br.

*F39* **NAIAD** Frigate. Br.

*F40* **SIRIUS** Frigate. Br.

*F41* **VICENTE YANEZ PINZON** Frigate. Sp.

*F42* **PHOEBE** Frigate. Br.

*F42* **LEGAZPI** Frigate. Sp.

*F42* **BONDIA** Store Ship. Am.

*F43* **TORQUAY** Frigate. Br.

*F44* **LAURENTIA** Store Ship. Am.

*F45* **MINERVA** Frigate. Br.

*F46* **KISTNA** Frigate. In.

*F47* **DANAE** Frigate. Br.

*F48* **DUNDAS** Frigate. Br.

*F49* **PICTOR** Store Ship. Am.

*F51* **DESCUBIERTA** Corvette. Sp.

*F52* **JUNO** Frigate. Br.

*F52* **ARCTURUS** Store Ship. Am.

*F53* **UNDAUNTED** Frigate. Br.

*F54* **HARDY** Frigate. Br.

*F54* **ZELIMA** Store Ship. Am.

*F55* **WAIKATO** Frigate. NZ.

*F55* **ALUDRA** Store Ship. Am.

*F56* **ARGONAUT** Frigate. Br.

*F56* **DENEBOLA** Store Ship. Am.

*F57* **ANDROMEDA** Frigate. Br.

*F57* **REGULUS** Store Ship. Am.

*F58* **HERMIONE** Frigate. Br.

*F58* **RIGEL** Store Ship. Am.

*F59* **CHICHESTER** Frigate. Br.

*F59* **VEGA** Store Ship. Am.

*F60* **JUPITER** Frigate. Br.

*F60* **SIRIUS** Store Ship. Am.

*F61* **LLANDAFF** Frigate. Br.

*F61* **ATREVIDA** Corvette. Sp.

*F61* **PROCYON** Store Ship. Am.

*F62* **PRINCESA** Corvette. Sp.

*F62* **BELLATRIX** Store Ship. Am.

*F63* **SCARBOROUGH** Frigate. Br.

*F63* **DIANA** Corvette. Sp.

*F64* **NAUTILUS** Corvette. Sp.

*F65* **TENBY** Frigate. Br.

*F65* **VILLA DE BILBAO** Corvette. Sp.

*F69* **BACCHANTE** Frigate. Br.

*F71* **SCYLLA** Frigate. Br.

*F73* **EASTBOURNE** Frigate. Br.

*F75* **CHARYBDIS** Frigate. Br.

*F77* **BLACKPOOL** Frigate. Br. (NZ).

*F79* **KARLSKRONA** Frigate. Sw.

*F80* **DUNCAN** Frigate. Br.

*F83* **ULSTER** Frigate. Br.

*F84* **EXMOUTH** Frigate. Br.

*F85* **KEPPEL** Frigate. Br.

*F87* **NIGERIA** Frigate. Ng.

*F88* **MALCOLM** Frigate. Br.

*F91* **MURRAY** Frigate. Br.

*F94* **PALLISER** Frigate. Br.

*F97* **RUSSELL** Frigate. Br.

*F99* **LINCOLN** Frigate. Br.

*F101* **YARMOUTH** Frigate. Br.

*F103* **LOWESTOFT** Frigate. Br.

*F104* **DIDO** Frigate. Br.

*F106* **BRIGHTON** Frigate. Br.

*F107* **ROTHESAY** Frigate. Br.

*F108* **LONDONDERRY** Frigate. Br.

*F109* **LEANDER** Frigate. Br.

*F110* **CAUVERY** Frigate. In.

*F111* **OTAGO** Frigate. NZ.

*F113* **FALMOUTH** Frigate. Br.

*F114* **AJAX** Frigate. Br.

*F115* **BERWICK** Frigate. Br.

*F117* **ASHANTI** Frigate. Br.

*F119* **ESKIMO** Frigate. Br.

*F122* **GURKHA** Frigate. Br.

*F124* **ZULU** Frigate. Br.

*F125* **MOHAWK** Frigate. Br.

*F126* **PLYMOUTH** Frigate. Br.

*F127* **PENELOPE** Frigate. Br.

*F129* **RHYL** Frigate. Br.

*F131* **NUBIAN** Frigate. Br.

*F133* **TARTAR** Frigate. Br.

*F137* **BEAS** Frigate. In.

*F138* **RAPID** Frigate. Br.
*F139* **BETWA** Frigate. In.
*F140* **TALWAR** Frigate. In.
*F143* **TRISHUL** Frigate. In.
*F144* **KIRPAN** Frigate. In.
*F145* **PRESIDENT PRETORIUS** Frigate. SA.
*F146* **KUTHAR** Frigate. In.
*F147* **PRESIDENT STEYN** Frigate. SA.
*F148* **TARANAKI** Frigate. NZ.
*F149* **KHUKRI** Frigate. In.
*F150* **PRESIDENT KRUGER** Frigate. SA.
*F157* **VRYSTAAT** Frigate. SA.
*F159* **WAKEFUL** Frigate. Br.
*F197* **GRENVILLE** Frigate. Br.
*F212* **GNEISENAU** Frigate. Ge.
*F213* **SCHARNHORST** Frigate. Ge.
*F220* **KOLN** Frigate. Ge.
*F221* **EMDEN** Frigate. Ge.
*F222* **AUGSBURG** Frigate. Ge.
*F223* **KARLSRUHE** Frigate. Ge.
*F224* **LUBECK** Frigate. Ge.
*F225* **BRAUNSCHWEIG** Frigate. Ge.
*F232* **GAJABAHU** Frigate. Ce. (May not have Number on hull)
*F300* **OSLO** Frigate. No.
*F301* **JOSE MARTI** Frigate. Cu.
*F301* **BERGEN** Frigate. No.
*F302* **ANTONIO MACEO** Frigate. Cu.
*F302* **TRONDHEIM** Frigate. No.
*F303* **MAXIMO GOMEZ** Frigate. Cu.
*F303* **STAVANGER** Frigate. No.
*F304* **NARVIK** Frigate. No.
*F331* **DIOGO GOMES** Frigate. Po.
*F332* **NUNO TRISTAO** Frigate. Po.
*F335* **PERO ESCOBAR** Frigate. Po.
*F336* **ALVARES CABRAL** Frigate. Po.
*F337* **PACHECO PEREIRA** Frigate. Po.
*F341* **ESBERN SNARE** Frigate. Da.
*F344* **BELLONA** Corvette. Da.
*F345* **DIANA** Corvette. Da.
*F346* **FLORA** Corvette. Da.
*F347* **TRITON** Corvette. Da.
*F348* **HVIDBJORNEN** Frigate. Da.
*F349* **VAEDDEREN** Frigate. Da.
*F350* **INGOLF** Frigate. Da.
*F351* **FYLLA** Frigate. Da.
*F352* **PEDER SKRAM** Frigate. Da.
*F353* **HERLUF TROLLE** Frigate. Da.
*F364* **LACHLAN** Survey Ship. NZ. (Number might not appear on hull)
*F422* **HAWAEA** Frigate. NZ.
*F432* **GOOD HOPE** Frigate. SA.
*F433* **HANG TUAH** Frigate. My.
*F451* **MELLA** Frigate. Do.
*F470* **CACHEU** Corvette. Po.
*F472* **ALMIRANTE PEREIRA DA SILVA** Escort. Po.
*F473* **ALMIRANTE GAGO COUT-INHO** Frigate. Po.
*F474* **ALMIRANTE MAGALHAES CORREIA** Escort. Po.
*F478* **VASCO DA GAMA** Frigate. Po.
*F479* **D. FRANCISCO DE AL-MEIDA** Frigate. Po.

*F480* **COMANDANTE JOAO BELO** Escort. Po.
*F481* **COMANDANTE HERMENE-GILDO CAPELO** Frigate. Po.
*F482* **COMANDANTE ROBERTO IVENS** Frigate. Po.
*F483* **COMANDANTE SAGADURA CABRAL** Frigate. Po.
*F540* **PIETRO DE CRISTOFARO** Corvette. It.
*F541* **UMBERTO GROSSO** Corvette. It.
*F542* **AQUILA** Corvette. It.
*F543* **ALBATROS** Corvette. It.
*F544* **ALCIONE** Corvette. It.
*F545* **AIRONE** Corvette. It.
*F546* **LICIO VISINTINI** Corvette. It.
*F547* **CRISALIDE** Corvette. It.
*F548* **FARFALLA** Corvette. It.
*F549* **BOMBARDA** Corvette. It.
*F550* **SALVATORE TODARO** Corvette. It.
*F552* **CANOPO** Frigate. It.
*F553* **CASTORE** Frigate. It.
*F554* **CENTAURO** Frigate. It.
*F555* **CIGNO** Frigate. It.
*F561* **IBIS** Corvette. It.
*F564* **SCIMITARRA** Corvette. It.
*F565* **SIBILLA** Corvette. It.
*F566* **GRU** Corvette. It.
*F569* **CHIMERA** Corvette. It.
*F570* **URANIA** Corvette. It.
*F571* **GABBIANO** Corvette. It.
*F572* **FLORA** Corvette. It.
*F574* **PELLICANO** Corvette. It.
*F575* **CORMORANO** Corvette. It.
*F578* **BAIONETTA** Corvette. It.
*F579* **SFINGE** Corvette. It.
*F580* **ALPINO** Frigate. It.
*F581* **CARABINIERE** Frigate. It.
*F590* **ALDEBARAN** Frigate. It.
*F591* **ALTAIR** Frigate. It.
*F592* **ANDROMEDA** Frigate. It.
*F593* **CARLO BERGAMINI** Frigate. It.
*F594* **VIRGINIO FASAN** Frigate. It.
*F595* **CARLO MARGOTTINI** Frigate. It.
*F596* **LUIGI RIZZO** Frigate. It.
*F597* **VEDETTA** Patrol Vessel. It.
*F602* **TRANSVAAL** Frigate. SA.
*F703* **ACONIT** G.M. Frigate. Fr.
*F708* **AL MOUNA** G.M. Frigate. Mo.
*F724* **MALGACHE** G.M. Frigate. Fr.
*F725* **VICTOR SCHOELCHER** Frigate. Fr.
*F726* **COMMANDANT BORY** Frigate. Fr.
*F727* **AMIRAL CHARNER** Frigate. Fr.
*F728* **DOUDART DE LA GREE** Frigate. Fr.
*F729* **BALNY** Frigate. Fr.
*F733* **COMMANDANT RIVIERE** Frigate. Fr.
*F740* **COMMANDANT BOUR-DAIS** Frigate. Fr.
*F748* **PROTET** Frigate. Fr.
*F749* **ENSEIGNE DE VAISSEAU HENRY** Frigate. Fr.
*F761* **LE CORSE** Frigate. Fr.
*F762* **LE BRESTOIS** Frigate. Fr.

*F763* **LE BOULONNAIS** Frigate. Fr.
*F764* **LE BORDELAIS** Frigate. Fr.
*F765* **LE NORMAND** Frigate. Fr.
*F766* **LE PICARD** Frigate. Fr.
*F767* **LE GASCON** Frigate. Fr.
*F768* **LE LORRAIN** Frigate. Fr.
*F769* **LE BOURGUIGNON** Frigate. Fr.
*F770* **LE CHAMPENOIS** Frigate. Fr.
*F771* **LE SAVOYARD** Frigate. Fr.
*F772* **LE BRETON** Frigate. Fr.
*F773* **LE BASQUE** Frigate. Fr.
*F774* **L'AGENAIS** Frigate. Fr.
*F775* **LE BEARNAIS** Frigate. Fr.
*F776* **L'ALSACIEN** Frigate. Fr.
*F777* **LE PROVENCAL** Frigate. Fr.
*F778* **LE VENDEEN** Frigate. Fr.
*F802* **VAN SPEIJK** Frigate. Du.
*F803* **VAN GALEN** Frigate. Du.
*F804* **TJERK HIDDES** Frigate. Du.
*F805* **VAN NES** Frigate. Du.
*F814* **ISAAC SWEERS** Frigate. Du.
*F815* **EVERTSEN** Frigate. Du.
*F817* **WOLF** Frigate. Du.
*F818* **FRET** Frigate. Du.
*F819* **HERMELIJN** Frigate. Du.
*F820* **VOS** Frigate. Du.
*F821* **PANTER** Frigate. Du.
*F822* **JAGUAR** Frigate. Du.
*FB101* **CAPOTILLO** Lighthouse and Buoy Tender. Do.
*FL5* **Y857** Rescue Vessel. Ge.
*FL6* **Y858** Rescue Vessel. Ge.
*FL7* **Y859** Rescue Vessel. Ge.
*FL8* **Y860** Rescue Vessel. Ge.
*FL9* **Y861** Rescue Vessel. Ge.
*FL10* **Y862** Rescue Vessel. Ge.
*FL11* **Y863** Rescue Vessel. Ge.
*FS1* **MARS** Combat Store Ship. Am.
*FS2* **SYLVANIA** Combat Store Ship. Am.
*FS3* **NIAGARA FALLS** Combat Store Ship. Am.
*FS4* **WHITE PLAINS** Combat Store Ship. Am.
*FS5* **CONCORD** Combat Store Ship. Am.
*FS6* **SAN DIEGO** Combat Store Ship. Am.
*FS7* **SAN JOSE** Combat Store Ship. Am.
*G12* **GARCIA D'AVILA** Oiler. Bz.
*G15* **CUSTODIO DE MELLO** Transport. Bz.
*G16* **BARROSO PEREIRA** Transport. Bz.
*G17* **POTENGI** Oiler. Bz.
*G19* **RAZA** Oiler. Bz.
*G20* **RIJO** Oiler. Bz.
*G21* **ARY PARREIRAS** Transport. Bz.
*G22* **SOARES DUTRA** Transport. Bz.
*G24* **BELMONTE** Repair Ship. Bz.
*G27* **MARAJO** Oiler. Bz.
*G38* **GC38** Patrol Vessel. Me.
*G153* **COMPASS ISLAND** Experimental Navigational Ship. Am. Pennant number might be *EAG 153*
*GC1* **SAVANNAH** Coast Guard Vessel. Haiti.

*GC2* **16 AOUT 1946** Coast Guard Vessel. Haiti.

*GC5* **ARTIBONITE** Coast Guard Vessel. Haiti.

*GC7* **MOUNT MCKINLEY** Amphibious Force Flagship. Am.

*GC7* **AMIRAL KILLICK** Coast Guard Vessel. Haiti.

*GC8* **LA CRETE A PIERROT** Coast Guard Vessel. Haiti.

*GC9* **VERTIERES** Coast Guard Vessel. Haiti.

*GC10* **DESSALINES** Coast Guard Vessel. Haiti.

*GC11* **ELDORADO** Amphibious Force Flagship. Am.

*GC11* **JUAN B. AZOPARDO** Frigate. Ar.

*GC11* — Coast Guard Vessel. Cu.

*GC12* **ESTES** Amphibious Force Flagship. Am.

*GC12* **SPIRO** Survey Ship. Ar.

*GC13* — Coast Guard Vessel. Cu.

*GC14* — Coast Guard Vessel. Cu.

*GC16* **POCONO** Amphibious Force Flagship. Am.

*GC17* **TACONIC** Amphibious Force Flagship. Am.

*GC19* **BLUE RIDGE** Amphibious Force Flagship. Am.

*GC20* **MOUNT WHITNEY** Amphibious Force Flagship. Am.

*GC21* **LYNCH** Survey Patrol Craft. Ar.

*GC22* **TOLL** Survey Patrol Craft. Ar.

*GC23* **EREZCANO** Survey Patrol Craft. Ar.

*GC32* — Coast Guard Vessel. Cu.

*GC33* — Coast Guard Vessel. Cu.

*GC34* — Coast Guard Vessel. Cu.

*GC101* **LEONCIO PRADO** Coast Guard Vessel. Cu.

*GC102* **DONOTIVO** Coast Guard Vessel. Cu.

*GC102* **BETELGEUSE** Coast Guard Vessel. Do.

*GC103* **MATANZAS** Coast Guard Vessel. Cu.

*GC104* **ORIENTE** Coast Guard Vessel. Cu.

*GC106* **LAS VILLAS** Coast Guard Vessel. Cu.

*GC107* **HABANA** Coast Guard Vessel. Cu.

*GC108* **PINAR DEL RIO** Coast Guard Vessel. Cu.

*GEH1* **PLAINVIEW** Research Vessel: Hydrofoil. Am.

*GMR1* **ANNAPOLIS** Major Communications Relay Ship. Am.

*GMR2* **ARLINGTON** Major Communications Relay Ship. Am.

*GOR3* **ROBERT D. CONRAD** Oceanographic Research Ship. Am.

*GOR4* **JAMES S. GILLISS** Oceanographic Research Ship. Am.

*GOR5* **CHARLES H. DAVIS** Oceanographic Research Ship. Am.

*GOR6* **SANDS** Oceanographic Research Ship. Am.

*GOR7* **LYNCH** Oceanographic Research Ship. Am.

*GOR9* **THOMAS G. THOMPSON** Oceanographic Research Ship. Am.

*GOR10* **THOMAS WASHINGTON** Oceanographic Research Ship. Am.

*GOR12* **DE STEIGUER** Oceanographic Research Ship. Am.

*GOR13* **BARTLETT** Oceanographic Research Ship. Am.

*GOR16* — Oceanographic Research Ship. Am. (Catamaran)

*GOR314* **KIMBLA** Oceanographic Research Ship. Au.

*GPV901* **BANKS** general Purpose Vessel. Au.

*GS19* **SHELDRAKE** Survey Ship. Am.

*GS25* **JOHN G. KELLAR** Survey Ship. Am.

*GS26* **SILAS BENT** Survey Ship. Am.

*GS27* **KANE** Survey Ship. Am.

*GS29* **CHAUVENET** Survey Ship. Am.

*GS32* **HARKNESS** Survey Ship. Am.

*GTR5* **LIBERTY** Research Ship. Am.

*H12* **JOSE BONIFACIO** Transport and Survey Ship. Bz.

*H21* **SIRIUS** Survey Ship. Bz.

*H22* **CANOPUS** Survey Ship. Bz.

*H31* **ARGUS** Survey Ship. Bz.

*H32* **ORION** Survey Ship. Bz.

*H33* **TAURUS** Survey Ship. Bz.

*HL02* **TAKUYO** Survey Ship. Ja.

*HL03* **MEIYO** Surveying Vessel. Ja.

*HM04* **HEIYO** Surveying Vessel. Ja.

*HM05* **TENYO** Surveying Vessel. Ja.

*HM06* **KAIYO** Surveying Vessel. Ja.

*HQ04* **TUY DONG** Patrol Vessel. Vietnam.

*HQ06* **VAN DON** Patrol Vessel. Vietnam.

*HQ07* **DONG DA II** Patrol Vessel. Vietnam.

*HQ08* **CHI LANG II** Patrol Vessel. Vietnam.

*HQ09* **KY IIOA** Patrol Vessel. Vietnam.

*HQ10* **NHUT TAO** Patrol Vessel. Vietnam.

*HQ11* **CHI LINH** Escort. Vietnam.

*HQ114* **HAM TU II** Coastal Minesweeper. Vietnam.

*HQ115* **CHU'O'NG-DU'O'** Coastal Minesweeper. Vietnam.

*HQ116* **BACH DANG II** Coastal Minesweeper. Vietnam.

*HQ225* **NO THAN** Landing Ship. Vietnam.

*HQ226* **LINH KIEM** Landing Ship. Vietnam.

*HQ227* **LE VAN BINH** Landing Ship. Vietnam.

*HQ228* **DOAN NGOC TANG** Landing Ship. Vietnam.

*HQ229* **LUU PHU THO** Landing Ship. Vietnam.

*HQ230* **NGUYEN NGOC LONG** Landing Ship. Vietnam.

*HQ231* **NGUYEN DUC BONG** Landing Ship. Vietnam.

*HQ327* **LONG DAO** Landing Ship. Vietnam.

*HQ328* **THAN TIEN** Landing Ship. Vietnam.

*HQ329* **THIEN KICH** Landing Ship. Vietnam.

*HQ330* **LOI CONG** Landing Ship. Vietnam.

*HQ331* **TAM SBT** Landing Ship. Vietnam.

*HQ400* **HAT GIANG** Landing Ship. Vietnam.

*HQ401* **HAN GIANG** Landing Ship. Vietnam.

*HQ402* **LAM GIANG** Landing Ship. Vietnam.

*HQ403* **NINH GIANG** Landing Ship. Vietnam.

*HQ404* **HUONG GIANG** Landing Ship. Vietnam.

*HQ405* **TIEN GIANG** Landing Ship. Vietnam.

*HQ406* **HAU GIANG** Landing Ship. Vietnam.

*HQ470* — Oiler. Vietnam. (May have number 470 on bow without letters)

*HQ471* — Oiler. Vietnam.

*HQ533* — Landing Craft. Vietnam.

*HQ534* — Landing Craft. Vietnam.

*HQ325* — Landing Craft. Vietnam.

*HQ537* — Landing Craft. Vietnam.

*HQ538* — Landing Craft. Vietnam.

*IX501* **ELK RIVER** Ocean Range Support Ship. Am.

*J12* — Motor Launch. Tu.

*J13* — Motor Launch. Tu.

*J14* — Motor Launch. Tu.

*J15* — Motor Launch. Tu.

*J16* **OLAND** Destroyer. Sw.

*J16* Motor Launch. Tu.

*J17* **UPPLAND** Destroyer. Sw.

*J18* **HALLAND** Destroyer. Sw.

*J18* Motor Launch. Tu.

*J19* **SMALAND** Destroyer. Sw.

*J19* Motor Launch. Tu.

*J20* **OSTERGOTLAND.** Sw.

*J20* Motor Launch. Tu.

*J21* **SODERMALAND** Destroyer. Sw.

*J22* **GASTRIKLAND** Destroyer. Sw.

*J23* **HALSINGLAND** Destroyer. Sw.

*J28* **PIRAJU** Seaward Defence Boat. Bz.

*J30* **PIRANHA** Seaward Defence Boat. Bz.

*J32* **PIRAQUE** Seaward Defence Boat. Bz.

*K08* **ENGADINE** Helicopter Support Ship. Br. (RFA)

*K1* Landing Craft. Sp.

*K2* Landing Craft. Sp.

*K3* Landing Craft. Sp.

*K4* Landing Craft. Sp.

*K5* Landing Craft Sp.

*K260* **BETELGEUSE** Cargo Ship. Am.

*K283* **WYANDOT** Stores Ship. Am.

*KA19* **THUBAN** Attack Cargo Ship. Am.

*KA54* **ALGOL** Attack Cargo Ship. Am.

*KA56* **ARNEB** Attack Cargo Ship. Am.

*KA57* **CAPRICORNUS** Attack Cargo Ship. Am.

*KA61* **MULIPHEN** Attack Cargo Ship. Am.

*KA93* **YANCEY** Attack Cargo Ship. Am.

*KA94* **WINSTON** Attack Cargo Ship. Am.

*KA97* **MERRICK** Attack Cargo Ship. Am.

*KA103* **RANKIN** Attack Cargo Ship. Am.

*KA104* **SEMINOLE** Attack Cargo Ship. Am.

*KA106* **UNION** Attack Cargo Ship. Am.

*KA107* **VERMILLION** Attack Cargo Ship. Am.

*KA108* **WASHBURN** Attack Cargo Ship. Am.

*KA112* **TULARE** Attack Cargo Ship. Am.

*KA113* **CHARLESTON** Attack Cargo Ship. Am.

*KA114* **DURHAM** Attack Cargo Ship. Am.

*KA115* **MOBILE** Attack Cargo Ship. Am.

*KA116* **ST. LOUIS** Attack Cargo Ship. Am.

*KA117* **EL PASO** Attack Cargo Ship. Am.

*KS1* **CASTOR** General Stores Issue Ship. Am.

*KS4* **POLLUX** General Stores Supply Ship. Am.

*KS32* **ALTAIR** General Stores Issue Ship. Am.

*KS33* **ANTARES** General Stores Issue Ship. Am.

*L10* **FEARLESS** Assault Ship. Br.

*L11* **INTREPID** Assault Ship. Br.

*L144* **SYROS** Tank Landing Ship. Gk.

*L153* **NAFKRATOUSSA** Dock Landing Ship. Gk.

*L154* **IKARIA** Tank Landing Ship. Gk.

*L157* **RODOS** Tank Landing Ship. Gk.

*L158* **LIMNOS** Tank Landing Ship. Gk.

*L161* **IPOPLIARKHOS GRIGORO-POULOS** Medium Landing Ship Gk.

*L162* **IPOPLIARKHOS TOURNAS** Medium Landing Ship. Gk.

*L163* **IPOPLIARKHOS SANIOLOS** Medium Landing Ship. Gk.

*L164* **IPOPLIARKHOS ROUSSEN** Medium Landing Ship. Gk.

*L165* **IPOPLIARKHOS CRYSTAL-IDIS** Medium Landing Ship. Gk.

*L166* **IPOPLIARKHOS MERLIN** Medium Landing Ship. Gk.

*L171* **PINIOS** Tank Landing Ship. Gr.

*L172* **LESBOS** Tank Landing Ship. Gr.

*L179* **SAMOS** Tank Landing Ship. Gr.

*L195* **CHIOS** Tank Landing Ship. Gr.

*L700* **LCM700** Tank Landing Craft. Br.

*L701* **LCM701** Tank Landing Craft. Br.

*L702* **LCM702** Tank Landing Craft. Br. (Attached to HMS "Fearless" and has *F3* on bows)

*L703* **LCM703** Tank Landing Craft. Br.

*L704* **LCM704** Tank Landing Craft. Br.

*L705* **LCM705** Tank Landing Craft. Br.

*L706* **LCM706** Tank Landing Craft. Br.

*L707* **LCM707** Tank Landing Craft. Br.

*L708* **LCM708** Tank Landing Craft. Br.

*L3209* **SIR LANCELOT** Transport. RFA. Br.

*L709* **LCM709** Landing Craft. rBr.

*L710* **LCM710** Landing Craft. Br.

*L711* **LCM711** Landing Craft. Br.

*L750* **KROKODIL** Landing Ship. Ge.

*L751* **EIDECHSE** Landing Ship. Ge.

*L752* **SALAMANDER** Landing Ship. Ge.

*L753* **VIPER** Landing Ship. Ge.

*L760* **FLUNDER** Landing Ship. Ge.

*L761* **KARPFEN** Landing Ship. Ge.

*L762* **LACHS** Landing Ship. Ge.

*L763* **PLOTZE** Landing Ship. Ge.

*L764* **ROCHEN** Landing Ship. Ge.

*L765* **SCHLEI** Landing Ship. Ge.

*L766* **STOR** Landing Ship. Ge.

*L767* **TUMMLER** Landing Ship. Ge.

*L768* **WELS** Landing Ship. Ge.

*L769* **ZANDER** Landing Ship. Ge.

*L788* **BUTT** Landing Ship. Ge.

*L789* **BRASSE** Landing Ship. Ge.

*L790* **BARBE** Landing Ship. Ge.

*L791* **DELPHIN** Landing Ship. Ge.

*L792* **DORSCH** Landing Ship. Ge.

*L793* **FELCHEN** Landing Ship. Ge.

*L794* **FORELLE** Landing Ship. Ge.

*L795* **INGER** Landing Ship. Ge.

*L796* **MAKRELLE** Landing Ship. Ge.

*L797* **MURANE** Landing Ship. Ge.

*L798* **RENKE** Landing Ship. Ge.

*L799* **SALM** Landing Ship. Ge.

*L1312* **LOKOJA** Landing Craft. Ng.

*L3004* **SIR BEDIVERE** Logistic Ship. Br.

*L3005* **SIR GALAHAD** Logistic Ship. Br.

*L3011* **MAGAR** Landing Ship. In.

*L3044* **NARVIK** Tank Landing Ship. Br.

*L3209* **SIR LANCELOT** Logistic Ship. Br.

*L3507* **LCM3507** Tank Landing Ship. Br.

*L3508* **LCM3508** Tank Landing Ship. Br.

*L3515* **STALKER** Tank Landing Ship. Br.

*L3522* **TRACKER** Tank Landing Ship. Br.

*L4002* **AGHEILA** Landing Craft. Br.

*L4037* **AKYAB** Landing Craft. Br.

*L4041* **ABBEVILLE** Landing Craft. Br.

*L4061* **AUDEMER** Landing Craft. Br.

*L4062* **AACHEN** Landing Craft. Br.

*L4073* **ARDENNES** Landing Craft. Br.

*L4074* **ANTWERP** Landing Craft. Br.

*L4085* **AGEDABIA** Landing Craft. Br.

*L4086* **ARROMANCHES** Landing Craft. Br.

*L4097* **ANDALNES** Landing Craft. Br.

*L4128* **AREZZO** Landing Craft. Br.

*L4164* **ARAKAN** Landing Craft. Br.

*L9003* **ARGENS** Landing Ship. Fr.

*L9004* **BIDASSOA** Landing Ship. Fr.

*L9005* **ODET** Landing Ship. Fr.

*L9006* **CHELIFF** Landing Ship. Fr.

*L9007* **TRIEUX** Landing Ship. Fr.

*L9008* **DIVES** Landing Ship. Fr.

*L9009* **BLAVET** Landing Ship. Fr.

*L9021* **OURAGAN** Landing Ship, Assault. Fr.

*L9022* **ORAGE** Landing Ship, Assault. Fr.

*L9070* **EDIC 7** Landing Craft. Fr.

*L9071* **EDIC 8** Landing Craft. Fr.

*L9091* **EDIC 1** Landing Craft. Fr.

*L9092* **EDIC 2** Landing Craft. Fr.

*L9093* **EDIC 3** Landing Craft. Fr.

*L9094* **EDIC 4** Landing Craft. Fr.

*L9095* **EDIC 5** Landing Craft. Fr.

*L9096* **EDIC 6** Landing Craft. Fr.

*L9097* **ISSOLE** Landing Craft. Fr.

*L9609* — Landing Craft. Du.

*LA5* **MAIMON** Survey Launch. Do.

*LC71* **QUITO** Gunboat. Ec.

*LC72* **GUAYAQUIL** Gunboat. Ec.

*LDG101* **ALFANGE** Landing Craft. Po.

*LDM101* — Landing Craft. Po.

*LDM102* — Landing Craft. Po.

*LDM103* — Landing Craft. Po.

*LDM201* — Landing Craft. Po.

*LDM202* — Landing Craft. Po.

*LDM203* — Landing Craft. Po.

*LDM204* — Landing Craft. Po.

*LDM205* — Landing Craft. Po.

*LDM301* — Landing Craft. Po.

*LDM302* — Landing Craft. Po.

*LDM303* — Landing Craft. Po.

*LDM304* — Landing Craft. Po.

*LDM305* — Landing Craft. Po.

*LDM306* — Landing Craft. Po.

*LDM307* — Landing Craft. Po.

*LDM308* — Landing Craft. Po.

*LDM309* — Landing Craft. Po.

*LDM310* — Landing Craft. Po.

*LDM311* — Landing Craft. Po.

*LDM312* — Landing Craft. Po.

*LDM313* — Landing Craft. Po.

*LDM401* — Landing Craft. Po.

*LDM402* — Landing Craft. Po.

*LDM403* — Landing Craft. Po.

*LDM404* — Landing Craft. Po.

*LDM405* — Landing Craft. Po.

*LDM406* — Landing Craft. Po.

*LDM407* — Landing Craft. Po.

*LDM408* — Landing Craft. Po.

*LDP103* — Landing Craft. Po.

*LDP104* — Landing Craft. Po.
*LDP105* — Landing Craft. Po.
*LDP106* — Landing Craft. Po.
*LDP107* — Landing Craft. Po.
*LDP108* — Landing Craft. Po.
*LDP109* — Landing Craft. Po.
*LDP201* — Landing Craft. Po.
*LDP202* — Landing Craft. Po.
*LDP203* — Landing Craft. Po.
*LDP204* — Landing Craft. Po.
*LDP205* — Landing Craft. Po.
*LDP206* — Landing Craft. Po.
*LDP207* — Landing Craft. Po.
*LDP208* — Landing Craft. Po.
*LDP209* — Landing Craft. Po.
*LDP210* — Landing Craft. Po.
*LDP211* — Landing Craft. Po.
*LDP212* — Landing Craft. Po.
*LDP213* — Landing Craft. Po.
*LDP301* — Landing Craft. Po.
*LDP302* — Landing Craft. Po.
*LDP303* — Landing Craft. Po.
*LDP304* — Landing Craft. Po.
*LL01* **WAKAKUSA** Tender. Ja.
*LL11* **HOKUTO** Tender and buoy Vessel. Ja.
*LL12* **GINGA** Tender and buoy Vessel. Ja.
*LL13* **KAIO** Tender and buoy Vessel. Ja.
*LM3001* **LSM 3001** Landing Ship. Ja. (Number amidships)
*LT30* Motor Torpedo Boat. Sp.
*LT31* Motor Torpedo Boat. Sp.
*LT32* Motor Torpedo Boat. Sp.
*M01* **BIDASOA** Fleet Minesweeper. Sp.
*M-01* **ALVSNABBEN** Minelayer. Sw.
*M02* **NERVION** Fleet Minesweeper. Sp.
*M03* **LEREZ** Fleet Minesweeper. Sp.
*M04* **TAMBRE** Fleet Minesweeper. Sp.
*M05* **SEGURA** Fleet Minesweeper. Sp.
*M06* **TER** Fleet Minesweeper. Sp.
*M3* **ROBINSON** Minesweeper. Ar.
*M4* **GRANVILLE** Minesweeper. Ar.
*M11* **JAVARI** Coastal Minesweeper. Ar.
*M11* **YOGAGA** Inshore Minesweeper. Gh.
*M11* **GUARDIARO** Fleet Mine - sweeper. Sp.
*M12* **AFADZATO** Inshore Mine - sweeper. Gh.
*M12* **TINTO** Fleet Minesweeper. Sp.
*M13* **EUME** Fleet Minesweeper. Sp.
*M14* **JURUENA** Coastal Mine - sweeper. Bz.
*M14* **ALMANZORA** Fleet Mine - sweeper. Sp.
*M15* **NAVIA** Fleet Minesweeper. Sp.
*M15* — Inshore Minesweeper. Sw. (Launch type)
*M16* **EJURA** Coastal Minesweeper. Gh.
*M16* **GUADALHORCE** Fleet Mine - sweeper. Sp.
*M16* — Inshore Minesweeper. Sw. (Launch type)

*M17* **EO** Fleet Minesweeper. Sp.
*M19* — Inshore Minesweeper. Sw. (Launch type)
*M20* — Inshore Minesweeper. Sw. (Launch type)
*M21* **NALON** Coastal Minesweeper. Sp.
*M21* — Inshore Minesweeper. Sw. (Launch type)
*M22* **LLOBREGAT** Coastal Minesweeper. Sp.
*M22* — Inshore Minesweeper. Sw. (Launch type)
*M23* **JUCAR** Coastal Minesweeper. Sp.
*M23* — Inshore Minesweeper. Sw. (Launch type)
*M24* **ULLA** Coastal Minesweeper. Sp.
*M24* — Inshore Minesweeper. Sw. (Launch type)
*M25* **MINA** Coastal Minesweeper. Sp.
*M25* — Inshore Minesweeper. Sw. (Launch type)
*M26* **EBRO** Coastal Minesweeper. Sp.
*M26* — Inshore Minesweeper. Sw. (Launch type)
*M27* **TURIO** Coastal Minesweeper. Sp.
*M28* **DUERO** Coastal Minesweeper. Sp.
*M29* **SIL** Coastal Minesweeper. Sp.
*M31* **GENIL** Coastal Minesweeper. Sp.
*M31* — Minelaying Tender. Ys.
*M32* **ODIEL** Coastal Minesweeper. Sp.
*M32* — Minelaying Tender. Ys.
*M33* — Minelaying Tender. Ys.
*M41* **ORUST** Inshore Minesweeper. Sw.
*M42* **TJORN** Inshore Minesweeper. Sw.
*M43* **HISINGEN** Inshore Mine - sweeper. Sw.
*M44* **BLACKAN** Inshore Mine - sweeper. Sw.
*M45* **DAMMAN** Inshore Mine - sweeper. Sw.
*M46* **GALTEN** Inshore Minesweeper. Sw.
*M47* **GILLOGA** Inshore Minesweeper. Sw.
*M48* **RODLOGA** Inshore Mine - sweeper. Sw.
*M49* **SVARTLOGA** Inshore Mine - sweeper. Sw.
*M51* **HANO** Coastal Minesweeper. Sw.
*M52* **TARNO** Coastal Minesweeper. Sw.
*M53* **TJURKO** Coastal Minesweeper. Sw.
*M54* **STURKO** Coastal Minesweeper. Sw.
*M55* **ORNO** Coastal Minesweeper. Sw.
*M56* **UTO** Coastal Minesweeper. Sw.
*M57* **ARKO** Coastal Minesweeper. Sw.
*M58* **SPARO** Coastal Minesweeper. Sw.
*M59* **KARLSO** Coastal Minesweeper. Sw.

*M60* **IGGO** Coastal Minesweeper. Sw.
*M61* **STYRSO** Coastal Minesweeper. Sw.
*M62* **SKAFTO** Coastal Minesweeper. Sw.
*M63* **ASPO** Coastal Minesweeper. Sw.
*M64* **HASSLO** Coastal Minesweeper. Sw.
*M65* **VINO** Coastal Minesweeper. Sw.
*M66* **VALLO** Coastal Minesweeper. Sw.
*M67* **NAMDO** Coastal Minesweeper. Sw.
*M68* **BLIDO** Coastal Minesweeper. Sw.
*M89* **BHATKAL** Inshore Minesweeper. In.
*M103* — Inshore Minesweeper. Ys.
*M105* — Inshore Minesweeper. Ys.
*M106* — Inshore Minesweeper. Ys.
*M109* — Inshore Minesweeper. Ys.
*M111* Inshore Minesweeper. Ys.
*M112* Inshore Minesweeper. Ys.
*M113* Inshore Minesweeper. Ys
*M114* Inshore Minesweeper. Ys.
*M115* Inshore Minesweeper. Ys.
*M116* Inshore Minesweeper. Ys.
*M117* Inshore Minesweeper. Ys.
*M118* Inshore Minesweeper. Ys.
*M119* Inshore Minesweeper. Ys.
*M120* Inshore Minesweeper. Ys.
*M121* Inshore Minesweeper. Ys.
*M140* Inshore Minesweeper. Ys.
*M141* Inshore Minesweeper. Ys.
*M142* Inshore Minesweeper. Ys.
*M143* Inshore Minesweeper. Ys.
*M144* Inshore Minesweeper. Ys.
*M151* **HRABRI** Coastal Minesweeper. Ys.
*M152* **SMELI** Coastal Minesweeper. Ys.
*M153* **SLOBODNI** Coastal Mine - sweeper. Ys.
*M154* **SNAZNI** Coastal Minesweeper. Ys.
*M228* **KONKAN** Minesweeper. In.
*M233* **INVERELL** Escort Minesweeper. NZ.
*M241* **KICHLI** Coastal Minesweeper. Gr.
*M242* **KISSA** Coastal Minesweeper. Gr.
*M245* **DORIS** Coastal Minesweeper. Gr.
*M246* **AIGLI** Coastal Minesweeper. Gr.
*M247* **DAPHNI** Coastal Minesweeper. Gr.
*M248* **AIDON** Coastal Minesweeper. Gr.
*M257* **SAMSUN** Coastal Mine - sweeper. Tu.
*M258* **SINOP** Coastal Minesweeper. Tu.
*M259* **SURMENE** Coastal Mine - sweeper. Tu.
*M260* **SEDDULBAHR** Coastal Mine - sweeper. Tu.
*M263* **SILIFKE** Coastal Minesweeper. Tu.

M264 **SAROS** Coastal Minesweeper. Tu.

M265 **SIGACIK** Coastal Minesweeper. Tu.

M266 **SAPANCA** Coastal Minesweeper. Tu.

M267 **SARIYER** Coastal Minesweeper. Tu.

M291 **PIETERMARITZBURG** Escort Minesweeper. SA.

M297 **SPA** Coastal Minesweeper. Be.

M304 **WATERWITCH** Inshore Survey Ship. Br.

M311 **SAUDA** Coastal Minesweeper. No.

M312 **SIRA** Coastal Minesweeper. No.

M313 **TANA** Coastal Minesweeper. No.

M314 **ALTA** Coastal Minesweeper. No.

M315 **OGNA** Coastal Minesweeper. No.

M316 **VOSSO** Coastal Minesweeper. No.

M317 **GLOMMA** Coastal Minesweeper. No.

M331 **TISTA** Coastal Minesweeper. No.

M332 **KVINA** Coastal Minesweeper. No.

M334 **UTLA** Coastal Minesweeper. No.

M348 **STAWELL** Escort Minesweeper. NZ.

M353 **KIAMA** Escort Minesweeper. NZ.

M392 **SANTA MARIA** Escort Minesweeper. Po.

M401 **S.ROQUE** Coastal Minesweeper. Po.

M402 **RIBEIRA GRANDE** Coastal Minesweeper. Po.

M403 **LAGOA** Coastal Minesweeper. Po.

M404 **ROSARIO** Coastal Minesweeper. Po.

M405 **PONTA DELGADA** Coastal Minesweeper. Po.

M406 **HORTA** Coastal Minesweeper. Po.

M407 **ANGRA DO HEROISMO** Coastal Minesweeper. Po.

M408 **VILA DO PORTO** Coastal Minesweeper. Po.

M409 **SANTA CRUZ** Coastal Minesweeper. Po.

M410 **VELAS** Coastal Minesweeper. Po.

M411 **LAJES** Coastal Minesweeper. Po.

M412 **S.PEDRO** Coastal Minesweeper. Po.

M415 **S.JORGE** Ocean Minesweeper. Po.

M416 **PICO** Ocean Minesweeper. Po.

M417 **GRACIOSO** Ocean Minesweeper. Po.

M418 **CORVO** Ocean Minesweeper. Po.

M470 **TEMSE** Inshore Minesweeper. Be.

M471 **HASSELT** Inshore Minesweeper. Be.

M472 **KORTRIJK** Inshore Minesweeper. Be.

M473 **LOKEREN** Inshore Minesweeper. Be.

M474 **TURNHOUT** Inshore Minesweeper. Be.

M475 **TONGEREN** Inshore Minesweeper. Be.

M476 **MERKSEM** Inshore Minesweeper. Be.

M477 **OUDENAERDE** Inshore Minesweeper. Be.

M478 **HERSTAL** Inshore Minesweeper. Be.

M479 **HUY** Inshore Minesweeper. Be.

M480 **SERAING** Inshore Minesweeper. Be.

M481 **TOURNAI** Inshore Minesweeper. Be.

M482 **VISE** Inshore Minesweeper. Be.

M483 **OUGREE** Inshore Minesweeper. Be.

M484 **DINANT** Inshore Minesweeper. Be.

M485 **ANDENNE** Inshore Minesweeper. Be.

M500 **AYVALIK** Escort Minesweeper. Tu.

M501 **ALANYA** Escort Minesweeper. Tu.

M502 **AMASRA** Escort Minesweeper. Tu.

M503 **FINIKE** Escort Minesweeper. Tu.

M522 **TRABZON** Coastal Minesweeper. Tu.

M523 **TERME** Coastal Minesweeper. Tu.

M524 **TIREBOLU** Coastal Minesweeper. Tu.

M525 **TEKIRDAG** Coastal Minesweeper. Tu.

M569 **KLORDYB** Inshore Minesweeper. Da.

M570 **VEJDYB** Inshore Minesweeper. Da.

M571 **AAROSUND** Coastal Minesweeper. Da.

M572 **ALSSUND** Coastal Minesweeper. Da.

M573 **EGERNSUND** Coastal Minesweeper. Da.

M574 **GRONSUND** Coastal Minesweeper. Da.

M575 **GULDBORGSUND** Coastal Minesweeper. Da.

M576 **OMOSUND** Coastal Minesweeper. Da.

M577 **ULVSUND** Coastal Minesweeper. Da.

M578 **VILSUND** Coastal Minesweeper. Da.

M579 **ASVIG** Inshore Minesweeper. Da.

M580 **MOSVIG** Inshore Minesweeper. Da.

M581 **SANDVIG** Inshore Minesweeper. Da.

M582 **SAELVIG** Inshore Minesweeper. Da.

M609 **NARVIK** Ocean Minesweeper. Fr.

M610 **OUISTREHAM** Ocean Minesweeper. Fr.

M612 **ALENCON** Ocean Minesweeper. Fr.

M613 **BERNEVAL** Ocean Minesweeper. Fr.

M614 **BIR HACHEIM** Ocean Minesweeper. Fr.

M615 **CANTHO** Ocean Minesweeper. Fr.

M616 **DOMPAIRE** Ocean Minesweeper. Fr.

M617 **GARIGLIANO** Ocean Minesweeper. Fr.

M618 **MYTHO** Ocean Minesweeper. Fr.

M619 **VINH LONG** Ocean Minesweeper. Fr.

M620 **BERLAIMONT** Ocean Minesweeper. Fr.

M621 **ORIGNY** Ocean Minesweeper. Fr.

M622 **AUTUN** Ocean Minesweeper. Fr.

M623 **BACCARAT** Ocean Minesweeper. Fr.

M624 **COLMAR** Ocean Minesweeper. Fr.

M631 **PAVOT** Coastal Minesweeper. Fr.

M632 **PERVENCHE** Coastal Minesweeper. Fr.

M633 **PIVOINE** Coastal Minesweeper. Fr.

M634 **RENONCULE** Coastal Minesweeper. Fr.

M635 **RESEDA** Coastal Minesweeper. Fr.

M638 **ACACIA** Coastal Minesweeper. Fr.

M639 **ACANTHE** Coastal Minesweeper. Fr.

M640 **ACONIT** Coastal Minesweeper. Fr.

M667 **AJONC** Coastal Minesweeper. Fr.

M668 **AZALEE** Coastal Minesweeper. Fr.

M669 **BEGONIA** Coastal Minesweeper. Fr.

M670 **BLEUET** Coastal Minesweeper. Fr.

M671 **CAMELIA** Coastal Minesweeper. Fr.

M672 **CHRYSANTHEME** Coastal Minesweeper. Fr.

M673 **COQUELICOT** Coastal Minesweeper. Fr.

M674 **CYCLAMEN** Coastal Minesweeper. Fr.

M675 **EGLANTINE** Coastal Minesweeper. Fr.

M676 **GARDENIA** Coastal Minesweeper. Fr.

M677 **GIROFLEE** Coastal Minesweeper. Fr.

M678 **GLAIEUL** Ocean Minesweeper. Fr.

M679 **GLYCINE** Ocean Minesweeper. Fr.

M680 **JACINTHE** Ocean Mine-sweeper. Fr.
M681 **LAURIER** Ocean Minesweeper. Fr.
M682 **LILAS** Ocean Minesweeper. Fr.
M683 **LISERON** Ocean Mine-sweeper. Fr.
M684 **LOBELIA** Ocean Minesweeper. Fr.
M685 **MAGNOLIA** Ocean Mine-sweeper. Fr.
M686 **MARGUERITE** Ocean Mine-sweeper. Fr.
M687 **MIMOSA** Ocean Mine-sweeper. Fr.
M688 **MUGUET** Ocean Mine-sweeper. Fr.
M691 — Patrol Launch. Fr.
M701 **SIRIUS** Coastal Minesweeper. Fr.
M702 **RIGEL** Coastal Minesweeper. Fr.
M703 **ANTARES** Coastal Mine-sweeper. Fr.
M704 **ALGOL** Coastal Minesweeper. Fr.
M705 **ALDEBARAN** Coastal Mine-sweeper. Fr.
M706 **REGULUS** Coastal Mine-sweeper. Fr.
M707 **VEGA** Coastal Minesweeper. Fr.
M708 **CASTOR** Coastal Mine-sweeper. Fr.
M709 **POLLUX** Coastal Minesweeper. Fr.
M710 **PEGASE** Coastal Mine-sweeper. Fr.
M726 **LA DUNKERQUOISE** Coastal Minesweeper. Fr.
M727 **LA MALOUINE** Coastal Mine-sweeper. Fr.
M728 **LA BAYONNAISE** Coastal Minesweeper. Fr.
M729 **LA PAMPOLAISE** Coastal Minesweeper. Fr.
M730 **LA DIEPPOISE** Coastal Minesweeper. Fr.
M731 **LA LORIENTAISE** Coastal Minesweeper. Fr.
M734 **CROIX DU SUD** Coastal Minesweeper. Fr.
M735 **ETOILE POLAIRE** Coastal Minesweeper. Fr.
M736 **ALTAIR** Coastal Minesweeper. Fr.
N737 **CAPRICORNE** Coastal Mine-sweeper. Fr.
M740 **CASSIOPE** Coastal Mine-sweeper. Fr.
M741 **ERIDAN** Coastal Minesweeper. Fr.
M742 **ORION** Coastal Minesweeper. Fr.
M743 **SAGITTAIRE** Coastal Mine-sweeper. Fr.
M744 **ACHERNAR** Coastal Mine-sweeper. Fr.
M745 **PROCYON** Coastal Mine-sweeper. Fr.
M746 **ARCTURUS** Coastal Mine-sweeper. Fr.

M747 **BETELGEUSE** Coastal Mine-sweeper. Fr.
M748 **PERSEE** Coastal Minesweeper. Fr.
M749 **PHENIX** Coastal Minesweeper. Fr.
M750 **BELLATRIX** Coastal Mine-sweeper. Fr.
M751 **DENEBOLA** Coastal Mine-sweeper. Fr.
M752 **CENTAURE** Coastal Mine-sweeper. Fr.
M753 **FOMALHAUT** Coastal Mine-sweeper. Fr.
M754 **CANOPUS** Coastal Mine-sweeper. Fr.
M755 **CAPELLA** Coastal Mine-sweeper. Fr.
M756 **CEPHEE** Coastal Minesweeper. Fr.
M757 **VERSEAU** Coastal Mine-sweeper. Fr.
M758 **ARIES** Coastal Minesweeper. Fr.
M759 **LYRE** Coastal Minesweeper. Fr.
M765 **MERCURE** Coastal Mine-sweeper. Fr.
M771 **TULIPE** Inshore Minesweeper. Fr.
M772 **ARMOISE** Inshore Mine-sweeper. Fr.
M773 **VIOLETTE** Inshore Mine-sweeper. Fr.
M774 **OEILLET** Inshore Mine-sweeper. Fr.
M775 **PAQUERETTE** Inshore Mine-sweeper. Fr.
M776 **JASMIN** Inshore Minesweeper. Fr.
M781 **AUBEPINE** Inshore Mine-sweeper. Fr.
M782 **CAPUCINE** Inshore Mine-sweeper. Fr.
M783 **HORTENSIA** Inshore Mine-sweeper. Fr.
M784 **GERANIUM** Inshore Mine-sweeper. Fr.
M785 **HIBISCUS** Inshore Mine-sweeper. Fr.
M786 **DAHLIA** Inshore Minesweeper. Fr.
M787 **JONQUILLE** Inshore Mine-sweeper. Fr.
M788 **MYOSOTIS** Inshore Mine-sweeper. Fr.
M789 **PETUNIA** Inshore Mine-sweeper. Fr.
M801 **DOKKUM** Coastal Mine-sweeper. Du.
M802 **HOOGEZAND** Coastal Mine-sweeper. Du.
M803 **WILDERVANK** Coastal Mine-sweeper. Du.
M804 **STEENWIJK** Coastal Mine-sweeper. Du.
M805 **GIETEN** Coastal Minesweeper. Du.
M806 **ROERMOND** Coastal Mine-sweeper. Du.
M807 **WAALWIJK** Coastal Mine-sweeper. Du.

M808 **AXEL** Coastal Minesweeper. Du.
M809 **NAALDWIJK** Coastal Mine-sweeper. Du.
M810 **ABCOUDE** Coastal Mine-sweeper. Du.
M811 **AALSMEER** Coastal Mine-sweeper. Du.
M812 **DRACHTEN** Coastal Mine-sweeper. Du.
M813 **OMMEN** Coastal Mine-sweeper. Du.
M814 **MEPPEL** Coastal Mine-sweeper. Du.
M815 **GIETHOORN** Coastal Mine-sweeper. Du.
M816 **LOCHEM** Coastal Mine-sweeper. Du.
M817 **VENLO** Coastal Minesweeper. Du.
M818 **DRUNEN** Coastal Mine-sweeper. Du.
M819 **GOES** Coastal Minesweeper. Du.
M820 **WOERDEN** Coastal Mine-sweeper. Du.
M822 **LEERSUM** Coastal Mine-sweeper. Du.
M823 **NAARDEN** Coastal Mine-sweeper. Du.
M824 **SNEEK** Coastal Minesweeper. Du.
M826 **GRIJPSKERK** Coastal Mine-sweeper. Du.
M827 **HOOGEVEEN** Coastal Mine-sweeper. Du.
M828 **STAPHORST** Coastal Mine-sweeper. Du.
M829 **ELST** Coastal Minesweeper. Du.
M830 **SITTARD** Coastal Mine-sweeper. Du.
M841 **GEMERT** Coastal Mine-sweeper. Du.
M842 **VEERE** Coastal Minesweeper. Du.
M843 **LISSE** Coastal Minesweeper. Du.
M844 **RHENEN** Coastal Mine-sweeper. Du.
M845 **BEEMSTER** Coastal Mine-sweeper. Du.
M846 **BOLSWARD** Coastal Mine-sweeper. Du.
M847 **BEDUM** Coastal Minesweeper. Du.
M848 **BEILEN** Coastal Minesweeper. Du.
M849 **BORCULO** Coastal Mine-sweeper. Du.
M850 **BORNE** Coastal Minesweeper. Du.
M851 **BRUMMEN** Coastal Mine-sweeper. Du.
M852 **BREUKELEN** Coastal Mine-sweeper. Du.
M853 **BLARICUM** Coastal Mine-sweeper. Du.
M854 **BRIELLE** Coastal Mine-sweeper. Du.
M855 **BRESKENS** Coastal Mine-sweeper. Du.

M856 **BRUINISSE** Coastal Mine -
sweeper. Du.
M857 **BOXTEL** Coastal Minesweeper.
Du.
M858 **BROUWERSHAVEN** Coastal
Minesweeper. Du.
M868 **ALBLAS** Inshore Mine -
sweeper. Du.
M869 **BUSSELMAKER** Inshore
Minesweeper. Du.
M870 **LACOMBLE** Inshore Mine -
sweeper. Du.
M871 **VAN HAMEL** Inshore Mine -
sweeper. Du.
M872 **VAN STRAELEN** Inshore
Minesweeper. Du.
M873 **VAN MOPPES** Inshore Mine-
sweeper. Du.
M874 **CHOMPFF** Inshore Mine -
sweeper. Du.
M875 **VAN WELL GROENEVALD**
Inshore Minesweeper. Du.
M876 **SCHULING** Inshore Mine -
sweeper. Du.
M877 **VAN VERSENDAAL** Inshore
Minesweeper. Du.
M878 **VAN DER WEL** Inshore
Minesweeper. Du.
M879 **VAN T'HOFF** Inshore Mine-
sweeper. Du.
M880 **MAHU** Inshore Minesweeper.
Du.
M881 **STAVERMAN** Inshore Mine-
sweeper. Du.
M882 **HOUTEPEN** Inshore Mine -
sweeper. Du.
M883 **ZOMER** Inshore Minesweeper.
Du.
M902 **VAN HAVERBEKE** Coastal
Minesweeper. Be.
M903 **A. F. OUFOUR** Ocean Mine-
sweeper. Be.
M906 **BREYDEL** Ocean Mine -
sweeper. Be.
M907 **ARTEVELDE** Ocean Mine -
sweeper. Be.
M908 **G. TRUFFAUT** Ocean Mine-
sweeper. Be.
M909 **F. BOVESSE** Ocean Mine-
sweeper. Be.
M910 **DIEST** Coastal Minesweeper. Be.
M911 **EEKLO** Coastal Minesweeper.
Be.
M912 **LIER** Coastal Minesweeper. Be.
M913 **MAASEIK** Coastal Mine -
sweeper. Be.
M917 **CHARLEROI** Coastal Mine -
sweeper. Be.
M918 **ST. NIKLAAS** Coastal Mine-
sweeper. Be.
M919 **ST. TRUIDEN** Coastal Mine-
sweeper. Be.
M920 **DIKSMUIDE** Coastal Mine-
sweeper. Be.
M921 **HERVE** Coastal Minesweeper.
Be.
M922 **MALMEDY** Coastal Mine -
sweeper. Be.
M923 **BLANKENBURGHE** Coastal
Minesweeper. Be.
M924 **LAROCHE** Coastal Mine -
sweeper. Be.

M925 **DE PANNE** Coastal Mine -
sweeper. Be.
M927 **SPA** Coastal Minesweeper.
Be.
M928 **STAVELOT** Coastal Mine -
sweeper. Be.
M929 **HEIST** Coastal Minesweeper.
Be.
M930 **ROCHEFORT** Coastal Mine-
sweeper. Be.
M931 **KNOKKE** Coastal Mine -
sweeper. Be.
M932 **NIEUWPOORT** Coastal Mine-
sweeper. Be.
M933 **KOKSIJDE** Coastal Mine -
sweeper. Be.
M934 **VERVIERS** Coastal Mine -
sweeper. Be.
M935 **VEURNE** Coastal Mine -
sweeper. Be.
M1050 **MIRA** Minesweeper. Ge.
(Number on superstructure)
M1051 **CASTOR** Minesweeper. Ge.
(Number on superstructure)
M1052 **KREBS** Minesweeper. Ge.
(Number on superstructure)
M1053 **ORION** Minesweeper. Ge.
(Number on superstructure)
M1054 **POLLUX** Minesweeper. Ge.
(Number on superstructure)
M1055 **SIRIUS** Minesweeper. Ge.
(Number on superstructure)
M1056 **RIGEL** Minesweeper. Ge.
(Number on superstructure)
M1057 **REGULUS** Minesweeper. Ge.
(Number on superstructure)
M1058 **MARS** Minesweeper. Ge.
(Number on superstructure)
M1059 **SPICA** Minesweeper. Ge.
(Number on superstructure)
M1060 **SKORPION** Minesweeper.
Ge. (Number on superstructure)
M1061 **STIER** Minesweeper. Ge.
(Number on superstructure)
M1062 **SCHUTZE** Minesweeper. Ge.
(Number on superstructure)
M1063 **WAAGE** Minesweeper. Ge.
(Number on superstructure)
M1064 **DENEB** Minesweeper. Ge.
(Number on Bridge)
M1065 **JUPITER** Minesweeper. Ge.
(Number on superstructure)
M1066 **PEGASUS** Minesweeper. Ge.
(Number on Bridge)
M1067 **ATAIR** Minesweeper. Ge.
(Number on superstructure)
M1068 **ALGOL** Minesweeper. Ge.
(Number on superstructure)
M1069 **WEGA** Minesweeper. Ge.
(Number on superstructure)
M1070 **GOTTINGEN** Coastal Mine-
sweeper. Ge.
M1071 **KOBLENZ** Coastal Mine -
sweeper. Ge.
M1072 **LINDAU** Coastal Mine -
sweeper. Ge.
M1073 **SCHLESWIG** Coastal Mine-
sweeper. Ge.
M1074 **TUBINGEN** Coastal Mine-
sweeper. Ge.
M1075 **WETTLAR** Coastal Mine -
sweeper. Ge.

M1076 **PADERBORN** Coastal Mine-
sweeper. Ge.
M1077 **WEILHEIM** Coastal Mine-
sweeper. Ge.
M1078 **CUXHAVEN** Coastal Mine-
sweeper. Ge.
M1079 **DUREN** Coastal Mine -
sweeper. Ge.
M1080 **MARBURG** Coastal Mine -
sweeper. Ge.
M1081 **KONSTANZ** Coastal Mine -
sweeper. Ge.
M1082 **WOLFSBURG** Coastal Mine-
sweeper. Ge.
M1083 **ULM** Coastal Minesweeper.
Ge.
M1084 **FLENSBURG** Coastal Mine-
sweeper. Ge.
M1085 **MINDEN** Coastal Mine -
sweeper. Ge.
M1086 **FULDA** Coastal Mine -
sweeper. Ge.
M1087 **VOLKLINGEN** Coastal Mine-
sweeper. Ge.
M1090 **PERSEUS** Minesweeper. Ge.
(Number on superstructure)
M1091 **STEINBACK** Minesweeper.
Ge.
(Number on superstructure)
M1092 **PLUTO** Minesweeper. Ge.
(Number on superstructure)
M1093 **NEPTUN** Minesweeper. Ge.
(Number on superstructure)
M1094 **WIDDER** Minesweeper. Ge.
(Number on superstructure)
M1095 **HERKULES** Minesweeper.
Ge.
(Number on superstructure)
M1096 **FISCHE** Minesweeper. Ge.
(Number on superstructure)
M1097 **GEMMA** Minesweeper. Ge.
(Number on superstructure)
M1098 **CAPELLA** Minesweeper. Ge.
(Number on superstructure)
M1099 **URANUS** Minesweeper. Ge.
(Number on superstructure)
M1102 **SNIPE** Coastal Minesweeper.
Au.
M1103 **KILMOREY** Coastal Mine -
sweeper. Br.
M1104 **ALVERTON** Coastal Mine -
sweeper. Br.
M1105 **CLYDE** Coastal Minesweeper.
Br.
M1107 **BEACHAMPTON** Coastal
Minesweeper. Br.
M1109 **KILLIECRANKIE** Coastal
Minesweeper. Br.
M1110 **BILDESTON** Coastal Mine-
sweeper. Br.
M1113 **BRERETON** Coastal Mine -
sweeper. Br.
M1114 **BRINTON** Coastal Mine -
sweeper. Br.
M1115 **BRONINGTON** Coastal
Minesweeper. Br.
M1117 **THAMES** Coastal Mine -
sweeper. Br.
M1118 **CALTON** Coastal Mine -
sweeper. Br.
M1120 **CAUNTON** Coastal Mine -
sweeper. Br.

*M1121* **CURLEW** Coastal Minesweeper. Au.

*M1124* **ST. DAVID** Coastal Minesweeper. Br.

*M1125* **CUXTON** Coastal Minesweeper. Br.

*M1126* **MONTROSE** Coastal Minesweeper. Br.

*M1127* **MAHAMIRU** Coastal Minesweeper. My.

*M1129* **OULSTON** Coastal Minesweeper. Br.

*M1130* **HIGHBURTON** Coastal Minesweeper. Br.

*M1132* **BLAXTON** Coastal Minesweeper. Br.

*M1133* **BOSSINGTON** Coastal Minesweeper. Br.

*M1134* **KINABALU** Coastal Minesweeper. My.

*M1135* **FENTON** Coastal Minesweeper. Br.

*M1136* **CURZON** Coastal Minesweeper. Br.

*M1137* **FLOCKTON** Coastal Minesweeper. Br.

*M1138* **FLORISTON** Coastal Minesweeper. Br.

*M1139* **HAWK** Coastal Minesweeper. Au.

*M1140* **GAVINTON** Coastal Minesweeper. Br.

*M1141* **GLASSERTON** Coastal Minesweeper. Br.

*M1142* **KAAPSTAD** Coastal Minesweeper. SA.

*M1143* **LEDANG** Coastal Minesweeper. My.

*M1144* **PRETORIA** Coastal Minesweeper. SA.

*M1146* **VENTURER** Coastal Minesweeper. Br.

*M1147* **HUBBERSTON** Coastal Minesweeper. Br.

*M1149* **BADMINTON** Coastal Minesweeper. Br.

*M1150* **INVERMORISTON** Coastal Minesweeper. Br.

*M1151* **IVESTON** Coastal Minesweeper. Br.

*M1152* **TEAL** Coastal Minesweeper. Au.

*M1153* **KEDLESTON** Coastal Minesweeper. Br.

*M1154* **KELLINGTON** Coastal Minesweeper. Br.

*M1155* **MONKTON** Coastal Minesweeper. Br.

*M1157* **KIRKLISTON** Coastal Minesweeper. Br.

*M1158* **LALESTON** Coastal Minesweeper. Br.

*M1159* **LANTON** Coastal Minesweeper. Br.

*M1161* **LEVERTON** Coastal Minesweeper. Br.

*M1163* **TAHAN** Coastal Minesweeper. My.

*M1164* **MADDISTON** Coastal Minesweeper. Br.

*M1165* **MAXTON** Coastal Minesweeper. Br.

*M1166* **NURTON** Coastal Minesweeper. Br.

*M1168* **JERAI** Coastal Minesweeper. My.

*M1172* **BRINCHANG** Coastal Minesweeper. My.

*M1173* **MERSEY** Coastal Minesweeper. Br.

*M1174* **PUNCHESTON** Coastal Minesweeper. Br.

*M1175* **NORTHUMBRIA** Coastal Minesweeper. Br.

*M1179* **SEFTON** Coastal Minesweeper. Br.

*M1180* **SHAVINGTON** Coastal Minesweeper. Br.

*M1181* **SHERATON** Coastal Minesweeper. Br.

*M1182* **SHOULTON** Coastal Minesweeper. Br.

*M1185* **GULL** Coastal Minesweeper. Au.

*M1187* **UPTON** Coastal Minesweeper. Br.

*M1188* **WALKERTON** Coastal Minesweeper. Br.

*M1189* **WASPERTON** Coastal Minesweeper. Br.

*M1190* **CUDDALORE** Coastal Minesweeper. In.

*M1191* **CANNONORE** Coastal Minesweeper. In.

*M1192* **WILKIESTON** Coastal Minesweeper. Br.

*M1193* **WOLVERTON** Coastal Minesweeper. Br.

*M1194* **THAMES** Coastal Minesweeper. Br.

*M1195* **WOTTON** Coastal Minesweeper. Br.

*M1196* **YARNTON** Coastal Minesweeper. Br.

*M1197* **KARWAR** Coastal Minesweeper. In.

*M1198* **ASHTON** Coastal Minesweeper. Br.

*M1199* **BELTON** Coastal Minesweeper. Br.

*M1200* **SOBERTON** Coastal Minesweeper. Br.

*M1201* **KAKINADA** Coastal Minesweeper. In.

*M1204* **STUBBINGTON** Coastal Minesweeper. Br.

*M1205* **WISTON** Coastal Minesweeper. Br.

*M1207* **JOHANNESBURG** Coastal Minesweeper. SA.

*M1208* **LEWISTON** Coastal Minesweeper. Br.

*M1209* **CHAWTON** Coastal Minesweeper. Br.

*M1210* **KIMBERLEY** Coastal Minesweeper. SA.

*M1211* **HOUGHTON** Coastal Minesweeper. Br.

*M1212* **PORT ELIZABETH** Coastal Minesweeper. SA.

*M1213* **MOSSELBAAI** Coastal Minesweeper. SA.

*M1214* **WALVISBAAI** Coastal Minesweeper. SA.

*M1215* **EAST LONDON** Coastal Minesweeper. SA.

*M1216* **SOLENT** Coastal Minesweeper. Ge.

*M1250* **VEGESACK** Coastal Minesweeper. Ge.

*M1251* **HAMELN** Coastal Minesweeper. Ge.

*M1252* **DETMOLD** Coastal Minesweeper. Ge.

*M1253* **WORMS** Coastal Minesweeper. Ge.

*M1254* **SIEGEN** Coastal Minesweeper. Ge.

*M1255* **PASSAU** Coastal Minesweeper. Ge.

*M1498* **WINDHOEK** Coastal Minesweeper. SA.

*M1499* **DURBAN** Coastal Minesweeper. SA.

*M2002* **AVELEY** Inshore Minesweeper. Br.

*M2010* **ISIS** Inshore Minesweeper. Br.

*M2603* **ARLINGHAM** Inshore Minesweeper. Br.

*M2610* **TODAK** Inshore Minesweeper. My.

*M2614* **BUCKLESHAM** Inshore Minesweeper. Br.

*M2615* **CARDINHAM** Inshore Minesweeper. Br.

*M2616* **CHELSHAM** Inshore Minesweeper. Br.

*M2618* **COBHAM** Inshore Minesweeper. Br.

*M2619* **DARSHAM** Inshore Minesweeper. Br.

*M2620* **DAVENHAM** Inshore Minesweeper. Br.

*M2621* **DITTISHAM** Inshore Minesweeper. Br.

*M2622* **DOWNHAM** Inshore Minesweeper. Br.

*M2624* **ELSENHAM** Inshore Minesweeper. Br.

*M2625* **ETCHINGHAM** Inshore Minesweeper. Br.

*M2626* **EVERINGHAM** Inshore Minesweeper. Br.

*M2627* **GERONG** Inshore Minesweeper. My.

*M2628* **FLINTHAM** Inshore Minesweeper. Br.

*M2629* **DAMERHAM** Inshore Minesweeper. Br.

*M2630* **FRITHAM** Inshore Minesweeper. Br.

*M2631* **GLENTHAM** Inshore Minesweeper. Br.

*M2635* **HAVERSHAM** Inshore Minesweeper. Br.

*M2636* **LASHAM** Inshore Minesweeper. Br.

*M2637* **HAVINGHAM** Inshore Minesweeper. Br.

*M2651* **HOLNIS** Inshore Minesweeper. Ge.

*M2671* **FRAUENLOB** Inshore Minesweeper. Ge.

*M2672* **NAUTILUS** Inshore Minesweeper. Ge.

*M2673* **GEFION** Inshore Mine - sweeper. Ge.

*M2674* **MEDUSA** Inshore Mine - sweeper. Ge.

*M2675* **UNDINE** Inshore Mine - sweeper. Ge.

*M2676* **MINERVA** Inshore Mine - sweeper. Ge.

*M2677* **DIANA** Inshore Minesweeper. Ge.

*M2678* **LORELY** Inshore Mine - sweeper. Ge.

*M2679* **ATLANTIS** Inshore Mine - sweeper. Ge.

*M2680* **ACHERON** Inshore Mine - sweeper. Ge.

*M2705* **BIMLIPTAN** Inshore Minesweeper. In.

*M2706* **LEDSHAM** Inshore Mine - sweeper. Br.

*M2707* **BASSEIN** Inshore Mine - sweeper. In.

*M2708* **LUDHAM** Inshore Mine - sweeper. Br.

*M2713* **NETTLEHAM** Inshore Minesweeper. Br.

*M2714* **OCKHAM** Inshore Mine - sweeper. Br.

*M2716* **PAGHAM** Inshore Mine - sweeper. Br.

*M2717* **FORDHAM** Inshore Minesweeper. Br.

*M2722* **RACKHAM** Inshore Mine - sweeper. Br.

*M2724* **SHIPHAM** Inshore Mine - sweeper. Br.

*M2727* **SAXLINGHAM** Inshore Minesweeper. Br.

*M2728* **SHRIVENHAM** Inshore Minesweeper. Br.

*M2733* **THAKEHAM** Inshore Minesweeper. Br.

*M2735* **TONGHAM** Inshore Minesweeper. Br.

*M2737* **WARMINGHAM** Inshore Minesweeper. Br.

*M2778* **WOLDINGHAM** Inshore Minesweeper. Br.

*M2780* **WOODLARK** Inshore Survey Ship. Br.

*M2781* **PORTISHAM** Inshore Minesweeper. Br.

*M2783* **ODIHAM** Inshore Mine - sweeper. Br.

*M2784* **PUTTENHAM** Inshore Minesweeper. Br.

*M2785* **BIRDHAM** Inshore Minesweeper. Br.

*M2787* **ABBOTSHAM** Inshore Minesweeper. Br. —

*M2788* **GEORGEHAM** Inshore Minesweeper. Br.

*M2790* **THATCHAM** Inshore Minesweeper. Br.

*M2791* **SANDRINGHAM** Inshore Minesweeper. Br.

*M2792* **POLSHAM** Inshore Mine - sweeper. Br.

*M2793* **THORNHAM** Inshore Minesweeper. Br.

*MB1* **No. 1** Minesweeping Boat. Ja. (Number amidships and also *701* on bows)

*MB2* **No. 2** Minesweeping Boat. Ja. (Number amidships and also *702* on bows)

*MB3* **No. 3** Minesweeping Boat. Ja. (Number amidships and also *703* on bows)

*MB4* **No. 4** Minesweeping Boat. Ja. (Number amidships and also *704* on bows)

*MB5* **No. 5** Minesweeping Boat. Ja. (Number amidships and also *705* on bows)

*MB6* **No. 6** Minesweeping Boat. Ja. (Number amidships and also *706* on bows)

*MCS1* **CATSKILL** Mine Counter Measures Support Ship. Am.

*MCS2* **OZARK** Mine Counter Measures Support Ship. Am.

*MGB101* Motor Gunboat. Bm.

*MGB102* Motor Gunboat. Bm.

*MGB104* Motor Gunboat. Bm.

*MGB105* Motor Gunboat. Bm.

*MGB106* Motor Gunboat. Bm.

*MGB108* Motor Gunboat. Bm.

*MGB110* Motor Gunboat. Bm.

*MHV69* Inshore Minesweeper. Da.

*MHV70* Patrol Boat. Da.

*MHV71* Patrol Boat. Da.

*MHV72* Patrol Boat. Da.

*MHV81* Inshore Minesweeper. Da.

*MHV82* Inshore Minesweeper. Da.

*MHV83* Inshore Minesweeper. Da.

*MOC1201* Repair Craft. It.

*MOC1202* Repair Craft. It.

*MP17* **WOOD** Ca. RCMP Marine Division

*MSF1* **COMMANDANTE PEDRO CAMPBELL** Escort Vessel. Ur.

*N04* **AKTION** Minelayer. Gr.

*N05* **AMVRAKIA** Minelayer. Gr.

*N13* **MINER III** Controlled Minelayer. Br.

*N21* **ABDIEL** Minelayer. Br.

*N39* **LINDORMEN** Coastal Minelayer. Da.

*N40* **LAALAND** Coastal Minelayer. Da.

*N41* **LOUGEN** Coastal Minelayer. Da.

*N42* **LANGELAND** Coastal Minelayer. Da.

*N47* **TYR** Coastal Minelayer. No.

*N48* **GOR** Coastal Minelayer. No.

*N49* **BRAGE** Coastal Minelayer. No.

*N50* **ULLER** Coastal Minelayer. No.

*N51* **BORGEN** Coastal Minelayer. No.

*N80* **FALSTER** Minelayer. Da.

*N81* **FYEN** Minelayer. Da.

*N82* **MOEN** Minelayer. Da.

*N83* **SJAELLAND** Minelayer. Da.

*N100* **MARMARIS** Coastal Minelayer. Tu.

*N101* **MARDOGAN** Coastal Minelayer. Tu.

*N102* **MERIC** Coastal Minelayer. Tu.

*N103* **MERSIN** Coastal Minelayer. Tu.

*N104* **MUREFTE** Coastal Minelayer. Tu.

*N105* **MEHMEDCIK** Coastal Minelayer. Tu.

*N108* **NUSRET** Minelayer. Tu.

*N120* **BOCHUM** Minelayer. Ge.

*N121* **BOTTROP** Minelayer. Ge.

*NO5* **KLONGYAI** Patrol Vessel. Th.

*NO6* **TAKBAI** Patrol Vessel. Th.

*NO7* **KANTANG** Patrol Vessel. Th.

*NO11* **TRAD** Patrol Vessel. Th.

*NO12* **PUKET** Patrol Vessel. Th.

*NO13* **PATTAN** Patrol Vessel. Th.

*NO21* **SURASDRA** Patrol Vessel. Th.

*NO22* **CHANDHABURI** Patrol Vessel. Th.

*NO25* **RAYONG** Patrol Vessel. Th.

*NO31* **CHUMPORN** Patrol Vessel. Th.

*OE1* **SACRAMENTO** Combat Support Ship. Am.

*OE2* **CAMDEN** Combat Support Ship. Am.

*OE3* **SEATTLE** Combat Support Ship. Am.

*OE4* **DETROIT** Combat Support Ship. Am.

*OE5* — Combat Support Ship. Am.

*OG1* **PATAPSCO** Gasoline Tanker. Am.

*OG7* **ELKHORN** Gasoline Tanker. Am.

*OG8* **GENESEE** Gasoline Tanker. Am.

*OG9* **KISHWAUKEE** Gasoline Tanker. Am.

*OG11* **TOMBIGBEE** Gasoline Tanker. Am.

*OG50* **CHEWAUCAN** Gasoline Tanker. Am.

*OG55* **NESPELEN** Gasoline Tanker. Am.

*OG56* **NOXUBEE** Gasoline Tanker. Am.

*OG1* **WICHITA** Replenishment Oiler. Am.

*OR2* **MILWAUKEE** Replenishment Oiler. Am.

*OR3* **KANSAS CITY** Replenishment Oiler. Am.

*OR4* — Replenishment Oiler. Am.

*OR5* **WABASH** Replenishment Oiler. Am.

*OR6* — Replenishment Oiler. Am.

*OSS01* **OCEANOGRAPHER** Survey Ship. Am.

*OSS03* **RESEARCHER** Survey Ship. Am.

*P-01* **MEJILLON** Patrol Vessel. Ve.

*P-02* **CALAMAR** Patrol Vessel. Ve.

*P-03* **ALCATRAZ** Patrol Vessel. Ve.

*P-04* **ALBATROS** Patrol Vessel. Ve.

*P-05* **PETREL** Patrol Vessel. Ve.

*P-06* **PATHFINDER** Survey Craft. Ng.

*P-06* **CARACOL** Patrol Vessel. Ve.

*P-07* **PULPO** Patrol Vessel. Ve.

*P-08* **CAMARON** Patrol Vessel. Ve.

*P 09* **SAPELE** Minesweeper Motor Launch. Ng.

P-09 **TOGOGO** Patrol Vessel. Ve.
P4 **DISCOVERY BAY** Patrol Boat. Jm.
P5 **HOLLAND BAY** Patrol Boat. Jm.
P6 **MANATEE BAY** Patrol Boat. Jm.
P10 **CHALLENGER** Survey Craft. Ng.
P-10 **GAVIOTA** Patrol Vessel. Ve.
P11 **PENELOPE** Survey Ship. Ng.
P13 **ELMINA** Seaward Defence Boat. Gh.
P14 **KOMENDA** Seaward Defence Boat. Gh.
P14 **PLOTARKHIS ARSLANO-GLOU** Patrol Vessel. Gr.
P19 **AIOLUS** Patrol Boat. Gr.
P20 **ASTRAPI** Patrol Boat. Gr.
P20 Patrol Boat. Gh.
P21 **SHARP** Motor Torpedo Boat. Et.
P21 **ANDROMEDA** Fast Patrol Boat. Gr.
P21 — Patrol Boat. Gh.
P22 **BARRACUDA** Motor Torpedo Boat. Et.
P22 **INIOHOS** Fast Patrol Boat. Gr.
P22 Patrol Boat. Gh.
P23 **KASTOR** Fast Patrol Boat. Gr.
P23 Patrol Boat. Gh.
P24 **KYKONOS** Fast Patrol Boat. Gr.
P25 **PICASSOS** Fast Patrol Boat. Gr.
P26 **TOXOTIS** Fast Patrol Boat. Gr.
P32 **HEROINA** Frigate. Ar.
P33 **SARANDI** Frigate. Ar.
P34 **KRIS** Patrol Boat. My.
P36 **SUNDANG** Patrol Boat. My.
P37 **BADEK** Patrol Boat. My.
P38 **RENCHONG** Patrol Boat. My.
P39 **TOMBAK** Patrol Boat. My.
P40 **LEMBING** Patrol Boat. My.
P41 **SERAMPANG** Patrol Boat. My.
P42 **PANAH** Patrol Boat. My.
P43 **KERAMBIT** Patrol Boat. My.
P44 **BELEDAU** Patrol Boat. My.
P45 **KELEWANG** Patrol Boat. My.
P46 **RENTAKA** Patrol Boat. My.
P47 **SRI PERLIS** Patrol Boat. My.
P48 **PANGLIMA** Seaward Defence Boat. Sg.
P49 **SRI JOHOR** Patrol Boat. My.
P53 **ANTIPLOIARKHOS LASKOS** Patrol Vessel. Gr.
P57 **PLOIARKHOS MELETOPOU-LOS** Patrol Vessel. Gr.
P69 **KOALA** Boom Defence Vessel. Au.
P70 **ANTIPLOIARKHOS PEZO-POULOS** Patrol Vessel. Gr.
P80 **KANGAROO** Boom Defence Vessel. Au.
P82 Motor Torpedo Boat. Ar.
P84 Motor Torpedo Boat. Ar.
P84 **AITAPE** Patrol Craft. Au.
P90 **ATTACK** Patrol Craft. Au.
P94 **PLOTARKHIS HARIDAKIS** Patrol Vessel. Gr.
P95 **PLOTARKHIS VLACHAVAS** Patrol Vessel. Gr.
P96 **PLOTARKHIS CHANTZIKON-STANDIS** Patrol Vessel. Gr.
P111 — Support Gunboat. Cambodia.
P111 **SULTAHISAR** Patrol Vessel. Tu.

P112 **DEMIRHISAR** Patrol Vessel. Tu.
P113 **YARHISAR** Patrol Vessel. Tu.
P114 **AKHISAR** Patrol Vessel. Tu.
P115 **SIVRIHISAR** Patrol Vessel. Tu.
P116 **KOCHISAR** Patrol Vessel. Tu.
P121 **BAFRA** Escort Minesweeper. Tu.
P122 **BEYKOZ** Escort Minesweeper. Tu.
P123 **BEYLERBEYI** Escort Mine-sweeper. Tu.
P125 **BODRUM** Escort Minesweeper. Tu.
P126 **BORNOVA** Escort Mine-sweeper. Tu.
P127 **BOZCADA** Escort Mine-sweeper. Tu.
P128 **BUYUKDERE** Escort Mine-sweeper. Tu.
P129 **BANDIRMA** Escort Mine-sweeper. Tu.
P130 **BARTIN** Escort Minesweeper. Tu.
P140 **RAJSHAHI** Fast Patrol Boat. Pk.
P141 **JESSORE** Fast Patrol Boat. Pk.
P142 **COMILLA** Fast Patrol Boat. Pk.
P143 **SYLHET** Fast Patrol Boat. Pk.
P150 **PERKASA** Fast Patrol Boat. My.
P151 **HANDALAN** Fast Patrol Boat. My.
P152 **GEMPITA** Fast Patrol Boat. My.
P153 **PENDEKAR** Fast Patrol Boat. My.
P179 **KILTON** Frigate. In.
P190 **LAYMOOR** Boom Defence Vessel. Br.
P191 **LAYBURN** Boom Defence Vessel. Br.
P201 **BARBAIN** Boom Defence Vessel. Br.
P202 **BARFOOT** Boom Defence Vessel. Br.
P204 **BARHILL** Boom Defence Vessel. Br.
P214 **BARBECUE** Boom Defence Vessel. Br.
P215 **BARNDALE** Boom Defence Vessel. Br.
P216 **BARGLOW** Boom Defence Vessel. Br.
P232 **BARMOND** Boom Defence Vessel. Br.
P233 **ANDROMEDA** Coastal Patrol Vessel. Gr.
P241 **BARNARD** Boom Defence Vessel. Br.
P259 **BARRINGTON** Boom Defence Vessel. Br.
P282 **BARFOAM** Boom Defence Vessel. Br.
P284 **MOORSMAN** Boom Defence Vessel. Br.
P285 **SOMERSET** Boom Defence Vessel. SA.
P287 **BARCAROLLE** Boom Defence Vessel. Br.
P294 **BARFOIL** Boom Defence Vessel. Br.

P301 **AG 1** Boom Defence Vessel. Tu.
P302 **AG 2** Boom Defence Vessel. Tu.
P303 **AG 3** Boom Defence Vessel. Tu.
P304 **AG 4** Boom Defence Vessel. Tu.
P305 **KALDIRAY** Boom Defence Vessel. Tu.
P306 **AG 5** Boom Defence Vessel. Tu.
P308 **LS 10** Motor Launch. Tu.
P309 **LS 11** Motor Launch. Tu.
P301 **LS 12** Motor Launch. Tu.
P311 **MTB 1** Motor Torpedo Boat. Tu.
P312 **MTB 2** Motor Torpedo Boat. Tu.
P313 **MTB 3** Motor Torpedo Boat. Tu.
P314 **MTB 4** Motor Torpedo Boat. Tu.
P315 **MTB 6** Motor Torpedo Boat. Tu.
P317 **MTB 7** Motor Torpedo Boat. Tu.
P318 **MTB 8** Motor Torpedo Boat. Tu.
P319 **MTB 9** Motor Torpedo Boat. Tu.
P320 **MTB 10** Motor Torpedo Boat. Tu.
P321 **AB 1** Motor Launch. Tu.
P322 **AB 2** Motor Launch. Tu.
P323 **AB 3** Motor Launch. Tu.
P324 **AB 4** Motor Launch. Tu.
P326 **AB 6** Motor Launch. Tu.
P327 **AB 7** Motor Launch. Tu.
P339 **LS 9** Motor Launch. Tu.
P343 **TJELD** Motor Torpedo Boat. No.
P344 **SKARV** Motor Torpedo Boat. No.
P345 **TEIST** Motor Torpedo Boat. No.
P346 **JO** Motor Torpedo Boat. No.
P347 **LOM** Motor Torpedo Boat. No.
P349 **HAVK** Motor Torpedo Boat. No.
P350 **FALK** Motor Torpedo Boat. No.
P351 **RAPP** Motor Torpedo Boat. No.
P352 **RASK** Motor Torpedo Boat. No.
P353 **KVIKK** Motor Torpedo Boat. No.
P354 **KJAPP** Motor Torpedo Boat. No.
P355 **SNAR** Motor Torpedo Boat. No.
P356 **SNOGG** Motor Torpedo Boat. No.
P357 **RAVN** Motor Torpedo Boat. No.
P360 **ANTARES** Patrol Launch. Po.
P361 **LIRA** Patrol Launch. Po.
P362 **ORION** Patrol Launch. Po.
P363 **BELLATRIX** Patrol Launch. Po.
P364 **CANOPUS** Patrol Launch. Po.
P365 **DENEB** Patrol Launch. Po.

P366 **ESPIGA** Patrol Launch. Po.
P367 **FOMALHAUT** Patrol Launch. Po.
P368 **POLLUX** Patrol Launch. Po.
P369 **REGULUS** Patrol Launch. Po.
P370 **RIO MINHO** Patrol Launch. Po.
P371 **TETE** Patrol Launch on Zambesi River. Po.
P372 **ARGOS** Patrol Launch. Po.
P373 **CASSIOPEIA** Patrol Launch. Po.
P374 **DRAGAO** Patrol Launch. Po.
P375 **ESCORDIAO** Patrol Launch. Po.
P376 **HIDRA** Patrol Launch. Po.
P377 **ALTAIR** Patrol Launch. Po.
P378 **RIGEL** Patrol Launch. Po.
P379 **PEGASO** Patrol Launch. Po.
P380 **SKREI** Motor Torpedo Boat. No.
P381 **HAI** Motor Torpedo Boat. No.
P382 **SEL** Motor Torpedo Boat. No.
P383 **HVAL** Motor Torpedo Boat. No.
P384 **LAKS** Motor Torpedo Boat. No.
P385 **KNURR** Motor Torpedo Boat. No.
P386 **DELFIN** Motor Torpedo Boat. No.
P387 **LYR** Motor Torpedo Boat. No.
P388 **GRIBB** Motor Torpedo Boat. No.
P389 **GEIR** Motor Torpedo Boat. No.
P390 **ERLE** Motor Torpedo Boat. No.
P401 Patrol Boat. Abu Dhabi.
P500 **FLYVEFISKEN** Motor Torpedo Boat. Da.
P501 **HAJEN** Motor Torpedo Boat. Da.
P502 **HAVKATTEN** Motor Torpedo Boat. Da.
P503 **LAXEN** Motor Torpedo Boat. Da.
P504 **MAKRELEN** Motor Torpedo Boat. Da.
P505 **SVAERDFISKEN** Motor Torpedo Boat. Da.
P506 **FALKEN** Motor Torpedo Boat. Da.
P507 **GLENTEN** Motor Torpedo Boat. Da.
P508 **GRIBBEN** Motor Torpedo Boat. Da.
P509 **HOGEN** Motor Torpedo Boat. Da.
P510 **SOLOVEN** Motor Torpedo Boat. Da.
P511 **SORIDDEREN** Motor Torpedo Boat. Da.
P512 **SOBJORNEN** Motor Torpedo Boat. Da.
P513 **SOHESTEN** Motor Torpedo Boat. Da.
P514 **SOHUNDEN** Motor Torpedo Boat. Da.
P515 **SOULVEN** Motor Torpedo Boat. Da.
P521 **WILLEMOES** Motor Torpedo Boat. Da.
P530 **DAPHNE** Seaward Defence Boat. Da.
P531 **DRYADEN** Seaward Defence Boat. Da.

P532 **HAVMANDEN** Seaward Defence Boat. Da.
P533 **HAVFRUEN** Seaward Defence Boat. Da.
P534 **NAJADEN** Seaward Defence Boat. Da.
P535 **NYMFEN** Seaward Defence Boat. Da.
P536 **NEPTUN** Seaward Defence Boat. Da.
P537 **RAN** Seaward Defence Boat. Da.
P538 **ROTA** Seaward Defence Boat. Da.
P568 **VIBEN** Motor Torpedo Boat. Da.
P580 **CASTOR** Patrol Launch. Po.
P580 **PRINCIPE** Patrol Vessel. Po.
P582 **MADEIRA** Patrol Vessel. Po.
P585 **S. TOME** Patrol Vessel. Po.
P586 **S. VICENTE** Patrol Vessel. Po.
P587 **MAIO** Patrol Vessel. Po.
P588 **PORTO SANTO** Patrol Vessel. Po.
P589 **S. NICOLAU** Patrol Vessel. Po.
P590 **BRAVA** Patrol Vessel. Po.
P591 **FOGO** Patrol Vessel. Po.
P592 **BOAVISTA** Patrol Vessel. Po.
P593 **SANTO ANTAO** Patrol Vessel. Po.
P594 **SANTA LUZIA** Patrol Vessel. Po.
P595 **AZEVIA** Fishery Protection Launch. Po.
P596 **BICUDA** Fishery Protection Launch. Po.
P597 **CORVINA** Fishery Protection Launch. Po.
P598 **DOURADA** Fishery Protection Launch. Po.
P599 **ESPADILHA** Fishery Protection Launch. Po.
P630 **L'INTREPIDE** Patrol Vessel. Fr.
P635 **L'ARDENT** Patrol Vessel. Fr.
P637 **L'ETOURDI** Patrol Vessel. Fr.
P638 **L'EFFRONTE** Patrol Vessel. Fr.
P639 **LE FRONDEUR** Patrol Vessel. Fr.
P640 **LE FRINGANT** Patrol Vessel. Fr.
P641 **LE FOUGUEUX** Patrol Vessel. Fr.
P642 **L'OPINIATRE** Patrol Vessel. Fr.
P643 **L'AGILE** Patrol Vessel. Fr.
P644 **L'ADROIT** Patrol Vessel. Fr.
P645 **L'ALERTE** Patrol Vessel. Fr.
P646 **L'ATTENTE** Patrol Vessel. Fr.
P647 **L'ENJOUE** Patrol Vessel. Fr.
P648 **LE HARDI** Patrol Vessel. Fr.
P680 **ASTROLABE** Survey Ship. Fr.
P681 **BOUSSOLE** Survey Ship. Fr.
P682 **ALIDADE** Survey Ship. Fr.
P683 **OPTANT** Survey Ship. Fr.
P706 Patrol Launch. Fr.
P730 **LA COMBATTANTE** Patrol Vessel. Fr.
P751 **VC 1** Seaward Patrol Craft. Fr.
P752 **VC 2** Seaward Patrol Craft. Fr.
P753 **VC 3** Seaward Patrol Craft. Fr.
P760 **VC 10** Seaward Patrol Craft. Fr.

P761 **ISTIQLAL** Patrol Craft. Tu.
P780 **OISEAU DES ISLES** Motor Launch. Fr.
P802 **BALDER** Patrol Vessel. Du.
P804 **FREYR** Patrol Vessel. Du.
P805 **HADDA** Patrol Vessel. Du.
P806 **HEFRING** Patrol Vessel. Du.
P950 **SLEIPNER** Patrol Vessel. No.
P951 **AEGER** Patrol Vessel. No.
P955 Motor Torpedo Boat. No.
P956 Motor Torpedo Boat. No.
P957 Motor Torpedo Boat. No.
P958 Motor Torpedo Boat. No.
P960 **STORM** Gunboat. No.
P961 **BLINK** Gunboat. No.
P962 **GLIMT** Gunboat. No.
P963 **SKJOLD** Gunboat. No.
P964 **TRYGG** Gunboat. No.
P965 **KJEKK** Gunboat. No.
P966 **DJERV** Gunboat. No.
P967 **SKUDD** Gunboat. No.
P968 **ARG** Gunboat. No.
P969 **STEIL** Gunboat. No.
P970 **BRANN** Gunboat. No.
P971 **TROSS** Gunboat. No.
P972 **HVASS** Gunboat. No.
P973 **TRAUST** Gunboat. No.
P974 **BROTT** Gunboat. No.
P975 **ODD** Gunboat. No.
P976 **PIL** Gunboat. No.
P977 **BRASK** Gunboat. No.
P978 **ROKK** Gunboat. No.
P979 **GNIST** Gunboat. No.
P980 **LYN** Gunboat. No.
P1114 **DARK GLADIATOR** Fast Patrol Boat. Br.
P1115 **DARK HERO** Fast Patrol Boat. Br.
P1130 **CENTAURO** Patrol Launch. Po.
P1132 **JUPITER** Patrol Launch. Po.
P1133 **VENUS** Patrol Launch. Po.
P1134 **MARTE** Patrol Launch. Po.
P1134 **SAGITARIO** Patrol Launch. Po.
P1135 **MERCURIO** Patrol Launch. Po.
P1136 **SATURNO** Patrol Launch. Po.
P1137 **URANO** Patrol Launch. Po.
P1138 **ALGOL** Patrol Launch. Po.
P1148 **DOM ALEIXO** Patrol Launch. Po.
P1156 **ALVOR** Patrol Launch. Po.
P1157 **ALBUFEIRA** Patrol Launch. Po.
P1158 **ALJEZUR** Patrol Launch. Po.
P3102 **NYATI** Seaward Defence Boat. Ke.
P3104 **BECKFORD** Seaward Defence Boat. Br.
P3105 **GELDERLAND** Seaward Defence Boat. SA.
P3106 **IBADAN II** Seaward Defence Boat. Ng.
P3110 **SPC 3110** Patrol Craft. In.
P3110 **SIMBA** Patrol Craft. Ke.
P3111 **BONNY** Seaward Defence Boat. Ng.
P3112 **SPC 3112** Patrol Craft. In.
P3112 **CHUI** Patrol Craft. Ke.
P3113 **DROXFORD** Seaward Defence Boat. Br.

*P3117* **KINGSFORD** Seaward Defence Boat. Br.
*P3117* **SPC 3117** Patrol Craft. In.
*P3117* **NDOVU** Patrol Craft. Ke.
*P3118* **SPC 3118** Patrol Craft. In.
*P3119* **SAPELE** Seaward Defence Boat. Ng.
*P3120* **NAUTILUS** Seaward Defence Boat. SA.
*P3125* **RIJGER** Seaward Defence Boat. SA.
*P3126* **HAERLEM** Seaward Defence Boat. SA.
*P3127* **OOSTERLAND** Seaward Defence Boat. SA.
*P3137* **ENUGU** Seaward Defence Boat. Ng.
*P3138* **SRI KEDAH** Patrol Craft. My.
*P3139* **SRI SELANGOR** Patrol Craft. My.
*P3140* **SRI PERAK** Patrol Craft. My.
*P3141* **SRI PAHANG** Patrol Craft. My.
*P3142* **SRI KELANTAN** Patrol Craft. My.
*P3143* **SRI TRENGGANU** Patrol Craft. My.
*P3144* **SRI SABAH** Patrol Craft. My.
*P3145* **SRI SARAWAK** Patrol Craft. My.
*P3146* **SRI NEGRI SEMBILAN** Patrol Craft. My.
*P3147* **SRI MELAKA** Patrol Craft. My.
*P3148* **SRI TANJONG MERANG** Patrol Craft. My.
*P3333* Fast Patrol Boat. Au.
*P3502* Patrol Craft. My.
*P3504* **MUTIARA** Despatch Vessel. My.
*P3517* **SDML 3517.** Seaward Defence Motor Launch. Pk.
*P3520* **SDML 3520** Seaward Defence Motor Launch. Pk.
*P3551* **MAKO** Patrol Craft. NZ.
*P3552* **PAEA** Patrol Craft. NZ.
*P3553* **KAHAWAI** Seaward Patrol Craft. NZ.
*P3554* **MARORO** Seaward Patrol Craft. NZ.
*P3555* **TAMURE** Seaward Patrol Craft. NZ.
*P3556* **TAKAPU** Seaward Patrol Craft. NZ.
*P3562* **PARORE** Seaward Patrol Craft. NZ.
*P3563* **KAUPARU** Seaward Patrol Craft. NZ.
*P3564* **KOURA** Seaward Patrol Craft. NZ.
*P3565* **HAKU** Seaward Patrol Craft. NZ.
*P3566* **TARAPUNGA** Seaward Patrol Craft. NZ.
*P3567* **MANGA** Seaward Patrol Craft. NZ.
*P6058* **ILTIS** Motor Torpedo Boat. Ge. (Number on bridge)
*P6059* **JAGUAR** Motor Torpedo Boat. Ge. (Number on bridge)
*P6060* **LEOPARD** Motor Torpedo Boat. Ge. (Number on bridge)
*P6061* **LUCHS** Motor Torpedo Boat. Ge. (Number on bridge)
*P6062* **WOLF** Motor Torpedo Boat. Ge. (Number on bridge)
*P6063* **TIGER** Motor Torpedo Boat. Ge. (Number on bridge)
*P6064* **PANTHER** Motor Torpedo Boat. Ge. (Number on bridge)
*P6065* **LOWE** Motor Torpedo Boat. Ge. (Number on bridge)
*P6066* **FUCHS** Motor Torpedo Boat. Ge. (Number on bridge)
*P6067* **MARDER** Motor Torpedo Boat. Ge. (Number on bridge)
*P6068* **SEEADLER** Motor Torpedo Boat. Ge. (Number on bridge)
*P6069* **ALBATROS** Motor Torpedo Boat. Ge. (Number on bridge)
*P6070* **KONDOR** Motor Torpedo Boat. Ge. (Number on bridge)
*P6071* **GREIF** Motor Torpedo Boat. Ge. (Number on bridge)
*P6072* **FALKE** Motor Torpedo Boat. Ge. (Number on bridge)
*P6073* **GEIER** Motor Torpedo Boat. Ge. (Number on bridge)
*P6074* **BUSSARD** Motor Torpedo Boat. Ge. (Number on bridge)
*P6075* **HABICHT** Motor Torpedo Boat. Ge. (Number on bridge)
*P6076* **SPERBER** Motor Torpedo Boat. Ge. (Number on bridge)
*P6077* **KORMORAN** Motor Torpedo Boat. Ge. (Number on bridge)
*P6082* **WEIHE** Motor Torpedo Boat. Ge. (Number on bridge)
*P6083* **KRANICH** Motor Torpedo Boat. Ge. (Number on bridge)
*P6084* **ALK** Motor Torpedo Boat. Ge. (Number on bridge)
*P6085* **STORCH** Motor Torpedo Boat. Ge. (Number on bridge)
*P6086* **PELIKAN** Motor Torpedo Boat. Ge. (Number on bridge)
*P6087* **HAHER** Motor Torpedo Boat. Ge. (Number on bridge)
*P6088* **ELSTER** Motor Torpedo Boat. Ge. (Number on bridge)
*P6089* **REIHER** Motor Torpedo Boat. Ge. (Number on bridge)
*P6090* **PINGUIN** Motor Torpedo Boat. Ge. (Number on bridge)
*P6091* **DOMMEL** Motor Torpedo Boat. Ge. (Number on bridge)
*P6092* **ZOBEL** Motor Torpedo Boat. Ge. (Number on bridge)
*P6093* **WIESEL** Motor Torpedo Boat. Ge. (Number on bridge)
*P6094* **DACHS** Motor Torpedo Boat. Ge. (Number on bridge)
*P6095* **HERMELIN** Motor Torpedo Boat. Ge. (Number on bridge)
*P6096* **NERZ** Motor Torpedo Boat. Ge. (Number on bridge)
*P6097* **PUMA** Motor Torpedo Boat. Ge. (Number on bridge)
*P6098* **GEPARD** Motor Torpedo Boat. Ge. (Number on bridge)
*P6099* **HYANE** Motor Torpedo Boat. Ge. (Number on bridge)
*P6100* **FRETTCHEN** Motor Torpedo Boat. Ge. (Number on bridge)
*P6101* **OZELOT** Motor Torpedo Boat. Ge. (Number on bridge)
*P6111* **THETIS** Corvette. Ge. (Number on superstructure)
*P6112* **HERMES** Corvette. Ge. (Number on superstructure)
*P6113* **NAJADE** Corvette. Ge. (Number on superstructure)
*P6114* **TRITON** Corvette. Ge. (Number on superstructure)
*P6115* **THESEUS** Corvette. Ge. (Number on superstructure)
*P9783* Rhine Patrol Boat. Fr.
*P9784* Rhine Patrol Boat. Fr.
*P9785* Rhine Patrol Boat. Fr.
*P9786* Rhine Patrol Boat. Fr.
*P9787* Rhine Patrol Boat. Fr.
*P9788* Rhine Patrol Boat. Fr.
*PA31* **MONROVIA** Attack Transport. Am.
*PA32* **CALVERT** Attack Transport. Am.
*PA36* **CAMBRIA** Attack Transport. Am.
*PA38* **CHILTON** Attack Transport. Am.
*PA44* **FREMONT** Attack Transport. Am.
*PA45* **HENRICO** Attack Transport. Am.
*PA194* **SANDOVAL** Attack Transport. Am.
*PA208* **TALLADEGA** Attack Transport. Am.
*PA213* **MOUNTRAIL** Attack Transport. Am.
*PA215* **NAVARRO** Attack Transport. Am.

*PA220* **OKANOGAN** Attack Transport. Am.

*PA222* **PICKAWAY** Attack Transport. Am.

*PA237* **BEXAR** Attack Transport. Am.

*PA248* **PAUL REVERE** Attack Transport. Am.

*PA249* **FRANCIS MARION** Attack Transport. Am.

*PC01* **HATSUNAMI** Patrol Craft. Ja.

*PC02* **AYANAMI** Patrol Craft. Ja.

*PC03* **ISONAMI** Patrol Craft. Ja.

*PC04* **URANAMI** Patrol Craft. Ja.

*PC05* **KYONAMI** Patrol Craft. Ja.

*PC06* **OKINAMI** Patrol Craft. Ja.

*PC07* **TAMANAMI** Patrol Craft. Ja.

*PC08* **SUZUNAMI** Patrol Craft. Ja.

*PC09* **CHIYONAMI** Patrol Craft. Ja.

*PC1* **MALDONADO** Patrol Craft. Ur.

*PC10* **HAYANAMI** Patrol Craft. Ja.

*PC11* Patrol Craft. Et.

*PC11* **HATSUZUKI** Patrol Craft. Ja.

*PC12* Patrol Craft. Et.

*PC12* **HANAZUKI** Patrol Craft. Ja.

*PC13* Patrol Craft. Et.

*PC13* **KIYOZUKI** Patrol Craft. Ja.

*PC14* Patrol Craft. Et.

*PC14* **MOCHIZUKI** Patrol Craft. Ja.

*PC15* Patrol Craft. Et.

*PC15* **NIIZUKI** Patrol Craft. Ja.

*PC16* **SUZUTSUKI** Patrol Craft. Ja.

*PC17* **TERUZUKI** Patrol Craft. Ja.

*PC18* **URAZUKI** Patrol Craft. Ja.

*PC19* **WAKAZUKI** Patrol Craft. Ja.

*PC20* **YAMAZUKI** Patrol Craft. Ja.

*PC21* **HARUZUKI** Patrol Craft. Ja.

*PC22* **NATSUZUKI** Patrol Craft. Ja.

*PC23* **AKIZUKI** Patrol Craft. Ja.

*PC24* **FUYUZUKI** Patrol Craft. Ja.

*PC25* **MUTSUKI** Patrol Craft. Ja.

*PC30* **SHINONOME** Patrol Craft. Ja.

*PC31* **HATAGUMO** Patrol Craft. Ja.

*PC32* **MAKIGUMO** Patrol Craft. Ja.

*PC33* **YAEGUMO** Patrol Craft. Ja.

*PC34* **ASAGUMO** Patrol Craft. Ja.

*PC35* **NATSUGUMO** Patrol Craft. Ja.

*PC36* **TATSUGUMO** Patrol Craft. Ja.

*PC37* **HANAYUKI** Patrol Craft. Ja.

*PC38* **MINEYUKI** Patrol Craft. Ja.

*PC39* **ISOYUKI** Patrol Craft. Ja.

*PC40* **MATSUYUKI** Patrol Craft. Ja.

*PC41* **SHIMAYUKI** Patrol Craft. Ja.

*PC42* **TAMAYUKI** Patrol Craft. Ja.

*PC43* **HAMAYUKI** Patrol Craft. Ja.

*PC44* **YAMAYUKI** Patrol Craft. Ja.

*PC45* **KOMAYUKI** Patrol Craft. Ja.

*PC46* **UMIGIRI** Patrol Craft. Ja.

*PC47* **ASAGIRI** Patrol Craft. Ja.

*PC75* **FUENTEALBA** Patrol Craft. Ch.

*PC76* **ODGER** Patrol Craft. Ch.

*PC109* **HIRYU** Patrol Craft. Ja.

*PC618* **WEATHERFORD** Submarine Chaser. Am.

*PC706* **MYO HYANG SAN** Patrol Vessel. Ko.

*PC707* **O TAE SAN** Patrol Vessel. Ko.

*PC708* **KUM CHONG SAN** Patrol Vessel. Ko.

*PC709* **SOL AK** Patrol Vessel. KO.

*PCH1* **HIGH POINT** Hydrofoil Submarine Chaser. Am.

*PCR855* **REXBURG** Training Experimental Ship. Am.

*PCR857* **MARYSVILLE** Training Experimental Ship. Am.

*PD101* **ALMIRANTE PADILLA** Destroyer Transport. Co.

*PE201* **CARIBE** Patrol Escort. Cu.

*PE302* **SIBONEY** Patrol Escort. Cu.

*PF1* **MONTEVIDEO** Frigate Training Ship. Ur.

*PF31* **IQUIQUE** Frigate. Ch.

*PF32* **COVADONGA** Frigate. Ch.

*PG37* **CASMA** Corvette. Ch.

*PG38* **CHIPANA** Corvette. Ch.

*PG39* **PAPUDO** Corvette. Ch.

*PGM69* Motor Gunboat. Li.

*PGM102* Motor Gunboat. Li.

*PGM401* Patrol Gunboat. Bm.

*PGM402* Patrol Gunboat. Bm.

*PGM403* Patrol Gunboat. Bm.

*PGM404* Patrol Gunboat. Bm.

*PGM405* Patrol Gunboat. Bm.

*PGM406* Patrol Gunboat. Bm.

*PL01* **MUROTO** Patrol Vessel. Ja.

*PL02* **DAIO** Patrol Vessel. Ja.

*PL12* **OJIKA** Patrol Vessel. Ja.

*PL11* **NOJIMA** Patrol Vessel. Ja.

*PL13* **ERIMO** Patrol Vessel. Ja.

*PL14* **SATSUMA** Patrol Vessel. Ja.

*PL21* **KOJIMA** Patrol Vessel. Ja.

*PL31* **IZU** Patrol Vessel. Ja.

*PL32* **MIURU** Patrol Vessel. Ja.

*PL107* **SOYA** Patrol Vessel. Ja.

*PM* Medium Patrol Vessel. Ja.

*PM01* Medium Patrol Vessel. Ja.

*PM02* **MIYAKE** Patrol Vessel. Ja.

*PM03* **SADO** Patrol Vessel. Ja.

*PM04* **REBUN** Patrol Vessel. Ja.

*PM05* **IKI** Patrol Vessel. Ja.

*PM06* **OKI** Patrol Vessel. Ja.

*PM07* **GENAKI** Patrol Vessel. Ja.

*PM08* **HACHIJO** Patrol Vessel. Ja.

*PM09* **AMAKUSA** Patrol Vessel. Ja.

*PM10* **OKUSHIRI** Patrol Vessel. Ja.

*PM11* **KUSAKAKI** Patrol Vessel. Ja.

*PM12* **RISHIRI** Patrol Vessel. Ja.

*PM13* **NOTO** Patrol Vessel. Ja.

*PM14* **HEKURA** Patrol Vessel. Ja.

*PM15* **MIKURA** Patrol Vessel. Ja.

*PM16* **KOSHIKI** Patrol Vessel. Ja.

*PM17* **HIRADO** Patrol Vessel. Ja.

*PM18* **CHIFURI** Medium Patrol Vessel. Ja.

*PM19* **KUROKAMI** Medium Patrol Vessel. Ja.

*PM20* **KOZU** Medium Patrol Vessel. Ja.

*PM21* **SHIKINE** Medium Patrol Vessel. Ja.

*PM22* **DAITO** Medium Patrol Vessel. Ja.

*PN13* Oiler. Ys.

*PN17* Oiler. Ys.

*PR2* **SALTO** Patrol Vessel. Ur.

*PR3* **RIO NEGRO** Patrol Vessel. Ur.

*PS* are Japanese Coast Guard small patrol vessels.

*PS01* **KUMA** Small Patrol Vessel. Ja.

*PS02* **FUJI** Small Patrol Vessel. Ja.

*PS03* **TENRYU** Small Patrol Vessel. Ja.

*PS04* **ISUZU** Small Patrol Vessel. Ja.

*PS05* **ISHIKARI** Small Patrol Vessel. Ja.

*PS06* **SAGAMI** Small Patrol Vessel. Ja.

*PS07* **OYODO** Small Patrol Vessel. Ja.

*PS08* **ABUKUMA** Small Patrol Vessel. Ja.

*PS09* **KUZURYU** Small Patrol Vessel. Ja.

*PS10* **KIKUCHI** Small Patrol Vessel. Ja.

*PS11* **MOGAMI** Small Patrol Vessel. Ja.

*PS12* **YOSHINO** Small Patrol Vessel. Ja.

*PS13* **NOSHIRO** Small Patrol Vessel. Ja.

*PS14* **KISO** Small Patrol Vessel. Ja.

*PS15* **SHINANO** Small Patrol Vessel. Ja.

*PS16* **CHIKUGO** Small Patrol Vessel. Ja.

*PS17* **KUMANO** Small Patrol Vessel. Ja.

*PS18* **NAGARA** Small Patrol Vessel. Ja.

*PS19* **TONE** Small Patrol Vessel. Ja.

*PS20* **KITAKAMI** Small Patrol Vessel. Ja.

*PS31* **TSUKUBA** Small Patrol Vessel. Ja

*PS32* **HIDAKA** Small Patrol Vessel. Ja.

*PS33* **HIMAYA** Small Patrol Vessel. Ja.

*PS34* **TSURUGI** Small Patrol Vessel. Ja.

*PS35* **ROKKO** Small Patrol Vessel. Ja.

*PS36* **TAKANAWA** Small Patrol Vessel. Ja.

*PS37* **AKIYOSHI** Small Patrol Vessel. Ja.

*PS38* **KUNIMI** Small Patrol Vessel. Ja.

*PS39* **TAKATSUKI** Small Patrol Vessel. Ja.

*PS40* **AKAGI** Small Patrol Vessel. Ja.

*PS41* **KAMUI** Small Patrol Vessel. Ja.

*PS42* **BIZAN** Small Patrol Vessel. Ja.

*PS43* **ASHITAKA** Small Patrol Vessel. Ja.

*PS44* **KURAMA** Small Patrol Vessel. Ja.

*PS45* **IBUKI** Small Patrol Vessel. Ja.

*PS46* **TOUMI** Small Patrol Vessel. Ja.

*PS51* **TOKACHI** Small Patrol Vessel. Ja.

*PS52* **TATSURA** Small Patrol Vessel. Ja.

*PS53* **TESHIO** Small Patrol Vessel. Ja.

*PS54* **YAHAGI** Small Patrol Vessel. Ja.

*PS55* **SUMIDA** Small Patrol Vessel. Ja.

*PS56* **CHITOSE** Small Patrol Vessel. Ja.

*PS57* **SORACHI** Small Patrol Vessel. Ja.

*PS58* **YUBARI** Small Patrol Vessel. Ja.

*PS59* **HORONAI** Small Patrol Vessel. Ja.

*PS60* **MATSUURA** Small Patrol Vessel. Ja.

*PS61* **SENDAI** Small Patrol Vessel. Ja.

*PS62* **AMAMI** Small Patrol Vessel. Ja

*PS63* **NATORI** Small Patrol Vessel. Ja.

*PS64* **KARATSU** Small Patrol Vessel. Ja.

*PS100* **KABASHIMA** Medium Patrol Vessel. Ja.

*PS102* **HAMACHIDORI** Medium Patrol Vessel. Ja.

*PS103* **ASACHIDORI** Small Patrol Vessel. Ja.

*PS104* **MIOCHIDORI** Small Patrol Vessel. Ja.

*PS105* **TOMOCHIDORI** Small Patrol Vessel. Ja.

*PS107* **SAWACHIDORI** Small Patrol Vessel. Ja.

*PS115* **HARUCHIDORI** Small Patrol Vessel. Ja.

*PT7* Motor Torpedo Boat. Ja.

*PT8* Motor Torpedo Boat. Ja.

*PT9* Motor Torpedo Boat. Ja.

*PT10* Motor Torpedo Boat. Ja.

*Q2* **BAHIA AGUIRRE** Transport. Ar.

*Q4* **GENERAL SAN MARTIN** Icebreaker—Research Ship. Ar.

*Q6* **BAHIA BUEN SUCESO** Transport. Ar.

*Q8* **BAHIA THETIS** Transport. Ar.

*Q8* **CAPITAN CANEPA** Survey Ship. Ar.

*Q10* **USHUAIA** Survey Ship. Ar.

*Q21* **INGENIERO IRIBAS** Repair Ship. Ar.

*Q54* **BDI-1** Infantry Landing Craft. Ar.

*Q57* **BDI-4** Infantry Landing Craft. Ar.

*Q68* **BDI-15** Infantry Landing Craft. Ar.

*Q69* **BDM-1** Medium Landing Craft. Ar.

*Q70* **BDM-2** Medium Landing Craft. Ar.

*R05* **EAGLE** Aircraft Carrier. Br. On Island Superstructure

*R06* **CENTAUR** Aircraft Carrier. Br. On Island Superstructure

*R07* **ALBION** Commando Carrier. Br. On Island Superstructure

*R08* **BULWARK** Commando Carrier. Br. On Island Superstructure

*R09* **ARK ROYAL** Aircraft Carrier. Br. On Island Superstructure

*R1* **DUK SOO** Repair Ship—Landing Craft. Ko.

*R5* **VULCAN** Repair Ship. Am.

*R6* **AJAX** Repair Ship. Am.

*R7* **HECTOR** Repair Ship. Am.

*R8* **JASON** Repair Ship. Am.

*R9* **DELTA** Repair Ship. Am.

*R-11* **FELIPE LARRAZABAL** Tug. Ve.

*R12* **BRIAREUS** Repair Ship. Am.

*R12* **HERMES** Aircraft Carrier. Br. On Island Superstructure

*R-12* **FERNANDO GOMEZ** Tug. Ve.

*R13* **AMPHION** Repair Ship. Am.

*R-13* **GENERAL JOSE FELIX RIBAS** Tug. Ve.

*R14* **CADMUS** Repair Ship. Am.

*R14* **LAURINDO PITTA** Tug. Bz.

*R14* **BERGANTIN** Tug. Do.

*R15* **SANTANA** Tug. Do.

*R16* **MERCEDES** Tug. Do.

*R17* **RIO HAINA** Tug. Do.

*R18* **CONSUELO** Tug. Do.

*R19* **CALDERAS** Tug. Do.

*R21* **TRITO** Tug. Do.

*R22* **KLONDIKE** Repair Ship. Am.

*R22* **TRIDENTE** Tug. Bz.

*R23* **TRIFUNO** Tug. Bz.

*R23* **MARKAB** Repair Ship. Am.

*R32* **QUILMES** Tug. Ar.

*R33* **GUAYCURU** Tug. Ar.

*R41* Motor Launch. Cu.

*R42* Motor Launch. Cu.

*R44* **IFUGAO** Tug. Pi.

*R51* **CAYAMBE** Fleet Tug. Ec.

*R52* **COTOPAXI** Fleet Tug. Ec.

*R53* **SANGAY** Fleet Tug. Ec.

*R96* **ARROMANCHES** Aircraft Carrier. Fr.

*R97* **JEANNE D'ARC** Helicopter Carrier. Fr.

*R98* **CLEMENCEAU** Aircraft Carrier. Fr.

*R99* **FOCH** Aircraft Carrier. Fr.

*RA1* Tug. Sp.

*RA2* Tug. Sp.

*RA3* Tug. Sp.

*RA4* Tug. Sp.

*RA5* Tug. Sp.

*RB4* **ZEUS** Repair Ship. Am.

*RB5* **MIDAS** Repair Ship. Am.

*RB7* **SARPEDON** Repair Ship. Am.

*RB8* **TELAMON** Repair Ship. Am.

*RC2* **NEPTUNE** Cable Ship. Am.

*RC3* **AEOLUS** Cable Ship. Am.

*RC4* **THOR** Cable Ship. Am.

*RG4* **TUTUILA** Repair Ship. Am.

*RL1* **ACHELOUS** Repair Ship. Am.

*RL2* **AMYCUS** Repair Ship. Am.

*RL7* **ATLAS** Repair Ship. Am.

*RL8* **EGERIA** Repair Ship. Am.

*RL9* **ENDYMION** Repair Ship. Am.

*RL23* **SATYR** Repair Ship. Am.

*RL24* **APHINX** Repair Ship. Am.

*RL30* **ASKARI** Repair Ship. Am.

*RL31* **BELLEROPHON** Repair Ship. Am.

*RL37* **INDRA** Repair Ship. Am.

*RL38* **KRISHNA** Repair Ship. Am.

*RR10* Patrol Vessel. Sp.

*RR11* Tug. Sp.

*RR15* Tug. Sp.

*RR16* Tug. Sp.

*RR19* Patrol Vessel. Sp.

*RR20* Patrol Vessel. Sp.

*RR28* Patrol Vessel. Sp.

*RR29* Patrol Vessel. Sp.

*RR50* Tug. Sp.

*RR51* Tug. Sp.

*RR52* Tug. Sp.

*RR53* Tug. Sp.

*RR54* Tug. Sp.

*RR55* Tug. Sp.

*RS6* **ESCAPE** Salvage Vessel. Am.

*RS7* **GRAPPLE** Salvage Vessel. Am.

*RS8* **PRESERVER** Salvage Vessel. Am.

*RS22* **CURRENT** Salvage Vessel. Am.

*RS23* **DELIVER** Salvage Vessel. Am.

*RS24* **GRASP** Salvage Vessel. Am.

*RS25* **SAFEGUARD** Salvage Vessel. Am.

*RS38* **BOLSTER** Salvage Vessel. Am.

*RS39* **CONSERVER** Salvage Vessel. Am.

*RS40* **HOIST** Salvage Vessel. Am.

*RS41* **OPPORTUNE** Salvage Vessel. Am.

*RS42* **RECLAIMER** Salvage Vessel. Am.

*RS43* **RECOVERY** Salvage Vessel. Am.

*RS210* **10 DE OCTUBRE** Rescue and Salvage Ship. Cu.

*RSD1* **GYPSY** Salvage Lifting Vessel. Am.

*RSD2* **MENDER** Salvage Lifting Vessel. Am.

*RST1* **LAYSAN ISLAND** Salvage Tender. Am.

*RST3* **PALMYRA** Salvage Tender. Am.

*RVA5* **FABIUS** Repair Ship. Am.

*RVA6* **MEGARA** Repair Ship. Am.

*RVE4* **CHLORIS** Repair Ship. Am.

*S11* **FULTON** Submarine Tender (N). Am.

*S12* **SPERRY** Submarine Tender (N). Am.

*S13* **GRIFFIN** Submarine Tender. Am.

*S14* **PELIAS** Submarine Tender. Am.

*S15* **BUSHNELL** Submarine Tender. Am.

*S16* **HOWARD W. GILMORE** Submarine Tender Am.

*S17* **NEREUS** Submarine Tender. Am.

*S18* **ORION** Submarine Tender. Am.

*S19* **PROTEUS** Submarine Tender. Am.

*S22* **EURYALE** Submarine Tender. Am.

*S23* **AEGIR** Submarine Tender. Am.

*S33* **SIMON LAKE** Submarine Tender. Am.

*S34* **CANOPUS** Submarine Tender. Am.

*S36* **L.Y.SPEAR** Submarine Tender. Am.

*S37* **DIXON** Submarine Tender. Am.

*S38* Submarine Tender. Am.

*SF10* **BERTHA** Lighthouse Tender. Cu.

*SR21* **PIGEON** Submarine Rescue Ship. Am.

*SR22* **ORTOLAN** Submarine Rescue Ship. Am.

*T-13* **LOS MONJES** Landing Ship. Ve.

*T-14* **LOS ROQUES** Landing Ship. Ve.

*T-15* **LOS FRAILES** Landing Ship. Ve

*T-16* **LOS TESTIGOS** Landing Ship. Ve.

*T-18* **GUAYANA** Landing Ship. Ve.
*T31* **JAMBELI** Landing Ship. Ec.
*T32* **TARQUI** Landing Ship. Ec.
*T32* Torpedo Boat. Sw.
*T33* Torpedo Boat. Sw.
*T34* Torpedo Boat. Sw.
*T35* Torpedo Boat. Sw.
*T36* Torpedo Boat. Sw.
*T37* Torpedo Boat. Sw.
*T38* Torpedo Boat. Sw.
*T39* Torpedo Boat. Sw.
*T40* Torpedo Boat. Sw.
*T41* Torpedo Boat. Sw.
*T41* **ATAMUALPA** Water Carrier. Ec.
*T42* **CALICUCHIMA** Supply Ship. Ec.

*T42* Torpedo Boat. Sw.
*T43* Torpedo Boat. Sw.
*T44* Torpedo Boat. Sw.
*T45* Torpedo Boat. Sw.
*T46* Torpedo Boat. Sw.
*T47* Torpedo Boat. Sw.
*T48* Torpedo Boat. Sw.
*T49* Torpedo Boat. Sw.
*T50* Torpedo Boat. Sw.
*T51* Torpedo Boat. Sw.
*T52* Torpedo Boat. Sw.
*T53* Torpedo Boat. Sw.
*T54* Torpedo Boat. Sw.
*T55* Torpedo Boat. Sw.
*T56* Torpedo Boat. Sw.
*T102* **PLEJAD** Motor Torpedo Boat. Sw.
*T103* **POLARIS** Motor Torpedo Boat. Sw.
*T104* **POLLUX** Motor Torpedo Boat. Sw.
*T105* **REGULUS** Motor Torpedo Boat. Sw.
*T106* **RIGEL** Motor Torpedo Boat. Sw.
*T107* **ALDEBARAN** Motor Torpedo Boat. Sw.
*T108* **ALTAIR** Motor Torpedo Boat. Sw.
*T109* **ANTARES** Motor Torpedo Boat. Sw.
*T110* **ARCTURUS** Motor Torpedo Boat. Sw.
*T111* **ARGO** Motor Torpedo Float. Sw.
*T112* **ASTREA** Motor Torpedo Boat. Sw.
*T121* **SPICA** Motor Torpedo Boat. Sw.
*T122* **SIRIUS** Motor Torpedo Boat. Sw.
*T123* **CAPELLA** Motor Torpedo Boat. Sw.
*T124* **CASTOR** Motor Torpedo Boat. Sw.
*T125* **VEGA** Motor Torpedo Boat. Sw.

*T126* **VIRGO** Motor Torpedo Boat. Sw.
*T127* Motor Torpedo Boat. Sw.
*T128* Motor Torpedo Boat. Sw.
*T129* Motor Torpedo Boat. Sw.
*T130* Motor Torpedo Boat. Sw.
*T131* Motor Torpedo Boat. Sw.
*T132* Motor Torpedo Boat. Sw.
*T201* Motor Torpedo Boat. Bm.
*T202* Motor Torpedo Boat. Bm.
*T203* Motor Torpedo Boat. Bm.
*T204* Motor Torpedo Boat. Bm.
*T205* Motor Torpedo Boat. Bm.
*T884* **TF102** Torpedo Recovery Boat. Ge.
*T913* Landing Craft. Cambodia
*T914* Landing Craft. Cambodia
*T915* Landing Craft. Cambodia
*TA2* **YONG MUN** Tug. Ko.
*TA3* **DO BONG** Tug. Ko.
*TA11* **ARAGON** Transport. Sp.
*TA21* **CASTILLA** Transport. Sp.
*TA181* **ACCOKEEK** Tug. Am.
*TA184* **KALMIA** Tug. Am.
*TA185* **KOKA** Tug. Am.
*TA186* **CAHOKIA** Tug. Am.
*TA187* **SALISH** Tug. Am.
*TA188* **PENOBSCOT** Tug. Am.
*TA190* **SAMOSET** Tug. Am.
*TA192* **TILLAMOOK** Tug. Am.
*TA193* **STALLION** Tug. Am.
*TA195* **TATNUCK** Tug. Am.
*TA196* **MAHOPAC** Tug. Am.
*TA204* **WANDANK** Tug. Am.
*TA208* **SAGAMORE** Tug. Am.
*TA209* **UMPQUA** Tug. Am
*TA210* **CATAWBA** Tug. Am.
*TA213* **KEYWADIN** Tug. Am.
*TA240* **ATA 240** Tug. Am.
*TD01* **TARQUI** Landing Ship. Ec.
*TD02* **JAMBELI** Landing Ship. Ec.
*TF67* **APACHE** Fleet Tug. Am.
*TF72* **KIOWA** Fleet Tug. Am.
*TF75* **SIOUX** Fleet Tug. Am.
*TF76* **UTE** Fleet Tug. Am.
*TF84* **CREE** Fleet Tug. Am.
*TF85* **LIPAN** Fleet Tug. Am.
*TF86* **MATACO** Fleet Tug. Am.
*TF91* **SENECA** Fleet Tug. Am.
*TF92* **TAWASA** Fleet Tug. Am.
*TF96* **ABNAKI** Fleet Tug. Am.
*TF98* **ARIKARA** Fleet Tug. Am.
*TF100* **CHOWANOC** Fleet Tug. Am.
*TF101* **COCOPA** Fleet Tug. Am.
*TF103* **HITCHITI** Fleet Tug. Am.
*TF105* **MOCTOBI** Fleet Tug. Am.
*TF106* **MOLALA** Fleet Tug. Am.
*TF108* **PAKANA** Fleet Tug. Am.
*TF110* **QUAPAW** Fleet Tug. Am.
*TF113* **TAKELMA** Fleet Tug. Am.
*TF114* **TAWAKONI** Fleet Tug. Am.
*TF149* **ATAKAPA** Fleet Tug. Am.
*TF156* **LUISENO** Fleet Tug. Am.
*TF157* **NIPMUC** Fleet Tug. Am.
*TF158* **MOSOSPELEA** Fleet Tug. Am.
*TF159* **PAIUTE** Fleet Tug. Am.
*TF160* **PAPAGO** Fleet Tug. Am.
*TF161* **SALINAN** Fleet Tug. Am.
*TF162* **SHAKORI** Fleet Tug. Am.
*TF163* **UTINA** Fleet Tug. Am.

*TGI* **TENGGIRI** Patrol Vessel. Ia. (This is abbreviation of name and not pendant number which is *309*)
*TS1* **EDENTON** Tug. Am.
*TS2* **BEAUFORT** Tug. Am.
*TS3* **BRUNSWICK** Tug. Am.
*U10* **ALMIRANTE SALDHANA** Oceanographic Research Ship. Bz.
*U16* **PARAGUACO** River Monitor. Bz.
*U17* **PARNAIBA** River Monitor. Bz.
*U20* **RIO DOCE** River Gunboat. Bz.
*U21* **RIO DAS CONTAS** River Gunboat. Bz.
*U22* **RIO FORMOSO** River Gunboat. Bz.
*U23* **RIO REAL** River Gunboat. Bz.
*U24* **RIO TURVO** River Gunboat. Bz.
*U25* **RIO VREDE** River Gunboat. Bz.
*U26* **CUSTODIO DE MELLO** Training Ship/Transport. Bz.
*U27* **BAEPENDI** Frigate. Bz.
*U28* **BAURU** Frigate. Bz.
*U30* **BENAVENTE** Frigate. Bz.
*U31* **BRACUI** Frigate. Bz.
*U32* **BOCAINA** Frigate. Bz.
*V15* **IMPERIAL MARINHEIRO** Fleet Tug/Corvette. Bz.
*V16* **IGUATEMI** Fleet Tug/Corvette. Bz.
*V17* **IPIRANGA** Fleet Tug/Corvette. Bz.
*V18* **FORTE DE COIMBRA** Fleet Tug/Corvette. Bz.
*V19* **CABOLCO** Fleet Tug/Corvette. Bz.
*V20* **ANGOSTURA** Fleet Tug/Corvette. Bz.
*V21* **BAHIANA** Fleet Tug/Corvette. Bz.
*V22* **MEARIM** Fleet Tug/Corvette. Bz.
*V23* **PURUS** Fleet Tug/Corvette. Bz.
*V24* **SOLIMOES** Fleet Tug/Corvette. Bz.
*V27* Patrol Boat. Sw.
*V57* Patrol Boat. Sw.
*VM1* **NORTON SOUND** Guided Missile Support Ship. Am.
*W4* **GLACIER** Coast Guard—Icebreaker. Am.
*W21* **NIOBE** Inshore Minesweeper. Ge
*W22* **HANSA** Inshore Minesweeper. Ge.
*W23* **ARIADNE** Inshore Minesweeper. Ge.
*W24* **FREYA** Inshore Minesweeper. Ge.
*W25* **VINETA** Inshore Minesweeper. Ge.
*W26* **HERTHA** Inshore Minesweeper. Ge.
*W27* **NYMPHE** Inshore Minesweeper. Ge.
*W28* **NIXE** Inshore Minesweeper. Ge.
*W29* **AMAZONE** Inshore Minesweeper. Ge.
*W30* **GAZELLE** Inshore Minesweeper. Ge.

*W31*  **BIBB** Coast Guard Cutter. Am.
*W32*  **CAMPBELL** Coast Guard Cutter. Am.
*W33*  **DUANE** Coast Guard Cutter. Am.
*W35*  **INGHAM** Coast Guard Cutter. Am.
*W37*  **SPENCER** Coast Guard Cutter. Am.
*W37*  **TANEY** Coast Guard Cutter. Am.
*W38*  **STORIS** Coast Guard Cutter. Am.
*W39*  **OWASCO** Coast Guard Cutter. Am.
*W40*  **WACHUSETT** Coast Guard Cutter. Am.
*W41*  **CHAUTAUQUA** Coast Guard Cutter. Am.
*W42*  **SEBAGO** Coast Guard Cutter. Am.
*W44*  **WACHUSETT** Coast Guard Cutter. Am.
*W44*  **UWI** Coastal Patrol Boat Ge.
*W45*  **TM 2** Coastal Patrol Boat. Ge.
*W53*  **TM 3** Coastal Patrol Boat. Ge.
*W54*  **TM 4** Coastal Patrol Boat. Ge.
*W55*  **TM 5** Coastal Patrol Boat. Ge.
*W60*  **MANITOU** Coast Guard Tug. Am.
*W61*  **KAW** Coast Guard Tug. Am.
*W62*  **BALSAM** Coast Guard Tug. Am.
*W64*  **ESCANABA** Coast Guard Cutter. Am.
*W65*  **WINONA** Coast Guard Cutter. Am.
*W66*  **KLAMATH** Coast Guard Cutter. Am.
*W67*  **MINNETONKA** Coast Guard Cutter. Am.
*W68*  **ANDROSCOGGIN** Coast Guard Cutter. Am.
*W69*  **MENDOTA** Coast Guard Cutter. Am.
*W70*  **PONTCHARTRAIN** Coast Guard Cutter. Am.
*W71*  **APALACHEE** Coast Guard Cutter. Am.
*W71*  Torpedo Boat. Ge.
*W72*  **YANKTON** Coast Guard Tug. Am.
*W73*  **MOHICAN** Coast Guard Tug. Am.
*W83*  **MACKINAW** Coast Guard Tug. Am.
*W86*  **CALUMET** Coast Guard Tug. Am.
*W87*  **HUDSON** Coast Guard Tug. Am.
*W88*  **NAVESINK** Coast Guard Tug. Am.
*W89*  **TUCKAHOE** Coast Guard Tug. Am.
*W90*  **ARUNDEL** Coast Guard Tug. Am.
*W91*  **MAHONING** Coast Guard Tug. Am.
*W92*  **NAUGATUCK** Coast Guard Tug. Am.
*W93*  **RARITAN** Coast Guard Tug. Am.

*W96*  **CHINOOK** Coast Guard Tug. Am.
*W97*  **OJIBWA** Coast Guard Tug. Am.
*W98*  **SNOHOMISH** Coast Guard Tug. Am.
*W99*  **SAUK** Coast Guard Tug. Am.
*W116*  **TRITON** Coast Guard Cutter. Am.
*W147*  **MORRIS** Coast Guard Cutter. Am.
*W150*  **AVOYEL** Coast Guard Tug. Am.
*W153*  **CHILUA** Coast Guard Tug. Am.
*W165*  **CHEROKEE** Coast Guard Tug. Am.
*W166*  **TAMAROA** Coast Guard Tug. Am.
*W167*  **ACUSHNET** Coast Guard Tug. Am.
*W168*  **VOCONA** Coast Guard Tug. Am.
*W186*  **KUKUI** Coast Guard Supply Ship. Am.
*W194*  **MODOC** Coast Guard Tug. Am.
*W202*  **COMANCHE** Coast Guard Tug. Am.
*W203*  **ARBUTUS** Coast Guard Tender. Am.
*W212*  **FIR** Coast Guard Tender. Am.
*W220*  **HOLLYHOCK** Coast Guard Tender. Am.
*W224*  **JUNIPER** Coast Guard Tender. Am.
*W227*  **LILAC** Coast Guard Tender. Am.
*W237*  **MISTLETOE** Coast Guard Tender. Am.
*W252*  **WALNUT** Coast Guard Tender. Am.
*W270*  **CACTUS** Coast Guard Tender. Am.
*W277*  **COWSLIP** Coast Guard Tender. Am.
*W278*  **STATEN ISLAND** Coast Guard Icebreaker. Am.
*W279*  **EASTWIND** Coast Guard Icebreaker. Am.
*W280*  **SOUTHWIND** Coast Guard Icebreaker. Am.
*W281*  **WESTWIND** Coast Guard Icebreaker. Am.
*W282*  **NORTHWIND** Coast Guard Icebreaker. Am.
*W283*  **BURTON ISLAND** Coast Guard Icebreaker. Am.
*W284*  **EDISTO** Coast Guard Icebreaker. Am.
*W289*  **WOODBINE** Coast Guard Tender. Am.
*W290*  **GENTIAN** Coast Guard Tender. Am.
*W291*  **LAUREL** Coast Guard Tender. Am.
*W292*  **CLOVER** Coast Guard Tender. Am.
*W293*  **FIREBUSH** Coast Guard Tender. Am.
*W295*  **EVERGREEN** Coast Guard Tender. Am.
*W296*  **SORREL** Coast Guard Tender. Am.

*W300*  **CITRUS** Coast Guard Tender. Am.
*W301*  **CONIFER** Coast Guard Tender. Am.
*W302*  **MADRONA** Coast Guard Tender. Am.
*W303*  **TUPELO** Coast Guard Tender. Am.
*W305*  **MESQUITE** Coast Guard Tender. Am.
*W306*  **BUTTONWOOD** Coast Guard Tender. Am.
*W307*  **PLANETREE** Coast Guard Tender. Am.
*W308*  **PAPAW** Coast Guard Tender. Am.
*W309*  **SWEETGUM** Coast Guard Tender. Am.
*W328*  **MAGNOLIA** Coast Guard Tender. Am.
*W329*  **IVY** Coast Guard Tender. Am.
*W330*  **JONQUIL** Coast Guard Tender. Am.
*W331*  **HEATHER** Coast Guard Tender. Am.
*W332*  **WILLOW** Coast Guard Tender. Am.
*W370*  **CASCO** Coast Guard Cutter. Am.
*W374*  **ABSECON** Coast Guard Cutter. Am.
*W375*  **CHINCOTEAGUE** Coast Guard Cutter. Am.
*W377*  **ROCKAWAY** Coast Guard Cutter. Am.
*W379*  **UNIMAK** Coast Guard Cutter. Am.
*W381*  **BARATARIA** Coast Guard Cutter. Am.
*W383*  **CASTLE ROCK** Coast Guard Cutter. Am.
*W384*  **COOK INLET** Coast Guard Cutter. Am.
*W385*  **TANAGER** Coast Guard Cutter. Am.
*W386*  **MCCULLOCH** Coast Guard Cutter. Am.
*W387*  **GRESHAM** Coast Guard Cutter. Am.
*W388*  **BASSWOOD** Coast Guard Tender. Am.
*W389*  **BITTERSWEET** Coast Guard Tender. Am.
*W390*  **BLACKHAW** Coast Guard Tender. Am.
*W391*  **BLACKTHORN** Coast Guard Tender. Am.
*W392*  **BRAMBLE** Coast Guard Tender. Am.
*W394*  **HORNBEAM** Coast Guard Tender. Am.
*W395*  **IRIS** Coast Guard Tender. Am.
*W396*  **MALLOW** Coast Guard Tender. Am.
*W397*  **MARIPOSA** Coast Guard Tender. Am.
*W399*  **SAGEBRUSH** Coast Guard Tender. Am.
*W400*  **SALVIA** Coast Guard Tender. Am.
*W401*  **SASSAFRAS** Coast Guard Tender. Am.

*W402* **SEDGE** Coast Guard Tender. Am.
*W403* **SPAR** Coast Guard Tender. Am.
*W404* **SUNDEW** Coast Guard Tender. Am.
*W405* **SWEETBRIAR** Coast Guard Tender. Am.
*W406* **ACACIA** Coast Guard Tender. Am.
*W407* **WOODBRUSH** Coast Guard Tender. Am.
*W410* **COURIER** Coast Guard Training Ship. Am.
*W615* **RELIANCE** Coast Guard Cutter. Am.
*W616* **DILIGENCE** Coast Guard Cutter. Am.
*W617* **VIGILANT** Coast Guard Cutter. Am.
*W618* **ACTIVE** Coast Guard Cutter. Am.
*W619* **CONFIDENCE** Coast Guard Cutter. Am.
*W620* **RESOLUTE** Coast Guard Cutter. Am.
*W621* **VALIANT** Coast Guard Cutter. Am.
*W622* **COURAGEOUS** Coast Guard Cutter. Am.
*W623* **STEADFAST** Coast Guard Cutter. Am.
*W624* **DAUNTLESS** Coast Guard Cutter. Am.
*W625* **VENTUROUS** Coast Guard Cutter. Am.
*W626* **DEPENDABLE** Coast Guard Cutter. Am.
*W627* **VIGOROUS** Coast Guard Cutter. Am.
*W628* **DURABLE** Coast Guard Cutter. Am.
*W629* **DECISIVE** Coast Guard Cutter. Am.
*W630* **ALERT** Coast Guard Cutter. Am.
*W641* **AZALEA** Coast Guard Tender. Am.
*W642* **BUCKTHORN** Coast Guard Tender. Am.
*W685* **RED WOOD** Coast Guard Tender. Am.
*W686* **RED BEECH** Coast Guard Tender. Am.
*W687* **RED BIRCH** Coast Guard Tender. Am.
*W899* **LAMAR** Coast Guard Training Ship. Am.
*Y42* **LAKE LANAO** Water Carrier. Pi.
*Y43* **LAKE NAUJAN** Oiler. Pi.
*Y300* **BARSO** Da.
*Y298* **SEAL** Diving Tender. Au.
*Y369* **ALHOLM** Inshore Minesweeper. Da.
*Y370* **BIRKHOLM** Inshore Minesweeper. Da.
*Y371* **ERTHOLM** Inshore Minesweeper. Da.
*Y372* **FYRHOLM** Inshore Minesweeper. Da.
*Y374* **LINDHOLM** Inshore Minesweeper. Da.

*Y383* **TEJSTEN** Patrol Craft. Da.
*Y384* **MAAGEN** Patrol Craft. Da.
*Y385* **MALLEMUKKEN** Patrol Craft. Da.
*Y386* **ASKO** Inshore Minesweeper. Da.
*Y387* **BAAGO** Inshore Minesweeper. Da.
*Y388* **ENO** Inshore Minesweeper. Da.
*Y389* **HJORTO** Inshore Minesweeper. Da.
*Y390* **LYO** Inshore Minesweeper. Da.
*Y391* **MANO** Inshore Minesweeper. Da.
*Y604* **ARIEL** Transport. Fr.
*Y661* **KORRIGAN** Transport. Fr.
*Y710* **SYLPHE** Transport. Fr.
*Y712* **TREBERON** Transport. Fr.
*Y800* **PASSAT** Tug. Ge.
*Y801* **PELLWORM** Tug. Ge.
*Y806* **TF 25** Torpedo Recovery Boat. Ge.
*Y807* **TF 26** Torpedo Recovery Boat. Ge.
*Y803* **BLAUORT** Tug. Ge.
*Y812* **LUTJE HORN** Tug. Ge.
*Y813* **MELLUM** Tug. Ge.
*Y814* **KNECHTSAND** Tug. Ge.
*Y815* **SCHARHORN** Tug. Ge.
*Y816* **VOGELSAND** Tug. Ge.
*Y817* **NORSTRAND** Tug. Ge.
*Y818* **TRISCHEN** Tug. Ge.
*Y819* **LANGENESS** Tug. Ge.
*Y820* **SYLT** Tug. Ge.
*Y821* **FOHR** Tug. Ge.
*Y822* **AMRUM** Tug. Ge.
*Y823* **NEUWERK** Tug. Ge.
*Y824* **BORKUM** Oiler. Ge.
*Y825* **EUTIN** Oiler. Ge.
*Y826* **JEVERLAND** Oiler. Ge.
*Y827* **FRANKENLAND** Oiler. Ge.
*Y828* **EMSLAND** Oiler. Ge.
*Y829* **MUNSTERLAND** Oiler. Ge.
*Y830* **SAUERLAND** Supply Ship. Ge.
*Y831* **PFALZERLAND** Supply Ship. Ge.
*Y832* **SIEGERLAND** Supply Ship. Ge.
*Y835* **TF 105** Torpedo Recovery Boat. Ge.
*Y843* **PLANET** Survey Ship.
*Y861* **FL 9** Coastal Patrol Boat. Ge.
*Y862* **FL 10** Coastal Patrol Boat. Ge.
*Y863* **FL 11** Coastal Patrol Boat. Ge.
*Y878* **HELMHOLTZ** Degaussing Vessel. Ge.
*Y879* **HANS BURKNER** Corvette. Ge.
(Number on superstructure)
*Y883* **TF 101** Torpedo Recovery Boat. Ge.
*Y884* **TF 102** Torpedo Recovery Boat. Ge.
*Y885* **TF 103** Torpedo Recovery Boat. Ge.
*Y886* **TF 104** Torpedo Recovery Boat. Ge.
*Y889* **RUDOLF DIESEL** Trials Vessel. Ge.
*Y890* **EF 1** Trials Vessel. Ge.
*Y8037* **BERKEL** Tug. Du.
*Y8038* **DINTEL** Tug. Du.

*Y8039* **DOMMEL** Tug. Du.
*Y8040* **IJSSEL** Tug. Du.
*Y8050* **URANIA** Training Ship. Du.
*Y8101* **HOBEIN** Training Ship. Du.
*Y8102* **HENDRIK KARSSEN** Training Ship. Du.
*YP654* Navigation Training Craft. Du.
*YP655* Navigation Training Craft. Du.
*YP656* Navigation Training Craft. Du.
*YP657* Navigation Training Craft. Du.
*YP658* Navigation Training Craft. Du.
*YP659* Navigation Training Craft. Du.
*YP660* Navigation Training Craft. Du.
*YP661* Navigation Training Craft. Du.
*YP662* Navigation Training Craft. Du.
*YP663* Navigation Training Craft. Du.
*YP664* Navigation Training Craft. Du.
*YP665* Navigation Training Craft. Du.
*YP666* Navigation Training Craft. Du.
*YP667* Navigation Training Craft. Du.
*YP668* Navigation Training Craft. Du.
*YT104* **ANCUD** Tug. Ch.
*YT105* **MONREAL** Tug. Ch.
*YT107* **UGARTE** Tug. Ch.
*YT120* **REYES** Tug. Ch.
*YT127* **CAUPOLICAN** Tug. Ch.
*YT128* **CORTEZ** Tug. Ch.
*01* **ANTIOQUIA** Destroyer. Co.
*01* **AETOS** Frigate. Gr.
*01* **DEDALO** Helicopter Carrier. Sp.
*02* **QUEENBOROUGH** Frigate. Au.
*03* **QUIBERON** Frigate. Au.
*03* **ALMIRANTE PADILLA** Destroyer. Co.
*04* **QUICKMATCH** Frigate. Au.
*05* **VEINTE DE JULIO** Destroyer. Co.
*06* **ASPIS** Destroyer. Gr.
*07* **DONG DA II** Escort. VN.
*08* **VENDETTA** Destroyer. Au.
*08* **CHI LANG II** Escort. VN.
*09* **KY HOA** Escort. VN.
*1* **ACHELOUS** Repair Ship. Am.
*1* **BROOKE** G.M. Escort. Am.
*1* **CARRONADE** Inshore Fire Support. Am.
*1* **COVE** Inshore Minesweeper. Am.
*1* **FLAGSTAFF** Patrol Gunboat. Am.
*1* **GLOVER** Escort Research Ship. Am.
*1* **NORFOLK** Frigate. Am.
*1* **NORTHAMPTON** Command Ship. Am.
*1* **RALEIGH** Amphibious Transport Dock. Am.
*1* **VALCOUR** Flagship. Am.
*1* **CABO SAN BARTOLOME** Landing Ship. Ar.
*1* **COMMANDANTE GENERAL IRIGOYEN** Patrol Vessel. Ar.
*1* **NEUQUEN** Minesweeper. Ar.
*1* **KALA I** Landing Craft. Fi.
*1* **NUOLI I** Fast Patrol Boat. Fi.
*1* **VASAMA I** Fast Patrol Boat. Fi.
*1* **TANDJUNG NUSANIE** Landing Ship. Ia.
*1* **No. 1** Patrol Boat. Iq.
*1* **KU RYON** Oil Barge. Ko.
*1* **ANGHTONG** Landing Ship. Th.
*1* **OGC I** Coast Guard Ship. Th.
*1* **PRAB** Landing Craft. Th.
*1* **SARASIN** Patrol Vessel. Th.
*1* **SICHANG** Transport. Th.

2 **AMYCUS** Repair Ship. Am.
2 **CAPE** Inshore Minesweeper. Am.
2 **CHARLES F. ADAMS** G.M. Destroyer. Am.
2 **IWOJIMA** Amphibious Assault Ship. Am.
2 **MONTEREY** Auxiliary Air Transport. Am.
2 **RAMSEY** G.M. Escort. Am.
2 **TUCUMCARI** Patrol Gunboat. Am.
2 **VANCOUVER** Amphibious Transport Dock. Am.
2 **WRIGHT** Command Ship. Am.
2 **RIO NEGRO** Minesweeper. Ar.
2 **COMMANDANTE GENERAL ZAPIOLA** Patrol Vessel. Ar
2 **KALA 2** Transport. Fi.
   (Number on bridge)
2 **NUOLI 2** Fast Patrol Boat. Fi.
   (Number on bridge)
2 **VASAMA 2** Fast Patrol Boat. Fi.
   (Number on hull)
2 **No. 2** Patrol Boat. Ia.
2 **CHUN-JI** Oiler. Ko.
2 **LSM 2** Landing Ship. Sp.
2 **CHANG** Landing Ship. Th.
2 **CHULA** Oiler. Th.
2 **PAI** Landing Ship. Th.
2 **PRASAE** Frigate. Th.
2 **SATAKUT** Landing Ship. Th.
2 **THAYANCHON** Patrol Vessel. Th.
2 **SUKOTHAI** Armoured Gunboat. Th.
3 **CABOT** Auxiliary Aircraft Transport. Am.
3 **GALVESTON** G.M. Light Cruiser. Am.
3 **JOHN KING** G.M. Destroyer. Am.
3 **LA SALLE** Amphibious Transport Dock. Am.
3 **OKINAWA** Amphibious Assault Ship. Am.
   (On Funnel)
3 **SCHOFIELD** G.M. Escort. Am.
3 **TARGETEER** Drone Aircraft Catapult Control. Am.
3 **LA ARGENTINA** Cruiser. Ar.
3 **KALA 3** Transport. Fi.
   (On Bridge)
3 **NUOLI 3** Fast Patrol Boat. Fi.
   (On Bridge)
3 **NO.3** Patrol Boat. Iq.
3 **LSM 3** Landing Ship. Sp.
3 **CGC 3** Coastguard Vessel. Th.
3 **KRAM** Landing Ship Th.
3 **MAEKLONG** Frigate. Th.
3 **MATRA** — Th.
3 **NAKA** Gunboat. Th.
3 **PANGAN** Landing Ship. Th.
3 **PIN KLAO** Destroyer Escort. Th.
3 **GOYENA** Patrol Vessel. Ar.
3 **CHUBUT** Minesweeper. Ar.
4 **AUSTIN** Amphibious Transport Dock. Am.
4 **CHLORIS** Repair Ship Am.
4 **LAWRENCE** G.M. Destroyer. Am.
4 **LITTLE ROCK** G.M. Light Cruiser. Am.
4 **TALBOT** G.M. Escort. Am.
4 **ZEUS** Repair Ship. Am.

4 **WILLIS A LEE** Frigate. Am.
4 **CABO SAN GONZALO** Tank Landing Ship. Ar.
4 **GENERAL BELGRANO** Cruiser. Ar.
4 **TIERRA DEL FUEGO** Coastal Minelayer. Ar.
4 **TOMPSON** Patrol Vessel. Ar.
4 **KALA 4** Transport. Fi.
   (On Bridge)
4 **NUOLI 4** Fast Patrol Boat. Fi.
   (On Superstructure)
4 **No. 4** Patrol Boat. Iq.
4 **BANGPAKONG** Frigate. Th.
4 **CGC-4** Cutter. Th.
4 **PHALI** Patrol Vessel. Th.
4 **YO 4** Oiler. Th.
5 **CLAUDE V. RICKETTS** G.M. Destroyer. Am.
5 **FABIUS** Repair Ship. Am.
5 **MIDAS** Repair Ship. Am.
5 **OGDEN** Amphibious Transport Dock. Am.
5 **OKLAHOMA CITY** G.M Cruiser. Am.
5 **PRINCETON** Amphibious Assault Ship. Am.
5 **RICHARD L. PAGE** G.M. Escort. Am.
5 **TERROR** Mine Warfare Ship. Am.
5 **WILKINSON** Frigate. Am.
5 **NUEVE DE JULIO** Cruiser. Ar.
5 **DIAGUITA** Patrol Vessel. Ar.
5 **KALA 5** Transport. Fi.
   (On Bridge)
5 **NUOLI 5** Fast Patrol Boat. Fi.
   (On Bridge)
5 **ROYTTA** Inshore Minesweeper. Fi.
5 **YO-5** Oil Barge. Korea.
5 **CGC 5** Coast Guard Vessel. Th.
5 Patrol Vessel. Th.
5 **KLONGYAI** Patrol Vessel. Th.
5 **KUT** Landing Craft. Th.
5 **LADYA** Coastal Minesweeper. Th.
5 **SUKRIP** Patrol Vessel. Th.
5 **CHACO** Minesweeper. Ar.
6 **BARNEY** G.M. Destroyer. Am.
6 **DULUTH** Amphibious Transport Dock. Am.
6 **JULIUS A. FURER** G.M. Escort. Am.
6 **FARRAGUT** G.M. Frigate. Am.
6 **MEGARA** Repair Ship. Am.
6 **ORLEANS PARISH** Tank Landing Ship. Am.
6 **PROVIDENCE** G.M. Light Cruiser. Am.
6 **FORMOSA** Minesweeper. Ar.
6 **BUENOS AIRES** Destroyer. Ar.
6 **CABO SAN ISIDRO** Tank Landing Craft. Ar.
6 **YAMANA** Patrol Vessel. Ar.
6 **KALA 6** Transport Craft. Fi.
   (On Bridge)
6 **NUOLI 6** Fast Patrol Boat. Fi.
   (On Superstructure)
6 **BANGKEO** Coastal Minesweeper. Th.
6 **CGC 6** Coast Guard Vessel. Th.
6 **CHAN** Water Carrier. Th.
6 **TONGPLIU** Patrol Vessel. Th.
7 **ATLAS** Repair Ship. Am.

7 **CHANTICLEER** Submarine Rescue Ship. Am.
7 **CLEVELAND** Amphibious Transport Dock. Am.
7 **ELKHORN** Petrol Carrier. Am.
7 **GUADALCANAL** Amphibious Assault Ship. Am.
   (On Funnel)
7 **HENRY B. WILSON** G.M. Destroyer. Am.
7 **LUCE** G.M. Frigate. Am.
7 **SARPEDON** Repair Ship. Am.
7 **SPRINGFIELD** G.M. Light Cruiser. Am.
7 **CHIRIGUANO** Patrol Vessel. Ar.
7 **ENTRE RIOS** Destroyer. Ar.
7 **NUOLI 7** Fast Patrol Boat. Fi.
   (On Bridge)
7 **KANTANG** Patrol Vessel. Th.
7 **BALEARES** Destroyer Escort. Sp.
7 **KLED KEO** Transport. Th.
7 **LIULOM** Patrol Vessel. Th.
7 **TADINDENG** Coastal Minesweeper. Th.
8 **COUCAL** Submarine Rescue Ship. Am.
8 **DUBUQUE** Amphibious Transport Dock. Am.
8 **EGERIA** Repair Ship. Am.
8 **FRANKLIN** Auxiliary Aircraft Transport. Am.
8 **GENESEE** Petrol Carrier. Am.
8 **KULA GULF** Aircraft Ferry. Am.
8 **LYNDE MCCORMICK** G.M. Destroyer. Am.
8 **MACDONOUGH** G.M. Frigate. Am.
8 **TELAMON** Repair Ship. Am.
8 **TOPEKA** G.M. Light Cruiser. Am.
8 **SANAVIRON** Patrol Vessel. Ar.
8 **NUOLI 8** Fast Patrol Boat. Fi.
8 **ANDALUCIA** Destroyer Escort. Sp.
8 **DONCHEDI** Coastal Minesweeper Th.
8 **LONGLOM** Patrol Vessel. Th.
8 **MATAPHON** Landing Craft. Th.
8 **SC 8** Patrol Boat. Th.
8 **SATTAHIB** Patrol Vessel. Th.
9 **BUNKER HILL** Auxiliary Aircraft Transport. Am.
9 **CAPE GLOUCESTER** Aircraft Ferry. Am.
9 **COONTZ** G.M. Frigate. Am.
9 **DENVER** Amphibious Transport Dock. Am.
9 **ENDYMION** Repair Ship. Am.
9 **ESSEX** Support Aircraft Carrier. Am.
9 **FLORIKAN** Submarine Rescue Vessel. Am.
9 **GUAM** Amphibious Assault Ship. Am. (On Funnel.)
9 **LONGBEACH** G.M. Cruiser (N). Am.
9 **TOWERS** G.M. Destroyer. Am.
9 **SAN JUAN** Destroyer. Ar.
9 **NUOLI 9** Fast Patrol Boat. Fi.
   (On Bridge)
9 **LCU 9** Landing Craft. Th.
9 **CATALUNA** Destroyer Escort. Sp.
10 **ALBANY** G.M. Cruiser. Am.

10 **GREENLET** Submarine Rescue Ship. Am.
10 **JUNEAU** Amphibious Transport Dock. Am.
10 **KING** G.M. Frigate. Am.
10 **SAMPSON** G.M. Destroyer. Am.
10 **LEYTE** Auxiliary Aircraft Transport. Am.
10 **TRIPOLI** Amphibious Assault Ship. Am.
10 **YORKTOWN** Support Aircraft Carrier. Am. (On Superstructure)
10 **CABO SAN PIO** Tank Landing Ship. Ar.
10 **SAN LUIS** Destroyer. Ar.
10 **NUOLI 10** Fast Patrol Boat. Fi. (On Bridge)
10 **ASTURIAS** Destroyer Escort. Sp.
10 **MUL 10** Mining Tender. Sw.
10 **ARDANG** Landing Craft. Th.
10 **NHUT TAO** Escort. VN.
11 **CHICAGO** G.M. Cruiser. Am.
11 **CORONADO** Amphibious Transport Dock. Am.
11 **INTREPID** Support Aircraft Carrier. Am.
11 **MAHAN** G.M. Frigate. Am.
11 **VAMPIRE** Destroyer. Au.
11 **NEW ORLEANS** Amphibious Assault Ship. Am.
11 **PHILIPPINE SEA** Auxiliary Aircraft Transport. Am.
11 **SELLERS** G.M. Destroyer. Am.
11 **TOMBIGBEE** Petrol Carrier. Am.
11 **VELLA GULF** Aircraft Ferry. Am.
11 **MISIONES** Destroyer. Ar.
11 **NUOLI II** Fast Patrol Boat. Fi. (On Bridge)
11 **BYBLOS** Patrol Boat. Le.
11 **ES SABIQ** Seaward Patrol Boat. Mo.
11 **AMAZONAS** River Gunboat. Pe.
11 **ESTREMADURA** Destroyer Escort. Sp.
11 **MUL II** Mining Tender. Sw.
11 **CGC II** Coast Guard Cutter. Th.
11 **PHETRA** Landing Craft. Th.
11 **RANG KWIEN** Tug. Th.
11 **T.11** Gunboat. Th.
11 **TRAD** Patrol Vessel. Th.
11 **CHI LINH** Escort. VN.
11 **SPLIT** Destroyer. Ys.
12 **COLUMBUS** G.M. Cruiser. Am.
12 **HORNET** Support Aircraft Carrier. Am.
12 **INCHON** Amphibious Assault Ship. Am.
12 **PENGUIN** Salvage Ship. Am.
12 **ROBISON** G.M. Destroyer. Am.
12 **DAHLGREN** G.M. Frigate. Am.
12 **SHREVEPORT** Amphibious Transport Dock. Am.
12 **SIBONEY** Aircraft Ferry. Am.
12 **TARAWA** Auxiliary Aircraft Transport. Am.
12 **SANTA CRUZ** Destroyer. Ar.
12 **HERCULES II** Tug. Do.
12 **TAN YANG** Tug. Cs.
12 **NUOLI 12** Fast Patrol Boat. Fi. (On Superstructure)
12 **SIDON** Patrol Boat. Le.

12 **LORETO** River Gunboat. Pe.
12 **LAGUNA** Escort. Pi.
12 **MUL 12** Mining Tender. Sw.
12 **KOLUM** Landing Craft. Th.
12 **PUKET** Patrol Vessel. Th.
12 **T.12** Gunboat. Th.
12 **NGOC HOI** Escort. VN.
13 **CASA GRANDE** Dock Landing Ship. Am.
13 **HOEL** G.M. Destroyer. Am.
13 **KITTIWAKE** Submarine Rescue Ship. Am.
13 **NASHVILLE** Amphibious Transport Dock. Am.
13 **WILLIAM V. PRATT** G.M. Frigate. Am.
13 **GUACANAGARIX** Tug. Do.
13 **NUOLI 13** Fast Patrol Boat. Fi. (On Bridge)
13 **BEYROUTH** Patrol Boat. Le.
13 **MARANON** River Gunboat. Pv.
13 **MUL 13** Mining Tender. Sw.
13 **HALSINGBORG** Frigate. Sw.
13 **CGC 13** Coast Guard Vessel. Th.
13 **PATTANI** Patrol Vessel. Th.
13 **T.13** Gunboat. Th.
13 **TALIBONG** Landing Craft. Th.
14 **BUCHANAN** G.M. Destroyer. Am.
14 **PETREL** Submarine Rescue Ship. Am.
14 **RENDOVA** Aircraft Ferry. Am.
14 **RUSHMORE** Dock Landing Ship. Am.
14 **TRENTON** Amphibious Transport Dock. Am.
14 **TICONDEROGA** Attack Carrier. Am.
14 **CABO SAN VICENTE** Tank Landing Ship. Ar.
14 **BLANCO ENCALADA** Destroyer. Ch.
14 **LO YANG** Destroyer. Cs.
14 **UCAYALI** River Gunboat. Pv.
14 **TARLAC** Escort. Pi.
14 **KALMAR** Frigate. Sw.
14 **MUL 14** Mining Tender. Sw.
14 **CGC 14** Coast Guard Vessel. Th.
15 **BERKELEY** G.M. Destroyer. Am.
15 **PONCE** Amphibious Transport Dock. Am.
15 **PREBLE** G.M. Frigate. Am.
15 **RANDOLPH** Attack Carrier. Am.
15 **SHADWELL** Dock Landing Ship Am.
15 **SUNBIRD** Submarine Rescue Vessel. Am.
15 **COCHRANE** Destroyer. Ch.
15 **HAN YANG** Destroyer. Cs.
15 **AGUASCALIENTES** Oiler. Me.
15 **AMERICA** River Gunboat. Pe.
15 **MOUNTAIN PROVINCE** Patrol Boat. Pi.
15 **MUL 15** Mining Tender. Sw.
15 **CGC 15** Coast Guard Vessel. Th.
16 **CABILDO** Dock Landing Ship. Am.
16 **JOSEPH STRAUSS** G.M. Destroyer. Am.
16 **LEAHY** G.M. Frigate. Am.
16 **LEXINGTON** Training Aircraft Carrier. Am.

16 **TRINGA** Submarine Rescue Vessel. Am.
16 **HSUEN YANG** Destroyer. Cs.
16 **VELOS** Destroyer. Gr.
16 **TLAXCALA** Oiler. Me.
16 **ALERT** Patrol Boat. Pi.
16 **MUL 16** Mining Tender. Sw.
16 **CGC 16** Coast Guard Vessel. Th.
17 **CATAMOUNT** Dock Landing Ship. Am.
17 **CONYNGHAM** G.M. Destroyer. Am.
17 **HARRY E. YARNELL** G.M. Frigate. Am.
17 **SADOR** Aircraft Ferry. Am.
17 **NAN YANG** Destroyer. Cs.
17 **SURIGAO** Patrol Boat. Pi.
17 **MUL 17** Mining Tender. Sw.
18 **COLONIAL** Dock Landing Ship. Am.
18 **PANDEMUS** Repair Ship. Am.
18 **SEMMES** G.M. Destroyer. Am.
18 **WARDEN** G.M. Frigate. Am.
18 **WASP** Support Aircraft Carrier. Am.
18 **RIVEROS** Destroyer. Ch.
18 **AN YANG** Destroyer. Cs.
18 **MUL 18** Mining Tender. Sw.
19 **COMSTOCK** Dock Landing Ship. Am.
19 **DALE** G.M. Destroyer. Am.
19 **POINT CRUZ** Aircraft Ferry. Am.
19 **HANCOCK** Attack Carrier. Am.
19 **TATTNALL** G.M. Destroyer. Am.
19 **BLUE RIDGE** Amphibious Warfare Ship. Am.
19 **WILLIAMS** Destroyer. Ch.
19 **KUN YANG** Destroyer. Cs.
19 **CAVITE** Patrol Boat. Pi.
19 **MUL 19** Mining Tender. Sw.
20 **BENNINGTON** Support Aircraft Carrier. Am.
20 **DONNER** Dock Landing Ship. Am.
20 **GOLDSBOROUGH** G.M. Destroyer. Am.
20 **RICHMOND K. TURNER** G.M. Frigate. Am.
20 **SKYLARK** Submarine Rescue Ship. Am.
20 **MOUNT WHITNEY** Amphibious Force Flagship. Am.
20 **BROWN** Destroyer. Ar.
20 **MURATURE** Corvette. Ar.
20 **DOXA** Destroyer. Ar.
20 **ISABELA** Tug. Do.
20 **MALAMPAY SOUND** Patrol Boat. Pi.
21 **COCHRANE** G.M. Destroyer. Am.
21 **FORT MANDAN** Dock Landing Ship. Am.
21 **GRIDLEY** G.M. Frigate. Am.
21 **RABAUL** Aircraft Ferry. Am.
21 **ESPORA** Destroyer. Ar.
21 **KING** Corvette. Ar.
21 **MELBOURNE** Aircraft Carrier. Au.
21 **TAI KANG** Frigate. Cs.
21 **DROR** Patrol Boat. Is.
21 **LIEUTENANT MALGHAGH** Landing Craft. Mo.
21 **INDEPENDENCIA** Transport. Pv.
21 **VELARDE** Fast Patrol Boat. Pv.

*21*   **MOUNT SAMAT** Command Ship; Presidential Yacht. Pi.
*21*   **SURASDRA** Patrol Vessel. Th.
*21* **KOTOR** Destroyer. Ys.
*22*   **BENJAMIN STODDERT** G.M. Destroyer. Am.
*22* **ENGLAND** G.M. Frigate. Am.
*22* **FORT MARION** Dock Landing Ship. Am.
*22* **ROSALES** Destroyer. Ar.
*22* **SANTILLANA** Fast Patrol Boat. Pe.
*22* **NOGAH** Patrol Vessel. Is.
*22* **AL BACHIR** Patrol Vessel. Mo.
*22* **BOHOL** Escort. Pi.
*22* **CHANDHABURI** Patrol Vessel. Th.
*22* **PULA** Destroyer. Ys.
*23* **HALSEY** G.M. Frigate. Am.
*23*   **RICHARD E. BYRD** G.M. Destroyer. Am.
*23*   **ROBERT H. SMITH** Destroyer Minelayer. Am.
*23* **SATYR** Repair Ship. Am.
*23* **TINIAN** Aircraft Ferry. Am.
*23* **TAI HO** Frigate. Cs.
*23* **DE LOS HEROS** Fast Patrol Boat. Pe.
*23* **RAYONG** Patrol Vessel. Th.
*24* **PLATTE** Oiler. Am.
*24* **REEVES** G.M. Frigate. Am.
*24* **THOMAS E. FRASER** Destroyer Minelayer. Am.
*24* **SPHINX** Repair Ship. Am.
*24* **WADDELL** G.M. Destroyer. Am.
*24* **TAI TSANG** Frigate. Cs.
*24* **HERRERA** Fast Patrol Boat. Pv.
*24* **BATANGAS** Escort. Pi.
*25*   **BAINBRIDGE** G.M. Destroyer (N.). Am.
*25*   **SAN MARCOS** Dock Landing Ship. Am.
*25*   **SHANNON** Destroyer Minelayer. Am.
*25* **SABINE** Oiler. Am.
*25* **TAI HU** Frigate. Cs.
*25* **TIRTSA** Patrol Boat. Is.
*25* **LARREA** Fast Patrol Boat. Pv.
*25* **NUEVA ECIJA** Escort. Pi.
*26* **BELKNAP** G.M. Frigate. Am.
*26*   **HARRY F. BAUER** Destroyer Minelayer. Am.
*26*   **TORTUGA** Dock Landing Ship. Am.
*26* **SERRANO** Escort. Ch.
*26* **TAI CHAO** Frigate. Cs.
*26*   **SANCHEZ CARRION** Fast Patrol Boat. Pv.
*27*   **ADAMS** Destroyer Minelayer. Am.
*27*   **JOSEPHUS DANIELS** G.M. Frigate. Am.
*27*   **WHETSTONE** Dock Landing Ship. Am.
*27* **ORELLA** Destroyer Escort. Ch.
*27* **CAPIZ** Escort. Pi.
*28*   **THOMASTON** Dock Landing Ship. Am.
*28*   **TOLMAN** Destroyer Minelayer. Am.
*28* **WAINWRIGHT** G.M. Frigate. Am.
*28* **RIQUELME** Destroyer. Ch.

*28* **THYELLA** Destroyer. Gr.
*28* **CEBU** Escort. Pi.
*29*   **HENRY A. WILEY** Destroyer Minelayer. Am.
*29* **JOUETT** G.M. Frigate. Am.
*29*   **PLYMOUTH ROCK** Dock Landing Ship. Am.
*29* **URIBE** Destroyer. Ch.
*29* **NEGROS OCCIDENTAL** Escort. Pi.
*30* **ASKARI** Repair Ship. Am.
*30* **FORT SNELLING** Dock Landing Ship. Am.
*30* **HORNE** G.M. Frigate. Am.
*30* **SHEA** Destroyer Minelayer. Am.
*30* **CHEMUNG** Oiler. Am.
*30* **LEYTE** Escort. Pi.
*31*   **BELLEROPHON** Repair Ship. Am.
*31*   **BON HOMME RICHARD** Attack Carrier. Am.
*31* **DECATUR** Destroyer. Am.
*31* **POINT DEFIANCE** Dock Landing Ship. Am.
*31* **STERETT** G.M. Frigate. Am.
*31* **IQUIQUE** Frigate. Ch.
*31* **BARRANQUILA** River Gunboat. Co.
*31* **IERAX** Frigate. Gr.
*31* **TARABLOUS** Patrol Boat. Le.
*31* **AL MOUNA** Frigate. Mo.
*31* **PANGASINAN** Escort. Pi.
*31* **CHUMPHONE** Patrol Vessel. Th.
*32*   **JOHN PAUL JONES** Destroyer. Am.
*32*   **LINDSEY** Destroyer Minelayer. Am.
*32*   **SPIEGEL GROVE** Dock Landing Ship. Am.
*32*   **WILLIAM H. STANDLEY** G.M. Frigate. Am.
*32* **GUADALUPE** Oiler. Am.
*32* **COVADONGA** Frigate. Ch.
*32* **LIEUTENANT RIFFI** Patrol Vessel. Mo.
*32* **ILOILO** Escort. Pi.
*33* **ALAMO** Dock Landing Ship. Am.
*33* **FOX** G.M. Frigate. Am.
*33* **GWIN** Destroyer Minelayer. Am.
*33*   **KEARSARGE** Support Carrier. Am.
*33*   **PLOVER** Coastal Minesweeper. Am.
*33* **SOMERS** Destroyer. Am.
*33* **HWA SHAN** Destroyer Escort. Cs.
*33* **CARTAGENA** River Gunboat. Co.
*34* **BIDDLE** G.M. Frigate. Am.
*34*   **HERMITAGE** Dock Landing Ship. Am.
*34* **ORISKANY** Attack Carrier. Am.
*34* **PARSONS** Destroyer. Am.
*34* **CHIMBOTE** Landing Ship. Pv.
*35* **BENEWAH** Depot Ship. Am.
*35* **MITSCHER** Destroyer. Am.
*35*   **MONTICELLO** Dock Landing Ship. Am.
*35* **TRUXTON** G.M. Frigate (N). Am.
*35* **AZOPARDO** Frigate. Ar.
*35* **FU SHAN** Destroyer Escort. Cs.
*35* **RIOHACHA** River Gunboat. Co.
*35* **PAITA** Landing Ship. Pv.
*36* **CALIFORNIA** Frigate. Am.

*36* **ANCHORAGE** Dock Landing Ship. Am.
*36* **ANTIETAM** Support Carrier. Am.
*36* **COLLETON** Depot Ship. Am.
*36*   **JOHN S. MCCAIN** G.M. Destroyer. Am.
*36* **KENNEBEC** Oiler. Am.
*36* **PIEDRABUENA** Frigate. Ar.
*36* **LU SHAN** Destroyer Escort. Cs.
*36* **LETICIA** River Gunboat. Co.
*36* **LOMAS** Landing Ship. Pv.
*37*   **COMMENCEMENT BAY** Aircraft Ferry. Am.
*37*   **CORSON** Seaplane Tender. Am. (Preceded by Air Force insignia)
*37* **ECHOLS** Depot Ship. Am.
*37* **INDRA** Repair Ship. Am.
*37* **PORTLAND** Dock Landing Ship. Am.
*37*   **WILLIS A. LEE** G.M. Destroyer. Am.
*37* **TOBRUK** Destroyer. Au.
*37* **CASMA** Corvette. Ch.
*37* **ARAUCA** River Gunboat. Co.
*37* **SHOA SHAN** Destroyer Escort. Cs.
*37* **ATICO** Landing Ship. Pv.
*38*   **DANIEL T. GRIFFIN** Transport. Am.
*38* **KRISHNA** Repair Ship. Am.
*38*   **DUXBURY BAY** Seaplane Tender. Am. (Preceded by Air Force insignia)
*38* **PENSACOLA** Dock Landing Ship. Am.
*38* **SHANGRI-LA** Attack Carrier. Am.
*38* **WILKINSON** G.M. Destroyer. Am.
*38* **PERTH** Destroyer. Au.
*38* **CHIPANA** Corvette. Ch.
*38* **TAI SHAN** Destroyer Escort. Cs.
*38* **HAIFA** Destroyer. Is.
*38* **BULACAN** Landing Ship. Pi.
*39* **MERCER** Depot Ship. Am.
*39* **MOUNT VERNON** Landing Ship Dock. Am.
*39* **LSD 39** Landing Ship. Am.
*39* **HOBART** Destroyer. Au.
*39* **ALBLAY** Landing Ship. Pi.
*39* **HENG SHAN** Destroyer Escort. Cs.
*40* **CARD** Aircraft Ferry. Am.
*40* **LSD 40** Landing Ship. Am.
*40* **NUECES** Depot Ship. Am.
*40* **MISAMIS ORIENTAL** Landing Ship. Pi.
*41* **CORE** Aircraft Ferry. Am.
*41*   **GREENWICH BAY** Seaplane Tender. Am. (Preceded by Air Force insignia)
*41* **MIDWAY** Attack Carrier. Am.
*41* **MATTAPONI** Oiler. Am.
*41* **BRISBANE** Destroyer. Au.
*41* **ISABELA** Landing Ship. Pi.
*42* **BRETON** Aircraft Ferry. Am.
*42*   **FRANKLIN D. ROOSEVELT** Attack Carrier. Am.
*42* **WEI YUAN** Escort. Cs.
*42* **YARDEN** Coast Guard Cutter. Is.
*42* **YAFFO** Destroyer. Is.
*42* **LAKE LANAO** Water Carrier. Pi.
*43* **BITTERN** Coastal Minesweeper. Am.

43 **CORAL SEA** Attack Carrier. Am.
43 **CROATAN** Aircraft Ferry. Am.
43 **TAPPAHANNOCK** Oiler. Am.
43 **CIUDAD DE QUIBDO** Transport. Co.
43 **KANG SHAN** Destroyer Escort. Cs.
43 **LAKE NAUJAN** Oiler. Pi.
43 **HORMUZ** Oiler. Ir.
44 **YARKON** Patrol Boat. Is.
44 **IFUGAO** Tug. Pi.
45 **YARRA** Frigate. Au.
45 **LAUIS LEDGE** Lighthouse Tender. Au.
46 **DORCHESTER** Depot Ship. Am.
46 **PARRAMATTA** Frigate. Au.
46 **LENGEM** Water Carrier. Ir.
46 **BOJEADUR** Lighthouse Tender. Pi.
47 **FULMAR** Coastal Minesweeper. Am.
47 **KINGMAN** Depot Ship. Am.
47 **NECHES** Oiler. Am.
47 **YUNG CHIA** Fleet Minesweeper. Cs.
47 **PEARL BANK** Landing Craft. Pi.
48 **VANDERBURGH** Depot Ship. Am.
48 **STUART** Frigate. Au.
48 **YUNG HSIU** Fleet Minesweeper. Cs.
48 **CAMARINES SUR** Patrol Boat. Pi.
49 **DERWENT** Frigate. Au.
49 **SULU** Patrol Boat. Pi.
50 **CHEWAUCAN** Petrol Carrier. Am.
50 **YUNG FEN** Minelayer. Cs.
50 **LA UNION** Patrol Boat. Pi.
50 **KO JIN** Escort. Ko.
51 **ASHTABULA** Oiler. Am.
51 **RO RYANG** Patrol Vessel. Ko.
51 **ANTIQUE** Patrol Boat. Pi.
51 **TRIGLAV** Frigate. Ys.
52 **MATTABESSET** Petrol Carrier. Am.
52 **CACAPON** Oiler. Am.
52 **MYONG RYANG** Escort. Ko.
52 **MASBATE** Patrol Boat. Pi.
52 **BIOKOVO** Frigate. Ys.
53 **SUISUN** Seaplane Tender. Am. (Preceded by Air Force insignia)
53 **CALIENTE** Oiler. Am.
53 **HAN SAN** Escort. Ko.
53 **MISAMIS OCCIDENTAL** Patrol Vessel. Pi.
53 **GROM** Destroyer. Ph.
54 **CHIKASKIA** Oiler. Am.
54 **LEON** Frigate. Gr.
54 **TOMAS MARTIN** Escort. Me.
54 **WICHER** Destroyer. Ph.
54 **UCKA** Frigate. Ys.
55 **LANING** Transport. Am.
55 **NESPELEN** Petrol Carrier. Am.
55 **YUNG PING** Coastal Minesweeper. Cs.
55 **OK BO** Escort. Ko.
55 **ZAMBALES** Coastal Minesweeper. Pi.
56 **AUCILLA** Oiler. Am.
56 **TURKEY** Coastal Minesweeper. Am.

56 **YUNG AN** Coastal Minesweeper. Cs.
56 **LONCHI** Destroyer. Gr.
56 **ZAMBOANGA DEL NORTE** Coastal Minesweeper. Pi.
57 **MARIAS** Oiler. Am.
57 **YUNG NIEN** Coastal Minesweeper. Cs.
57 **PYOK PA** Escort. Ko.
57 **YACHI** Patrol Vessel. Pi.
58 **BROADBILL** Fleet Minesweeper. Am.
58 **SISKIN** Coastal Minesweeper. Am.
58 **MANATEE** Oiler. Am.
58 **YUNG CHUAN** Coastal Minelayer. Cs.
58 **RYUL PO** Escort. Ko.
59 **FORRESTAL** Attack Aircraft Carrier. Am.
59 **FOSS** Escort. Am.
59 **ANZAC** Destroyer. Au.
59 **YUNG HSIN** Coastal Minesweeper. Cs.
59 **SA CHON** Patrol Vessel. Ko.
59 **YANGA** Patrol Vessel. Pi.
60 **SARATOGA** Attack Aircraft Carrier. Am.
60 **NANTAHALA** Oiler. Am.
60 **LIENTUR** Patrol Vessel. Ch.
60 **ZACATECAS** Transport. Me.
60 **YUNDI** Patrol Boat. Pi.
61 **CASTILLA** Destroyer Escort. Am.
61 **IOWA** Battleship. Am. (Not in commission)
61 **PHEASANT** Fleet Minesweeper. Am.
61 **RANGER** Attack Aircraft Carrier. Am.
61 **LEUCOTON** Patrol Vessel. Ch.
61 **ASHDOD** Landing Craft. Is.
61 **DUMAN** Patrol Vessel. Ko.
61 Patrol Vessel. Sw.
61 **AGUSAN** Patrol Vessel. Pi.
62 **INDEPENDENCE** Attack Aircraft Carrier. Am.
62 **NEW JERSEY** Battleship. Am.
62 **TALUGA** Oiler. Am.
62 **LAUTARO** Patrol Vessel. Ch.
62 **MAMONAL** Oiler. Co.
62 **AGUIRRE** Escort. Pv.
62 **CATAN DUANES** Patrol Boat. Pi.
62. Patrol Boat. Sw.
63 **MISSOURI** Battleship. Am. (Not in commission)
63 **KITTYHAWK** Attack Aircraft Carrier. Am.
63 **CHIPOLA** Oiler. Am.
63 **SANCHO JIMENO** Oiler. Co.
63 **NAVARINO** Destroyer. Gr.
63 **ASHKELON** Landing Craft. Is.
63 **TAE DONG** Patrol Vessel. Ko.
63 **RODRIQUEZ** Escort. Pv.
63 Patrol Boat. Sw.
63 **ROMBLON** Patrol Boat. Pi.
64 **CONSTELLATION** Attack Aircraft Carrier. Am.
64 **STARLING** Fleet Minesweeper. Am.
64 **WISCONSIN** Battleship. Am. (Not in commission)

64 **TOLOVANA** Oiler. Am.
64 **ANTONIO DE AREVALO** Oiler. Co.
64 **PALAWAN** Patrol Boat. Pi.
64 Patrol Boat. Sw.
65 **ENTERPRISE** Attack Carrier (N). Am.
65 **PASADENA** Cruiser. Am.
65 **COVENAS** Oiler. Co.
65 **NIKI** Destroyer. Gr.
65 **ACHZIV** Landing Craft. Is.
65 **NAKTONG** Patrol Vessel. Ko.
65 **BATANES** Landing Craft. Pi.
65 Patrol Boat. Sw.
66 **AMERICA** Attack Carrier. Am.
66 **WU SHENG** Escort. Ch.
66 **IMCHIN** Patrol Vessel. Ko.
66 Patrol Vessel. Sw.
67 **APACHE** Fleet Tug. Am.
67 **JOHN F. KENNEDY** Attack Carrier. Am.
67 **CHU YUNG** Escort. Cs.
67 **PANTHIR** Frigate. Gr.
67 **AKLAN** Repair Ship. Pi.
67 Patrol Boat. Sw.
68 **BALTIMORE** Cruiser. Am.
68 **MO LING** Patrol Vessel. Cs.
68 **NIMITZ** Aircraft Carrier. Am.
68 **GALVEZ** Patrol Vessel. Pv.
68 **ORIENTAL MINDORO** Landing Ship. Pi
68 Patrol Boat. Sw.
69 **DWIGHT D. EISENHOWER** Aircraft Carrier. Am.
69 **BOSTON** Cruiser. Am.
69 **DIEZ CANSECO** Patrol Vessel. Pe.
69 **RIZAL** Escort. Pi.
69 Patrol Boat. Sw.
70 **CANBERRA** G.M. Cruiser. Am.
70 **PAVLIC** Transport. Am.
70 **PING CHING** Patrol Vessel. Cs.
70 **QUEZON** Escort. Pi.
70 Patrol Boat. Sw.
71 **ODIUM** Transport. Am.
71 **QUINCY** Cruiser. Am.
71 **ANDAGOYA** Tug. Co.
71 **QUITO** Gunboat. Ec. (May be *LC 71* on hull)
71 **KYONG KI** Escort. Ko.
71 **VILLAR** Destroyer. Pv.
72 **JACK C. ROBINSON** Transport. Am.
72 **KIOWA** Fleet Tug. Am.
72 **PITTSBURGH** Cruiser. Am.
72 **PEDRO DE HEREIDA** Tug. Co.
72 **KANG WON** Escort. Ko.
72 **GUISE** Destroyer. Pv.
72 **CAMIGUIN** Hydrofoil Patrol Boat. Pi.
73 **ST. PAUL** Cruiser. Am.
73 **CHUNG NAM** Frigate. Ko.
73 **SIQUIJOR** Hydrofoil Patrol Boat. Pi.
73 **MODE** Frigate. Sw.
74 **BONTOC** Hydrofoil Patrol Boat. Pi.
75 **HELENA** Cruiser. Am.
75 **SIOUX** Fleet Tug. Am.
75 **BALER** Hydrofoil Patrol Boat. Pi.
75 **MUNIN** Frigate. Sw.
76 **UTE** Fleet Tug. Am.

76 **DATO KALANTIAN** Destroyer Escort. Pi.
78 **BULL** Transport. Am.
78 **COHOES** Netlayer. Am.
78 **MALMO** Frigate. Sw.
79 **LIMASAWA** Supply Ship. Pi.
80 **GUACOLDA** Motor Torpedo Boat. Ch.
80 **NUEVA VISCAYA** Patrol Vessel. Pi.
81 **FRESIA** Motor Torpedo Boat. Ch.
81 **GUARDIAMARINAZICARI** Salvage Vessel. Ar.
81 **KYONG NAM** Transport. Ko.
81 **ALMIRANTE GRAU** Cruiser. Pv.
81 **NORRKOPING** Frigate. Sw.
82 **QUIDORA** Motor Torpedo Boat. Ch.
82 **ASAN** Escort Transport. Ko.
82 **CORONEL BOLOGNESI** Cruiser. Pv.
83 **CHICKASAW** Fleet Tug. Am.
83 **TEGUALDA** Motor Torpedo Boat. Ch.
83 **UNG PO** Escort Transport. Ko.
85 **KYONG BUK** Escort Transport. Ko.
86 **ANTELOPE** Gunboat. Am.
86 **HOLLIS** Transport. Am.
86 **MATACO** Fleet Tug. Am.
86 **CHUN NAN** Escort Transport. Ko.
87 **READY** Gunboat. Am.
87 **CHR JU** Escort Transport. Ko.
88 **CROCKETT** Gunboat. Am.
88 **CALOOSAHATCHEE** Oiler. Am.
89 **MARATHON** Gunboat. Am.
89 **ASPIRANTE GOICOLEA** Landing Ship. Ch.
89 **TENIENTE MIGUEL SILVA** Tug. Co.
90 **CANON** Gunboat. Co.
90 **KIRWIN** Transport. Co.
90 **JOVES FIALLO** Tug. Co.
91 **SENECA** Fleet Tug. Am.
91 **ASPIRANTE IZAZA** Landing Ship. Ch.
91 **CHUNG MU** Destroyer. Ko.
91 Gunboat. Th.
92 **REGISTER** Transport. Am.
92 **TACOMA** Gunboat. Am.
92 **TAWASA** Fleet Tug. Am.
92 **ASPIRANTE MOREL** Landing Ship. Ch.
92 **SEOUL** Destroyer. Ko.
93 **WELCH** Gunboat. Am.
93 **GRUMETE TELLEZ** Landing Craft. Ch.
93 **PUSAN** Destroyer. Ko.
94 **CHEHALIS** Gunboat. Am.
94 **OROMPELLO** Landing Craft. Ch.
95 **DEFIANCE** Gunboat. Am.
95 **GRUMETE BOLADOS** Landing Craft. Ch.
96 **ABNAKI** Fleet Tug. Am.
96 **BENICIA** Gunboat. Am.
96 **GRUMETE DIAZ** Landing Craft. Ch.
97 **ALLAGASH** Oiler. Am.
97 **SURPRISE** Gunboat. Am.
97 Patrol Boat. Ceylon.
98 **ARIKARA** Fleet Tug. Am.
98 **GRAND RAPIDS** Gunboat. Am.

98 Ex **TRUXTON** Transport. Am.
99 **CANISTEO** Oiler. Am.
99 **BEACON** Gunboat. Am.
99 **CHOWANOC** Fleet Tug. Am.
100 **DOUGLAS** Gunboat. Am.
100 **RINGNESS** Transport. Am.
100 **CAPE BRETON** Escort Maintenance Ship. Ca.
100 **CHUKAWAN** Fleet Oiler. Am.
101 **AMSTERDAM** Cruiser. Am.
101 **COCOPA** Fleet Tug. Am.
101 **HERALD** Fleet Minesweeper. Am.
101 **KNUDSON** Transport. Am.
101 **GREEN BAY** Gunboat. Am.
101 **CAPE SCOTT** Escort Maintenance Ship. Ca.
101 **CAPITAN BINNEY** C.G Vessel. Co.
101 **ORION** Survey Ship. Ec.
101 **RIGEL** C.G Vessel. Co.
101 **HARUKAZE** Destroyer. Ja.
102 **PORTSMOUTH** Cruiser. Am.
102 **BETELGEUSE** C.G Vessel. Do.
102 **YUKIKAZE** Destroyer. Ja.
102 Torpedo Boat. Ys.
103 **HITCHITI** Fleet Tug. Am.
103 **WILKES BARRE** Cruiser. Am.
103 **PROCION** C.G Vessel. Do.
103 **AYANAMI** Destroyer. Ja.
103 Torpedo Boat. Ys.
104 **PILOT** Fleet Minesweeper. Am.
104 **ISONAMI** Destroyer. Ja.
105 **MOCTOBI** Fleet Tug. Am.
105 **PIONEER** Fleet Minesweeper. Am.
105 **MISPILLION** Oiler. Am.
105 **FUKIANG** Submarine Chaser. Cs.
105 **URANAMI** Destroyer. Ja.
105 **CAPITAN ALSINA** Rescue Launch. Do.
106 **FARGO** Cruiser. Am.
106 **MOLALA** Fleet Tug. Am.
106 **WALTER B. COBB** Transport. Am.
106 **NAVASOTA** Oiler. Am.
106 **BELLATRIX** C.G Vessel. Do.
106 **SHIKINAMI** Destroyer. Ja.
107 **MUNSEE** Fleet Tug. Am.
107 **PASSUMPSIC** Oiler. Am.
107 **MURASAME** Destroyer. Ja.
108 **HSIANG KIANG** Submarine Chaser. Cs.
108 **HARRY L. CORL** Transport. Am.
108 **PAWCATUCK** Oiler. Am.
108 **YUDACHI** Destroyer. Ja.
108 **CAPELLA** C.G Vessel. Do.
108 Torpedo Boat. Ys.
109 **WACCAMAW** Oiler. Am.
109 **CHIH KIANG** Submarine Chaser. Cs.
109 **HARUSAME** Destroyer. Ja.
110 **JULIUS A. RAVEN** Transport. Am.
110 **QUAPAW** Fleet Tug. Am.
110 **TAKANAMI** Destroyer. Ja.
111 **SAGE** Fleet Minesweeper. Am.
111 **LI-KIANG** Submarine Chaser. Cs.
111 **ONAMI** Destroyer. Ja.
112 **MAKINAMI** Destroyer. Ja.

113 **TAKELMA** Fleet Tug. Am.
113 **SACKVILLE** Research Ship. Ca.
113 **KUNG KIANG** Submarine Chaser. Cs.
113 **YAMAGUMO** Destroyer. Ja.
114 **TAWAKONI** Fleet Tug. Am.
114 **BLUETHROAT** Research Ship. Ca.
114 **PO KIANG** Submarine Chaser. Cs.
114 **MAKIGUMO** Destroyer. Ja.
115 **CHUNG KIANG** Submarine Chaser. Cs.
115 **ASAGUMO** Destroyer. Ja.
115 Torpedo Boat. Ys.
116 **CHUNG KIANG** Submarine Chaser. Cs.
116 **MINEGUMO** Destroyer. Ja.
116 Torpedo Boat. Ys.
117 **CHU KIANG** Gunboat. Cs.
119 **BEVERLY W. REID** Transport. Am.
119 **TUNG KIANG** Submarine Chaser. Cs.
119 Torpedo Boat. Ys.
120 **KLINE** Transport. Am.
120 **SWAY** Fleet Minesweeper. Am.
120 **HSI KIANG** Submarine Chaser. Cs.
120 Torpedo Boat. Ys.
121 **BLUEBIRD** Coastal Minesweeper. Am.
121 **RAYMOND W. HERNDON** Transport. Am.
122 **CORMORANT** Coastal Minesweeper. Am.
122 **OREGON CITY** Cruiser. Am.
122 **SCRIBNER** Transport. Am.
122 **SWIFT** Fleet Minesweeper. Am.
122 **JUAN LUCIO** Motor Launch. Co.
122 **PEI KIANG** Submarine Chaser. Cs.
122 Torpedo Boat. Ys.
123 **DIACHENKO** Transport. Am.
123 **SYMBOL** Fleet Minesweeper. Am.
123 **ALFONSO VARGAS** Motor Launch. Co.
123 **LIU KIANG** Submarine Chaser. Cs.
123 **RIOS** Tug. Pv.
124 **HORACE A. BASS** Transport. Am.
124 **ROCHESTER** Cruiser. Am.
124 **THREAT** Fleet Minesweeper. Am.
124 **FRITZ HAGALE** Motor Launch. Co.
124 **HAN KIANG** Submarine Chaser. Cs.
124 Torpedo Boat. Ys.
125 **ALBERTO RESTREPO** Motor Launch. Co.
125 **TO KIANG** Submarine Chaser. Cs.
125 Torpedo Boat. Ys.
126 **HUMBERTO CORTES** Motor Launch. Co.
126 Torpedo Boat. Ys.
127 **BEGOR** Transport. Am.
127 Torpedo Boat. Ys.

128 **VELOCITY** Fleet Minesweeper. Am.
128 **CARLOS GALINDO** Motor Launch. Co.
129 **EDSALL** Escort. Am.
130 **BREMERTON** Cruiser. Am.
130 **JACOB JONES** Escort. Am.
130 **PALACE** Motor Launch. Co.
131 **FALL RIVER** Cruiser. Am.
131 **HAMMAN** Escort. Am.
132 **BALDUCK** Transport. Am.
132 **CALLAO** Transport. Pv.
133 **BURDO** Transport. Am.
133 **TOLEDO** Cruiser. Am.
133 **TRIUNFANTE** Motor Launch. Co.
134 **DES MOINES** Cruiser. Am.
134 **POPE** Escort. Am.
134 **INDEPENDENTE** Motor Launch. Co.
134 **PC 134** Patrol Craft. Ys.
135 **LOS ANGELES** Cruiser. Am.
135 **WEISS** Transport. Am.
135 **AGUILA** Helicopter Support. Ch.
135 **VOLADORA** Motor Launch. Co.
136 **TORMENTOSO** Motor Launch. Co.
136 **UNANUE** Tug. Pv.
137 **HERBERT C. JONES** Escort. Am.
137 **VALEROSA** Motor Launch. Co.
138 **DOUGLAS J. HOWARD** Escort. Am.
138 **DILIGENTE** Motor Launch. Co.
138 **SAN MARTIN** Coastal Mine - sweeper. Pe.
139 **FARQUHAR** Escort. Am.
139 **SALEM** Cruiser. Am.
139 **VENGADORA** Motor Launch. Co.
140 **J. R. Y. BLAKELEY** Escort. Am.
141 **HILL** Escort. Am.
141 **MANTILLA** Water Carrier. Pv.
143 **NEOSHO** Oiler. Am.
144 **MISSISSINEWA** Oiler. Am.
144 **WORCESTER** Cruiser. Am.
145 **HUSE** Escort. Am.
145 **ROANOKE** Cruiser. Am.
145 **HASSAYAMPA** Oiler. Am.
146 **INCH** Escort. Am.
146 **KAWISHIWI** Oiler. Am.
147 **BLAIR** Escort. Am.
147 **TRUCKEE** Oiler. Am.
148 **NEWPORT NEWS** Cruiser. Am.
148 **PONCHATOULA** Oiler. Am.
149 **ATAKAPA** Fleet Tug. Am.
149 **CHATELAIN** Escort. Am.
149 **QUINTE** Coastal Minesweeper. Ca.
150 **NEUNZER** Escort. Am.
150 **OPHIR** Torpedo Boat. Is.
151 **POOLE** Escort. Am.
151 **FORTUNE** Coastal Minesweeper. Ca.
151 **SHVA** Torpedo Boat. Is.
151 **MOLLENDO** Oiler. Pv.
152 **PETERSON** Escort. Am.
152 **JAMES BAY** Coastal Mine - sweeper. Ca.
152 **TARSHISH** Torpedo Boat. Is.
153 **TALARA** Oiler. Pv.
156 **LUISENO** Fleet Tug. Am.

154 **DUCHESS** Destroyer. Au.
154 **RESOLUTE** Coastal Minesweep- er. Ca.
154 **SECHURA** Oiler. Pv.
157 **NIPMUC** Fleet Tug. Am.
157 Torpedo Boat. Ys.
158 **MOSOSPELEA** Fleet Tug. Am.
159 **FUNDY** Coastal Minesweeper. Ca.
158 **ZORRITOS** Oiler. Pv.
159 **PAIUTE** Fleet Tug. Am.
159 **FUNDY** Coastal Minesweeper. Ca.
159 **LOBITOS** Oiler. Pv.
159 Torpedo Boat. Ys.
160 **PAPAGO** Fleet Tug. Am.
160 **CHIGNECTO** Coastal Mine - sweeper. Ca.
160 **YUNG CHI** Coastal Mine - sweeper. Cs.
160 **ALAMGIR** Destroyer. Pk.
160 **MAHMOOD** Coastal Mine - sweeper. Pk.
161 **SALINAN** Fleet Tug. Am.
161 **THUNDER** Coastal Mine - sweeper. Ca.
171 **YUNG LO** Coastal Mine - sweeper. Cs.
161 **GORGONA** Tender. Co.
161 **AKIZUKI** Destroyer. Ja.
161 **BADR** Destroyer. Pk.
162 **LEVY** Escort. Am.
162 **SHAKORI** Fleet Tug. Am.
162 **COWICHAN** Coastal Mine - sweeper. Ca.
162 **TERUZUKI** Destroyer. Ja.
162 **JAHANGIR** Destroyer. Pk.
162 Torpedo Boat. Ys.
163 **MCCONNELL** Escort. Am.
163 **UTINA** Fleet Tug. Am.
163 **MIRAMICHI** Coastal Mine - sweeper. Ca.
163 **AMATSUKAZE** Destroyer G.M. Ja.
163 **KHAIBAR** Destroyer. Pk.
164 **OSTERHAUS** Escort. Am.
164 **CHALEUR** Coastal Minesweeper. Ca.
164 **SHAH JAHAN** Destroyer. Pk.
164 Torpedo Boat. Ys.
164 **TAKATSUKI** Destroyer. Ja.
165 **COUNSEL** Minesweeper. Am.
165 **PARKS** Escort. Am.
165 **KIKUZUKI** Destroyer. Ja.
165 Torpedo Boat. Ys.
166 **MOCHIZUKI** Destroyer. Ja.
167 **ACREE** Escort. Am.
167 **NAGATSUKI** Destroyer. Ja.
167 **MOSHAL** Coastal Minesweeper. Pk.
167 Torpedo Boat. Ys.
168 **NEW LISKEARD** Ocean - ographic Research Ship. Ca.
170 **FORT FRANCES** Ocean - ographic Research Ship. Ca.
170 Torpedo Boat. Ys.
171 **ENDEAVOUR** Oceanographic Research Ship. Ca.
172 **COONER** Escort. Am.
172 **QUEST** Oceanographic Research Ship. Ca.
174 Torpedo Boat. Ys.

179 **ALLEGHENY** Tug. Am.
180 **TRUMPETER** Escort. Am.
180 **PORTE ST. JEAN** Gate Vessel. Ca.
180 **GRANBY** Diving Depot Ship. Ca.
181 **ACCOKEEK** Tug. Am.
181 **STRAUB** Escort. Am.
183 **PORTE ST. LOUIS** Gate Vessel. Ca.
183 **ARIAKE** Destroyer. Ja.
184 **KALMIA** Tug. Am.
184 **PORTE DE LA REINE** Gate Vessel. Ca.
184 **YUUGURE** Destroyer. Ja.
185 **KOKA** Tug. Am.
185 **PORTE QUEBEC** Gate Vessel. Ca.
186 **CAHOKIA** Tug. Am.
186 **PORTE DAUPHINE** Gate Vessel. Ca.
187 **SALISH** Tug. Am.
188 **PENOBSCOT** Tug. Am.
190 **FALCON** Coastal Minesweeper. Am.
190 **SAMOSET** Tug. Am.
191 **COFFMAN** Escort. Am.
191 **FRIGATE BIRD** Coastal Mine- sweeper. Am.
191 (*G. 191*) **SPOKANE** Sonar Test Ship. Am.
191 **TUNG HAI** Dock Landing Ship. Cs.
192 **HUMMING BIRD** Coastal Minesweeper. Am.
192 **TILLAMOOK** Tug. Am.
193 **JACANA** Coastal Minesweeper. Am.
193 **STALLION** Tug. Am.
194 **KING BIRD** Coastal Mine - sweeper. Am.
195 **LIMPKIN** Coastal Minesweeper. Am.
195 **TATNUCK** Tug. Am.
196 **MAHOPAC** Tug. Am.
196 **MEADOW LARK** Coastal Minesweeper. Am.
197 **PARROT** Coastal Minesweeper. Am.
198 **PEACOCK** Coastal Minesweeper. Am.
199 **PHOEBE** Coastal Minesweeper. Am.
199 Torpedo Boat. Ys.
200 Torpedo Boat. Is.
201 **SHRIKE** Coastal Minesweeper. Am.
201 **CHUNG HAI** Landing Ship. Cs.
201 **SILIWANGI** Destroyer. Ia.
201 Torpedo Boat. Is.
201 **AKEBONO** Destroyer. Ja.
201 Torpedo Boat. Ys.
202 **EICHENBERGER** Escort. Am.
202 Torpedo Boat. Is.
202 **IKAZUCHI** Destroyer. Ja.
202 **KUM SEONG** Patrol Vessel. Ko.
203 **THRASHER** Coastal Mine - sweeper. Am.
203 **CHUNG TING** Landing Ship. Cs.
203 **RESTAURACION** Patrol Vessel. Do.
203 **SANDJAJA** Destroyer. Ia.

203 Torpedo Boat. Is.
203 **INAZUMA** Destroyer. Ja.
204 **WANDANK** Tug. Am.
204 **THRUSH** Coastal Minesweeper. Am.
204 **CHUNG HSI** Landing Ship. Cs.
204 **INDEPENDENCIA** Patrol Vessel. Do.
204 Torpedo Boat. Is.
205 **ST. LAURENT** Destroyer. Ca.
205 **VIREO** Coastal Minesweeper. Am.
205 **CHUNG CHIEN** Landing Ship. Cs.
205 **LIBERTAD** Patrol Vessel. Do.
205 Torpedo Boat. Is.
205 **HWA SEONG** Patrol Vessel. Ko.
206 **WARBLER** Coastal Mine-sweeper. Am.
206 **SAGUENAY** Destroyer. Ca.
206 **CHUNG CHI** Landing Ship. Cs.
207 **WHIPPORWILL** Coastal Mine-sweeper. Am.
207 **SKEENA** Destroyer. Ca.
208 **SAGAMORE** Tug. Am.
208 **WIDGEON** Coastal Mine-sweeper. Am.
208 **CHUNG SHUN** Landing Ship. Cs.
209 **UMPQUA** Tug. Am.
209 **WOODPECKER** Coastal Mine-sweeper. Am.
209 **CHUNG LIEN** Landing Ship. Cs.
210 **CATAWBA** Tug. Am.
210 **CHUNG YUNG** Landing Ship. Cs.
211 **ISUZU** Destroyer Escort. Ja.
212 **MOGAMI** Destroyer Escort. Ja.
213 **KEYWADIN** Tug. Am.
213 **KITAKAMI** Destroyer Escort. Ja.
214 **SYDNEY** Aircraft Transport. Au.
214 **01** Destroyer Escort. Ja.
215 **CRUISE** Fleet Minesweeper. Am.
215 **STALWART** Destroyer Tender. Au.
215 **CHUNG YU** Landing Ship. Cs.
215 **CHIKUGO** Frigate. Ja.
216 **CHUNG KUANG** Landing Ship. Cs.
216 **UNDEN** Water Carrier. Sw.
217 **COOLBAUGH** Escort. Am.
217 **FRYKEN** Water Carrier. Sw.
218 **CHUNG CHIH** Landing Ship. Cs.
219 **CHUNG HSI** Landing Ship. Cs.
220 **FRANCIS M. ROBINSON** Escort. Am.
221 **CHUNG CH'UAN** Landing Ship. Cs.
221 **MARANAO** Tug. Pi.
222 **CHUNG SHENG** Landing Ship. Cs.
222 **IGOROT** Tug. Pi.
223 **CHUNG FU** Landing Ship. Cs.
223 **MANGYAN** Tug. Pi.
224 **ALGONQUIN** Destroyer. Ca.
224 **CHUNG CHENG** Landing Ship. Cs.
225 **CHUNG CHIANG** Landing Ship. Cs.
226 **CRESCENT** Destroyer Escort. Ca.

226 **CHUNG SHIH** Landing Ship. Cs.
227 **CHUNG MING** Landing Ship. Cs.
228 **CHUNG SUO** Landing Ship. Cs.
229 **OTTAWA** Destroyer Escort. Ca.
229 **CHUNG WAN** Landing Ship. Cs.
230 **MARGAREE** Destroyer Escort. Ca.
230 **CHUNG BANG** Landing Ship. Cs.
231 **HODGES** Escort. Am.
231 **CHUNG YEA** Landing Ship Cs.
233 **FRASER** Destroyer Escort. Ca.
234 **ASSINIBOINE** Destroyer Escort. Ca.
235 **CHAUDIERE** Destroyer Escort. Ca.
236 **GATINEAU** Destroyer Escort. Ca.
238 **STEWART** Escort. Am.
239 **STURTEVANT** Escort. Am.
240 **MOORE** Escort. Am.
241 **KEITH** Escort. Am.
241 **MEI CHIN** Landing Ship. Cs.
242 **TOMICH** Escort. Am.
243 **MEI I** Landing Ship. Cs.
244 **OTTERSTETTER** Escort. Am.
245 **SLOAT** Escort. Am.
245 **MEI HENG** Landing Ship. Cs.
246 **MEI HUNG** Landing Ship. Cs.
247 **STANTON** Escort. Am.
247 **MEI SUNG** Landing Ship. Cs.
248 **MEI HO** Landing Ship. Cs.
248 **SWASEY** Escort. Am.
249 **MARCHAND** Escort. Am.
249 **MEI CHIEN** Landing Ship. Cs.
250 **HURSH** Escort. Am.
250 **MEI HWA** Landing Ship. Cs.
251 **CAMP** Escort. Am.
251 **MEI CHEN** Landing Ship. Cs.
252 **MEI KUN** Landing Ship. Cs.
253 **PETTIT** Escort. Am.
253 **MEI PING** Landing Ship. Cs.
254 **RICKETTS** Escort. Am.
254 **MEI WEN** Landing Ship. Cs.
255 **SELLSTROM** Escort. Am.
255 **MEI HAN** Landing Ship. Cs.
256 **ST. CROIX** Destroyer. Ca.
256 **MEI LO** Landing Ship. Cs.
257 **RESTIGOUCHE** Destroyer. Ca.
258 **KOOTENAY** Destroyer. Ca.
259 **TERRA NOVA** Destroyer. Ca.
260 **COLUMBIA** Destroyer. Ca.
260 **TIPPU SULTAN** Frigate. Pk.
261 **MACKENZIE** Destroyer. Ca.
261 **LIEN CHU** Landing Craft. Cs.
261 **WAKABA** Radar Experimental Ship. Ja.
261 **TUGHRIL** Frigate. Pk.
262 **SASKATCHEWAN** Destroyer. Ca.
262 **LIEN LI** Landing Craft. Cs.
262 **ASAHI** Destroyer Escort. Ja.
262 **ZULFIQUAR** Survey Ship. Pk.
263 **YUKON** Destroyer. Ca.
263 **LIEN SHENG** Landing Craft. Cs.
263 **HATSUHI** Destroyer Escort Ja.
264 **LIEN CHENG** Landing Craft. Cs.
265 **ANNAPOLIS** Destroyer. Ca.
265 **LIEN HUA** Landing Craft. Cs.

266 **NIPIGON** Destroyer. Ca.
266 **LIEN CHING** Survey Ship. Cs.
271 **LIEN CHIH** Landing Craft. Cs.
271 **BLYSKAWICA** Destroyer. Ph.
272 **LIEN JEN** Landing Craft. Cs.
273 **LIEN YUNG** Landing Craft. Cs.
275 **SHAHBAZ** Coastal Mine-sweeper. Ir.
275 **PELIKANEN** Tender. Sw.
276 **SHAHROKH** Coastal Mine-sweeper. Ir.
280 **IROQUOIS** Destroyer. Ca.
281 **HURON** Destroyer. Ca.
281 **KUSU** Drone Target Carrier. Ja.
282 **ATHABASKAN** Destroyer. Ca.
282 **NARA** Training Frigate. Ja.
283 **ALGONQUIN** Destroyer. Ca.
283 **KASHI** Training Frigate. Ja.
284 **MOMI** Training Frigate. Ja.
285 **SUGI** Patrol Frigate. Ja.
286 **MATSU** Training Frigate. Ja.
287 **VANCE** Escort. Am.
287 **NIRE** Patrol Frigate. Ja.
288 **KAYA** Patrol Frigate. Ja.
289 **UME** Training Frigate. Ja.
290 **SAKURA** Training Frigate. Ja.
291 **SIMORGH** Coastal Mine-sweeper. Ir.
292 **KARKAS** Coastal Minesweeper. Ir.
293 **KAEDE** Training Frigate. Ja (Moored)
294 **BUNA** Training Frigate. Ja. (Moored)
294 **MADADGAR** Tug. Pk.
295 **KEYAKI** Patrol Frigate. Ja.
296 **TOCHI** Training Frigate. Ja.
297 **LADYA** Coastal Minesweeper. Th.
298 **MAKI** Training Frigate. Ja.
301 **SIRIO** Landing Ship. Do.
301 **HARISCHI** Inshore Minesweeper. Ir.
301 **KARI** Patrol Boat. Ja.
301 **NAPO** River Gunboat. Pv.
302 **HSIN KAO** Oiler. Cs.
302 **SAMANA** Landing Craft. Do.
302 **SINGAMANGARADJA** Destroyer. Ia.
302 **RIAZI** Inshore Minesweeper. Ir.
302 **KIJI** Patrol Vessel. Ja.
303 **ENRIQUILLO** Landing Craft. Do.
303 **TAKA** Patrol Vessel. Ja.
304 **SZU MING** Oiler. Cs.
304 **WASHI** Patrol Vessel. Ja.
305 **PROWESS** Training Ship. Am.
305 **KAMOME** Patrol Vessel. Ja.
306 **SPECTER** Fleet Minesweeper. Am.
306 **SWANSEA** Escort. Ca.
306 **KUAI CHI** Oiler. Cs.
306 **TSUBAME** Patrol Vessel. Ja.
306 **PCF 306** Patrol Boat. Pi.
307 **CHANG PEI** Oiler. Cs.
307 **MISAGO** Patrol Vessel. Ja.
307 **PCF 307** Patrol Boat. Pi.
308 **HAYABUSA** Patrol Vessel. Ja.
308 **PCF 308** Patrol Boat. Pi.
309 **UMITAKA** Patrol Vessel. Ja.
309 **PCF 309** Patrol Boat. Pi.
309 Motor Launch. Tu.
310 **OTAKA** Patrol Vessel. Ja.

310 **PCF 310** Patrol Boat. Pi.
311 **PCF 311** Patrol Boat. Pi.
311 **SUPERIOR** Fleet Minesweeper. Am.
311 **WULING** Transport. Cs.
311 **MIZUTORI** Patrol Vessel. Ja.
311 **SI HUNG** Rocket Landing Ship. Ko.
312 **YAMADORI** Patrol Vessel. Ja.
313 **TIEN CHU** Transport. Cs.
313 **OTORI** Patrol Vessel. Ja.
314 **CHAMPION** Fleet Minesweeper. Am.
314 **KASASAGI** Patrol Vessel. Ja.
315 **CHIEF** Fleet Minesweeper. Am.
315 **TIEN SHAN** Destroyer Escort. Cs.
315 **CHIU HUA** Transport. Cs.
315 **HATSUKARI** Patrol Vessel. Ja.
316 **COMPETENT** Fleet Minesweeper. Am.
316 **UMIDORI** Patrol Vessel. Ja.
317 **DEFENSE** Fleet Minesweeper. Am.
317 **JOYCE** Escort. Am.
317 **CHUNG SHAN** Transport. Cs.
317 **WAKATAKA** Patrol Vessel. Ja.
318 **DEVASTATOR** Fleet Minesweeper. Am.
318 **KIRKPATRICK** Escort. Am.
318 **KUMATAKA** Patrol Vessel. Ja.
319 **GLADIATOR** Fleet Minesweeper. Am.
319 **SHIRATORI** Patrol Vessel. Ja.
320 **IMPECCABLE** Fleet Minesweeper. Am.
320 **MENGES** Escort. Am.
320 **HIYODORI** Patrol Vessel. Ja.
321 **MOSLEY** Escort. Am.
322 **SPEAR** Fleet Minesweeper. Am.
323 **PRIDE** Escort. Am.
324 **FALGUT** Escort. Am.
326 **THOMAS J. GARY** Escort. Am.
328 **FINCH** Escort. Am.
329 **KRETCHMER** Escort. Am.
330 **O'REILLY** Escort. Am.
332 **PRICE** Escort. Am.
333 **STRICKLAND** Escort. Am.
334 **FORSTER** Escort. Am.
335 **DANIEL** Escort. Am.
336 **ROY O'HALE** Escort. Am.
336 **SHUNG SHAN** Repair Ship. Cs.
337 **DALE W. PETERSON** Escort. Am.
339 **JOHN C. BUTLER** Escort. Am.
340 **ARDENT** Fleet Minesweeper. Am.
340 **O'FLAHERTY** Escort. Am.
341 **RAYMOND** Escort. Am.
342 **RICHARD W. SUESENS** Escort. Am.
342 **TA WU** Tug. Cs.
343 **TA MING** Tug. Cs.
344 **BLANCO COUNTY** Landing Ship. Am.
345 **TA YU** Tug. Cs.
346 **EDWIN A. HOWARD** Escort. Am.
347 **TA SHUEH** Tug. Cs.
348 **KEY** Escort. Am.

349 **GENTRY** Escort. Am.
353 **DOYLE C. BARNES** Escort. Am.
354 **KENNETH M. WILLETT** Escort. Am.
356 **LLOYD E. ACREE** Escort. Am.
357 **GEORGE A. DAVIS** Escort. Am.
358 **MACK** Escort. Am.
360 **JOHNNIE HUTCHINS** Escort. Am.
361 **NIEUGIETY** Patrol Vessel. Ph.
362 **ROLF** Escort. Am.
362 **YANG MING** Survey Ship. Cs.
362 **GROZNY** Patrol Vessel. Ph.
363 **PRATT** Escort. Am.
363 **ZAWZIETY** Patrol Vessel. Ph.
364 **ROMBACH** Escort. Am.
364 **ZWROTNY** Patrol Vessel. Ph.
365 **ZWINNY** Patrol Vessel. Ph.
366 **ZRECNY** Patrol Vessel. Ph.
367 **FRENCH** Escort. Am.
367 **WYTRWALY** Patrol Vessel. Ph.
368 **CZUINY** Patrol Vessel. Ph.
370 **JOHN L. WILLIAMSON** Escort. Am.
379 **ROSELLE** Fleet Minesweeper. Am.
381 **SCOTER** Fleet Minesweeper. Am.
382 **RAMSDEN** Escort. Am.
383 **MILLS** Escort. Am.
384 **RHODES** Escort. Am.
384 **SPRIG** Fleet Minesweeper. Am.
386 **SAVAGE** Escort. Am.
386 **TERCEL** Fleet Minesweeper. Am.
387 **VANCE** Escort. Am.
388 **LANCING** Escort. Am.
389 **DURANT** Escort. Am.
390 **CALCATERRA** Escort. Am.
390 **WHEATEAR** Fleet Minesweeper. Am.
391 **CHAMBERS** Escort. Am.
392 **MERRILL** Escort. Am.
394 **SWENNING** Escort. Am.
395 **WILLIS** Escort. Am.
396 **JANSSEN** Escort. Am.
398 **COCKRILL** Escort. Am.
399 **STOCKDALE** Escort. Am.
400 **HISSEM** Escort. Am.
400 **BRAS D'OR** Hydrofoil. Ca.
401 **BIG BLACK RIVER** Landing Ship. Am.
401 **HO CHUN** Landing Craft. Cs.
401 **CRISTOBAL COLON** Corvette. Do.
401 **CHIHAYA** Submarine Rescue Ship. Ja.
402 **HO CH'UNG** Landing Craft. Cs.
402 **JUAN ALEJANDRO ACOSTA** Corvette. Do.
403 **HO CHENG** Landing Craft. Cs.
403 **JUAN BAUTISTA CAMBIASO** Corvette. Do.
404 **GERARDO JANSSEN** Corvette. Do.
404 **HO CHUNG** Landing Craft. Cs.
405 **DENNIS** Escort. Am.
405 **BROADKILL RIVER** Landing Ship. Am.
405 **HO CHANG** Landing Craft. Cs.

405 **JUAN BAUTISTA MAGGIOLO** Corvette. Do.
406 **EDMONDS** Escort. Am.
406 **HO CHEN** Landing Craft. Cs.
407 **HO CHIH** Landing Craft. Cs.
409 **CLARION RIVER** Landing Ship. Am.
409 **LA PRADE** Escort. Am.
411 **STAFFORD** Escort. Am.
411 **HAMANA** Oiler. Ja.
412 **DES PLAINES RIVER** Landing Ship. Am.
414 **LE RAY WILSON** Escort. Am.
415 **LAWRENCE C. TAYLOR** Escort. Am.
416 **MELVIN R. NAWMAN** Escort. Am.
417 **OLIVER MITCHELL** Escort. Am.
418 **TABBERER** Escort. Am.
419 **ROBERT F. KELLER** Escort. Am.
420 **LELAND E. THOMAS** Escort. Am.
421 **AGILE** Ocean Minesweeper. Am.
421 **CHESTER T. O'BRIEN** Escort. Am.
422 **AGGRESSIVE** Ocean Minesweeper. Am.
422 **MAYO** Destroyer. Am.
423 **DUFILHO** Escort. Am.
424 **BOLD** Ocean Minesweeper. Am.
424 **NIBLACK** Destroyer. Am.
425 **BULWARK** Ocean Minesweeper. Am.
426 **CONFLICT** Ocean Minesweeper. Am.
427 **CONSTANT** Ocean Minesweeper. Am.
428 **DASH** Ocean Minesweeper. Am.
429 **DETECTOR** Ocean Minesweeper. Am.
430 **DIRECT** Ocean Minesweeper. Am.
431 **DOMINANT** Ocean Minesweeper. Am.
432 **DYNAMIC** Ocean Minesweeper. Am.
432 **KEARNEY** Destroyer. Am.
433 **ENGAGE** Ocean Minesweeper. Am.
434 **EMBATTLE** Ocean Minesweeper. Am.
435 **ENDURANCE** Ocean Minesweeper. Am.
435 **GRAYSON** Destroyer. Am.
436 **ENERGY** Ocean Minesweeper. Am.
437 **ENHANCE** Ocean Minesweeper. Am.
437 **WOOLSEY** Destroyer. Am.
438 **CORBESIER** Escort. Am.
438 **ESTEEM** Ocean Minesweeper. Am.
439 **CONKLIN** Escort. Am.
439 **EXCEL** Ocean Minesweeper. Am.
440 **ERICSSON** Destroyer. Am.
440 **EXPLOIT** Ocean Minesweeper. Am.
441 **EXULTANT** Ocean Minesweeper. Am.

441 **WILKES** Destroyer. Am.
441 **WILLIAM SEIVERLING** Escort. Am
441 Torpedo Boat. It.
442 **FEARLESS** Ocean Minesweeper. Am.
443 **FIDELITY** Ocean Minesweeper. Am.
443 **KENDALL C. CAMPBELL** Escort. Am.
443 **SWANSON** Destroyer. Am.
443 Torpedo Boat. It.
444 **FIRM** Ocean Minesweeper. Am.
444 **GOSS** Escort. Am.
444 Torpedo Boat. It.
445 **FORCE** Ocean Minesweeper. Am.
446 **FORTIFY** Ocean Minesweeper. Am.
447 **GUIDE** Ocean Minelayer. Am.
448 **ILLUSIVE** Ocean Minesweeper. Am.
448 **LA VALLETTE** Destroyer. Am.
449 **HANNA** Escort. Am.
449 **IMPERVIOUS** Ocean Minesweeper. Am.
450 **JOSEPH E. CONNOLLY** Escort. Am.
451 **MELLA** Training Ship. Do.
451 **HOA GIANG** Training Ship. VN.
452 **GREGORIO LUPERON** Frigate. Do.
453 Torpedo Boat. It.
453 **CAP. GENERAL PEDRO SANTANA** Frigate. Do.
455 **HAMBLETON** Destroyer. Am.
455 **IMPLICIT** Ocean Minesweeper. Am.
456 **INFLICT** Ocean Minesweeper. Am.
457 **LOYALTY** Ocean Minesweeper. Am.
458 **LUCID** Ocean Minesweeper. Am.
459 **NIMBLE** Ocean Minesweeper. Am.
460 **NOTABLE** Ocean Minesweeper. Am.
461 **OBSERVER** Ocean Minesweeper. Am.
461 **HAYATOMO** Minesweeper Tender. Ja.
462 **FITCH** Destroyer. Am.
462 **PINNACLE** Ocean Minesweeper. Am.
463 **PIVOT** Ocean Minesweeper. Am.
464 **PLUCK** Ocean Minesweeper. Am.
466 **PRIME** Ocean Minesweeper. Am.
467 **REAPER** Ocean Minesweeper. Am.
468 **RIVAL** Ocean Minesweeper. Am.
469 **SAGACITY** Ocean Minesweeper. Am.
470 **SALUTE** Ocean Minesweeper. Am.
471 **SKILL** Ocean Minesweeper. Am.
472 **VALOR** Ocean Minesweeper. Am.
472 Torpedo Boat. It.

473 **VIGOR** Ocean Minesweeper. Am.
473 Torpedo Boat. It.
474 **VITAL** Ocean Minesweeper. Am.
474 Torpedo Boat. It.
475 **HUDSON** Destroyer. Am.
478 **STANLEY** Destroyer. Am.
479 **STEVENS** Destroyer. Am.
481 Torpedo Boat. It.
481 **TSUGARU** Cable & Minelayer. Ja.
488 **CONQUEST** Ocean Minesweeper. Am.
489 **GALLANT** Ocean Minesweeper. Am.
489 **MERVINE** Destroyer. Am.
490 **LEADER** Ocean Minesweeper. Am.
490 **QUICK** Destroyer. Am.
490 **FOLGORE** Motor Gunboat. It.
491 **FARENHOLT** Destroyer. Am.
491 **PERSISTANT** Ocean Minesweeper. Am.
491 **LAMPO** Motor Gunboat. It.
491 **ERIMO** Minelayer & Minesweeper. Ja.
492 **PLEDGE** Ocean Minesweeper. Am.
492 **BALENO** Motor Gunboat. It.
493 **CARMICK** Destroyer. Am.
493 **FRECCIA** Motor Gunboat. It.
494 **DOYLE** Destroyer. Am.
494 **STURDY** Ocean Minesweeper. Am.
494 **SAETTA** Motor Gunboat. It.
495 **SWERVE** Ocean Minesweeper. Am.
495 **DARDO** Motor Gunboat. It.
496 **MCCOOK** Destroyer. Am.
496 **VENTURE** Ocean Minesweeper. Am.
496 **STRALE** Motor Gunboat. It.
497 **FRANKFORD** Destroyer. Am.
499 **FULMINE** Motor Gunboat. It.
500 **CAM RANH** Landing Ship. VN.
501 **ELK RIVER** Ocean Engineering Range Support Ship. Am.
501 **SCHROEDER** Destroyer. Am.
501 **DA NANG** Landing Ship. Vietnam.
501 **PBR 501** Patrol Boat. Ys.
502 **SIGSBEE** Destroyer. Am.
502 Coastal Minesweeper. Cs.
502 **THI NAI** Landing Ship. VN.
502 **PBR 502** Patrol Boat. Ys.
503 Coastal Minesweeper. Cs.
503 **KWANG CHE** Coastal Minesweeper. Ko.
503 **VUNG TAU** Landing Craft. VN.
503 **PBR 503** Patrol Boat. Ys.
504 **PBR 504** Patrol Boat. Ys.
505 **PBR 505** Patrol Boat. Ys.
506 **PBR 506** Patrol Boat. Ys.
507 **PBR 507** Patrol Boat. Ys.
508 **ACME** Ocean Minesweeper. Am.
508 **GILLIGAN** Escort. Am.
508 **PROVIDER** Operational Support Ship. Ca.
508 **PBR 508** Patrol Boat. Ys.
509 **ADROIT** Ocean Minesweeper. Am.

509 **BULLOCH COUNTY** Landing Ship. Am.
509 **PROTECTOR** Operational Support Ship Ca.
509 **PBR 509** Patrol Boat. Ys.
510 **ADVANCE** Ocean Minesweeper. Am.
510 **HEYLIGER** Escort. Am.
510 **PRESERVER** Operational Support Ship. Ca.
510 **PBR 510** Patrol Boat. Ys.
511 **AFFRAY** Ocean Minesweeper. Am.
511 **FOOTE** Destroyer. Am.
511 **PT 511** Motor Torpedo Boat. Cs.
511 **PBR 511** Patrol Boat. Ys.
512 **LAMOILLE RIVER** Landing Ship. Am.
512 **PT 512** Motor Torpedo Boat. Cs.
512 **PBR 512** Patrol Boat. Ys.
513 **TERRY** Destroyer. Am.
513 **LARAMIE RIVER** Landing Ship. Am.
513 **KIM CHON** Coastal Minesweeper. Ko.
513 **PBR 513** Patrol Craft. Ys.
514 **PBR 514** Patrol Craft. Ys.
515 **CADDO COUNTY** Landing Ship. Am.
515 **OWYHEE RIVER** Landing Ship. Am.
515 **PBR 515** Patrol Boat. Ys.
516 **LAYMORE** Research Vessel. Cd.
516 **PBR 516** Patrol Boat. Ys.
519 **ABILITY** Ocean Minesweeper. Am.
519 **DALY** Destroyer. Am.
519 **KUM HWA** Coastal Minesweeper. Ko.
520 **ALACRITY** Ocean Minesweeper. Am.
520 **KIM PO** Coastal Minesweeper. Ko.
521 **ASSURANCE** Ocean Minesweeper. Am.
521 **HAI LI** Patrol Craft. Cs.
521 **KOCHANG** Coastal Minesweeper. Ko.
522 **RED RIVER** Landing Craft. Am.
522 **HAI NING** Patrol Craft. Cs.
522 **KUM SAN** Coastal Minesweeper. Ko.
523 **MSO 523** Ocean Minesweeper. Am.
523 **HAI YAO** Patrol Craft. Cs.
523 **KO HUNG** Coastal Minesweeper. Ko.
524 **MSO 524** Ocean Minesweeper Am.
524 **HAI WEI** Patrol Craft. Cs.
525 **CAROLINE COUNTY** Landing Ship. Am.
525 **MSO 525** Ocean Minesweeper. Am.
525 **HAI AN** Patrol Craft. Cs.
525 **KUM KOK** Coastal Minesweeper. Ko.
526 **MSO 526** Ocean Minesweeper. Am.
526 **HAI CHING** Patrol Craft. Cs.
526 **NAM YANG** Coastal Minesweeper. Ko.

527 **MSO 527** Ocean Minesweeper. Am.

527 **HA DONG** Coastal Minesweeper. Ko.

528 **MSO 528** Ocean Minesweeper. Am.

528 **MULLANY** Destroyer. Am.

529 **MSO 529** Ocean Minesweeper. Am.

530 **MSO 530** Ocean Minesweeper. Am.

530 **TRATHEN** Destroyer. Am.

531 **EDWARD H. ALLEN** Escort. Am.

531 **HAZELWOOD** Destroyer. Am.

531 **MSO 531** Ocean Minesweeper. Am.

531 **SMOKEY RIVER** Landing Craft. Am.

532 **CHASE COUNTY** Landing Ship. Am.

532 **MSO 532** Ocean Minesweeper. Am.

533 **CHEBOYGAN COUNTY** Landing Ship. Am.

533 **HOWARD F. CLARK** Escort. Am.

533 **MSO 533** Ocean Minesweeper. Am.

534 **MCCORD** Destroyer. Am.

534 **MSO 534** Ocean Minesweeper. Am.

534 **SILVERSTEIN** Escort. Am.

535 **LEWIS** Escort. Am.

535 **MSO 535** Ocean Minesweeper. Am.

535 **MILLER** Destroyer. Am.

536 **MSO 536** Ocean Minesweeper. Am.

536 **OWEN** Destroyer. Am.

536 **WHITE RIVER** Landing Ship. Am.

537 **MSO 537** Ocean Minesweeper. Am.

537 **RIZZI** Escort. Am.

537 **THE SULLIVANS** Destroyer. Am.

538 **MSO 538** Ocean Minesweeper. Am.

538 **OSBERG** Escort. Am.

538 **STEPHEN POTTER** Destroyer. Am.

539 **LCU 539** Landing Craft. Am.

539 **WAGNER** Escort; Radar Picket. Am.

540 **TWINING** Destroyer. Am.

540 **VANDIVIER** Escort; Radar Picket. Am.

541 **YARNALL** Destroyer. Am.

543 **CHIANG HSIU** Patrol Craft. Cs.

544 **CHIANG TING** Patrol Craft. Cs.

545 **CHIANG MING** Patrol Craft. Cs.

546 **CHIANG LIEN** Patrol Craft. Cs.

547 **COWELL** Destroyer. Am.

547 **CHIANG P'ING** Patrol Craft. Cs.

548 **CHIANG FENG** Patrol Craft. Cs.

548 **TA TUNG** Tug. Cs.

549 **CHIANG KUNG** Patrol Craft. Cs.

550 **CHIANG LUN** Patrol Craft. Cs.

550 **VITTORIO VENETO** G.M. Cruiser. It.

551 **CHESTERFIELD COUNTY** Landing Ship. Am.

551 **CHIANG CH'ENG** Patrol Craft. Cs.

551 **GIUSEPPE GARIBALDI** G.M. Cruiser. It.

551 **PBR 551** Patrol Vessel. Ys.

553 **ANDREA DORIA** G.M. Cruiser. It.

554 **FRANKS** Destroyer. Am.

554 **CAIO DUILIO** G.M. Cruiser. It.

448 **LAWS** Destroyer. Am.

562 **ROBINSON** Destroyer. Am.

563 **ROSS** Destroyer. Am.

564 **ROWE** Destroyer. Am.

566 **STODDARD** Destroyer. Am.

567 **WATTS** Destroyer. Am.

568 **WREN** Destroyer. Am.

575 **MCKEE** Destroyer. Am.

577 **ALEXANDER J. LUKE** Escort. Am.

578 **ROBERT I. PAYNE** Escort. Am.

578 **WICKES** Destroyer. Am.

580 **L. B. KNOX** Escort. Am.

581 **MCNULTY** Escort. Am.

581 **P'AO.101** Patrol Craft. Cs.

581 **PBR 581** Patrol Craft. Ys.

583 **CHURCHILL COUNTY** Landing Ship. Am.

584 **CHARLES J. KIMMEL** Escort. Am.

584 **P'AO 104** Patrol Craft. Cs.

585 **HARADEN** Destroyer. Am.

587 **BELL** Destroyer. Am.

587 **THOMAS F. NICKEL** Escort. Am.

587 **P'AO 107** Patrol Craft. Cs.

588 **BURNS** Destroyer. Am.

588 **LCU 588** Landing Craft. Am.

588 **P'AO 408** Patrol Craft. Cs.

589 **IZARD** Destroyer. Am.

589 **TINSMAN** Escort. Am.

590 **MC 590** Motor Gunboat. It.

591 **P'AO 111** Patrol Vessel. Cs.

591 **MC 591** Motor Gunboat. It.

592 **P'AO 112** Patrol Vessel. Cs.

592 **MC 592** Motor Gunboat. It.

593 **P'AO 113** Patrol Vessel. Cs.

593 **MC 593** Motor Gunboat. It.

594 **HART** Destroyer. Am.

594 **P'AO 114** Patrol Craft. Cs.

595 **METCALF** Destroyer. Am.

595 **P'AO 115** Patrol Craft. Cs.

596 **SHIELDS** Destroyer. Am.

596 **P'AO 116** Patrol Craft. Cs.

598 **BANCROFT** Destroyer. Am.

599 **LCU 599** Landing Craft. Am.

600 **BOYLE** Destroyer. Am.

600 **PHU DU** Motor Gunboat. VN.

601 **CHAMPLIN** Destroyer. Am.

601 **CLARKE COUNTY** Landing Craft. Am.

601 **ATADO** Coastal Minesweeper. Ja.

601 **TAE CHO** Landing Ship. Ko.

601 **TIEN MOI** Motor Gunboat. VN.

602 **CLEARWATER** Landing Ship. Am.

602 **MEADE** Destroyer. Am.

602 **ITSUKI** Coastal Minesweeper. Ja.

602 **YEU DO** Landing Ship. Ko.

602 **MINH HOA** Motor Gunboat. VN.

603 **MURPHY** Destroyer. Am.

603 **YASHIRO** Coastal Minesweeper. Ja.

603 **KIEN YANG** Motor Gunboat. VN.

604 **PARKER** Destroyer. Am.

604 **KASADO** Coastal Minesweeper. Ja.

604 **KEO NGUA** Motor Gunboat. VN.

605 **SHISAKA** Coastal Minesweeper. Am.

605 **KA DUK** Landing Ship. Ko.

605 **KIM QUI** Motor Gunboat. VN.

606 **CAGHLAN** Destroyer. Am.

606 **KANAWA** Coastal Minesweeper. Ja.

606 **KU MOON** Landing Ship. Ko.

606 **MAY RUT** Motor Gunboat. VN.

607 **FRAZIER** Destroyer. Am.

607 **SAKITO** Coastal Minesweeper. Ja.

607 **SAKITO** Coastal Minesweeper. Ja.

607 **BIYOUP** Landing Ship. Ko.

607 **NAM DU** Motor Gunboat. VN.

608 **GANGSEVOORT** Destroyer. Am.

608 **LCU 608** Landing Craft. Am.

608 **HABUSHI** Coastal Minesweeper. Ja.

608 **PUNG DO** Landing Ship. Ko.

608 **HOA LU** Motor Gunboat. VN.

609 **GILLESPIE** Destroyer. Am.

609 **KOOZU** Coastal Minesweeper. Ja.

609 **WOLMI** Landing Ship. Ko.

609 **TO YEN** Motor Gunboat. VN.

610 **HOBBY** Destroyer. Am.

610 **TATARA** Coastal Minesweeper. Ja.

610 **KI RIN** Landing Ship. Ko.

610 **DINH HAI** Motor Gunboat. VN.

611 **TSUKUMI** Coastal Minesweeper. Ja.

611 **NEUNG RA** Landing Ship. Ko.

611 **TRUONG SA** Motor Gunboat. VN.

612 **MIKURA** Coastal Minesweeper. Ja.

612 **SIN-MI** Landing Ship. Ko.

612 **THAI BINH** Motor Gunboat. VN.

613 **LAUB** Destroyer. Am.

613 **SHIKINE** Coastal Minesweeper. Ja.

613 **ULRYUNG** Landing Ship. Ko.

613 **THI TU** Motor Gunboat. VN.

614 **MACKENZIE** Destroyer. Am.

614 **HIRADO** Coastal Minesweeper. Am.

615 **MCLANAHAN** Destroyer. Am.

615 **KOSHIKI** Coastal Minesweeper. Ja.

616 **NIELDS** Destroyer. Am.
616 **HATAKA** Coastal Minesweeper. Ja.
617 **ORDRONAUX** Destroyer. Am.
617 **KARATO** Coastal Minesweeper. Ja.
618 **DAVISON** Destroyer. Am.
618 **HARIO** Coastal Minesweeper. Ja.
619 **EDWARDS** Destroyer. Am.
619 **MUTSURE** Coastal Mine - sweeper. Ja.
620 **CHIBURI** Coastal Minesweeper. Ja.
621 **JEFFERS** Destroyer. Am.
621 **OOTSU** Coastal Minesweeper. Ja.
622 **KUDAKO** Coastal Minesweeper. Ja.
623 **RISHIRI** Coastal Minesweeper. Ja.
624 **REBUN** Coastal Minesweeper. Ja.
625 **AMAMI** Coastal Minesweeper. Ja.
626 **SATTERLEE** Destroyer. Am.
626 **URUME** Coastal Minesweeper. Ja.
627 **THOMPSON** Destroyer. Am.
627 **MINASE** Coastal Minesweeper. Ja.
628 **IBUKI** Coastal Minesweeper. Ja.
629 **ABBOT** Destroyer. Am.
629 **KATSURA** Coastal Minesweeper. Ja.
630 **BRAINE** Destroyer. Am.
630 **TAKAMI** Coastal Minesweeper. Ja.
631 **P'AO 1** Patrol Craft. Cs.
631 **IOU** Coastal Minesweeper. Ja.
632 **COWIE** Destroyer. Am.
632 **P'AO 2** Patrol Craft. Cs.
633 **P'AO 3** Patrol Craft. Cs.
634 **DORAN** Destroyer. Am.
634 **P'AO 4** Patrol Craft. Cs.
635 **P'AO 5** Patrol Craft. Cs.
636 **P'AO 6** Patrol Craft. Cs.
637 **GHERARDI** Destroyer. Am.
637 **P'AO 7** Patrol Craft. Cs.
638 **HERNDON** Destroyer. Am.
638 **P'AO 8** Patrol Craft. Cs.
639 **GENDREAU** Escort. Am.
639 **P'AO 9** Patrol Craft. Cs.
640 **FIEBERLING** Escort. Am.
640 **P'AO 10** Patrol Craft. Cs.
641 **TILLMAN** Destroyer. Am.
641 **WILLIAM C. COLE** Escort. Am.
641 **P'AO 11** Patrol Craft. Cs.
642 **P'AO 12** Patrol Craft. Cs.
643 **DAMON M. CUMMINGS** Escort. Am.
643 **SIGOURNEY** Destroyer. Am.
643 **P'AO 13** Patrol Craft. Cs.
645 **STEVENSON** Destroyer. Am.
646 **STOCKTON** Destroyer. Am.
646 **P'AO 16** Patrol Craft. Cs.
647 **THORN** Destroyer. Am.
649 **ALBERT W. GRANT** Destroyer. Am.
650 **CAPERTON** Destroyer. Am.
651 **YASHIMA** Coastal Mine - sweeper. Ja.

652 **HASHIMA** Coastal Mine - sweeper. Ja.
653 **KNAPP** Destroyer. Am.
653 **TSUSHIMA** Coastal Mine - sweeper. Ja.
654 **BEARSS** Destroyer. Am.
654 **LCU 654** Landing Craft. Am.
654 **TOSHIMA** Coastal Mine - sweeper. Ja.
655 **JOHN HOOD** Destroyer. Am.
659 **DASHIELL** Destroyer. Am.
660 **BULLARD** Destroyer. Am.
660 **LCU 660** Landing Craft. Am
661 **KIDD** Destroyer. Am.
662 **BENNION** Destroyer. Am.
665 **BRYANT** Destroyer. Am.
665 **JENKS** Escort. Am.
666 **BLACK** Destroyer. Am.
666 **LCU 666** Landing Craft. Am.
667 **CHAUNCEY** Destroyer. Am.
667 **LCU 667** Landing Craft. Am.
667 **WISEMAN** Escort. Am.
669 **COTTEN** Destroyer. Am.
671 **GATLING** Destroyer. Am.
672 **HEALY** Destroyer. Am.
674 **HUNT** Destroyer. Am.
674 **LCU 674** Landing Craft. Am.
679 **MCNAIR** Destroyer. Am.
680 **MELVIN** Destroyer. Am.
681 **GILLETTE** Escort. Am.
681 **FANG 1** Patrol Craft. Cs.
682 **PORTERFIELD** Destroyer. Am.
682 **FANG SAN** Patrol Craft. Cs.
683 **STOCKHAM** Destroyer. Am.
684 **FANG SEU** Patrol Craft. Cs.
685 **PICKING** Destroyer. Am.
685 **FANG CHI** Patrol Craft. Cs.
686 **HALSEY POWELL** Destroyer. Am.
686 **FANG LIU** Patrol Craft. Cs.
687 **UHLMANN** Destroyer. Am.
687 **FANG PA** Patrol Craft. Cs.
688 **REMEY** Destroyer. Am.
690 **NORMAN SCOTT** Destroyer. Am.
691 **MERTZ** Destroyer. Am.
692 **ALLEN M. SUMNER** Destroyer. Am.
693 **MOALE** Destroyer. Am.
694 **INGRAHAM** Destroyer. Am.
696 **SPANGLER** Escort. Am.
696 **HATSUTAKA** Inshore Mine - sweeper. Ja.
697 **CHARLES S. SPERRY** Destroyer. Am.
698 **AULT** Destroyer. Am.
699 **MARSH** Escort. Am.
699 **WALDRON** Destroyer. Am.
699 **HAYATORI** Inshore Mine - sweeper. Ja.
700 **HIYODORI** Inshore Mine - sweeper. Ja.
701 **JOHN W. WEEKS** Destroyer. Am.
701 **OSMOS** Escort. Am.
701 **No. 1** Minesweeping Boat. Ja. (Also has *MB1* on hull amidships)
702 **HANK** Destroyer. Am.
702 **No. 2** Minesweeping Boat. Ja. (*MB2* on hull)
703 **HOLTON** Escort. Am.

703 **WALLACE L. LIND** Destroyer. Am.
703 **No. 3** Minesweeping Boat. Ja. (Also has *MB3* on hull amidships)
704 **BORIE** Destroyer. Am.
704 **CRONIN** Escort. Am.
704 **No. 4** Minesweeping Boat. Ja. (Also has *MB4* on hull amidships)
705 **COMPTON** Destroyer. Am.
705 **FRYBARGER** Escort. Am.
705 **MULTATULI** Submarine Support Ship. Ia.
705 **No. 5** Minesweeping Boat. Ja. (Also has *MB5* on hull amidships)
706 **GAINARD** Destroyer. Am.
706 **No. 6** Minesweeping Boat. Ja. (Also has *MB6* on hull amidships)
707 **SOLEY** Destroyer. Am.
708 **HARLAN R. DICKSON** Destroyer. Am.
709 **HUGH PURVIS** Destroyer. Am.
710 **GEARING** Destroyer. Am.
711 **EUGENE A. GREENE** Destroyer. Am.
713 **KENNETH D. BAILEY** Destroyer. Am.
714 **WILLIAM R. RUSH** Destroyer. Am.
715 **DE KALB COUNTY** Landing Ship. Am.
715 **HAMILTON** Coast Guard Cutter. Am.
715 **WILLIAM M. WOOD** Destroyer. Am.
716 **DALLAS** Coast Guard Cutter. Am.
716 **WILTSIE** Destroyer. Am.
717 **MELLON** Coast Guard Cutter. Am.
717 **THEODORE E. CHANDLER** Destroyer. Am.
718 **CHASE** Coast Guard Cutter. Am.
718 **HAMNER** Destroyer. Am.
719 **BOUTWELL** Coast Guard Cutter. Am.
719 **EPPERSON** Destroyer. Am.
720 **SHERMAN** Coast Guard Cutter. Am.
721 **GALLATIN** Coast Guard Cutter. Am.
722 **DODGE COUNTY** Landing Ship. Am.
722 **MORGENTHAU** Coast Guard Cutter. Am.
723 **RUSH** Coast Guard Cutter. Am.
723 **WALKE** Destroyer. Am.
724 **LAFFEY** Destroyer. Am.
724 **JARVIS** Coast Guard Cutter. Am.
725 **O'BRIEN** Destroyer. Am.
725 **MUNRO** Coast Guard Cutter. Am.
727 **DE HAVEN** Destroyer. Am.
728 **MANSFIELD** Destroyer. Am.
729 **LYMAN K. SWENSON** Destroyer. Am.
730 **COLLETT** Destroyer. Am.
731 **MADDOX** Destroyer. Am.

734 **PURDY** Destroyer. Am.
742 **FRANK KNOX** Radar Picket Destroyer. Am.
742 **HILBERT** Escort. Am.
742 **LCU 742** Landing Ship. Am.
743 **LAMONS** Escort. Am.
743 **SOUTHERLAND** Destroyer. Am.
744 **BLUE** Destroyer. Am.
744 **KYNE** Escort. Am.
745 **SNYDER** Escort. Am.
746 **TAUSSIG** Destroyer. Am.
750 **MCCLELLAND** Escort. Am.
752 **ALFRED A. CUNNINGHAM** Destroyer. Am.
753 **JOHN R. PIERCE** Destroyer. Am.
755 **JOHN A. BOLE** Destroyer. Am.
756 **BEATTY** Destroyer. Am.
757 **PUTNAM** Destroyer. Am.
758 **DUVAL COUNTY** Landing Ship. Am.
758 **STRONG** Destroyer. Am.
759 **LOFBERG** Destroyer. Am.
760 **JOHN W. THOMASON** Destroyer. Am.
761 **BUCK** Destroyer. Am.
762 **FLOYD COUNTY** Landing Ship. Am.
762 **HENLEY** Destroyer. Am.
763 **WILLIAM C. LAWE** Destroyer. Am.
764 **LLOYD THOMAS** Destroyer. Am.
765 **EARL K. OLSEN** Escort. Am.
765 **KEPPLER** Destroyer. Am.
767 **OSWALD** Escort. Am.
768 **LCU 768** Landing Craft. Am.
770 **LOWRY** Destroyer. Am.
775 **WILLARD KEITH** Destroyer. Am.
776 **JAMES C. OWENS** Destroyer. Am.
777 **ZELLARS** Destroyer. Am.
777 **THE PRESIDENT** Command Ship. Pi.
778 **MASSEY** Destroyer. Am.
779 **DOUGLAS H. FOX** Destroyer. Am.
780 **LCU 780** Landing Craft. Am.
780 **STORMES** Destroyer. Am.
780 **LOON** Patrol Craft. Ca.
781 **CORMORANT** Patrol Craft. Ca.
781 **ROBERT K. HUNTINGTON** Destroyer. Am.
782 **ROWAN** Destroyer. Am.
783 **GURKE** Destroyer. Am.
783 **MALLARD** Patrol Craft. Ca.
784 **MCKEAN** Destroyer. Am.
785 **HENDERSON** Destroyer. Am.
786 **GARRETT COUNTY** Landing Ship. Am.
786 **RICHARD B. ANDERSON** Destroyer. Am.
787 **JAMES E. KYES** Destroyer. Am.
788 **HOLLISTER** Destroyer. Am.
789 **EVERSOLE** Destroyer. Am.
790 **SHELTON** Destroyer. Am.
793 **CASSIN YOUNG** Destroyer. Am.
795 **GUNASON** Escort. Am.
796 **MAJOR** Escort. Am.
798 **VARIAN** Escort. Am.

800 **JACK W. WILKE** Escort. Am.
800 **PORTER** Destroyer. Am.
803 **LCU 803** Landing Craft. Am.
805 **CHEVALIER** Destroyer. Am.
806 **HIGBEE** Destroyer. Am.
708 **BENNER** Destroyer. Am.
807 **UN BONG** Landing Ship. Ko.
808 **DENNIS J. BUCKLEY** Destroyer. Am.
808 **DUK BONG** Landing Ship. Ko.
809 **BI BONG** Landing Ship. Ko.
810 **KAE BONG** Landing Ship. Ko.
812 **WEE BONG** Landing Ship. Ko.
813 **SU YONG** Landing Ship. Ko.
815 **BUK HAN** Landing Ship. Ko.
816 **HWA SAN** Landing Ship. Ko.
817 **CORRY** Destroyer. Am.
818 **NEW** Destroyer. Am.
819 **HAMPSHIRE COUNTY** Landing Ship. Am.
819 **HOLDER** Destroyer. Am.
820 **RICH** Destroyer. Am.
821 **HARNETT COUNTY** Landing Ship. Am.
821 **JOHNSTON** Destroyer. Am.
822 **HARRIS COUNTY** Landing Ship. Am.
822 **ROBERT H. MCCARD** Destroyer. Am.
823 **SAMUEL B. ROBERTS** Destroyer. Am.
824 **BASILONE** Destroyer. Am.
824 **HENRY COUNTY** Landing Craft. Am.
825 **CARPENTER** Destroyer. Am.
825 **HICKMAN COUNTY** Landing Craft. Am.
826 **AGERHOLM** Destroyer. Am.
827 **ROBERT A. OWENS** Destroyer. Am.
829 **MYLES C. FOX** Destroyer. Am.
830 **EVERETT F. LARSON** Destroyer. Am.
831 **GOODRICH** Destroyer, Radar Picket, Am.
832 **HANSON** Destroyer. Am.
833 **HERBERT J. THOMAS** Destroyer. Am.
835 **CHARLES P. CECIL** Destroyer. Am.
836 **GEORGE K. MACKENZIE** Destroyer. Am.
836 **HOLMES COUNTY** Landing Craft. Am.
837 **SARSFIELD** Destroyer. Am.
838 **ERNEST G. SMALL** Destroyer, Radar Picket. Am.
838 **HUNTERDON COUNTY** Landing Ship. Am.
839 **IREDELL COUNTY** Landing Ship. Am.
839 **POWER** Destroyer. Am.
840 **GLENNON** Destroyer. Am.
841 **NOA** Destroyer. Am.
842 **FISKE** Destroyer. Am.
843 **WARRINGTON** Destroyer. Am.
844 **PERRY** Destroyer. Am.
845 **BAUSSELL** Destroyer. Am.
846 **JENNINGS COUNTY** Landing Ship. Am.
846 **OZBOURN** Destroyer. Am.

847 **ROBERT L. WILSON** Destroyer. Am.
848 **JEROME COUNTY** Landing Ship. Am.
849 **RICHARD E. KRAUS** Destroyer. Am.
850 **JOSEPH P. KENNEDY Jr.** Destroyer. Am.
851 **RUPERTUS** Destroyer. Am.
852 **LEONARD F. MASON** Destroyer. Am.
853 **CHARLES H. ROAN** Destroyer. Am.
854 **KEMPER COUNTY** Landing Ship. Am.
858 **FRED T. BERRY** Destroyer. Am.
859 **NORRIS** Destroyer. Am.
860 **MCCAFFERY** Destroyer. Am.
860 **TELUKWADJO** Landing Craft. Ia.
861 **HARWOOD** Destroyer. Am.
861 **TELUKWEDA** Landing Craft. Ia.
862 **VOGELGESANG** Destroyer. Am.
862 **TELUKKATURAI** Landing Craft. Ia.
863 **STEINAKER** Destroyer. Am.
863 **TELUKWORI** Landing Craft. Ia.
864 **HAROLD J. ELLISON** Destroyer. Am.
864 **AMAHAI** Landing Craft. Ia.
865 **CHARLES R. WARE** Destroyer. Am.
866 **CONE** Destroyer. Am.
866 **LCM 8** type Landing Craft. Am.
866 **MARICH** Landing Craft. Ia.
867 **STRIBLING** Destroyer. Am.
868 **BROWNSON** Destroyer. Am.
868 **PIRU** Landing Craft. Ia.
868 **TELUK LANGSA** Landing Ship. Ia.
869 **ARNOLD J. ISBELL** Destroyer. Am.
869 **TELUK AMBOINA** Landing Ship. Ia.
870 **FECHTELER** Destroyer. Am.
870 **TELUK BAYUR** Landing Ship. Ia.
871 **DAMATO** Destroyer. Am.
871 **LCU 871** Landing Craft. Am.
871 **TELUK KAU** Landing Ship. Ia.
872 **FORREST ROYAL** Destroyer. Am.
872 **TELUK MENADO** Landing Ship. Ia.
873 **HAWKINS** Destroyer. Am.
874 **DUNCAN** Destroyer. Am.
875 **HENRY W. TUCKER** Destroyer. Am.
876 **ROGERS** Destroyer. Am.
877 **PERKINS** Destroyer. Am.
878 **VESOLE** Destroyer. Am.
879 **LEARY** Destroyer. Am.
880 **DYESS** Destroyer. Am.
881 **BORDELON** Destroyer. Am.
882 **FURSE** Destroyer. Am.
883 **NEWMAN K. PERRY** Destroyer. Am.
884 **FLOYD B. PARKS** Destroyer. Am.
885 **JOHN R. CRAIG** Destroyer. Am.
886 **ORLECK** Destroyer. Am.

887 **BRINKLEY BASS** Destroyer. Am.
888 **STICKELL** Destroyer. Am.
889 **O'HARE** Destroyer. Am.
890 **MEREDITH** Destroyer. Am.
893 **LCU 893** Landing Craft. Am.
901 **LITCHFIELD COUNTY** Landing Ship. Am.
901 **TJEPU** Oiler. Ia.
902 **LUZERNE COUNTY** Landing Ship. Am.
902 **KIMHAE** Supply Ship. Ko.
902 **PLADJU** Oiler. Ia.
903 **SAMBU** Oiler. Ia.
903 **WAKEWAN** Supply Ship. Ko.
904 **BUNJU** Oiler. Ia.
905 **MADERA COUNTY** Landing Ship. Am.
905 **WAEKWAN** Supply Ship. Ko.
907 **MOCK PO** Supply Ship. Ko.
908 **KUN SAN** Supply Ship. Ko.
909 **MA SAN** Supply Ship. Ko.
921 **HALMAHERA** Transport. Ia.
922 **MOROTAI** Transport. Ia.
924 **NUSA TELU** Transport. Ia.
925 **BANGGAI** Transport. Ia.
926 **TRITON** Salvage Vessel. Ia.
928 **RAKATA** Tug. Ia.
931 **FORREST SHERMAN** Destroyer. Am.
933 **BARRY** Destroyer. Am.
934 **LAMPO BATANG** Tug. Ia.
935 **TAMBORA** Tug. Ia.
936 **BROMO** Tug. Ia.
937 **DAVIS** Destroyer. Am.
938 **JONAS INGRAM** Destroyer. Am.
940 **MANLEY** Destroyer. Am.
941 **DU PONT** Destroyer. Am.
942 **BIGELOW** Destroyer. Am.
943 **BLANDY** Destroyer. Am.
944 **MULLINNIX** Destroyer. Am
945 **HULL** Destroyer. Am.
946 **EDSON** Destroyer. Am.
948 **MORTON** Destroyer. Am.
950 **RICHARD S. EDWARDS** Destroyer. Am.
951 **TURNER JOY** Destroyer. Am.
963 **SPRUANCE** Destroyer. Am.
980 **MEEKER COUNTY** Landing Ship. Am.
983 **MIDDLESEX COUNTY** Landing Ship. Am.
1001 **SHIN SONG** Escort. Ko.
1002 **PCE 1002** Escort. Ko.
1003 **PCE 1003** Escort. Ko.
1006 **DEALEY** Destroyer. Am.
1006 **BURUDJULASAD** Survey Ship. Ia.
1014 **CROMWELL** Destroyer. Am.
1015 **HAMMERBERG** Destroyer. Am.
1021 **COURTNEY** Destroyer. Am.
1022 **LESTER** Destroyer. Am.
1023 **EVANS** Destroyer. Am.
1024 **BRIDGET** Destroyer. Am.
1025 **BAUER** Destroyer. Am.
1026 **HOOPER** Destroyer. Am.
1027 **JOHN WILLIS** Destroyer. Am.
1028 **VAN VOORHIS** Destroyer. Am.
1029 **HARTLEY** Destroyer. Am.

1030 **JOSEPH K. TAUSSIG** Destroyer. Am.
1032 **MONMOUTH COUNTY** Landing Ship. Am.
1033 **CLAUD JONES** Destroyer. Am.
1034 **JOHN R. PERRY** Destroyer. Am.
1035 **CHARLES BERRY** Destroyer. Am.
1036 **MCMORRIS** Destroyer. Am.
1037 **BRONSTEIN** Destroyer. Am.
1038 **MCCLOY** Destroyer. Am.
1040 **GARCIA** Escort. Am.
1041 **BRADLEY** Escort. Am.
1043 **EDWARD MCDONNELL** Escort. Am.
1044 **BRUMBY** Escort. Am.
1045 **DAVIDSON** Escort. Am.
1045 **LCU 1045** Landing Craft. Am.
1047 **VOGE** Escort. Am.
1048 **SAMPLE** Escort. Am.
1049 **KOELSCH** Escort. Am.
1050 **ALBERT DAVID** Escort. Am.
1051 **O'CALLAHAN** Escort. Am.
1052 **KNOX** Escort. Am.
1053 **ROARK** Escort. Am.
1054 **GRAY** Escort. Am.
1055 **HEPBURN** Escort. Am.
1056 **CONNOLE** Escort. Am.
1057 **RATHBURNE** Escort. Am.
1058 **MEYERKORD** Escort. Am.
1059 **W. S. SIMS** Escort. Am.
1060 **LANG** Escort. Am.
1061 **PATTERSON** Escort. Am.
1062 **WHIPPLE** Escort. Am.
1063 **REASONER** Escort. Am.
1064 **LOCKWOOD** Escort. Am.
1065 **STEIN** Escort. Am.
1066 **MARVIN SHIELDS** Escort. Am.
1066 **NEW LONDON COUNTY** Landing Ship. Am.
1067 **FRANCIS HAMMOND** Escort. Am.
1067 **NYE COUNTY** Landing Ship. Am.
1068 **VREELAND** Escort. Am.
1069 Escort. Am.
1069 **ORLEANS REACH** Landing Ship. Am.
1070 **DONNES** Escort. Am.
1071 **BADGER** Escort. Am.
1072 **BLAKELEY** Escort. Am.
1073 Escort. Am. No Name Yet
1073 **OUTAGAMIE COUNTY** Landing Ship. Am.
1074 **HAROLD E. HOLT** Escort. Am.
1075 **TRIPPE** Escort. Am.
1076 **FANNING** Escort. Am.
1076 **PAGE COUNTY** Landing Ship. Am.
1077 **OUELLET** Escort. Am.
1077 **PARK COUNTY** Landing Ship. Am.
1078 **JOSEPH HEWES** Escort. Am.
1079 **BOWEN** Escort. Am.
1080 **PAUL** Escort. Am.
1081 **AYLWIN** Escort. Am.
1082 Escort. Am. No Name Yet
1082 **PITKIN COUNTY** Landing Ship. Am.
1083 Escort. Am.

1083 **PLUMUS COUNTY** Landing Ship. Am.
1084 Escort. Am.
1084 **POLK COUNTY** Landing Ship. Am.
1085 Escort. Am. No Name Yet
1086 Escort. Am. No Name Yet
1087 Escort. Am. No Name Yet
1088 Escort. Am. No Name Yet
1088 **PULASKI COUNTY** Landing Ship. Am.
1089 Escort. Am. No Name Yet
1090 Escort. Am. No Name Yet
1091 Escort. Am. No Name Yet
1092 Escort. Am. No Name Yet
1093 Escort. Am. No Name Yet
1094 Escort. Am. No Name Yet
1095 Escort. Am. No Name Yet
1096 Escort. Am. No Name Yet
1096 **ST. CLAIR COUNTY** Landing Ship. Am.
1097 Escort. Am. No Name Yet
1098 Escort. Am. No Name Yet
1099 Escort. Am. No Name Yet
1100 Escort. Am. No Name Yet
1101 Escort. Am. No Name Yet
1122 **SAN JOAQUIN COUNTY** Landing Ship. Am.
1123 **SEDGWICK COUNTY** Landing Ship. Am.
1124 **LCU 1124** Landing Craft. Am.
1126 **SNOHOMISH COUNTY** Landing Ship. Am.
1141 **STONE COUNTY** Landing Ship. Am.
1146 **SUMMIT COUNTY** Landing Ship. Am.
1148 **SUMNER COUNTY** Landing Ship. Am.
1150 **SUTTER COUNTY** Landing Ship. Am.
1153 **TALBOT COUNTY** Landing Ship. Am.
1156 **TERREBONNE PARISH** Landing Ship. Am.
1157 **TERRELL COUNTY** Landing Ship. Am.
1158 **TIOGA COUNTY** Landing Ship. Am.
1159 **TOM GREEN COUNTY** Landing Ship. Am.
1160 **TRAVERSE COUNTY** Landing Ship. Am.
1161 **VERNON COUNTY** Landing Ship. Am.
1162 **WAHKIAKUM COUNTY** Landing Ship. Am.
1163 **WALDO COUNTY** Landing Ship. Am.
1164 **WALWORTH COUNTY** Landing Ship. Am.
1165 **WASHOE COUNTY** Landing Ship. Am.
1166 **WASHTENAW COUNTY** Landing Ship. Am.
1167 **WESTCHESTER COUNTY** Landing Ship. Am.
1168 **WEXFORD COUNTY** Landing Ship. Am.
1169 **WHITFIELD COUNTY** Landing Ship. Am.

1170 **WINDHAM COUNTY** Landing Ship. Am.

1171 **DE SOTO COUNTY** Landing Ship. Am.

1173 **SUFFOLK COUNTY** Landing Ship. Am.

1174 **GRANT COUNTY** Landing Ship. Am.

1175 **YORK COUNTY** Landing Ship. Am.

1176 **GRAHAM COUNTY** Landing Ship. Am.

1177 **LORRAIN COUNTY** Landing Ship. Am.

1178 **WOOD COUNTY** Landing Ship. Am.

1179 **NEWPORT** Landing Ship. Am.

1180 **MANITOWOC** Landing Ship. Am.

1181 **SUMTER** Landing Ship. Am.

1182 **FRESNO** Landing Ship. Am.

1183 **PEORIA** Landing Ship. Am.

1184 **FREDERICK** Landing Ship. Am.

1185 **SCHENECTADY (LST 1185)** Landing Ship. Am.

1186 **CAYUGA (LST 1186)** Landing Ship. Am.

1187 **TUSCALOOSA (LST 1187)** Landing Ship. Am.

1188 **SAGINAW (LST 1188)** Landing Ship. Am.

1189 **SAN BERNARDINO (LST 1189)** Landing Ship. Am.

1190 **BOULDER (LST 1190)** Landing Ship. Am.

1191 **RACINE (LST 1191)** Landing Ship. Am.

1192 **LST 1192** Landing Ship. Am.

1193 **LST 1193** Landing Ship. Am.

1194 **LST 1194** Landing Ship. Am.

1195 **LST 1195** Landing Ship. Am.

1196 **LST 1196** Landing Ship. Am.

1197 **LST 1197** Landing Ship. Am.

1198 **LST 1198** Landing Ship. Am.

1241 **LCU 1241** Landing Craft. Am.

1348 **LCU 1348** Landing Craft. Am.

1387 **BEAUFORT** Submarine Chaser. Am.

1387 **LCU 1387** Landing Craft. Am.

1430 **LCU 1430** Landing Craft. Am.

1451 **LCU 1451** Landing Craft. Am.

1459 **LCU 1459** Landing Craft. Am.

1462 **LCU 1462** Landing Craft. Am.

1463 **LCU 1463** Landing Craft. Am.

1466 **LCU 1466** Landing Craft. Am.

1467 **LCU 1467** Landing Craft. Am.

1468 **LCU 1468** Landing Craft. Am.

1469 **LCU 1469** Landing Craft. Am.

1470 **LCU 1470** Landing Craft. Am.

1471 **LCU 1471** Landing Craft. Am.

1472 **LCU 1472** Landing Craft. Am.

1473 **LCU 1473** Landing Craft. Am.

1475 **LCU 1475** Landing Craft. Am.

1476 **LCU 1476** Landing Craft. Am.

1477 **LCU 1477** Landing Craft. Am.

1481 **LCU 1481** Landing Craft. Am.

1482 **LCU 1482** Landing Craft. Am.

1483 **LCU 1483** Landing Craft. Am.

1484 **LCU 1484** Landing Craft. Am.

1485 **LCU 1485** Landing Craft. Am.

1486 **LCU 1486** Landing Craft. Am.

1487 **LCU 1487** Landing Craft. Am.

1488 **LCU 1488** Landing Craft. Am.

1489 **LCU 1489** Landing Craft. Am.

1490 **LCU 1490** Landing Craft. Am.

1491 **LCU 1491** Landing Craft. Am.

1492 **LCU 1492** Landing Craft. Am.

1493 **LCU 1493** Landing Craft. Am.

1494 **LCU 1494** Landing Craft. Am.

1495 **LCU 1495** Landing Craft. Am.

1497 **LCU 1497** Landing Craft. Am.

1498 **LCU 1498** Landing Craft. Am.

1499 **LCU 1499** Landing Craft. Am.

1500 **LCU 1500** Landing Craft. Am.

1525 **LCU 1525** Landing Craft. Am.

1535 **LCU 1535** Landing Craft. Am.

1536 **LCU 1536** Landing Craft. Am.

1537 **LCU 1537** Landing Craft. Am.

1539 **LCU 1539** Landing Craft. Am.

1547 **LCU 1547** Landing Craft. Am.

1548 **LCU 1548** Landing Craft. Am.

1559 **LCU 1559** Landing Craft. Am.

1576 **LCU 1576** Landing Ship. Am.

1576 **LCU 1576** Landing Craft. Am.

1582 **LCU 1582** Landing Craft. Am.

1608 **LCU 1608** Landing Craft. Am.

1609 **LCU 1609** Landing Craft. Am.

1610 **LCU 1610** Landing Craft. Am.

1611 **LCU 1611** Landing Craft. Am.

1612 **LCU 1612** Landing Craft. Am.

1613 **LCU 1613** Landing Craft. Am.

1614 **LCU 1614** Landing Craft. Am.

1615 **LCU 1615** Landing Craft. Am.

1616 **LCU 1616** Landing Craft. Am.

1617 **LCU 1617** Landing Craft. Am.

1618 **LCU 1618** Landing Craft. Am.

1619 **LCU 1619** Landing Craft. Am.

1620 **LCU 1620** Landing Craft. Am.

1621 **LCU 1621** Landing Craft. Am.

1622 **LCU 1622** Landing Craft. Am.

1623 **LCU 1623** Landing Craft. Am.

1624 **LCU 1624** Landing Craft. Am.

1625 **LCU 1625** Landing Craft. Am.

1627 **LCU 1627** Landing Craft. Am.

1628 **LCU 1628** Landing Craft. Am.

1629 **LCU 1629** Landing Craft. Am.

1630 **LCU 1630** Landing Craft. Am.

1631 **LCU 1631** Landing Craft. Am.

1632 **LCU 1632** Landing Craft. Am.

1633 **LCU 1633** Landing Craft. Am.

1634 **LCU 1634** Landing Craft. Am.

1635 **LCU 1635** Landing Craft. Am.

1636 **LCU 1636** Landing Craft. Am.

2001 **LCU 2001** Landing Craft. Am.

2002 **LCU 2002** Landing Craft. Am.

2003 **LCU 2003** Landing Craft. Am.

2004 **LCU 2004** Landing Craft. Am.

2005 **LCU 2005** Landing Craft. Am.

2006 **LCU 2006** Landing Craft. Am.

3501 **KATORI** Training Ship. Ja.

3515 **STALKER** Landing Ship. Br.

3522 **TRACKER** Landing Ship. Br.

4001 **OOSUMI** Landing Ship. Ja.

4001 **ML 4001** Patrol Boat. Li.

4002 **SHIMOKITA** Landing Ship. Ja.

4002 **ML 4002** Patrol Boat. Li.

4003 **SHIRETOKO** Landing Ship. Ja.

5001 **FUJI** Icebreaker & Research Ship. Ja.

5301 **DR 301** General Purpose Vessel. It.

5302 **DR 302** General Purpose Vessel. It.

5303 **DR 303** General Purpose Vessel. It.

5304 **ALICUDI** Netlayer. It.

5304 **DR 304** General Purpose Vessel. It.

5305 **DR 305** General Purpose Vessel. It.

5305 **FILICUDI** Netlayer. It.

5306 **DR 306** General Purpose Vessel. It.

5307 **DR 307** General Purpose Vessel. It.

5308 **DR 308** General Purpose Vessel. It.

5309 **DR 309** General Purpose Vessel. It.

5310 **DR 310** General Purpose Vessel. It.

5311 **DR 311** General Purpose Vessel. It.

5312 **DR 312** General Purpose Vessel. It.

5313 **DR 313** General Purpose Vessel. It.

5314 **DR 314** General Purpose Vessel. It.

5315 **DR 315** General Purpose Vessel. It.

5316 **DR 316** General Purpose Vessel. It.

5400 **ANEMONE** Coastal Minesweeper. It.

5401 **AZALEA** Coastal Minesweeper. It.

5402 **M5402** Coastal Minesweeper. It.

5403 **BIANCOSPINO** Coastal Minesweeper. It.

5404 **DALIA** Coastal Minesweeper. It.

5405 **FIORDALSIO** Coastal Minesweeper. It.

5406 **GARDENIA** Coastal Minesweeper. It.

5407 **GERANIO** Coastal Minesweeper. It.

5408 **MAGNOLIA** Coastal Minesweeper. It.

5409 **MUGHETTO** Coastal Minesweeper. It.

5410 **NARCISO** Coastal Minesweeper. It.

5411 **OLEANDRO** Coastal Minesweeper. It.

5412 **ORCHIDEA** Coastal Minesweeper. It.

5413 **PRIMULA** Coastal Minesweeper. It.

5414 **TULIPANO** Coastal Minesweeper. It.

5415 **VERBENA** Coastal Minesweeper. It.

5416 **GLADIOLO** Coastal Minesweeper. It.

5430 **SALMONE** Ocean Minesweeper. It.

5431 **STORIONE** Ocean Minesweeper. It.

5432 **SGOMBRO** Ocean Minesweeper. It.

5433 **SQUALO** Ocean Minesweeper. It.

| | | |
|---|---|---|
| *5450* **ARAGOSTA** Inshore Mine - sweeper. It. | *5509* **GELSO** Coastal Minesweeper. It. | *9853* **MASTINO** Support Gunboat. It. |
| *5451* **ARSELLA** Inshore Mine - sweeper. It. | *5510* **LARICE** Coastal Minesweeper. It. | *9854* **MOLOSSO** Support Gunboat. It. |
| *5452* **ASTICE** Inshore Minesweeper. It. | *5511* **NOCE** Coastal Minesweeper. It. | *9855* **SEGUGIO** Support Gunboat. It. |
| *5453* **ARTINIA** Inshore Mine - sweeper. It. | *5512* **OLMO** Coastal Minesweeper. It. | *9856* **SPINONE** Support Gunboat. It. |
| *5454* **CALAMARO** Inshore Mine - sweeper. It. | *5513* **ONTANO** Coastal Mine - sweeper. It. | *95300* **CAPE SMALL** Coast Guard Patrol Vessel. Am. |
| *5455* **CONCHIGLIA** Inshore Mine - sweeper. It. | *5514* **PINO** Coastal Minesweeper. It. | *95301* **CAPE CORAL** Coast Guard Patrol Vessel. Am. |
| *5456* **DROMA** Inshore Minesweeper. It. | *5515* **PIOPPO** Coastal Minesweeper. It. | *95302* **CAPE HIGGON** Coast Guard Patrol Vessel. Am. |
| *5457* **GAMBERO** Inshore Mine - sweeper. It. | *5516* **PLATANO** Coastal Mine - sweeper. It. | *95303* **CAPE UPWRIGHT** Coast Guard Patrol Vessel. Am. |
| *5458* **GRANCHIO** Inshore Mine - sweeper. It. | *5517* **QUERCIA** Coastal Mine - sweeper. It. | *95304* **CAPE GULL** Coast Guard Patrol Vessel. Am. |
| *5459* **MITILO** Inshore Minesweeper. It. | *5519* **MANDORLO** Coastal Mine - sweeper. It. | *95305* **CAPE HATTERAS** Coast Guard Patrol Vessel. Am. |
| *5460* **OSTRICA** Inshore Mine - sweeper. It. | *5521* **BAMBU** Coastal Minesweeper. It. | *95306* **CAPE GEORGE** Coast Guard Patrol Vessel. Am. |
| *5461* **PAGURO** Inshore Mine - sweeper. It. | *5522* **EBANO** Coastal Minesweeper. It. | *95307* **CAPE CURRENT** Coast Guard Patrol Vessel. Am. |
| *5462* **PINNA** Inshore Minesweeper. It. | *5523* **MANGO** Coastal Minesweeper. It. | *95308* **CAPE STRAIT** Coast Guard Patrol Vessel. Am. |
| *5463* **POLIPO** Inshore Minesweeper. It. | *5524* **MOGANO** Coastal Mine - sweeper. It. | *95309* **CAPE CARTER** Coast Guard Patrol Vessel. Am. |
| *5464* **PORPORA** Inshore Mine - sweeper. It. | *5525* **PALMA** Coastal Minesweeper. It. | *95310* **CAPE WASH** Coast Guard Patrol Vessel. Am. |
| *5465* **RICCO** Inshore Minesweeper. It. | *5526* **ROVERE** Coastal Minesweeper. It. | *95311* **CAPE HEDGE** Coast Guard Patrol Vessel. Am. |
| *5466* **SCAMPO** Inshore Mine - sweeper. It. | *5527* **SANDALO** Coastal Mine - sweeper. It. | *95312* **CAPE KNOX** Coast Guard Patrol Boat. Am. |
| *5467* **SEPPIA** Inshore Minesweeper. It. | *5531* **AGAVE** Coastal Minesweeper. It. | *94313* **CAPE MORGAN** Coast Guard Patrol Boat. Am. |
| *5468* **TELLINA** Inshore Minesweeper. It. | *5532* **ALLORO** Coastal Minesweeper. It. | *95314* **CAPE FAIRWEATHER** Coast Guard Patrol Boat. Am. |
| *5469* **TOTANO** Inshore Minesweeper. It. | *5533* **EDERA** Coastal Minesweeper. It. | *95316* **CAPE FOX** Coast Guard Patrol Boat. Am. |
| *5501* **ABETE** Coastal Minesweeper. It. | *5534* **GAGGIA** Coastal Minesweeper. It. | *95317* **CAPE JELLISON** Coast Guard Patrol Boat. Am. |
| *5502* **ACACIA** Coastal Minesweeper. It. | *5535* **GELSOMINO** Coastal Mine - sweeper. It. | *95319* **CAPE ROMAIN** Coast Guard Patrol Boat. Am. |
| *5503* **BETULLA** Coastal Minesweeper. It. | *5536* **GIAGGIOLO** Coastal Mine - sweeper. It. | *95320* **CAPE STARR** Coast Guard Patrol Boat. Am. |
| *5504* **CASTAGNO** Coastal Mine - sweeper. It. | *5537* **GLICINE** Coastal Minesweeper. It. | *95321* **CAPE CROSS** Coast Guard Patrol Boat. Am. |
| *5505* **CEDRO** Coastal Minesweeper. It. | *5538* **LOTO** Coastal Minesweeper. It. | *95322* **CAPE HORN** Coast Guard Patrol Boat. Am. |
| *5506* **CIUEGO** Coastal Minesweeper. It. | *5539* **MIRTO** Coastal Minesweeper. It. | *95324* **CAPE SHOALWATER** Coast Guard Patrol Boat. Am. |
| *5507* **FAGGIO** Coastal Minesweeper. It. | *5540* **TIMO** Coastal Minesweeper. It. | *95326* **CAPE CORWIN** Coast Guard Patrol Boat. Am. |
| *5508* **FRASSINO** Coastal Mine - sweeper. It. | *5541* **TRIFOGLIO** Coastal Mine - sweeper. It. | *95328* **CAPE HENLOPEN** Coast Guard Patrol Boat. Am. |
| | *5542* **VISCHO** Coastal Minesweeper. It. | *95332* **CAPE YORK** Coast Guard Patrol Boat. Am. |
| | *9851* **ALANO** Support Gunboat. It. | |
| | *9852* **BRACCO** Support Gunboat. It. | |

# SUBMARINE PENDANT OR IDENTIFICATION NUMBERS

| | | |
|---|---|---|
| *S01* **G7.** Sp. | *S78* **POSEIDON.** Gr. | *S185* **U6.** Ge. |
| *S09* **POSEIDON.** Gr. | *S86* **TRIAINA.** Gr. | *S187* **U8.** Ge. |
| *S11* **RIO GRANDE DO SUL.** Bz. | *S160* **NARVAL.** Po. | *S188* **U9.** Ge. |
| *S-11* **CARITE.** Ve. | *S163* **ALBACORA.** Po. | *S189* **U10.** Ge. |
| *S12* **BAHIA.** Bz. | *S164* **BARRACUDA.** Po. | *S190* **U11.** Ge. |
| *S12* **HUMAITA.** Bz. | *S165* **CACHALOTE.** Po. | *S191* **U12.** Ge. |
| *S15* **RIACHUELO.** Bz. | *S166* **DELFIM.** Po. | *S300* **ULA.** No. |
| *S21* **D2.** Sp. | *S180* **U1.** Ge. | *S301* **UTSIRA.** No. |
| *S22* **D3.** Sp. | *S181* **U2.** Ge. | *S302* **UTSTEIN.** No. |
| *S31* **ALMIRANTE GARCIA DE LOS REYES.** Sp. | *S183* **U4.** Ge. | *S303* **UTVAER.** No. |
| | *S184* **U5.** Ge. | *S304* **UTHAUG.** No. |

| | | | | | |
|---|---|---|---|---|---|
| S305 | SKLINNA. No. | 44 | IQUIQUE. Pv. | 484 | ODAX. Am. |
| S306 | SKOLPEN. No. | 71 | TANIN. Is. | 485 | SIRAGO. Am. |
| S307 | STADT. No. | 72 | OJIBWA. Ca. | 486 | POMODON. Am. |
| S308 | STORD. No. | | (May not be on boat) | 487 | REMORA. Am. |
| S309 | SVENNER. No. | 73 | ONONDAGA. Ca. | 490 | VOLADOR. Am. |
| S315 | KAURA. No. | | (May not be on boat) | 503 | PIETRO CALVI. It. |
| S316 | KINN. No. | 73 | RAHAV. Is. | 505 | BAGNOLINI. It. |
| S317 | KYA. No. | 74 | OKANAGAN. Ca. | 506 | TOTI. It. |
| S318 | KOBBEN. No. | | (May not be on boat) | 507 | ALFREDO CAPPELLINI. It. |
| S319 | KUNNA. No. | 74 | DOLPHIN. Is. | 508 | FRANCESCO MOROSINI. It. |
| S320 | NAEHVALEN. Da. | 75 | RAINBOW. Ca. | 510 | LEONARDO DA VINCI. It. |
| S321 | NORDKAPEREN. Da. | 75 | LEVIATHAN. Is. | 511 | ENRICO TAZZOLI. It. |
| S326 | DELFINEN. Da. | 130 | GHAZI. Pk. | 511 | OYASHIO. Ja. |
| S327 | SPAEKHUGGEREN. Da. | 240 | ANGLER. Am. | 512 | ALUGORO. Ia. |
| S328 | TUMLEREN. Da. | 244 | CAVALLA. Am. | 512 | EVANGELISTA TORRICELLI. It. |
| S329 | SPRINGEREN. Da. | 246 | CROAKER. Am. | 513 | DANDOLO. It. |
| S330 | BIRINCI INONU. Tu. | 269 | RASHER. Am. | 514 | MOCENIGO. It. |
| S331 | IKINCI INONU. Tu. | 302 | SABALO. Am. | 521 | HAYASHIO. Ja. |
| S332 | SAKARYA. Tu. | 315 | SEALION. Am. | 522 | AMBERJACK. Am. |
| S333 | CANAKKALE. Tu. | 318 | BAYA. Am. | 522 | WAKASHIO. Ja. |
| S334 | GUR. Tu. | 319 | BECUNA. Am. | 523 | GRAMPUS. Am. |
| S340 | PREVEZE. Tu. | 322 | BLACKFIN. Am. | 523 | NATSUSHIO. Ja. |
| S341 | GERBE. Tu. | 323 | CAIMAN. Am. | 524 | PICKEREL. Am. |
| S342 | TURGUT REIS. Tu. | 324 | BLENNY. Am. | 524 | FUYUSHIO. Ja. |
| S343 | PIRI REIS. Tu. | 328 | CHARR. Am. | 525 | GRENADIER. Am. |
| S344 | HIZIR REIS. Tu. | 330 | BUGARA. Am. | 555 | DOLPHIN. Am. |
| S603 | L'ARTEMIS. Fr. | 337 | CARBONERO. Am. | 561 | OSHIO. Ja. |
| S610 | LE FOUDROYANT. Fr. | 339 | CATFISH. Am. | 562 | ASASHIO. Ja. |
| S611 | LE REDOUTABLE. Fr. | 340 | ENTEMEDOR. Am. | 563 | TANG. Am. |
| S612 | LE TERRIBLE. Fr. | 341 | CHIVO. Am. | 563 | HARUSHIO. Ja. |
| S631 | NARVAL. Fr. | 342 | CHOPPER. Am. | 564 | TRIGGER. Am. |
| S632 | MARSOUIN. Fr. | 343 | CLAMAGORE. Am. | 564 | MICHISHIO. Ja. |
| S633 | DAUPHIN. Fr. | 344 | COBBLER. Am. | 565 | WAHOO. Am. |
| S634 | REQUIN. Fr. | 346 | CORPORAL. Am. | 565 | ARASHIO. Ja. |
| S635 | ARETHUSE. Fr. | 347 | CUBERA. Am. | 566 | TROUT. Am. |
| S636 | ARGONAUTE. Fr. | 349 | DIODON. Am. | 567 | GUDGEON. Am. |
| S637 | ESPADON. Fr. | 350 | DOGFISH. Am. | 568 | HARDER. Am. |
| S638 | MORSE. Fr. | 351 | GREENFISH. Am. | 569 | ALBACORE. Am. |
| S639 | AMAZONE. Fr. | 352 | HALFBEAK. Am. | 571 | NAUTILUS. Am. |
| S640 | ARIANE. Fr. | 365 | HARDHEAD. Am. | 572 | SAILFISH. Am. |
| S641 | DAPHNE. Fr. | 368 | JALLAO. Am. | 573 | SALMON. Am. |
| S642 | DIANE. Fr. | 377 | MENHADEN. Am. | 574 | GRAYBACK. Am. |
| S643 | DORIS. Fr. | 382 | PICUDA. Am. | 575 | SEAWOLF. Am. |
| S645 | FLORE. Fr. | 385 | BANG. Am. | 576 | DARTER. Am. |
| S646 | GALATEE. Fr. | 391 | POMFRET. Am. | 577 | GROWLER. Am. |
| S648 | JUNON. Fr. | 392 | STERLET. Am. | 578 | SKATE. Am. |
| S649 | VENUS. Fr. | 394 | RAZORBACK. Am. | 579 | SWORDFISH. Am. |
| S650 | PSYCHE. Fr. | 395 | REDFISH. Am. | 580 | BARBEL. Am. |
| S651 | SIRENE. Fr. | 396 | RONQUIL. Am. | 581 | BLUEBACK. Am. |
| S655 | GYMNOTE. Fr. | 398 | SEGUNDO. Am. | 582 | BONEFISH. Am. |
| S802 | WALRUS. Du. | 401 | TJAKRA. Ia. | 583 | SARGO. Am. |
| S803 | ZEELEUW. Du. | 402 | SEA FOX. Am. | 584 | SEADRAGON. Am. |
| S804 | POTVIS. Du. | 402 | NANGGALA. Ia. | 585 | SKIPJACK. Am. |
| S805 | TONIJN. Du. | 403 | ATULE. Am. | 586 | TRITON. Am. |
| S808 | DOLFIJN. Du. | 406 | SEA POACHER. Am. | 587 | HALIBUT. Am. |
| S809 | ZEEHOND. Du. | 407 | SEA ROBIN. Am. | 588 | SCAMP. Am. |
| SA51 | Sp. | 410 | THREADFIN. Am. | 590 | SCULPIN. Am. |
| SA52 | Sp. | 416 | TIRU. Am. | 591 | SHARK. Am. |
| | | 417 | TENCH. Am. | 592 | SNOOK. Am. |
| | | 418 | THORNBACK. Am. | 594 | PERMIT. Am. |
| *No Flag Superior* | | 419 | TIGRONE. Am. | 595 | PLUNGER. Am. |
| 1 | MACKEREL. Am. | 420 | TIRANTE. Am. | 596 | BARB. Am. |
| 2 | MARLIN. Am. | 421 | TRUTTA. Am. | 597 | TULLIBEE. Am. |
| 3 | BARRACUDA. Am. | 423 | TORSK. Am. | 598 | GEORGE WASHINGTON. Am. |
| 11 | SANTA FE. Ar. | 424 | QUILLBACK. Am. | 599 | PATRICK HENRY. Am. |
| 12 | SANTIAGO DEL ESTERO. Ar. | 425 | TRUMPET FISH. Am. | 600 | THEODORE ROOSEVELT. Am. |
| 12 | 'R' class. Eg. (ex USSR) | 426 | TUSK. Am. | 601 | ROBERT E. LEE. Am. |
| 20 | THOMPSON. Ch. | 476 | RUNNER. Am. | 602 | ABRAHAM LINCOLN. Am. |
| 21 | SIMPSON. Ch. | 478 | CUTLASS. Am. | 603 | POLLACK. Am. |
| 41 | DOS DE MAYO. Pv. | 480 | MEDREGAL. Am. | 604 | HADDO. Am. |
| 42 | ABTAO. Pv. | 481 | REQUIN. Am. | | |
| 43 | ANGAMOS. Pv. | 483 | SEA LEOPARD. Am. | | |

| 605 | PERMIT. Am. |
| 606 | TINOSA. Am. |
| 607 | DACE. Am. |
| 608 | ETHAN ALLEN. Am. |
| 609 | SAM HOUSTON. Am. |
| 610 | THOMAS A. EDISON. Am. |
| 611 | JOHN MARSHALL. Am. |
| 612 | GUARDFISH. Am. |
| 613 | FLASHER. Am. |
| 614 | GREENLING. Am. |
| 615 | GATO. Am. |
| 616 | LAFAYETTE. Am. |
| 617 | ALEXANDER HAMILTON. Am. |
| 618 | THOMAS JEFFERSON. Am. |
| 619 | ANDREW JACKSON. Am. |
| 620 | JOHN ADAMS. Am. |
| 621 | HADDOCK. Am. |
| 622 | JAMES MONROE. Am. |
| 623 | NATHAN HALE. Am. |
| 624 | WOODROW WILSON. Am. |
| 625 | HENRY CLAY. Am. |
| 626 | DANIEL WEBSTER. Am. |
| 627 | JAMES MADISON. Am. |
| 628 | TECUMSEH. Am. |
| 629 | DANIEL BOONE. Am. |
| 630 | JOHN C. CALHOUN. Am. |
| 631 | ULYSSES S. GRANT. Am. |
| 632 | VON STEUBEN. Am. |
| 633 | CASIMIR PULASKI. Am. |
| 634 | STONEWALL JACKSON. Am. |
| 635 | SAM RAYBURN. Am. |
| 636 | NATHANAEL GREENE. Am. |
| 637 | STURGEON. Am. |
| 638 | WHALE. Am. |
| 639 | TAUTOG. Am. |
| 640 | BENJAMIN FRANKLIN. Am. |
| 641 | SIMON BOLIVAR. Am. |
| 642 | KAMEHAMEHA. Am. |
| 643 | GEORGE BANCROFT. Am. |
| 644 | LEWIS AND CLARK. Am. |
| 645 | JAMES K. POLK. Am. |
| 646 | GRAYLING. Am. |
| 647 | POGY. Am. |
| 648 | ASPRO. Am. |
| 649 | SUNFISH. Am. |
| 650 | PARGO. Am. |
| 651 | QUEENFISH. Am. |
| 652 | PUFFER. Am. |
| 653 | RAY. Am. |
| 654 | GEORGE C. MARSHALL. Am. |
| 655 | HENRY L. STIMSON. Am. |
| 656 | GEORGE WASHINGTON CARVER. Am. |
| 657 | FRANCIS SCOTT KEY. Am. |
| 658 | MARIANO G. VALLEJO. Am. |
| 659 | WILL ROGERS. Am. |
| 660 | SAND LANCE. Am. |
| 661 | LAPON. Am. |
| 662 | GURNARD. Am. |
| 663 | HAMMERHEAD. Am. |
| 664 | SEA DEVIL. Am. |
| 665 | GUITARRO. Am. |
| 666 | HAWKBILL. Am. |
| 667 | BERGALL. Am. |
| 668 | SPADEFISH. Am. |
| 669 | SEAHORSE. Am. |
| 670 | FINBACK. Am. |
| 671 | NARWHAL. Am. |
| 672 | PINTADO. Am. |
| 673 | FLYING FISH. Am. |
| 674 | TREPANG. Am. |
| 675 | BLUEFISH. Am. |
| 676 | BILLFISH. Am. |
| 677 | DRUM. Am. |
| 678 | ARCHERFISH. Am. |
| 679 | SILVERSIDES. Am. |
| 680 | REDFISH. Am. |
| 681 | BATFISH. Am. |
| 682 | TUNNY. Am. |
| 683 | PARCHE. Am. |
| 684 | CAVALLA. Am. |
| 802 | SAVA. Ys. |
| 810 | NERETVA. Ys. |
| 811 | SUTJESKA. Ys. |
| 812 | ULJANIK. Ys. |
| Abb. | ABBORREN. Sw. |
| Bav. | BAVERN. Sw. |
| Del. | DELFINEN. Sw. |
| Dra. | DRAKEN. Sw. |
| F1 | Sp. |
| F2 | Sp. |
| For. | FORELLEN. Sw. |
| Gad. | GADDEN. Sw. |
| Gri. | GRIPEN. Sw. |
| Haj. | HAJEN. Sw. |
| Ila. | ILLERN. Sw. |
| Lax. | LAXEN. Sw. |
| Mak. | MAKRILLEN. Sw. |
| Nor. | NORDKAPAREN. Sw. |
| Sal. | SALEN. Sw. |
| Sbj. | SJOBJORNEN. Sw. |
| Sha. | SJOHASTEN. Sw. |
| Shu. | SJOHUNDEN. Sw. |
| Sik. | SIKEN. Sw. |
| Sle. | SJOLEJONET. Sw. |
| Sor. | SJOORMEN. Sw. |
| Spg. | SPIGGEN. Sw (Might not have number on ship) |
| Spr. | SPRINGAREN. Sw. |
| Utn. | UTTERN. Sw. |
| Val. | VALEN. Sw. |
| Vgn. | VARGEN. Sw. |
| X1 | XI. Am. |
| Y880 | WILHELM BAUER. Ge. |

# Naval Aviation

The majority of aircraft in this section are ship-borne but one or two are land based. These are put in because they *can* be operated at sea. The purpose of this section is to assist in the recognition of warships by identifying their aircraft.

The abbreviations of nationalities are the same as for ships. Dimensions are the span followed by the overall length. The speed given is the maximum at average cruising height. For the **helicopters** only the overall length of the fuselage is given. The speed given is the maximum speed, in knots, at sea level.

## SHIP-BORNE NAVAL AIRCRAFT
### (The drawings are not to scale)

**1. DOUGLAS A-4 SKYHAWK.** Am. Attack Bomber. 27'6" x 42'11". One turbojet. 612 m.p.h. Served with the U.S. Navy since 1956. Several thousand completed. Type shown is the A-4E for the US Navy. Latest type is the A-4M. The only really significant external difference in the latest marks is a prominent bulge aft of the cockpit.
*Operators:* U.S. Navy, U.S. Marines, Royal Australian Navy (A-4G). Also operates as a land-based aircraft with other air forces.

**2. GRUMMAN F-14. TOMCAT.** Am. All weather Fighter. No dimensions available. 1,650 m.p.h. Two turbofans. Note the variable geometry wings and small canard surfaces from the fixed part of the wing. Will replace the Phantom in U.S. Naval service. Should be operational in 1973.

**3. McDONNELL DOUGLAS F-4 PHANTOM II.** Am. All weather Fighter. 38'4" x 57'11". Two turbojets. 1,400 m.p.h. Very versatile aircraft. In U.S. Navy service since 1962. Drawing shows the F-4K version for the Royal Navy. This is externally very similar to the latest U.S. Navy version; the F-4J. *Operators:* U.S. Navy, U.S. Marines, British Fleet Air Arm (FG.Mk.I). Also operated by land-based forces including the U.S. Air Force and the R.A.F. Will be replaced in U.S. Naval service in the mid 70's.

**4. NORTH AMERICAN ROCKWELL RA-5C VIGILANTE.** Am. Tactical reconnaissance Aircraft. 53' x 75'10". Two turbojets. 1,400 m.p.h. A few of the earlier A-5B (attack bomber) version are still in service but most have been converted to RA-5C standard. *Operated* by the U.S. Navy.

**5. HAWKER SIDDELEY HARRIER.** Br. Strike and reconnaissance Fighter. 25'3" x 46'4". One turbofan. 680-720 m.p.h. Became *operational* with the R.A.F. in 1969. Has undergone sea trials on British warships. *Operated* by the U.S. Marines as the AV-8A. India and Italy have also shown interest.

**6. SEPECAT JAGUAR.** Br./Fr. Tactical Fighter. 27'10" x 53'11". Two turbofans. 1,120 m.p.h. The Jaguar is a joint Anglo-French aircraft in five different versions. The drawing shows the Jaguar "M" version for the French Navy for service aboard their aircraft carriers.

**7. LING - TEMCO - VOUGHT F - 8 CRU - SADER.** Am. Intercepter Fighter. 35'8" x 54'6". One turbojet. Over 1,000 m.p.h. The Crusader has been operational in the U.S. Navy since 1957. There are many different versions including the RF-8G reconnaissance version. The drawing shows the F-8E version.
*Operators:* U.S. Navy, U.S. Marines, French Navy (F-8E(FN) ).

**8. LING - TEMCO - VOUGHT A - 7 CORSAIR II.** Am. Attack Bomber. 38'9" x 46'2". One turbofan. 600 m.p.h. Can carry a very large load of external ordinance. Became operational in the U.S. Navy in 1967. Latest Navy version is the A-7E.
*Operated* by the U.S. Navy and also land-based by the U.S.A.F.

**9. GRUMMAN A-6 INTRUDER.** Am. Attack Bomber. 53' x 54'7". Two turbojets. 600 m.p.h. Entered service with the U.S. Navy in 1963. Drawing shows the original A-6A version. There is also a KA-6 tanker version and an EA-6 electronics countermeasures version (see No. 10).
*Operated* by the U.S. Navy and Marine Corps.

**10. GRUMMAN EA-6B INTRUDER.** Am. Electronic Countermeasures Aircraft. 53' x 59'5". Two turbojets. 600 m.p.h. The head on view and plan are much the same as number 9. There is also the EA-6A which has the same details but with a conventional type cockpit like the A-6A (number 9).

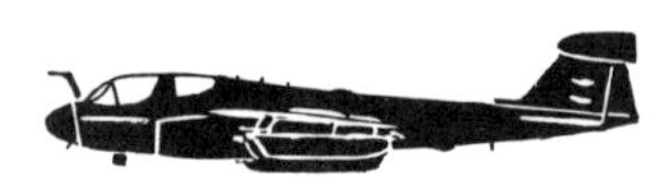

## 11. HAWKER SIDDELEY BUCCANEER.
Br. Low level strike Aircraft. 44' x 62'5". Two turbofans. 700 m.p.h. In service since 1962. The drawing shows the latest version the S Mk. 2.
*Operated* by the Fleet Air Arm and the R.A.F.

## 12. DOUGLAS EA-3B SKYWARRIOR. Am.
Electronics Countermeasures Aircraft. 72'5" x 76'4". Two turbojets. 550 m.p.h. The world's largest carrier borne aircraft. Entered service with the U.S. Navy as an attack bomber in 1957. It is now principally used as an electronics countermeasures aircraft, reconnaissance aircraft (RA-6) and flight refueller (KA-6).

## 13. DASSAULT ETENDARD. Fr. Strike
Fighter and tactical reconnaissance aircraft. 31'6" x 47'3". One turbojet. 670 m.p.h. Entered service in 1962. The IV-M version is a strike fighter, some have facilities for in-flight refuelling. The IV-P version is a reconnaissance version. Note the nose refuelling probe. The Etendard IV-M will be replaced by the Jaguar "M" in the near future.

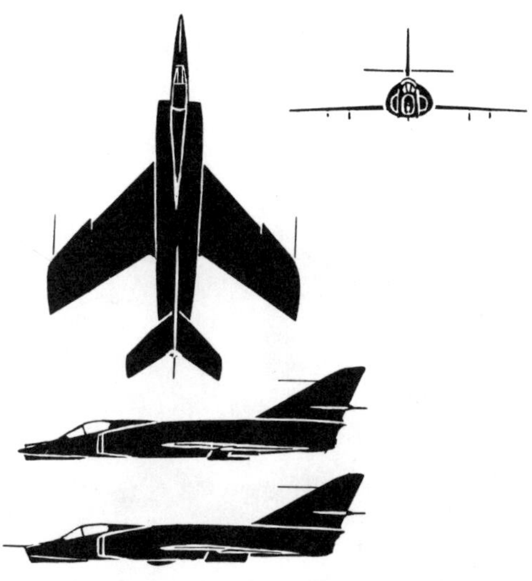

## 14. HAWKER SIDDELEY SEA VIXEN. Br.
All weather strike Fighter. 50' x 55'7". Two turbojets. 650 m.p.h. The original version (FAW.Mk.1) entered service in 1959. The present operational type (FAW.Mk.2), shown above, entered service in 1964. The long tail booms are very distinctive. Being replaced in F.A.A. by Phantoms.

**15. AERMACCHI MB 326**. It. Trainer/Attack Aircraft. 35'7" x 34'11". One turbojet. 520 m.p.h. Although this Italian aircraft serves in many air forces throughout the world it is only used by one Naval air service—*ARGENTINA.* Argentina will eventually operate 24 of this type which at the moment are land based.

**16. HAWKER SIDDELEY SEA HAWK**. Br. Fighter-Bomber. 39' x 39'8". One turbojet. 500 m.p.h. First became operational with the Royal Navy in 1950. Only the *Indian Navy* now use this aircraft operationally. They use former Fleet Air Arm F Mk.6's as shown above. They are likely to be replaced shortly.

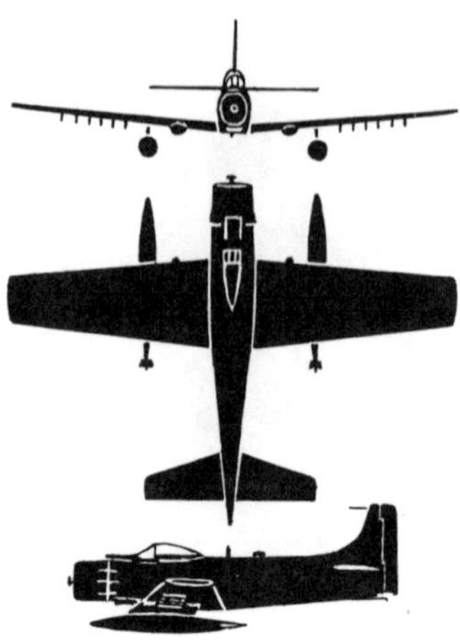

**17. DOUGLAS A-I SKYRAIDER**. Am. Tactical Attack Bomber. 50'9" x 38'10". One radial piston engine. 300 m.p.h. Although first flown in 1944 the Skyraider was kept in front line service with the U.S. Navy until recently because of its ability to carry large underwing loads. It has now, however, practically disappeared from the U.S. Navy. The drawing shows the last version; the A-IJ. It is still operated by the U.S.A.F. and other Air Forces.

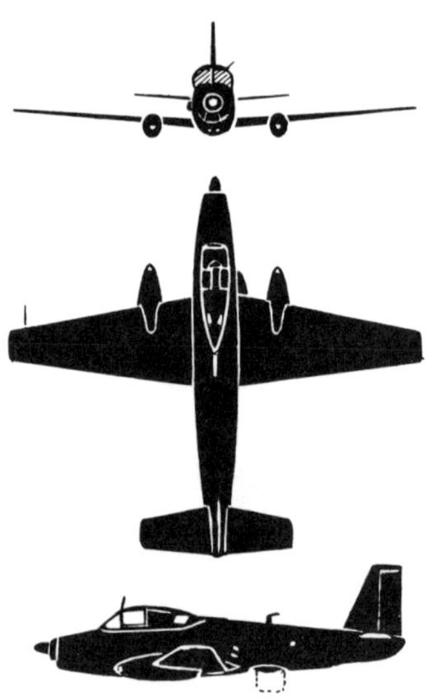

**18. BREGUET ALIZE**. Fr. Reconnaissance and anti-submarine Aircraft. 51'2" x 45'6". One turboprop. 290 m.p.h.
*Operators:* French Navy (75), Indian Navy (12).

**19. FAIREY GANNET.** Br. Early warning
Aircraft. 54'6" x 44'. One double turboprop.
250 m.p.h. The Gannet was originally an
anti-submarine aircraft and a small number
of the anti-submarine and training version
are still operated by the Fleet Air Arm for COD
(courier on board) duties. The type shown is
the AEW Mk.3. They were manufactured
1958-61.
*Operated* (C.O. Deck) by the British Fleet
Air Arm.

**20. GRUMMAN E-2A HAWKEYE.** Am.
Early Warning Aircraft. 80'7" x 56'4". Two
turboprops. 300 m.p.h. Manufactured 1961-
67. Latest development is the E-2B. The huge
radome is prominent from all angles.
The **GRUMMAN C-2A GREYHOUND** is a
transport version which, despite the absence
of the radome and a fatter fuselage is similar
in most respects to the Hawkeye. Both
aircraft are operated solely by the U.S. Navy.

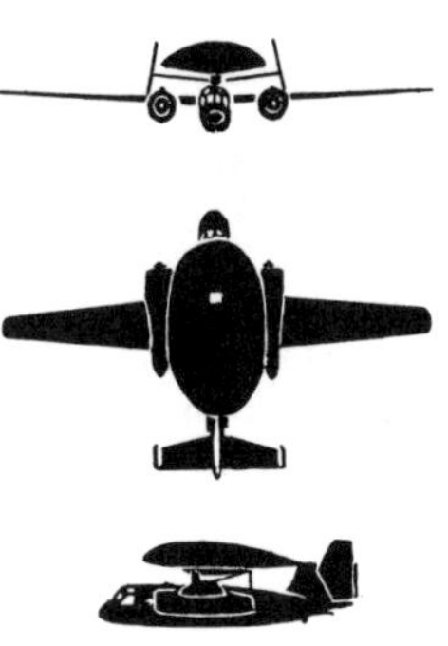

**21. GRUMMAN E-I TRACER.** Am. Airborne
Early Warning Aircraft. 72'7" x 45'4". Two
piston engines. 200 m.p.h. Derived from the
C-I Trader (see number 22). Being replaced
by the larger Hawkeye (number 20). The
version shown is the E-IB.

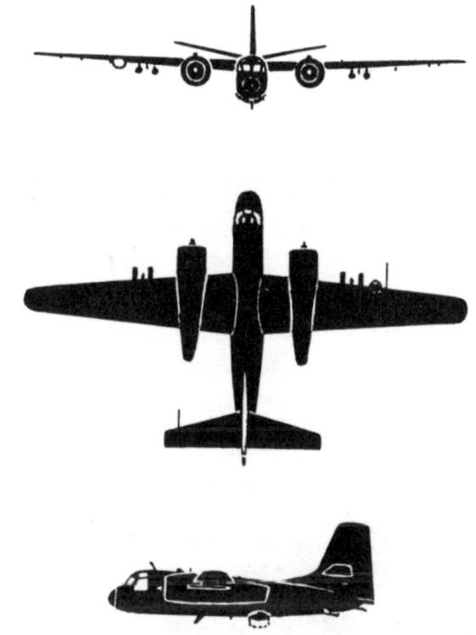

**22. GRUMMAN S-2 TRACKER.** Am. Anti-
submarine Aircraft. 72'7" x 43'6". Two radial
piston engines. 200 m.p.h. These were largely
replaced by helicopters in the U.S. Navy. Various versions are flown by the following Navies:
Argentina, Australia, Brazil. Some are also
operated by land based Navies and Air forces.
The drawing shows the S-2D versions. Some
of the early versions have a small radome over
the cabin.
Similar to the Tracker is the **GRUMMAN C-I
TRADER,** which is operated by the U.S. Navy
as a carrier onboard delivery transport but is
being succeeded by the larger C-2A Greyhound.

# NAVAL HELICOPTERS

**23. BOEING-VERTOL SEA KNIGHT.** Am. Transport and Utility Helicopter. 44′10″. Two shaft turbine engines. 150 knots. Operated as a carrier borne aircraft by the U.S. Navy and Marine Corps. The design is basically the Vertol 107 and has been adopted as a land based helicopter by the Swedish and Japanese Navies as well as the Canadian Armed Forces. In U.S. Navy and Marines service it is designated the CH-46 and UH-46 (illustrated).

**26. SIKORSKY SH-3 SEA KING.** Am. Anti-submarine and Transport Helicopter. 72′-8″ x 62′. Two shaft turbines. 140 knots. Basically the Sikorsky S-61 design. Operators (carrier borne): U.S. Navy, Canadian Navy (CHSS-2), Spanish Navy. The Royal Navy version is manufactured in the U.K. and is called the WESTLAND SEA KING H.A.S. Mk. 1. It has a prominent dorsal radome which is indicated by dotted lines in the drawing. The Italian and Japanese Navies also operate the Sea King.

**24. SUD AVIATION SUPER FRELON.** Fr. Heavy assault and anti-submarine Helicopter. 76′7″. Three shaft turbines. 150 knots. The anti-submarine version used by the French Navy (and the South African Air Force) is known as the SA-321G. As a land based helicopter the Super Frelon is also operated by the Israeli Air Force.

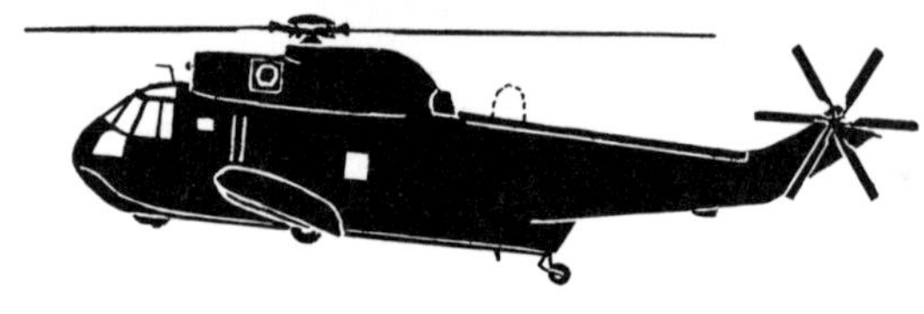

**27. KAMAN UH-2 SEASPRITE.** Am. Rescue and General Purpose Helicopter. 52′2″. Two shaft turbines. 140 knots. The original version of the Seasprite entered service in 1962. The early versions were all single engined but the latest version (the UH-2C) is twin engined and the remaining older aircraft are being retrospectively modified to this standard. A gunship version of the UH-2C, the HH-2C, has a minigun turret forward and many other alterations (shown by dotted lines in the drawing).

**25. SIKORSKY CH-53 SEA STALLION.** Am. Heavy Assault, Transport and Rescue Helicopter. 88′3″. Two shaft turbines. 190 knots. Entered service with the U.S. Marine Corps in 1966. Also operated by the U.S.A.F. as the HH-53.

**28. WESTLAND WESSEX.** Br. Anti-submarine, Assault and General Purpose Helicopter. 65'9" x 56'. Two shaft turbines. 115 knots. Many versions of this well-known helicopter exist. The one shown is the Wessex HU. Mk. 5. This is the commando assault version for the Royal Navy. Note the rocket tubes and missiles forward. Another distinctive Royal Navy version is the Mk. 3 anti-submarine Wessex with prominent dorsal radome. The Wessex also serves with the Australian Navy and many inland forces.

The Wessex is derived from the American **Sikorsky S-58** (called Seabat in U.S. Navy service). This has one piston engine which gives its nose a distinctive shape from the Wessex. Also serves with the Navies of ARGENTINA and FRANCE and land-based Navies and Air Forces.

**29. WESTLAND WHIRLWIND.** Br. Rescue and General Purpose Helicopter. 62'4" x 44'2". One shaft turbine. 104 knots. The drawing shows the Series 3 Whirlwind as operated by the Brazilian Navy. The Royal Navy use the HAR. Mk. 9 version for plane guard and search-and-rescue operations. The Spanish Navy use the old series 2 Whirlwinds which are piston engined and have a nose like the one shown in the inset.

The American **SIKORSKY S-55** is also piston engined and serves with the ARGENTINEAN and SPANISH Navies as well as many land based forces.

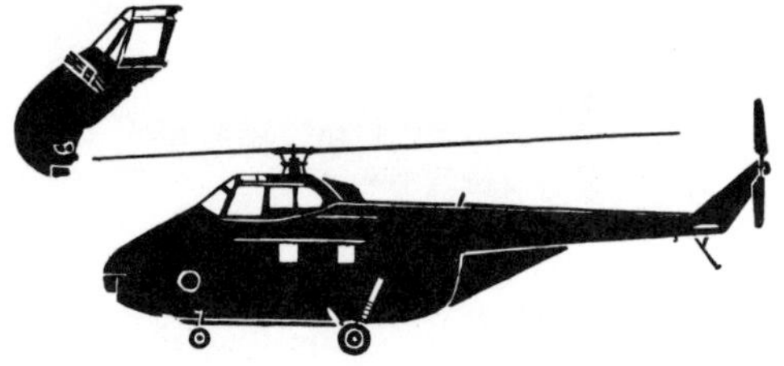

**30. WESTLAND WG.13. LYNX** Br. Anti-submarine Search and Strike and General Purpose Helicopter. 38'3". Two shaft turbines. 150 knots. This versatile helicopter is due to come into service shortly aboard Royal Navy destroyers and frigates. A training version is also proposed. It will replace the smaller Wasp helicopter. A version will also be used by the Royal Marines.

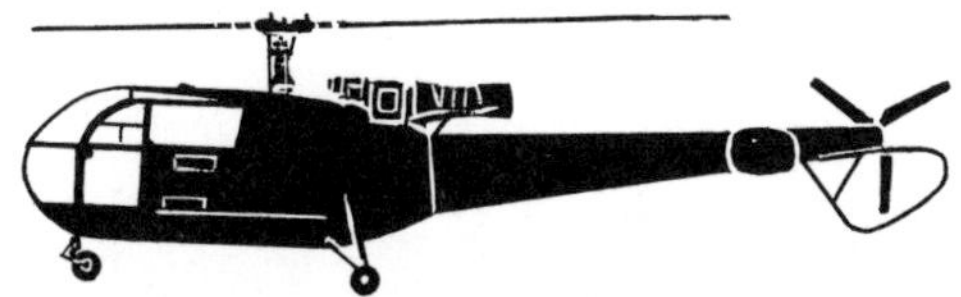

**31. SUD AVIATION ALOUETTE III.** Fr. Rescue and General Purpose Helicopter. 32'9". One shaft turbine. 114 knots. This very popular helicopter is operated by, or on order for, a large number of air forces. France (Aeronavale) is the principal naval operator and uses them for plane guard duties aboard her carriers. In this role the Alouette III is normally fitted with floats. Other naval operators include Brazil and Denmark.

**32. AGUSTA-BELL AB 204B.** Am./It. Anti-submarine and General Purpose Helicopter. 42'7". One shaft turbine. 120 knots. This is a version of the American Bell UH-IB built in Italy. It is *operated* in the anti-submarine role by the Navies of Italy, Spain and the Netherlands.

The very similar **BELL UH-I IROQUOIS** general purpose helicopter (not anti-submarine) is operated by the U.S. Marines and the Australian Navy.

**33. WESTLAND WASP.** Br. Anti-submarine Helicopter. 40'4" x 30'6". One shaft turbine. 105 knots. This helicopter is standard equipment for most Royal Navy frigates although it will eventually be replaced by the WG.13 (number 30). It is also *operated* by the following Navies: Australia, Brazil, Netherlands, New Zealand, South Africa.

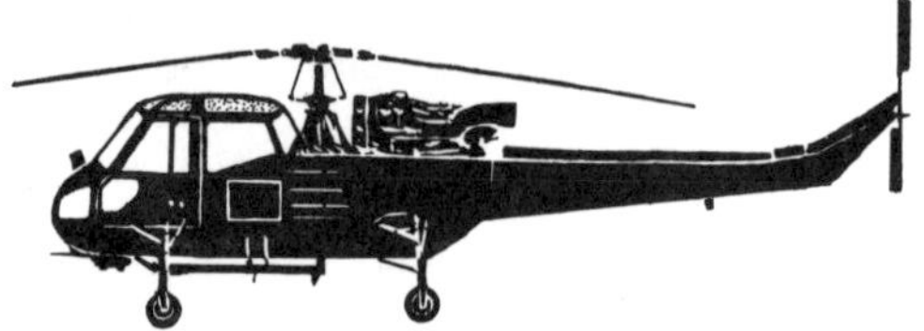

**34. AGUSTA A.106.** It. Anti-submarine Attack Helicopter. 26'3". One shaft turbine. 100 knots. Production of this light helicopter for the Italian Navy started in 1970. A slightly larger version (the A.106B) is being developed although it is not known if this will serve in the Italian Navy. At present the Italian Navy are the sole operators of this type.

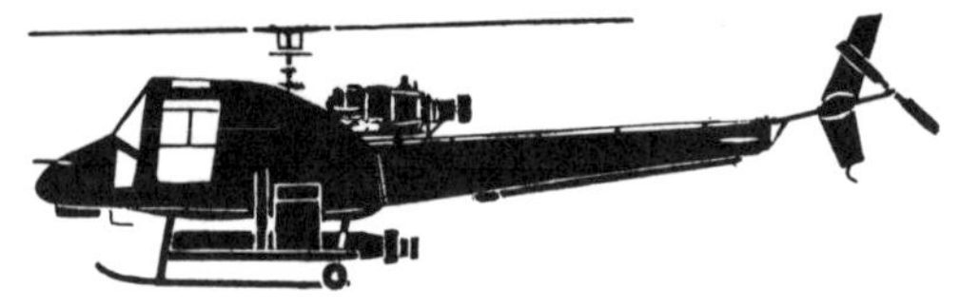

**35. KAMOV Ka-25 (HORMONE).** Ru. Anti-submarine Attack Helicopter. 32'3". Two shaft turbines. 130 knots. The prototype of this helicopter was the Ka-20 (NATO code name "HARP"). It is used by the Soviet Navy aboard their helicopter carriers "Moskva" and "Leningrad". The large radome forward and the three fins aft make it very distinctive.

**36. KAMOV Ka-15 (HEN).** Ru. General Purpose Light Helicopter. 19'6". One radial piston engine. 81 knots. This type serves with the Soviet Navy aboard their warships although as it has been in military service for at least 15 years it is probably becoming obsolete.

**37. AGUSTA-BELL AB.47J.** It. Anti-submarine and General Purpose Helicopter. 32'5". One piston engine. 95 knots. The AB.47J is built in Italy under licence from the U.S.A. and is developed from the AB.47G (see number 38). The drawing does not show the special anti-submarine version. It is *operated* by the Navies of Italy and Spain.

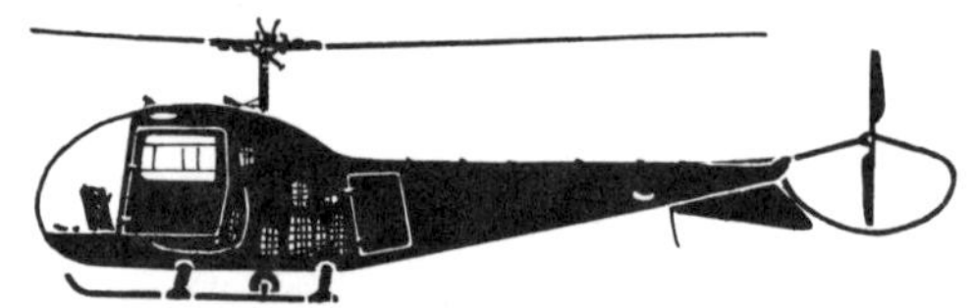

**38. BELL 47G (SIOUX).** Am. Light Communications and General Purpose Helicopter. 32'7". One piston engine. 95 knots. There is a large range of types in the Bell 47 series but the 47G is the principal one. It is also built under licence in Italy and the United Kingdom. It is *operated* by the following Navies: Argentina, Italy, Chile, Mexico, Peru, Uruguay. The Royal Marines also operate a British built version which can be described as the Westland Sioux AH1.

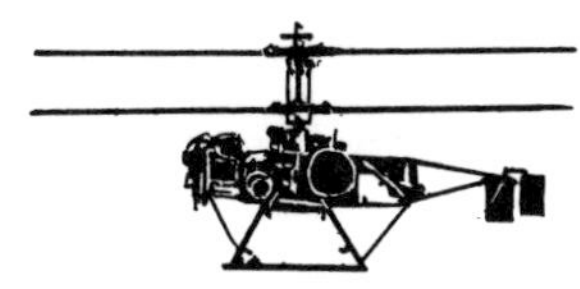

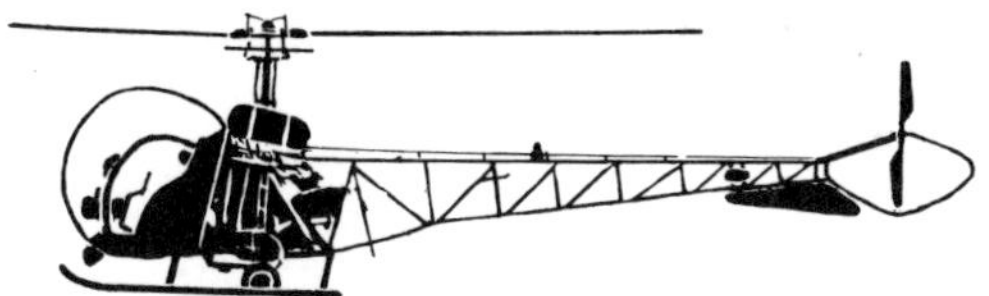

**39. GYRODYNE QH-50.** Am. Anti-submarine Helicopter Drone. 12'11". One shaft turbine. 80 knots. This pilotless drone forms the weapon carrying part of the DASH (Drone Anti-Submarine Helicopter) system on some U.S. Navy ships. The version shown is the QH-50C. A later version, the QH-50D, does not have the extended tail shown in the drawing. The drone is controlled entirely from the ship and can carry one or two torpedoes. They have also been used for air-sea rescue. *Operators:* U.S. Navy, Japanese Maritime Self Defence Force.

# Index

The first numbers or sets of numbers refer to the silhouette drawings and those after the comma refer to the grey drawings.

Where only one number is shown, it almost invariably refers to a submarine and will be found in the 2nd (grey) section, although on occasion it may be the number of a vessel illustrated by a solid silhouette but not repeated in the other section.

In cases of countries having more than one ship of the same name, the type of vessel is indicated. Letters M.S.A. after Japanese ships indicate that they are units of the Maritime Safety Agency and not of the regular Navy or Defence Force.

Bremerton (Am) 199, 36
Brereton (Br) 376/596, 689/691
Breskens (Am) 468, 698
Breton (Am) 17, 15
Breukelen (Am) 468, 698
Breydel (Be) 504, 680
Briareus (Am) 1115, 1039
Bridget (Am) 220, 277
Brielle (Am) 468, 698
Brighton (Br) 113, 196
Brinchang (My) 596, 689
Brinkley Bass (Am) 88, 96
Brinton (Br) 596, 689
Brisbane (Aus) 62, 81
Bristol (Br) 45, 169
Britannia (Br) 1087, 1016
Britannic (Br) 1195, 860
Broadbill (Am) 394, 148
Broadkill River (Am) 219, 646
Brodick (Br) 1228, 1250
Bronington (Br) 595, 690
Bronstein (Am) 287, 180
Brooke (Am) 281, 178
Brott (No) 550, 437
Brouwershaven (Du) 468, 698
Brown (Ar) 143, 105
Brown Ranger (Br) 1272, 1191
Brownson (Am) 88, 96
Bruang (Ia) 546, 474
Bruinisse (Am) 468, 698
Brumby (Am) 286, 177
Brummen (Du) 468, 698
Brunswick (Am) 1114, 793
Bryanston (Ng) 385, 440
Bryant (Am) 150, 106
Bryce Canyon (Am) 849, 1043
BS 1 (Sp) 1032, 1306
Bubara (Ia) 566, 450B
Buccaneer (Au) 485, 422
Buchanan (Am) 87, 80
Buck (Am) 144, 100
Bucklesham (Br) 329, 720
Buckley class (Am) etc. 516, 271
Buenos Aires (Ar) 238, 135
Bugara (Am) 927
Buk Han (Ko) 133, 635
Bulacan (Th) 132, 620
Bulgia (Du) 640, 452
Bullard (Am) 150, 106
Bulldog (Br) 808, 824
Bullfinch (Br) 888, 808
Bulloch County (Am) 132, 620
Bulwark (Am) 503, 678
Bulwark (Br) 20, 9
Bunju (Ia) 1156, 1174
Burlnyi (Rus) 139/140, 90/91
Burns (Am) 150, 106
Burton Island (Am) 846, 1001
Burudjulasad (Ia) 38, 375
Bushnell (Am) 828, 731
Bussard (EG) 574, 468
Bussard (Ge) 546, 474
Bussemaker (Du) 718, 706
Bustler (Br) 1030, 1300
Butt (Ge) 318, 366
Butte (Am) 876, 745
Butternut (Am) 1105
Buttonwood (Am) 883, 1087
Buyukdere (Tu) 754, 346
Byblos (Le) 583, 569

C class submarine (Ru) 916

C. D. Howe (Ca) 792, 999
CGC 11 (Th) 655, 438
CGC 13 (Th) 361, 434
CGC 14 (Th) 361, 434
CGC 15 (Th) 361, 434
CGC 16 (Th) 361, 434
C. P. Edwards (Ca) 1287, 1231
CR1 (Sp) 1078, 800
Cabildo (Am) 707, 611
Cabo San Bartolome (Ar) 270, 633
Cabo San Gonzalo (Ar) 270, 633
Cabo San Isidro (Ar) 270, 633
Cabo San Pio (Ar) 270, 633
Cabo San Vicente (Ar) 270, 633
Caboclo (Bz) 949, 1327
Cabrales (Ch) 1037, 1322
Cacapon (Am) 1176, 1136
Cachalot (Br) 905
Cachalote (Po) 907
Cache (Am) 1177, 1160
Cacheu (Po) 343, 349
Cactus (Am) 883, 1087
Cadmus (Am) 849, 1043
Cahokia (Am) 855, 1308
Caiman (Am) 897
Caio Duilio (It) 628, 76
Cairn (Br) 922, 1326
Calamar (Ve) 411, 409
Calamaro (It) 688, 720
Calcaterra (Am) 523, 278
Caldy (Br) 878, 1098
Caliente (Am) 1176, 1136
California (Am) 639, 186
California (Me) 260, 282
Callao (Pv) 1092, 1065
Calliope (Fr) 384, 702
Caloosahatchee (Am) 1139, 1135
Cam Ranh (VN) 132, 620
Camarines sur (Pi) 576, 470
Camaron (Ve) 411, 409
Cambria (Am) 834, 1044
Camden (Am) 1322, 1277
Camelia (Fr) 468, 698
Camiguin (Pi) 676, 586
Camp (Am) 524, 278
Campbell (Am) 477, 317
Camsell (Ca) 1235, 1268
Canakkale (Tu) 923
Canarias (Sp) 227, 44
Canberra (Am) 770, 162
Candarli (Tu) 395, 149
Candido Perez (Sp) 589, 480
Canisteo (Am) 1139, 1135
Cannanore (In) 776, 689
Canon (Am) 78, 413
Canopo (It) 295, 122
Canopus (Am) 1328, 862
Canopus (Bz) 860, 817
Canopus (Fr) 597, 693
Canopus (Po) 307, 525
Canterbury (NZ) 97, 191
Cantho (Fr) 507, 682
Cap. General Pedro Santana (Do) 262, 307
Capable (Br) 1026, 1320
Cape (Am) 715, 705
Cape Breton (Ca) 1123, 1066
Cape Carter (Am) 362, 431
Cape Coral (Am) 362, 431
Cape Corwin (Am) 363, 430
Cape Cross (Am) 363, 430
Cape Current (Am) 362, 431
Cape Fairweather (Am) 724, 432

Cape Fox (Am) 724, 432
Cape George (Am) 362, 431
Cape Gloucester (Am) 16, 22
Cape Gull (Am) 362, 431
Cape Hatteras (Am) 362, 431
Cape Hedge (Am) 362, 431
Cape Henlopen (Am) 363, 430
Cape Higgon (Am) 362, 431
Cape Jellison (Am) 724, 432
Cape Knox (Am) 724, 432
Cape Morgan (Am) 724, 432
Cape Newagen (Am) 724, 432
Cape Horn (Am) 363, 430
Cape Romain (Am) 724, 432
Cape Scott (Ca) 1123, 1066
Cape Shoalwater (Am) 363, 430
Cape Small (Am) 362, 431
Cape Starr (Am) 724, 432
Cape Strait (Am) 362, 431
Cape Upright (Am) 362, 431
Cape Wash (Am) 362, 431
Cape York (Am) 363, 430
Capella (Do) 553 555
Capella (Fr) 597, 693
Capella (Ge) 386, 400
Capella (Sw) 46, 497
Caperton (Am) 150, 106
Capitan Alsina (No) 773, 549
Capitan Beotegui (Do) 1288, 1201
Capitan Binney (Co) 699, 449
Capitan Cabral (Py) 370, 602
Capitan Canepa (Ar) 895, 1104
Capitan Miranda (Ur) 1007, 1020
Capitan N. Arvelo (Do) 1288, 1201
Capiz (Pi) 411, 409
Capotillo (Do) 1024, 1082
Caprera (It) 437, 630
Caprice (Br) 163, 244
Capricorne (Fr) 597, 693
Capricornus (Am) 838, 1057
Capucine (Fr) 330, 720
Carabiniere (It) 217, 176
Caracol (Ve) 411, 409
Carbonero (Am) 927
Card (Am) 29, 30, 16
Cardak (Tu) 395, 149
Careful (Br) 1026, 1320
Caribe (Cu) 453, 360
Carite (Ve) 895
Carlo Bergamini (It) 215, 183
Carlo Margottini (It) 215, 183
Carlos E. Restrepo (Co) 723, 415
Carlos Galindo (Co) 44, 572
Carmick (Am) 154, 138
Caroline County (Am) 133, 635
Carpenter (Am) 90, 95
Carronade (Am) 237, 645
Carsamba (Tu) 395, 149
Cartagena (Co) 127, 599
Carvalho Araujo (Po) 344, 343
Casa Grande (Am) 707, 611
Casabianca (Fr) 282, 113
Casamance (Se) 313, 483
Cascade (Am) 819, 739
Casimir Pulaski (Am) 871
Cassard (Fr) 100, 110
Cassin Young (Am) 150, 106
Cassiope (Fr) 597, 693
Castagno (It) 468, 698
Castilla (Pv) 167, 266
Castilla (Sp) 838, 1057
Castle Rock (Am) 479, 316

Fuyushio (Ja) 934
Fuyuzuki (Ja) 784, 554
Fyen (Da) 51, 776
Fylla (Da) 341, 777
Fyrholm (Da) 918, 1351
G class (Ru) 886
G 7 (Sp) 951
G. Truffaut (Be) 504, 680
Gabbiano (It) 406, 345
Gaddan (Sw) 947
Gaggia (It) 468, 498
Gainard (Am) 155, 104
Gajabahu (Ce) 530, 288
Galatea (Br) 91, 191
Galatee (Fr) 907
Galeb (Ys) 864, 772
Gallant (Am) 503, 678
Gallatin (Am) 606, 211
Gallup (Am) 78, 413
Galten (Sw) 1206, 1343
Galveston (Am) 769, 38
Galvez (Pv) 394, 148
Gambero (It) 688, 720
Ganga (In) 116, 253
Gannet (Ca) 1264, 1267
Gansevoort (Am) 159, 140
Garcia (Am) 286, 177
Gardenia (Fr) 468, 698
Garganey (Br) 1017, 798
Garigliano (Fr) 507, 682
Garonne (Fr) 1330, 849
Garrett County (Am) 133, 635
Gascoyne (Au) 347, 294
Gastrikland (Sw) 256, 128
Gatineau (Ca) 525, 228
Gato (Am) 877
Gavington (Br) 595, 690
Gaviota (Ve) 411, 409
Gavril Saritshev (Ru) 1012, 827
Gazelle (Ge) 380, 704
Gaziantep (Tu) 161, 137
GC 11 (Cu) 311, 553
GC 13 (Cu) 311, 553
GC 14 (Cu) 311, 553
GC 32 (Cu) 311, 553
GC 33 (Cu) 311, 553
GC 34 (Cu) 311, 553
GC 38 (Me) 411, 409
Gearing (Am) 88, 96
Gefion (Ge) 380, 704
Geier (Ge) 546, 474
Geiger (Am) 901, 1006
Geir (No) 555, 513
Geisomino (It) 468, 698
Gelderland (Du) 283, 69
Gelderland (SA) 385, 440
Gelibolu (Tu) 157, 137
Gelso (It) 468, 698
Gemert (Du) 597, 693
Gemlik (Tu) 161, 137
Gemma (Ge) 386, 400
Gempita (My) 611, 503
Gendreau (Am) 76/80, 271
General Alexander M. Patch (Am) 882, 958
General Belgrano (Ar) 200, 43
General H. H. Arnold (Am) 1164, 865
General Hoyt S. Vandenberg (Am) 1164, 865
General John Pope (Am) 966, 959
General Jose de Austria (Ve) 277, 219
General Jose Trinidad Moran (Ve) 239, 218
General Juan Jose Flores (Ve) 239, 218

General Maurice Rose (Am) 882, 958
General Nelson M. Walker (Am) 882, 958
General Rafael Reyes (Co) 126, 448
General San Martin (Ar) 959, 992
General Simon B. Buckner (Am) 882, 958
General Vasques Cobe (Co) 126, 448
General W. H. Gordon (Am) 966, 959
General William O. Darby (Am) 882, 959
General William Weigel (Am) 966, 959
Genesee (Am) 1325, 1283
Geniere (It) 143, 105
Genil (Sp) 382, 701
Genkai (Ja) 497, 1122
Gentian (Am) 883, 1087
Gentry (Am) 164a, 247
George Bancroft (Am) 871
George C. Marshall (Am) 871
George E. Davis (Am) 164A, 274
George Eastman (Am) 1124, 1051
George K. Mackenzie (Am) 88, 96
George Washington (Am) 872
George Washington Carver (Am) 871
Gephard (Ge) 546, 474
Gera (EG) 229, 372
Geranium (Fr) 330, 720
Gerardo Jansen (Do) 75, 339
Gharbia (Eg) 442, 676
Ghasm (Ir) 320, 665
Ghazi (Pk) 925
Gherardi (Am) 154, 138
Giaggiolo (It) 468, 698
Gidrolog (Ru) 953, 675
Giethoorn (Du) 597, 693
Gifford (Ng) 385, 440
Gigrometr (Ru) 1194, 835
Gihad (Su) 599, 481
Gillespie (Am) 159, 140
Gillette (Am) 76/80, 271
Gilligan (Am) 164A, 274
Gilloga (Sw) 1206, 1343
Ginga (Ja) 1021, 1084
Giresun (Tu) 157, 137
Girl class (Br) 922, 1326
Giroflee (Fr) 468, 698
Giuseppe Garibaldi (It) 179, 166
Glacier (Am) 841, 1002
Gladiator (Am) 394, 148
Glaieul (Fr) 468, 698
Glamorgan (Br) 188, 62
Glasserton (Br) 596, 689
Glennon (Am) 88, 96
Glenten (Da) 541, 472
Glicine (It) 468, 698
Glimt (No) 550, 487
Globus (Ru) 1194, 835
Glomma (No) 468, 698
Glover (Am) 279, 179
Glucksburg (Ge) 1131, 847
Glycine (Fr) 468, 698
Gneisenau (Ge) 463, 255
Gnevnyi (Ru) 633, 88
Gnist (No) 550, 487
Godavari (In) 116, 253
Godetia (Be) 387, 778
Golcuk (Tu) 1145, 1180
Gold Ranger (Br) 1272, 1191
Goldeneye (Br) 1017, 798
Goldsborough (Am) 87, 80
Gomati (In) 116, 253
Good Hope (SA) 476, 295
Goodrich (Am) 190, 97
Gor (No) 67, 151

Gordy class (RC) 197, 248
Gordyi (Ru) 633, 88
Gorgona (Co) 960, 781
Gorizont (Ru) 1194, 835
Goss (Am) 164a, 274
Gota Lejon (Sw) 59, 55
Gottingen (Ge) 378, 684
Graciosa (Po) 507, 682
Graemsay (Br) 878, 1098
Graham County (Am) 273, 618
Grampus (Am) 897
Grampus (Br) 905
Granby (Ca) 529, 282A
Granchio (It) 688, 720
Grand Canyon (Am) 849, 1043
Grand Rapids (Am) 78, 413
Grant County (Am) 273, 618
Granville S. Hall (Am) 1124, 1051
Grapple (Am) 993, 1301
Grasp (Am) 993, 1301
Gray (Am) 280, 181
Grayback (Am) 896
Grayling (Am) 876
Grayson (Am) 160, 141
Great Sitkin (Am) 913, 1056
Green Bay (Am) 78, 413
Green Rover (Br) 1271
Greenfish (Am) 899
Greenlet (Am) 1015, 1285
Greenling (Am) 877
Greenville Victory (Am) 906, 1048
Gregorio Luperon (Do) 264, 307
Greif (Ge) 546, 474
Gremyashchyi (Ru) 633, 88
Grenadier (Am) 897
Grenville (Br) 734, 200
Gresham (Am) 479, 316
Grey Rover (Br) 1271, 1188
Gribb (No) 555, 513
Gribben (Da) 541, 472
Gridley (Am) 642, 74
Griffin (Am) 1094, 1045
Grillon (Fr) 1078, 800
Grim (Sw) 679, 670
Grimmen (EG) 321, 643
Grinder (Br) 951, 1325
Gripen (Sw) 929
Gripor (Br) 951, 1325
Grisslan (Sw) 943
Grom (Ph) 103, 93
Grom (Ru) 645, 83
Groningen (Du) 284, 68
Gronsund (Da) 468, 698
Growler (Am) 896
Grozny (Ph) 449, 387
Grozny (Ru) 645, 83
Gru (It) 406, 345
Gryf (Ph) 865, 775
Guacolda (Ch) 559, 527
Grumete Bolados (Ch) 323, 656
Grumete Diaz (Ch) 323, 656
Grumete Tellez (Ch) 323, 656
Guadalcanal (Am) 10, 14
Guadalhorce (Sp) 482, 371
Guadalupe (Am) 1176, 1136
Guam (Am) 10, 14
Guanjuato (Me) 259, 332
Guardfish (Am) 877
Guardiamarina Zicari (Ar) 1005, 1102
Guardiaro (Sp) 482, 371
Guayaquil (Ec) 455, 423
Guayas (Ec) 262, 307

Jana (Ru) 804, 809
Janssen (Am) 234, 269
Jarvis (Am) 606, 211
Jasmin (Fr) 330, 720
Jasmine (Mg) 511, 147
Jason (Am) 824, 733
Jastrab (Ph) 443, 306
Jaureguiberry (Fr) 187, 109
Javier Quiroga (Sp) 411, 409
Jeanne D'Arc (Fr) 28. 32
Jeffers (Am) 154, 138
Jennings County (Am) 133, 635
Jerai (My) 596, 689
Jerome County (Am) 133, 635
Jerong (My) 329, 722
Jessore (Pk) 571, 485
Jo (No) 555, 513
Johann L. Kruger (Eg) 1254, 1342
Johan Mansson (Sw) 1065, 840
Johanna Van Der Merwe (SA) 907
Johannesburg (SA) 595, 690
John A. Bole (Am) 144, 100
John A. Macdonald (Ca) 900, 996
John Adams (Am) 871
John C. Butler (Am) 164A, 274
John C. Calhoun (Am) 871
John Cabot (Ca) 806, 811
John F. Kennedy (Am) 26, 26
John Hood (Am) 150, 106
John King, 87, 80
John L. Williamson (Am) 164A, 274
John Marshall (Am) 870
John Paul Jones (Am) 105, 59
John R. Craig (Am) 88, 96
John R. Perry (Am) 66, 77
John R. Pierce (Am) 155, 104
John S. McCain (Am) 291, 58
John W. Thomason (Am) 144, 100
John W. Weeks (Am) 155, 104
John Willis (Am) 220, 277
Johnnie Hutchins (Am) 164A, 274
Johnston (Am) 88, 96
Jonas Ingram (Am) 186, 99
Jonquille (Fr) 330, 720
Jorge Juan (Sp) 143, 105
Jose Marti (Cu) 241, 307
Josef Romer (EG) 610, 515
Joseph E. Connolly (Am) 164A, 274
Joseph Hewes (Am) 280, 181
Joseph K. Taussig (Am) 220, 277
Joseph P. Kennedy Jr. (Am) 88, 96
Joseph Strauss (Am) 87, 80
Josephus Daniels (Am) 629, 73
Josiah Willard Gibbs (Am) 736, 315
Jouett (Am) 629, 73
Joumouria (Tn) 565, 539
Joyce (Am) 523, 278
Juan Alejandro Acosta (Do) 75
Juan B. Azopardo (Ar) 474, 309
Juan Bautista Cambiaso (Do) 75, 339
Juan Bautista Maggiolo (Do) 75, 339
Juan De La Cosa (Sp) 1011, 1023
Juan Lucio (Co) 44, 572
Jucar (Sp) 382, 701
Juist (Ge) 858, 1299
Julius A. Furer (Am) 281, 178
Jumna (In) 625, 306
Juneau (Am) 119, 607
Juniper (Am) 942, 1080
Juno (Br) 97, 191
Junon (Fr) 907
Jupiter (Br) 97, 191

Jupiter (Gr) 386, 400
Jupiter (Po) 310, 526
Jupiter (Sp) 244, 325
Jurua (Bz) 732, 700
Juruena (Bz) 732, 700
Ka Duk (Ko) 680, 660
Kaakkuri (Fi) 712, 453
Kaapstad (SA) 595 690
Kaarhu (Fi) 1085, 982
Kadmath (In) 288, 390
Kaduna (Ng) 385, 440
Kae Bong (Ko) 133, 635
Kahawai (NZ) 669, 565
Kahnamuie (Ir) 408, 217
Kaio (Ja) 1023, 1085
Kaiyo (Ja) 700, 1128
Kakinda (In) 776, 689
Kala 1 (Fi) 618, 657
Kala 2 (Fi) 618, 657
Kala 3 (Fi) 618, 657
Kala 4 (Fi) 618, 657
Kala 5 (Fi) 618, 657
Kala 6 (Fi) 618, 657
Kalahitam (Ia) 353, 411
Kaldiray (Tu) 983, 794
Kalmar (Sw) 70, 131
Kalmia (Am) 855, 1308
Kalvari (In) 900
Kalymnos (Gr) 469, 696
Kamehameha (Am) 871
Kamome (Ja) 351, 394
Kamorta (In) 288, 390
Kamui (Ja) 743, 1126
Kan Tang (RC) 429, 397
Kanawa (Ja) 594, 714
Kandheri (In) 900
Kang Shan (Cs) 253, 281
Kang Won (RC) 167, 266
Kanin Class (Ru) 223, 86
Kanjar (In) 900
Kankakee (Am) 1178, 1144
Kansas City (Am) 1320, 1278
Kantang (Th) 393, 145
Kapitan Belousov (Ru) 1084, 976
Kapitan Melechov (Ru) 1084, 976
Kapitan Voronin (Ru) 1084, 976
Karanj (In) 900
Karato (Ja) 594, 714
Karatsu (Ja) 494, 1113
Karho (Fi) 1085, 982
Kari (Ja) 300, 469
Karjala (Fi) 591, 465
Karkas (Ir) 382, 701
Karl Liebknecht (EG) 162, 259
Karl Marx (EG) 162, 259
Karl Marx-Stadt (EG) 229, 372
Karl Meseberger (EG) 335, 494
Karlskrona (Sw) 69, 132
Karlso (Sw) 467, 703
Karlsruhe (Ge) 213, 175
Karpfen (Ge) 318, 666
Kartal (Tu) 546, 474
Karteria (Gr) 469, 696
Karwar (In) 776, 689
Kasado (Ja) 594, 714
Kasasagi (Ja) 500, 395
Kashin class (Ru) 278, 84
Kasirga (Tu) 546, 474
Kastor (Gr) 555, 513
Kaszub (Ph) 954
Katchall (In) 288, 390
Katori (Ja) 218, 223

Katsura (Ja) 594, 714
Katula (Ia) 449, 387
Kaura (No) 941
Kaveri (In) 254, 304
Kavrati (In) 288, 390
Kawishiwi (Am) 1129, 1134
Kawkab (Abu Dhabi) 419, 446
Kaya (Ja) 263, 308
Kazbek class (Ru) 1152, 1164
Kearney (Am) 160, 141
Kearsarge (Am) 2, 24
Kedah class (My) 420, 424
Kedleston (Br) 596, 689
Keihassalmi (Fi) 231, 373
Keith (Am) 234, 269
Kelalang (Ia) 353, 411
Kelewang (My) 420, 424
Kellar (Am) 1113, 829/830
Kellington (Br) 376/596, 689
Kemper County (Am) 133, 635
Kendall C. Campbell (Am) 164A. 274
Kennebec (Am) 1178, 1144
Kenneth D. Bailey (Am) 190, 97
Kenneth M. Willett (Am) 164A, 274
Kent (Br) 188, 62
Keo Ngua (VN) 455, 428
Keppel (Br) 752, 205
Keppler (Am) 68, 96
Kerambit (My) 420, 424
Kerkyra (Gr) 469, 696
Kersaint (Fr) 636, 111
Keta (Gh) 407, 417
Key (Am) 164A 274
Keya (Ja) 263, 308
Keyaki (Ja) 246, 308
Keyvan (Ir) 724, 432
Keywadin (Am) 855, 1308
Khaderi (In) 900
Khaibar (Pk) 207, 235
Khariton Laptev (Ru) 1012, 827
Khariton Laptev (Ru) (Icebreaker) 1042,
975
Khobi (Ru) 1201, 1196
Khukri (In) 752, 205
Ki Duk (Ko) 680, 660
Ki Rin (Ko) 680, 660
Kiama (NZ) 527, 351
Kiarny (Am) 160, 141
Kichli (Gr) 382, 701
Kidd (Am) 150, 106
Kien Vang (VN) 455, 428
Kiev (Ru) 807, 974
Kiilsa (Fi) 712, 453
Kiji (Ja) 351, 394
Kikuchi (Ja) 356, 1121
Kikuzuki (Ja) 638, 71
Kilauea (Am) 876, 745
Kildin class (Ru) 180, 87
Kilic Ali Pasa (Tu) 192, 237
Killiecrankie (Br) 596, 689
Kilmorey (Br) 596, 689
Kilton (In) 288, 390
Kim Chon (Ko) 469, 696
Kim Hae (Ko) 1306, 1255
Kim Po (Ko) 469, 696
Kim Qui (VN) 455, 428
Kimberley (SA) 595, 690
Kimbla (Au) 940, 804
Kinabalu (My) 596, 689
Kinbrace (Br) 875, 800B
King (Am) 290, 78
King (Ar) 235, 330

King Bird (Am) 468, 698
Kingarth (Br) 875, 800B
Kingman (Am) 276, 665
Kingsford (Br) 1260, 800C
Kingsport (Am) 1100, 1050
Kinloss (Br) 1260, 800C
Kinn (No) 941
Kinterbury (Br) 1308, 1227
Kiowa (Am) 851, 1287
Kirkliston (Br) 376/595, 690
Kirkpatrick (Am) 523, 278
Kirov (Ru) 255, 54
Kirpan (In) 752, 205
Kirwin (Am) 260, 282
Kishwaukee (Am) 1325, 1283
Kiso (Ja) 356, 1121
Kissa (Gr) 382, 701
Kistna (In) 254, 304
Kitakami (Ja) 298, 264
Kitakami (Ja) (M.S.A.) 493, 1120
Kittiwake (Am) 1015, 1285
Kitty Hawk (Am) 26, 26
Kiyozuki (Ja) 784, 554
Kjapp (No) 758, 521
Kjekk (No) 550, 487
Klamath (Am) 251, 354
Klondike (Am) 1101, 1042
Klongyai (Th) 392, 145
Knapp (Am) 150, 106
Knokke (Be) 468, 698
Knorr (Am) 1112, 841
Knox (Am) 280, 181
Knudson (Am) 260, 282
Knurr (No) 555, 513
Ko Hung (Ko) 382, 701
Kobben (No) 941
Koblenz (Ge) 378, 684
Kochang (Ko) 469, 696
Kochisar (Tu) 726, 408
Koelsch (Am) 286, 177
Koje (Ko) 396, 148
Kojima (Ja) 492, 1110
Kojin (Ko) 453, 360
Koka (Am) 855, 1308
Koksijde (Be) 468, 698
Kola (Ru) (Oiler) 1268, 1189
Kola (Ru) 191, 92
Köln (Ge) 213, 175
Kolum (Th) 323, 656
Komar class (Ru) 309, 495
Komenda (Gh) 385, 440
Kompas (Ph) 413, 393
Kompas (Ru) 1194, 835
Komsomolets (Ru) 184, 53
Konda (Ru) 1274, 1195
Kondor (Ge) 546, 474
Kondor (Ph) 949
Konkan (In) 533, 347
Konstanz (Ge) 378, 684
Kootenay (Ca) 525, 228
Koozu (Ja) 594, 714
Korawakka (Ce) 671, 566
Kormoran (Ge) 546, 474
Kormoran (Ph) 443, 386
Kortrijk (Be) 330, 720
Kosa Minin (Ru) 183, 52
Koshiki (Ja) 594, 714
Koshiki (Ja) (M.S.A.) 497, 1122
Koskelo (Fi) 694, 536
Kosmonaut Vladimir Komarov (Ru) 1317, 866
Kotlin class (Ru) 139/40, 90/91

Kotlin-Sam (Ru) 141, 89
Kotor (Ys) 170, 240
Koura (NZ) 669, 565
Kozu (Ja) 489, 1116
Krake class (EG) 229, 372
Krakowiak (Ph) 954
Kraljavica class (Ys) 566, 480B
Kram (Th) 680, 659
Kranich (EG) 574, 468
Kranich (Ge) 546, 474
Krapu (Ia) 556, 480B
Krassin (Ru) 1060, 977
Krebs (Ge) 386, 400
Kresta (Ru) 630, 173
Kresta II class (Ru) 630, 174
Kretchmer (Am) 539, 278
Kris class (My) 420, 424
Krishna (Am) 1200, 640
Krogulec (Ph) 443, 386
Krokodil (Ge) 680, 659
Kromantse (Gh) 407, 417
Kronstadt (Ru) (A) (Bu) (Cu) (RC) (Rm) 449, 387
Krupny class (Ru) 633, 88
K'un Ming (RC) 162, 259
Ku Hoa (VN) 439, 681
Ku Moon (Ko) 680, 660
Ku Ryong (Ko) 1293, 1203
Kuai Chi (Cs) 1150, 1158
Kuban (Ru) 1068, 769
Kudako (Ja) 594, 714
Kuei Lin (RC) 162, 259
Kuei Yang (RC) 162, 259
Kuikka (Fi) 694, 536
Kujawiak (Ph) 954
Kukui (Am) 1266, 1218
Kula Gulf (Am) 16, 22
Kum Chong San (Ko) 411, 409
Kum Hwa (Ko) 469, 696
Kum Kok (Ko) 382, 701
Kum San (Ko) 382, 701
Kuma (Ja) 356, 1121
Kumano (Ja) 356, 1121
Kumataka (Ja) 500, 395
Kun Yang (Cs) 143, 105
Kung Kiang (Cs) 585, 405
Kunimi (Ja) 743, 1126
Kunna (No) 941
Kuns San (Ko) 1306, 1255
Kuovi (Fi) 712, 453
Kuparu (NZ) 669, 565
Kurama (Ja) 743, 1126
Kurki (Fi) 712, 453
Kurokami (Ja) 489, 1116
Kurtaran (Tu) 853, 1288
Kusakaki (Ja) 497, 1122
Kusu (Ja) 246, 308
Kut (Th) 680, 659
Kuthar (In) 752, 205
Kuzuryu (Ja) 356, 1121
Kvikk (No) 758, 521
Kvina (No) 468, 698
Kwang Che (Ko) 469, 696
Kwang Kuo (RC) 619, 455
Kya (No) 941
Kykonos (Gr) 555, 513
Kynda class (Ru) 645, 83
Kyne (Am) 167, 266
Kyonami (Ja) 784, 554
Kyong Buk (Ko) 253, 281
Kyong Ki (Ko) 167, 266
Kyong Nam (Ko) 253, 281

L class tankers (Ru) 1310, 1187
L 51 (Sw) 685, 658
L 52 (Sw) 685, 658
L 53 (Sw) 685, 658
L 54 (Sw) 685, 658
L 55 (Sw) 685, 658
LCM 700-LCM 711 (Br) 683, 652
LCM 3507 (Br) 683, 652
LCM 3508 (Br) 683, 652
LCU 539 (Am) 323, 656
LCU 588 (Am) 523, 656
LCU 599 (Am) 323, 656
LCU 608 (Am) 323, 656
LCU 654 (Am) 323, 656
LCU 660 (Am) 323, 656
LCU 666 (Am) 323, 656
LCU 667 (Am) 323, 656
LCU 674 (Am) 323, 656
LCU 763 (Gr) 323, 656
LCU 766 (Gr) 323 656
LCU 768 (Am) 323, 656
LCU 780 (Am) 323, 656
LCU 803 (Am) 323, 656
LCU 827 (Gr) 323, 656
LCU 852 (Gr) 323, 656
LCU 871 (Am) 323, 656
LCU 893 (Am) 323, 656
LCU 971 (Gr) 323, 656
LCU 1045 (Am) 323, 656
LCU 1124 (Am) 323, 656
LCU 1229 (Gr) 323, 656
LCU 1241 (Am) 323, 656
LCU 1348 (Am) 323, 656
LCU 1379 (Gr) 323, 656
LCU 1382 (Gr) 323, 656
LCU 1387 (Am) 323, 656
LCU 1430 (Am) 323, 656
LCU 1451 (Am) 323, 656
LCU 1459 (Am) 323, 656
LCU 1462 (Am) 323, 656
LCU 1466 (Am) 682, 654
LCU 1467 (Am) 682, 654
LCU 1468 (Am) 682, 654
LCU 1469 (Am) 682, 654
LCU 1470 (Am) 682, 654
LCU 1471 (Am) 682, 654
LCU 1472 (Am) 682, 654
LCU 1473 (Am) 682, 654
LCU 1475 (Am) 682, 654
LCU 1476 (Am) 682, 654
LCU 1477 (Am) 682. 654
LCU 1481 (Am) 682, 654
LCU 1482 (Am) 682, 654
LCU 1483 (Am) 682, 654
LCU 1484 (Am) 682, 654
LCK 1485 (Am) 682, 654
LCU 1486 (Am) 682, 654
LCU 1487 (Am) 682, 654
LCU 1488 (Am) 682, 654
LCU 1489 (Am) 682, 654
LCU 1490 (Am) 682, 654
LCU 1491 (Am) 682, 654
LCU 1492 (Am) 682, 654
LCU 1493 (Am) 682, 654
LCU 1494 (Am) 682, 654
LCU 1495 (Am) 682, 654
LCU 1497 (Am) 682, 654
LCU 1498 (Am) 682, 654
LCU 1499 (Am) 682, 654
LCU 1500 (Am) 682, 654
LCU 1525 (Am) 682, 654
LCU 1536 (Am) 682, 654

LCU 1537 (Am) 682, 654
LCU 1539 (Am) 682, 654
LCU 1547 (Am) 682, 654
LCU 1548 (Am) 682, 654
LCU 1559 (Am) 682, 654
LCU 1576 (Am) 682, 654
LCU 1582 (Am) 682, 654
LCU 1596 (Cs) 682, 654
LCU 1597 (Cs) 682, 654
LCU 1598 (Cs) 682, 654
LCU 1600 (Cs) 682, 654
LCU 1601 (Cs) 682, 654
LCU 1608 (Am) 682, 654
LCU 1609 (Am) 682, 654
LCU 1610 (Am) 674, 667
LCU 1611 (Am) 674, 667
LCU 1612 (Am) 674, 667
LCU 1613 (Am) 674, 667
LCU 1614 (Am) 674, 667
LCU 1615 (Am) 674, 667
LCU 1616 (Am) 674, 667
LCU 1617 (Am) 674, 667
LCU 1618 (Am) 674, 667
LCU 1619 (Am) 674, 667
LCU 1620 (Am) 674, 667
LCU 1621 (Am) 674, 667
LCU 1622 (Am) 674, 667
LCU 1623 (Am) 674, 667
LCU 1624 (Am) 674, 667
LCU 1625 (Am) 681, 653
LCU 1626 (Bm) 681, 1626
LCU 1627 (Am) 674, 667
LCU 1628 (Am) 674, 667
LCU 1629 (Am) 674, 667
LCU 1630 (Am) 674, 667
LCU 1631 (Am) 674, 667
LCU 1632 (Am) 674, 667
LCU 1633 (Am) 674, 667
LCU 1634 (Am) 674, 667
LCU 1635 (Am) 674, 667
LCU 1636 (Am) 674, 667
LCU 2001 (Td) 682, 654
LCU 2002 (Td) 682, 654
LCU 2003 (Td) 682, 654
LCU 2004 (Td) 682, 654
LCU 2005 (Td) 682, 654
LCU 2006 (Td) 682, 654
LS 9 (Tu) 654, 439
LS 10 (Tu) 654, 439
LS 11 (Tu) 654, 439
LS 12 (Tu) 654, 439
LSM 1 (Sp) 680, 659
LSM 2 (Sp) 680, 659
LSM 3 (Sp) 680, 659
LSM 3001 (Ja) 680 659
LSMR 1 (In) 651, 627
LSMR 2 (In) 651, 627
LSP 1-6 (Ec) 697, 445
LT 30 (Sp) 660, 476
LT 31 (Sp) 660, 476
LT 32 (Sp) 660, 474
L. Y. Spear (Am) 1321, 861
L'Adroit (Fr) 410, 407
L'Agenais (Fr) 510/634, 261
L'Agile (Fr) 434, 406
L'Alerte (Fr) 410, 407
L'Alsacien (Fr) 509, 262
L'Ardent (Fr) 410, 407
L'Attentif (Fr) 410, 407
L'Effronte (Fr) 410, 407
L'Enjoue (Fr) 410, 407
L'Esperance (Fr) 1255, 1337

L'Etourdi (Fr) 410, 407
L'Intrepide (Fr) 410, 407
L'Opiniatre (Fr) 434, 406
La Argentina (Fr) 137, 48
La Bayonnaise (Fr) 777, 694
La Bourdonnais (Fr) 187, 109
La Charente (Fr) 1159, 1154
La Combattante (Fr) 339, 489
La Crete a Pierrot (Ha) 724, 432
La Dieppoise (Fr) 777, 694
La Dunkerquoise (Fr) 777, 694
La Galissonniere (Fr) 151, 112
La Lorientaise (Fr) 777, 694
La Malouine (Fr) 777, 694
La Paimpolaise (Fr) 777, 694
La Pataia (Ar) 1002, 1010
La Prade (Am) 164A, 274
La Recherche (Fr) 1233, 856
La Salle (Am) 96, 609
La Saone (Fr) 1155, 1138
La Seine (Fr) 1155, 1138
La Union (Pi) 576, 470
La Vallette (Am) 150, 106
Laaland (Da) 1298, 461
Labo class (EG) 322, 648
Labrador (Br) 922, 1326
Labrador (Ca) 886, 1000
Lac Chambon (Fr) 1291, 1206
Lac Tchad (Fr) 1291, 1206
Lac Tonle-Sap (Fr) 1291, 1206
Lachlan (NZ) 738, 283
Lachs (Le) 318, 666
Lacomble (Du) 718, 707
Ladava (Au) 485, 422
Ladjura (Ia) 449, 387
Ladya (Th) 382, 701
Lae (Au) 485, 422
Lafayette (Am) 871
Laffey (Am) 144, 100
Lagoa (Po) 596, 689
Laguna (Pi) 301, 486A
Lahn (Ge) 388, 321
Lajes (Po) 468, 698
Lake Lanao (Pi) 1292, 1202
Lake Naujan (Pi) 1292, 1202
Laks (No) 555, 513
Laleston (Br) 776, 689
Lam Ciane (VN) 680, 659
Lama (Ru) 1201, 854
Lamar (Am) 427, 358
Lamoille River (Am) 219, 646
Lamons (Am) 167, 266
Lampo (It) 367, 399
Lanciere (It) 149, 103/107
Lane (Am) 280, 181
Langeland (Da) 1205, 460
Langeoog (Ge) 858, 1299
Laning (Am) 260, 282
Lansing (Am) 523, 278
Lapai (Ia) 449, 387
Lapon (Am) 876
Larak (Ir) 320, 665
Laramie River (Am) 219, 646
Larice (It) 468, 698
Laroche (Br) 468, 698
Larrea (Pv) 520, 421
Las Aves (Ve) 944, 1026
Las Villas (Cu) 582, 480A
Lasham (Br) 329, 722
Lassen (Am) 914, 1060
Laub (Am) 159, 140
Lauis Ledge (Pi) 1246, 1256

Laurel (Am) 883, 1087
Laurier (Fr) 468, 698
Lautaro (Ch) 855, 1308
Lawrence (Am) 87, 80
Lawrence C. Taylor (Am) 164A, 274
Lans (Am) 150, 106
Laxen (Da) 542, 473
Laxen (Sw) 947
Layburn (Br) 1018, 796
Laymoor (Br) 1018, 796
Laymore (Ca) 1230, 1258
Lazar Kaganovich (Ru) 964, 961
Le Basque (Fr) 510, 260
Le Bearnais (Fr) 510/634, 261
Le Bordelais (Fr) 536, 263
Le Boulonnais (Fr) 536, 263
Le Bourguignon (Fr) 510, 260
Le Brestois (Fr) 536, 263
Le Breton (Fr) 510/634, 261
Le Champenois (Fr) 510, 260
Le Corse (Fr) 536, 263
Le Foudroyant (Fr) 873
Le Fougueux (Fr) 434, 406
Le Fringant (Fr) 410, 407
Le Gascon (Fr) 510, 260
Le Hardi (Fr) 410, 407
Le Lorrain (Fr) 510, 260
Le Normand (Fr) 510/635, 260
Le Picard (Fr) 510, 260
Le Provencal (Fr) 509, 262
Le Ray Wilson (Am) 164A, 274
Le Redoubtable (Fr) 873
Le Savoyard (Fr) 510, 260
Le Terrible (Fr) 873
Le Van Binh (VN) 577, 662
Le Vendeen (Fr) 509, 262
Le Vigilant (Iv) 423, 427
Leader (Am) 503, 678
Leahy (Am) 642, 74
Leander (Br) 91, 191
Leary (Am) 88/89, 96
Lech (Ge) 388, 321
Ledane (My) 596, 689
Ledokol (Ru) 1042, 975
Legazpi (Sp) 166, 328
Leipzig (EG) 229, 372
Leland E. Thomas (Am) 164A, 274
Lemadang (Ia) 556, 480B
Lembine (My) 420, 424
Lengeh (Ir) 1273, 1199
Lenin (Ru) 924, 969
Leninakan (Ru) 1310, 1187
Leningrad (Ru) 14, 33
Leningrad (Ru) (Icebreaker) 807, 974
Leninsky Komsomol (Ru) 914
Lentra class (Ru) 1252, 1340
Leon (Gr) 265, 267
Leonard F. Mason (Am) 88, 96
Leonardo da Vinci (It) 926
Leoncio Prado (Ca) 501, 457
Leopard (Br) 124, 189
Lepard (Ce) 546, 474
Lepanto (Sp) 150, 106
Lerez (Sp) 538, 370
Lesbos (Gr) 133, 635
Leslie L. B. Knox (Am) 164A, 274
Lester (Am) 220, 277
Leticia (Co) 579, 600
Leverton (Br) 596, 689
Leviathan (Is) 912
Levy (Am) 167, 266
Lewis & Clark (Am) 871

Missouri (Am) 765, 34
Mitilo (It) 688, 720
Mitscher (Am) 291, 58
Miura (Ja) 706, 1109
Miyake (Ja) 488, 1119
Mizar (Am) 1307, 1212
Mizutori (Ja) 500, 395
Mo Ling (Cs) 396, 148
Moale (Am) 144, 100
Mobile (Am) 833, 1036
Mocenigo (It) 911
Mochizuki (Ja) 638, 71
Mochizuki (Ja) (M.S.A.) 784, 554
Mock Po (Ko) 1306, 1255
Moctobi (Am) 851, 1287
Mode (Sw) 86, 258
Modoc (Am) 1052, 1308
Moen (Da) 51, 776
Mogami (Ja) 297, 264
Mogami (Ja) (M.S.A.) 356, 1121
Mogano (It) 468, 498
Mohawk (Br) 61, 129
Molala (Am) 868, 1287
Molders (Ge) 53, 82
Molosso (It) 236, 661
Moma class (Ru) 793, 834
Momare (Ia) 449, 387
Momin (Pk) 382, 701
Monkton (Br) 596, 689
Monmouth County (Am) 133, 635
Montante (Po) 705, 623
Montcalm (Ca) 1222, 1270
Monterey (Am) 7, 17
Montevideo (Ur) 340, 310
Monticello (Am) 57, 610
Montmorency (Ca) 1236, 1271
Montrose (Br) 595, 690
Moore (Am) 234, 369
Moorhen (Br) 1259, 800A
Moorland (Br) 1259, 800A
Moorpout (Br) 1259, 800A
Moorsman (Br) 1259, 800A
Mordogan (Tu) 268, 783
Moresby (Au) 1327, 822
Morgenthau (Am) 606, 211
Mornar (Ys) 233, 389
Morris (Am) 464, 1091
Mors (Ph) 442, 676
Morse (Fr) 898
Morton (Am) 186, 99
Morvan (Fr) 929, 1009
Mosel (Ge) 222, 320
Moselle (Fr) 1096, 1004
Moshal (Pk) 382, 701
Moskva (Ru) 14, 33
Moskva (Ru) (Icebreaker) 807, 974
Mosley (Am) 234, 369
Mosospelea (Am) 851, 1287
Mosselbai (SA) 595, 690
Mosvig (Da) 717/718, 706
Mount Hood (Am) 876, 745
Mount Katmai (Am) 913, 1056
Mount McKinley (Am) 836, 740
Mount Samat (Pi) 349, 357
Mount Vernon (Am) 609
Mount Whitney (Am) 13, 31
Mountrail (Am) 910, 1046
Mowe (EG) 574, 468
Mubarak (Pk) 382, 701
Muguet (Fr) 468, 698
Muhafiz (Pk) 382, 701
Mujahid (Pk) 382, 701

Mukhtar (Pk) 382, 701
Mul II (Sw) 962, 782
Mul 12 (Sw) 797, 764
Mul 13 (Sw) 797, 764
Mul 14 (Sw) 797, 764
Mul 15 (Sw) 797, 764
Mul 16 (Sw) 797, 764
Mul 17 (Sw) 797, 764
Mul 18 (Sw) 797, 764
Mul 19 (Sw) 797, 764
Muliphen (Am) 838, 1057
Mullany (Am) 143, 105
Mullinix (Am) 186, 98
Multatuli (Ia) 871, 1062
Munin (Sw) 86, 258
Munro (Am) 606, 211
Munsif (Pk) 382, 701
Munsterland (Ge) 1184, 1140
Murane (Ge) 318, 666
Murasame (Ja) 257, 119
Murature (Ar) 235, 330
Murefte (Tu) 268, 783
Murman (Ru) 989, 973
Murmansk (Ru) 183, 52
Murmansk (Ru) (Icebreaker) 807, 974
Muroto (Ja) 850, 1124
Murphy (Am) 159, 140
Murray (Br) 752, 205
Murshed (Ku) 714, 420
Murtaya (Fi) 1085, 982
Muskingum (Am) 1316, 1219
Mutsuki (Ja) 665, 550
Mutsure (Ja) 594, 714
Myles C. Fox (Am) 88/89, 96
Myo Hyang San (Ko) 411, 409
Myong Ryang (Ko) 453, 360
Myosotis (Fr) 330, 720
Mysore (In) 142, 47
Mytho (Fr) 507, 682

N class (Ru) 914
N. B. McLean (Ca) 973, 967
NR-1 (Am) 883
Naaldwiyk (Du) 597, 693
Naarden (Au) 597, 693
Nafkratoussa (Gr) 707, 611
Nagakyay (Bm) 417, 593
Nagara (Ja) 493, 1120
Nagatsuki (Ja) 784, 71
Naghdi (Ir) 408, 217
Naiad (Br) 97, 191
Najade (Ge) 652, 374
Najaden (Da) 722
Naka (Th) 577, 662
Naktong (Ko) 241, 307
Nalon (Sp) 382, 701
Nam Du (VN) 455, 428
Nam Yang (Ko) 382, 701
Namdo (Sw) 467, 703
Nan Chang (RC) 108, 380
ex Nan Chang (RC) 531, 588
Nan Yang (Cs) 159, 140
Nanggala (Ia) 918
Nantahala (Am) 1176, 1136
Napo (Pv) 243, 605
Naporistyi (Ru) 139/140, 90/91
Narhvalen (Da) 939
Narval (Fr) 898, 928
Narvik (Fr) 504, 680
Narvik (No) 405, 216
Narwhal (Am) 876
Narwhal (Br) 905

Nasami (Ja) 1304, 1254
Nashville (Am) 119, 607
Nasr (Eg) 416, 350
Nastoychivyi (Ru) 139/140, 90/91
Nasty type (No, Gr) 555/756, 507/513
Natal (SA) 737, 296
Nathan Hale (Am) 871
Nathanael Greene (Am) 781
Natori (Ja) 494, 1113
Natsugumo (Ja) 785, 559
Natsushio (Ha) 934
Natsuzuki (Ja) 784, 554
Nautilus (Am) 891
Nautilus (Ge) 380, 704
Nautilus (SA) 385, 440
Nautilus (Sp) 338, 363
Navak (Ir) 780, 530
Navarinon (Gr) 150, 106
Navarro (Am) 910, 1046
Navasota (Am) 1139, 1135
Navia (Sp) 482, 371
Navmachos (Gr) 749, 337
Navarat (Bm) 417, 593
Ndovu (Ke) 521, 425
Neches (Am) 1178, 1144
Neckar (Ge) 222, 320
Negros Occidental (Pi) 452, 359
Neosho (Am) 1129, 1134
Neptun (Da) 722
Neptun (Ge) 386, 400
Neptun class (Ru) 937, 805
Neptune (Am) 992, 806
Neptuno (Sp) 242, 324
Neretva (Ys) 945
Nereus (Am) 828, 731
Nervion (Sp) 538, 370
Nerz (Ge) 546, 474
Nespelen (Am) 1325, 1283
Neung Ra (Ko) 680, 660
Neunzer (Am) 234, 269
Neuquen (Ar) 595, 690
Neaustrashimyi (Ru) 55, 85
New (Am) 88, 96
New Jersey (Am) 765, 34
New London County (Am) 132, 620
New Orleans (Am) 10, 14
Newman K. Perry (Am) 88, 96
Newport (Am) 965, 606
Newport News (Am) 771, 163
Ngoc Hoi (VN) 453, 360
Nguyen Duc Bong (VN) 577, 662
Nguyen Ngoc Long (VN) 577, 662
Nhong Sarhai (Th) 869, 1108
Nhut Tao (VN) 439, 681
Niagara Falls (Am) 867, 1038
Nields (Am) 159, 140
Nienburg (Ge) 1131, 847
Nieugiety (Ph) 449, 387
Nieustrashimyi (Ru) 55, 85
Nieuwport (Be) 468, 698
Nigeria (Ng) 176, 319
Niizuki (Ja) 784, 554
Niki (Gr) 161, 137
Nikolai Stolbov (Ru) 822, 749
Nikolai Zubov (Ru) 1012, 827
Nilgiri (In) 97, 191
Nimble (Am) 503, 678
Nimble (Br) 1026, 1320
Ninh Giang (VN) 680, 659
Niobe (Ge) 327, 717
Nipigon (Ca) 342, 229
Nipmuc (Am) 851, 1287

Phenix (Fr) 597, 693
Phetra (Th) 323, 656
Philippine Sea (Am) 2, 24
Phoebe (Am) 468, 698
Phoebe (Br) 97, 191
Phoenix (Am) 906, 1048
Phosamton (Th) 274A/375, 337
Phu Du (VN) 455, 428
Piaui (Bz) 150, 106
Pickaway (Am) 910, 1046
Pickerel (Am) 899
Picking (Am) 143, 105
Pico (Po) 507, 682
Pictor (Am) 911, 1054
Picuda (Am) 897
Piedmont (Am) 825, 730
Piedrabeuna (Ar) 85, 331
Pietermaritzburg (SA) 375, 337
Pietro Calvi (It) 936
Pietro Cavezzale (It) 249, 314
Pietro de Cristofaro (It) 89, 230
Pigassos (Gr) 555, 513
Pigeon (Am) 866, 787
Pil (No) 550, 487
Piloto Pardo (Ch) 794, 760
Pin Klao (Th) 167, 266
Pinar del Rio (Cu) 582, 480A
Pine Island (Am) 1091, 742
Ping Ching (Cs) 396, 148
Pinguin (Ge) 546, 174
Pinios (Gr) 272, 624
Pinna (It) 688, 720
Pinnacle (Am) 503, 678
Pino (It) 468, 698
Pintado (Am) 876
Pintail (Br) 1017, 798
Pioneer (Am) 394, 148
Pioneer Valley (Am) 1177, 1160
Pionier (EG) 41, 541
Pioppo (It) 468, 698
Piraju (Bz) 698, 412
Piranha (Bz) 698, 412
Piraque (Bz) 698, 412
Piri Reis (Tu) 923
Pirttisaari (Fi) 1090, 1295
Piscataqua (Am) 1181, 1167/1168
Pitkin County (Am) 133, 635
Pittsburgh (Am) 199  36
Pivoine (Fr) 468, 498
Pivot (Am) 503, 678
Piyale Pasa (Tu) 192, 237
Plainview (Am) 703, 580
Plamannyi (Ru) 139/140, 90/91
Plamyonny (Ru) 633, 88
Planetree (Am) 883, 1087
Platano (It) 468, 698
Platte (Am) 1176, 1136
Pledge (Am) 503, 678
Plejad (Sw) 548, 475
Ploiarkhos Meletopoulous (Gr) 600, 471
Plotarkhis Arslanoglou (Gr) 600, 471
Plotarkhis Chantzikonstandis (Gr) 600, 471
Plotarkhis Maridakis (Gr) 236, 661
Plotarkhis Vlachavas (Gr) 236, 661
Plotze (Ge) 318, 666
Plover (Am) 469, 696
Pluck (Am) 503, 678
Plumas County (Am) 132, 620
Plumleaf (Br) 1173, 1147
Plunger (Am) 877
Pluto (Ge) 386, 400
Pluton (Sp) 1157, 1171

Plymouth (Br) 92, 195
Plymouth Rock (Am) 57, 610
Po (It) 1146, 1182
Po Kiang (Cs) 585, 405
Pocono (Am) 1118, 740
Poel (EG) 1143, 1179
Pogy (Am) 876
Point Arden (Am) 303, 545
Point Arena (Am) 303, 545
Point Baker (Am) 303, 545
Point Banks (Am) 303, 545
Point Barnes (Am) 303, 545
Point Barron (Am) 958, 756
Point Barrow (Am) 303, 545
Point Batan (Am) 303, 545
Point Bannett (Am) 303, 545
Point Bonita (Am) 303, 545
Point Bridge (Am) 303, 545
Point Brower (Am) 303, 545
Point Brown (Am) 303, 545
Point Camden (Am) 303, 545
Point Carrew (Am) 303, 545
Point Caution (Am) 303, 545
Point Charles (Am) 303, 545
Point Chico (Am) 303, 545
Point Clear (Am) 303, 545
Point Comfort (Am) 303, 545
Point Countess (Am) 303, 545
Point Cruz (Am) 16, 22
Point Cypress (Am) 303, 545
Point Defiance (Am) 57, 610
Point Divide (Am) 303, 545
Point Doran (Am) 303, 545
Point Dume (Am) 303, 545
Point Ellis (Am) 303, 545
Point Estero (Am) 303, 545
Point Evans (Am) 303, 545
Point Francis (Am) 303, 545
Point Franklin (Am) 303, 545
Point Gammon (Am) 303, 545
Point Glass (Am) 303, 545
Point Glover (Am) 303, 545
Point Grace (Am) 303, 545
Point Grey (Am) 303, 545
Point Hannon (Am) 303, 545
Point Harris (Am) 303, 545
Point Herron (Am) 303, 545
Point Heyer (Am) 303, 545
Point Highland (Am) 303, 545
Point Hobart (Am) 303, 545
Point Hope (Am) 303, 545
Point Hudson (Am) 303, 545
Point Huron (Am) 303, 545
Point Jackson (Am) 303, 545
Point Jefferson (Am) 303, 545
Point Judith (Am) 303, 545
Point Kennedy (Am) 303, 545
Point Knoll (Am) 303, 545
Point Ledge (Am) 303, 545
Point Lobos (Am) 303, 545
Point Lomas (Am) 303, 545
Point Lookout (Am) 303, 545
Point Martin (Am) 303, 545
Point Mast (Am) 303, 545
Point Munroe (Am) 303, 545
Point Morone (Am) 303, 545
Point Nowell (Am) 303, 545
Point Orient (Am) 303, 545
Point Partridge (Am) 303, 545
Point Richmond (Am) 303, 545
Point Roberts (Am) 303, 545
Point Sal (Am) 303, 545

Point Slocum (Am) 303, 545
Point Spencer (Am) 303, 545
Point Steele (Am) 303, 545
Point Stuart (Am) 303, 545
Point Swift (Am) 303, 545
Point Thatcher (Am) 303, 545
Point Turner (Am) 303, 545
Point Verde (Am) 303, 545
Point Warde (Am) 303, 545
Point Welcome (Am) 303, 545
Point Wells (Am) 303, 545
Point White (Am) 303, 545
Point Whitehorn (Am) 303, 545
Point Winslow (Am) 303, 545
Point Young (Am) 303, 545
Pointer (Br) 922, 1326
Polarfront 1 (No) 1072, 338
Polarfront 11 (No) 1072, 338
Polaris (Sw) 548, 475
Polemistis (Gr) 749
Polimar 1 (Me) 364, 447
Polimar 2 (Me) 364, 447
Polimar 3 (Me) 364, 447
Polipo (It) 688, 720
Polk County (Am) 133, 635
Pollack (Am) 877
Pollux (Fr) 597, 693
Pollux (Ge) 386, 400
Pollux (Po) 307, 525
Pollux (Sw) 548, 475
Polnocny (Ru) (In) (Eg) (Ph) 651, 627
Polnocny II (Ru) 632, 627
Polyarnik (Ru) 1170, 1176
Polyus (Ru) 1120, 815
Pomfret (Am) 897
Pomodon (Am) 897
Ponce (Am) 123, 608
Ponchatoula (Am) 1129, 1134
Ponta Delgada (Po) 468, 698
Pontchartrain (Am) 251, 354
Poole (Am) 234, 269
Poolster (Du) 1128, 846
Pope (Am) 234, 269
Porpoise (Br) 905
Porpora (It) 688, 720
Port Elizabeth (SA) 595, 690
Port Said (Eg) 81, 252
Porte Dauphine (Ca) 1207, 1350
Porte de la Reine (Ca) 1207, 1350
Porte Quebec (Ca) 1207, 1350
Porte St. Jean (Ca) 1207, 1350
Porte St. Louis (Ca) 1207, 1350
Porter (Am) 150, 106
Porterfield (Am) 150, 106
Portisham (Br) 330, 720
Portland (Am) 109
Porto Santo (Po) 434, 406
Portsmouth (Am) 203, 37
Poseidon (Gr) 924
Poti class (Ru) 650, 466
Potosi (Me) 259, 322
Potsdam (EG) 229, 372
Potvis (Du) 890
Power (Am) 88, 96
Prab (Th) 320, 665
Prairie (Am) 825, 730
Prasae (Th) 241
Prat (Ch) 200, 43
Pratt (Am) 164A, 274
Prebble (Am) 290, 78
Preserver (Am) 993, 1301
President Kruger (SA) 111, 194

San Luis (Ar) 238, 135
San Marco (It) 293, 65
San Marcos (Am) 707, 611
San Martin (Pv) 511, 147
Sanaviron (Ar) 1053, 1311
Sanchez Carrion (Pv) 520, 421
Sancho Timeno (Co) 1182, 1167
Sanctuary (Am) 1324, 1280
Sand Lance (Am) 876
Sandalo (It) 468, 698
Sandjaja (Ia) 103, 93
Sandoval (Am) 910, 1046
Sands (Am) 1113, 829/830
Sandvig (Da) 717/718, 706
Santa Antao (Po) 434, 406
Santa Barbara (Am) 876, 745
Santa Caterina (Bz) 150, 106
Santa Cruz (Ar) 238, 135
Santa Cruz (Po) 468, 698
Santa Fe (Ar) 920
Santa Luza (Po) 434, 406
Santa Maria (Po) 459, 1099
Santiago del Estero (Ar) 924
Santillana (Pv) 520, 421
Santo Antao (Po) 434, 406
Sapanca (Tu) 382, 701
Sapele (Ng) 385, 440
Sarasin (Th) 411, 409
Saratoga (Am) 19, 25
Sargo (Am) 878
Sarmiento de Gamboa (Sp) 446, 327
Sarner (Tu) 382, 701
Saros (Tu) 382, 701
Sarpedon (Am) 1200, 640
Sarsfield (Am) 88, 96
Sasha (Ru) 381, 709
Saskatchewan (Ca) 525, 228
Sassafras (Am) 883, 1087
Sassnitz (EG) 229, 372
Satakut (Th) 320, 665
Satsuma (Ja) 496, 1111
Sattahib (Th) 393, 145
Satterlee (Am) 160, 141
Saturno (Po) 310, 526
Satyr (Am) 1200, 640
Sauda (No) 468, 698
Sauerland (Ge) 1295, 1225
Saugatuck (Am) 1177, 1160
Savage (Am) 524, 278
Savarona (Tu) 967, 960
Savitri (In) 781, 533
Sawachidori (Ja) 741, 1123
Sawunggaling (Ia) 103, 93
Scamp (Am) 879
Scampo (It) 688, 720
Scarabee (Fr) 1078, 800
Scarborough (Br) 110, 194
Scharnhorst (Ge) 230, 305
Schenectady (Am) 965, 606
Schleie (Ge) 318, 666
Schleswig ( Ge) 378, 681
Schleswig-Holstein (Ge) 214, 61
Schofield (Am) 281, 178
Schroeder (Am) 150, 106
Schuiling (Du) 718, 707
Schutze class (Ge) 386/412, 466/711
    400/401, 402/403
Schuyler Otis Bland (Am) 1099, 1035
Schuylkill (Am) 1177, 1160
Schwalbe II class (EG) 56, 482
Schwarzwald (Ge) 870, 1074
Schwedt (EG) 321, 634

Scimitar (Br) 666, 504
Scimitarra (It) 406, 345
Scorpion (Fr) 1105, 797
Scoter (Am) 394, 148
Sculpin (Am) 879
Scylla (Br) 97, 191
Sea Devil (Am) 876
Sea Fox (Am) 897
Sea Giant (Br) 978, 1331
Sea Leopard (Am) 897
Sea Lift (Am) 879, 1034
Sea Poacher (Am) 897
Sea Robin (Am) 897
Sea Salvor (Br) 1005, 1102
Seadragon (Am) 878
Seahorse (Am) 876
Seal (Au) 689/776, 724
Sealion (Am) 920
Sealion (Br) 905
Seattle (Am) 1322, 1277
Seawolf (Am) 931
Sebago (Am) 251, 354
Sebka (My) 611, 503
Sechura (Pv) 1165, 1170
Seddulbahir (Tu) 382, 701
Sedge (Am) 883, 1087
Sedgwick County (Am) 133, 635
Seeadler (Ge) 546, 474
Segugio (It) 236, 661
Segundo (Am) 924
Segura (Sp) 538, 370
Sel (No) 555, 513
Sellers (Am) 87, 80
Seminole (Am) 838, 1057
Semmes (Am) 87, 80
Semyon Chelyuskin (Ru) 1042, 975
Sendai (Ja) 494, 1113
Seneca (Am) 851, 1287
Senegal (Se) 582/589, 480
Senja (No) 481, 376
Seoul (Ko) 150, 106
Sep (Ph) 917
Separacion (Do) 439, 681
Seppia (It) 688, 720
Seraing (Be) 330, 720
Serampang (My) 420, 424
Sergeant Andrew Miller (Am) 906, 1048
Sergeant Archer T. Gammon (Am) 906,
    1048
Sergeant Jack J. Pendleton (Am) 906, 1048
Sergeant Morris E. Crain (Am) 906, 1048
Sergeant Truman Kimbro (Am) 906, 1048
Serigala (La) 546, 474
Seriotyi (Ru) 103, 93
Seriozynyi (Ru) 103, 93
Serrano (Ch) 252, 281
Seruwa (Ce) 671, 566
Severn (Am) 1176, 1136
Serviola (Sp) 996, 1338
Seyma (Ru) 1301, 1196
Sfendoni (Gr) 143, 105
Sfinge (It) 406, 345
Sgombro (It) 504, 680
Shaab (Su) 599, 481
Shadwell (Am) 707, 611
Shah Jahan (Pk) 164, 245
Shahbas (Ir) 382, 701
Shahrokh (Ir) 382, 701
Shakori (Am) 851, 1287
Shangri-La (Am) 2, 24
Shannon (Am) 155, 104
Sharada (In) 672, 532

Shark (Am) 879
Shark (Et) 760, 520
Sharyu (In) 781, 533
Shavington (Br) 596, 689
Shawnee Trail (Am) 1160, 1160
Shea (Am) 155, 104
Sheldrake (Am) 395/721, 149
Shelton (Am) 174, 96
Shenandoah (Am) 849, 1043
Sheraton (Br) 376, 595, 690
Sherman (Am) 606, 211
Shershen class (Ru and Eg) 337, 491
Shields (Am) 150, 106
Shikinami (Ja) 153, 120
Shikine (Ja) 594, 714
Shikine (Ja) (M.S.A.) 489, 116
Shimokita (Ja) 133, 635
Shin Song (Ko) 396, 148
Shinano (Ja) 356, 1121
Shinonome (Ja) 785, 559
Shipham (Br) 330, 720
Shiratori (Ja) 500, 395
Shiretoko (Ja) 133, 635
Shisaka (Ja) 594, 714
Shoa Shan (Cs) 352, 281
Short Splice (Am) 1315, 1220
Shoshone (Am) 1138 1150
Shoulton (Br) 776, 689
Shreveport (Am) 119, 607
Shrike (Am) 468, 698
Shushuk (Pr) 907
Shva (Is) 586, 523
Si Hung (Ko) 219, 646
Sibilla (It) 406, 345
Sibir (Ru) 810, 768
Sibiryakov (Ru) 969, 962
Siboney (Am) 16, 22
Siboney (Cu) 453, 360
Sichang (Th) 1167, 1183
Sidi Fradj (Ag) 469, 696
Sidon (Le) 583, 569
Siegen (Ge) 377, 688
Sierra (Am) 825, 730
Siete de Agosto (Co) 637, 126
Sigacik (Tu) 382, 301
Sigourney (Am) 150, 106
Sigsbee (Am) 150
Siken (Sw) 947
Sil (Sp) 382, 701
Silifke (Tu) 382, 701
Siliwangi (Ia) 103, 93
Silma (Fi) 1317
Silnij class (Ru) 1041, 1304
Silversides (Am) 876
Silverstein (Am) 164A, 274
Simba (Ke) 521, 425
Simcoe (Ca) 1251, 1273
Simon Bolivar (AM) 871
Simon Lake (Am) 1328, 862
Simon van der Stel (SA) 73, 241
Simorgh (Ir) 382, 701
Simpson (Ch) 895/920
Sin Mi (Ko) 680, 660
Sine-Saloum (Se) 313, 483
Singa (Ia) 546, 474
Singamangaradja (Ia) 103, 93
Sinop (Tu) 382, 701
Sioux (Am) 851, 1287
Siquijor (Pi) 676, 586
Sir Bedevere (Br) 1212, 614
Sir Galahad (Br) 1212, 614
Sir Geraint (Br) 1212, 614

Suffolk County (Am) 273, 618
Suffren (Fr) 134, 170
Sugi (Ja) 263, 308
Sukanya (In) 672, 532
Sukothai (Th) 515, 594
Sukrip (Th) 411, 409
Sultan Hasanudin (Ia) 455A, 182
Sultanhisar (Tu) 726, 408
Sulu (Pi) 576, 470
Sumida (Ja) 496, 1112
Summit County (Am) 133, 635
Sumner County (Am) 133, 635
Sumter (Am) 965, 606
Sunbird (Am) 1015, 1285
Sunchon (Ko) 396, 148
Sundang (My) 420, 424
Sundew (Am) 883, 1087
Sundsvall (Sw) 47, 130
Sunfish (Am) 876
Superior (Am) 326/439, 681/712
Superman (Br) 978, 1331
Supply (Av) 1187, 1133
Surapati (Ia) 168, 220
Surasdra (Th) 461, 250
Surcouf (Fr) 100, 110
Surfbird (Am) 721, 149
Suribachi (Am) 831, 1059
Surmene (Tu) 382, 701
Surovyi (Ru) 103, 93
Surprise (Am) 78, 413
Susa (Ly) 611, 503
Sutjeska (Ys) 945
Sutlej (In) 625, 306
Sutter County (Am) 133, 635
Suvarna (In) 781, 533
Suzunami (Ja) 784, 554
Suzutsuki (Ja) 784, 554
Svaerdfisken (Da) 542, 473
Svartan (Sw) 943
Svartloga (Sw) 1206, 1343
Svenner (No) 941
Sverdlov (Ru) 183, 52
Svetlnyiare (Ru) 139/40, 90/91
Svetlyi (Ru) 139/140, 90/91
Svir (Ru) 1323, 1333, 1282
Svobodnyi (Ru) 103, 93
Swan (Au) 93, 192
Swanson (Am) 160, 141
Swasey (Am) 234, 269
Swatow class (RC) 609, 516
Sway (Am) 394, 148
Sweetbriar (Am) 883, 1087
Sweetgum (Am) 883, 1087
Swenning (Am) 234, 269
Swerve (Am) 503, 678
Swift (Am) 394, 148
Swin (Br) 875, 800B
Switha (Br) 878, 1098
Sword Knot (Am) 1280, 858
Swordfish (Am) 878
Sydney (Au) 24, 7
Sylhet (Pk) 571, 485
Sylvania (Am) 867, 1038
Symbol (Am) 394, 148
Syros (Gr) 133, 635
Syu Ch'ing Shan (RC) 133, 635

T 1 (M-A-2) Am 1297, 1205
T 11 (Th) 455, 428
T 12 (Th) 455, 428
T 13 (Th) 455, 428
T 32 (Sw) 649, 506

T 33 (Sw) 649, 506
T 34 (Sw) 649, 506
T 35 (Sw) 649, 506
T 36 (Sw) 649, 506
T 37 (Sw) 649, 506
T 38 (Sw) 649, 506
T 39 (Sw) 649, 506
T 40 (Sw) 649, 506
T 42-T 56 (Sw) 55, 505
T 43 (Ru) (A) (Ia) (Eg) (Ph) (RC) (Bu)
    (Sy) 442, 676
T 43 (Radar Picket) (Ru) 537, 356
T 58 class (Ru) 71, 674
T 61-T 70 (Sw) 315, 575
T 201 (Bm) 562, 509
T 202 (Bm) 562, 509
T 203 (Bm) 562, 509
T 204 (Bm) 562, 509
T 205 (Bm) 562, 509
T 301 (Ru) (Al) (Bu) (Eg) (Ia) (Rm)
    441, 686
T 914 (Cambodia) 323, 656
T 915 (Cambodia) 323, 656
T-AGOR 16 (Am) 1089, 839
TM 41 (Ru) 1302, 1198
TM 42 (Ru) 1302, 1198
TM 43 (Ru) 1302, 1198
Ta Chen (RC) 1224, 1253
Ta Pie Shan (RC) 133
Ta Shueh (Cs) 855, 1308
Ta Tung (Cs) 851, 1287
Ta Yu (Cs) 855, 1308
Tabberer (Am) 164A, 274
Tacoma (Am) 78, 413
Taconic (Am) 1118, 740
Tadindaeng (Th) 382, 701
Tae Cho (Ko) 680, 660
Tae Dong (Ko) 241, 301
Tafelberg (SA) 1179, 1137
Tahan (My) 596, 689
Tahchin (Th) 241, 307
Tahmadou (Ir) 626, 564A
Tahmass (Is) 558, 529
Tai Chao (Cs) 167, 266
Tai Ho (Cs) 167, 266
Tai Hsing Shan (RC) 133, 635
Tai Hu (Cs) 167, 266
Tai Shan (Cs) 253, 281
Tai Tsang (Cs) 167, 266
Tai Yuan (RC) 844, 169
Taiyuan (Cs) 164A, 274
Tajo (Sp) 382, 701
Taka (Ja) 351, 394
Takami (Ja) 594, 714
Takanami (Ja) 153, 120
Takanawa (Ja) 743, 1126
Takapu (NZ) 669, 565
Takatsuki (Ja) 638, 71
Takatsuki (Ja) (M.S.A.) 743, 1126
Takbai (Th) 395, 145
Takelma (Am) 851, 1287
Takuyo (Ja) 884, 1125
Talara (Pv) 1175, 1166
Talbot (Am) 281, 178
Talbot County (Am) 438, 619
Talibong (Th) 323, 656
Talladega (Am) 910, 1046
Tallin class (Ru) 55, 85
Talluah (Am) 1177, 1160
Taluga (Am) 1176, 1136
Talwar (In) 109, 194
Tam Sbt (VN) 269, 665

Tamanami (Ja) 784, 554
Tamandare (Bz) 201, 42
Tamaron (Am) 853, 1287
Tambre (Sp) 538, 370
Tamure (NZ) 669, 565
Tamyr (Ru) 793, 834
Tana (No) 468, 698
Tanager (Am) 391, 150
Tandjung Nusanie (Ia) 133, 635
Taney (Am) 477, 317
Tang (Am) 950
Tanin (Is) 953
Tappahannock (Am) 1179, 1144
Tarablous (Le) 549, 537
Taranaki (NZ) 94, 196
Tarapunga (NZ) 669, 565
Tarawa (Am) 2, 24
Tarawa (Ce) 671, 566
Tarbatness (Br) 874, 746
Tarek Ben Said (Sy) 354, 398
Tarentule (Fr) 1105, 797
Tarik (Eg) 240, 303
Tarlac (Pi) 301, 486A
Tarmo (Fi) 1043/1074, 908
Tarn (Fr) 1095, 1071
Tarnan (Sw) 943
Tarno (Sw) 584, 715
Tarqui (Ec) 680, 659
Tarshish (Is) 586, 523
Tartar (Br) 63, 129
Tartu (Fr) 187, 109
Tatara (Ja) 594, 714
Tatnuck (Am) 855, 1308
Tatsugumo (Ja) 785, 559
Tatsuta (Ja) 487, 1115
Tattnall (Am) 87, 80
Taurus (Bz) 952, 833
Taussig (Am) 144, 100
Tautog (Am) 876
Tavi (Fi) 712, 453
Tawakoni (Am) 851, 1287
Tawasa (Am) 851, 1287
Teal (Au) 776, 790
Tecumseh (Am) 871
Tegualda (Ch) 559, 527
Tehuantepec (Me) 260, 282
Teide (Sp) 1153, 1173
Teist (No) 555, 513
Tejsten (Da) 1106, 1347
Tekirdag (Tu) 777, 694
Telamon (Am) 1200, 640
Telkka (Fi) 712, 453
Tellina (It) 688, 720
Teluk Bayur (Ia) 133, 635
Teluk Kau (Ia) 133, 635
Teluk Langsa (Ia) 133, 635
Teluk Menado (Ia) 133, 635
Temerario (Sp) 398, 133
Temse (Be) 330, 720
Tenacity (Br) 613, 493
Tenby (Br) 112, 194
Tench (Am) 897
Tenggiri (Ia) 411, 409
Tenryu (Ja) 356, 1121
10 De Octubre (Cu) 859, 1318
Ter (Sp) 538, 370
Tercel (Am) 394, 148
Terek (Ru) 1323/1333, 1282
ex Terek (Ru) 1064, 774
Terme (Tu) 777, 694
Terra Nova (Ca) 499, 227
Terrebone Parish (Am) 132, 620

Terror (Am) 826, 728
Terrell County (Am) 132, 620
Terry (Am) 150, 106
Teruzuki (Ja) 209, 118
Teruzuki (Ja) (M.S.A.) 784, 554
Teshio (Ja) 490, 1118
Tete (Po) 957, 595
Thai Binh (VN) 455, 428
Thakeham (Br) 330, 720
Thamrin (Ia) 803, 1075
Than Tien (VN) 269, 665
Thayanchon (Th) 411, 409
The President (Pi) 885, 1027
The Sullivans (Am) 150, 106
Theodore E. Chandler (Am) 88, 96
Theodore Roosevelt (Am) 872
Theseus (Ge) 652, 374
Thetis (Ge) 652, 374
Thetis (Gr) 1016, 799
Thi Nai (VN) 132, 620
Thi Tu (VN) 455, 428
Thien Kich (VN) 269
Thoaban (Abu Dhabi) 419, 446
Thomas A. Edison (Am) 870
Thomas E. Fraser (Am) 155, 104
Thomas F. Nickel (Am) 164A, 274
Thomas G. Thompson (Am) 1113, 829/830
Thomas Grant (Br) 1244, 1236
Thomas J. Gary (Am) 523, 278
Thomas Jefferson (Am) 870
Thomas Washington (Am) 1075, 830
Thomaston (Am) 57, 610
Thompson (Am) 154, 138
Thomson (Ch) 895
Thor (Am) 968, 726
Thor (Ic) 1204, 851
Thorn (Am) 160, 141
Thornback (Am) 897
Thrasher (Am) 468, 698
Threadfin (Am) 897
Threat (Am) 394, 148
Throsk (Br) 1308, 1227
Thrush (Am) 468, 698
Thuban (Am) 838, 1057
Thule (Sw) 1045, 985
Thunder (Ca) 691, 695
Thyella (Gr) 150, 106
Ticonderoga (Am) 2, 24
Tideflow (Br) 1187, 1133
Tidepool (Br) 1186, 1132
Tidereach (Br) 1187, 1133
Tidespring (Br) 1186, 1132
Tidesurge (Br) 1187, 1133
Tidewater (Am) 849, 1043
Tien Chue (Cs) 1093, 1069
Tien Giang (VN) 680, 659
Tien Moi (VN) 455, 428
Tien Shan (Cs) 253, 281
Tierra Del Fuego (Ar) 595, 690
Tiger (Br) 136, 45
Tiger (Ge) 546, 474
Tigrone (Am) 925
Tillamook (Am) 855, 1308
Tillman (Am) 160, 141
Timo (It) 468, 698
Tinian (Am) 16, 22
Tinosa (Am) 877
Tinsman (Am) 164A, 274
Tinto (Sp) 482, 371
Tioga County (Am) 131, 620
Tippu Sultan (Pk) 433, 243
Tir (In) 502, 289

Tiran (Ir) 724, 432
Tirante (Am) 926
Tirebolu (Tu) 777, 694
Tirtsa (Is) 312, 561
Tiru (Am) 899
Tista (No) 468, 698
Tjakalang (Ia) 411, 409
Tjakra (Ia) 918
Tjeld (No) 555, 513
Tjerk Hiddes (Du) 91A, 190
Tjorn (Sw) 1210, 1348
Tjurko (Sw) 584, 715
Tjutjut (Ia) 449, 387
Tlaxcala (Me) 1293, 1203
To Kiang (Cs) 585, 405
To Yen (VN) 455, 428
Toba (Ar) 1028, 1323
Tobruk (Au) 177, 232
Tobruk (Ly) 454, 418
Todak (Ia) 556, 480B
Todak (My) 329, 722
Tofino (Sp) 847, 1015
Togogo (Ve) 411, 409
Tokachi (Ja) 487, 1115
Toledo (Am) 199, 36
Toll (Ar) 366, 435
Tolman (Am) 155, 104
Tolovana (Am) 1176, 1136
Tom Green County (Am) 132, 620
Tomas Marin (Me) 453, 360
Tombak (My) 420, 424
Tombigbee (Am) 1325, 1283
Tomich (Am) 234, 269
Tomochidori (Ja) 741, 1123
Ton class (Br) 376/595/596/776,
  689/690/691
Tondar (Ir) 780, 530
Tondbad (Ir) 780, 530
Tone (Ja) 493, 1120
Tongeren (Be) 330, 720
Tongham (Br) 688, 723
Tongkol (Id) 449, 387
Tongpliu (Th) 411, 409
Tonijn (Du) 890
Topeka (Am) 768, 41
Tor (Sw) 1043, 980
Torani (Ia) 411, 409
Torquay (Br) 111, 194
Torrens (Au) 93, 192
Tortuga (Am) 707, 611
Tortuguero (Do) 439, 681
Toshima (Ja) 468, 698
Totano (Ia) 688, 720
Toti (It) 911
Toufan (Ir) 780, 530
Toumi (Ja) 743, 1126
Tournai (Be) 330, 720
Tousan (Ir) 780, 530
Tovda (Ru) 818, 734
Towers (Am) 87, 80
Town class (Pk) 571, 485
Toxotis (Gr) 555, 513
Trabzon (Tu) 777, 694
Tracker (Br) 272, 624
Tracy (Ca) 1213, 1275
Trad (Th) 461, 250
Transvaal (SA) 456, 297
Trathen (Am) 143, 105
Traust (No) 550, 487
Trave (Ge) 861, 1336
Traverse County (Am) 132, 620
Tree class (Am etc) 1105, 797

Trenton (Am) 123, 608
Trepang (Am) 876
Triaina (Gr) 924
Tribal class (Br) 61/63, 129
Tridente (Bz) 1052, 1308
Trieux (Fr) 271, 626
Trifoglio (It) 468, 698
Trigger (Am) 950
Triglav (Ys) 457, 256
Tringa (Am) 1015, 1285
Trinity (Tr) 484, 423
Triong Sa (VN) 455, 428
Tripoli (Am) 10, 14
Trippe (Am) 280, 181
Trishul (In) 109, 194
Tritao (Bz) 1052, 1308
Triton (Am) 869
Triton (Da) 455A, 182
Triton (Ge) 652, 374
Triton (Sp) 247, 329
Triumph (Br) 11, 13
Triunfo (Bz) 1052, 1308
Trondheim (No) 405, 216
Tropik (Ru) 1194, 835
Tross (No) 550, 487
Trout (Am) 950
Truckee (Am) 1129, 1134
Trumpeter (Am) 167, 266
Trumpetfish (Am) 899
Truong Sa (VN)
Trutta (Am) 897
Truxton (Am) 121, 185
Trygg (No) 550, 487
Tsubame (Ja) 351, 394
Tsugaru (Ja) 1318, 813
Tsukuba (Ja) 701, 560
Tsukumi (Ja) 594, 714
Tsurugi (Ja) 743, 1126
Tsushima (Ja) 468, 698
Tubingen (Ge) 378, 684
Tucumcari (Am) 572, 583
Tughril (Pk) 433, 243
Tukan (Ph) 443, 386
Tulare (Am) 893, 1037
Tulipe (Fr) 330, 720
Tullibee (Am) 875
Tumleren (Da) 909
Tummler (Ge) 318, 666
Tummler class (EG) 557/564, 542/543
Tung Hai (Cs) 707, 611
Tung Kiang (Cs) 585, 405
Tunny (Am) 876
Tupelo (Am) 883, 1087
Tur (Po) 442, 676
Turgut Reis (Tu) 923
Turia (Sp) 382, 701
Turkey (Am) 469, 496
Turner Joy (Am) 186, 98
Turnhout (Be) 330, 720
Tursas (Fi) 1208, 1339
Turunmaa (Fi) 590, 465
Tuscaloosa (Am) 965, 606
Tusk (Am) 897
Tutuila (Am) 827, 1052
Tuy Dong (VN) 411, 409
25 De Julio (Ec) 253, 281
Twining (Am) 150, 105
Tyne (Br) 823, 735
Typhoon (Br) 1035, 1305
Tyr (No) 67, 151
U 1 (Ge) 940
U 2 (Ge) 940

U 4 (Ge) 939
U 5 (Ge) 939
U 6 (Ge) 939
U 7 (Ge) 939
U 8 (Ge) 939
U 9 (Ge) 921
U 10 (Ge) 921
U 11 (Ge) 921
U 12 (Ge) 921
Ucayali (Pv) 435
Uda (Ru) 1333, 1282
Uhlman (Am) 143, 105
Uisko (Fi) 976, 1096
Ula (No) 941
Uljanik (Ys) 945
Ulla (Sp) 468, 698
Uller (No) 67, 151
Ulm (Ge) 378, 684
Ulryung (Ko) 680, 660
Ulster (Br) 750, 204
Ulvsund (Da) 468, 698
Ulysses S. Grant (Am) 871
Umberto Grosso (It) 89, 230
Umidori (Ja) 500, 395
Umitaka (Ja) 350, 395
Umpqua (Am) 855, 1308
Un Bong (Ko) 133, 635
Unanue (Pv) 1052, 1308
Undaunted (Br) 473, 199
Undine (Ge) 380, 704
Ung Po (Ko) 253, 281
Unimak (Am) 479, 316
Union (Am) 838, 1057
Uplifter (Br) 875, 800B
Uppland (Sw) 118, 251
Upshur (Am) 901, 1006
Upton (Br) 596, 689
Uranami (Ja) 153, 120
Uranami (Ja) (M.S.A.) 784, 554
Urania (It) 406, 345
Urano (Po) 310, 526
Uranus (Ge) 386, 400
Urazuki (Ja) 784, 554
Uribe (Ch) 252, 281
Uruguay (Uv) 167, 266
Urume (Ja) 594, 714
Ushuaia (Ar) 990, 1105
Usumacinta (Me) 260, 282
Ute (Am) 851, 1287
Uthaug (No) 941
Utina (Am) 851, 1287
Utla (No) 468, 698
Uto (Sw) 584, 715
Utrecht (Du) 284, 68
Utsira (No) 941
Utstein (No) 941
Uttern (Sw) 929
Utvaer (No) 941
Uusimaa (Fi) 162, 259
V 1 (Rm) 449, 387
V 2 (Rm) 449, 387
V 3 (Rm) 449, 387
V 21 (Sp) 790, 547
V 57 (Sw) 725, 385
VC 1 (Fr) 567, 538
VC 2 (Fr) 567, 538
VC 3 (Fr) 567, 538
VC 10 (Fr) 567, 538
VMV 11 (Fr) 472, 444
VMV 13 (Fr) 472, 444
VP 212 (Cambodia) 575, 562
VR 1 (Cambodia) 760, 520

VR 11 (Cambodia) 760, 520
Vaedderen (Da) 341
Valcour (Am) 117, 311
Valday (Ru) 953, 675
Valen (Sw) 929
Valiant (Am) 299, 465A
Valiant (Br) 885
Valkyrien (No) 475, 285
Vallo (Sw) 467, 703
Valor (Am) 503, 678
Vammen (Am) 107, 273
Vampire (Au) 115, 224
Van Bochove (Du) 1227, 1247
Van de Wel (Du) 718, 707
Van Don (VN) 411, 409
Van Galen (Du) 91A, 190
Van Hamel (Du) 718, 707
Van Haverbeke (Be) 504, 680
Van Moppes (Du) 718, 707
Van Nes (Du) 91A, 190
Van Speijk (Du) 91A, 190
Van Straelen (Du) 718, 707
Van 'T Hoff (Du)
Van Versendaal (Du) 718, 707
Van Voorhis (Am) 220, 277
Van Well Groenevald (Du) 718, 707
Vance (Am) 523, 278
Vancouver (Am) 96, 609
Vancouver (Ca) 873, 1007
Vandenburgh (Am) 276, 665
Vandivier (Am) 106, 279
Vanguard (Am) 1329, 864
Vanya (Ru) 323, 713
Vargen (Sw) 929
Varian (Am) 76/80, 271
Varma (Fi) 1043/1074, 980
Varyag (Ru) 645, 83
Vasama 1 (Fi) 305/563, 511/512
Vasama 2 (Fi) 305/563
Vasco da Gama (Po) 430, 302
Vasco Nunez Pinzon (Sp) 446, 327
Vasilii Veresovoi (Ru) 822, 749
Vasily Golovnin (Ru) 1012, 827
Vasily Poyarkhov (Ru) 1042, 975
Vasily Pronchishchev (Ru) 1042, 975
Vauquelin (Fr) 282, 113
Vdoknovenyi (Ru) 139/140, 90/91
Vdumchivi (Ru) 103, 93
Vedetta (It) 410, 407
Veere (Du) 597, 693
Vega (Am) 832, 1058
Vega (Fr) 597, 693
Vega (Po) 307, 525
Vega (Sw) 46, 497
Vegesack (Ge) 377, 688
Veinte de Julio (Co) 637, 126
Veinticino de Mayo (Ar) 9, 11
Velarde (Pv) 520, 421
Velas (Po) 468, 698
Vella Gulf (Am) 16, 22
Velocity (Am) 394, 148
Velos (Gr) 143, 105
Vendetta (Au) 165, 225
Vendetta (It) 410, 407
Venlo (Du) 597, 693
Venture (Am) 503, 678
Venturer (Br) 596, 689
Venturous (Am) 299, 465A
Venus (Fr) 907
Venus (Po) 310, 526
Vermillion (Am) 838, 1057
Vernon County (Am) 132, 620

Verseau (Fr) 597, 693
Vertieres (Ha) 724, 432
Verviers (Be) 468, 698
Vesole (Am) 88, 96
Vesuvio (It) 1218, 1224
Vesuvius (Am) 913, 1056
Veurne (Be) 468, 698
Vicente Yanez Pinzon (Sp) 166, 328
Victor Schoelcher (Fr) 390, 207
Victoria (Am) 907, 1049
Victoria (Ca) 355, 443
Vidal (Br) 1071, 820
V 16 class (Da) 717/718, 706
Viggen (Sw) 943
Vigilant (Am) 299, 465A
Vigilante (Am) 313, 483
Vigor (Am) 503, 678
Vigorous (Am) 299, 465A
Viima (Fi) 365, 416
Vikrant (In) 22, 5
Viktor Kotelnikov (Ru) 821, 749
Vila do Porto (Po) 468, 698
Villa de Bilbao (Sp) 338, 363
Villapando (Me) 368, 454
Villar (Pv) 143, 105
Vilsund (Da) 468, 698
Vinh Long (Fr) 507, 682
Vino (Sw) 467, 703
Violette (Fr) 330, 720
Viper (Ge) 680, 659
Vireo (Am) 468, 698
Virginio Fasan (It) 215, 183
Virgo (Am) 838, 1057
Virgo (Sw) 46, 497
Visby (Sw) 47, 130
Vischio (It) 468, 698
Vise (Be) 330, 720
Vital (Am) 503, 678
Vittorio Veneto (It) 631, 75
Vityaz (Ru) 1001, 814
Vladimir Ilyich (Ru) 963, 964
Vladimir Rusanov (Ru) 1042, 975
Vladimir Trefolev (Ru) 1059, 790
Vladivostock (Ru) 807, 974
Vneta (Ge) 380, 704
Voge (Am) 286, 177
Vogelgesang (Am) 88, 96
Voima (Fr) 1003, 903
Volador (Am) 899
Volkhov (Ru) 1152, 1164
Volklingen (Ge) 378, 684
Volturno (It) 1146, 1182
Volynets (Ru) 972, 963
Von Steuben (Am) 871
Vos (Du) 588, 362
Vosper Thornycroft Mk7 Frigate (Ly) 333, 213
Vosso (No) 468, 698
Vozmuschenny (Ru) 139/140, 90/91
Vrazumitelnyi (Ru) 103, 93
Vreeland (Am) 280, 181
Vrystaat (SA) 751, 201
Vulcan (Am) 824, 733
Vulcano (Sp) 244, 325
Vun Tau (Th) 132, 620
Vung Tau (VN) 132, 620
Vytegra (Ru) 518, 734
Vyuga (Ru) 1042, 975
W class (Ru) 918, 949
W F/R class (Ru) 908/915
W. S. Sims (Am) 280, 181
Waage (Ge) 386, 400

Founded 1957

# THE SHIP RECOGNITION CORPS

*Past Presidents:*
Admiral the Lord Mountevans, 1956-57
Admiral of the Fleet the Viscount Cunningham of Hyndhope, 1957-63
Admiral of the Fleet Sir Philip Vian, 1966-68

---

*President:*
Vice-Admiral Sir John Gray, K.B.E., C.B.

**THE SHIP RECOGNITION CORPS** is a volunteer, civilian force and receives the goodwill and practical, but not financial, support of the Ministry of Defence.

Its objects are :—

(a)   To build up a nucleus of trained observers who would be of value in an emergency as instructors in visual recognition.

(b)   To encourage an interest in, and knowledge of, ships and the country's dependence upon them.

In spite of changed conditions of warfare very great importance is placed on ship recognition and as an Admiralty memorandum states "PRACTICE IN RECOGNITION IS ESSENTIAL IN PEACE-TIME."

Membership is open to men aged **18** years and upwards and there is a junior section, SHIP SPOTTERS, for those aged 13 to 18.

**For further particulars write to :—
The Director at 67, New Dover Road, Canterbury, Kent.**